RETAILING

Dale M. Lewison
University of Akron

M. Wayne DeLozier
Nicholls State University

RETAILING

Third Edition

MERRILL PUBLISHING COMPANY
A Bell & Howell Information Company
Columbus   Toronto   London   Melbourne

Published by Merrill Publishing Company
A Bell & Howell Information Company
Columbus, Ohio 43216

This book was set in Italia.

Administrative Editor: Pamela B. Kusma
Developmental Editor: Jim Kilgore
Production Coordinator: Molly Kyle
Art Coordinator: James Hubbard
Cover Designer: Cathy Watterson
Text Designer: Cynthia Brunk

Library of Congress Catalog Card Number: 88-63212
International Standard Book Number: 0-675-20984-6
Printed in the United States of America
1 2 3 4 5 6 7 8 9 — 93 92 91 90 89 88

Cover Photo: David Phillips
Title page photo: Larry Hamill.

Text photos: Part opening color photos, Larry Hamill;
background photo, Jake Raj/The Image Bank. Text
photos: p. 145 *top right, bottom left, bottom right,*
pp. 291, 293, 313, 479, 505, 636, Tim Cairns—Cobalt
Productions/Merrill; p. 145 *top left,* pp. 295, 299, 647,
Michael Pogony—Photographic Communications/Merrill.
All other photos, Larry Hamill.

PREFACE

Courses in retailing have never been stronger offerings than they are now. A primary reason for their popularity is the job-oriented student. With the seller's market of the sixties and seventies turning into a buyer's market of the eighties and nineties, students today are concerned about getting good jobs. The need for courses that enhance their chances of finding entry-level management positions explains the increase in course offerings and higher enrollments in retailing courses.

Goal for the Text

With students demanding more job-oriented subjects, basic courses such as retailing should continue to have a steady growth. Students as well as the business community view retailing as a practical, operations-oriented discipline. Accordingly, operations-oriented policies, methods and procedures *must* be an integral part of a retailing course. Academic credibility requires, however, that course materials be couched within a conceptual, theoretical framework. *To meet these dual needs, the goal for this third edition of* Retailing *has been to strike a balance between academic credibility and the basic, operations-oriented needs of the job-seeking student.*

Plan for the Text

The organization and plan for the text, combined with many features from previous editions and several new features, accomplish this goal. The book is organized into six parts, divided into 24 chapters that provide comprehensive yet brief learning modules. The book covers all major topics: consumers; retail site location; designing, staffing, and organizing; developing the retail offering and getting the merchandise into the store; developing and controlling the merchandise plan; setting and adjusting retail prices; promotional activities; the importance of environmental influences in retail business; and retail financial statements and operations control. All chapters have been thoroughly updated and carefully reviewed to include the most recent developments in the field and to reinforce the decision-making approach.

Special features that help achieve the book's goals include:

1. A new chapter on Services Retailing, one of the fastest growing areas in the nation's economy, has been written expressly for this edition and appears in Part Six.
2. A new decision-making framework has been developed throughout the text and provides the basis for discussion of all fundamental retailing topics.
3. We have doubled the number and variety of cases for discussion and analysis in this edition.

Learning Aids

1. Chapter opening outlines that preview the important topics covered in each chapter help students organize their reading of the chapter.
2. Learning objectives guide students' reading and help them identify important ideas for review and application.
3. Brief, end-of-chapter summaries reflect the chapter objectives and streamline students' review of major concepts.
4. Key terms and concepts, including both

technical and nontechnical items, are provided
to guide students' review process for tests and
greater understanding.

5. Each chapter concludes with a listing of Related
Readings to direct students toward even more
interesting and challenging readings in retailing.

6. The text is enhanced throughout with exhibits
(graphs, tables, illustrations) created especially
for this book or derived from authoritative
sources. The graphic treatment consists of full-
color artwork and many color photographs that
enhance textual presentation.

7. The learning aids system is reinforced by a
bibliography of standard works in the retailing
area, encompassing both academic and trade
sources.

8. The author and subject indexes provide the
student with an accurate reference to all key
ideas and concepts in the text.

Ancillaries and Supplements

Instructor's Manual: The Instructor's Manual
contains complete lecture outlines, answers to the
discussion questions, and teaching notes for the
cases.

Student Study Guide: A new student guide is also
available to provide exercises and additional
examples and insights into retailing.

Transparency Masters: 190 transparency masters
of key illustrations from the text are available to all
adopters.

Test Bank: A test bank of over 2,000 true-false
and multiple-choice questions is also available to
adopters.

Casebook: For this edition, Dale Lewison has
developed a separate book of 30 cases for
additional reading. The casebook can be ordered
from the publisher and used to complement this
text, or the *Essentials of Retailing* text that appears
this year from Merrill for the first time.

ACKNOWLEDGMENTS

This book would not have been possible without the valuable support of many people. Therefore, we wish to thank the following professors for reviewing the manuscript: Dr. Larry Gresham, Texas A & M University; Jack Sheeks, Ed.D., Broward Community College; Ken Evans, Arizona State University; Ken Fontz, Youngstown State University; Jim Burke, Santa Rosa Junior College; John Lloyd, Monroe Community College; and Karen Schaeffer, University of Delaware.

Also, I wish to extend my appreciation for the helpful suggestions of reviewers in the earlier stages of manuscript preparation: Dave Snyder, Pennsylvania State University: Lewis J. Neisner, SUNY at Buffalo; John B. Gifford, Miami University; Dr. Robert Solomon, Stephen F. Austin State University; John J. Porter, West Virginia University; William Piper, University of Wisconsin; Rebecca Kaminsky Shidel, Bauder Fashion College; Morton Cooper, Cleveland State University; Paul Gulbicki, Middlesex Community College; Del Clayton, Spalding University; Jean Shanneyfelt, Edison State Community College; Ethel Fishman, Fashion Institute of Technology; and Myrna Glenny, Fashion Institute of Design and Merchandising. With such qualitative input from so many knowledgeable people in the field of retailing, I believe this book can fulfill students' needs for a basic understanding of both the theoretical and the practical applications of retailing.

For his support and encouragement, special appreciation goes to James W. Dunlap, Dean of the College of Business Administration at the University of Akron. Special thanks also to the staff of the Marketing Department at the University of Akron; to Pat Johnson, who oversaw all the original production of this revision; to my graduate assistants, Dan Gilmore and Sandra Rapp, for their research efforts; and to my student assistant, Nannette Elrod, for her numerous contributions.

Additionally, we wish to thank the editors of Merrill Publishing for their support in this project, specifically Pam Kusma and Jim Hubbard. Finally, we are indebted to our students, who, through the questions and comments, guide us in the teaching of the basics of retailing.

BRIEF CONTENTS

CONTENTS

**PART SIX
ADDITIONAL CONSIDERATIONS: JUDGING
AND EXPLORING OPPORTUNITIES**

23

Service Retailers: Exploring Growth Opportunities   666

24

Retailing Careers: Judging Career Opportunities   686

CASES

RETAILING

PART ONE
Retail Strategies: Delineating the Dimensions of Retailing

1

Objectives

- [ ] Appreciate the complexities of operating a retail business.
- [ ] Distinguish retailers and their activities from other marketing institutions.
- [ ] Describe the importance of retailing within our nation's economy.
- [ ] Discuss the retailer's problem of striking a balance between the customer's merchandising needs and the retailer's performance needs.
- [ ] Explain what merchandising factors are involved with offering the right product. . .in the right quantities. . .in the right place. . .at the right time. . .at the right price. . .by the right appeal.
- [ ] Identify the role of operating and financial ratios in establishing performance standards for retailers.

The Nature of Retailing

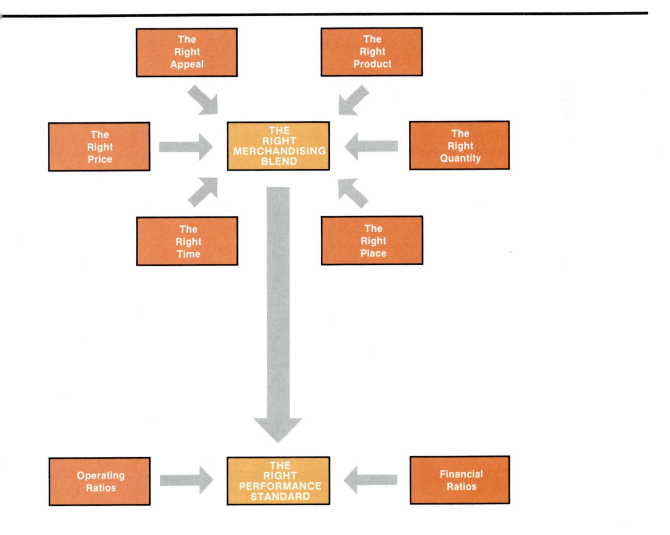

Successful retailing is a complex undertaking. "Over the years, the myth has grown that if you are not qualified or trained for any specific field you can 'make it' in retailing. After all, retailing is neither art nor science, it's sheer common sense."[1] Although common sense is a definite asset to any retailer, common sense is not enough to survive in the competitive world of retailing. The days when "rules of thumb" were sufficient to run a successful retail business have long since disappeared.

In many respects, retailing requires greater skill for survival than most other business enterprises do. Successful retailers combine the creative aspects of art with the rigid requirements of science. Retailing activities such as advertising, personal selling, merchandising, and interior store design are as much an art as a science. Other activities such as inventory control, market research, and financial accounting demand the discipline of a science.

One reason the myth of retailing has existed for so long is the misguided perception of the ease with which a person can enter the field. A retailer is not required by law to have any formal education or other qualifications to open a business. The only requirement is that an owner have a business license. Also, because the initial capital investment for starting a limited retail operation can be relatively small (compared to that for some manufacturers and wholesalers), virtually anyone can enter some form of retail operation. As a result, most business start-ups each year are retail stores. In reality, a number of formidable entry barriers restrict one from starting a retail business, including (1) stiff competition from large, integrated retail organizations, (2) sophisticated management skills needed to solve complex and dynamic problems, and (3) escalating costs of physical, human, and financial resources.

The real challenge of retailing, however, is not entering the field, but knowing how to *stay* in business—this is the critical task. The failure rate among retailers is extremely high. Although figures vary, Dun & Bradstreet estimates that approximately two out of every four retailers fail within the first year.

WHAT IS RETAILING?

The Retailer

The many definitions of retailing all share the same basic thought: **Retailing** is the business activity of selling goods or services to the final consumer. A **retailer** is any business establishment that directs its marketing efforts toward the final consumer for the purpose of selling goods or services. The key words in this definition are "the final consumer." A business selling the same product to two different buyers may in one instance perform a retailing activity but in the other instance *not* perform a retailing activity. As an example, assume that you buy a chandelier to hang in your living room. In this case, the lighting company has made a retail sale. On the other hand, assume that a home builder walks into the same store, purchases the same chandelier, and installs it in a home he or she is building. In this case, the lighting company did not make a retail sale, because the chandelier was not sold to the final consumer (user) of the product. Thus, a sale is a retail sale when the ultimate consumer purchases the product. What distinguishes a retail sale from other types of sales is the buyer's *reason* for buying. If the buyer purchases the product for personal use, the sale is considered a retail sale. If the buyer purchases the product for resale at a profit or to use in a business, the sale is *not* a retail sale. Instead, it is a business sale.

In the preceding example, is the lighting company a retailer? The answer depends on the amount of business the company does with *final* consumers. According

Retailing is the art and science of selling goods and services to the final consumer.

to the U.S. Bureau of the Census in its *Census of Retailing*, a retailer is any business establishment whose retail store can make both retail and business (nonretail) sales but is classified as a retailer when its retail sales exceed 50 percent of its total sales.

The Retail Level

Retailers are referred to as "middlemen" or "intermediaries." Both references suggest that retailers occupy a position "in the middle of" or "between" two other levels. In fact, retailers do occupy a middle position. They purchase, receive, and store products from producers and wholesalers to provide consumers with convenient locations for buying products.

As shown in Figure 1−1, retailers are part of a chain, or channel, that enables the movement of products from producer markets to local customers. This chain of business is called a marketing channel. A **marketing channel** is a team of marketing institutions that directs a flow of goods or services from the producer to the final consumer. Generally, the team consists of a producer, one or more wholesalers, and many retailers.

Although the retailer's role within the marketing channel team is covered more extensively in Chapter 3, at this point it is useful to examine some different operating characteristics distinguishing retailers from other members of the channel team (producers and wholesalers):

1. Retailers sell in smaller quantities (individual units) on a more frequent basis, whereas the less frequent typical order quantity sold by wholesalers and producers is much larger (cases and truck load lots).
2. Retailers' place of business is open to the general consuming public, but producers and wholesalers do not normally make over-the-counter sales to the general public (factory and wholesaler outlets are exceptions).
3. Retailers charge higher per-unit prices than those commonly associated with producers and wholesalers (loss leaders are a notable exception).
4. Retailers tend to use a one-price policy, whereas producers and wholesalers make more extensive use of variable prices based on some form of discounting structure.

FIGURE 1–1
The marketing channel

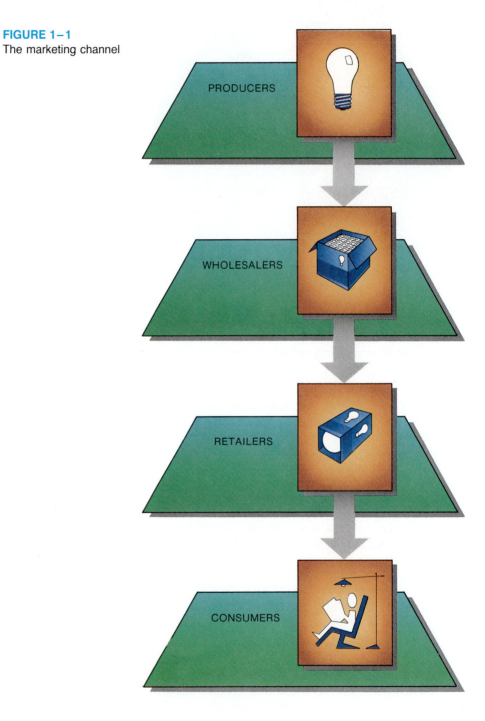

5. Retailers rely on consumers to make the initial contact by visiting the store or placing mail or telephone orders, whereas producers and wholesalers employ outside sales representatives to make initial sales contacts (at-home retailing is a notable exception).
6. Retailers place greater emphasis on the external and internal atmospherics of their physical facilities and fixtures as major merchandising tools.

Retailers place greater emphasis on internal atmospherics than do wholesalers.

Retailing has a profound effect on our society and the people it comprises. The large number of establishments engaging in retail activities, the number of people those establishments employ, and the tremendous sales volume they generate indicate the importance of retailing within our society.

Retail establishments (individual operating units) outnumber the combined total of the other two major members of the distribution channel, manufacturers and wholesalers. As Figure 1–2 shows, 1.285 million retail establishments operate within the U.S. economy, compared with 329,000 manufacturers and 404,000 wholesalers. In relative terms, there are approximately 3.9 retail establishments for each manufacturing establishment and 3.1 retailers for every wholesaler.

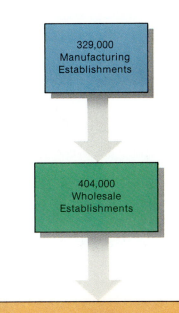

FIGURE 1–2
Number of establishments within the channel of distribution (source: U.S. Department of Commerce, *Statistical Abstract of the United States,* 105th ed. [Washington, D.C.: U.S. Department of Commerce, 1985], 518)

329,000 Manufacturing Establishments

404,000 Wholesale Establishments

1,285,000 Retail Establishments

Retailing's significance for the nation's economic welfare is reflected by the status of the retail industry as an employer of U.S. workers. Figure 1−3 portrays 1985 employment figures by industry. Retailing is the third largest employer, exceeded only by the manufacturing and service sectors. Retailers provide employment for approximately one of every six workers. If past trends continue, retail employment is expected to exceed twenty million persons by the end of the decade.

Total retail sales, as well as per capita retail sales, have netted steady gains over the last nineteen years (see Figure 1−4). Total retail sales in 1985 were about $1,374

FIGURE 1−3

Employment by industry, 1985 (source: U.S. Department of Commerce, *Statistical Abstract of the United States,* 107th ed. [Washington, D.C.: U.S. Government Printing Office, 1987], 388)

Number employed	Industry	Percentage employed
3,179,000	Agriculture, Forestry	3.0%
939,000	Mining	1.0%
6,987,000	Construction	6.5%
20,879,000	Manufacturing	19.5%
7,548,000	Transportation, Communications, Public Utilities	7.0%
4,341,000	Wholesale Trade	4.0%
17,955,000	Retail Trade	17.0%
7,005,000.	Finance, Insurance and Real Estate	6.5%
33,322,000	Services	31.0%
4,995,000	Public Administration	4.5%

Year	Total Retail Sales ($ Billions)	Annual Percentage Change (%)	Per Capita Retail Sales ($)
1967	293.0	—	1,484
1968	324.4	10.7	1,627
1969	346.7	6.9	1,722
1970	368.4	6.3	1,806
1971	406.2	10.3	1,964
1972	449.1	10.6	2,146
1973	509.5	13.4	2,411
1974	541.0	6.2	2,536
1975	588.1	8.7	2,729
1976	677.4	11.8	3,022
1977	725.2	10.3	3,300
1978	806.9	11.3	3,633
1979	899.4	11.5	4,005
1980	960.8	6.8	4,228
1981	1,043.5	8.6	4,546
1982	1,074.6	3.0	4,636
1983	1,174.0	9.3	5,018
1984	1,293.1	10.1	5,468
1985	1,373.9	6.3	5,755

FIGURE 1–4

Total and per capita retail sales, 1967 to 1985 (in current dollars)

Source: U.S. Department of Commerce, *Statistical Abstract of the United States,* 107th ed. (Washington, D.C.: U.S. Government Printing Office, 1987), 756.

billion, compared to total retail sales of $293 billion in 1967. Per capita retail sales increased from $1,484 to $5,755 during the same time period. These figures increase in significance when one considers that retail sales account for approximately 45 percent of personal income.

Retail store sales by type of business are shown in Figure 1–5. The dominance of our stomachs and our love of the automobile are readily apparent in our spending. Combined food and drink sales account for 30.1 percent of total retail sales, and automotive-related expenditures exceed 29 percent.

THE PROBLEM OF RETAILING

The retailer's problem is how to maintain a proper balance between the ability of the firm's merchandising programs to meet the needs of targeted consumers satisfactorily and the ability of the firm's administrative plans to meet the retailer's need to operate effectively and efficiently. Just as the scales of justice must judge the rights and responsibilities of two disputing parties, the "scale of retailing" must weigh the product and service needs of the customer against the operational and financial needs of the retailer. A successful retail business strikes a balance between the customer's merchandising needs and the retailer's performance standards (see Figure 1–6). In other words, a successful retail management team consists of both "out-front" merchandisers and "behind the scenes" operations managers, a problem that is at the heart of the marketing concept.

FIGURE 1–5
Estimated sales of all retail stores, by kind of business, as a percentage of total retail sales, 1985 (source: U.S. Department of Commerce, *Current Business Reports, 1985 Retail Trade,* [Washington, D.C.: U.S. Government Printing Office], 3)

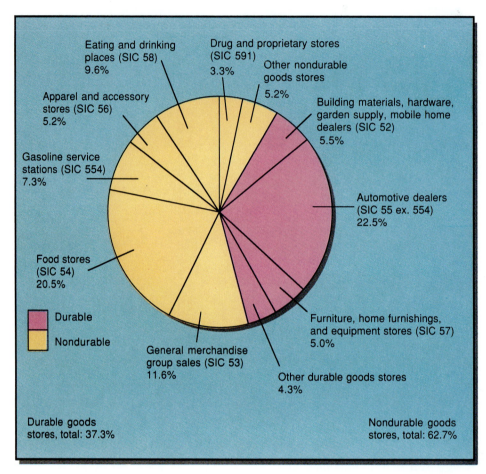

FIGURE 1–6
The scales of retailing

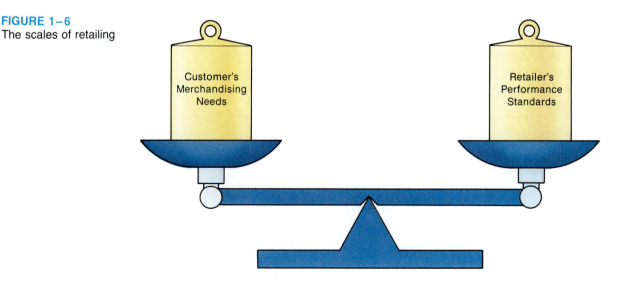

The Marketing Concept

The **marketing concept** is the philosophy that the overall goal of every business organization is to satisfy consumer needs at a profit. Before the general acceptance of the marketing concept, the role of marketing in most businesses was either "to sell what we have produced" or "to sell what we have bought." A firm adopting the marketing concept, however, strives to sell what the customer wants. "It is the willingness to recognize and understand the consumer's needs and wants and a willingness to adjust any of the marketing mix elements . . . [product, price, place, promotion] . . . to satisfy those needs and wants."[2] The marketing concept, then, stresses keying supply to demand rather than keying demand to supply. The equally important objective in addition to customer satisfaction, of course, is profit. Without profit, the firm cannot stay in business to satisfy anyone's needs. Retailers who adopt the marketing concept are neither exclusively customer driven nor profit driven; rather, they seek a workable balance between these two important goals.

For the retailer, more so than any other marketing institution, adoption of the marketing concept is an immediate problem. Because the retailer deals with consumers on a day-to-day basis, it is more directly affected than wholesalers and producers by the need to deliver consumer satisfaction at a profit. The retailer is the first to reap the benefits of consumer satisfaction but also the first to bear the brunt of consumer dissatisfaction. As described by Stanley Marcus, of Neiman-Marcus Co., "satisfaction means that customers come back."[3] Research indicates that "96 percent of dissatisfied customers never complain to the company."[4] Instead, sixty to ninety percent of them simply switch stores or brands. Insofar as it costs five times as much to attract a new customer as it does to retain an existing one, it makes sense for a store to try to ensure customer satisfaction.

Satisfying the customer at a profit is not a simple task, however. By definition, the solution to the marketing concept—and to the problem of retailing—demands the solution of two other problems: the right merchandising blend and the right performance standards.

The right **merchandising blend** matches the ingredients of the retailer's merchandising program with the decisions the consumer faces in making the right choice. Figure 1–7 illustrates this problem. The right blend includes the following six ingredients:

☐ Offering the right product
☐ In the right quantities
☐ In the right place
☐ At the right time
☐ At the right price
☐ By the right appeal

THE RIGHT MERCHANDISING BLEND

The right blend is thus the one that satisfies both customer and retailer. The right choice is the set of decisions that best satisfies the consumer's needs before, during, and after the purchase decision.

The Right Product

What makes a product "right" is a unique composite of three product elements—merchandising utilities, intrinsic qualities, and augmenting extras. Figure 1–8 portrays the concept of the **right product**.

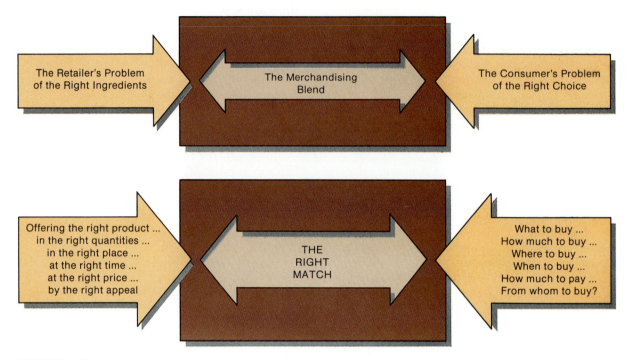

FIGURE 1–7

The problem of the right merchandising blend

Merchandising Utilities

The merchandising utilities associated with each product provide the foundation for building the right product offering. A product's **merchandising utilities** are benefits the consumer seeks in buying, using, and possessing the product. Stated differently, a product's merchandising utilities are satisfactions that either are *perceived* (a woman feels her new suit makes her look more distinguished), *real* (other people think she looks more distinguished in her new suit), *functional* (a woman's new suit is a comfortable fit), or *psychological* (she believes the new suit makes her look thinner). We must then ask what the retailer is really selling. Is it deodorant or security, cosmetics or hope, club membership or acceptance? "Without a unique point of view, general merchandise becomes commodity."[5] From the merchandising utilities perspective, the retailer is selling the expected benefits of security, hope, and acceptance.

Intrinsic Qualities

The tangible aspects of a product are also important in the consumer's evaluation of what makes a product right. **Intrinsic qualities** are the inherent physical attributes such as product form, features, materials, and workmanship that satisfy consumer needs. The intrinsic qualities of a product are important because they determine whether the product is capable of doing what it is supposed to do, looking the way it is supposed to look. These qualities determine the utility of the product. Intrinsic qualities strongly influence the consumer's perception of a product's quality, suitability, and durability. Some aspects that determine a product's intrinsic qualities are style, design, shape, weight, color, and material.

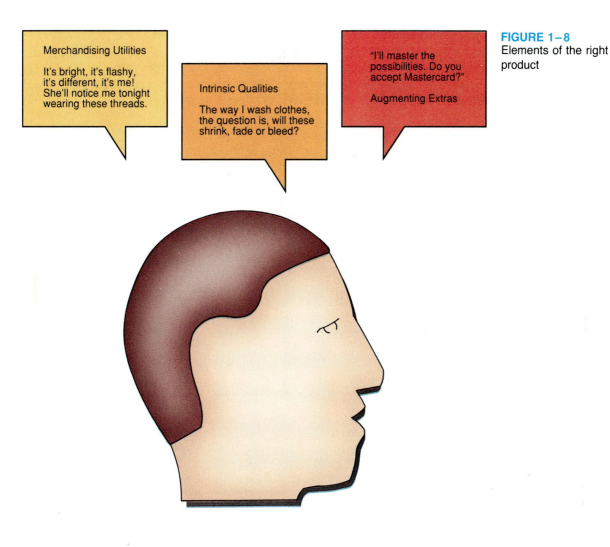

FIGURE 1–8
Elements of the right product

Augmenting Extras

Augmenting extras are auxiliary product dimensions that provide supplementary benefits to the customer. Warranties, delivery, installation, packaging, instructions, and alterations are some of the major extras that can greatly enhance the customer's satisfaction with the product. The type and extent of the benefits such extras provide depend on the customer's buying and usage behavior. For example, the additional benefit of convenience can be provided by offering home delivery and packages with handles. "One of the hottest trends of the past few years is actually a revival of a very old service—home delivery."[6] The resurgence of this augmenting extra is a result of (1) time-constrained consumers who have extensive career commitments; (2) the "me," baby boom generation, who has become accustomed to instant gratification; and (3) increased competitive actions of retailers looking for ways to differentiate themselves.[7] A customer's need for additional security and reassurance when making a purchase decision can be augmented by warranties, maintenance contracts, and liberal return policies.

The Right Quantity

The **right quantity** is the exact match between the consumer's buying and using needs and the retailer's buying and selling needs. Factors the retailer must consider in determining the right quantity are (1) the number of units, (2) the size of units, (3) the unit measurements, and (4) the unit needs.

Number of Units

For some consumers, a single unit is the right quantity: one tube of toothpaste, one pack of cigarettes, one can of Coke, or one box of bandages. For other consumers, multiple-unit quantities are the right quantity: two tubes of toothpaste, a carton of cigarettes, a six-pack of Coke, or a home first-aid kit.

A single tube of toothpaste might be the right quantity if the retailer knows that consumers either are not concerned about price, are unmarried, have only one bathroom, or shop frequently. However, a retailer whose customers are price sensitive, married, have more than one bathroom, or shop infrequently should offer larger quantities at a price savings per unit. For example, the retailer could offer two tubes of toothpaste for $1.39 instead of one tube for $.75. Burger King is attempting to capitalize on the "finger-foods" trend by introducing a new product in the "right number and size of units." Burger Bundles is a product package consisting of one--ounce burgers in $1.19 three-packs and $2.38 six-pack cartons. A twelve-pack is also under consideration.[8]

Sizes of Units

Products come in many sizes: small, medium, large, and extra large; short, regular, and long; king, queen, and regular; super, jumbo, and superjumbo; individual and family. Retailers know that the "size" labels they carry affect the kind of clientele they attract and the sales they make. A shrewd clothing retailer, for example, knows that the right size for Bill is "extra large," but the right size for Mary is one for the "full-figured woman." "Thirty percent of American women wear plus sizes, making full-figure fashions the hottest new market in the business."[9] K Mart has added a new line of Jordache clothing for bigger women. Spiegel's upscaled "For You" catalog for larger women is a successful market introduction. The Limited, Inc., has two specialty store formats that target women who need special-sized apparel: Lane Bryant and Sizes Unlimited. The right size, then, is the size that fits the customer's needs, both physically and psychologically. And even though the sizes consumers desire are usually predictable, without proper inventory control, retailers can lose many sales by stocking the wrong sizes.

Unit Measurement

Quantities are expressed in various units of measurement: inches, feet, yards, and miles; centimeters, decimeters, meters, and kilometers; ounces, pounds, and English tons; grams, kilograms, and metric tons; pints, quarts, and gallons; liters and dekaliters. Retailers realize, at least for the present, that most Americans think the inch, pound, and quart are the right quantities and the centimeter, kilogram, and liter are the wrong quantities. Recent government efforts at metric education, however, could soon make metric measurements acceptable quantity expressions.

Unit Need

Unit need refers to the purchase-quantity decisions that both retailers and consumers must make. In the consumer's purchase decision process, buying too few units of a particular product means personal or family dissatisfaction, and buying too many units results in waste or leftovers. Buying just enough, however, provides personal and family satisfaction.

The retailer's decision about quantity is in many ways more critical than the consumer's. A retailer that does not purchase enough risks stockouts and therefore lost sales. Purchasing too much causes overstocking and subsequently higher inventory carrying costs and very likely reduced profit margins if markdowns are necessary. Buying the proper quantity therefore leads to customer satisfaction and higher retail profits.

The Right Place

A retailer trying to determine the **right place** should consider the following place factors in making the decision: (1) market area, (2) market coverage, and (3) store layout and design.

A **market** is a geographic area where buyers and sellers meet to exchange money for products and services. The right marketplace for retailers is the area containing enough people to allow retailers to satisfy consumer needs at a profit. The retailer's marketplace can range from one block to several hundred miles, and it can range from thousands of miles, even countries, to a corner in a small rural crossroad town. To find the "right" market area, the retailer must consider (1) **regional markets,** (2) **local markets,** (3) **trading areas,** and (4) **site**.

Market Areas

Regional markets. For the retailer the regional market may be the entire nation or the right part of the country. Chain retailers, however, must evaluate different parts of the country to determine where to locate new stores. Many chain retailers face the decision of whether to expand into or increase their representation within various parts of the United States. "Many geographic areas are targets for continued expansion, even though more than sufficient retail store space exists—the Sunbelt and especially the Southeast are overstored and overcentered. The East and West Coasts are in balance, neither overstored nor understored. Areas of understoring include Michigan, Illinois, part of Massachusetts, and New Jersey."[10] In essence, everyone in the last decade was focusing on the Sunbelt, hence, the need to rebuild and refurbish the Rustbelt.

Local markets. At the local level, retailers must determine the right town and the right part of town. For some retailers the right town is one with a minimum population of 100,000. Large megastore merchandisers, such as Sam's Warehouse Clubs, or hypermarket retailing formats, such as Meijer and Carrefour, need a large population base to develop the sales volume they need to operate their stores profitably. On the other hand, smaller retailers are less concerned with total population but rather with the size and demographic composition of a *segment* of the population. In some cases, a smaller town might be the preferred local market if it represents a better competitive environment. For example, Best Buy Co., a Minneapolis/St. Paul operator of consumer electronics superstores, is expanding into smaller cities, such as Sioux Falls, S.D., which are not as tempting to other superstore competitors.[11] The local market strategy of Family Dollar Stores (a general merchandise discounter) and Food Lion (a supermarket) is to locate in small rural towns with minimal price competition.

The right part of town for some retailers is the central city; for others, the suburbs. An office supply store probably would not succeed in a residential suburb, and a nursery probably would not flourish downtown. Some retailers cater to upper- and middle-income consumers who often cluster in suburbs; others cater to lower-income consumers who often live in or near the inner city. Zayre, a discounter, targets lower-income innercity urban customers. Bloomingdale's selects intercity locations that cater to the upscaled, upper-income urbanite.

Trading areas.   Once the right local market has been chosen, the retailer must determine the right shopping area or the right shopping center. Some retailers go it alone, relying on their own abilities to draw customers. A convenience food store located near a residential neighborhood is an example. Other retailers rely on the drawing power of a cluster of stores. They believe that by grouping together in shopping centers or associating with anchor stores (such as department stores, discount houses, and supermarkets), they can create the "right" place. For Bob Evans, a family restaurant chain in eleven eastern and midwestern states, the right trading area is incorporated into its "I-75 strategy." This plan calls for restaurants to be located on a major interstate highway and within the immediate vicinity of a major shopping center or mall with a minimum of 50,000 residents living within a five-mile radius of the proposed location.[12]

Site.   For the freestanding retailer, the right site allows the store to intercept customers on their way to work or on their way home; is readily accessible to consumers from the standpoints of approaching, entering, and exiting; and is visible to passing consumer traffic. Within a shopping mall, the right site may be on the ground floor or at one end of the mall, or it may avoid customers who are incompatible with the operation (i.e., with complementary neighboring retailers). A pet shop, for example, might discourage potential patrons of a bridal boutique.

Market Coverage

The right place may be every place, a few places, or a single place. As part of the "right place" decision, retailers must decide whether they want **intensive market coverage, selective market coverage,** or **exclusive market coverage** (Figure 1–9).

Intensive market coverage.   With an intensive strategy, the retailer selects and uses as many retail outlets as are justified to obtain "blanket" coverage of an entire market

Intensive Coverage:
"Everyplace"

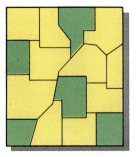

Selective Coverage:
"A Few Places"

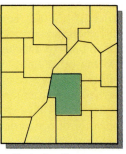

Exclusive Coverage:
"A Place"

area. Generally, convenience-goods retailers use an intensive market strategy. (Convenience goods are products and services consumers want to purchase with a minimum of effort; examples are snack foods and soft drinks.) A good strategy for a convenience food chain (such as 7-Eleven stores) might be to locate a store on every major traffic artery leading into each important residential area in town. Because the retailer who employs an intensive coverage strategy must try to serve *all* customers within a given market area, the right place is *everyplace*. The ultimate intensive market coverage is to offer home delivery. Domino's Pizza has become the second largest chain in the pizza industry by offering home delivery convenience under the theme "one call does it all." Its success has forced number-one Pizza Hut to adopt a similar strategy in many of its markets.[13]

Selective market coverage. When a retailer sells shopping goods, the logical strategy is to cover selective markets. (Shopping goods are products that consumers want to compare for style, price, or quality before making a purchase decision; examples are clothing, furniture, and appliances.) For these products a retailer should choose enough locations to ensure adequate coverage of selected target markets. The number of outlets the retailer establishes in the selective coverage strategy should equal the number of market segments served. Generally speaking, chain retailers such as apparel stores, department stores, hardware stores, discount-department stores, auto repair shops, and drugstores follow a selective market coverage strategy. In this case, the right place is the *select* place.

Exclusive market coverage. In an exclusive market coverage strategy, the retailer elects to use one location to serve either an entire market area or some major segment of that market. An exclusive strategy is ideal for retailers who sell specialty goods. (Specialty goods are those that consumers are willing to put forth considerable effort to obtain.) Specialty goods manufacturers often enter into exclusive arrangements with certain retailers. The advantages to manufacturers are more intense selling efforts on the part of their retailers and an exclusive, high-quality image for their products. By the same token the exclusive retailer enjoys several advantages. Among the advantages are (1) the retailer's store image is enhanced because of the exclusive merchandise and (2) no *direct* competition exists for the *brands* of merchandise carried. For these retailers the right place is *a* place. Many specialty stores dealing in well-known, prestigious products such as Mercedes-Benz, Jaguar, and Steuben Glass use this form of market coverage.

In sum, market coverage is related to the nature of the retailer's product mix. As shown in Figure 1–10, retailers attempt to achieve intensive coverage when their product mix is convenience oriented. At the other end of the continuum, using one outlet (exclusive coverage) is most appropriate when merchandising specialty goods. An intermediate strategy (selective coverage) is used when shopping goods predominate the product mix.

Store Layout and Design

Store layout and design are two essential elements to consider in creating the right shopping atmosphere for the chosen target market. The retailer should consider floor locations, shelf positions, in-store location, and display location.

Floor location. In some department stores the right place in a store for a product, department, display, event, or activity may be either the basement, the first floor, or

FIGURE 1–10

The relationship between market coverage and product mix

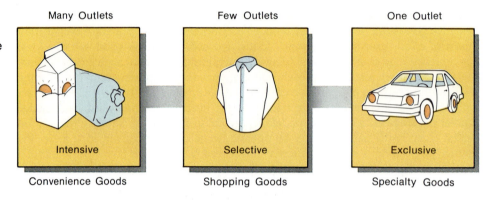

the top floor. Customers often think of the basement as the "bargain basement," the first floor as the "main floor," and the top floor as the "exclusive floor." The right floor is the one that is most consistent with where customers think things should be and where the retailer can provide the level of service consumers expect.

Shelf position.   Retail merchandisers and marketers generally agree that the best place to shelve merchandise is at **eye level**. Placing merchandise at eye level is especially important when the retailer wants to attract new or additional sales. For example, in a supermarket, Campbell often will place several popular varieties of its soups such as tomato, chicken noodle, and vegetable beef at *non–eye-level* positions. These soups are in great demand and customers will seek them out. New varieties and slower-selling varieties, however, often are positioned at eye level to generate additional sales.

In-store location.   The right place within a store for a product, a customer service, or a display is the one that best conforms to customer in-store traffic patterns. The right place therefore might be either in front, in back, along the sides, or in the center. The in-store layout of most supermarkets, for example, is based on the "ring of perishables" principle. Food retailers know that consumers purchase their perishables (eggs, milk, butter, meat, vegetables, etc.) every week. By placing perishables in a ring around the store (sides and back), supermarket retailers have learned that they can draw customers into other sections of the store. Supermarkets using this technique greatly increase the chances that customers will pass by and purchase other products in the store's total merchandise offering. Supermarket managers believe that the result of their strategy is additional impulse sales—purchases the consumer did not plan to make. Wellpet, a pet-care specialty chain in Oregon and northern California, uses a similar principle in its stores, where a wood veneer pathway guides customers through the store, thereby enhancing customer exposure to the firm's total product line.[14]

Another strategy some retailers use is the attractors and interceptors strategy. Many department stores place merchandise such as men's suits, better women's wear, and other big-ticket items in the back of the store to act as attractors, drawing customers through the entire length of the store. In the process, customers are intercepted by departments carrying complementary product lines, such as shirts, scarves, and jewelry. Because the interceptor items normally produce a higher percentage of profit per unit for the store, this layout strategy contributes to the store's overall profit rate.

Display location.   Retailers use displays to draw attention to their product offerings. The right place must be found for them. Whether at end-of-aisle, at the checkout stand, or a freestanding location near high-traffic areas, the right place is the "visible" place for these special displays. For example, supermarkets often place their weekly features of cakes, cookies, and pies at highly visible, end-of-the-aisle sites where frequently purchased items such as breads, buns, and rolls are located.

Within the display itself, "right is also right": the best position within a display is the right side. The right-side bias is based on the belief that most consumers view a display from right to left. So right is "right" because it is the first place consumers look.

The Right Time

The right time to sell is when consumers are willing to buy. Because time affects different types of consumers differently, retailers must develop retailing strategies that coincide with consumer buying times. With two-income families approaching fifty percent, time is a commodity that has become scarce. People are willing to buy time to make life simpler. Time convenience is an issue that cannot be ignored by retailers in their tactical and strategic plans.[15] Some particular times that retailers consider in developing time strategies are (1) calendar times, (2) seasonal times, (3) life times, and (4) personal times.

Calendar Times

In the category of calendar times, consider times of the day, times of the week, times of the month, and times of the year. Because consumers' behavior is largely geared to these times, any one of these times can be an opportune time for the retailer.

Times of the day.   Whether morning, noon, afternoon, or evening, many retailers have businesses with daily peak periods. Restaurants, for example, have definite

The right place for special displays is where they are most visible.

"right times" of the day: breakfast, lunch, and dinner times. For most restaurants these are the only times for sales and profits. "Bennigan's, a unit of Pillsbury Co., puts stopwatches on its restaurants' tables and promises to serve in 15 minutes or [the meal is] free. Pizza Hut offers a second pizza free if the first takes more than five minutes."[16] In essence, the lunch hour has become the third rush hour. Evenings are "most times" for motion picture theaters. By reducing prices for the afternoon matinee, however, the theater manager can make afternoons a "sometimes" for some moviegoers. Morning and afternoon rush hours are the right times for some retailers who want to intercept consumers going to and from work.

Times of the week.   Certain days of the week are better times to sell some products than other days. Sunday is the right time of the week for some consumers because they have free time to shop. On the other hand, Sunday might not be the right time for other consumers, because for them it is "God's time" or in their area it is an illegal time (where Sunday closing laws are in effect). Blue Monday is often a poor time for a retailer, because the consumer's mood usually is bad at the start of a new work week.

Times of the month.   Paydays and bill-paying day are two examples of times of the month of which every retailer should be aware. Paydays are usually once, twice, or four times a month, and they could very well be the most important times for the retailer regardless of when they occur. With money in their pockets, consumers are most susceptible to advertising, new merchandise, and old merchandise clearance sales. Bill-paying days are the right time to collect on past credit sales. However, they usually are poor times for making sales.

Times of the year.   Holiday seasons often represent the "best times" of the year for retailers. Christmas, Easter, Thanksgiving, Memorial Day, Labor Day, and New Year's Eve are "special times" for consumers, and provide special opportunities to retailers. For many retailers, back-to-school time is second only to Christmas in its potential to generate sales.

Seasonal Times

Consumers' buying patterns change with the seasons of the year. These are not only spring, summer, fall, and winter but perhaps football, basketball, and baseball seasons; or planting, growing, and harvesting seasons; or even opera, social, and theater seasons. Most retailers know which times are best for selling seasonal goods in their geographic and cultural region. Retailers also know that the best part of the season is the beginning of the season, when they can sell goods at full markup. They also know that during the middle and latter part of the season, consumers are thinking about the next season, and therefore the retailer must mark down the prices on certain merchandise.

Life Times

In everyone's life there are special times—births, weddings, graduations, and many more—that are rare times for the retailer to make a special effort to sell merchandise. They are also the right time for the retailer because consumers are in one of their

(opposite) Back to school is the right time of year for many retailers. (Courtesy of Gold Circle Stores)

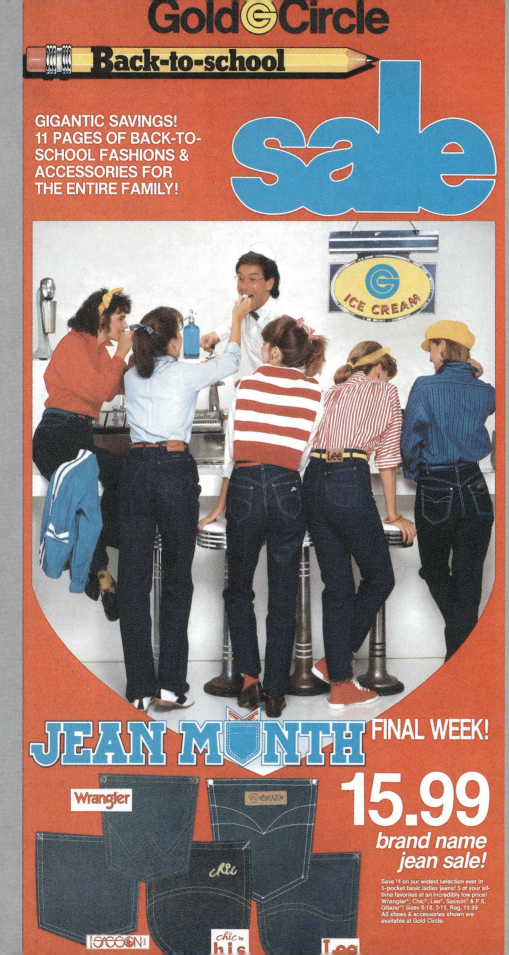

most susceptible buying moods. At these times the retailer can generate additional sales by "trading up" the consumer, that is, inducing the customer to buy a higher--quality, higher-price, or markup product or to add features and extras to the selection.

Personal Times

Every consumer experiences working times, leisure times, and maintenance times. Every retailer should be sensitive to the merchandising times of the weekday, the weekend, the workday, and the day off. A building materials firm that caters to the home handyman, for example, makes most sales on Friday and Saturday. A company that produces many sporting goods, AMF, advertises that "we make weekends."

For the retailer, all of the times just discussed can be either good or bad times, fast or slow times, profitable or unprofitable times. In summary, a right time is any time that helps the retailer either avoid losing sales or create new sales that ordinarily would not have been made.

The Right Price

The **right price** is the amount consumers are willing to pay and retailers are willing to accept in exchange for merchandise and services. Consumers experience various forms of prices in the marketplace. They encounter odd prices, even prices, prices with coupons, sticker prices, bid prices, bargain prices, status prices, sales prices, manufacturers' suggested list prices, and retailers' prices, among many other price forms. Like consumers, retailers also face different forms of prices. There are markup prices, markdown prices, price lines, base prices, unit prices, package prices, promotional prices, regular prices, loss-leader prices, illegal prices, and prices that include accessories.

In developing a pricing strategy, the retailer must price merchandise low enough to generate sales but high enough to cover costs and make a fair profit. At the same time the retailer must consider pricing products in a manner consistent with consumers' expectations. F.A.O. Schwartz, a purveyor of pricey playthings, operates under the assumption that there is a large market for fashion toys. Buyers of expensive toys are not motivated as much by price as by the product.[17] Unique products, special services, and exciting store atmospherics equals successful prestige pricing. For example, $25 may be the subjective value a consumer places on a pair of tire chains in July, but in January that same person may agree that $40 is okay. On the other hand, many consumers would rather be stuck in the snow than pay $75 for the chains.

The right price is one that is satisfactory to the customer not only before the sale but after the sale as well. A consumer who is willing to pay a "premium" price for a product generally expects premium performance. If the product does not display this expected level of performance, the customer might not ever buy products from the same retailer again. Because retailers depend heavily on repeat business, not meeting consumers' performance expectations would be disastrous for most retailers.

Finally, the right price must be competitive—if not with all competitors, then at least with those in the same trading area or with those who have similar operations. Competitive pricing means setting a price that is about the same as that found in similar stores within the same trading area.

(opposite) The right appeal is one that reaches its target market.

WESTIES™

The right shoe
at the right time...

Because timing is everything.

The Right Appeal

The **right appeal** represents the **right message** to the **right audience** through the **right media**. Though the product, place, and price are right, the retailer will not be successful unless it can communicate its offering effectively to its target market. The retailer must inform and persuade consumers that its product mix precisely meets their particular needs. In making the right appeals, the retailer's problem is how to identify the target audience, create the appropriate message, and select the best medium of communication.

The Right Message

The right message is the right thing to say (the right message *content*) presented in the right *manner*. The right message content emphasizes what consumers are most concerned about and explains how the retailer's offerings can satisfy those concerns. For example, homemakers deciding among supermarkets may be more concerned with what they buy and how much they pay (e.g., selection and value) than from whom, where, and when they buy. In this case the best message emphasizes the *what* and *how much*. When deciding among furriers, however, the same individuals may be more concerned with what and from whom they buy (e.g., quality and status) and less concerned with where and when they buy and how much they pay. Brooks Brothers, the "paragon of pin stripes," sells only private-label merchandise to the image-conscious moneyed consumer at selected locations within up-scale shopping malls and avenues.[18] In this situation the retailer should emphasize the *what* and *from whom*.

The retailer must determine which purchase factors are most important to the consumer's buying decision and emphasize those appeals in the message. After gathering consumer information, a retailer may decide to make a **product appeal**, emphasizing the rightness of its products for consumers; a **patronage appeal**, emphasizing the rightness of the store, location, and hours; or a **price appeal**. Or, the retailer may make a combined appeal if it thinks several "right choice" elements are important to the consumer.

In structuring the message content, the retailer must also choose between direct action and indirect action. **Direct-action messages** urge the consumer to come to the store now either to take advantage of a sale or to redeem a coupon. **Indirect-action messages,** on the other hand, have long-run goals. They attempt to change consumers' attitudes toward the retailer by cultivating its image as the "right" place for the consumer to buy (e.g., "When you think of fine furniture, think of us"). Both types of messages have advantages and disadvantages. Direct-action messages usually result in immediate sales but normally do not encourage regular patronage. Indirect-action messages encourage regular patronage, but the retailer must invest considerable time and money to develop it.

The retailer must not only present the right message content but also present it in the right manner, by choosing either a logical or an emotional approach. Using the **logical approach,** a retailer makes a factual presentation about its offering and then shows consumers why buying from that source is the "right" choice. For example, a retailer might say, "Compare prices, and you'll see why you should shop with us." A retailer that uses an **emotional approach** speaks not to what consumers think, but to what they feel (pride, fear, etc.). Retailers that create emotional appeals in their messages try to incite the following among consumers:

1. Sense of loyalty ("Shop your local hometown merchants")
2. Sense of security ("We sell only brand-name merchandise")

3. Sense of fair play ("Please, before you buy, check our. . .")
4. Sense of tradition and stability ("Serving you from the same location for 25 years")
5. Sense of adventure ("A new shopping experience. . .")
6. Sense of success (". . .the largest dealer in the state")
7. Sense of belonging ("Shop with us, where only the discriminating shop"), among other target emotions

The Right Audience

The right message must be directed to the right audience. In seeking to determine the right audience, the retailer can make one of two choices—either pursue the mass-market audience or pursue one or more target-market audiences.

Mass-market audience. A retailer that decides to appeal to all of the consumers within a market area should use a broad appeal to the mass market. By using a broad appeal the retailer hopes to attract a few customers from all segments of the market. The message must be general enough to appeal to a wide range of consumers and their needs but specific enough to stimulate consumers to action.

Target-market audience. The retailer may decide to appeal to a select group of customers within a market area. The process of dividing a market into smaller sub-sets is called *market segmentation,* and the market segment to which the retailer directs its appeal is the *target market.* Any market can be segmented along the lines of various characteristics. The three most common of these are demographic characteristics, patronage motives, and psychographic profiles.

Demographic characteristics include age, sex, income, race, occupation, family structure, and social class. A record store targeting upper-income teenagers is an example of a retailer segmenting the market by demographic characteristics (in this case, age and income). "The entry of fashion into children's wear has created opportunities for market segmentation. Children's retail shops run the gamut from the well-rounded Kids 'R' Us, whose supermarket-size stores discount favored national brands, to GapKids, an off-shoot of The Gap Stores Inc. Just as Benetton 012 and Esprit Kids take their style cues from their adult namesakes, GapKids offers junior versions of the Gap's colorful sportswear.[19] Patronage motives describe consumers' shopping and buying habits. How much they buy, when, where, what, and why they buy are all patronage market dimensions. A retailer catering to working mothers who buy after work is an example of a target market selected on the basis of patronage characteristics. Mother's Work is a specialty apparel retailer focusing on pregnant career women.

Psychographic profiles are composite "pictures" of different consumer life-styles—living patterns that are the result of a consumer's activities, interests, and opinions. This patterned style of living stems from an individual's perceptions and attitudes; it represents a behavioral profile of an individual's psychological makeup. Both conforming and nonconforming life-styles are behavioral reactions to expected and accepted modes of living. To illustrate, one local tavern might appeal to politically inactive sedentary gentlemen who believe a woman's place is in the home and that hunting and fishing are adventurous men's activities. Another local tavern, however, might cater to men who actively participate in rugged athletic sports such as football, who feel that women should have equal opportunities and responsibilities, and who are politically active. Regardless of which target market the retailer selects, the right message appeals to the needs and desires of its chosen market segment.

tradition
quality and value for 30 years

**Famous maker sport shirts
comparable in quality at $25**

A stock-up price on long sleeve, patterned sport shirts from two prestigious names. Polyester/cotton, sizes S-M-L-XL. First quality.

marshalls price
9⁹⁹

**Famous maker twill pants
comparable in quality at $40**

From a leading sportswear name, belted slacks for dress or casual. Assorted colors, in polyester/cotton twill. Sizes 32 to 40. First quality.

marshalls price
16⁹⁹

**Famous maker dress shirts
comparable in quality at $20**

Terrific value on these long sleeve, machine wash-and-dry polyester/cotton dress shirts. Assorted patterns. Sizes 14½ to 17. First quality.

marshalls price
9⁹⁹

**Famous maker dress pants
comparable in quality at $35**

A collection of famous maker gabardines in polyester/wool. Plain or pleated fronts. Assorted colors. Sizes 30 to 40. First quality.

marshalls price
16⁹⁹

Designer and famous maker ties. First quality. Pre-ticketed by the famous makers at 8.50 to $20.   **marshalls price 4.99 to 8.99**

The Right Media

The means by which a retailer communicates its product offering to consumers is just as important as the content. Typically, a retailer has several choices in reaching an audience: newspapers, television, radio, magazines, telephone, direct mail, window displays, outdoor signs, in-store demonstrations, and personal sales representatives. The right medium for the retailer effectively and economically reaches the largest portion of the mass or target audience.

Having discussed those elements of the right merchandising blend, let us now examine the other half of the equation for a successful retail organization—the **right performance standards**.

THE RIGHT PERFORMANCE STANDARDS

Retailers must have some means by which to judge both the operational and financial performance of their firms. Several operating and financial ratios can aid their judgment. These ratios concisely express the relationship between elements in the income statement and the balance sheet. Because these ratios have gained wide acceptance within the general business community as well as within specific retail trades, they have become trade standards by which retailers can judge their individual performances against national and trade norms. These standard ratios are published annually (or more frequently) by private firms such as Dun & Bradstreet, trade organizations such as the National Retail Merchants Association, and public agencies such as the Small Business Administration. Within individual retail organizations, historical comparisons can be made between current ratios and past ratios. The availability of these external and internal standards helps each retailer to make meaningful judgments on the firm's operating efficiency and financial ability. Ratio analysis provides a "snapshot" of the relative health of the retailer's operating and financial condition and serves as a control to identify conditions deviating from established norms.

Operating Ratios

Retailers compute some ratios to gain insight into the firm's operating performance. Retailers use **operating ratios** to compute relationships between elements in the income statement. Ratio computations simply divide one element of the income statement (e.g., operating profit) by another element (e.g., net sales). A standard practice is to convert ratios into percentages by multiplying the results by 100. Of particular concern to most retailers are operating ratios involving net sales (i.e., operating profit divided by net sales). Operating ratios are discussed in Chapter 7.

Financial Ratios

Financial ratios identify relationships among elements of a balance sheet or between a balance sheet element and an element in the income statement. The most widely used financial ratios are those reported by Dun & Bradstreet. These key performance measurements help the retailer make meaningful comparisons between the firm's financial performance and the national median performance of similar retailers. These ratios are also useful in establishing realistic financial objectives. In evaluating the firm's performance against these national norms, however, the retailer must recognize that the firm's individual circumstances might prohibit direct comparison. The ratios of retailing are used as basic reference points and not as absolute guidelines for

(opposite) The right price continues to be satisfactory to the customer after the sale.

judging financial performance levels for a given retail firm. Chapter 7 provides more in-depth coverage of financial ratios in the discussion of managing the firm's resources.

SUMMARY

At first glance retailing might appear to be a simple task, but the successful operation of a retail store is, in fact, a very complex and difficult undertaking—a truth vividly illustrated by the number of retail enterprises that fail each year.

A retailer is a business organization within a marketing channel of distribution that makes most of its sales to final consumers. Retailers differ from other marketing institutions in that they (1) sell in small quantities on a more frequent basis, (2) open their place of business to the general public, (3) charge higher per-unit prices, (4) use a one-price policy, (5) rely on consumers to make the initial contact, and (6) use store atmospherics as a major merchandising tool. Evidence of their importance lies in the number of retail establishments and the many people they employ.

The basic task of retailing is to balance the product and service needs of the consuming public with the operational and financial needs of the retail organization; in other words, find the right merchandising blend to ensure the right performance standards. Elements of the retailer's right blend are offering the right products in the right quantities, in the right place, at the right time, at the right price, by the right appeal. Performance standards can be expressed in terms of operating ratios and financial ratios.

KEY TERMS AND CONCEPTS

augmenting extras	price appeal
direct-action message	product appeal
emotional approach	regional market
exclusive market coverage	retailer
eye-level merchandising	retailing
financial ratios	right appeal
indirect-action message	right audience
intensive market coverage	right media
intrinsic qualities	right message
local market	right performance standards
logical approach	right place
market	right price
marketing channel	right product
marketing concept	right quantity
merchandising blend	right time
merchandising utilities	selective market coverage
operating ratios	site
patronage appeal	trading area

REVIEW QUESTIONS

1. What is retailing?
2. Describe the marketing channel of distribution. Where does the retailer fit into this organization?

3. How do retailers differ from other members of the marketing channel of distribution?
4. What is the problem of retailing?
5. Define the marketing concept and discuss how it relates to the problem of retailing.
6. List the six ingredients of the right merchandising blend.
7. What makes a product right? Describe each element.
8. Discuss the consequences the retailer faces in misjudging unit need.
9. What is the "right place" in terms of regional and local markets, trading areas, and site?
10. Compare and contrast intensive, selective, and exclusive market coverage.
11. Why is eye-level merchandising an important concept in making display decisions?
12. Why is "right is right" in positioning products within a display?
13. Identify the opportune times on a retailer's calendar.
14. What is the right price?
15. Describe the three types of message appeals used in creating the right appeal.
16. How do direct-action messages differ from indirect-action messages?
17. Compare and contrast operating ratios and financial ratios.

ENDNOTES

1. Ruth A. Keyes and Ronald A. Cushman, *Essentials of Retailing* (New York: Fairchild, 1977), 6.
2. Franklin S. Houston, "The Marketing Concept: What It Is and What It Is Not," *Journal of Marketing* 50 (April 1986): 86.
3. Joe Agnew, "Marcus on Marketing: Profits are By-products of Rendering Satisfactory Customer Service." *Marketing News,* 10 April 1987, 16.
4. Dale R. Harley, "Customer Satisfaction Tracking Improves Sales Productivity, Morale of Retail Chains," *Marketing News,* 22 June 1984, 15.
5. Muriel J. Adams, "Robots In The Future?" *Stores* (April 1988): 40.
6. "Home Delivery: An Old Idea Born Again." *Meretrends* (Winter 1987): 4–5.
7. Ibid.
8. Patricia Winters, "What's on the Doorstep of BK? It's Burger Bundles." *Advertising Age,* 12 Jan. 1987, 1.
9. Patricia Strand, "Big Idea Links K Mart, Jordache." *Advertising Age,* 2 March 1987, 58.
10. Joan E. Primo and Howard L. Green, "To Mall or Not to Mall: Where Retail Opportunities Lie." *Marketing News,* 10 Feb. 1988, 10.
11. Mary J. Pitzer, "Electronics 'Superstores' May Have Blown a Fuse." *Business Week,* 8 June 1987, 90, 94.
12. Joe Agnew, "Breakfast Only Image Shed as Bob Evans Flees the Farm." *Marketing News,* 5 June 1987, 13.
13. See Raymond Serafin, "Escalating Pizza Wars Move to the Streets." *Advertising Age,* 14 April 1986, 26. Also, see Kevin T. Higgins, "Home Delivery is Helping Pizza to Battle Burgers." *Marketing News,* 1 Aug. 1986, 1.
14. "Wellpet: Felix and Fido Create Its Niche." *Chain Store Age Executive* (September 1986): 74.
15. Susan Benway, "Presto! The Convenience Industry: Making Life a Little Simpler." *Business Week,* 27 April 1987, 86.
16. Robert Johnson and Dae Tononarive, "Eatery Chains Pour on Speed at Lunchtime." *The Wall Street Journal,* 1 Feb. 1988.
17. Amy Dunkin, "F.A.O. Schwartz: A Short Move—and Big Plans." *Business Week,* 27 April 1986, 32–33.
18. Mark Maremont, "Marks & Spencer Pays a Premium for Pinstripes." *Business Week,* 18 April 1988, 67.
19. Jonathan B. Levine and Amy Dunkin, "Toddlers in $90 Suits? You Gotta Be Kidding." *Business Week,* 21 Sept. 1987, 52.

RELATED READINGS

Adams, Muriel J., "Robots in the Future." *Stores* (April 1988): 41.

Cronin, J. Joseph, Jr., and Joyce, Mary L., "An Investigation Between Marketing and Financial Strategies in Retail Firms." In *Developments in Marketing Science, Proceedings,* edited by J.D. Lindquist, 288–93. Academy of Marketing Science, 1984.

Dickinson, Roger, "Innovations in Retailing." *Retail Control* (June–July 1983): 30–54.

Greensmith, Denis S., "New Retail Strategies for a Changing World Business Environment." *Retail Control* (June–July 1984): 2–17.

Hawes, Jon M., and Varble, Dale L., "The Marketing Concept and Organizational Goals." In *Marketing: The Next Decade, Proceedings,* edited by D.M. Klein and A.E. Smith, 131–34. Southern Marketing Association, 1985.

Hinnefeld, Edwin, "Competing in a Changing Retail Marketplace." *Retail Control* (September 1983): 9–19.

Hirschman, Elizabeth C., "Aesthetics, Ideologies, and the Limits of the Marketing Concept." *Journal of Marketing* 47 (Summer 1983): 45–55.

"Kolter: Rethink the Marketing Concept." *Marketing News,* 14 Sept. 1984, 1, 22, 24.

Kornblum, Warren, "Survival Tactics for Retailers." *Retail Control* (August 1984): 29–41.

Lusch, Robert F., and Laczniak, Gene R., "The Evolving Marketing Concept, Competitive Intensity and Organizational Performance." *Journal of the Academy of Marketing Science* 15 (Fall 1987): 1–13.

Marcus, Stanley, "Retailing's Urgent Need for Creativity as Viewed by Stanley Marcus." *Retail Control* (February 1984): 19–27.

Nason, Robert W., and Bitta, Albert J. Della, "The Incidence and Consumer Perceptions of Quantity Surcharges." *Journal of Retailing* 59 (Summer 1983): 40–54.

Sharma, Subhash, and Mahajan, Vijay, "Early Warning Indicators of Business Failure." *Journal of Marketing* 44 (Fall 1980): 80–89.

Sheth, Jagdish, N., "Emerging Trends for the Retailing Industry." *Journal of Retailing* 59 (Fall 1983): 6–18.

Turpin, Miles, "In Search of Retail Marketing Excellence." *Retail Control* (August 1984): 11–26.

2

Objectives

☐ Appreciate the need for strategic retail management and planning.

☐ Develop an organizational mission statement that can serve as a focus for the firm's current and future activities.

☐ Construct the organizational objectives for achieving the organization's mission.

☐ Conduct a portfolio analysis and classify different business units on the basis of their market and cash flow positions.

☐ Identify the various types of growth and performance opportunities and evaluate the appropriate strategies associated with each type of opportunity.

☐ Discuss the basic components of the retailing plan.

Strategic Retail Management

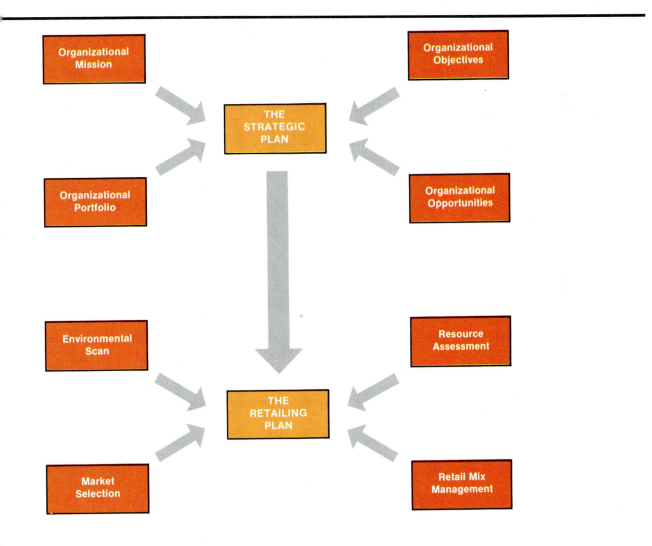

Some retail organizations have been slow to adopt strategic planning as part of their management effort. Retailers are traditionally action oriented and more concerned with short-run problems and results. "Historically, retailing has tended to emphasize the tactical rather than the strategic."[1] For example, within the department store business, merchants rather than strategists dominated the ranks of top management. Merchandising was the appropriate driving force of the business, during the introduction and growth stages of its retail life cycles; however, in a mature economy with intensive competition, strategic thinking and execution become essential.[2] Their resistance to and skepticism of the long-run character of strategic planning are based on a number of factors that differentiate retailing from other business enterprises. Some of the more commonly cited factors are (1) rapid and unpredictable changes in the retail market, (2) intense and diverse competition, (3) shorter retail institutional life cycles, (4) unstable economic climate, and (5) the need for flexibility in the face of the changing retailing scene.[3] As Rosenbloom points out, however, "Careful analysis and planning over a relatively long period are the necessary requisites for the development of successful long-term strategies—even in the fast-paced and rapidly changing world of retailing."[4]

STRATEGIC RETAIL MANAGEMENT

Planning is essential if the retail organization is to survive and prosper in the competitive environment associated with consumer markets. **Strategic retail management** is the process of planning the organization, implementation, and control of all the firm's activities. It involves making both strategic and tactical decisions for different levels within an organization. The strategic management process consists of two major components: the strategic plan and the retailing plan. The schematic diagram at the start of this chapter illustrates the relationship between these two plans and identifies the major activities under each plan.

Before discussing each of these plans, it is instructive to examine the issue of strategic versus tactical planning as it relates to the various levels (corporate, strategic business unit, store, department, and product line) within the retail organization. *Corporate planning* is conducted by the corporate headquarters management team and is directed at developing an overall plan for the entire organization. The corporate planning process is strategic because it establishes the general framework for the firm's actions over an extended period of time. As a broad statement based on experience, intuition, and analytical judgment, the corporate plan outlines the organization's general business intent. *Business planning* involves developing a course of action for each of the **strategic business units** (SBUs) within the retail organization. An SBU is a business division with "a clear market focus, an identifiable strategy, and an identifiable set of competitors."[5] Business planning identifies the role of each SBU in the overall corporate strategy.

> In retailing enterprise, SBUs are probably best defined in terms of types of stores or store formats and market areas. For general merchandise retailers, it may be desirable to define SBUs even more narrowly in terms of merchandise categories within their stores . . . the object of dividing a company's operations into SBUs is to permit a detailed strategic appraisal of such units.[6]

The planning process continues with the development of plans for each store, department, and product line within each SBU. *Store, department, and product line planning* is more tactical than strategic. It focuses more on current problems and decisions faced in implementing SBU and corporate strategy.

Figure 2–1 presents planning levels for a large retail organization. Planning at the corporate level is conducted by upper-level management for The May Depart-

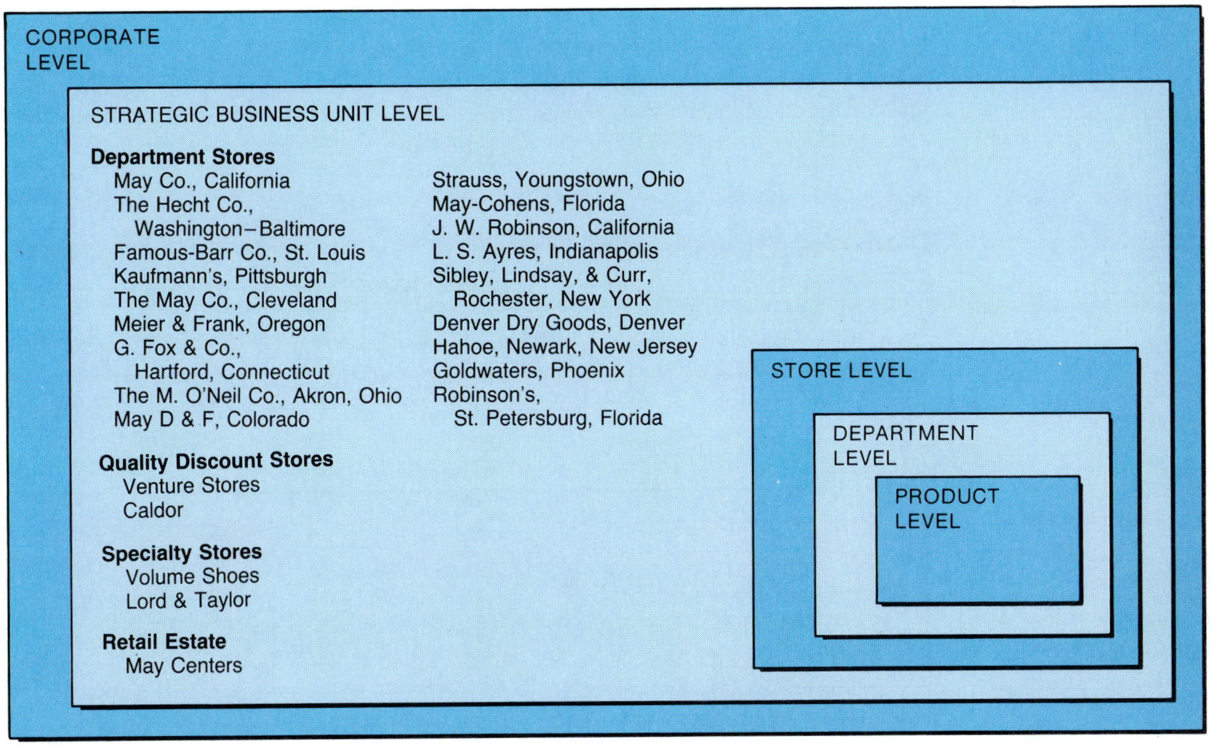

CORPORATE LEVEL

STRATEGIC BUSINESS UNIT LEVEL

Department Stores

May Co., California
The Hecht Co.,
   Washington–Baltimore
Famous-Barr Co., St. Louis
Kaufmann's, Pittsburgh
The May Co., Cleveland
Meier & Frank, Oregon
G. Fox & Co.,
   Hartford, Connecticut
The M. O'Neil Co., Akron, Ohio
May D & F, Colorado

Strauss, Youngstown, Ohio
May-Cohens, Florida
J. W. Robinson, California
L. S. Ayres, Indianapolis
Sibley, Lindsay, & Curr,
   Rochester, New York
Denver Dry Goods, Denver
Hahoe, Newark, New Jersey
Goldwaters, Phoenix
Robinson's,
   St. Petersburg, Florida

Quality Discount Stores

Venture Stores
Caldor

Specialty Stores

Volume Shoes
Lord & Taylor

Retail Estate

May Centers

STORE LEVEL

DEPARTMENT LEVEL

PRODUCT LEVEL

FIGURE 2–1
Business planning levels: The May Department Stores Co.

ment Stores Company in their corporate headquarters in St. Louis. Corporate plans set the parameters for the business plans developed by each of the firm's SBUs (business segments and operating divisions). Using the corporate and business plans as guidelines, store, merchandise, and department managers develop tactical plans for each store, department, and product line. In a small retail organization such as a local chain or independent retail operator, the entire planning process may be conducted by one or a small group of individuals in a single location.

Keeping in mind that planning can be both strategic and tactical and occurs at several levels within the organization, we now turn our attention to a more comprehensive examination of the strategic plan and the retailing plan. The discussion of the strategic plan emphasizes the large, diversified retail organization; the retailing plan is more applicable to a single retail business or any SBU regardless of size and composition.

THE STRATEGIC PLAN

Strategic planning aims to develop a long-term course of action that will provide an overall sense of direction for a retail organization's business activities. The strategic plan is a grand design or blueprint for ensuring success in all of the organization's business endeavors. A strategic plan is directed at achieving a strategic fit between the organization's capabilities (present and future) and its environmental opportunities (present and future). A good fit positions the organization to enable it to sustain competitive assets and overcome competitive liabilities, as well as to anticipate external environmental changes and identify needed internal organizational adjustments.

The development of an organization's strategic plan is a process that consists of (1) establishing the organization's mission, (2) identifying the organization's objectives, (3) evaluating the organization's portfolio of SBUs, and (4) assessing the organization's opportunities. Figure 2–2 illustrates the process of developing a strategic plan.

Organizational Mission

The **mission statement** is a generalized yet meaningful expression of the organization's future direction. It is a commitment to future actions. As a statement of intended future actions, the organizational mission has numerous tasks to perform.

First, a mission statement identifies both the business and customer domains wherein the organization operates or plans to operate. A well-defined mission will answer such business domain questions as "What *is* our business?" "What *will* our

FIGURE 2–2

The strategic plan

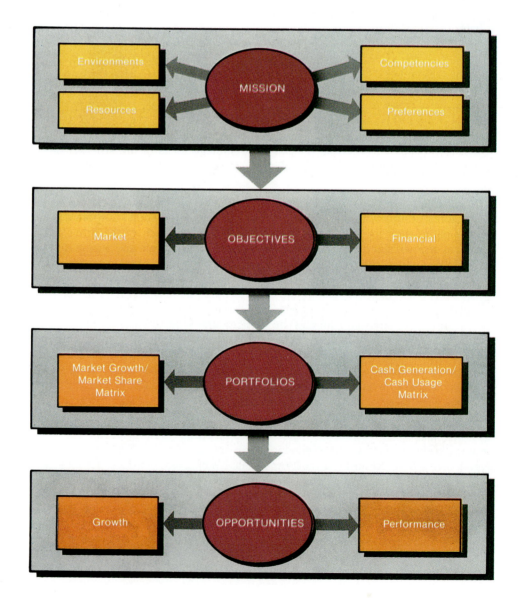

business be?" and "What *should* our business be?" Corresponding questions in the customer domain are "Who *is* our customer?" "Who *will* our customer be?" and "Who *should* our customer be?" As Figure 2–3 illustrates, strategic gaps grow between each of these business and customer domain questions as one moves from the present to the future. These gaps represent the difference between current, expected, and desired performances, and as such, they indicate the possible need for changing the strategic plan of the organization.

Second, a mission statement identifies the organization's responsibilities toward the people with whom it interacts. Retailing has been described as a people business, and the mission statement should recognize this orientation. In its 1980 mission statement, the Dayton Hudson Department Store Co. reaffirmed its commitment to people through (1) serving *customers* by offering better service than competitors; (2) serving *communities* by contributing to a strong, healthy environment; (3) serving *shareholders* by providing a superior return on their investment; and (4) serving *employees* by offering rewarding careers.

Third, a mission statement provides a general blueprint for accomplishing the organizational mission. The May Department Stores Co.'s mission statement used a symbol for communicating its mission of excellence in retailing by meeting its general objective: "top quartile performance" as measured by "return on common stockholders' investment." The May mission symbol is a pyramid whose base is formed by the associates who make up the organization. The May Co. said it plans to achieve its general mission and objective by "building a strong organization and setting clear strategy."[7] The organizational foundation of the firm's pyramid is directed at developing a superior general management, cultivating an innovative corporate culture, and securing the best talent in retailing. The strategy focus of the firm will be on productivity, merchandise impact, genuine customer service, sound pricing practices,

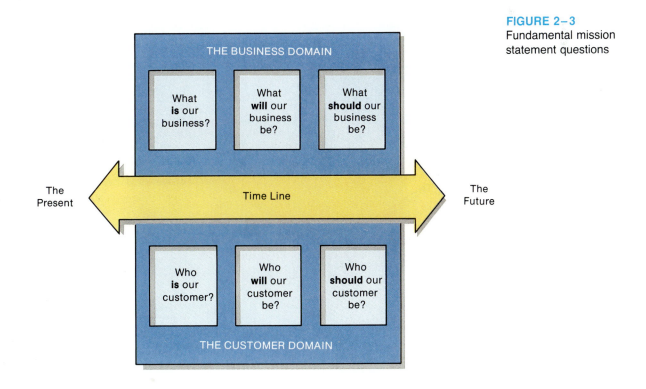

FIGURE 2–3
Fundamental mission statement questions

vital sales promotions, visually exciting stores, and efficient systems (see Figure 2–4).

The statement of the organizational mission is developed by taking several factors into account. These factors include environmental considerations, resource considerations, distinctive competencies, and managerial preferences.

Environmental Considerations

The retail organization must accommodate and react to several different environments that present both opportunities and threats. Some of the major components of an organization's environment are suppliers, marketing intermediaries, customers, competitors, and the public (see Figure 2–5).

As a marketing intermediary, the retail organization has an internal environment within which the daily operation of the firm must be successfully completed. The strengths and weaknesses of the organization's structure and personnel must be accounted for when developing mission statements. The planning process should involve all levels of the organization to ensure a full commitment from all affected parties.

As a team member in the marketing channel of distribution, the mission statement must also address the needs of suppliers and customers. The retailer's mission should recognize the need for a "coordinated effort" and a "cooperative spirit" in conducting channel affairs. Retail organizations that have adopted the marketing concept (customer satisfaction at a profit) will, as a matter of course, consider the expectations of their targeted markets and make provisions within the mission statement for gaining buyer acceptance of the firm's programs.

Retailing activities are not conducted within a vacuum; the mission statement therefore must recognize the existence of competitors and the expectations of the

FIGURE 2–4

The mission pyramid of The May Department Stores Co. (source: The May Department Stores Co. annual report, 1983)

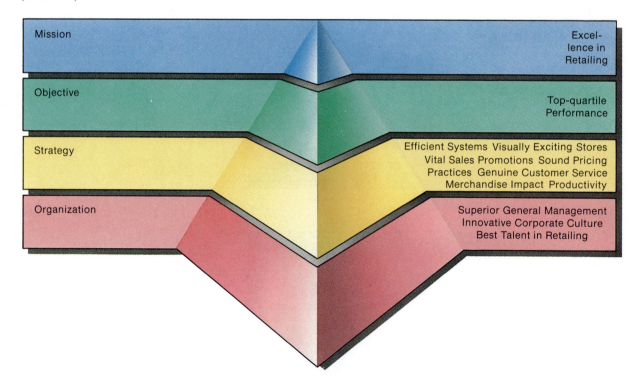

Mission	Excellence in Retailing
Objective	Top-quartile Performance
Strategy	Efficient Systems Visually Exciting Stores Vital Sales Promotions Sound Pricing Practices Genuine Customer Service Merchandise Impact Productivity
Organization	Superior General Management Innovative Corporate Culture Best Talent in Retailing

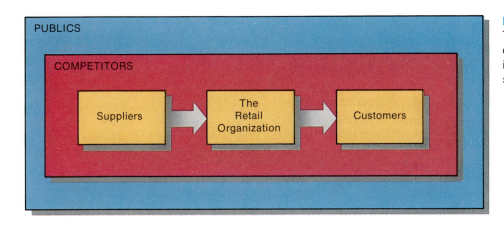

FIGURE 2–5
The environments to be considered in developing organizational missions

general public. The strategic planning process must devote considerable attention to positioning the retail organization relative to competition. The general public's perception of the retail organization is also vital to acceptance of the firm's activities. The goal of serving the public need by being a responsive corporate citizen meeting its social responsibilities also needs to be addressed within the mission statement.

Resource Considerations

The mission statement must be realistic. The extent of that realism depends on the resources available to the retail organization. Because resources are essential to implement the firm's current and future strategies, the mission statement should recognize the problems associated with acquiring, maintaining, and using resources. The resource base to consider in developing the mission statement consists of (1) the financial assets and liabilities of the firm, (2) the organizational composition and structure of the management team, (3) the human resource component in terms of supporting personnel, and (4) the physical plant—store facilities, fixtures, and equipment.

Distinctive Competencies

A careful assessment of practically any retail organization will reveal certain merchandising and operating capabilities that distinguish it from competing organizations. Distinctive competencies might occur in such areas as visual merchandising, exclusive supplier relationships, customer communications and sales promotions, unique store imagery, inventory planning and control systems, organization integration, product assortments, market coverage, or store atmospheres. The list of possible distinctive competencies is almost endless. For example, the Walt Disney Company is testing its first retail outlet outside of its own theme park. One test store is a tourist location (i.e., distinctive competency) having a festival atmosphere with high tourist foot traffic (e.g., San Francisco's Pier 39 tourist attraction).[8] In any case, distinctive competencies are solid foundations for suggesting future strategies in a mission statement.

Managerial Preferences

Additional considerations in developing a mission statement include the merchandising and operating preferences of the organization's cadre of managers. The type and extent of managerial expertise (e.g., mass merchandise vs. specialty retailing) will vary among retail organizations; therefore, it is both logical and practical to consider management strengths when planning the organization's future directions. In addition, managerial intuition should not be overlooked when plotting a new and innovative course of action and finding unique methods of strategy implementation.

Organizational Objectives

An **organizational objective** can be defined as a strategic position to be attained or a purpose to be achieved by the retail organization and/or one of its strategic business units. It is an aim or end-of-action statement toward which the retail organization's efforts are directed. As such, organizational objectives need to be stated in quantitative, realistic, and consistent terms. By stating objectives in *quantitative* terms (e.g., increase total sales volume by twelve percent next year), these expressions provide a specific measurement or target for judging performance. Performance must be based on a *realistic* assessment of the firm's environments, resources, and markets. For example, it would be wishful thinking to set an objective of a fifty percent increase in annual sales volume for a retail enterprise in a mature market. Finally, organizational objectives need to be *consistent*. A retailer simply cannot expect to minimize costs while maximizing sales volume.

Chapter 1 introduced the concept of the "scales of retailing"—the desirability of striking a balance between satisfying the customer's merchandising needs and meeting the retailer's need of a satisfactory financial performance. The two major categories of organizational objectives reflect this balance: the market objectives of customer patronage and competitive position and the financial objectives of profitability and productivity. Figure 2–6 presents a typology of organizational objectives.

Market Objectives

Market objectives are aimed at securing customer patronage and achieving competitive positions within the general marketplace. Market objectives are realized by carefully planned merchandising programs that can satisfy the consumer's psychological, social, and personal needs.

Sales volume. Sales volume increases are a commonly identified objective. A sales growth objective is typically expressed as a certain percentage increase (e.g., fifteen percent) for a particular strategic business unit (e.g., store) over a defined time period (e.g., next year). It is an expansion objective that involves additional commitment of the organization's resources and the foregoing of short-term profits for long-term gains. Increases in total sales volume might be achieved by (1) adding new operating units, (2) increasing advertising expenditures, (3) improving a product/service offering, (4) lowering prices, or (5) making other merchandising adjustments (e.g., added convenience) that can increase customer satisfaction.

Another type of sales volume objective is to increase the average customer sale. Increasing the total amount spent by each customer during a store visit should have a direct and positive effect on total sales. Kinney Shoes, a subsidiary of F.W. Woolworth Co., repositioned its women's shoes to appeal to working women who are willing and able to spend more on fashionable dress shoes; the goal was to increase the average sale by ten to fifteen percent.[9] Personal selling and various sales promotion methods are used to increase the amount of the average sale.

Customer traffic. Many retailers believe that if they can attract customers into the store, then they can obtain desired sales through customer exposure to the direct merchandising efforts of the organization. Their objectives thus are to increase (1) the

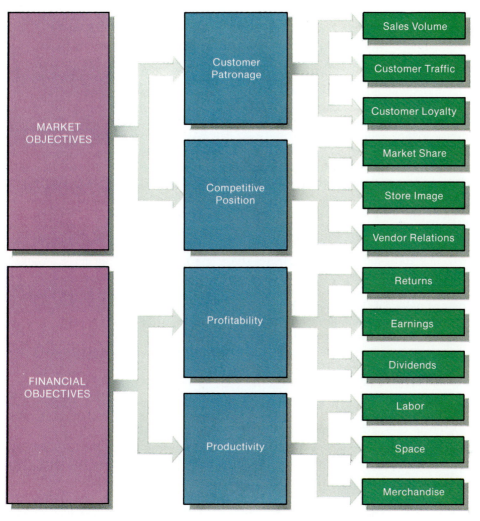

FIGURE 2–6
A typology of organizational objectives

total number of customers visiting the store during a specific time period; (2) the total complement of various types of customers attracted into the store (e.g., low-, middle-, and upper-income consumers); and/or (3) the magnitude of specific customer groups targeted for special attention (e.g., professional women). "Safeway, by offering the added convenience of instore banking to its present and potential customers, enhances its prospects of increased store traffic and customer patronage (market penetration)."[10] Possible strategies to increase the total number of customer visits include additional mass advertising, sales promotions, and special-event merchandising. Offering a range of pricing points and a wider selection of merchandise are two means by which the firm can expand its appeal to a more extensive customer base. Offering unique services, specialty merchandise lines, and personal selling from sales representatives who have appropriate expertise can increase the traffic of targeted customer groups.

Customer loyalty. A customer loyalty objective is aimed at improving return trade. Repeat business is essential to almost any retail operation because for many it represents store loyalty. The average number of store visits or purchases during a defined time period is one means of measuring return trade. Ideally, a worthy objective is to develop a high preference level for the organization and its merchandising programs. Obviously, the key to store loyalty is customer satisfaction. Retailers should understand the realities of customer loyalty—it "is the absence of something better."[11] Customer loyalty is something the retailer has to earn and keep on earning.

The type and quality of services provided to the customer are important strategic considerations in developing customer loyalty. A retail organization often develops strategies based on the *completeness* of the service offering: essential services (basic to the retailer's operation) and expected services ("extras" that help distinguish the retailer's service mix). Service quality is generally expressed in terms of the service levels offered by competitors—better transactional efficiency, better service availability, and less trouble in service execution. "Don't get caught in the trap of being an upscaled store with low-end service. Today's customers want and expect good service because their time is limited and more valuable."[12]

Market share.   Market share objectives are the most commonly used form of expressing competitive position. **Market share** is a measure of a retail organization's sales position relative to all competitors within the same market. It is calculated by dividing a retail organization's total sales by total market sales for a defined business type or product line category. In expanding market areas, *market share growth* could well be an appropriate objective (e.g., increase market share by six percent over the duration of this planning period). On the other hand, retail organizations operating in mature and stable market areas generally call for the more moderate objective of *market share maintenance* (e.g., protect our current market share against the aggressive actions of all competitors).

Store image.   An *image* is the mental conception of something held in common by members of a group. **Store image** is the mental picture of a retail organization as viewed by customers and the general public. Store image includes both the "functional" or physical properties of the store as well as its "psychological attributes"—a sense of belonging or a feeling of friendliness.[13] Because the term "store" is used here in its most generalized meaning, to the consumer, store image is a symbolic representation of the basic attributes, orientations, and activities of the organization. Originally, Pier I Imports appealed to the hippies or beatniks; its image suggested you had to drive a VW or wear a tie-dyed shirt to get into the store. Today, the firm has upscaled the business format to appeal to customers whose tastes have become more sophisticated.[14] Retailers establish image objectives because they realize that consumers tend to categorize people, places, and things in relative terms (e.g., bigger, better, faster, easier, and sooner). By offering wider product selections, higher quality products, better price values, more convenient locations, easier credit terms, and faster service, retailers can competitively position themselves in the minds of consumers. By careful planning it is possible to position the organization in an imagery niche that clearly distinguishes it from its competitors.

Vendor relations.   Carving out a viable competitive position includes a supply side that a retail organization's statement of objectives should also recognize. Prudent retail organizations strive to ensure that they are well positioned with respect to both established vendors (e.g., to be considered a preferred account by desired vendors) and new emerging sources (e.g., to engage in a systematic search for suppliers of new and innovative products). Retailers also must cooperate and coordinate their activities with other members of the marketing channel of distribution.

The "functional" properties and "psychological attributes" of these restaurants give each a different store image.

Financial Objectives

Financial objectives are directed at ensuring that the retail organization operates profitably and productively. Financial objectives provide quantifiable standards by which the organization's performance will be judged. Targeted returns, earnings, and dividends are three common profitability goals. "The three most critical resources to be managed in a traditional retail enterprise are merchandise, space, and labor."[15]

Returns. The monetary return the retail organization desires can be stated in terms of return on sales or assets. These profit-based objectives reflect what management expects in return for its efforts. A *return on sales* (net profit divided by net sales) objective identifies what percentage of the average sales dollars should be profit. For example, an objective of twenty percent could be the targeted net profit return on net sales. To realize a fair return on the organization's asset investment, a *return on assets* (net profit divided by total assets) objective is frequently included in the organization's statement of objectives.

Earnings.   Objectives should also reflect the performance of the organization relative to stockholders' interests. A targeted *earnings per share* of common stock can be established as an objective to show the amount of earnings available to the owners of common stock. A desired objective of $4 per share of common stock could be the targeted earnings/share ratio.

Dividends.   A designated proportion of the earnings that will actually be allocated to stockholders can also serve as an objective. *Dividends* are a measure of the return to common stock owners representing the return on their investment (this statement does not reflect any increase or decrease in the market value of the common stock). For example, a retailer could set as its objective a $2 dividend yield on each share of common stock.

Labor.   The productivity of the organization's labor pool can be measured by dividing net sales by the total number of employees or by dividing net sales by the total number of worker hours of labor; the latter measure would take into account the productivity of both full- and part-time employees. Another view of labor productivity can be obtained by examining buying and selling expenses as a percentage of net sales (see Figure 2−7, columns [a] and [b]). Retailing can be a labor-intensive business; hence, the contribution of human resources must be recognized and productivity performance standards established. Many retailers also recognize that turnover adversely affects labor productivity and therefore strive to reduce this phenomenon by setting employee satisfaction objectives aimed at increasing employee retention.

Space.   One of the retailer's most important resources is the merchandising and operating space available. Most retail organizations attempt in their plans to maximize their selling space and its productivity. Sales/productivity ratios are established for stores as well as for individual department and product line areas. Space productivity is measured by dividing net sales or gross margin by the most appropriate expression of area. Some examples of sales/space or margin/space productivity ratios are (1) net sales per square foot of selling space (see column [c] of Figure 2−7), (2) net sales per cubic foot of display area, (3) net sales per linear foot of shelf space, and (4) gross margin dollars per square foot.

Merchandise.   *Inventory turnover* is the most widely used criterion for measuring the productivity of merchandise; it can be defined as the number of times (e.g., four times) during a specific time period (e.g., a year) that the average stock on hand is sold. The desired objective is to achieve the highest possible inventory turnover rate for the type of merchandise being sold and the additional resources that must be used to improve turnover rates. Obviously, convenience goods will have higher stock turns than specialty goods; therefore, an annual turnover objective of three turns for specialty goods could be considered as productive as fifteen yearly turns for convenience goods. Column (d) of Figure 2−7 shows department store stock turn rates by merchandise line; the highest turns are associated with female apparel and accessories, a fact that helps explain why department stores focus on these merchandise categories. An objective of increasing the turnover rate by increasing advertising or adding more sales personnel may prove productive if increased expenditures do not exceed the additional profits derived from such a strategy.

Merchandise Line	(A) Selling Salaries, Percentage of Sales (%)	(B) Buying Salaries, Percentage of Sales (%)	(C) Net Sales Per Square Foot of Selling Space ($)	(D) No. of Stock Turns at Retail
Female apparel	5.9	2.0	129	3.4
Female accessories	7.9	2.4	179	2.7
Men's and boy's apparel and accessories	6.5	1.7	141	2.6
Infant's and children's clothing and accessories	8.4	3.5	96	2.7
Shoes	9.7	NA*	178	1.9
Cosmetics and drugs	8.0	2.4	241	2.1
Recreation	8.7	3.6	106	2.0
Home furnishings	8.2	2.0	74	1.8
All other merchandise	9.7	NA*	118	4.9

Source: Adapted from David P. Schulz, "New MOR: New Data," *Stores* (January 1988): 123.
*NA, not available.

FIGURE 2–7
Merchandising/operating results, 1986: All department stores over $2 million

Other Objectives

In addition to market and financial objectives, retail organizations often identify many objectives that relate to their social responsibilities. Such social objectives include supporting charitable causes, providing educational opportunities, assuming an equitable tax burden, and participating in professional and social organizations and events.

Organizational Portfolio

The third stage in developing a strategic plan is to review the organization's portfolio of strategic business units. An **organizational portfolio** is the collection of strategic business units held and managed by a retail organization. The portfolio approach to retail planning is becoming an increasingly important method used by the diversified retail organization. Portfolio analysis is appealing because it suggests, but does not dictate, specific courses of action to achieve a balanced mix of businesses that will provide the maximum long-run benefits from scarce cash and managerial resources.[16] As Hall observed, "the total portfolio of businesses is managed by allocating capital and managerial resources to serve the interests of the firm as a whole in order to achieve balanced growth in sales, earnings, and asset mix with an acceptable and controlled level of risk."[17] Portfolio analysis is not in and of itself a strategy, however; rather, it is an analytical tool to provide perspective on the organization's current situation (where it is now) and to suggest possible courses of action for the future (where it wants to be).[18] A commonly used portfolio approach is the growth/share matrix developed by the Boston Consulting Group (BCG).

BCG Portfolio Approach

The **BCG portfolio approach** is best illustrated by the use of two matrices: the market growth/market share matrix (see Figure 2–8) and the cash generation/cash usage matrix (see Figure 2–9). The former is used to illustrate current market positions of

FIGURE 2–8

Market growth/market share matrix

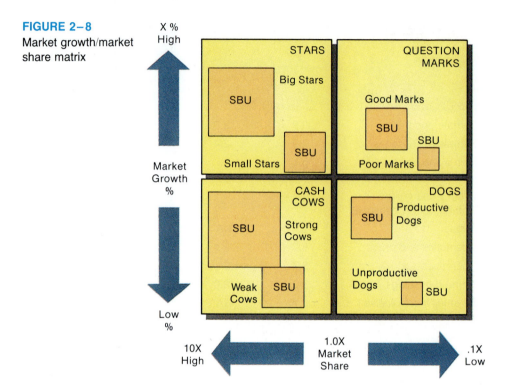

each strategic business unit, whereas the latter identifies each SBU's net cash flow position.

Market growth/market share matrix. In Figure 2–8, the vertical axis identifies the annual growth rate (percentage) of each SBU's operating market. The logic of including market growth rate in such an analysis is based on the benefits to be derived from the experience curve. As the organization gains more experience, it can reduce costs and realize greater business unit profits. The sales growth rate ranges from a low of zero percent to a high of whatever percentage is appropriate (e.g., twenty-five percent). A rate of eight to twelve percent is generally considered to be quite good in most industries.

The horizontal axis indicates the relative market share of the SBU, a ratio of SBU share of the market to that of the largest competitor. Market share is considered important, based on research indicating that profitability of an SBU is directly related to its market share. A "logarithmic scale is used for market share that goes from 1/10 the size of the competition to 10 times that of the largest competitor. Thus, business units located to the right of the value 1.0 are smaller than competition and those to the left are larger."[19] The size of each square in the matrix shows each SBU's dollar sales, and the location of each SBU square indicates its competitive market share position for various growth rate markets. The size and location of each SBU square simply suggest different financial and marketing needs.

To facilitate analysis of the growth/share matrix, it is arbitrarily divided into four quadrants classifying SBUs as one of four different types of businesses—stars, cash cows, question marks, or dogs. **Stars** are SBUs having a high market share within a high-growth market. These businesses are market leaders within their respective industries. As Figure 2–8 shows, stars can be big or small, depending on the sales volume and share of the market. **Cash cows** are SBUs having a high market share within a low-growth market. Like stars, cash cows also have a dominant or leader position; unfortunately, this position occurs in a less desirable market. Some cows are stronger than others, based on the sales volume, market share, and the growth characteristics of their market (see Figure 2–8). SBUs with a low market share in a high-growth market are classified as **question marks;** these are often also called *problem children* because they offer considerable promise if given the attention they need. Depending on the amount of promise it shows, an SBU might be considered a good mark (reasonable chance for increasing market share and sales volume with an acceptable resource investment) or a poor mark (market share and sales volume increases are unlikely within acceptable resources commitments). **Dogs** are SBUs that have a low market share within a low-growth market. Their prospects for the future are dim; nevertheless, dogs can be productive if they find a market niche and produce an acceptable profit level.

Cash generation/cash usage matrix. The net cash flow situation for stars, cash cows, question marks, and dogs is shown in Figure 2–9. The vertical axis shows cash usage (low to high), and the horizontal axis portrays cash generation (low to high). Stars are both high users and generators of cash, but their net cash flow tends to be negative because they require considerable cash to expand with their growing market and maintain or improve their market share. Cash cows are the key to the organization's cash flow problems. Given the low market growth rate, fewer expenditures are needed to maintain market position; cash cows therefore tend to be net cash generators. The SBU cash cow provides the bulk of the cash to finance stars' and question marks' marketing operations. Question marks typically use more cash than they produce. If the organization decides that a question mark is capable of becoming

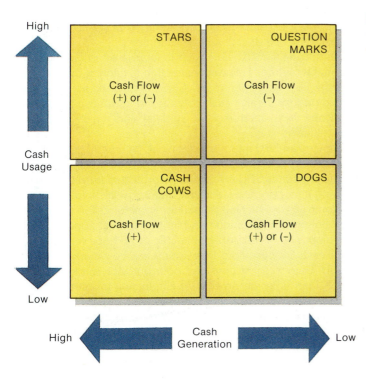

FIGURE 2–9
Cash generation/cash usage matrix

a star, then it must provide the cash needed to capture additional market share. Dogs can produce either a positive or negative net cash flow. Properly niched within a secure market segment, some dogs can provide some cash that can be used to finance stars and question marks. Other dogs are unproductive because of their vulnerable position in no-growth markets; in such cases, they can become "cash traps" and a lost cause. Day described an overall strategy for this type of portfolio analysis:

> The long-run health of the corporation depends on having some businesses that *generate* cash (and provide acceptable reported profits), and others that *use* cash to support growth. Among the indicators of overall health are the size and vulnerability of the "Cash Cows" (and the prospects for the "Stars," if any), and the number of "Problem Children" and "Dogs." Particular attention must be paid to those businesses with large cash appetites. Unless the company has abundant cash flow, it cannot afford to sponsor many such businesses at one time. If resources (including debt capacity) are spread too thin, the company simply will wind up with too many marginal businesses and suffer a reduced capacity to finance promising new business entries or acquisitions in the future.[20]

Resource allocation matrix.   The combined information provided in the market/growth share matrix and the cash generation/usage matrix suggests ways to allocate financial resources. As Figure 2–10 illustrates, for each different category of SBU (stars, cash cows, question marks, and dogs), two or more of the five following possible allocation alternatives are suggested:

1. Building involves increasing an SBU's market share. The decision to build an SBU typically requires cash infusion. The building alternative is used to expand smaller stars into bigger stars and to transform promising question marks into stars.

2. Holding involves maintaining an SBU's market share. The decision to hold is a defensive posture by which the organization will protect and reinforce its current market share. The goal is to make big stars productive in terms of positive net cash flow and to keep strong cash cows producing a large cash flow.

3. Harvesting involves milking an SBU of its cash to finance other SBU alternatives that seem to have a brighter future. This cash extraction is often at the expense of the long-run survival of the SBU being harvested. Given the drastic nature of this alternative, it should be used only for weaker cash cows and dogs whose futures are extremely dim with little hope of maintenance or survival and where additional resource investment is unjustifiable.

4. Niching involves moving an SBU into a market niche (segment) in which the fit between resource requirements and available resources is more acceptable. The goal is to find a market niche where the SBU is reasonably protected from the actions of competitors while allowing it to generate sufficient long-term sales volumes and profits to justify the repositioning costs. Niching is used for some question marks and dogs that demonstrate the potential for a unique and limited market appeal.

5. Divesting involves disposing of SBUs that offer little or no hope of improving either their market share or cash flow position. Divestment can be accomplished by selling or liquidating the SBU. Unproductive dogs and poor question marks are both candidates for divestiture. K Mart is in the process of eliminating investments with little or no return. The sale of most S.S. Kresge and Jupiter variety stores signals K Mart's total graduation to discount retailing. Earlier, K Mart closed its unprofitable Designer Depot operation and sold its investment in the restaurant industry (Furr's Cafeterias and Bishop Buffets).[21]

RESOURCE ALLOCATION STRATEGIES

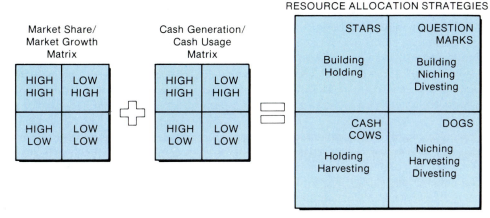

Market Share/
Market Growth
Matrix

HIGH HIGH	LOW HIGH
HIGH LOW	LOW LOW

Cash Generation/
Cash Usage
Matrix

HIGH HIGH	LOW HIGH
HIGH LOW	LOW LOW

STARS Building Holding	QUESTION MARKS Building Niching Divesting
CASH COWS Holding Harvesting	DOGS Niching Harvesting Divesting

FIGURE 2–10

Strategies for allocating organizational resources

Organizational Opportunities

Portfolio analysis allows the retail organization to assess its current situation (what its business is) and to identify possible future courses of action (what its business should be) for various strategic business units. After completion of the portfolio analysis, the decision to target some SBUs for extinction (harvesting) or replacement (divesting) while others are targeted for maintenance (holding) and growth (building) often leaves a strategic gap between the current and desired performance of the retail organization; in other words, projected sales will fall short of desired sales (see Figure 2–11). To fill this strategic gap, retail management must take advantage of any opportunities for better growth and/or improved performance. In the department store industry, "Opportunities for new stores in different cities are limited now. So, expansion-minded chains are forced to seek market share and sales growth by acquiring existing stores in other cities."[22]

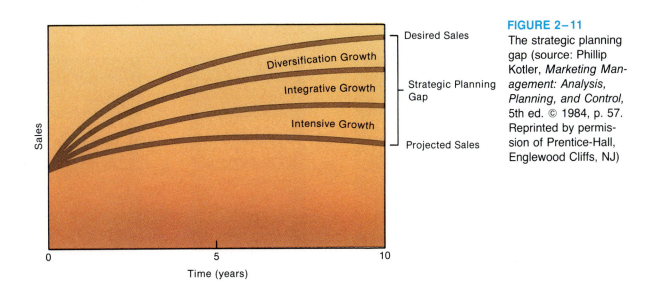

FIGURE 2–11

The strategic planning gap (source: Phillip Kotler, *Marketing Management: Analysis, Planning, and Control,* 5th ed. © 1984, p. 57. Reprinted by permission of Prentice-Hall, Englewood Cliffs, NJ)

Growth Opportunities

Long-term corporate survival "depends upon the organization's ability to redirect organizational efforts in response to environmental change and to increase the firm's resources through investment in profitable growth opportunities."[23]

Kotler identified three types of growth opportunities—intensive, integrative, and diversification. Figure 2–12 illustrates these opportunities and identifies the appropriate strategies to be used in pursuing a particular type of opportunity.

Intensive growth.   Opportunities found within the organization's current portfolio of businesses are referred to as **intensive growth** opportunities. As shown in Figure 2–12, three possible strategies can improve the performance of existing SBUs: **market penetration, market development, and product development**. Figure 2–13 outlines the objective for each of these intensive growth strategies and identifies some of the tactics and methods retailers use in implementing these strategies.

Integrative growth.   Opportunities can take the form of backward, forward, and horizontal integration. In the case of opportunities for integrative growth, the organization's efforts focus on building or acquiring SBUs related to the organization's current portfolio of SBUs. An **integration strategy** aims to increase sales by incorporating one or more levels of the marketing channel of distribution into the organization's operations. **Backward integration** involves seeking ownership and/or control of supply systems (e.g., a retailer acquiring a wholesaler or manufacturer). Avon Products, Inc., which grew to be the world's largest cosmetic marketer peddling beauty door-to-door, is pursuing a backward integration strategy (they acquired Giorgio Inc., the Beverly Hills fragrance company) to broaden its distribution into department stores (a modified horizontal integration strategy.[24] **Horizontal integration** is achieved by seeking ownership and/or control of competitors at the same level within the marketing channel. The merger of Sears Automotive Centers and Western Auto Supply Co. allowed Sears to become the second largest retailer in the auto parts industry.[25] Many manufacturers (Sherwin-Williams) and wholesalers (True Value Hardware) have engaged in **forward integration** by developing or acquiring retail businesses and operating them as part of their strategic marketing efforts. Esprit de

FIGURE 2–12
Types of growth opportunities

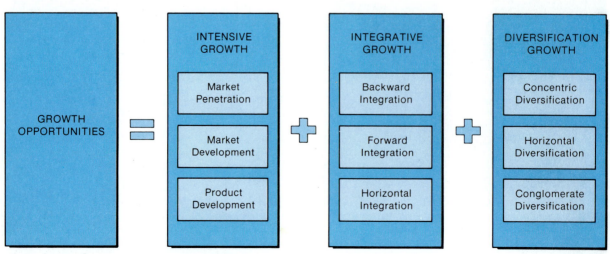

Strategy	Objective	Tactics	Methods
Market penetration	To increase the sales productivity of current SBU stores within existing markets	Increase patronage level of current customers by increasing the frequency of store visits and the amount of the average sale per customer visit Stimulate trial visits among nonpatrons who reside in existing trading areas Entice customers who currently patronize competing outlets with existing trading areas	Increase advertising and sales promotion activities Expand product and service mix Use suggestive selling techniques Engage in trade-up selling techniques Develop special event merchandising programs Offer lower prices
Market development	To increase sales by expanding existing store operations into new markets	Open new geographic markets Appeal to new market segments Expand into new market levels	Locate and develop new store sites within new trading areas Develop new product, service, price, and image programs that appeal to different consumer groups Offer products and services to wholesaling and manufacturing organizations
Product development	To increase sales within existing markets by developing new product/service mixes	Increase sales by replacing old product lines with new product lines Increase sales by adding new product lines and items	Adjust product variety and assortment to create a more differentiated product mix Add the more desirable product items that are normally associated with another type of retailer Develop general-purpose product mix by combining two or more broad product lines

FIGURE 2–13
Intensive growth strategies

Corp. is building a network of franchised and company-owned retail stores; this funky fashion design company is changing its channels of distribution.[26]

Diversification growth. When the retail organization adds attractive SBUs whose business nature and format are dissimilar to current SBUs, the company is engaged in **diversification growth**. Concentric, horizontal, and conglomerate diversification are three different diversifying strategies for increasing sales. **Concentric diversification** tries to attract new customers by adding businesses having technological or marketing similarities with existing businesses. The objective of **horizontal diversification** is to increase sales by adding SBUs that appeal to the organization's current customers even though they are not technologically related to its current businesses. The joint venture of IBM, CBS, and Sears in developing a videotex service is a good example of concentric diversification: computer and information processing by IBM, picture and text transmission by CBS, and retailing and merchandising by Sears.[27] Finally, the retail organization can diversify by adding new businesses that are totally unrelated to its current SBUs in hopes of appealing to entirely new markets. Both Sears and J.C. Penney have engaged in **conglomerate diversification**. Sears, for example, has diversified extensively into the area of financial services with insurance (Allstate), real estate (Coldwell Banker), and stock brokerage (Dean Witter Reynolds). Melville, a shoe manufacturer, has become a diversified giant with nearly 6,000 retailing outlets including Marshalls (discount clothing stores), CVS (drugstores), and Kay-Bee Toy & Hobby Shops.[28]

Performance Opportunities

A number of opportunities exist for improving the organization's profits and productivity through more efficient usage of organizational resources—financial, human, and facilities. The previous discussion on organizational objectives identified the need to achieve acceptable performance in (1) return on sales and assets, (2) earnings per share, (3) labor and space productivity, and (4) inventory turnover. Improved operational and managerial efficiencies are the key to achieving desired performance standards. Toys 'R' Us, The Limited, Wal-Mart, and May Department Stores are among an elite group of national retailers whose size, market clout, and efficiency have positioned them to succeed. These "power retailers" are fast and focused and have been on the cutting edge of merchandising and operating developments.[29]

    The value of strategic planning is that it provides a systematic method for analyzing the economic and competitive prospects for the retail organization and for charting a long-term course of action. The retail organization, however, must guard against having the strategic planning process become "less of a creative thinking exercise and more of a bureaucratic process," and retail management should not "confuse strategy with planning and implementation."[30] Without safeguards, the strategic planning process can lose contact with the external world of customers and competitors and the internal world of line managers who must implement designated strategies. The key to a successful strategic plan is the implementation of the retailing plan.

THE RETAILING PLAN

The **retailing plan** is an organized framework of activities directed at implementing the strategies identified in the strategic plan. It addresses the operational questions of why, what, when, where, and how specific retail business activities are to be accomplished. The retailing plan tends to be more tactical than the strategic plan because of its limited scope and specific character. Typically, retailing plans are developed for each SBU and its stores, departments, and product lines.

    The process of retail planning is a cyclical activity involving four stages: (1) conducting **environmental scans,** (2) preparing **resource assessments,** (3) making **market selections,** and (4) **developing retailing mixes**. As Figure 2–14 illustrates, the retail planning cycle depends on a review of the strategic plan. At each stage of the retail planning process the retail planner must review the guidelines in the strategic plan to ensure congruency with those guidelines.

    The remainder of this text is devoted to the issues and concerns associated with implementing and controlling the activities that a retailing plan comprises. Figure 2–15 shows a model of the retailing plan that will be used as the general organiza-

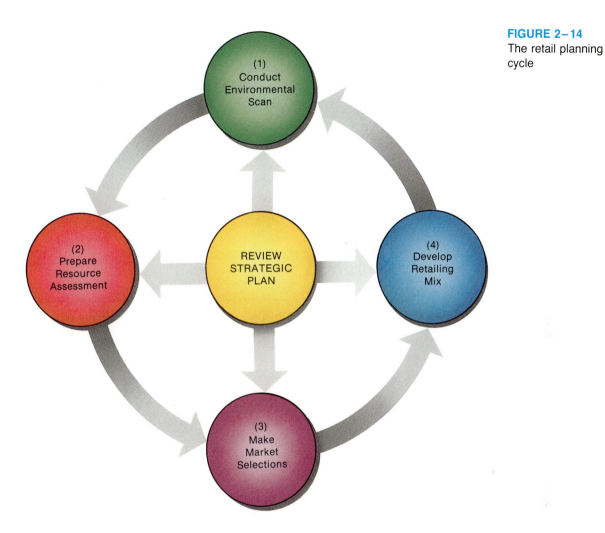

FIGURE 2–14
The retail planning cycle

tional framework for the discussion of retailing throughout this text. It identifies the major areas of concern at each stage of the retail planning cycle.

In Part Two, the Environmental Scan, the uncontrollable environments of retailing are analyzed regarding the competitive behavior of retail institutions (Chapter 3), the buying behavior of consumers (Chapter 4), and the protective and prohibitive nature of the regulatory environment (Chapter 5). Part Two concludes with a discussion on the retail information system (Chapter 6), the methodology used in gathering and analyzing information about the environments of retailing.

Part Three focuses on appraising the retailer's resources. Effective, efficient use of the organization's financial (Chapter 7), organizational and human (Chapter 8), and facilities (Chapter 9) resources are highlighted in this topical coverage on resource assessments.

Identification, evaluation, and selection of retail markets are covered in Part Four. Analyzing regional and local markets (Chapter 10) and assessing retail trading areas (Chapter 11) are part of the general issue of market segmentation and the need to target selected market segments.

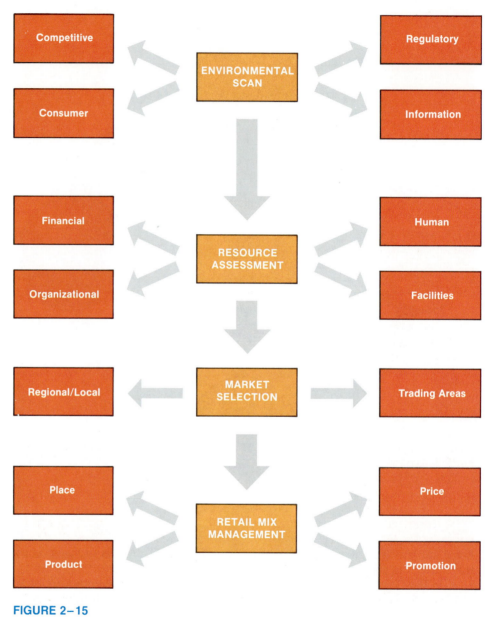

FIGURE 2–15
The retailing plan

Part Five discusses the management of the retailing mix—place, product, price, and promotion. The retailer's place of business, the retail site, is the focus of Chapter 12. The product dimension of the retailing mix is covered in Chapters 13 through 18. Discussions of the product mix (Chapter 13) and service mix (Chapter 14) are supported by an examination of the buying (Chapter 15), procuring (Chapter 16), planning (Chapter 17), and controlling (Chapter 18) processes. The pricing dimension is covered in the discussion of setting and adjusting retail prices (Chapter 19). The last dimension of the retailing mix is promotion, including retail advertising (Chapter 20), personal selling (Chapter 21), and retail displays, sales promotions, and publicity (Chapter 22). Evaluating retail service marketing and retail employment opportunities is the topic for Part Six.

SUMMARY

Strategic retail management is the process of planning the organization's survival and growth. Planning is conducted at corporate, SBU, store, department, and product-line levels of the organization. The retail organization's strategic plan is an overall business plan developed for the entire firm that involves (1) identifying the organizational mission, (2) establishing organizational objectives, (3) conducting an organizational portfolio analysis, and (4) evaluating organizational opportunities.

The mission statement is a generalized yet meaningful expression of the organization's future direction. Its three tasks are to identify (1) the business and customer domains within which the organization operates, (2) the organization's responsibilities toward the people with whom it interacts, and (3) the blueprint for accomplishing the organizational mission. Mission statements are developed according to environmental and resource considerations, distinctive competencies, and managerial preferences.

Organizational objectives identify the specific purposes that the firm is to achieve. Most retail organizations identify two general sets of objectives, market and financial. Market objectives aim at securing customer patronage (sales volume, customer traffic, and customer service objectives) and achieving competitive positions within the general marketplace (market share, store image, and vendor relations objectives). Financial objectives establish goals for profitability (returns, earnings, and dividends) and productivity (labor, space, and merchandise).

Organizational portfolio analysis involves reviewing the SBUs that the total business interest of a diversified retail organization comprises. The most commonly used portfolio approach is the market growth/market share matrix developed by the BCG. A portfolio analysis allows the retail organization to assess its current situation (what its business is), and to identify possible future courses of action (what the business should be).

The final step in developing a strategic plan is to identify and evaluate potential opportunities for continued organizational growth and improved organizational performance. Growth opportunities can be identified as intensive (market penetration, market development, and product development), integrative (backward, forward, and horizontal integration), and diversifying (concentric, horizontal, and conglomerate diversification). Performance opportunities include more efficient use of financial, human, and facility resources.

The retailing plan is an organizational framework of activities directed at implementing the strategies identified in the strategic plan. It is a cyclical process involving environmental scans, resource assessments, market selections, and retailing mix management.

KEY TERMS AND CONCEPTS

backward integration

Boston Consulting Group (BCG) portfolio approach

cash cows

concentric diversification

conglomerate diversification

diversification growth

dogs	mission statement
environmental scan	organizational objectives
financial objectives	organizational portfolio
forward integration	product development
horizontal diversification	question marks
horizontal integration	resource assessment
integration strategy	retailing mix management
intensive growth	retailing plan
market development	stars
market objectives	store image
market penetration	strategic business unit (SBU)
market selection	strategic plan
market share	strategic retail management

REVIEW QUESTIONS

1. Explain why many retailers have exhibited resistance to and skepticism about strategic planning.
2. What is strategic retail management? Describe its two major components. Define each.
3. At what level does strategic and tactical planning occur? How is each planning level different from the others?
4. Characterize a strategic plan. Describe its purposes.
5. What are the four elements of the strategic planning process? Define each.
6. Describe the three tasks of an organizational mission.
7. Identify the factors to be considered in developing an organizational mission. Briefly describe each factor.
8. There are six types of market objectives. Provide a brief description and example of each.
9. List the six types of financial objectives. Provide a brief description and example of each.
10. Describe the BCG market growth/market share matrix approach to portfolio analysis.
11. What are the five possible alternatives for the allocation of financial resources as identified in the BCG portfolio approach? Discuss each alternative.
12. What three strategies are associated with integrative growth opportunities? Briefly describe each.
13. Compare and contrast concentric diversification, horizontal diversification, and conglomerate diversification.
14. What specific questions does the retailing plan address?

ENDNOTES

1. Julian Yudelson, "Critical Success Factors: Just What the Doctor Ordered for Today's Retail Management Headaches," *Retail Control* (June/July 1987): 45.
2. See Walter K. Levy, "Department Stores, The Next Generation: Form and Rationale," *Retailing Issues Letter* 1 (1987): 1.
3. Bert Rosenbloom, "Strategic Planning in Retailing: Prospects and Problems," *Journal of Retailing* 56 (Spring 1980): 110.
4. Ibid., 108.
5. Derek Abell and John S. Hammond, *Strategic Market Planning* (Englewood Cliffs, NJ: Prentice-Hall, 1979), 10.
6. Robert D. Buzzell and Marc K. Drew, "Strategic Management Helps Retailers Plan for the Future," *Marketing News,* 7 March 1980, 1.

7. The May Department Stores Co. annual report, 1982, 1.

8. Marcy Magiera, "Disney Tries Retailing," *Advertising Age,* 1 June 1987, 80.

9. Teri Agins, "Kinney Polishing Image for Its Line of Women's Shoes," *The Wall Street Journal,* 30 March 1988.

10. P. "Ragan" Varadarajan and Daniel Rajaratnam, "Symbiotic Marketing Revisited," *Journal of Marketing* 50 (Jan. 1986): 11.

11. Joseph Pereira, "Zayre Corp.'s Most Important Task Is to Re-Store Itself," *The Wall Street Journal,* 11 March 1988.

12. Sallie Hook, "Retailers Turn to Narrowcasting to Survive." *Marketing News,* 15 Feb. 1988, 9.

13. David Mazursky and Jacob Jacoby, "Exploring the Development of Store Images," *Journal of Retailing* 62 (Summer 1986): 146–147.

14. Shannon Thurmond, "Pier I Sets Its Course," *Advertising Age,* 22 Feb. 1988, 30.

15. Robert F. Lusch, "The New Algebra of High Performance Retail Management," *Retail Control* (Sept. 1986): 15–16.

16. George S. Day, "Diagnosing the Product Portfolio," *Journal of Marketing* 41 (April 1977): 29.

17. William K. Hull, "SBUs: Hot New Topic in the Management of Diversification," *Business Horizons* (Feb. 1978): 18.

18. "The New Breed of Strategic Planners," *Business Week,* 17 Sept. 1986, 66.

19. Douglas J. Dalrymple and Leonard J. Parsons, *Marketing Management: Strategy and Cases,* 3d ed. (New York: John Wiley & Sons, 1983): 35.

20. Day, "Diagnosing the Product Portfolio," 31.

21. Patricia Strand, "K Mart Pares Unprofitable Units," *Advertising Age,* 13 April 1987, 22.

22. Michael Totty, "Expansion-Minded Dillards Is Catching Some Attention," *The Wall Street Journal,* 16 March 1988.

23. Christie H. Paksoy and J.B. Wilkinson, "An Analysis of Retail Diversification Strategies Among U.S. Retailers." In *Marketing in an Environment of Changes, Proceedings,* edited by R.L. King, 165. (Southern Marketing Association, 1986).

24. Amy Dunkin, "Big Names Are Opening Doors for Avon," *Business Week,* 1 June 1987, 96.

25. Kate Fitzgerald, "Sears May Go Incognito," *Advertising Age,* 28 March 1988, 4.

26. Cleveland Horton, "Esprit to Skirt Retail Clients by Setting up Its Own Stores," *Advertising Age,* 26 Jan. 1987, 12.

27. Varadarajan and Rajaratnam, "Symbiotic Marketing Revisited," 12.

28. Frank McCoy, "Melville's New Crew Aims to Get Back to Speed," *Business Week,* 13 July 1987, 94.

29. Amy Dunkin and Michael Oneal, "Power Retailers," *Business Week,* 21 Dec. 1987, 86.

30. "The New Breed of Strategic Planners," 62.

Berens, John S. "The Marketing Mix, the Retailing Mix, and the Use of Retail Strategy Continue." In *Developments in Marketing Science, Proceedings,* edited by J.C. Rogers, III, 323–27. Academy of Marketing Science, 1983.

Berry, Leonard L., and Gresham, Larry G. "Relationship Retailing: Transforming Customers into Clients." *Business Horizons* 29 (November–December 1986): 43–47.

Bivins, Jacquelyn. "Diversification: Retailers Reach Out." *Chain Store Age Executive* (March 1985): 25, 28, 31–32.

Cravens, David W. "Strategic Forces Affecting Marketing Strategy." *Business Horizons* (September–October 1986): 77–86.

Cronin, J. Joseph, Jr. "Determinants of Retail Profit Performance: A Consideration of Retail Marketing Strategies." *Journal of the Academy of Marketing Science* 13 (Fall 1985): 40–53.

Cronin, J. Joseph, Jr., and Skinner, Steven J. "The Marketing—Finance Interface: The Impact of Marketing Objectives and Financial Conditions on Retail Profitability." In *Develop-*

RELATED READINGS

ments in *Marketing Science, Proceedings*, edited by N.K. Malhotra, 182–86. Academy of Marketing Science, 1985.

Feinberg, Richard A., Koscica, Donna, and Recobs, Stephen J. "Strategic Planning: What the Top 100 Stores Say." *Retail Control* (October 1983): 9–21.

Horr, David A. "How the Independent Store Can Benefit from Strategic Planning." *Retail Control* (March 1984): 40–48.

Ingene, Charles A. "Productivity and Functional Shifting in Spatial Retailing: Private and Social Perspectives." *Journal of Retailing* 60 (Fall 1984): 15–36.

Karch, Nancy, "The New Strategic Era in Retailing," *Retail Control* (November 1985): 10–19.

Kelly, J. Patrick, and George, William R. "Strategic Management Issues for the Retailing of Services." *Journal of Retailing* 58 (Summer 1982): 26–43.

Kerin, Roger A., and Varaiya, Nikhil. "Mergers and Acquisitions in Retailing: A Review and Critical Analysis." *Journal of Retailing* 61 (Spring 1985): 9–34.

Kerin, Roger A., and Varaiya, Nikhil. "Value-Based Planning in Retailing." *Journal of Retailing* 61 (Winter 1985): 5–9.

Klokis, Holly. "Retailing's Grande Dame: Cloaked in New Strategies." *Chain Store Age Executive* (March 1985): 18–20.

Knee, Derek, and Walters, David. *Strategy in Retailing: Theory and Application*. Oxford: Phillip Allan, 1985.

Lincoln, Doug, and McCain, Gary. "Marketing Decision-Making Problems Faced by Small Business Retailers." *Journal of the Academy of Marketing Science* 13 (Summer 1985): 183–197.

Lovelock, Christopher H., and Weinberg, Charles B. "Retailing Strategies for Public and Nonprofit Organizations." *Journal of Retailing* 59 (Fall 1983): 93–115.

Lusch, Robert F., and Moon, Soo Young. "An Exploratory Analysis of the Correlates of Labor Productivity in Retailing." *Journal of Retailing* 60 (Fall 1984): 37–61.

Mason, J. Barry, Mayer, Morris L., and Koh, Anthony. "Functional Marketing Plan Development in Department Store Retailing." *Journal of the Academy of Marketing Science* 13 (Summer 1985): 161–182.

Mason, Todd. "That Neiman-Marcus Mystique Isn't Traveling Well." *Business Week*, 8 July 1985, 44–45.

May, Eleanor G., Ress, C. William, and Salmon, Walter J. *Future Trends in Retailing: Merchandise Line Trends and Store Trends 1980–1990*. Cambridge, MA: Marketing Science Institute, 1985.

Powell, Judith D., and Bitner, Larry N. "Retail Expansion: Where on the Continuum of Control." In *Marketing in An Environment of Change, Proceedings*, edited by R.L. King, 161–64. Southern Marketing Association, 1986.

Ring, Lawrence J. "Retail Positioning: A Multiple Discriminant Analysis Approach." *Journal of Retailing* 55 (Spring 1979): 25–36.

Russell, Lloyd J. "Strategic Planning: What's Wrong with Retailer Strategies?" *Retail Control* (September 1983): 2–8.

Schulz, David P. "Retail Expansion." *Stores* (August 1985): 19–24.

Sheth, Jagdish N., and Frazier, Gary L. "A Margin Return Model for Strategic Market Planning." *Journal of Marketing* 47 (Spring 1983): 100–109.

Soldner, Helmut. "Conceptual Models for Retail Strategy Formulation." *Journal of Marketing* 44 (Fall 1976): 47–56.

Trombella, William L. "An Empirical Approach to Marketing Strategy for the Small Retailer." *Journal of Small Business* (October 1976): 55–58.

PART TWO
Environmental Scan: Analyzing the Environments of Retailing

3

Objectives

☐ Describe the marketing channel of distribution and understand the role of the retailer within this organizational system.

☐ Identify and discuss the four major types of retail competition.

☐ Recognize the different types of retailing institutions that the retailing community comprises.

☐ Identify the organizational and operational traits that characterize each type of retailer.

☐ Discuss the principal product, price, place, and promotional strategies each type of retailer employs.

☐ Discern the relative advantages and disadvantages that accrue to each type of retailer.

☐ Identify and discuss the theories of retail institutional change that are used to explain past evolution and predict future developments in retailing.

The Competitive Behavior of Retail Institutions

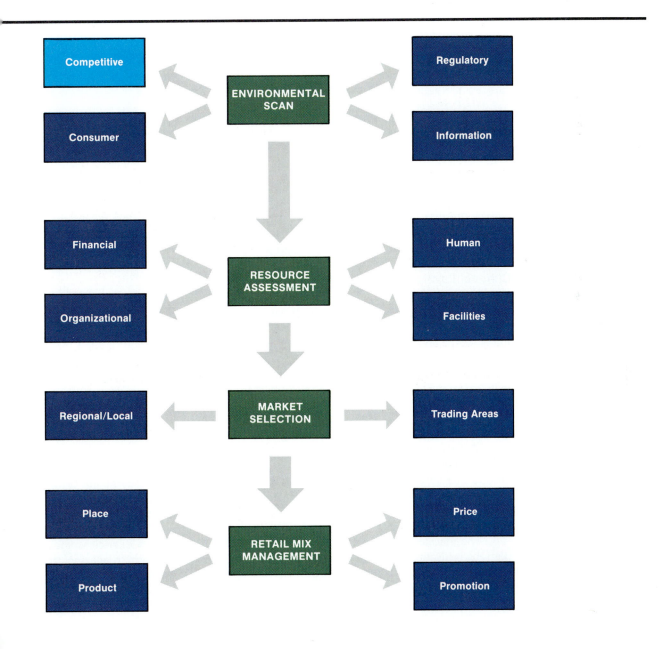

Retailing is an intensely competitive industry, a "24-hour-a-day-war." To survive and prosper, retailers must compete aggressively, create a differential advantage over competitors, and give consumers a reason to shop at their stores.[1]

Successful retailers historically have used multidimensional market strategies in developing a differential advantage in the marketplace. Merchandise quality, selection, assortment, and services typically have been used in conjunction with prices to build store traffic and loyalty.[2]

One of the most dramatic developments in today's world of retailing is the number of alternative types of stores available to consumers. "By and large, people have a wide repertoire of stores that they patronize. And they are open to all kinds of retail alternatives. So a store is not simply competing with other stores in its own retail category. It's competing with retailers across the board."[3]

In this chapter we extend our understanding of retailing beyond our own personal experiences; we will survey the broad spectrum of competitive retail business formats. Specifically, we will examine the following:

☐ Structure and composition of the marketing channel of distribution
☐ Methods and procedures of classifying retailing institutions
☐ Types and levels of retail competition
☐ Strategies and tactics of competing retail business formats
☐ Changing and adopting character of retail competition

THE NATURE OF MARKETING CHANNELS

The goal of a **marketing channel** of distribution is to have the right product. . .in the right quantities. . .in the right place. . .at the right time. The marketing channel's actions are directed at bringing together producers and their respective customers. The marketing channel can be described as a multilevel structure made up of channel teams whose interactions coordinate channel flows through channel teamwork.

Channel Levels

Marketing channels can be characterized by a number of different structural designs defined by the inclusion or exclusion of various intermediaries. The producer has a number of alternative channel structures to reach consumers. As Figure 3–1 illustrates, there are three basic alternative channel structures: extended, limited, and direct. The first alternative is to use an **extended channel** by marketing through both wholesalers and retailers. In this case, producers rely on wholesalers to reach retailers that, in turn, will stock their products and sell them to final consumers. Because there usually are fewer wholesalers than retailers in a marketing channel, this option allows the producer to spend less time and money cultivating the necessary channel contacts to reach the ultimate consumers.

The second alternative for a producer is the **limited channel**; that is, to use only retailers, thereby eliminating the wholesaler. A growing number of producers of such products as automobiles, furniture, appliances, and other big-ticket items are using the limited channel. Also, manufacturers of "perishable" products such as clothing (which goes out of style quickly) and fresh and frozen foods (which spoil rapidly) frequently use a limited channel.

The third alternative is the **direct channel**. In this case, the producer eliminates both the retailer and the wholesaler. By using door-to-door, television, magazine, or direct-mail selling techniques, these producers market directly to final consumers. Examples of products distributed that way include Electrolux Vacuum Cleaners, Avon Cosmetics, and Fuller Brushes.

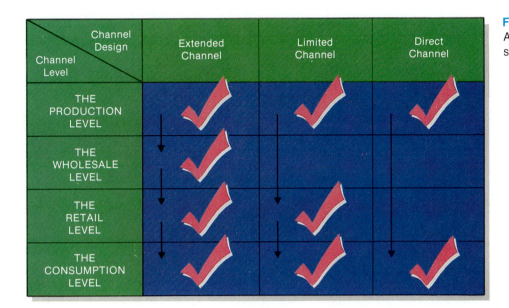

FIGURE 3–1
Alternative channel structures

Although a producer may choose not to use another team member in the channel, it can never eliminate the functions that must be performed at each channel level. In other words, *it can eliminate the retailer, but not the retail level and the retail functions.* Thus, producers who sell directly to consumers have taken over, but not eliminated, retailer operations at the retail level. Such producers become both wholesalers and retailers.

Channel Teams

Channel teams include both full- and limited-number institutions supported by facilitating nonmember institutions. Membership in the marketing channel team is based on the nature of an institution's transactional involvements and whether members assume title to the goods involved in the transaction. A *full-member institution* is a wholesaler or retailer directly involved in the purchase and/or sale of products and that takes title to the products involved in the transaction. Merchant wholesalers and nearly all retailers have full membership in the channel team. *Limited-member institutions* are marketing intermediaries with a direct involvement in purchase/sales transactions that do not take title to the involved product. Agent wholesalers hold limited team membership, as do retailers when they engage in consignment selling. A number of organizations provide a wide range of support functions; these *nonmember facilitating institutions* assist the team effort by providing specialized advertising, research, transportation, storage, financial, risk-taking, and/or consulting services. These facilitators neither take title to goods involved in a transaction nor become directly involved in sales and/or purchase of those goods.

Channel Interactions

Interactions between participants within the marketing channel of distribution can take several forms. As intermediaries, wholesalers and retailers must successfully complete a number of tasks for each other and their clientele to accomplish distribution and transactional functions most efficiently and effectively. These interactive tasks include buying, selling, breaking bulk, creating assortments, stocking, delivering, extending credit, informing, consulting, and transferring titles and payments (see Figure 3–2).

Channel Flows

A marketing channel can be likened to a pipeline, or conduit, that guides the movement of entire marketing programs between channel participants. Although the flow of physical goods is the channel flow most commonly recognized by the general public, other types of flows are equally important to delivering a successful marketing effort. The five major types of channel flows follow:

1. **Physical flow**—the actual movement of a physical product from one channel participant to another
2. **Ownership flow**—transferring title (right of ownership and usage) from one channel participant to another
3. **Information flow**—the two-way communication of useful data between channel participants
4. **Payment flow**—the transfer of monies from one channel participant to another as compensation for services rendered and/or goods delivered

FIGURE 3–2
Interactive tasks performed by the channel team

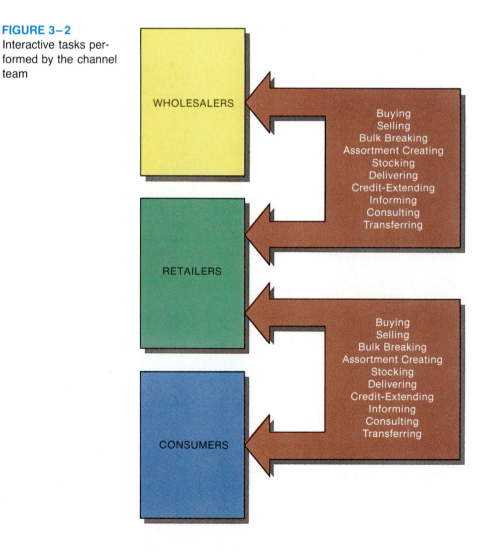

5. **Promotion flow**—the flow of persuasive communication directed at influencing the decisions of consumers (consumer promotion) and other channel participants (trade promotion)

The nature and degree of involvement with each of these flows for any given channel participant will vary depending on the structure of the channel. In most channel structures, however, retailers have a direct involvement in each of these flows and play a key role in successful channel flow management.

Channel Teamwork

As a social interactive system, the marketing channel is subject to the behavioral processes inherent in all such systems. The behavior of each channel participant affects all other participants; hence, the need for channel teamwork. Good teamwork results in a cooperative spirit and a coordinated effort; poor teamwork nets channel disruptions and conflict. To ensure good teamwork the channel of distribution needs to be integrated. **Channel integration** is the process of incorporating all channel members into one channel system and uniting them under one leadership and one set of goals. As Chapter 2 showed, channel integration can be accomplished through backward integration of retailers and wholesalers, forward integration of producers and wholesalers, and horizontal integration of each channel member within its respective channel level.

Channel integration ends the segregation of intermediary operations and their functional tasks. As Figure 3–3 shows, channel integration can take the form of a highly integrated vertical marketing system or a modestly integrated conventional marketing channel. A **vertical marketing system** is "*a professionally managed and centrally programmed network, pre-engineered to achieve operating economies and maximum market impact.*"[4] The advantage of this type of system is that it allows the

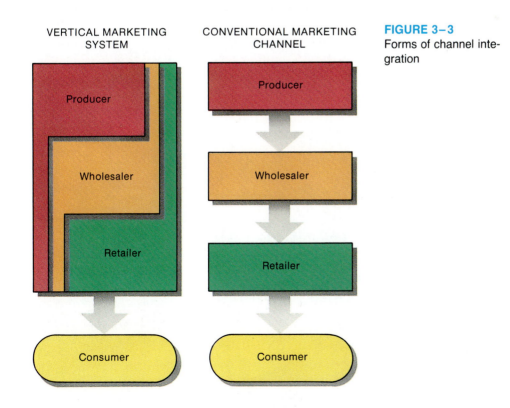

VERTICAL MARKETING SYSTEM

CONVENTIONAL MARKETING CHANNEL

FIGURE 3–3
Forms of channel integration

channel team to achieve technological, managerial, and promotional leverages through integrating and synchronizing the five channel flows.[5] A vertical marketing system can be established using persuasive administrative powers, legally binding contractual agreements, and partial or total ownership of channel members.

In a vertical marketing system, each channel member assumes the functions and tasks that will best support the entire channel system. As a team member, the retailer operates within the retail level of distribution and provides most of the team-

There are many different ways to classify retailers, and some classifications overlap.

work at that level. Some, however, engage in operations at the wholesale and even the production levels of the marketing channel. Sears, Roebuck & Co., for example, conducts extensive operations at both the wholesale and production levels of the channel. Sears buys a large portion of its products from manufacturers in which it has part ownership. Also, individual stores obtain most of their merchandise from Sears' wholesale distribution facilities.

A **conventional marketing channel** is a loosely aligned, independently owned and operated channel team. The chief advantage of this type of an arrangement is the freedom each member has in conducting business. The disadvantages of conventional channels include (1) the failure to achieve economies of scale, (2) the instability of the arrangement as a result of the ease of channel entry and exit, and (3) the limited levels of cooperation and coordination as a result of the greater autonomy of participating members. In short, the conventional marketing channel is becoming an outdated mode of operation for most retailers. The exceptions are the smaller, more specialized retailers that need their freedom of action to target specialty markets.

THE NATURE OF
RETAIL
COMPETITION

Retailers compete with one another on the basis of their product, place, price, and promotion strategies. These strategies are directed at securing the attention and patronage of ultimate consumers and serve as the focus for retail competitive actions. As described by *Business Week* magazine, "power retailers" are highly competitive organizations who succeed by sharply defining their customer base and fully understanding what their target customer wants. What the customer wants is the feeling that the retailer is on the cutting edge and that there is good reason to visit them frequently.[6] In assessing the competitive structure faced by a particular retailer, two dimensions of competition must be examined: the type of competition and the levels of competition.

Types of Competition

Retail competition is more complex than just two similar stores competing against each other. Figure 3–4 shows the four different types of retail competition: intratype,

FIGURE 3–4
Types of competition

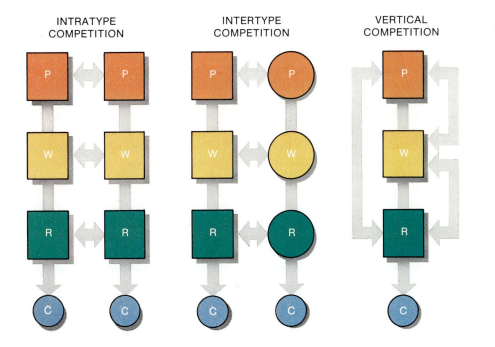
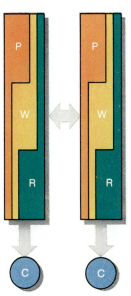

INTRATYPE COMPETITION   INTERTYPE COMPETITION   VERTICAL COMPETITION   SYSTEMS COMPETITION

FIGURE 3–5
The top 50 retail chains

Chains	1986 Sales ($ Millions)	1986 Earnings as Percentage of Sales (%)	Existing Units (1985)
1. Sears, Roebuck[a]	27,074	2.7	1,047
2. K mart	23,812	2.4	3,782
3. Safeway[c]	20,311	NA	1,909
4. Kroger	17,123	0.3	735
5. American Stores	14,021	1.0	1,498
6. J.C. Penney	13,390	3.4	1,793
7. Wal-Mart	11,909	3.8	1,029
8. Federated Dept. Stores	10,512	2.7	631
9. May Dept. Stores	10,328	3.7	2,766
10. Dayton Hudson	9,259	3.4	475
11. Winn-Dixie[d]	8,225	1.4	1,262
12. Southland	8,039	3.3	8,137
13. A&P	7,835	1.2	1,200
14. F.W. Woolworth	6,501	3.3	6,309
15. Lucky	6,441	34.5	579
16. Supermarkets General[c]	5,508	1.1	310
17. Albertson's	5,380	1.9	452
18. Zayre	5,351	1.7	1,092
19. Melville	5,262	4.5	5,833
20. Army/Air Force Exchange	5,187	4.4	5,441
21. R.H. Macy[c,d]	4,653	4.4	87
22. Allied Stores[e]	4,435	NA	697
23. Montgomery Ward	4,383	2.4	295
24. Carter Hawley Hale	4,090	0.0	302
25. Stop & Shop	3,872	1.0	275

intertype, vertical, and systems competition. **Intratype competition** involves the competition between two or more retailers using the same type of business format. For example, in a regional shopping mall we often see several small independent women's apparel shops competing with one another. Competition between two or more retailers using different types of business formats to sell the same type of merchandise is referred to as **intertype competition**. A supermarket (Safeway) and a discount store (Wal-Mart) attempting to sell Crest toothpaste to the same customer are engaging in intertype competition. **Vertical competition** is the competition between a retailer and a wholesaler or producer that is attempting to make retail sales to the retailer's customers. For example, if a retailer were to stock and sell a product line that the manufacturer was also offering through a catalog operation, the retailer and manufacturer would be engaged in vertical competition. Many manufacturers sell their goods directly to consumers through their own outlets located in factory outlet malls. Bass Shoes, Calvin Klein Sportswear, and Palm Beach, Inc., makers of Evan Picone and Giant sportswear, are just a few examples of producers who are in vertical competition with their retail outlets.[7] The final type of competition occurs between entire marketing channel systems. **Systems competition** is the competition between two or more vertical marketing systems. The competition between McDonald's, Burger King, and Wendy's is between three highly integrated marketing systems at all levels of the distribution channel.

FIGURE 3–5
continued

Chains	1986 Sales ($ Millions)	1986 Earnings as Percentage of Sales (%)	Existing Units (1985)
26. Publix	3,797	2.2	307
27. Walgreen[f]	3,661	2.8	1,273
28. The Limited	3,143	7.2	2,682
29. Von's	3,000	NA	NA
30. Grand Union	2,746	1.2	369
31. Revco[c,d]	2,743	2.1	2,031
32. Jack Eckerd[c]	2,700	NA	1,596
33. Radio Shack	2,687	NA	4,863
34. Price[d]	2,667	2.2	25
35. Wickes[a]	2,656	NA	565
36. Giant Food	2,528	1.8	142
37. Service Merchandise	2,527	NA	313
38. Batus	2,500	NA	197
39. Toys 'R' Us	2,445	6.2	338
40. Food Lion	2,407	2.6	388
41. Circle K	2,289	2.2	NA
42. Lowe's	2,283	2.3	300
43. Super Valu[a]	2,269	2.5	170
44. Best Products	2,142	NA	205
45. Mercantile Stores	2,028	5.5	82
46. Ames	1,888	1.4	463
47. Dillard	1,851	4.0	115
48. Rite Aid	1,757	4.4	1,586
49. Fred Meyer	1,688	1.3	93
50. Long's	1,635	2.4	222

NA, not available
Profit/earnings ratios are based on primary per share earnings as reported by the companies for the most recent four quarters. Extraordinary items generally are excluded.
[a]Retail only.
[b]Operating earnings, retail.
[c]Company has gone private during last twelve months.
[d]Fiscal year ended in summer of 1986.
[e]Acquired in last twelve months.
[f]Formerly American Can.
Source: Reprinted by permission from *Chain Store Age Executive*, August 1987, pp. 11–12. Copyright © Lebhar-Friedman, Inc., 425 Park Avenue, New York, New York 10022.

Levels of Competition

The level of competition a retailer faces in any market area is a function of the number, size, and quality of competitors within that area. Ideally, the retailer who faces a few small competitors is better off than the retailer who must compete against either a large number of small competitors or a few large competitors. The number and size of competitors can be determined with reasonable accuracy; Figure 3–5 shows the number (existing units) and size (sales volume) of the top fifty retail chains. The quality of each competitor is difficult to measure and analyze. The aggressiveness and effectiveness of competitors are important determinants of the level of competition for a market area. In the following pages, the competitiveness and effectiveness of various types of retailers are examined in detail.

THE COMPETITIVE STRATEGIES OF RETAILERS

Retailers can be classified on the basis of their ownership, merchandise, size, affiliation, contractual, location, service, organizational, and operational characteristics. The diversity and complexity of business formats found within the retailing industry preclude developing a mutually exclusive classification that clearly differentiates each type of retailer. For example, specialty and department stores can be distinguished on the basis of their respective merchandise mix; however, each might also be classified as a chain, affiliated, or integrated operation. Figure 3–6 outlines the multiplicity of characteristics that classify retail institutions.

FIGURE 3–6
Classifying retail institutions

A. By ownership of establishment
  1. Single-unit independent stores
  2. Multiunit retail organizations
    a) chain stores
    b) branch stores
  3. Manufacturer-owned retail outlets
  4. Consumers' cooperative stores
  5. Farmer-owned establishments
  6. Company-owned stores (industrial stores) or commissaries
  7. Government operated stores (post exchanges, state liquor stores)
  8. Public utility company stores (for sale of major appliances)
B. By kind of business (merchandise handled)
  1. General merchandise group
    a) department stores
    b) dry goods, general merchandise stores
    c) general stores
    d) variety stores
  2. Single-line stores (e.g., grocery, apparel, furniture)
  3. Specialty stores (e.g., meat markets, lingerie shops, floor coverings stores)
C. By size of establishment
  1. By number of employees
  2. By annual sales volume
D. By degree of vertical integration
  1. Nonintegrated (retailing functions only)
  2. Integrated with wholesaling functions
  3. Integrated with manufacturing or other form-utility creation
E. By type of relationship with other business organizations
  1. Unaffiliated
  2. Voluntarily affiliated with other retailers
    a) through wholesaler-sponsored voluntary chains
    b) through retailer cooperation
  3. Affiliated with manufacturers by dealers franchises

F. By method of consumer contact
  1. Regular store
    a) leased department
  2. Mail order
    a) by catalog selling
    b) by advertising in regular media
    c) by membership club plans
  3. Household contacts
    a) by house-to-house canvassing
    b) by regular delivery route service
    c) by party plan selling
G. By type of location
  1. Urban
    a) central business district
    b) secondary business district
    c) string street location
    d) neighborhood location
    e) controlled (planned) shopping center
    f) public market calls
  2. Small city
    a) downtown
    b) neighborhood
  3. Rural stores
  4. Roadside stands
H. By type of service rendered
  1. Full service
  2. Limited service (cash-and-carry)
  3. Self-service
I. By legal form of organization
  1. Proprietorship
  2. Partnership
  3. Corporation
  4. Special types
J. By management organization or operational technique
  1. Undifferentiated
  2. Departmentalized

Source: T. N. Beckman, W. R. Davidson, and W. W. Talarzyk, *Marketing*, 9th ed. (New York: Ronald Press Co., 1973), 239.

This section discusses the competitive strategies of various retail institutions from the perspective of twelve general types of retail operations. In reading this chapter, you should keep in mind the variety and complexity of retail characteristics as shown in Figure 3–6.

Specialty Store Retailing

Specialty store retailers "specialize" in the merchandise or service they offer a consumer. Specialty stores vary significantly in their degree of merchandise specialization. *Single-line specialty stores* offer only one or a very few closely related product lines. For example, retailers that specialize in either jewelry, shoes, hardware, furniture, or apparel are single-line specialty retailers. *Limited-line specialty stores* specialize in more than single-line specialty stores—within a single line of merchandise. For example, the retailer that specializes in either men's, women's, or children's shoes is a limited-line specialty store. Some retailers even limit their merchandise line to one manufacturer's brand, such as The Levi's Place, and the Lazy Boy Shop. Within any given merchandise line, retailers can specialize on the basis of price (e.g., discount or off-price), size (e.g., tall or big men's), quality (e.g., exclusive), style (e.g., early American), or fashion (e.g., new wave).

Figure 3–7 identifies the top specialty store chains in terms of sales volume. Of the top fifty specialty stores, twenty-one are apparel outlets; eight specialize in consumer electronics; six are shoe stores; four merchandise toys; two sell either books, textiles, or sporting goods; and the remaining five members of the Top 50 Club are a jewelry, furniture, giftware, record, and hard goods specialty chain.

A key tactic in the specialty retailer's product strategy is merchandise assortment. Although specialty stores carry only a limited variety of products, they offer consumers the opportunity to choose from a deep assortment within each line. The large number of brands, models, styles, sizes, and colors within each product line is the principal means by which specialty retailers attract customers. In general, the more specialized the retailer, the greater the depth of the product assortment. A specialty store might stock national brands, designer labels, private labels, or some combination of these products. Most specialty stores also stress the quality of their customer support services as part of its customer offering

Specialty retailers can be either high-margin operations (The Limited), or low-margin (T.J. Maxx) operations. Specialty retailers normally operate in varying size facilities with decor and layouts that complement the nature of their merchandise and support their mode of operation. Specialty retailers are found in a variety of locations including large shopping centers, downtown malls, specialty malls, and string/strip developments along major traffic arteries.

Specialty stores' promotions stress the uniqueness and distinctiveness of their product offerings and the depth of selection they offer the consumer. In final analysis, the product, price, place, and promotional strategies of the specialist are directed at serving the needs of a more targeted and homogeneous market segment. The specialty retailer attempts to serve all consumers in one or a limited number of market segments.

Department Store Retailing

Department stores are large retailing institutions that carry a wide variety of merchandise lines with a reasonably good selection within each line. What distinguishes the department store is its organizational structure, specifically the high degree of "departmentalization." From an operational standpoint, most of the basic functions of buying, selling, promoting, and servicing are conducted entirely or at least in part at the department level. Also, accounting and control procedures are organized on a

FIGURE 3–7

The top 50 specialty store chains

Rank	Company/Chain (Headquarters)	Type	Sales ($000,000s)	Units
1.	The Limited	Apparel	3,143	2,682
2.	Mervyn's	Apparel	2,862	175
3.	Radio Shack[a]	Consumer Electronics	2,700	4,795
4.	Toys 'R' Us	Toys	2,445	295
5.	Marshall's	Apparel	1,410	261
6.	Petrie Stores	Apparel	1,198	1,478
7.	Circuit City	Consumer Electronics	1,011	87
8.	T.J. Maxx	Apparel	1,010	226
9.	Zale[b]	Jewelry	939	1,216
10.	Volume Shoe	Shoe	934	2,210
11.	Gap Inc.[c]	Apparel	848	724
12.	Levitz	Furniture	831	101
13.	Kinney Shoe	Shoe	700	1,535
14.	Highland Superstores	Consumer Electronics	656	53
15.	Waldenbooks	Books	650	944
16.	Brown Shoe	Shoe	630	1,324
17.	Herman's[d]	Sporting Goods	630	205
18.	Child World	Toys	629	134
19.	Businessland[a]	Consumer Electronics	600	95
20.	B. Dalton[e]	Books	585	820
21.	Foot Locker	Shoe	572	765
22.	Edison Bros. Shoe	Shoe	570	1,403
23.	Ross Stores	Apparel	534	121
24.	Casual Corner	Apparel	530	702
25.	Charming Shoppes[f]	Apparel	521	678

[a]Estimates for fiscal year ended June 30, 1987, for US company-owned stores.
[b]Continuing operations only, for fiscal year ended March 31, 1987.
[c]Includes 65 Banana Republic and 10 GapKids stores.
[d]Estimate for fiscal year ended April 30, 1987.
[e]Acquired by Barnes & Noble in November 1986.
[f]For fiscal year ended July 16, 1986.
[g]Cyclops Corp. now 83% owned by Dixon PLC.

departmental basis. The advantages of this type of organization are that it allows both *functional* (buying, selling, etc.) and *merchandise* (apparel, shoes, etc.) specialization, while at the same time gaining the economies of scale associated with a large retailing operation.

Some department stores are local independents (see Figure 3–8); others are part of a national chain (e.g., Sears and J.C. Penney) or an ownership group (e.g., see Figure 3–9).

Some department stores limit their departmentalization to a few (less than 30) broad merchandise lines, whereas others departmentalize into many (more than 100) very limited merchandise groups. Whatever the degree of departmentalization, department stores commonly divide merchandise into "hard" and "soft" line departments. Home furnishings is an example of a broad, hard-line department that could be further departmentalized into consumer electronics, floor coverings, furniture, major appliances, and decorative furnishings. The women's department is a soft line that can be further departmentalized by creating separate departments for dresses, footwear, hosiery, lingerie, jewelry, and ladies' accessories. Department stores offer

FIGURE 3–7

continued

Rank	Company/Chain (Headquarters)	Type	Sales ($000,000s)	Units
26.	Alexanders'	Apparel	520	14
27.	Silo Electronics[g]	Consumer Electronics	494	119
28.	Kay Bee	Toys	487	639
29.	Thom McAn	Shoe	484	1,033
30.	Lechmere	Hard Goods	476	17
31.	Federated Group	Consumer Electronics	430	65
32.	Hartmarx Specialty[h]	Apparel	415	230
33.	C.R. Anthony	Apparel	412	268
34.	Brooks Fashion	Apparel	412	777
35.	Musicland[i]	Records	412	525
36.	Burlington Coat[j]	Apparel	392	87
37.	Crazy Eddie	Consumer Electronics	353	34
38.	Loehmann's	Apparel	351	90
39.	Edison Apparel	Apparel	334	1,072
40.	Bealls	Apparel	325	150
41.	County Seat	Apparel	325	301
42.	Oshman's[k]	Sporting Goods	323	315
43.	Hit or Miss	Apparel	320	461
44.	House of Fabrics	Textiles	316	707
45.	Pic 'n Save	Apparel	305	101
46.	Spencer Gifts[1]	Giftware	302	439
47.	McDuff-Scott[a]	Consumer Electronics	300	294
48.	Ups 'N' Downs[m]	Apparel	300	667
49.	Hancock[n]	Textiles	290	325
50.	Lionel	Toys	288	65

[h]For year ended Nov. 30, 1986.
[i]Includes Sam Goody, Licorice Pizza, and Discount Records stores.
[j]For fiscal year ended Nov. 1, 1986.
[k]Includes 27 Abercrombie & Fitch stores.
[1]Includes mail-order sales as well as results of Intrigue jewelry and A2Z—The Best of Everything stores.
[m]Includes sales of Caren Charles, Petite Sophisticate, and August Max.
[n]Prior to spinoff by Lucky Stores in May 1987.
Source: David P. Schulz, "The Top 100 Specialty Stores," *Stores* (August 1987): 26–27.

FIGURE 3–8

The top 10 independent department stores

Organization (Location)	Sales Volume ($ Millions)	Number of Units
Dillard's (Little Rock, AR)	1,851	115
Nordstrom (Seattle)	1,630	53
Woodward & Lothrop (Washington, D.C.)	497	16
Carson Pirie Scott (Chicago)	435	20
Strawbridge & Clothier (Philadelphia)	410	12
P.A. Bergner (Milwaukee)	391	34
McRae's (Jackson, MS)	331	29
Jacobson's (Jackson, MI)	308	20
Elder-Beerman (Dayton, OH)	287	26
Boscou's (Reading, PA)	270	11

Source: David P. Schulz, "The Top 100 Department Stores," *Stores* (July 1987): 13–16.

Chain and Division(s)	Sales Volume ($ Millions)	Number of Units
Federated Department Stores		
Bloomingdales (New York)	1,050	16
Abraham and Straus (Brooklyn)	779	15
Foley's (Houston)	1,107	37
Burdine's (Miami)	810	29
Bullock's (California)	752	28
Rich's (Atlanta)	691	20
Lazarus (Cincinnati)	905	32
Filene's (Boston)	391	16
Goldsmith's (Memphis)	174	6
Boston Stores (Milwaukee)	131	8
I. Magnin (San Francisco)	317	26
Dayton Hudson		
Dayton Hudson (Minneapolis)	1,566	37
May Department Stores		
May Co. (California)	814	34
Hecht Co. (Washington, D.C.)	624	22
Famous-Barr (St. Louis)	495	17
Kaufman's (Pittsburgh)	455	14
May Co. (Cleveland)	248	10
Meier & Frank (Portland)	226	8
G. Fox & Co. (Hartford)	264	9
M. O'Neil Co. (Akron)	182	9
May D&F (Denver)	175	10
Strouss (Youngstown)	104	8
May-Cohens (Jacksonville)	80	6
Lord & Taylor (New York)	865	45
J.W. Robinson (California)	586	24
L.S. Ayres (Indianapolis)	440	25
Sibley, Lindsay & Curr (Rochester)	192	14
Denver Dry Goods (Denver)	151	12
Hahne (Newark)	153	8
Goldwaters (Phoenix)	157	9
Robinson's (St. Petersburg)	136	10
Mercantile Stores		
Gayfer's (Mobile)	350	12
McAlpin (Cincinnati)	325	9
Castner-Knott (Nashville)	225	11
Jones Store (Kansas City)	220	8
Joslin's (Denver)	215	11
Gayfer's (Montgomery)	175	6
Bacons/Roots (Louisville)	160	7

a wide selection of brand-name and designer-label merchandise. Because of the competition from off-price retailers, however, "many department stores have developed private-label programs that enable them to offer exclusive merchandise and receive higher profits than for brand name merchandise."[8]

Several inherent advantages to departmental organization aid the retailer in developing and implementing a product strategy. First, department managers are in

FIGURE 3–9
continued

Chain and Division	Sales Volume ($ Millions)	Number of Units
Mercantile Stores *(continued)*		
J.B. White (Augusta)	145	7
Lion (Toledo)	120	3
Hennesey's (Billings)	75	5
Allied Stores		
Jordon Marsh (New England)	537	19
The Bon (Seattle)	490	39
Joske's (Texas)	349	27
Sterns (New Jersey)	484	24
Maas Bros. (Tampa)	332	21
Jordon Marsh (Florida)	251	17
Pomeroy's (Pennsylvania)	149	16
Bonwit Teller (New York)	157	13
Miller & Rhoads (Richmond)	138	17
Donaldson's (Minneapolis)	181	15
Garfinckel's (Washington)	112	10
Miller's (Knoxville)	107	12
Read's (Bridgeport)	111	6
Block's (Indianapolis)	86	10
Cain Sloan (Nashville)	64	4
Carter Hawley Hale		
The Broadway (California)	1,045	43
Emporium Capwell (San Francisco)	710	22
Neiman-Marcus (Dallas)	850	22
John Wanamaker (Philadelphia)	433	16
Weinstock's (Sacramento)	236	12
Thalheimer's (Richmond)	360	24
Broadway-Southwest (Phoenix)	210	13
Bergdorf Goodman (New York)	120	1
R.H. Macy & Co.		
Macy's (New Jersey)	1,440	24
Macy's (New York)	1,575	22
Macy's (California)	1,335	25
Macy's (Atlanta)	605	16
Batus (retail group)		
Saks Fifth Avenue (New York)	1,005	44
Marshall Field's (Chicago)	925	25
Ivey's (Charlotte, FL)	275	25

Source: Adapted from David P. Schulz, "Stores' Annual Ranking," *Stores* (July 1987): 13–18.

a good position to supervise and control each individual product line closely. Second, sales personnel operating at the departmental level are directly in touch with consumers' needs, buying problems, and special concerns. Third, a departmental organization allows the retailer to segment the consumer market. Figure 3–10 illustrates how retailers can use store departmentalization to satisfy a particular market segment's needs. Chicago's Carson Pirie Scott & Co. has made a major statement of its targeting strategy by creating Corporate Level, a separate department tailored to the needs and wants of executive and professional women. Not just any working woman will be targeted, only those with individual incomes of at least $25,000.[9] To attract the

FIGURE 3–10
Market segmentation
through store depart-
mentalization

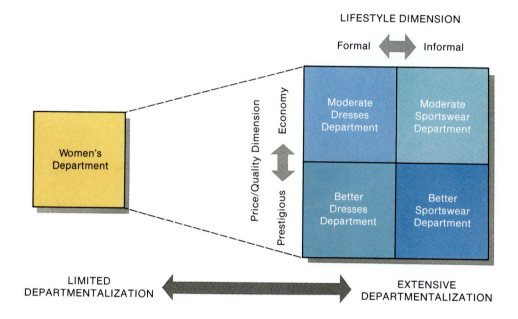

professional woman, Corporate Level offers a mix of goods and services; "a customer can buy a wardrobe, get a haircut, and drop off the dry cleaning."[10]

Department stores usually are high-margin operations. Because of the high operating expenses (30 to 40 percent of sales) stemming from the store's organizational structure, service offering, physical facilities, and high-risk merchandise, margins between merchandise costs and retail selling prices must be substantial to ensure a fair profit. Department stores normally appeal to middle- and upper-income consumers. To appeal to such a diverse group of consumers, some department stores have at least three pricing points. "Low or economy" prices are directed at the lower- to middle-income consumer; "midline" prices appeal to those who want neither the lowest nor the highest priced merchandise; "prestige" prices are aimed at the upper-income consumer who desires the best. These good, better, and best price lines not only allow the department store to project a broad price appeal, but also help consumers to make price and quality comparisons. Some upscaled department stores, like Bloomingdale's and Nieman Marcus, focus their attention on the middle and upper pricing points.

Department stores typically occupy high-rent locations within major commercial centers. The place strategy of most department stores has been to locate in an "anchor" (end) position at one or more major suburban shopping centers. The exterior and interior motifs of the average department store are designed to create a prestige image. Externally, the architectural form might communicate either bigness, success, uniqueness, strength, security, elegance, or any number of store images. Internally, the store's layout, fixtures, and decor create consumer buying moods by appealing to all the customers' sensory modes of sight, sound, smell, taste, and touch.

The department store's principal promotional appeals are product selection and quality, service offerings, and shopping atmosphere. Nordstrom's of Seattle has become the model for good service, and as a result, it enjoys the highest sales per square foot of any department store: $310 versus the industry average of $150. Nordstrum's service is based on having highly motivated sales associates—"an attitude, a kind of caring on the part of everybody in the store."[11] Each of these appeals is directed toward enhancing the prestige image of the department store. "A well-honed identity helps persuade customers that they are getting their money's worth even if the department store is higher priced than some of its rivals. Bloomingdale's is renowned as a yuppie emporium where trendiness makes up for higher prices. Macy's aims for the shopper on a budget who is interested in wide assortment and name brands. A reputation for quality merchandise, hassle-free returns, and a more personal service may still draw a value-conscious crowd."[12] Both product and institutional advertising are an integral part of the department store's strategy to favorably influence potential consumers. Although advertisements feature several carefully selected products, every department store advertising campaign subtly communicates the message that "this is the place to shop." Department stores like to create the "big event" by developing shopping themes consistent with the customer's moods and needs, the seasons or current events, the merchandise, and the store's environment. For example, Bloomingdale's likes to stage multimillion-dollar extravaganzas honoring individual countries' crafts.

Chain Store Retailing

In retailing, the term *chain* is used in a variety of ways. As commonly used, a chain store is any retail organization that operates multiple outlets. To be properly classified as a chain, however, a retail organization must meet several additional criteria. What distinguishes chain operations from similar types of operations are the number of units (stores), the merchandise mix, and the form of ownership and control.

Technically, any retail organization that operates more than one unit can be classified as a chain. However, the *Census of Business* considers chains as retail organizations that operate 11 or more units. A workable compromise is to discuss chain organizations as *small chains* (two to ten units) and *large chains* (eleven or more units). Another criterion for classifying a conglomeration of stores as a chain is that each unit in the chain must *sell similar lines of merchandise*. So long as the product is basically the same, a chain store organization could be a multiunit operation of specialty stores, discount stores, department stores, or food stores. The third criterion used to determine if a group of stores is a chain is whether there is a *central form of ownership and control*. With central ownership, the parent organization has control over all operating and merchandising aspects of the entire chain of stores.

Traditionally, chain stores offer highly standardized merchandise. Frequently, the home office establishes a basic stock list in which the standard items on the list are typically staple merchandise items that have a relatively high market demand and turnover rate. The merchandise items are the most popular brands, styles, models, sizes, and colors as perceived by the store's targeted consumers. Store-to-store variation in product mix is receiving considerable attention. Montgomery Ward has launched its specialty store strategy in which seven specialty shops (e.g., apparel, appliance, automotive, home care, home electronics, home store, and recreation and leisure) have been developed. A given Ward's store may get two, three, or up to all seven shops, depending on the marketplace characteristics. Store to store merchandise variations are allowed but tightly controlled.[13]

In recent years, many of the larger chain organizations have engaged in "private-label" branding (the retailer's brand) as part of their overall product strategy. In some cases, a few of the private brands of very large chains have become, in effect, national brands. For example, most consumers think of Sears' "Craftsman" and "Kenmore" brands as high-quality, national brands. In the apparel lines, Sears is aggressively merchandising its Stefanie Powers career collection, its Cheryl Tiegs sportswear line, and its Arnie (Palmer) menswear.[14] By virtue of the fact that Sears' operations are national in scope, many more of their private labels are viewed in the same perspective.

Economies of scale are an important part of the chain's central buying policies. By buying in large quantities, often directly from the manufacturer, chain stores receive substantial quantity discounts. Large-quantity purchases also reduce the cost of merchandise, because the chains can take advantage of lower transportation rates on carload and truckload shipments. An additional benefit associated with large-scale purchases are *promotional allowances* (payments that chains receive from suppliers to help defray the cost of advertising the suppliers' products). The net result of the chain's centralized buying policies is that it can acquire merchandise at the lowest costs in the retailing industry.

Several advantages accrue to chain store operations. First, by operating a large number of stores within a particular market, chains can exert substantial control over their stores and achieve economies of scale through a centralized distribution system. The result is high turnover rates and few stockouts and overstocks. Second, chains can spread risk over many different stores in many different markets. Third, chain organizations obtain benefits from vertically integrating their channels of distribution. Sears, for example, obtains approximately 50 percent of its merchandise from manufacturers in which it has equity interest (partial ownership). Finally, chain operations enjoy the advantage of a high level of consumer recognition. The use of a standardized sign and architectural motif reinforces consumers' awareness of the chain and what it has to offer.

Chain stores usually promote both their store image and their individual products. Generally, chains promote the standardized nature of their operations and therefore the consistency (product quality, customer service, etc.) of their product offerings from store to store. Chains also commonly promote their convenience and large number of locations available to their customers. Many chains stress the reliability of buying from a large national or regional firm. Finally, with multiple locations within a given market, chain stores can effectively use the most expensive media (television) and exposure time (prime time).

Discount Store Retailing

The **discount store** is a retailing institution that sells a wide variety of merchandise at less than traditional retail prices. Targeted to meet the needs of the economy-minded consumer, the discount store uses mass-merchandising techniques that enable it to offer discount prices as its major consumer appeal. The discount store sells namebrand (national or manufacturers' brands) and private-label merchandise at prices that consumers easily recognize as below traditional prices. The discount store carries a fairly complete variety of hard and/or soft goods. In its drive for high turnover, the typical discounter stocks only the most popular brands, styles, models, sizes, and colors, along with its own private labels. In general, the product strategy of the discount store is to carry many different product lines but limit the amount of selection within each line.

A few nationally well-known brands in key product line areas are an integral part of the discounter's product strategy. In selling national brands, the discounter takes advantage of the fact that consumers know the going price for various products. Thus, it sells most of its merchandise to the price-conscious shopper. Also, selling national brands below suggested manufacturer's retail price greatly enhances the store's discount image. This image helps the discounter convince the general public that its large selection of private labels are also a good value. To capitalize on its value image, K mart is installing five distinctive private label lines of women's clothing; they range from the classically styled Hunter's Glen label to the dressier Jaclyn Smith line; K mart wants to sell customers something more than pantyhose, hairspray, and school supplies.[15]

The discounter's service offering is limited to services necessary to run the operation. Traditionally cash-and-carry businesses, most major discount chains now offer credit services. Sales personnel are used in departments (jewelry, camera, etc.) that absolutely need them. Store personnel also include those who staff information booths, return and credit approval counters, and checkouts.

The pricing strategy of the conventional discount store promotes the highest possible turnover rate. A high rate of stock turns is the key to success and profitability for the discount retailer. Although the amount of the discount varies greatly from one product line to another, it is large enough for the majority of the consuming public to recognize it as a discount.

Conventional discounters select suburban locations convenient to the large, middle-class consumer market; discount houses frequently serve as anchors for community shopping centers and, in some rare cases, as the major anchors of a regional shopping center. An exception to this strategy is Wal-Mart, which became the seventh largest retailer by following a location strategy of "selling name-brand merchandise at a discount in small-town America."[16] The typical discounter operates out of a modern one-story building ranging in area from 20,000 to 150,000 square feet. The store size depends on the local market size. Many discount stores create a carnival-like environment through their store decor and special sales events. Tile floors, plain pipe racks, bargain tables and bins, and rows of shelving are the primary ways for these discounters to display their merchandise. Centralized checkout areas are a prominent part of all discount operations. Some leased departments and high-ticket item departments have localized checkouts.

Most discount stores are aggressive advertisers. Discounters use a broad message appeal highlighting variety, selection, and especially price. Newspapers are the discounter's principal medium, but television and radio advertising are increasing. Another key promotional strategy discounters use to inform and persuade the consumer is the point-of-purchase display. Bargain tables, bins, and stacks greet consumers as they enter, check out, and exit. End-of-aisle and main-aisle displays intercept shoppers as they travel through the store. In-store loudspeaker announcements of unadvertised specials are used to draw customers throughout the store.

Off-Price Retailing

Off-price retailers are specialty retailers that sell both soft goods and/or hard goods at price levels (20 to 60 percent) below regular retail prices. There are two general types of off-price operations: (1) **factory outlet** stores or direct manufacturers' outlets (e.g., Levi Strauss, Manhattan's Brand Name Fashion Outlet, Burlington Coat Factory Warehouse, and Bass Shoes), which sell their own seconds, overruns, and pack-aways from last season, and (2) *independents* (e.g., Loehmann's, T.J. Maxx, Marshall's, and Clothestime), who buy seconds, irregulars, canceled orders, overages, or leftover goods from manufacturers or other retailers.[17] A key concept in the off-price retailer's strategy is selling designer labels and branded merchandise; consumers know if the price is an "off-price" if they can make price comparisons on like goods.

The off-price retailer's mode of operation can be described as follows:

- ☐ Low buying prices, often lower than for conventional discounters and lower than could be expected on the basis of quantity discounts

- A high proportion of established, often designer, brands from manufacturers that seek the highest prices they can get for distressed and leftover merchandise, overruns, and irregulars
- Merchandise often of higher quality than usually found in "discount stores"
- A changing and unstable assortment in that the customer can't confidently predict exactly what the retailer will have on a given day—a major factor distinguishing off-pricing from simple discounting
- Customer services varying from minimal to extensive, sometimes including wrapping, exchange, refunds, and credit card acceptance
- Variety ranging from very narrow (for example, men's suits) to very broad (for example, family apparel)[18]

One explanation for the ability of off-price retailers to secure favorable terms is that they tend to pay promptly and do not ask for such extras as advertising allowances, return privileges, and markdown adjustments.

On the selling side, off-price retailers strive to keep their overhead low to maintain lower margins. Operating expenses are reduced by operating out of modest facilities located in strip malls, where rent is half that charged by large shopping centers.

A variation of the off-price retailer is the **close-out store**—an outlet that specializes in the retailing of a wide variety of merchandise obtained through close-outs, retail liquidations, and bankruptcy proceeds. "The merchandise mix varies, depending on wholesale buying opportunities that arise, but fall into certain broad categories, including household products, small appliances, toys, snack foods, and health and beauty aids."[19] An 80/20 product mix (hardgoods to softgoods) is common for close-out operations.[20] Like other off-pricers, close-out stores strive to keep operating expenses at a minimum. Consolidated Stores of Columbus, Ohio, operators of Odd Lots and Big Lots stores, Job Lot Trading of New York, and Pick 'n' Save of Los Angeles, are the major players in this form of off-price retailing.

Supermarket Retailing

Supermarket retailing as we know it began in the early 1900s, when Piggly Wiggly experimented with the self-service method of food retailing. Today, food store sales (over $300 billion) account for one fifth of all retail sales in the United States. No commonly accepted definition of a supermarket exists because of the wide range of business formulas used in this industry. One common definitional classification of supermarkets follows:

- *Conventional supermarket:* a self-service grocery store that offers a full line of groceries, meat, and produce with at least $2 million in annual sales
- *Superstore:* a modern, upgraded version of the conventional supermarket with at least 30,000 square feet in total area and more than $8 million in annual sales; offers an expanded selection of nonfoods and service departments (e.g., deli, bakery, seafood)
- *Food and drug combo:* combination of superstore and drugstore under a single roof and common checkout; drugstore merchandise represents at least one third of the selling area and a minimum of 15 percent of store sales
- *Warehouse store:* a low-margin grocery store that combines reduced variety, lower service levels, simpler decor, streamlined merchandising presentation, and aggressive prices
- *Superwarehouse store:* a high-volume hybrid of the superstore and the warehouse store offering full variety, quality perishables, and low prices

☐ *Limited-assortment store:* a very "bare bones," low-price grocery store that eliminates services and carries fewer than 1,000 items with few, if any, perishables[21]

The market share of each of these formats is shown in Figure 3–11. The growth of the economy (price-oriented) and extended (selection-oriented) formats are at the expense of the more traditional supermarket operation.

The products offered by a supermarket include a relatively broad variety and complete assortment of dry groceries, fresh meats, produce, and dairy products. In recent years, the basic food lines have been supplemented by a variety of prepared food lines (the deli department) and nonfood lines. By adding prepared foods, the supermarkets hoped to negate the threat posed by the fast-food restaurants. The addition of "carry-out services" and "eating-in areas" for such foods as deli products, fresh bakery products, and fast-food restaurant lines (e.g., hamburgers, hot dogs, chicken, tacos, and fish) represents a direct effort to obtain a large share of this eating-out business.

By broadening their merchandise lines to include nonfood products, supermarkets have successfully increased sales and profits. With large numbers of customers moving through their stores each week, this product strategy has resulted in numerous sales of convenience and shopping goods. Today, supermarket's upgraded and upscaled operations include such nonfood lines as prescription drugs, small appliances, linens, auto accessories, books, magazines, clothing, flowers, and housewares. Recently, many supermarkets have added numerous services—including dry cleaning, post-office, banking, tailoring, medical, dental, insurance, and legal services. If the "scrambling" process continues, the supermarket of the future could well become the modern version of the "general store."

Supermarkets are low-margin operations that depend on very high stock turnover rates to sustain profits. Operating out of clean, modern facilities (an extremely important patronage motive for most food shoppers), the supermarket is basically a

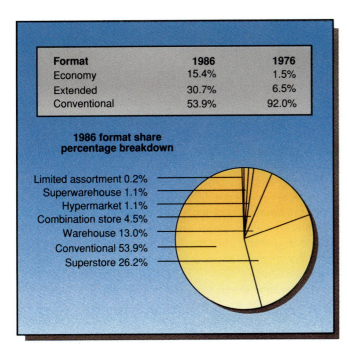

Format	1986	1976
Economy	15.4%	1.5%
Extended	30.7%	6.5%
Conventional	53.9%	92.0%

1986 format share percentage breakdown

Limited assortment 0.2%
Superwarehouse 1.1%
Hypermarket 1.1%
Combination store 4.5%
Warehouse 13.0%
Conventional 53.9%
Superstore 26.2%

FIGURE 3–11
U.S. supermarkets' format share (source: Cynthia Valentino, "In a fragmented market." Reprinted with permission of *Advertising Age*, 4 May 1987. Copyright © Crain Communications, Inc.)

self-service operation offering few free services with the exception of parking and bagging. Although some supermarkets accept credit cards and offer tote services to automobiles, cash and carry is the preferred method of doing business. The most distinguishing promotional characteristic of supermarkets is the weekly advertising of loss or low-price leaders (products sold below or at cost). Leader pricing is aimed at attracting consumers into the store, where it is hoped they will purchase the rest of their weekly shopping list at full markup prices.

Convenience Store Retailing

The modern-day version of the corner "mom and pop" grocery store is the **convenience store**. As its name suggests, the convenience store offers customers a convenient place to shop. In particular, it offers time convenience by being open longer and during the inconvenient early morning and late night hours, and place convenience by being a small, compact, fast-service operation that is close to consumers' homes and places of business. Their time and place convenience appeals are suggested in their trade names—7-Eleven, Stop-N-Go, Majik Markets, Quik-Pik, Minit Markets, and Jiffy.

The basic premise of the convenience store is capturing fill-in or emergency trade—after the consumer has forgotten to purchase a needed product during the planned weekly trips to the supermarket or has unexpectedly run out of a needed product before the next planned supermarket trip. Because these stores are frequently located between the consumer's home and the nearest supermarket, they serve as effective "interceptors" of fill-in and emergency trade.

Convenience stores carry both food and nonfood merchandise lines. Like supermarkets, convenience stores have broadened their basic product mix to include items such as motor oil, toys, prepared foods (7-Eleven's Hot-To-Go), firewood, ice drinks, and self-service gasoline. Product assortment within each line is very limited. Major national brands dominate the product line, although some of the major chain organizations offer private labels in beverages and some canned goods.

Because they provide time and place utilities, convenience stores charge appreciably higher prices than other stores. From a promotional viewpoint, the store's sign and location are the most important weapons in the war to attract consumers. The convenience store's facilities include buildings that range from 1,000 to 3,200 square feet and parking areas that accommodate five to fifteen cars. Store layouts are designed to draw customers through the store to increase impulse purchasing. To accomplish this, convenience store managers place high-volume items (e.g., beer and soft drinks) at or near the back of the store.

Contractual Retailing

Independent retailers often attempt to achieve economies of operations and an increased market presence by integrating their operations with other retailers and wholesalers. By entering contractual arrangements, retailers can formalize the rights and obligations of each party in the contract. The terms of the contract can, and often do, cover all aspects of the retailer's product, place, price, and promotional activities. Contractual retailing exists in several forms, but the four most common forms are retailer-sponsored cooperative groups, wholesaler-sponsored voluntary chains, franchised retailers, and leased departments.

The **retailer-sponsored cooperative group** is a contractual organization formed by many small independent retailers and usually involves the common ownership of a wholesaler. Originally formed to combat competition from large chain organizations, this type of contractual system allows the small independent to realize economies of scale by making large-quantity group purchases. The contractual agreement usually requires individual members to concentrate their purchases of products from the cooperative wholesaler and, in turn, receive some form of patronage refund. Associated Grocers and Certified Grocers are two large food wholesalers having cooperative contractual arrangements with independent food retailers.

The **wholesaler-sponsored voluntary chain** is a contractual arrangement in which a wholesaler develops a merchandising program that independent retailers voluntarily join. By agreeing to purchase a certain amount of merchandise from the wholesaler, the retailer is assured of lower prices. These lower prices are possible because the wholesaling organization can buy in larger quantities with the knowledge that it has an established market. The Independent Grocers Alliance (IGA) and Super Valu Stores, Inc., are both food wholesalers that sponsor voluntary chains. Other examples include Western Auto in the automotive and household-accessories market and Ben Franklin in the variety store market.

A large and growing percentage of retail marketing is conducted today through a franchise system, a form of retailing in which a parent company (franchisor) obtains distribution of its products, services, or methods through a network of contractually affiliated dealers (franchisees). The International Franchise Association defines **franchising** as "a continuing relationship in which the franchisor provides a licensed privilege to do business, plus assistance in organizing, training, merchandising, and management in return for a consideration from the franchisee."[22] In other words, what the franchisor offers the franchisee is a patterned way of doing business that includes product, price, place, and promotional strategies.

In practice, this means that the franchisee is the owner of his or her own business, distributing the goods or services of the franchisor and paying for that privilege through an initial fee and/or a percentage of future sales or profits. Though the franchisee owns the business, the franchisor usually exercises control over some aspects of its operation to ensure conformity to the franchisor's proven methods and standards for products, services, quality, and methods.

In return for the fees and royalties paid by the franchisee, the franchisor may provide some or all of the following services: (1) location analysis and counseling; (2) store development, including lease negotiations; (3) store design and equipment purchasing; (4) initial employee and management training, and continuing management counseling; (5) advertising and merchandising counsel and assistance; (6) standardized procedures and operations; (7) centralized purchasing with consequent savings; (8) financial assistance in the establishment of the business; (9) an exclusive territory in which to operate; and (10) the goodwill and recognition of a widely known brand or tradename.

Franchisors expect franchisees to conform to the business pattern and also to provide them with some form of compensation for their right to use the franchise. Franchisor compensation usually involves either one or a combination of the following:

1. *Initial franchise fee*—a fee that the franchisor charges up front for the franchisee's right to own the business and to receive initial services
2. *Royalties*—an operating fee imposed on the franchisee's gross sales
3. *Sales of products*—profits the franchisors make from sales to franchisees of raw and finished products, operating supplies, furnishings, and equipment
4. *Rental and lease fees*—fees that franchisors charge for the use of their facilities and equipment
5. *Management fee*—a fee that franchisors charge for some of the continuous services they provide the franchisee[23]

Business in the franchise system is thriving, both in terms of retail sales of goods and services through franchise outlets and in the growth of the number of franchises themselves. Retail sales of franchising companies in 1987 were estimated at $515.2 billion, or about 33 percent of total U.S. retail sales.[24] The Naisbitt Group, a national forecasting firm, predicts that by the year 2005 franchising will become a $1 trillion industry and account for 50 percent of all retail sales.[25]

Among the primary advantages of owning a franchise unit are that it usually requires less capital to set up a franchise than it would to start up independently; it is often unnecessary to possess knowledge about a particular type of business because of franchisor training programs; and business risk is frequently reduced because of the recognition and goodwill of the franchisor's name and product and through the initial and continued help the franchisor provides in running the business. Franchising, however, should not be considered an easy and failure-proof way to financial success. The franchisee faces a number of disadvantages. First, the relationship between the franchisor and franchisee usually involves control over many aspects of the franchisee's business operations, and some owners find that this overly inhibits their creativity and independence. Second, to acquire a blue-chip franchise such as a McDonald's or Pizza Hut requires considerable financial resources and high royalty payments. Someone wishing to purchase a McDonald's in 1986, for instance, was required to have $140,000 in unborrowed funds plus the ability to obtain outside financing for an additional $160,000 to $200,000, on top of which were added royalty and advertising fees of 15 percent of sales.[26] Third, the success of each individual franchise unit depends on the workings of the parent company, and even the best managers can find their business—and investment—jeopardized if trouble develops in the franchisor's operations. For example, more than 50 Arthur Treacher's Fish and Chips franchises went bankrupt in the mid-1980s after the parent company sold out to a new owner, who promptly changed practices and policies. Finally, experts urge those thinking of purchasing a franchise to remember that it is usually much more a full-time job than an investment, with most new owners finding themselves putting in well above an average work week. Said the president of the International Franchise Association: "Franchising brings opportunities, not miracles."[27]

Today, there are over 2,000 franchise companies involved in almost every type of retail business area, from molars to mufflers, as evidenced by The American Dental Centers joining Midas shops on the scene. In the 1980s, firms starting franchise operations for the first time were adding to this total at a rate of over 200 per year.

Franchise companies can be divided into two main types. The first are called *product or trade-name franchises* and are characterized by franchised dealers that carry one company's product line and identify their business with that company and product. Examples of this type include automobile dealers, gasoline stations, and soft drink bottlers. Together, product franchises accounted for an estimated 71 percent of franchise sales in 1987, though this percentage has been slowly decreasing. These types of operations are often referred to as manufacturer-sponsored and wholesaler-sponsored retailers (see Figure 3–12).

The second type is called *business format franchising,* or service firm-sponsored retailer, a system in which the franchisee not only carries the franchisor's products and trade name but the entire business format itself, from merchandising to store design (see Figure 3–12). Most aspects of the franchisee's operations are coordinated to ensure a certain and consistent image that is designed to appeal to particular market segments. This category includes restaurants (McDonald's), auto repair shops (MAACO), personal and business services (H&R Block), and many others, and is increasing at a much greater rate than product franchises. Sales in 1987 were an estimated $171 billion, compared with $141 billion in 1985, a 21-percent

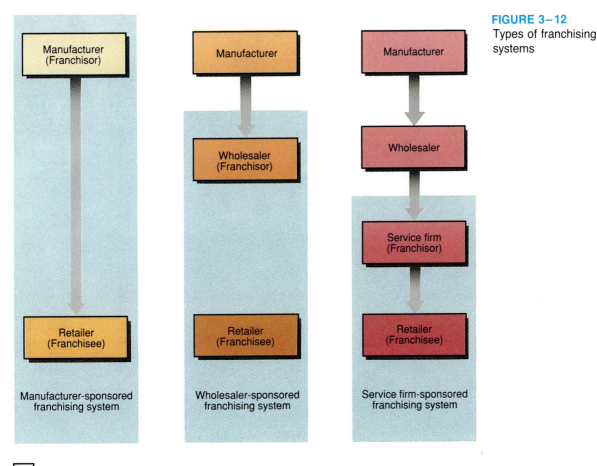

FIGURE 3–12
Types of franchising systems

☐ = Franchised System

increase. Estimated sales for 1987 for various kinds of franchised businesses are shown in Figure 3–13.

The rapid rate of franchise sales growth experienced in the past three decades is expected to continue. This trend will be fueled by the entrance of many new and small companies into the franchise system, attracted by both the ability to expand rapidly despite limited company capital and the competitive advantages that franchising often can provide. Growing customer preference for convenience and consistent quality—two of franchising's principal strengths—should also accelerate franchise growth. Another important factor will be increasing activity by U.S. franchisors in foreign markets, a pattern that has developed significantly in the 1980s.

Much of the increase in domestic franchise sales is expected to come from the service sector. With the average age of the U.S. population rising and the increasing number of two-earner families, forecasters see further creation of franchise opportunities in such areas as maid services, repair and home remodeling, carpet and other cleaning services, and various maintenance functions.

Franchises specializing in business services are expected to grow at an even faster rate, a product of the so-called "age of information" and the increasing preference of many firms to contract out functions they once performed internally. Growth is expected to come in franchises supplying services for businesses such as

	Establishments (No.)		Sales ($000s)	
Kinds of Franchised Business	Company Owned	Franchise Owned	Company Owned	Franchise Owned
Total, all franchising	90,952	407,543	76,292,106	515,049,824
Automobile and truck dealers	0	27,750	0	305,617,000
Automotive products and services	5,214	35,157	4,503,595	8,406,869
Business aids and services	6,495	54,822	2,390,135	13,154,421
Accounting, credit, collection agencies, and general business systems	23	2,572	4,283	207,502
Employment services	1,865	4,107	1,455,125	2,109,520
Printing and copying services	142	5,831	35,656	1,188,017
Tax preparation	3,392	4,868	257,520	227,281
Real estate	335	15,822	89,700	5,832,465
Miscellaneous business services	738	21,622	547,851	3,589,636
Construction, home improvements, maintenance and cleaning services	776	21,389	1,443,857	3,493,430
Convenience stores	9,654	6,922	7,720,141	5,082,990
Educational products and services	537	8,567	140,560	710,637
Restaurants (all types)	26,293	60,106	10,376,297	37,574,835
Gasoline service stations	21,060	95,940	17,083,000	77,824,000
Hotels, motels, and campgrounds	1,206	7,372	4,945,493	11,783,961
Laundry and drycleaning services	269	2,888	52,931	372,115
Recreation, entertainment, and travel	484	8,460	881,605	2,309,470
Rental services (auto–truck)	2,479	9,041	3,737,836	2,800,299
Rental services (equipment)	511	2,392	292,385	524,000
Retailing (nonfood)	11,617	39,108	7,838,512	17,340,000
Retailing (food other than convenience stores)	3,742	19,795	3,134,185	8,508,334
Soft drink bottlers	122	1,128	1,603,000	18,429,000
Miscellaneous	493	6,706	138,574	1,118,463

[a]1987 data estimated by respondents.

Source: U.S. Department of Commerce, *Franchising in the Economy 1985–1987* (January 1987): 27.

FIGURE 3–13
Franchising in the
economy: 1987[a]

accounting, advertising, packaging and shipping, consulting, security, personnel, and copying and printing. Though there are currently many independent firms supplying these services to local business, some see them giving way to national or regional franchise operations in the coming years. Projected growth in various retail franchising categories is illustrated in Figure 3–14.

Other specific types of franchises targeted by the Commerce Department for above-average growth throughout the 1980s include weight control centers, hair salons, temporary help services, printing and copying services, medical centers, and clothing stores.[28]

Leased departments are retailers that operate departments (usually in specialized lines of merchandise) under contractual arrangements with conventional retail stores. Many supermarkets and department stores, for example, lease space to outside organizations to sell magazines (as in supermarkets) and auto supplies and

FIGURE 3–14

Top franchise industries: Projected growth

Business Category	Sales ($ millions)		Annual Growth (%)
	1985	1990	
Restaurants (all types)	48,926	86,109	12.0
Retailing (nonfood)	18,790	33,560	12.3
Hotels/motels/campgrounds	14,631	22,511	9.0
Convenience stores	12,309	19,377	9.5
Business services	12,076	21,282	12.0
Automotive products and services	10,604	15,944	8.5
Food retailing (other than convenience stores)	10,370	14,544	7.0
Rental services (auto–truck)	5,282	8,900	11.0
Construction and home services	3,720	9,255	20.0
Recreation/entertainment/travel	1,840	6,573	29.0
Total	138,548	238,055	11.5

Source: Reprinted by permission, *Nation's Business*, February 1986. Copyright 1986, U.S. Chamber of Commerce.

shoes (as in many department and discount stores). The most frequently leased-out departments are beauty salon, books, cameras, candy, costume jewelry, electronics, family shoes, fine jewelry, furs, and photo.[29] The lessor usually furnishes space, utilities, and basic in-store services necessary to the lessee's operation. In turn, the lessee agrees to provide the personnel, management, and capital necessary to stock and operate a department with carefully defined merchandise. Generally, the contract calls for the lessee to pay the lessor either a flat monthly fee, a percentage of gross sales, or some combination of the two.

Warehouse Retailing

The typical **warehouse** retailing operation involves some combination of warehouse and showroom facilities. In some cases, these facilities are located in separate but adjacent areas; in others, the warehouse and showroom are combined into one large physical structure. Generally, the warehouse retailer uses warehouse principles to reduce operating expenses and thereby offer discount prices as a primary customer appeal. Five types of warehouse retailers can be identified: warehouse showroom, catalog showroom, home center, hypermarkets, and warehouse clubs.

The **warehouse showroom** is generally a single-line hard-goods retailer that stocks merchandise such as furniture, appliances, or carpeting. To help the consumer make price comparisons with conventional home-furnishing retailers, the warehouse showroom typically stocks only well-known, nationally advertised brands. These retailers set up sample merchandise displays in showrooms so potential consumers can get an idea of what the products will look like in their homes. After making a selection, consumers immediately receive the merchandise in shipping cartons from the completely stocked adjacent warehouse. Although they prefer the "cash-and-carry" mode of operation, most warehouse retailers offer credit, delivery, and installation services. Warehouse retailers provide these services at an additional fee over the selling price. Because of space and delivery requirements, plus the need to attract consumers from a large market area, warehouse showroom locations usually are freestanding sites near major traffic intersections such as interstate highway systems.

The **catalog showroom** is a warehouse retailer featuring hard goods such as housewares, small appliances, jewelry, watches, toys, sporting goods, lawn and garden equipment, luggage, stereos, televisions, and other electronic equipment at a discount. The distinguishing feature of the catalog showroom is that a merchandise catalog is combined with the showroom and an adjacent warehouse as part of the retailer's operation. By adding a catalog of products to showroom products, the retailer provides consumers with both an in-store and at-home method of buying merchandise.

Catalogs, which are generally issued biannually, sometimes incorporate a unique method of illustrating the discounted price. List prices appear in plain bold numerals while the actual discounted prices are the last several digits of a code. This method often accentuates the discount nature of the price by forcing the customer to calculate the difference. The price tags on the sample merchandise on display in the showroom incorporate the same pricing method. As with the warehouse showroom, the catalog showroom features nationally branded merchandise that facilitates consumer price comparisons with conventional hard-goods retailers.

For consumers, the typical shopping trip to a catalog showroom involves (1) filling out an order form using the merchandise/price code found on either the showroom price tag or in the catalog, (2) ordering and paying for merchandise at a cashier's desk, and (3) picking up the merchandise at a pick-up desk. The pick-up desk is directly connected to an adjacent warehouse containing a complete stock of merchandise. Best Products, Consumers' Distributing, and Service Merchandise are the three companies that account for the bulk of catalog showroom sales.[30]

The modern **home center** combines the traditional hardware store and lumberyard with a self-service home-improvement center. The typical merchandise mix includes a wide variety and deep assortment of building materials, hardware, paints, plumbing and heating equipment, electrical supplies, power tools, garden and yard equipment, and other home-maintenance supplies. Some home centers have also expanded their merchandise offerings to include household appliances and home furnishings. Home centers usually have large showrooms that display sample merchandise (large, bulky items) and complete stock (small, standardized items). Consumers purchase showroom sample merchandise by placing an order at the order desk, and clerks pull the order from adjacent warehouse stocks. Customers simply serve themselves with showroom stock. While appealing to all home owners, the home center has been particularly successful in appealing to the "do it yourselfer." By providing customers with information on materials and equipment and by offering "how-to" services, home centers have developed a strong customer following. Major home center operators include Mr. How, Home Depot Inc., K mart's Builders' Square, Payless Cashways, and Handy Dan.

The **hypermarket** is a general-merchandise warehouse retailer that stocks and sells food products and a wide variety of both hard and soft goods. Operating out of a warehouse, the hypermarket displays offerings in wire baskets, metal racks, wooden bins, and simple stacks of merchandise that often reach heights of 12 to 15 feet. A self-service retailer with central checkouts and a sophisticated system of materials handling, the hypermarket attempts to underprice traditional retailers by as much as 15 to 20 percent. A European innovation, the hypermarket is making inroads into U.S. retailing. One example is the 245,000-square-foot hypermarket that Meijer, Inc., built near Detroit. Recent entries into the hypermarket field include Bigg's in Cincinnati (joint venture between French-based Euromarche and American-based SuperValue) and Wal-Mart's new Hypermart USA in Texas.[31]

Warehouse clubs are "huge outlets open to members only and typically sell merchandise at 20 to 40 percent below prices at supermarkets and discount stores."[32] As a special type of discount house, warehouse clubs are also referred to as wholesale clubs, membership clubs, and wholesale centers.[33] The principal play-

| Company | Number of Outlets | Membership Policy | |
		Wholesale	Retail
B.J.'s Wholesale Club (Zayre)	8	$30 annual fee; up to two additional memberships $10 each	5% markup
Buyers Club	2	[not available]	
Club Mart of America	1	[not available]	
Club Wholesale (Elixir)	2	$25 annual fee	5% markup
Costco Wholesale Club	21	$25 annual fee	5% markup
Metro Cash & Carry of Illinois	3	No fee	5% markup
Money's Worth	1	$25 annual fee	5% markup
Pace Membership Warehouse	15	$25 annual fee	5% markup
Price Club	24	$25 annual fee	Either $15 annual fee and 5% markup or $25 annual fee without 5% markup
Price Savers (Kroger)	5	$25 annual fee	5% markup
Sam's Wholesale Club	23	$25 annual fee	5% markup
Super Saver	9	[not available]	
The Warehouse Club (joint partnership with W.R. Grace)	7	$25 annual fee	5% markup
The Wholesale Club	5	$25 annual fee	5% markup
Wholesale Plus	1	$25 annual fee	5% markup
Value Club	5	$25 annual fee	$5 fee and 5% markup

Source: Jack G. Kaikati, "The Boom in Warehouse Clubs," *Business Horizons* (March–April 1987): 72. Compiled from: Molly Brauer, "Membership Retailing Trend Taking Off," *Chain Store Age Executive,* November 1984: 18; and Joseph H. Ellis, *The Warehouse Club Industry: An Update* (New York: Goldman Sachs & Co., July 25, 1986).

FIGURE 3–15
The warehouse club merchandisers

ers in the warehouse club market are identified in Figure 3–15. Most warehouse clubs have a two-tiered membership plan: (1) wholesale members who pay an annual fee and must be operators of small businesses and (2) group members who usually pay about 5 percent above the ticket price of the merchandise. The principal retail mix strategies are as follows:

☐ Product mix—a vast array of product categories but a limited selection of the best selling brands, sizes, and models in each category
☐ Service mix—cash and carry business with limited hours and no amenities (e.g., bathrooms)
☐ Place mix—large (100,000 square feet) bare-bones facilities (warehouse) located in out-of-the-way low-rent locations
☐ Price mix—rock-bottom wholesale prices that produce paper-thin gross margin profits (10 to 11 percent)
☐ Promotional mix—minimal advertising (less 1/2 percent of sales) supported by minimal sales support, visual merchandising, and sales incentives

Nonstore Retailing

Nonstore retailing involves retailers that do not use conventional store facilities as part of their standard mode operation. Nonstore, direct marketing methods are used to target a select group of consumers.[34] A major strategy of the nonstore retailer is to take the "store" (i.e., party, catalog, videodisc) to the customer rather than wait for the customer to come to the retailer (i.e., store). Nonstore retailers include a wide variety of retailing formats; Figure 3–16 identifies those formats.

At-home retailing is the market approach of making personal contacts and sales in the consumers' homes. This form of retailing offers the consumer the ultimate in *place convenience* and, with some planning on the part of the salesperson (such as making an appointment), can provide an equal amount of *time convenience*. At-home retailing provides several other advantages to the consumer. First, it is a highly

FIGURE 3–16
Nonstore retailing
formats

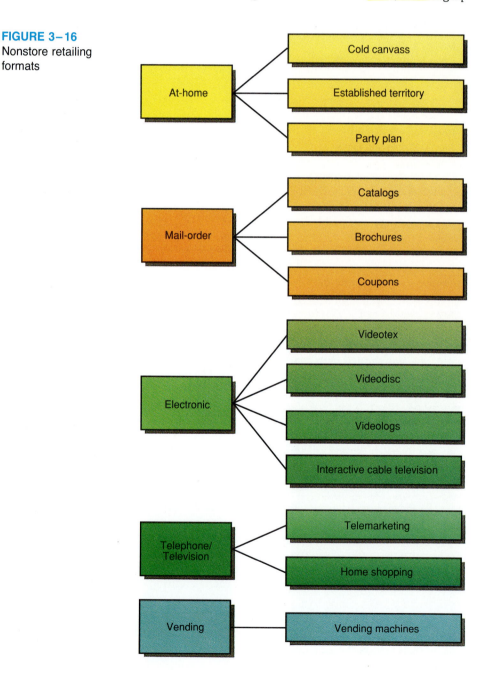

personalized service because of the one-on-one relationship between the customer and salesperson. Second, at-home retailing aids consumers in making a product evaluation before the purchase by letting them try the product in a home setting. Next, it saves the consumer the time and effort of going to the store, searching for needed merchandise, and waiting in checkout lines. Finally, this type of retailing usually includes home delivery, which appeals to most customers, especially the elderly.

At-home retailing also offers the seller certain advantages, including (1) no direct competition because the seller presents its products in "isolation" in the home, where consumers cannot make direct comparisons with similar products; (2) avoidance of uncontrollable intermediaries; and (3) elimination of investments in stores and other facilities, because sales representatives are compensated on a commission basis and pay their own expenses.

The at-home method of retailing, also referred to as "door-to-door" and "house-to-house" selling, exists in several forms. The three principal forms are the cold-canvass, the established territory or route, and the party plan. The *cold-canvass method* involves soliciting sales door-to-door without either advanced selection of homes or prior notice to potential consumers of an intended sales call. Vacuum cleaners, magazines, and books are some of the more common products sold by the cold-canvass method. The *established territory method* assigns salespeople to prescribed geographical areas, in which they must make their door-to-door sales and delivery calls at regular, predetermined time intervals. Some of the best-known users of the established territory method are Avon (cosmetics), Fuller Brush (household products), Stanley Home Products (household products), and Sarah Coventry (jewelry). The *party plan method* of at-home retailing requires a salesperson to make sales presentations in the home of a host or hostess who has invited potential customers to a "party." Usually, the party plan includes various games and other entertainment activities in which participants receive small, inexpensive gifts. Closing the sale occurs when the salesperson takes orders from the people attending the party. As a reward for holding the party, the host or hostess receives either cash or gifts from the salesperson. Tupperware and Wearever Aluminum Products make extensive use of the party method. Toys, books, home-decorating products, household goods, jewelry, health and beauty aids, and apparel are just a few of the products sold in this manner.

Mail-order sales to the final consumer was a $33.6 billion business in 1987.[35] **Mail-order retailers** are business formats that contact prospective customers by mail, receive their orders by mail, and/or make their deliveries by mail. Mail-order operations vary significantly in terms of their merchandise lines and operations (i.e., methods of customer contact, order placement, and delivery arrangements). As we shall see, "mail-order" probably is a misnomer for the modern mail-order retailer.

Mail-order operations differ tremendously in the variety and assortment of merchandise lines they offer the mail-order customer. Three important types of mail-order operations have been identified. The *general merchandise mail-order house* is a mail-order retailer offering a wide variety of merchandise lines. The depth of the assortment within each merchandise line varies among houses and among lines. Sears, J.C. Penney, and Spiegel of Chicago all operate general merchandise mail-order operations. The second type of mail-order operation is the *novelty mail-order retailer* whose lines are often limited to unusual products not normally carried by conventional retailers. Frequently, the novelty operator directs merchandise appeals to a small market segment. For example, intimate wearing apparel, unusual reading materials, specialized sporting equipment, exotic foods, unusual hobby equipment, and novel gifts are the kind of merchandise that novelty mail-order retailers sell. The

Sharper Image is an excellent example of this type of cataloger. The third type of mail-order retailing is the *supplementary mail-order operations of department and specialty stores.* Many conventional department and specialty stores offer mail-order service for the convenience of their customers. The Neiman-Marcus Christmas catalog and the "Hot Properties" life-style catalog by Marshall Field exemplify this type of mail-order retailing.[36]

Because of different operating characteristics, three forms of mail-order retailing have emerged. They are catalogs, brochures, and coupons. Any given mail-order retailer can use one or any combination of these three forms.

Catalog operations involve the use of specially prepared catalogs that present the retailer's merchandise both visually and verbally. Basic product assortment (sizes, colors, materials, styles, models, etc.) and pricing information are included along with directions stating how to order on the order blanks provided. Modern catalog operations allow the customer to place orders by mail, telephone, or in person at a catalog desk. In addition, catalog operations offer a variety of delivery arrangements such as mail, parcel post, express service, customer pickup, and store delivery.

Some retailers use a brochure form of mail-order retailing by preparing a small booklet or leaflet that they mail to potential consumers. The distinguishing feature of this type of brochure is that it usually displays only a limited number of product items that can attract consumer attention and interest. These interesting and attention-getting brochures usually emphasize either the innovative nature or the good value of the product.

The coupon form of mail-order retailing involves using magazine and newspaper advertisements. Advertisements featuring special merchandise and mail-order coupons are placed in magazines and newspapers that appeal to specific market segments. To some extent, most magazines and newspapers segment their markets either geographically (regional or local editions) or psychographically (subscribers to specialty publications usually have certain common activities, interests, and opinions).

Electronic retailing via electronic and video systems is in the innovation stage of the retail life cycle. Although a large number of potential electronic retailing options exist and the number of options are expected to expand as new technologies are brought on line, retailers are currently focusing their attention on videotex, videodisc, videologs, and interactive cable television.

Videotex is "an interactive electronic system in which data and graphics are transmitted from a computer network over telephone or cable lines and displayed on a subscriber's TV or computer-terminal screen."[37] The basic components and interactions of a videotex system appear in Figure 3–17. Shopping with a videotex system consists of selecting from a series of choices, called menus, that are displayed on the screen. For example, a shopper narrows down the choice by selecting from a menu of product lines and product items (brands, styles, sizes, colors, prices, and so on). In addition to at-home shopping, videotex systems can provide subscribers a wide selection of services including news, weather, sports, financial, and consumer information; at-home banking, reservations, and travel information; electronic encyclopedias and magazines, videocoupons and educational/instructional games; directories; real-estate and employment listings; home energy management; security, medical, and fire monitoring; and electronic mail/messaging.

Videodisc "is an interactive electronic system that uses flat optical discs capable of storing vast amounts of information in the form of moving pictures, still pictures, printed pages, and sound—for display on a TV screen."[38] One such system is the "Electronic Bed and Bath Fashion Center" developed by the J.P. Stevens Co., an in-store videodisc, text, and printer information system that allows consumers to see and purchase virtually the entire product line. "A printout from the Stevens unit gives

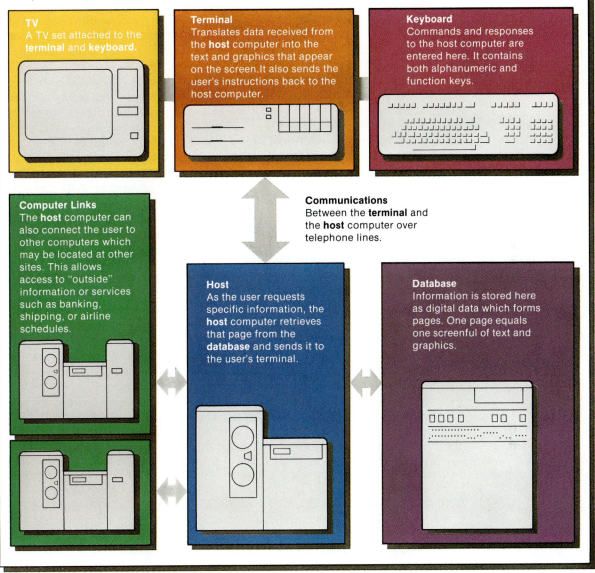

THE VIDEOTEX SYSTEM
A central computer controls the videotex systems. Users communicate with the **host** computer to request information from the **database** which is then sent to the home **terminal.**

TV
A TV set attached to the **terminal** and **keyboard.**

Terminal
Translates data received from the **host** computer into the text and graphics that appear on the screen. It also sends the user's instructions back to the host computer.

Keyboard
Commands and responses to the host computer are entered here. It contains both alphanumeric and function keys.

Communications
Between the **terminal** and the **host** computer over telephone lines.

Computer Links
The **host** computer can also connect the user to other computers which may be located at other sites. This allows access to "outside" information or services such as banking, shipping, or airline schedules.

Host
As the user requests specific information, the **host** computer retrieves that page from the **database** and sends it to the user's terminal.

Database
Information is stored here as digital data which forms pages. One page equals one screenful of text and graphics.

a record of the entire order for the customer. . .the customer is helped at the console by a store salesperson specially trained by Stevens. After she punches all her keypad buttons, she is given the order printout, which must be taken to a cashier for completion of the sale."[39]

Videologs are shop-at-home videotapes. In essence, it is the next wave of catalog shopping. "Customers either receive the video for free by mail or pay a fee that is credited toward any purchase."[40] A third distribution alternative is to make the videologs available free-of-charge to customers through video stores; however, the video must be returned to the video store. Videologs can be produced to reflect product usage, consumers' life-styles, or any other merchandising theme that might

FIGURE 3–17
Basic components and interactions of a videotex system (source: Tom Mach, "High-Tech Opportunities Getting Closer to Home," *Advertising Age,* 16 [April 1984]. Copyright Crain Communications Inc. Reprinted by permission.)

prove successful. The two-fold sight and sound appeal provides a competitive edge over the sight-oriented printed catalog.

Interactive cable television provides the ultimate in shopping convenience; it "permits viewers to purchase merchandise displayed on their television screens and charge the cost to a credit card or bank account by punching a keypad."[41] Warner-Amex Cable Communications QUBE service in Columbus, Ohio, is one example of this type of electronic retailer.

Telephone (telemarketing) and the telephone/television (home shopping) business formats are two more methods of nonstore retailing that are experiencing impressive growth rates. In recent years, the **telemarketing**—the selling of goods and services through telephone contact—has helped some retailers increase service satisfaction by providing greater customer convenience. For customers who want to avoid traffic congestion and parking problems, telephone shopping is a desirable alternative. This form of retailing also can be of service to shut-ins, the elderly, parents with babysitting problems, working people who do not have time to shop, and consumers who do not like to shop. Figure 3–18 profiles the "teleshopping-prone" consumer and the "ideal product" for teleshopping.

Retailers' major reasons for using telephone retailing are that it (1) provides customers with information on new merchandise and upcoming sales events, (2) allows customers to order merchandise that retailers are willing to deliver to the customers' homes, and (3) gives consumers a convenient way to hold merchandise that they can pick up at a later date.

Home shopping combines two of America's favorite pastimes—watching television and going shopping. A price-value–oriented retailing operation, *home shopping* is a business format whereby: (1) merchandise items are displayed, described, and demonstrated on television; (2) customers order the merchandise by calling a toll-free number; (3) customers pay for the order by credit cards, C.O.D., or check; (4) the retailer (home-shopping network) delivers the merchandise by United Parcel Service (UPS) or some other parcel post company; and (5) the retailer typically offers money-back guarantees if the merchandise is returned within 30 days.[42] The principal players in the shop-by-television game are: (1) Home Shopping Network, Inc., Clearwater, Florida; (2) Television Auction Shopping Program, Inc., of San Jose,

FIGURE 3–18
Teleshopping profiles

Profile of the "teleshopping-prone" consumer	Profile of the "ideal product" for teleshopping
• younger female who:	• a product that:
• is part of a two-career household	• has a strong brand with identifiable model number
• has heavy demands on her time	• comes in a few standard sizes
• is affluent	• does not need special customization and prepurchase service
• has above-average education	• does not involve considerable sensual experience in customer evaluation process
• takes risks	• has a low bulk to value ratio
• seeks information	• has a medium-to-low level of complexity
• uses direct mail	• has a limited number of attributes important to consumer decision making
• is technology-fluent	• is nonperishable and not subject to price negotiation at point-of-sale
	• is a planned-purchase-type product

Source: "Videotex to Curtail Canada In-Store Retailing; Study Predicts 15% Home Penetration by 1990," *Marketing News*, 25 November 1983, 20.

California; and (3) Cable Value Network of Minneapolis, Minnesota. An analysis of the largest system, Home Shopping Network (HSN), found that:

1. Seventy-five percent of the merchandise offered by HSN consisted of manufacturers' overruns and closeouts, and the overstock inventory of wholesalers and retailers.
2. Twenty-five percent of the goods sold is special-order merchandise, much of it from foreign sources of supply.
3. The product mix is 25 percent jewelry, 15 to 20 percent electronics and phones, 15 percent soft goods, and the miscellaneous items contributes the remainder of the mix.
4. Fifty to seventy-five percent gross margins on jewelry and soft goods with price points of $30 to $70.[43]

Consumer demand for greater time and place convenience and concurrent technological developments spurred the successful introduction and market expansion of the self-contained, automatic vending machine in the late 1940s. Rather than competing with store retailing, **vending machine retailing** became a complement of the store's operations by vending products that are usually a nuisance to handle within conventional store operations. On a much smaller scale, vending machines are similar to convenience store retailing in that they usually serve to meet the "fill-in," "emergency," and "after- or off-hour" needs of consumers.

Products that vending machines dispense have several characteristics in common. They typically are small, branded, and standardized products of low-unit value. Candies, soft drinks, hot beverages, and cigarettes are the most popular vending machine items. Among other food products commonly sold in vending machines are milk, snack foods, bakery products, and sandwiches. Nonfood products frequently sold by vending machines include life insurance policies for air travel, postage stamps, newspapers, ice, health and beauty aids, and some novelty items. One of the most significant developments in the use of vending machines is in the field of entertainment. Jukeboxes, pinball machines, and electronic games have greatly expanded the sales potential of vending operations.

THE CHANGING CHARACTER OF RETAIL INSTITUTIONS

Retailing and the institutions of retailing are still undergoing numerous changes in response to numerous environmental trends. Innovative merchandising strategies and operational methods are constantly being developed to meet these competitive challenges. What the future will bring to the everchanging retailing world is a matter of speculation. Given that "the past is the key to the future," however, some retailing experts have identified patterns of competitive change that they express as theories of retail institutional change. Four of the more commonly accepted theories are the wheel of retailing, the dialectic process, the retail accordion, and the theory of natural selection.

Wheel of Retailing

One of the most widely recognized theories of retail institutional change is the **wheel of retailing**. First hypothesized by Malcolm P. McNair, the wheel of retailing states that the dynamics of institutional change are a "more or less definite cycle"; the cycle "begins with the bold new concept, the innovation" and ends with "eventual vulnerability. . .to the next fellow who has a bright idea."[44] A careful examination of the wheel theory reveals three distinct phases to each cycle and that a pattern of cycles will develop over a period of time. Figures 3–19 and 3–20 illustrate the three

FIGURE 3–19
The wheel of retailing

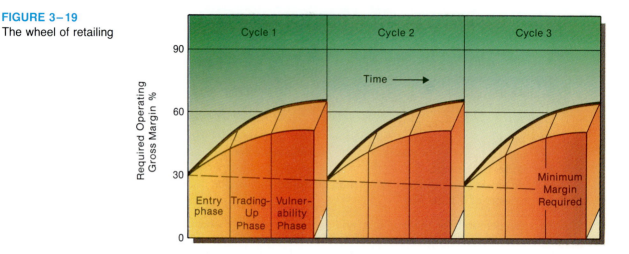

phases of entry, trading up, and vulnerability and how each cycle might be repeated to form a wavelike pattern.

Entry Phase

In the first phase of the cycle, an innovative retailing institution enters the market as a low-status, low-price competitor. By reducing operating expenses to a minimum, the new institution can operate at a gross margin substantially below (e.g., 30 percent as opposed to 50 percent) the required gross margins of the more established retailers in the market. Operating expenses usually are maintained at low levels by (1) offering minimal customer services, (2) providing a modest shopping atmosphere in

FIGURE 3–20
The retailer and the
wheel of retailing

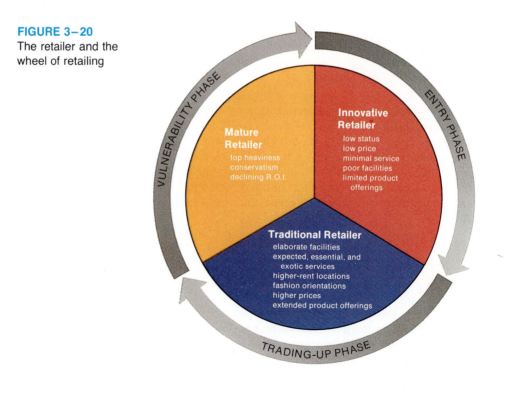

terms of exterior and interior facilities, (3) occupying low-rent locations, and (4) offering limited product mixes. Generally, market entry is easier for retailers selling low-margin, high-turnover products. Although consumers and competitors consider the innovative institution low-status, it does gain market penetration primarily on the basis of price appeals. Once the new form of retailing has become an established competitor, it enters the second phase of the cycle.

Trading-Up Phase

Emulators quickly copy the successful innovation because of its success and market acceptance. The competitive actions of these emulators force the original innovative business to differentiate itself by engaging in the process of trading up. The trading-up phase of the cycle involves various changes to upgrade and distinguish the innovative institution.[45] Trading up usually takes the form of acquiring more elaborate facilities, offering expected and exotic as well as essential services, and locating in high-rent neighborhoods. Also, product lines frequently are traded up to include high markup items, often with a fashion orientation. The end result of the trading-up phase is that the original innovative institution matures into a higher-status, higher-price operation with a required operating gross margin comparable to that of many established competitors. In other words, the innovative institution matures into a traditional retail institution.

Vulnerability Phase

With maturity, the now-established innovative institution enters a phase "characterized by top-heaviness, conservatism, and a decline in the rate of return on investments."[46] Eventually, the original innovator becomes vulnerable "to the next fellow who has a bright idea and who starts his business on a low-cost basis, slipping in under the (price) umbrella that the old-line institutions have hoisted."[47] The entry of a new low-price innovator into the retail market signals the end of one cycle and the beginning of a new competitive cycle.

In practice, the theory of the wheel of retailing has been used to explain numerous changes in the institutional structure of U.S. retailing. In the food industry, the independent corner grocery store was replaced to a large extent by the chain grocery store, which in turn, became vulnerable to the competition of the supermarket operation. A second commonly cited example of the "wheel" concept is the emergence of the department store innovation as an alternative to the small specialty retailer, and its subsequent vulnerability to discount retailers. Recently, some discount retailers have progressed far enough into the trading-up phase that they, in turn, are becoming vulnerable to discount warehouses, showroom operations, and off-price retailers.

Dialectic Process

The **dialectic process** is a "melting pot" theory of retail institutional change in which two substantially different competitive forms of retailing merge together into a new retailing institution, a composite of the original two forms. Figure 3–21 illustrates the dialectic process, involving a thesis (the established institutional form), an antithesis (the innovative institutional form), and a synthesis (the new form drawn from the other two). The dynamics of the dialectic process, as outlined by Maronick and Walker, are as follows:

> In terms of retail institutions, the dialectic model implies that retailers mutually adapt in the face of competition from "opposites." Thus, when challenged by a competitor with a differential advantage, an established institution will adopt strategies and tac-

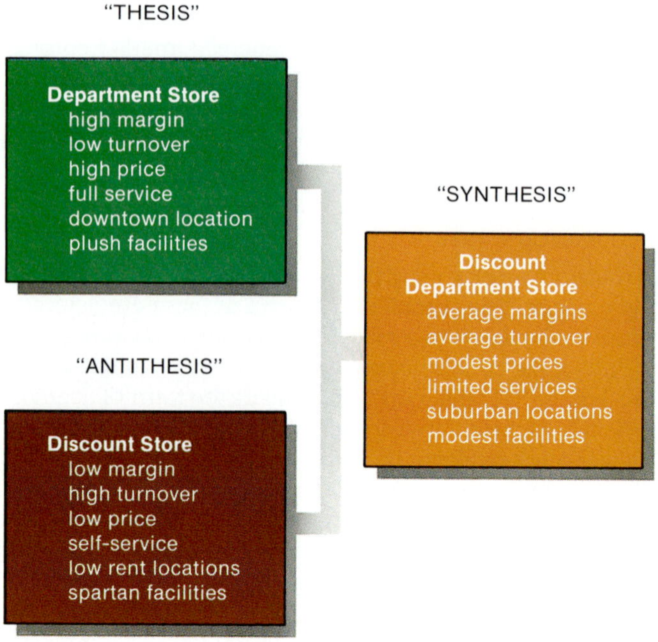

FIGURE 3–21
The dialectic process

"THESIS"

Department Store
high margin
low turnover
high price
full service
downtown location
plush facilities

"SYNTHESIS"

Discount Department Store
average margins
average turnover
modest prices
limited services
suburban locations
modest facilities

"ANTITHESIS"

Discount Store
low margin
high turnover
low price
self-service
low rent locations
spartan facilities

tics in the direction of that advantage, thereby negating some of the innovator's attraction. The innovator, meanwhile, does not remain unchanged. Rather, as McNair noted, the innovator over time tends to upgrade or otherwise modify products and institutions. In doing so, he moves toward the "negated" institution. As a result of the mutual adaptions, the two retailers gradually move together in terms of offerings, facilities, supplementary services, and prices. They thus become indistinguishable or at least quite similar and constitute a new retail institution, termed the synthesis. This new institution is then vulnerable to "negation" by new competitors as the dialectic process begins anew.[48]

Retail Accordion

The **retail accordion** theory (also known as the general-specific-general process) is based on the premise that the changing character of retail competition stems from strategies that alter the width (selection) of the merchandise mix.[49] Historically, retail institutions have evolved from general store (offering a wide variety of merchandise) to the specialty store (offering a limited variety of merchandise) back to general-line stores and so on. The term accordion is used to suggest the alternating expansion and contraction of the retailer's merchandise mix. As described by Ralph Hower in his book, *The History of Macy's of New York:*

> Throughout the history of retail trade (as, indeed in all business evolution) there appears to be an alternating movement in the dominant method of conducting operations. One swing is toward the specialization of the function performed on the merchandise handled by the individual firm. The other is away from such specialization toward the integration of related activities under one management or the diversification of products handled by a single firm.[50]

Figure 3–22 provides one author's interpretation of the retail accordion.

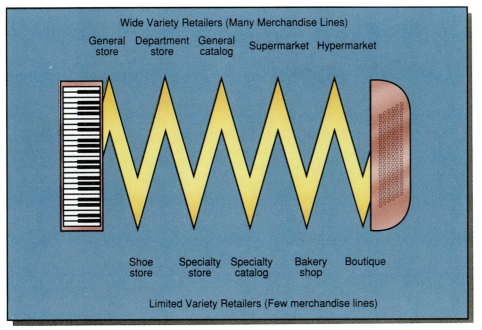

FIGURE 3–22
The retail accordion
theory

Natural Selection

The concept of the "survival of the fittest" is the central theme in Darwin's theory of **natural selection**. Environmental suitability and adaptive behavior are necessary traits for the long-term survival of a species. The species most willing and able to adapt to changing environmental conditions is the one most likely to prosper and grow. An unwillingness or inability to change could result in a species stagnation or possible extinction. As an economic species, competitive retailers are both willing and able to change and adapt to the environmental conditions under which they operate. The potential list of environmental conditions that might require adaptive behavior on the part of the retailer is almost endless. In general terms, the dynamic environments of retailing include changes in the social, cultural, political, legal, technological, economical, and competitive structure of the marketplace. Required adaptions by retailers might include alterations in the product, price, place, and/or promotional mix offered to the retailer's targeted consumers.

SUMMARY

The retailer is a member of a marketing channel of distribution whose actions are directed at bringing producers and their respective customers together. The marketing channel is a multilevel structure (extended, limited, and direct channels) made up of channel teams (full, limited, and nonmember institutions) whose interactions (buying, selling, etc.) coordinate channel flows (physical, ownership, information, payment, and promotion) through channel teamwork.

The retailer must operate in a very complex competitive environment. Retail competition can take one of several forms: intratype, intertype, vertical, and systems. Retailers also face different levels of competition as defined by the number, size, and quality of competitors.

The various types of retailing institutions are distinguishable on the basis of product-line variety, organizational structure, price appeals, customer convenience, and many other criteria. Based on the variety of product lines offered and their organizational structure, retailers are classified as either specialty or department stores. Chain stores are multiunit retailers that use a high degree of centralization in their operations. The discounter and off-price retailer emphasize price by offering nationally branded and designer merchandise at below market prices. A major development in food retailing has been the supermarket with its emphasis on a complete, self-serve product offering. Time and place convenience distinguish the convenience store in its efforts to provide the "fill-in" and "emergency" needs of consumers. Some retailers try to formalize their relationships with suppliers and other retailers by entering a contractual arrangement. The retailer-sponsored cooperative group, the wholesaler-sponsored voluntary chain, the franchising organization, and the leased department are all examples of contractual retailing. Other retailers tend to stress a certain method of operation. Warehouse showrooms, catalog showrooms, and home centers are retailers that employ warehouse methods of operation. At-home, mail-order, telephone, electronic, and vending machine retailing are nonstore retailers that attempt to serve potential customers where they live, work, and play.

Theoretically, retail institutions undergo certain competitive changes over time. Four theories that help to explain these competitive changes are the wheel of retailing, the dialectic process, the retail accordion theory, and the theory of natural selection.

KEY TERMS AND CONCEPTS

at-home retailing	mail-order retailing
catalog showroom	marketing channel
chain store	natural selection
channel integration	nonstore retailing
close-out store	off-price retailer
convenience store	ownership flow
conventional marketing channel	payment flow
department store	physical flow
dialectic process	promotion flow
direct channel	retail accordion
discount store	retailer-sponsored cooperative group
electronic retailing	specialty store
extended channel	supermarket
factory outlet	systems competition
franchising	telemarketing
home center	vending machine retailing
hypermarket	vertical competition
information flow	vertical marketing systems
intertype competition	warehouse club
intratype competition	warehouse showroom
leased department	wheel of retailing
limited channel	wholesaler-sponsored voluntary chain

1. Describe the three basic alternative channel structures. Provide an example of each alternative.
2. Define the five major types of channel flows.
3. Identify the four types of retail competition. Illustrate and describe each type of competition and provide two nontext examples of each type.
4. How are retailers classified? Identify the classification criteria and the types of retailers within each classification group. Provide trade examples (e.g., Sears, Ace Hardware, etc.) of each type of retailer.
5. What distinguishes specialty store retailing from other forms of retailing? Describe the key merchandising strategies employed by the specialty retailer.
6. Develop a profile of the operational and merchandising strategies of department stores.
7. Compare and contrast the merchandising tactics of the conventional discounter and the off-price retailer. How are they alike and how do they differ?
8. How are supermarkets attempting to negate the competitive threat posed by the fast-food industry? What other competitive merchandising trends are currently being employed by the supermarket industry to be more competitive?
9. What is contractual retailing? Describe the four types of contractual retailers.
10. Describe the similarities and differences of the various types of warehouse retailers.
11. What are the customer and retailer advantages and disadvantages of at-home shopping. Do the advantages and disadvantages vary with the form of at-home retailing?
12. Why do retailers use telephone retailing?
13. Outline the differences between videotex, videodisc, and videolog methods of electronic retailing.
14. What is the basic premise of the wheel of retailing theory of institutional change? Characterize the three phases of the wheel.
15. What does the dialectic model of retail institutional change imply?
16. How does the concept of "survival of the fittest" describe the competitive conditions faced by retailers?

1. Avijit Ghost, "Customer Service: The Key to Successful Retailing," *The Channel of Communication* 3 (Winter 1988): 1.
2. Joseph Barry Mason, "Redefining Excellence in Retailing," *Journal of Retailing* 62 (Summer 1986): 115.
3. Belinda Hulin-Sakin, "Value Heads Up the New Shopper List," *Advertising Age,* July 1983, 16.
4. Bert C. McCammon, Jr., "Perspectives for Distribution Programming," in *Vertical Marketing Systems,* ed. Louis P. Bucklin (Glenview, IL: Scott, Foresman, and Co., 1970), 43.
5. Ibid.
6. Amy Dunkin and Michael Oneal, "Power Retailers," *Business Week,* 21 Dec. 1987, 86–89, 92.
7. Lois Therrien and Amy Dunkin, "The Wholesale Success of Factory Outlet Malls," *Business Week,* 3 Feb. 1986, 92, 94.
8. Gail Hutchinson Kirby and Rachel Dardis, "Research Note: A Pricing Study of Women's Apparel in Off-Price and Department Stores," *Journal of Retailing* 62 (Fall 1986): 329.
9. Joanne Cleaver, "New Leader Directs Carson's Rebuilding," *Advertising Age,* 9 Aug. 1984, 16.
10. Amy Dunkin, "How Department Stores Plan to Get the Registers Ringing Again," *Business Week,* 18 Nov. 1985, 66–67.
11. Joan O'C. Hamilton, "Why Rivals Are Quaking as Nordstrom Heads East," *Business Week,* 15 June 1987, 99–100.
12. 12.Anthony Ramirez, "Department Stores Shape Up," *Fortune,* 1 Sept. 1986, 51–52.
13. "Specialty Store Strategy," *Stores* (October 1985): 58.

14. Michael Oneal, "Can Sears Get Sexier But Keep the Common Touch?" *Business Week,* 6 July 1987, 93–95.
15. Russell Mitchell, "How They're Knocking the Rust Off Two Old Chains," *Business Week,* 8 Sept. 1986, 45.
16. Todd Mason, "Sam Walton of Wal-Mart: Just Your Basic Homespun Billionaire," *Business Week,* 14 Oct. 1985, 143.
17. "Off-Pricers Grab Growing Retail Market Share," *Marketing News,* 3 March 1987, 9, 14.
18. Ibid.
19. Jules Abend, "Closing in on Closeouts," *Stores* (March 1986): 21.
20. "Consolidated Ups Share of Close-Out Market," *Chain Store Age Executive* (April 1987): 98.
21. "There's One for All," *Advertising Age,* Oct. 1983, M11; *Competitive Edge* (Barrington, IL: Willard Bishop Consulting Economists, June 1983).
22. U.S. Department of Commerce, *Franchise Opportunities Handbook* (Washington, D.C.: U.S. Government Printing Office, November 1986): XXIX.
23. Louis W. Stern and Adell I. El-Ansary, *Marketing Channels* (Englewood Cliffs, N.J.: Prentice-Hall, 1988), 341.
24. U.S. Department of Commerce, *Franchising in the Economy 1985–1987* (Washington, D.C.: U.S. Government Printing Office, January 1987): 15.
25. Thomas Petzinger, Jr., "So You Want to Get Rich?" *The Wall Street Journal,* 15 May 1987.
26. U.S. Dept. of Commerce, *Franchise Opportunities Handbook:* 141.
27. Ellen Paris, "Franchising—Hope or Hype?" *Forbes* 138 (Dec. 15, 1987): 43.
28. U.S. Department of Commerce, *Franchising in the Economy:* 6.
29. Lewis A. Spalding, "On Leased Departments," *Stores* (September 1987): 42.
30. Kimberly Carpenter, "Catalog Showrooms Revamp to Keep Their Identity," *Business Week,* 10 June 1985, 117.
31. Iris S. Rosenberg, "Hypermarkets Now!" *Stores* (March, 1988): 54–61.
32. Frank E. James, "Big Warehouse Outlet Breaks Traditional Rules of Retailing," *Wall Street Journal,* 22 Dec. 1983, 21.
33. This description of warehouse clubs is based on the excellent article by Jack G. Kaikati, "The Boom in Warehouse Clubs," *Business Horizons* (March/April 1987): 68–73.
34. Jean C. Darian, "In-Home Shopping: Are There Consumer Segments?" *Journal of Retailing* 63 (Summer 1987): 163–186.
35. Janice Steinberg, "Cacophony of Catalogs Fills All Niches," *Advertising Age,* 26 Oct. 1987, S-1.
36. Cara S. Trayer, "Retailers, Catalogers Cross Channels," *Advertising Age,* 26 Oct. 1987, S-8.
37. "Videotex: What It's All About," *Marketing News* (November 1983): 16.
38. Louis W. Stern and Adel I. El-Ansary, *Marketing Channels,* 3d ed. (Englewood Cliffs, N.J.: Prentice-Hall, 1988), 81.
39. JoAn Paganetti, "High-Tech Ads Gleam to Service with a Smile," *Advertising Age,* 25 July 1983, M24.
40. Wayne Walley, "Home Shopping Moves Onto Tape," *Advertising Age,* 16 Nov. 1987, 76.
41. Stern and El-Ansary, *Marketing Channels,* 81.
42. Betsy Lammerding, "Shopping by TV a Big Turn-On for Many Buyers," *Akron Beacon Journal,* 25 Jan. 1987, A-1, A-15.
43. Jules Abend, "Electronic Selling," *Stores* (November 1986): 23.
44. Malcolm P. McNair, "Significant Trends and Developments in Post War Period," in *Competitive Distribution in a Free, High-Level Economy, and Its Implications for the Universities,* ed. A.B. Smith (Pittsburgh: University of Pittsburgh Press, 1958): 18.
45. Arieh Goldman, "The Role of Trading-Up in the Development of the Retailing System," *Journal of Marketing* 39 (January 1975): 54–62.
46. Arieh Goldman, "Institutional Changes in Retailing: An Updated 'Wheel of Retailing' Theory," in *Foundations of Marketing Channels,* ed. A.G. Woodside, J.T. Sims, D.M. Lewison, and I.F. Wilkinson (Austin, TX: Lone Star, 1978), 193.

47. McNair, "Significant Trends and Developments," 18.

48. Thomas J. Maronick and Bruce J. Walker, "The Dialectic Evolution of Retailing," in *Proceedings: Southern Marketing Association,* ed. Burnett Greenburg (1974), 147.

49. See Stanley C. Hollander, "Notes On the Retail Accordion," *Journal of Retailing* 42 (Summer 1966), 20–40, 54.

50. Ralph Hower, *The History of Macy's of New York 1858–1919* (Cambridge, MA: Harvard University Press, 1943), 73.

Adams, Muriel J. "Hot New Retail Formats." *Stores* (February 1988): 34–44.

Agnew, Joe. "Home shopping: TV's Hit of the Season." *Marketing News,* 13 March 1987, 1.

Bahn, Kenneth D., and Granzin, Kent L. "Benefit Segmentation in the Restaurant Industry." *Journal of the Academy of Marketing Science* 13 (Summer 1985): 226–247.

Barmash, Isadore. "DD: Deep Discounting." *Stores* (March 1985): 22–26.

Barmash, Isadore. "The Warehouse Clubs," *Stores* (September 1985): 14–21.

Bucklin, Louis P. "Technological Change and Store Operations: The Supermarket Case." *Journal of Retailing* 56 (Spring 1980): 3–15.

Carpenter, Kimberley. "Catalog Showrooms Revamp to Keep Their Identity." *Business Week,* 10 June 1985, 117, 120.

Cohen, William A. "The Future of Direct Marketing." *Retailing Issues Letter* 1 (November 1987): 1–3.

"Combos Take the Lead in Performance Race." *Chain Store Age Executives* (June 1985): 10–26.

Deiderick, Terry E., and Dodge, H. Robert. "The Wheel of Retailing Rotates and Moves." In *Marketing: Theories and Concepts for an Era of Change, Proceedings,* edited by J. Summey, R. Viswanathan, R. Taylor, and K. Glynn, 149–52. Southern Marketing Association, 1983.

"Department Stores 'Specialize' in Competitive Maneuvers." *Marketing News,* 15 Feb. 1988, 14.

Dwyer, F. Robert, and Oh, Sejo. "The Consequences of Intertype Competition on Retail and Interfirm Behavior." In *1987 AMA Educators' Proceedings,* edited by Susan P. Douglas et al., 23–28. American Marketing Association, 1987.

English, Wilke D. "The Impact of Electronic Technology Upon the Marketing Channel." *Journal of the Academy of Marketing Science* 13 (Summer 1985): 57–71.

Festervand, Troy A., Snyder, Don R., and Tsalikis, John D. "Influence of Catalog vs. Store Shopping and Prior Satisfaction on Perceived Risk." *Journal of the Academy of Marketing Science* 14 (Winter 1986): 28–36.

Gehrt, Kenneth C. "Nonstore Retailing: Theoretically Based Selection of Household Predictor Variables and Considerations of Situational Predictor Variables." In *1986 AMA Educators' Proceedings,* edited by T. Shimp et al., 172–5. American Marketing Association, 1986.

Goldstucker, Jac L., Stanley, Thomas J., and Moschis, George P., "How Consumer Acceptance of Videotex Services Might Affect Consumer Marketing." In *AMA Educators' Proceedings,* edited by R.W. Belk et al., 200–204. American Marketing Association, 1984.

Henderson, Bruce D. "The Anatomy of Competition." *Journal of Marketing* 47 (Spring 1983): 7–11.

Hirschman, Elizabeth C. "Intertype Competition among Department Stores." *Journal of Retailing* 55 (Winter 1979): 20–34.

Ingene, Charles A. "Intertype Competition: Restaurants versus Grocery Stores." *Journal of Retailing* 59 (Fall 1983): 49–75.

Klippel, R. Eugene, Anderson, Robert L., and Sweeney, Timothy W. "Direct Marketing Via High-Technology: Is There A Market?" In *Developments in Marketing Science, Proceedings,* edited by J.M. Hawes and G.B. Glisan, 418–22. Academy of Marketing Science, 1987.

RELATED READINGS

Korgaonkar, Pradeep K. "Consumer Preferences for Catalog Showrooms and Discount Stores." *Journal of Retailing* 58 (Fall 1982): 76–88.

Korgaonkar, Pradeep K., and Smith, Alan E. "Psychographic and Demographic Correlates of Electronic In-Home Shopping and Ranking Service." In *1986 AMA Educators' Proceedings,* edited by Terence A. Shimp et al., 167–70. American Marketing Association, 1986.

Patton, Charles R., and DeLozier, M. Wayne. "The Wheel of Retailing Keeps Spinning: Supermarkets Continue to Evolve." In *Developments in Marketing Science, Proceedings,* edited by J. D. Lindquist, 349–52. Academy of Marketing Science, 1984.

Robbins, John E., Speh, Thomas W., and Mayer, Morris L. "Retailers' Perceptions of Channel Conflict Issues." *Journal of Retailing* 58 (Winter 1982): 46–67.

Rosenberg, Larry J., and Hirschman, Elizabeth C. "Retailing Without Stores." *Harvard Business Review* 58 (July–August 1980): 103–12.

Schul, Patrick L., Little, Taylor E., Jr., and Pride, William M. "Channel Climate: Its Impact on Channel Members' Satisfaction." *Journal of Retailing* 61 (Summer 1985): 9–38.

Schulz, David P. "New Expansion Paths." *Stores* (August 1987): 58–68.

Sharma, Subhash, Bearden, William O., and Teel, Jessee E. "Differential Effects of In-Home Shopping Methods." *Journal of Retailing* 59 (Winter 1983): 29–52.

Sibley, Stanley D., and Michie, Donald A. "An Exploratory Investigation of Cooperation in a Franchise Channel." *Journal of Retailing* 58 (Winter 1982): 23–45.

Strand, Patricia. "Meijer Hyper in Midwest Markets." *Advertising Age,* 15 Feb. 1988, 62MW.

Urbany, Joel E., and Talarzyk, W. Wayne. "Videotex: Implications for Retailing." *Journal of Retailing* 59 (Fall 1983): 76–92.

Wintzer, Fred W., Jr. "The Future of Off-Price Retailing." *Retail Control* (January 1985): 21–26.

4

Outline

THE MARKET
Structure of Buying Populations
Nature of Buying Behavior

CONSUMER MARKETS

POPULATION ANALYSIS

DEMOGRAPHIC ANALYSIS
The Aging Population
The Shrinking Household
The Working Woman
The Diversified Minorities

GEOGRAPHIC ANALYSIS
Regional Markets
Metro Geography
Nonmetro Geography

CONSUMER BUYING BEHAVIOR

BUYING CONSIDERATIONS
Product Tangibility
Product Durability
Product Availability

BUYING SITUATIONS
Consumer Population
Consumer Requirements
Consumer Potential

BUYING CENTERS

BUYING INFLUENCES
Psychological Factors
Personal Factors
Social Factors

BUYING PROCESS
Stage 1: Problem Recognition
Stage 2: Information Search
Stage 3: Alternative Evaluation
Stage 4: Purchase Decision
Stage 5: Postpurchase Evaluation

BUYING SCENES

Objectives

☐ Delineate the structure of buying populations and nature of buying behavior.

☐ Identify and explain U.S. population trends.

☐ Describe the major demographic population trends and their impact on retailing practices.

☐ Discuss the major geographic population patterns and their effect on retailing strategies.

☐ Understand the concept of product tangibility, durability, availability, and its impact on consumer buying behavior.

☐ Explain the concept of market potential and discuss the elements of the market potential equation.

☐ Describe the psychological, personal, and social factors that influence consumer buyer behavior.

☐ Outline and discuss the five stages of the consumer buying process.

The Buying Behavior
of Consumers

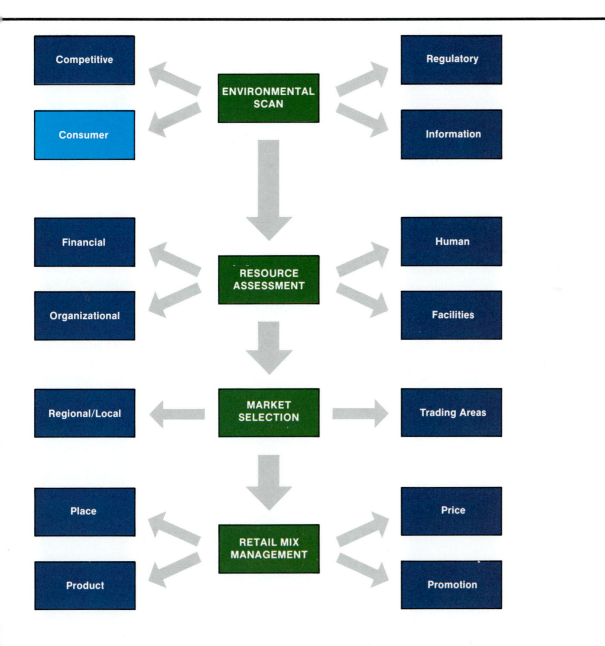

T he marketplace is the battleground for the recognition, acceptance, and adoption of various merchandising programs offered by competing retailers. An understanding of the marketplace and its behavior is essential to any successful marketing effort. After you have completed studying this chapter, you will have a deeper appreciation of the terrain in which the battle for profitable sales must be fought. More importantly, you will possess more of the information needed to develop a viable retailing plan and wage a successful merchandising campaign.

THE MARKET

Fundamental to an understanding of the marketplace and its behavior is a definition of a market. The term *market* can be used in conjunction with a variety of places (i.e., going to the farmers' market or a trade show), products (i.e., the bond or housing market), levels (i.e., the wholesale or retail market), and activities (i.e., an individual who markets a good or a service). In this text, however, the term *market* has a precise meaning and usage. As shown in Figure 4–1, a **market** is a group of actual and potential buyers at a given time and place whose actions lead to an exchange of goods and services or create the potential for an exchange process. In essence, a market is a buying population and its corresponding buying behavior. An appreciation of the concept of a market dictates an understanding of both the structure of buying populations and the nature of their buying behavior.

Structure of Buying Populations

Buying populations can be classified into one of two groups—consumer markets or organizational markets. **Consumer markets** are composed of individuals and/or households who are the ultimate consumers of goods and services. **Organizational markets** are composed of industrial firms, resellers, and governments who represent intermediate consumers of goods and services. This market accounts for the nonretail

FIGURE 4–1
A market definition

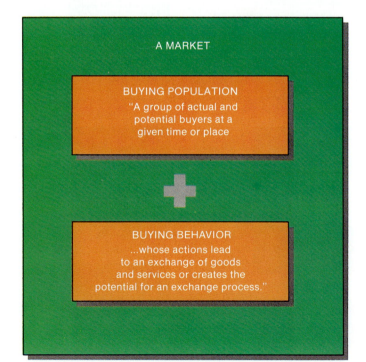

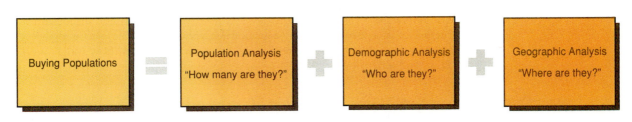

FIGURE 4–2
The structure of buying populations

sales made by retailers. The discussion in this chapter, however, is limited to consumer markets and their impact on retail decisions. Regardless of consumer type, the structure of buying populations needs to be examined in terms of "how many are they" (population analysis), "who are they" (demographic analysis), and "where are they" (geographic analysis). (See Figure 4–2.)

Nature of Buying Behavior

The second part of the market equation (see Figure 4–1) is buying behavior. Buyers act in a variety of ways when faced with a market situation that requires a purchase decision. The nature of buying behavior comprises a number of issues. An analysis of buying behavior is directed at answering the questions of "what buyers buy," "how much buyers buy," "who does the buying," "why buyers buy," "how buyers buy," and "where buyers buy" (see Figure 4–3).

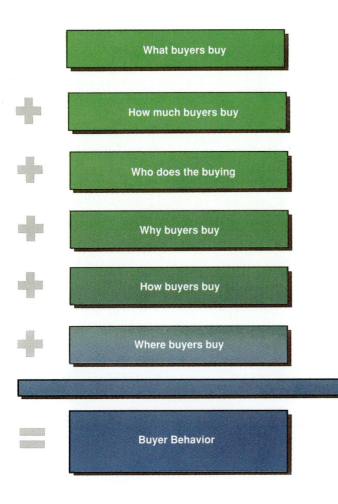

FIGURE 4–3
The nature of buying behavior

The remainder of this chapter is devoted to an examination and discussion of the structure of consumer markets (e.g., population, demographic, and geographic analysis) and the nature of consumer buying behavior (e.g., what, how much, who, why, how, and where buyers buy).

CONSUMER MARKETS

The consumer market is made up of ultimate consumers. Who are they? **Ultimate consumers** are individuals who purchase goods and services for their own personal use or for use by members of their household. The purchase intent of an ultimate consumer is to consume the utility of a product. As discussed in Chapter 1, sales to the ultimate consumer represent retail sales transacted by retailers, service firms, and to a lesser extent, wholesalers and other organizations.

POPULATION ANALYSIS

In this discussion of population analysis, we will examine the question of "how many ultimate consumers are there?" The actual and potential market for any particular product is determined in part by **total population**—the total number of persons residing within an area at a given time. An area's total population is determined by relationships between birthrates and deathrates and immigration and emigration rates. As illustrated in Figure 4–4, births and immigration are net contributors to an area's population whereas deaths and emigration reduce total population.

The past and projected population growth rates of the United States exhibit some noteworthy differences from world population growth experiences. Although the United States did experience a population "boom" for almost two decades, the nation celebrated its bicentennial by reaching **zero population growth** (ZPG); that is, the fertility rate fell below 2.0 children per average woman of childbearing age (fifteen to forty-four years). Fertility rates have increased somewhat during the 1980s but are projected to decline again during the 1990s.

The total population of the United States continued to grow in spite of its declining fertility rates. Several factors contributed to this growth. First, the average life expectancy of the average American has increased as a result of improvements in diet and medical care. Second, the baby boom during the post-World War II years increased the number of women of childbearing age during the ZPG years. Finally, both legal and illegal immigration has swelled the nation's population figure as the United States continues to represent a better way of life for many peoples of the world.

The ebb and tide of U.S. population growth has and will continue to have profound merchandising implications. As each new population wave breaks over the retailing system, new target market opportunities emerge that require continuous and innovative adjustments. Classic examples of this adjustment process can be found in the baby products industry. The Gerber Company and Johnson & Johnson were both left with volatile markets as the birthrate fell from record highs following WWII to record lows during the ZPG years of the mid-1970s. Gerber answered the challenge

FIGURE 4–4
Determinants of total population

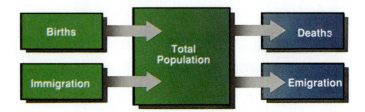

by altering the exclusivity of its business. In contrast to its former slogan, today "babies are *not* Gerber's only business"; Gerber now markets insurance programs to "golden agers." In addition, Gerber diversified out of baby foods by "buying a maker of nursery lamps and other novelty items; a producer of cribs, dressers, and youth beds; and Biltrite Juvenile Products Co., which makes strollers, high chairs and carriages. . . .Gerber has also snapped up. . .the leading maker of car seats" for children.[1] Johnson & Johnson responded to the unsettling nature of their markets by repositioning their baby products for usage by adults. Their success in persuading adults to use baby shampoo and baby powder is evidenced by the large number of "me-too" products that competitors have introduced into the market.

Other companies have also adjusted to the changing baby business. In response to few children per family and the resulting desire for and the ability to buy additional and more upscaled products, the Health-Tex division of Chesebrough-Ponds stresses fashion for kids at moderate prices. Along the same theme, such fashionable items as Christian Dior Pajamas, Izod shirts, Norma Kamali jumpsuits, and Pierre Cardin diaper covers are being marketed for children. Retailers reacted to these population changes by: (1) altering the width and depth of their product lines, (2) adjusting the amount and location of display space devoted to a particular product item, (3) changing the type and amount of promotional support used to enhance sales of certain products, and (4) adapting product-line pricing points to current market expectations.

DEMOGRAPHIC ANALYSIS

Who is the "average American" or the "typical American family"? In past years reasonably descriptive profiles were possible. Today under novel family, marriage, living, and working arrangements, the average or typical profile is considerably less representative of the population as a whole. This section addresses the question of who the ultimate consumers are in terms of their demographic makeup. **Demography** is the study of statistics that are used to describe a population. Each person can be characterized in terms of age, sex, education, income, occupation, race, nationality, family size, and family structure. These individual characteristics can be aggregated into relatively homogeneous profiles of population groupings that represent consumer market segments and the opportunity to tailor a firm's marketing efforts to one or more of these segments (see Figure 4–5).

In the following discussion, we shall examine some of the more pronounced shifts in the demographic makeup of the U.S. population and the changes in marketing strategies and tactics that will be required to accommodate those shifts. Although demographic shifts are treated individually, you should be aware that all or most of these changes are interrelated.

The Aging Population

The American population is aging as a result of a declining fertility rate and an increasing life expectancy. Consumer markets in the 1980s have been reshaped by the same baby boom generation that has had such a profound effect on marketing strategies for the last 30 years. It is the age group that created the 1950s infant market, the 1960s teenage market, the 1970s young adult market, and the 1980s middle-aged market. The realignment of the nation's population by age group is pictured in Figure 4–6.

As Figure 4–6 shows, the **youth market** (17 and under) is in the process of registering a notable 7.63 percent decrease; from 34.11 to 26.48 percent of the total U.S. population. Although this decline has signaled a de-emphasis in the youth-

FIGURE 4–5
The market segmentation view of the total market

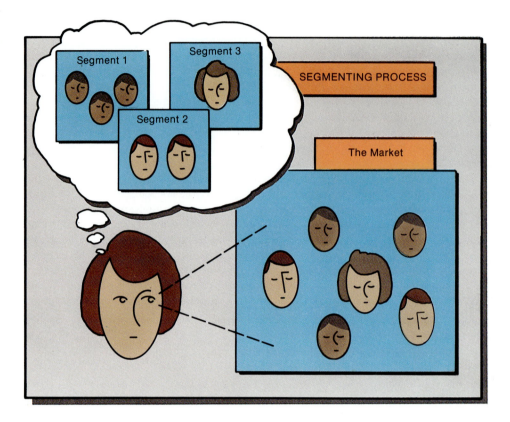

FIGURE 4–6
Percentage change in total population by age group, 1970 to 1990 (source: U.S. Census Bureau, *Projections of the Population of the U.S., 1977 to 2050* [Washington, D.C.: U.S. Government Printing Office])

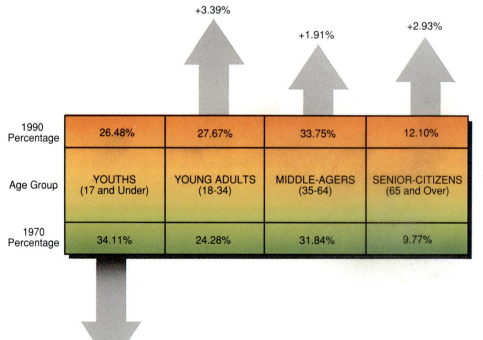

	YOUTHS (17 and Under)	YOUNG ADULTS (18-34)	MIDDLE-AGERS (35-64)	SENIOR-CITIZENS (65 and Over)
	+3.39%	+1.91%	+2.93%	
1990 Percentage	26.48%	27.67%	33.75%	12.10%
1970 Percentage	34.11%	24.28%	31.84%	9.77%

oriented marketing that has held center-stage since WWII, the absolute size of this age group (approximately one fourth of the population) still makes it a formidable retail market. The importance of the youth market to most retailers is twofold. First, older youths have billions of dollars for discretionary spending on both nondurable and durable goods.[2] Important teen-oriented expenditures include fast foods, sporting equipment, casual clothing, audio and visual entertainment products, soft drinks, and personal accessories. Second, youths of all ages are major influencers on the buying behavior of their parents. They play an important role in deciding what products and brands are purchased, as well as when and where purchases are made. From the retailer's viewpoint, perhaps the most difficult aspect of merchandising this age group is the multiplicity of consumer life-styles and the dynamics of change that are associated with each life-style segment. It can be a very faddish world.

The coming of age of the baby boom generation is reflected in the significant growth (see Figure 4–6) of the **young-adults market** (ages eighteen to thirty-four). Within this age group, it is the older half (ages twenty-five to thirty-four) that accounts for the vast majority of this group's growth. Some demographers have painted a somewhat bleak picture for these tail-ended members of the baby boom. With entry- and lower-level employment positions bulging with earlier baby boomers, these later cohorts are experiencing difficulties in satisfying career aspirations. Nevertheless, this age group will still seek to satisfy the needs associated with early adulthood. The demand for housing will continue to increase for both the single-family homes and apartments that cater to the growing number of single-adult, one-child, and childless households. Smaller domiciles and limited incomes suggest that successful merchandising to this group in the future will require smaller multipurpose appliances, do-it-yourself products, and durable household furnishings.

As seen in Figure 4–6, a modest increase (from 31.28 to 33.75 percent of the total U.S. population) is projected through 1990 for the **middle-aged market** (ages thirty-five to sixty-four). Beyond 1990, the relative size of this age group will continue to expand as late baby boomers enter middle age. Early middle agers (thirty-five to forty-four), the fastest-growing market throughout the 1980s, can typically be characterized as a higher-income, free-spending group whose purchase motives are directed more at quality, durability, and variety. Today's late middle agers (forty-five to sixty-four) contain a large number of empty-nest families wherein the parents feel free to spend on themselves and seem less intent on leaving an estate for their offspring. This attitudinal change reveals a big market for new retirement products, a trend that has not gone unnoticed by the financial community. In the 1980s, these affluent families will stimulate retail sales of top-of-the-line big-ticket items in a wide variety of product lines, such as autos and home furnishings. In general, consumers in their middle years will heighten demand for entertainment, travel, recreation, adult education, and other convenience- and experience-oriented goods and services. A major plus in retailing to this group is that they tend to have more established careers and community roots; therefore, they are less likely to move and represent a stationary market segment that is conducive to target marketing efforts.

A significant increase in the **senior-citizens market** will occur over the next several decades. According to the Census Bureau estimates, the percentage of the population aged sixty-five and over is expected to increase from 11.4 percent in 1981 to 13.1 percent in 2000 and 21.7 percent in 2050. Marketers should also take note that the market potential of the upper end of the senior-citizens market will be notably greater in the future. For example, the percentage of the population aged eighty-five and over is projected to grow from 1.0 percent in 1981 to 1.9 percent in 2000 and 5.2 percent in 2050. The senior-citizen market has changed drastically in recent years. Because of the fact that people are living longer, a life span of 20 to 25 years following retirement, they are faced with a wide variety of buying concerns. Aged-based merchandising strategies are often inappropriate because it is usually a mistake to sell products to older people by telling them it's a product designed for the elderly. A more effective strategy is to sell product benefits that fit the interests and aspirations of this age group. "Marketers should avoid age typing products in their messages."[3] In product and service lines such as food, housing, clothing, transportation, health care, personal care, and recreation, the senior-citizen's share of the market is greater than that suggested by their numbers. Sears is wooing customers over fifty with their Mature Outlook Club. It provides special services and discounts on everything from eyeglasses to lawnmowers.[4]

The Shrinking Household

While the total number of households is expected to increase dramatically (from approximately 63 million in 1970 to 96 million in 1990), the size of each individual household is expected to shrink. The shrinking household is well illustrated by the changing mix of household types. As depicted in Figure 4–7, the number of traditional family-type households will decrease by 11.1 percent between 1970 and 1990, while the individual nonfamily household will increase by the same percentage. Further evidence of the shrinking household is the increased number of "male–no wife" (+0.3 percent) and "female–no husband" (+3.5 percent) family-type households. It is also worth noting that the number of single-male households will more than double (from 6.4 to 13.6 percent). Government projections are that the average family size will slip from 3.3 persons in 1978 to 3.0 in 1990; the average household size has decreased from 3.14 in 1970 to 2.66 persons in 1987.[5] When one considers that a major portion of this changing household makeup is associated with the middle-age groups of thirty-five to forty-four and forty-five to fifty-four year olds, there is a strong underpinning for booming retail sales in household goods and services. Typically, these middle agers are the most lavish spenders in that they spend 27 percent more on goods and services than the average domicile. Some of the more direct merchandising impacts of the shrinking household lie with product design and packaging. The old adage that "bigger is better" is simply an inappropriate strategy for accommodating this demographic trend.

The Working Woman

Merchandising strategies that cater to working women will become increasingly more important during the next several decades. The participation rate of women in the

FIGURE 4–7
Changing mix of household types, 1970 to 1990

Household Type	Year (%)	
	1970	1990
Family type	81.2	70.1
Husband and Wife	70.6	55.7
Male, no wife	1.9	2.2
Female, no husband	8.7	12.2
Nonfamily type	18.8	29.9
Male	6.4	13.6
Female	12.4	16.3

Source: U.S. Census Bureau, *Projections of the Number of Households and Families, 1979 to 1995*, Series P-25, No. 805 (Washington, D.C.: U.S. Government Printing Office).

nation's workforce has increased dramatically since the post-WWII period. In 1950, women accounted for 29.6 percent of the total labor force. By 1990, their participation is expected to account for about one half of the U.S. work force. The changing needs and roles of working women have had a major impact on their buying behavior. Let's examine these alterations in buying behavior by viewing working women in their role as a working partner, a head of household, and a working person.

As an equal working partner within a marriage, the "work wife" has shed the stereotypical role of the chief purchasing agent for most of the family's household needs. Today, a teamwork trend is emerging, where the wife and husband share the responsibilities for the decisions on and procurement of household requirements. For the retailer, this shared purchasing behavior requires targeting the products, prices, promotions, and distribution channels toward the team rather than the individual wife or husband. Joint satisfaction of both partners will become an increasingly important factor in future successful merchandising tactics.

Being the head of a single, separated, widowed, or divorced household, the working woman has become the decision maker and procurer of both traditional household purchases and nontraditional purchases of goods and services. For example, in her role as head of a household, the working woman is becoming an increasingly important consideration in the marketing of homes (apartments, condominiums, and houses); financial services (banking, investment, and retirement programs); and professional services (law, tax, and insurance). In this role, she is solely responsible for purchase decisions that formerly were either made by or shared with her partner. With more female household heads in the workplace, the traditional distinction between women-dominated purchases (i.e., food and clothing) and men-dominated purchases (i.e., investment and insurance) is fading rapidly.

Employee responsibilities and employer expectations are an integral part of any job. In an attempt to meet these responsibilities and expectations, the product—service needs and the buying behavior of working women have undergone dynamic changes. As an illustration, the professional woman requires a professional wardrobe that is sufficient in size and consistent in character with her profession. In contrast with the housewife who is a "special occasion" buyer of "better dresses and suits," the professional woman is required to make such purchases on a regular and frequent basis. As such, the working woman tends to be a "wardrobe builder" in that each new clothing purchase is often viewed in terms of how well it can be integrated into her current wardrobe. Durability of each new clothing purchase tends to be a very important purchase motive for the professional, whose usage rate of the item is notably greater than a purchase made for occasional use. Nordstrom's, the Seattle-based department store, has developed an executive shopping club called 'Personal Touch,' which provides a full range of services from fashion consultants to hair care.[6] The professional working woman also has a specialized need for "tools of her trade"; these tools may consist of briefcases, appointment books, tape recorders, record-keeping ledgers, or a home personal computer.

The Diversified Minorities

The concept that the United States is one large "melting pot" where all ethnic groups are assimilated into the American culture simply is an inappropriate and inoperative assumption for the retailer. Not only are there nonassimilated geographic concentrations of ethnic minorities (e.g., Hispanics in Miami and Los Angeles), within each of the major minority markets (Hispanic and black Americans) there are numerous

"McDonald's® is music to my ears."

"I started out as a freelance arran[ger]
composer and one of the first natio[nal]
spots I ever produced was for McDonal[d's]
Then I formed my own company and t[hey]
gave me enough work to get me over [the]
hump and establish myself in the busin[ess].
At the time, McDonald's was one of [the]
first advertisers to produce commerc[ials]
directed to the Black consumer on s[uch]
a large scale. As a result, I was abl[e to]
open the door for a lot of talented Bl[ack]
musicians and singers who had ne[ver]
worked professionally before
McDonald's really opened up the busin[ess]
for many people in this town. A[nd]
we're all still working for McDonal[d's].
And that's gre[at]."

McDonald's continues to support Black-ow[ned]
businesses and individuals in communicatio[n].
Morris "Butch" Stewart and his Joy[Art]
Productions is one of them. And his wor[k is]
music to our e[ars].

Morris "Butch" Stewart
Joy Art Music Production
Chicago, IL.

WE'RE INVOLVED.

McDona[ld's]

© 1985 McDonald's Corp[oration]

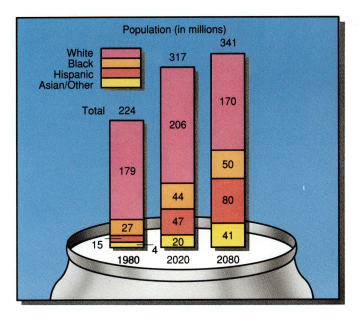

Population (in millions)

White
Black
Hispanic
Asian/Other

Total   224   317   341

179   206   170

27   44   47   50   80

15   20   41
4

1980   2020   2080

FIGURE 4–8
A changing population:
Sometime in the next
century, blacks, Asians,
and Hispanics will out-
number whites (source:
"Selling To The New
America." Reprinted
with permission, *INC.*
Magazine [July 1987],
p. 45. Copyright © 1987
by INC. Publishing
Company, 38 Commer-
cial Walk, Boston MA
02110)

market segments. As with so many other American markets, success in reaching minority markets requires market segmentation and the tailoring of the firm's retailing mix. "Penney's hispanic TV commercials bear little resemblance to their general market counterparts. The English-language spots tend to be fast-paced and contemporary, often show just one individual. The hispanic spots always focus on the family—usually the extended family."[7] Mass-marketing strategies will find limited application in appealing to most minority markets. "What 'minority' consumers respond to most eagerly is a level of respect—targeted advertising, bilingual salespeople, and special events all help to break down barriers. But their long-term value is to confirm for minorities that they are welcome and valued not just as consumers, but as people—and as Americans."[8]

The major trend that characterizes minority markets is their growth both in number and income. Ethnic minority groups are increasing faster than the population as a whole. The number of blacks in the nation could almost double between now and 2080; during this time their share of the total population would increase from 12 to 18 percent.[9] Hispanics are the fastest growing ethnic group in the U.S.; by 2080 the number of Hispanics is expected to exceed the number of blacks (see Figure 4–8). By 1990, blacks are expected to comprise 12.6 percent of the total population, and Hispanics are projected to account for 10.7 percent of the nation's people.

Few markets are growing as fast as the Hispanic and Asian markets. Annual income for these market segments will almost double between 1980 and 1990, and that trend is expected to continue on into the year 2000 (see Figure 4–9). The total minority market in 2000 is expected to be close to $800 billion. In addition to a demographic diversity, minority groups show considerable variance in their life-styles as defined by the activities they engage in, what interests them, and the opinions they hold.

Targeting the black consumer. (Courtesy of McDonald's Corporation)

FIGURE 4–9

A changing market-place: If it's growing markets you seek, few are growing faster than the Hispanic and Asian markets (source: "Selling To The New America." Reprinted with permission, *INC*. Magazine [July 1987], p. 45. Copyright © 1987 by INC. Publishing Company, 38 Commercial Walk, Boston MA 02110)

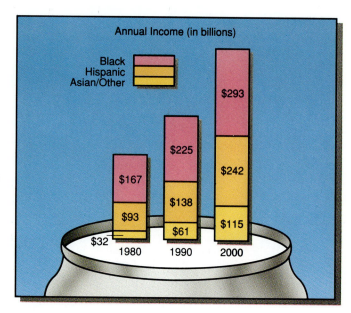

GEOGRAPHIC ANALYSIS

Americans tend to be a very mobile society. It is estimated that approximately one American in five moves every year. Therefore, a necessary part of any successful marketing program is the identification of current geographic population patterns and future shifts in those patterns. This discussion concerns the issue of where consumers are today and where consumers will be tomorrow.

Regional Markets

The dimensions of a market area are defined by several factors, one of the more important is *population density*—the number of persons living within a delineated geographic area. By knowing how many people occupy an area, the retailer has one major element in the equation for determining the consumption potential of that area. Our examination of regional patterns and shifts of U.S. population can be delineated in terms of the nine census regions and the fifty states. According to the Census Bureau, one third of the nation's population now lives in the South. The second largest concentration of population is in the North Central region; it contains 26 percent of the nation's population. Following in order of size of population are the Northeast region (21.6 percent) and the West (19 percent). Of the ten largest states, three are in the Northeast (New York, Pennsylvania, and New Jersey), three are in the North Central (Illinois, Ohio, and Michigan), three are in the South (Texas, Florida, and North Carolina), and one is in the West (California). The South is the only region that is not represented in the ten least-populated states. One-half of the least populated states are in the West (Idaho, Nevada, Montana, Wyoming, and Alaska), three states are in the Northeast (New Hampshire, Delaware, and Vermont), and two sparsely populated states are in the North Central region (North and South Dakota). Judging from these patterns, it appears that the previous population dominance of the Northeastern/Great Lakes manufacturing belt has been replaced by a somewhat more even regional distribution of population.

If the old adage is true that "retailers follow markets," then retailers are shifting their attention toward the West and South. The ten fastest growing states (percentage change) during the seventies and eighties were all in the West (Nevada, Arizona, Wyoming, Utah, Alaska, Idaho, Colorado, and New Mexico) and the South (Florida and Texas). A similar trend emerges when we view population change in terms of absolute numbers of people. California, Texas, and Florida are the most powerful population magnets. Other major absolute population gainers include Arizona, Georgia, North Carolina, Washington, Virginia, Colorado, and Tennessee.

What do these population shifts mean to the retailer? Regional differences stimulate new expenditure patterns. Different climates, life-styles, and customs necessitate modification of existing merchandising programs and development of new retailing strategies. From the more formal life-styles of the northeast to the informality of western living, from the more rigorous climates of the north to the moderate environs of the south, from southern fried chicken to New England boiled lobster, the retailer is faced with different customer expectations requiring different marketing tactics.

Metro Geography

America is an urbanized society; 75 percent of the nation's population lives within one of the 318 metropolitan areas. This is almost a complete reversal from 1880, when three out of four Americans lived in largely rural areas. Metro-area residents are of two types: urbanites who dwell in the central cities and suburbanites who live in the suburbs that surround the core city. The suburbs continued to dominate the population growth pattern of the metro areas. While the percentage increase for all metropolitan areas registered approximately 10 percent, suburbanites increased 18 percent while gains in central city populace were almost stagnant at 0.1 percent.

Nonmetro Geography

Nonmetro markets consist of the many small hamlets, villages, and towns that dot the nation's countryside together with the rural farm areas. Since 1800, the population of nonmetro areas has been declining, largely as a result of migration to the metropolitan areas. However, during the 1970s, the migration process reversed itself as nonmetro markets experienced both a population growth and a net in-migration.

In the migrational interchange of population between metro and nonmetro markets, the nonmetro areas experienced a net gain. A number of reasons have been cited as explanations for this turnabout. Nonmetro areas appear to be attracting population because of (1) more casual life-styles, (2) greater opportunity for outdoor experiences, (3) slower pace of living, (4) lower cost of living, (5) less competitive environment, and (6) changing preferences from cultural amenities to physical environmental amenities.

Consumer **buying behavior** is the manner in which consumers act, function, and react to various situations involving the purchase of a good or service or the acceptance of an idea. Effective retailing requires both an understanding and an appreciation of the buying behavior of consumers. "Real consumer insight means understanding more about your target (market) than your competitor does."[10] Retailers require such buying behavior information as what and how much consumers buy, who does the buying, and how, and where consumers buy (see Figure 4–10). This section examines the ultimate consumer's actual act of buying and the situations and influences that impact on the consumer's choice of retailers and their products and services.

CONSUMER BUYING BEHAVIOR

FIGURE 4–10
The dimensions of consumer buying behavior

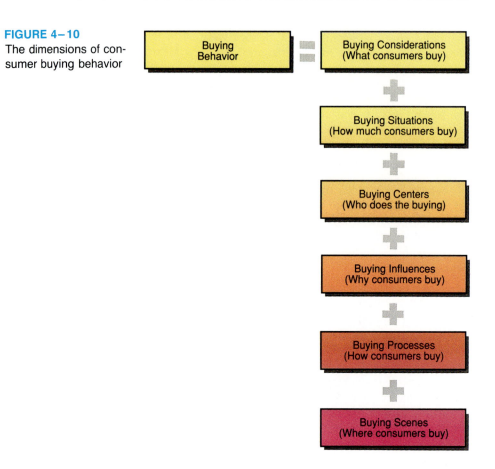

BUYING CONSIDERATIONS

"What do consumers buy?" is the first question that needs to be answered if we are to gain an understanding of consumer buying behavior. Consumers buy products. **Products** are bundles of benefits capable of satisfying consumer wants and needs. A product can be "anything" that can be offered to a market as a need and want satisfier. Consumers have "benefit expectations" that need to be realized in buying, using, and possessing products. Successful products are those that provide the tangible and/or intangible features necessary for the realization of the consumer's expectations of benefits. Viewed in this broad perspective, the retailer has great latitude in planning and implementing the "basic offering" that is to be presented to the consuming public. To enhance our conception of what is a product, marketers have developed several classifications based on various product and/or buyer behavior dimensions. Let's look at the dimensions of tangibility, durability, and availability (see Figure 4–11).[11]

Product Tangibility

Tangibility is the degree to which an item has physical and material properties that are capable of being perceived. The sense of touch is generally considered to be the

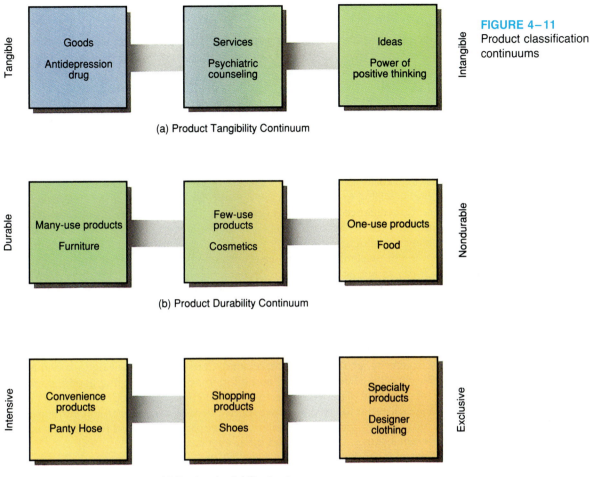

FIGURE 4–11
Product classification
continuums

(a) Product Tangibility Continuum

(b) Product Durability Continuum

(c) Product Availability Continuum

deciding factor in determining tangibility. Tangible products can be held, hefted, and felt; intangible products cannot be touched.

Product tangibility ranges from goods to services to ideas (see Figure 4–11a). **Goods** are tangible items defined by their size, shape, and weight together with their chemical and/or biological makeup. This book is a good example of a tangible item, as is the chair you are sitting in and the desk where you are sitting. **Services** are largely intangible activities that typically involve the application of human skills within a consumer problem-solving context. A service may or may not be associated with the sale of a good. Services range from personal services like hair styling and massages to professional services such as medical attention and legal advice, from household services of housekeeping and gardening to automotive services of maintenance and repair, from recreational services of amusement parks and campgrounds to cultural services of plays and concerts; the list is almost endless. **Ideas** are concepts and ways of thinking about a particular event or situation. These highly intangible products are often extensions of the opinions, attitudes, and interests of the person marketing the idea. Ideas are often categorized as business, religious, political, social, or personal expressions of conceptual thinking.

Product Durability

Durability is the ability of something to endure or to last. **Durables** are products that are capable of surviving many uses. An automobile is a durable good that can provide the transportation function for 100,000 miles or more assuming proper maintenance. Appliances and home furnishings are additional examples of durables. **Nondurables** are perishable products that are used up in one or a few uses. Faddish goods, services, and ideas last for a short period of time with a limited useful life. Figure 4–11b illustrates the continuum of product durability.

Product Availability

Product availability is a means of classifying products on the amount of effort the consumer is willing to exert to secure a particular good, service, or idea (see Figure 4–11c). **Convenience products** are those that the consumer is not willing to spend time, money, and effort in locating, evaluating, and procuring. Consumers expect convenience products to be readily available. If a particular brand of a convenience product is not available, the consumer will select another brand. Bread, cigarettes, and soft drinks are all examples of convenience goods, while dry cleaning and automotive maintenance are typical convenience services. "By the early 1990's more than half of all families will wield two paychecks—with more money to spend and less time to spend it." The convenience goods and services industry can expect to continue its past steady growth rate.[12]

Shopping products are products for which consumers want to make price, quality, suitability, and/or style comparisons. Consumers are willing to spend a considerable amount of time, money, and effort in securing shopping goods; therefore, these goods can be distributed selectively. What constitutes shopping products varies from one consumer to another; however, we usually think of clothing, furniture, and linens as shopping goods. In a similar vein, people shop around for ideas by attending different lectures, churches, and other events.

Specialty products are those in which the consumer's buying behavior is directed at securing a particular good, service, or idea without regard to time, effort, or expense. The consumer will not accept a substitute; therefore, they will expend whatever effort is required to procure the product. For example, a specialty good may be a specific branded good such as Lagerfeld cologne or a company product line such as Royal Copenhagen figurines. For the individual who insists on a particular hair stylist and is willing to travel to, wait for, and pay whatever the price, that service is a specialty service to that consumer. Given the insistent character of the consumer, specialty products tend to be exclusively distributed in a very limited number of outlets.

BUYING SITUATIONS

Consumer Population

This discussion of buying situations focuses on how much consumers buy. Viewed from the perspective of the individual consumer, the question of how much he or she buys is a function of his or her needs and desires plus the ability, willingness, and authority to buy. Taking a broader market perspective, how much consumers will buy in total is the problem of determining **market potential**—a market's total capacity to consume a given good, service, or idea. As seen in Figure 4–12, market potential equals the consuming population within a market plus the consumption requirements and potential of that population. Let's examine each of these elements of the market potential equation.

A market's total capacity to consume is, in part, a function of the total number of consumption units that make up that market. Therefore, the first step in determin-

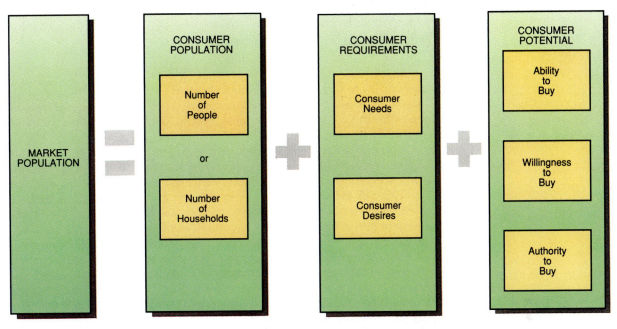

FIGURE 4-12
Market potential as the capacity to consume

ing market potential is to obtain an accurate count of the number of consumption units. However, before consumption units can be counted, they must be defined. The definition of a consumption unit will depend on the type of product that is the focus of the market potential determination. The "number of persons" is the most appropriate population count when market potential is being determined for such personal goods and services as clothing and accessories, health and beauty aids, or medical and legal services. On the other hand, a count of the "number of households" or "the number of residential units" probably is more indicative of a market's consumption capacity for hardware and household goods, furniture, and appliances, lawn and garden equipment, or plumbing and heating services. Although these population figures are important, they must be qualified in terms of their likelihood of a purchase either now or in the near future.

Consumer Requirements

Prerequisites to the consumer buying process are needs and desires; they motivate and direct the buying activities of consumers. Although the distinction between needs and desires is open to debate, the main difference is in their essentiality. **Needs** are essential physiological or psychological requirements necessary to the general physical and mental welfare of the consumer. **Desires** are more akin to wishes, in that they are conscious impulses toward objects or experiences that hold promise of enjoyment in their attainment. However, the attainment of desires is less essential to the consumer's well-being than is the satisfaction of needs.

Consumer Potential

Consumers must distinguish between having a need or desire for a product and buying it. Many consumers have product needs (i.e., a new toaster) that go unsatisfied and desires (i.e., a new Porsche) that go unfulfilled. The essential difference between needing or desiring a product and buying it is the consumer's ability, willingness, and authority to purchase the needed or desired good, service, or idea. With respect to product purchases, the list of what each of us *would* like to buy is far more extensive than the list of what we are *willing* and *able* to buy.

Ability to Buy

A consumer's ability to buy is his or her **buying power**—the financial resources that are available to the consumer for making purchases. The determining elements of buying power are the consumer's spendable income, asset position, and available credit.

There are many different expressions of income. **Total income** refers to the total amount of money received from salaries, wages, interest investments, pensions, and profit-making activities. Average family income in 1987 is about $33,000, up from $17,125 in 1950, in today's dollars.[13] Unfortunately, not all of an individual's or family's total income is available for spending as the individual or family pleases—taxes have to be paid, savings accounts need to be enhanced, and basic living expenses need to be covered. To accommodate for these unavoidable expenditures, additional income expressions are in common usage. **Disposable income** is the income that remains after taxes and other required payments (e.g., Social Security) have been deducted from total income. It is the total amount of money that is available for spending and saving. Although disposable income is an appropriate and useful expression of available income for the retailer of essential goods and services, it is not a useful tool in examining the capacity of a market to consume nonessential or luxury goods and services. The expression *discretionary income* therefore has been developed. **Discretionary income** is that portion of an individual's or family's disposable income that remains after purchasing the basic necessities of life—food, clothing, and shelter. Consumers are free to purchase whatever they want to with their discretionary income. Marketers of many recreation, entertainment, household, automotive, and personal products depend on the amount of discretionary income for satisfactory sales volumes.

The relationships between type of income and consumer expenditure patterns are stated in terms of laws developed from the work of Ernest Engel, a nineteenth-century German statistician. Briefly, these laws state that as a family's income increases, the following result:

1. The percentage of that income spent on food decreases.
2. The percentage of that income spent on clothing is roughly constant.
3. The percentage of that income spent on housing and household operations remains roughly constant.
4. The percentage of that income spent on luxury and other goods increases.

Credit and assets are the second and third buying power determinants.

Credit is (1) the borrowing power of a consumer, (2) an amount of money that is placed at a consumer's disposal by a financial or other institution, and (3) a time allowed for payment for goods and services sold on trust. **Assets** are anything of value that is owned by an individual. The role of assets in determining buying power is twofold: (1) they can be converted to cash and (2) they are a major factor in determining the amount of credit that borrowers are willing to extend.

Willingness to Buy

A consumer may have a need and the ability to satisfy that need, yet, for a number of reasons, may be unwilling to make a purchase decision. As consumers, our willingness to buy or not to buy a product is related to the many influences that impact on us and the way in which we make purchase decisions. Psychologically, we may or may not be motivated to make a purchase, or our perception of a product is such that we do not feel it is capable of meeting our needs. From a personal standpoint, a product may not be congruent with our self-image or our life-style. On the other hand, our willingness to buy may be based on whether a product meets our "belongingness" need to be accepted by our family, peer groups, or social class. Finally, our willingness to buy or not to buy may slow our actual buying process. We may postpone a purchase because we need more information about the product or more time to evaluate the information we already have.

Authority to Buy

Even with the ability and willingness to buy, a certain degree of authorization must be present before a consumer will finalize the purchase decision. Authority to buy can be of either a formal or an informal type. Formal authorization consists of the consumer meeting various eligibility requirements such as age, residency, and occupation constraints. Minors cannot legally purchase alcoholic beverages. Nonresidents of a state are ineligible for many services provided by state and local governments. Many social and professional organizations make available their products only to members of certain occupations (e.g., American Medical Association or Wisconsin Bar Association).

Informal authorization for making purchases is an expected courtesy when more than one individual is involved and when the purchase can be classified as being of major importance (special occasion or expensive). For example, when either a husband or wife is considering the purchase of a new automobile, the other partner would expect to be consulted before the purchase is made. The family vacation decision as to what, where, and when is one in which informal approval and/or input is expected by all family members.

BUYING CENTERS

A pertinent question in any study of buying behavior is "Who does the buying?" To answer this question, marketers have developed the concept of a buying center. A **buying center** is a basic unit of consumption that engages in the buying process. In consumer products marketing, the basic consumption units tend to be either individuals or households. In certain situations, individuals buy products for their own consumption with no or little regard for the needs or opinions of others. In other situations, purchases are made for a household by one of its members. In a household that is buying, purchase decisions are based on collective needs and influenced by most or all of the members of the household.

The distinction between individual and household buying centers is important in studying buyer behavior and developing merchandising programs that are appropriate to that behavior. In the following sections, we look at the influences on the individual and household buying behavior and the processes that are employed in making purchases by these two types of buying centers.

BUYING INFLUENCES

Why do consumers buy what, when, where, and how they buy? Marketers, like psychologists, do not fully understand the "whys" of human behavior. Although we have a fair understanding of what factors influence behavior, our knowledge of how those factors interact to influence behavior is limited. The human mind is often compared to a "black box"; we know the inputs (stimuli) and the outputs (responses) but not the inner workings of the mind (processes) with respect to the transformation of inputs and outputs. Nevertheless, by detecting patterned buying responses that emerge from planned marketing stimuli, retailers can draw inferences about the processing system of the human mind. One viewpoint on the nature of retailing is that it is the art and science of creating and delivering a package of stimuli (products, prices, promotions, and places) that is capable of producing consistent patterns of buying behavior. Fortunately, or unfortunately depending on your perspective, retailing is still more art than science.

In this section we explore the many interacting factors that impact on buying behavior and serve as a basis for formulating marketing strategies and tactics. Figure 4–13 is an overview of the major determinants of the buying behavior of the ultimate consumer.

Psychological Factors

The field of psychology has contributed greatly to the marketer's quest for explanations to the "whys" of consumer behavior. Motivation, perception, learning, and attitude are four major psychological factors that influence consumers in the determination of their buying choices.

Motivation

Preceding any action is the mental process of motivation. The act of buying starts with a motive. **Motivation** refers to the process by which consumers are moved or incited to action. Motivation starts with stimulated needs that lead to aroused tensions and result in goal-directed actions. A basic tenet of psychology is "look behind the behavior." What retailers have found when they have examined the buying choices of consumers are unsatisfied needs. A **need** is the lack of something that is necessary to the well-being of the individual. Needs are the basic source of buyer behavior, but they must be stimulated before the consumer is driven to action. Activation of a need is the result of some internal or external stimulus that arouses tensions. A headache

FIGURE 4–13
Determinants of consumer buying behavior

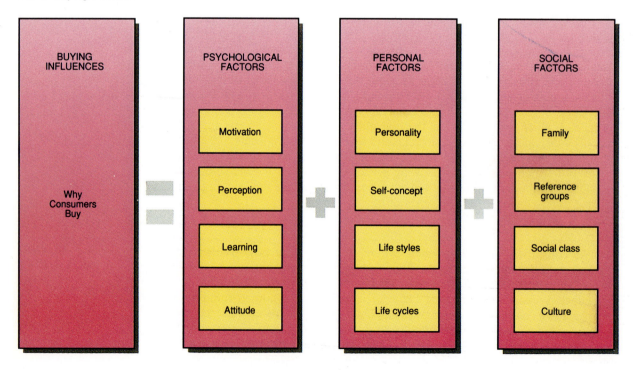

is an internal stimulus that creates an uncomfortable feeling (an aroused tension) that activates the goal-directed action of taking aspirin for relief from the headache (the need). An external stimulus might be a department store advertisement announcing the arrival of the latest fall fashions; this cue may stimulate our need to be noticed as a contemporary dresser, thereby promoting the action of purchasing something distinctive to wear.

Having portrayed motivation as a needs-based process, a further explanation of the nature and intensity of human needs is required. Needs have been categorized in a variety of ways; one of the more widely accepted need classification schemes is that of the psychologist Abraham H. Maslow (see Figure 4–14). According to Maslow, human needs are hierarchical and can be rank-ordered on the basis of their motivational power. Lower-order needs, those that are related to our physiological well-being, are basic innate needs that must be satisfied before higher-order needs can emerge as strong motivators of our behavior. Higher-order needs are learned needs that are largely psychological in nature. Although higher-order needs are secondary to physiological needs, once these basic needs are satisfied, psychological needs will emerge as extremely important motivators of consumer behavior. Let's explore Maslow's hierarchy of needs.

Physiological needs are life-sustaining and creature comforts that need to be reasonably satisfied before the search for fulfillment of higher-order needs. Food, fluids, shelter, rest, waste elimination, and clothing are all basic to the physiological

FIGURE 4–14
The hierarchy of needs

well-being of the individual. In reading this text, for example, your thirst for knowledge and an "A" on the next exam may be secondary to your need for sleep if you were out partying half the night. On the other hand, if you are well rested, your concern (aroused tension) over improving your grade point (need) may encourage you to review this chapter several times in order to earn a grade of "B" or better on the next exam (goal-directed action). However, one thing you can be sure of—once you have satisfied either or both of these needs, other needs will arise (i.e., getting a date for the weekend).

Safety needs are satisfied by feelings of security and stability. To be secure, a person must feel free from physical harm or danger. Product and service retailers that focus on the need for protection include those that sell smoke- or burglar-alarm systems, insurance and retirement plans, exercise and health programs, warranties and guarantees, and caffeine-free, sugar-free, and salt-free foods and beverages. Stability is an equally important factor in meeting the need for safety. Generally, people feel more secure when there is a reasonable amount of order and structure in their lives. The often heard expressions "I need to simplify my life" or "I need to get organized" are directed at obtaining relief from the tensions that are aroused by an unstructured, unorganized, and chaotic life-style. Simplification and organization are both excellent concepts to be used by retailers in developing product lines, designing store and display layouts, creating advertising appeals, and establishing pricing points.

As social creatures, we all have social needs—the desire for love, belongingness, affection, and friendship. Because of our relatively affluent society, social needs have become powerful motivators of our behavior and influential organizers of our perceptions. Capitalizing on this need to "be accepted" or to "fit in," retailers structure many merchandising strategies around the need for satisfying relationships with family, friends, peers, and reference groups. Social need gratification influences where we live, what we wear, what organizations we belong to, what stores we patronize, and how much we are willing to pay.

Esteem needs involve consumer aspirations regarding prestige, recognition, admiration, self-respect, success, and achievement. An individual who seeks to fulfill esteem needs wants to "stand out" as contrasted to the social need to "fit in." In satisfying esteem needs, a consumer is more likely to (1) purchase "limited edition" merchandise (i.e., collectable figurines); (2) patronize distinctive outlets (i.e., specialty shops); (3) respond to individualist retail promotions (i.e., image-building advertisements); and (4) react in a less price-sensitive manner (i.e., prestige price preference). The retailer's task in meeting esteem needs is to make the consumer feel special and appreciated.

"Doing what you are capable of doing" is a phrase that summarizes an individual's need for self-actualization. The desire for self-fulfillment is the highest order need; it reflects the desire to reach one's full potential as an individual—"what you can be, you must be." A good example of an industry directed toward helping consumers realize their potential are the numerous motivational books, tapes, seminars, and programs designed to provide the means for realizing self-actualization. By combining the self-actualization need of self-fulfillment with the social need of recognition, the retailer has target-market opportunities for a wide range of goods and services of a conspicuous nature.

This ad appeals to social needs of love and belongingness to influence store patronage behavior. (Courtesy of Chess King; Jan Schoenbrun, art director)

Perception

How motivated consumers act out the buying process is determined, in part, by their perceptions of the buying situation. **Perception** is the process by which consumers attach meaning to incoming stimuli by forming mental pictures of persons, places, and objects. An individual's perception is how he or she views the world. The basic perceptual process consists of receiving, organizing, and interpreting stimuli. *Stimulus reception* is accomplished through the five senses of sight, sound, taste, touch, and smell. For most people, the sense of sight is the most used and developed sense mode, a fact that retailers should keep in mind when planning all aspects of their retailing mix. Exposure is the key to receiving stimuli; perception follows exposure. A major tactic in any retailing program is the inclusion of plans for gaining buyer exposure for the firm's product offering.

Stimulus organization is a mental data processing system whereby incoming stimuli (data) are organized into descriptive categories. Received stimuli must be simplified through organization if they are to be mentally converted into meaningful information that can be useful in problem solving, that is, making purchase decisions. Individuals vary greatly in their ability to mentally receive, store, and organize stimuli; hence, their interpretations of stimuli exhibit equal variance.

Stimulus interpretation is the process of assigning meaning to stimuli. When the consumer attaches meaning to something he or she has sensed, the perceptual process is completed. Interpretation of stimuli is accomplished by the mental comparison of what is sensed to what the individual knows or feels from previous experience. Having reviewed how we perceive, let's examine how we tend to be selective about what we perceive.

Selectivity is a natural phenomenon occurring within the perceptual process of receiving (selective exposure), organizing (selective retention), and interpreting (selective distortion) stimuli. "What you see [hear, feel, taste, and smell] is what you get. But what consumers actually perceive is always vastly different from the actual stimuli presented—not sometimes, not usually, but ALWAYS!"[14] The selectivity of perception is a key factor in explaining why different people have different perceptions of the same stimuli. **Selective exposure** is the act of limiting the type and amount of stimuli that are received and admitted to awareness. It is a screening process that allows us to select only the stimuli that interest us. For example, most consumers watch only certain types of television programming or read selected sections of their local newspaper. **Selective retention** is the act of remembering only the information that individual wants to remember. Individuals tend to retain information that is consistent with their feelings, beliefs, and attitudes. Information that is conflicting is likely to be forgotten. **Selective distortion** is the act of misinterpreting incoming stimuli to make them consistent with the individual's beliefs and attitudes. By changing incoming information, people can create a harmonious relationship between that information and their mind-set and avoid the tension that results from not having one's beliefs supported by new inputs. For example, if we like a particular retail store because of its friendly sales personnel, we might distort the fact that their higher prices are not competitive. The selectivity of perception places a considerable strain on the retailer who must get messages admitted to awareness without being misinterpreted or forgotten.

Learning

The logical extension of the motivational and perceptual process is learning. A considerable amount of human behavior is learned. **Learning** is the process of acquiring knowledge through past experiences. Behavioral psychologists view learning as a stimulus-response mechanism wherein drives, cues, and responses interact to produce a learned pattern of behavior. A **drive** is whatever impels behavior; it arises from a strongly felt inner need that requires action. A fear of failure, for example, may drive an insecure individual to work longer and more efficiently. **Cues** are external stimuli that direct consumers toward specific objects that can satisfy basic needs and reduce drives. To illustrate, an advertisement promoting a new book on time management is likely to catch the attention of an unsure individual who is looking for ways to improve his or her work efficiency. **Responses** are the actions taken to reduce a cue stimulated drive. In a buying situation, these actions typically include identifying, trying, evaluating, and selecting purchase alternatives. To continue the example, our fearful individual may respond by visiting the bookstore and after previewing the book may or may not decide to buy it.

The extent to which an individual learns from this stimulus-response mechanism is influenced by three factors: reinforcement, repetition, and participation. *Reinforcement* is the comparing of anticipated results with the actual results experienced from a chosen response. If actual results compare favorably with anticipated results, response reinforcement occurs and learning takes place. *Repetition* is the act of repeating a past experience. Learning is enhanced by performing the same action several times. *Participation* is the active involvement in the learning process. An active role in any activity generally results in the acquisition of more knowledge about that activity.

The retailer's efforts regarding the learning process should be directed at enhancing reinforcement, repetition, and participation. Reinforcement may take the form of return and allowance policies that confirm the retailer's intent to correct product deficiencies. Frequent advertisements that expose the consumer to the retailer's products and services is a commonly employed tactic used in supporting the learning process through repetition. Free samples, trial sizes, and demonstrations are participation devices used in marketing to guide the consumer's learning process toward the retailer's products.

Attitudes

An **attitude** is an evaluative mental orientation that provides a predisposition to respond in a certain fashion. People use their attitudes as evaluative mechanisms to pass judgment (i.e., good or bad, right or wrong) and as orientation mechanisms to focus that judgment on particular persons, places, things, or events. Attitudes can perform an important simplification function of the buying process by providing the consumer with a preset way to respond to the object of the attitude. For example, if Bob thinks that department stores are overpriced, he can avoid shopping there.

What is the makeup of an attitude? Figure 4–15 portrays the three basic components of an attitude—cognitive, affective, and behavior. The **cognitive component** consists of what the consumer believes about an object based on available information and knowledge. Essentially, a cognition is what is known about the object and its attributes. Feelings, not beliefs, are the focal point of the **affective component**—the emotions a consumer feels about an object. The third element of an attitude is the **behavior component**—the predisposition to respond in a certain way to the object based on one's beliefs and feelings.

Attitude formation is the result of past experiences. Attitudes are learned through interactions with family members and a wide range of peer and reference groups. People often adopt the prevailing attitudes of their associates. The learning of an attitude takes one of several forms: (1) trial and error (purchasing and using a product), (2) visual observation (watching a product demonstration), and (3) verbal

FIGURE 4–15
Components of an attitude (mind set)

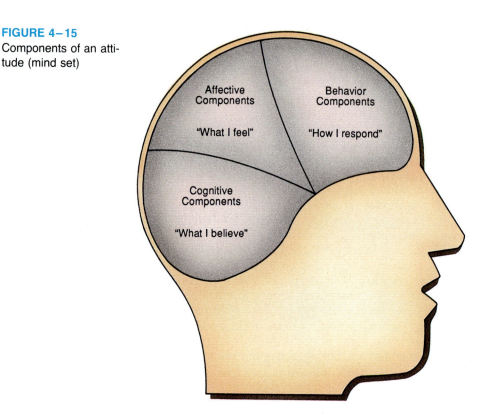

communications (listening to the product opinions of others). Through involvement in trial and error, visual observation, and verbal communication experiences of consumers, retailers can influence attitude formation.

Personal Factors

An individual's personality, self-concept, life-style, and position in the life cycle are all personal factors that impact on that individual's buying behavior (see Figure 4–13). We continue our exploration of the "whys" of consumer behavior by discussing each of the four personal factors.

Personality

Everyone has a personality; unfortunately, there is considerable disagreement as to what it is and to what extent it influences buying behavior. Because of its complex nature, personality is perhaps best defined in general terms; therefore, **personality** is a general response pattern used by individuals in coping with their environment. For example, an individual may be positive or negative, pessimistic or optimistic, aggressive or passive, independent or dependent, sociable or unsociable, and friendly or withdrawn. Logically, the existence of a particular personality trait will affect an individual's buying behavior. For example, a person with a pessimistic personality will approach buying situations with a considerable amount of doubt whereas an optimistic individual should be more impulsive and confident about buying choices. Market researchers, however, have been largely unsuccessful in their efforts to find significant statistical relationships between personalities and buying behavior. The junior customer—who and what is she? Demographically, she is eighteen to twenty-five years old, a high school girl, or a college student, or a young career woman. Her personality is complex, as described by one writer, "She is sexy and innocent, fickle, fun loving and fashion crazed; she is moody, wild for music, and demands to be entertained; she loves to be courted, but refuses to be loyal; she hasn't much money, never spends her dollars on long term investments, but splurges on instant fads; she's a non-conforming conformist who rebels daily against the establishment, but yearns just as much to be exactly the same as every one of her peers."[15] Most department stores and specialty shops have been mystified by the consumer group and continue to look for the right definition.

Self-Concept

Who are we? One answer to that question is that we are what we perceive ourselves to be; that is, our **self-concept**—the set of perceptions that people have of themselves within a social context. Each individual has a general awareness of his or her capabilities and attributes and how they are perceived within a social setting. The self-concept consists of four parts:

1. Real self—the way you actually are
2. Ideal self—how you would like to be
3. Looking-glass self—how you think others see you
4. Self-image—how you see yourself

As illustrated in Figure 4–16, our self-image is to some extent a composite of the real, ideal, and looking-glass selves. The importance of the self-concept to retailers in understanding consumer behavior is twofold; first, consumers often purchase products and/or brands that they feel support and reinforce their self-concept, and second, consumers never consciously purchase products that are incompatible with their self-concept. For example, the "contemporary conservative" pictured in Figure 3–15 may purchase a blue blazer with gray slacks because it is consistent with each of his

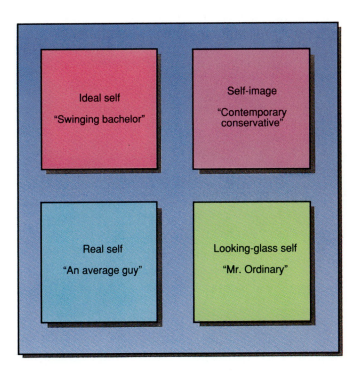

FIGURE 4–16
The four parts of the self-concept

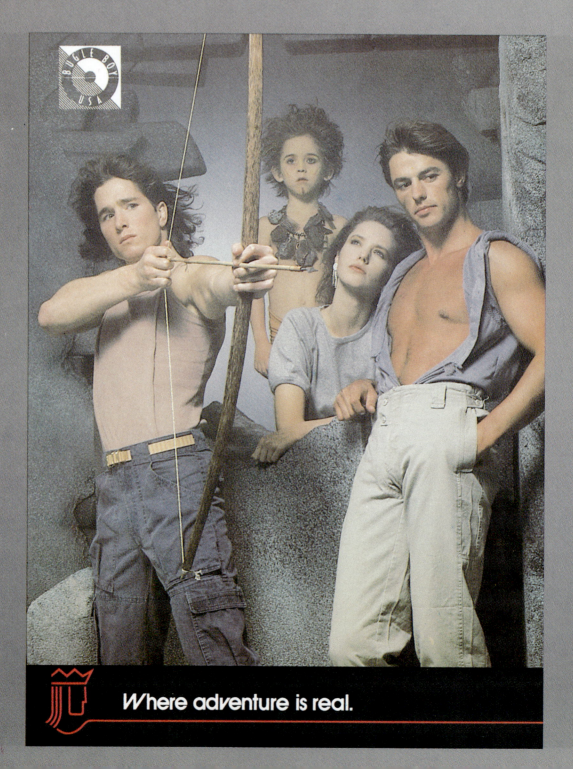

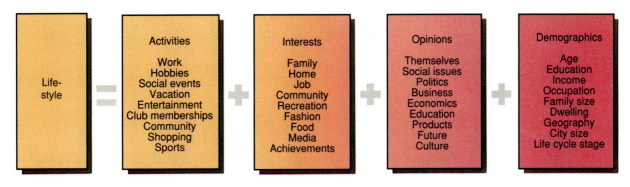

FIGURE 4–17
Dimensions of life-style (source: Joseph T. Plummer, "The Concept and Application of Life-Style Segmentation," *Journal of Marketing* 38 [January 1974]: 34)

"selfs"; such an apparel selection would allow this individual to fantasize about being a swinging bachelor (what he would like to be) while preserving his image as an average (what he really is) and ordinary (what others see him as) guy. One major use of the self-concept by retailers is in the creation of advertising appeals. By directing an advertising message to such self-images as the "homebody," the "good provider," the "budding scholar," and the "professional," the retailer has an additional tool for targeting selected consumer markets, developing product lines, planning price tactics, and designing store layouts.

Life-Styles

Some people lead an active life, others have **life-styles** that are more sedentary. Some people's are centered around their home and family; others center their lives around jobs, organizations, hobbies, or events. Couch Potatoes and their couch potatoes life-style "involves members of the baby boom generation who are simultaneously settling down while becoming bored with nightlife and its related expenses—found it trendy to stay home."[16] A consumer's life-style affects what, when, where, how, and why they buy. Life-style can be defined as *the way consumers live*. It is a patterned style of living that stems from the individual's needs, perceptions, and attitudes; as such, it represents a behavioral profile of the individual's psychological makeup. How consumers choose to live is also a reflection of the influences exerted by family members, peers, and other groups. Both conforming and nonconforming life-styles are behavioral reactions to what are expected and accepted modes of living.

Life-style analysis (psychographics) is an attempt by marketing researchers to develop consumer profiles based on consumers' ways of living. Life-style profiles are composite pictures of the consumer's **activities, interests, and opinions (AIO)**, together with their demographic makeup. Figure 4–17 identifies a commonly used enumeration of AIO variables. To develop life-style profiles, consumers are asked to respond to a multitude of AIO statements by indicating their degree of agreement or disagreement with those statements (see Figure 4–18). By finding patterned responses to AIO statements (e.g., strong agreement with all statements that reflect favorably on work-oriented activities, job-related interests, and probusiness opinions), the retailer is better able to identify market segments and to target marketing programs.

Life-style analysis tends to be special-purpose research; that is, it is directed at determining life-style profiles relative to a particular market, product, or retailing

This ad appeals to the consumer's self-concept. (Courtesy of Chess King; Jan Schoenbrun, art director)

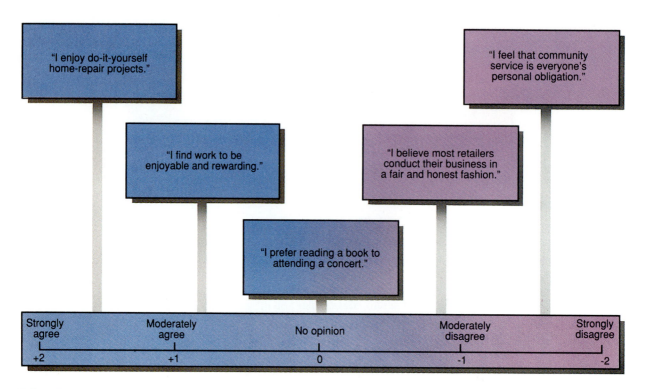

FIGURE 4–18

AIO statements (activities, interests, and opinions)

program. As an illustration, let's assume that a retailer wants to develop a fashion merchandising program based on life-style dimensions. After having administered a series of AIO statements to a represented sample, the following life-style profiles emerge:

1. The "perfectionist"—a career-oriented, free-spirited, active fashion leader who is concerned with uniqueness and individuality to support her avant-garde image; an individual who can be nonconforming and impractical when in an adventurous mood
2. The "traditionalist"—a job-oriented, conforming fashion follower who is extremely label-conscious and interested in being accepted as well as presenting a dignified and practical image

Having identified two distinct market segments based on life-style dimensions, the retailer can choose to (1) appeal to the perfectionist by offering the most advanced fashion apparel, stocking only one of each type of garment and timing new arrivals every week or (2) appeal to the traditionalist by offering stylish yet accepted fashions, stocking well-established labels and displays in practical combinations (outfits) of apparel. "Lifestyle analysis is not a panacea. . .but used well, psychographics can give us that critical bit of insight we need for added leverage in the marketplace."[17]

Life Cycle

Are you single, married, widowed, or divorced; are you with or without children; and are you young, middle-aged, or elderly? These are some of the factors that determine which stage of the life cycle you are in. The **life cycle** is a description of the changes that occur in an individual's demographic, psychographic, and behavioristic profile while progressing through a series of stages during his or her life time. The life cycle starts with the singles stage and ends with the retired solitary survivor of a family. The nine stages of the life cycle and their key demographic, psychographic, and behavioristic elements are portrayed in Figure 4–19. The differences in buyer behavior can often be explained by very practical considerations. Families with children buy toys, large families buy large-sized packages, and empty-nest families are in a position to more readily afford luxury products and services. A recent development in the family life cycle has been the delayed exit from the nest by older children or the coming home to roost by the offspring who might wish to boost buying power; with no or reduced rent, these "late nesters" have considerably greater disposable income.[18]

Social Factors

Conformity to group expectations is a basic element of human behavior. Much of what we do is directed at gaining acceptance from other people, so it is with our buying behavior. We buy certain products, select particular brands, and patronize certain stores because we want the approval and support of others. The importance of group influences on individual buying behavior is great. Human interactions affect our motivation, perception, and learning processes and help shape our attitudes, personality, self-concept, and life-style. The following discussion examines the impact of the family, reference groups, social class, and culture on our individual buying behavior (see Figure 4–13).

The Family

A family can be described in terms of the *nuclear family,* consisting of a father, mother, and their children, or as the *extended family,* which includes the nuclear family plus grandparents, aunts, uncles, and cousins. Regardless of how the family unit is defined, it represents one of the most important social factors impacting on our buying behavior. The importance of the family to planning merchandising strategies lies in the fact that (1) every family member's behavior is strongly influenced by the interactions that occur within the family; (2) every family represents both a buying and consuming unit within our economy; and (3) as more and more children boost buying power by returning to the family nest, that consuming unit has increased purchasing capabilities.[19]

Family influences on individual buyer behavior stem from childhood. Consciously or unconsciously, we adopt many of our parents' attitudes, values, morals, and ways of doing things. These basic orientations remain with us long after we have left our family of origin. As we establish a new family by getting married and having children, the influences of our spouse and children assume a primary role of importance in the acquisition of new orientations and the development of new behavioral patterns.

Family buying roles are a key issue in understanding consumer behavior. From a merchandising perspective, a consumer is often not an individual but a family represented by an individual. Therefore, retailers must recognize and understand the various roles played by various family members within a given purchase situation. Five specific roles have been identified as follows:

1. Initiator—the family member who first recognizes the problem
2. User—the family member who will actually use or consume the product or service
3. Decision maker—the family member who decides what will be bought and at what time, place, and source

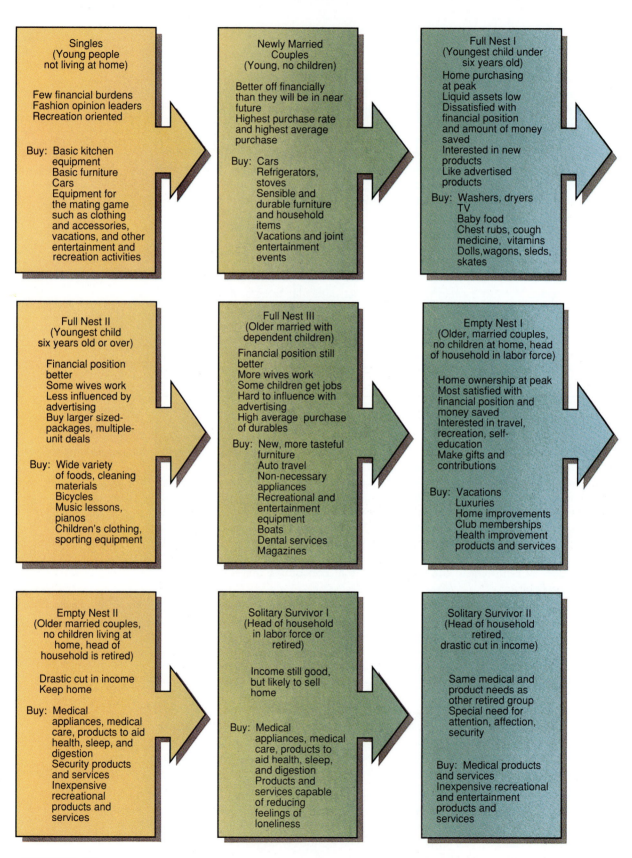

FIGURE 4-19

The life-cycle progression (source: William D. Wells and George Gubar, "Life Cycle Concept In Marketing Research," *Journal of Marketing Research* 3 [November 1966]: 362)

4. Decision influencer—the family member who has input to affect the choice of the decision maker
5. Purchasing agent—the family member who actually visits the store and makes the purchase

To be effective, a merchandising program must take into account each family member and their respective roles. For example, the retailer's persuasive and informational advertising might be directed at (1) the initiator to create awareness, (2) the decision influencer and decision maker to develop comprehension and conviction, (3) the user to provide reinforcement, and (4) the purchasing agent to guide shopping trip behavior. Role specialization in family buying is common in most families. Although some purchase decisions are made jointly or independently, other purchases are dominated by either the husband or wife. With the increase of working mothers, many teens are taking on adult buying roles of decision maker and purchasing agent. "While both parents may be the breadwinners, teenagers now are the bread buyers."[20]

Reference Groups

Reference groups provide individuals with a "frame of reference" in making such purchase decisions as what and where to buy. A **reference group** is a group that serves as a model or standard for an individual's behavior and attitudes. An individual may develop associations with such reference groups as friends, colleagues, co-workers, clubs, and associations.

Reference group influences on purchase behavior vary by product and brand. Purchases of highly conspicuous and visible products such as clothing, furniture, and automobiles are strongly influenced by reference groups. The importance of peer group influence in the purchase of fashion is shown in Figure 4–20. If the brand name, style, or design is uniquely conspicuous, reference group influences become an important decision factor. The retailer's image as the "right or in place" for a particular reference group can also be an important consideration in deciding what retailer to patronize. The colorful and distinctive clothing offered by Esprit and the unusual and adventurous apparel sold by the Banana Republic are both good examples of retailers who have been successful with a specialty business format in which reference group influence is a key focal point for merchandising decisions. The distinctive package of a distinctive retailer may be as important as the product in a group gift-giving situation.

FIGURE 4–20
Setting the style on campus: When it comes to fashion, most college students are influenced by their friends (source: Elys McLean-Ibrahim, "What makes workers succeed." *USA Today* [September 1987], pB-1. Copyright © 1987 USA TODAY. Reprinted with permission)

Social Class

Based on occupation, education, place of residence (i.e., prestige of neighborhood), income, and wealth, social scientists have developed societal, rank-ordered groupings of individuals and families known as **social classes**. The higher the class rank, the higher the status (greater prestige) of the class. A widely used classification scheme of American social classes is that developed by W. Lloyd Warner. His scheme consists of six levels ranging from upper-upper class to lower-lower class. The Warner classification is reported in Figure 4–21.

A number of generalizations can be made concerning the marketing implications stemming from our social class groupings. They include the following:

Upper-upper class consumers typically do not engage in conspicuous consumption; rather, they tend to be governed by conservative tastes and a selective buying process. They represent potential markets for unique and expensive products (e.g., "originals" in fashion apparel). Patronage motives tend toward personalized services and individualistic merchandising at exclusive retailers. The buying patterns of this class often serve as a reference point for the consumption activities of lower classes.

Lower-upper class consumers engage in conspicuous consumption of a wide range of highly visible personal, recreational, and household products and services. This buying behavior is often directed at impressing lower social classes. A primary consideration of lower-upper class purchase behavior is social acceptability of their peer class and the acceptance of the upper-upper class; in other words, much of this class's buying behavior is directed at achieving status.

Upper-middle class consumers are quality-conscious purchasers of products that are acceptable to the upper class; hence, they tend to be cautious consumers of prestigious products that communicate "who they are" to others. On the other hand, they also tend to be venturesome in their willingness to try new products and seek out new places to shop. For the upper-middle class, their home is the center of their personal and social life and therefore is a focus for their buyer behavior.

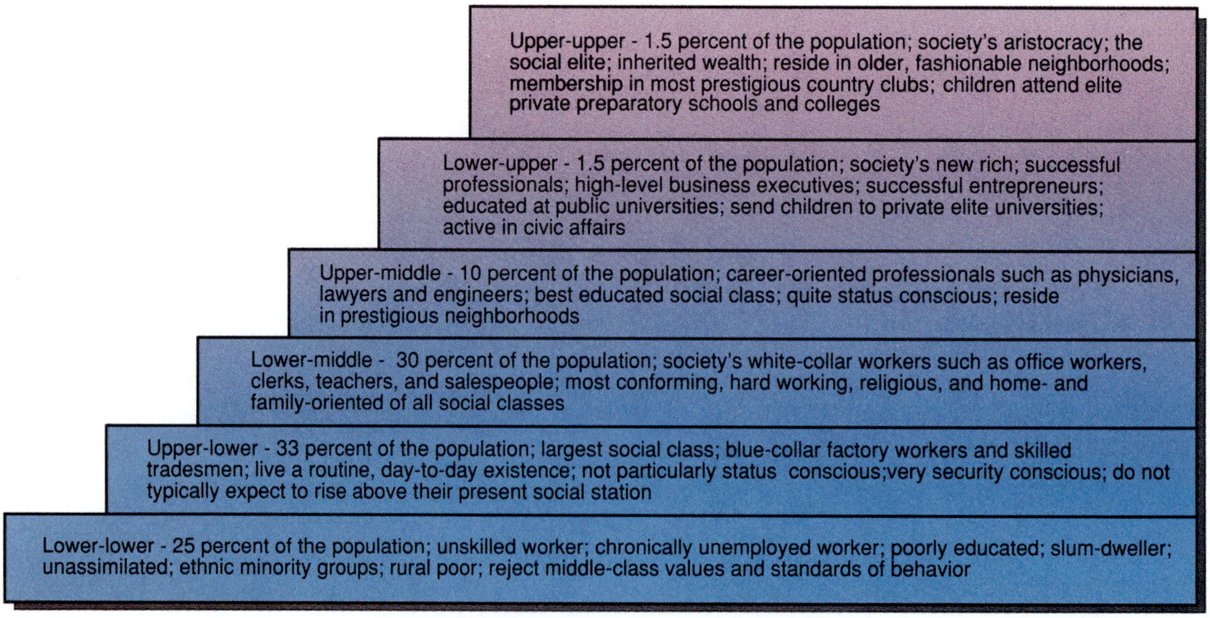

FIGURE 4–21

The staircase of social classes (source: Adapted from W. Lloyd Warner, *American Life, Dream and Reality* [Chicago: University of Chicago Press, 1953])

Upper-upper - 1.5 percent of the population; society's aristocracy; the social elite; inherited wealth; reside in older, fashionable neighborhoods; membership in most prestigious country clubs; children attend elite private preparatory schools and colleges

Lower-upper - 1.5 percent of the population; society's new rich; successful professionals; high-level business executives; successful entrepreneurs; educated at public universities; send children to private elite universities; active in civic affairs

Upper-middle - 10 percent of the population; career-oriented professionals such as physicians, lawyers and engineers; best educated social class; quite status conscious; reside in prestigious neighborhoods

Lower-middle - 30 percent of the population; society's white-collar workers such as office workers, clerks, teachers, and salespeople; most conforming, hard working, religious, and home- and family-oriented of all social classes

Upper-lower - 33 percent of the population; largest social class; blue-collar factory workers and skilled tradesmen; live a routine, day-to-day existence; not particularly status conscious;very security conscious; do not typically expect to rise above their present social station

Lower-lower - 25 percent of the population; unskilled worker; chronically unemployed worker; poorly educated; slum-dweller; unassimilated; ethnic minority groups; rural poor; reject middle-class values and standards of behavior

Lower-middle class consumers focus a considerable amount of buying behavior around maintaining a respectable home within a do-it-yourself context. They tend to be quite value conscious in that they seek an acceptable relationship between lower prices and good quality. Standardization is a key factor in their buying behavior; they therefore purchase products of standard design from traditional retail operations.

Upper-lower class consumers are less concerned with purchasing products that enhance status and are more concerned with buying goods and services for personal enjoyment. In comparison to other classes above them, this class spends a lower portion of their incomes on housing and a higher proportion of their income on household goods. They tend to be impulsive buyers yet remain loyal to previously bought brands that they believe to be a reflection of good quality. As heavy users of credit, this class is hesitant to try new retail outlets.

Lower-lower class consumers use credit extensively and impulsively to purchase highly visible products of a personal nature. They prefer well-known brands and local stores with easy credit terms.

Culture

The final social influence on our behavior is the cultural environment within which the consumer lives. **Culture** is the sum total of knowledge, attitudes, symbols, and patterns of behavior that are shared by a group of people and transmitted from one generation to the next. Cultural traits include (1) profound beliefs (e.g., religious); (2) fundamental values (e.g., achievements); and (3) customs (e.g., ladies first). Because cultural environmental influences are a major determinant of human behavior, it is essential for the retailer to adapt and conform merchandising programs to the cultural heritage of his or her chosen markets.

The American culture is undergoing dynamic changes that have a profound effect on consumption patterns and buying behavior. For some products and firms, ongoing cultural trends spell new opportunities and merchandising success; for others, it equates to new threats and possible market failure. In developing and implementing merchandising programs, the retailer must ascertain the type and extent of influence exerted by the cultural traits of the local market area.

BUYING PROCESS

Being loved and accepted, overcoming loneliness and insecurity, or gaining status and prestige are all problems that consumers attempt to solve in part by engaging in buying activities. Individuals make purchase decisions by passing through the five stages of what we can call the consumer buying process. The **consumer buying process** is the sum total of the sequential parts of problem recognition, information search, alternative evaluation, purchase decision, and postpurchase evaluation. The duration and extent to which an individual gets involved in any one stage of the buying process varies greatly, depending on such factors as urgency of need, frequency of purchase, importance of purchase, and so on. A preview of each stage is presented in the following discussion; see if you can recognize these stages in your own buying behavior.

Stage 1: Problem Recognition

A felt discrepancy between an ideal state of affairs and the actual state of affairs starts the consumer's buying process by creating an awareness that a problem exists. Problem recognition is, then, a feeling that things are not what they should be. Internally felt physiological and psychological needs are tension-producing stimuli that create an awareness that something is lacking. In addition, external cues attract and direct the consumer's attention toward the recognition that he or she is unsatisfied with his or her state of affairs. Exposure to the retailer's stores, products, advertisements, merchandising incentives, personal selling efforts, and price structures are all potential reminders to consumers of unfulfilled needs and wants.

Based on importance, cost, knowledge, and/or experience factors, there are three types of problem-solving situations—extensive, limited, and routinized problem solving. **Extensive problem solving** involves a buying situation in which the consumer is considering the purchase of an important and costly product under the unfavorable circumstances of having no knowledge or experience with the product. First-time purchases, once-in-a-lifetime purchases, and highly infrequent purchases are all buying situations that require extensive consumer effort in achieving a satisfactory solution. Providing useful and readily available information and reducing risk and uncertainty of the purchase are key variables to be considered by the retailer when developing merchandising tactics to assist the consumer faced with an extensive problem-solving situation.

Limited problem solving occurs when the consumer has some knowledge and experience with purchasing and using the product under consideration. The problem may or may not involve an important purchase and/or costly product. In either case, the buyer is able to limit the range of considerations (e.g., brands, sizes, colors, materials, and so on) because of existing knowledge and previous experience. The retailer's task is to discover which limited decision factors are being used in making product selections, then use these selective factors as focal points in developing appropriate product, price, distribution, and promotion strategies.

Routinized problem solving involves making the same purchase decision time after time. Consumers purchase many products frequently and regularly. Typically, these purchases tend to involve products of lower importance and cost that arise as repurchase needs. The typical weekly grocery list represents this type of purchase. Consumers simply repeat a previous purchase decision with little thought or deliberation because they feel there is no reason to change.

Stage 2: Information Search

Gathering information and gaining experience make up the second stage of the consumer buying process. A *low-level information search* involves an increased awareness of readily available information. The consumer pays closer attention to advertisements, store displays, sales pitches, and comments of others in an effort to gather additional information to supplement existing product knowledge. A *high-level information search* consists of a conscientious effort to seek out and gather new and supplementary information from new and existing sources. It involves actively talking with, reading from, and observing information sources that will be useful to an extensive problem-solving situation involving re-evaluation and reinforcement purchases.

Stage 3: Alternative Evaluation

Product, brand, and store information needs to be processed before it is useful in the evaluation of purchase alternatives. Consumers use a variety of criteria in making different purchase decisions. What evaluation criteria would you use in purchasing a tube of toothpaste, a desk lamp, a winter coat, a color television, and a new automobile? A comprehensive list of evaluative criteria consumers use in purchasing these products is far too complex and extensive to fully enumerate here; however, a general list of potential evaluation criteria is presented in Figure 4–22.

FIGURE 4–22
Product, brand, and
store evaluation criteria

I. Product Evaluation Criteria
    A. Functional Features
       1. Size
       2. Shape
       3. Weight
       4. Material
       5. Workmanship
    B. Aesthetic Features
       1. Color
       2. Texture
       3. Odor
       4. Taste
       5. Sound
       6. Style
    C. Service Features
       1. Delivery
       2. Alteration
       3. Installation
       4. Warranty
       5. Maintenance
    D. Psychological Features
       1. Prestige
       2. Image
       3. Acceptability
       4. Safety
       5. Security
       6. Uniqueness

II. Merchandising Evaluation Criteria
    A. Price Features
       1. Selling Price
       2. Perceived Value
       3. Credit Terms
    B. Place Features
       1. Convenience
       2. Availability
       3. Prestige
    C. Promotional Features
       1. Labels
       2. Logos
       3. Packages

III. Personal Evaluation Criteria
    A. Compatability Considerations
       1. Substitutive
       2. Complement
       3. Different
    B. Appropriateness Considerations
       1. Life-Style
       2. Life Cycle
    C. Other Considerations
       1. Durability
       2. Suitability
       3. Quality

Criteria do not carry the same weight or have the same importance in deciding on a purchase. In some cases we are simply interested in having the product do what it was designed to do (e.g., clean and polish, cool or heat); therefore, we place greater weight on the functional features of the product. In other cases, our needs may be more social in character; hence, we emphasize the psychological features of the product or brand and the personal considerations of the product's or brand's appropriateness to our life-style and circle of friends. In essence, for a given purchase, criteria may be weighted along an importance scale as illustrated in Figure 4–23.

Stage 4: Purchase Decision

The purchase decision is actually two decisions—*if* and *when*. The "if decision" deals with the issue of whether or not to make a purchase. Based on the previous evaluation stage, the consumer may decide that there are several products, brands, or stores that are capable of resolving the problem identified in the first stage of the buying process—*the buy decision*. On the other hand, the consumer may conclude that of the known alternatives evaluated, none meet minimum expectations for need satisfaction—*the no-buy decision*. A no-buy decision terminates the current cycle of the buying process; the consumer can either dismiss the problem or start the buying process anew with hopes of gaining a different perspective on the problem.

The "when decision" is concerned with deciding whether to make an immediate purchase or to wait until some future date. A *decision to proceed* with the purchase may stem from urgently felt needs, currently available opportunities, and other circumstances that mediate against delaying the decision. A *decision to post-*

FIGURE 4–23
Criteria-weighting scale

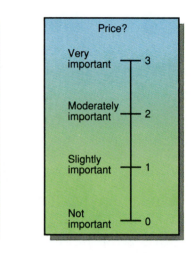
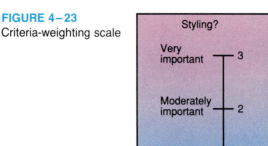

pone a purchase is frequently associated with a high level of perceived risk. The consumer becomes anxious because of the importance, cost, and/or uncertainty of the decision.

Stage 5: Postpurchase Evaluation

The purchasing of a product does not end the consumer buying process. Once a purchase has been made, the consumer proceeds to re-evaluate the decision in an attempt to judge whether or not he or she made the right (e.g., best or acceptable) decision. Essentially, the postpurchase evaluation stage consists of comparing the actual performance of the product/service or the actual experience with the store with the expected or hoped for performance or experience. The basic question to be answered by the consumer in the postpurchase evaluation stage is "Did the product or store relieve aroused tensions stemming from felt needs?" In other words, "Did the product or store solve the problem?" An affirmative answer promotes *postpurchase satisfaction* and encourages the consumer to repeat the purchase behavior at the same outlet when the same or similar problem arises. A negative answer results in *postpurchase dissonance*—being dissatisfied with the purchase and the process that led to it. To relieve the feelings of uneasiness that are associated with an unsatisfactory product, the consumer may engage in a variety of actions: (1) discard the product and write it off as a bad experience; (2) obtain some type of an allowance from the retailer, thereby increasing the product's perceived value; (3) return the product to the retailer and attempt to improve on their purchase decision process; and (4) write the retailer off as a poor place to shop.

Often consumers have mixed feelings concerning their purchases—a mild case of postpurchase dissonance. In such cases they attempt to confirm a right decision or at least an acceptable decision by (1) seeking positive comments from others, (2) distorting information so that it fits the purchase decision, and (3) emphasizing positive information and de-emphasizing negative data.

BUYING SCENES

The final buyer behavior issues to be considered are buying scenes—where consumers buy. A **buying scene** is the actual place where consumers complete a purchase transaction. There are four possible buying scenes: (1) a retail store, (2) a consumer's home, (3) a consumer's workplace, and (4) a parasite point of consumption. Americans make a majority of their purchases by visiting a retail store or re-

These are examples of the four buying scenes.

sponding to in-the-home marketing efforts. While a consumer's place of work is a place of production, not consumption, some retailers (e.g., hair stylists and food vendors) have had success by providing the consumer with a high level of time and place convenience. Snap-on-Tool Corp. uses step vans to take its products to the customer.[21] Convenience is also the key for successfully marketing a limited number of products at "parasite" scenes (e.g., newspaper stand at a restaurant, hot dog vendor at a football game, and magazine rack at an airport). A rapidly growing example of this retail format is the pushcart market, or temporary, seasonal tenants found in various malls, marketplaces, and airports. Hickory Farms of Ohio operates more than 1,000 such operations in addition to its 500 stores. The temporary nature of such activities is illustrated by the fact that the Jubilee Market at Jackson Brewery in New Orleans offers one-week leases.[22]

SUMMARY

A market is a buying population and its corresponding buying behavior. Buying populations can be classified into one of two groups—consumer markets (ultimate consumers of goods and services) and organizational markets (intermediate consumers of goods and services). The structure of buying populations was examined from the perspective of population analysis, demographic analysis, and geographical analysis. Population analysis answers the question "How many are they?" The total population of a consumer market determined in part the actual and potential market for a particular market. Demographic analysis answers the question "Who are they?" Demography is the study of statistics that are used to describe a population. People can be described in terms of age, sex, education, income, occupation, race, nationality, family size, and structure. Major demographic trends are (1) an aging population, (2) a shrinking household, (3) a changing role for women, and (4) an increasing role of many diversified minorities. Geographic analysis answers the question "Where are they?" People move, therefore markets change. Some important geographic trends and patterns are: (1)population is shifting from the north and eastern U.S. to the south and western sectors of the country, (2) America is an urbanized society (e.g., 75 percent urbanized), (3) there are more suburbanites than urbanites, and (4) nonmetro areas are making a comeback.

Buying behavior is the manner in which consumers act, function, and react to various situations involving the purchase of a good or service or the acceptance of an idea. The dimensions of consumer buying behavior include understanding buying considerations, situations, centers, influences, processes, and scenes. Buying consideration is concerned with the question "What do consumers buy?" Consumers buy products—bundles of benefits capable of satisfying consumer wants and needs. Products are viewed in terms of their tangibility (goods, services, or ideas); durability (durables and nondurables); and availability (convenience, shopping, and specialty products).

Buying situations are concerned with the question "How much do consumers buy?" The answer is a function of the individual's needs and desires together with the individual's ability to buy (the financial resources—income, credit, assets—that are available to the consumer); willingness to buy (psychological, personal, and social reasons for buying); and authority to buy (formal and informal authorization). Buying centers deal with the issue "Who does the buying?" A buying center is a basic unit of consumption that engages in the buying center. Basic consumption units tend to be either individual or household.

"Why consumers buy" is the question of concern in the discussion of buying influences. The major influences of consumer buying behavior include psychological, personal, and social factors. Motivation, perception, learning, and attitudes are the four major psychological factors that influence consumers in the determination of the buying choices. An individual's personality, self-concept, life-style, and position in the life cycle are all personal factors that have an impact on his or her buying behavior. Conformity to group expectations (family, reference groups, social class, and culture) is the basic premise behind the impact of social factors on consumer buying behavior.

The buying process is the sum total of the sequential arts of problem recognition, information search, alternative evaluation, purchase decision, and postpurchase evaluation. In other words, the buying process answers the question "How do consumers buy?" "Where consumers buy" is described by the four buying scenes. A buying scene is the actual place where consumers complete a purchase transaction; it can be at a retail store, a consumer's home, a consumer's workplace, or a parasite point of consumption.

KEY TERMS AND CONCEPTS		
activities, interests, and opinions (AIO) statements	buying center	
affective component	buying power	
attitudes	buying scenes	
assets	cognitive component	
behavior component	consumer buying process	
buying behavior	consumer markets	
	convenience products	

credit	perception
cues	personality
culture	physiological needs
demography	products
desires	reference groups
discretionary income	responses
disposable income	routinized problem solving
drive	safety needs
durables	selective distortion
esteem needs	selective exposure
extensive problem solving	selective retention
family buying roles	self-actualization
goods	self-concept
ideas	senior-citizens market
learning	services
life cycle	shopping products
life-style	social class
limited problem solving	social needs
market	specialty products
market potential	total income
middle-aged market	total population
motivation	ultimate consumers
needs	young-adults market
nondurables	youth market
organizational markets	zero population growth

REVIEW QUESTIONS

1. A market is comprised of two major components. What are they? Provide a brief description.
2. Who are ultimate consumers? What are their purchase intentions?
3. What is demography? A demographic description is based on what variables?
4. Profile the changing age structure of the U.S. population. Discuss the impact of these changes on the retailing of goods.
5. How is the U.S. household mix changing? Is it good or bad news for American retailers? Explain.
6. What are the three working women roles? Describe the impact of these roles on the merchandising of goods and services.
7. Illustrate the basic geographic shifts in the distribution of the nation's population.
8. Define product. Develop a graphic presentation of the various product classifications. Provide a description of each product class.
9. Describe the determinants of consumer buying power.
10. Identify the elements of the motivational process. Distinguish between the various types of needs that direct individual consumer behavior.
11. How is perception accomplished? Delineate between the various forms of selectivity that are portrayed in the perception process.
12. Discuss the stimulus-response mechanisms inherent in the learning process.
13. What are attitudes used for? Describe the components that make up an attitude.
14. Who are we? Identify and define the four parts of the self-concept.

15. Life-style profiles are composite pictures of what factors? How do life-styles affect buying behavior?
16. Portray the various roles that various family members might play relative to a given purchase situation.
17. Outline the various stages of the consumer buying process.

ENDNOTES

1. John A. Byrne and Paul B. Brown, "Those Unpredictable Babies," *Forbes* (November 1982): 206.
2. Selina S. Guber, "The Teenage Mind," *American Demographics* (August 1987): 44.
3. David B. Wolfe, "The Ageless Market," *American Demographics* (July 1987): 28.
4. Paul B. Brown, "Last Year It Was Yuppies—This Year It's Their Parents," *Business Week,* 10 March 1986, 68.
5. Heidi E. Capousis, "Household Size Shrinks," *USA Today,* 15 Oct. 1987, A-1.
6. Janet Wallach, "Career Dressing," *Stores* (January 1987): 51.
7. Lori Keslar, "Efforts by Big Retailers Gaining Notice," *Advertising Age,* 8 Feb. 1988, 5–6.
8. Joel Kotkin, "Selling to the New America," *INC* (July 1987): 47.
9. Dwight Johnson, "Black Population: Present and Future," *Black Enterprise* (July 1987): 39.
10. "2000," *Chain Store Age Executive* (May 1987): 22.
11. Martin L. Bell, "Some Strategy Implications of a Matrix Approach to the Classification of Marketing Goods and Services," *Journal of the Academy of Marketing Sciences* 14 (Spring 1986): 13–20.
12. Susan Benway, "Presto! The Convenience Industry: Making Life a Little Simpler," *Business Week,* 27 April 1987, 86.
13. "Standard of Living Rate Increasing 20% Per Decade," *Marketing News,* 13 Feb. 1987, 3.
14. Robert B. Settle and Pamela L. Alreck, "Knowing Your Consumer Inside and Out," *Marketing Communications* (March 1987): 50.
15. Janet Wallach, "The Junior Customer: Who Is She, and What Does She Want?" *Stores* (January 1988): 53.
16. Joe Agnew, "Targeting the Couch Potato," *Marketing News,* 15 Feb. 1988, 1.
17. Bickley Townsend, "Psychographic Glitter and Gold," *American Demographics* (November 1985): 79.
18. Nancy Giges, "Prodigal Offspring Boost Buying Power by Returning to Roost," *Advertising Age,* 2 March 1987, 36.
19. Ibid.
20. "If Both Parents Are Bread Winners, Teenagers Often Are the Bread Buyers," *Marketing News,* 13 Feb. 1987, 5.
21. "Step Vans Serve as Store on Wheels," *Marketing News* (June 1987): 6.
22. Eric C. Peterson, "Temporary Tenants," *Stores* (January 1987): 144; Barbara Bryan, "Airport Retailing," *Stores* (July 1987): 37; "Airport Retailers Expected to Reach New Sales Heights," *Marketing News,* 15 Feb. 1988, 23.

SELECTED READINGS

Bartos, Rena. "Over 49: The Invisible Consumer Market." *Harvard Business Review* 58 (January–February 1980): 140–49.

Bellenger, Danny N., and Korgaonkar, Pradeep K. "Profiling the Recreational Shopper." *Journal of Retailing* 56 (Fall 1980): 77–92.

Bivins, Jacquelyn. "Adult Boom: The Aging of the Wundergeneration." *Chain Store Age Executive* (May 1985): 27–30.

Blackwell, Roger D., and Talarzyk, W. Wayne. "Lifestyle Retailing: Competitive Strategies for the 1980s." *Journal of Retailing* 59 (Winter 1983): 7–28.

Bruner, Gordon C. "Problem Recognition Styles and Search Patterns: An Empirical Investigation." *Journal of Retailing* 62 (Fall 1986): 281–97.

Cobb, Cathy J., and Hoyer, Wayne D. "Planned Versus Impulse Purchase Behavior." *Journal of Retailing* 62 (Winter 1986): 384–409.

Gutman, Jonathan, and Mills, Michael K. "Fashion Life-Style, Self-Concept, Shopping Orientation and Store Patronage." *Journal of Retailing* 58 (Summer 1982): 64–86.

Hawes, Jon M., and Lumpkin, James R. "Perceived Risk and the Selection of a Retail Patronage Mode." *Journal of the Academy of Marketing Science* 14 (Winter 1987): 37–42.

Hirschman, Elizabath C., and Wallendorf, Melanie R. "Characteristics of the Cultural Continuum: Implications for Retailing." *Journal of Retailing* 58 (Spring 1982): 5–21.

Holak, Susan L., Lehmann, Donald R., and Sultan, Fareena. "The Role of Expectations in the Adoption of Innovative Consumer Durables: Some Preliminary Evidence." *Journal of Retailing* 63 (Fall 1987): 243–59.

Hyman, Michael R. "Long-Distance Geographic Mobility and Retailing Attitudes and Behaviors: An Update." *Journal of Retailing* 63 (Summer 1987): 187–204.

Kim, Chankon, and Khoury, Majeed. "Task Complexity and Contingent Information Processing in the Case of Couple's Decision Making." *Journal of the Academy of Marketing Science* 15 (Fall 1987): 32–43.

Korgaonkar, Pradeep K. "Consumer Shopping Orientations, Non-Store Retailers, and Consumer's Patronage Intentions: A Multivariate Investigation." *Journal of the Academy of Marketing Science* 12 (Winter–Spring 1984): 11–22.

Korgaonkar, P. K., Lund, Daulat; and Price, Barbara. "A Structural Equation Approach Toward Examination of Store Attitude and Store Patronage Behavior." *Journal of Retailing* 61 (Summer 1985): 39–60.

Lavin, Marilyn. "Husband–Wife Decision Making: A Theory-Based, Process Model." In *1985 AMA Educators' Proceedings,* edited by R. F. Lusch et al., 21–25. American Marketing Association, 1985.

Lumpkin, James R., and Greenberg, Barnett A. "Apparel-Shopping Patterns of the Elderly Consumer." *Journal of Retailing* 58 (Winter 1982): 68–89.

Lumpkin, James R., Greenberg, Barnett A., and Goldstucker, Jac L. "Marketplace Needs of the Elderly: Determinant Attributes and Store Choice." *Journal of Retailing* 61 (Summer 1985): 75–105.

Malhotra, Naresh K. "A Threshold Model of Store Choice." *Journal of Retailing* 59 (Summer 1983): 3–21.

Murphy, Patrick E., and Enis, Ben M. "Classifying Products Strategically." *Journal of Marketing* 50 (July 1986): 24–42.

Sirgy, M. Joseph, Samli, A. Coskun, Bahn, Kenneth, and Varvoglis, T. G. "Self-Concept and Retailing Strategy." In *Developments in Marketing Science, Proceedings,* edited by N. K. Malhotra, 2–6. Academy of Marketing Science, 1985.

Spiggle, Susan, and Sewall, Murphy A. "A Choice Sets Model of Retail Selection." *Journal of Marketing* 51 (April 1987): 97–111.

Tatzel, Miriam. "Skill and Motivation in Clothes Shopping: Fashion-Conscious, Independent, and Apathetic Consumers." *Journal of Retailing* 58 (Winter, 1982): 90–97.

Unger, Lynette S., Stearns, James M., and Lesser, Jack A. "Sources of Consumer Satisfaction with Retail Outlets: Issues and Evidence." In *Developments in Marketing Science, Proceedings,* edited by J. C. Rogers, III, 34–37. Academy of Marketing Science, 1983.

Westbrook, Robert A., and Black, William C. "A Motivation-Based Shopper Typology." *Journal of Retailing* 61 (Spring 1985): 78–103.

Williams, Terrell, Slama, Mark, and Rogers, John. "Behavioral Characteristics of the Recreational Shopper and Implications for Retail Management." *Journal of the Academy of Marketing Science* 13 (Summer 1985), 307–16.

Zeithaml, Valarie A., and Gilly, Mary C. "Characteristics Affecting the Acceptance of Retailing Technologies: A Comparison of Elderly and Nonelderly Consumers." *Journal of Retailing* 63 (Spring 1987): 49–68.

5

Outline

THE LEGAL ENVIRONMENT

THE LEGAL ASPECTS OF RETAIL COMPETITION
Present Restraints on Trade
Probable Restraints on Trade
Unfair Trade Practices

THE LEGAL ASPECTS OF STORE OPERATIONS
Store Organization and the Law
Personnel Management and the Law
Store Facilities and the Law

THE LEGAL ASPECTS OF RETAIL MERCHANDISING
Product Legalities
Price Legalities
Promotion Legalities
Distribution Legalities

Objectives

☐ Respect the legal complexities under which the retailer must operate.

☐ Understand the legal framework establishing the lawful limits within which retailing activities must be conducted.

☐ Identify and discuss the legal aspects of retail competition.

☐ Distinguish the legal aspects of retail store operations.

☐ Describe the legal aspects of retail merchandising.

The Regulatory Aspects
of Retailing

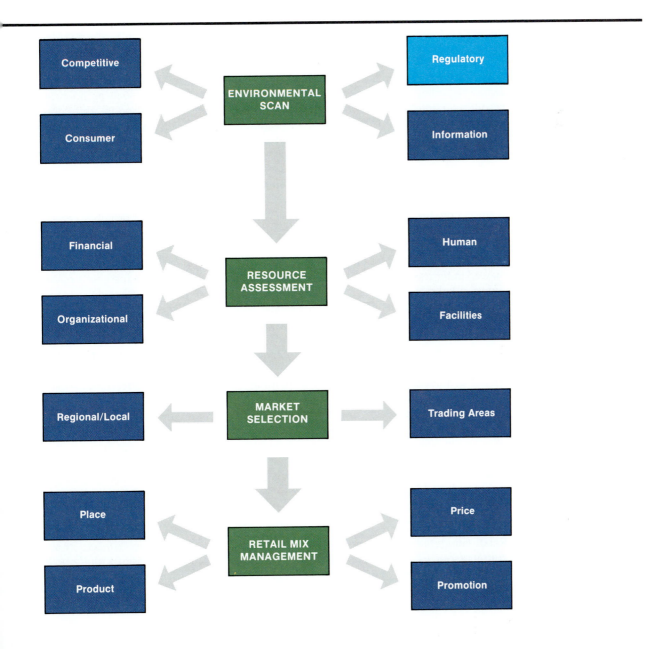

The legal aspects of retailing are an integral part of store operations. Legal considerations affect almost all aspects of the retailer's daily operations. To the retailer, these legal constraints are largely uncontrollable, at least in the short run. Equally noteworthy is the fact that the law constantly changes as a result of the political activities (lobbying, lawsuits, referenda, and negotiations) of a large number of concerned interest groups. To operate successfully *and* legally, the retailer must both understand and appreciate the legal environment.

THE LEGAL ENVIRONMENT

The legal environment is the framework that establishes the lawful limits within which retailing and other business activities must be conducted. It is the attempt by various governmental bodies to modify or control the retailer's behavior and activities through various statutory measures and regulatory instruments. The legal environment and the need for a legal framework are the result of the increasingly complex business and social climate.

Conflicts are bound to emerge from increased economic and social interdependence. Sources of conflict include disputes over competitive business practices; priorities regarding the use of scarce human and raw material, as well as financial resources; controls on environmental pollution and energy consumption; and rights and responsibilities of various members within a channel of distribution. Regardless of the sources of conflict, some rules of conduct must be established to settle conflicting issues and to guide future behavior. Creation and continual modification of the legal environment are ways to referee these conflicts.

The legal environment is often viewed as restrictive and prohibitive of business activities. In many respects the legal environment *is* restrictive. In some cases, it restricts how the retailer can conduct business, and in other cases, it prohibits certain business practices. The legal environment is also protective, however. It protects the retailer, the employee, the stockholder, the community, and the retailer's suppliers and competitors from unfair dealings. Overall, the legal environment should be viewed in terms of how well it balances the needs of the retailer with the needs of the public at large.[1]

The legal environment is defined by the actions of the legislative, executive, and judicial branches of federal, state, and local governments. As illustrated in Figure 5–1, the principal legal measures and regulatory instruments used in defining the environment are statutes, ordinances, administrative regulations, contracts, certificates, licenses, taxes, and emergency controls. In addition, governments have other means of influencing the general legal environment. Subsidies and government ownership are two examples.

In retailing, the legal environment has a direct bearing on the two basic components of any enterprise—store operations and store merchandising activities. It also directly affects the type and degree of retail competition. The remainder of this chapter examines the retailer's concerns with the legal aspects of retail competition, store operations, and retail merchandising. Figure 5–2 summarizes the major legal issues to be addressed in this chapter.

THE LEGAL ASPECTS OF RETAIL COMPETITION

Retail competition involves the actions of one retailer against other retailers in securing resources and the patronage of consumers. Competitive actions include both the actual operation of the store and retailers' merchandising strategies and tactics. Governments make laws to ensure that these competitive actions are conducted under equitable rules and circumstances. What is fair or equitable naturally is open to

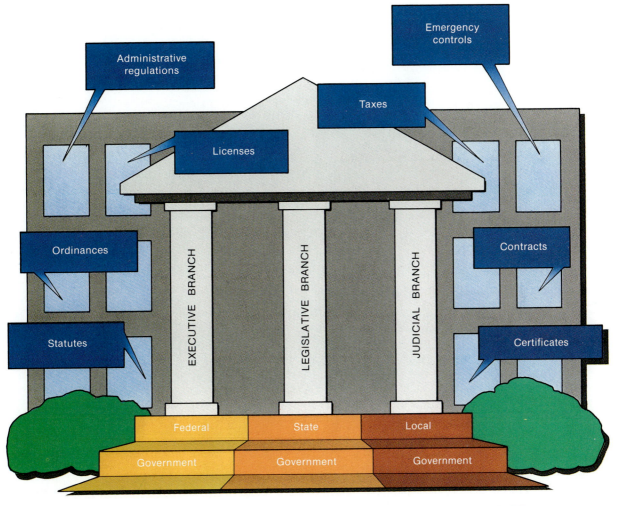

FIGURE 5–1
The legal environment

interpretation; generally the court system and various governmental regulatory agencies make such interpretations. One effort to create and maintain a competitive business environment has taken the form of antitrust legislation.

Antitrust legislation is a set of laws directed at preventing unreasonable "restraints on trade" and "unfair trade practices" to foster a competitive environment. According to "what" exactly it is preventing and "when" it seeks to prevent it, government's antitrust legislation aims to protect consumers and business from (1) present restraints on trade, (2) probable restraints on trade, and (3) unfair trade practices. Figure 5–3 identifies the principal legislative measures (laws) associated with each classification.

Present Restraints on Trade

The federal government, in an attempt to control big business's control or restraint of free trade, passed the **Sherman Antitrust Act** in 1890. The existence of cartels, pools, and trade associations during the post-Civil War years led to fear that big business might control prices and supplies of products in the marketplace. In passing the Sherman Antitrust Act, the federal government restricted the size and economic

FIGURE 5–2
The retailer and the law

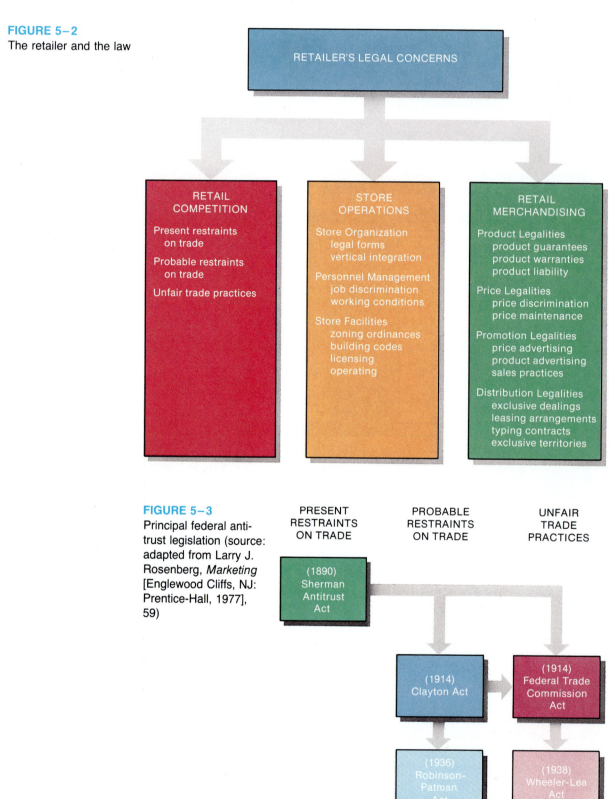

FIGURE 5–3
Principal federal antitrust legislation (source: adapted from Larry J. Rosenberg, *Marketing* [Englewood Cliffs, NJ: Prentice-Hall, 1977], 59)

power of any given organization, with the purpose of correcting existing—and preventing future—unreasonable restraints on trade. Sections 1 and 2, the key provisions of the act, state that every contract, combination, or conspiracy in restraint of trade is illegal and that all monopolies or attempts to monopolize are also illegal. Because of the vague language of the Sherman Antitrust Act, however, the Supreme Court ruled that the company's act must constitute an *unreasonable* restraint of trade to be unlawful. This ruling has become known as the "rule of reason," making the Sherman Antitrust Act ineffective because each case had to be tried against the rule of reason. Later legislation filled the gaps in the Sherman Act.

Probable Restraints on Trade

To overcome the shortcomings of the Sherman Antitrust Act, several pieces of federal legislation were passed to curtail competitive actions that *might* lead to restraints on trade if allowed to continue. In essence, these legislative amendments were enacted to prevent rather than correct restraints of trade. The first of these legislative amendments was the Clayton Act passed by Congress in 1914. The **Clayton Act** dealt with several specific anticompetitive actions such as price discrimination, tying contracts, exclusive dealings, and interlocking boards of directors (each of these actions will be discussed later in the chapter). It declared such actions illegal where the effect may be to "substantially lessen competition" or "tend to create a monopoly." With passage of the Clayton Act, the government no longer had to prove that either a restraint of trade or a monopoly existed. Instead, it was sufficient to show that a *probable* restraint of trade or monopoly *might* result if certain competitive actions were allowed to continue.

The **Robinson-Patman Act** of 1936 amended the Clayton Act by broadening the scope and clarifying the meaning of unlawful competition. Under the Robinson-Patman Act, unlawful competition included any competitive action that would tend "to injure, destroy, or prevent competition." Subsequent interpretation extended the intent of the law to include injury to "competitors." The major thrust of the Robinson-Patman Act was directed at various means of price discrimination.

Unfair Trade Practices

In 1914, Congress passed the **Federal Trade Commission (FTC) Act,** prohibiting unfair trade practices that could be injurious to either competition or competitors. To determine what constitutes fair and unfair trade practices, the FTC was established as a quasi-judicial agency having limited judicial powers. In 1938, Congress amended the 1914 Act by passing the **Wheeler-Lea Act,** banning unfair and deceptive business acts or practices. The significance of this amendment is that it outlaws unfair and deceptive activities regardless of their effects on competition or competitors. Armed with this amendment, the FTC has become, for most retailers, the single most important regulatory agency. The rules and regulations the FTC administers affect primarily deceptive advertising and sales practices.

The procedures the FTC uses to enforce these rules and regulations include (1) individual-firm or industrywide conferences to secure voluntary compliance, (2) consent orders whereby the firm or industry agrees to abandon an unfair trade practice, and (3) formal court action to force the firm or industry to comply with FTC decisions. The first two procedures have been so successful in preventing and correcting unfair or deceptive trade practices that reliance on formal legal action has been significantly reduced.

THE LEGAL ASPECTS OF STORE OPERATIONS

Government regulations and controls extend to all aspects of the physical operations of the store. In "running" the store, the retailer must follow laws pertaining to its organizational structure, store personnel, physical facilities, and other aspects of the operation.

Store Organization and the Law

In establishing, expanding, contracting, and discontinuing a retail business, the law imposes certain restrictions and controls. The influence of the law plays an especially important role in store organization.

Legal Forms of Retail Organization

Three basic forms of business organization are recognized by law: the sole proprietorship, the partnership, and the corporation. The **sole proprietorship** is a business owned and managed by a single individual. Having its origins in common law, the sole proprietorship is the simplest legal form of organization. The principal legal advantages of this form of organization are the following:

1. No formal legal requirement—except for a business license, so the retailer does not have to obtain authorization from state or federal governments to form the business
2. Greater flexibility in operations—the retailer is not expected to meet the maze of state regulations imposed on corporations
3. Single taxation—all profits taxed at once as personal income

Unlimited liability is the major legal limitation of a sole proprietorship. Unlimited liability means that the sole proprietor assumes total responsibility for all debts stemming from the business and that responsibility extends to current and future *personal as well as business assets*. In other words, not only is the proprietor's business in jeopardy should the business fail in some way, but personal assets also can be seized to cover bad debts.

When two or more persons form a business without incorporating, the business is a *partnership*. Partnerships can consist of any number of partners whose share and control of the business is determined at the time the organization is formed. In a **general partnership,** all partners take part in the control and operation of the partnership; hence, all partners can be held jointly and severally liable for the debts of the partnership. The unlimited liability of all general partners represents substantial personal risk, since each partner is legally liable for the actions of all other partners. When one partner makes a business commitment, it is legally binding on all of the other partners. Not only are commonly owned business assets therefore subject to legal judgments, but also each of the other partners' personal assets can be used to pay off the business liabilities of another partner.

An alternative partnership arrangement is the **limited partnership**. This is a legal form of organization with one or more members of the partnership contributing capital to the formation and running of the partnership, but these limited partners do not take part in managing the firm's retail operations. The main advantage of the limited partnership is that the personal assets of limited partners may not be reached by creditors of the partnership. In exchange for this limited liability, the limited partner foregoes control over the running of the partnership.

A **corporation** is a legal business entity authorized by state law to operate as a single person even though it may consist of many persons. Limited liability is the principal legal advantage of this type of organization. The liability of any given owner (shareholder) is limited to equity money, or the amount of stock owned. The nonlegal advantages of being able to raise investment capital and to engage in a greater degree of operational and managerial specialization are equally important incentives that lead many retailers to use a corporate form of organization. Corporations, however, are subject to a greater number of legal controls (e.g., public financial accountability, public stockholders' meetings, certificates of incorporation) and possibly double taxation (the corporation pays a corporate income tax and stockholders pay personal income tax on any dividends they receive).

Limitations on Vertical Integration

The law places certain limitations on any retailer's attempts to integrate vertically. **Vertical integration** is the merger of two organizations from different levels within a channel of distribution. Examples of vertical integration are the merger of a retailer and a wholesaler or a retailer and a producer. **Mergers** occur when one firm acquires the stocks or assets of another firm. Mergers are regulated by Section 7 of the Clayton Act (1914) as amended by the Celler-Kefauver Act (1950). These acts prohibit any company from acquiring the stocks or assets of other firms in any line of commerce in any part of the country if the effect is to substantially reduce competition or tend to create a monopoly. The federal government views mergers as monopolistic when they tend to either close out other retailers from a source of supply or close out other suppliers from a market area.

Personnel Management and the Law

The law protects the retail employee in a variety of ways. Because of this, a store's personnel manager must be acquainted with the legal environment surrounding job discrimination, working conditions, and various compensation requirements.

Job Discrimination

Equal employment opportunity is a civil right. The **Civil Rights Act of 1964** makes job discrimination illegal if it is based on the applicant's or employee's sex, race, color, creed, age, or national origin. Essentially, the intent of the Civil Rights Act is to eliminate both intentional and inadvertent discriminatory employment practices. It charges the Equal Employment Opportunity Commission (EEOC) with administering the act, and it charges each employer with the implicit obligation to discover discriminatory practices and to eliminate them.

The two most prevalent forms of employment discrimination are personal and systematic. *Personal discrimination* occurs when the personal biases of an individual in authority enter the decision-making process in employment matters to the detriment of applicants or employees. *Systematic discrimination* is the unintentional and inadvertent discrimination resulting from policies, practices, and decision-making criteria that negatively affect protected classes. In all areas of staffing (job description and specification, recruitment and selection, training and supervision, evaluation and compensation), the retailer must take every precaution to ensure compliance with the intent of the law.

To eliminate discriminatory employment criteria and measurements (age, sex, race, etc.), the retailer should follow two basic guidelines to help ensure compliance with the law: consistency and supportability. *Consistency* means treating all employees and job applicants in a uniformly fair and equitable manner. Also, all actions taken by the retailer for or against an employee should be carefully *documented and supported* on the basis of legally defensible economic and/or social terms. If an employer can show due cause through documentation for firing an employee, promoting an employee, or creating a new position for an employee, then the employer probably has reasonably safe ground for actions and employees are likely to be protected from bias and job discrimination.

Figure 5–4 illustrates the complexity of the equal employment opportunity issue. The legalities of preemployment questions alone clearly indicate that the retailer must proceed with great caution to ensure full compliance with the various laws, administration rulings, and judicial interpretations of the laws concerning equal employment opportunity.

Working Conditions and Compensation

Numerous legal requirements govern the conditions under which retail employees work. Of importance to the retailer are wage and hour requirements, restrictions on the use of child labor, provisions regarding equal pay, workers' compensation, and unemployment benefits.

The **Fair Labor Standards Act** (FLSA) of 1938 sets the legal requirements for both minimum wages and maximum working hours. It also governs the use of child labor and contains an equal-pay provision. Initially, the act did not affect retail businesses; however, later amendments (1966) established a minimum hourly wage for all retail organizations with annual sales of $250,000 and above. The FLSA also established a forty-hour work week. Employees working in excess of this maximum are entitled to overtime benefits (extra compensation). While more retailers are increasingly feeling the impact of FLSA, there are several exceptions. For example, executive, administrative, and professional employees, family-owned and -operated retail stores, and in some cases the employees of certain types of retailing establishments (restaurants, motion picture theaters, auto dealerships, among others) can be exempt from the provisions of the FLSA. Retailers can apply for and receive a certificate from the Department of Labor that allows them to pay full-time students 85 percent of the hourly minimum wage.

The use of child labor is also restricted by the FLSA. The law determines the age at which minors can work, the type of job (hazardous versus nonhazardous occu-

FIGURE 5–4
Legal and illegal preemployment questions (source: The New York State Division of Human Rights, January 1982)

Here is a series of questions that the New York State Division of Human Rights has compiled as being lawful and unlawful preemployment inquiries. As New York appears to be stricter than most states and the federal government, by following these recommendations, lawyers suggest that a company may be less likely to find itself in difficulty with the authorities because of preemployment inquiries.

Subject	Lawful*	Unlawful
Race or Color:		Inquiry into complexion or color of skin Coloring
Religion or Creed:		Inquiry into applicant's religious denomination, religious affiliations, church parish, pastor, or religious holidays observed Applicant may not be told "This is a (Catholic, Protestant, or Jewish) organization"

(continued)

Subject	Lawful*	Unlawful
National Origin:		Inquiry into applicant's lineage, ancestry, national origin, descent, parentage, or nationality Nationality of applicant's parents or spouse What is your mother tongue?
Sex:		Inquiry as to sex Do you wish to be addressed as Mr.? Mrs.? Miss? or Ms.?
Marital Status:		Are you married? Are you single? Divorced? Separated? Name or other information about spouse Where does your spouse work? What are the ages of your children, if any?
Birth Control:		Inquiry as to capacity to reproduce, advocacy of any form of birth control or family planning
Age:	Are you between 18 and 70 years of age? If not, state your age.	How old are you? What is your date of birth?
Disability:	Do you have any impairments, physical, mental, or medical, that would interfere with your ability to perform the job for which you have applied? If there are any positions or types of positions for which you should not be considered, or job duties you cannot perform because of physical, mental, or medical disability, please describe.	Do you have a disability? Have you ever been treated for any of the following diseases . . . ?
Arrest Record:	Have you ever been convicted of a crime? Give details	Have you ever been arrested?
Name:	Have you ever worked for this company under a different name? Is any additional information relative to change of name, use of an assumed name, or nickname necessary to enable a check on your work record? If yes, explain.	Original name of an applicant whose name has been changed by court order or otherwise Maiden name of a married woman If you have ever worked under another name, state name and dates.
Address or Duration of Residence:	Applicant's place of residence How long a resident of this state or city?	
Birthplace:		Birthplace of applicant Birthplace of applicant's parents, spouse, or other close relatives

(continued)

Subject	Lawful*	Unlawful
Birthdate:		Requirement that applicant submit birth certificate, naturalization, or baptismal record Requirement that applicant produce proof of age in the form of a birth certificate or baptismal record
Photograph:		Requirement or option that applicant affix a photograph to employment form at any time before hiring
Citizenship:	Are you a citizen of the United States? If not a citizen of the United States, do you intend to become a citizen of the United States? If you are not a United States citizen, have you the legal right to remain permanently in the United States? Do you intend to remain permanently in the United States?	Of what country are you a citizen? Whether an applicant is naturalized or a native-born citizen; the date when the applicant acquired citizenship Requirement that applicant produce naturalization papers or first papers Whether applicant's spouse or parents are naturalized or native-born citizens of the United States; the date when such parents or spouse acquired citizenship
Language:	Inquiry into languages applicant speaks and writes fluently	What is your native language? Inquiry into how applicant acquired ability to read, write, or speak a foreign language
Education:	Inquiry into applicant's academic, vocational, or professional education and the public and private schools attended	
Experience:	Inquiry into work experience	
Relatives:	Name of applicant's relatives, other than a spouse, already employed by this company	Names, addresses, ages, numbers, or other information concerning applicant's spouse, children, or other relatives not employed by the company
Notice in Case of Emergency:		Name and address of person to be notified in case of accident or emergency
Military Experience:	Inquiry into applicant's military experience in the Armed Forces of the United States or in a State Militia Inquiry into applicant's service in United States Army, Navy, etc.	Inquiry into applicant's general military experience
Organizations:	Inquiry into applicant's membership in organizations the applicant considers relevant to his or her ability to perform the job	List all clubs, societies, and lodges to which you belong.
Driver's License:	Do you possess a valid driver's license?	Requirement that applicant produce a driver's license prior to employment

Source: The New York State Division of Human Rights, January 1982.

pations) minors can take, and when they can work (hours, days, etc.). Also, the FLSA equal-pay provision prohibits wage differentials for doing work requiring equal skill, effort, and responsibility. Legal wage differentials are justified on the basis of training, education, and experience.

The **Williams-Steiger Occupational Safety and Health Act** of 1970 established the Occupational Safety and Health Administration (OSHA). This agency is charged with enforcing the provisions of the act—to have each employer "furnish. . .a place of employment which is free from recognized hazards that cause or are likely to cause death or serious physical harm to employees." Compliance officers from OSHA make unannounced workplace inspections to ensure compliance. Any citations issued after an inspection identify the nature of the alleged violations and the time set for abatement. In addition to requiring corrective actions, OSHA may issue monetary penalties depending on the seriousness of the violation.

Workers' compensation is an employee accident and disability insurance program required under various state laws. It covers the employee who is accidentally injured while working or who is unable to work as a result of a disease associated with a particular occupation. While these programs vary between states, they generally provide for medical expenses and basic subsistence during the period of disability. Both public (state-operated) and private (insurance company) programs are available to companies and employees in most states. The insurance premiums that retailers pay for these programs represent a substantial operating expense, so they must be planned for and managed with considerable care.

Unemployment compensation is a tax levied by the state on each retailer's payroll. The state uses the revenue to create an unemployment fund for the retailer. Qualified former employees of the retailer can draw unemployment benefits from the fund, the amount and duration of which are prescribed by state law. Employees who are either laid off or fired usually qualify for benefits; employees who simply quit usually do not qualify. Unemployment tax usually ranges from 3 to 5 percent of the retailer's payroll, but under some circumstances it can be less if the employer has a low rate of firings and layoffs.

Store Facilities and the Law

A number of local regulations have direct bearing on the retailer's facilities. Zoning ordinances, building codes, licensing requirements, and operating requirements are the most common forms of local controls on the retailer's facilities and operations.

Zoning Ordinances

Zoning ordinances are controls that local governments place on land use by regulating the type of activities and buildings located in certain areas. Land is zoned according to residential, commercial, and industrial uses. By controlling the use of land, local governments offer the retailer (1) protection against undesirable neighbors by ensuring that land users are properly situated in relation to one another, (2) assurance that an orderly growth of business will occur in only those areas zoned for business activities, and (3) certainty that adequate government services, such as trash removal, street maintenance, and police protection, will be available to businesses.

Sometimes, however, ordinances can unduly restrict development of new businesses. In an attempt to limit competition and to gain or preserve a competitive advantage, some local governments pass anti-new-business zoning ordinances, protecting already established, and sometimes influential, local businesses.

Building Codes

Local governments enact numerous regulations affecting the design and construction of retail facilities. Design regulations include local authority over the (1) size of the building relative to the size of the site; (2) height of the building; (3) number of entrances and exits; (4) architectural style (some communities, such as Santa Fe, New Mexico, require businesses to conform to a particular style); and (5) safety features such as plumbing, electricity, and fire protection.

Construction regulations control both the methods and the materials used in construction. Public safety and convenience, such as access for the handicapped, are two major guidelines local governments use in developing construction regulations. Associated with building codes are inspection requirements that retailers must meet before they can open the facility to the public.

Licensing Requirements

Retailers usually must meet two types of local licensing requirements before they can begin operations. Many local communities require retailers to obtain a **general business license** before they can operate a business. In most cases, it is nothing more than a registration fee to operate a business. A major purpose of the general business license is to generate a source of revenue for a community. A **special business license** applies to either the sale of certain types of products (e.g., guns, prepared foods, drugs, gasoline) or the operation of a particular type of retail organization (e.g., vending machines, door-to-door selling, telephone selling, various types of personal services). A recent U.S. Supreme Court case ruled that local ordinances or licenses cannot be too restrictive; for example, unreasonable door-to-door time restrictions were found unconstitutional because they violated free-speech rights.[2]

Operating Requirements

Many of the retailer's day-to-day operations also are controlled by state and local regulations. In some states and communities, a host of "**blue laws**" regulate everything from operating hours (such as "sundown laws" that prohibit the sale of liquor after sundown) and days (Sunday closing laws that limit the types of goods consumers can purchase on Sunday) to operating locations (prohibiting the sale of certain products such as liquor and beer within a prescribed distance of a church, school, or some other community facility).[3] Retailers should learn which blue laws affect their business, the legal and social implications of such laws on the business, and where and when they can operate successfully and legally. In addition, local ordinances regulate trash pickup, snow removal, sign placement, the number and width of entrances and exits (curb cuts), customers' minimum age (e.g., for liquor), and many others.

THE LEGAL ASPECTS OF RETAIL MERCHANDISING

Legal requirements govern all aspects of the retailer's merchandising efforts. Strategies in pricing, promoting, and distributing products must fall within certain legal limits.

Product Legalities

As a reseller of products, the retailer assumes three major responsibilities in the areas of product guarantees, product warranties, and product liability. Because of these responsibilities, retailers incur additional operating expenses; however, sales volume can offset these expenses and help a retailer establish a reliable and dependable reputation.

Product Guarantees

Product guarantees are policy statements by retailers expressing their general reasonability for the products they sell. Some retailers offer very broad guarantees, such as "complete satisfaction or your money back." Other retailers limit their guarantee statements to certain aspects of the product (e.g., six months from date of purchase). Often consumers and retailers disagree about what is guaranteed; "consumers interpret satisfaction to apply not only to the products they acquire but also to the shopping experience that results in these acquisitions."[4] Given these customer expectations and the legal requirement to fulfill the general intent of any guarantee made, the retailer needs to carefully monitor all guarantee statements.

Product Warranties

A **warranty** is a specific statement by the seller of the quality or performance capabilities of the product and the exact terms under which the seller will take action to correct product deficiencies. There are two basic types of warranties—expressed and implied. **Expressed warranties** are written and oral statements that the seller makes to consumers about a product and performance and that the retailer is legally obligated to honor. While written statements of fact are expressed in fairly specific terms and subject to precise interpretation, oral statements of fact and promises are more difficult to interpret. A fine line distinguishes oral promises from mere sales talk. Often the distinction is made on the basis of whether the statements made during a sale are an expression of opinion or of fact. Courts have recognized the difference between "puffing" and promise. To avoid being charged with engaging in unfair competitive acts, the retailer must be careful that its sales "puffery" is not construed as a legally binding promise of product performance. The same care must be applied to all of the retailer's advertisements.

puffery

Implied warranties are the seller's implied or "intended" promises of product performance, even though they were not actually expressed in either written or oral form. Under the Uniform Commercial Code, every sale is subject to a warranty of merchantability and a warranty of title. The "warranty of merchantability" implies that all merchandise that retailers offer for sale is fit for the purpose for which it was sold. A clothes dryer that scorches clothes is not fit for its intended purpose, for example. The "warranty of title" implies that the seller has offered the buyer a free and clear title to the product. Consumers have the right to assume that they own the product and have full use of it without fear of repossession. That assumption is not valid, however, when the consumer elects to purchase an item from a questionable source (e.g., a car from "Midnight Auto Sales").

The most significant piece of federal legislation concerning warranties in recent years is the Magnuson-Moss Warranty Act of 1975. This act greatly strengthens consumers' rights by substantially increasing the responsibilities of retailers and other sellers of products under warranty. Of importance to retailers are the first three regulations the FTC issued under this act. They require retailers to (1) provide consumers with warranty information before they buy the product, (2) disclose the terms of the product warranty in "simple and readily understood language," and (3) establish and maintain procedures for handling customer complaints.

Product Liability

The retailer, as well as the manufacturer, can be held liable for an unsafe product. The retailer's **product liability** can result from either failing to inform the customer of the dangers associated with using the product; misrepresenting the product as to how, when, and where it should be used; or selling a product that results in injury as a result of its failure to meet warranty standards. Much confusion exists over the exact nature of the retailer's product liability. The retailer's best protection is to provide the consumer with adequate product safety information, to correctly represent the product, and to obtain adequate liability insurance.

Price Legalities

The most regulated aspect of a retailer's merchandising program is pricing. Government regulations influence prices that the retailer pays the supplier, prices the retailer charges customers, the conditions under which prices are set or adjusted, and the impact of the retailer's prices on the competitive structure of the marketplace.

Price Discrimination

In a very broad sense, **price discrimination** covers a number of situations involving pricing arrangements under various buying and selling circumstances. The law recognizes both illegal and legal price discrimination. *Illegal pricing* potentially exists when different prices are offered or received under similar circumstances, or when similar prices are offered or received under different circumstances. *Price discrimination* can be legally justified when different prices are offered or received under different circumstances. Obviously, the degree of the price differential, the exact nature of the circumstances, and their effects on all parties involved determine the precise legalities of the situation. Retailers become involved with price discrimination in a number of ways. As illustrated in Figure 5–5, the retailer can be both a victim and a perpetrator of price discrimination as a result of both buying activities with suppliers and selling activities with consumers. Each of these circumstances will be examined individually.

When a supplier treats one retailer unequally or differently from the way it treats other retailers, the one retailer becomes a potential victim of price discrimination. As defined by Section 2 of the Robinson-Patman Act, unequal treatment or price discrimination is illegal when its effect "may be to substantially lessen competition or tend to create a monopoly. . .or to injure, destroy, or prevent competition." Price

FIGURE 5–5
The retailer's involvement with price discrimination

PRICE DISCRIMINATION AGAINST	THE RETAILER'S ROLE IN PRICE DISCRIMINATION	
	Victim	Perpetrator
Buying Activities Supplier Interactions	product discrimination quantity discrimination allowance discrimination service discrimination	coercive buying dummy brokerage
Selling Activities Customer Interactions		predatory pricing price fixing

discrimination against retailers can result when a supplier treats one retailer differently from others with respect to product characteristics, quantity discounts, special allowances, and special services.

Product characteristics.   It is unlawful for any business either to discriminate directly or indirectly in price among different purchasers of commodities of like grade and quality. *Competing retailers are entitled to pay the same price for the same type of merchandise.* While the meaning of "like grade and quality" is ambiguous, courts have generally interpreted the phrase to mean that there must be clearly distinguishable differences in either materials or workmanship. Courts have generally found products with minor differences in materials and workmanship to be of "like grade and quality." Thus, where minor differences exist, sellers run the risk of price discrimination if they sell to different buyers at different prices under similar circumstances.

Quantity discounts.   The general principle is that *all competing retailers are entitled to pay the same price for the same quantity of "like" merchandise.* Suppliers often try to encourage volume buying by offering their customers (retailers) discount prices for large-quantity orders. However, even this form of seller inducement is illegal unless the seller can show that the lower prices for volume buyers result from a cost savings from producing and selling the larger quantity.

Sellers offer quantity discounts in two ways—cumulative and noncumulative. *Cumulative* quantity discounts apply to customers' purchases over an extended time. For example, if a buyer purchases a certain quantity of merchandise over a twelve-month period, the seller will give the buyer a discount on any additional purchases. *Noncumulative* quantity discounts apply only to a single large-volume purchase. Recent court rulings have clarified the legalities of noncumulative and cumulative discounts. Because cumulative discounts do not represent cost savings equal to those of noncumulative discounts, the courts ruled that cumulative discounts cannot be as large.

Special allowances.   The Robinson-Patman Act makes it unlawful for a seller to grant payment of any special allowances for any services that a retailer might provide to attempt to sell, advertise, or distribute a product, unless those allowance payments are also made available to all competing retailers on proportionately equal terms. Therefore, *all competing retailers are entitled to the same opportunities to receive the same allowance payments for providing the same special services.* Of special interest to the retailer is the "push money" that various suppliers provide. Push money is money that suppliers pay the retailer's sales personnel for making a special selling effort on their brands. Push money is legal if the same incentives are available to all competing retailers, if the retailer gives its consent, and if it does not reduce competition or severely affect competitive products.

Special services.   It is unlawful for a supplier to provide retailers with services and facilities that aid them in selling merchandise unless those same favors are made available to all competing retailers on proportionately equal terms. Thus, *all competing retailers are entitled to receive the same support in services and facilities to sell the same goods.* Regulatory agencies have permitted the use of substitute services or facilities. When the original service or facility offer is impractical for competing retailers, regulatory agencies have allowed sellers to substitute different, but equal, services or facilities more suitable to their operations.

Price-discrimination defenses.   Although each of the seller activities discussed could lead to price-discrimination suits, the Robinson-Patman Act contains provisions for a legal defense for price differentials. Cost justification and good faith are two of the common defenses.

The *cost-justification defense* makes it lawful to charge retailers different prices if the supplier can justify those price differences on the basis of its cost of doing business with each competing retailer. If it costs a supplier more to do business with one retailer than another, then the supplier can legally charge that retailer a higher price. The courts have placed the burden of proof on the seller, however, and have been quite particular about which costs (e.g., overhead) the seller can include in estimates and how cost calculations can be made.

The *good-faith defense* makes it lawful for a seller to discriminate in price if such action is done in good faith to meet an equally low price of a competitor. The essential factor in using the good-faith defense is whether the discriminatory price was necessary to meet competition rather than an offensive move to beat competition. Defensive price discrimination is legal; offensive price discrimination is illegal.

The retailer assumes the role of a perpetrator of illegal price discrimination when it uses coercive buying techniques or deceptive brokerage practices to obtain a lower price than that available to competing retailers. **Coercive buying** is the retailer's use of financial, distribution, marketing, and other powers to gain lower prices from sellers. Since some retailing organizations are larger than their suppliers, they are in a position to force favorable but unfair price treatment. However, under Section 2(f) of the Robinson-Patman Act, it is unlawful for a retailer to knowingly receive or induce a discriminatory price or special allowance and service. Thus, a "giant" retailer making a supplier sell merchandise at unfairly low prices is breaking a law and could cause legal action to be taken against the retailer.

Deceptive brokerage activities involve the establishment and use of "dummy" brokerage firms to secure a brokerage allowance from suppliers, giving retailers an unfair purchase-price advantage. A dummy brokerage firm is a brokerage company owned and operated by a retailer but that represents itself as an independent operation. As such, the brokerage firm does not charge its parent retailing firm a brokerage fee for bringing the buyer and seller together, and such "savings" in brokerage fees are passed on to the retailer. In this situation, the retailer with a dummy brokerage firm pays less for merchandise and therefore can sell products at a lower price, thus creating an unfair competitive advantage. Section 2(c) of the Robinson-Patman Act makes it unlawful for a company to receive brokerage allowances (fees and/or discounts) unless the broker is completely independent of both the supplier and retailer.

Retailers can also run the risk of price discrimination in selling activities by engaging in predatory pricing and price fixing. **Predatory pricing** is a pricing tactic whereby the retailer charges customers different prices for the same merchandise in different markets to eliminate competition in one or more of those markets. Such pricing practices are illegal except when the firm can show a cost justification. **Price fixing** is an illegal pricing activity in which several retailers establish a fixed retail selling price for a particular product line within a market area. The illegality of price fixing is established by both the Sherman Antitrust Act and the Federal Trade Commission Act.

Resale Price Maintenance

Resale price maintenance legislation, commonly referred to as "fair-trade laws," was designed to permit manufacturers and wholesalers to set retail prices by requiring retailers to sign contracts agreeing to sell their products at the "suggested" prices. The primary purpose of these laws was to protect the small, independent retailer who could not compete effectively on a price basis with the large chains and discount operations.

With the changing economic environment and the rampant inflation of the 1970s, however, Congress removed the enabling legislation, wiping out the fair trade laws that still existed in 21 states. The question of "fair trade" has resurfaced in recent years. At issue is whether some degree of resale price maintenance should be allowed. One survey indicated that most business executives support free-market principles over a fair-trade doctrine (see Figure 5–6).

Although **resale price maintenance** is no longer legal, a limited type of resale price maintenance exists in some states in the form of **unfair trade practice acts**. These state laws regulate the right of retailers to sell either below cost or at cost plus some minimum markup (e.g., cost plus 5 percent). The intent of these laws is to preserve competition by eliminating predatory price cutting and loss-leader selling (the use of a below-cost price on a popular item to attract customers into the store).[5] These laws vary from state to state, depending on the definition of costs, the minimum required markups, if any, and the products covered by such laws. As a rule, unfair trade practice laws have been ineffective as a result of enforcement problems and the large number of exceptions. Typical exemptions permitting sales below cost include clearance sales, closeout sales, business liquidation sales, sales to relief agencies or for charitable purposes, and sales of products with deteriorating marketability (such as seasonal, damaged, and perishable goods).

Promotion Legalities

Freedom of speech for the retailer is not without its limitations. Numerous laws govern what retailers may communicate to their customers and how they may com-

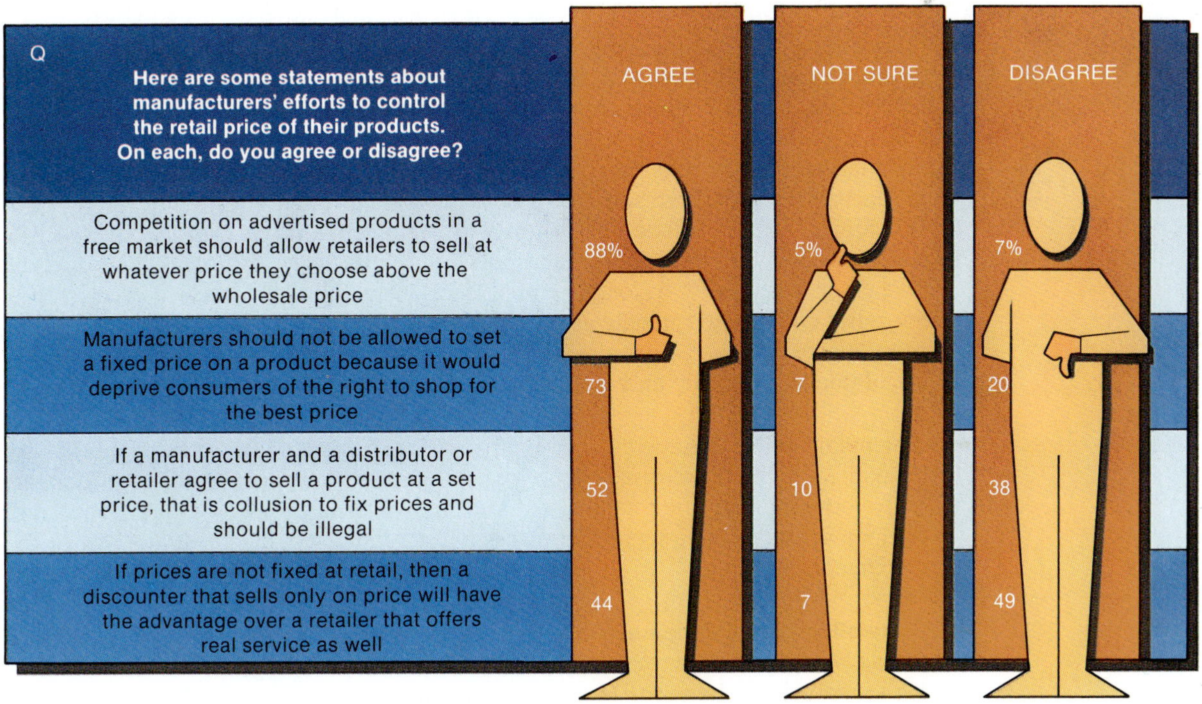

FIGURE 5–6
How business views fair trade (source: "Resounding Support for Price Competition," Reprinted from the November 14, 1983 issue of *Business Week* by special permission, © 1983 by McGraw-Hill, Inc.)

Q Here are some statements about manufacturers' efforts to control the retail price of their products. On each, do you agree or disagree?	AGREE	NOT SURE	DISAGREE
Competition on advertised products in a free market should allow retailers to sell at whatever price they choose above the wholesale price	88%	5%	7%
Manufacturers should not be allowed to set a fixed price on a product because it would deprive consumers of the right to shop for the best price	73	7	20
If a manufacturer and a distributor or retailer agree to sell a product at a set price, that is collusion to fix prices and should be illegal	52	10	38
If prices are not fixed at retail, then a discounter that sells only on price will have the advantage over a retailer that offers real service as well	44	7	49

municate it. Legal restrictions influence all aspects of the retailer's promotional efforts—advertising, sales promotions, and personal selling. The principal legal vehicles through which the federal government regulates promotional activities are the Federal Trade Commission Act (1914) and the Wheeler-Lea Amendment to that act. Together these laws make it illegal for a retailer to engage in any unfair method of competition or unfair or deceptive act or practice in commerce. If retailers are caught using either deceptive price advertising, deceptive product advertising, or misleading personal sales information, the FTC can take legal action against them.

Deceptive Price Advertising

Retailers can express price information in a number of confusing and misleading ways. For example, prices expressed as the "suggested retail price," the "original price," the "regular price," "our price and our competitor's price," "two for the price of one," "buy one and get one free," "50 percent off," and "reduced one half" all can be used to mislead consumers into believing they are receiving a better price or a larger discount than is actually being offered. The FTC has established several guidelines for the use of such pricing terms to prohibit **deceptive price advertising**.

Former-price comparisons.   The retailer that uses such pricing terms as "originally," "usually," or "regularly" is using a former-price comparison that suggests an item is selling at a price lower than its former price. To avoid charges of deceptive price advertising, the retailer should determine whether the former price was well established as the original, usual, or regular selling price. When the former price is established, the retailer's advertisements can inform consumers that the "new" price is a discount price. If the former price was not established, the retailer cannot make a former-price comparison. Also, for a sale price to be legal, the price reduction should be for a specific and reasonable period of time and be accompanied by a price increase at the end of the sales period.

Competitive-price comparisons.   When making an advertising claim that its prices are lower than its competitors', the retailer must establish that the competitors' prices are, in fact, prices that they regularly and typically charge. In addition, under FTC guidelines, the competitive-price comparison must be made on identical products. If the retailer wishes to make competitive-price comparisons on similar but not identical products, then the advertisement must make it clear to the consumer that the price comparison is being made on "comparable" and not "identical" products. The FTC guidelines allow the retailer to make price comparisons on comparable products of "like grade and quality" as long as it clearly states that different products of essentially the same quality and quantity are being compared. Hence, a retailer can make price comparisons between a private-label brand and a nationally advertised brand if they are of the same quality and quantity.

Free merchandise.   Advertisements offering free merchandise represent a price reduction, since the offer usually depends on the consumer meeting certain conditions (e.g., "buy one, get one free"). These promotional pricing practices are not considered deceptive if the advertisement clearly states the conditions under which the merchandise is "free."

Cents-off pricing.   When a retailer's advertisement contains a cents-off coupon, it should be based on the regular price. If the retailer raises the product's price to inflate the coupon value, then the FTC will consider this kind of promotional effort deceptive.

Another deceptive act is the retailer's failure to stock sufficient quantities of the coupon product to meet the normal demand associated with such a sale. The FTC does consider "rain checks" (for the same or comparable product at a later date at the same price) an adequate substitute when an unusual demand or out-of-stock problem unexpectedly arises; however, if retailers use rain checks in conjunction with planned shortages of advertised products hoping that only a small percentage of the rain checks will be redeemed, they are engaging in a deceptive practice. As with free merchandise offerings, any conditional aspects of the cents-off offering (e.g., quantity limitations) must be clearly stated in the advertisement.

Deceptive Product Advertising

Deceptive product advertising involves making a false or misleading claim about the physical makeup of the product, the appropriate uses for the product, or the benefits from using the product, as well as using packages and labels that tend to mislead the customer about the exact contents, quality, or quantity of the package. In April of 1987, several state attorneys-general asked McDonald's to "cease and desist" further "use of print ads extolling the quality and nutritional makeup of its foods or face legal action for violating state false-advertising statutes. . .it charges that one ad's claim that 'our sodium is down across the menu' is false because the ad mentions four products for which the sodium content has not been lowered."[6] Several laws have been enacted to control the various claims about the physical makeup of the product. Among these laws are the Wool Products Labeling Act (1941), the Fur Products Labeling Act (1952), the Flammable Fabrics Act (1953), and the Textile Fiber Products Identification Act (1960).

Other legislation has been directed at identifying appropriate product usage. For example, the Child Protection and Toy Safety Act of 1965 instructs manufacturers to identify the appropriate age group for a particular toy. Armed with the Wheeler-Lea Amendment (known as the Truth in Advertising Act), the FTC has taken an active role in correcting false claims concerning product benefits. The agency's major weapon has been the concept of corrective advertising, which requires companies to use promotional messages correcting these previous false claims.

Finally, the Fair Package and Labeling Act of 1966 was drafted to prevent companies from using deceptive packaging and labeling methods. Companies must properly label the contents, ingredients, net quantity, and name and address of the manufacturer on the package. Also, the act contains guidelines regarding deceptive package sizes and shapes as well as the misleading use of printed material on packages.

Deceptive Sales Practices

The law also places restrictions on several kinds of personal selling that constitute **deceptive sales practices**. One is called **bait and switch**. The "bait" is an advertised low price on a product that the retailer does not really intend to sell.[7] The "switch" involves personal selling techniques that induce the customer to buy a higher-priced product that will provide the retailer with greater profits. These selling techniques involve (1) making disparaging remarks about the product, (2) either failing to stock the product or planning a stockout, (3) refusing to show or demonstrate the product to the consumer on some false pretense, or (4) denying credit arrangements in conjunction with the sale of the product. To protect the consumer, the FTC can require any retailer to make good any "bait" offer extended to consumers.

A legal issue related to sales transactions involves deceptive credit contracts. In 1960, Congress passed the **Truth-in-Lending Act**, requiring full disclosure of credit terms. Retailers must give borrowers a disclosure statement detailing the exact terms of their contract. Terms such as the loan amount, finance charges, annual percentage rate, miscellaneous charges, number of payments, the amount of each payment, and description of any property held by the lender as security must be clearly stated in the disclosure statement. Additional legal requirements of retail lenders have been enacted through amendments to protect the consumer further. These amendments state the following:

1. Monthly statements (bills) must include information (address and telephone number) about where inquiries about them can be made.
2. Consumers have sixty days to lodge complaints concerning billing errors; retailers have thirty days to reply to the complaint and must make a reasonable effort to resolve each complaint.
3. All credit arrangements containing a "free period" provision require retailers to mail monthly statements fourteen days before assessment of finance charges.
4. Credit payments must be credited to the customer's account on the day that they are received.
5. Issuers of credit cards cannot restrict the retailer from offering the final consumer a cash discount.[8]

In 1980, Congress passed the *Truth in Lending Simplification and Reform Act*. In adopting the act, Congress sought to simplify for both creditors and consumers the complex provisions surrounding the Truth-in-Lending Act. The later act simplified both the disclosure forms and the regulations governing the extension of credit.[9]

Distribution Legalities

Retailers often enter into agreements with suppliers that might give them a competitive edge in the marketplace. These agreements are legal under some circumstances but illegal under others. Some of these competitively advantageous, but potentially illegal, arrangements are exclusive dealings, anticompetitive leasing arrangements, tying contracts, and exclusive territories.

Exclusive Dealings

Exclusive dealings are arrangements between retailers and suppliers in which the retailer agrees to handle only the supplier's products or no other products that pose direct competition. Benetton, the upscaled apparel retailer, requires no fees or royalties from their independent licenses; however, each shopkeeper "agrees to sell only Benetton-made goods through one of several standard store formats."[10] Such agreements are not illegal per se; however, Section 3 of the Clayton Act declares exclusive dealings to be illegal where the effect of such arrangements may be to substantially lessen competition or to create a monopoly. The courts have generally viewed exclusive dealings as illegal when they exclude competitive products from a large share of the market and when they represent a large share of the total sales volume for a particular product type.

Anticompetitive Leasing Arrangements

A variation of exclusive dealings involves several forms of **anticompetitive leasing arrangements**. The purpose of the contracts is to limit the type and amount of competition a particular retailer faces within a given area. Generally associated with shopping centers, anticompetitive leasing arrangements grant some retailers certain rights such as "(1) the right to be the only retailer of its kind, (2) the right to reject or accept the opportunity to operate an additional outlet in a shopping center where it already has one, (3) the right to prohibit or control the entrance of tenants into shopping centers, and (4) the right to restrict the business operations of other tenants in shopping centers."[11] Under Section 5 of the Federal Trade Commission Act, the FTC has the power to enforce rules prohibiting one retailer in a shopping center from limiting the competitive activities of another retailer.

Tying Contracts

Tying contracts are conditional selling arrangements between retailers and suppliers in which a supplier agrees to sell a retailer a highly sought-after line of products if the retailer will agree to buy additional product lines in return (usually those not frequently sought) from the same supplier. An extended version of the tying contract concept is **full-line forcing**, when the supplier requires the retailer to carry the supplier's full line of products if the retailer wishes to carry any part of that line. The FTC views both tying contracts and full-line forcing as illegal when the supplier has sufficient coercive powers to force compliance.

The most serious problems involving tying arrangements are those associated with franchise retailing. Quite often, franchise agreements contain provisions requiring the franchisee to purchase all raw materials and supplies from the franchisor. The courts generally consider tying provisions of a franchise agreement legal as long as there is sufficient proof that these arrangements are necessary to maintain quality control. Otherwise, they are viewed as unwarranted restraints of competition.

Exclusive Territories

Exclusive territories are agreements under which a supplier grants a retailer the exclusive right to sell its products within a defined geographic area. In return, the retailer agrees not to sell the product anywhere except within the agreed-upon area. In essence, a geographic monopoly is created for a particular product line. For obvious reasons, these territorial arrangements are generally viewed as unlawful systems of distribution. The law does not, however, prevent suppliers and retailers from establishing territorial responsibilities as long as they are not exclusive and do not restrict the resale of products.

SUMMARY

Legal considerations are an integral part of the retailer's daily operations. The retailer must consider the legal aspects of retail competition, store operations, and retail merchandising within the legal environment created by federal, state, and local legislative, executive, and judicial branches of government.

The legal aspects of competition deal with attempts by various governmental bodies to correct present restraints on trade and to prevent probable trade restraints and unfair trade practices. The major laws dealing with maintaining a competitive environment are the Sherman Antitrust Act, the Clayton Act, the Robinson-Patman Act, the Federal Trade Commission Act, and the Wheeler-Lea Act.

The legal forms of store organization (sole proprietorship, partnership, and corporation); the limitations of vertical integration; the laws governing personnel management (job discrimination, working conditions, and compensation requirements); and the restrictions on store facilities (zoning ordinances, building codes, licensing requirements, and operating requirements) are all central legal issues in store operations.

The legal aspects of merchandising require the retailer to carefully consider the legalities of its product, price, promotion, and distribution mix. Guarantees, warranties, and liability are three of the more important legalities associated with the product. Price discrimination in terms of product characteristics, quantity discounts, and special allowances or services, together with resale price maintenance activities, are the retailer's chief legal concerns regarding price. Deceptive price and product advertising and deceptive sales practices are illegalities of promotion that retailers must avoid. Finally, the laws pertaining to distribution call for careful consideration of exclusive dealings, anticompetitive leasing arrangements, tying contracts, and the use of exclusive territories.

KEY TERMS AND CONCEPTS

anticompetitive leasing arrangements	mergers
antitrust legislation	partnership
bait and switch	predatory pricing
blue laws	price discrimination
Civil Rights Act	price fixing
Clayton Act	product guarantees
coercive buying	product liability
corporation	product warranties
deceptive brokerage activities	resale price maintenance
deceptive credit contracts	retail competition
deceptive price advertising	Robinson-Patman Act
deceptive product advertising	Sherman Antitrust Act
deceptive sales practices	sole proprietorship
exclusive dealings	special business license
exclusive territories	Truth-in-Lending Act
expressed warranties	tying contracts
Fair Labor Standards Act	unemployment compensation
Federal Trade Commission Act	unfair trade practice acts
full-line forcing	vertical integration
general business license	Wheeler-Lea Act
general partnership	Williams-Steiger Occupational Safety and Health Act
implied warranties	workers' compensation
limited partnership	

REVIEW QUESTIONS

1. Whose actions define the retailer's legal environment?
2. What is antitrust legislation?
3. What action was taken to overcome the shortcomings of the Sherman Antitrust Act? Be specific.
4. Compare and contrast the legal and operational advantages and disadvantages of a sole proprietorship, partnership, and corporate forms of retail organization.
5. What are the two most prevalent forms of employment discrimination? Describe each.

6. Which two basic guidelines should a retailer follow to ensure compliance with the provisions of the Civil Rights Act?
7. What is OSHA? Describe the primary responsibility of this governmental agency.
8. What is workers' compensation? Whom does it cover?
9. Who qualifies for unemployment compensation?
10. Why do local governments enact zoning ordinances? What are the benefits and limitations for the retailer?
11. What two types of local licensing requirements do retailers usually have to meet before they can begin operations? Define each.
12. Compare and contrast product guarantees with product warranties.
13. What are the two basic types of warranties? Describe each type.
14. Under what conditions can the retailer be held liable for an unsafe product?
15. What is price discrimination?
16. When is price discrimination illegal?
17. Describe the two legal defenses for price discrimination.
18. What techniques or practices constitute illegal price discrimination? Describe each technique or practice.
19. To avoid charges of deceptive price advertising when using former- and competitive-price comparisons, the retailer should follow which practices?
20. What is deceptive product advertising?
21. What is the major weapon the FTC uses in correcting false claims concerning product benefits? Explain.
22. Describe the sales practice of bait and switch. When is it illegal?
23. Identify the requirements of the Truth-in-Lending Act.
24. Compare and contrast the distribution arrangements of exclusive dealings, tying contracts, and exclusive territories. When are they illegal?

ENDNOTES

1. See Charles F. Rule, "An Antitrust Bill of Goods." *The Wall Street Journal,* 5 Feb. 1988, 7.
2. Diane Schneidman, "Door-to-Door Time Restrictions Found Unconstitutional," *Marketing News,* 13 March 1987, 4.
3. Joe Agnew, "Small Retailers Help Retain North Dakota Sunday Blue Law." *Marketing News,* 13 March 1987, 8.
4. Sandra L. Schmidt and Jerome B. Kernam, "The Many Meanings (and Implications) of 'Satisfaction Guaranteed'," *Journal of Retailing* 61 (Winter 1985): 89.
5. See Willard F. Mueller and Thomas W. Paterson, "Effectiveness of State Sales-Below-Cost Laws: Evidence from the Grocery Trade." *Journal of Retailing* 62 (Summer 1986): 166–169.
6. Scott Hume, "Big Mac attacked." *Advertising Age,* 4 May 1987, 110.
7. See Susan M. Thomas, Doris C. Van Doren, and Louise W. Smith, "Bait and Switch May Be Getting Passe; Consumers Want Information Respect." *Marketing News,* 15 Feb. 1988, 3.
8. See Sheldon Feldman, *Compliance with Simplified Truth in Lending by Retailers—Review of 1981 Changes in the Act and Regulation* 2 (New York: National Retail Merchants Association, 1981), 1–41; *Fair Credit Billing Act—Summary of Federal Reserve Board Regulation* (New York: National Retail Merchants Association, 1981): 1–19.
9. Ibid.
10. Amy Dunkin, "Why Some Benetton Shopkeepers Are Losing Their Shirts," *Business Week,* 14 March 1988, 78.
11. Louis W. Stern and Adel I. El Ansary, *Marketing Channels,* 2d ed. (Englewood Cliffs, NJ: Prentice-Hall, 1982): 368.

RELATED READINGS

"Antitrusters Revive 'Fair Trade'." *Chain Store Age, General Merchandise Edition* (February 1982): 35–36.

Boedecker, Karl A., and Morgan, Fred. W. "The Channel Implications of Product Liability Developments." *Journal of Retailing* 56 (Winter 1980): 59–72.

Crawford, Carol T. "The Federal Trade Commission and Consumer Protection." *Retail Control* (November 1984): 43–57.

Cromartie, Jane. "New Trends in Robinson-Patman Enforcement: Implications for the Marketing Manager." In *Marketing: Theories and Concepts for an Era of Change, Proceedings,* edited by J. Summey, R. Viswanathan, R. Taylor, and K. Glynn, 64–66. Southern Marketing Association, 1983.

Davis, Jennifer, and Renforth, William. "Consumer Product Warranties: Has the Magnuson-Moss Act Affected Their Readability?" In *Marketing: Theories and Concepts for an Era of Change, Proceedings,* edited by J. Summey, R. Viswanathan, R. Taylor, and K. Glynn, 194–97. Southern Marketing Association, 1983.

Emamalizadeh, Hossein. "Bait-and-Switch Advertising: A Conceptual Approach." In *Developments in Marketing Science, Proceedings,* edited by J.C. Rogers, III, 470–72. Academy of Marketing Science, 1983.

Houston, Michael J. "Minimum Markup Laws: An Empirical Assessment." *Journal of Retailing* 57 (Winter 1981): 98–113.

Hunt, Shelby O., and Nevin, John R. "Tying Agreements in Franchising." *Journal of Marketing* 39 (July 1975): 20–26.

Lambert, Zarrel V. "Consumer Alienation, General Dissatisfaction, and Consumerism Issues: Conceptual and Managerial Perspectives." *Journal of Retailing* 56 (Summer 1980): 3–24.

"The Liability Explosion." *Chain Store Executive* (April 1981): 54–56.

Marks, Norton E., and Inlow, Neely S. "Robinson Patman Act: Actions and Decisions 1961 to 1986." In *Marketing In An Environment of Change, Proceedings,* edited by R.L. King, 348–52. Southern Marketing Association, 1986.

Seesel, John H. "Off-Price Retailing: Regulatory Issues." *Retail Control* (November 1983): 55–61.

Stern, Louis W., and Eovaldi, Thomas L. *Legal Aspects of Marketing Strategy.* Englewood Cliffs, NJ: Prentice-Hall, 1984.

Turk, Michael A., and Cooke, Ernest F. "What Is False, Deceptive, or Misleading Advertising?" In *Developments in Marketing Science, Proceedings,* edited by J.D. Lindquist, 249–53. Academy of Marketing Science, 1984.

Welch, Joe L. *Marketing Law.* Tulsa, OK: Petroleum Publishing Co., 1980.

Wiener, Joshua L. "The Inferences Consumers Draw from a Warranty: Did They Become More Accurate after the Magnuson-Moss Act?" In *1985 AMA Educators' Proceedings,* edited by R.F. Lusch et al., 309–12. American Marketing Association, 1985.

6

Objectives

☐ Describe how to reduce the risks of doing business through an adequate retailing information system.

☐ Determine what information is available, what information is needed, how information is gathered and processed, and where information is obtained.

☐ Productively use information in retail problem-solving and decision-making situations.

☐ Recognize the key considerations in effective management of the retailing information system.

☐ Design, implement, and manage a retail research project.

☐ Understand and appreciate the role of the electronic data processing system within the retailing information system.

The Retail Information System

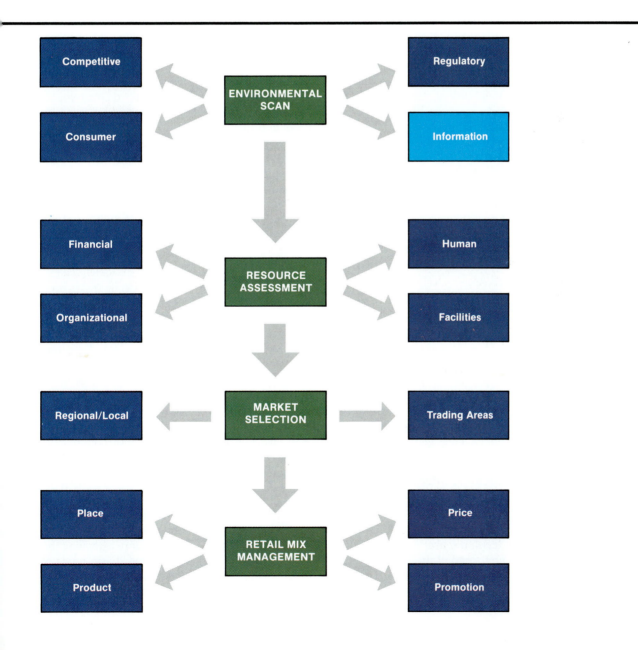

The retailer must learn how to reduce the risks of doing business to succeed in today's complex, dynamic retailing environment. Basing decisions on reliable information is perhaps the single most effective way to reduce business risks. Because good information is the precursor to effective decision making and problem solving, this chapter appears early in the text.

THE RETAILER'S NEED TO KNOW

"No organization, retailing included, can be effectively managed without some type of information system. Decisions based on an absence of information are decisions for disaster."[1] Retailers need to know what information is available, what information is needed, how and where information can be obtained, and how to use productively the information received. The kinds of information in which the retailer is interested are those that can make problem solving and decision making as effective as possible. "Retail information strategies and systems of the future will . . . help management consider all of the customer purchase factors in making its decisions: in-store price promotions, consumer expendable income, seasonal influences, in-store personal selling, advertising, number of brands, number of shoppers, display space, brand positioning, availability of goods."[2] This is but a limited listing of the retailer's information needs regarding consumers and their behavior.

In *Future Shock,* Alvin Toffler develops the thesis that society and technology are changing so rapidly that the reverberations disorient and confuse all members of society.[3] This constant state of environmental flux continually tests the retailer's ability to manage a retailing information system. Successful information systems are, by necessity, future oriented. A major function of any information system is to predict today what is going to happen tomorrow. Equally important is the capability of the information system to reduce the time span required to make a decision. The adage, "He who hesitates is lost" is all too true in retailing, where fast adaptation to new market opportunities is necessary.

THE RETAILING INFORMATION SYSTEM

Because successful retailing starts with the possession and proper use of business information, many retailers have developed and implemented some form of **retailing information system (RIS)**. An RIS is an interacting organization of people, machines, and methods designed to produce a regular, continuous, and orderly flow of information necessary for the retailer's problem-solving and decision-making activities. The RIS is a planned, sequential flow of information tailored to the needs of a particular retail operation. As shown in Figure 6–1, the four basic activities of the RIS are locating, gathering, processing, and utilizing pertinent retailing information.

Locating Information

The fundamental purpose of the RIS is to provide a framework for gathering input (information) from both the retailer's external and internal environments so that the retailer can develop the best possible output ("correct" decisions). In the first stage the decision maker must locate information relevant to its business. Before activating the first stage of an RIS, however, the retailer must understand the two basic *types* of information and the two *sources* from which this information can be derived. The two types of information are secondary and primary information, and the two sources of information are external and internal information.

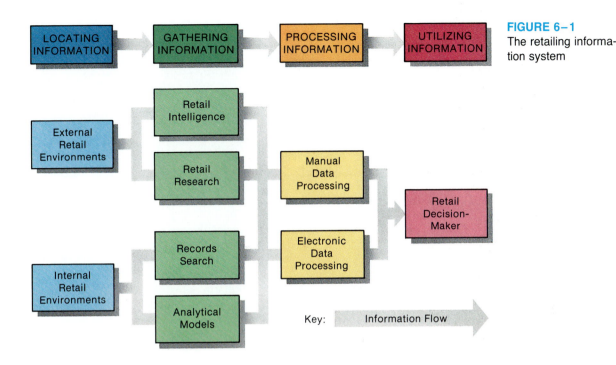

FIGURE 6–1
The retailing informa-
tion system

Types of Information

Secondary information is existing information that has been collected for another
purpose and that is often published. Although secondary information is collected for
some other purpose, a retailer often can adapt this information to its own needs.
Given the tremendous wealth of secondary information collected and published by
government agencies, trade associations, and other research groups, the chance of
finding useful information for other purposes is very high. Even though secondary
information might not fit the retailer's *precise needs,* a major function of the RIS is to
convert this information into a reservoir of useful knowledge. As is true with any type
of information, secondary information has advantages and disadvantages (see Figure
6–2).

    Primary information is new information the retailer collects for a specific pur-
pose tailored to its needs. Original data are collected using survey, panel, laboratory,
and statistical techniques. Sometimes the retailer collects primary information because it can find no secondary sources to help make an important decision. At other
times, the retailer obtains primary information to corroborate the secondary information gathered.

    By using primary information, the retailer overcomes most of the disadvantages
associated with secondary information. Primary information is generally more accurate, more current, and more suitable to the retailer's problem at hand. Unfortunately,
primary information is usually more costly and time-consuming to obtain. Additionally, to gain the advantages of primary information, a retailer normally must be willing
to invest in specialized equipment and personnel to gather the information.

Sources of Information

The retailer has two sources of information—external and internal. **External information** is information obtained from outside the firm. It originates from formal (li-

FIGURE 6–2

The advantages and disadvantages of secondary information

DISADVANTAGES

Lack of Suitability

Suitability is the "match" between pertinent secondary information and the information needs of the retailer. Where there is a lack of suitability, there is a poor match between the secondary information and the retailer's information needs. Lack of suitability can be the result of either geographic or class conformity. Geographic conformity is concerned with whether the information is broken down by geographic units (census areas, cities, counties, states, etc.) which are consistent with the retailer's needs. Class conformity is concerned with how information is classified and defined, as well as what units of measurements are used in measuring each class. Sales, for example, can be defined as gross *or* net sales per square *or* linear foot.

Lack of Accuracy

Secondary data can be inaccurate for a number of reasons: (1) a considerable amount of secondary information is reported without sufficient comment on how, when, and under what circumstances the information was collected and tabulated; (2) some secondary sources get their information from other sources, with the result being third-hand information for the retailer, for whom the problems of accuracy are substantially increased; and (3) secondary information was collected for a specific purpose and frequently that purpose was to promote a particular idea, position, or organization. By definition and design, such information is biased and often inaccurate.

Obsolescence

The usefulness of secondary information is sometimes limited by its obsolescence. In the time it takes to collect, tabulate, and publish secondary information, it can become quite dated. Census information, for example, is collected at 5-, 7-, and 10-year intervals, depending on the particular type of census.

ADVANTAGES

Less Costly

Secondary information generally costs less to obtain than primary information. By using published sources of information, the very expensive collecting, editing, and tabulating phases can be avoided. The use of unpublished secondary information requires a more extensive search process; however, such information usually can be obtained at costs below primary information. Many governmental agencies and trade associations provide vast amounts of information either free of charge or at some minimal charge. Private commercial sources normally charge substantial fees; nevertheless, due to their operating economies and efficiencies, they frequently can provide secondary information at rates lower than the costs of the retailer doing it.

Greater Speed and Availability

Secondary information often can be obtained immediately or in a matter of days, whereas the collection of primary information can take several weeks or months. When the firms's decision makers require at least some information, secondary information may be the only feasible alternative.

Greater Familiarity

Since the firm's managers have been exposed at one time or another to many of the standard types of secondary information, they tend to be more comfortable with that information because they are more aware of its uses and its limitations.

Possible Greater Credibility

Secondary information has greater credibility when the original source is highly credible. Sources with questionable reputations are usually perceived as having less credible information.

brary, government, trade, and commercial) organizations and from informal (supplier, competitor, and consumer) sources. With the great variety of outside sources, the task of locating and collecting external information often is very tedious and time-consuming.

Internal information is information found within the firm. For example, various departments and divisions generate a wide range of information in the normal course of their operations. It comes from a variety of sources such as operating statements, sales records, expense records, purchasing and inventory records, accounts receivable and payable records, and prior written reports. Other information can be obtained from employee surveys and employment records. By applying certain statistical and analytical procedures, the retailer can generate additional information.

Gathering Information

Once the information has been located, the second stage is to gather it. Figure 6–3 represents a taxonomy of information-gathering methods including retail intelligence, retail research, records search, and analytical models. This section briefly defines and describes each of the methods. Later in the chapter, retail intelligence and retail research will be discussed in more depth.

Retail intelligence is any method or combination of methods used to obtain external secondary information. To keep the firm's decision makers current, the retailing information system must be able to monitor the daily developments of the marketplace. Retail intelligence involves search procedures to comb libraries and government and trade sources for pertinent information regularly and systematically. For a fee, additional retail intelligence can be secured from various commercial organizations that specialize in monitoring certain aspects of the marketplace.

Retail research involves the use of a set of scientific procedures to gather external primary information from consumers, suppliers, and competitors. Typically, retail research is project oriented and directed at a particular decision-making or problem-solving situation. Two major characteristics of retail research are that (1) it is conducted in a fragmented, intermittent fashion and (2) a computer usually processes the data. Surveys, panels, and laboratory experiments are the most common information-gathering techniques used in retail research.

Records search includes all methods used in gathering internal secondary information. The firm's internal accounting system and its various operational control subsystems can provide a wealth of information on all aspects of the retailer's operations. A records search can generate information on both past and current per-

DIMENSIONS OF INFORMATION		Types of Information	
		Secondary	Primary
Sources of Information	External	retail intelligence	retail research
	Internal	records search	analytical models

FIGURE 6–3

A taxonomy of information-gathering methods

formances and activities. Such internal records contain information on sales, expenses, inventories, purchases, potential vendors, and a host of other factors. They also indicate a great deal about the relationship between these factors and the retailer's products, prices, promotions, facilities, and personnel.

Analytical models are various statistical and quantitative methods that researchers use internally to generate primary information. Used mostly by large retailers, analytical models employ mathematical techniques to find the best solution to a particular problem. Retailers use analytical models to estimate a trading area's sales potential, to evaluate an advertising campaign, to predict operating expenses under various circumstances, and to analyze stocking and handling procedures. Essentially, analytical models generate primary information from secondary information using a complex set of quantitative procedures.

Processing Information

After locating and gathering information, the RIS must be able to process the information effectively. The information-processing system consists of (1) selecting and preparing input; (2) evaluating, storing, and retrieving processed information; and (3) preparing and disseminating output. As shown in Figure 6–1, the information-processing system can be either manual or electronic.

Manual data processing uses human labor to process information. The typical hardware of such a system usually consists of typewriters, calculators, filing cabinets, and hand-carried files. The software usually consists of written instructions on how each of the processing functions should be conducted. For small retailers, manual data processing is practical and can be effective if the system is carefully developed and maintained.

Electronic data processing is a computer-based system of processing information. The computer is the principal piece of hardware used in preparing, evaluating, storing, retrieving, and disseminating information. It has three major components—an input system, a central processing unit, and an output system. The software consists of the instructional procedures for programming the computer. Traditionally, only large retailing organizations could afford a computer-based electronic data processing system. With the recent development of the personal computer, electronic data processing is becoming a more accessible option for all retailers.

Utilizing Information

No matter how well the RIS accomplishes the tasks of locating, gathering, and processing information, the total system is a failure if the decision maker does not fully utilize the information. Information, the principal input into every decision-making and problem-solving situation, is crucial to the retailer in establishing goals and objectives, identifying and analyzing alternatives, developing plans, and making recommendations and decisions. To avoid "muddling through" problems and making decisions with crude rules of thumb and rough approximations, reliable and pertinent information must be available and must be used.

| RETAIL INTELLIGENCE | Gathering retail intelligence from library, government, association, and commercial sources provides the retailer with information about the legal, political, social, economic, and technological environments. For any one of these sources, the information can be published or reported in the form of books, monographs, reports, periodicals, bulletins, tapes, films, or several types of special publications. Additionally, unpublished retail intelligence can be secured if the researcher knows what to look for |

and how to find it. The prudent strategy in this case is to seek help from someone familiar with unpublished sources of information.

Library Sources of Retail Intelligence

The library not only is a source of information on a wide variety of subjects but also frequently serves as a means for locating other sources of retail intelligence. For the retailer seeking external secondary information, the library is a good starting point. Library research skills are developed by using the library and becoming familiar with its information retrieval systems (e.g., card catalogs and visual display terminals). A number of excellent reference guides contain potential sources of retail intelligence (see Figure 6–4). Also, many libraries have specialized personnel (e.g., government documents librarian), trained in finding specific information.

Government Sources of Retail Intelligence

The most prolific compilers of external secondary information are federal, state, and local governments. While government sources collect and disseminate an enormous amount of information on a wide variety of subjects, the types of information retailers use most often are census and registration data.

Census Information

The U.S. Bureau of the Census of the Department of Commerce regularly conducts nine different censuses. These constitute the most important sources of external secondary information for most businesses. In addition to the volume of information they contain, Census Bureau reports are quite accurate, particularly in light of the monumental work involved in collecting data from so many sectors of the U.S. economy.

FIGURE 6–4
Selected reference guides

Business Periodicals Index
> A cumulative subject index to English-language periodicals in the fields of accounting, advertising and public relations, automation, banking, communications, economics, finance and investment, insurance, labor, management, marketing, taxation, and specific businesses, industries, and trades.

Wall Street Journal Index
> A monthly index with annual cumulations prepared by M. Dow Jones and Company from the final eastern edition of the *Wall Street Journal*. The index consists of two parts: corporate news and general news.

New York Times Index
> A semimonthly subject index with annual cumulations covering every subject reported in the final late city edition of the *New York Times*. Contains brief abstracts of news stories classified by subject, geographic, association, institution, and company headings.

Monthly Catalog of U.S. Government Publications
> A monthly subject index to publications of the various branches of government. A condensed biweekly version, *Selected U.S. Government Publications*, contains a list of business-related publications that have general application to most businesses.

Reader's Guide to Periodical Literature
> A semimonthly author, subject, and title index of approximately 130 general, nontechnical U.S. publications.

The nine censuses produced by the federal government follow:

- Census of Population
- Census of Housing
- Census of Governments
- Census of Agriculture
- Census of Construction
- Census of Business
- Census of Manufacturing
- Census of Mineral Industries
- Census of Transportation

The *Census of Population* and the *Census of Housing* contain a vast amount of detailed information broken down according to predefined geographical reporting units. Information for both censuses is reported by states, counties, cities, and various urban area classifications. Within urban areas, population and housing characteristics are available on a very localized level. Urban areas are subdivided into census tracts, enumeration districts, and census blocks for reporting purposes. In addition to population, housing counts, and density measurements (persons or units per area), each census contains an extensive amount of information concerning each person or unit. For example, the *Census of Population* provides statistics on the demographic makeup of a given reporting area, such as statistics on age, sex, race, education, occupation, income, marital status, living arrangements, and family structure of the population. The *Census of Housing* gives additional information on the occupancy status and the financial and structural characteristics of the housing stock.

The *Census of Governments* describes the operating characteristics of all levels of government—federal, state, and local. The economic censuses of agriculture, construction, business, manufacturing, mineral industries, and transportation are presented by geographical areas and by Standard Industrial Classification (SIC) system codes. States, counties, and cities (in some cases) are the most common reporting units for the economic censuses. The SIC is a standardized code that categorizes industries into major groups and subclassifies them into highly descriptive groups. Each of the economic censuses enumerates the number of establishments as well as information on their sales, expenditures, number of employees, size of operation, and types of facilities and equipment they use in their operations. The most important economic census for the retailer is the *Census of Business,* consisting of three parts: "Retail Trade," "Wholesaler Trade," and "Selected Services."

Registration Information

All levels of government at various times require individuals and organizations to register and report activities in which they are engaged. This routinely collected data can provide the retailer with a tremendous amount of useful information if the retailer knows how and where to secure it. Some of the more common forms of registration include public records on (1) births, (2) deaths, (3) marriages, (4) school enrollments, (5) income, (6) sales tax payments, (7) automobile and recreational vehicle registration, and (8) general and special business licenses and crime statistics. This list of registration information is far from comprehensive; it merely illustrates the kinds of information that retailers can get from public records.

Additional Information

At all levels of government, various departments and agencies produce a mountain of information pertaining to their areas of responsibility. The *County and City Data*

Book provides information on a variety of topics of interest to the retailer. This source contains economic and social facts on local areas such as counties, cities, metropolitan areas, urbanized areas, and unincorporated places of 25,000 or more inhabitants in the United States. The Small Business Administration (SBA) publishes a number of aids directed at specific problems retailers frequently encounter. These aids take one of several forms: (1) Small Marketer's Aids, (2) Management Aids, (3) Small Business Bibliographies, (4) Small Business Management Series, (5) Starting and Managing Series, and (6) nonseries publications.

Association Sources of Retail Intelligence

A third major source of external secondary information is the large group of trade and professional associations that collect and publish highly specialized information. It would be difficult to find a subject that one or more of these groups or associations could not provide information on. Their charges for information range from free to various organization membership fees and publication subscription rates. To contact these organizations, the retailer can consult the *World Almanac* (which lists over 1,100 associations in the United States), the *Encyclopedia of Associations* (with more than 16,000 names), or the *Writer's Guide* (which lists the names and addresses of literally thousands of magazines).

Most associations publish either a magazine, a journal, or a newsletter; they usually issue special reports, maintain files of information, and send out promotional literature as well. Figure 6–5 lists some of the more important trade and professional associations and publications of particular interest to retailers. In using information from these associations, the retailer should remember that some of these sources promote special interests and therefore contain certain biases.

Commercial Sources of Retail Intelligence

The need for marketing information has led many firms into the business of providing it commercially. Commercial sources make a business out of collecting, tabulating, analyzing, and reporting information. *Bradford's Directory* lists more than 350 firms engaged in the commercial gathering and selling of information. Typically, commercial information sources provide either a standardized information service or a service tailored to the informational needs of a particular customer.

Standardized information services provide a prescribed type of information continuously and regularly. Figure 6–6 illustrates several examples of standardized information sources and the types of information they provide. *Tailored information services* provide customized information for the specific needs of the retailer. These services are typically performed on either a single occasion or an irregular, contractual basis.

Retail research is the systematic process of gathering and analyzing primary, external information about consumers, suppliers, and competitors. It is conducted on a project-by-project basis and directed at a particular problem-solving or decision-making situation. The main purpose of research is to obtain specific information to help reduce the risks of making a decision. Conducting research can be an expensive and time-consuming venture, so each research project must be selected carefully on the basis of its potential for providing meaningful, useful information.

Research projects that have proven to be productive ventures for the retailer in the past include studies on (1) consumer attitudes toward the retailer and its merchandising efforts, (2) consumer purchase motives and preferences, (3) demographic and psychographic profiles of both customers and noncustomers, (4) buyer-behavior patterns and their relationships to the retailer's mode of operations, (5) service and

**RETAIL
RESEARCH**

Trade and Professional Associations

American Booksellers Association	National Association of Retail Grocers
American Management Association	National Association of Variety Stores
American Marketing Association	National Home Furnishing Association
American Retail Federation	National Industrial Conference Board
Automotive Parts and Accessories Association	National Jewelers of America
Better Business Bureau	National Lumber and Building Materials Association
Chamber of Commerce	National Retail Furniture Association
International Franchise Association	National Retail Hardware Association
Mass Retailing Institute	National Retail Merchants Association
Menswear Retailers of America	National Shoe Retailers Association
National Appliance and Radio-TV Dealers Association	National Sporting Goods Association
National Association of Retail Druggists	Sales and Marketing Executives
	Urban Land Institute

Trade and Professional Publications

Advertising Age	*Journal of Advertising Research*
American Fabrics and Fashions	*Journal of Marketing*
Auto Merchandising News	*Journal of Marketing Research*
Business Week	*Journal of Retailing*
California Apparel News	*Juvenile Merchandising*
Chain Store Age	*Luggage and Leather Goods*
Clothes	*Mart Magazine*
Curtain, Drapery and Bedspread Magazine	*Merchandising Week*
Dealerscope (Appliances)	*Modern Jeweler*
Discount Merchandiser	*Office Products News*
Drug Topics	*Progressive Grocer*
Earnshaw's Infants, Girls, and Boyswear Review	*Publishers Weekly*
Floor Covering Weekly	*Retail Advertising Week*
Florist	*Sales and Marketing Management*
Fortune	*Sports Merchandiser*
Furniture News	*Sporting Goods Business*
Hardware Age	*Stores*
Hardware Merchandiser	*Visual Merchandising*
Harvard Business Review	*Volume Retail Merchandising*
Home and Auto	*Women's Wear Daily*

FIGURE 6–5
Association sources of
retail intelligence

performance records of suppliers, (6) price and cost comparisons between suppliers, (7) merchandising and operational strengths and weaknesses of competitors, and (8) employee perceptions of the company and its dealings with them. Retail research also provides information on the sales potential and customer acceptance of product lines, advertising and personal selling effectiveness, locational attributes of the retailer's outlets, and consumer service and price perceptions. To conduct research, a basic understanding of the scientific method is useful.

The Scientific Method

The **scientific method** is a set of procedures that allows the retailer to gather and analyze data in a systematic, controlled fashion. It is perhaps the most commonly

FIGURE 6–6
Selected examples of
standardized informa-
tion sources

Survey of Buying Power .... Sales and Marketing Executives	Information on population, retail sales by store group, and effective buying income.
Market Survey .... The Editor and Publisher Market Guide	Information on the number of retail stores and their sales, population, disposable personal income, number of households, and household income.
Retail Index .... A. C. Nielsen Co.	Information on retail sales by product class and brand, purchases by retailers, retail inventories and stock turn, and retail and wholesale prices.
Consumer Panel .... Market Research Corporation of America	Information on product and brand sales by type of consumer, type of household, and type of retailer.
Supermarket Audit .... Market Research Corporation of America	Information on in-store type and amount of stock, prices of products, and shelf space assignments.
Channel Survey .... Selling Areas-Marketing, Inc.	Information on movements of products from suppliers to retailers.
Television Index .... A. C. Nielsen Co.	Information on size of television audience, viewing habits, flow of audience, and cost per 1,000 homes reached.
Media Survey .... Audit Bureau of Circulation	Information on readership of newspaper and magazine ads.
Media Survey .... Standard Rate and Data Service	Information on advertising rates for various media.

used method of producing defensible results and drawing reliable conclusions. The accepted stages of the scientific method follow:

- ☐ Identifying the problem
- ☐ Developing a hypothesis
- ☐ Collecting information
- ☐ Analyzing information
- ☐ Drawing conclusions

Its objectivity in the midst of creative and mechanical processes gives the scientific method its unusual level of acceptance.

The Creative Process

The creative aspect of the scientific method consists of identifying problems and developing hypotheses, the most critical part of any research project. The *problem-identification process* requires the retailer to clearly identify the problem and then state it in precise terms. Problem statements are made in the form of a declarative sentence ("The problem is to determine the relationship. . . .") or expressed as a question ("What is the relationship between . . .?"). Perhaps the importance of the problem-identification process is best expressed by the old saying "A problem well defined is a problem half solved." Problem identification demands more than basic knowledge and skills; it demands creative perception and insight and the ability to look beyond the "symptoms" of a problem in an effort to find its causes.

The *hypothesis-development* process is the most important stage in the scientific method. It is the stage that characterizes the whole process of scientific investigation by focusing that investigation. In developing a hypothesis, the researcher formulates a definite position that will be either accepted or rejected in the analysis stage. In essence, the hypothesis is nothing more than a statement of the researcher's tentative solution to the identified problem. A hypothesis takes a known fact and proposes a relationship one step beyond existing knowledge. Once the hypothesis has been developed, it is considered "cast in concrete." Based on the outcome of the analysis, the researcher's decision is automatic: either to accept or to reject the hypothesis. The hypothesis can be expressed in statistical or verbal terms. The important factor in developing any hypothesis is to express explicitly the researcher's objectives, whether statistical or verbal. Moreover, once the hypothesis has been stated, the rest of the research process becomes largely mechanical.

The Mechanical Process

Compared to the creative stages of the scientific method, the last three stages (collection, analysis, and conclusion) are largely mechanical. In the *information-collection process,* the researcher must select and use one or more research methods, such as survey, observation, or experimental, in association with a research instrument such as a questionnaire. This process also involves the use of some form of scientific sampling. While collecting information is a laborious mechanical task, it does produce highly visible results that satisfy the basic human desire to have something to show for one's efforts.

The *information-analysis process* consists of several mechanical activities. The first is to prepare the information for analysis. Examples are editing and tabulating raw data. The second step is to calculate statistical expressions such as percentages, averages, and measures of central tendency. The third activity is to observe the relationships between these statistical expressions. For example, the researcher might want to observe similarities and differences between the statistics. The fourth step is testing the degree of relationship between the statistical expressions. The degree of relationship can be determined through a variety of statistical tests that measure how significant the differences are and how strongly data are associated. These four steps in information analysis should be followed in sequence.

Drawing conclusions is the final stage of the scientific method and should evolve naturally from the problem-identification, hypothesis-development, information-collection, and analysis stages. Conclusions usually state whether the hypothesis was accepted or rejected, together with an operational interpretation of the results. Because the retailer's decisions are based on the final conclusions of the research, the research analyst should take considerable care to present the results clearly, concisely, and professionally.

Collecting Primary Information

The following discussion identifies and examines the most common of the various methods and instruments used to collect information in retail research.

Research Methods

Retail analysts use three basic methods in collecting external primary information: surveys, observation, and experimentation. The method depends on the nature of the research problem. In some cases, they might employ all three methods in one project.

The survey method. Using the **survey method,** the researcher systematically gathers information directly from the appropriate respondents. Generally, in the survey method the researcher uses a questionnaire administered either in person, over the telephone, or by mail. The *personal interview* is a face-to-face question-and-answer session between the interviewer and the respondent. Interviewers can contact respondents either at their homes or places of employment or at public places (street corners, shopping centers, retail stores). Typically, the personal interview consists of these steps:

1. Identification—a statement of who is conducting the interview, what the survey is about, for whom it is being conducted, and why it is being conducted
2. Permission—a request of the respondent for an interview
3. Administration—when the interviewer asks a predetermined list of questions and records the respondent's answers
4. Closure—the terminating step in which the interviewer thanks the respondent for his or her cooperation

Two other survey methods retailers use are the telephone survey and the mail survey. In a *telephone survey,* retailers phone potential respondents at their homes. Successful telephone interviews take no more than three or four minutes of the respondent's time. The basic survey steps of identification, permission, administration, and closure are essentially the same for telephone surveys as they are for personal surveys.

Mail surveys differ from personal interviews and telephone surveys in that the questionnaire is administered in writing. The potential respondent in a mail survey receives and returns the questionnaire by mail. The survey director also can administer the survey by attaching questionnaires to products or packages, passing them out in a store or on the street, or placing them in newspapers. In these cases, respondents are asked to return the questionnaire in a self-addressed, postage-paid envelope. Because the questionnaire is in written form and the interviewer is not available to ask or answer questions, the questionnaire should be short and simple and have complete instructions.

In determining which survey method to use, the retailer must select the method most appropriate to the problem under investigation. To help the retailer select the best survey method, Figure 6–7 summarizes the relative strengths and weaknesses of each.

The observation method. Researchers can obtain significant amounts of primary information simply by observing consumers' behavior. **Observation** is a method of recording some aspect of consumers' overt behavior by either personal or mechanical means. What the consumer does, not says, is the principal focus of the observation method. The advantages of this method are that it (1) eliminates any interviewer bias associated with the survey method and (2) does not require the respondent's cooperation. The major disadvantage of the observation method is that the retailer cannot investigate the consumer's motives, attitudes, beliefs, and feelings. If the retailer uses this method, it must decide what observation and recording techniques to use, the setting in which to make the observation, and whether to inform consumers that they are being observed. Each of these decisions is outlined in Figure 6–8. In some situations, the retailer might find it beneficial to combine the observation method with the survey method. For example, by first observing the consumers' behavior patterns, the retailer might obtain a more objective assessment of what actions the consumer actually took and then, through a follow-up survey, learn why the consumer took those actions.

Selection Criteria	Survey Method		
	Personal Interview	Telephone Survey	Mail Survey
Cost:[1] What is the most expensive method of collecting information?	Most expensive	Intermediate	Least expensive
Speed: What is the fastest method of collecting information?	Slowest method	Fastest method	Intermediate
Accuracy: What is the most accurate method of collecting information?	Most accurate	Intermediate	Least accurate
Volume: Which method is capable of collecting the most information?	Most information	Least information	Intermediate
Response rate: Which method results in the highest number of completed interviews?	Highest response	Intermediate	Lowest response
Flexibility: What method is most capable of adjusting to changing interviewing conditions?	Most flexible	Intermediate	Least flexible
Sample control:[2] Which method is capable of securing the best representative sample of the total population?	Intermediate	Worst representation	Best representation
Interview control: What method provides the interviewer the greatest amount of control over the interview situation?	Greatest control	Intermediate	Least control
Administrative control: Which method provides the retailer the greatest amount of control over the actions of the interviewer?	Least control	Intermediate	Greatest control

[1]Where the sample is scattered over a wide geographic area.
[2]Assumes an accurate mailing list.
Source: Adapted from K. L. McGown, *Marketing Research: Text and Cases* (Cambridge, MA: Winthrop Publishers, 1979), 135.

FIGURE 6–7
Determining which survey method to use

The purchase intercept technique.   By combining the observation method with the survey (self-report) method, the **purchase intercept technique (PIT)** capitalizes on "the advantages of observation (e.g., accuracy and objectivity) and the significant information gained through self-report (e.g., information about why the specific behavior takes place)."[4] The PIT is an in-store information-gathering technique consisting of the following steps:

1. Observe customer in-store shopping behavior.
2. Record pertinent shopping behavior information.
3. Interview customer immediately (at the time of observable product selection or other significant behavior trait under study—reaction to displays and signs) about their purchase or shopping behavior.[5]

The experimentation method.   **Experimentation** is a technique that researchers use to determine a cause-and-effect relationship between two or more factors. An experiment is usually conducted under controlled conditions; that is, the factors under

Decision	Description	Example
Observation methods:		
1. Direct	Observing current behavior	Watching the number of consumers who stop to inspect a store display
2. Indirect	Observing past behavior	Counting the number of store-branded products (e.g. Sears) found in the consumer's home
Recording methods:		
1. Personal	Recording observations by hand	Logging customer reactions to a sales presentation by visually observing and manually recording the process
2. Nonpersonal	Recording observations mechanically or electronically (counters, cameras, sensors)	Measuring television viewing habits using an "audiometer," measuring pupil dilation while an advertisement is viewed as an indication of interest using a "perceptoscope," and using an "eye camera" to measure eye movement of a consumer as he or she views a display
Observation setting:		
1. Natural	Observing behavior in an unplanned and real setting	Observing the customer's natural and unobstructive trip behavior through the store
2. Artificial	Observing behavior in a planned and contrived setting	Observing sales personnel reaction to various customer "plants" who dress in a different fashion (e.g. well-dressed or shabbily dressed)
Observation organization:		
1. Structured	Observing specific behavior patterns	Observing the actions of only female customers who purchase a particular product
2. Unstructured	Observing general behavior patterns	Observing all of the actions of all customers regardless of who they are or what they buy
Observation situation:		
1. Disguised	Observing behavior without the person being aware that he or she is being observed	Using a two-way mirror to observe how customers inspect a display
2. Nondisguised	Observing behavior in an open fashion, thereby allowing the person to be aware that he or she is being observed	Following the customer around the store to observe shopping patterns

FIGURE 6–8
Using the observation method

study are manipulated while all other factors are held constant. For example, a retailer might increase the price of a product by $5.00 to see what effect the price change had on sales and profits, while holding constant all other factors, such as location, amount of shelf space, advertisements, and in-store displays. A number of experimental designs are illustrated in Figure 6–9.

The before-after design *without* a control group measures the dependent factor (sales volume) before and after the factor has been manipulated (e.g., change from a middle- to end-of-aisle display). The researcher assumes that the difference in sales volume is caused by the change in location, since all other factors affecting the sale of the product were held constant (see Figure 6–9a).

The before-after design *with* control group is essentially the same as the design just described except that a control group is used to determine if any changes in sales volume would have occurred regardless of any manipulation. For example, in Figure 6–9b, Store A's sales volume is measured before and after an advertising campaign

FIGURE 6–9
Experimental research designs

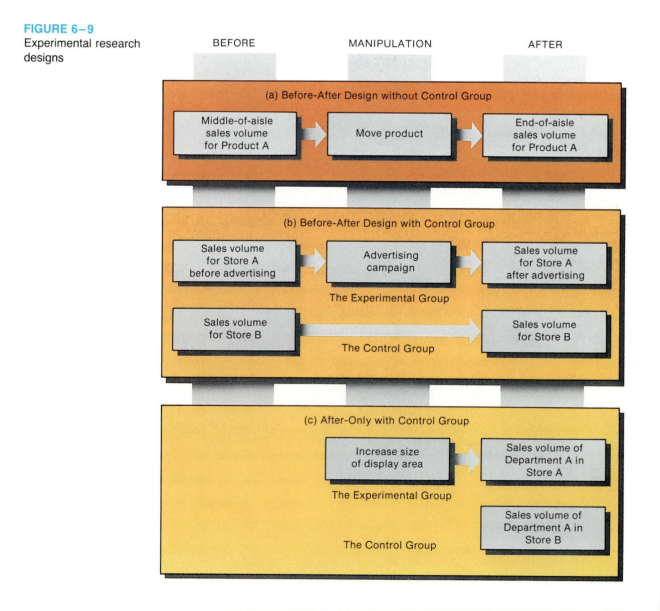

to determine the effects of advertising. To prove that all changes in sales volume are the result of advertising, any changes in the sales volume of control Store B, which is unaffected by the advertising campaign, are also measured over the same period of time. If control Store B experienced no change in sales volume, then the researcher can more comfortably state that changes in sales volume for Store A are the result of the advertising campaign, everything else being equal.

The after-only *with* control group design is the most widely used design because of its simplicity and ease of implementation. As shown in Figure 6–9c, it involves measuring the dependent factor (sales volume of Department A in Store A) for one group that has been manipulated (increased size of display area) and comparing it with the same dependent factor (sales volume of Department A in Store B) for the control group that was not manipulated.

In general, the major advantage of using the experimentation method is that it systematically demonstrates cause-and-effect relationships. High costs, artificial settings, and the difficulties of controlling all the factors that might influence the results of the experiment are its principal limitations.

Research Instruments

By far the most widely used research instrument in retail research is the questionnaire. This discussion therefore is limited to this particular instrument. The four major factors a researcher must carefully consider are structuring, wording, and sequencing questions and scaling answers in the questionnaire.

Structuring questions. Questions can be either open-ended (unstructured) or closed-ended (structured). Open-ended questions allow respondents to answer questions in their own words, thereby providing greater freedom in communicating their responses. Used extensively in motivation research, the open-ended question allows respondents to project their feelings about the retailer's merchandising and operational activities. Retailers can use a number of open-ended or projective techniques. One is the **word-association test**—a set of words or phrases to which respondents must give their immediate reactions:

Retailer (Interviewer)	Consumer (Respondent)
Store	Clean
Products	Good selection
Services	Courteous salespeople
Prices	Low

A second projective technique is the **sentence-completion test,** which simply asks respondents to finish a set of sentences. Examples follow:

Store personnel should be _____.
Store advertising should stress _____.
Store convenience is a matter of _____.

A third open-ended questionnaire is the **narrative projection test** in which the researcher provides respondents with a descriptive situation and asks them to write a paragraph in response.[6] An example of a descriptive situation the researcher might give respondents is the following:

> **A neighbor asks you what is the best store in town for buying draperies and why you think it is best. What would you tell her?**

Respondents would then write their reactions to this description.

The fourth projection technique is the **thematic apperception test**. In this test, respondents are shown a cartoon, drawing, or picture and then asked to put themselves into the situation and tell a story about what is happening or what they would do:

> A picture showing one customer observing a poorly dressed elderly woman placing merchandise into a pocket.

A typical response to this picture might be, "She lives on welfare, has very little money, and must resort to shoplifting."

The major purpose of most **open-ended questionnaires** is to explore and identify potential problems and to obtain information that could be included in a structured research study. Because of the numerous difficulties in classifying and interpreting the results of open-ended questions, many retailers prefer to use structured questioning. The closed-ended questionnaire meets this need.

The closed-ended questionnaire is a highly structured format giving respondents a set of answers from which to choose. The three most common closed-ended questionnaires are in the form of dichotomous, multiple-choice, or rank-ordered questions.

Dichotomous questions limit a respondent's answer to only one of two choices. Examples of dichotomous questions follow:

> Is our store the closest food store to your home?
> _____ Yes   _____ No
> Is price the most important factor in comparing products?
> _____ True   _____ False

Multiple-choice questions provide several possible answers from which the respondent can select the best answer:

> What is your favorite type of television program?
> _____ Sports
> _____ News
> _____ Comedy
> _____ Mystery
> _____ Drama
> _____ Variety
> _____ Other
>
> What is your approximate income?
> _____ Under $15,000
> _____ $15,000 $24,999
> _____ $25,000 $34,999
> _____ Over $35,000

The third type of structured question is the **rank-ordered question,** in which the respondent is asked to rank a list of factors in order of their importance. An example of a rank-ordered question is the following:

> Please rank the following store services in terms of their importance in attracting you as a customer. Let 1 be the most important service, 2 the second most important service, and so on until each service has been ranked.
>
> _____ Easy credit terms
> _____ Liberal return policy
> _____ Free home delivery

_____ Free layaway service
_____ Good repair service
_____ Long store hours

Many researchers prefer structured questions because they are easier to tabulate and analyze and because they eliminate the ambiguity of answers and the interpretation problems of unstructured questions. The major disadvantage of structured questions is that they limit the amount and type of answers the respondent can make.

Scaling answers.   To overcome the high cost and interpretation problems associated with unstructured questions and to gain more information than structured questions provide, many researchers prefer to use questions whose answers reflect the relative degree of the respondent's attitudes and opinions on a subject. The two most commonly used scales in retail research are Likert's summated ratings scale and Osgood's semantic differential.

Likert's summated rating scale measures attitudes and opinions by asking respondents to indicate their extent of agreement or disagreement with a list of statements concerning the issue being studied.[7] The answers to several statements concerning a clothing store's merchandise offering could be scaled as follows:

	Strongly Agree	Agree	Undecided	Disagree	Strongly Disagree
The Castle Shop Stocks a wide assortment of products	(+2)	(+1)	(0)	(−1)	(−2)
Stocks only high-quality products	(+2)	(+1)	(0)	(−1)	(−2)

The responses for each statement are given a numerical weight of either +2, +1, 0, −1, and −2, or 5, 4, 3, 2, and 1. An overall measure of opinion and attitudes is determined either by summing all subjects' responses to a particular statement or by summing one subject's responses for all statements.

One of the most popular scaling instruments in recent years is the semantic differential. The **semantic differential rating scale** is a set of seven-point, bipolar scales that measure the meanings and attitudes that people have regarding some object.[8] The respondent is asked to mark one of seven positions on a scale with ends identified by opposite descriptive terms. For example, the retailer that wants to obtain information concerning the appearance of its store might use the following scale:

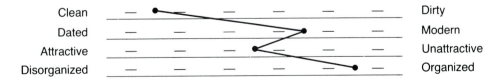

Each position of the semantic scale is assigned a numerical value that can be used to calculate arithmetic means for all respondents' answers to each scale. These figures can be used to profile a store's image, as illustrated by the connected lines.

Wording of questions. If questions are leading, ambiguous, poorly worded, or use a vocabulary with which respondents are unfamiliar, then the resulting answers will not be especially helpful—perhaps even meaningless. To help the researcher avoid wording problems, the following guidelines should be observed:

1. Keep each question as short as possible.
2. Limit each question to one idea.
3. Use simple, concise language.
4. Avoid technical or "buzz" words.
5. Ask questions that have answers the respondent can be expected to know and remember.
6. Ask personal questions in a generalized way.

These guidelines along with common sense will help the researcher avoid many pitfalls in wording questions.

Sequencing of questions. Once the researcher has carefully worded the questionnaire, the next step is to order the questions. To sequence questions, use the following three guidelines:

1. Use an attention getter and an interest grabber for the opening question.
2. Ask general questions first, specific questions last.
3. Place personal questions at the end of the questionnaire.

Order is an important aspect of developing any questionnaire because the sequence can affect the final results.

Sampling Procedures

After selecting the type of research method and the instrument, the retailer must decide on the sampling procedure to use in collecting information. That is, once the retailer has decided "what" information is needed and "how" it is to be obtained, it then must determine "who" to ask to obtain the desired information. The "who" in this case is a **sample,** or some portion of a predefined population. A **population** is the total membership of a defined group of individuals or items. For example, a population could be defined as either all potential consumers or all actual consumers of a particular product. Researchers use samples instead of an entire population because it is too costly and time-consuming to observe or survey an entire population. With proper sampling procedures, the researcher can draw valid conclusions about the attitudes, opinions, makeup, or behavior of the total population without contacting its entire membership. The retailer's sampling procedures follow three essential steps: (1) identifying the sampling frame, (2) determining the size of the sample, and (3) selecting the sample items.

Identifying the sample frame. The first step in sampling is to either create or find a list of individuals included in the defined population being investigated. From this list the sample will be drawn. For example, the list could be names of retail businesses listed in the phone book, names and addresses of all adults (aged 18 and over) living within a defined trading area, or a list of a store's credit card holders. The sample frame must be carefully identified to obtain meaningful and appropriate information.

Determining the sample size. Sample size is the number of people the researcher wants to survey. A large sample normally results in greater accuracy and more reliable information; however, as the size of the sample increases, so do the costs of obtaining the sample. If scientific sampling procedures are followed carefully, small samples such as 400 or 500 people can provide satisfactory results and reliable information. (Almost any marketing research text explains the necessary procedures for calculating the required sample size for a predetermined level of reliability.)

Selecting the sample item. The last sampling procedure is to select the sample, determining how the sample items or individuals are to be chosen. There are two general types of samples—probability and nonprobability. In a **probability sample,** each individual in the total population has a known chance of being selected. In a **nonprobability sample,** each individual in the total population does not have a known and equal chance of being selected, but the researcher controls selection. Whenever possible, the researcher should use a probability sample, because it provides more reliable results and permits the use of more sophisticated analytical techniques. Figure 6–10 identifies and briefly defines the various types of probability and nonprobability samples.

Analyzing Primary Information

The retailer's second major concern in conducting retail research is to analyze the collected information. We cannot describe here all the possible techniques for ana-

---

Probability Samples

1. *Simple random:* A sampling procedure in which one sample is drawn from the entire population, with each individual or item having an equal probability of being selected.
2. *Stratified random:* A sampling procedure in which the population is first subdivided into groups based on some known and meaningful criteria (e.g., sex, age). Then a simple random sample is drawn for each subgroup.
3. *Cluster or area:* A sampling procedure in which geographical areas (e.g., census tracts or blocks) are randomly selected. Then a simple random sample is used to select a certain number of individuals or items (e.g., houses) from each of the selected geographical areas.
4. *Systematic:* A sampling procedure in which the first individual or item of a sampling frame is selected randomly. Then each subsequent individual or item is selected at every *n*th interval (e.g., every fifth item on the list).

Nonprobability Samples

1. *Convenience:* A sampling procedure in which each sample individual or item is selected at the convenience of the researcher (e.g., whoever walks in the store).
2. *Judgment:* A sampling procedure in which each sample individual or item is selected by the researcher based on an idea of what constitutes a representative sample (e.g., every seventh person who walks past the display counter).
3. *Quota:* A sampling procedure in which the researcher divides the total population into several segments based on some factor believed to be important (e.g., sex and age). Then the researcher arbitrarily selects a certain number (quota) from each segment (e.g., selects five females over age 40, five females under age 40, five males over age 40, and five males under age 40).

FIGURE 6–10
Types of probability and nonprobability samples

lyzing information, but Figure 6–11 identifies the basic approaches researchers use to analyze information.

Researchers use summarization procedures to simplify and organize information into meaningful descriptive measurements. **Statistical inferences** are used to make interpretations from a sample about the total population under study. **Bayesian analysis** attempts to combine managerial judgment and objective information to assess dollars-and-cents consequences of alternative decisions. **Mathematical programming** involves the use of mathematics to find optimal solutions to problems, whereas **simulation** uses mathematics to develop models of retailing situations and to provide solutions "by inserting various values of parameters and observing results."[9] A more complete description of each of these approaches together with their respective techniques can be found in most marketing research textbooks.

ELECTRONIC DATA PROCESSING SYSTEM

Processing information is the third basic activity of the retailing information system. An integral part of this processing activity is the **electronic data processing system (EDPS)**. Electronic data processing is that part of the information processing system built around a computer. As illustrated in Figure 6–12, the EDPS consists of three basic elements: the input, the computer, and the output. The computer's ability to process large volumes of data with incredible speed and accuracy makes it a valuable tool. Properly used, electronic data processing can be extremely efficient for many retail operations.

The Input

Any system must have the right input in the right form with the right directions if it is to produce the desired results. This is especially true when putting data into the computer. The input element of an EDPS requires the retailer to carefully select and prepare the data and provide the computer with instructions on exactly what to do with the data.

The data selected as input depend on the retailer's needs. Before feeding any data into the computer, the retailer must clearly identify what information is needed, for what purpose, when, and in what form. If the retailer has clearly identified the

FIGURE 6–11
Processing techniques for information analysis

1. Summarization procedures
    Percentages
    Measures of central tendency
    Trend analysis (time series)
	4. Mathematical programming
	    Linear programming
	    Nonlinear programming
	    Critical path scheduling

2. Statistical inference
    Estimation
    Hypothesis testing
    Analysis of associative data
	5. Simulation
	    Micro models
	    Organization models
	    System models

3. Bayesian analysis
    Prior
    Preposterior
    Posterior	

Source: Keith K. Cox and Ben M. Enis, *The Marketing Research Process* (Pacific Palisades, CA: Goodyear Publishing, 1972), 351.

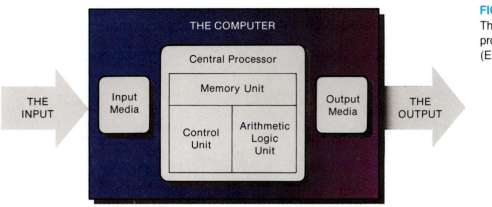

FIGURE 6–12
The electronic data processing system (EDPS)

problem, data selection has already been predetermined. The actual data to be put into the EDPS can come from any of the previously discussed sources—retail intelligence, retail research, internal records, or analytical models. After the right data have been selected, they must be prepared to meet the input requirements of the computer.

The computer is fussy. It will accept only data in its own machine language. The basic machine languages of the computer consist of binary numbers—various combinations of ones and zeros. To communicate with the computer, several binary arrangements are substituted for numbers, letters, and other special characters. After the data are transformed into machine language, the next step is to feed the data into the computer. The data can be fed into the computer in batches or in a continuous fashion (real time). In **batch processing** the retailer waits until considerable amounts of data have been collected and then processes the entire batch at one time (e.g., at the end of the day or week). **Real-time processing** involves continuous feeding of data from input devices connected directly to the computer. It allows immediate processing of all data.

Regardless of the processing method, all input must be accompanied by instructions to the computer about what to do with the data. In many cases these instructions simply ask the computer to recall earlier, more detailed instructions. Instructions to the computer are in the form of computer programs that the retailer can write or obtain as part of a "software package" from either the manufacturer of the computer or various software firms. Computer programs are written in a number of languages. Figure 6–13 describes some of the more common languages.

The Computer

The heart of the electronic data processing system is the computer, an information processing machine. For a computer to be functional, it must consist of three hardware components: an *input medium* for feeding information into a *central processor unit* (CPU) that stores and manipulates information and an *output medium* for delivering the results (see Figure 6–12).

Based on the number of input and output devices that can be handled simultaneously, the amount of storage or memory, and the speed of processing, computers fall into three categories. (1) **Mainframe computers** are large machines with large CPUs and vast amounts of memory. They can handle a large number of terminals simultaneously and have incredibly fast processing speeds. (2) **Microcomputers** are small personal computers with self-contained CPUs and a single, attached input

Small computers have been multiplying like frenzied gerbils in recent years, and so have computer languages, the stuff from which all computer programs are built. Lest you sound ignorant next time the cocktail-hour conversation turns to the latest in software, here's a brief rundown on some of the most popular languages.

ALGOL. ALGOrithmic Language. Granddaddy of 'em all, ALGOL has been around for years and is said to be particularly well suited to number-type applications. Numerous "improvements" on this program have been written over the years, some of them of dubious utility. However, one computer jock referred to ALGOL 60 (written in 1960, in case you wonder) as "a great improvement on all its successors."

APL. A Programming Language. APL was designed for mathematical applications. It uses a lot of symbols that permit complex instructions to be economically expressed. Statements that might take dozens of lines in other languages can be squeezed into one in APL. Widely available on mainframe computers, it is seldom used on microcomputers.

BASIC. Beginners' All-purpose Symbolic Instructional Code. BASIC, originally developed at Dartmouth College for instructional purposes, has become the language most widely used on microcomputers.

COBOL. COmmon Business Oriented Language. Originally developed by the Department of Defense, COBOL is used around the world for business applications such as accounting, bookkeeping and inventory control.

In itself an admirably no-nonsense language, COBOL unfortunately inspired would-be computer comedians to come up with numerous lame puns as names for their own languages, such as CUBOL (Computer Usage Business Oriented Language) and the unbelievably tortured SNOBOL (StriNg Oriented symBOlic Language). These in turn gave rise to such gems as LISP (LISt Processing), PRONTO (PROgram for Numerical Tool Operation) and MUMPS (Multi-User Multi-Processing System).

FORTRAN. FORmula TRANslator. One of the earliest computer languages, FORTRAN was originally developed to make it easier to program complex scientific and engineering equations, although it's been used at one time or another for just about everything. Considered a bit old-fashioned by the avant-garde of the computer world, FORTRAN nonetheless has the advantage of being the closest thing the data processing biz has to a universal language.

PASCAL. Named for Blaise Pascal, the famous mathematician and philosopher. The comer among computer languages. Pascal may soon become more popular than BASIC. Powerful and versatile, it is said to be extremely easy to learn, although you'd never know it from looking at a program.

In a quote from a book on Pascal, it read: "FORTRAN has the rugged simplicity of a Model T Ford, and BASIC displays a childlike naivete, but Pascal exhibits the elegant simplicity that derives from economy and rightness of concept." Uh-huh.

PL/1. Programming Language 1 is a name universally regarded as an example of typical IBM arrogance, inasmuch as hundreds of languages preceded it. It must be admitted, however, that something called Programming Language 143 lacks something in the way of snappiness. PL/1 is IBM's attempt to combine the business capabilities of COBOL with the mathematical finesse of FORTRAN.

Source: Ed Zohi, "Let's Get Down to BASICs." Reprinted with permission of *Advertising Age,* 14 Nov. 1983. Copyright Crain Communications Inc.

FIGURE 6–13
Common computer languages

terminal. While these home computers have limited memory and processing speeds, they nevertheless have many of the processing capabilities associated with mainframes. Use ranges from sophisticated desktop computers to portable typewriter-size models. (3) **Minicomputers** are medium-sized computers designed for business use. They are capable of handling several terminals. Minis have memory and processing speeds sufficient for most small business systems.[10]

Computers can accept data via punched cards, punched paper tapes, magnetic tapes, teletypes, and optical scanners. Thus, the input medium can be any one or combination of the following: card readers, tape readers, teletypewriters, and wand readers.

The central processor consists of three basic units: a memory unit for internal storage of data and instruction, an arithmetic logic unit for making the necessary mathematical computations, and a control unit for guiding the operations of the other two units. The principal output media available to the retailer are those that produce printouts and visual displays. Output in the form of punched cards and magnetic tapes also is available for storing data for future use.

The output from the EDPS should be meaningful information. The whole purpose of an EDPS is to process raw data into useful information. The application of electronic data processing to the retailer's merchandising and operating activities can be quite extensive, depending on the retailer's willingness to invest in the equipment, facilities, and personnel necessary for its operation.

Computer Applications in Retailing

"The computer has been used to improve retailers' inventory control, payroll, general ledger, merchandise reporting, purchase order management and accounts payable."[11] In addition to these conventional uses of the computer in retailing operations, "there are numerous innovative applications that can help the retail manager exploit market opportunities."[12] Some of the more innovative applications include the following:

- **Electronic point-of-sale systems** involve cash registers that allow the retailer to quickly transcribe, validate, and collect sales information that ties specific purchases to certain consumers, thereby improving its segmentation strategies.
- **Electronic funds-transfer systems** allow customers to use a bank card in making purchases by electronically transferring funds from their account to the store's account[13]; these transactions (size and nature) can be linked to demographic and psychographic information and used by the retailer in developing target market strategies.
- **Electronic pushbutton questionnaire systems** involve the use of a computer to conduct in-store customer surveys. One such system is TELLUS, which allows the retailer to conduct surveys on performance levels, store image, and other consumer perceptions.

Retailing opportunities created by innovative computer-based technologies include the following:

- Advanced teleshopping systems will enable consumers to sit at home and use their video screens and keypads to select merchandise, arrange for payment, and express satisfaction/dissatisfaction to channel members after purchase.
- Centralized retail establishments will allow consumers to shop at home or in electronic malls and receive overnight delivery.
- Buyers in centralized offices will be able to randomly ask consumers about their opinions on new fashions and other trendy merchandise.
- Complete customer profiles, both demographic and psychographic, could be keyed with major purchasing habits by product class and brand to provide the ultimate in direct marketing promotion.
- The delivery of retail repair services will become more productive when electronic and mechanical products are diagnosed in the home over phone lines connected to retailers' diagnostic computers.

☐ With the proliferation of electronic media, retailers will be excluded from mass market advertising blitzes; consumers could request and prescreen product information from a "retailer service bureau" that will rate each retailer.

☐ Retailers will service customers twenty-four hours a day, thereby eliminating the "hours of operation" limitation; retailers will provide consumers with the ability to shop at their leisure.

☐ Shopping motives will change as electronic technology eliminates or equalizes certain retail attributes; consumers' perceived images of retailers will be based on product assortment and price.[14]

SUMMARY

Information is the key to reducing the risks associated with retail decision making and problem solving. Retailers need to know what information they need, what information is available, how to gather information, where to obtain information, and how to use information once it has been obtained.

The retailing information system consists of four basic activities: locating, gathering, processing, and utilizing information. Locating information requires the retailer to be acquainted with the various types (primary and secondary) and sources (external and internal) of information. In gathering information, the retailer engages in the four basic activities of retail intelligence, retail research, records search, and constructing analytical models. Having located and gathered the necessary information, the retailer then processes it, using either manual or electronic data processing techniques. Each of the three preceding steps is useless unless the retailer utilizes the information in daily operations.

Retail intelligence is any method or combination of methods used to obtain external secondary information. The principal sources of retail intelligence are libraries, government publications (e.g., census and registration information), association information (trade and professional organizations), and commercial providers (those that make a business out of collecting, analyzing, and reporting information).

Retail research uses a set of scientific procedures to gather external primary information from consumers, suppliers, and competitors. These scientific procedures are best described in the five stages of the scientific method: (1) identifying problems, (2) developing hypotheses, (3) collecting information, (4) analyzing information, and (5) drawing conclusions. Collection of primary information is accomplished using research methods such as surveys, observations, and experiments. Sampling procedures are crucial in conducting primary retail research. The retailer must develop the skills for identifying the sample frame, determining the sample size, and selecting the sample item. The last issue in retail research is analyzing primary information; summarization procedures, statistical inferences, Bayesian analysis, mathematical programming, and simulation all are used in the analysis process.

Electronic data processing systems are computer-based procedures for analyzing information. The retailer requires sound input, computer, and output systems to process information effectively.

KEY TERMS AND CONCEPTS

analytical models

batch processing

Bayesian analysis

dichotomous question

electronic data processing system (EDPS)

electronic funds-transfer systems

electronic point-of-sale systems

electronic pushbutton questionnaire systems

experimentation	purchase intercept technique (PIT)
external information	rank-ordered question
internal information	real-time processing
Likert's summated rating scale	records search
mainframe computer	retail intelligence
manual data processing	retail research
mathematical programming	retailing information system (RIS)
microcomputer	sample
minicomputer	scientific method
multiple-choice question	secondary information
narrative projection test	semantic differential rating scale
nonprobability sample	sentence-completion test
observation	simulation
open-ended questionnaires	statistical inferences
population	survey
primary information	thematic apperception test
probability sample	word-association test

REVIEW QUESTIONS

1. Define RIS. What are the four basic activities of an RIS?
2. Compare and contrast secondary and primary information. What are their relative advantages and disadvantages?
3. Compare and contrast external and internal sources of information.
4. Identify and define the four information-gathering methods.
5. What are the two types of systems used in processing information? Briefly describe each.
6. How do the two general forms of commercial sources of retail intelligence differ?
7. What are the five stages of the scientific method? Describe the major task to be accomplished in each stage.
8. What are the three basic methods of collecting external primary information? Define each method.
9. Characterize the personal interview process. How should a personal interview be conducted?
10. How do mail surveys differ from personal and telephone surveys?
11. How are mail surveys administered?
12. Develop a graphic presentation of the three experimental designs used by researchers.
13. Describe the four open-ended or projective techniques for collecting primary information.
14. Develop a questionnaire that explores why a consumer has selected a particular product brand. Use each of the three types of closed-ended questions in developing your questionnaire.
15. What guidelines should be followed to avoid the many pitfalls in wording questionnaire items?
16. How should questions be sequenced?
17. What is a sample frame?
18. Describe briefly the various types of probability and nonprobability samples.
19. In an EDPS, what is the difference between batch and real-time processing?
20. Compare and contrast the mainframe computer, microcomputer, and minicomputer.
21. What is TELLUS?

ENDNOTES

1. Robert F. Lusch, "Recent Retailing Texts: A Comparative Review," *Journal of Marketing* 43 (Fall 1979): 152.
2. "New Focus on Marketing," *Stores* (September 1986): 44.
3. Alvin Toffler, *Future Shock* (New York: Random House, 1970).
4. Shelby H. McIntyre and Sherry D. F. G. Bender, "The Purchase Intercept Technique (PIT) in Comparison to Telephone and Mail Surveys," *Journal of Retailing* 62 (Winter 1986): 364.
5. Ibid.
6. See Sharon L. Hollander, "Projective Techniques Uncover Real Consumer Attitudes," *Marketing News,* 4 Jan. 1988, 34.
7. See R. A. Likert, "A Technique for the Measurement of Attitudes," *Archives of Psychology* 140 (1932).
8. See C. E. Osgood, C. J. Suci, and P. H. Tannenbaum, *The Measurement of Meaning* (Urbana, IL: University of Illinois Press, 1957); William Mindak, "Fitting the Semantic Differential to the Marketing Problem," *Journal of Marketing* 25 (April 1981): 28–33.
9. Keith D. Cox and Ben M. Enis, *The Marketing Research Process* (Pacific Palisades, CA: Goodyear Publishing, 1972): 350.
10. See Antonia Stone, "Getting Out of the Maze—A Basic Primer Cuts Through the Jargon," *Advertising Age,* 11 April 1983, M42; "A Glossary of Computer Terms," *Advertising Age,* 11 April 1983, M42.
11. Duane L. Davis and Mary Joyce, "Some Retailers Snooze, While Others Use New Technologies to Gain Marketing Edge," *Marketing News,* 22 November 1981, 1.
12. Ibid.
13. See Paul A. Suneson and Ernest R. Cadotte, "Research Suggests Automated Polling Machines Yield Reliable and Valid Data," *Marketing News,* 6 Jan. 1984, 8.
14. Davis and Joyce, "Some Retailers Snooze," 17.

RELATED READINGS

Achabal, Dale D., and McIntyre, Shelby H. "Information Technology Is Reshaping Retailing." *Journal of Retailing* 63 (Winter, 1987): 321–325.

Albaum, Gerald. "Do Source and Anonymity Affect Mail Survey Results." *Journal of the Academy of Marketing Science* 15 (Fall, 1987): 74–81.

Bennett, Amanda. "Once a Tool of Retail Marketers, Focus Groups Gain Wider Usage." *The Wall Street Journal,* 3 June 1986, 33.

Bolger, Joseph P. "Dealing with the Micro Computer Revolution at J. C. Penney." *Retail Control* (October 1984): 40–49.

"Electronicstore Debuts." *Marketing News,* 24 May 1985, 1, 42.

Greenwald, Mathew, and Katosh, John P. "How to Track Changes in Attitudes." *American Demographics* (August 1987): 46–47.

Hawes, Jon M., Varble, Dale L., and d'Amico, Michael F. "Increasing Mail Survey Response Rates." In *Developments in Marketing Science, Proceedings,* edited by N. K. Malhotra, 394–98. Academy of Marketing Science, 1985.

Holbrook, Morris B. "On the Importance of Using Real Products in Research on Merchandising Strategy." *Journal of Retailing* 59 (Spring 1983): 4–20.

Horr, David A., and Barker, William E. "Choosing Your First Computer System." *Retail Control* (March 1984): 46–54.

Joseph, Anthony M. "EPP Strategies: New Options, New Challenges." *Retail Control* (August 1983): 44–64.

Langer, Judith. "Getting to Know the Customer Through Qualitative Research." *Management Review* (April 1987): 42–46.

Lillie, John M. "A CEO's Perspective on the Changing Role of MIS." *Retail Control* (September 1987): 1–10.

McFarlan, F. Warren. "Information Technology Changes the Way You Compete." *Harvard Business Review* 12 (May–June, 1984): 98–103.

McFarlan, F. Warren. "The Computer: Your Strategic Business Weapon." *Retail Control* (February 1986): 2–28.

Malhotra, Naresh K. "Modeling Store Choice Based on Censored Preference Data." *Journal of Retailing* 62 (Summer 1986): 128–44.

Prasad, V. Kanti, Casper, Wayne R., and Schieffer, Robert J. "Alternatives to the Traditional Retail Store Audit: A Field Study." *Journal of Marketing* 48 (Winter 1984): 54–61.

Schulz, David P. "EFTS Status Report." *Stores* (March 1985): 61–63.

Seiberling, Steve, Taylor, Steve, and Ursic, Michael. "Open Ended Question V. Rating Scale: An Empirical Comparison." In *Developments in Marketing Science, Proceedings,* edited by J. C. Rogers, III, 440–45. Academy of Marketing Science, 1983.

"Toffler on Marketing." *Marketing News,* 15 March 1985, 1, 30–31.

Tse, David K. C. "Retail Store Image Research—A Critical Review." In *Developments in Marketing Science, Proceedings,* edited by J. C. Rogers, III, 28–33. Academy of Marketing Science 1983.

Zikmund, William G. *Exploring Marketing Research,* 2d ed. New York: The Dryden Press, 1985.

PART THREE
Appraising the Retailer's Resources

7

Outline

THE RETAILER'S FINANCIAL RECORDS

THE RETAILER'S FINANCIAL STATEMENTS
The Income Statement
The Balance Sheet
The Financial Status Checklist

PERFORMANCE ANALYSIS
Operating Ratios
Financial Ratios

CAPITAL MANAGEMENT
Capital Requirements
Types of Financing
Sources of Funding

EXPENSE MANAGEMENT
Expense Classification
Expense Allocation
Expense Budgeting

Objectives

☐ Defend the need for fiscal control as an essential ingredient in any successful retail operation.

☐ Identify and define the basic financial records required to accomplish fiscal control.

☐ Discuss the concept of profit and its impact on retailing activities.

☐ Prepare a basic income statement for a retailing enterprise.

☐ Prepare a basic balance sheet for a retailing enterprise.

☐ Analyze and evaluate the operational and financial performance of a retail firm.

☐ Explain how to generate and maintain sufficient capital to conduct a retail business.

☐ Describe the procedures for managing the retailer's operating expenses.

Financial Management: Managing and Controlling the Retailer's Finances

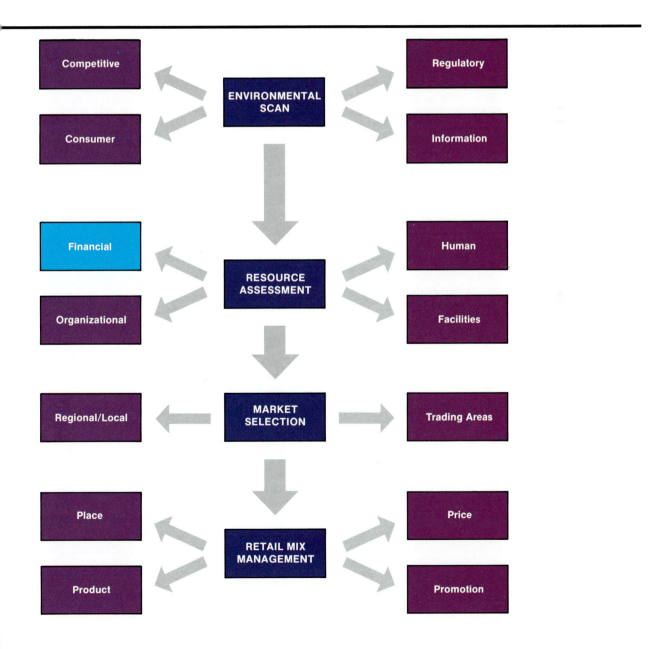

Fiscal control is an essential ingredient to the success of any retail operation. To develop and maintain a viable retail enterprise, the retailer must control the financial health of the firm. Many retailers encounter financial trouble in spite of respectable sales volumes. A common cause of such trouble is insufficient planning and control of the firm's financial affairs. Before the retailer can improve operations, it must be fully aware of the present state of operations. This chapter examines the retailer's financial system. As Figure 7–1 illustrates, the retailer's financial system consists of (1) developing and maintaining good financial records, (2) preparing and analyzing financial statements, (3) constructing and evaluating financial performance ratios, (4) obtaining and managing capital funds, and (5) planning and controlling operating expenses. Each of these tasks is examined in this chapter.

THE RETAILER'S FINANCIAL RECORDS

Size and operational complexities of the retail firm determine the type and level of sophistication of the financial record keeping system the retailer uses. Most retailers, however, maintain a number of ledger accounts. "An **account** is a record of the increases and decreases in one type of asset, liability, capital, income, or expense. A book or file in which a number of accounts are kept together is a **ledger** [emphasis added]."[1] The following basic ledger accounts or records are fairly standard:

- ☐ Cash receipts—record the cash received
- ☐ Cash disbursements—record the firm's expenditures
- ☐ Sales—record and summarize monthly income
- ☐ Purchases—record the purchases of merchandise bought for processing or resale
- ☐ Payroll—records the wages of employees and their deductions, such as income tax and social security
- ☐ Equipment—records the firm's capital assets, such as equipment, office furniture, and motor vehicles
- ☐ Inventory—records the firm's investment in stock, needed to arrive at a true profit on financial statements and for income tax purposes
- ☐ Accounts receivable—record the balances that customers owe to the firm
- ☐ Accounts payable—record what the firm owes its creditors and suppliers[2]

THE RETAILER'S FINANCIAL STATEMENTS

To gain a clear picture of the firm's financial position, the retailer must prepare two standard financial statements: the income statement and the balance sheet. The **income statement** (also referred to as the profit and loss statement, operating statement, or earnings statement) is a picture of the retailer's profits or losses over a period of time; it summarizes the firm's income and expenses. The **balance sheet** is a picture of the firm's assets, liabilities, and net worth on a given date; it summarizes the basic accounting equation of assets equal liabilities plus net worth.

The Income Statement

To understand fully the many dimensions of profit, the retailer must have some procedure for organizing these dimensions. The retail accounting procedure known as the income statement is an excellent means for organizing and understanding the many facets of profit. The income statement summarizes the retailer's financial activity for a given period. The principal objective of the income statement is to show whether the retailer had a profit or a loss. Before examining the various considerations in preparing an income statement, we shall first review the basic profit concept.

FIGURE 7–1
The retailer's financial system

The Profit Concept

The concept of profit is viewed in many different ways. It can be thought of as (1) the money the retailer gains over time as the result of buying and selling activities; (2) the retailer's reward or return for ideas, work, and investment; (3) the means of assuring the long-term continuation of the retailer's business; (4) the measure of the retailer's success; (5) what the retailer must pay income tax on; and (6) the performance criterion by which the retailer can be judged or evaluated.

The term *profit* is a relative word that can be determined and expressed in a variety of ways, depending on the context in which it is used. For example, profit can be expressed as either operating or net profit, dollar or percentage profit, or before- or after-tax profit. Also, profit can be expressed in relation to sales, selling space, number of transactions, net worth, and average inventory investment.

Preparation of the Income Statement

Time, unit, and usage are three important variables retailers must consider in preparing the income statement. *Time* considerations concern when income statements are prepared. Federal and state income tax regulations require that the retailer prepare at least an annual income statement. By preparing the income statement more frequently, however, the retailer can maintain closer control over operations.

Unit considerations influence how many income statements are prepared and at what organizational level. For the small, independent retailer, a single income statement should suffice for the entire store. For a departmentalized chain store operation, income statements are prepared for the department and store unit as well as for the entire chain organization. As with more frequent preparation, greater control of operations is the primary advantage of preparing income statements for each of the retailer's operating units.

Usage considerations involve the type of format to use in preparing income statements. A retailer should select an appropriate standardized format, since standardization will allow the retailer to (1) compare current income statements to previous statements and (2) analyze trends in sales, expenses, profits, and losses.

Elements of the Income Statement

Every income statement has at least nine basic elements, regardless of the size, type, or organizational structure of the retail enterprise. Figure 7–2 illustrates the nine elements and the relationships among them, and it shows that the elements of an income statement can be divided into two major groups: income measurements and income modifications.

Income measurements are different expressions of the monetary gain the retailer realizes from retailing activities. The exact nature of each income measure-

FIGURE 7–2
Elements of the income statement

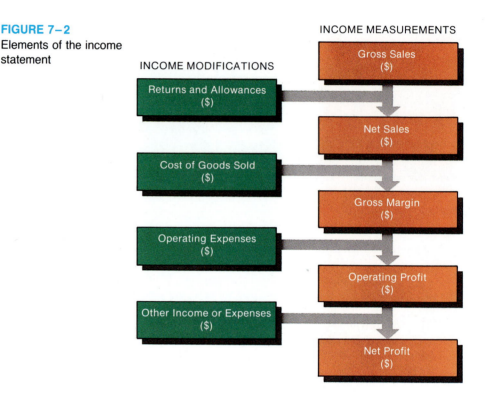

INCOME MODIFICATIONS | INCOME MEASUREMENTS

Gross Sales ($)

Returns and Allowances ($)

Net Sales ($)

Cost of Goods Sold ($)

Gross Margin ($)

Operating Expenses ($)

Operating Profit ($)

Other Income or Expenses ($)

Net Profit ($)

ment depends on where it appears in the income statement and the income modifications that have been applied in calculating it. Figure 7–2 shows five income measurements—gross sales, net sales, gross margin, operating profit, and net profit. In essence, each income expression represents the monetary gain the retailer realizes before making certain adjustments.

Income modifications are monetary additions or reductions applied to one income measurement to calculate another measurement of income. These income modifications simply reflect normal adjustments required by the operating characteristics of the retailer. Most income modifications are reductions; they represent the various costs the retailer incurs in conducting the business, and they are necessary to arrive at the retailer's true income—the bottom line of the income statement or net profit before taxes. In one case, an income modification represents an addition to a measurement of income. This "other income" usually represents income the retailer generates outside normal retailing activities. As illustrated in Figure 7–2, there are four general income modifications—returns and allowances, cost of goods sold, operating expenses, and other income or expenses.

The basic format for the income statement is shown in Figure 7–3. The retailer must carefully follow the format to maintain the correct relationships between the basic statement elements.

Gross sales. Gross sales can be defined as the total dollar revenues the retailer receives from the sale of merchandise and services. The gross sales figure, which includes both cash and credit sales, is obtained by first posting in a sales ledger all cash and credit sales at the price actually charged customers, then totaling those sales for the appropriate accounting period. The gross sales figure is the starting point from which all other income measurements are calculated. This figure is important be-

FIGURE 7–3
Format of the income
statement

```
Gross sales ................................... $_____
    — Returns and allowances .... $_____
Net sales ...................................... $_____
    — Cost of goods sold ......... $_____
Gross margin ................................. $_____
    — Operating expenses ....... $_____
Operating profit ............................. $_____
    ± Other income or expenses .. $_____
Net profit before taxes ..................... $_____
```

FIGURE 7–3
Format of the income
statement

cause it reflects the total dollar amount that not only must cover all of the retailer's costs of doing business but also must provide a reward (profit) for conducting that business.

To better understand the gross sales figure, many retailers calculate a number of ratios and make a number of comparisons. The relationship of gross sales per square foot or per employee can greatly enhance the retailer's understanding of its sales picture and the operation's efficiency.

While gross sales relationships provide insight into the retailer's operations, these insights can be greatly enhanced by comparing the gross sales figure with both internal and external records. For example, by comparing current gross sales figures with the same figures for previous accounting periods, the retailer can identify sales gains or losses as well as any emerging sales patterns or trends. By examining trade data, the retailer can also compare its gross sales performance with that of similar retail operations.

Returns and allowances.   Not all customer purchases are finalized with the initial sale. Some customers will become dissatisfied with their purchases and will expect the retailer to make some sort of adjustment. **Returns from customers** and **allowances to customers,** two means by which retailers adjust for customer dissatisfaction, represent cancellation of sales; therefore, the gross sales figure must be adjusted to reflect the cancellations. While some returns and allowances are expected, excessive returns and allowances can be a major problem.

Returns and allowances can be expressed in percentage terms and compared with previous years or with industrywide averages. The retailer can use the following formula to compute the return and allowance percentage:

$$\text{return and allowance percentage} = \frac{\text{returns and allowances in dollars}}{\text{net sales dollars}}$$

Analyzing returns and allowances is important because it helps the retailer to identify areas of customer dissatisfaction and to prevent additional expenses associated with those returns and allowances.

Net sales.   **Net sales,** the income measurement that results when returns and allowances are subtracted from gross sales, represent the amount of merchandise the retailer actually sold during the accounting period. Most retailers perform the same type of analysis on net sales as they do on gross sales; they calculate net sales per square foot, average net sales, and net sales per employee group. In addition, they make both internal comparisons with past accounting periods and external comparisons with trade averages.

Cost of goods sold.   The value of the merchandise the retailer sells during any given accounting period is the **cost of goods sold.** The cost of goods sold is a function of six factors: beginning inventory, net purchases, transportation charges, ending inventory, cash discounts earned, and alteration and workroom costs. The format for calculating total cost of goods sold is illustrated in Figure 7–4. As shown, the calculating procedures consist of determining total goods handled, gross cost of goods sold, net cost of goods sold, and total cost of goods sold.

The first step in calculating cost of goods sold is to determine the total amount of goods handled during the accounting period. **Total goods handled** is the value of the beginning inventory plus net purchases and transportation charges during the accounting period. **Beginning inventory** is the dollar value of the inventory the retailer has on hand at the beginning of the accounting period (usually the value of the ending inventory for the previous period).

Net purchases are calculated by subtracting from gross purchases the returns to and allowances from suppliers. **Gross purchases** are expressed in terms of "billed costs" to the retailer, and they represent the invoice cost minus any trade and/or quantity discounts granted by the supplier. **Returns to vendors** occur when the retailer returns merchandise to the supplier, and **allowances from vendors** occur when the retailer receives a downward price adjustment from the supplier. **Transportation charges** are costs the retailer incurs in getting the merchandise to the store from the supplier's place of business. In addition to the actual transit charges, handling costs and insurance in transit must be included if the retailer is responsible for these charges.

The second step in calculating cost of goods sold is determining **gross cost of goods sold.** Total goods handled (computed in the first step) minus ending inventory equals gross cost of goods sold (see Figure 7–4). **Ending inventory** is the value of the goods the retailer has on hand at the end of the accounting period; however, the value of the ending inventory may not be worth what the retailer originally paid for it. The value of the ending inventory may have increased or decreased, depending on general marketplace conditions and the retailer's individual operating conditions. For example, increases or decreases in the value of the retailer's inventory will occur as a result of increases and decreases in wholesale prices.

FIGURE 7–4

Calculating cost of
goods sold

```
Opening inventory . . . . . . . . . . . . . . . . . . . . . . ($)
     + Net purchases . . . . . . . . . . . . . . . . . . . . ($)
     + Transportation charges . . . . . . . . . . . . ($)

Total goods handled . . . . . . . . . . . . . . . . . . . ($)
     − Ending inventory . . . . . . . . . . . . . . . . . ($)

Gross cost of goods sold . . . . . . . . . . . . . . . ($)
     − Cash discounts earned . . . . . . . . . . . . ($)

Net cost of goods sold . . . . . . . . . . . . . . . . . ($)
     + Alteration and workroom costs . . . . . ($)

Total cost of goods sold . . . . . . . . . . . . . . . . ($)
```

Ending inventory must be examined to determine its true worth. Incorrect inventory valuation can result in a number of adverse effects. An undervalued ending inventory understates profits for the current accounting period but overstates profits for the next accounting period. An overvalued ending inventory overstates profits for the current accounting period but understates profits of the next accounting period. Incorrect inventory also leads to overpaying or underpaying taxes during a given accounting period.

Several different methods can determine the value of an ending inventory (e.g., cost and retail methods); each of these methods will be discussed in detail in Chapter 18. For present purposes, the objective of any valuation of inventory is to obtain a conservative estimate. Original cost or current market value, whichever is lower, provides the best conservative estimate of inventory. For example, if the ending inventory had cost the retailer $9,000 and the current market value of that inventory is appraised at $11,000, the retailer values it at the lower cost of $9,000. On the other hand, if the current market value has declined to $7,000, then the market value of $7,000 is used.

If cash discounts earned by the retailer are subtracted from gross cost of goods sold, the remainder is **net cost of goods sold** (see Figure 7–4). The retailer earns **cash discounts** if it makes full payment of the invoice within a prescribed period of time. (Chapter 15 discusses cash discounts in detail.) Because cash discounts represent a reduction in the cost of goods sold, they must be deducted from gross cost of goods sold to arrive at the net cost of goods sold.

By adding alteration and workroom costs to net cost of goods sold, the retailer can arrive at the **total cost of goods sold**. Frequently, merchandise must be altered to meet the consumer's needs. This creation of "form utility" by the retailer adds to the cost of the merchandise, and this cost must be included in the calculation of the total cost of goods sold. Alteration and workroom costs include not only materials and labor costs but also operating supplies and expenses directly involved.

Gross margin.   **Gross margin** is defined as the dollar difference between the retailer's net sales and the total cost of goods sold (see Figure 7–3). It represents the funds available for covering operating expenses and generating a profit. Gross margin is sometimes referred to as *gross profit,* although this term is misleading because gross margin dollars might not be sufficient to cover expenses, let alone provide a profit. The relationship between gross margin and cost of goods sold for various kinds of business is shown in Figure 7–5.

Gross margins for department stores averaged about 40 percent of net sales in 1986; specialty stores' gross margins were slightly better at about 41 percent.[3] The best and the worst gross margin performance for various types of merchandise lines within department and specialty stores are shown in Figure 7–6.

Operating expenses.   Every retailer incurs certain expenses (payroll, rent, utilities, supplies, etc.) in operating a business. To realize a profit, the retailer's **operating expenses** must be less than the gross margin figure identified in the previous discussion. Therefore, every retailer must fully understand the management of operating expenses. In 1986, department store's operating expenses were about 34 percent of total store sales; specialty stores tended to have operating expenses that are 2 to 3 percent higher.[4]

Operating profit.   The difference between gross margin and operating expenses is the retailer's **operating profit** (see Figure 7–3). It is what remains after the retailer has covered the cost of goods sold and its cost of doing business. Operating profit defines

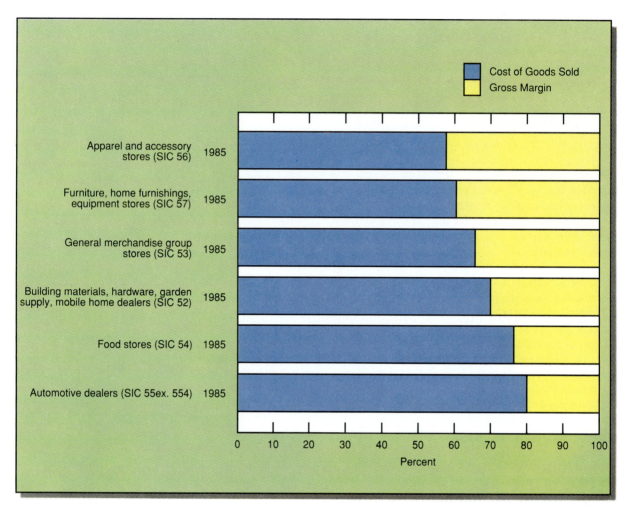

FIGURE 7–5

Estimated gross margin and cost of goods sold as a percentage of sales, by selected kinds of business: 1985 SIC - standard industrial classification. (source: U.S. Department of Commerce, *Current Business Reports,* 1985 Retail Trade, 12)

productivity of the capital and labor invested in the retail store; it is derived from retail management's skill in maintaining a reasonable spread between operating expenses and gross margin.[5] For any given operating unit within the retailer's organization (e.g., a department within a store), operating profit represents the final expression of profit. Operating profit, however, is not the figure that determines the retailer's tax liability; net profit must be determined by considering other income and expenses associated with the operation.

Other income and/or expenses.   The final modification to the income statement is considering other income the retailer receives and other expenses incurred in conducting the business. **Other income** can be defined as additional revenues that result from retailing activities other than the buying and selling of goods and services. Rent from a leased department, interest on installment credit, and interest on deposited bank funds are all examples of other income that must be added to operating profit to obtain the retailer's net profit. Before the retailer can compute the final net sales figure, however, some additional expenses must be deducted from the operating profit figure. Interest paid by the retailer on borrowed funds is an example of **other expenses**.

Department Stores				
Gross Margin				
Rank Best	Net Sales (%)	Rank Worst	Net Sales (%)	
1. Intimate daywear	50.4	1. Audio-visual, musical	15.9	
2. Neckwear, rainwear, belts, handkerchiefs	49.7	2. Home electronics	16.1	
3. Costume jewelry	49.3	3. Photo equipment	16.6	
4. Men's and boys' accessories	49.0	4. Major appliances	20.5	
5. Intimate nightwear	47.9	5. All other merchandise	28.0	
6. Women's small leather goods	47.3	6. Housewares, small appliances	29.6	
7. Ladies' gloves	47.2	7. Books, stamps and coins	30.2	
8. Handbags	46.6	8. Sporting goods	32.6	
9. Loungewear and robes	46.2	9. Toys, hobby goods, games	33.8	
10. Men's and boys' furnishings	46.0	10. Misc. men's and boys' apparel and accessories	35.9	

Specialty Stores				
Gross Margin				
Rank Best	Net Sales (%)	Rank Worst	Net Sales (%)	
1. Intimate daywear	49.8	1. Linens and domestics	37.6	
2. Ladies' gloves	47.8	2. Men's and boys' clothing	38.2	
3. Neckwear, rainwear, belts and handkerchiefs	46.3	3. Girls' clothing, underwear, and accessories	38.2	
4. Costume jewelry	44.9	4. Cosmetics, toiletries and fragrances	38.5	
5. Men's and boys' furnishings	44.4	5. Loungewear and robes	38.8	
6. Hosiery	44.1	6. Infants' and toddlers' apparel and furniture	38.9	
7. Junior sportswear	42.3	7. Junior dresses	39.3	
8. Intimate nightwear	42.2	8. Women's, misses' and junior suits	39.4	
9. Women's and misses' sportswear	41.7	9. Women's and misses' dresses	40.3	
10. Men's and boys' sportswear	41.5	10. Handbags	40.6	
11. Little boys' (ages 4–7) wear	41.5			

Source: David P. Schulz, "New MOR: New Data," *Stores* (January 1988), pp. 124, 126. Reprinted by permission of *Stores*. Copyright by National Retail Merchants Association.

FIGURE 7–6
Gross margins—the best and the worst

Net profit.   **Net profit** is operating profit plus other income and minus other expenses (see Figure 7–3). Net profit is the figure on which the retailer pays income tax, and it is usually referred to either in terms of "net profit before taxes" or "net profit after taxes."

The Balance Sheet

The second accounting statement used in reporting financial information is the balance sheet—a statement of the retailer's financial condition as of a given date. In its most basic form, the balance sheet summarizes the relationship among the retailer's assets, liabilities, and net worth. The following equation shows this basic balance sheet relationship:

$$assets = liabilities + net\ worth$$

The balance sheet is prepared to show what the retailer owns (the amount and distribution of assets), what the retailer owes (the amount and distribution of liabilities), and what the retailer is worth (the difference between assets and liabilities). By comparing the current year's balance sheet to those of previous years, the retailer can identify any changes in the firm's financial position and determine whether any operational improvements are possible.

A typical balance sheet format, illustrated in Figure 7−7, consists of two major parts. The first part lists assets; the second part lists the retailer's liabilities and states the equity position (the net worth of the owners). As Figure 7−7 shows, the total assets figure always equals the sum of total liabilities plus net worth.

The Retailer's Assets

The first part of the balance sheet reports the retailer's asset position. An **asset** is anything of value owned by the retail firm. Assets are categorized into two groups: current assets and fixed assets.

FIGURE 7−7
Balance sheet format

Assets		
Current assets		
Cash	$10,000	
Accounts	15,000	
Merchandise inventory	90,000	
Supply inventory	5,000	
Total current assets		$120,000
Fixed assets		
Building (less depreciation)	75,000	
Fixtures and equipment (less depreciation)	25,000	
Total fixed assets		100,000
Total assets		220,000

Liabilities and net worth		
Current liabilities		
Accounts payable	$25,000	
Payroll payable	10,000	
Taxes payable	5,000	
Notes payable	15,000	
Total current liabilities		$55,000
Fixed liabilities		
Mortgage payable	50,000	
Notes payable	20,000	
Total fixed liabilities		70,000
Net worth		
Capital surplus	85,000	
Retained earnings	10,000	
Total net worth		95,000
Total liabilities and net worth		$220,000

Current assets include all items of value that the retailer can easily convert into cash within a relatively short time, usually within one year or less. In addition to cash on hand, current assets include accounts receivable, merchandise inventory, and supply inventory. Accounts receivable are amounts that customers *owe* the retailer for goods and services. Frequently, the retailer reduces the accounts receivable figure by some fixed percentage (based on past experience) to take into account customers that will eventually default on their payments. The retailer makes this adjustment to avoid overstating assets. The value of the merchandise on hand at the time of preparing the balance sheet is a part of the retailer's current assets. Stating the merchandise inventory in terms of "cost or current market value, whichever is lower" is a more conservative approach that helps the retailer avoid overstating its assets. Supply inventory reflects operating supplies on hand that have been paid for but not used; in effect, they represent prepaid expenses. The retailer arrives at the total current asset figure by totaling cash on hand, accounts receivable, merchandise inventory, and supply inventory (see Figure 7–7).

Fixed assets are those that require a significant length of time to convert into cash (more than one year). These long-term assets include buildings, fixtures (e.g., display racks), and equipment (e.g., delivery trucks). The value of fixed assets is expressed in terms of their cost to the retailer minus an assigned depreciation. This depreciation is necessary because fixed assets have a limited useful life; therefore, depreciation better reflects their true value. The depreciation also helps to avoid overstating the retailer's total assets. Some retailers include a fixed asset value (not illustrated) for such intangibles as goodwill or the store loyalty the retailer has developed. The value assigned to intangible assets is usually minimal.

Total assets equal current assets plus fixed assets (see Figure 7–7).

The Retailer's Liabilities

Part two of the balance sheet reflects the retailer's liabilities and net worth. A **liability** is a debt owed to someone. On the balance sheet, liabilities represent a legitimate claim against the retailer's assets. Liabilities are classified as either current or long-term.

Current liabilities are short-term debts that must be paid during the current fiscal year. Included in the current liabilities column are accounts payable, payroll payable, and notes payable that are due within one year. Accounts payable represent money owed to suppliers for goods and services they have provided. Payroll payable is money owed to store employees for labor performed. Principal and interest the retailer owes on a bank loan (notes payable) and taxes the retailer owes local, state, and federal governments (taxes payable) are classified as current liabilities.

Long-term liabilities are long-term indebtedness. Mortgages and long-term notes and bonds not due during the current fiscal year are the most common long-term liabilities. Another category sometimes treated as a long-term liability is a reserve account to provide the retailer with funds for emergencies. The total liability figure is computed by combining the current and long-term liabilities.

The Retailer's Net Worth

Net worth represents the owner's equity in the retail business and is defined by the following equation:

$$net\ worth = total\ assets - total\ liabilities$$

Another way to look at net worth is to view it as the owner's share of the firm's total assets.

FIGURE 7–8
Financial status check-
list for retailers

Daily
1. cash on hand
2. bank balance (business and personal funds kept separate)
3. daily summary of sales and cash receipts
4. all errors in recording collections on accounts corrected
5. a record maintained of all monies paid out, by cash or check

Weekly
1. accounts receivable (action taken on slow payers)
2. accounts payable (advantage taken of discounts)
3. payroll (records include name and address of employee, social security number, number of exemptions, date ending the pay period, hours worked, rate of pay, total wages, deductions, net pay, check number)
4. taxes (sales, withholding, social security, etc.) paid and reports to state and federal government completed on time

Monthly
1. all journal entries classified according to like elements (these should be generally accepted and standard for both income and expense) and posted to general ledger
2. income statement for the month available within a reasonable time—usually 10 to 15 days following the close of the month
3. balance sheet accompanying the income statement, showing assets (what the business has), liabilities (what the business owes), and the investment of the owner
4. bank statement reconciled (that is, the owner's books are in agreement with the bank's record of the cash balance)
5. petty cash account in balance (that is, the actual cash in the petty cash box, plus the total of the paid-out slips that have not been charged to expense, total the amount set aside as petty cash)
6. all federal tax deposits, withheld income and FICA taxes, and state taxes made
7. accounts receivable aged—i.e., 30, 60, 90 days, etc., past due (all bad and slow accounts pursued)
8. inventory control worked to remove dead stock and order new stock (What moves slowly? Reduce. What moves fast? Increase.)

Source: Adapted from John Cotlon, *Keeping Records in Small Business,* Small Marketers Aids No. 155 (Washington, D.C.: Small Business Administration, May, 1974), 8.

The Financial Status Checklist

To achieve sound fiscal control over the retail operation, the retailer must maintain accurate and timely records and statements. Figure 7–8 illustrates a **financial status checklist** of the kinds of financial information retailers need and how frequently (daily, weekly, and monthly) they should compile this information. By carefully checking the status of each financial record on a frequent, regular basis, retailers can identify problem situations and take the necessary action to correct or eliminate them.

PERFORMANCE ANALYSIS

The income statement and the balance sheet provide the retailer with a wealth of data. To convert these data into meaningful information, retailers rely on **ratio analysis**—an examination of the relationship between elements in the income statement and/or the balance sheet. A number of different ratios and relationships can assist retailers in appraising the firm's past and present performances and can provide some insight into the firm's future performances. By making comparisons among the firm's past ratios and the ratios of similar national and local firms, the retailer can constructively evaluate the firm's performance. Ratios can be grouped into two general categories: operating ratios and financial ratios.

Operating Ratios

Operating ratios express relationships between elements of the income statement. They are used to judge how efficiently the retailer generates sales and manages expenses. To obtain operating ratios, one element of the retailer's income statement must be divided by another element and multiplied by 100. To illustrate the use of operating ratios, we use Figure 7–9. This figure uses information from an income statement (see Figure 7–9a) to calculate several operating ratios (see Figure 7–9b)

FIGURE 7–9
The use of operating ratios

(a) 1986 Income Statement: The Smart Shop

Gross sales		$220,000
− Returns and allowances	$ 4,000	
Net sales		$216,000
− Cost of goods sold	$104,000	
Gross margin		$112,000
− Operating expenses	$ 80,000	
Operating profit		$ 32,000
+ Other income	$ 1,000	
− Other expenses	$ 3,000	
Net profit		$ 30,000

(b) 1986 Operating Ratios The Smart Shop

Ratio	Calculation	Interpretation
$\dfrac{\text{Gross sales}}{\text{Net sales}}$	$\dfrac{\$220,000}{\$216,000} \times 100$	Gross sales equal 102 percent of net sales.
$\dfrac{\text{Cost of goods sold}}{\text{Net sales}}$	$\dfrac{\$104,000}{\$216,000} \times 100$	Cost of goods sold equals 48.1 percent of net sales.
$\dfrac{\text{Gross margin}}{\text{Net sales}}$	$\dfrac{\$112,000}{\$216,000} \times 100$	Gross margin equals 51.9 percent of net sales.
$\dfrac{\text{Operating expenses}}{\text{Net sales}}$	$\dfrac{\$ 80,000}{\$216,000} \times 100$	Operating expenses equal 37 percent of net sales.
$\dfrac{\text{Operating profit}}{\text{Net sales}}$	$\dfrac{\$ 32,000}{\$216,000} \times 100$	Operating profit equals 14.8 percent of net sales.
$\dfrac{\text{Net profit}}{\text{Net sales}}$	$\dfrac{\$ 30,000}{\$216,000} \times 100$	Net profit equals 13.9 percent of net sales.

that show the basic relationship between net sales and (1) gross sales, (2) cost of goods sold, (3) gross margin, (4) operating expenses, (5) operating profit, and (6) net profit. By making historical comparisons with past years, the retailer can detect any positive or negative changes that might be significant in judging operating efficiency. Comparisons with trade data allow the retailer to determine whether significant differences exist between its operation and national operating norms.

Financial Ratios

Financial ratios express relationships between the elements of a balance sheet or between a balance sheet element and an element in the income statement. These ratios are used to identify relative strengths and weaknesses in the retailer's financial status and to discover trends that will affect future performance capabilities. Liquidity, leverage, and profitability ratios are the three key financial areas of concern.

Liquidity Ratios

Liquidity determines whether the retailer can meet payment obligations as they mature. It is the state of possessing sufficient liquid assets that can be quickly and easily converted to cash to meet scheduled payments or to take advantage of special merchandising opportunities. **Liquidity ratios** answer the question of "how solvent is the retailer?" The current ratio and the quick ratio are the two most common measures of a retailing enterprise's solvency or insolvency.

The **current ratio** represents the retailer's ability to meet current debts with current assets; it is computed by dividing current assets by current liabilities (see previous definitions of current assets and liabilities). While the desired current ratio will depend on the nature of the retailer's operation (i.e., high volume, high turnover operations do not require as high a ratio as low volume, low turnover retailers), a current ratio of 2:1, $2 of current assets to $1 of current liabilities, is the most common benchmark used in retailing. Low current ratios suggest liquidity problems; high ratios indicate good long-term solvency. If a retailer's current ratio is too high, however, it might indicate that management is not using its assets to their fullest potential.

The **quick ratio** is a more severe measure of the retailer's liquidity position. It measures the retailer's ability to meet current payments with assets that can be immediately converted to cash. To calculate the quick ratio (also referred to as the acid test), simply divide the firm's quick assets by its current liabilities. Quick assets include cash, readily marketable securities, notes receivable, and accounts receivable.[6] Typically, a quick ratio of 1:1 is deemed satisfactory for most retailing organizations.

Leverage Ratios

Owner financing versus creditor financing is addressed by leverage ratios. A **leverage ratio** measures the relative contributions of owners and creditors in the financing of the firm's operations. One type of leverage ratio is the **debt ratio**—total debt (current plus long-term liabilities) divided by total assets (current plus fixed assets). The higher the ratio, the greater the role of creditors in the firm's total financing. Within reason, owners like to limit their own financial investment; hence they prefer high debt ratios while creditors prefer the lower risks associated with more moderate debt ratios.

To compare what the retail firm owes to what it owns, management can compute the **debt/net worth ratio**—a measure of the retailer's ability to cover both creditor and owner obligations in case of liquidation. Total debt divided by tangible net worth equals the debt to net worth ratio (i.e., current liabilities plus long-term liabilities minus capital plus capital stock plus earnings surplus plus retained earnings minus intangible assets).[7] Higher debt/net worth ratios result in greater risk to creditors and greater difficulty for owners in securing credit. A high ratio suggests possible undercapitalization and overextension in terms of credit.

Profitability Ratios

An overall assessment of a retailer's performance in terms of profit can be obtained from the **Strategic Profit Model (SPM)**. The SPM is

$$\frac{\text{profit}}{\text{margin}} \times \frac{\text{asset}}{\text{turnover}} = \frac{\text{return on}}{\text{assets}} \times \frac{\text{financial}}{\text{leverage}} = \frac{\text{return on}}{\text{net worth}}$$

where **profit margin** is net profit (after taxes) divided by net sales. This ratio measures the after-tax profit per dollar of sales. **Asset turnover** is net sales divided by total assets. This ratio measures the productivity of the firm with respect to asset utilization. **Return on assets** is net profit (after taxes) divided by total assets. This ratio measures the return on all funds invested in the firm by both owners and creditors. **Financial leverage** is total assets divided by net worth. This ratio is a measure of the relative owner/creditor contributions in the firm's capital structure. **Return on net worth** is net profit (after taxes) divided by net worth. This ratio measures the return on funds invested in the firm by its owners.

Profitability goals can be established by setting a target rate of return on net worth. Profit performance can be judged by how well the firm achieves its targeted return. What constituted a high performer in the retail industry has varied considerably over the last few decades; the definition of high performance increased from 4.4 percent return on net worth in 1960 to 10.0 percent in 1980.[8] To improve its return on net worth ratio, a retailer can strive to improve profit margins, increase asset turnover rate, or seek higher leverage ratios.

A widely used source of financial ratios are those reported by Dun & Bradstreet in its publication *Industry Norms and Key Business Ratios*. An example of these ratios is shown in Figure 7–10. These key performance measurements help the retailer make meaningful comparisons between the firm's financial performance and the national median performance of similar retailers. These ratios are also useful in establishing realistic financial objectives.

CAPITAL MANAGEMENT

A major concern of every retailer is how to create and maintain sufficient capital to conduct business. Careful financial planning and control are means to alleviate this concern. Few retailers, if any, have enough money available at all times to finance daily business operations and meet long-term investment requirements. Hence, the retailer's ability to *obtain* money and to secure *credit* is essential to sustaining a healthy financial situation.

Capital management involves planning and controlling the retailer's **equity capital** (what the retailer owns) and **borrowed capital** (money the retailer has obtained from outside sources). The following discussion examines the retailer's capital requirements, types of retail financing, and various sources of funds.

Capital Requirements

A retailer needs money for a variety of purposes. **Fixed capital** is money needed to purchase such physical facilities as buildings, fixtures, and equipment. This type of

	SIC 5271 Mobile Home Dealers (no breakdown)		SIC 5311 Department Stores (no breakdown)		SIC 5331 Variety Stores (no breakdown)		SIC 5399 Misc Genl Mdse Stores (no breakdown)	
	1986 (1205 Estab)		1986 (1032 Estab)		1986 (810 Estab)		1986 (2160 Estab)	
	$	%	$	%	$	%	$	%
Cash	49,667	10.0	103,633	9.3	23,136	12.5	28,211	12.5
Accounts receivable	34,270	6.9	199,465	17.9	4,072	2.2	17,152	7.6
Notes receivable	5,463	1.1	6,686	0.6	740	0.4	1,580	0.7
Inventory	246,845	49.7	499,219	44.8	113,830	61.5	113,296	50.2
Other current	23,840	4.8	50,145	4.5	4,627	2.5	8,802	3.9
Total current	360,086	72.5	859,148	77.1	146,406	79.1	169,041	74.9
Fixed assets	57,117	11.5	118,119	10.6	20,545	11.1	27,985	12.4
Other noncurrent	79,467	16.0	137,062	12.3	18,139	9.8	28,663	12.7
Total assets	496,671	100.0	1,114,329	100.0	185,090	100.0	225,689	100.0
Accounts payable	21,357	4.3	110,319	9.9	22,581	12.2	21,666	9.6
Bank loans	5,960	1.2	18,944	1.7	2,221	1.2	2,708	1.2
Notes payable	51,157	10.3	41,230	3.7	6,848	3.7	6,996	3.1
Other current	185,258	37.3	117,005	10.5	18,879	10.2	21,215	9.4
Total current	263,732	53.1	287,497	25.8	50,530	27.3	52,586	23.3
Other long term	59,104	11.9	160,463	14.4	26,098	14.1	23,472	10.4
Deferred credits	4,967	1.0	2,229	0.2	—	—	—	—
Net worth	168,868	34.0	664,140	59.6	108,463	58.6	149,632	66.3
Total liab & net worth	496,671	100.0	1,114,329	100.0	185,090	100.0	225,689	100.0
Net sales	1,151,895	100.0	1,605,242	100.0	354,211	100.0	388,734	100.0
Gross profit	245,354	21.3	569,861	35.5	117,952	33.3	120,896	31.1
Net profit after tax	31,101	2.7	32,105	2.0	17,711	5.0	17,882	4.6
Working capital	96,354	—	571,651	—	95,876	—	116,455	—

Ratios	UQ	MED	LQ	UQ	MED	LQ	UQ	MED	LQ	UQ	MED	LQ
Solvency												
Quick ratio (times)	0.5	0.2	0.1	2.4	1.2	0.4	1.3	0.4	0.2	2.6	0.9	0.3
Current ratio (times)	1.8	1.3	1.1	6.2	3.2	2.1	6.7	3.4	2.1	9.7	4.1	2.1
Curr liab to nw (%)	57.1	156.7	353.6	15.8	38.5	85.4	15.3	37.5	91.6	7.9	23.5	63.7
Curr liab to inv (%)	80.8	103.6	121.7	29.8	54.0	86.7	19.0	36.9	60.5	15.6	37.0	68.9
Total liab to nw (%)	86.0	197.6	410.2	19.7	64.4	151.9	19.3	55.6	146.9	11.7	34.5	99.6
Fixed assets to nw (%)	16.8	38.1	77.4	6.7	19.9	54.2	7.3	18.4	40.2	6.5	18.6	45.8
Efficiency												
Coll period (days)	3.7	8.3	21.7	8.9	30.1	57.9	1.5	4.0	10.7	3.3	10.1	24.1
Sales to inv (times)	5.9	4.2	2.9	6.2	4.6	2.9	5.3	3.6	2.4	7.1	4.2	2.5
Assets to sales (%)	29.4	43.4	71.2	39.2	50.6	69.1	32.3	44.5	65.2	30.0	47.4	77.6
Sales to nwc (times)	30.3	13.4	6.1	6.2	3.9	2.6	6.9	4.1	2.7	7.4	4.2	2.3
Acct pay to sales (%)	0.5	1.1	2.8	2.6	4.7	7.5	3.0	5.0	8.8	1.8	3.9	7.4
Profitability												
Return on sales (%)	5.6	2.2	0.5	4.2	1.8	0.2	8.2	4.1	1.5	8.0	3.0	0.7
Return on assets (%)	8.2	3.3	0.3	6.9	3.6	0.5	16.2	8.3	2.8	13.7	6.0	1.5
Return on nw (%)	32.9	11.7	1.5	13.2	6.7	1.1	31.6	15.9	5.8	23.1	9.7	2.5

Source: *Industry Norms and Key Business Ratios.* (1986–87 Edition) © Dun and Bradstreet Credit Services, 1987)

FIGURE 7–10
The ratios of retailing

capital requirement represents long-term investments that tie up capital for extended periods. **Working capital** is money needed to meet day-to-day operating costs. It is used to pay the rent and utility bills, to purchase inventories, and to cover payroll expenses. **Liquid capital** is money held in reserve for emergency situations, usually in the form of cash or disposable securities (e.g., stocks, bonds, certificates of deposit).

The amount of fixed, working, and liquid capital required by a particular retail operation is a function of the size and nature of that operation. Capital requirements for larger retailers are greater than those for smaller retailers, other things being equal. Upscale retail operations featuring complete product assortments, plush facilities, personal selling, and many services have a greater need for capital than retailers offering limited product assortments, spartan facilities, and limited services.

In planning capital requirements for *existing* operations, a retailer can consult past company records and adjust for anticipated additional needs for capital. For the *new* retail establishment, estimating capital requirements presents greater problems. Given the lack of any previous company records, the new retailer must rely on outside sources of information (e.g., financial institutions, trade associations, and the Small Business Administration).

Types of Financing

The first step a retailer takes in securing capital funds is determining what kind of money is needed. The retailer's purpose for the money (e.g., for use as fixed, working, or liquid capital) determines the type of financing. There are three types of financing: short-, intermediate-, and long-term credit. **Short-term credit** is money the retailer can borrow for less than one year. Lending institutions provide retailers with short-term loans primarily for working capital. For example, banks extend short-term credit to retailers to purchase next season's inventory. In such cases, the loans are self-liquidating because they generate sales dollars. **Intermediate-term credit** usually is offered for periods longer than one year but less than five years. Retailers secure such loans to finance smaller, fixed capital expenditures (e.g., fixtures and equipment). **Long-term credit** takes the form of loans that retailers secure for periods greater than five years. Typically, retailers use long-term financing to purchase major fixed capital investments such as buildings and land. For both intermediate- and long-term credit, the retailer must make periodic installment payments (monthly, quarterly, or annually) from earnings.

Sources of Funding

To obtain funds, retailers can turn to a number of sources, including equity, vendors, lending institutions, and the government. Determining which source to use depends on the type of financing the retailer needs, the nature and size of the business, and the retailer's particular financial condition. Most retailers find it necessary to tap several sources of funds.

Equity sources of funds are obtained by selling part ownership in the business. Equity sales allow the retailer to raise funds without borrowing money or having to pay interest and repay a loan. Investors in a retail business are individuals willing to accept a certain amount of risk (i.e., the amount of their investment) for potential long-term gains. Before selling equity shares, however, the retailer should determine how much control over the business would be relinquished by making the sale.

Vendors, who supply retailers with merchandise, are frequently used as sources for short-term credit. This form of "trade credit" is made available by vendors when they extend dating terms—the amount of time the retailer has to pay the net invoice price for a shipment of merchandise. By extending dating terms to 60, 90, and even 120 days, the vendor is effectively financing the retailer's inventory for that period. Favorable dating terms often give the retailer time to sell the merchandise before having to pay for it.

Lending institutions are sources of short- and long-term retail financing. Commercial banks, credit associations, and insurance companies are the most common lending institutions willing to make loans to credit-worthy retailers. When lending institutions make short-term working capital loans, they expect repayment immediately after they have served the purpose for which the loan was made. For example, a seasonal inventory loan must be repaid at the end of the season. The lender carefully specifies repayment and other terms associated with fixed capital loans in written contractual agreements.

Commercial lending institutions make both secured and unsecured loans. Retailers with good credit ratings can often get unsecured loans on their signature alone. To obtain outside institutional financing, the retailer must demonstrate good knowledge of business trends, possess reliable sales forecasts, have a keen appreciation of the marketplace, and produce superb merchandising plans.[9] Figure 7–11 identifies the various methods by which a loan can be secured.

Government sources of funds are usually the only viable alternative for the small retailer whose credit rating is either uncertain or not established. The Small Business Administration (SBA) was established to provide consulting services for small business enterprises on a number of business activities. The SBA also is entrusted with the responsibility of making available financial resources for small businesses, including retailers, that have exhausted all other avenues (e.g., traditional sources such as banks) for financing. The SBA provides financing by acting as a (1) "guarantor," guaranteeing a loan made by a bank to a retailer, or (2) "lender," directly lending money to retailers when local banks will not.

EXPENSE MANAGEMENT

Expense management is the planning and control of operating expenses. To ensure an operating profit, operating expenses must be less than the retailer's gross margin. The retailer that fails to plan and control operating expenses risks losing financial control over an important segment of the business. Expense management entails three basic planning and control activities: classifying expenses, allocating expenses, and budgeting expenses.[10]

Expense Classification

All planning and control activities require careful identification and classification of every relevant factor. Hence, the first step in expense management is to recognize the various costs of doing business and to classify these costs into logical groupings based on some common feature. In retailing, four fundamental perspectives on operating expenses will lead to different classifications. They are sales, control, allocation, and accounting perspectives.

Sales Perspective

One way to look at operating expenses is to see how such expenses are affected by sales. From a sales perspective, operating expenses are classified as fixed and variable. **Fixed expenses** are usually fixed for a given period of time (e.g., the life of a contract, or a planning or operating period). Expenses are classified as fixed when they remain the same regardless of the sales volume. As sales increase or decrease, fixed expenses remain constant.

Endorser	A third party signs a note to bolster the retailer's credit. If the retailer fails to pay the note, the bank expects the endorser to make the payments.
Comaker	A third party creates an obligation jointly with the retailer. The bank can collect directly from either the retailer or the comaker.
Guarantor	A third party guarantees the payment of a note by signing a guaranty commitment.
Assignment of leases	An arrangement in which the bank automatically receives the rent payments from a leasing agreement made between a retailer and a third party. Used in franchising to finance buildings.
Warehouse receipts	An arrangement in which the bank accepts commodities as security by lending money on a warehouse receipt. Such loans are generally made on staple merchandise that can be readily marketed.
Floor-planning	An arrangement in which banks accept a trust receipt for display merchandise as collateral. Used for securing loans on serial-numbered merchandise (automobiles, appliances, boats). When the retailer signs a trust receipt, it (1) acknowledges receipt of the merchandise, (2) agrees to keep the merchandise in trust for the bank, and (3) promises to pay the bank as soon as the merchandise is sold.
Chattel mortgage	An arrangement in which the bank accepts a lien on a piece of new equipment as security for the loan needed to buy the equipment.
Real estate	An arrangement in which the bank accepts a mortgage on real estate as collateral for a loan.
Accounts receivable	An arrangement in which the bank accepts accounts receivable (money owed the retailer) as collateral for a loan. Under the *notification plan* the retailer's customers are informed by the bank that their accounts have been assigned to the bank and all payments are made to the bank. Under the *nonnotification plan,* the retailer's customers are not informed of the assignment to the bank. The customer continues to pay the retailer who, in turn, pays the bank.
Savings accounts or life insurance	An arrangement in which the bank extends a loan to a retailer that assigns to the bank a savings account or the cash value of a life insurance policy as collateral.
Stocks and bonds	An arrangement in which the bank accepts as collateral marketable stocks and bonds. Usually the bank will accept as collateral only a certain percentage of the current market value of the stock or bond.

Source: Adapted from *ABCs of Borrowing,* Management Aids No. 170 (Washington, D.C.: Small Business Administration, April, 1977) 2–3.

FIGURE 7–11
Methods for securing a retail loan

Expenses that vary with the volume of sales are called **variable expenses**. As sales increase or decrease, variable expenses also increase or decrease. Although the relationship between sales and expenses is not always directly proportional, they are sufficiently related that the retailer can reasonably predict changes in operating expenses. By being attentive to specific relationships between a variable expense and sales, the retailer can identify opportunities for increasing profits. For example, initial increases in advertising expenditures could increase sales to such a degree that profit increases are greater than the advertising expense.

Control Perspective

The second way to look at operating expenses is to see whether a particular expense is controllable. As the name implies, **controllable expenses** are those over which the retailer has direct control. Retailers can adjust these expenses as warranted by operating conditions. For example, part-time help can be reduced during slack sales periods.

Uncontrollable expenses are outlays over which retailers have no control and that, in the short run, they cannot adjust to current operating needs. Expenses incurred as a result of long-term contractual arrangements are uncontrollable over the short run. Given their adaptability, controllable expenses should be the focus of the retailer's attention. Daily or weekly monitoring of these expenses helps maintain operating expenses at acceptable levels.

Allocation Perspective

In using the allocation perspective, the retailer looks at operating expenses to see if they can be directly attributed to some operating unit. Many retailers find it useful for purposes of analysis and control to allocate operating expenses to various operating units, such as store units or departmental units.

Under this approach, retailers classify operating expenses as either direct or indirect expenses. **Direct expenses** are those directly attributable to the operations of a department or some other defined operating unit. If the retailer eliminated a department or unit, then the direct expenses associated with that department would also be eliminated. Salaries and commissions of departmental sales personnel are examples of direct expenses. Expenses not directly attributable to the operations of a department are classified as **indirect expenses**. These costs cannot be eliminated if a particular department is dropped. Indirect expenses are general business expenses a retailer incurs in running the entire operation.

Accounting Perspective

A final way to look at operating expenses is to classify them into well-defined groups that the retailer can use to identify year-to-year trends for each expense class and to make comparisons with trade averages of similar retailers. This expense classification system helps the retailer to identify, analyze, and initiate controls for expenses that are out of line with either last year's figures or those of similar retailers. Using the accounting approach, the retailer can classify operating expenses using either a natural division of expenses or expense-center accounting.

Using the **natural division of expenses,** the retailer classifies expenses on the basis of the kind of expense each is, without regard for (1) which store functions (e.g., selling, buying, or receiving) incurred the expense, or (2) where (e.g., store or department) the expense was incurred. The natural division method of expense classification is used primarily by small- and medium-sized retailers looking for simple yet acceptable means of classifying expenses. The natural classification of expenses as recommended by the National Retail Merchants Association appears in Figure 7–12.

The second accounting method for classifying operating expenses is **expense-center accounting**. An expense center is a functional center within the store's operation or a center of a certain store activity. The center incurs expenses in the process of providing its assigned functions or performing its required activities. Expense-center accounting is a system of classifying operating expenses into such functional

Natural Division 01—*Payroll*

Includes all items of compensation for services actually rendered by employees of a company—wages, salaries, commissions, promotion money, bonuses, prizes, and vacation, sick, and holiday payments.

Natural Division 02—*Allocated Fringe Benefits*

Includes a transfer account to allocate fringe benefits out of their appropriate expense centers to all other expense centers with a payroll natural division.

Natural Division 03—*Media Costs*

Includes all cost of media—the cost of newspaper, periodical, program, streetcar and billboard space, the cost of radio and television time, and the cost of direct mail advertising.

Natural Division 04—*Taxes*

Includes all state and local taxes (excluding taxes based on income), unemployment, social security and disability taxes, and government license fees.

Natural Division 06—*Supplies*

Includes the cost of items consumed in the operation of the business—stationery and related items, wrapping, packaging, cleaning, and repairing materials, and heating, cooling, lighting, and other power expenses.

Natural Division 07—*Services Purchased*

Includes charges for all nonprofessional services rendered by outsiders that aid, supplement, or substitute for the normal routine activity of the store—cleaning, delivery, shopping, detective, alarm, armored car, statistical, typing, and collection services.

Natural Division 08—*Unclassified*

Includes all expenses not otherwise classified as chargeable to another natural division.

Natural Division 09—*Travel*

Includes all expenses resulting from domestic (local or out of town) and foreign travel of all employees of the company for business purposes—transportation, hotel bills, meals, tips, and incidentals.

Natural Division 10—*Communications*

Includes all expenses relative to the cost of store and central organization communications—local and long distance telephone services and postage.

Natural Division 11—*Pensions*

Includes all expenses relating to pensions, retirement allowances, pension funds, insured and trusteed plans, and direct payments to retired employees.

Natural Division 12—*Insurance*

Includes the cost of all insurance.

Natural Division 13—*Depreciation*

Includes depreciation of the original cost of the capital assets employed in the operation of the business—building, leasehold improvements, equipment, furniture, and fixtures.

Natural Division 14—*Professional Services*

Includes the cost of any service of a highly specialized and professional character furnished by outside organizations—legal, accounting, appraisal, management service, architectural, and survey fees.

Natural Division 16—*Bad Debts*

Includes actual bad debts written off or the provision relating to an allowance for doubtful accounts; it also includes losses due to bad checks and fraudulent purchases, less recoveries.

Natural Division 17—*Equipment Rentals*

Includes the costs of all equipment rented or leased and is restricted to expense centers where equipment represents a significant investment in the center's operations.

Natural Division 18—*Outside Maintenance and Equipment Service Contracts*

Includes the costs of outside contractual arrangements for servicing and maintaining equipment.

Natural Division 20—*Real Property Rentals*

Includes expenses incurred or rent paid for real estate used in the operation of the business.

Natural Division 90—*Expense Transfers In*

Natural Division 91—*Expense Transfers Out*

Natural Division 92—*Credits and Outside Revenues*

Source: Adapted from *Retail Accounting Manual, Revised* (New York: Financial Executives Division, National Retail Merchants Association, 1978), III-3.

FIGURE 7–12
Natural division of expenses

or activity classes as management, direct selling, customer services, and so on. The National Retail Merchants Association has identified 44 major expense centers, shown in Figure 7–13. Expense-center accounting is used most frequently by large, departmentalized retailers.

In using the expense-center accounting system, the retailer follows a two-step procedure. The first step is to classify operating expenses according to natural divisions. The second step is to cross-classify each of the natural expenses with each of the 23 expense centers. As illustrated in Figure 7–14, the retailer can use expense-center accounting to identify, analyze, and control operating expenses either by the kind or type of expense (i.e., natural divisions) or by the function or activity that incurred the expense (i.e., expense center). Typically, the expense-center accounting system provides greater detail in classifying operating expenses than do other methods. After operating expenses have been classified, the retailer's second task is to allocate expenses to each of the operating units, such as departments within a store or stores within a chain organization.

A comparative expense distribution between department stores and specialty retailers is shown in Figure 7–15. While several similarities exist, several differences are noteworthy: (1) department store expenses are higher for services/operations, sales promotions, and merchandise receiving/storage, and (2) specialty stores spent a greater percentage on property/ equipment, company management, and accounting/management information systems.[11]

Expense Allocation

The small retailer views operating expenses from the standpoint of the entire store and therefore gives little thought to the problem of allocating operating expenses to various operating units. Because most small retailers operate their businesses as a whole rather than as several individual operating units, there is usually no need for expense allocation. On the other hand, large retailers that are either departmentalized or multiunit (chain) operations have a great need for examining the operating expenses of individual operating units.

Three methods by which retailers allocate operating expenses to operating units are (1) the net profit plan, (2) the contribution plan, and (3) the net profit contribution plan. Figure 7–16 illustrates each of these expense allocation plans. Several points are notable. First, the bottom line for a departmental income statement is its operating profit. However, this profit expression is often referred to as the department net profit. Second, the allocation methods are quite similar; the principal differences are in treatment of indirect expenses and calculation criteria for the operating unit.

Net Profit Plan

When employing the **net profit plan,** the retailer allocates all direct and indirect expenses. Direct expenses are directly attributed to the particular department that incurred them. Indirect expenses are not *directly* attributed to a particular department, but instead are allocated to departments based on a prejudged set of criteria. Figure 7–17 lists common criteria for retailers. To illustrate, the salary of a department manager would be considered a direct expense that could be allocated to the department. The salary of the store manager would be an indirect expense to any given department, however, and the store manager's salary could be allocated to various departments based on each department's percentage of total net sales.

As shown in Figure 7–16, the department's gross margin minus both the department's direct and indirect expenses equals the department's net profit. The treatment of each department as a profit-producing center has the advantage of providing a "hard-figure" (net profit) evaluation of departmental operations and en-

FIGURE 7–13
Major expense centers

010   Property and equipment
  020   Real estate, buildings, and building equipment
  030   Furniture, fixtures, and nonbuilding equipment
100   Company management
  110   Executive office
  130   Branch management
  140   Internal audit
  150   Legal and consumer activities
200   Accounting and management information
  210   Control management, general accounting, and statistical
  220   Sales audit
  230   Accounts payable
  240   Payroll and time-keeping department
  280   Data processing
300   Credit and accounts receivable
  310   Credit management
  330   Collection
  340   Accounts receivable and bill adjustment
  350   Cash office
  360   Branch/store selling location offices
400   Sales promotion
  410   Sales promotion management
  420   Advertising
  430   Shows, special events, and exhibits
  440   Display
500   Service and operations
  510   Service and operations management
  530   Security
  550   Telephones and communications
  560   Utilities
  570   Housekeeping
  580   Maintenance and repairs
600   Personnel
  610   Personnel management
  620   Employment
  640   Training
  660   Medical and other employee services
  670   Supplementary benefits
700   Merchandise receiving, storage, and distribution
  710   Management of merchandise receiving, storage, and distribution
  720   Receiving and marking
  730   Reserve stock storage
  750   Shuttle services
800   Selling and supporting services
  810   Selling supervision
  820   Direct selling
  830   Customer services
  840   Selling support services
  860   Central wrapping and packing
  880   Delivery
900   Merchandising
  910   Merchandising management
  920   Buying
  930   Merchandise control

Source: *Retail Accounting Manual, Revised* (New York: Financial Executives Division, National Retail Merchants Association, 1978), III-3.

FIGURE 7–14

Expense-center ac-
counting system

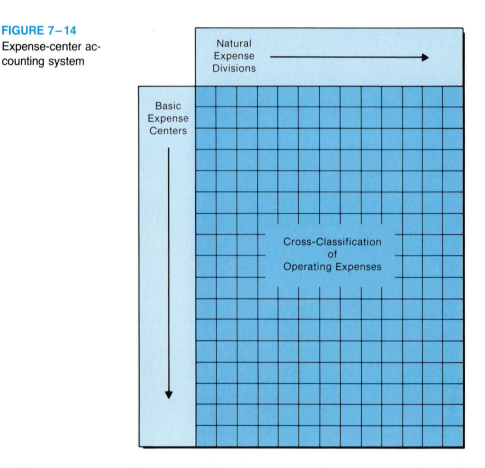

courages each department to be expense-control conscious. On the other hand,
unfair or questionable allocations of indirect expenses to the department can distort
the department's profit picture and create considerable dissatisfaction among departmental managers whose careers are on the line.

Contribution Plan

The **contribution plan** can be characterized as follows: (1) direct expenses are allocated to the departments that incurred them, and (2) indirect expenses are not
allocated to departments, but instead to a general expense account. The department's
contribution is defined as the department's gross margin minus its direct expenses.
Again referring to Figure 7–16, we see that each department is judged on the basis
of its contribution to the store. The sum of the contributions from each department is
treated as a "reservoir" to cover the indirect expenses in the general expense account
and to provide an operating profit for the store.

Net Profit Contribution Plan

Using the **net profit contribution plan,** the retailer calculates both the department's net
profit and its contribution (see Figure 7–16). This plan involves a two-step procedure. First, the department's contribution is calculated by subtracting the department's direct expenses from its gross margin. Second, the department's net profit is
calculated by subtracting the department's indirect expenses from its contribution.

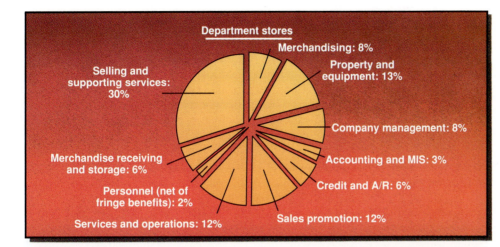

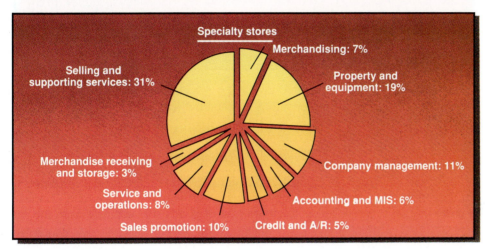

FIGURE 7–15
Expense distribution for department and specialty stores (percentage of total expenses) (source: David P. Schulz, "86: Better for Some," *Stores* [November 1987]: 94. Reprinted by permission of *Stores*. Copyright National Retail Merchants Association)

The combination net profit contribution plan allows examination of departmental performance from both the contribution and net profit perspectives.

Expense Budgeting

An **expense budget** is a plan or a set of guidelines that a retailer uses to control operating expenses. It is an estimate or a forecast of the amount of money needed during a given accounting period to operate the business. Essentially, the expense budget is a continuation of the retailer's total budgetary process. Just as merchandise budgets are developed to plan and control expenditures for merchandise items, the major purpose of expense budgets is to plan and control the amount of money the retailer spends in merchandising those items.

An annual expense budget for the entire store is the normal starting point in expense control. The annual budget is then broken down into monthly and weekly expense plans. While small retailers typically operate on a storewide expense budget, larger departmentalized retailers usually find it necessary to prepare departmental expense budgets separately from the store budget.

In practice, expense budgets should act as a general game plan, not as a straitjacket of unbreakable rules. As a plan of action, budgets must be flexible enough

FIGURE 7–16
Allocating operating
expenses

```
Net profit plan
   Department gross margin ...................................... ($)
     – Direct expenses of the department .......................... ($)
     – Indirect expenses charged to department .................... ($)
   Department net profit ........................................ ($)*

Contribution plan
   Department gross margin ...................................... ($)
     – Direct expenses of the department .......................... ($)
   Contribution of the department ............................... ($)*

Net profit contribution plan
   Department gross margin ...................................... ($)
     – Direct expenses of the department .......................... ($)
   Contribution of the department ............................... ($)*
     – Indirect expenses charged to department .................... ($)
   Department net profit ........................................ ($)*
*Measurement used to evaluate departmental performance.
```

for management to adjust as conditions warrant, but rigid enough to provide meaningful guidance.

One of the first steps in preparing an expense budget is to determine an overall expense figure for the prescribed operating period. This figure is a general estimate of the amount of money the retailer will have available to cover operating expenses. The estimate can be figured simply with these two steps: (1) secure a net sales estimate for the forthcoming period (obtained from the merchandising budget) and (2) make a gross margin estimate by subtracting a cost of goods sold estimate from the net sales estimate. This estimated gross margin represents the amount of money available to cover operating expenses plus achieve an operating profit. By subtracting the desired level of operating profit from gross margin, the retailer has an estimate of money that should be available to cover both fixed and variable expenses. In some cases, retailers take the process one step further. Because fixed expenses are generally known and fairly constant, they are deducted to determine the amount of money that can be allocated to variable expenses.

Several specific budgetary procedures have been developed for expense planning and control. The retailer can elect to use any one of three approaches to expense

FIGURE 7–17
Selected expense-center allocation criteria

Type of Expense	Allocation Criteria
Property and equipment	Weighted floor space
Company management	Net sales
Accounting and management information	Gross sales
Credit and accounts receivable	Number of transactions
Sales promotion	Number of displays
Personnel	Number of employees
Merchandise receiving storage and distribution	Number of invoices
Selling and supporting services	Number of units
Merchandising	Net sales

budgeting: zero-based budgeting, fixed-based budgeting, and productivity-based budgeting.

Zero-Based Budgeting

As the name implies, under **zero-based budgeting,** each operating department or unit starts with no allocated operating expenses. To secure operating funds, each operating department must justify its need for each expense item on the budget. While past expenditures may be considered supporting evidence, management does not accept past expenditures as total justification for future expense allocations. To obtain operating funds, department personnel must use justifications based on current merchandising plans, market conditions, competitive atmospheres, and operating requirements. Although zero-based budgeting is generally time-consuming and costly, it does force each operating department to reevaluate its expenses and to define the needs and benefits that should be derived from each expenditure. Zero-based budgeting is the most appropriate way to establish an expense budget for a new retailer or a new department.

Fixed-Based Budgeting

In the **fixed-based budgeting** process, each expense (e.g., payroll, supplies) is budgeted at a specific dollar amount. The predetermined amount is based on past experience as well as on evaluating the need for incurring the expense in the forthcoming budgeting period. A fixed-based budgeting form is illustrated in Figure 7–18. To facilitate control, the retailer should fill in the form for both the budgeted and the actual expenditure in the current budget period, as well as complete a year-to-date summary.

    The form also provides space for the retailer to report variances between actual and budgeted amounts in both dollars and percentages. Management carefully scrutinizes these variances; when they exceed either a predetermined dollar or percentage amount, the manager of the operating department should examine and correct the situation and submit either a written or oral report to the supervisor. The example in Figure 7–18 shows that the manager of the receiving department appears to be controlling the department's expenses quite adequately. Although the current period

FIGURE 7–18

Fixed-based budgeting form

Period: Third Quarter			Store: 12			Expense Center:	721-Receiving			
Natural Division			**Current Period**				**Year-to-Date**			
			Amount		Variance		Amount		Variance	
No.	Expense		Actual	Budget	Dollar	Percent	Actual	Budget	Dollar	Percent
01	Payroll		4,000	4,000	00	00	12,000	12,000	00	0.0
06	Supplies		1,000	800	(200)	(25)	2,600	2,400	(200)	(8.3)
07	Services Purchased		500	600	100	16.7	1,400	1,800	400	22.2
10	Communications		100	100	00	00	270	300	30	10.0
	Total		5,600	5,500	(100)	1.8	16,270	16,500	230	1.4

Natural Division		Period: April		Store: 12		Expense Center: 410—		Sales Promotion
		Unit Sales						
No.	Expense	500	1000	1500	2000	2500	3000	3500	4000
01	Payroll	$2,000	$2,000	$2,500	$2,500	$3,000	$3,500	$4,000	$4,500
03	Advertising	500	1,000	1,500	2,000	2,500	3,000	3,500	4,000
06	Supplies	500	550	600	700	800	1,000	1,200	1,400
	Total	$3,000	$3,550	$4,600	$5,200	$6,300	$7,500	$8,700	$9,900

FIGURE 7–19
Productivity-based budgeting form

shows the department slightly over budget, the year-to-date expenses are slightly below the budgeted amount.

Productivity-Based Budgeting

Expense budgets based on levels of productivity provide a high degree of flexibility in the budgetary process. Under a **productivity-based budget,** the retailer prepares a series of expense budgets to correspond to various sales levels (or some other productivity measure). As illustrated in Figure 7–19, an increase in unit sales automatically increases the amount budgeted for each item in the department's expense budget. Given that numerous operating expenses are either directly or indirectly related to sales, a budget based on sales productivity should help the retailer make operational adjustments to meet changing market conditions. Some retailers think that a productivity-based budget is the most appropriate approach to expense budgeting, especially when reliable sales estimates are difficult to make or when there is a high likelihood for extreme sales variations. Essentially, this budget approach allows the retailer to allocate limited financial resources based on actual need, as opposed to anticipated requirements.

SUMMARY

A key means of gaining retailing success is fiscal control. To ensure an adequate degree of control over financial affairs, the retailer must develop and maintain a set of financial records that provide a broad picture of the firm's financial condition. A typical set of records includes a separate record for each of the following: sales, cash receipts, cash disbursements, purchases, payroll, equipment, inventory, accounts receivable, and accounts payable. The retailer then uses these records to prepare two essential financial statements: the income statement and the balance sheet.

The income statement summarizes the retailer's financial activity for a stated accounting period. It is prepared to show the profit (or loss) a retailer has made during an accounting period. The income statement is a systematic set of procedures that helps the retailer identify five income measurements: gross sales, net sales, gross margin, operating profit, and net profit.

The balance sheet is a statement of the retailer's financial condition on a given date. It summarizes the basic relationship between the retailer's assets, liabilities, and net worth. The balance sheet gets its name from its principal objective of showing how the sides of the accounting equation (assets = liabilities + net worth) are balanced.

The financial status checklist provides a means for retailers to check the status of each financial record or statement and identify financial problems requiring corrective action.

In performance analysis, the retailer must make judgments on the firm's operating and financial performance. By using several standardized operating and financial ratios, the retailer can compare performance, on either a historical basis or a trade basis, to national norms.

Capital management involves planning of and controlling the retailer's equity capital (what the retailer owns) and borrowed capital (what the retailer owes). A retailer needs money for a variety of reasons, including funds for fixed, working, and liquid capital requirements. The type of financing a retailer needs depends on its capital requirements. Short-term credit is used when the retailer needs working capital, whereas intermediate- and long-term credit are used to meet fixed capital requirements. Equity sales, vendor credit, and loans from lending institutions and government agencies are the major sources of funds for the retailer.

Expense management entails three basic planning and control activities: classifying, allocating, and budgeting expenses. Logical groupings of operating expenses are essential to planning and control. Expenses can be classified on the basis of sales (variable or fixed), control (controllable or uncontrollable), or allocation (direct or indirect) characteristics, and according to accounting procedures (natural division of expenses or expense-center accounting). In departmentalized or chain store organizations, operating expenses must be allocated to various operating units. Expense allocation is accomplished by using the net profit plan, the contribution plan, and the net profit contribution plan. An expense budget is used to plan and control operating expenditures. The retailer can elect to use one of several budgeting procedures: zero-based, fixed-based, or productivity-based.

KEY TERMS AND CONCEPTS

account	direct expenses
allowances from vendors	ending inventory
allowances to customers	equity capital
asset	expense budget
asset turnover	expense-center accounting
balance sheet	financial leverage
beginning inventory	financial ratios
borrowed capital	financial status checklist
cash discounts	fixed asset
contribution plan	fixed-based budgeting
controllable expenses	fixed capital
cost of goods sold	fixed expenses
current asset	gross cost of goods sold
current liability	gross margin
current ratio	gross purchases
debt/net worth ratio	gross sales
debt ratio	income measurements

income modifications	operating ratios
income statement	other expenses
indirect expenses	other income
intermediate-term credit	productivity-based budgeting
ledger	profit margin
leverage ratios	quick ratio
liability	ratio analysis
liquid capital	return on assets
liquidity ratios	return on net worth
long-term credit	returns from customers
long-term liability	returns to vendors
natural division of expenses	short-term credit
net cost of goods sold	Strategic Profit Model (SPM)
net profit	total assets
net profit contribution plan	total cost of goods sold
net profit plan	total goods handled
net purchases	transportation charges
net sales	uncontrollable expenses
net worth	variable expenses
operating expenses	working capital
operating profit	zero-based budgeting

REVIEW QUESTIONS

1. Identify the nine basic ledger accounts.
2. Explain the purpose of an income statement. How does a balance sheet differ from an income statement?
3. List the nine elements of an income statement. Define each element.
4. Outline the steps used in calculating cost of goods sold.
5. Why is a balance sheet prepared?
6. How do current assets differ from fixed assets?
7. How do current liabilities differ from long-term liabilities? Cite examples of each type of liability.
8. Define net worth.
9. What is ratio analysis?
10. What relationships are expressed by operating ratios and financial ratios?
11. How does the current ratio differ from the quick ratio?
12. Describe what a leverage ratio measures.
13. What are fixed, working, and liquid capital needed for?
14. Briefly describe the three types of financing.
15. What are the retailer's primary sources of financing?
16. How can expenses be classified? Identify and define the eight expense classifications.
17. Discuss how large retailers allocate operating expenses to operating units.
18. Identify the three approaches to expense budgeting. Briefly describe each approach.

ENDNOTES

1. Robert C. Ragan, *Financial Recordkeeping for Small Stores,* Small Business Management Series No. 32 (Washington, D.C.: Small Business Administration, 1976): 5.
2. Irving M. Cooper, *Accounting Services for Small Service Firms,* Small Marketers Aids No. 126 (Washington, D.C.: Small Business Administration, March 1977): 3.

3. David P. Schulz, "86: Better for Some," *Stores* (November 1987): 92.
4. Ibid.
5. Ernest H. Risch, "Operating Profit in the Conventional Department Store: A Statistical Prognosis," *Retail Control* (January 1986): 40.
6. See Norman M. Scarborough and Thomas W. Zimmerer, *Effective Small Business Management* (Columbus, OH: Charles E. Merrill, 1988): 170.
7. Ibid., 171.
8. Robert F. Lusch, *Management of Retail Enterprises* (Boston: Kent Publishing Co., 1982): 25.
9. Gordon E. Pillsbury, "Management of Financing," *Retail Control* (February 1986): 54.
10. Nathan Katz, "12 Keys to Effective Expense Control," *Retail Control* (February 1987): 11–21.
11. David P. Schulz, "86: Better for Some," 94.

Abend, Jules. "Increasing Profitability." *Stores* (June 1985): 22–32.
Abend, Jules. "Asset Management Tactics." *Stores* (June 1987): 77–82, 86.
Achabal, Dale D., Heineke, John M., and McIntyre, Shelby H. "Issues and Perspectives on Retail Productivity." *Journal of Retailing* 60 (Fall 1984): 107–27.
Christensen, Kenneth. "Expense Budgeting and Control for Productivity." *Retail Control* (August 1983): 26–37.
Cronin, J. Joseph, Jr., Ingram, Thomas N., and Skinner, Steven J. "The Impact of Financial Conditions on the Relationship Between Margin-Turnover and Profit Performance." In *Marketing Comes of Age, Proceedings,* edited by David M. Klein and Allen E. Smith, 138–41. Southern Marketing Association, 1984.
Cronin, J. Joseph, Jr., and Skinner, Steven J. "Marketing Outcome, Financial Conditions, and Retail Profit Performance." *Journal of Retailing* 60 (Winter 1984): 9–22.
Curhan, Ronald C., Salmon, Walter J., and Buzzell, Robert D. "Sales and Profitability of Health and Beauty Aids and General Merchandise in Supermarkets." *Journal of Retailing* 57 (Spring 1983): 77–99.
Higgins, Robert C., and Kerin, Roger A. "Managing the Growth—Financial Policy Nexus in Retailing." *Journal of Retailing* 59 (Fall 1983): 19–48.
Hise, Richard T., Kelly, J. Patrick, Gable, Myron, and McDonald, James B. "Factors Affecting the Performance of Individual Chain Store Units." *Journal of Retailing* 59 (Summer 1983): 22–39.
Ingene, Charles A. "Labor Productivity in Retailing." *Journal of Marketing* 46 (Fall 1982): 75–90.
Kelly, William D. "An Approach to Expense Control." *Retail Control* (December 1982): 2–8.
Risch, Ernest H. "Operating Profit in the Conventional Department Store: A Statistical Prognosis." *Retail Control* (January 1986): 28–60.
Rizzi, Joseph. "Return on Investment as a Measure of Asset Management." *Retail Control* (September 1983): 20–26.
Schulz, David P. "New MOR: New Data." *Stores* (January 1988): 123–126.
Siegel, Joel G., and Akel, Anthony. "Monitoring the Financial Health of Independent Stores." *Retail Control* (November 1984): 35–42.
Steven, Michael T. "Methods of Analyzing and Improving Store Profitability." *Retail Control* (March 1985): 49–55.
Stevens, Robert E. "Using Accounting Data to Make Decisions." *Journal of Retailing* 51 (Fall 1975): 23–28.
Waybright, George. "GMROI: Get More Return on Investments." *Retail Control* (October 1984): 2–10.

RELATED READINGS

8

Objectives

☐ Develop organizational objectives that can provide focus for the structure and activities of the retail firm.

☐ Identify the organizational tasks necessary to realize the firm's organizational objectives.

☐ Explain the basic principles of organization that are an inherent part of any effective retail structure.

☐ Distinguish among the organizational patterns of various types of retailers.

☐ Write a job description and develop specifications for each position.

☐ Identify potential sources of store employees and describe the criteria and methods for screening job applicants.

☐ Understand and use the basic techniques for matching job requirements with employee attributes.

☐ Specify the different procedures used in training and supervising store personnel.

☐ Discuss when to evaluate, what to evaluate, and how to evaluate employees and their performances.

☐ Evaluate the various methods used in compensating store personnel.

Organization Management: Organizing and Staffing the Retail Firm

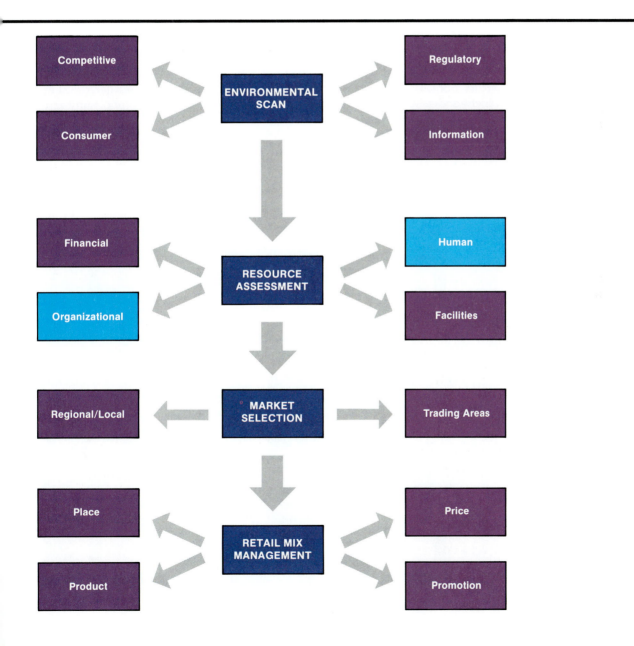

People make a successful business! However, organization is essential to any group of people having a common purpose or goal. Whether the group is an army, a church, a football team, or a retail business, organization is the binding force that coordinates, channels, and propels the group toward its stated mission.

Retailers use a vast number of different organizational structures to organize their people. All retailing organizations, however, incorporate certain common organizational elements and principles structured around one of several basic organizational forms. This chapter examines these organizational elements, principles, and forms, and presents the general organizational patterns that small independent retailers, department store retailers, and chain store retailers use in organizing groups of people. In addition, this chapter looks at the retailer's staffing process. Figure 8–1 illustrates the issues of retail organization and the eight steps of the retail staffing process.

ELEMENTS OF RETAIL ORGANIZATION

The particular organizational foundation a retail firm adopts depends on several factors. Some of these factors are (1) the type of merchandise to be offered, (2) the variety and assortment of the merchandise stocked, (3) the type and number of customer services performed, (4) the type and number of locations used, (5) the availability and quality of personnel employed, and (6) the legal requirements and/or restrictions. Given this vast array of influential factors, the firm's organization must center around specific organizational objectives and tasks.

FIGURE 8–1

The organizational and human resource components of the retailing plan

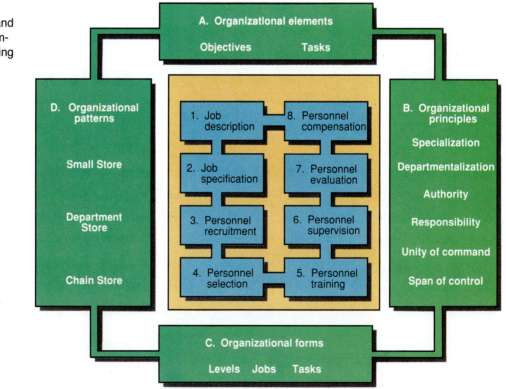

Organizational Objectives

In retailing, the firm's organizational foundation focuses on achieving the firm's objectives. Establishing well-defined organizational objectives is an important step because it forces the retailer to think through what the firm is trying to accomplish, where the firm is going, and how the firm intends to get there. In addition, organizational objectives provide a realistic orientation to the retailer's planning process as well as a means of evaluating the firm's past performance and its current status.

Three levels of organizational objectives correspond to the three general levels of retail management (see Figure 8–2). They are (1) strategic objectives developed by top managers at the strategic level of management, (2) operational objectives identified by middle managers within the administrative level of management, and (3) functional objectives that direct front-line managers at the operational management level.

Strategic objectives are general, long-term goals that the retail firm intends to pursue. Essentially, a strategic objective identifies an overall mission that the firm's management wishes to realize. **Operational objectives** are general, long-term operational requirements necessary to achieve a strategic objective. Operational objectives establish the general framework within which a particular merchandising or operating function can be identified. **Functional objectives** are specific task objectives that

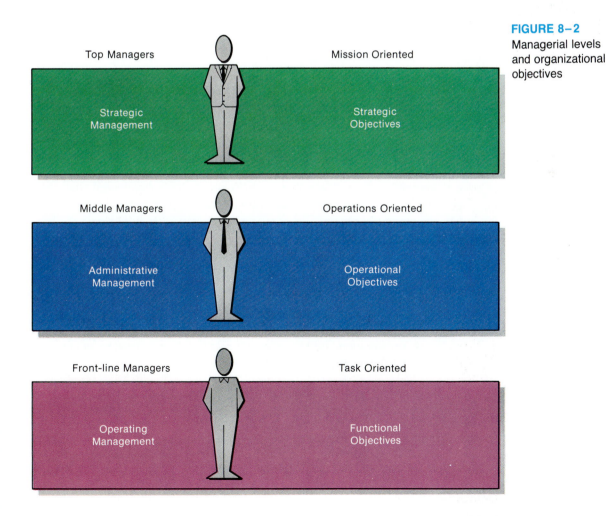

FIGURE 8–2

Managerial levels and organizational objectives

Top Managers   Mission Oriented

Strategic Management   Strategic Objectives

Middle Managers   Operations Oriented

Administrative Management   Operational Objectives

Front-line Managers   Task Oriented

Operating Management   Functional Objectives

Strategic Objectives	Operational Objectives	Functional Objectives
To appeal to the "perfectionist," the "updated," the "traditionalist," and the "establishment" consumer	To offer the "perfectionist" consumer the most advanced fashion apparel	To ensure the "perfectionist" consumer a new and fresh selection of fashionables by stocking only one garment in each size category (e.g., Misses 4–14) and by timing new arrivals every week
	To offer the "updated" consumer new styles that have gained wide acceptance	To ensure the "updated" consumer stylish yet not extreme fashion apparel by stocking a limited selection of last season's perfectionist styles in Misses sizes 4–16
	To offer the "traditionalist" and the "establishment" consumer well-established yet fashionable apparel	To ensure the "traditionalist" and "establishment" consumer a complete selection of stylish yet dignified fashion apparel by stocking a representative offering of well-established designer labels in Misses sizes 8–20

FIGURE 8–3
Examples of organizational objectives

identify a specific function and how it is to be accomplished. The unique value of functional objectives is their quantifiability, which makes them especially useful in planning, executing, and controlling a particular retailing activity. Figure 8–3 provides examples of strategic, operational, and functional objectives for an upscale specialty retailer of women's apparel. The objectives in Figure 8–3 identify not only the target markets, but also how to serve them in terms of product offering and assortment.

Organizational Tasks

In developing the retail organization, the retailer must identify and assign the various tasks necessary to realize the firm's stated organizational objectives. The number of organizational tasks that can be identified is large. Figure 8–4 lists the basic organizational tasks inherent to any retail organization. Although the list of tasks in Figure 8–4 can help a retailer develop a general organizational structure, a more detailed description of tasks must be made in assigning responsibilities and authority to each position in the organization. Additionally, the retailer should develop written job descriptions for each job classification.

PRINCIPLES OF RETAIL ORGANIZATION

There are several basic principles of organization that every retailer should consider in establishing a retail organization. Organizational principles that are particularly appropriate to the retail firm are the principles of specialization and departmentalization, of lines of authority and responsibility, of unity of command, and of span of control. By applying these principles, retailers can avoid managerial confusion and employee discontent.

FIGURE 8–4

Basic organizational
tasks

1. **Operating the store**
   a. Recruiting store personnel
   b. Training store personnel
   c. Supervising store personnel
   d. Planning information systems
   e. Meeting legal obligations
   f. Designing store facilities
   g. Maintaining store facilities
   h. Ensuring store security

2. **Finding the best location**
   a. Analyzing regional markets
   b. Assessing trading areas
   c. Appraising site locations

3. **Developing the merchandise mix**
   a. Determining consumer product needs
   b. Evaluating product alternatives
   c. Planning product-mix strategies
   d. Determining consumer-service requirements
   e. Evaluating service alternatives
   f. Planning service-mix levels

4. **Buying the merchandise**
   a. Identifying sources of supply
   b. Contacting sources of supply
   c. Evaluating sources of supply
   d. Negotiating with sources of supply

5. **Procuring the merchandise**
   a. Ordering merchandise
   b. Receiving merchandise
   c. Checking merchandise
   d. Marking merchandise
   e. Stocking merchandise

6. **Controlling the merchandise**
   a. Planning sales
   b. Planning stocks
   c. Planning reductions
   d. Planning purchases
   e. Planning markups
   f. Planning margins
   g. Controlling inventories
   h. Taking inventory
   i. Valuating inventory
   j. Evaluating inventory

7. **Pricing the merchandise**
   a. Setting prices
   b. Adjusting prices

8. **Promoting the merchandise**
   a. Planning advertising strategies
   b. Selecting advertising media
   c. Preparing advertisements
   d. Designing promotional displays
   e. Planning promotional events
   f. Gaining favorable publicity
   g. Managing the personal-selling effort

Specialization and Departmentalization

Specialization and departmentalization are inherent parts of any efficient retail organizational structure. With job **specialization,** employees concentrate their efforts on a limited number of tasks. Retailers have learned that specialization improves the speed and quality of employee performance.

Departmentalization, an extension of the specialization principle, occurs when tasks and employees are grouped together into departments to achieve the operating efficiencies of specialization for a group performing similar tasks. Specialization and departmentalization can be based on *product type* (such as apparel, home furnishings, and appliances), *activity* (such as buying, selling, and stocking), *activity location* (such as main store, branch store, and warehouse) and *consumer type* (such as household consumer and business customers). In choosing which of these bases to use in departmentalizing the store, a retailer should select the one providing management with the best level of control and producing the highest employee efficiency.

Authority and Responsibility

Lines of authority and responsibility are the organizational principle that each store employee (managerial and nonmanagerial) should be given the authority to accomplish whatever responsibilities have been assigned to that individual. Figure 8–5 demonstrates the relationship between the responsibilities and the authority of a sales manager whose general charge is to direct the customer service, personnel, sales, merchandising, and operations activities of a department to achieve sales goals and to maximize profit. To assume certain responsibilities and accomplish them most efficiently, an employee must be given the necessary authority to call on whatever resources are necessary to complete the task.

An equally important aspect of this principle is that all members of the organization know and respect the established lines of authority and responsibility. A retailer's "chain of command" comprises lines of authority that link together the various managerial levels of the organization. Line and staff relationships are the linkages that join management levels and create organizational hierarchies. **Line relationships** are

FIGURE 8–5
Authority should equal responsibility

Department Sales Manager's Responsibilities	Equals	Department Sales Manager's Authority
1. to ensure that the store's customer service standards and policies are maintained		1. to direct customer service standards and procedures; make customer adjustments
2. to provide (ensure) adequate floor coverage while controlling personnel budgets		2. to assign personnel within area; prepare weekly personnel schedule; request additional personnel
3. to ensure that the physical appearance of the area is visually appealing and orderly		3. to determine the merchandising set-up of area; request the removal or addition of fixtures; request and followup maintenance services
4. to communicate selling trends and other merchandise information to merchants and associates		4. to request sales and merchandising information; analyze current reports and information
5. to supervise the receipt, movement, maintenace, and display of merchandise on the selling floor and in the stockroom area		5. to determine merchandising set-up of selling-floor area; coordinate merchandising set-up of stockroom area; maintain a merchandise-movement information file
6. to ensure that advertised merchandise is available and properly priced, ticketed, and displayed		6. to communicate information about advertised merchandise to Central Stock, Receiving, and/or the merchandising staff; make necessary price and/or ticket changes
7. to shop the competition		7. to visit the competition to determine competitive pricing; communicate and/or adjust price changes for competition
8. to lead, delegate, control, discipline, and train associate employees		8. to establish, monitor, and appraise selling personnel on standards of performance; enforce store policies and procedures; communicate all information pertinent to the department operation
9. to maintain inventory control		9. to inspect and approve all paperwork within area; ensure that adjustments are properly recorded

affiliations among managers at different organizational levels or between a manager and a subordinate within the same level who are directly responsible for achieving the firm's strategic, operational, and/or functional objectives. In a line relationship, the manager has direct authority over the subordinate. On an organizational chart, line relationships typically are shown as solid lines. **Staff relationships** are advisory or supportive and appear on organizational charts as broken lines. Staff employees are typically specialists with expertise in a particular area of concern (e.g., legal affairs, taxation, or market analysis), and their primary function is to assist line managers to realize their objectives. To avoid confusion, duplication of effort, and territorial disputes, an organization needs to distinguish clearly the responsibilities and authority of each line manager and supportive staff.

Unity of Command

The principle of **unity of command** states that the organizational structure of the retail firm should ensure that each store employee should be directly accountable to only one immediate supervisor at any one time for any given task. Most employees find it difficult if not impossible to satisfy several superiors at the same time. It is not unusual for different supervisors to want subordinates to accomplish a particular task in a different way at a different time. The store employee who must serve several masters at one time is often confused, inefficient, and frustrated.

Span of Control

Every organization must determine how many subordinates one person can manage. One rule of thumb suggested by authorities on management is that the ideal number of subordinates ranges from four at the highest levels to twelve at the lowest levels of organization. The principle of **span of control** sets guidelines for the number of subordinates a superior should control, depending on the level within the organization and the nature of the tasks being performed. Three of the guidelines follow:

1. As employees' tasks become more complex and unstandardized, their supervisor's span of control should narrow.
2. Where supervisors and employees are highly competent and well trained, the supervisor's span of control can be broader.
3. Where tasks are highly centralized in one location, a person can supervise more subordinates than if the tasks are scattered throughout a location.

These guidelines suggest the latitudes within which organizers vary the "4–12" rule for supervisors. In retailing, these guidelines can help determine the size of the various merchandising and operating departments and divisions.

FORMS OF RETAIL ORGANIZATION

The organizational structure of the retail firm can assume many different forms. To help employees understand the organizational structure, the retailer prepares organizational charts that show the formal relationships existing between various parts of the organization. Organizational charts also describe the hierarchy of authority, the areas of responsibility, the span of control, the type and degree of specialization and departmentalization, and the reporting relationships among employees at different levels.

In planning an organizational structure, the retailer must ask two critical questions. The first is how many organizational *levels* are needed for effective and efficient operation of the firm; the second, how the various tasks should be organized into *areas of responsibility* (jobs) and how many of these areas should be designated.

Number of Organizational Levels

The number of levels separating the firm's top manager from its lowest-level employee can be viewed as a hierarchy of organizational levels. Firms that limit the number of organizational levels to one or two levels are using a **flat organizational structure** as illustrated in Figure 8–6a. Small, independent retailers and low-margin retailers attempting to keep their operating expenses at the lowest possible level typically use a flat organizational structure. In addition to lower operating expenses, the flat organizational structure allows direct communications with employees, higher employee morale, and quicker reaction time to problems that may arise. A flat organizational structure is often a wide organizational structure, however, which means the supervisor might have too many people to manage at one time.

Vertical, or tall, organizational structures have many layers of supervisor–subordinate relationships. As illustrated in Figure 8–6b, a large number of levels separates top management from employees at the bottom of the organization. Large retailers (e.g., department stores) and multiunit retailers (e.g., chain stores) typically use a taller organizational structure. The impersonal nature, lack of direct communications, and rigidity associated with a large number of organizational levels are the primary limitations of such organizations. These limitations may be offset by

FIGURE 8–6
The number of organizational levels

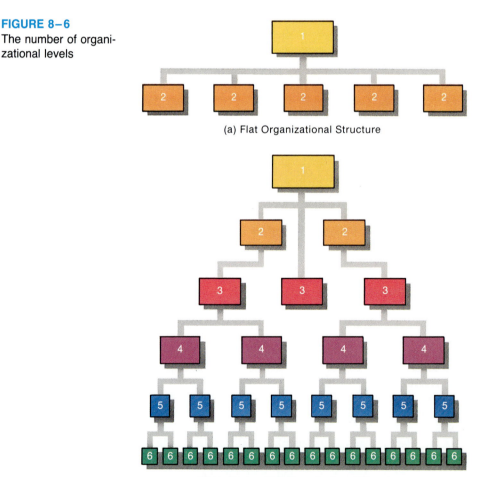

(a) Flat Organizational Structure

(b) Vertical or Tall Organizational Structure

the benefits of having well-defined areas of responsibility and gaining increased supervision over employees and their assigned tasks.

Job and Task Organization

The exact form of organizational structure of any retailer depends on how the retailer classifies jobs that employees must perform. A retailer can classify jobs on the basis of their functional nature, geographic location, product involvement, or some combination of the three. Using the **functional approach** to retail organizational structure, the retailer groups tasks and classifies jobs according to such functional areas as store operations, buying and selling merchandise, promotional activities, or recruiting and training store personnel. In essence, the functional approach is one of task and job specialization in one or more general functions.

Small, independent retailers usually have a two-function organizational structure, thereby limiting specialization. As illustrated in Figure 8–7a, merchandising and store operations are the first two functional divisions that retailers usually create. As their firms become larger and more complex, retailers will create additional functional divisions. In the three-function organizational structure, shown in Figure 8–7b, retailers add a third division to the basic merchandising and operating divisions, typically one of the following: a financial controls division, a sales promotion division, or a personnel division. Although Figure 8–7 illustrates only the two- and three-function organizations, it is not unusual for the retailer to create four, five, or more functional divisions. (Four- and five-function organizations are illustrated and discussed under department store organizational patterns.)

The **geographic approach** to organizational structure is one in which the retailer organizes tasks and assigns jobs on the basis of where those tasks and jobs are performed. Multiunit retailers (such as chain stores) frequently use the geographic

FIGURE 8–7
Functional organizational structures

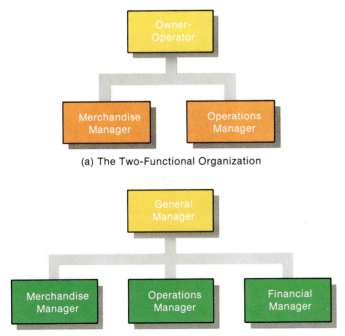

(a) The Two-Functional Organization

(b) The Three-Functional Organization

FIGURE 8–8
Geographic organiza-
tion structure

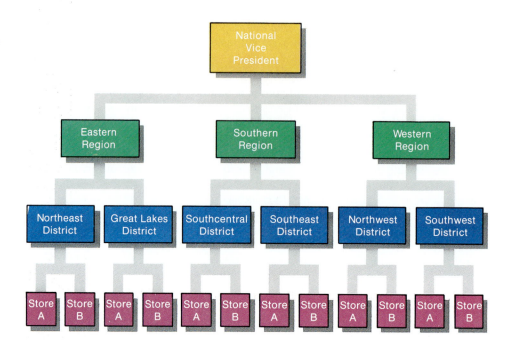

approach. The geographic size of the retailer's market influences both the number of organizational levels and the degree of market specialization at each level. A multiunit retailer with a limited number of stores within a concentrated geographic market usually has only two levels (the main store with several branch stores) and a local market specialization (neighborhood or community). On the other hand, large chain organizations with many stores operating all over the country typically form organizational structures with several levels and various degrees of market specialization. Figure 8–8 illustrates a national retail firm that uses the geographic approach of organization.

In the **product approach** to retail organizational structure, the retailer organizes the store by product line. This organizational form centers around task and job specialization to meet the consumers' buying needs for certain products. For many shopping and specialty goods, for example, consumers think, shop, and buy in terms of product groupings. Figure 8–9 illustrates a family apparel store organized around the general product lines of women's, men's, and children's apparel and accessories.

PATTERNS OF RETAIL ORGANIZATION

Over the years various retail organizational patterns have emerged as the result of the diverse sizes and natures of firms. To characterize these patterns, we shall look at the organizational structures of small, independent retailers, department store retailers, and chain store retailers.

Small Store Organization

Many retailers began business as a one-person, owner-operator shop. In these cases, the owner-operator was the organization. As such, the individual had the responsibility and authority for all organizational tasks. As the firm grew, the owner-operator hired additional store personnel to handle the increasing number of complex tasks that accompany a larger, more formal organizational structure.

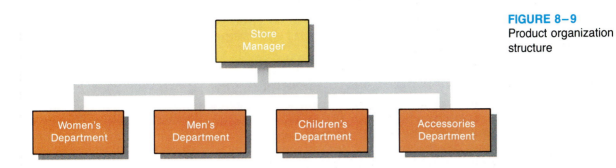

FIGURE 8–9
Product organization structure

The typical organizational structure of the small, independent retailer has previously been characterized as flat, typically with two levels and a general organization and a limited amount of specialization. As illustrated in Figure 8–10, the owner-manager develops store and personnel policies; administers expense, sales, and merchandising budgets; and oversees accounting and other control procedures. In most small retail firms, however, it is common for the owner-manager to become directly involved with many of the routine merchandising tasks and day-to-day operations.

Also illustrated in Figure 8–10 are the two most common functional divisions that small retailers use: the merchandising and operations divisions. The merchandise manager usually is a salesperson with considerable experience in merchandising and has been an employee for a long time. Typically, this person is assigned the responsibilities of buying and selling the firm's merchandise. The operations manager is an employee who assumes the responsibilities for recruiting and supervising store personnel; for planning, securing, and maintaining store facilities, equipment, and supplies; and for many of the back-room activities of receiving and stocking merchandise and overseeing the activities of the office staff.

Department Store Organization

Department store organizations are more formal and complex than small retailers'. As mentioned earlier, the organizational structure of department stores is taller and more

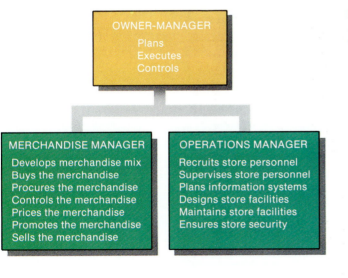

FIGURE 8–10
Small, independent retail organization

specialized than small retail stores. To understand department store organization, we shall examine the Mazur Plan of retail organization and its functional and geographic modifications.

The Mazur Plan

Most retailing experts date modern retail organizational structures from 1927, when an investment banker named Paul Mazur introduced his ideas on how to structure a retail store.[1] The **Mazur Plan** divides the retail organization into four functional divisions: finance, merchandising, promotion, and operations. Each division manager has specific responsibilities (see Figure 8–11).

The *finance manager's* chief responsibilities are to control the firm's assets and to ensure that sufficient working capital is available for each of the firm's functional divisions. In particular, the finance manager is responsible for (1) developing and maintaining accounting and other record-keeping systems; (2) planning and controlling physical inventory, merchandise budgets, and expense budgets; and (3) preparing financial reports for the firm's general management, government agencies, and trade organizations.

The *general merchandising manager* is responsible primarily for supervising the firm's buying and selling activities. An equally important responsibility is to coordinate these activities with those of the finance, promotions, and operations managers. Given the consumer orientation of retailing, the general merchandise division is usually the most important functional area within the organization.

The *promotions manager* is responsible for directing the firm's persuasive communications to consumers. Specifically, the promotions manager oversees all advertising, sales promotional activities (e.g., fashion shows, demonstrations), interior and window displays, public relations, and publicity. In addition, the promotions manager handles consumer feedback and directs advertising research in companies that conduct these activities.

The *operations manager* is generally responsible for all the physical operations of the store that are not directly assigned to one of the other divisions. Major tasks

FIGURE 8–11
The Mazur Plan for department store organization

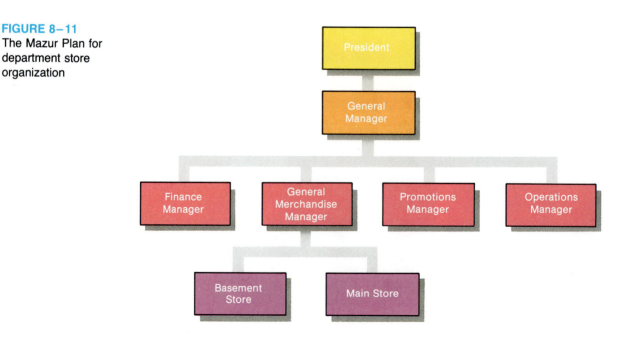

assigned to the store operations division are facilities development and maintenance; customer services and assistance; receiving, checking, marking, and stocking of incoming merchandise; store security; and general store housekeeping. Recruiting, training, and evaluating store personnel also are responsibilities assigned to the operations manager in a four-function organization.

Functional modifications. The two most common functional modifications in the Mazur Plan are (1) changing the number of functional divisions and (2) separating the buying and selling functions. In changing the Mazur Plan, department stores most often create a five-function organization by establishing a personnel division, equal in status to the other four divisions. Other functional activities that retailers might consider for separate divisional status are distribution, real estate and construction, and catalog operations.

According to the Mazur Plan, the buying and selling functions both fall under the direct supervision of the general merchandise manager. Some retailing experts argue, however, that these functions should be separated. Proponents of separation believe that (1) buying and selling require different skills, talents, and training; (2) selling activities suffer because buying takes up a considerable amount of the buyer's time spent away from the store; (3) feedback on consumer needs can be handled better by a well-developed and maintained merchandise-control system; (4) greater flexibility in the use of sales and buying personnel is possible when these individuals specialize in either selling or buying activities; and (5) in-store grouping of merchandise should be based on selling, not buying, activities. Those who argue against separation of buying and selling activities, however, hold that (1) the buyer must have direct contact with customers to determine their needs; (2) if the individuals who buy the merchandise are responsible for selling it, they will therefore exercise greater care in buying activities; and (3) it is easier to assign responsibility for the department's profit performance if buying and selling are conducted by the same person, because the buyer cannot blame the seller for not putting out the necessary selling effort, and the seller cannot blame the lack of a good profit performance on buying mistakes. Both sides of the issue offer valid arguments. (The combination and separation of buying and selling activities in department stores are discussed later in conjunction with branch store organizations.)

Geographic modifications. When department stores began to "branch out" into other geographic areas, they necessitated several additional changes in the basic Mazur Plan.[2] These new organizational arrangements, based on geographical modifications, were the main-store approach, the separate-store approach, and the equal-store approach.

With the **main-store approach** to branch organization, the parent organization (the main store) exercises control over branch stores. As illustrated in Figure 8–12, main-store managers of finance, general merchandise, promotion, and operations are responsible for supervising the same functions in the branch stores as at the main store. Under this organizational plan, main-store buyers and their assistants are responsible for securing merchandise for the main store and all branches. Sales activities in the main store are under the direct supervision of buyers, whereas sales activities in all branch stores are the responsibility of branch sales managers. In essence, those who use the main-store approach treat branch stores as sales organizations, performing merchandise and operation functions from within the main store.

Used by department stores in the initial stages of expansion, the main-store approach is most appropriate when (1) there are only a few branches; (2) customer

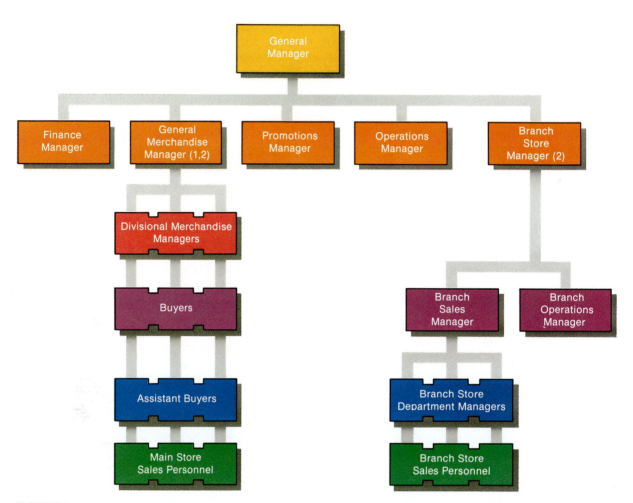

FIGURE 8–12

The main-store approach to branch department-store organization

preferences and the merchandise mix are fairly similar for the main and branch stores; (3) branch stores are located near the main store; and (4) main-store management and supporting staff can comfortably supervise branches without overextending themselves.

The **separate-store approach** to branch department-store organization treats each branch as an independent operation with its own organizational structure of managers, buyers, and sales personnel. Under this plan, branch-store management assumes both the merchandising responsibilities of buying and selling and the routine responsibilities of operating the branch store. As shown in Figure 8–13, each branch has its own store manager as well as personnel, merchandise, and operations managers, who operate separately from the parent organization. Although the parent organization has little direct involvement in the day-to-day operations of the branch store, it does have the general responsibilities of serving in an advisory and policy-making capacity.

The separate-store approach generally is used by department stores that have four to seven branches approximately the size of the main store. The major advantage of this approach is that each branch has great flexibility in tailoring its merchandise and operations to meet the needs of its local clientele. The principal disadvantages are (1) a loss in economies of scale in buying; (2) an increase in operating costs because of additional management and staff needs; (3) increased difficulties in main-

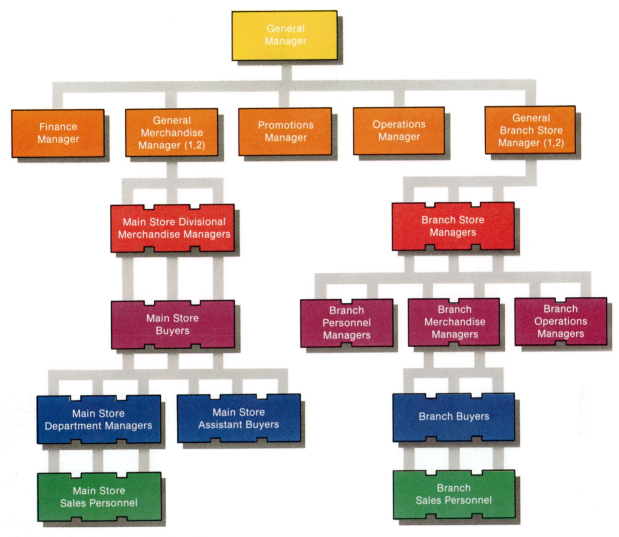

1 = buying function   2 = selling function

taining a consistent image from store to store; and (4) increased problems of coordination (e.g., stock transfers, promotion activities, etc.).

In response to the increasing number of branch stores, retailers have developed an alternative strategy to the separate- store approach. Instead of the decentralized authority and responsibility of the separate-store approach, the **equal-store approach** emphasizes centralization of authority and responsibility. Under the equal-store plan, all major managerial functions are controlled from a central headquarters. The finance, merchandise, promotions, and operations functions are under the direct supervision of headquarters managers. This approach has two unique features. First, the buying and selling functions are separated; the buying function remains a centralized activity under the general merchandise manager, and the selling function becomes a decentralized activity under the manager of stores. Second, all stores (main and branches) are treated equally as basic sales units (see Figure 8–14). The equal-store plan attempts to combine the advantages of centralized buying (economies of scale) with the advantages of localized selling (target market selling).

FIGURE 8–13
Separate-store approach to branch department-store organization

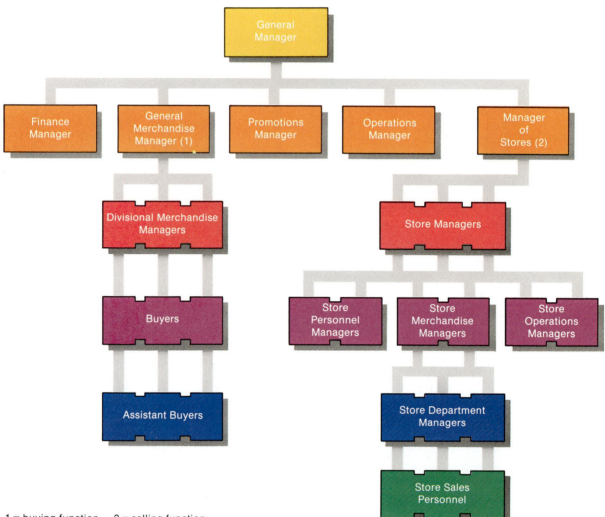

1 = buying function   2 = selling function

FIGURE 8–14

Equal-store approach to branch department-store organization

Chain Store Organization

Chain store organizations vary considerably in size, geographic spread, local markets, product mix, and number of operating units. Although all of these factors influence how a chain store will organize, three distinctive elements characterize all chain store organizations: centralization, specialization, and standardization.

Centralization is the concentration of policy and decision making in one location, either called *central headquarters* or the *home office*. Within the chain-store organizational structure, the authority and responsibilities for most operating and merchandising functions are assigned to home office management personnel. Greater effectiveness and cost reductions are two important reasons why chains like F. W. Woolworth pursue a centralization policy.[3] The primary exception is sales, which are under the decentralized control of local management. In recent years chain store organizations have tended to adopt limited decentralization. Thus, more and more functional authority and responsibility are being given to regional and divisional levels of the organization. The main reason behind this change is the gigantic size of many chain store retailers (see Figure 8–15).

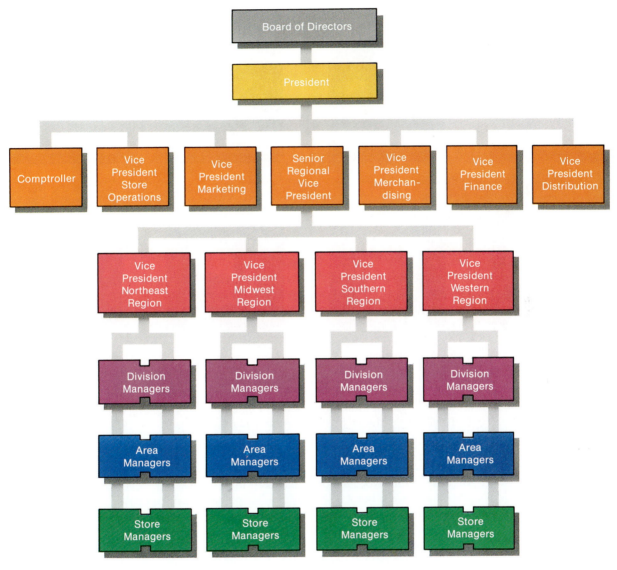

FIGURE 8-15
Chain store organization

A high degree of **specialization** is another distinguishing feature of chain store organizations. Typically, the chain store incorporates a greater number of functional divisions in its organizational structure. In addition to the four basic functional divisions of finance, merchandising, operations, and promotions, many chain stores include one or more of the following functional divisions: distribution (traffic and warehousing), marketing, real estate and construction, personnel, and industrial relations. Some large chains also specialize geographically.

The third distinguishing feature of chain organizations is a high degree of **standardization,** or similarities between the operating and merchandising operations of the business. To support standardization, chain store management establishes an elaborate system of supervision and control mechanisms to keep fully informed. Through standardization, the chain projects a consistent company image and minimizes total costs of doing business.

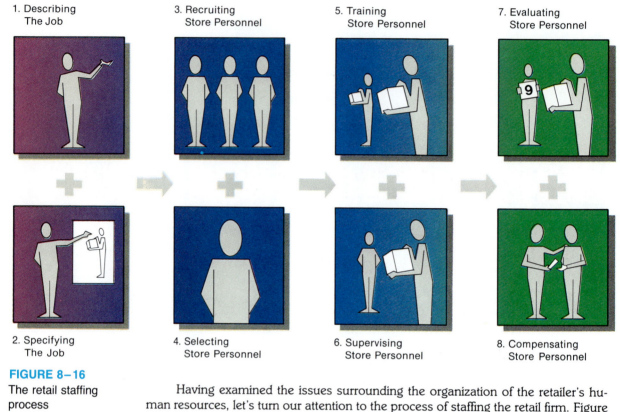

1. Describing
The Job

3. Recruiting
Store Personnel

5. Training
Store Personnel

7. Evaluating
Store Personnel

2. Specifying
The Job

4. Selecting
Store Personnel

6. Supervising
Store Personnel

8. Compensating
Store Personnel

FIGURE 8–16
The retail staffing
process

Having examined the issues surrounding the organization of the retailer's human resources, let's turn our attention to the process of staffing the retail firm. Figure 8–16 illustrates the eight steps of the staffing process.

DESCRIBING THE JOB

The first step in the staffing process is to develop a well-defined and clearly expressed **job description**. Not only does this step force the retailer to carefully determine its personnel needs, but it also provides the potential employee with a means of evaluating the job. Before writing a job description, the retailer should conduct a job analysis to determine (1) specific job-performance objectives and standards; (2) the tasks, duties, and responsibilities of the job; and (3) the skills, aptitudes, experience, education, and physical abilities that potential employees must possess to meet the minimum job requirements.[4] Figure 8–17 illustrates a job-analysis questionnaire for a retail salesperson.

After the job analysis is completed, the retailer can write a job description containing the following items: (1) the job title (e.g., sales representative, assistant store manager); (2) the job location (e.g., store, department); (3) the job position and relationships with the firm's organizational structure (e.g., identify superiors and subordinates, if any); and (4) job description (i.e., duties and responsibilities). Figure 8–18 presents a typical job description for a sales manager position.

SPECIFYING THE JOB

To meet federal, state, and local regulations on hiring practices, many retailers provide potential employees with a written job specification. A **job specification** clearly states the minimum qualifications a person must have to obtain the job applied for. Qualification criteria include education and training requirements and/or basic knowledge and skill requirements. Because of recent legislation, retailers need to recognize

Salesperson

Job Title: _____

Supervisor's Position: _____

Store Department: _____

Store Name _____

Location: _____

Approvals: _____ (Incumbent)

_____ (Supervisor)

1. *Major Function:* (Write a brief statement on the reason for the job's existence).
2. *Dimensions:* (This section should give pertinent statistics about the job. What is the individual sales volume? What are the department and store sales volumes? What are the numbers of sales people on the floor, on average, during store-opening time?)
3. *Merchandise:* (List here the lines sold—number and/or types of merchandise.)
4. How is the department merchandised?
5. Does merchandise need fitting or alterations?
6. Are deliveries involved?
7. List specific duties:
   a.
   b.
   c.
   etc.
8. Who assigns, reviews, and/or approves work?
9. What responsibility or decision-making authority have you?
10. Do you prepare reports and, if so, what are they and what are they used for?
11. Do you operate or service any equipment, fixtures or machinery?
12. What is the hardest part of the job?
13. What experience is necessary to perform the job adequately?
14. How long does it take to learn the job adequately?
15. How would you describe the working conditions in which you perform?
16. Additional useful information.

Source: Jon Laking and Robin Roark, *Retailing Job Analysis and Job Evaluation* (New York: Personnel Division, National Retail Merchants Association, 1975), 6–7

FIGURE 8–17

Job-analysis questionnaire

that they might be asked to prove that their qualifying criteria are directly related to successful performance in the positions outlined in their job descriptions. To avoid costly lawsuits, they must establish the validity of the relationship between job success and the stated job qualifications. Before filling any position, the retailer should protect itself by gathering evidence that the job qualifications actually enable an employee to meet job expectations. The retailer must avoid certain illegal conditions for employment in writing job qualifications, such as any requirement related either directly or indirectly to the applicant's race, age, creed, color, sex, religion, or national origin.

Recruiting is the active search for qualified employees. The astute manager recruits personnel by aggressively *seeking* lists of qualified prospects, *screening* large numbers of applicants, and *maintaining* a pool of prospective employees. Successful

RECRUITING STORE PERSONNEL

Job title:	Sales manager
Job location:	Men's shoe department Walnut Valley Branch Selmer's Department Stores
Job position:	Reports to assistant store manager
Job description:	To achieve sales goals by setting and maintaining customer service standards, training and motivating a professional sales staff, and maintaining merchandise presentation standards.
Job objectives:	1. To work as a partner with the merchandise analyst to develop sales plans and to reach sales goals within the area of responsibility.
	2. To ensure that the store's customer service standards and policies are maintained.
	3. To train, develop, motivate, and appraise the sales associates working within the area of responsibility.
	4. To work as a partner with the merchandise analyst and assistant store manager in developing stock assortments and quantities.
	5. To verify that the appearance and presentation of merchandise on the selling floor adhere to the visual merchandising guidelines.
	6. To ensure that selling services provide appropriate floor coverage to meet or exceed productivity goals.
	7. To communicate with the branch store coordinator, assistant store manager, and merchandise analyst concerning floor presentation.
	8. To ensure that advertised merchandise is properly priced, ticketed, and displayed and to ensure that sales associates are aware of this merchandise.
	9. To control merchandise inventories, including but not limited to receiving, pricing, transfers, price changes, security, and damages.
	10. To conduct all stock counts.
	11. To supervise the control of sales register media and cash register shortage.
	12. To shop the competition.
	13. To input information into major sale resumes.
	14. To disseminate all pertinent information to all sales associates including night contingents.
	15. To ensure the correct documentation of time sheets within the area.
	16. To implement credit promotions and other programs in the area.

FIGURE 8–18

A typical job description

recruiting is the process of knowing where to look, what to look for, and how to find qualified people.

Finding Employees

Several internal and external sources can provide the names and general backgrounds of prospective employees. Internal sources include lists of current and past employees as well as employee recommendations. *Current employees* should not be overlooked if they possess the necessary qualifications for the job. Promotions and transfers are not only a means of finding qualified persons, but also a way to improve employee morale by demonstrating that advancement is possible within the firm. *Past employees* with satisfactory service records are an internal source of employees that retailers often overlook. By maintaining files on past employees (full- and part-time), the personnel manager has access to prospective employees who could be productive immediately with minimal training. The third internal source comprises *employee recommendations*. Frequently, the firm's employees know of friends, relatives, and acquaintances who are in the job market and have the necessary skills and training to fill a position. Neiman-Marcus has a hiring bonus program for employees who recommend qualified persons who are hired and stay for a prescribed period of time.[5]

External sources of prospective employees come from advertisements, employment agencies, educational institutions, and unsolicited applications. *Advertisements* in newspapers, trade publications, and professional papers and journals are common methods of attracting applicants. These printed media frequently devote sections to employment opportunities at certain times or in particular issues. Private and public *employment agencies* are also sources of prospective employees. Two advantages of using employment agencies are that they provide initial screening for a large number of prospects and that they maintain the retailer's anonymity during the initial stages of the recruiting process. Before using the services of a private or government employment agency, the retailer should determine the agency's fee structure and which party is responsible for paying the fee—the employer or the employee.

The third external source of prospective employees is *educational institutions*. Career counselors at most high schools often can provide a list of suitable prospects for part-time and entry-level positions. Placement offices at junior colleges and four-year colleges and universities are always eager to supply retailers and other businesses with the names and qualifications of prospective employees for low- and middle-management positions. Walk-ins and mail-ins represent *unsolicited applications* that retailers should keep on file and periodically review when a job becomes available. One additional external source of employees is *pirating*—hiring an employee who works for a noncompeting retailer. The major advantage of pirating is the retailing experience the prospective employee undoubtedly has. However, the retailer should proceed cautiously when hiring another retailer's employee.

Screening Applicants

In the screening process, personnel managers examine the applicant's qualifications to determine whether the person has the requisite background and capabilities to perform the job. The most common criteria retailers use in the initial screening process are educational background, ability to communicate in oral and written form, experience in working with people, and knowledge, experience, or skills to perform a particular activity (e.g., typing). Other screening criteria retailers use indirectly and subjectively are personal appearance, general attitude, motivation, and personality.

From the list of qualified applicants, the retailer must select the individual best suited to the job. Matching job requirements to employee attributes is the point of the selection step of the staffing process. In finding the best match, the retailer has available several methods of generating additional information on the prospective employee before deciding to make an offer. These methods include application forms, personal interviews, reference checks, testing instruments, and physical examinations.

Application Forms

All retailers should require each prospective employee to complete an application form as a prerequisite for further processing. Application forms provide the retailer

SELECTING STORE PERSONNEL

with preliminary information on each applicant and (1) serve as a means of checking minimum qualifications during initial screening; (2) provide basic information to guide the interviewer during the personal interview process; (3) allow a preliminary check on the applicant's ability to follow instructions; and (4) provide background information for a permanent record if the applicant is hired.[6] A typical application form provides space for the applicant's name, address, telephone number, employment history (when and where the applicant has previously worked, levels of compensation, and reasons for leaving previous jobs), formal education and training, personal health history, and demographic information allowed by state and federal regulations. The application form also usually includes space for a list of personal references. Although the retailer should carefully review all the information on the application form, special attention should be given to *omissions* and *job changes*. What is *not* on the application form can be as important as what *is* on it. The retailer should seek clarification of all omissions on application forms. A careless or deceptive omission can tell the retailer a great deal about the character of the prospective employee. Frequent job changes without good cause can also reveal something about the applicant's character.

Reference Checks

After the retailer has initially screened prospective employees' application forms and eliminated those who are unqualified, the references of the remaining prospects should be contacted. Although most references the applicants list are favorably biased, they do give the retailer a way to verify the accuracy and completeness of the applicant's form. Telephone calls to references normally provide more complete and honest evaluations than do letters, mainly because of the immediate and personal two-way communications telephone conversations allow. Telephone contact gives the retailer a chance to ask questions about issues of particular concern. To reinforce reference checks, many retailers contact former employers, teachers, and other individuals who might have specific knowledge of the applicant's character and abilities. Some retailers even check applicants' credit by calling local credit bureaus.

Personal Interviews

Retailers use personal interviews to question and observe applicants in a face-to-face situation. Formal, highly structured interviews have the advantage of establishing the relative roles of each party in the interview, permitting a controlled interviewing environment, and facilitating complete, effective information gathering. Informal and unstructured interviews help the applicant to relax, to talk freely, and to act naturally— thereby allowing the interviewer to view the applicant in an unguarded state. Most retailers prefer to compromise by injecting enough formality and structure into the interview to promote efficiency but not enough to create undue tension in the applicant. The number of interviews usually depends on the level of the position to be filled. When retailers are trying to fill upper-level managerial positions, they normally interview each applicant several times; for entry-level positions, one interview generally suffices.

The location of any interview should be private and in pleasant surroundings. Both factors help to relax the prospective employee and give the retailer a chance to see the applicant in a natural setting. The length of an interview may be from a few minutes for low-echelon, part-time employees to several days for the applicant who is interviewing for a high-level management position. Many retailers find it advantageous to have the applicant interview with several of the firm's managers so they can elicit several opinions of the applicant's qualifications.

The personal interviewing process should fully comply with state and federal equal employment opportunity regulations. Questions asked in the interview must be job-related and necessary to judging the applicant's qualifications and abilities. To avoid charges of discrimination, the retailer should construct a list of questions to use in the interviewing process and have the store's legal department review it for any possible discriminatory inquiries. Figure 8–19 identifies several questions concerning past job experiences, current job expectations, and personal goals and ambitions that could be legally asked in an interview.

Testing Instruments

In the hiring process, some retailers use testing instruments to evaluate prospective employees. These instruments are pencil-and-paper tests that applicants take to demonstrate their abilities to handle a job. Although the validity and usefulness of these instruments have been debated, many retailers believe they provide valuable insights into a person's qualifications for employment.

Retailers use two general types of instruments to evaluate their applicants: psychological tests and achievement tests. **Psychological tests** are instruments de-

FIGURE 8–19
What an interviewer can ask

About past job experiences
- Can you give me an example of your abilities to manage or supervise others?
- What are some things you would like to avoid in a job? Why?
- What are some of the things on your job you feel you have done particularly well or in which you have achieved the greatest success?
- What were some of the things about your last job that you found difficult to do?
- In what ways do you feel your present job has developed you to take on even greater responsibilities?
- What do you feel has been your greatest frustration or disappointment on your present job and why do you feel this way?
- What are some of the reasons that are prompting you to consider leaving your present job?
- What are some of the things about which you and your supervisor might occasionally disagree?

About current job expectations
- What do you see in this job that makes it appealing to you that you do not have in your present job?
- How do you evaluate our company as a place to build your future?
- What would you say there is about this job that is particularly appealing to you?
- What aspects of this job do you find undesirable?
- What are some of the first things you need to know about before you could really step in and do your assignment justice?

About personal goals and ambitions
- Where do you see yourself going from here?
- What are your long-term career objectives?
- What is it you have going for you that might make you successful on the job?
- Who or what in your life would you say influenced you most with regard to your career objectives?
- What would you say are some of the basic factors that motivate you?
- How would you describe yourself as a person?
- What things give you the greatest satisfaction?

signed to measure an applicant's personality, intelligence, aptitudes, interests, and supervisory skills. Regardless of which tests are used, the retailer needs trained personnel to administer and interpret the results.

Achievement tests are questionnaires designed to measure a person's basic knowledge and skills. Tests that measure an applicant's ability to do basic arithmetic computations or to operate mechanical devices, such as cash registers, typewriters, and calculators, are examples. Generally, retailers prefer achievement tests to psychological tests because they are easier to administer and interpret. Also, most retailers believe that achievement tests are more valid than psychological tests because the statistical relationship between the skills they measure and job success is stronger—a particularly important consideration in light of recent court rulings regarding equal employment opportunities. Target discount stores uses an assessment center (AC) concept in which a series of simulated experiences provides the potential employee with "an opportunity to demonstrate competencies in certain areas. What distinguishes it from testing per se is testing looks at intellectual capability, past background, and tries to forecast the future. . .the AC puts the candidate in an actual experience—one that will be encountered at retail—then measures performance."[7]

Physical Examinations

Some retailers require applicants to undergo a physical examination. Usually this examination is requested only after the applicant has been judged the most qualified person for the job. Some states have laws requiring a physical examination for employees who handle food and drug products. In addition, some firms' health, life, and disability insurance programs require exams. Testing for drug usage and acquired immune deficiency syndrome (AIDS) is also an issue being addressed by some retailers.

Final Selection

Ultimately, the retailer must make a final selection among the qualified applicants. No absolute, totally objective method can determine the most qualified person; rather, the final selection is largely a subjective choice based on all available information. An experienced personnel manager with good intuition is perhaps one of the most valuable assets a firm can have for selecting employees who will make a significant contribution over an extended period. Objective tests, experience, and good personal judgment are the tools a personnel manager needs to make the final selection.

TRAINING STORE PERSONNEL

The fifth step in the staffing process is employee training. Training programs are needed not only for new employees, but also for existing employees to update their knowledge and skills. Training programs are designed to help both the employer and employee reach mutually beneficial goals.

Regardless of the retailer's individual situation, however, every sound retail training program should address three basic questions. These elements are *what type* of training the employee should have, *where* the training should take place, and *how* the training should be done. Figure 8–20 identifies these basic elements.

What Training to Give

Two basic kinds of training that both new and old employees need are organization orientation and functional training. **Organization orientation** is a program that either initiates new employees or updates old employees on the general organizational

FIGURE 8–20
Elements of a retail training program

WHAT	Organizational orientation
	Functional training
WHERE	On the job—decentralized training
	Off the job—centralized training
HOW	Individual methods
	"on your own"
	programmed learning
	Sponsor method
	Group methods
	lectures
	demonstrations
	case studies
	role playing
	Executive training programs

structure of the firm and its policies, rules, and regulations. It also acquaints employees with the company's history, objectives, and future expectations. Essentially, an organization orientation program makes employees aware of what the firm is trying to accomplish and how it plans to accomplish it. One aim of this program is to improve employees' morale and to make them feel they are members of the "team."

Functional training is a program that develops and expands the basic skills and knowledge employees need to perform their jobs successfully. Training sessions on selling techniques, customer service procedures, and inventory control are three examples of functional training directed at improving basic employee skills. Increasing employees' knowledge of the company's product lines and helping them to understand customer purchase motives are examples of knowledge-oriented, functional training.

Where to Train

The second element of the training program concerns where training is to take place and under whose supervision. Normally, training occurs either on the job during regular working hours, off the job during scheduled training periods, or in some combination of both. **On-the-job training** is a decentralized approach that occurs on the sales floor, in the stockroom, or in some other work environment where employees are performing their jobs. The trainee usually is under the direct supervision of the department manager or some other designated person responsible for handling the training program. **Off-the-job training** is conducted in centralized training classrooms away from the employees' work environment. In centralized classrooms, the trainer can use various learning aids (e.g., films, demonstrations, and role playing) under controlled conditions, allowing the employee to focus on the learning experience without interruption.

How to Train

The third element in the retailer's training program is how each employee should be instructed; that is, which methods the retailer should use in the training process. As Figure 8–20 outlines, there are four general training methods: individual, sponsor, group, and executive. In the **individual training method,** employees "train" themselves. One individual training method is the "on your own" approach. In this training situation the employee is put on the job and expected to learn by trial and error, observation, and asking questions. In essence, this sink-or-swim approach includes no formal training. Although the retailer bears no training costs in the short run, the total costs in the long run could be substantial because of potential low employee productivity, high employee turnover, employee errors, and dissatisfied customers because of improper service.

An alternative method retailers use is programmed learning, which uses a highly structured format. First, employees study a unit of material. Second, they respond to a series of questions (true/false, multiple-choice, fill-in-the-blank, etc.) on the material they have read. Third, they receive immediate feedback on their performance in answering the questions. Fourth, they continue to repeat the first three steps until they master the material. Once employees achieve an acceptable competence level on a unit of material, they move on to the next level of instruction. Repetition is the key to **programmed learning**. These training devices are available in both written (paper-and-pencil) and machine (mechanical and computer) form.

The **sponsor method of training** uses an experienced employee to assume part or all of the responsibility for training a new employee. Most retailers believe that this one-on-one approach is the best method for teaching new employees the basic skills of selling, buying, promotion, and so forth. The sponsor's responsibilities also extend to introducing the employee to fellow workers, evaluating the employee's progress, and providing advice on the employee's problems and concerns. Successful sponsor training programs involve sponsors who volunteer for the assignment and are compensated for their efforts (e.g., with money or time off).

Group training methods involve the simultaneous training of several employees through lectures (or discussion, films, or slides), demonstrations (on sales or marking and stock presentations), case studies (e.g., oral and written problem-solving situa-

On-the-job training takes place in the environment where the employee will work.

tions), role-playing activities (e.g., a sales or customer complaint situation),[8] and computer simulations,[9] and interactive videos.[10] Large retailers use group training in centralized training facilities with specialized personnel. Group training sessions may last from five to ten minutes to update existing employees on new policies to as long as several days of classes on a wide variety of subjects. The advantage of group training is the low cost of training several employees at one time; the principal drawback is the lack of individual attention.

Executive training programs (ETPs) are educational sessions directed at supervisors, managers, and executives. Common among large department store and chain organizations, ETPs are designed to recruit personnel who have executive potential and to provide them with the opportunity to gain management experience. The typical ETP is a step-by-step training procedure whereby the executive trainee gains practical management experience by progressing from low- to higher-level management positions.

Figure 8–21 illustrates the ETP for Dayton Hudson department stores. As shown in Figure 8–21, Dayton Hudson creates two separate but parallel routes to

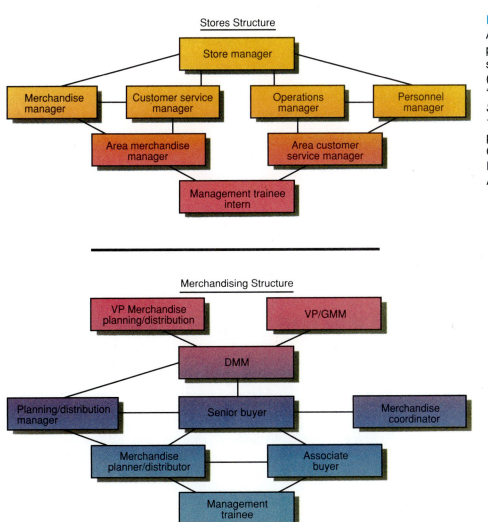

FIGURE 8–21

An executive training program—Dayton Hudson department stores (source: Jules Abend, "The Fast Track," *Stores* [September 1985]: 63. Reprinted by permission of *Stores*. Copyright by National Retail Merchants Association)

senior management. This example shows several alternative routes that a trainee might follow. An executive trainee is first promoted to either an associate buyer or an area sales manager position. The progression from that point varies according to the individual and the company's needs. The amount of time one spends at any position depends on individual ability, the type and complexity of the position, and the number of positions open at any given time. Lower-level positions usually involve several months of training, whereas middle- and upper-level positions frequently necessitate several years' experience. By moving potential executives from one position to another, the retailer gives them complete exposure to all or most of the firm's operations, policies, and procedures.

Many large retail organizations also have special executive development programs for new and existing employees with extensive educational backgrounds and experience. These programs normally include orientation programs, project assignments, executive seminars, and sponsorship programs with one of the firm's top executives. Many companies also encourage a wide range of self-development activities.

SUPERVISING STORE PERSONNEL

Supervision is the process of directing, coordinating, and inspecting the efforts of store employees to attain both company and individual goals. Effective supervisors can successfully satisfy the needs of the retailer (such as quality job performance, company loyalty, satisfactory profits) and the needs of the employee (such as fair treatment, a decent standard of living, a chance for advancement). The key to good supervision is knowing how to motivate employees. **Motivation** is the drive that moves people to act. Employees are driven to excel in a variety of ways. Some employees are motivated by money, others by praise, and still others possibly by the promise of free time to spend with their families. "There is no doubt that money can be a strong incentive for employee productivity, but it may not be a sufficient condition for it. The link between pay and performance is a bit more complex than the simple formulation that incentive pay increases motivation and performance."[11] The supervisor must discover the key that motivates each employee.

How to Motivate

Frederick Herzberg offered one method of motivation in his theory of satisfiers and dissatisfiers.[12] **Satisfiers** are employment factors that produce pleasurable reactions within people's work lives. Herzberg found that the primary employment satisfiers were a challenging job, recognition of achievement, a responsible position, a chance for advancement, and professional and personal growth. In essence, motivation factors are conditions that enhance the employee's needs for self-esteem and self-actualization.

Dissatisfiers are employment factors that make workers unhappy with their job, leading to high turnover and weak performance. Oversupervision, poorly developed work rules, undesirable working conditions, restrictive company policies, and inadequate wages and fringe benefits are common examples of dissatisfiers. In general, dissatisfiers are closely associated with an individual's physiological and security needs. Given Herzberg's findings, the answer to the question "How to motivate?" is to eliminate conditions that generate dissatisfiers and initiate programs and policies that promote satisfiers.

How to Supervise

The optimal level of employee supervision depends largely on how motivated employees are. Two opposing schools of thought on the amount of supervision that employers should exercise are the "heavy-handed" approach and the "light-handed" approach. Those who support the **heavy-handed** approach assume that employees are lazy, passive, self-centered, and irresponsible. With these assumptions, they maintain that employers must closely supervise and control their employees to motivate them to work toward company goals and to assume responsibilities. Retailers that subscribe to this school of thought view economic inducements as the primary means of motivation (McGregor's Theory X).[13] In particular, some retailers consider the heavy-handed approach the only way to motivate people in the lower-level positions of their stores. In modern society, however, the heavy-handed approach may not apply.

A more contemporary view of motivation and supervision is the **light-handed** approach. Retailers that support this view believe that providing employees with a favorable work environment can create a situation in which employees will obtain job satisfaction and their personal goals by directing their efforts toward the firm's needs (McGregor's Theory Y). Retailers that use the light-handed approach think that close supervision and control are unnecessary. Employees, they feel, will assume their responsibilities and, in part, supervise themselves if a desirable social and psychological environment is present. The previously discussed satisfiers are the keys to creating this desirable social and psychological condition. Within this kind of working environment, less supervision produces better job performance.

A summary of Douglas McGregor's two contrasting models of motivation, Theory X and Theory Y, appears in Figure 8–22.

FIGURE 8–22
McGregor's Theory X and Theory Y models of motivation

Theory X states that efficiency will be high when:

- Authority flows down a hierarchical chain in which each subordinate has but one supervisor or manager.
- Work is divided into the smallest number of sets of similar functions.
- Span of management is kept small, but balanced against the number of levels of management.
- Jobs are carefully defined and the worker is hired to fit the job.

Theory X assumes that:

- Most people prefer to be directed and have little desire for responsibility and creativity.
- Motivation occurs only at an economic level. The worker is resistant to change.
- People must be closely supervised. They have a short time span of responsibility. People are by nature indolent.
- People can be considered alike as units of production. No differentiation of jobs to utilize different interests and capacities is desirable. The worker is self-centered and indifferent to organizational needs.

Theory Y states that efficiency will be high when:

- Authority and communication flow in all directions in both formal and informal systems.
- Work is varied and enriched.
- Span of management is as broad as possible as long as major objectives can be achieved.
- Tasks are grouped into different meaningful jobs to accommodate individual talents and capacities.

Theory Y assumes that:

- Workers are social beings who can work together for organizational and personal goals.
- Capacity for creativity is present to some degree in everybody. Needs at the level above the economic level are powerful motivators.
- People desire self-fulfillment through directing their own activities and participating in setting their own objectives.
- Workers achieve their fullest potential when their aspirations and job challenges are matched to their capabilities.

Source: Norman M. Scarborough and Thomas W. Zimmerer, *Effective Small Business Management* (Columbus: Charles E. Merrill Publishing Co., 1984), 503

FIGURE 8–23
Employee evaluation
factors

Performance characteristics	Personal attributes
Job knowledge	Enthusiasm
Quality of work	Loyalty
Quantity of work	Dependability
Organizing capabilities	Leadership
Supervision requirements	Maturity
Promptness	Stability
Peer relationships	Creativity
Customer relations	Honesty
Analytic abilities	Initiative

EVALUATING STORE PERSONNEL

The seventh step in the store staffing process is the development of personnel evaluation procedures. Each store employee, regardless of position or level, should be periodically evaluated. The purposes of personnel evaluations are (1) to determine compensation, (2) to recommend or deny promotions and transfers, and (3) to justify demotions and terminations. Conducted constructively, personnel evaluations can be used to motivate employees, to improve store morale, to generate information for planning purposes, to encourage employee self-development, and to improve communications between the employee and employer. In developing the store's personnel evaluation methods and procedures, the retailer should decide when to evaluate, what to evaluate, and how to evaluate.

When to Evaluate

A smart retailer evaluates personnel continuously. It would be unfair to judge an employee's contribution and performance at the end of an arbitrary time period, such as the end of the fiscal year. Instead, retailers should provide their employees with immediate feedback on their progress. This informal feedback, however, should also be accompanied by an established, formal evaluation in which employees receive a detailed account of their job performance.[14] Formal evaluations tell employees exactly what their status is. It is not unusual for new employees to be evaluated weekly or monthly. Established lower-level employees, however, are typically evaluated on a formal basis every six months, while annual evaluations for upper-level management and executive personnel are the norm.

What to Evaluate

Retailers have learned that the most important employee factors to evaluate are performance-demonstrated skills and personal attributes. These factors appear to relate most closely to employee success. Examples of such characteristics appear in Figure 8–23. Figure 8–24 identifies those traits that executives believe are most important to employee success.

In selecting evaluation criteria and their respective measuring instruments, the retailer must consider the legal ramifications of each decision and the influence of any labor union that might be involved. It often is a good policy to seek advice regarding the legality of the employee evaluation system. In areas where unionization of labor is present, management consults with appropriate union representatives before formulating evaluation methods and procedures.

How to Evaluate

Retailers use a variety of methods for evaluating store personnel; the method used depends on the degree of objectivity and formality that the retailer wants. Figure

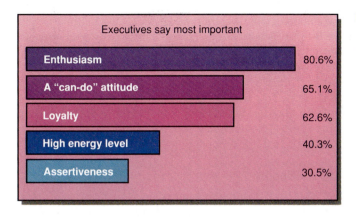

Executives say most important	
Enthusiasm	80.6%
A "can-do" attitude	65.1%
Loyalty	62.6%
High energy level	40.3%
Assertiveness	30.5%

FIGURE 8–24
Employee traits that executives believe are most important to employee success (source: Elys McLean-Ibrahim. "What makes workers succeed." *USA Today* (September 25, 1987). p. B–1. Copyright © 1987 *USA Today*. Reprinted with permission.)

8–25 identifies several objective employee evaluation methods, which are based largely on factual and measurable criteria, and subjective methods, which are based on the evaluator's perceptions, feelings, and prejudices. Formal methods are regularly scheduled evaluations; informal methods follow no set schedule, and the criteria and procedures may or may not be known to the employee.

Formal Objective Evaluation Methods

Formal objective employee evaluation procedures include performance records and management by objectives (MBO) procedures. Performance records are quantitative measures of the employee's performance and include such varied statistics as (1) total sales dollars, (2) total number of sales transactions, (3) number of customer complaints, (4) number of merchandise returns and their dollar value, (5) number of times an employee is absent or late for work, and (6) net sales per working hour or per hourly wage. By comparing the employee's performance against the store average for any one of these criteria, the retailer can identify above-, at-, and below-average performers. These MBO procedures set measurable performance objectives for employees that should match their job descriptions. Employees are then evaluated on how well they achieved their objectives. Using MBO procedures has the advantage of drawing the employee into the evaluation process and thereby encouraging self-development and self-evaluation. The employee is asked (1) to set objectives in specific terms, (2) to determine the method of accomplishment, (3) to set an accomplishment time frame, and (4) to determine the measure of accomplishment.

Formal Subjective Evaluation Methods

Rating scales and checklists constitute two of the more common **formal subjective employee evaluation methods**. The typical procedure is to identify and list several

Degree of Formality \ Degree of Objectivity	Objective	Subjective
Formal	performance records MBO (management by objectives)	rating scales checklists
Informal	professional shoppers	intuition

FIGURE 8–25
Store personnel evaluation methods

criteria in checklist form. The evaluator may weight the individual criteria according to their importance (see Figure 8–26). Typical scales are (1) satisfactory or unsatisfactory; (2) below average, average, or above average; and (3) poor, fair, average, good, and excellent. Given the subjective character of these ratings, many retailers prefer to have several supervisors rate each employee. The average of these ratings forms the basis for the employee's evaluation. To obtain additional viewpoints, some retailers ask fellow employees to rate one another. When using rating scales, retailers should recognize the central tendency effect—the tendency of evaluators to rate everyone at or near the midpoint of the scale.

Informal Objective Evaluation Methods

The most common **informal objective evaluation method** in retailing is to employ professional or mystery shoppers.[15] Professional shoppers are people who wander into a store to "shop" for merchandise in a "typical" way. Actually, they are professional investigators who attempt to learn how a retailer's employees behave toward them. This evaluation method should not be the *basis* of employee evaluation but a *supplement* to the retailer's assessment of employees' job performance.

Informal Subjective Evaluation Methods

Informal subjective evaluation methods have no structure and rely heavily on the supervisor's intuition. Although a supervisor's feelings and perceptions might represent a correct evaluation of an employee, the lack of objectivity and formality leaves such a method open to criticism by both employees and outside concerns (e.g., the Fair Labor Standards Law). A constant danger in using intuition as an evaluative method is the "halo effect" or the "good old boy syndrome." An employee who is a good person is not necessarily contributing effectively to the firm's efforts; in fact, such considerations often lead to other employees' accusations of favoritism.

Regardless of the method used to evaluate store personnel, employees should be made aware of the method (its criteria, measurements, and procedures), given feedback after each evaluation, and permitted to appeal the evaluation.

COMPENSATING STORE PERSONNEL

Equitable compensation is an integral part of the retailer's staffing process. A well-designed compensation package is not only an important factor in rewarding past performance but also an important incentive for future performance.[16] Compensation methods include the straight-salary plan, the straight-commission plan, the salary plus commission plan, and the salary plus bonus plan. Long-term incentives (top level management), annual bonuses (midlevel management) and short-term incentives (sales personnel) are all becoming more important in all retail compensation practices.[17]

Straight-Salary Plan

The **straight-salary plan** is a fixed amount of compensation for a specified work period such as a day, week, month, or year. For example, an employee's salary might be set at $200 per week or $4 per hour. For the retailer, the straight-salary plan offers the advantages of easy administration and a high level of employer control. Under the straight-salary plan, the retailer can expect employees to engage in non-selling activities such as stocking and housekeeping. For the employee, the straight-salary plan has a known level of financial security and stability. The disadvantages of this plan for the retailer are (1) limited incentives to increase employee performance,

Employee's name _____   Date _____

Employee's title _____   Supervisor _____

Instructions: Please review the performance of the employee whose name is listed above on each of the following items. In order to guide you in your rating, the five determinants of performance have been defined.

Rating Points

5 OUTSTANDING
A truly outstanding employee whose achievements are far above acceptable. Has consistently performed far beyond established objectives and has made significant contributions beyond current position. Requires minimal direction and supervision. (Relatively few employees would be expected to achieve at this level.)

4 SUPERIOR
An above-average employee whose performance is clearly above acceptable. Has usually performed beyond established objectives and, at times, has made contributions beyond responsibilities of present position. Requires less than normally expected degree of direction and supervision.

3 AVERAGE
A fully acceptable employee who consistently meets all requirements of position. Has consistently met established objectives in a satisfactory and adequate manner. Performance requires normal degree of supervision and direction. (The majority of employees should be at this level.)

2 BELOW AVERAGE
A somewhat below-average employee whose performance, while not unsatisfactory, cannot be considered fully acceptable. Generally meets established objectives and expectations, but definite areas exist where achievement is substandard. Performance requires somewhat more than normal degree of direction and supervision.

1 UNACCEPTABLE
A far-below-average employee whose performance is barely adequate to meet the requirements of the position. Generally performs at a level below established objectives with the result that overall contribution is marginal. Performance requires an unusually high degree of supervision. (This level is considered acceptable only for employees new to the job.)

JOB CRITERIA   POINTS

1. Amount of work. Consider here only the **quantity** of the employee's output.   _____
   Supervisor's comments:

2. Quality of work. Consider how well the employee does each job assigned. Include your   _____
   appraisal of such items as accuracy, thoroughness, and orderliness.
   Supervisor's comments:

3. Cooperation. How well does this employee work and interact with you and coworkers   _____
   for the accomplishment of organization goals?
   Supervisor's comments:

4. Judgment. Consider this employee's ability to reach sound and logical conclusions.   _____
   Supervisor's comments:

FIGURE 8–26
A formal subjective employee evaluation form

5. Initiative. The energy or aptitude to originate action toward organization goals.   _____
   Supervisor's comments:

6. Job knowledge. How well does the employee demonstrate an understanding of the   _____
   basic fundamentals, techniques, and procedures on the job?
   Supervisor's comments:

7. Interest in job. Does the employee demonstrate a real interest in the job and the orga-   _____
   nization?
   Supervisor's comments:

8. Ability to communicate. How well does this employee exchange needed information   _____
   with others in the work group and with supervisors?
   Supervisor's comments:

9. Dependability. Consider the employee's absences, tardiness, punctuality, timeliness in   _____
   completing job assignments, and the amount of supervision required.
   Supervisor's comments:

10. Adaptability. Consider the degree to which this employee demonstrates adjustment to   _____
    the varying requirements of the job.
    Supervisor's comments:
                                                              TOTAL POINTS   _____

    Supervisor's general comments:

Instructions: After you have rated the employee and made whatever comments you feel are pertinent to each
criterion and the overall evaluation, schedule a meeting to review each item with the employee. An employee
wishing to make comments about the evaluation should be asked to do so in the following space.

Employee's comment:

Date: _____

Supervisor present (Name): _____

Employee's signature: _____ Date: _____

Notice to employee: Signing the form does not imply that you either agree or disagree with the evaluation.

Source: Norman M. Scarborough and Thomas W. Zimmerer, *Effective Small Business Management* (Columbus: Charles E. Merrill Publishing Co.,
1984), 521–23.

FIGURE 8–26, *continued*

(2) fixed costs that result in a high wage cost/sales ratio, and (3) lack of downward salary adjustments during periods of sales decline. Retailers typically use straight-salary plans when a job involves a considerable amount of customer service and nonselling time, such as stocking, receiving, clerking, and checking out.

Straight-Commission Plan

Under a **straight-commission plan**, a store employee receives a percentage of what he or she sells. The commission percentage is either fixed (e.g., 5 percent on all sales) or variable (e.g., 6 percent on high-margin lines and 3 percent on low-margin lines). In some cases, the time of year determines the commission (e.g., 4 percent during the Christmas season or the annual clearance sale). Retailers may calculate an employee's commission on the basis of *net sales* (gross sales dollars minus dollar value of returned merchandise). Retailers that use straight-commission plans are those that sell big-ticket items such as automobiles, furniture, appliances, and jewelry. It also is the common method for compensating door-to-door salespersons.

The major advantage of a straight-commission plan is the monetary incentive it creates for employees; however, this incentive often causes several problems. Salespeople on commission often become overly aggressive in trying to make a sale. High-pressure selling is also a temptation when commission sales are involved. By exerting undue pressure on the customer to buy now (as opposed to later, when a different salesperson might be serving the customer), the sale could be lost to the retailer forever. Also, commission sales tempt many salespeople to practice trading up the customer to more expensive merchandise. However, when trading up leads to a large number of returns, not only does the salesperson lose the commission, but the retailer also loses a sale and very likely the goodwill of the store's clientele.

For the commissioned salesperson, the straight-commission plan has the weaknesses of financial insecurity and instability. To overcome these limitations, many retailers have established "drawing accounts" that allow employees to draw a fixed sum of money at regular intervals against future commissions.

Salary Plus Commission Plan

As the name implies, the **salary plus commission plan** provides employees with a salary and a commission. There are a number of variations to this plan. The *straight salary/single commission* variation uses a base salary (e.g., $200 per week) plus (1) a single commission (e.g., 1/2 percent) on all net sales up to the sales quota and a larger commission (e.g., 2 percent) on all sales in excess of sales quota, *or* (2) a commission only on net sales that exceed the quota. As a general rule, the base salary constitutes the greatest share of the employee's total compensation. To offer greater sales incentive, however, a retailer can increase the commission rate to make commission income a significantly higher proportion of the employee's total income.

The strengths of this plan are that it provides employees with financial security and stability while helping the retailer to control and motivate personnel. Although the combination plan is more difficult to administer, its benefits generally outweigh its costs.

Salary Plus Bonus Plan

A popular method for compensating middle-management personnel (such as department managers, store managers, and buyers) is **salary plus bonus plan,** which

Retail firms have recently begun to offer employees
the use of physical fitness centers as a fringe benefit.

involves a straight monthly salary supplemented by either semiannual or annual
bonuses for exceeding performance goals. Performance goals and related bonuses
usually are set by upper management for each operating unit and usually are expressed in the form of increased sales or profits, decreased operating costs, or some
other measure of the operating unit's productivity. The most common problems
associated with the salary plus bonus plan are employees' difficulty in understanding
such plans and administrators' difficulty in setting up the performance criteria and
measurement instruments to make the system work.

Fringe Benefits

The employee's total compensation package also includes fringe benefits, which vary
greatly from one retail firm to another. In recent years, fringe benefits have become
more important in the retailer's efforts to attract and keep qualified personnel. Fringe
benefits are much more important for middle- and upper-level positions than for
entry-level positions. As unionization of lower-level personnel becomes more common, however, benefit packages at that level will become more significant.

Among the most popular fringe benefits are (1) insurance programs covering
life, health, accident, and disability; (2) sick leave; (3) personal leave time; (4) holiday
leave and paid vacations; (5) pension plans; (6) profit sharing; (7) employee discounts; (8) recreation facilities; (9) coffee breaks; (10) employee parties; and (11)
team sponsorships. Fringe benefits are becoming a more important form of compensation in today's leisure-oriented society, with the goal of making employees
happy, content, and loyal to the store. Additional perks for company executives
include club memberships, company cars, financial counseling, and spouse travel.[18]

SUMMARY

Retailers use numerous different structures to organize their people, tasks, and operations. In retailing, the firm's organization is directed at accomplishing certain strategy objectives (general, long-term goals); operational objectives (long-term operational requirements to obtain strategy objectives); and functional objectives (specific task-oriented objectives). Also, retailers must organize in such a manner that the basic operational tasks of planning and controlling the product, price, promotion, and place can be facilitated readily.

The retailer should consider several basic principles of organization in developing the structure of the firm. Of particular interest are the organizational principles of specialization and departmentalization, lines of authority and areas of responsibility, unity of command, and span of control.

Many retailers prepare charts to illustrate their form of retail organization. Some retail organizational structures are characterized by a limited number of levels (flat organizations), while others incorporate many levels of organization (vertical structures). Organizational forms are strongly influenced by how retailers classify jobs and tasks. Depending on the firm, jobs and tasks can be classified on the basis of their functional, geographic, or product relationships; also, a combination of these three factors can be used in job and task classification.

Patterns of retail organization vary considerably between the simple structures of the small, independent retailer and the often complex organization of the department and chain store retailer. Centralization, specialization, and standardization are the key characteristics of chain store organizational structures, while the Mazur Plan, and its variations characterize department store organizations.

A key ingredient in any successful retail operation is its personnel. Merchandising and operational plans are of limited value without loyal, productive employees. All retailers face the problem of finding and keeping good people.

The staffing process consists of eight steps. First, describing the job includes developing job descriptions and conducting job analyses. Second, specifying the job involves writing job classifications that not only outline the responsibilities of the position but also avoid charges of unfair employment practices. Third, recruiting store personnel includes both finding and screening potential employee candidates. The fourth step in the staffing process is selection. From the list of qualified applicants, the retailer selects individuals best suited to the job by carefully reviewing application forms, personal interviews, reference checks, testing instruments, and physical examinations.

Training store personnel is the fifth step in the staffing process. It requires the retailer to know what to train (organization orientation and functional or task training), where to train (on the job or off the job), and how to train (individual training method, programmed learning, sponsor or group training methods). Executive training programs are sessions directed at store supervisors, managers, and executives. The sixth step is supervision. An important supervising task is motivation. One method of motivating employees is to eliminate conditions that generate job dissatisfaction and to initiate programs that promote satisfaction. Supervising can be approached in a heavy-handed manner (close supervision) or in a light-handed fashion (limited supervision).

Evaluating store employees constitutes the seventh step in the staffing process. The retailer must address such issues as when to evaluate, what to evaluate, and how to evaluate personnel. Finally, the retailer must determine the type of compensation system to use. Alternatives are the straight-salary plan, straight-commission plan, salary plus commission plan, and salary plus bonus plan, all of which might involve various fringe benefits.

KEY TERMS AND CONCEPTS

achievement tests

centralization

departmentalization

dissatisfier

equal-store organization

executive training programs (ETPs)

flat organizational structure

formal objective employee evaluations

formal subjective employee evaluations

functional approach to organizational structure

functional objectives

functional training

geographic approach to organizational structure

group training method

heavy-handed supervision

individual training method

informal objective employee evaluations

informal subjective employee evaluations

job description

job specification

light-handed supervision

line relationships

lines of authority

lines of responsibility

main-store organization

Mazur Plan

motivation

off-the-job training

on-the-job training

operational objectives

organization orientation

product approach to organizational structure

programmed learning

psychological tests

salary plus bonus plan

salary plus commission plan

satisfier

separate-store organization

span of control

specialization

sponsor training method

staff relationships

standardization

straight-commission plan

straight-salary plan

strategic objectives

supervision

unity of command

vertical organizational structure

REVIEW QUESTIONS

1. Identify the three levels of organizational objectives. Define each and describe its relationship to the general levels of retail management.
2. Describe the organizational principles of specialization and departmentalization.
3. Distinguish between line and staff relationships.
4. Discuss the principle of unity of command.
5. What is the ideal span of control?
6. What determines the number of subordinates a superior should control?
7. Why use a flat organizational structure?
8. Which factors determine the number of functional divisions within a retail organization?
9. Identify the four functional divisions in the Mazur Plan of retail organization.
10. Why should the buying and selling functions be separated?
11. Compare and contrast the main-store, separate-store, and equal-store approaches to branch department-store organization.
12. Cite the distinguishing elements of a chain store organization. Discuss each distinctive element.
13. Discuss why a written job specification should be given to a potential employee.
14. Identify the internal and external sources of prospective employees.
15. What is the most effective way to check an applicant's references?

16. List the advantages to using a formal, highly structured interviewing process.

17. Characterize the two general types of testing instruments used in evaluating applicants.

18. How do on-the-job and off-the-job training differ?

19. Identify the methods available to the retailer for training employees. Briefly describe each method.

20. What are satisfiers and dissatisfiers? How do they affect employee motivation?

21. Compare and contrast McGregor's Theory X and Theory Y.

22. How are formal objective employee evaluations conducted? Describe the two methods.

23. Professional shoppers are used to conduct which type of employee evaluation?

24. Cite the disadvantages of the straight-salary compensation plan.

25. Discuss the problems that result from the monetary incentive created by the straight-commission plan.

26. How does the straight salary/single commission plan differ from the straight salary/quota commission plan?

ENDNOTES

1. Paul M. Mazur, *Principles of Organization Applied to Modern Retailing* (New York: Harper & Row, 1927).

2. See for example, Carole Sloan, "Merchandising the Branches," *Stores* (January 1988): 71–74.

3. "Centralization Pays for Woolworths," *Stores* (June 1985): 26.

4. Neil M. Ford, "Recruitment and Selection—Are There Easy Answers," *Sales Management Bulletin* 2 (Summer 1987): 3–4.

5. Jules Abend, "Taking Care of Your Own," *Stores* (November 1987): 98.

6. Robert F. Hartley, "The Weighted Application Blank," *Journal of Retailing* 46 (Spring 1970): 32–40.

7. "The Score on Psycho Testing," *Stores* (September 1985): 63.

8. See J. B. Robinson, "Role Playing as a Sales Training Tool," *Harvard Business Review* (May–June 1987): 34–35.

9. See "Trainees Build Skills in Risk-Free Contest." *Chain Store Age Executive* (June 1987): 56, 58.

10. See Robert Neff, "Videos Are Starring in More and More Training Programs," *Business Week,* 7 Sept. 1987, 108–109.

11. Richard A. Feinberg, Richard Widdows, and Amy Rummel, "Paying For Performance: What You Need to Know," *Retail Control* (April–May 1987): 40–41.

12. Frederick Herzberg, "One More Time: How Do You Motivate Employees?" *Harvard Business Review* 46 (January–February 1968): 53–62.

13. See Douglas McGregor, "The Human Side of Enterprise," in *Leadership and Motivation: Essays of Douglas McGregor,* edited by W. G. Bennis and E. Schein (Cambridge, MA: MIT Press, 1966).

14. See Charles L. Brown, "Staff Assessment and Evaluation Techniques," *Retail Control* (March 1987): 53–60.

15. See William Lundstrom and Cliff Scott, "Mystery Shoppers as a Salesperson Training Tool: Once Is Not Enough," in *Marketing: The Next Decade, Proceedings,* edited by D. M. Klein and A. E. Smith, 170–171 (Southern Marketing Association, 1985); also see "Mystery Shoppers Provide Check on Customer-Service Experience," *Marketing News,* 5 June 1987, 5; also see Art Palmer and Robert Morey, "Retail Sales Check Evaluation Methods," *Developments in Marketing Science, Proceedings,* edited by J. M. Hawes and G. B. Glisan, 330–334 (Academy of Marketing Science, 1987).

16. James R. Terborg and Gerardo R. Ungson, "Group-Administered Bonus Pay and Retail Store Performance: A Two-Year Study of Management Compensation," *Journal of Retailing* 61 (Spring 1985): 63.

17. Jules Abend, "A Bonus Does Pay Off," *Stores* (July 1987): 69.

18. "Hewitt: Long-Term Incentives Grow, Bonuses Shrink," *Stores* (July 1987): 74.

RELATED READINGS

Allmon, Dean E., and Garrott, Stephen. "Retail Personnel Turnover: A Predictive Demographic Model." In *1984 Proceedings,* edited by J. R. Lumpkin and J. C. Crawford, 50–52. Southwestern Marketing Association, 1984.

Brief, Arthur P. *Managing Human Resources in Retail Organizations.* Lexington, MA.: Lexington Books, 1984.

Cayer, Maurice. "Common Sense Ways for Selecting Better People." *Retail Control* (February 1985): 13–36.

Darden, William R., Hampton, Ronald D., and Boatwright, Earl W. "Investigating Retail Employee Turnover: An Application of Survival Analysis." *Journal of Retailing* 63 (Spring 1987): 69–88.

Dubinsky, Alan J., and Skinner, Steven J. "Impact of Job Characteristics on Retail Salespeople's Reactions to Their Jobs." *Journal of Retailing* 60 (Summer 1984): 35–62.

Dubinsky, Alan J., and Skinner, Steven J. "Turnover Tendencies Among Retail Salespeople: Relationships with Job Satisfaction and Demographic Characteristics." In *AMA Educators' Proceedings,* edited by R. W. Belk et al., 153–57. American Marketing Association, 1984.

Gable, Myron and Hollon, Charles. "Employee Turnover of Managerial Trainees in a Department Store Chain." *Retail Control* (January 1984): 54–61.

Gable, Myron, Hollon, Charles J., and D'angello, Frank. "Predicting Voluntary Managerial Trainee Turnover in a Large Retailing Organization from Information on Employment Application Blank." *Journal of Retailing* 60 (Winter 1984): 43–63.

Gifford, John B. and Norris, Donald G. "Research Note: Ethical Attitudes of Retail Store Managers: A Longitudinal Analysis." *Journal of Retailing* 63 (Fall 1987): 298–311.

Hampton, Ron, Dubinsky, Alan J., and Skinner, Steven J. "A Model of Sales Supervisor Leadership Behavior and Retail Salespeople's Job-Related Outcome." *Journal of the Academy of Marketing Science* 14 (Fall 1986): 33–43.

Hansen, Stephen W. "Restructuring for Organizational Efficiency." *Retail Control* (August 1983): 20–25.

Horney, Bryan. "Implementing a Management Control System." *Retail Control* (March 1984): 18–32.

James, Donald L., Stoeberl, Philipp A., and Schniederjans, Marc J. "Coping Strategies for Managing: The Ineffective Subordinate in Retailing Management." *Akron Business and Economic Review* (Fall 1986): 7–19.

Judd, L. Lynn. "Owner/Manager's Age and Retailing Experience: Do They Influence Business Strategies and Success?" In *Developments in Marketing Science, Proceedings,* edited by J. C. Rogers, III, 12–16. Academy of Marketing Science, 1983.

Klatt, Lawrence, Murdick, Robert G., and Schuster, Frederick. *Human Resource Management.* Columbus, OH: Charles E. Merrill, 1985.

Lake, Marjorie A. "Recruiting." *Stores* (April 1982): 63–71.

Lucas, George H., Jr. "The Relationships Between Job Attitudes, Personal Characteristics, and Job Outcomes: A Study of Retail Store Managers." *Journal of Retailing* 61 (Spring 1985): 35–62.

Miller, John D., and Wilson, George. "An Evolving Department Store Structure: A Case Study for the 90's." *Retail Control* (February 1984): 46–55.

Randolph, W. Alan. *Understanding and Managing Organizational Behavior.* Homewood, IL: Richard D. Irwin, 1985.

Redding, Dennis C. "Developing Successors in Senior Management." *Retail Control* (January 1987): 2–33.

Ringel, Lance. "Buyer Training." *Stores* (April 1981): 47–48.

Skinner, Steven J., Dubinsky, Alan J., and Cronin, J. Joseph, Jr. "Sex Differences in Retail Salespeople's Attitudinal and Behavior Responses." In *Marketing Comes of Age, Proceedings,* edited by David M. Klein and Allen E. Smith, 131–33. Southern Marketing Association, 1984.

Still, Leonie V. "Part-Time versus Full-Time Salespeople: Individual Attributes, Organizational Commitment, and Work Attitudes." *Journal of Retailing* 59 (Summer 1983): 55–79.

"Teamwork Pays Off at Penney's." *Business Week,* 12 April 1982, 107–8.

Teas, R. Kenneth. "Performance-Reward Instrumentalities and the Motivation of Retail Salespeople." *Journal of Retailing* 58 (Fall 1982): 4–26.

9

Objectives

☐ Appreciate the physical and psychological impact that store facilities have on customer attraction, employee morale, and store operations.

☐ Distinguish design features vital in creating a desirable store image, in targeting the appropriate consumer group, and in communicating the right impression.

☐ Understand design features necessary to create a store atmosphere conducive to buying.

☐ Identify and explain the major considerations in planning store exteriors capable of stopping and attracting customers.

☐ Specify and discuss the key features of the store's interior and their role in creating an inviting, comfortable, and convenient facility.

☐ Appreciate the need for an aggressive security program.

☐ Identify the various types of security problems and recognize their causes.

☐ Distinguish between various devices and techniques employed by thieves.

☐ Outline the methods used by retailers in detecting and preventing criminal activities.

☐ Discuss the procedures used in apprehending and prosecuting criminals.

Facilities Management: Designing and Securing the Retail Store

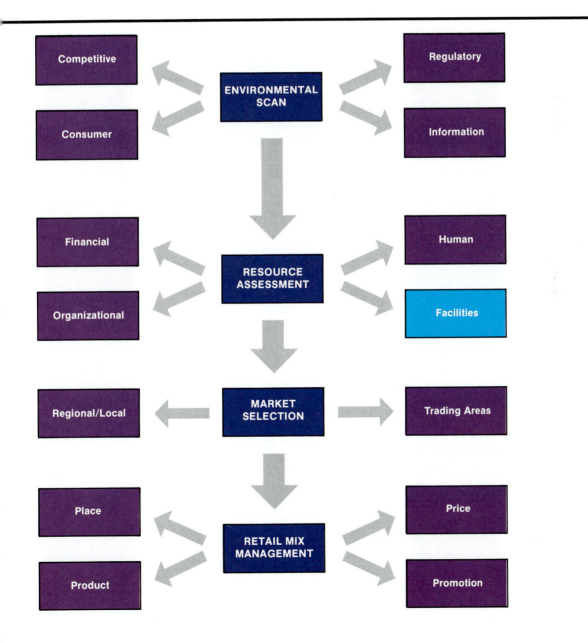

A store and its immediate area create the environment within which a retailer must operate. It is an environment that either attracts or repels potential customers. Accordingly, the retailer must make a concentrated effort to ensure that the store's environment is conducive both to retail operations and to consumer's shopping needs. The elements of store design and store security discussed in this chapter include the physical aspects of the store's exterior and interior design, the problems of customer theft, employee and supplier pilferage, bad checks and credit cards, and burglary and robbery. First, however, this chapter examines the psychological aspects of the retailer's facilities and the environment they create.

THE STORE'S ENVIRONMENT

In selecting and developing a store's environment, the retailer must consider its *physical* and *psychological* impacts on customer attraction, employee morale, and store operations. Store operations and customer shopping are both enhanced by a well-planned and well-designed setting. To appeal to the fashion-conscious, upscaled shopper, Macy's upgraded its New York flagship store "by creating a theatrical environment enhanced by colorful displays and high-tech lighting and audio presentations."[1] A store's physical environment is a composite of the tangible elements of form reflected in the way land, building, equipment, and fixtures are assembled for the convenience and comfort of both customers and retailer. Equally important is the store's psychological environment—the perceived atmosphere the retailer creates. In essence, a store's psychological environment is the mental image of the store produced in customers' minds. A store's effectiveness and uniqueness lie in the retailer's ability to plan, create, and control both the store's physical and psychological setting. The psychological impressions a store makes on consumers depend on the store's image and buying atmosphere. "For a consumer to want to go to a store . . . he or she is going to need a reason. . . . Retailers will have to offer a theatrical approach."[2] "One important aspect of all theater is escapism, and for many shoppers, the retail store can offer that quick escape. Ralph Lauren is an escapist design, pseudo British."[3]

Creating a Store Image

Creating a **store image** should be one of the retailer's principal concerns. The fact that it represents to the consumer a composite picture of the retailer makes image one of the most powerful tools in attracting and satisfying consumers. Creating an image, however, is a very difficult task. An image is a mental picture that forms in the human mind as a result of many different stimuli. These stimuli include the retailer's physical facilities, the store's location, product lines, service offering, pricing policies, and promotional activities.

A store's image is its personality. It is how the consumer *sees* the store as well as what the consumer *feels* about the store. It is important, therefore, that retailers know and plan what they want the consumer to see and feel. A retailer can choose from among many different images; some of the most common follow:

- ☐ Prestigious or economical
- ☐ Contemporary or traditional
- ☐ Swinging or subdued
- ☐ Family or singles
- ☐ Formal or informal
- ☐ Friendly or reserved
- ☐ Restful or active

The store's exterior and interior are key factors in the retailer's image-creating efforts. *Externally*, the position of the store on the site, its architectural design, its store front, and the placement of signs, entrances, and display windows all contribute to the store's image. *Internally*, a store's image can be created, in part, by the layout of departments and traffic aisles, the use of store displays, and the selection of store fixtures and equipment. No standard combinations of external and internal store factors can produce a given image.

In designing the image-creating features of the store's physical facilities, the retailer must work with a particular target consumer in mind. Neither the retailer nor the store can be all things to all people. Likewise, neither can a single image be created that will appeal to *all* consumers. Therefore, a store's facilities should be tailored to the psychological and physical needs of a selected customer group.

The physical facilities of a retail store can be an important vehicle for nonverbal communication. The importance of communicating the right impression assumes that the store's personality helps "position" one retailer against other retailers, thereby facilitating the store-selection process for consumers.

For example, a high-fashion image is the right impression if the retailer has decided to position the store's personality to well-to-do shoppers. Communicating the right impression, then, is a problem of how best to use physical facilities to convey to consumers what the retailer wants them to see and feel.

Creating a Buying Atmosphere

To create an atmosphere conducive to buying, a retailer should establish in the consumer a frame of mind that promotes a buying spirit. Even the economy-minded consumer wants something more than a shopping atmosphere with only the bare essentials. Today's shoppers, regardless of their principal shopping motives, are drawn to safe, attractive, and comfortable shopping environments. The store's atmosphere should be an agreeable environment for both the consumer and the

These two stores have completely different buying atmospheres.

retailer. Some congenial yet stimulating atmospheres might include the following characteristics:

Different lines and shapes give various impressions to store displays and contribute to the overall atmosphere of the store layout.

- ☐ Quiet and plush for the prestige shopper
- ☐ Safe but engaging for the elderly shopper
- ☐ Friendly and loud for the youthful shopper
- ☐ Clean and cheerful for the family shopper
- ☐ Formal and pleasant for the professional shopper

The retailer wants to influence the consumer's mood by creating an atmosphere that will positively influence buying behavior. An appealing buying atmosphere uses cues that appeal to the consumer's five senses of sight, hearing, smell, touch, and taste. Waldenbooks, Inc., is introducing its WaldenKids stores, which sell books and educational toy and games. The WaldenKids stores mimic a playground; "kids can even crawl into the store through a carpeted tunnel. Inside, children are greeted by a video monitor playing cartoon fairy tales—painted primary red, yellow, and blue—toys from computer games to wooden railroads are just waiting for eager little hands."[4]

Sensory cues can be strongly reinforced if they are structured around shopping themes that unify and organize the store's atmosphere. For example, in one store, "Walls, ceilings, beams, and posts were made of laminated layers of pine, with two natural, gray stains used to help create focal points along the walls for various merchandise categories. Special floor coverings used the most dramatic element . . . the 8,500-gallon pond supports about 16 trout and provides the visual centerpiece for the new addition . . . large windows, skylights, and . . . the trout pond all contribute to the out-of-doors feeling."[5] The following sections discuss how a retailer can use sensory appeals to effect a favorable store image and pleasant shopping environment.

Sight Appeal

The sense of sight provides people with more information than any other sense mode and therefore must be classified as the most important means by which retailers can

appeal to consumers. For present purposes, and for the sake of simplicity, **sight appeal** can be viewed as the process of imparting stimuli, resulting in perceived visual relationships. Size, shape, and color are three primary visual stimuli a retailer can use to arouse the consumer's attention. Visual relationships are interpretations made by the "mind's eye" from visual stimuli consisting of harmony, contrast, and clash. *Harmony* is "visual agreement"; *contrast,* "visual diversity"; and *clash,* "visual conflict" that can occur among the many parts of any display, layout, or physical arrangement. In any given situation, either harmony, contrast, or clash may be the best way to create an appealing shopping atmosphere. Harmonious visual relationships are generally associated with a quieter, plusher, and more formal shopping setting, whereas contrasting and clashing visual relationships can promote an exciting, cheerful, or informal atmosphere. To control these environmental impressions, the retailer must understand the basics of visual stimuli.

Size perceptions.   The sheer physical size of a store, a display, a sign, or a department can communicate many things to many people. Size can communicate relative importance, success, strength, power, and security. Some consumers feel more secure when they buy from large stores because they believe that large stores are more capable and more willing to fix, adjust, or replace faulty merchandise. Other consumers prefer larger stores because of the prestige they associate with such operations. A smaller store, display, or department may not be perceived as being as important, successful, or powerful as its larger counterparts, but it could be viewed as more personal, intimate, or friendly.

Size is a key element in creating harmony, contrast, and clash. To achieve a harmonious atmosphere in a store department or display, the retailer should maintain a consistent size relationship among the various elements. Using moderately different size elements can create contrast among different departments within the store or different displays within the department. Clashing relationships can be created by using substantially different size elements.

Shape perceptions.   Shapes arouse certain emotions within buyers. In planning store layouts and in designing store displays, the retailer should recognize that the vertical line gives "a rigid, severe, and masculine quality to an area. It expresses strength and stability . . . gives the viewer an up-and-down eye movement . . . tends to heighten the area, gives the illusion of increased space in this direction."[6] Horizontal lines promote a feeling of rest, relaxation, and repose, while diagonal lines connote action and movement and sometimes give the illusion of instability.[7] Curved lines suggest a feminine atmosphere and add a flowing movement that directs the eye to a display or department. Equally important in facilities planning is the similarity or dissimilarity of shapes. "For the creation of perfect harmony in a display, shapes that correspond exactly to one another are used exclusively. Inharmonious or dissimilar shapes may be used in a display to create contrast and, in some instances, a point of emphasis."[8]

Color perceptions.   Color makes the first impression on someone looking at an object. Color is often what catches customers' eyes, keeps their attention, and stimulates them to buy. The U.S. consumer is becoming increasingly color conscious. For most customers, if the color is wrong, all is wrong.

The psychological impact of color is the result of the three color properties of hue, value, and intensity. *Hue* is the name of the color. *Value* is the lightness or darkness of a hue. Darker values are referred to as "shades," while lighter values are called "tints." The brightness or dullness of a hue is its *intensity.* For the retailer, color psychology is important not only in selling merchandise but also in creating the proper atmosphere for selling that merchandise.

Display harmony (visual agreement) and clash (visual conflict) affect consumer buying moods.

The impact of color psychology becomes apparent as soon as we classify *hues* into "warm" and "cool" tones. The warm colors (red, yellow, and orange) and the cool colors (blue, green, and violet) symbolize different things to different consumer groups. Figure 9–1 identifies some of the associations and symbols consumers attach to colors. Warm colors give the impression of a comfortable, informal atmosphere. Cool colors, on the other hand, project a formal, aloof, icy impression. When used properly, however, both warm and cool colors can create a relaxing yet stimulating atmosphere in which to shop.

Red is one of the most stimulating colors and should be used with considerable care. Too much red can be overpowering; it should thus be used as an accent color rather than a basic background color. To attract attention and to stimulate buyer action, red frequently appears in building signs, fixtures, and displays. Two exceptions to using red only as an accent color are restaurants and cocktail lounges, where red is thought to stimulate people's appetites. Christmas and Valentine's Day are two holiday seasons when red is an appropriate display color. Shades of red are also appropriate for certain decorative themes, such as carnivals and sports.

Yellow, like red, is a stimulating color that must be used with caution. Yellow's principal asset is its visibility at long distances, which makes shades of yellow a logical color selection for signs, walls, and poorly lit areas. The time to use yellow is in the spring, particularly around Easter. Yellow is also considered a color for children, so it is appropriate for decorating infants', children's, and toy departments.

Orange is used sparingly because of its high intensity and its tendency to clash with other colors. Most often thought of as a fall color (fall foliage, harvest, and Halloween), orange is used primarily for accent and not as a basic decorative color. Orange, like yellow, is a children's color and livens up a children's department by evoking warm, cheerful surroundings.

FIGURE 9–1
Perceptions of colors

Warm Colors			Cool Colors		
Red	Yellow	Orange	Blue	Green	Violet
Love	Sunlight	Sunlight	Coolness	Coolness	Coolness
Romance	Warmth	Warmth	Aloofness	Restful	Retiring
Sex	Cowardice	Openness	Fidelity	Peace	Dignity
Courage	Openness	Friendliness	Calmness	Freshness	Rich
Danger	Friendliness	Gaiety	Piety	Growth	
Fire	Gaiety	Glory	Masculine	Softness	
Sinful	Glory		Assurance	Richness	
Warmth	Brightness		Sadness	Go	
Excitement	Caution				
Vigor					
Cheerfulness					
Enthusiasm					
Stop					

Blues are associated with the cool, blue sky and the calm, blue sea. As a result, retailers use blues to create a calm, relaxing shopping atmosphere. Shades of blue often appear in men's departments since this color also connotes masculinity. In addition, blue works well as a trim and as a basic background.

Like blue, *green* suggests many pleasant associations—the newness and freshness of spring and the peace and restfulness of the great outdoors. Many experts believe that green is probably the single most popular and accepted color. Its soft and relaxing qualities make green an ideal choice for many uses. Green is perceived as a spacious color and is therefore useful for making small areas appear larger. Its softness also helps accentuate displayed merchandise.

Violet is little used in retail displays, except to achieve special effects. Too-extensive use of this hue is thought to dampen shoppers' spirits.

The lightness and darkness of colors create optical illusions that retailers can use to modify the store's physical characteristics. Generally, lighter colors make a room or an object appear larger, while darker colors create an illusion of smallness. Light neutral tones (e.g., beige) are popular as fixture colors because they are perceived as warm and soft and do not detract from the displayed merchandise. On the other hand, darker colors have attention-grabbing ability; for example, by using darker colors at the back of a store, a retailer can draw consumers' attention to that area and increase the flow of customer traffic throughout the store.

The brightness and dullness of different physical facilities also affect the buying atmosphere. As with color value, color intensity can create illusions. Bright colors make the facilities appear larger than do duller colors. A bright color tends to create an illusion of hardness, however, whereas a dull color appears softer. As a rule, children react more favorably to brighter colors; hence, these colors' widespread use in children's departments. Adults, on the other hand, prefer softer tones, which may explain why so many retailers use pastels.

Sound Appeal

Sound can either enhance or hinder a store's buying atmosphere. In planning store facilities, it is as important to avoid undesirable sounds as it is to create desirable ones. Disturbing noises detract from a store's appeal, whereas pleasant sounds can attract customers.

Packaging relies heavily on the psychological effects of colors.

Sound avoidance. Obtrusive sounds distract consumers, interrupting the buying process. Whether these sounds originate inside or outside the store, they must be either controlled or eliminated. The clicking of heels on a hard floor surface, the humming of an air conditioner, the rattling of a jackhammer in the street outside, or the blaring music of the record shop next door may represent sound "pollution" to a retailer's selling efforts. Certain buying decisions require considerable thought, and disruptive noises during this thought process are irritating, possibly causing the loss of a sale or a long-term customer.

Noise avoidance is a problem tailor-made for physical facilities planning. Careful use of architectural design, construction materials, equipment, and interior decors can eliminate or at least substantially reduce most obtrusive sounds. For example, clicking heels can be eliminated by heavy, durable carpeting, humming air conditioners can be strategically positioned away from selling areas, and rattling jackhammers and undesirable external music can be neutralized by proper insulation. Lower ceilings and sound-absorbing partitions and fixtures reduce unwanted sounds even further.

Sound creation. To create an atmosphere that encourages buying, the retailer can use **sound appeal** in a variety of ways. Sound can be a mood setter, an attention getter, and an informer. Music can relax the customer, promote a buying spirit, set the stage for a particular shopping theme (e.g., a Mexican fiesta), or remind the customer of a special season or holiday (particularly Christmas), as well as provide a generally pleasant background of familiar sounds. Music must complement the selling scene, though, not detract from it. The type (rock, classical, soul, etc.) and volume of music must be suitable to the retailer's consuming public. "If a store chooses to play music, the selection should match its image and audience—music should enhance the environment, not overwhelm it. In Ralph Lauren's Madison Avenue store the stereo plays Vivaldi and jazz in the morning and Frank Sinatra at 5 P.M."[9]

Sound has been employed as an attention getter under a variety of circumstances. Attention-getting sound can draw customers to a particular display or department. Noise-making toys are effective in attracting both children and adults to the toy department. A principal attention-getting device of stereo departments is the quality of sound emanating from the area. K Mart stores draw attention to their "specials" by loud announcements: "Attention K Mart shoppers." Finally, fast, convenient, and pleasurable shopping requires that the customer have sufficient information about the store, its merchandise, and its operations. Frequently, the retailer must inform the consumer about where to go, when to go, how to get there, and what is available. Because this basic information is a prerequisite to the buying process, the *informer* role of sound is a key element in creating a buying atmosphere. The Music Sampler is an interactive kiosk that "lets customers listen to musical excerpts from new releases while watching a video slide show for each album."[10] Like bookstore customers, record store customers will now be able to browse the records before buying.

Scent Appeal

The creation of **scent appeal** is a problem similar in scope to the sound-appeal problem—how to avoid unpleasant odors and how to create pleasant scents. Stale, musty, and foul odors offend everyone and are sure to create negative impressions. Inadequate ventilation, insufficient humidity control, and poorly placed and maintained sanitation facilities are frequent causes of undesirable odors. Store facilities should be designed to minimize these problems or eliminate them entirely. Pleasurable scents, on the other hand, are key ingredients in creating atmospheric conditions that induce the customer to buy. A well-placed fan in a bakery shop, candy store, or

Note the selection of colors for this children's department.

delicatessen attracts the passerby to these almost unavoidable pleasurable scents of products that are frequently bought on impulse. Retailers of foods, tobacco, flowers, perfumes, and other scented products know the value of exposing their customers' noses to the scents. A store should smell like it is supposed to smell. Some stores, such as a drugstore, should smell clean and antiseptic. For others, such as an antique store, a dusty, musty smell could enhance the buying atmosphere.

Touch Appeal

At one point in the history of retailing, the vending machine was considered the retailing store of the future. Today, although the vending machine is admittedly an important retailer of some standardized products, it is still an unacceptable way to sell most goods. The vending machine's lack of acceptance is, to a large extent, the direct result of its inability to provide **touch appeal**. For most products, personal inspection—handling, squeezing, and cuddling—is a prerequisite to buying. Consider the Charmin example: "It's so squeezably soft." Before buying a product, the average consumer must at least hold it, even if it cannot be removed from its package. Many consumers have become upset because supermarkets now prepackage so many of their fruits, vegetables, and meats in hopes of reducing product damage inflicted by "the squeezers." In general, however, store layouts, fixtures, equipment, and displays must encourage and facilitate the consumer's sense of touch. The chances of a sale increase substantially when the consumer handles the product. The expression "I just couldn't put it down" underscores the importance of getting the consumer to pick up a product.

Good facilities planning not only encourages the consumer to pick up the product, it also helps protect the product. Displays and fixtures should be designed (1) to provide consumers with samples to handle, thereby protecting products for sale from unnecessary handling, and (2) to provide product protection from normal store dust and dirt.

This display appeals directly to several of the physical senses.

Taste Appeal

For some food retailers, offering the consumer a taste might be a necessary condition for buying. This is often the case with specialty foods such as meats, cheeses, and bakery and dairy products. Hickory Farms and Baskin Robbins are two specialty food retailers that use **taste appeal** as part of their selling operations. In designing in-store displays, such retailers provide potential customers with a sample of the product under clean and sanitary conditions.

Theme Appeal

Many retailers find that a *shopping theme* helps provide a focus in planning physical facilities. Theme appeal is a useful vehicle around which to organize the five sensory appeals. Any number of themes can be employed. Common themes center around natural and holiday seasons, historical periods, current issues (energy, environment), and special events (anniversaries). Shopping themes can be organized either on a storewide, department, or product-line basis.

THE STORE'S EXTERIOR

First impressions are so important they are often the swing factor in a consumer's decision to stop at one store or another. Frequently, a consumer's first impression about a store is produced by the exterior. The store's exterior is a key factor in stopping and attracting new customers and retaining existing customers. The major considerations in planning store exteriors are the store's position, architecture, sign, and front.

These shopping themes make appeals to the physical senses, and have both strengths and limitations.

The Store's Position

How and where the store is positioned on the site affects the retailer's ability to attract customers. In evaluating existing store facilities or planning future site layouts, the retailer should consider at least these three questions: (1) How visible is the store? (2) Is the store compatible with its surroundings? and (3) Are store facilities placed for consumer convenience?

Ensuring Store Visibility

For the physical exterior to accomplish its goals of stopping, attracting, and inviting customers to shop, customers must see it. A visible store becomes part of the consumer's mental map of where to shop for a certain product or service. Visual awareness of a store's existence has the short-run benefit of alluring impulse shoppers and the long-run benefit of attracting future customers who develop a particular need for the retailer's products. Simply put, people shop more frequently at stores they are aware of, and **store visibility** is an important factor in developing that awareness. Ideally, a store should be positioned so that it is clearly visible from the major traffic arteries (foot and/or vehicle) adjacent to the site. The retailer improves the store's visibility by using the three interacting factors of setback, angle, and elevation to advantage.

Setback. Reduced visibility can result either from setting the store too far back from a traffic artery or from positioning it too close to the street. Ideally, a store should be set back far enough to give passersby a broad perspective of the entire store, but close enough to let them read major signs and see any window displays.

Angle. Visual impressions also can be enhanced or hindered by the angle of the store relative to a traffic artery. In positioning the store, a retailer should place the building at an angle to the traffic artery that maximizes exposure. Since the store's front is designed to stop and attract potential customers, it should face the major traffic artery. When a store's back or sides are visible to passersby, they too should be attractive and informative.

Elevation. The elevation of a site can place the retailer's store above or below the main traffic artery level. Elevation problems can be partially overcome by landscaping and the use of signs; however, such problems always translate into visibility problems for retailers that need exposure. Most consumers do not see stores that are too high or too low. These stores are also perceived as having accessibility problems.

Designing Site Compatibility

Fitting the store to the natural lay of the land and the natural habitat can reap substantial benefits for the retailer in terms of visual impressions. In designing for **site compatibility,** the retailer should consider several issues. First, the size of the facility should be appropriate to the size of the site. Placing an oversized building on a small site produces a distorted sense of proportion that is visually disturbing to customers and noncustomers alike. Second, architectural design and construction materials should demonstrate a harmonious relationship with the immediate environment. And, finally, a certain amount of open space greatly enhances the appearance of an attractive store.

Planning Consumer Convenience

In planning the store's on-site position, the retailer should consider how the position affects consumer convenience. The retailer might ask a number of questions. Does the store's position allow enough parking spaces and permit easy access to them? Can cars and trucks turn around in the parking lot? Does the position permit safe, convenient pedestrian traffic? Does the position enhance or hinder pedestrian access to the store?

The Store's Architecture

Architecture is a major factor both in making the right impression on the consumer and in developing an efficient retail operation. In most cases the store's architecture is a compromise between these two objectives.

Making an Impression

The store's architectural motif can convey any number of different impressions as well as communicate a considerable amount of information. A certain architectural style can indicate the size and prestige of the retailer's operation, the nature of the retailer's principal product line (e.g., Taco Bell), and the retailer's affiliation (standard store designs used by chain operations, such as McDonald's). In addition, architectural design can support a central theme or focal point for the retailer's merchandising activities. For example, a *marketplace* theme can be suggested architecturally by the use of open space—open store fronts, central squares, and shopping stalls standing out in the open.

Designing a Functional Facility

The impression-creating elements of the architecture must be balanced against the functional needs of retailer and consumer. Functional considerations that are paramount in the store's design are *costs, energy efficiency, security, operational efficiency,* and *customer convenience.*

Rapidly rising land, construction, and materials costs have made the retailer's attempt to differentiate a store from the competition increasingly difficult. Additionally, architectural freedom is limited by the costs associated with maintenance; conversely, architectural designs that reduce maintenance costs often limit customer convenience and store attractiveness.

With increased energy prices, the retailer has an overriding obligation to minimize energy costs. Energy-saving construction methods include lower ceilings, less window space, proper air circulation, controlled entrances and exits, and proper insulation.

Because of the rising crime rate, modern retailers have had to design facilities that increase store security. In their architectural plans, retailers include such security

Note the different impressions projected by the architectural motifs of these store facilities.

features as reduced window space, elimination of unexposed areas, controlled entrances and exits, proper lighting, limited exposure of high-value products, and security devices such as television monitors, two-way mirrors, and observation areas.

Another architectural design consideration is operational efficiency. The best allocation of store space for operational activities is where there is easy movement for customers, sales personnel, and merchandise, and where the retailer can gain maximum product exposure. Of the objectives in architectural design, maximizing selling areas and creating the highest level of product exposure are the chief concerns. With new government regulations and public pressure, the retailer must ensure that all possible physical barriers to handicapped consumers are removed. Physical barriers can also present problems for the elderly and the consumer with small children.

The Store's Sign

A store's sign (marquee) is often the first "mark" of the retailer that a potential customer sees. It serves the two key purposes of identifying the store and attracting the consumer's attention.

This sign both attracts attention and concisely communicates a maximum of information.

Identifying the Store

Signs provide the potential customer with the "who, what, where, and when" of the retailer's offering. Signs identify *who* the retailer is by a name, logo, or some other symbol. Sears, Safeway, and Holiday Inn are immediately recognized by most consumers. Equally recognizable are McDonald's golden arches and Kentucky Fried Chicken's big bucket. Signs can also convey something more to the consumer about who the retailer is. Consider the different impressions that a sign reading "Joe's Bar and Grill" communicates as opposed to one for the "Olde English Pub." Signs also inform consumers about *what* the retailer's operation is. They transmit information concerning the type of retail operation (department store, supermarket, catalog showroom), the nature of the product line (food, hardware, clothing, gifts), the extent of the service offering (full-service bank, self-service gasoline station), and the character of the pricing strategy (discount prices, family prices). Signs inform the consumer *where* the retailer is located and in some cases how to get there (e.g., "Located at 5th and Main," or "Take the next right and follow Washington Avenue for one block"). Finally, some retailers use signs to inform the consumer *when* they are willing to provide service or when they are open (e.g., 24 hours).

Attracting Consumer Attention

The store's sign should create awareness, generate interest, and invite the consumer to try the store. The size, shape, color, lighting, and materials all contribute to the sign's distinctiveness and its abilities to create awareness and interest. The special design of McDonald's golden arches has helped it become one of the most highly recognized signs in the United States.

The Store's Front

A store's front is the first major impression that consumers have of a store. The three primary design elements in a facade are storefront configuration, window displays, and store entrances.

Storefront Configurations

The three basic storefront configurations are the straight, angled, and arcade fronts. As illustrated in Figure 9–2, the **straight front** is a **store configuration** that runs parallel to the sidewalk, street, mall, or parking lot. Usually the only break in the front is a small recess for an entrance. This storefront design is operationally efficient because it does not reduce interior selling space. It lacks consumer appeal, however, because it is monotonous and less attractive than either of the other two configurations.

Window-shoppers can inspect only a small part of any display from any one position when retailers use the straight-front configuration. Reflective glare from windows can inhibit window-shopping, while heavy foot traffic and little privacy deter in-store shopping.

The **angled-front configuration** overcomes the monotony of the straight front by positioning the store's front at a slight angle to the traffic arteries. To create a more attractive and interesting front, retailers that use the angled-front approach place windows and entrances off-center or at one end of the store's front. Angled fronts also give the window shopper a better viewing angle of the merchandise in the window and reduce window glare. The entrance in an angled front is usually located at the most recessed part, to funnel and direct consumers into the store. It provides more

FIGURE 9–2
Storefront configurations

The Straight Front

The Angled Front

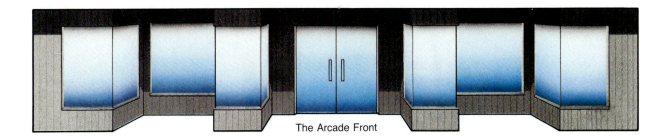

The Arcade Front

protection for the window-shopper than the straight front. The main limitation of the angled front is that it reduces the interior space the retailer can devote to selling.

The **arcade front** is characterized by several recessed windows and/or entrances. Its advantages are that it (1) increases the store's frontage exposure and display areas; (2) provides the shopper with several protected areas for window shopping; (3) increases the privacy under which the shopper can inspect window displays; (4) creates an attractive, relaxing atmosphere for the shopper; and (5) reduces glare for a substantial part of the store front. Its disadvantages are that it considerably reduces interior space for selling and displaying merchandise; it requires a substantial investment in construction and materials; and it requires a professional display staff to make full use of the arcade concept of window settings.

Window Displays

The number, size, depth, and type of windows a store has can substantially alter its exterior appearance and the general impression it produces on consumers. To create the desired impression, the retailer can use one or a combination of the elevated, ramped, shadow box, or island displays.

Elevated windows are display windows with floors of varying heights. The floor elevations range from 12 to 36 inches above sidewalk level. The choice of floor height depends on the kind of merchandise and the elevation necessary to place the display at the typical shopper's eye level. Small merchandise such as shoes, jewelry, books, and cosmetics normally are displayed in windows with a floor elevation of 36 inches, whereas large merchandise such as clothing displayed on mannequins usually appears in windows with a floor elevation of 12, 18, or 24 inches. Elevated windows give consumers an excellent visual perspective of the retailer's merchandise and also protect the glass from damage that might otherwise occur at sidewalk levels. The retailer can use one of three backings for elevated windows: open-backed, which permit the consumer to view the store's interior; closed-back, which prevent that view; and partial-back, which allow the consumer to see only part of the store's interior.

Ramped windows are standard display windows having a display floor higher in back than in front. The floor ramp either is a wedge or is tiered, while the backing may be either open, partially opened, or closed. The principal advantage of the ramped display window is the greater visual impact of merchandise displayed in the rear.

Shadow box windows are small, box-like display windows set at eye-level heights. They are usually completely enclosed and focus the shopper's attention on a selected line of merchandise. Jewelry stores use this type of window display extensively.

Island windows are four-sided display windows isolated from the rest of the store. Used in conjunction with the arcade storefront configuration, the island window can effectively highlight merchandise lines from all angles. This display advantage can become a disadvantage, however, if the retailer does not carefully select and position merchandise.

Store Entrance

Retailers should design store entrances for the customer's *safety, comfort, and convenience,* as well as for guiding the customer into the store. Design considerations for store entrances include (1) good lighting, (2) flat entry surfaces (no steps), (3) nonskid materials, (4) easy-to-open doors (slide away or air curtains), (5) little or no entrance

Explain why these window displays are effective or ineffective.

clutter, such as merchandise tables, and (6) doors wide enough for people carrying large parcels. In addition, store entrances must meet all access regulations for the handicapped.

THE STORE'S INTERIOR

The store's interior must contribute to the retailer's basic objectives of minimizing operating expenses while maximizing sales and customer satisfaction. To accomplish these goals, the store's interior not only must be inviting, comfortable, and convenient for the customer, it must also permit the retailer to use interior space efficiently and effectively.

The Store's Space

Not all of the interior space is of equal value when judged against its revenue-producing capabilities. The consumer's in-store shopping responses to different interior arrangements vary substantially. Specifically, the value of any unit of store space will vary with the floor location, with the area position within each floor, and with its location relative to various types of traffic aisles. Many retailers recognize these variations in the value of store space and allocate total store rent to sales departments according to where they are located and how valuable each space is.

Floor Values

The value of space in multilevel stores decreases the further it is from the main or entry-level floor. Although experts have different opinions on exactly how to allocate rental costs to each floor, they all agree that sales areas on the main floor should be charged a higher rent than sales areas in the basement or on the second, third, and higher floors (see Figure 9–3). The additional customer exposure associated with entry-level floors justifies both the greater sales expectations (value of space) and the higher rent allocation of total store rent by floors.

Area Values

The value of space also varies depending on where customers enter and how they traverse the store. In assigning value to interior store areas (and in making rent allocations), the retailer should consider the following three factors. First, the most exposed area of any floor is the immediate area surrounding the entrance. Second, most consumers tend to turn right when entering the store or floor. Third, a general rule of thumb is that only one quarter of the store's customers will go more than halfway into the store. Based on these three considerations, Figure 9–4 provides one of several variations for allocating store rents to a floor area. Another rule of thumb in assigning rent allocations is the **4-3-2-1 rule** (see Figure 9–5).

FIGURE 9–3
Rent allocation by floors

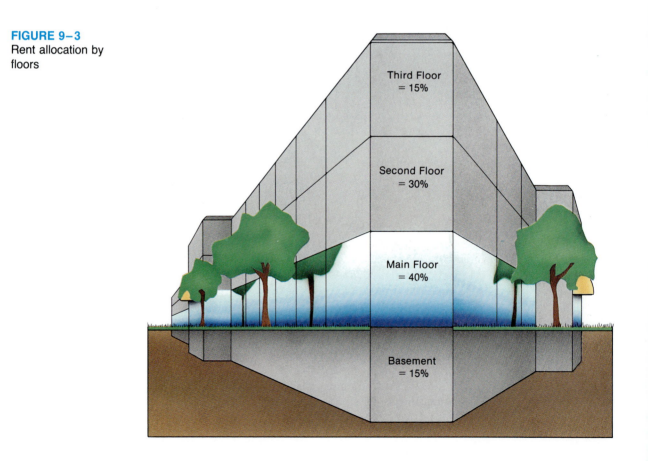

FIGURE 9–4
Rent allocations by
areas

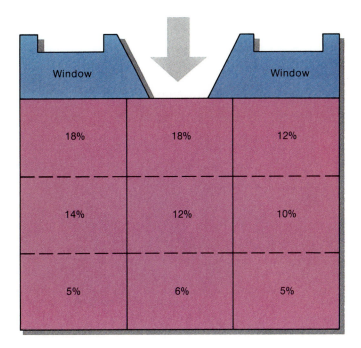

Window		Window
18%	18%	12%
14%	12%	10%
5%	6%	5%

Aisle Values

Because merchandise located on primary traffic aisles greatly benefits from increased customer exposure, the retailer should assign a higher value and a higher rent to space along these aisles than to that along secondary aisles. To illustrate, Figure 9–6 classifies interior store space into high-, medium-, and low-rent areas based on their position relative to primary and secondary traffic aisles. As illustrated, a high-rent area is one exposed to two primary traffic aisles, while a low-rent area is exposed only to

FIGURE 9–5
The 4-3-2-1 rule

The decline in value of store space from front to back of the shop is expressed in the 4-3-2-1 rule. This rule assigns 40 percent of a store's rental cost to the front quarter of the shop, 30 percent to the second quarter, 20 percent to the third quarter, and 10 percent to the final quarter. Similarly, each quarter of the store should contribute the same percentage of sales revenue.

For example, suppose that a small department store anticipates $120,000 in sales this year. Each quarter of the store should generate the following sales volume:

Front quarter	$120,000 · .40 =	$ 48,000
Second quarter	120,000 · .30 =	36,000
Third quarter	120,000 · .20 =	24,000
Fourth quarter	120,000 · .10 =	12,000
Total		$120,000

Source: Norman M. Scarborough and Thomas W. Zimmerer, *Effective Small Business Management* (Columbus: Charles E. Merrill Publishing Co., 1984), 339.

FIGURE 9–6
Rent allocations based on traffic aisles

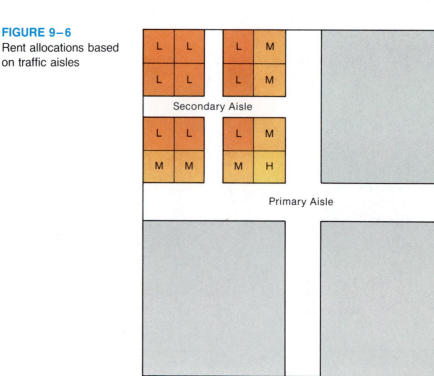

H = High-Rent Area   M = Medium-Rent Area   L = Low-Rent Area

secondary aisles. Medium-rent areas are exposed to one primary and one secondary aisle.

The Store's Layout

A store's interior can be divided into two general areas according to usage: nonselling areas and selling areas. Store size averages for various types of retailers, and the typical amount of space devoted to selling activities, are shown in Figure 9–7. Selling space usually accounts for 75 to 80 percent of the total space available.

Nonselling Areas

A nonselling area is space devoted to customer services, merchandise processing, and management and staff activities. Figure 9–8 identifies some common nonselling areas.

An important consideration in planning a store's interior is where to locate nonselling areas. The four general approaches to locating nonselling areas capable of satisfying both customer-convenience and employee-productivity needs are the sandwich, core, peripheral, and annex approaches. The **sandwich approach** involves using one floor of a multilevel store for nonselling activities (see Figure 9–9a). The **core approach** is the concept of locating all nonselling areas within a central core area surrounded by selling areas (see Figure 9–9b). The **peripheral approach** locates nonselling areas around the exterior of the store or floor (see Figure 9–9c). The **annex approach** locates all nonselling activities away from the sales floor in a non-

Type of Retailer	Average Total Store Size: Square Feet (%)	Average Selling Space Available: Square Feet (%)
Supermarkets	48,800 (100)	36,209 (74.2)
Department stores	148,300 (100)	119,975 (80.9)
Discount stores	88,700 (100)	69,097 (77.9)
Apparel specialty stores	21,200 (100)	16,536 (78.0)
Drug stores	14,300 (100)	11,440 (80.0)
Home centers	28,300 (100)	22,753 (80.4)

FIGURE 9-7
Store size and selling space for selected retailing formats

Source: Reprinted by permission from "Annual Decision-Makers' Digest," *Chain Store Age Executive* (July 1987), pp. 36-37. Copyright © Lebhar-Friedman, Inc. 425 Park Avenue, New York, NY 10022.

FIGURE 9-8
Selected examples of nonselling areas

CUSTOMER SERVICE AREAS

Checkout areas
Dressing rooms
Wrapping desk
Complaint desk
Credit desk
Catalog desk
Repair counter
Return desk
Rest rooms
Restaurants

MERCHANDISE SERVICE AREAS

Receiving areas
Checking areas
Marking areas
Stocking areas
Merchandise control areas
Alteration and work rooms

MANAGEMENT/STAFF AREAS

Offices
Lounges
Locker rooms
Conference rooms
Classrooms
Training areas

selling annex. Usually, the annex is an appendage to the back of the store (see Figure 9–9d).

Selling Areas

Selling space is the area of the store devoted to the display of merchandise and the interaction between customers and store personnel. In planning the store's interior selling areas, the designer must organize merchandise into logical selling groups and allocate space, locate merchandise, and design layouts that are conducive to both the selling function and efficient overall operations.

FIGURE 9–9
General approaches to locating nonselling areas

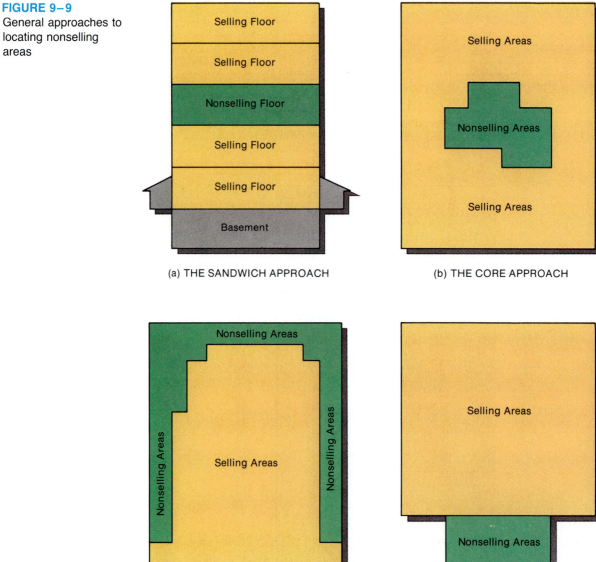

(a) THE SANDWICH APPROACH

(b) THE CORE APPROACH

(c) THE PERIPHERAL APPROACH

(d) THE ANNEX APPROACH

Grouping merchandise. Better merchandise *planning,* greater merchandise *control,* and a more *personalized shopping atmosphere* are three important reasons for assembling merchandise into some type of natural grouping. A logical grouping of merchandise also helps customers find, compare, and select merchandise suited to their needs. The most common criteria the retailer uses are (1) functional (footwear, underwear, outerwear), (2) storage and display (racks, bins, shelves, or dry, refrigerated, frozen), and (3) target-market consumer criteria (men's, women's, children's, or economy minded, prestige oriented, convenience directed). The key points retailers must ensure in grouping merchandise are that the customer understands and appreciates the organization and that merchandise groupings are consistent with efficient operating principles. Figure 9–10 illustrates the floor plan and merchandise grouping of Hypermarket USA, Wal-Mart's entry into the hypermarket business in Garland, Texas.

Allocating space. After a retailer has grouped merchandise according to some logical criteria, selling space must be allocated to each merchandise group. Given that each store has a limited amount of space, the retailer must select some method to allocate selling space. One method is the *model stock method,* whereby the retailer

FIGURE 9–10
Merchandise groupings and floor plan hypermarket USA (source: *Stores* [March 1988]: 56. Reprinted by permission of *Stores.* Copyright by National Retail Merchants Association.)

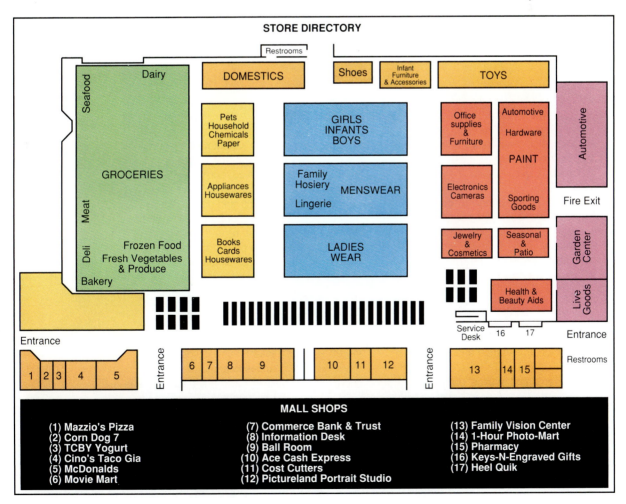

determines the amount of floor space needed to stock a desired assortment of merchandise for each grouping. For the more important merchandise groupings, the retailer allocates a sufficient amount of space to achieve the desired assortment. Merchandise groupings of lesser importance are allocated space based on their assortment needs and the remaining available space.

A second method by which retailers allocate selling space is the *sales/ productivity ratio*. This method allocates selling space on the basis of sales per square foot for each merchandise group. Figure 9–11 identifies some of the best and worst merchandise lines for department and specialty stores in terms of sales-per-square-foot performance. Some retailers use profit per square foot as the basis of space allocation. Merchandise groups with lower sales or profit productivity are assigned space on an availability and needs basis.

Locating merchandise.   Where on the sales floor to put each merchandise group is the third factor in planning the sales floor. Criteria that retailers consider are rent-paying ability, consumer buying behavior, merchandise compatibility, seasonality of demand, space requirements, and display requirements.[11] *Rent-paying ability* is the contribution that a merchandise group can generate in sales to pay the rent for the area to which it is assigned. Other things being equal, merchandise groups with the highest rent-paying ability are located in the most valuable space.

FIGURE 9–11
The best and the worst merchandise performers based on sales per square foot

Department Stores			
Sales per Square Foot			
Rank Best	Sales ($)	Rank Worst	Sales ($)
1. Fine jewelry and watches	332.00	1. Millinery	36.00
2. Cosmetics, fragrances, toiletries	221.00	2. Gifts, Christmas decorations	51.50
3. Costume jewelry	204.00	3. Notions and closet accessories	53.00
4. Ladies' gloves	187.50	4. Floor coverings	55.00
5. All shoes	178.50	5. Window and furniture coverings	56.00
6. Ladies' small leather goods	158.50	6. Linens and domestics	70.00
7. Men's and boys' sportswear	158.00	7. Toys, hobby goods, games	71.50
8. Men's and boys' furnishings	154.00	8. Furniture and bedding	74.50
9. Hosiery	151.00	9. Little boys' (ages 4–7) wear	81.00
10. Women's and misses' sportswear	148.00	10. Lamps, pictures, mirrors	82.00
Specialty Stores			
Sales per Square Foot			
Rank Best	Sales ($)	Rank Worst	Sales ($)
1. Cosmetics, toiletries and fragrances	340.00	1. Infants' and children's clothing and accessories	108.00
2. Women's and misses' dresses	271.00	2. Men's and boys' apparel and accessories	142.00
3. Women's and misses' sportswear	252.00	3. Women's, misses' and junior coats	173.00
		4. Junior sportswear	179.00
		5. Hosiery	184.00

Source: David P. Schulz, "New MOR: New Data," *Stores* (January 1988): 124, 126. Reprinted by permission of *Stores*. Copyright by National Retail Merchants Association.

Consumer buying behavior criteria are based on the recognition that consumers are willing to spend different amounts of time and effort in searching for merchandise. For example, the retailer should place impulse and convenience goods in areas with high exposure (major aisles, checkout stands, etc.) because customers will not exert much effort to find them. In contrast, the retailer should locate shopping and specialty goods in less accessible areas, because consumers' purchase intents are well established and they will exert the necessary effort to find them.

The degree of relationship between various merchandise groups is termed *merchandise compatibility*. This concept states that closely related merchandise should be located together to promote complementary purchases. For example, the sale of a man's suit will increase the chances of selling men's ties and shirts if those products are located close to and are visible from the men's suit department.

Merchandise characterized by *seasonality of demand* is often accorded highly valuable, visible space during the appropriate season. In addition, merchandise groups with different seasonal selling peaks are often placed together to allow the retailer to expand or contract these lines without major changes in the store's layout. Examples are Christmas toys, lawn and garden equipment, women's coats, and women's dresses.

Space requirements for each merchandise group also must be considered in making in-store location decisions. For example, merchandise groups that require large amounts of floor space (e.g., a department store's furniture department) use less valuable space either at the rear of the store, on an upper floor or in the basement, or in an annex. Normally, the bulky nature of such products cannot justify their placement in higher-rent locations.

Display requirements also influence where the retailer places a particular group of merchandise. For example, merchandise such as clothing, which must be hung to display it, probably is located along the sides of walls or at the rear of the store, where it will not interfere with the customer's needs for convenience and comparison shopping and the retailer's selling and operating needs.

Designing layouts.   When designing sales floor layouts, the retailer must consider the arrangement of merchandise, fixtures, displays, and traffic aisles so that they accommodate the spatial and locational requirements of different merchandise groups. Selling floor layouts are extremely important because they strongly influence in-store traffic patterns, shopping atmosphere, shopping behavior, and operational efficiency. Some of the factors the retailer must consider in designing the sales floor layout include the following:

> *Type of displays* (shelves, tables, counters) and *fixtures* (stands, easels, forms, platforms)
> *Size* and *shape* of fixtures
> *Permanence* of displays and fixtures
> *Arrangement* (formal or informal balance) of displays and fixtures
> *Width* and *length* of traffic aisles
> *Positioning* of merchandise groups, customer services, and other customer attractions

Three basic layout patterns are the grid, free-form, and boutique layouts. The **grid layout** is a rectangular arrangement of displays and aisles that generally run parallel to one another. As illustrated in Figure 9–12, the grid layout represents a formal arrangement in which the size and shape of display areas and the length and width of the traffic aisles are homogeneous throughout the store. Although the retailer can develop various modifications in this layout to create variety and to respond to operational needs, this grid pattern essentially retains its formal arrangement. One new upscaled version of the grid layout is Level 6, the home furnishings department of Carson Pirie Scott's flagship store in Chicago:

> It is described as "a creative, functional and personal way to shop for home furnishings and accessories. . . . a splendid new excitement center that's brimming with color, home fashions and flair."
>
> "It" is the new sixth floor—or "Level 6"—of Carson Pirie Scott's State Street store in Chicago, slated to hold its grand opening in early July. And whatever else it may be, there is no doubt it is unique.
>
> Beginning with the layout of Level 6, Carson's has created an environment designed to highlight and emphasize the merchandise itself. The walls, ceiling and floor are all white and devoid of extraneous decor. Previously hidden windows allow natural light to flow in, so the merchandise colors read true.
>
> Now here's where Level 6 deviates from the beaten track of department store merchandising: Near the elevators, customers pick up a shopping cart or basket to hold their selections as they shop. Not precisely the metal supermarket variety, though. Carson's shopping carts and baskets are custom-lacquered in six bright colors to add to the fun of the floor.
>
> And, if shopping carts denote checkout stands to most people, they will not be surprised to see 12 such lanes, including an express lane, at one end of the floor. Additional cash register stations, however, are also spread at various locations throughout the floor, "for your convenience," Carson's is saying.
>
> To create an all-new shopping experience on Level 6, Carson's has also replaced the traditional counters and showcases with nine freestanding merchandise islands, located in the center of the floor. Each island houses a different merchandise classification—including china, glass, silver, gifts, stoneware, cutlery, gadgets, electrics, cookware, sheets, towels, table linens.
>
> The islands are each made up of two facing "U" shapes, the outside of which is covered with mirrors and display fixtures for merchandise presentation, and the inside of which contains all the stock, for customers to walk in and pick up, unaided.
>
> New, custom-made fixtures highlight the outer displays, such as rod sculptures in silver and white for sheets, and pedestals in marble, black, white or gray lacquer and laminate for place settings.
>
> Around the window walls, Carson's has installed a series of vignettes, highlighting changing themes and merchandise. These rooms—which include such themes as party goods, kids' linens, Chicago designers, and a corner rotunda of luxury linens—are meant to be shopped, and customers are invited to pick up any item they see on display.

Figure 9–13 illustrates this twist in the old supermarket layout. Used most frequently by supermarkets and convenience, variety, and discount stores, the grid layout offers several advantages. First, it allows the most efficient use of selling space of any of the layout patterns. Second, it simplifies shopping by creating clear, distinct traffic aisles. Third, it promotes the image of a clean, efficient shopping atmosphere. Fourth, it facilitates routine and planned shopping behavior as well as self-service and self-selection by creating a well-organized environment. And, finally, it allows more efficient operations by simplifying the stocking, marking, and housekeeping tasks, and reduces some of the problems connected with inventory and security control. The major disadvantage of the grid layout is the sterile shopping atmosphere it creates. For this reason, the grid pattern is simply inappropriate for most shopping- and specialty-goods retailers.

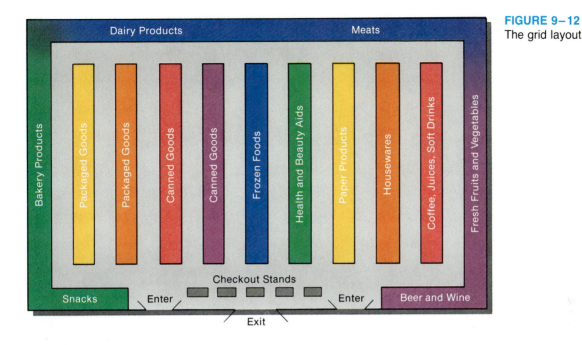

FIGURE 9–12
The grid layout

The **free-form layout,** on the other hand, arranges displays and aisles in a free-flowing pattern (see Figure 9–14). This layout employs a variety of different sizes, shapes, and styles of displays, together with fixtures positioned in an informal, unbalanced arrangement. The main benefit retailers derive from the free-form layout is the pleasant atmosphere it produces—an easy-going environment that promotes window-shopping and browsing. This comfortable environment increases the time the customer is willing to spend in the store and results in an increase in both planned and unplanned purchases. These benefits of a superior shopping atmosphere are

FIGURE 9–13
Retail floor plan (source: "Carson's Level 6: Supermarket Style," *Stores* [August 1985]: 62–63. Reprinted by permission of *Stores.* Copyright by National Retail Merchants Association.)

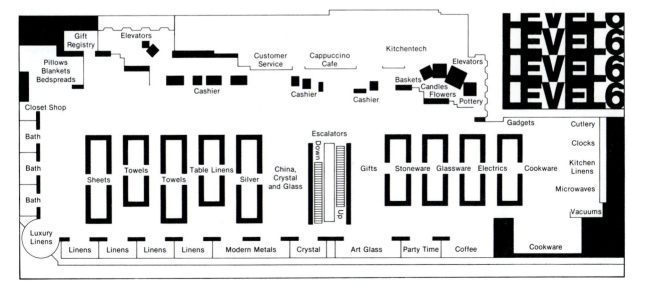

FIGURE 9–14
The free-form layout

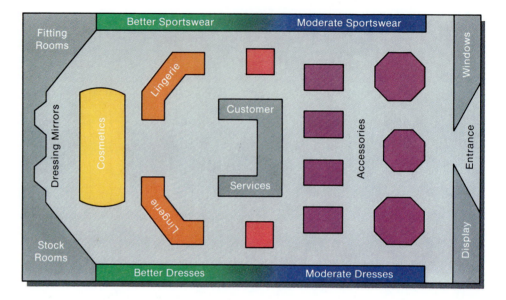

partially offset by the increased cost of displays and fixtures, high labor requirements, additional inventory and security control problems, and the wasted selling space that normally accompany a free-form layout.

The *boutique layout* arranges the sales floor into individual, semiseparate areas, each built around a particular shopping theme. The boutique layout illustrated in Figure 9–15 shows the sales floor divided into several small specialty shops. Carson Pirie Scott changed the second floor of its flagship store into a 60,000-square-foot mall of specialty stores called "Metropolis on 2." Each of the 26 separate stores has its own signage, display fixtures, and shopping bags—in other words, its own identity.[12] By using displays and fixtures appropriate to a particular shopping theme

FIGURE 9–15
The boutique layout

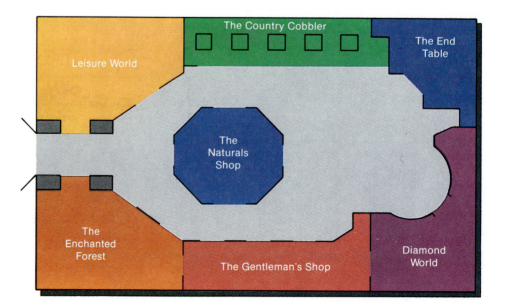

and by stocking the boutique according to this theme, the retailer can create an unusual and interesting shopping experience; for example:

> It's a bird, it's a plane, it's a—a Superman boutique in Macy's Herald Square Store in New York!
>
> The boutique is a joint venture by DC Comics and Licensing Co. of America, both Warner Communications companies.
>
> At the center of the boutique is a life-size figure of Clark Kent standing in a phone booth. Video monitors show Superman movies, and famous sayings about the Man of Steel ("Able to leap tall buildings in a single bound") decorate the valance.
>
> The boutique sells items designed for children and adults, and is a way to commemorate Superman's 50th anniversary, which is being celebrated until June, according to Cheryl Rubin, licensing sales manager for DC Comics.
>
> Products include comic books, J. G. Hook's "Krypton Clothing Co." T-shirts, Una Donna pop-up watches and S-shield pins, Pajama Corp. of America boys' and girls' pajamas and playsuits, Victor P. Handal backpacks and baseball caps, Aladdin lunchboxes, Design Look calendars, posters by Portal Publications, and Dynatoy International's "Power Shirts."
>
> Batman and Wonder Woman, other characters in DC Comics, greeted customers when the store opened and handed out ballots for a drawing. The winner will become a character in a superman comic book.[13]

A "Leisure World" boutique might include such an unconventional merchandise assortment as sporting goods, exercise equipment, home electronics (computer games, stereos, televisions), and art and music supplies. The "Naturals Shop" could feature apparel and food products along with home furnishings, all made from natural materials. To reinforce the theme, fixtures could be constructed from natural, unfinished woods. Boutique layouts have essentially the same advantages and disadvantages as free-form layouts.

STORE SECURITY

Customer theft, employee pilferage, burglary, and robbery are everyday facts of life that every retailer must face and protect against. Collectively, these protective measures are called store security, which must include not only the store and its merchandise, but also its customers and employees. This section describes how a retailer can detect and prevent many of the losses that might result from criminal activities such as shoplifting by customers, pilferage by employees and suppliers, passing of bad checks and credit cards, and thefts by burglary and robbery. While estimates vary greatly, about five cents out of every dollar spent in a retail store goes to cover the losses resulting from these criminal activities and the security measures used to prevent them. As indicated in Figure 9–16, 42 percent of all losses can be attributed to employee theft, 31 percent to shoplifting, 23 percent to poor paperwork control, and 4 percent to vendors.

CUSTOMER THEFT

Shoplifting is the act of pilfering merchandise from a store display by customers and individuals posing as customers. To *pilfer* is to commit or practice petty theft. This form of petty thievery can account for 30 to 40 percent of all stock losses the retailer suffers. Unfortunately for the store's customers, retail prices must be set high enough to cover these losses. Shoplifting occurs in three basic ways: (1) outright theft of merchandise, (2) alteration of the retailer's price tag to reflect a lower price, and (3) switching or substituting a lower price tag for the original tag.

FIGURE 9–16
Retailers' losses
1986 breakdown of re-
tail "shrinkage"—
losses attributed to
theft and other prob-
lems (source:
"Retailers' Losses,"
The Wall Street Journal
[15 May 1987].
Reprinted by permis-
sion of *The Wall Street
Journal.* © Dow Jones
& Company 1987. All
rights reserved.)

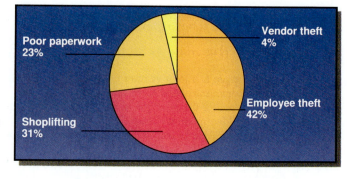

Shoplifter Types and Reasons

Shoplifters fall into two general categories: the amateur who steals to satisfy physical or psychological needs and the professional who steals for a living. An **amateur shoplifter** may be anyone. Usually they neither look nor act the part. They range from juveniles to homemakers, kleptomaniacs to vagrants, and alcoholics to drug addicts. **Professional shoplifters** are in the business for the money. Professionals makes their livelihood by stealing and then reselling the merchandise. They cause serious losses for the retailer because they focus their activities on high-value merchandise that is easy to fence but difficult to trace and recover.

Shoplifting Devices and Techniques

The amateur and the professional use a variety of devices in shoplifting. The main purpose of shoplifting devices is to conceal both the actual act of stealing and the merchandise once it has been stolen. Shoplifting devices include various types of clothing (e.g., coats, "booster" panties, wide-top boots, and other loose-fitting garments) and parcels (e.g., booster boxes, purses, umbrellas, newspapers, magazines, and shopping, school, and knitting bags). The shoplifter might also hide stolen merchandise (e.g., jewelry) in merchandise actually purchased (e.g., box of candy).

Shoplifters use a number of techniques in their pilfering activities. Shoplifters who employ these techniques can be characterized as the booster, the diverter, the blocker, the sweeper, the walker, and the wearer.

The Booster

The **booster** is a shoplifter who shoves merchandise into concealed areas of parcels and/or clothing. Booster boxes are carefully constructed boxes that appear to be authentic, tightly wrapped packages, but contain trap doors that allow the shoplifter to slip merchandise into the box quickly and easily. Other booster devices are *booster hooks* and *bags* securely fastened to the inside of a large, bulky coat; the shoplifter simply slips merchandise onto the hooks or into the bags and walks away. Some shoplifters use *booster coats* constructed to conceal merchandise. Still others wear *booster panties*, loose-fitting bloomers that are fastened tightly around the knees and worn under bulky clothing. The shoplifter drops merchandise into them at the waist.

Decide how effective these security devices might be in preventing and detecting shoplifting.

The Diverter

The **diverter** is one member of a team of shoplifters who attempts to divert the attention of the store's personnel while a partner shoplifts. Diverters use several techniques to attract store personnel's attention, including (1) engaging the salesperson in conversation, (2) creating an attention-grabbing disturbance, and (3) requesting merchandise that requires the salesperson to go to the stockroom. If the diverter manages to draw attention, the shoplifter partner can secure the merchandise and be out of the store before anyone realizes what has happened.

The Blocker

Obstructing the vision of store personnel while they or a partner shoplift is the principal technique of **blockers.** In a team effort, the blocker simply stands between the salesperson and a shoplifting partner. Working as a single, the blocker might employ a topcoat draped over the arm to shield the shoplifting activities of the other hand.

The Sweeper

The **sweeper** simply brushes merchandise off the counter into a shopping bag or some other type of container. Typically, sweepers reach over a counter, apparently to examine a piece of merchandise, but in the process of bringing the arm back, sweep merchandise off the counter and into the container.

The Walker

Some shoplifters have perfected the technique of walking naturally while carrying concealed merchandise between their legs. The **walker** is usually a woman. Shoplifters who have developed this skill are capable of carrying, in a completely natural way, both small items such as jewelry and large items such as small appliances.

The Wearer

The **wearer** tries on merchandise, then wears it out of the store. The *open-wearer* is a bold shoplifter who tries on a hat, coat, or some other piece of clothing, removes the tags, and then openly wears it while shopping and exiting the store. It is the boldness of this technique that makes it successful. *Under-wearers* steal clothing items by wearing them under their own loose outerwear. The most common technique is to take several items into the fitting room but return fewer to the racks.

Other Techniques

Several other shoplifting techniques also are used by both amateur and professional shoplifters. The **carrier** walks in, picks up a large piece of merchandise, removes the tags, affixes a fake sales slip, and walks out. **Self-wrappers** use their own wrapping paper to wrap store merchandise before removing it from the store. And the **price changer** pays for the merchandise but only after taking a shoplifter's reduction by altering or switching the store's price tag or by removing the store tag and substituting a realistic fake.

Shoplifting Detection and Prevention

The retailer's security program should include both shoplifting detection and shoplifting prevention measures. Detecting shoplifters is largely a matter of good observation. Successful detection involves knowing what to look for and where to look. Training store employees to be better observers not only increases the chances of detecting actual shoplifting activities but also increases the likelihood of discouraging potential shoplifters. These are basic observation rules for spotting shoplifting activities.

> **Watch the eyes**. Professional shoplifters avoid looking at the merchandise they are about to steal; their eyes are searching for possible observers. Amateur shoplifters, on the other hand, often focus undue attention on the merchandise they are about to steal.

> **Watch the hands**. Shoplifters and magicians have one thing in common; both rely on sleight-of-hand. It is equally important to watch *both* hands. While one hand may be visibly handling merchandise on top of the counter, the other hand may be busily engaged in shoplifting activities.

> **Watch the body**. Unnatural body movements are more common with amateur shoplifters than with professionals, who have been trained to use smooth, fluid body movements.

Watch the clothing. Loose and bulky clothing are trademarks of a potential shoplifter. When the clothing is out of season (e.g., winter clothing in the summer), when it appears to be inconsistent with the individual wearing it (e.g., large, bulky clothing on a small person), and when it is inconsistent with the weather (e.g., a raincoat on a bright sunny day), the likelihood that the customer is a potential shoplifter is substantially increased.

Watch for devices. Anything the customer carries is a potential concealment device. If the object appears out of place, such as an umbrella on a sunny day or gloves on a warm day, store personnel should pay special attention to the individual.

Watch for groups. Amateur teenage shoplifters often travel in groups or gangs; while two or three members divert attention, the other members shoplift.

Watch for loiterers. Many amateur shoplifters must work up the nerve to steal. In doing so, they frequently loiter around the area containing the merchandise they have targeted for the theft. Professionals also must wait for the opportunity to shoplift. Excessive time spent inspecting exposed merchandise is a good telltale sign of potential shoplifting activities.

Watch for switches. Shoplifters often work in pairs. One shoplifts the merchandise and then passes it on to a partner. Telephone booths, restrooms, and restaurants are favorite switching places for this team effort, so they should be scrutinized.

To facilitate observation and detection, many retailers use devices such as mirrors, observation towers, closed-circuit television, and electronic bugs (see Figure 9–17).

Prevention is the best way to control losses from shoplifting. Without good prevention, the retailer's reputation as "easy pickings" travels fast. While some retailers employ door guards, floor walkers, and mechanical detection devices, the best prevention measures are well-trained, observant employees. Training store employees in the following basic security measures creates the best arsenal to combat shoplifting.

Be aware. Store employees should be aware of all individuals in their areas of responsibility. Anonymity is the shoplifter's friend. Suspicious individuals should be reported to the appropriate security personnel.

Be visible. Store employees should attempt to maintain a high profile in terms of visibility. Shoplifting opportunities are notably reduced in the shoplifter's mind when store personnel are readily visible.

Be alert. Regardless of their activities (selling, stocking, housekeeping), store employees should be alert to the actions of others in the department. The store employee who appears to be "on the lookout" will discourage all but the boldest of shoplifters.

Be available. When a store employee is busy with a customer and another customer is examining merchandise, the latter's presence should be acknowledged by saying, "I'll be with you in a minute." This acknowledgement can tend to discourage the shoplifter.

Be organized. Shoplifting opportunities can be reduced by keeping a minimum amount of merchandise on open counters, returning all merchandise to its proper place after showing it to customers, keeping all high-value merchandise in secured display cases when not showing it, removing all merchandise from

FIGURE 9–17
Observation methods
(source: adapted from
M. E. Williams, "Theft:
Stores Fight Back: For
Retailers, 'tis the Sea-
son to be Wary," Copy-
right 1984, *USA Today*.
Reprinted with permis-
sion.)

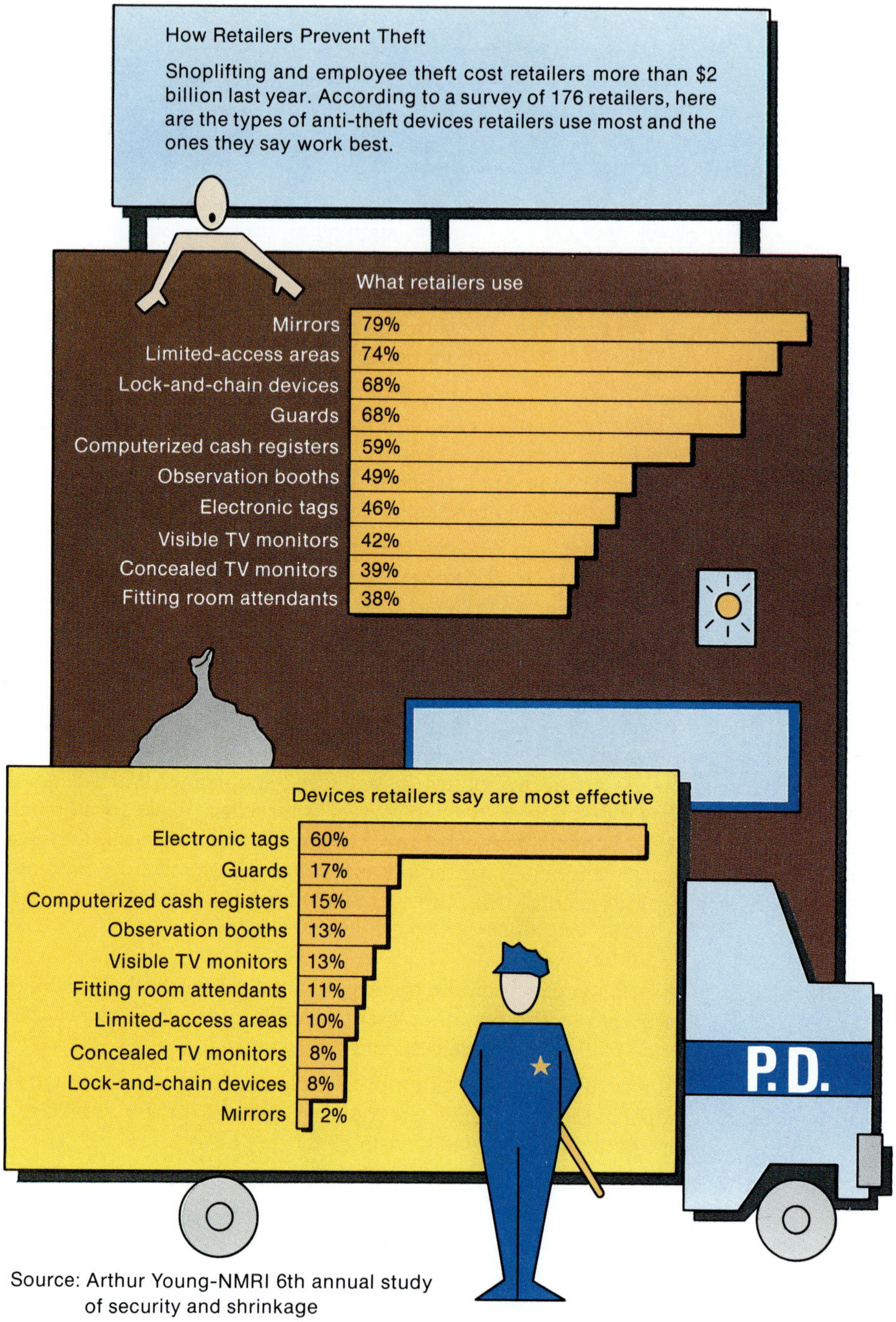

How Retailers Prevent Theft

Shoplifting and employee theft cost retailers more than $2
billion last year. According to a survey of 176 retailers, here
are the types of anti-theft devices retailers use most and the
ones they say work best.

What retailers use

Mirrors	79%
Limited-access areas	74%
Lock-and-chain devices	68%
Guards	68%
Computerized cash registers	59%
Observation booths	49%
Electronic tags	46%
Visible TV monitors	42%
Concealed TV monitors	39%
Fitting room attendants	38%

Devices retailers say are most effective

Electronic tags	60%
Guards	17%
Computerized cash registers	15%
Observation booths	13%
Visible TV monitors	13%
Fitting room attendants	11%
Limited-access areas	10%
Concealed TV monitors	8%
Lock-and-chain devices	8%
Mirrors	2%

P.D.

Source: Arthur Young-NMRI 6th annual study
of security and shrinkage

fitting rooms, and using a check-in and check-out system for all merchandise taken into a fitting room. Detecting shoplifting activities is easier when displays are neatly organized.

Shoplifter Apprehension and Prosecution

Approaching, apprehending, and prosecuting an individual for shoplifting is a tricky business. State and local laws differ concerning the apprehension and prosecution of shoplifters. A number of general rules are appropriate in dealing with any shoplifting situation.

Rule 1: Be Absolutely Certain

Before approaching or accusing an individual of shoplifting, the retailer should be as certain as possible that the individual has pilfered merchandise. Ideally, the person observing the pilferage should be able to identify both the pilfered items and where they were concealed.

Rule 2: Use Trained Personnel

Only trained personnel (e.g., security personnel or store manager) who are familiar with the legalities and techniques of apprehension should attempt to apprehend shoplifters. Store employees who observe actual pilferage of merchandise should notify the proper store security people and should keep the shoplifter in sight at all times to ensure that the pilfered merchandise is not paid for or discarded between the time of the theft and the apprehension by security personnel.

Rule 3: Pick the Right Place

Good judgment is needed to know where to apprehend the shoplifter. In some cases it is best to wait until the shoplifter has left the store because (1) it can improve the store's legal case in prosecuting the shoplifter, and (2) it may avoid a scene or commotion in front of the store's legitimate customers, who might misunderstand what is happening. In other cases, in-store apprehension is preferred when high-value merchandise is involved or when the shoplifter might successfully leave the store. In many states, the law considers concealment of merchandise an illegal act of shoplifting.

Rule 4: Make a Positive Approach

Suspected shoplifters should be approached positively and firmly. Strong-arm tactics, however, should be avoided. The Super Market Institute recommends the following approach:

> One of the common problems in confronting shoplifters is getting them to admit the theft. In most cases approaching the person with "Pardon me, but haven't you got an item you haven't reported?" will get good results. The customer may profess innocence, but if the manager can point out exactly where the item is hidden the guilty person will usually admit it and produce the item. Take advantage of the surprise element and act quickly and positively.[13]

Rule 5: Observe Legal Rights

In apprehending shoplifters the retailer must observe the suspect's legal rights. Undue harassment or force will eliminate any chance of successful prosecution. Use of excessive force, false accusation, search without consent, undue restraint, and public embarrassment are all actions that are viewed as mistreatment of suspects that could lead to successful civil actions.[14]

Rule 6: Call the Police

The police, not the retailer, are duly authorized agents of the law. If the retailer decides to detain the suspect for any reason, the police should be called immediately.

Rule 7: Prosecute When Warranted

Most retailers agree that professional shoplifters should be fully prosecuted at every opportunity where evidence is sufficient for a reasonable chance of conviction. Many retailers like to examine the individual circumstances surrounding each case of amateur shoplifting. Other retailers feel that failure to prosecute amateur shoplifters simply encourages other amateurs to shoplift.

EMPLOYEE PILFERAGE

Employee pilferage represents serious losses for many retailers. Employee theft accounts for approximately 42 to 44 percent of retail shrinkage.[15] It is not unusual for losses from employee theft to exceed those from all other forms of theft. Perhaps the single most important factor contributing to these losses is the retailer's belief that trusted employees do not and will not steal. Recognizing that the problem exists and understanding why and how employees pilfer are the first steps in developing a security program to detect and prevent losses resulting from **employee pilferers**.

Types and Reasons

Employee pilferage takes one of two forms: theft of merchandise and theft of money. Opportunity and need are the two most commonly cited factors responsible for the honesty or dishonesty of employees. In the face of easy and continuous opportunities to pilfer, just about any employee could be expected to take advantage of the situation. By reducing the opportunity to pilfer, the retailer can go a long way to help keep honest employees honest. Some employees may think they need to steal to meet their basic financial obligations. Employees who are intentionally or unintentionally underpaid are prime candidates for "making up the difference" through a self-help program of pilfering.

Devices and Techniques

Like most thieves, the employee who pilfers money and/or merchandise develops definite patterns or modes of operation. Based on these operational modes, profiles can be developed that characterize typical methods of employee pilferage. The most common profiles include the eater, the smuggler, the discounter, the dipper, the embezzler, the partner, and the stasher.

The Eater

The **eater** is the employee who samples the retailer's food and beverage lines or supplements lunch with a soft drink or dessert. Unfortunately, what starts out as a free snack often leads to a six-course feast. For the food store, restaurant, and cocktail lounge, the eater (or drinker) can literally eat up the profits. The only "free lunch" should be one the retailer grants employees under specific and strict guidelines.

The Smuggler

The **smuggler** is the employee who takes merchandise out of the store by whatever means are available. Many retailers might be surprised to learn how much merchandise is carried out the back door in trash cans and bags. The smuggler also uses coats, lunch boxes, purses, and various other types of bags and packages to conceal and transport merchandise from the store's premises.

The Discounter

The **discounter** feels entitled to give unauthorized discounts to friends and relatives. By charging $10 for a $16 pair of slacks, the employee may satisfy a "special" customer but certainly not at a profit for the retailer. Other employees give their friends and relatives unauthorized discounts with free merchandise or "two for one" sales. The friend or relative who receives two for the price of one is sure to spread the word among other friends and relatives. Before long, the employee is in a compromising position with few alternatives other than to quit the job.

The Dipper

The **dipper** is the store employee who steals money by dipping into the cash register or mishandles cash in some other way, such as making short rings, fraudulent refunds, or false employee discounts. A *short ring* occurs when the employee fails to ring a sale on the cash register or rings less than the purchase amount. In either case, the employee pockets whatever money is left over from the transaction. Regular occurrences of either shortages or overages are perhaps the best clue to possible short rings and the employee's inability to keep track of what has been pilfered.

The *fraudulent refund* is the second method the dipper uses to steal money. By writing up refund tickets for merchandise that has not been returned, the dipper can pocket the entire amount of the refund. To use this method the dipper must have access to refund slips and the authority to issue refunds. *False employee discounts* also allow the dipper to pilfer cash; the employee simply rings up a regular customer sale as an employee-discount sale and pockets the difference. If employees are allowed a 10-percent discount, a $10 false employee-discount sale would net the dipper $1.

The Embezzler

The **embezzler** is most often a highly trusted employee who takes advantage of that trust to divert the retailer's funds for either permanent or temporary use. Obviously, permanent diversion of funds is an outright theft; equally dishonest, and illegal, however, is temporary diversion of funds for personal use. Some of the simpler embezzlement schemes are (1) adding the names of relatives and fictitious employees to the payroll and collecting "their" multiple paychecks; (2) creating dummy suppliers and falsifying purchase orders, then collecting for fictitious shipments; (3) accepting kickbacks from suppliers for inflated purchases; (4) padding expense accounts; (5) falsifying overtime records; and (6) using company supplies and facilities (postage stamps, long distance calls, etc.) for personal use.

The Partner

The **partner** is a store employee who does not actually pilfer the merchandise or money, but who supplies outside individuals with information (such as security procedures) or devices (such as keys) that increase the likelihood of successful theft. In return, the store employee receives a cut of the pilfered merchandise.

The Stasher

The **stasher** is the store employee who hides merchandise in a secure place inside the store. Later in the selling season, when the merchandise is marked down for clearance, the employee removes the stashed merchandise from its hiding place and purchases it at the discount price. Essentially, the store employee has pilfered the difference between the original price of the merchandise and the discounted price.

Detection and Prevention

To combat employee pilferage, the retailer's security program should include (1) creating a security atmosphere, (2) using security personnel, and (3) establishing security policies.

Creating a Security Atmosphere

One of the most effective methods of controlling employee theft is to create a general store atmosphere in which not even the slightest degree of dishonesty is tolerated and where honesty and integrity are rewarded. The first step in creating a security atmosphere is to stop employee theft before it starts by carefully screening employees before they are hired and by properly training them after they are employed. Some retailers require each prospective employee to take a polygraph (lie-detector) test as a prerequisite to being hired.

The second step in creating a security atmosphere is for management to set the example. By engaging in dishonest or questionable behavior, the manager sets the tone for an atmosphere that can lead to employee pilferage. If the manager is not subject to various security measures, why should employees tolerate them?

A third step is to create a work environment that is free from unnecessary temptation. Establishing and enforcing good security policies can substantially reduce opportunities for employee theft.[16] Many retailers hold awareness-raising seminars for managers to assist them in identifying theft opportunities.

Finally, an important step toward creating a security atmosphere is to establish an environment that makes employees feel like trusted and respected members of a team. By being aware of and interested in employees' problems, needs, and aspirations, the retailer can develop a personal relationship that encourages honesty and loyalty.

Using Security Personnel

To detect, discourage, and prevent employees from pilfering, some retailers use several types of security personnel. Stationing *uniformed guards* at employee entrances/exits and requiring employees to check in and out of the store reduce opportunities for removing merchandise from the store. The threat of search on a random basis can serve as a major deterrent to employee theft.

Retailers also use **undercover shoppers** to check on the honesty of employees. Posing as a legitimate customer, an undercover shopper can often detect the activities of the eater, the discounter, and the dipper. By informing store employees that such undercover security personnel are present in the store, the retailer has activated an effective preventive measure.

Additional security measures include **silent witness programs** that reward employees with cash for anonymous tips on theft activities of other employees. Tips are transmitted to a third party, who relays the information to the employer.

Establishing Security Policies

Retailers have established a number of store security policies to control employee theft. The following policies aim at controlling employee pilferage.

1. All packages, bags, trash cans, and other devices for concealing merchandise are subject to unannounced random inspection.
2. All store employees (including management personnel) will enter and leave the store by designated entrances and exits.
3. All customers' discounts must be specifically approved by the store manager.
4. All sales must be registered, and each customer must be given a sales receipt.
5. All customer returns and refunds must be approved by the department or store manager.
6. All sales involving employee discounts must be approved by the store manager.
7. All cash registers and cash boxes are subject to regularly scheduled checks as well as random unscheduled checks.
8. All records (sales, purchase, expense, etc.) are audited regularly and randomly.
9. All sales personnel are assigned individual cash draws and are responsible for their security.
10. All refund slips, sales slips, price tags, and other recording instruments are sequentially numbered and assigned to the store employee who, in turn, is responsible for their proper use.
11. All employee purchases must be made during regular working hours.
12. All locks are changed periodically and new keys issued only to authorized personnel.
13. All employee purses, handbags, lunch boxes, packages, and coats will be kept off the sales floor and out of the stockroom. Central locker facilities will be provided for their security.
14. All store facilities, supplies, and equipment are to be used for store business only. Personal use of such facilities, equipment, and supplies is forbidden.
15. All employees are forbidden to accept any favor, gift, or other unauthorized consideration for any reason from any supplier.
16. All employees are responsible for keeping accurate records on all transactions.
17. All payments above a specific limit require a countersignature.
18. All employees caught pilfering will be fired and prosecuted.

Apprehension and Prosecution

The same rules apply in approaching, apprehending, and prosecuting employee pilferers as apply for shoplifters: (1) be absolutely certain, (2) use trained personnel, (3) pick the right place, (4) make a positive approach, (5) observe legal rights, (6) call the police, and (7) prosecute when warranted.

SUPPLIER PILFERAGE

When developing a store security program, the retailer must remember that suppliers have some of the same security problems with dishonest employees as does the retailer. Therefore, it is prudent to take security precautions against pilfering by supplier representatives. The retailer is very vulnerable to pilfering activities of delivery personnel. These activities include (1) **short counts**—delivering fewer items than were listed on the purchase order and signed for on the invoice—and (2) **merchandise removal**—stealing merchandise from receiving, checking, stocking, and selling areas. In the latter case, dishonest delivery personnel have readily accessible concealment devices, such as empty boxes, delivery carts, and bulky work clothes. There are numerous security requirements and procedures to reduce and eliminate pilferage by supplier personnel, some of which are listed here.

1. Establish a receiving area (preferably in the rear of the store) for accepting all incoming merchandise.
2. Supervise all deliveries made directly to the sales floor and/or stockroom.
3. Limit the number of entrances to the receiving area and secure them with locks, alarms, surveillance equipment, etc.
4. Control entry and exit to the receiving area by restricting the area to authorized store personnel only or to individuals who are under the direct supervision of authorized employees.
5. Inform all delivery personnel that they and their equipment are subject to random inspection while they are on the store's premises.
6. Check all incoming shipments using one of the many available checking procedures.
7. Document all incoming shipments as to contents, weight, size, condition of shipment, and any other information pertaining to the supplier, the shipment, and conditions of acceptance.
8. Accept only shipments from suppliers that agree to make necessary adjustments resulting from inaccurate, damaged, or otherwise unacceptable merchandise.
9. Avoid collusion between supplier personnel and store personnel by developing adequate auditing procedures.

BAD CHECKS

Accepting checks in exchange for merchandise has become an essential part of most retailers' service offering. Accepting bad checks, however, is not part of that service. A bad check is, of course, not honored for payment when the retailer presents it to the designated bank. The retailer's security program must include safeguards against accepting worthless checks and appropriate procedures for recovering losses resulting from such exchanges.

Types and Reasons

In exchange for merchandise, the customer may present a number of different kinds of checks: personal, two-party, payroll, government, blank, counter, and travelers'. Any one of these checks can represent a bad check. Bad checks can be stolen and falsely endorsed, written on bank accounts with insufficient funds, and written on nonexistent or closed bank accounts. Also, a check can be bad if the customer stops payment on the check, or intentionally or unintentionally fills it out incorrectly, or the bank simply does not accept a particular type of check (e.g., a blank check). Given this number of possibilities for accepting a bad check, the retailer must carefully develop detection and prevention measures.

Detection and Prevention

It is virtually impossible to avoid some bad checks. Through proper detection and prevention measures, however, the retailer can keep bad check losses at a minimum.

Inspect Checks

Clues to worthless checks are often contained on the checks themselves. By carefully examining each check not only for fraudulent information but for simple, honest mistakes in writing, the retailer can help avoid accepting checks that are intentionally or unintentionally bad. The following guidelines should be observed in accepting and cashing checks:

1. Do not accept checks on nonlocal banks unless clear identification of the customer can be made.
2. Do not accept undated or postdated checks.
3. Do not accept checks with a date more than 30 days old.
4. Do not accept two-party or counter checks.
5. Do not accept checks on which the numerical amount does not agree with the written amount.
6. Do not accept checks that are not written legibly.
7. Do not accept checks in excess of the amount of purchase.
8. Do not accept payroll checks on which the company's name is stamped or typed. It should be a printed check.
9. Do not accept payroll checks on an unknown company.
10. Do not accept payroll checks unless they are endorsed exactly as the name appears on the face of the check.

When the customer is well known, strict adherence to these guidelines may not be necessary, though only the store manager should make exceptions. After determining that the check is okay, it is then necessary to determine whether the customer offering the check is the right person (see Figure 9–18).

FIGURE 9–18

Spotting the bad check artist

- Does the age of the customer match with the identification? Birthdate on ID seem correct for the customer? Is customer with a driver's license old enough to drive?
- Does the sex shown on the ID match the customer? Does the name on check and identification match the sex of the presenter?
- If photo identification is shown, does the picture look reasonably like the customer, allowing for aging and cosmetic changes, such as hair coloring?
- Is the customer nervous? Or appear to be in a rush? Does the customer hesitate when signing the check or when asked to verbally repeat the address or phone number?
- Is the customer shopping in a "high risk" merchandise department? These might include: jewelry; consumer electronics; appliances; and other merchandise categories where goods can be sold quickly for cash. Your own store's experiences will help you determine where you are most at risk.
- Is the transaction too rapid for the type of merchandise selected? For example, does the customer fail to ask about warranty, delivery, layaway, or other questions which frequently arise in connection with the merchandise being purchased?

Source: *Check Acceptance Policies and Procedures,* Credit Management Division, National Retail Merchants Association, New York, 1984, 9.

Require Identification

No check should be accepted without proper identification. Many retailers require at least two pieces of acceptable identification. Driver's licenses, automobile registration cards, credit cards, and employment identification cards are most accepted by retailers. Some retailers will not cash checks unless the customer has at least one piece of identification with a current photograph.

Establish a System

The retailer should establish a system that clearly states check-cashing policies. Employees and customers alike should be informed of the types of checks that are acceptable and the conditions under which the retailer will accept them. Some retailers have created check-cashing systems that employ various recording devices and registration methods. Some retailers use the *thumbprint system,* which imprints a customer's thumb on the back of the check. If the check is bad, later identification is possible. With the *registration system,* retailers request that their customers register identification information at some prior time with the store's credit or customer-service office. Once registered, the customer receives a check-cashing ID card. All pertinent information concerning the customer is gathered at the time of registration and verified by the central office. When paying by check, the customer simply shows the ID to the salesclerk, who records the ID number on the check and compares the check signature with the ID signature.

BAD CREDIT CARDS

Sales charged to stolen, fictitious, cancelled, and expired credit cards cause substantial losses for retailers each year.[17] To reduce these costs, a good policy for retailers is to exercise as much care in accepting credit cards as in cashing checks. In accepting both third-party credit cards (bank cards, entertainment cards, etc.) and the store's own credit cards, the following procedures are recommended:

1. Check credit card against "stolen card" list.
2. Check credit card against "cancelled card" list.
3. Check credit card expiration date.
4. Compare signature on credit card with that on credit slip.
5. Obtain approval of all credit card sales above a specific amount.
6. Fill in all required information on each credit slip (date of purchase, itemized list and amounts of purchases, sales tax charges, and total amount of purchases).
7. Submit all credit card sales for immediate processing.

BURGLARY AND ROBBERY

Retail stores are prime targets for burglary and robbery because they are less secure than most other businesses. This lack of security results from carelessness as well as from the general nature of the retailing business (which often requires some isolated locations, evening hours, exposed cash in registers, etc.). While retailers can do little to alter the nature of their business, they can initiate security measures to make their stores a less desirable target for burglary and robbery and reduce their harmful impact. **Burglary** is defined as "any unlawful entry to commit a felony or a theft, even though no force is used to gain entrance."[18] **Robbery** is "stealing or taking anything of value by force, or violence, or by use of fear."[19] Given the steady increase in the number of burglaries and robberies in recent times, the retailer's security program must incorporate careful measures to prevent such crimes.

Preventing Burglary

Burglars usually operate under cover of darkness, after the store is closed. They gain entry by picking locks, forcing doors or windows open, using duplicate keys, or hiding in the store until it closes. Most security measures are directed at (1) preventing the burglar from gaining entry to the store, (2) securing all high-value merchandise, and (3) informing police and other security personnel of all successful and unsuccessful attempts at entry. Most retailers use locks and lights to discourage attempts at entry, safes to secure valuables, and alarms to warn police.

Security Locks

Good security locks offer protection in a number of ways. First, they discourage the less-skilled burglar from attempting entry. Second, they are generally "pick proof," thereby requiring the burglar to make a forced entry, which is riskier because of the time it takes, the noise it makes, and the evidence it leaves. Third, by making it necessary for the burglar to use force to enter the store, the retailer is protected by insurance because most burglary insurance policies require evidence of forced entry.

Security Safes

Some skilled burglars can gain undetected entry to the store regardless of the preventive measures the retailer uses. These highly skilled burglars, however, usually are interested only in high-value merchandise or cash. A burglar-resistant safe can create another major obstacle to attempted theft. The safe should be well lighted, and usually near the front of the store where it is visible from the outside. To boost security, the retailer can bolt the safe to the floor or set it in concrete. Even when the building is reasonably secure and safe, the retailer can further discourage burglary attempts by "keeping the cupboard bare." All excess cash should be banked every day.

Security Alarms

Security alarms serve a number of purposes. They discourage some burglars from attempting entry, they detect the entry of those who do not know they are there or who do not know how to circumvent them, and they notify the police or a private security agency that an illegal entry has been made. The silent, central-station burglary alarm system gives the best protection. Retailers can choose from several alarm-sensing devices: (1) radar motion detectors, (2) invisible photo beams, (3) ultrasonic sound detectors, and (4) vibration detectors.

In addition to locks, safes, and alarms, retailers located in high-crime areas might also consider using heavy window screens (removable metal grating), burglar-resistant glass (shatterproof), watchdogs, private security patrols, and security lights. Savings from fewer thefts and reduced insurance premiums can offset the additional cost of these security measures.

Handling Robbery

Although burglary can result in substantial losses of money and merchandise, robbery is far more serious because it always holds the potential of loss of life as well as property. By definition, robbery is a violent crime in which one person uses force, or the threat of it, against another individual. Perhaps the most disturbing aspect of robbery is that many robberies are committed for very small sums of cash or merchandise, often by individuals who are extremely unstable (e.g., drug addicts). Training employees to cope with robbers and limiting the opportunities for robbery help to ensure the well-being of store personnel and to reduce property losses.

Training Employees

The retailer's first concern in developing any robbery security program is to train store employees to handle the actual robbery situation. The following procedures and instructions can help:

1. Remain as calm as possible.
2. Make no sudden moves.
3. Reassure robbers that they can expect full cooperation in every way.
4. Make no attempt to be a hero by trying to apprehend the robber.
5. Give robbers whatever they want when they want it.
6. Attempt to make mental notes on the robber's description (height, weight, hair and eye color, complexion, voice, clothing, and any other distinguishing characteristics).
7. Remain stationary until the robber has completely exited the premises. Then call the police and the store's management.
8. Talk only to the police and store manager regarding the robbery situation and the robber.

Reducing Risks

Several preventive measures might well reduce the number of robbery attempts as well as losses suffered from robberies. To reduce the risk of robbery, the retailer should heed the following guidelines:

1. Keep as little cash in each cash register as possible and remove excess cash from the register frequently.
2. Maintain a minimum level of operating cash in the store. Bank all excess cash.
3. Use armored-car service for making bank deposits. If using armored car service is impractical, vary bank trip routes and times.
4. Keep store safes locked at all times. Do not leave a safe open during operating hours.
5. Use two people to open and close the store—one for the actual opening and closing of the store and the other as an outside security lookout.
6. Exercise extreme caution when someone asks you to make an emergency opening during hours the store is closed. Before going to the store, call the police and make sure they will be there for the unscheduled opening.

Establish the Defense

Antirobbery defense systems are directed at discouraging and apprehending the robber. Some of the more common robbery-protection systems include panic buttons, till traps, video systems, and cash-control devices.[20] Panic buttons are hidden alarm devices that silently alert the police or security company that a robbery is in progress. Most security experts recommend placing buttons in several locations to increase the chances of their being activated. Till traps are devices installed in cash register drawers that trigger a silent alarm when the last dollar bill is removed from the till. In-house video systems are highly visible closed-circuit TV monitors trained on the cash register. They serve the dual purpose of discouraging potential robbers and providing police with pictures of an actual robbery. "Where there is money, there are robberies."[21] To correct this situation, retailers can install cash-control devices that accept currency deposits and dispense cash on an irregular basis. Keeping small amounts of cash in the till discourages robbery.

One of the most valuable ways the retailer can attract customers is by the appearance of the store and its immediate surroundings. The store's environment has both physical and psychological repercussions in the battle for the customer's attention and for efficient operations. By identifying the desired image, targeting the right consumer, and communicating the right impression, the retailer creates a store image that is right for shopping and working. Appeals to the five senses promote a favorable buying atmosphere. Sight, sound, smell, touch, and taste appeals have an obvious influence on the consumer's buying behavior.

Communication with the consumer is facilitated by the store's exterior. How and where the store is positioned on the site affect the retailer's ability to attract customers. The store should be positioned so that it is visible to the consumer, compatible with the natural environment, and convenient for on-site movement of people and vehicles. The store's architecture should incorporate features that make a good impression while remaining functionally efficient. The store's sign serves two purposes: identifying the store and attracting consumer attention. Because the store's facade often creates the consumer's first impression, the appropriate configuration, attractive window displays, and accessible store entrances are essential.

The store's interior should minimize operating expenses while maximizing sales activities and customer satisfaction. In planning store layouts, the retailer must consider that all space is not equal in sales-producing potential. Also, wise use of non-selling space helps the retailer meet consumers' service needs.

Store security calls for developing the necessary safeguards for the store and its merchandise by initiating programs for detecting and preventing losses resulting from shoplifting by customers, pilfering by employees and suppliers, passing of bad checks and credit cards, and burglary and robbery.

Shoplifting is the theft of merchandise by customers or individuals posing as customers. There are basically two types of shoplifters: those who steal from need and for psychological reasons (amateurs) and those who steal for a living (professionals). Several shoplifting devices and techniques can be enumerated: the booster, the diverter, the blocker, the sweeper, the walker, and the wearer. The best means of detecting shoplifters is good observation—knowing what to look for and where to look. In addition to well-trained personnel, retailers use convex mirrors, one-way mirrors, observation towers, closed-circuit television, and electronic "bugs" to aid in the detection process. Retailers should apprehend shoplifters in full compliance with the law and prosecute shoplifters when conditions warrant.

Store employees do steal; losses from employee pilferage exceed those from shoplifting. Opportunity and need are the two most critical causes for this type of theft. The eater, the smuggler, the discounter, the dipper, the embezzler, the partner, and the stasher are all types of dishonest employees who pilfer merchandise and money. The retailer can reduce this form of theft by creating an atmosphere of honesty, by using security personnel, and by establishing strict security policies.

The retailer's security program must also extend to procedures for controlling pilferage by suppliers, for guarding against bad checks and credit cards, and for reducing opportunities for burglary and robbery.

amateur shoplifters

angled-front configuration

annex approach

arcade-front configuration

the blocker

the booster

boutique layout

burglary

the carrier	scent appeal
core approach	the self-wrapper
the dipper	shadow box windows
the discounter	shoplifting
the diverter	short counts
the eater	sight appeal
elevated windows	silent witness programs
the embezzler	site compatibility
4-3-2-1 rule	the smuggler
free-form layout	sound appeal
grid layout	the stasher
merchandise compatibility	store image
merchandise removal	store visibility
the partner	straight-front configuration
peripheral approach	the sweeper
pilferers	taste appeal
the price changer	theme appeal
professional shoplifters	touch appeal
ramped windows	undercover shoppers
robbery	the walker
sandwich approach	the wearer

REVIEW QUESTIONS

1. What is store image?
2. List three types of visual relationships. Briefly describe each type.
3. How are large and small sizes perceived?
4. Describe the emotions or feelings consumers associate with horizontal lines, vertical lines, and slanted lines.
5. Explain the psychological impact of color.
6. What illusions are created by bright colors?
7. Identify the three uses for sound in creating a buying atmosphere.
8. What is site compatibility? How is it achieved?
9. What three factors determine a store's visibility? Explain.
10. Discuss design considerations for a functional facility.
11. Describe the who, what, where, and when functions of a retail store sign.
12. Compare and contrast the three basic storefront configurations.
13. What is the 4-3-2-1 rule?
14. Describe the four general approaches to locating nonselling areas.
15. Compare and contrast the model stock and sales productivity methods of allocating selling space.
16. How can seasonality of demand affect the in-store location of merchandise?
17. Describe the three basic layout patterns. What are the strengths and weaknesses of each pattern?
18. Identify the three basic ways by which shoplifting is accomplished.
19. Discuss the shoplifting devices used by the booster.
20. How does the diverter distract the attention of sales personnel?
21. Who are walkers?
22. How does the price changer secure unauthorized price reductions?
23. List the eight basic rules for spotting shoplifting activities.
24. Describe the major devices retailers use in observing and detecting shoplifters.

25. What are the two most commonly cited factors for explaining the dishonesty of employees?
26. Who is the discounter?
27. How does the dipper dip? Discuss the three types of dipping.
28. What are the two most common methods of supplier pilferage?
29. How does burglary differ from robbery?
30. What antirobbery defense system might the retailer use to help discourage or apprehend robbers?

ENDNOTES

1. Amy Dunkin, "Taking Macy's Out From Under the Magnifying Glass," *Business Week,* 4 Nov. 1985, 26.
2. Muriel J. Adams, "Robots in the Future," *Stores* (April 1988): 41.
3. Ibid.
4. Russell Mitchell, "Waldenbooks Tries Hooking Young Bookworms," *Business Week,* 11 May 1987, 48.
5. "Design Lends Sense of Theater to Mail-Order Firm's Home Town Store," *Marketing News,* 1 Feb. 1985, 26.
6. Kenneth H. Mills and Judith E. Paul, *Applied Visual Merchandising* (Englewood Cliffs, NJ: Prentice-Hall, 1982), 47.
7. Ibid., 47–48.
8. Kenneth H. Mills and Judith E. Paul, *Create Distinctive Displays* (Englewood Cliffs, NJ: Prentice-Hall, 1974), 61.
9. Sallie Hook, "All the Retail World's a Stage," *Marketing News,* 31 July 1987, 16.
10. Cyndee Miller, "Interact Updates Old 'listening booth' Concept in Record Stores," *Marketing News* (January 1988): 4.
11. See William R. Davison, Daniel J. Sweeney, and Ronald W. Stampfl, *Retailing Management* (New York: John Wiley & Sons, 1985), 205–6.
12. "Carson's Specialty," *Stores* (October 1986): 52.
13. "Man of Steel Has His Own Boutique," *Marketing News* (23 Oct. 1987): 8. Reprinted by permission of the American Marketing Association.
14. *Super Market Institute, How to Control Pilferage and Bad Check Losses* (Chicago: Super Market Institute), 5.
15. See James Cleary, Jr., *Prosecuting the Shoplifter* (Boston: Butterworths, 1986): 27.
16. Larry Hansen, "Thwarting the In-House Thief," *USA Today,* 16 Nov. 1984, 1B.
17. See Peter D. Berlin, "A Shrinkage Success Story—Herman's World of Sporting Goods," *Retail Control* (November 1986): 37–43.
18. See "Preventing Credit Card Fraud," *Stores* (September 1985): 38, 40.
19. Discussion based on S. J. Curtis, *Preventing Burglary and Robbery Loss, Small Marketers Aids,* No. 134 (Washington, D.C.: Small Business Administration, 1968).
20. Ibid., 2.
21. See David Rowe, "Robbery," *Video Store* 5 (July 1983), 32–33.
22. Ibid., 32.

RELATED READINGS

Abend, Jules. "Shortages." *Stores* (June 1982): 48–57.
Abend, Jules. "Why, What, and How Some Steal." *Stores* (January 1982): 71–77.
"Chains Fortifying Shrinkage Defenses." *Chain Store Age* (January 1981): 53–57.
Cooper, Donald, Clare, Donald, and Korgaonkar, Pradeep. "Retailers' Evaluation of Electronic Article Surveillance (EAS) System: An Exploratory Study." In *Developments in Marketing Science, Proceedings,* edited by N. K. Malhotra, 238–41. Academy of Marketing Science, 1985.
Deevey, Robert J. "Modifying Store Layout to Minimize Shrinkage." *Retail Control* (January 1985): 10–20.

Donovan, Robert J., and Rossiter, John R. "Store Atmosphere: An Environmental Psychology Approach." *Journal of Retailing* 58 (Spring 1982): 34–57.

Evans, Brian A. "Preventing Internal Theft." *Retail Control* (September 1982): 21–29.

French, Warren A., Crask, Melvin R., and Mader, Fred H. "Retailers' Assessment of the Shoplifting Problem." *Journal of Retailing* 60 (Winter 1984): 108–15.

Goldfinger, Jack I. "Pilferage Loss Resulting in Short Shipments." *Retail Control* (November 1982): 31–32.

Guffey, Hugh J., Jr., Harris, James, R., and Laumer, J. Ford, Jr. "Shopper Attitudes toward Shoplifting and Shoplifting Preventive Devices." *Journal of Retailing* 55 (Fall 1979): 75–89.

Jewell, Thomas R. "Excess Space: J. C. Penney's Solution." *Retail Control* (January 1984): 28–33.

Klokis, Holly. "Confessions of an Ex-Shoplifter." *Chain Store Age Executive* (February 1985): 15–18.

Markin, Rom J., Lillis, Charles M., and Narayana, Chem L. "Social-Psychological Significance of Store Space." *Journal of Retailing* 52 (Spring 1976): 43–54.

Miller, Joseph H., Jr., and Budden, Michael C. "Biorhythm and Shoplifting: An Empirical Investigation." In *1985 Educators' Proceedings,* edited by R. F. Lusch et al., 56–58. American Marketing Association, 1985.

Milliman, Ronald E. "Using Background Music to Affect Behavior of Supermarket Shoppers." *Journal of Marketing* 46 (Summer 1982): 86–91.

Rosen, Mark, and Zingman, Mitchell, S. "Coping with Bad Checks: Legal Remedies." *Retail Control* (November 1983): 25–29.

Schulz, David. "How Much is Enough?" *Stores* (June 1985): 72–75.

Schulz, David P. "Computer-Aided Design." *Stores* (March 1985): 47–48, 74.

"Supermarket Design Takes Bold Strides." *Chain Store Age Executive* (May 1985): 37, 40, 43.

"Taking the High-Tech Approach to Pilferage." *Chain Store Age Executive* (February 1985): 55–56.

Whalen, Bernie. "Threshold Messaging Touted as Antitheft Measure." *Marketing News* (15 March 1985): 5–6.

Wilkes, Robert. "Fraudulent Behavior by Consumers." *Journal of Marketing* 42 (October 1978): 67–74.

PART FOUR
Market Selection:
Evaluating Retail Markets

10

Objectives

☐ Appreciate the considerable impact that the retail-location decision has on all other aspects of the retailer's business.

☐ Characterize a market and describe its components.

☐ Explain why retail location is a problem of market segmentation.

☐ Employ standardized criteria to delineate and describe regional and local market areas.

☐ Evaluate regional and local market areas by sales potential and operational suitability.

☐ Select regional and local market areas capable of meeting the sales and operational needs of a particular retailing firm.

Analyzing Regional and Local Markets

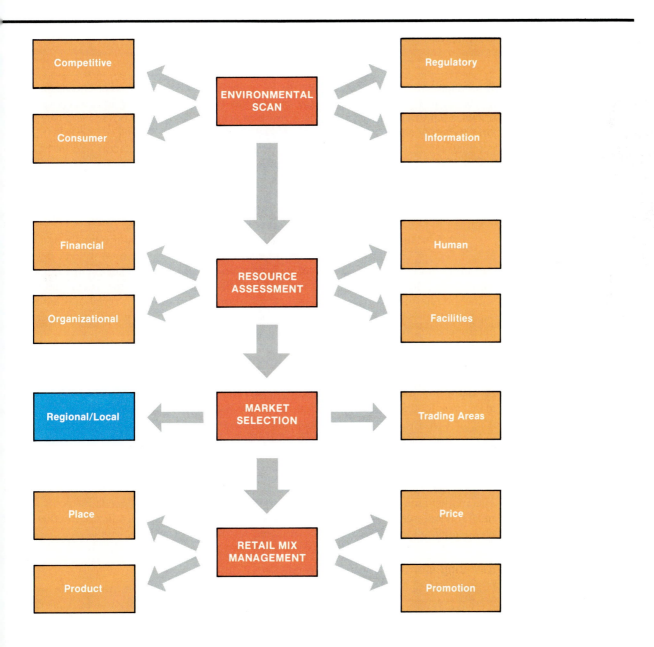

The importance of location decisions cannot be overstated. Because of its tremendous impact on virtually all other operational decisions, the location decision is perhaps the single most important operational decision a retailer makes. A retailer that selects a poor location will always be at a competitive disadvantage. To overcome a poor location (a struggle that is not always successful), the retailer must make substantial adjustments in the product, price, and promotional mixes. Because these adjustments usually are expensive to implement, they adversely affect the firm's profits.[1] On the other hand, selecting a good location enhances the chances of success because it allows greater flexibility in developing the product, price, and promotional mixes. Given the long-term commitment, the substantial financial investments, and the effects on the retailing mix, the retailer must consider the location problem extremely carefully.

This chapter discusses the nature of markets and how they can be subdivided into more meaningful and operational segments. It also covers how to identify, evaluate, and select regional and local markets.

THE MARKET

The definition of a market is fundamental to understanding the market and its behavior. In this discussion, the term *market* has a precise meaning and usage. As discussed in Chapter 4, a **market** is a group of actual and potential buyers at a given time and place whose actions lead to an exchange of goods and services or create the potential for an exchange. In essence, a market is a buying population and its behavior. Buying populations can be classified into one of two groups: **consumer markets**—individuals and/or households that are the ultimate consumers of goods and services, and **organizational markets**—industrial firms, resellers, and governments that represent intermediate consumers of goods and services. This discussion is limited to the consumer market and its impact on retail location.

Retail location is a problem of **market segmentation**—viewing the total market as a collection of heterogeneous consumers and subdividing the total market into consumer market segments. Market segmentation starts with the belief that there are identifiable differences among a product's various consumers and that these differences are relevant to their buying and store-patronage behavior. The goal of market segmentation is to identify smaller, homogeneous submarkets within the larger, heterogeneous mass market. Stated differently, the market segmenter views the market as consisting of several demand curves—one for each market segment or consumer subgroup.

The major tasks associated with segmenting markets appear in Figure 10–1. By identifying, evaluating, and selecting retail market and trading areas, the retailer is in fact segmenting the total mass market on the basis of geographic dimensions. This chapter examines identification, evaluation, and selection methods for analyzing regional and local markets. Figure 10–2 outlines the basic procedures for analyzing regional and local markets.

THE MARKET-AREA IDENTIFICATION PROCESS

The market-area identification process involves delineating and describing general retail market areas. There are two major steps in this process: (1) selecting market-area identification criteria and (2) identifying regional and local markets.

Selecting Identification Criteria

Retailers use several criteria to identify retail market areas. Two common criteria are market potential and retail operations. Using the **market potential approach**, retailers

FIGURE 10-1
Market-segmentation tasks

IDENTIFYING MARKET SEGMENTS

Task 1: To disaggregate total market by identifying significant differences between consumers and their buying behavior

Task 2: To regroup disaggregated consumers into homogeneous submarkets by identifying meaningful commonalities between consumers and their buying behavior

EVALUATING MARKET SEGMENTS

Task 3: To determine whether the identified market segments are meaningful

Task 4: To determine whether the identified market segments are serviceable

SELECTING MARKET SEGMENTS

Task 5: To determine which market segments offer the most attractive opportunities

Task 6: To determine which market segments offer the most feasible opportunities

select criteria that reflect the support (in sales, number of customers, etc.) that a geographic area will provide a given retail operation. In a **retail operations approach,** the retailer examines factors that might enhance or limit operations.

The Market Potential Approach

In using the market potential approach, the retailer identifies segmenting criteria specific to its class of goods (i.e., retailer-specific criteria). Whereas certain segmenting criteria are useful to one retailer, the same criteria may be of no use to another retailer. The major areas from which retailer-specific criteria are drawn are (1) population, (2) housing, (3) buyer behavior, and (4) physical environment.

Population characteristics are the most common segmenting criteria. As illustrated in Figure 10-3, a retailer can describe any geographic area (state, county, city, etc.) by any combination of population characteristics. Although total population figures and population densities are of primary importance, the retailer can get a more detailed profile of a market by examining education, age, income, sex, occupation, religion, race, nationality, and family characteristics data. The retailer's purpose is to

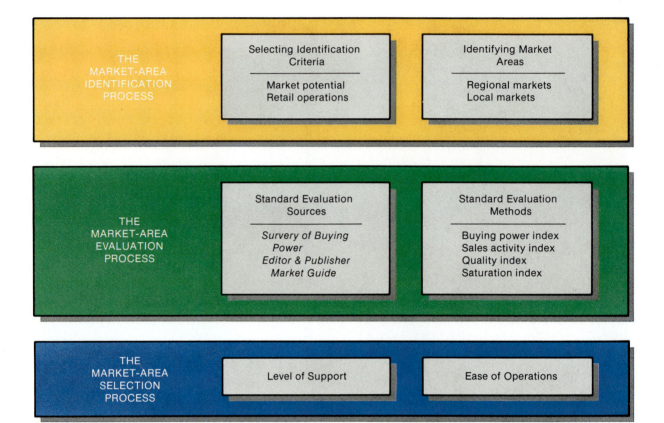

FIGURE 10–2

The basic procedures for analyzing regional and local markets

match a market's population characteristics to the population characteristics of people who desire its goods and services.

Retailers can get population and demographic data from the *Census of Population*. For more current data, retailers can consult the *Current Population Survey,* which provides estimates and projections on a variety of population characteristics.

Housing characteristics are an important criterion for some retailers in determining profitable markets. Hardware retailers, home-improvement centers, and home-furnishings stores are examples of retailers that rely on data on the housing market. Figure 10–4 illustrates some of the more important housing characteristics that retailers use to identify lucrative market areas. To locate these data, retailers turn to the *Census of Housing* and the *Annual Housing Survey.* Also, the Census Bureau produces several special publications, such as *Current Housing Reports* and *Current Construction Reports.* At the local level, retailers examine building permits to determine economic activity affecting their businesses.

Buyer behavior characteristics also are extremely useful in identifying and segmenting retail markets, as Figure 10–5 illustrates. Among such characteristics are store loyalty, consumer psychographics, store patronage reasons, usage rates, lifestyles, benefits sought, and purchase situations. Although buyer behavior characteristics provide retailers with the most useful information to make location decisions, the data are neither easy to measure nor to obtain. (The various dimensions of buyer behavior were discussed in Chapter 4.)

Another way retailers measure market potential is to examine an area's physical environment. Differing characteristics of their physical environments influence peo-

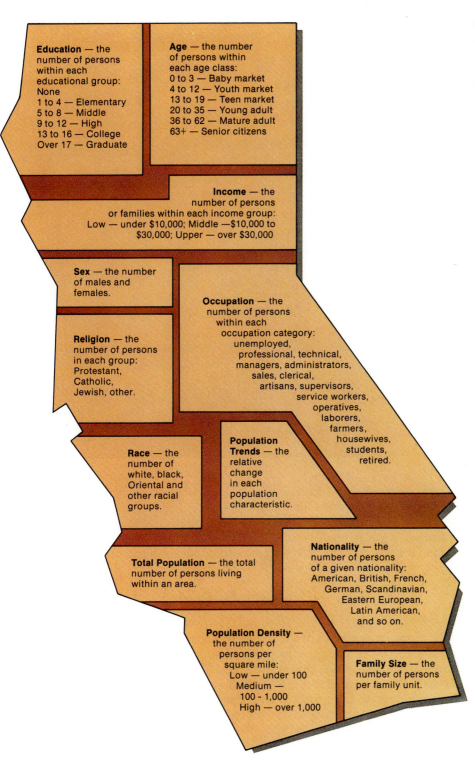

Education — the number of persons within each educational group:
None
1 to 4 — Elementary
5 to 8 — Middle
9 to 12 — High
13 to 16 — College
Over 17 — Graduate

Age — the number of persons within each age class:
0 to 3 — Baby market
4 to 12 — Youth market
13 to 19 — Teen market
20 to 35 — Young adult
36 to 62 — Mature adult
63+ — Senior citizens

Income — the number of persons or families within each income group:
Low — under $10,000; Middle —$10,000 to $30,000; Upper — over $30,000

Sex — the number of males and females.

Religion — the number of persons in each group: Protestant, Catholic, Jewish, other.

Occupation — the number of persons within each occupation category: unemployed, professional, technical, managers, administrators, sales, clerical, artisans, supervisors, service workers, operatives, laborers, farmers, housewives, students, retired.

Race — the number of white, black, Oriental and other racial groups.

Population Trends — the relative change in each population characteristic.

Total Population — the total number of persons living within an area.

Nationality — the number of persons of a given nationality: American, British, French, German, Scandinavian, Eastern European, Latin American, and so on.

Population Density — the number of persons per square mile:
Low — under 100
Medium — 100 - 1,000
High — over 1,000

Family Size — the number of persons per family unit.

FIGURE 10–3
Using population characteristics as criteria in identifying market areas

FIGURE 10–4

Using housing characteristics as criteria in identifying market areas

ple's choices of clothing, housing, foods, and forms of recreation, as well as their preferences among many other products, services, and activities. Certainly, physical environment influences *when* consumers buy products or use services and thereby determines when markets occur—or at least when they are most profitable. Since *physical environment characteristics* are easy to measure and obtain, they are excellent criteria for segmenting markets for many products such as skis, suntan lotion, lip balm, fertilizer, and so forth.

The Retail Operations Approach

In identifying market areas, the location specialist must take into account the nature of the retailer's operations. A profitable retail store is one that not only serves a consumer market of high potential but also operates in a market that allows for efficiency and competitiveness. Several factors that directly influence the retailer's chances to operate successfully are (1) distribution, (2) competition, (3) promotion, and (4) legal considerations.

Distribution factors. A crucial problem for all retailers is to get the product into the store. This problem area involves inventory control—overstocks increase carrying costs, whereas stockouts cause lost sales and customer ill will. The retailer must consider transportation and handling costs, delivery time, and reliability of delivery services. To identify potential market areas, the retailer also must consider the loca-

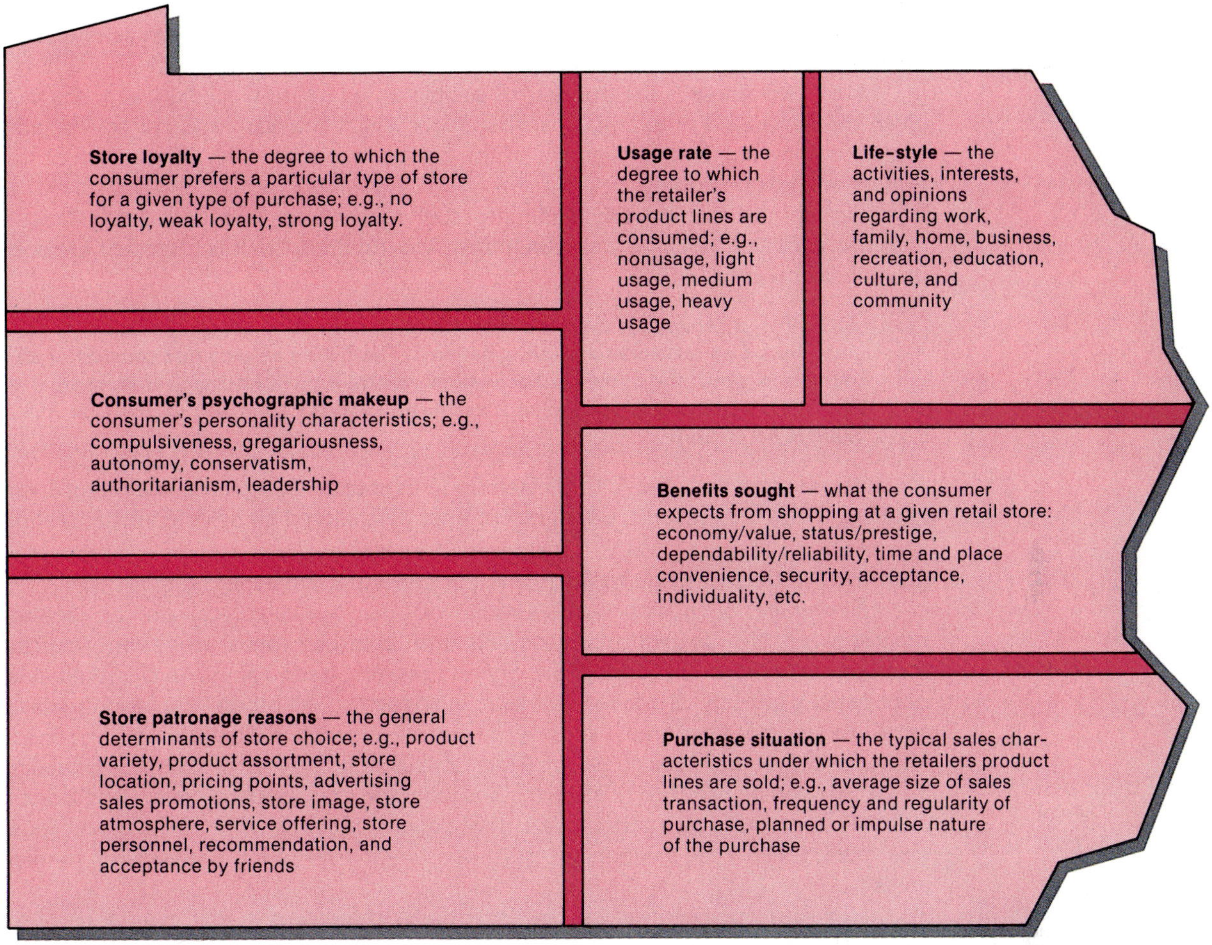

Store loyalty — the degree to which the consumer prefers a particular type of store for a given type of purchase; e.g., no loyalty, weak loyalty, strong loyalty.

Usage rate — the degree to which the retailer's product lines are consumed; e.g., nonusage, light usage, medium usage, heavy usage

Life-style — the activities, interests, and opinions regarding work, family, home, business, recreation, education, culture, and community

Consumer's psychographic makeup — the consumer's personality characteristics; e.g., compulsiveness, gregariousness, autonomy, conservatism, authoritarianism, leadership

Benefits sought — what the consumer expects from shopping at a given retail store: economy/value, status/prestige, dependability/reliability, time and place convenience, security, acceptance, individuality, etc.

Store patronage reasons — the general determinants of store choice; e.g., product variety, product assortment, store location, pricing points, advertising sales promotions, store image, store atmosphere, service offering, store personnel, recommendation, and acceptance by friends

Purchase situation — the typical sales characteristics under which the retailers product lines are sold; e.g., average size of sales transaction, frequency and regularity of purchase, planned or impulse nature of the purchase

FIGURE 10–5
Using buyer behavior characteristics as criteria in identifying market areas

tion and delivery practices of suppliers and the market area's ability to support distribution facilities.

Competitive factors. It is imperative that the retailer take into account the reality of the competition when identifying market areas. Competition varies from one area to another according to type, number, and size of competitors. Types, levels, and competitive strategies of various retailing formats were discussed in Chapter 3. As a quick review of that chapter would indicate, retail competition is very complex; hence, the market area specialist must carefully audit all competitors, regardless of their form.

Promotional factors. A retailer that depends heavily on promotional activities can identify market areas by analyzing the advertising media within each market area and the behavior of competitive retailers. Media selectivity and coverage are both important. With respect to **media selectivity,** the retailer should look at **geographic selectivity** (the ability of a medium to target a specific geographic market area such as a city or a part of a city) and **class selectivity** (the ability of a medium to target specific kinds of people who have certain common characteristics). In other words, most advertising media are "targeted" to serve certain geographical areas and to appeal to certain groups of consumers. For example, a radio station serves only the geographical area defined by its transmitting power, antenna system, frequency on the dial, and other local conditions. If the station happens to follow a "pop" format, certain listeners will be attracted by the format.

Media coverage is the number of people an advertising medium reaches in a given market area. For example, a newspaper might provide excellent coverage in one county by reaching 90 percent of the homes but cover only 30 percent of the homes in a distant county.

Perhaps the simplest way to identify retail market areas by broadcasting stations is to use data generated by a research firm. The Arbitron Co. has identified **areas of dominant influence (ADIs):**

> [An ADI is] a geographic market design which defines each market, exclusive of another, based on measurable viewing patterns. The ADI is an area that consists of all counties in which the home market stations receive a preponderance of viewing. Each county in the U.S. (excluding Alaska) is allocated exclusively to only one ADI. There is no overlap.

A similar research firm, the A. C. Nielsen Co., has created **designated marketing areas (DMAs)**. A DMA represents a geographic area best served by selected broadcasting stations. Both ADIs and DMAs are supported with a wealth of audience information from their respective research firms and the individual broadcasting stations.

Newspaper circulation is still another criterion by which retailers can identify market areas. Newspaper circulation falls into three categories: *city zone, retailing zone,* and *all others.* Frequently, the city and retailing trade zones are classified as a newspaper's primary circulation markets, whereas the "all others" category (usually small towns and rural areas) represents outside circulation or secondary markets. Newspapers generally are considered local media, but there is considerable flexibility in the circulation patterns relative to the geographic areas they cover. The zoned editions of some large metropolitan newspapers, together with many small local newspapers, allow the location specialist considerable freedom in identifying market areas.

Magazine circulation is yet another media characteristic that can be used to identify retail markets. Because magazines generally have a smaller impact than newspapers on the retailer's promotional program, their use in market-area identification is limited. Nevertheless, the geographic (sectional or regional) editions of many nationally circulated magazines provide a convenient means of identifying market areas for the growing number of upscaled, image-minded retailers (e.g., Bloomingdale's, Neiman-Marcus, and Macy's) who are going "national."

Legal factors.   The final group of criteria that retailers use to identify market areas are state and local legal requirements. Land-use regulation in the form of *zoning restrictions, building codes,* and *signing requirements* has a direct bearing on the success of a retailer's operation. State and local taxes on the firm's *real estate, personal property,* and *inventory* can have an equally important impact on the cost of operation. Retailers must also meet certain *licensing requirements* to conduct a business. License availability and cost are necessary considerations; additional limitations can include legal constraints that affect *store hours, local minimum wage laws,* and *Sunday closing laws.*

Identifying Market Areas

Market areas come in all sizes, shapes, and descriptions. The dimensions of a market area depend on several factors, such as population density and media coverage. The two general problems facing the location specialist are (1) how to identify regional markets and (2) how to identify local markets. These two problems and their particular components are illustrated in Figure 10–6.

Identifying regional markets consists of determining the "right region" of the country and the "right part of the region." The geographic extent of a regional market is not fixed and could include either one state or a multistate area. For many small, independent retailers, the regional market problem is not a concern. They often have narrowed their choice of regions to the ones in which they currently live or work. For the chain organization or for the retailer that intends to expand, however, the starting point in the location-decision process is to identify regional and subregional markets.

As shown in Figure 10–6, the local market problem is how to find the "right town" and the "right part of town." For our purposes, "town" refers to any size urban center that can be associated with a particular regional or subregional market.

Regional Markets

Most business organizations have regionalized the United States in some way. Regional classification schemes suggest that people perceive social, cultural, and eco-

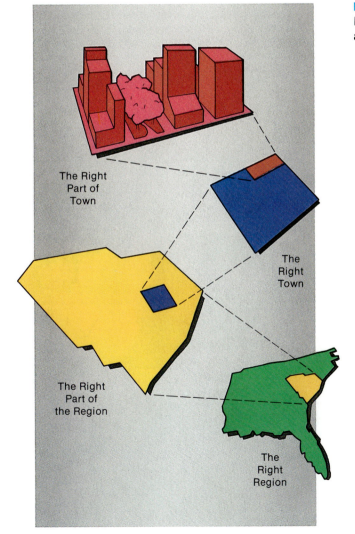

FIGURE 10–6
Identification of regional and local market areas

The Right Part of Town

The Right Town

The Right Part of the Region

The Right Region

nomic differences among various parts of the country. The retailer should try to identify and analyze these perceived differences.

Regional markets based on census areas.   Perhaps the most widely used regional classification system is one developed by the U.S. Census Bureau. As shown in Figure 10–7, the Census Bureau divides the United States into nine census regions. The relative importance of this **census market** classification scheme is evident from the fact that many public and private organizations use this system as the organizational framework for their information reporting and analyzing process. Two private organizations that use this classification are of particular interest to the retailer: the *Survey of Buying Power,* published annually by *Sales and Marketing Management,* and Standard Rate and Data Service's monthly rate and data publication, *Spot Television.*

Regional markets based on communication areas.   Regional markets can be identified on the basis of various types of media coverage—**communication markets**. In the case of the broadcast media, a 50,000-watt radio station like WGN in Chicago is capable of providing the retailer with multistate regional coverage. On the other hand, a 5,000-watt station like KVI in Seattle/Tacoma covers only a subregional market because its output is restricted to the western portion of the state of Washington. The large-area coverage by WGN is appropriate to a multiunit retailer (such as K Mart) that has operations in each of the states WGN covers.

FIGURE 10–7

Census regions as defined by the Census Bureau

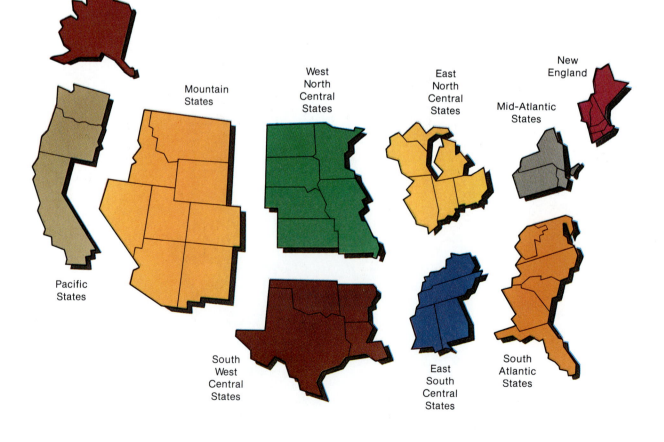

Introducing 27 small bites of the Big Apple.

For a small businessman, New York can be a big place. A little too big, perhaps. Even for a businessman who's not so small.

So, the New York News, New York's largest newspaper, has taken it upon itself to cut the New York market down to size.

More accurately, we've cut it down to sizes. 27 of them. It's as if New York were made up of 27 small towns, each with its own demographic character. Now an advertiser can have a preprint inserted in The Sunday News and have that preprint delivered only to the market or markets vital to him.

We call this new marketing concept ZIM.

Who's ZIM?

ZIM stands for Zoned Insert Marketing. It marries the ever increasing power and popularity of inserts with the precision and flexibility of direct mail. So, while we may call it ZIM, we think you'll call it terrific.

ZIM vs. the P.O.

When you insert a message in an envelope and send it through the mail, you can hardly count on it reaching all your customers at virtually the same time. You can count on that with ZIM, however.

And you can count on spending less money too. For ZIM costs just a fraction of what direct mail costs.

You spend less, you waste less.

With ZIM you can buy the full run of The Sunday News. Any combination of zones, or just one zone. That's anywhere from a circulation of 2½ million to as little as 35,000.

You can match your distribution. And speak only to those New Yorkers who speak your language. So you're not throwing money away on people who'll throw your message away.

And you're not biting off more of the Big Apple than you can chew.

In other words, ZIM lets you be anything you want in the Big Apple. From small potatoes to a big cheese.

ZIM lets you test. Anything.

You can test copy with ZIM by running different strategies in similar zones.

You can test zones with ZIM. By running the same copy strategies in different zones.

You can also change copy according to local conditions and regulations.

Add all that to the couponing capabilities inherent in inserts and you have a testing device that truly makes the grade.

Us and ZIM.

It's appropriate that the newspaper that can give you more New Yorkers than anyone else can also give you as few as you want.

But that's not the whole News story.

We can give you the highest level of penetration in the city, the highest level of penetration in the suburbs. Or both.

And with our Instant Market Data service with its on-line computer facility, we can tell you an awful lot about our readers by income, occupation and product use.

What's more, we can particularize census data by zip code information for any zone or combination of zones.

So, not only do we offer you the use of ZIM, but we can also help you make even better use of it.

You and ZIM.

A phone call to your News sales rep or our research department (212-682-1234) can get you a specific breakdown for each zone by population, circulation and percent of household coverage.

A phone call to Jim (ZIM) Ruddy (212-682-1234) can get you information on the maximums, the minimums, the costs and the variety of insert sizes, from catalogs on down. Also, the uses, applications and combinations available with ZIM.

Maybe ZIM is just the thing to help keep you from getting chewed up in the Big Apple.

SUNDAY ● NEWS
NEW YORK'S PICTURE NEWSPAPER
Today... you really need it!

FIGURE 10–8

Regional and local markets as delineated by newspaper circulation (Courtesy of New York Daily News, Inc.)

Print media also provide good operational definitions of regional and subregional markets. Figure 10–8 shows the multistate regional coverage of the *New York News*. By dividing the total New York regional markets into 27 zones (a process referred to as *zoned insert marketing*), the regional market is effectively segmented into subregional markets. Figure 10–8 discusses some of the operational advantages of subregional market-area segmentation.

Magazines also recognize the value of regional and subregional classifications. *Newsweek,* for example, has segmented the U.S. market into five regions—Western, West Central, East Central, Eastern, and Southern—and three of these regional markets are segmented further into subregional markets. *USA Weekend* uses what it calls "geodemographic marketing,"[2] to divide the country into "nine nations" or intranational markets based on demographic and life-style characteristics (Figure 10–9). Regional and subregional issues of magazines such as *Newsweek* and *USA Weekend* provide regional and local retailers with an opportunity to advertise in prestigious publications to reach an upper-bracket audience within a selective geographic area.

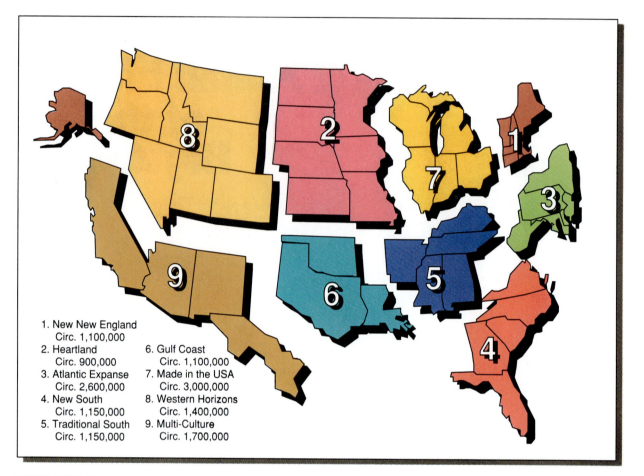

1. New New England
   Circ. 1,100,000
2. Heartland
   Circ. 900,000
3. Atlantic Expanse
   Circ. 2,600,000
4. New South
   Circ. 1,150,000
5. Traditional South
   Circ. 1,150,000
6. Gulf Coast
   Circ. 1,100,000
7. Made in the USA
   Circ. 3,000,000
8. Western Horizons
   Circ. 1,400,000
9. Multi-Culture
   Circ. 1,700,000

FIGURE 10-9
Market segmentation using geodemographic data

Local Markets

Finding the "right town" and the "right part of town" constitutes the local market identification problem. Faced with an array of thousands of urban centers, the retail location specialist must use some organized method to identify local markets.[3]

Function markets: The right town. Urban centers often are classified on the basis of the types of economic activities they support. Although most urban centers are multifunctional, one or two functions (such as manufacturing and retailing) tend to dominate a local economy. Most cities have "acquired a distinction for the real or reputed dominance of one function or another."[4] These urban centers are known as **functional markets** based on the functions they perform. By classifying urban centers, the location specialist can obtain a broad overview of each center as a potential retail market. Urban centers tend to take on a certain character or atmosphere that reflects how the population makes its living.

ABC markets: The right town. A second method of classifying urban centers is to group or rank them on the basis of population, retail sales, employment levels, disposable income, number of households, and a host of other factors. Figure 10-10 identifies the fifty largest metro markets based on 1991 projected population; Figure 10-11 projects the largest markets based on household income. Many retailing

FIGURE 10–10

The 50 Largest Metro Markets Based On 1991 Projected Population

1991 Rank	Metro Market	Projected 1991 Pop. (Thous.)	Projected % Change 1986–91	1991 Rank	Metro Market	Projected 1991 Pop. (Thous.)	Projected % Change 1986–91
1.	Los Angeles-Long Beach	8,869.6	+ 6.7%	27.	San Francisco	1,649.6	+ 4.2
2.	New York	8,713.0	+ 2.2	28.	Kansas City	1,582.3	+ 3.7
3.	Chicago	6,187.9	+ 0.4	29.	San Jose, CA	1,484.5	+ 5.4
4.	Philadelphia	4,884.2	+ 1.2	30.	Sacramento	1,450.9	+11.2
5.	Detroit	4,412.7	+ 1.2	31.	Cincinnati	1,421.0	+ 0.1
6.	Boston-Lawrence-Salem- Lowell-Brockton	3,752.9	+ 0.8	32.	Fort Worth-Arlington	1,420.3	+15.9
7.	Washington, DC	3,744.8	+ 5.7	33.	New Orleans	1,402.8	+ 4.1
8.	Houston	3,567.9	+10.4	34.	Milwaukee	1,400.5	+ 0.4
9.	Atlanta	2,800.3	+10.1	35.	Norfolk-Virginia Beach- Newport News, VA	1,394.9	+ 6.7
10.	Nassau-Suffolk, NY	2,738.7	+ 2.8	36.	San Antonio	1,378.6	+10.2
11.	Dallas	2,666.3	+12.1	37.	Columbus, OH	1,334.4	+ 2.5
12.	St. Louis	2,498.7	+ 1.9	38.	Bergen-Passaic, NJ	1,311.1	+ 0.6
13.	San Diego	2,466.0	+11.2	39.	Fort Lauderdale-Hollywood- Pompano Beach	1,280.0	+ 9.6
14.	Minneapolis-St. Paul	2,445.9	+ 5.3	40.	Indianapolis	1,247.2	+ 2.3
15.	Baltimore	2,374.7	+ 3.0	41.	Portland, OR	1,188.3	+ 2.5
16.	Anaheim-Santa Ana	2,341.3	+ 7.5	42.	Charlotte-Gastonia-Rock Hill	1,140.3	+ 6.4
17.	Riverside-San Bernadino, CA	2,325.2	+15.9	43.	Salt Lake City-Ogden	1,139.5	+ 8.3
18.	Phoenix	2,221.4	+15.9	44.	Hartford-New Britain- Middletown-Bristol, CT	1,126.5	+ 2.6
19.	Tampa-St. Petersburg- Clearwater, FL	2,133.9	+11.4	45.	Oklahoma City	1,081.0	+ 8.9
20.	Pittsburgh	2,103.4	− 1.7	46.	Monmouth-Ocean, NJ	1,033.1	+ 7.9
21.	Oakland	2,070.6	+ 6.2	47.	Orlando, FL	1,031.4	+14.7
22.	Newark	1,905.4	+ 0.3	48.	Rochester, NY	1,005.4	+ 1.3
23.	Miami-Hialeah	1,901.7	+ 6.5	49.	Nashville, TN	995.8	+ 6.3
24.	Seattle	1,860.5	+ 5.8	50.	Middlesex-Somerset- Hunterdon, NJ	983.6	+ 4.0
25.	Cleveland	1,823.2	− 1.6				
26.	Denver	1,796.3	+ 8.9				

Source: Sales & Marketing Management's *1987 Survey of Buying Power—Part II.* © Sales & Marketing Management.

operations employ population and demographic analysis to determine each market's sales potential for a particular line of merchandise or a given type of retail operation. Based on their sales volume potential, urban centers can be classified in descending order as either **A, B, or C markets**. The exact definition of what constitutes an A, B, or C market varies from one retailing organization to another, because each retailing organization uses different decision variables. Nevertheless, the purpose of identifying various-sized markets is to help the retailer adjust the business format to meet the consumption needs of a particular market.

Markets designated as A markets can provide the highest levels of support for retailers. Typically, A markets have the sales potential to support large operating units and/or a multiple number of operating units. J. C. Penney, for example, defines A markets as those "where the sales potential for 'department store type merchandise' exceeds $100 million in sales."[5] In an A market, the J. C. Penney organization often operates several large (100,000 to 200,000 or more square feet), full-line department stores, as well as several smaller, limited-line soft-goods outlets. Because of the tremendous potential of an A market, the retailer can develop a wide range from a

FIGURE 10–11

The 50 Largest Metro Markets Based on 1991 Projected Household Income

1991 Rank	Metro Market	1991 Average Household EBI	1991 Rank	Metro Market	1991 Average Household EBI
1.	Bridgeport-Stamford-Norwalk-Danbury, CT	$73,851	26.	Minneapolis-St. Paul	$54,770
2.	Nassau-Suffolk, NY	71,637	27.	Kenosha, WI	53,862
3.	Lake County, IL	68,624	28.	Chicago	53,679
4.	Washington, DC	64,031	29.	Santa Barbara-Santa Maria-Lompoc	53,676
5.	Middlesex-Somerset-Hunterdon, NJ	63,163	30.	Aurora-Elgin, IL	53,529
6.	San Jose	62,556	31.	Wichita, KS	53,426
7.	Bergen-Passaic, NJ	62,337	32.	Seattle	53,416
8.	Grand Forks, ND	61,138	33.	Lincoln, NE	53,370
9.	Oxnard-Ventura, CA	60,662	34.	Portsmouth-Dover-Rochester, NH	53,264
10.	Trenton, NJ	60,216	35.	Omaha	53,216
11.	Anaheim-Santa Ana, CA	59,777	36.	Richland-Kennewick-Pasco, WA	53,086
12.	San Francisco	58,959	37.	San Diego	52,969
13.	Newark	58,615	38.	Santa Cruz, CA	52,437
14.	Midland, TX	58,599	39.	Topeka	52,392
15.	Honolulu	58,043	40.	Wilmington, DE	52,281
16.	Anchorage	56,403	41.	Kalamazoo, MI	52,108
17.	Boston-Lawrence-Salem-Lowell-Brockton	56,325	42.	Rochester, MN	52,013
18.	Hartford-New Britain-Middletown-Bristol, CT	56,282	43.	Dallas	51,877
19.	Oakland	56,269	44.	Ann Arbor, MI	51,375
20.	Monmouth-Ocean, NJ	56,094	45.	Grand Rapids, MI	51,152
21.	Poughkeepsie, NY	55,918	46.	Salinas-Seaside-Monterey, CA	51,111
22.	Brazoria, TX	55,655	47.	Denver	51,096
23.	Manchester-Nashua, NH	55,493	48.	Iowa City	51,007
24.	New London-Norwich, CT	55,004	49.	Peoria, IL	50,659
25.	New Haven-Waterbury-Meriden, CT	54,999	50.	West Palm Beach-Boca Raton-Delray Beach, FL	50,615
				U.S. Average	**$45,362**

Source: Sales & Marketing Management's *1987 Survey of Buying Power—Part II.* © Sales & Marketing Management.

broad assortment to a highly specialized one. In addition, A markets provide retailing environments that can support pricing, advertising, and personal-selling strategies that range from discount to prestige pricing, mass to direct advertising, and store to in-home selling.

From Baton Rouge, Louisiana, to Lancaster, Ohio, many medium-sized cities offer adequate sales potential for a wide variety of retailing activities. Although lacking the sales potential of the A market, the B market is still strong for most types and sizes of store operations. The J. C. Penney organization defines a B market as having the "potential of racking up 'department store type merchandise' sales of between $25 million and $100 million."[6] Typically, a B market would not warrant a full-line department store operation unless special circumstances prevailed in the market. Usually, a B market calls for an extensively stocked soft-goods operation with limited lines of hard goods.

The C market is basically the small-town market. The potential of these smaller C markets is considerable. Many of the country's retailing giants in recent years have targeted these markets as major areas for expansion. This once-secure market domain of the small, independent retailer has felt the impact of the entry of such large multiline chain retailers as K Mart, Wal-Mart, and TG&Y. Towns with potential sales of "department store type merchandise" of less than $25 million are classified by Penney's as *C* markets, but J. C. Penney management does not necessarily view *C* markets as small. According to the company, "J. C. Penney started out in small towns, is still in small towns, and is planning to go into more small towns."[7]

Intraurban markets: The right part of town.   For most retailers, there are literally "right" and "wrong" parts of town. An urban center is not simply a homogeneous mass; rather, it is a heterogeneous grouping of people and activities, making up **intraurban markets** that can have a profound effect on a retailer's operations.

The internal structure of urban centers is composed of many recognizable areas, including the downtown and the suburbs; shopping centers and strip shopping developments; ethnic and racial areas; residential, commercial, and industrial areas; and low-, middle-, and high-income areas. To facilitate understanding of the internal structure of cities, this chapter examines several theories of urban structure based on *land-use patterns*. Over time, these patterns emerge when certain activities (such as commercial, industrial, and residential) tend to dominate the land use of particular areas in and around the urban center. To describe these patterns, retailing analysts have proposed several theories; of these, the three most recognized are (1) the concentric zone theory, (2) the sector theory, and (3) the multiple-nuclei theory.

Concentric zone theory asserts that the internal structure of a city develops as a series of concentric zones, each characterized by a particular set of activities. As illustrated in Figure 10–12a, there are five basic zones; each one "under conditions of normal city growth tends to extend its area by invading the next outer zone. The process has been likened to outward movement of ripples when one tosses a stone into a still pond."[8]

The first zone, *the central business district (CBD),* is the center of a city's social and economic life. Typically, the zone is divided into the inner and outer CBD. The land-use pattern of the inner CBD usually consists of several identifiable districts, each supporting a predominant economic activity. Common districts are retail, financial, hotel and entertainment, government, and general office complex. The outer CBD is composed of commercial businesses that cannot afford the high rent associated with the inner CBD. Businesses typically in the outer CBD include wholesaling, "low-rent" retailing, and transportation activities.

As the name implies, the *zone of transition* is in a state of transition, from residential to nonresidential land use. The encroachment of light and heavy industry results in deteriorated housing and the formation of slum areas. "The inner belt of the zone is likely to be a business and light manufacturing district, and the outer boundary a ring of retrogressing neighborhoods from which, as people become more prosperous, they escape into Zone 3."[9] Low incomes and high crime rates make this zone undesirable for most retailers.

The *zone of independent workers' homes,* a blue-collar, residential area, is populated by low- to middle-income groups that often cluster in ethnic neighborhoods. Although their housing is usually of the moderately or low priced or tract type, the residents take considerable local pride in maintaining a well-kept neighborhood. With few exceptions, commercial activities tend to be limited to neighborhood corner retailers and small retailing clusters.

Middle-class Americans dominate the *zone of better residences*. The population of this zone is likely to include white-collar workers (independent businesspeople, professional people, clerical staff, and salespersons). At strategic points, business clusters are interspersed with single- and multiple-family dwelling units. A major shopping mall is likely to be found at the intersection of primary traffic arteries.

The *commuters' zone* is composed of many small cities and towns that ring a central city. Often referred to as "bedroom" or "dormitory" cities, these small urban centers house primarily middle- and higher-income people who commute to work in the central city. Spot development of commercial and industrial land appears primarily along major traffic arteries.

A second theory of land-use patterns is the **sector theory,** which hypothesizes that residential land-use patterns are essentially "wedges or sectors radiating from the center of the city along the lines of transportation."[10] Whereas the theory deals primarily with residential land use, the sector concept also incorporates commercial and industrial land use. The wedge-shaped land-use patterns hypothesized in this theory result from rent patterns.

FIGURE 10–12
Theories of urban structure

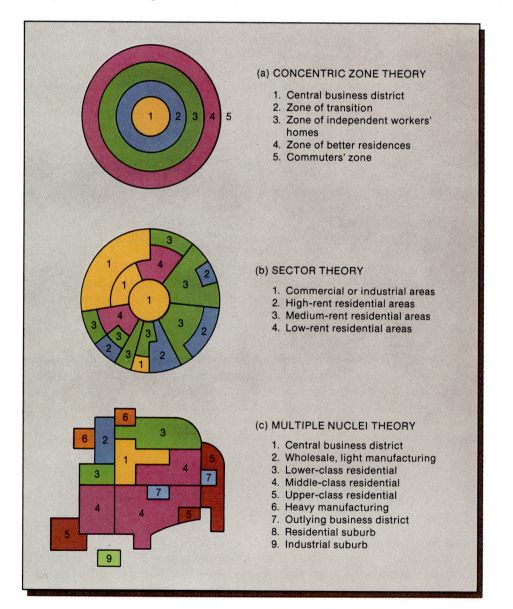

(a) CONCENTRIC ZONE THEORY

1. Central business district
2. Zone of transition
3. Zone of independent workers' homes
4. Zone of better residences
5. Commuters' zone

(b) SECTOR THEORY

1. Commercial or industrial areas
2. High-rent residential areas
3. Medium-rent residential areas
4. Low-rent residential areas

(c) MULTIPLE NUCLEI THEORY

1. Central business district
2. Wholesale, light manufacturing
3. Lower-class residential
4. Middle-class residential
5. Upper-class residential
6. Heavy manufacturing
7. Outlying business district
8. Residential suburb
9. Industrial suburb

> The highest rent areas of a city tend to be located in one or more sectors of the city. There is a gradation of rentals downward from these high rental areas in all directions. Intermediate rental areas, or those ranking next to the highest rental areas, join the high rent area on one or more sides, and tend to be located in the same sectors as high rental areas. Low rent areas occupy other entire sectors of the city from the center to the periphery.[11]

Because people from different rent areas tend to migrate, a continually changing pattern of wedge-shaped areas occurs. The key to these changing patterns is the high-rent areas. As people from the high-rent areas move outward from the central city and away from industrial and commercial areas, the city is pulled in the same direction. The result of this migration is the evolution of residential areas from high- to middle- to low-rent areas, as shown in Figure 10–12b.

A third theory of land-use patterns is the **multiple-nuclei theory,** which states that there are several identifiable centers of activities within a city, with each specializing in a given activity such as retailing, wholesaling, government, or education. Development of these centers does not necessarily correspond to a set pattern; in fact, any number of land-use patterns can develop. Figure 10–12c illustrates one possible land-use pattern.

THE MARKET-AREA EVALUATION PROCESS

After identifying potential market areas, the retail location specialist must evaluate each one. The identification process itself should have provided considerable insight into the various capacities of each area to support a given type of retail organization. The evaluation process involves collecting and analyzing data pertinent to a particular retailer's operation.

Standard Evaluation Sources

In evaluating retail market areas, retailing analysts primarily use two major sources: the *Survey of Buying Power* and the *Editor & Publisher Market Guide.* Both contain vast amounts of data for estimating a retail market's potential sales.

Survey of Buying Power

The **Survey of Buying Power** is an annual publication compiled by the editors of *Sales and Marketing Management* magazine. Surveys are divided into two parts. Part I consists of four sections: (1) survey highlights, (2) national and regional summaries, (3) metro area, county, and city data by states, and (4) the Canadian survey of buying power. Part II of the survey (1) provides an analysis of changes in metropolitan markets, (2) makes five-year projections for metropolitan markets, (3) evaluates newspaper and TV markets, and (4) discusses merchandise-line sales. While the survey contains a great deal of information that is useful to the retailer, three basic categories of information are of particular interest to the retail location specialist attempting to evaluate potential market areas. Those three categories are population, retail sales, and effective buying income. Each is further divided into subcategories to provide additional, detailed information on smaller geographic units. These figures help the retailer identify and evaluate all the market-area problems previously discussed, with the exception of the "right part of town."

The survey contains information for all census regions, states, metro areas, counties, and cities. Although the population and retail sales figures reported in the survey are self-explanatory, the expression *effective buying income* requires additional explanation. As used in the survey, effective buying income is all personal income (wages, salaries, rental income, dividends, interest, pension, welfare) less federal, state, and local personal taxes, contributions for social security insurance, and nontax payments (fines, fees, penalties). In essence, effective buying income is the rough equivalent of disposable personal income; that is, the spendable income available to the consumer.

The raw population, retail sales, and income figures provide the location specialist with a demographic overview of the *absolute* sales potential of various market areas. By comparing each identified market area to others, the location specialist can develop "relative" measures of each market's potential. In addition, the retailer can use this survey information to develop several relevant measures of a market's potential in terms of percentages, averages, ratios, and indices.

Editor & Publisher Market Guide

The second standard source of information for evaluating market areas is **Editor & Publisher Market Guide**. Although similar in some aspects to the *Survey of Buying Power,* the yearly editions provide additional and different information about market areas. Besides standard information on population, income, households, farm products, and retail sales for states, metro areas, counties, and cities, the guide provides specific features for each city.

Rand McNally Commercial Atlas & Marketing Guide

The third source, Rand McNally's **Commercial Atlas & Marketing Guide,** also provides a wealth of information, much of it in a very useful format—maps. Population, income, buying power, and sales data are available by states, trading areas, metropolitan statistical areas, and zip codes. This source gives a general overview (maps) or a specific detailed presentation (tables) of a number of different regional and local market areas.

Standard Evaluation Methods

The previous section described two standard evaluation sources that retailers use to obtain market information; this section discusses several standard *methods* for evaluating market areas: the buying power index, the sales activity index, the quality index, and the index of retail saturation.

Buying Power Index

The **buying power index,** published annually in the *Survey of Buying Power,* is "a measurement of a market's ability to buy."[12] The index is constructed using three criteria:

1. The market area's population expressed as a percentage of the total U.S. population
2. The market area's retail sales expressed as a percentage of total U.S. retail sales
3. The market area's effective buying income expressed as a percentage of the total U.S. effective buying income

The index does not equally weight each criterion as an indicator of a market area's ability to buy. Instead, each is weighted according to its perceived importance— population by 2, retail sales by 3, and effective buying income by 5. The buying power index (BPI) is calculated as follows:

$$BPI = \frac{(\text{pop.} \times 2) + (\text{retail sales} \times 3) + (\text{effect. buying inc.} \times 5)}{10\ (\text{the sum of the weights})}$$

The higher the index value, the greater the market area's ability to buy and therefore to support retailing activities. Although the BPI provides a good estimate of the spendable income within a market area, it does not indicate the area's "distribution of income," "stability of income," or "income trends." As described by the editors of *Survey of Buying Power,* the index "is most useful in estimating the potential for mass products sold at popular prices. The further a product is removed from the mass market, the greater is the need for a BPI to be modified by more discriminating factors—income, class, age, sex, etc."[13]

Sales Activity Index

The *Survey of Buying Power* also reports the standardized **sales activity index (SAI):** "a measure of the per capita retail sales of an area compared with those of the nation."[14] Although the SAI is reported for the nine census regions and for each state within those regions, it can be calculated for any geographic subdivision contained in the survey. The SAI is calculated as follows:

$$SAI = \frac{\text{market area's \% of U.S. retail sales}}{\text{market area's \% of U.S. population}}$$

Because the numerator (retail sales) reflects all sales made in an area regardless of where the consumer is from and the denominator (population) includes only those people who live in the area, the sales activity index does not specify whether a market area's sales activity is the result of the shopping activities of area residents, nonresidents, business concerns, or some combination. "A high index may, therefore, indicate a strong influx of nonresident shoppers, heavy buying by business concerns, heavy buying by residents, or all three."[15]

Quality Index

A third index prepared by *Sales and Marketing Management* and reported in the *Survey of Buying Power* is the **quality index.** As described by the publishers, the quality index achieves the following:

> . . . shows the extent to which the market's quality is above or below par (represented by 100). If a market's percent of the national population, which can be taken to represent par, is divided into the buying power index, it yields the quality index. A high index could reflect either above-average buying power or a strong influx of shoppers from outside the area, or both.[16]

Index of Retail Saturation

The **index of retail saturation (IRS)** is a measure of the potential sales per square foot of store space for a given product line within a particular market area.[17] As a market-area evaluation tool, it incorporates both consumer demand and competitive supply. Essentially, the index is the ratio between a market area's capacity to consume and its capacity to retail. The formulation of the index of retail saturation is expressed as

$$IRS = \frac{(C)(RE)}{RF}$$

where

IRS = index of retail saturation for a given product
line(s) within a particular market area

FIGURE 10–13
Market-area evaluation
using the index of retail
saturation

	Market Area		
	A	B	C
Number of customers (C)	40,000	50,000	70,000
Retail expenditures (RE)	$10	$12	$10
Retail facilities (RF)	10,000	12,000	15,000
Index of retail saturation (IRS)	$40.00	$50.00	$46.67

C = number of customers in a particular market for a given product line

RE = retail expenditures—the average dollar expenditure for a given product line(s) within a particular market area

RF = retail facilities—the total square feet of selling space allocated to a given product line(s) within a particular market area

To illustrate, assume that a retail operation needs sales of $45 per square foot of selling space for a given product line to operate profitably. Also assume that the retailer is currently examining three potential market areas (see Figure 10–12). Market area A can be eliminated from further consideration because it does not meet the $45 minimum sales per square foot criterion. Both markets B and C meet the minimum sales criterion. If all other location considerations are equal, however, market B would be preferable to C because it offers the retailer more ($3.33 higher) sales potential per square foot of selling space.

The index of retail saturation allows the retailer to classify market areas on the basis of their competitive situation—understored, overstored, or saturated.[18] **Understored market areas** are those in which the capacity to consume exceeds the capacity to retail. In other words, there are too few stores and/or too little selling space devoted to a product line to satisfy consumer needs. **Overstored market areas** occur when the capacity to retail exceeds the capacity to consume. In this situation, retailers have devoted too much space to a particular product line. Finally, a **saturated market area** is one in which the capacity to retail equals the capacity of buyers to consume a product line. In this case, demand for and supply of a given product line are in equilibrium. The understored market area obviously offers the best opportunity for the retailer seeking a new location. During the last several years, retailers like IKEA, Scandinavian home furnishing; Carrefour, European hypermarket; and Chas. A. Stevens, women's apparel have all located in Philadelphia because they considered it understored.[19]

THE MARKET-AREA SELECTION PROCESS

On completing the market-area identification and evaluation processes, the retailer must select a regional and local market. There are no simple decision rules to aid the retailer in selection. The basis of the location decision varies with types of retailers, operational characteristics, and stated objectives. At this point, the retailer's *judgment* is the critical factor. Ultimately, the retailer should select the regional and local markets that provide sufficient levels of support (sales potential) conducive to the firm's operational needs. Generally, the market area a retailer selects represents a compromise among several promising but different market situations.

A market consists of buying populations and their buying behavior. Consumer and organizational markets are the two market types from which retailers secure their business. Retail location is a problem of market segmentation—the process of dividing the total market into more meaningful and homogeneous market segments.

The retail-location problem is multidimensional. The retailer must identify, evaluate, and select a market area to support a particular operation. The market-area identification process involves two tasks. The first is determining which criteria to use in segmenting markets. Both market criteria (population, housing, buyer behavior, and physical environment characteristics) and retail operation criteria (distribution, competition, promotion, and legal characteristics) are useful in identifying retail market areas.

The second task is to identify market areas. Market areas can be delineated as regional markets ("the right region" and the "right part of the region") and local markets (the "right town" and the "right part of town"). Based on census areas, communication areas, functional markets, ABC markets, and intraurban markets, the retailer can identify several regional and local market areas.

The market-area evaluation process is an attempt to ascertain a market area's relative potential. Although the retailer is free to develop original sources and methods of evaluation, several standard sources (such as the *Survey of Buying Power* and the *Editor & Publisher Market Guide*) and standard methods (such as the buying power index, quality index, sales activity index, and index of retail saturation) are readily available.

Finally, the market-area selection process requires the retailer to choose (1) regional and local markets that provide potential sales large enough to support a firm's operations and (2) retailing environments that will enhance operations. In the selection process, the retailer has no magical "rules of thumb" for arriving at a final decision. Instead, the retailer must use judgment and experience to select a market area from the several alternatives that have been identified and evaluated.

ABC markets

areas of dominant influence (ADIs)

buying power index

census markets

class selectivity

Commercial Atlas & Marketing Guide

communication markets

concentric zone theory

consumer markets

designated marketing areas (DMAs)

direct competitors

Editor & Publisher Market Guide

functional markets

geographic selectivity

index of retail saturation (IRS)

indirect competitors

intraurban markets

level of competition

market

market potential approach

market segmentation

media coverage

media selectivity

multiple-nuclei theory

organizational markets

overstored market area

quality index

retail operations approach

sales activity index (SAI)

saturated market area

sector theory

Survey of Buying Power

understored market area

REVIEW QUESTIONS

1. What is a market?
2. Describe how consumer markets differ from organizational markets.
3. Outline the market-segmentation process. What are the major tasks to be accomplished in segmenting markets?
4. What are the four criteria used to segment markets based on market potential?
5. Compare and contrast direct and indirect competitors.
6. How might geographic selectivity and class selectivity be used to identify promotional market areas?
7. What two standardized areas are used in identifying retail markets based on the coverage by broadcast stations?
8. Describe the nine census regions that make up the U.S. market.
9. Define ABC markets. Characterize each of these markets.
10. Describe the concentric zone theory of intraurban markets.
11. Compare and contrast the sector and multiple-nuclei theories of intraurban structure.
12. What does the buying power index measure?
13. How is the sales activity index determined? What does it show?
14. Describe the quality index.
15. How is the formulation of the index of retail saturation expressed?
16. What are the three market-area classifications as defined by the index of retail saturation?
17. On what basis are regional and local markets selected?

ENDNOTES

1. Louis W. Stern and Frederick D. Sturdivant, "Customer-Driven Distribution Systems," *Harvard Business Review* (July–August 1987): 34.
2. See Dwight J. Shelton, "Birds of a Geodemographic Feather Flock Together," *Marketing News,* 28 Aug. 1987, 13.
3. See Peter S. Carusone and Brenda J. Moscove, "Special Marketing Problems of Smaller City Retailing," *Journal of the Academy of Marketing Science* 13 (Summer 1985): 198–211.
4. Raymond E. Murphy, *The American City—An Urban Geography* (New York: McGraw-Hill, 1966): 114.
5. "JCP/Stores—What Makes Penney Run," *Chain Store Age* (December 1977): 141.
6. Ibid., 155.
7. Ibid., 165.
8. Murphy, *The American City,* 209.
9. Ibid., 208.
10. Ibid., 211.
11. *The Structure and Growth of Residential Neighborhoods in American Cities* (Washington, D.C.: U.S. Federal Housing Administration, 1976): 76.
12. 1987 *Survey of Buying Power, Sales, and Marketing Management,* 27 July 1987, C-3.
13. Ibid.
14. Ibid., C-5.
15. Ibid.
16. Ibid.
17. The following discussion is based on Bernard J. LaLonde, "New Frontiers in Store Location," *Supermarket Merchandising* (February 1963): 110.
18. Ibid.
19. "Retailers Buy into Philadelphia," *Advertising Age,* 28 March 1988, 48MW.

RELATED READINGS

Bellenger, Danny, Robertson, Dan H., and Hirschman, Elizabeth C. "Age and Education as Key Correlates of Store Selection for Female Shoppers." *Journal of Retailing* 52 (Winter 1976): 71–78.

Bush, Ronald H., Tatham, Ronald L., and Hair, Joseph F., Jr. "Community Location Decisions by Franchisors: A Comparative Analysis." *Journal of Retailing* 52 (Spring 1976): 33–42.

Craig, C. Samuel, and Ghosh, Avijit. "Covering Approaches to Retail Facility Location." In *AMA Educators' Proceedings,* edited by R. W. Belk et al., 195–99. American Marketing Association, 1984.

Finn, Adam. "Characterizing the Attractiveness of Retail Markets." *Journal of Retailing* 63 (Summer 1987): 129–62.

Garreau, Joel. *The Nine Nations of North America.* New York: Avon Books, 1981.

Ghosh, Avijit, and Craig, C. Samuel. "Formulating Retail Location Strategy in a Changing Environment." *Journal of Retailing* 47 (Summer 1983): 56–68.

Ingene, Charles A. "Structural Determinants of Market Potential." *Journal of Retailing* 60 (Spring 1984): 5–36.

Joyce, Mary, and Guiltinan, Joseph. "The Professional Woman: A Potential Market Segment for Retailers." *Journal of Retailing* 54 (Summer 1978): 59–70.

Kramer, Jonathan M. "Benefits in the Use of Suburban Press for Large Metropolitan Buys." *Journal of Marketing* 41 (January 1977): 68–70.

Samli, A. Coskun, Riecken, Glen, and Yavas, Ugur. "Inter-Market Shopping Behavior and the Small Community: Problems and Prospect of a Widespread Phenomenon." *Journal of the Academy of Marketing Science* 11 (Winter–Spring 1983): 1–14.

Valentin, E. K. "Strategic Location Analysis: A Rudimentary Framework." In *1985 Educators' Proceedings,* edited by R. F. Lusch et al., 233–37. American Marketing Association, 1985.

Zeithaml, Valarie A. "The New Demographics and Market Fragmentation." *Journal of Marketing* 49 (Summer 1985): 64–73.

11

Objectives

- [ ] Define a retail trading area in terms of its operational dimensions.
- [ ] Describe the size, shape, and structural dimensions of retail trading areas.
- [ ] Understand and use various techniques for trading-area identification.
- [ ] Ascertain the gross and net adequacy of retail trading areas.
- [ ] Evaluate and select retail trading areas in accordance with established minimum criteria.

Retail Trading Areas: Identification, Evaluation, and Selection

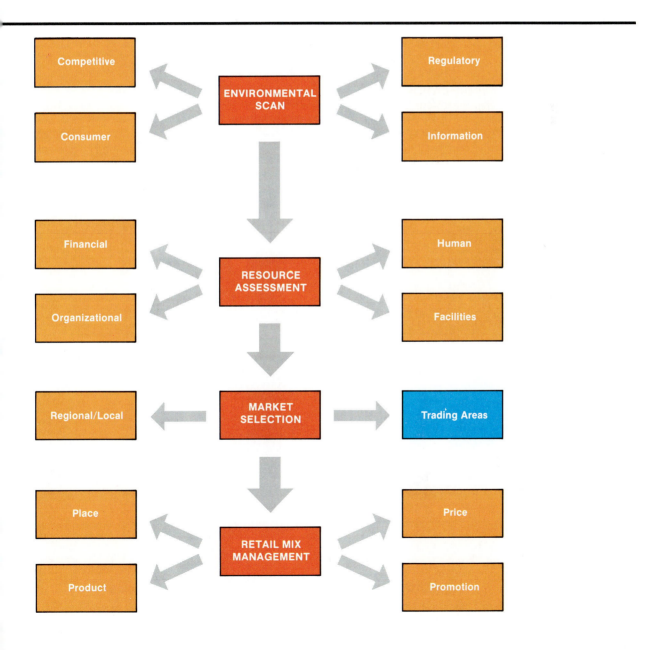

A critical element in determining a retailer's success is the ability to assess and acquire a good location. To achieve this objective, the retailer must *identify, evaluate,* and *select* retail trading areas to segment its consumer markets further. After identifying and evaluating local markets, the retailer must then segment them into *trading areas* (i.e., areas from which to attract potential customers). This chapter explains how to define and evaluate the retail trading area so as to operate profitably.

THE RETAIL TRADING AREA

A **retail trading area** is broadly defined as that area from which a store attracts its customers or obtains its business. Depending on the *kind* of retail operations, a retail trading area can be described more specifically in the following terms:

☐ *Drawing power*—the area from which a *shopping center* could expect to derive as much as 85 percent of its total volume
☐ *Per capita sales*—the area from which a *general merchandise store* can derive a minimum annual per capita sale of $1
☐ *Patronage probability*—the area from which potential customers come who have a probability greater than zero of purchasing a given class of products or services that either a retailer or group of retailers offers for sale
☐ *Retail operations*—the area from which either a marketing unit or group can operate economically, depending on volume, cost to operate, and cost to sell and/or deliver a good or service

FIGURE 11–1
Assessing retail trading areas

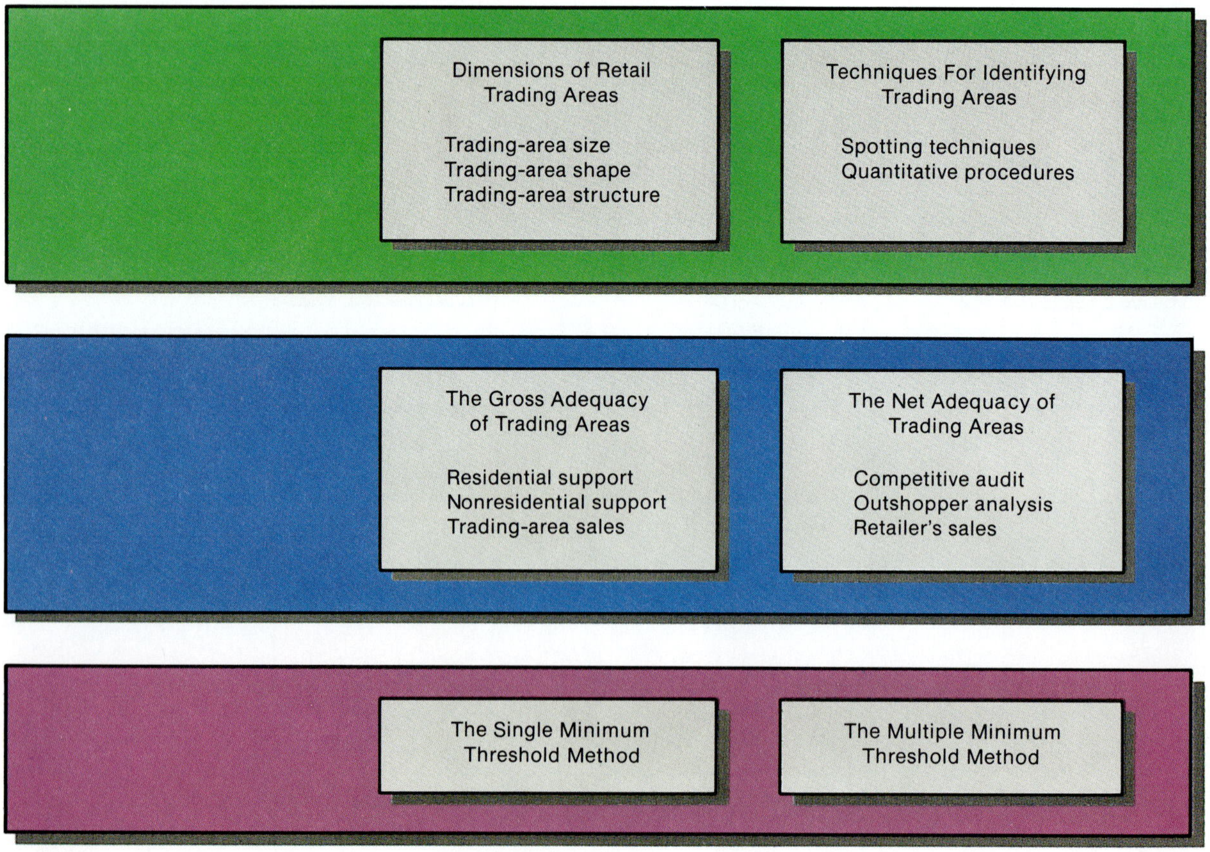

Dimensions of Retail Trading Areas

Trading-area size
Trading-area shape
Trading-area structure

Techniques For Identifying Trading Areas

Spotting techniques
Quantitative procedures

The Gross Adequacy of Trading Areas

Residential support
Nonresidential support
Trading-area sales

The Net Adequacy of Trading Areas

Competitive audit
Outshopper analysis
Retailer's sales

The Single Minimum Threshold Method

The Multiple Minimum Threshold Method

Two characteristics common to these four definitions are that (1) they identify an area from which retailers *draw customers* over a specific period of time and (2) they identify a *single focal point* (such as a town, a shopping center, or a single retail outlet) around which the trading area develops. Essentially, then, retail trading areas are "gravity areas"—retail sites to which consumers will gravitate or be pulled from an identifiable area.

The three purposes of any trading-area analysis are to determine the area from which the majority of the retailer's customers might come, the potential sales level of the area of majority support, and the source of support in terms of customers' needs. Given these purposes, the threefold problem of retailers is how (1) to identify several potential trading areas, (2) to evaluate these trading areas, and (3) to select a trading area (see Figure 11−1).

The Dimensions of Retail Trading Areas

THE TRADING-AREA IDENTIFICATION PROCESS

Retailers use three dimensions to describe a retail trading area: size, shape, and structure. Describing a trading area's dimensions is the first step in the retail trading-area identification process.

Trading-Area Size

Trading areas range in size from a few square blocks to a radius of many miles. The size of a trading area is a function of the cumulative effects of several *operational* and *environmental* factors. The two major operational factors are *type* and *size*. *Type of retail operation* means the kind of goods and services offered. Retailers that offer specialty and shopping goods will draw consumers from a wider geographic area than retailers that offer convenience goods, because consumers are willing to exert greater effort and to travel greater distances to buy specialty and shopping goods than to buy convenience goods. Macy's of Kansas City, for example, is able to draw customers from Manhattan, Kansas; this represents a trading area radius of 110 miles.[1]

The second operational factor, *store size,* is directly related to the retailer's trading-area size. That is, the larger the retail store and the greater its selection of merchandise, the larger its trading area will be. Because of their physical size and wide range of merchandise, Bloomingdale's of New York and Rich's of Atlanta are department stores with very large trading areas.

The second set of factors that determine the size of a retailer's trading area are environmental, including (1) the number, size, and type of *neighboring stores;* (2) the nature and activity of *competing stores;* and (3) the character of the *transportation network.*

A retailer that locates near other retailers often finds that the combined trading area of all the neighboring retailers in the cluster is larger than if the store were in an isolated location. Thus, a retailer that locates in a regional shopping mall shares more potential customers from a larger area than a retailer that locates either in a small, neighborhood shopping center or in an isolated, freestanding location.

The size of a retailer's trading area also depends on the location, size, and activity of competing stores. One large department store, for example, might locate next to another large department store to facilitate consumers' comparative shopping and thus draw from a larger geographic area. Consumers reason that by going to the geographic site of two similar stores, they probably will find what they are looking for.

The third environmental factor, the transportation network, strongly influences a retailer's ability to attract consumers from an area. The effect of traffic networks on the size of a retailer's trading area becomes apparent when we consider that stores located on major thoroughfares usually have larger trading areas than those located on secondary streets and roads. Thus, the number of traffic lanes, the number and nature of intersections (controlled or uncontrolled), the speed limit, and the presence or absence of barriers to uncongested movement all affect the size of the area from which a retailer can attract consumers.

Trading-Area Shape

Trading areas assume many different shapes, a result of three distinct factors: (1) transportation networks; (2) physical, social, and political barriers; and (3) location of competitors.[2]

Transportation networks. The shape of a trading area depends largely on the makeup of the transportation network near which a retailer is located. Because of the ease of movement along a major artery (such as an interstate) and the lack of physical barriers (such as traffic lights, traffic signs, and low speed limits), a store located along a major route should expect an elongated trading-area shape. Where two major arteries intersect, the shape of the trading area tends to be elongated along both major routes.

Physical, social, and political barriers. Although major transportation arteries extend a retailer's trading area, certain physical, social, and political barriers reduce these extensions. Figure 11−2 illustrates the influence of all three barriers on the shape of a retailer's trading area. First, the lake acts as a physical barrier to the trading area. Similar physical barriers include rivers, mountainsides, ocean, deserts, land formations, limited-access highways, and railroad tracks. Another kind of barrier that affects a trading area's shape is a social barrier. In this illustration, a high-crime area limits the retailer's trading area; another example might be an ethnic neighborhood whose inhabitants would never think of going outside the neighborhood to shop. Finally, *political* barriers can limit a retailer's trading area. A state line (perhaps because of higher and lower sales taxes) and the borders of counties (one that limits or does not allow the sale of certain merchandise) might greatly influence the shape of a retailer's trading area.

Location of competitors. Where competitors locate their stores influences the shape of a retailer's trading area. Figure 11−3 shows how competitors can cut into a

FIGURE 11−2

Effects of physical, social, and political barriers on the shape of a retailer's trading area

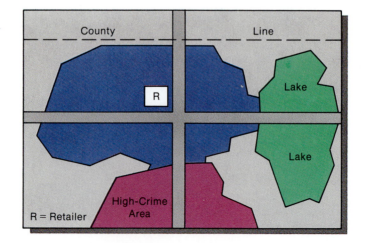

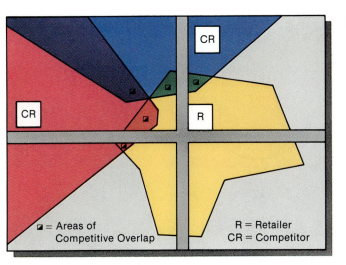

FIGURE 11–3
An example of how competitors affect a retailer's trading-area shape

retailer's trading area. A competitor's location, size, and type of operation all alter the shape of another retailer's trading area.

Trading-Area Structure

The third and final dimension of a retail trading area is structure. Trading-area structure is the comparative ability of a retailer or a cluster of retailers to attract customers from various distances or from various customer regions. Three trading-area structures are general, composite, and proportional.[3]

General trading areas.   **General trading areas** provide the majority of a retailer's business. The general trading area includes any and all customers who do, or might, buy any product line the retailer carries. Thus, a customer who purchases only perfume at the store is included in the retailer's general trading area along with a customer who buys perfume, dresses, shoes, handbags, and several other products (see Figure 11–4a).

Composite trading areas.   A **composite trading area** is a set of trading areas, each of which is structured according to the type of goods the retailer sells. Figure 11–4b illustrates the composite trading area for a store (or shopping center) selling convenience, shopping, and specialty goods. In this case, the retailer draws from a larger trading area for specialty goods than for shopping and convenience goods. The consumer's willingness to exert shopping effort, as described earlier, accounts for the composite-area boundary lines.

Proportional trading areas.   Whereas the composite trading area is based on the types of products retailers carry and the degree of consumer willingness to search for a product, a **proportional trading area** is based on the distance customers are from the store. The further customers are from the retail store, the less likely they are to patronize it. The closer customers are to the store, the greater the likelihood they will patronize it. These two statements define what retailers call the "distance decay function"—that is, the number of customers attracted to a given store decreases as their distance from the store increases. As illustrated in Figure 11–4c, three distance zones—primary, secondary, and fringe—constitute the proportional trading area.

The **primary trading zone** is the area around which a retailer can expect to attract 50 to 70 percent of its business. The primary trading area might be defined in

FIGURE 11–4
Trading-area structure

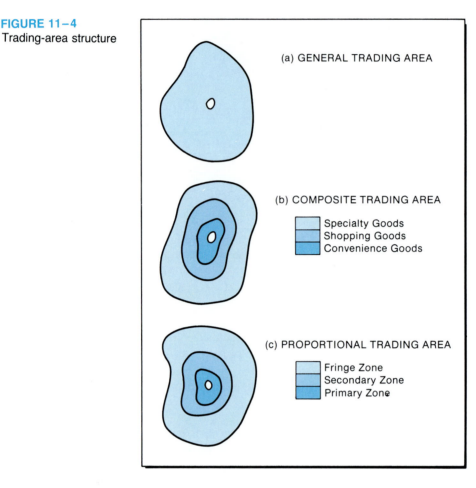

one of three ways: (1) the area closest to the store; (2) the area in which the retailer has a competitive advantage, such as customer convenience and accessibility; and (3) the area from which the retailer produces the highest per capita sales. The **secondary trading zone** surrounds the primary zone and generally represents 20 to 30 percent of the retailer's total sales volume. From the secondary zone, consumers usually select the store as their second or third shopping choice. The **fringe trading zone** is that area from which the retailer occasionally draws customers (5 to 10 percent of the business). Retailers generally attract customers from this zone either because "they just happened to be in the vicinity" or because they are extremely loyal to the store or its personnel.

Techniques for Identifying Trading Areas

Two general research approaches for identifying trading areas are spotting techniques and quantitative procedures. Quantitative approaches are more appropriate for the new or expanding retailer, while spotting techniques are more commonly used by the existing retailer seeking to determine the extent of its present trading area.

Spotting Techniques

Spotting techniques include several methods by which the retailer attempts to "spot" customer origins on a map. By carefully observing the magnitude and arrangement of these origins, the retailer can identify the dimensions of the trading area. Retailers normally define customer origins by home addresses, although customers' places of employment also are important. Some of the more common spotting techniques include surveys of customers' license plates, customer surveys, analyses of customer records, and studies of customer activities.

License plate surveys. By recording the license plate numbers of automobiles in the store's parking lot, retailers can obtain customer home addresses. Sampling should include checking license plates at different times of the day, different days of the week, and different weeks of the month to ensure a representative sample. The primary advantage of this technique is that it is relatively inexpensive to administer.[4] License plate surveys have several limitations, including the following: (1) there is no way to determine who actually drove the car to the store, or whether that car represents a regular customer or someone who just happened to be in the neighborhood; (2) a survey of license plates reveals no information on the shopping behavior of customers, such as what they bought, how much they bought, where they bought, why they bought, or if they bought anything at all; and (3) the number of purchasers in each car cannot be determined. Nevertheless, the relatively low cost and minimal time requirements of license plate surveys make them an attractive method for providing general information about a trading area.

Customer surveys. Either a personal interview, mail questionnaire, or telephone survey can provide information on who lives or works in a given area and who either current or potential customers are. Actual customers can be surveyed on the premises (within a particular store or shopping mall) by either personal interviews or take-home/mail-back questionnaires. Good surveying techniques must be employed to ensure an unbiased, representative sample. Customer surveys can provide a significant amount of information regarding demographics and shopping behavior; their limitations are cost, time, and the skill required to conduct them efficiently and effectively.

Customer records. Retailers have several ways to obtain addresses of current customers as well as additional valuable information. Customer credit, service, and delivery records contain a great deal of information if properly developed and maintained. From their records, retailers can find customer addresses and places of employment, ages, sex, family status, telephone numbers, and types and amounts of purchases. Although customer credit, service, and delivery records are a fast and inexpensive means of obtaining information, they are biased because cash customers, who require no services or delivery, are omitted from the analysis.

Customer activities. Any method that asks or requires customers to provide their names and addresses can help identify an existing or proposed trading area. Promotional activities such as contests and sweepstakes can be effective in obtaining names and addresses. Unfortunately, they tend to be biased toward the consumer who is willing to participate (sometimes, for example, the high-income consumer would not think it worth the time). Cents-off coupons that require the consumer to provide minimal information also have been used in identifying trading areas.

Quantitative Procedures

Retailers have used several quantitative procedures to delineate retail trading areas. The one most retailers use is the **retail gravitation concept,** which provides a measure of the potential interaction between various locations by determining the relative drawing power of each location.[5] Based on the relative drawing power of a location within an area, each area can be identified as part of a trading area (in some cases, areas can be shared by more than one location). Retailing analysts have developed several formulations of the gravitation concept, each of which uses a somewhat different procedure to identify trading areas. Two of the more widely recognized formulations are Converse's break-even point and Huff's probability model.

Converse's break-even point.   Converse developed a formula that allows the retailer to calculate the **break-even point** in miles between competing retail centers (stores, shopping centers, or cities).[6] In essence, Converse computes the break-even point as the point between the competing retailing centers where the probability of a consumer patronizing each retailing center is equal. This break-even point identifies the trading-area boundary line between competing retail trade centers. By identifying the break-even point between one retail center and all competing centers, the retailer can determine the trading area. The break-even point formula is expressed as

$$BP = \frac{d}{1 + \sqrt{\dfrac{P1}{P2}}}$$

where

BP = break-even point between the competing
retail centers in miles from the smaller center

d = distance between the two competing retail centers

$P1$ = population of the larger retail center

$P2$ = population of the smaller retail center

Both the distance and population expressions require further explanation. Although distance is normally measured in miles, recent studies show that many people think of distance in terms of travel time. Retail analysts can use travel time to replace miles for the distance between competing retail centers.

Populations ($P1$ and $P2$) can be expressed in several different ways. The total population in each center is the most common measurement. Another approach is to use the center's total number of retailers or the total retail square footage as the population measurement. Any measurement that reflects a retail center's ability to attract customers can be used as an expression of population. Figure 11–5 illustrates the identification of shopping center trading areas using Converse's break-even point method.

Huff's probability model.   The consumer choice of a retail store or shopping cluster is a complex decision-making process. The number and importance of store and cluster attributes used in the selection process vary with each shopper. Huff's model "was the first to suggest that market areas were complex, continuous, and probabilistic rather than the nonoverlapping geometrical areas of central place theory."[7] The basic premise of Huff's "shopper attraction" model is based on the following empirical regularities:

1. The proportion of consumers patronizing a given shopping area [cluster] varies with distance from the shopping area.

FIGURE 11–5
A problem using Converse's break-even point formula

The Problem:
Where are the break-even points between the following retail trade centers?

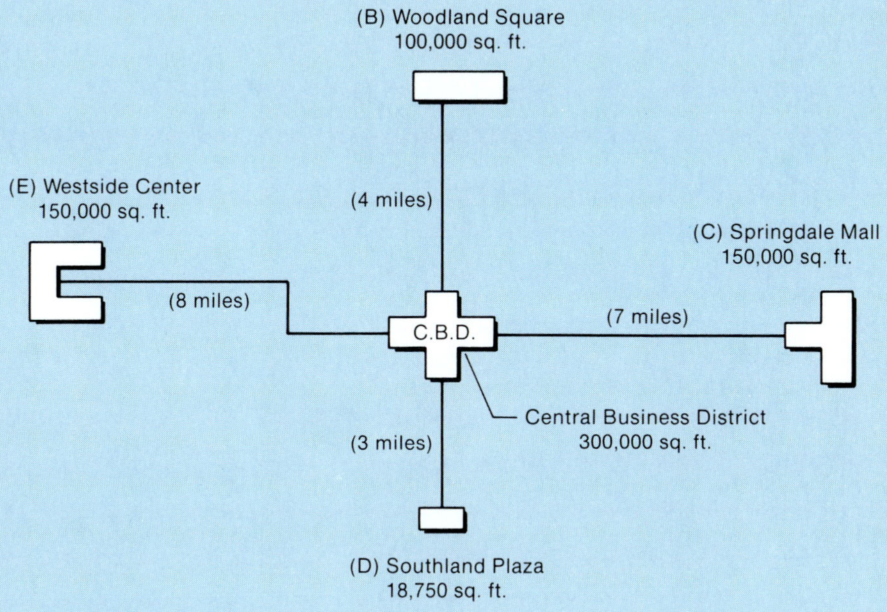

(B) Woodland Square
100,000 sq. ft.

(E) Westside Center
150,000 sq. ft.

(4 miles)

(C) Springdale Mall
150,000 sq. ft.

(8 miles)

C.B.D.

(7 miles)

Central Business District
300,000 sq. ft.

(3 miles)

(D) Southland Plaza
18,750 sq. ft.

The Calculation

$$BP_{AB} = \frac{4}{1 + \sqrt{\dfrac{300,000}{100,000}}} = \frac{4}{1 + \sqrt{3}} = \frac{4}{1 + 1.73} = \frac{4}{2.73} = 1.46$$

$$BP_{AC} = \frac{7}{1 + \sqrt{\dfrac{300,000}{150,000}}} = \frac{7}{1 + \sqrt{2}} = \frac{7}{1 + 1.41} = \frac{7}{2.41} = 2.90$$

$$BP_{AD} = \frac{3}{1 + \sqrt{\dfrac{300,000}{18,750}}} = \frac{3}{1 + \sqrt{16}} = \frac{3}{1 + 4} = \frac{3}{5} = .60$$

$$BP_{AE} = \frac{8}{1 + \sqrt{\dfrac{300,000}{300,000}}} = \frac{8}{1 + \sqrt{1}} = \frac{8}{1 + 1} = \frac{8}{2} = 4.00$$

The Interpretation
The break-even point between Central Business District and
(1) Woodland Square is 1.46 miles from Woodland Square
(2) Springdale Mall is 2.90 miles from Springdale Mall
(3) Southland Plaza is .60 miles from Southland Plaza
(4) Westside Center is 4.00 miles from either Center, i.e., halfway between

FIGURE 11−6

Huff's probability model for defining and estimating a trading area

The model developed by D. L. Huff to measure the probability of consumers expected to be attracted to a particular shopping cluster can be formally expressed as follows:

$$P_{ij}^k = \frac{\dfrac{S_j^k}{(T_{ij})^\lambda}}{\displaystyle\sum_{j=1}^{n} \dfrac{S_j^k}{(t_{ij})^\lambda}} \qquad (1)$$

$$i = 1, 2, \ldots, m$$
$$j = 1, 2, \ldots, n$$
$$k = 1, 2, \ldots, p$$

where

P_{ij}^k = the probability of a consumer at a given origin i traveling to a particular shopping cluster j for a type k shopping trip

S_j^k = the size of the shopping cluster j devoted to shopping tip k (measured in square footage of retail selling area devoted to shopping trip k items)

T_{ij} = the travel time involved in getting from a consumer's point of origin i to a given shopping cluster j

λ = a parameter which is to be estimated empirically to reflect the effect of travel time on various kinds of shopping trips

m = the number of origins in the marketing area

n = the number of shopping clusters in the marketing area

P = the number of different types of shopping trips defined.

2. The proportion of consumers patronizing various shopping areas [clusters] varies with the breadth and depth of merchandise offered by each shopping area.

3. The distance that consumers travel to various shopping areas [clusters] varies for different types of products purchased.

4. The "pull" of any given shopping area [cluster] is influenced by the proximity of competing shopping areas.[8]

The Huff model computation is shown in Figure 11−6.

THE TRADING-AREA EVALUATION PROCESS

The basic problem of any trading-area evaluation is to answer two questions: (1) what is the total amount of business a trading area can generate now and in the future? and (2) what share of the total business can a retailer in a given location expect to attract? Although there is no standardized trading-area evaluation process, most evaluation procedures use the concepts of trading-area adequacy and trading-area potential to predict total trading-area business and the share of business a particular retailer can expect.

Trading-area adequacy is the ability of a trading area to support proposed and existing retail operations.[9] This support capability may be viewed in a gross as well

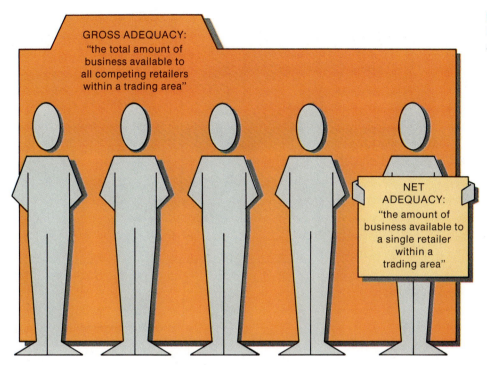

FIGURE 11–7
Elements of trading-area adequacy

as net form (see Figure 11–7). **Gross adequacy** is the ability of a trading area to support a retail operation without any consideration of retail competition. That is, the gross adequacy measures the total amount of business available to all competing retailers within a defined trading area. On the other hand, **net adequacy** is the ability of a trading area to provide support for a retailer after competition has been taken into account.

Finally, **trading-area potential** is the predicted ability of a trading area to provide acceptable support levels for a retailer in the future.

The Gross Adequacy of Trading Areas

Measuring gross adequacy determines a trading area's total *capacity to consume.* The capacity of a retail market to consume is a function of the total *number of consumers* within a trading area at any given time and their need, willingness, and ability to purchase a particular class of goods (see Figure 11–8). Unfortunately, it is not easy to determine consumers' need, willingness, and ability to buy a certain class of goods. To determine gross adequacy, the retailer must first consider appropriate consumption units (such as people, homes, businesses, and so forth) to count for a general class of goods. Second, the retailer must find an appropriate measure of a consumption unit's need, willingness, and ability to buy. To feel confident in their analyses, retailers must use one or more indicators of their potential buyers' behavior. Finally, the support capabilities of a trading area depend to some extent on sources outside the gross trading area.

Residential Support Levels

After sufficiently identifying the gross trading area, a retailer needs to concentrate on the most important source of business: the area's residents. To measure a trading area's potential consumers, the retailer must analyze population/demographic and household/residential variables.

FIGURE 11–8
The market potential
puzzle: Determinants of
a market's capacity to
consume

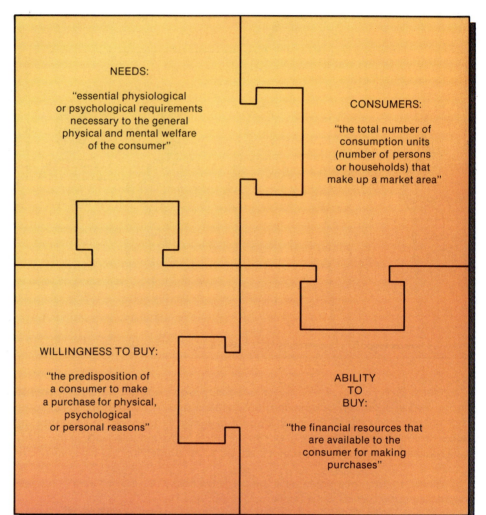

Population/demographic analysis.   A trading area's total capacity to consume is partly a function of the total number of people who reside in that trading area. It is important to obtain an accurate population count, because the total population figure plays a part in several quantitative estimates of gross and net adequacy; the population figure must be accurate to produce reliable estimates. Although total population figures are informative, many experts think these figures need to be qualified in terms of their demographic makeup.

The actual level of support for a given line of products or services that can be expected from persons living in the trading area may come, for example, from those who have an annual income of $15,000 or more and are between the ages of twenty and thirty-five. That is, a trading area's capacity to consume may not be directly related to its total population; instead, it may be a function of the number of people who have a certain demographic makeup—such as age, sex, income, occupation, and family status. For example, measurements such as the number of children (bike store), the number of women (women's clothing store), or the number of high-income homeowners (expensive home furnishings) indicate a population count that should produce more reliable gross adequacy estimates.

Evaluating gross adequacy is a matter of identifying demographic characteristics that best indicate the consumer's need, willingness, and ability to buy, and of obtaining a reliable count of the number of people who have the desired demographic makeup. At the local trading-area level, a good source of population and demographic information is the *Census of Population*.

Household/residential analysis. For some retailing operations, a trading area's capacity to consume is more directly related to the *number of households* or *residential units* than to the number of people in the area. For example, a count of household or residential units is probably more indicative than a population count of a trading area's consumption capacity for hardware, furniture, and appliance goods. This relationship simply reflects the fact that the household unit purchases many goods, and the consumer's home is the prime determinant of the need for certain product lines.

Definitions of household unit and residential unit are quite similar; the primary difference is the occupancy factor. *Households* are private dwelling units that include all persons occupying a particular house or apartment, whereas a *residential unit* is a housing unit occupied as separate living quarters, such as an apartment building. A count of households would produce a more reliable estimate of the existing capacity to consume, and a count of residential units might better reflect the potential consumption capacity, at least in terms of existing residential facilities. A household unit count by tracts and blocks can be obtained from the *Census of Population*. A residential unit count for either census tracts or blocks is available from the *Census of Housing* and can be checked through field observation and air photographs. To reflect their consumption capacity more accurately, each residential unit can be weighted by average value, size, type of construction, and characteristics noted in housing census reports and local building permits.

Nonresidential Support Levels

Although the vast majority of a trading area's consumption capacity comes from people who live in that area, some of the consumption support does not. Consumers who reside outside a trading area contribute significantly to that area's capacity to consume.

Most trading areas are characterized by daily inward, outward, and through migration of consumers who are attracted into the trading area for work, recreation, and other reasons, such as the need for professional services. Although these consumers might live many miles away, they do represent a significant portion of trade customers who visit the area. Some of these customers visit frequently and regularly (work trip); others visit infrequently and irregularly (recreation trip). Nevertheless, this external consumption capacity should be included in assessing a trading area's gross adequacy.

Although it is impossible to count accurately the number of consumers that make up the external consumption capacity, it *is* possible to count the number of nonresidential units likely to attract consumers to the trading area (e.g., retailers, wholesalers, manufacturers, offices, schools, churches). Since not all nonresidential units have equal consumption-generating abilities, each must be weighted according to its ability to generate traffic. Because some nonresidential units are more compatible with a retail enterprise than others, the weights a retailer assigns to each nonresidential unit should reflect the degree of consumer–retailer compatibility.

Although a weighted nonresidential unit count does not fully describe or measure the impact of "outsiders" on the volume of a trading area, it does provide a reasonable estimate of this impact. At the very least, it forces the retailer to consider the effects of nonresidential consumers in calculating trade-area gross adequacy.

Estimating Trading-Area Sales

Several methods are available to estimate trading-area sales. The two most widely used techniques are the corollary data method and the per capita sales method.

Corollary data method. The **corollary data method** assumes that an identifiable relationship exists between sales for a particular class of goods and one or more trading-area characteristics (such as population, residential units, etc.). Knowledge of these relationships helps retailers estimate total sales.

Per capita sales method. Retail sales figures by store groups and general merchandise categories are available from the *Survey of Buying Power* and *Editor & Publisher Market Guide,* respectively. Unfortunately, the localized nature of most retail trading areas makes it difficult to obtain sales data because identified trading areas rarely correspond to the reported geographical areas (states, metro areas, counties, and cities) found in these trade sources. Retailers can, however, get reasonably reliable estimates despite the lack of conformity in these secondary sources of information.

One method for estimating trading-area sales is the **per capita sales method**. The estimated trading-area sales for a general product line is a function of the per capita expenditures for that product line times the total population of that trading area. As discussed earlier, retailers can obtain reliable population counts from census materials and per capita expenditure figures from consumer surveys and trade-source estimates.

A consumer survey asks residents in a particular trading area how much they have spent on a given category of merchandise over a specified period. Although consumer surveys can provide detailed data, most retailers cannot afford the considerable time and money it takes to conduct them. Instead, retailers usually rely on trade-source estimates, which are much less expensive than consumer surveys, easier and faster for obtaining the desired data, and generally as accurate as most consumer surveys. Additionally, they include per capita expenditures for specific trading areas within local markets.

For example, a retailer can use the *Survey of Buying Power* to find an estimate of retail sales for a particular store group (such as food) for a particular geographic unit (such as a city) and divide that figure by the city's population to yield a per capita expenditure for food. The retailer can use this figure as the average per capita expenditure on food for *all* trading areas within the city and adjust it either upward or downward depending on knowledge of the particular trading area under examination. This figure is called the gross adequacy of a trading area. Gross adequacy, remember, is the estimated total sales for a particular product line in a specified trading area. The question the retailer must then answer is "What is my slice of the pie?"

The Net Adequacy of Trading Areas

To answer the preceding question, a retailer must estimate the net adequacy of the trading area. Net adequacy has been defined as the proportion of sales volume a retailer can expect to receive from the total sales in a trading area; that is, net adequacy is the percentage of gross adequacy (or market share) a retailer can expect to get. To determine net adequacy, a retailer must consider the trading area's *capacity to consume* and its *capacity to sell*.

The capacity to consume is the gross adequacy measurement. Having obtained a gross estimate of the trading area's sales volume capabilities, the retailer's problem is to find a method of allocating total sales volume to each of the trading area's existing and proposed competitors. This allocation process consists of (1) analyzing the competitive environment and (2) estimating each retailer's sales and market share.

To determine net adequacy, a retailer must first identify the competitive environment. To analyze the competitive environment, the retailer must examine the types of competition, the number and size of competitors, and the marketing mix of competitors. We discussed these characteristics in Chapter 10 in the analysis of regional and local markets; however, to assess a trading area's net adequacy requires certain refinements. To gain a clearer picture of the competitive environment, a retailer can use two methods: (1) a competitive audit and (2) an outshopper analysis.

Competitive Audit

A **competitive audit** is an arbitrary, composite rating of each competitor's product, service, price, place, and promotion mixes. An audit covers a wide range of activities including eyeballing competitors' floor space, checking ad results, getting information from media people and vendors, checking competitors' prices, and evaluating the competition's merchandise mix.[10] The purpose of a competitive audit is to assess the ability of competitors to provide a marketing mix that consumers desire within the trading area. The sum of all audits is a measurement of total competition.

Retailers use a competitive audit in several ways. First, they use it to measure the total competition within the trading area (the sum of all competitors times their competitiveness rating). Second, they derive a measure of each competitor's expected share of total trading-area sales. Third, they gain a picture of an unfulfilled product position or "niche" in the trading area. The latter information can help the retailer develop a marketing strategy.

Outshopper Analysis

Not all consumers who live within a trading area shop exclusively in that area. A group of consumers known as "outshoppers" frequently and regularly shop outside their local trading area. These consumers spend a considerable amount of time, money, and effort making inter–trading-area shopping trips. One analyst characterizes outshoppers and their shopping behavior this way:

> Some outshoppers are looking for economic gains resulting from lower prices in larger trading centers where assortments are better and the level of competition more intense. Some outshoppers simply *seek* the diversity of unfamiliar or more stimulating surroundings . . . demographically, outshoppers are younger (25–54 year age group), are relatively well educated (had some college), and the relative income is high . . . psychographically outshoppers are active, on the "go," urban-oriented housewives who are neither time-conscious nor store-loyal shoppers. They tend to manifest a distaste for local shopping and hence a strong preference for out-of-town shopping areas.[11]

To obtain an accurate estimate of total expected sales, the retailer must perform **outshopper analysis**, subtracting outshopping sales, referred to as "sales leakage," from the trading area's gross sales to arrive at a more realistic total sales volume for the trading area.

To estimate sales leakage that results from outshopping behavior, a retailer can either conduct consumer surveys or use standard adjustments. In using consumer surveys, the retailer asks trading-area consumers to estimate how much they spend locally on a particular class of goods as a percentage of their total expenditures for those goods. The retailer then can use this percentage to adjust the gross sales figure for the trading area. As noted in Chapter 6, however, consumer surveys are costly and time-consuming.

A simple and less expensive method is the standard adjustment. A standard adjustment figure depends on prevailing trading-area conditions. For example, if the trading area contains a large number of consumers who are similar to the demographic and psychographic profile of outshoppers, the retailer should make a standard downward adjustment (e.g., 5 percent) in gross sales. Other factors to consider in making standard adjustments are (1) the existence of major shopping centers outside the trading area that are within easy driving distance, (2) the presence of major traffic arteries that facilitate outshopping, and (3) the lack of a sufficient number of competing retailers to facilitate consumers' comparison shopping. Although estimates of outshopping are not always accurate, the retailer must consider these factors in making a conservative estimate of trading-area net adequacy.

Estimating the Retailer's Sales

After evaluating the competitive environment, a retailer can estimate each competitor's sales. To calculate a net adequacy (i.e., the trading-area market share) figure, the retailer can use either the "total sales method" or the "sales per square foot method." Both methods use a ratio of trading-area capacity to consume (gross adequacy) to trading area capacity to sell.

Total sales method.   With the **total sales method,** a retailer allocates an equal share of the trading area's total sales for a specific product category to each competing retailer. This calculation is shown in Figure 11–9. The advantage of this method is that it is simple and quick to calculate. A limitation, however, is the assumption that all competing retailers are equal and can generate an equal share of the trading-area sales. Because competing retailers devote different amounts of time, money, space, and effort to sales, the analyst must make adjustments to the "all are equal" assumption. The competitive audit, discussed earlier, can be used to make this adjustment.

Sales per square foot method.   Another method for allocating trading-area sales to competitors is the **sales per square foot method,** whereby the retailer computes a ratio of each retailer's floor space devoted to a specific product category to the total of all retail floor space for the product category in the trading area. The calculation procedure is illustrated in Figure 11–10. This method assumes that selling space is a good predictor of a retailer's competitiveness. Variations of this method substitute amount of shelf space (linear, square, or cubic feet), sales per employee, or sales per checkout counter for sales per square foot.

The Growth Potential of Trading Areas

Before completing the trading-area evaluation process, the retailer must answer an additional question: What does the future hold for the trading area? Because mar-

FIGURE 11–9
Total sales method for estimating a retailer's sales

Capacity to Consume
———————
Capacity to Retail (Sell)

=

Total Sales for Product Category
———————
Number of Retailers Selling Product Category*
*Includes proposed retail operations

=

Total Sales per Retailer for Product Category

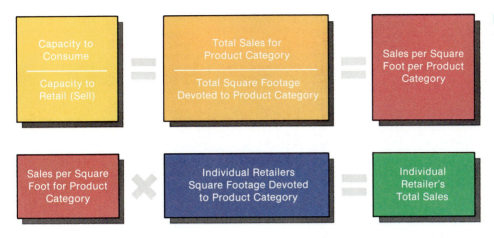

keting opportunities can change quickly, dynamically growing trading areas often become either static or declining markets. Without growth, the retailer either must fight to maintain present market share or be willing to survive on a smaller share. With growth, however, the retailer has an opportunity to expand sales and market share at a reasonable amount of cost and effort. Therefore, the final step in evaluating a retail trading area is to determine the area's future growth.

Because the future of a trading area is an outgrowth of past and current conditions, the retailer often can learn what to expect by examining those conditions. Visual observation of an area is a simple method of looking into the future. Although lacking scientific methodology, visual inspection of current activities can produce a useful picture of the future. A retailer should consider several factors:

1. New and expanding residential areas combined with older, stable neighborhoods provide a solid base for future growth.
2. An expanding commercial or industrial base signals growth opportunities.
3. A good balance between items 1 and 2 reflects a stable growth rate that avoids overdependence on limited economic activity.
4. A well-developed transportation network as well as proposed future transportation networks in the trading area contribute to a trading area's growth.
5. An involved local government that takes an interest in residential and business development is a great asset.
6. A progressive social and cultural environment (theaters, museums, zoos, etc.) is a healthy climate for business.

Figure 11–11 provides a checklist of these factors and how to use them in assessing the growth potential of a trading area.

To make the final selection of a trading area, the retailer must evaluate the alternatives in accordance with each of the following criteria, referred to as a "minimum threshold":

1. A stated minimum population having the desired demographic characteristics (such as 10,000 persons)
2. A stated minimum sales volume (such as $300,000 per year)
3. A stated minimum daily traffic count (such as 5,000 vehicles per day)

If a trading area does not meet at least one or a certain combination of these minimums, the retailer excludes it from further consideration.

THE TRADING-AREA SELECTION PROCESS

FIGURE 11–11

A simple checklist to evaluate a trading area's potential growth

FACTORS[1]	RATING SCALE[2]				
	Excellent (5)	Good (4)	Fair (3)	Poor (2)	Very Poor (1)
1					
2					
3					
4					
5					
6					

[1]Factors may be added to or deleted from this checklist depending upon local conditions.

[2]Total Rating Points	Trading Area Growth Potential
27 to 30	excellent
21 to 26	good
15 to 20	fair
10 to 14	poor
6 to 9	very poor

SUMMARY

A retail trading area is the area from which the retailer attracts all or most of its customers. The size, shape, and internal structure of a trading area depend on several factors. Trading-area size is directly related to (1) the type and size of the retailer's operation; (2) the number, size, and type of neighboring stores; (3) the nature and actions of competing stores; and (4) the character of the transportation network. The shape of a trading area is determined, in part, by the effects of the local network of transportation; by physical, social, and political barriers; and by the location of competitors. The internal structure of trading areas reflects the relative ability of either a single retailer or a cluster of retailers to attract customers from various distances or customer-source regions. Three internal trading-area structures are general, composite, and proportional.

The problem is how to identify, evaluate, and select trading-area alternatives. Retailers can identify potential trading areas through spotting techniques and quantitative procedures. The retailer determines the value of each trading area by first determining its gross and then its net adequacy. To refine the net adequacy further, it then assesses the future growth potential of each area. Gross adequacy is a measure of the trading area's total capacity to consume. This consumption capacity is a function of both residential (those who live inside the trading area) and nonresidential (those who live outside the trading area) consumers. Residential consumption is measured by population/demographic and household/residential-unit factors. The number and type of nonresidential units within a trading area are used to measure nonresidential consumption. Total trading-area sales can be estimated using either the corollary data method or the per capita sales method.

Net adequacy is the level of support a given retailer can expect to attract from the trading area. A retailer's expectations must depend on the relationship between a trading area's capacity to consume and its capacity to retail. Through a competitive audit, the retailer can ascertain within reliable limits the trading area's capacity to retail. The retailer can estimate the amount of sales it can expect to derive from the trading area by dividing the trading area's capacity to consume by its capacity to retail, using either the total sales method or sales per square foot method. Before selecting which trading-area alternatives to consider further, the retailer should determine the area's future growth potential.

KEY TERMS AND CONCEPTS

break-even point

competitive audit

composite trading area

corollary data method

fringe trading zone

general trading area

gross adequacy

net adequacy

outshopper analysis

per capita sales method

primary trading zone

proportional trading area

retail gravitation

retail trading area

sales per square foot method

secondary trading zone

spotting technique

total sales method

trading-area adequacy

trading-area potential

REVIEW QUESTIONS

1. What are the two characteristics common to most trading-area definitions?
2. What are the three purposes of any trading-area analysis?
3. How do the retailer's operations affect the size of a trading area?
4. Which factors have an impact on the shape of a retail trading area? Briefly explain each factor.
5. How are composite retail trading areas structured?
6. How much business can a retailer expect to receive from the secondary zone of a proportional trading area?
7. Describe the limitations of the license-plate survey method for identifying trading areas.
8. How is Converse's break-even point formula expressed? Define each part of the expression.
9. What are the components of trading-area adequacy? Define each.
10. What determines a trading area's capacity to consume? Describe each factor.
11. How might a retailer assess the impact of "outsiders" on a trading area's capacity to consume?
12. Describe the per capita sales method for estimating trading-area sales.
13. What two methods give a clearer picture of a trading area's competitive environment? Briefly describe each method.
14. Develop a demographic profile of the typical outshopper.
15. Describe the sales per square foot method of estimating a retailer's share of the total sales within a trading area.
16. What should a retailer consider when assessing the growth potential of a trading area?

ENDNOTES

1. Kevin T. Higgins, "Retail Strategies Always Evolving," *Marketing News,* 31 Jan. 1986, 6.
2. See Grady Tucker, "Site Selection Techniques and Evaluation," *Retail Control* (October 1986): 49.
3. See Ross L. Davies, *Marketing Geography* (Corbridge, Northumberland, England: Retailing and Planning Associates, 1976): 200–202.
4. Larry D. Crabtree, "Survey Car License Plates to Define Retail Trade Area," *Marketing News,* 4 Jan. 1985, 12.

5. See Howard L. Green, "Retail Sales Forecasting Systems," *Journal of Retailing* 62 (Fall 1986): 227–230.
6. Paul D. Converse, *Retail Trade Areas in Illinois,* Business Study No. 4 (Urbana, IL: University of Illinois, 1946): 30–31.
7. C. Samuel Craig, Avijit Ghosh, and Sara McLafferty, "Models of the Retail Location Process: A Review," *Journal of Retailing* 60 (Spring 1984): 15.
8. D. C. Huff, "Defining and Estimating a Trading Area," *Journal of Marketing* 28 (1964): 34.
9. Dale M. Lewison and Ray Robins, "A Model for Evaluating the Adequacy of a Retail Trading Area," in *Proceedings: Small Business Administration Directors Institute,* edited by David H. Hovey and Ronald S. Rubin (Small Business Administration Directors Institute, 1980).
10. Lewis A. Spalding, "Strategies for Share-Boosting," *Stores* (June 1986): 11.
11. Rom J. Markin, Jr., *Retailing Management,* 2d ed. (New York: Macmillan, 1971), 170; Fred D. Reynolds and William R. Darden, "International Patronage: A Psychographic Study of Consumer Outshoppers," *Journal of Marketing* 36 (October 1972): 50–54.

RELATED READINGS

Black, William C., Ostlund, Lyman E., and Westbrook, Robert A. "Spatial Demand Models in an Intrabrand Context." *Journal of Marketing* 49 (Summer 1985): 106–13.
Clithero, Joseph B., and Levenson, Lawrence A. "Urban Renewal Projects Pull Up Short of Revitalizing Downtown Retailing When They Only Entail Brick and Mortar." *Marketing News* (February 1985): 23.
Dove, Rhonda W. "Retail Store Selection and the Older Shopper." In *Marketing Comes of Age, Proceedings,* edited by David M. Klein and Allen E. Smith, 75–77. Southern Marketing Association, 1984.
Ghosh, Avijit. "The Value of a Mall and Other Insights from a Revised Central Place Model." *Journal of Retailing* 62 (Spring 1986): 79–97.
Ghosh, Avijit, and McLafferty, Sara L. "Locating Stores in Uncertain Environments: A Scenario Planning Approach." *Journal of Retailing* 58 (Winter 1982): 5–22.
Hawes, Jon M. "Winning the Battle for Intermarket Patronage." In *1985 Proceedings,* edited by J. C. Crawford and B. C. Garland, 196–200. Southwestern Marketing Association, 1985.
Hawes, Jon M., and Lumpkin, James R. "Understanding the Outshopper." *Journal of the Academy of Marketing Science* 12 (Fall 1984): 200–217.
Houston, Franklin S., and Stanton, John. "Evaluating Retail Trade Areas for Convenience Stores." *Journal of Retailing* 60 (Spring 1984): 124–36.
Hozier, George C., Jr., and Stem, Donald E., Jr. "Retail Patronage Loyalty as a Determinant of Consumer Outshopping Behavior." *Journal of the Academy of Marketing Science* 13 (Winter 1985): 32–46.
Ingene, Charles A., and Lusch, Robert F. "Market Selection Decisions for Department Stores." *Journal of Retailing* 56 (Fall 1980): 21–40.
Lewison, Dale M., and Zerbst, Robert A. "Trade Area Mix and Intensity Concepts for Evaluating Retail Site Alternatives." *Annals of Regional Science* 11 (July 1977): 86–96.
Lord, J. Dennis, and Mesimer, Douglas B. "Trade Area, Land Use Mix, and Diurnal Shifts in Store Patronage Patterns." *Akron Business and Economic Review* 13 (Fall 1982): 17–22.
Mahajan, Vijay, Sharma, Subhash, and Srinivas, D. "An Application of Portfolio Analysis for Identifying Attractive Retail Locations." *Journal of Retailing* 61 (Winter 1985): 19–34.
Nevin, John R., and Houston, Michael J. "Image as a Component of Attraction to Intraurban Shopping Areas." *Journal of Retailing* 56 (Spring 1980): 77–93.
Olsen, Janeen E., and Granzin, Kent L. "Consumer Logistics: The Location Subsystem." In *Developments in Marketing Science, Proceedings,* edited by N. K. Malhotra, 21–25. Academy of Marketing Science, 1985.

Papadopoulos, N. G. "Consumer Outshopping Research: Review and Extension." *Journal of Retailing* 56 (Winter 1980): 41–58.

Reindenbach, R. Eric, Cooper, M. Bixby, and Harrison, Mary Carolyn. "A Factor Analytic Comparison of Out Shopping Behavior in Larger Retail Trade Areas." *Journal of the Academy of Marketing Science* 12 (Winter–Spring 1984): 145–58.

Rust, Roland T., and Brown, Julia A. "Estimation and Comparison of Market Area Densities." *Journal of Retailing* 62 (Winter 1986): 410–30.

Stanley, Thomas J., and Korgaonkar, Pradeep. "Explaining Retail Trade in the Urban Environment." In *AMA Educators' Proceedings,* edited by R. W. Belk et al., 381–84. American Marketing Association, 1984.

Wee, Chow-Hou, and Pearce, Michael R. "Retail Gravitational Models: A Review with Implications for Further Research." In *Developments in Marketing Science, Proceedings,* edited by J. D. Lindquist, 300–305. Academy of Marketing Science, 1984.

Weisbrod, Glen E., Parcells, Robert J., and Kern, Clifford. "A Disaggregate Model for Predicting Shopping Area Market Attraction." *Journal of Retailing* 60 (Spring 1984): 65–83; (Fall 1984): 200–217.

PART FIVE
Retail Mix Management:
Implementing the Retailing Mix

12

Objectives

☐ Delineate and describe the four major ingredients of the retail mix.

☐ Classify and characterize the various types of site alternatives.

☐ Identify and use the five principles of site evaluation to assess the value of alternative sites.

☐ Describe and apply the basic method of retail site evaluation.

☐ Make a final site-selection decision through the process of elimination.

Place Strategy:
Selecting Retail Sites

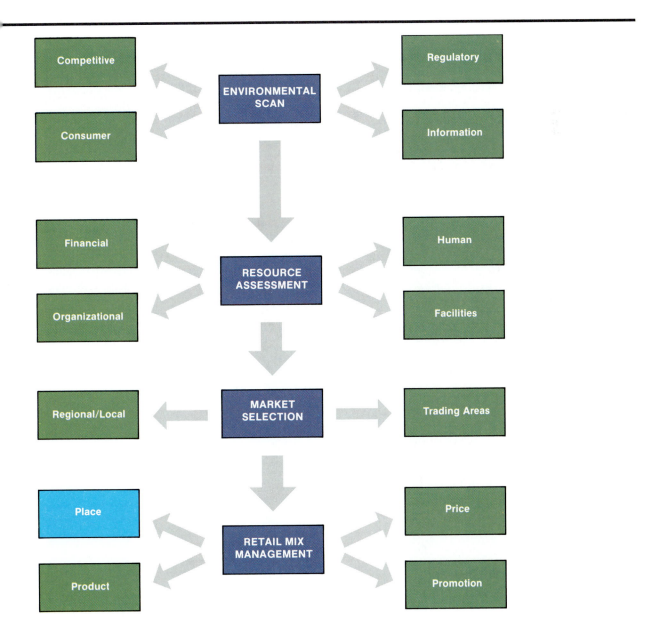

A primary concern of retail managers is to effectively manage the four major ingredients of the **retail mix,** commonly referred to as the 4 Ps of marketing: **place, product, price,** and **promotion.** Figure 12–1 illustrates the major ingredients of the retail mix and describes the decisions associated with each ingredient. Management must creatively combine the four ingredients into a successful merchandising mix consistent with the expectations and needs of the firm's targeted consumers. The retail mix represents the decisions over which the retail manager can exercise the most control. As markets and their environments change, the 4 Ps can be adjusted to meet new challenges. The next eleven chapters cover place, product, price, and promotion decisions. This chapter concerns selection of the right site.

A **retail site** is the actual physical location from which a retail business operates. Specialists in the retailing field comment that a retailer's site is one of the principal tools for obtaining and maintaining a competitive advantage through spatial monopoly. A given site is unique when its "positional qualities" serve a particular trading-area consumer in a way that no other site can match. Obviously, competing sites also are uniquely situated. The *retailer's site problem,* therefore, is how to identify, to evaluate, and to select the best available site alternative to profitably serve the needs of an identified trading-area consumer (see Figure 12–2).

THE SITE-IDENTIFICATION PROCESS

The first step in appraising retail site locations is to identify all potential site alternatives. The number of site alternatives in any given trading area can range from an extremely limited to a very large selection. Before attempting any formal evaluation, the retailer should screen the alternatives by asking three questions:

FIGURE 12–1
Ingredients of the retail mix

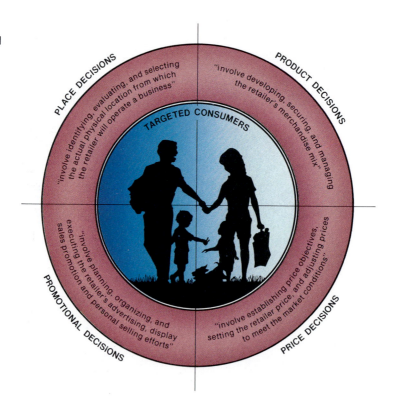

PLACE DECISIONS
"involve identifying, evaluating, and selecting the actual physical location from which the retailer will operate a business"

PRODUCT DECISIONS
"involve developing, securing, and managing the retailer's merchandise mix"

TARGETED CONSUMERS

PROMOTIONAL DECISIONS
"involve planning, organizing, and executing the retailer's advertising, display sales promotion and personal selling efforts"

PRICE DECISIONS
"involve establishing price objectives, setting the retailer price, and adjusting prices to meet the market conditions"

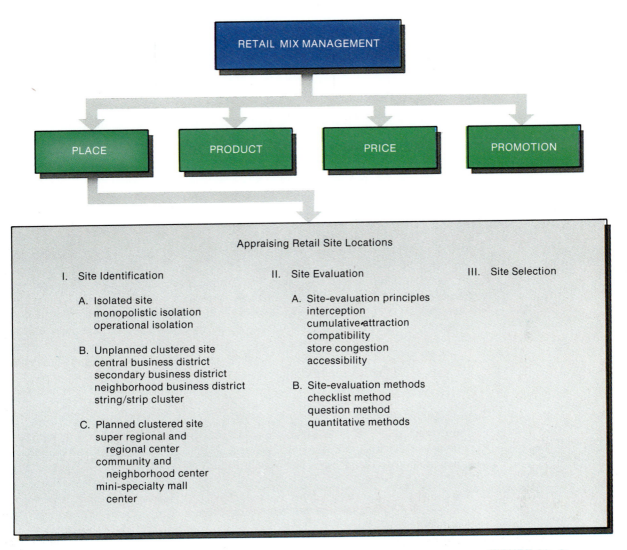

FIGURE 12–2
Appraising retail site locations

☐ **Availability**—Is the site available for rent or purchase?
☐ **Suitability**—Are the site and facilities of a suitable size and structure?
☐ **Acceptability**—Is the asking rental rate within the retailer's operating budget? Rent varies according to location, type, and size of retailing cluster, and market size and quality. While averages can be misleading, rents range from $5 to $15 per square foot for neighborhood centers, $8 to $20 for community centers, and $15 to $40 for regional centers.[1]

To be considered for further evaluation, a site alternative must meet all three screening criteria: it must be available, suitable, and acceptable.

Retail sites can be classified as either isolated or clustered. **Isolated sites** are retail locations that are geographically separated from other retailing sites. They can, however, be located next to other forms of economic and social activity. **Clustered sites** are retail locations that are either next to each other or in close proximity. From a shopping perspective, a cluster is two or more closely located retailers capable of sharing customers with minimal effort. Retail clusters are of two types: unplanned and planned. An *unplanned retail cluster* is the result of a natural evolutionary process; a *planned retail cluster* is the result of planning.

The Isolated Site

One site alternative is to "go it alone" by selecting an absolute location isolated from other retailers. The degree of physical isolation can range from "around the corner and down the block" to "far out on the outskirts of town." In relative location terms, an isolated site is situated so that it will not normally share consumer traffic with other retailers; however, its relative location offers certain advantages in attracting customers from other sources of business. Generally, the retailer that selects an isolated site is seeking to gain either a monopolistic or an operational advantage.

Monopolistic Isolation

Monopolistic isolation is a site that affords the retailer a uniquely convenient and accessible location to serve consumers. A monopolistically isolated site is isolated from competing retail sites but is uniquely situated for traffic-generating activities. Examples are a convenience-food store in a residential area, a neighborhood bar, a local service station, and a cafeteria located in an office complex. Exclusive airport locations, let under concessionaire agreements to the highest bidder, are excellent examples of monopolistic locations.[2] An example of monopolistic isolation familiar to students is the local campus bookstore.

Operational Isolation

Some retailers prefer to locate in isolated areas because they think it gives them greater flexibility in operating a retail business. A retailer that uses such an **operational isolation** strategy can achieve flexibility in a number of areas.

Site geography. Site alternatives that meet the size, shape, and terrain requirements of the retailer's operation constitute site geography. A home-improvement center, for example, normally requires a large, flat site to accommodate large showrooms and storage facilities.

Transportation network. Some site alternatives have transportation networks that generate good consumer traffic and also have good supply connections. A large warehouse-showroom retailer might consider locating the store at the junction of two major highway systems where customer traffic is high, but should also consider whether there is an adjacent railroad spur to handle large numbers of heavy, bulky products efficiently.

Type of facilities. Certain site alternatives permit installation of facilities that are conducive to the retailer's operations. The store's architectural motif, internal layout, fixturing, and atmosphere, as well as supporting facilities such as parking and signing, are all important considerations to any retailer. Most clustered locations have numerous facility restrictions, whereas isolation permits great freedom in design.

Operating methods. Some sites offer the retailer freedom of operation and avoidance of group rules that are common to shopping centers. Such restrictions include store operating hours, external displays, and cooperative advertising programs.

Operating costs.   A site must give the retailer the opportunity to operate within the business's cost constraints. A low-margin, high-turnover retailer (e.g., discount houses) needs to keep operating expenses low to offer discount prices. An isolated site can have low rental costs that help hold prices down.

Along with its advantages, an isolationist strategy has several disadvantages. First, the retailer must attract and hold its own customers. An isolationist strategy may cause the shopping goods retailer to encounter serious problems, since these consumers prefer either to compare brands or are one-stop shoppers. A second disadvantage is that retailers usually must design and build their own facilities. Only the largest retail organizations have the human and financial resources to engage in such activities. Third, the isolated retailer cannot share operating costs with neighboring establishments. Clustered locations allow retailers to share certain common ground costs such as maintenance, security, lighting, and snow and garbage removal.

The Unplanned Clustered Site

Before widespread urban planning and zoning laws, "unplanned" retailing clusters sprang up, many of which still exist. In cities where local zoning ordinances are not strictly enforced, they continue to form. Unplanned retailing clusters are often part of larger unplanned business districts where retailers can be either clustered together or scattered with no discernible pattern. The four general types of unplanned clusters are the central business district, the secondary business district, the neighborhood business district, and the string-strip shopping cluster.

Central Business District

The **central business district (CBD)** was, and in many cities still is, the single most important retailing cluster. A strong downtown retailing cluster is North Michigan Avenue in Chicago. In recent years this downtown area has attracted many of the nation's leading merchandisers: Bloomingdale's, Saks Fifth Avenue, Lord & Taylor, and Bonwit Teller from New York; I. Magnin from San Francisco; Neiman-Marcus from Dallas; and a host of other well-known specialty stores.[3] Since World War II,

Shopping in the central business district (CBD) offers both advantages and disadvantages.

however, the CBD has declined in its role as the city's principal place to shop. Among the commonly cited reasons for the CBD's decline are the following:

☐ Migration of middle- and upper-income consumers to the suburbs
☐ Development of fast, accessible intracity transportation networks, which allow people to live anywhere in the city and still work in the CBD
☐ General congestion in the CBD and its effects on free movement and accessibility
☐ Environmental pollution (air, noise, etc.) and its physiological effects
☐ General decay of the physical facilities in many downtown areas and its psychological effect
☐ High crime rates in and around the CBD
☐ Problems associated with the influx of low-income and ethnic groups into the areas immediately surrounding the CBD

Despite its problems and predictions of its extinction, the CBD and the retailing clusters within it have survived. In fact, some cities are experiencing a renaissance. Revitalized CBDs have resulted from the following efforts:

☐ Converting streets to pedestrian malls
☐ Modernizing physical facilities
☐ Reducing traffic congestion with one-way streets and modern traffic-control devices
☐ Constructing new middle- and upper-income residential complexes
☐ Renovating low-income residential areas
☐ Organizing commercial businesses to develop and promote the downtown area

Whereas some CBD revitalization projects have been extremely successful, others have failed. Successful revitalization projects include the Nicollet Mall in Minneapolis, Ghirardelli Square in San Francisco, Faneuil Hall Marketplace in Boston, and the Gallery at Market Street East in Philadelphia. The key to successful revitalization projects is not so much the development of new and existing facilities, but the creation of a safe and pleasant shopping atmosphere. "Festival marketplaces" have long been a key to reversing the flight from center cities and in developing the environment for a successful retail cluster.[4]

Secondary Business Districts

Most medium- and large-size cities have one or more **secondary business districts (SBDs),** located at the intersections of major traffic arteries. Some of these SBDs were originally the downtown areas of cities that were later incorporated into larger cities. Others represent the natural evolution of a retailing cluster to meet the convenience shopping needs of adjacent neighborhoods. As the name implies, these clusters are secondary to central business districts. They are similar to CBDs except they are much smaller. A typical SBD generally varies from 10 to 30 stores, radiating from one or more major intersections along primary traffic arteries.

The typical store mix of an SBD includes one or two branch department stores (or some other mass merchandiser) that serve as the principal consumer attraction; several specialty, shopping, and convenience goods retailers; and various service establishments. Often one or more large, nonretailing generators (e.g., hospital, office complex, university, manufacturing plant) are in the immediate vicinity of an SBD. These nonretailing establishments are usually important nonresidential sources of business.

Neighborhood Business Districts

The **neighborhood business district (NBD)** is a small retailing cluster that serves primarily one or two residential areas. The NBD generally contains four to five stores, usually including some combination of food and drug stores, gasoline service stations, neighborhood bars, self-service laundries, barber shops, beauty shops, and small, general-merchandise stores. The most common structural arrangement for the NBD is the "four-corners" layout, with a retailer situated on each corner. Although the four-corners layout is generally associated with secondary and residential streets, these streets represent the major "feeder" into the adjacent residential neighborhoods. The NBD is a logical alternative for a convenience retailer that wants to serve a particular neighborhood.

String/Strip Cluster

The **string/strip cluster** develops along a major thoroughfare and depends on the consumption activity of people who travel these busy thoroughfares.[5] The size of the string (or strip) is directly related to the average volume of traffic along a thoroughfare. Some strings stretch for miles along the heavily traveled arteries leading in and out of a CBD, whereas others are limited to one or two blocks along streets carrying a lower density of traffic. Examples of long strips are those with new and used car lots, rows of mobile home dealerships, strings of home-furnishings outlets, and a strand of side-by-side fast-food restaurants or collection of specialty shops.

The positional strengths of the string/strip cluster are their ability to achieve the following:

- ☐ Intercept consumers as they travel from one place to another
- ☐ Expose consumers to the retailer's operations
- ☐ Attract consumers on impulse
- ☐ Provide lower rents than central and secondary business districts

A recent development in the evolution of the string/strip cluster has been the "power strip," a clustering (planned or unplanned) of retailers next to or near major shopping malls.

This "power strip" is located near a major shopping mall and can readily intercept mall shoppers.

[These power strips] contain strong retail merchants, each being a destination-oriented shopping trip in its own right. Potential anchor tenants include off-price apparel merchants such as T.J. Maxx, promotional department stores such as Mervyn's or Main Street, children's stores such as Toys 'R' Us, Kids 'R' Us, or Child World, major consumer electronics chains such as Highland Superstores or Fretters, home centers such as Home Depot, and occasionally deep-discount drug stores such as F&M.[6]

The Planned Clustered Site

Over the last several decades, the growth of suburban populations has given retailers the opportunity to meet the needs of the suburban shopper. Originally, the basic problem was to develop an institution that could satisfy the shopping needs of a geographically dispersed market. The most common solution was (and still is) a one-stop shopping institution such as a planned shopping center. Through careful planning, a developer could offer a merchandise mix—products, services, prices—to meet most customer needs for convenience, shopping, and specialty goods.

A planned shopping center is a purposeful cluster of retail and service establishments at a location designed to serve a specific geographic, demographic, and psychographic market segment. Shopping centers vary in nature according to their

FIGURE 12–3

Sales performance for various types of retailers at different types of malls ($ sales per square foot)

Types of Retailers	Super Regional	Regional	Community	Neighborhood
Cameras	553	425	—	—
Jewelry	447	380	207	161
Key shop	362	—	—	—
Computers/calculators	359	—	130	—
Cookie shop	320	188	—	—
Leather shop	313	243	—	—
Film-processing store	295	217	165	141
Costume jewelry	294	274	—	—
Optometrist	287	175	150	—
Photocopy/fast printing	285	163	132	92
Tobacco	281	258	114	—
Candy and nuts	282	239	176	7
Radio/video/stereo	280	230	150	143
Records and tapes	245	229	148	—
Eyeglasses/optician	246	220	150	119
Athletic footwear	252	219	130	—
Superstore (over 30,000 sq. ft.)	—	—	318	307
Supermarket (over 6,000 sq. ft.)	—	—	291	279
Liquor and wine	159	—	186	170
Ladies' shoes	194	166	163	72
Drugstore	182	184	156	144
Fast food/carryout	262	215	155	148
Super drugstore	153	173	140	152
Ladies' specialty	189	169	118	138

Source: *Dollars & Cents of Shopping Centers: 1987* (ULI—the Urban Land Institute, 1987, 1200 18th St. NW, Washington, DC 20036).

FIGURE 12–4

Facilities' cost (total charges as a percentage of sales) for various types of retailers at different types of malls (%)

Types of Retailers	Super Regional	Regional	Community	Neighborhood
Ladies' ready-to-wear	9.91	9.12	8.04	7.92
Jewelry	8.08	7.56	7.06	—
Fast food/carryout	14.69	13.22	9.71	7.14
Men's wear	9.68	9.29	—	—
Ladies' shoes	11.34	10.77	—	—
Family shoes	10.41	12.03	8.69	—
Cards and gifts	13.09	12.12	11.36	—
Ladies' specialty	9.74	9.61	9.07	—
Men's and boys' shoes	11.12	—	—	—
Unisex/jeans shop	10.34	8.95	—	—
Books and stationery	9.49	9.06	—	—
Restaurant with liquor	—	—	7.59	8.50
Beauty	—	—	10.27	10.62
Medical/dental	—	—	9.32	10.39
Restaurant without liquor	—	—	7.59	9.23
Cleaners and dyers	—	—	—	12.57
Supermarket (over 6,000 sq. ft.)	—	—	—	1.51
Drugstore	—	—	—	3.88
Videotape rentals	—	—	—	12.61

Source: *Dollars & Cents of Shopping Centers: 1987.* (ULI—the Urban Land Institute, 1987, 1200 18th St. NW, Washington, DC 20036).

tenants and the size of the markets they serve. On the basis of type and size, shopping centers are classified as regional, community, neighborhood, and specialty centers. Figure 12–3 shows sales performance (sales per square foot) for various types of retailers at different types of malls. Occupancy costs (total charges equals rent plus common area maintenance [CAM] charges) as a percentage of sales are enumerated in Figure 12–4.

Super Regional and Regional Centers

Regional shopping centers serve regional markets varying in size according to the type of transportation network serving the center, the location of competing centers and unplanned business districts, the willingness of consumers to travel various distances to shop, and the tenant mix. The Urban Land Institute identifies two types of regional shopping centers: a **super regional shopping center** is built around at least three and often four major department stores; a **regional shopping center** is built around one or two full-line department stores. Typical sizes range from 400,000 to 600,000 square feet of gross leasable area (GLA) for the regional center to 750,000 to 1,000,000 square feet of GLA for the super regional center.

Regional and super regional centers provide consumers with an extensive assortment of convenience, shopping, and specialty goods as well as numerous personal and professional service facilities. The trend in tenant mix for shopping centers is "mixed-use developments" (MXDs). In addition to retailing establishments, these MXDs might include office buildings, recreational and entertainment facilities, residential units, hotels, government buildings, wholesaling, and light manufacturing.[7] This extensive assortment is achieved through a balanced tenancy of some 50 to 150 individual stores.

The tenant mix is very important; in the past, shopping malls were built around one or more major department stores whose size and advertising attracted customers to the center. The basic premise of the shopping center was that people would "walk up and down the malls to get to the different department stores, and as they walk, they look at the small stores to see what they like and what they want to buy."[8] Today, shopping centers and areas within shopping centers (wings) are being planned as "a collection of stores with a purpose rather than those (stores) offering undefined impulse shopping."[9] The modern mall has become a festival, tourist, theme, recreational, entertainment, and/or specialty center; it caters to multiple market segments including tourists, conventioneers, sports enthusiasts, shoppers, and to locals who are looking "to escape" for a few hours.[10]

While traditional department store anchors will continue as a major element in the shopping center's tenant mix, new and different anchors are becoming more important. Specialty store chains like Main Street and Mervyn's (apparel), IKEA (home furnishings), and Lechmere's (hard goods) are achieving anchor status. In some areas, "category killers" (aggressive, high-volume specialty superstores such as Toys 'R' Us, Circuit City, Cohoes, Crazy Eddie, and The Wiz), and catalog showrooms (e.g., Service Merchandise and Best) are assuming the role of anchors as a result of their ability to generate high traffic volumes and attract consumers from considerable distances. Equally important is the collection of specialty stores that complete the tenant mix. Each developer must find the right blend of: (1) general merchandise lines (e.g., apparel, shoes, gifts, food); (2) pricing points (e.g., exclusive, upper, middle, value); (3) life-styles and demographic specialties (e.g., Limited Express For Men, Gap Kids, Just Sweats, Banana Republic); and (4) national chains and local establishments.

Shopping centers are designed in a variety of shapes and arrangements. A given configuration must conform to the site's terrain and the tenants' space requirements, as well as provide ease of customer movement. While any number of configurations are possible, Figure 12–5 illustrates four basic shopping center configurations. The "I" plan is the simplest and most common regional shopping center configuration (Figure 12–5a). Although the "I" plan is efficient for retailer space requirements and customer movement, it does not create an interesting and exciting shopping environment.

For regional and super regional centers containing three or more major anchors, retailers can use either the "Y" plan (Figure 12–5b) or the "L" plan (Figure 12–5c). Examples of a modified "Y" plan include the TownEast Shopping Center in Mesquite, Texas, near Dallas; the Pompano Fashion Square in Pompano Beach, Florida; and the Santa Anita Fashion Park in Arcadia, California. Tysons Corner Center in Fairfax County, Virginia, and the North Park Mall in Dallas, Texas, represent modifications of the basic "L" plan.

The "X" plan serves as the basic configuration for the four-anchor, super regional center (Figure 12–5d). The best example of this configuration is Crossroads Center in Oklahoma City.

Regardless of the configuration, a key feature of most super regional and regional shopping centers is a central court. Some super regional centers also have several smaller secondary courts, each with its own character and decor. The importance of courts lies in their image-creating role. The central court is what consumers remember most often and most vividly. Hence, in recent years, more and more emphasis has been placed on court design. As one shopping center specialist writes:

> . . . concentrate on excellence in the design of courts—on such various exciting features as glass space-frame domes, special lighting fixtures, sculptural fountains,

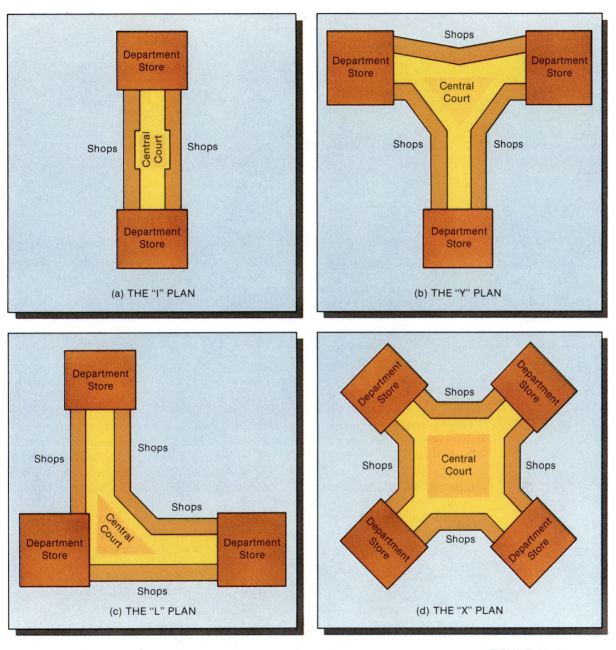

FIGURE 12–5
Shopping center configurations

landscaped areas, specially designed staircases, escalators, glass-enclosed elevators (for multilevel centers) and important art work. The design of the graphics—directional signs, banners, central symbols, and the choice of colors—also becomes an important element in the total impact on the shopper. . . . The main court, in addition to serving as an exciting place for the shopper to sit, relax, and meet friends, could also be designed for functional and profitable uses. In order to provide for this flexibility, permanent installations (i.e., fountains, plantings, artwork) should be placed so as to allow for large open areas for special events—concerts, auto and boat (as well as other large equipment) displays, art shows, and community programs. The idea of providing amphitheater-type seating in the main court adds to

Kiosks add to a mall's atmosphere and can be highly profitable retail operations.

the possibilities of arranging festive events for both the young and the older shopper.[11]

The third design consideration is the planning of mall areas. Mall areas are the center's traffic arteries; as such, they must facilitate movement and exchange of customers throughout the entire complex. The length and width of mall areas are prime considerations in planning for movement and exchange. "Where the distance from one major store to another is long (over 700 feet), there are both physical and psychological reactions to the 'tunnel' effect."[12] Several design features help overcome these negative reactions. The most common is a "break" in the mall approximately midway between major attractions, such as the central court; however, if the distance between the central court and each department store is too long, additional breaks may be required. Secondary court areas and slight angles in the mall that require shoppers to make short turns before they can see the remainder of the mall can be extremely effective in reducing the tunnel effect. Also, a series of small storefront setbacks starting at each end of the mall makes the mall appear shorter and wider.[13]

Besides customer movement and exchange, mall areas should facilitate shopping. "Generally the design of the malls and arcades leading to the main courts should strive for an intimate character and subdued atmosphere. The purpose is to have the shopper's eye attracted to the store displays."[14] Storefronts should afford the consumer some privacy for "window shopping" without jostling from passing pedestrian traffic. On the other hand, some mall designs incorporate "kiosks" to create the happy and busy atmosphere of an open marketplace. These freestanding booths with highly specialized product lines (greeting cards, cutlery items, T-shirts, candy) and services (minibanks, snack bars, utility cashiers) add a new dimension to the mall's shopping atmosphere and contribute substantially to profitability.

Community and Neighborhood Centers

Community and neighborhood shopping centers serve the market areas their names suggest. The **neighborhood shopping center** obtains its customers from one or a few neighborhoods within the immediate vicinity. Its trading area can be roughly defined as the area within a five-minute drive of the center, containing anywhere from 7,000 to 50,000 potential customers. The **community shopping center** serves a composite of many neighborhoods within a ten- to fifteen-minute drive from the center. The number of potential customers within its trading area ranges from 20,000 to 100,000. The community shopping center in a smaller city serves the entire city and often competes with the downtown area.

The size of the market areas for each of these centers is primarily a function of the center's number of stores and tenant mix. The neighborhood center usually has five to fifteen stores, with a supermarket as the principal tenant. Comprising largely convenience goods retailers, the neighborhood center sells products that meet the daily living needs of its local area. With a GLA ranging from 25,000 to 100,000 square feet, the neighborhood center frequently includes a hardware store, drugstore, and various personal-service retailers, such as beauty and barber shops.

The community center is considerably larger and more diverse in its mix of tenants than the neighborhood center. Containing from ten to thirty retail establishments with a total GLA of 75,000 to 300,000 square feet, the community center offers a wide range of shopping goods and convenience goods. It is likely to be anchored by one or more mass merchandising stores, the most common being junior department stores, discount stores, and discount department stores. Large supermarkets and variety stores also play an important role in attracting consumers to the community center.[15] Like regional centers, atmospherics are becoming more and more important in boosting customer traffic in community shopping centers. Varying roof lines, atriums, skylights, canopies, and landscaping are currently used to enhance the shopping atmosphere.[16]

The Specialty Shopping Center

The **specialty shopping center** essentially is a smaller cluster of specialty retailers that tends to be more focused in its target market.[17] Offering many of the same features as regional malls, these centers range in size from 100,000 to 300,000 square feet with fifteen to thirty specialty stores, boutiques, and service retailers. The largest store usually does not exceed 25,000 square feet. Specialty malls range from enclosed malls with a common architectural motif and decor (e.g., Discoveries in Oklahoma

These are two views of specialty malls.

City) to restored manufacturing plants, railroad stations, shipping docks, and warehouses (Quaker Square in Akron, Ohio, is a conversion of the original manufacturing plant and grain elevators of the Quaker Oats Company).

Additional preservation and restoration examples include Cincinnati's West 4th Street, Denver's Tivoli Union brewery, Bullock's old downtown department store in Los Angeles, the Alabama theater in Houston, and Pioneer Square in Seattle.[18] "There's a uniqueness in converting properties that you can't get in building new properties. . . .Old buildings are especially interesting to young, upwardly mobile people because of their sense of nostalgia."[19]

Another variation of the specialty mall is the "manufacturers' outlet mall." These malls specialize in off-price merchandising by the manufacturers themselves (e.g., seconds, irregulars, pack-aways) and in other forms of discounting. This type of mall tends to be located "along an interstate highway between a metropolitan area and a resort community or tourist attraction."[20]

THE SITE-EVALUATION PROCESS

The following sections discuss the site-evaluation process in two phases. The first section explains several principles of site evaluation and how retailers use them to assess the value of alternative sites. The second looks at several methods by which retailers evaluate alternative site locations.

Principles of Site Evaluation

Several consumer-oriented location principles help retailers evaluate site alternatives. While there are no standard criteria by which all sites can be judged, the following location principles provide the necessary framework for developing practical solutions to the problem of retail site evaluation. These location principles are (1) interception, (2) cumulative attraction, (3) compatibility, (4) store congestion, and (5) accessibility.

Principle of Interception

The principle of **interception** covers a site's positional qualities that determine its ability to "intercept" consumers as they travel from one place to another. Interception has two distinct elements: first, a "source region" from which consumers are drawn; second, a "terminal region" or consumer destination, a region to which consumers are drawn. Examples of source and terminal regions are residential areas, office complexes, industrial plants, business districts, and shopping centers. Any point between source and terminal regions can be considered a point of interception. In considering a site's interceptor qualities, the evaluator has both an identification and an evaluation problem. The identification problem consists of determining (1) the location of source and terminal regions, (2) the lines connecting those regions, and (3) appropriate points (sites) along the connection line. The evaluation problem is one of measuring the magnitude and quality of these regions, lines, and points. Thus, the evaluator's problem is how to determine whether a site is an efficient "intervening opportunity" between known source and terminal regions.

A different perspective of the interception principle is often expressed as the "concept of location vulnerability." In this case, the evaluator's job is to determine the source of a competitor's business and then locate a site that intercepts the competitor's customer flow. If such a location exists, the firm's competitor is vulnerable in terms of location, at least regarding one or more source regions.

It is difficult to measure interceptor qualities because of the numerous potential source and terminal regions, connecting lines, and interceptor points (sites) along these lines of movement. Location specialists often use traffic volume as a surrogate measurement of interception.

Principle of Cumulative Attraction

According to the principle of **cumulative attraction,** a cluster of similar and complementary retailing activities will generally have greater drawing power than dispersed and isolated stores engaging in the same retailing activities. Retail-location literature often refers to the cumulative attraction effects of the familiar "rows," "cities," and "alleys." In many large cities, certain types of retailing establishments tend to cluster in specific areas. Examples are the familiar automobile rows, mobile home cities, and restaurant alleys.

The evaluator's problem in this case is how to determine whether the retail operation can benefit from the cumulative drawing power of a site's immediate environment.

Principle of Compatibility

Retail **compatibility** refers to the "degree to which two businesses interchange customers."[21] As a rule, the greater the compatibility between businesses located in close proximity, the greater the interchange of customers and the greater the sales volume of each compatible business. Compatibility between retailers occurs when their merchandising mixes are complementary, as in the case of an apparel shop, shoe store, and jewelry store that are located very close to one another. If there are several apparel, shoe, and jewelry stores located in the same cluster, all the better! They are not only complementary, they also provide a healthy competitive situation that satisfies the customers' need for comparison shopping and thus provide greater customer interchange for the retailers. Sometimes shopping center managers reduce cross-shopping (i.e., customer exchange) because they spread "like establishments" (e.g., intratype competitors like shoe stores) throughout the mall, rather than concentrating them in one area of the mall.[22] As a rule, good comparative shopping opportunities benefit all concerned.

A high degree of compatibility is more likely to occur when the pricing structures of neighboring businesses are complementary. Other things being equal, there will be greater interchange of customers between one high-margin retailer and another than between a high-margin and a low-margin retailer. Equally important in site evaluation is determining whether neighboring businesses are compatible. An exclusive dress shop would be incompatible with a pet shop, for example, because of the odor and noise produced by the pets.

Principle of Store Congestion

At some point, the advantages of cumulative attraction and compatibility end, and the problems of site congestion begin. The principle of **store congestion** states that as locations become more saturated with stores, other business activities, and people, they become less attractive to additional shopping traffic. This phenomenon results from the limited mobility of people and cars in the area. Retailers should have learned this lesson from the original congested CBDs. While the excitement of the crowd can be a positive factor, the aggravation of a mob can be a limiting factor, discouraging customers from visiting the site. Thus, in the site-evaluation process, the retailer should estimate at what point the volume of vehicle and foot traffic would limit business, both in the present and the near future. In measuring store congestion, the retailer should recognize that "the shopper's tolerance for retail crowding may differ across types of retail establishments (for example, discount stores versus department stores) and shopping times (for example, Christmas season, weekends, lunch hour)."[23]

Principle of Accessibility

Perhaps the most basic of site-evaluation principles, the principle of **accessibility** states that the more easily potential consumers can approach, enter, traverse, and exit a site, the more likely they will visit the site to shop. Accessibility is a function of both physical and psychological dimensions. The physical dimensions of accessibility are tangible site attributes that either facilitate or hinder the actual physical movement of potential consumers in, through, or out of a site. Psychological dimensions of accessibility include how potential customers *perceive* the ease of movement toward and away from a site. If consumers believe that it is difficult, dangerous, or inconvenient to enter a site, then a psychological barrier has been created equal to any physical barrier. Retailers should consider both real and apparent barriers to accessibility.

Number of traffic arteries.   The number of traffic arteries adjacent to a site has a profound effect on the consumer's ability to approach and enter the site. Other things being equal, a corner site that is approachable from two traffic arteries is more accessible than a site served by a single traffic artery. Traffic arteries are not all equal, though. Major thoroughfares provide greater accessibility to trading areas than secondary, feeder, or side streets. Because their function is to provide access for local traffic, side streets are of less value to retailers.

Number of traffic lanes.   The more lanes in a traffic artery, the more accessible the site located on this artery. Multilane arteries are the consumer's first choice in selecting routes for most planned shopping trips. Multilanes often reduce the consumer's access to a site, however, especially with left turns. Given some drivers' hesitancy to turn left across traffic, wide roads create a psychological barrier, especially when consumers must cross two or more lanes of oncoming traffic. In essence, multilanes increase consumers' perceived risks.

Directional flow of traffic arteries.   The accessibility of any site is enhanced if the site is directly accessible from all possible directions. Any reduction in the number of directions from which the site can be approached has an adverse effect on accessibility. Usually, several traffic arteries adjacent to the site enhance accessibility. The location analyst should examine local maps to determine directional biases.

Number of intersections.   The number of intersections in the site's general vicinity has both positive and negative effects on accessibility. A large number of intersections offers consumers more ways to approach a site, but may also reduce accessibility because of slower speeds and the consumer's increased risk of an accident. Where intersections are plentiful, the role of traffic-control devices (such as traffic lights and stop signs) becomes critical.

Configuration of intersections.   Consumers generally perceive a site located on a three-corner or four-corner intersection as very accessible because these kinds of intersections are fairly standard; consumers are familiar with them and with negotiating them. When there are more than four corners at an intersection, consumers are

Uncrossable medians create both a physical and psychological barrier.

often confused by the "unstandardized" configuration. This "zone of confusion" exists across the entire intersection and presents the potential consumer with numerous conflict situations.

Type of median.   The type of median associated with each of the site's adjacent traffic arteries strongly influences accessibility. Some medians are crossable, while others are not. Generally, crossable medians increase accessibility, although in varying degrees. Medians that provide a "crossover lane" are more encouraging to potential consumers attempting site entry than those without a crossover lane. Crossable medians that force consumers to wait in a traffic lane until crossover is possible create a perceived danger. The driver often has to put up with horn honkers and has the fear of being "stuck out there." This situation results in a psychological deterrent to the site's accessibility.

Uncrossable medians are both a physical and psychological barrier to site entry. Elevated and depressed medians serve to physically separate traffic, but they also separate traffic psychologically. Potential consumers traveling on the right side of an uncrossable median tend to feel isolated from left-side locations and become more aware of right-side locations, where access is substantially easier.

Speed limit on traffic arteries.   The speed limit on a traffic artery influences a site's accessibility, since it determines the amount of time potential customers have in which to make a decision about entering a site. Expert opinions vary over what constitutes an ideal speed limit. The limit must be high enough to encourage consumers to use the route but low enough to allow them a safe and easy approach to the site. Most experts believe a speed limit between 25 and 40 mph is best.

Number and type of traffic-control devices.   Of the several different devices for controlling traffic, the most common are traffic lights, stop signs, rule signs, and guidance lines. In terms of accessibility, *traffic lights* have enormous effect at crossovers because of the protection left-turn arrows allow. Traffic lights may be more important for their psychological value than for their physical value. Consumers perceive retail sites with controlled crossovers as more accessible. "Free left turn" lights are extremely important to site accessibility.

Stop signs are another major accessibility improvement and can increase accessibility in two ways. First, the chances of creating consumer awareness of the retailer's location and product offering are higher if traffic "stoppers" force consumers to halt and look around. Second, stop signs help to space the flow of traffic. Psychologically, these breaks in traffic are extremely important to the potential customer attempting to cross over from a left-hand lane.

Traffic rule signs, in addition to speed limit signs, also influence site accessibility. Traffic signs prohibiting U-turns and left turns can reduce accessibility.

Finally, one effective way to reduce traffic confusion and to increase the actual and perceived safety and ease of entering a site is to employ *guidance lines* (turn- and through-arrows and traffic lines) to direct traffic. Guidance lines are especially important at intersection locations. Any means of traffic guidance that tells the consumer how and where to go enhances accessibility.

Size and shape of site.   The proposed site should be large enough to facilitate all four components of accessibility. Sufficient space should be available to allow ease of parking as well as turning and backing in and out without interfering with consumers who are entering and exiting the site. The shape of the site also can affect accessibility. The wider the site, the greater the exposure to passing traffic, thereby increasing consumer awareness of the retailer's location and activities. Finally, a site should be deep enough to allow ease of entry without interference from exiting traffic or other on-site traffic activities.

Methods of Site Evaluation

Analysts use several methods to evaluate retail site alternatives. Some of these methods are subjective, verbal descriptions of a site's worth; others provide objective, quantitative measurements. The subjective methods lack the qualities for good scientific decision making, while the latter methods require specialized skills and equipment. Certain methods, however, incorporate both simplicity and objectivity without the need for specialized training or equipment. One such methods is the checklist.

The Checklist Method

The **checklist method** provides the evaluator with a set of procedural steps for arriving at a subjective, yet quantitative, expression of a site's value. First, the evaluator enumerates the general factors that are usually considered in any site evaluation. A typical list of factors includes all or most of the site-evaluation principles: interception, cumulative attraction, compatibility, and accessibility. Second, for each general factor, the evaluator identifies several attribute measurements that reflect the location needs of the proposed retail operation. For example, interception, which is a key location attribute for most convenience retailers, can be divided into the volume and quality of vehicular and pedestrian traffic.

Third, each location attribute receives a subjective weight based on its relative importance to a particular type of retailer. A common weighting system assigns 3 to very important, 2 to moderately important, 1 to slightly important, and 0 to unimportant attributes. The fourth step is to rate each site alternative in terms of each location attribute. Any number of rating scales can be constructed; one possible scale might range from 1 to 10, with 1 as very poor and 10 as highly superior. To illustrate, a site alternative located on a major thoroughfare with a high volume of traffic throughout the day might be rated a 9 or a 10; another site alternative located on a traffic artery characterized by high volumes of traffic only during the morning and evening rush hours could be rated either a 5 or a 6.

Step five involves calculating a weighted rating for each attribute for each site alternative. The weighted rating is obtained by multiplying each attribute rating by its weight. Sixth, the weighted ratings for all attributes are added to produce an overall rating for each site alternative. Finally, the last step is to rank all evaluated alternatives in order of their overall ratings. Figure 12–6 illustrates the checklist method for evaluating one site alternative for a fast-food restaurant. If, for example, the numerical value of 236 is the highest of all evaluated alternatives, then from the standpoint of site considerations this alternative would be rated as the retailer's first choice. The checklist method has the advantages of being (1) easy to understand, (2) simple to construct, and (3) easy to use. In addition, it gives considerable weight to the opinions of location experts who know the firm and its locational requirements.

Quantitative Methods

Although beyond the scope of this book, several quantitative models can be used to evaluate retailer sites. Two of these are analog models and regression analysis. **Analog models** are used to make sales projections for new stores based on the sales

Evaluation Factor	Rating	Weight	Weighted Rating
Interception			
Volume of vehicular traffic	8	3	24
Quality of vehicular traffic	8	3	24
Volume of pedestrian traffic	3	3	9
Quality of pedestrian traffic	2	3	6
Cumulative attraction			
Number of attractors	4	1	4
Degree of attraction	5	1	5
Compatibility			
Type of compatibility	6	2	12
Degree of compatibility	7	1	7
Accessibility			
Number of traffic arteries	8	3	24
Number of traffic lanes	10	3	30
Directional flow of traffic	7	2	14
Number of intersections	7	2	14
Configuration of intersections	4	3	12
Type of medians	2	3	6
Speed limits of traffic arteries	5	3	15
Number/type of traffic-control devices	6	2	12
Size and shape of site	6	3	18
Overall site rating			236

FIGURE 12–6
The checklist method

*For definitions of evaluation factors, see the text discussion of site-evaluation criteria.

performances of existing stores. The chain retailer can approach the evaluation problem by finding the best "match" between the site characteristics of new site alternatives and those of a successful existing site. This matching process is usually quantified into a statistical model.

Ease of implementation is the principal advantage of an analog approach; however, this model suffers from two important drawbacks:

> One problem is that the results are dependent on the particular stores chosen as analogs and therefore rely heavily on the analyst's ability to make judicious selection of analogous stores. . . . The second, and perhaps more important difficulty, is that the method does not directly consider the competitive environment in evaluating the sites. The competitive situation is brought into consideration only through the selection of analog stores.[24]

Regression models are a more rigorous approach to the problem of site location; hence, they offer certain advantages over checklist and analog approaches. First, a regression model allows "systematic consideration of both trading area factors as well as site-specific elements in a single framework. Further, regression models allow the analyst to identify the factors that are associated with various levels of revenues from stores at different sites."[25] The basic multiple regression model for analyzing determinants of retail performance is expressed as a linear function of location (*L*), store attributes (*S*), market attributes (*M*), price (*P*), and competition (*C*):

$$Y = f(L,S,M,P,C)$$

THE SITE-SELECTION PROCESS

The final selection of a retail site is essentially a process of elimination. By analyzing regional and local markets, assessing retail trading areas, and appraising retail site locations, the range of choices has been narrowed to site alternatives consistent with the firm's objectives, operations, and future expectations. If markets, trading areas, and sites have all been carefully evaluated, the retailer should be able to arrive at the final location decision. Normally, the retailer will not select the optimal location, but rather a compromise location that has most of the desirable attributes.

In the end, no steps, procedures, or models can totally quantify the final site-selection process. Nevertheless, with the data generated and the analysis completed in market, trading-area, and site evaluations, the retailer has sufficient information to make a good site selection.

SUMMARY

To appraise retail site locations, the location analyst must determine each site's ability to interact with its trading area. The retailer's problem is how to identify, evaluate, and select a good site location.

The site-identification process is the first step in appraising retail site locations. After identifying all potential site alternatives, the evaluator then can initially screen each alternative in terms of availability, suitability, and acceptability. Retail site alternatives can be classified as either isolated or clustered. Isolated sites are retail locations geographically separated from other retailer sites; they normally will not share customers with other retailers. A retailer that selects an isolated site is seeking to gain either a monopolistic or an operational advantage.

Clustered sites are retail locations that are geographically adjacent to each other or in close proximity; normally they are capable of sharing customers with minimal effort on the part of the customer. Two types of clustered sites exist. The first, an unplanned retail cluster, is one that results from the natural evolutionary process of urban growth. It includes central business districts, secondary business districts, neighborhood business districts, and string/strip clusters. The second is the planned retail cluster and includes such clusters as regional, community, neighborhood, and mini-specialty shopping centers.

The second step in appraising retail site locations is site evaluation, based on site-evaluation principles and site-evaluation methods. Several principles used in evaluation are interception, cumulative attraction, compatibility, store congestion, and accessibility. The checklist method provides the basic framework for making both subjective and objective evaluations of retail site alternatives. Quantitative site-evaluation methods include analog models and regression analysis.

The final step in site appraisal is site selection. The process of elimination narrows the range of choices to site alternatives that are consistent with the firm's objectives, operations, and future expectations. Essentially, the task of site selection becomes one of selecting the best location from several acceptable alternatives.

KEY TERMS

acceptability

accessibility

analog models

availability

central business district (CBD)

checklist method

clustered sites

community shopping center

compatibility

cumulative attraction

interception

isolated sites

monopolistic isolation

neighborhood business district (NBD)

neighborhood shopping center

operational isolation

place decisions

price decisions

product decisions

promotion decisions

regional shopping center

regression models

retail mix

retail site

secondary business district (SBD)

specialty shopping center

store congestion

string/strip cluster

suitability

super regional shopping center

REVIEW QUESTIONS

1. What ingredients make up the retail mix? Briefly describe the decisions associated with each ingredient.
2. What three questions should the retailer ask in conducting an initial screening of site alternatives?
3. Why would a retailer select an isolated site?
4. What is the key to successfully revitalizing the CBD (central business district)?
5. Compare and contrast the SBDs and NBDs (secondary and neighborhood business districts).
6. What are the positional strengths of the string/strip retailing cluster?
7. What distinguishes a super regional from a regional shopping center?
8. Describe the four basic shopping center configurations.
9. How might a shopping center developer overcome the "tunnel" effect?
10. Compare and contrast a community and neighborhood shopping center.
11. What is a mini-specialty mall center?

12. Describe the site-evaluation principle of interception.
13. Why is cumulative attraction important?
14. How does the principle of compatibility affect the evaluation of a retail site?
15. Describe the role of traffic arteries and lanes in determining the accessibility of a site.
16. What role do the number and configuration of intersections play in creating an accessible site?
17. How do the number and type of traffic-control devices influence the accessibility of a retail site?
18. What are the seven steps of the checklist method of retail site evaluation?
19. Describe the two quantitative methods of retail site evaluation.

ENDNOTES

1. Eric C. Peterson, "Higher Rents? Downsize It," *Stores* (March 1986): 40.
2. See Barbara Bryan, "Airport Retailing," *Stores* (July 1986): 37–40.
3. "900 North Michigan Rises on Chicago Skyline," *Chain Store Age Executive* (April 1987): 30.
4. Joseph Weber, "Jim Rouse May Be Losing His Touch," *Business Week,* 4 April 1988, 33.
5. See "Retailers Are Taking to the Streets," *Chain Store Age Executive* (September 1987): 19–22.
6. Joan E. Primo and Howard L. Green, "To Mall or Not to Mall: Where Retail Opportunities Lie," *Marketing News,* 15 Feb. 1988, 10.
7. See Eric Peterson, "MXD—Mall Excitement," *Stores* (January 1986): 144–146, 151–152, and "New Focus Emerging," *Stores* (March 1987): 36–40.
8. "Building Up to the Year 2000," *Chain Store Age Executive* (May 1987): 44.
9. Ibid.
10. "Theme Centers Draw Multi-Market Customers," *Chain Store Age Executive* (May 1987): 98.
11. Louis G. Redstone, *New Dimensions in Shopping Centers and Stores* (New York: McGraw-Hill, 1973), 61, 68. Used by permission.
12. Ibid., 68.
13. Ibid.
14. Ibid.
15. Eric C. Peterson, "What's Working Now?" *Stores* (July 1987): 50.
16. See Eric C. Peterson, "Recipes For New Sites," *Stores* (March 1985): 70–72.
17. See Steven B. Weiner, "Off With Their Heads," *Forbes,* 9 Feb. 1987, 34–35.
18. Kurt Anderson, "Spiffing Up the Urban Heritage," *Time,* 23 Nov. 1987, 74.
19. Diane Schneidman, "Buildings Saved From Wrecker's Ball Enjoy Second Life as a Shopping Mall," *Marketing News,* 15 Feb. 1988, 7.
20. Primo and Green, "To Mall or Not to Mall," 10.
21. Richard L. Nelson, *The Selection of Retail Locations* (New York: F. W. Dodge, 1958), 66.
22. Marvin J. Rothenberg, "Mall Marketing Principles that Affect Merchandising," *Retail Control* (October 1986): 25.
23. See Sevgin Eroglu and Gilbert D. Harrell, "Retail Crowding: Theoretical and Strategic Implications," *Journal of Retailing* 62 (Winter 1986): 346–63.
24. C. Samuel Craig, Avijit Grosh, and Sara McLafferty, "Models of the Retail Location Process: A Review," *Journal of Retailing* 60 (Spring 1984): 21.
25. Ibid.

RELATED READINGS

Achabal, Dale, Gorr, Wilpen L., and Mahajan, Vijay. "Multiloc: A Multiple Store Location Decision Model." *Journal of Retailing* 58 (Summer 1982): 5–25.
Anderson, Patricia M. "Association of Shopping Center Anchors With Performance of a Nonanchor Specialty Chain's Stores." *Journal of Retailing* 61 (Summer 1985), 61–74.

Gill, James D., and Evans, Kenneth R. "Shopping Center Patronage Motives of Shopping Orientation Groups." In *1985 AMA Educators' Proceedings,* edited by R. F. Lusch et al., 202–8. American Marketing Association, 1985.

Goodchild, Michael F. "ILACS: A Location-Allocation Model for Retail Site Selection." *Journal of Retailing* 60 (Spring 1984): 84–100.

Hawes, Jon M., and Lewison, Dale M. "Retail Site Evaluation: An Examination of the Principle of Accessibility." In *AMA Educators' Proceedings,* edited by R. W. Belk et al., 280–84. American Marketing Association, 1984.

Lewison, Dale M., DeLozier, M. Wayne, and Robbins, Ray B. "Assessing the Accessibility of Retail Sites." In *Survival and Growth in the 1980's, Proceedings,* edited by R. D. Lewis, 139–48. Southwestern Small Business Institute Association, 1981.

Maronick, Thomas J., and Stiff, Ronald M. "The Impact of a Specialty Retail Center on Downtown Shopping Behavior." *Journal of the Academy of Marketing Science* 13 (Summer 1985): 292–306.

Parker, R. Stephen. "Shopping Center or Shopping Mall: A Study of Consumer Perception." In *Marketing: The Next Decade, Proceedings,* edited by D. M. Klein and A. E. Smith, 32–34. Southern Marketing Association, 1985.

Pearson, Michael M., Stoops, Glen T., and Wu, Bob T. W. "Identifying the Factors Contributing to Customers Driving Directly by a Competitor to Shop at the Host Store." In *Developments in Marketing Science, Proceedings,* edited by N. K. Malhotra and J. M. Hawes, 223–26. Academy of Marketing Science, 1986.

Peterson, Eric C. "Targeting the Market." *Stores* (July 1985): 62–65.

Taylor, Ronald D. "Multiple Regression Analysis as a Retail Site Selection Method: An Empirical Review." In *Developments in Marketing Science, Proceedings,* edited by V. V. Bellur, 184–87. Academy of Marketing Science, 1981.

Thompson, John S. *Site Selection.* New York: Chain Store Publishing Corporation, 1982.

Vaughn, Ronald L. "Site Location Demand Analysis: A Practical New Approach." In *Marketing: The Next Decade, Proceedings,* edited by D. M. Klein and A. E. Smith, 312–15. Southern Marketing Association, 1985.

Wee, Chow-Hou. "Complexity of Shopping Area Image: Its Factor Analytic Structure in Relation to the Effects of Familiarity and Size of the Area." In *Developments in Marketing Science, Proceedings,* edited by N. K. Malhotra, 196–201. Academy of Marketing Science, 1985.

13

Objectives

☐ Understand tactics used in developing a merchandise mix.

☐ Recognize retailers' need to market all of a product's dimensions.

☐ Understand and make the "which" and "how many" product decisions.

☐ Evaluate new and existing products and their impact on merchandising decisions.

☐ Acquire and evaluate sources of product information.

☐ Define and describe the various types of product-mix strategies.

☐ Discuss major emerging trends in the development of product mixes.

Product Strategy: Planning Merchandise Assortments

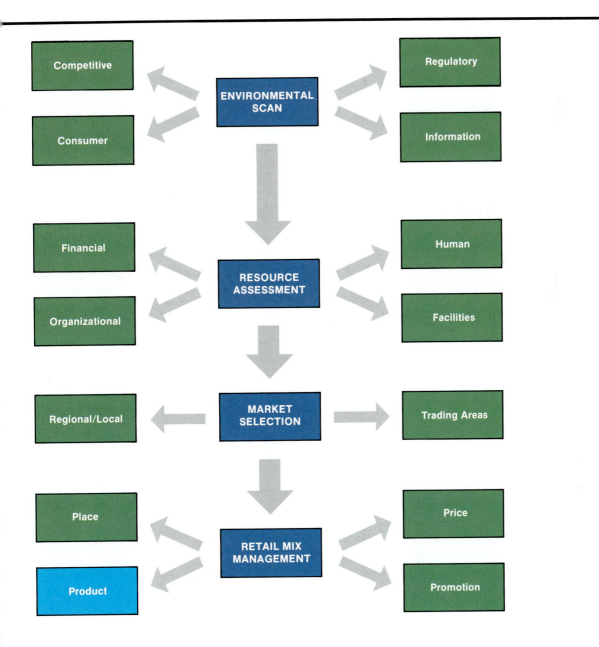

As identified in Chapter 1, the retailer's problem is how to find the "right blend" of marketing ingredients that satisfy the needs of the target market. The "right blend" is the best combination of the right product, at the right time, in the right quantities, at the right price, with the right appeal. The focus of this and the next five chapters is the offering of the right product in the right quantities within the context of the right place, time, price, and appeal.

THE MERCHANDISING PROCESS

Consumers patronize a particular retail outlet for many different reasons: its convenient location, friendly personnel, desirable prices, and pleasant shopping atmosphere. The patronage reason common to all customers for visiting a particular store, however, is the expectation of finding a product or a set of products that will fulfill some present or future need. In a general sense, fulfilling customer product expectations is what retail merchandising is all about.

Merchandising is the process of developing, securing, and managing the merchandise mix to meet the firm's marketing objectives. The *merchandise mix* refers to the retailer's total offering, be it goods or services or both. The *merchandising process,* as illustrated in Figure 13–1, consists of three stages. The first stage is developing the merchandise mix, which is composed of the product mix and the service mix. The retailer's concern here is to determine "what" and "how many" products and services to offer. Next, the retailer must secure the products. Stage two deals with this problem of buying and procuring the merchandise mix. In this stage, the retailer determines "from where," "when," and "how" to get products into the store. The final stage in the merchandising process is managing the merchandise mix. To ensure efficient, profitable operations, the retailer must plan and control the merchandise mix.

Developing the merchandise mix is a means for the retailer to segment the market and appeal to a select group of consumers. Just as the retail-location decision can segment a market geographically, merchandise-mix decisions can segment markets demographically and by behavioral dimensions. By buying, stocking, and selling a select combination of products and by offering a certain level of services, the retailer can appeal to consumers of a particular age, sex, occupation, race, or income level, as well as to other demographic groupings. Likewise, the retailer can develop the merchandise mix to appeal to certain *life-styles*—the "swinger," the "sophisticate," the "homebody"—or to certain *buyer–behavior patterns*—the brand-loyal consumer, the style-conscious consumer, the quality-minded consumer.

Equally important in the merchandising process is ensuring the firm's profitability. To accomplish this objective, the retailer must efficiently develop, secure, and control the merchandising process. The retailer should include in its mix products that contribute to the total profitability of the mix. To ensure profitable operations, the retailer must use a merchandise budget in which sales, stocks, reductions, purchases, markups, and margins are carefully planned. The final attempt to manage profitability is to control product inventories. One of the fastest ways "to end up in the red" is to mismanage the "back-room" operations.

The entire merchandising process is examined in this and the next five chapters; the remainder of this chapter describes factors that affect product mix. Figure 13–2 illustrates the retailer's main concerns in developing the product mix. Chapter 14 discusses the retailer's service mix. Problems in securing the merchandise mix and their solutions are handled in Chapter 15. The procurement, merchandise-planning, and merchandise-control processes are treated in Chapters 16, 17, and 18, respectively.

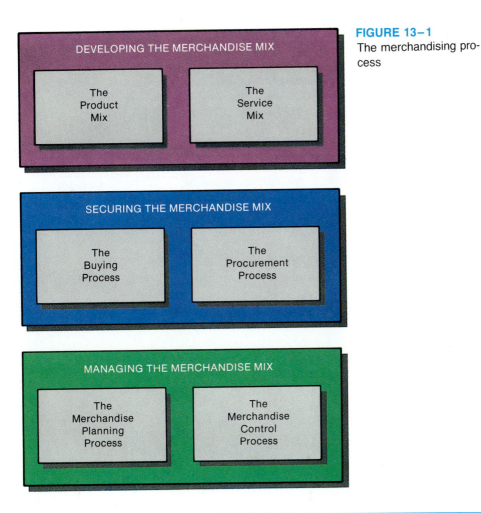

FIGURE 13–1
The merchandising process

THE PRODUCT MIX

To develop product mix, the retailer must first understand what a product really is. The product is not simply some item of merchandise with certain physical and functional attributes; it is something much more complex. Before we discuss the concept of product mix, let's first examine the "total-product concept."

Total-Product Concept

The **total-product concept** recognizes that a product is more than just the tangible object offered for sale. Retailers that sell "things" will soon discover that there is no one to sell them to. To be successful, the retailer must act on the premise that a product is more than just functional and aesthetic features; instead, it incorporates the various service features and psychological benefits conveyed by the product. In essence, the total-product concept acknowledges the need for retailers to market every one of a product's dimensions. The relationship among a product's many facets is illustrated in Figure 13–3. As shown, the total-product concept is the sum of all physical, extended, and generic products.

The Physical Product

The **physical product** encompasses both its functional and aesthetic features. A product's functional features include the tangible elements of size, shape, and weight,

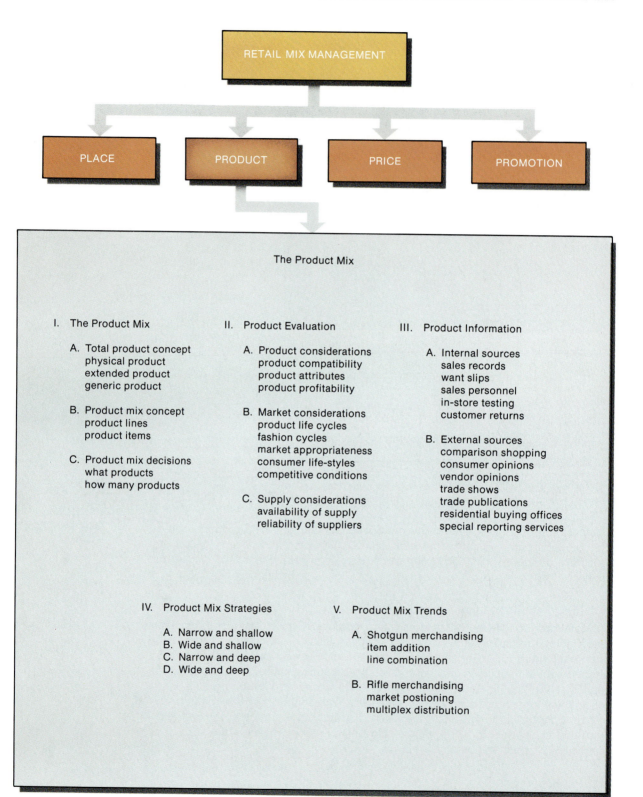

FIGURE 13–2
Developing and managing the product mix

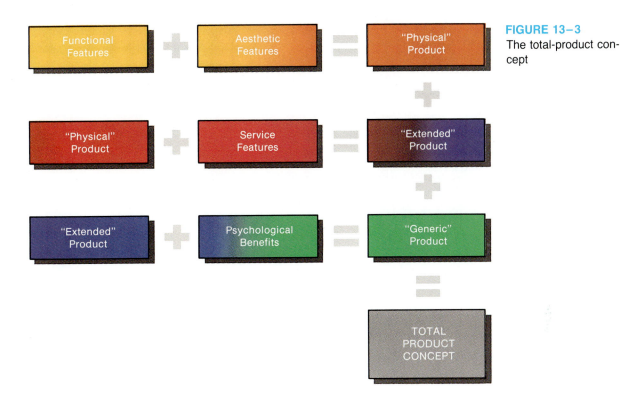

FIGURE 13–3
The total-product concept

together with its chemical and/or biological makeup. "Today, performance and fashion not only coexist, but in fact are quite dependent upon one another."[1] For example, athletic apparel must not only be fashionable but "offer benefits of qualities such as stretch, moisture-transport, and abrasion/wind-resistance . . . [and must be] lightweight, long-wearing, and easily washable."[2] Functional features are extremely important because they determine to a large extent how well the product will actually perform the functions it was designed to accomplish. If a product cannot clean and polish, or brighten and freshen, or cool and heat—in short, if it can't perform the basic function it was designed to do—then all other aspects of the product are severely diminished. The aesthetic features of a product are elements that appeal to the five senses. If a product does not look, smell, feel, sound, and/or taste "right," its merchandising qualities have been substantially reduced or eliminated. Consumers have strong preconceived ideas about how a product should look, smell, feel, sound, and taste. Wendy's "Give a little nibble" advertisement, which asks the customer to taste the meat—Is it dry and chewy? Or hot and juicy? Is it bland or is it tasty?—is directed at enhancing the perception of Wendy's hamburger as a desirable physical product.[3]

The Extended Product

The **extended product** surrounds the physical product with the whole set of service features provided as a conditional part of the sale. Service features are "extras" that might include delivery, alterations, installation, repairs, warranties, returns, adjustments, wrapping, telephone and mail ordering, or any other service that consumers want for purchase satisfaction. A retailer must determine which service features are *required* for the purchase decision and which are simply *desired* by the customer as an added product dimension. These requirements and desires then are incorporated into the retailer's product–service mix.

This display in a men's wear department illustrates a merchandise category.

The Generic Product

The final aspect of the total-product concept is the generic product. When consumers buy products, they seek something more than the physical and extended product: they expect to benefit in some way from the purchase. The **generic product** is defined as the extended product (functional, aesthetic, and service features) plus the expected psychological benefits that consumers derive from buying, using, and possessing the product. Consumers buy products to be beautiful, safe, thin, comfortable, and noticed, or to gain prestige, recognition, security, independence, love, or a host of other benefits. Retailers that recognize that a product's psychological endowments are as important as, if not more important than, the product itself will have considerably more to sell to their customer than just a physical product. People don't want lawn and garden tools; they want nice-looking lawns and gardens their families can play on and their neighbors can admire. To paraphrase Charles Revson of Revlon Cosmetics: We manufacture cosmetics; in the store, women seek hope and the promise of beauty.

Product-Mix Concept

The first step in operationalizing the total-product concept is to develop the product mix. The **product-mix concept** refers to the full range or mixture of products the retailer offers to consumers. The product mix represents "appropriate combinations" of products to meet the specific needs of one or more identified target markets. The number of appropriate mixes is nearly unlimited. As such, success often depends on whether the retailer can identify and operationalize a *new and appropriate mix*. In making product-mix decisions, the retailer must also recognize the degree of perishability of many products. What is an appropriate mix today might not be an appropriate mix tomorrow.

If the product mix represents "appropriate combinations," the obvious question becomes "appropriate combinations of what?" The answer is "appropriate combinations of product lines and product items." A **product line** is any grouping of related products. A **product item** refers to a specific product within a product line that is unique and clearly distinguishable from other products within and outside the product line.

Product Lines

Based on type and degree of relationship, product lines are often subdivided to facilitate the retailer's planning of a product mix. Products can be related in terms of (1) satisfying a particular need (e.g., health or beauty aids); (2) being used together (e.g., pieces of living room furniture); or (3) being purchased or used by a similar customer group (e.g., women's, men's, or children's wearing apparel). The degree to which products are related also can vary greatly from a close relationship to a remote relationship. There is no single method of subdividing product lines, nor is there common terminology for subdivisions.[4] For illustration here, the product line is subdivided into three groupings: merchandise group, merchandise class, and merchandise category.

A **merchandise group** is a broadly related line of products that retailers and consumers associate together according to end use. Examples of merchandise groups include such wide product combinations as furniture, appliances, home furnishings, housewares, wearing apparel, sporting goods, food products, personal-care products, and automotive products. Single-line retailers often are identified on the basis of these broad product groupings (e.g., hardware store, clothing store). Mass merchandisers frequently use merchandise groups to identify operating divisions.

A **merchandise class** is a closely related line of products within a merchandise group. This level more clearly distinguishes the particular consumer need, usage pattern, or behavior. Merchandise classes often correspond to the operating departments of a traditional department store and serve as a way to identify many specialty retailers (e.g., men's, women's, or children's wearing apparel).

A **merchandise category** is a specific line of products within a merchandise class; for example, sport and dress shirts within men's wearing apparel, lipstick and eye shadow within cosmetics, and sofas and end tables within living room furniture. This subdivision is important because products within merchandise categories are directly comparable and substitutable. It is the level within a product line at which consumer *comparison shopping* occurs.

An example of a product's three subdivisions (merchandise groups, classes, and categories) is illustrated in Figure 13-4. As shown, subdividing a product line is essentially a refinement process that helps simplify the retailer's problem of how (1) to target certain consumer groups, (2) to allocate store space and locations, (3) to develop efficient inventory control systems, and (4) to create a unique store image.

Product Items

Within a product line, a product item is distinguishable by its brand, style, size, color, material, price, or any combination of these factors. A *brand* is a distinctive grouping of products identified by a name, term, design, symbol, or any combination of these markings. Used to identify the products of a particular manufacturer or seller, brand is a common criterion in distinguishing both product lines and product items within lines. *Style* refers to the characteristic or distinctive form, outline, or shape of a

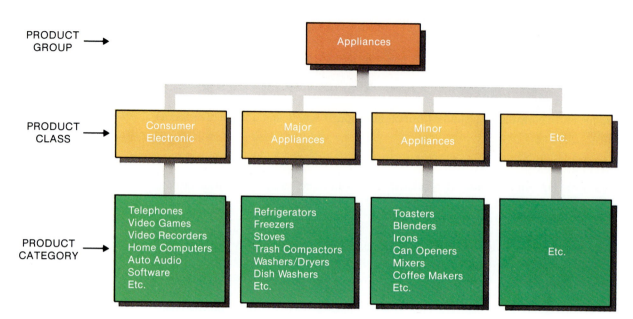

FIGURE 13–4
Product-line subdivisions

product item. As a unique mode of expression or presentation, style can be the principal criterion by which consumers distinguish one product item from another (e.g., clothing). Products also come in various sizes. *Size* can refer to the product's actual size (e.g., 42-long or X-large) or to the size of its package (e.g., family size, 12-ounce bottle). The physical magnitude, extent, and bulk of a product not only are distinguishing features that influence the consumer's purchase decision, they are also important factors in the retailer's decision to buy, stock, display, and shelve the product. *Colors, materials,* and *prices* are also important features in distinguishing one product item from another.

Product-Mix Decisions

In developing the product mix, the retailer faces two basic decisions: "Which product lines and items?" and "How many product lines and items?" A product is only "right" when it is "right" for all three merchandising activities of buying, stocking, and selling. If a product is easy to sell but creates extremely difficult buying and stocking problems, the retailer should seriously question whether to include it in the product mix!

Which Products?

No simple criteria determine whether a product line or item should be part of the product mix. The retailer must judge each product on its own merits relative to its particular situation. In considering "which products," the retailer should ask the following questions:

1. Is the product consistent with our current and proposed product mix?
2. Is it consistent with the store image we want to portray?
3. Will the product be appropriate to existing target markets or will it require development and cultivation of new market segments?
4. What level of sales support does the product require in terms of personal selling, advertising, and sales promotions?

5. What is the existing market potential and what growth potential does the product have?
6. How susceptible is the product to demand cycles and the actions of competitors?
7. Does the product require new fixturing or specialized storage facilities, or can it be properly displayed and stored with existing fixtures and facilities?

How Many Products?

Another basic problem for the retailer is the number of different product lines and items to include in the product mix. The retailer should ask and attempt to answer the following questions to decide "how many products."

1. Should we carry several product lines or specialize in one or a few lines?
2. How broad a selection (brands, styles, sizes) should we offer in each line?
3. How many different price lines should we offer?
4. Do we want a broad or limited market appeal?
5. Are there strong consumer preferences for certain brands and styles? If so, what are they?
6. What are the cyclical demand patterns (product, fashion, seasonal cycles) associated with the various product items?
7. What effect does an extensive or limited product offering have on inventory control and investment?

The "how many products" decision is two-dimensional, requiring decisions on both product variety and product assortment. **Product variety** is the number of different product lines the retailer stocks in the store. The retailer can engage in variety strategies ranging from a narrow variety of one or a few product lines to a wide variety encompassing a large number of product lines. **Product assortment** refers to the number of different product items the retailer stocks within a particular product line. Assortment strategies vary from shallow assortments of one or a few product items within each line to deep assortments having a large selection of product items within each line. The dimensions of the "how many products" decision are illustrated in Figure 13-5. (These variety and assortment strategies are discussed more fully later in the chapter.)

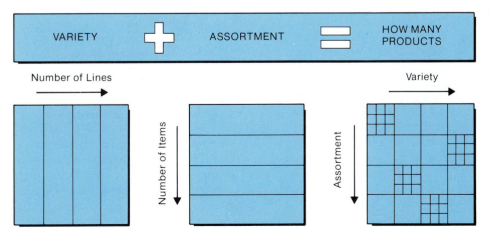

FIGURE 13-5
How many products?

PRODUCT EVALUATION

Retailers continually are besieged with a barrage of "new" and "improved" products and must evaluate each of these products before making any product-mix decision. Some require more extensive evaluation than others. Retailers use three sets of criteria to aid them in making "which" and "how many products" decisions: product, market, and supply considerations.

Product Considerations

Product considerations are those criteria directly concerned with the characteristics of the product itself. The three product considerations are compatibility, attributes, and profitability.

Product Compatibility

In developing a product mix, the retailer should consider **product compatibility**—the nature of the relationship between various product lines and between various product items within them. Based on the type of compatibility, retailers classify products as (1) substitutes, (2) complements, and (3) unrelated. The degree of product compatibility ranges from a perfect to a general relationship.

A **product substitute** is a product consumers use for the same general purpose as another product; it has the same basic functional attributes and meets the same basic consumer needs. A *perfect substitute* is a product consumers perceive as being essentially the same as another product. In this case, the consumer is totally indifferent about what product to buy and use. A *general substitute* is a product consumers perceive as being different from another product but that serves the same general purpose (e.g., Stove Top Stuffing instead of potatoes).

In deciding which products to sell, the retailer usually should avoid perfect substitutes. They divert sales from other products without adding anything in return. From the consumer's viewpoint, perfect substitutes do not even add the element of choice because a choice situation is unimportant. In addition, perfect substitutes complicate inventory control and increase handling costs. General substitutes present a different situation. For the homemaker whose family is tired of potatoes, the availability of a general substitute (dressing or rice) might preserve a lost sale (potatoes). General substitutes represent an increase in the selection a retailer offers consumers; as such, they can increase total sales.

The retailer must realize that many "new" products offered by manufacturers are often nothing more than "me-too" substitutes that add little, if anything, to the store's total sales. Whereas a selection of various me-too products is necessary for consumer comparison shopping, the retailer should review the product mix periodically to avoid an unprofitable proliferation of me-too merchandising.

A **product complement** is a product that is bought and used in conjunction with another product. A *perfect complement* is a product consumers must purchase because their original product purchase cannot function immediately or effectively without it (e.g., film is a perfect complement to a camera). *General complements* are products sold in conjunction with other products because they enhance or supplement the original purchase in some way. Apparel accessories that are color- and style-coordinated with a suit or dress are excellent examples of general complements. Both perfect and general complements are highly desirable additions to the retailer's product mix because they often represent additional, unplanned sales beyond the original, planned purchase. Also, consumers tend to be less sensitive about the price of complements; hence, retailers often sell them at above-average markups. As a rule, the depth of assortment for complements is rather extensive, and the chances for additional sales increase when consumers have a great selection.

Unrelated products are neither substitutes nor complements, but retailers seriously consider them for their product mix since they represent potential additional sales, theoretically at low risk and reasonable profit. Some impulse goods fit this description. Normally, unrelated products are not stocked in depth; rather, retailers often follow a strategy of "creaming," stocking and selling only the best-selling items. (The process of item additions and line combinations are discussed later in this chapter.)

Product Attributes

The attributes of the product itself strongly influence which and how many products retailers stock. Four **product attributes** to consider are product bulk, standardization, service requirements, and required selling method.

Product bulk is the weight or size of a product in relation to its value. Bulky products usually require substantial space, both on the sales floor and in the stockroom, and often require special handling. If only limited space is available, the retailer may have to forego stocking bulky products or limit the depth of selection. Furniture, appliances, lawn and garden equipment, and some home-improvement products are examples of bulky products. In addition, many bulky products typically are low in sales per square foot of floor space. In fact, some retailers have found that the space these bulky items occupy should be (and has been) turned over to more productive merchandise with higher sales per square foot.

Product standardization is the second product attribute retailers should consider in evaluating product attributes. Generally, standardized products fit into the retailer's routine operating procedures, whereas nonstandardized products often require special buying, stocking, and handling. Few products offer enough potential to the retailer to justify developing specialized merchandising skills. Unless the supplier is willing to make certain adjustments or provide considerable support, nonstandardized products should be excluded from the product mix.

Because products vary noticeably concerning *required service levels,* retailers should evaluate each product individually. If a required customer service (e.g., home delivery, home repair, or long-term credit) is not part of the retailer's normal service offering, the retailer should seriously consider the product's service requirements before adding it to the product line. It is seldom possible for a retailer to add a new service for a new product line and expect that line to be profitable.

Required selling methods are particular skills needed to sell a product. Some products call for a personal selling approach, while others can be sold on a self-

This camera store can sell both perfect and general complements to its primary product.

service basis. Generally, self-service retailers should not sell merchandise that requires personal selling. Likewise, an upscale retailer that stocks too many self-service items risks the prestige and product-quality image of the store.

Product Profitability

In determining the merits of a product, **product profitability** is one of the most important and complex criteria retailers use, since it can be expressed and measured in so many different ways. It is sufficient to state here that each product should make some contribution to profit; the contribution can be direct in the sense of per-unit profit or indirect by creating customer traffic and additional sales on other products.

Market Considerations

Retailers use market considerations as criteria to evaluate a product according to its compatibility with the retailer's markets and customers. Products should be examined relative to their life- or fashion-cycle stages, market appropriateness, life-style implications, and competitive positions.

Product Life Cycle

Products pass through several stages in their lifetime, each identified by its sales performance characteristics. This series of stages is called the **product life cycle (PLC)**. Knowing what stage a product is in helps the retailer judge both its existing and future sales potential. Also, the PLC stage suggests a particular retailing strategy. The four stages of the product life cycle are *introduction, growth, maturity,* and *decline.* Figure 13–6 illustrates one basic shape of the PLC as defined by sales-performance levels.

    In the *introductory stage,* products are characterized by low sales and losses, high risk, and high costs. Many products never make it out of the introductory stage. Thus, the retailer's risks are high. On the other hand, where manufacturers invest heavily in advertising to gain consumer awareness and acceptance and offer liberal returns and adjustments, the retailer's risk is substantially reduced. For many retailers, new products are essential to their avant-garde image and the necessary merchandising skill is to select only introductory products that are truly innovative. Another consideration for retailers is that the manufacturer may decide to limit distribution of the product to a few *exclusive* or several *selective* outlets. Faced with this situation, the retailer must decide to get in at once or be shut out permanently. A retailer that stocks introductory products should limit selection to a few key items until primary demand for the product has been established.

FIGURE 13–6
The product life cycle

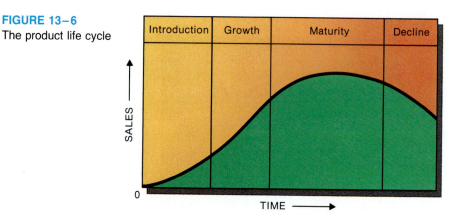

Most of the really successful new products have been just slightly ahead of their time. . . . They've caught the leading edge of a trend. But if they're too far ahead, they're not well understood and if they're too different, they require a habit change. To be a real success a product should be both better and different—a lot better and a little different.[5]

Almost without exception, the most desirable products for retailers are those in the *growth stage.* Products in the growth stage are characterized by accelerating sales, highest profit levels of any stage in the PLC, limited competitors in the market, and lower relative costs and risk. To satisfy the growing number of customers, retailers usually stock an extensive assortment of growth products. Figure 13–7 is an example of a product (cellular phones) that is in the growth stage.

In the *maturity stage,* sales increase at a slower rate and finally begin to level off. Characteristics of this stage are (1) a highly competitive market, (2) falling prices and margins, (3) more intensive advertising, and (4) lower profits. Most retailers should

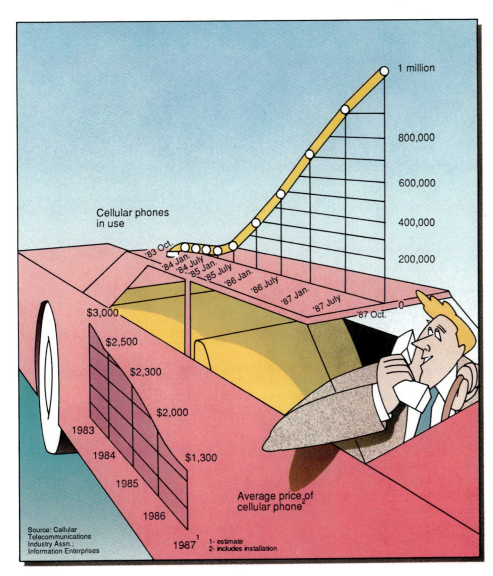

FIGURE 13–7
A product in the growth stage: Cellular phone usage (source: reprinted with permission from Sam Ward, *USA Today,* 14 Oct. 1987, B-1)

include or continue to include mature products in their product mix because consumers expect them.

As a rule, retailers do not include *declining products* in their product mix. Normally, retailers drop these products, if they have not done so already, because products in the decline stage are high-risk items. This stage is characterized by rapidly declining sales and profits (or losses) and little, if any, manufacturer support in promotion. Retailers that continue to stock declining products should only do so in limited quantities and assortments and only if demand is sufficient to yield a reasonable profit.

Fashion Cycle

Like the product life cycle, the **fashion cycle** is a conceptualization of the "life of a fashion." A fashion is a product that has distinctive attributes that are currently appropriate and represent the prevailing style. Fashion is a reflection of a society's cultural, social, and economic environment at one particular point. As one fashion expert writes, "Fashion trends reflect the changes in what a culture is thinking, feeling, and doing, both in work and recreation; how an era is behaving morally; and how stable or successful a country is financially."[6]

Major fashion houses frequently distinguish between their premium-priced collections, displayed at the New York and Paris fashion shows and sold to a limited number of wealthy clients, and their classification merchandise: lower priced, with a broader appeal, and incorporating the features of last year's collections. Profits derived from classification sales subsidize the development of collections, which cast a premium halo over the classification merchandise, for which, in turn, a premium price can be charged.[7] Fashions represent great opportunities for retailers, but also substantial risks. Fashionable products include the following:

- ☐ High-margin items that can provide above-average profits
- ☐ Shopping and specialty goods that consumers will spend time, money, and effort to find
- ☐ Products that enhance the retailer's general image and help generate consumer traffic
- ☐ A means of distinguishing a retailer's operation from the competition

Fashion-conscious consumers may be characterized as follows:

- ☐ Oriented toward the social world
- ☐ Gregarious and likable
- ☐ Active participants in society
- ☐ Self-assertive, competitive, and venturesome
- ☐ Attention seekers and self-confident
- ☐ Aesthetic-, power-, and status-oriented individuals[8]

The risk associated with fashion products comes from the uncertainty that surrounds both consumers' *level* of acceptance and the *duration* of their acceptance of the fashion. "The fashion industry thrives on the concept of psychological obsolescence. A major driving force for consumers is the continual search for newness and the discarding of the old."[9] One management tool retailers use to reduce the risks of including fashion products in their product mix is the *fashion cycle*. During its lifetime, a fashion passes through three stages: introduction, acceptance, and decline. From its beginning in the introductory stage to its obsolescence in the decline stage, the fashion innovation struggles to obtain customer acceptance and customer adoptions.

Fashion represents the prevailing style.

Customer acceptance of fashion varies significantly according to level of acceptance (as measured by sales) and the duration of that acceptance (as measured by weeks, months, years). Based on the two acceptance factors, four types of fashion cycles occur: flop, fad, ford, and classic (see Figure 13–8). A **flop** is a fashion cycle rejected by all consumer segments almost immediately. Other than for a few fashion innovators who try and then discard the fashion, a flop gains neither a significant level nor duration of acceptance. Flops are fashion items most retailers hope to avoid; they not only represent the financial loss of obsolete merchandise, they also tend to tarnish the retailer's image as a fashion leader. Some flops are inevitable—they are the realization of the risks that go with fashion merchandising.

A **fad** is a fashion that obtains a relatively high level of customer acceptance for a short time. It is quickly accepted but rejected with the same quickness (see Figure 13–9). Typically, the lifetime of a fad ranges from a few weeks to several months. Because a relatively large number of these items can be sold at substantial markups (consumers are somewhat price insensitive regarding fads) in a short period of time, fads are extremely profitable. They are also highly risky, however, because of the short duration of the cycle. To capitalize on a fad, the retailer must stock the item at the introductory or early part of the cycle.

A best-seller in fashion merchandising is referred to as a **ford**. A ford is also referred to as a "runner" or "hot item." Fords gain wide customer acceptance over extended periods of time. Because of their wide acceptance, long-term salability, and stable demand, fords usually are produced by many different manufacturers in a variety of price lines.[10] For the same reasons, nearly every retailer must include fords in the product mix or suffer loss of profits and loss of a fashion image. The miniskirt is an excellent example of a ford, lasting from 1965 to 1971. Men's leisure suits are another example of a ford.

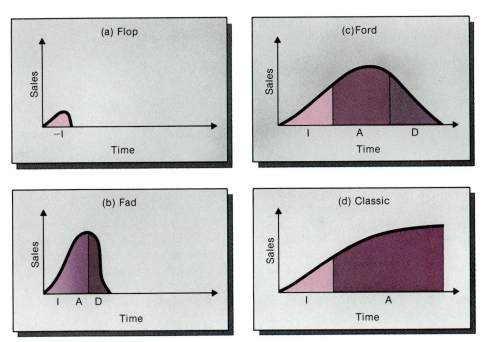

FIGURE 13–8
Types of fashion cycles

Key: I = Introductory Stage   A = Acceptance Stage   D = Decline Stage

FIGURE 13–9

Great fads of our time

How many do you remember? How many
did you own? How long did
you keep them?

Shmoos
Rubik's Cubes
Hula Hoops
Nehru jackets
Running
Pet Rocks
Puka beads
Love beads
Indian glass beads
3-D movies
The Lindy
Skateboards
Ankle bracelets
Coonskin caps
Telephone booth packing
Flubber (from the Disney flick
    The Absent-Minded Professor)
Slime (mutant son of Flubber)
Nautilus
Super Balls
Dickies
Clackers
Zoot suits
E.T.
Disco

Source: Adapted from Stephen Fried, "Summer Madness," *Philadelphia* August
1983, p. 122.

The "classic look," the "classic cut," and the "classic shape" describe a style trend that endures for many years (see Figure 13–10). The **classic** fashion has both a high level and a long duration of acceptance. Although a classic might undergo minor changes, it essentially looks the same. "The aging of the baby-boom generation has produced shifts in apparel demand. The fad orientation of the 1960s and early 1970s gave way to the 'preppie look' in the late 1970s. This look has evolved into a new approach to dressing, consisting of classically styled pieces in updated colors and traditional items combined in innovative ways. The 'layered look' and 'investment dressing' are terms fashion-conscious people use to describe these classically styled items."[11] The classic, even more than the ford, is an absolute must in the retailer's product mix. The decision relative to the classic is not whether to stock it, but rather which price line to stock from which supplier with which product features. The pantsuit, introduced as a fashionable women's garment in 1966, retains a high level of acceptance in almost all market segments. It has become a classic fashion because it fits the needs and life-styles of the modern woman, especially the working woman.

Several theories have been proposed to explain the process by which consumer groups adopt fashionable products. An understanding of this consumer adoption

Would you categorize these fashion items as flops, fads, fords, or classics?

FIGURE 13–10
Trend or fad? Guidelines for assessing trends and fads

- A new product is more likely to be a trend if it is consistent with the consumer's basic values and lifestyles. New products which produce value and lifestyle conflicts are more likely to be a fad!
- A new product is more likely to be a trend if it promotes a voluntary change in behavior that is derived from customer satisfaction. Products which force a behavioral change (e.g., adoption of inexpensive products during tough economic times) tend to be more fadish in nature.
- A new product stands a better chance of becoming a trend if it can be modified or expressed in different ways by different people. Fads are more rigid (e.g., exaggerated, extreme, and impractical hairstyles).
- A new product is more likely to be a trend if it is based on a good underlying theme (e.g., physical fitness). Fadish products are often based on a specific manifestation or expression of a basic theme (e.g., fadish diet). Specific manifestations come and go and often are replaced by other expressions of a basic theme.
- A new product is more likely to be a trend if it is supported by new developments in related areas (e.g., nutrition, physical fitness, nonsmoking, and stress reduction). If a new product stands alone, it is more likely to be a fad.

Source: Adapted from "Distinguishing Fads from Trends with 6 Research Guidelines," *Marketing News,* 21 January 1983, 3, 15.

process provides the retailer with one more tool by which to judge the appropriateness of a fashion to the targeted market. The three basic theories of fashion follow.

1. **Trickle-down theory** hypothesizes that new innovative fashions and styles originate in the upper socioeconomic classes and are passed down through the middle class to the lower socioeconomic consumer. European designers (i.e., Paris, London, Milan) are considered to be the usual origin for a given fashion cycle; however, American designers are becoming the original source with greater frequency.[12] Figure 13–11a illustrates and describes this theory.

2. **Trickle-up theory** states that some unusual fashions or styles are developed in the lower socioeconomic classes, picked up by the upper class, and finally adopted by the middle class (see Figure 13–11b). Blue jeans, the funky look, and the leather look are examples.

3. **Trickle-across theory** recognizes that a fashion or style can originate within any social class. Fashions and styles are marketed to opinion leaders within one or more social class levels; these opinion leaders are then instrumental in getting other members of the same social class to adopt the fashion or style. Hence, the fashion spreads horizontally through the population within the upper, middle, and/or lower social class.

FIGURE 13–11
Fashion adoption theories

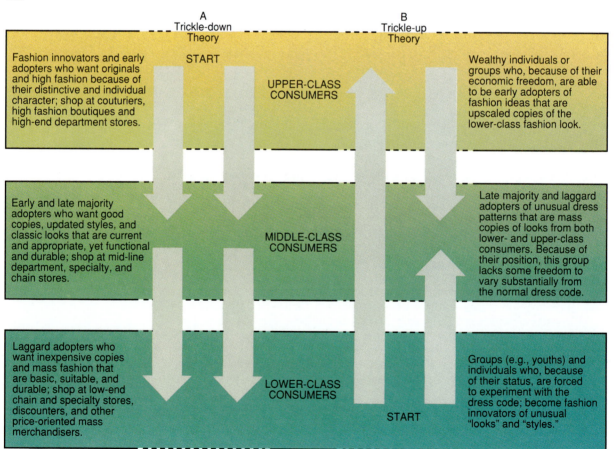

A
Trickle-down
Theory

B
Trickle-up
Theory

START

UPPER-CLASS
CONSUMERS

Fashion innovators and early adopters who want originals and high fashion because of their distinctive and individual character; shop at couturiers, high fashion boutiques and high-end department stores.

Wealthy individuals or groups who, because of their economic freedom, are able to be early adopters of fashion ideas that are upscaled copies of the lower-class fashion look.

MIDDLE-CLASS
CONSUMERS

Early and late majority adopters who want good copies, updated styles, and classic looks that are current and appropriate, yet functional and durable; shop at mid-line department, specialty, and chain stores.

Late majority and laggard adopters of unusual dress patterns that are mass copies of looks from both lower- and upper-class consumers. Because of their position, this group lacks some freedom to vary substantially from the normal dress code.

LOWER-CLASS
CONSUMERS

START

Laggard adopters who want inexpensive copies and mass fashion that are basic, suitable, and durable; shop at low-end chain and specialty stores, discounters, and other price-oriented mass merchandisers.

Groups (e.g., youths) and individuals who, because of their status, are forced to experiment with the dress code; become fashion innovators of unusual "looks" and "styles."

Market Appropriateness

Retailers should evaluate new-product candidates on their chances for success in the marketplace, that is, *market appropriateness*—how well the new product matches the consumption and buying needs of targeted consumers. Several characteristics that serve as good indicators of how well a product might be received by the retailer's current and potential customers are relative advantage, affinity, trial-ability, observability, and complexity.

Relative advantage is the extent to which the new product is perceived to be better than existing products. A product that offers clear-cut advantages or provides a more satisfying benefit package is more likely to attract the interest and patronage of the store's customers.

Affinity is the extent to which the new product is consistent with the consumer's current buying and usage behavior. Products that require noticeable behavioral modification are often viewed by consumers as being incompatible with their needs. A product that is consistent with the consumer's beliefs, values, and experiences is more likely to gain customer acceptance and a faster and higher rate of adoptions.

Trial-ability is the extent to which a new product can be tested on a trial basis. All new-product purchases involve some risk to the purchaser. Anything that substantially reduces the risk improves the chances for initial and subsequent purchases. A product that can be physically divided into small quantities and given as free samples or sold in trial sizes benefits from good trial-ability. If division is not possible, demonstrations and guarantees can reduce perceived risks.

Observability is the extent to which the consumer can see a new product's favorable attributes. If relative advantages are easily visible and can be easily described to others, the new product's probability of market success is greatly enhanced.

Complexity is the extent to which a new product can be easily understood or used. Products that require the consumer to invest considerable time and effort to reap any benefits will involve greater selling efforts and a slower rate of consumer adoptions.

Life-Styles

As discussed in Chapter 4, a life-style is a pattern of living shaped by psychological influences, social experiences, and demographic makeup. Knowing targeted consumers' activities, interests, and opinions makes retailers better able to select products that are consistent with both the consumer's life-style and the retailer's image. Developing product lines in accord with consumer living patterns is referred to as **life-style merchandising**. This method of product evaluation requires the retailer to do the following:

1. Identify target markets based on consumers' life-styles and their product, place, promotion, and price preferences.
2. Determine which life-style markets are consistent with the retailer's image and mode of doing business.
3. Evaluate which and how many products to carry based on their ability to satisfy certain life-style markets.

Many fashion retailers go to trade shows and producer markets looking for merchandise suited for their targeted consumers' life-style. One illustration of how retailers can characterize consumers' life-styles appears in Figure 13–12. Using this life-style scheme and others like it, retailers can select, purchase, and stock merchandise that matches their target consumers' life-styles.

"The Perfectionist"

- Age: 25–45
- Size: Misses 4–14
- A woman who is *first* in a fashion trend; has the most advanced taste of all customers—the "Fashion Leader."
- Active; worldly; career-oriented; involved; free-spirited; energy abounding.
- Inherently understands fashion . . . incorporates fashion into every aspect of her lifestyle.
- Uniqueness and individuality are her two main concerns—she depends on clothes as a means of self-expression.
- She is governed by her emotions. When in an adventurous mood, she seeks the most advanced fashions . . . always avant-garde, nonconforming, often impractical. When in a classic mood, her taste level is pure, clean, and sophisticated.
- She combines a mix of fashion looks to cover her variety of emotional and active lifestyle needs.
- She is extremely conscious of her body; chooses clothes to complement her figure.
- Demands and appreciates quality.
- Impressed by designers who style for her contemporary lifestyle.
- Not necessarily price conscious; buys what she desires.
- She is influenced by her surroundings when shopping.
- Does not respond well to markdowns or price promotions.
- Needs little salespeople attention.
- Expects new arrivals often.
- Buys impulsively.
- Loyal to a store wherever she feels her *mood runs free.*

"The Updated"

- Age: 25–60
- Size: Misses 4–16
- Desires fashion after it has been modified from its pure, advanced stages. Very often *this season's updated styles were last season's perfectionist styles.*
- Demands smart-looking items; stylish, yet not extreme.
- Working girl or woman; housewife; mother.
- Desires clothes that are functional additions to her wardrobe—multipurpose.
- Desires high degree of quality, practicality, and value for the price.

- Not necessarily label conscious.
- Will buy regular stock markdowns; responds only moderately to price promotions.
- Loyal to store that separates her look, supports her type, and puts her look together for her.
- Fastest-growing misses customer type.

"The Young Affluent"

- Age: 25–50
- Size: Misses 4–14
- Career woman, wife.
- Leads active social life; involved.
- Often attracted to designer labels.
- Ruled by current designer trends.
- Respects fine merchandise.
- Demands quality.
- Is an investment buyer; designer wardrobe builder.
- Taste level similar to updated customer, but not price conscious.

"The Traditionalist"

- Age: 26–65
- Size: Misses 8–20
- The conformist . . . likes fashion only after it is accepted.
- Less career-oriented; more job-oriented. Oftentimes office worker, teacher, housewife.
- Does not react to, or desire, fashion extremes.
- Extremely label conscious—loyal to those she has worn and liked in the past.
- Price conscious; quality aware.
- Very practical; demands ease of care.
- Very insecure about fashion in general—must have fashion put together for her.
- Fashion influenced by peers.
- Loyal to stores and professional salespeople who service her needs.
- Responds exceptionally well to price promotions and markdowns.
- Replacement customer; conservative taste.

"The Establishment"

- Age: 45+
- Size: Misses 8–20
- Older, refined woman—dignified.
- Active in community; holds prestigious position.
- An investment buyer; wardrobe builder.
- Loves fine workmanship, fabrics, and detail.
- Concerned with quality and value.
- Appreciates designer merchandise.
- Limitless buying ability.
- Seeks clothes that fill her needs.

Source: M. M. Cohn, Little Rock, AK.

FIGURE 13–12

Life-style merchandising

Competitive Conditions

To decide which products to include in or exclude from the product mix, the retailer must consider the competitive conditions under which the product is available. Two aspects of competitive conditions are type and degree of competition. Type of competition refers to whether the product is available to direct or indirect competitors. A **direct, or intratype, competitor** is one whose merchandising program is about the same as another retailer's. An **indirect, or intertype, competitor** is one whose merchandising program is noticeably different from that of a retailer of similar products.

A product that is available to direct competitors has no "distinctive" advantage to any retailer. In some cases, however, it might help a retailer to establish that the store's image is on par with its competitors', and therefore the retailer would want to promote comparison shopping. Adopting a product that is available to indirect competitors might either help or hurt the store's image. If upscale, indirect competitors stock the product, the retailer's image can be enhanced, but if downscale, indirect competitors stock the product, the retailer's image could be damaged.

The degree of competition refers to the number of competitors that are or will be stocking the product. **Competitive conditions** can be either **exclusive** (no competitors), **selective** (few competitors), or **intensive** (many competitors). Exclusive rights to a product offer several advantages. First, they help build an exclusive image by distinguishing the retailer's product mix from the competitors' mixes. Second, they permit greater freedom in merchandising products, since the retailer can worry less about what competitors are doing. Sears has exclusive product arrangements with the Walt Disney Co. and McDonald's, which are but two of the many exclusive arrangements Sears has initiated as it shifts emphasis from being a mass merchandiser toward a specialty retailer of exclusive products.[13] Suppliers, however, do not grant exclusive rights to products without expecting something in return, so retailers must have a clear understanding of the requirements they must meet to handle the product exclusively.

Selective competition is generally not as desirable as an exclusive arrangement. For retailers that want some limit on competition but still need comparable products to facilitate customer comparison shopping, a selective arrangement is the best alternative. Retailers normally have little incentive to stock a product when there is intense competition; however, they are often "forced" to carry intensively distributed products that are so readily available in competitive outlets because consumers expect them to be in stock.

The retailer's typical assortment strategy varies with competitive conditions. Retailers should carry a deep assortment of exclusive product items and a limited assortment of selective products. And, for intensively distributed products, retailers must resort to one of two strategies: (1) stock only the best-selling items to satisfy customers whose preferred item is not available and who will accept a substitute, or (2) stock a deep assortment to satisfy most customers and thereby create a store image of "complete selection."

Supply Considerations

In evaluating what and how many products to include in the product mix, the retailer should examine not only market conditions but also supply considerations, two of which are *availability* and the *reliability* of the supplier.

Availability of Supply

Before making a decision to stock a product, the retailer should study the product's **availability of supply**. Following are four basic questions the retailer should ask:

1. Is the product readily available through the retailer's normal channels of distribution?
2. Are alternative backup sources of supply available?
3. Will the product be available on a continuing basis?
4. What are the terms and conditions of sale under which the product is available?

Ideally, for the retailer to make a positive decision on a product candidate, the product should be available from normal channels, with sufficient alternative supply sources, and under terms and conditions consistent with the product's sales and profit potential.

Reliability of Supplier

In deciding whether to include a product in the product mix, a retailer should also evaluate the **reliability of the supplier**. The ease of getting the product into the store at the *right time,* in the *right quantities,* and in *good condition* is a necessary consideration. Criteria that describe a supplier's reliability include (1) shipping on time, (2) filling orders adequately, (3) maintaining adequate stocks (avoiding stockouts), and (4) adjusting orders to meet the retailer's changing needs. (Chapters 15 and 16 regarding buying and procurement give further information for choosing the right supplier.)

Brand Considerations

What's in a name? A great deal! Most consumers rely on brand names to distinguish among the massive numbers of product offerings by competing marketers; in essence, consumers use brand names to help them define their product and store choices. Retailers depend on brand names to distinguish themselves from competing retail organizations and to develop a cadre of loyal customers. Assuming the retailers' name(s) and brand(s) are associated with positive images created by user satisfaction, the store can position itself on the consumer's quality continuum (i.e., establish a reputation). Although branding can be viewed from a number of different perspectives, this chapter examines brand considerations in terms of no-names (generics) versus name-brand labels and manufacturer (national) brands versus store (private-label) brands. Finally, this chapter examines the merchandising of licensed products.

No-Name Generics Versus Name-Brand Labels

No-name generic products are unadvertised, lower-grade, no-frill brands that are offered as low-cost alternatives to name-brand merchandise.[14] These plain-packaged, starkly labeled products (i.e., list of contents) achieved record levels of sales during the high inflationary periods of the early 1980s. Generics are an expected part of the product mix in most supermarkets and drugstores. Therefore, the major decision concerns "how many" generic products to stock. Typically, food and drug retailers tend to increase the selection of generic products in stores located within market areas comprised of price-oriented consumers and during times of high inflation and economic recession when everyone's buying power is reduced. Given the somewhat questionable and unreliable quality of generic products, consumers tend to be more cautious with food than nonfood products. They are more careful "when it comes to products they ingest"[15]; hence, the selection of nonfood generics can be increased with lower selling risks. A final consideration in developing the generic product mix is the belief of some experts that selling generics simply cannibalizes the sale of more profitable private labels and manufacturers' brands. Those who hold this viewpoint recommend keeping generic stock at "bare-bones" levels.

Manufacturer (National) Brands Versus Store (Private) Brands

Manufacturer brands are products that are produced, owned, controlled, and sometimes distributed by the manufacturer (e.g., Ford, General Electric, Kellogg, IBM, Arrow). They are referred to as national brands because many of them have countrywide recognition created through national advertising programs. The national status of these manufacturer labels created the image of better and more consistent quality; to consumers they represent a known or "sure thing" with little or no purchase risk. Some manufacturer brands are in fact regional or local in scope and unknown outside their own area, and their quality may or may not be better than private-label merchandise. **Store, or private-label, brands** are items that are owned, controlled, merchandised, and sold through the retailer's own outlets (e.g., Kroger, Radio Shack, The Limited, and Sears). Historically, consumers often considered private labels as somewhat lower-quality, lower-status, and lower-priced merchandise, and many retailers directly or indirectly promoted this perceptional difference between house and national brands. For example, many department stores often stock the lower price points within a merchandise category with private-label items, whereas the prestige points are covered with designer labels (e.g., Christian Lacroix, Karl Lagerfeld, Geoffrey Beene, Calvin Klein, and Ralph Lauren) and bridge lines (e.g., Anne Klein II, Calvin Klein Classics, and Perry Ellis Portfolio). Brooks Brothers is the classic exception to this perception, and many department and specialty stores are emulating this traditional private-label retailer. For example, "The Limited . . . has made private-label merchandise a cornerstone of its strategy . . . [its] private brand Forenza and Outback Red combined are the third largest in sales of women's apparel in the country"[16]; "Macy's has boosted its private-label sales . . . to more than 20 in 1986 and currently has more than 50 in-house labels."[17]

The "which products" (manufacturer or store brand) decision will vary considerably with the different retailers' individual merchandising formats; however, the retail manager should consider the pros and cons of stocking manufacturer and private-label merchandise (see Figure 13–13).

Licensed Products

A product's greatest asset is often the intangible benefits and psychological symbols associated with its name. **Licensed products** are items that are designed and sold through identification with a famous individual or corporate name, title, logo, slogan, or fictional character; the owner of the name, logo, or character develops contractual arrangements permitting licensees to use that identification on products they make and sell. Cartoon characters (G.I. Joe), sports figures (Jim McMann), corporate logos (Playboy Clubs), fashion designers (Yves St. Laurent), and celebrities (Baryshnikov Bodywear) are just a few of the licensed product categories the retailer can consider for inclusion in the product mix. Figure 13–14 illustrates total sales of licensed merchandise by product types.

In choosing from the vast selection of licensed products, retailers and their buyers should be increasingly selective. The days of the almost guaranteed licensed product success have disappeared as the number of items has increased and their novelty has diminished.

Though licensed names with widespread media exposure can do very well, especially in the short run, most experts today recommend that a retailer evaluate

FIGURE 13–13
Retailer's viewpoint:
The pros and cons of
manufacturer and
private-label brands

Manufacturer Brands	
Pros	Cons
Presold to target consumers	Lower gross margins
Lower selling costs	Selling restrictions
Attracts new customers	Pricing restrictions
Helps create assortments	Advertising restrictions
Enhances store image	Create more brand loyalty than store loyalty
Allows comparison shopping	

Private-Label Brands	
Pros	Cons
Greater price flexibility	Higher selling costs resulting from demand stimulation
Higher gross margins	Greater financial risk resulting from greater involvement
No advertising restrictions	Expanded buying and procuring responsibilities and costs
Enhance store and store brand loyalty	
Better product quality control through specification buying	
Promotes distinctive store and product image	
No direct brand competition	

licensed goods as it would any other merchandise, looking first for quality, design, price, and compatibility with current store image and consumer wants—with or without the name. If those criteria are met, sales can be greatly enhanced as a result of the extremely fast customer recognition factor and personal identification with the image projected by the licensed name. Thus, for example, though the licensed Coca-

FIGURE 13–14
Licensed sales by
product category, 1986
(source: reprinted with
permission from the
June 1 1987 issue of
Advertising Age. Copy-
right © by Crain Com-
munications, Inc.)

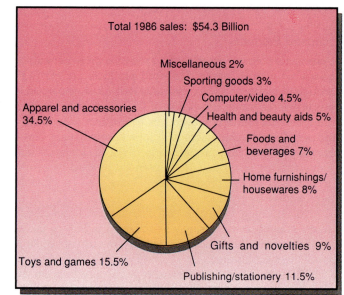

Total 1986 sales: $54.3 Billion

Miscellaneous 2%
Sporting goods 3%
Computer/video 4.5%
Health and beauty aids 5%
Foods and beverages 7%
Home furnishings/housewares 8%
Gifts and novelties 9%
Publishing/stationery 11.5%
Toys and games 15.5%
Apparel and accessories 34.5%

Cola clothing line has enjoyed enormous retail success since its introduction in 1986, retail executives attribute its popularity primarily to its quality, stylishness, and reasonable price, with the impact of the Coca-Cola name itself receiving only secondary credit.[18] The Coke example also illustrates the principle that retailers should look for an appropriate marriage between name and product; Coca-Cola's casual, good-times, active image and life-style associations provide an exceptional match with its licensed line of beach towels, sweatshirts, and other active wear. Illogical matches, such as the recently available G. I. Joe cake pan and James Bond 007 bagels (one baker figured he already had the 0's) should be avoided.

Despite retailers' best efforts to carry in their stores only the right mix of licensed lines, the enormity of the product selection and the basic uncertainty of exactly which licensed names will catch on make these choices very difficult. The desire of some image-conscious retailers to be the first in an area to merchandise hot new licenses adds additional pressure by emphasizing quick decisions. In response to these problems, some large department stores test market a licensed product or product line in a few stores before deciding whether to carry it throughout the entire chain. Another problem to consider when choosing which licenses to carry is the often accelerated product life cycles (to be discussed) of licensed goods. The retailer must be especially alert to timing the introduction and discontinuation of sales of a licensed product line. Many licensed products, such as designer clothing and Disney items, remain strong sellers for years, but others (e.g, those tied to currently popular celebrity names or one-time events like Halley's comet) can have sales that peak within months and then fall precipitously.

Several other licensing strategies are also available. One is called *direct licensing,* in which a retailer (usually a large chain) signs an exclusive agreement to carry licensed products and often takes an active role in their design and manufacture. Sears is considered the leader in this type of venture, as exemplified by its Cheryl Tiegs and Stephanie Powers clothing lines and, in 1987, the inauguration of a cooperative agreement with McDonald's for merchandising the McKids' brand of children's wear. K mart's Jaclyn Smith apparel line has also proven successful, but other chains have gotten poor results from direct-licensing programs, such as Federated Department Stores' failed Cacharel licensed sportswear.

Another popular technique for marketing licensed products is through in-store *boutiques,* where all goods of a given license are merchandised together, often using innovative visual displays and special promotions. The boutique strategy can both increase sales of the licensed goods and generate store traffic. Some retailers even base entire promotion campaigns around a licensed product line, a tactic used in 1986 by a group of sixteen J. C. Penney stores in the New York City area. Their month-long promotion, featuring 300-square-foot Disney shops, in-store appearances of Mickey Mouse and other Disney characters, showings of classic Disney film footage in the boutiques, and widespread publicity, was considered an enormous success and on some evenings brought thousands of additional shoppers into the stores.[19]

There are excellent sources of information to help retailers make product-mix decisions. Internal sources include sales records, want books and slips, sales personnel, in-store testing, and customer returns. External sources are comparison shopping, consumer opinions and behavior, vendors, trade shows, trade publications, residential buying offices, and special reporting services.

PRODUCT INFORMATION

Internal Sources

Sales Records

The most widely used internal source of product information must be the store's past sales for various product lines and items. Past sales records are especially useful for deciding about staple merchandise. As a result of the regular demand for staples, past demand often is the key to predicting future demand. On the other hand, cyclical demand patterns for fashion goods limit the usefulness of past sales for estimating future demand. The past may very well be the past for fashion goods and have little to do with what consumers want in the future. Although past sales data are useful in many situations, they are of limited or no use for new products.

Want Books and Slips

Another method for determining what customers want is to record their inquiries about (1) products the retailer does not stock and (2) products the retailer carries but that currently are out of stock. Salespeople can systematically record inquiries in want books or want slips. **Want books and slips** range from simple blank notebooks and slips of paper to printed books and forms.

Sales Personnel

Sales personnel are an excellent source of information. Because they have more direct contact with consumers than anyone in the firm, salespeople are in a position to observe why and how consumers buy. Reports from sales personnel must be viewed with caution, though, since they are subjective and tend to reflect the sales-person's own biases and preferences. Nevertheless, if properly encouraged, sales-people can give the retail manager information on how existing products are selling and insight into which products might sell in the future.

In-Store Testing

Retailers frequently use **in-store testing**, test marketing within their stores, to judge customer wants. Products are pretested by stocking a sample order and observing customer responses. If the product stimulates no interest, the retailer can dispose of the merchandise with minimal losses. If the product sells in sufficient quantities over a short period of time, the retailer can reorder a much larger quantity of the merchandise.

Customer Returns

Sometimes it is as important to find out what customers do not want as it is to find out what they do want. Store data on products customers return or require adjust-ment for provide valuable information on the product mix, but the retailer must try to discover why customers returned the merchandise to make the data useful.

External Sources

Comparison Shopping

A good outside source of information on what consumers want is what other stores sell them. Through **comparison shopping** at both competing and noncompeting stores, a retailer can often discover missed product opportunities and also inspect the merchandising techniques that competitors are using to move certain products successfully. Comparative checks should include examining the competitor's window and store displays, advertisements, promotions, featured products, prices, shelf quantities, and product appeals. Some retailers even hire people to pose as customers to discover what methods and appeals competitive salespeople are using in merchandising their products. By learning how competitors think, the retailer can distinguish between promotions used to promote fast movers and those used to move "dogs."

For "complete" information on what competitors are doing, many retailers use the "three-level comparison shopping" strategy. This strategy calls for retailers to shop at stores operating above, at, and below their own targeted market. Shopping at all three levels gives the retailer information on what products customers might want in the near future (above), what products they are currently buying (at), and what products are dated (below). This strategy helps retailers decide what products they should *add* in the near future and those they should quickly *delete* from their product mix.

Consumer Opinions and Behavior

Perhaps the most effective methods for determining consumer preferences are to ask and to observe. Asking consumers their opinions and observing their behavior yield first-hand information on what products consumers want and when, where, how, and why they want them. Three common methods for soliciting consumer opinions and observing consumer behavior are consumer surveys, consumer panels, and consumer counts.

Vendors

Being in contact daily with large numbers of retailers, vendors and their representatives have a wide range of experiences on which to base their product opinions. They are thus excellent sources of product information, although retailers must be somewhat wary of their reliability. As a rule, vendor information is accurate in a general sense; however, vendor representatives are often overly enthusiastic about their own products.

Trade Shows

Trade shows are occasions when manufacturers get together to exhibit their merchandise in one place. Trade shows range from exhibitions of a particular line of products to general merchandise displays. These events allow retailers to comparison shop, to talk to various vendor representatives, and to inspect displayed merchandise. They also give retailers an opportunity to talk about their experiences with various products, vendors, and merchandising programs.

Trade Publications

Trade publications are good sources of information because (1) they provide basic trade information and (2) they contain numerous advertisements of interest to the retailer. Trade publications have feature articles and special reports on topics such as new products, industry trends, merchandising tips, current developments, and legal and environmental issues.

Residential Buying Offices

Many retailers either rely on independent residential buyers or establish their own **residential buying offices** in major producer markets. Major producer markets (do-

Trade shows offer retailers a convenient way to compare vendors and merchandise.

mestic) in the apparel industry, for example, are New York, Dallas, and Los Angeles. A representative in producer areas keeps the retailer abreast of which products are available and which new products are in the offing.

Special Reporting Services

Retailers subscribe to numerous **specialized reporting services**. Frequently, these services offer information on certain product lines and merchandising activities (e.g., advertising, store displays, and facings). They provide retailers with information periodically (daily, weekly, monthly) in the form of newspapers, special reports, or flash reports, but the cost can be substantial. Moreover, depending on the reporting, the information can be dated.

PRODUCT-MIX STRATEGIES

The basic objective in planning product-mix strategies is to offer consumers an optimum number of product lines and an optimum number of product items within each line. The optimum number of lines and items a retailer should carry varies with the type and extent of the market served, as well as with operating capabilities. Several different optimal strategies are possible, depending on the retailer's circumstances. Figure 13–15 illustrates the four basic variety/assortment combination strategies: (1) narrow variety/shallow assortment, (2) wide variety/shallow assortment, (3) narrow variety/deep assortment, and (4) wide variety/deep assortment.

Narrow Variety/Shallow Assortment

A **narrow variety/shallow assortment strategy** offers consumers the most limited product selection (lines and items) of any of the combination strategies. Retail operations characterized by narrow variety/shallow assortment are unconventional. Vending machines that hold only two or three choices of soft drinks, door-to-door sales representatives who sell only one product line with a limited number of product features, and the newsstand that offers only one or two newspapers are examples of retail institutions that use the narrow variety/shallow assortment strategy. The key to merchandising this limited product-mix strategy successfully is *place and time con-*

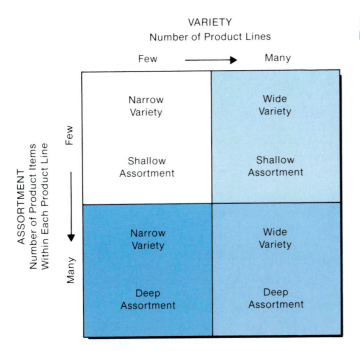

FIGURE 13–15
Product-mix strategies

venience. Because it offers a limited choice, the narrow variety/shallow assortment retailer must make its offering readily available where and when consumers want it. Generally, the narrow variety/shallow assortment strategy suffers from a poor image and little, if any, customer loyalty other than that generated by convenience. A limited product mix, however, does create certain benefits. It simplifies operations, makes inventory control problems insignificant, and minimizes facility requirements. A major benefit is the retailer's small investment in inventories.

Wide Variety/Shallow Assortment

The basic philosophy behind the **wide variety/shallow assortment strategy** is "stock a little of everything." The retailer offers a wide selection of different product lines but limits the selection of brands, styles, sizes, and so on within each line. Most variety stores (five and dime stores), general stores, and some discount houses follow this product-mix philosophy. McCrory, Ben Franklin, F. W. Woolworth and M. H. Lamston are the major U.S. operators of variety stores.[20] A wide and shallow product mix offers the advantages of appealing to a broad market, satisfying the consumer in terms of product availability if not product selection, promoting one-stop shopping, and permitting reasonable control over inventories. The disadvantages of this product-mix strategy are lost sales and customer disappointment with the lack of selection within lines, low inventory turnover rate on slow-moving product lines, weak store image, and limited store loyalty. A paradox of sorts can occur within the wide variety/narrow assortment strategy. A retailer that wants to project a prestige image might choose to stock many different high-priced product lines but limit the selection within each line to one or two unique items—originals or limited editions.

Narrow Variety/Deep Assortment

The "specialty" philosophy characterizes the **narrow variety/deep assortment strategy**. Some retailers try to appeal to a select group of consumers by offering only one or a few product lines with an excellent selection within each line. By offering a specialized mix of products supported by specialized personnel, the narrow variety/deep assortment retailer can develop a distinct store image and a loyal customer following. Additional advantages to the retailer follow:

☐ Rare sales losses as a result of an inadequate selection ofbrands, styles, sizes, colors, and materials
☐ Greater likelihood of a high level of repeat shopping
☐ Greater specialization in the buying, managing, and selling of a limited line of products
☐ Good economies of scale in ordering large quantities of the same product

The principal limitation of a specialty strategy is that successful operations *depend solely on a single or limited line of products.* "Putting all the eggs in one basket" creates a high risk for the retailer that sells in a very limited market. When adverse conditions occur in the market area, the specialty retailer suffers the most.

Wide Variety/Deep Assortment

The full-line department store best typifies the **wide variety/deep assortment strategy**. One-stop shopping is the basic philosophy of this all-inclusive product-mix strategy. A large number of product lines with supporting depth in each line allows the retailer to make a broad market appeal while satisfying most of the product needs of specific target markets. Few sales are lost as a result of an inadequate variety or assortment. Generally, satisfied customers develop store loyalty, leading to a high level of repeat shopping. Although retailers generally regard a wide variety/deep assortment strategy as the most desirable strategy from the viewpoint of selling, they also recognize the problems they must encounter in store operations. The most common problems are (1) the necessarily high level of investment in inventory to support such a diverse product mix; (2) the low stock-turnover rate associated with many marginal product lines; and (3) the large amount of space, fixtures, and equipment the retailer must have to properly merchandise such a wide range of products. In recent years, this strategy of trying to be "most things to most people" has placed the department store format in a vulnerable position as competitors attack from all directions (see Figure 13–16).

FIGURE 13–16
The vulnerable department store (source: reprinted with permission from Leonard L. Berry, "Editor's Corner," *Retailing Issues Letter* 1 [Arthur Andersen & Co. in conjunction with the Center for Retailing Studies, Texas A&M University, 1987]: 4)

To survive in the contemporary world of retailing, product mixes must be adapted rapidly and creatively to the dynamics of the marketplace. Future winners in the field of retailing will be those that can best identify consumers' emerging unsatisfied needs and develop innovative product-mix strategies to satisfy them. Two emerging product-mix trends of particular interest are shotgun merchandising and rifle merchandising.

PRODUCT-MIX
TRENDS

Shotgun Merchandising

Shotgun merchandising is the marketing strategy of broadening the retail offering to meet consumers' expanding needs. By expanding the number of product options, retailers try to increase the size of their total market by appealing to several submarkets—attempting to satisfy the specific needs of several individual market segments. In diversifying the product mix, the shotgun merchandiser attempts to develop a general-purpose mix that will satisfy the product needs of most consumers "pretty well." A retailer can either add new product items or combine major product lines to develop a general-purpose mix.

Item Addition

Item addition involves adding to one retailer's traditional product lines the more desirable product items normally associated with another type of retailer. Book, magazine, cosmetic, and apparel racks are item additions to the supermarket's primary product offerings. In the retailing industry, item addition is often referred to as *cherry picking,* because the product item additions are those retailers consider the cream of the crop—the best of the product line. Characteristics of these product items are (1) low risk because of reasonably sure sales, (2) relatively high turnover rates, (3) adequate margins for respectable profits, (4) minimal personal selling effort, (5) routine ordering and stocking procedures, and (6) relatively low per-unit prices with high levels of impulse and unplanned purchasing.

Retailers use the item-addition strategy on both a permanent and a temporary basis. Frequently, retailers add products on a trial basis to determine how well customers will receive them and whether the product additions provide sufficient profits with minimal operating difficulties. If these conditions are met, the retailer will add the product permanently. In other instances, some retailers engage in seasonal item-addition strategy. During Christmas, for example, retailers add "hot items" as potential gift selections, although they would not stock these items during other times of the year.

Line Combination

Line combination is the second shotgun strategy, in which the retailer combines two or more broad product lines into the store operation. The principle behind combining major merchandise lines is to provide consumers with a one-stop shopping opportunity for a wide range of products and therefore satisfy several needs under one roof. An example of a retail organization that uses the line-combination strategy is the superstore. The superstore combines many of the standard product lines of the supermarket, drugstore, variety store, and hardware store. With consumers demanding more and more convenience and with the soaring price of gasoline, superstores could be the wave of the future.

Rifle Merchandising

Rifle merchandising is a strategy of targeting a product offering to a select group of customers. Although the number of product lines is very selective—often only one or two lines—there is a large assortment of product items within each line. In essence, the rifle merchandiser employs a penetration strategy, concentrating product options within limited lines to serve "all" the individual needs of a given market segment for a particular line of products. Burlington Coat, Linens 'n Things, Herman's World of Sporting Goods, and Tower Records are superspecialists who are narrowly defining sharply focused retail formats that exemplify the rifle merchandising approach to the marketplace.[21] By concentrating on a limited line, the rifle merchandiser develops a specific-purpose mix that will satisfy very well all of the targeted consumers' specific needs for a given product. To create specific-purpose mixes, the rifle merchandiser uses one of two marketing strategies: either market positioning or multiplex distribution.

Market Positioning

Market positioning is the strategy of creating a "position" for a store and its product mix in the minds of consumers by relating it to other stores and their mixture of products. By specializing in certain product lines and by offering a choice within those lines, the rifle retailer hopes to establish a market niche and a particular market image. A long-time rifle merchandiser, The Gap, is repositioning itself to attract an older customer base. The Gap is changing its image from a teenaged jeans mecca to "one of America's largest retailers of casual and active sportswear for men and women." The new target market ranges from teenagers to the dodderers in their forties.[22] Creating an image leads the rifle merchandiser to program its entire operation so that the consumer will perceive it as occupying a unique position within a particular product category (see Figure 13–17). By focusing on certain product lines and developing highly complementary price, place, and promotional strategies, the rifle merchandiser attempts to achieve a dominant position in the sales of particular product lines. This strategy positions the store in the minds of consumers as one that "has it all" in a particular class of merchandise. Baskin-Robbins Ice Cream Shops, National Shirt Shops, Radio Shacks, Dunkin' Donut Shops, Blockbuster Videos, Bookshop, and Container Store are examples of multiunit retailers that have pursued a limited-line market-positioning policy.

Multiplex Distribution

"No single retailing approach is likely to be sufficient in the future simply because markets are diverging more and more with respect to wants, needs, and buying power. Therefore, a single way of doing business is unlikely to appeal to all market segments."[23] An extension of the market-positioning strategy is the **multiplex distribution strategy**. In the last decade, rifle merchandisers have begun to operate multiple types of outlets with individual product mixes serving multiple market segments.

In multiplex distribution, the rifle merchandiser aims at a number of different target markets. This specialized type of merchandiser accomplishes the task of serving several target markets using a "free-form" organization that permits it to develop a specialized product mix for each market segment. Operating under the assumption that no one individual store can please all consumers, the multiplex retailer simply

(Opposite page) This ad demonstrates the strategy of targeting products to a select group of consumers.

FIGURE 13–17

The corporate level: A market-positioning strategy

It used to be a dingy basement where shoppers rummaged through piles of bargain-priced clothes. But six months ago, Carson Pirie Scott & Co. transformed the 40,000-sq. ft. room into a colorful, mirrored space more befitting an exclusive shop in Beverly Hills than an 81-year-old department store in downtown Chicago. The new store-within-a-store is called Corporate Level, and it represents a bold attempt by Carson's to recapture the cream of the shopping masses—professional women who have fled department stores in search of high-quality merchandise and service.

Targeting the Career Woman

Carson's is not alone in its quest for the woman executive, who generally spends more on clothes than average shoppers. Many retailers provide wardrobe consultants for working women, and some have departments that sell "career" clothes. But Carson's approach is being heralded as one of the most comprehensive. . . .

Tailoring the Producer-Service Mix

What makes Corporate Level different is that almost everything a customer needs is in one place. Designer outfits are steps away from shoes and accessories. And a woman not only can buy clothes but have her shoes repaired and her hair styled, drop off dry cleaning, make photocopies, and eat a meal. For $50 annually, she gets an extra package of services that allows her to cash checks, reserve a meeting room, and use a fashion consultant.

Source: Jo Ellen Daily, "One-Stop Shopping for the Woman on the Go," *Business Week,* 18 March 1985, 116.

develops individual product mixes positioned to meet the needs of a given market segment. Big names in adult fashion are "begetting shops selling miniature versions of high fashions—Benetton's 012, for kids 0 to 12 years of age; GapKids with pint-size to teen-sized jeans . . . Laura Ashley's Mother and Child shops offering infants' and children's clothing and bedroom furnishings with the romantic look."[24] J. C. Penney has been one of the leading proponents of the free-form organization. Currently, the firm operates full-line department stores, limited-line soft-goods stores, insurance centers, discount stores, catalog desks and stores, and several foreign retail operations. The Limited also employs the free-form concept of multiplex distribution; its individual retailing formats include Limited Stores, Limited Express, Lane Bryant, Victoria's Secret, Lerner Stores, Sizes Unlimited, Henri Bendel, and Brylane Mail Order.

SUMMARY

Offering the right product in the right quantities in the right place at the right time at the right price and with the right appeal constitutes the merchandising process. The three stages of the merchandising process are developing the merchandise mix (product and service mix), securing the merchandising mix (buying and procurement process), and managing the merchandise mix (planning and controlling process).

To develop a product mix, the retailer must first understand the total-product concept. The total product is the sum of the product's functional, aesthetic, and service features plus the psychological benefits the customer expects from buying and using the product. Product mix refers to the full range of products a retailer offers to the consumer. It is composed of product lines (any grouping of related products) and product items (specific products within a product line that are clearly distinguishable). Product lines can be subclassified into merchandise groups, classes, and categories. Product items are different brands of products, differentiated by brand name, style, size, color, material, and price.

Product-mix decisions revolve around two separate but related decisions—which and how many products to stock. Deciding which products requires determining what product types are to be included in the product mix. Deciding how many products concerns developing product variety (number of different products to stock) and product assortment (number of different product items to stock in each product line).

Retailers use several criteria to decide which and how many products to carry: product compatibility, product attributes, product profitability, product life cycles, fashion cycles, product appropriateness, and competitive conditions. The retailer must also consider the availability of needed products and the reliability of suppliers.

The retailer can consult several sources of information to evaluate the merits of a product. Internal sources consist of sales records, want books and slips, sales personnel, in-store testing, and customer returns. External sources of information are comparison shopping, consumer opinions and behavior, vendors, trade shows, trade publications, residential buying offices, and special reporting services.

Regarding product mix, a retailer can use one of four variety/assortment strategies: narrow variety/shallow assortment, wide variety/shallow assortment, narrow variety/deep assortment, and wide variety/deep assortment. Correct selection of a product-mix strategy depends on the retailer's current or proposed variety/assortment situation.

Retailers are responding to the changing marketplace by employing either a shotgun or a rifle approach to merchandising. The shotgun merchandiser appeals to a combination of market segments by broadening its product lines through either product-item addition or product-line combination. The rifle merchandiser appeals to a target-market segment by using either a market-positioning strategy or a multiplex distribution system.

KEY TERMS AND CONCEPTS

affinity

availability of supply

classic

comparison shopping

complexity

direct and indirect competitors

exclusive, selective, and intensive competitive conditions

extended product

fad

fashion cycle

flop

ford

generic product

generics

in-store testing

item addition

licensed products

life-style merchandising

line combination

manufacturer brands

market positioning

merchandise category

merchandise class

merchandise group

merchandising

multiplex distribution strategy

narrow variety/deep assortment strategy

narrow variety/shallow assortment strategy

observability

physical product

product assortment

product attributes

product compatibility

product complement

product item

product life cycle (PLC)

product line

product-mix concept

product profitability

product substitute

product variety

relative advantage

reliability of supplier

residential buying offices

rifle merchandising

shotgun merchandising

specialized reporting services

store (private) brands

total-product concept

trade shows

trialability

trickle-across theory

trickle-down theory

trickle-up theory

unrelated products

want books and slips

wide variety/deep assortment strategy

wide variety/shallow assortment strategy

REVIEW QUESTIONS

1. Discuss the principal tasks to be accomplished within the merchandising process.
2. What is the total-product concept? Briefly describe each of the concept's components.
3. How do product lines differ from product items?
4. Describe the two basic decisions the retailer faces in developing the product mix.
5. Define product variety. How does it differ from product assortment?
6. Identify and describe the three basic classes of products based on product compatibility. Which of these classes of products should be included in the retailer's product mix?
7. How do the product attributes of bulk and standardization influence the retailer's decisions of which and how many products should be stocked?
8. What should the retailer's stocking strategy be for products in each of the four stages of the product life cycle?
9. Develop a profile of a fashion-conscious consumer.
10. Describe each of the four fashion cycles and discuss what the retailer's stock position should be relative to each cycle.
11. Discuss the three theories of fashion adoption.
12. Discuss the pros and cons of stocking manufacturer versus store brands.
13. Characterize the five product characteristics used in evaluating new product offerings relative to their market appropriateness.
14. What is life-style merchandising?
15. What are the internal sources of product information?
16. Describe the three-level comparison shopping strategy for gathering product information.
17. Identify the four basic variety/assortment combination strategies used in developing a retail product mix. Briefly describe each strategy.
18. What are the most common problems associated with a wide variety/deep assortment product mix strategy?
19. Compare and contrast the strategies of shotgun and rifle merchandising.
20. List the characteristics of the typical product-item addition.
21. How can retailers develop a market position for their stores and product mixes?
22. What is multiplex distribution? Give examples of retail organizations that use this strategy.

ENDNOTES

1. Fisher A. Rhymes, "The Fashion of Performance," *The FIT Review* 4 (Spring 1988): 30.
2. Ibid., 31.
3. Bob Garfield, "Images a Plus for Wendy's," *Advertising Age,* 13 April 1987, 30.
4. Penny Gill, "Bridge-(Wo)manship," *Stores* (October 1987): 20.

5. Anna Sobezynski, "New Product Success Can Be All in the Timing," *Advertising Age,* 3 May 1984, M15.
6. Kathryn M. Greenwood and Mary F. Murphy, *Fashion Innovation and Marketing* (New York: Macmillan, 1978), 57–58.
7. John A. Quelch, "Marketing the Premium Product," *Business Horizons* (May–June 1987): 44.
8. Miriam Tatzel, "Skill and Motivation in Clothes Shopping: Fashion-Conscious, Independent, and Apathetic Consumers," *Journal of Retailing* 58 (Winter, 1982): 91–92.
9. Sallie Hook, "Managers Must Know Conceptual Distinctions of Fashion Marketing," *Marketing News,* 8 May 1987, 23.
10. Miriam Tatzel, "Skill and Motivation," 56.
11. Walter J. Salmon and Karen A. Cmar, "Private Labels Are Back in Fashion," *Harvard Business Review* (May–June 1987): 102.
12. See Penny Gill, "European Designers," *Stores* (December 1987): 16–22.
13. 13.Scott Hume, "Sears Gains Exclusivity with Disney Contract," *Advertising Age,* 23 Nov. 1987, 63.
14. Amy Dunkin, "No-Frills Products: An Idea Whose Time Has Gone," *Business Week,* 17 June 1985, 64.
15. Ibid., 65.
16. Salmon and Cmar, "Private Labels," 99.
17. Ibid.
18. Penny Gill, "Look at Licensing," *Stores* (February 1986): 17.
19. "How Penney's Saluted Mickey and Friends," *Stores* (February 1987): 14.
20. "McCrory: Redefining the 5 & 10," *Chain Store Age Executives* (July 1987): 15.
21. "Hot Format for New Growth: Superspecialists," *Stores* (August 1987): 63.
22. Jules Abend, "Widening the Gap," *Stores* (November 1985): 95.
23. Jagdish N. Sheth, "Emerging Trends for the Retailing Industry," *Journal of Retailing* 59 (Fall 1983): 14.
24. Muriel J. Adams, "Hot New Retail Formats," *Stores* (February 1988): 34–35.

Dunkin, Amy. "No-Frills Products: An Idea Whose Time Has Gone." *Business Week,* 17 June 1985, 64–65.
Dunn, Mark G., Murphy, Patrick E., and Skelley, Gerald U. "Research Note: The Influence of Perceived Risk on Brand Preference for Supermarket Products." *Journal of Retailing* 62 (Summer 1986): 204–216.
Gill, Penny. "Merchandising Licensed Lines." *Stores* (February 1987): 12–20.
Jocoby, Jacob, and Olson, Jerry C. *Perceived Quality: How Consumers View Stores and Merchandise.* Lexington, MA: Lexington Books, 1984.
King, Charles W., and Ring, Lawrence J. "Market Positioning Across Retail Fashion Institutions: A Comparative Analysis of Store Types." *Journal of Retailing* 56 (Spring 1980): 37–55.
Levitt, Theodore. "Marketing Success Through Differentiation—Of Anything." *Harvard Business Review* 58 (January–February 1980): 83–91.
Lumpkin, James R., and McConkey, C. William. "Identifying Determinants of Store Choice of Fashion Shoppers." *Akron Business and Economic Review* 15 (Winter 1984): 30–35.
Mangone, Dominic M. "How to Measure Merchandise Profitability." *Retail Control* (October 1984): 11–20.
Mills, Michael K. "Strategic Retail Fashion Market Positioning: A Comparative Analysis." *Journal of the Academy of Marketing Science* 13 (Summer 1985): 212–225.
Pessemier, Edgar A. "Store Image and Positioning." *Journal of Retailing* 56 (Spring 1980): 94–106.
Schulz, David P. "New Expansion Paths." *Stores* (August 1987): 58–68.
Solomon, Michael R. *The Psychology of Fashion.* Lexington, MA: Lexington Books, 1985.
Wingate, Isabel, Gillespie, Karen, and Anderson, Mary. *Know Your Merchandise.* 5th ed. New York: McGraw-Hill, 1984.

RELATED READINGS

14

Outline

Objectives

☐ Comprehend the need to support the product mix with adequate customer services.

☐ Differentiate among consumer expectations for various services types and levels.

☐ Identify the principal objectives in providing customer services and discuss the factors that determine level of services required to meet those objectives.

☐ Name the major components of the service mix and explain how each component enhances the retailer's product mix and facilitates consumers' purchase decision making.

Service Strategy: Providing Sales Support Services

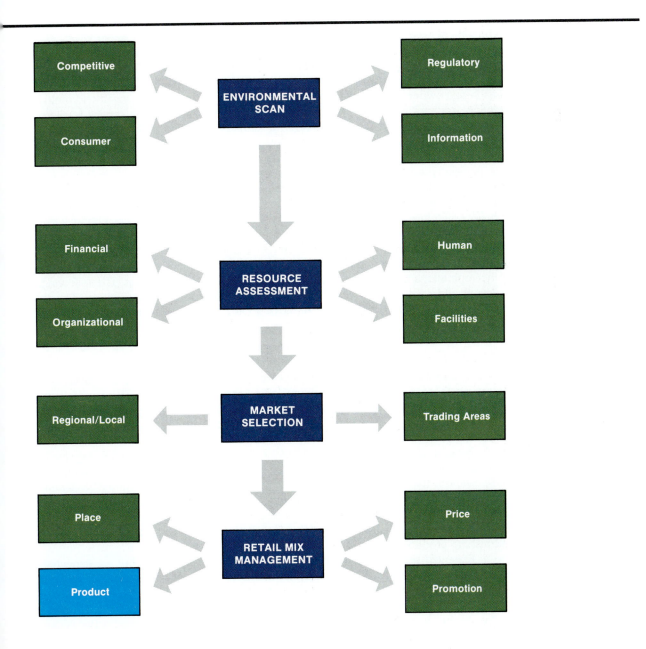

Often overlooked in the retailer's merchandise mix is the service mix. Consumers buy more than a physical product; in fact, consumers expect the retailer to perform certain services before, during, and after the sale. These services often are as important as, if not more important than, the product itself. "Retailing is a 'people' business. 'People service' makes the difference—It matters not whether a company sells fashion or food, upscale or downscale, in market focus. Study the most successful self-service retailers and what you will find is that service is a key to their success."[1] This chapter describes the role of the service mix in the retailer's total merchandise mix.

TYPES OF RETAIL SERVICES

The term *retail services* encompasses a wide variety of activities.[2] Retailers offer either primary services or complementary services. **Primary-service** retailers concentrate on rendering services to consumers and typically sell physical products as supplements to these services. Service is their reason for being in business. Examples of service retailers are banking, insurance, and real estate firms; firms that provide recreational and entertainment services; personal-care specialists ranging from hair stylists to health-spa owners; and establishments that provide home and auto repair and maintenance services. Retailers can obtain information on most of these service retailers from the "Selected Services" section of the *Census of Business*. (Chapter 23 examines the issue of services retailing in more depth.)

Many retailers view the services they offer as secondary or supplementary to the physical products they sell. These **complementary services** are neither their main function nor the reason these retailers are in business. Essentially, consumers and retailers consider supplementary services as "fringe benefits" that some, but not all, retailers offer in addition to their product mixes. Supplementary services enhance the retailer's merchandising program by providing "extras." Examples of supplementary services are delivery, credit, wrapping and packaging, parking, return privileges, installation, maintenance, repairs, alterations, some consulting services, and a host of other operations that only supplement the retailer's business format. The following sections address the fundamental problem of offering supplementary services. Figure 14–1 outlines the major concerns with developing and implementing a supplementary service mix.

THE RETAIL SERVICE PROBLEM

The basic problems retailers face in developing their service mix are essentially the same as those they encounter in developing their product mix. The service-mix decision entails determining "which services" and "how many services" they should offer consumers. Thus, retailers must decide on the level of services that will complement their product mix.

Based on relative importance, services can be classified as essential, expected, and optional. **Essential services** are basic and necessary to a particular retail operation; without them, it is unlikely that the retailer could survive. Although essential services vary from one type of operation to another, the following services are essential to most retailers: (1) maintaining store hours, (2) providing parking facilities, (3) handling customer complaints, (4) supplying information and assistance, and (5) furnishing product display facilities.

Expected services are not essential for the retailer to operate but are expected by consumers. Delivery, credit, and alterations are three services that consumers expect from appliance, furniture, and clothing retailers, respectively. **Optional services** are neither necessary to the retailer's operation nor expected by the customers. Although not as important as essential and expected services, optional services can

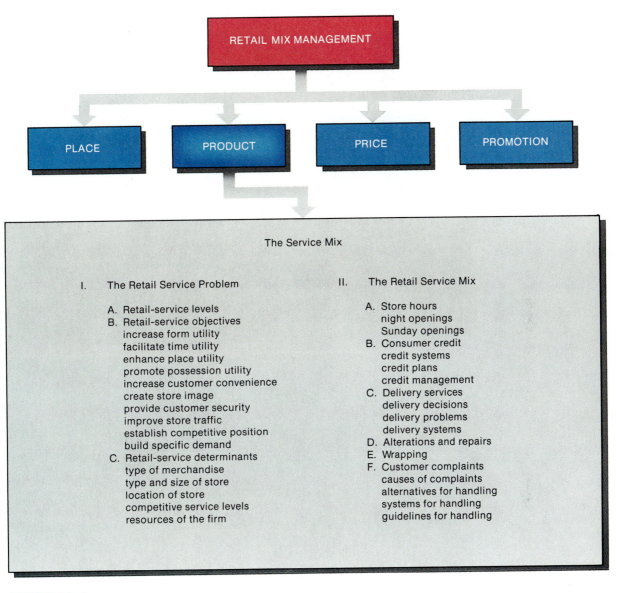

FIGURE 14–1
Developing and implementing the service mix

help a retailer develop a unique service offering and thereby distinguish itself. For example, "Rich's in Atlanta is offering automobile leasing . . . open and closed leasing contracts are available and financing is arranged. . . . Woodward & Lothrop has gone into the apartment-finding business in Washington, D.C., and environs. . . . Marshall Field has a corporate gift service."[3] McDonald's added stock repeater boards in selected restaurants where business people make up most of the morning trade.[4]

Retail Service Levels

A **service level** is the extent to which a retailer will provide consumers with "extra" help in purchasing a product. The level of service is a function of the type and number of services the retailer provides and the terms and conditions under which they are

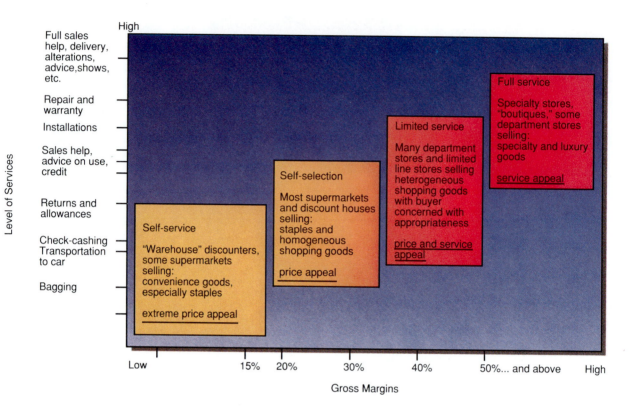

FIGURE 14–2
Retail service levels

FIGURE 14–3
Winning and losing in
the retail service game

Winning Service Retailers
Are noticeably more friendly, courteous and really care about customer satisfaction
Go out of their way to understand customer needs
Consider the smallest detail as critical
Know the business exceedingly well: Its products, its services, its procedures, and
how to get things done quickly and accurately
Shine under pressure, especially in solving customer problems
Adopt integrity as their byword
Exhibit genuine appreciation for patronage

Losing Service Retailers
Dehumanize the service delivery interaction by inattention or plastic profession-
alism
Regard questions or service requests as interruptions or nuisances
Often do not keep promises
Are poor troubleshooters and unskilled in rectifying problems promptly
Appear disorganized, inefficient, and waste the customer's time without noticeable
regret
Communicate in vague language

Source: George A. Rieder, " 'Show Me' : The Secret to Building a Service-Minded Culture," *Retailing Issues Letter*
(Center for Retailing Studies, Texas A&M University, June 1986):1.

provided (see Figure 14–2). Service levels range along a continuum from a low to a high service level. A low-service–level retailer offers only services that are essential to its operation. Although these services are typically essential to the consumer's purchase of the product, some retailers even assess a separate charge for them. "Over the last 20 years, prices for services have risen about 80% more than prices for goods . . . since automation has squeezed labor out of the manufacturing process, goods have become cheap and services expensive."[5] At the other end of the continuum, high-service–level retailers offer consumers expected and optional services. At this level, retailers offer all essential and expected services free of charge; optional services may entail a separate assessment. In addition to the number, type, and conditions of services, a number of differentiating characteristics separate the service winners from the service losers (Figure 14–3).

Retail Service Objectives

Increasing Form Utility

Retailers often receive products from suppliers that require final adjustments and assembly. Additional form-creating services that retailers offer include altering and tailoring for clothing products, installing appliances and home furnishings, engraving and personalizing jewelry, and assembling lawn and garden equipment.

Facilitating Time Utility

For some consumers the right time is now; they want immediate gratification. Consumer credit and extended store hours are two services retailers offer to create time utility. Other consumers are more concerned with saving time; for them, retailers can add time utility to their product mix by accepting telephone and mail orders or by providing carry-out services. Layaway services also add time utility by permitting the consumer to reserve a purchase for some future time when payment is more convenient. To strengthen its time utility service mix, K mart has introduced an automated layaway system. This computer-based system generates the layaway contract, handles customer payments, and maintains layaway records.[6] Finally, storage service (e.g., for furs) provides consumers with safe places to keep merchandise for future use.

Enhancing Place Utility

The best way to add place utility to a product mix is through convenient locations. Delivery services also form an essential part of some retailers' total product. Without home deliveries, most bulky products (e.g., furniture and appliances) would have no value to consumers who have no means to transport them. Some retailers offer catering services to enhance their products' place value.

Promoting Possession Utility

Possession utility is the satisfaction consumers receive from owning and using a product. To promote possession utility, retailers must provide consumers with information to facilitate the exchange of ownership process. Personal selling, fashion shows, information booths, complaint desks, bridal registries, and consultants are some of the informational services retailers offer. Additionally, retailers provide credit, cash, personal checks, and tender itemized receipts (an itemized list of products purchased by name or brand model, size, per-unit price, number of items purchased, date and time of purchase, and basic store information).

Increasing Customer Convenience

Services that provide customer convenience and comfort include packaging, bagging, free parking, check cashing, restaurants, snack bars, restrooms, lounges, parcel checking, push carts, water fountains, and complimentary coffee. Any service that helps customers get into the store, travel around the store, and stay in the store not only enhances customers' convenience but also increases the likelihood of planned purchases as well as additional, unplanned purchases. Shoppers at California-based Lucky Stores who want to pay in cash no longer have to withdraw money from their wallets or suffer through a time-consuming check-approval process. Instead, using a debit card, in just seven seconds customers can pay a retailer directly out of their checking accounts via an electronic funds transfer.[7]

Creating a Store Image

A retailer can use the service mix to pursue one of several image strategies. By offering a *full range of services,* the retailer can promote the image of being a full-service store with quality merchandise and prestige prices. Conversely, the retailer can choose to offer only services that are essential to the exchange process, thereby creating a no-frills, low-price image.

Providing Customer Security

Restroom attendants, properly lighted stores and parking facilities, and security guards all enhance the customer's feeling of a safe and secure environment. Perhaps equally important to most customers is product security, provided by such services as warranties, return privileges, allowances, and maintenance contracts.

Improving Store Traffic

Retailers frequently incorporate into their mix services intended solely to generate additional traffic through their stores. For example, some stores provide (1) rooms for public and private meetings; (2) space for various types of exhibits; (3) rental services for products that might not be related to their product mix; (4) post office, utility bill collection, and entertainment ticket facilities; (5) license bureaus; and (6) various types of professional services (e.g., tax, health, and personal care). All these services tend to draw into the store customers who might not otherwise be attracted. Macy's in San Francisco created the Hospitality Room for conventioneers who are visiting the city. These traffic-building services range from offering refreshments to shopping assistance.[8]

Establishing Competitive Position

Retailers can use services to establish either competitive parity or to create a competitive edge. To remain competitive, retailers offer many services because they are essential to the retailer's operation, competitors offer them, or customers expect them. To gain a competitive edge, some retailers offer services that are not essential to their operations or expected by consumers. A distinctive service mix can create competitive benefits that are long lasting and reasonably difficult to imitate.

Building Specific Demand

Although most services contribute either directly or indirectly to total demand, retailers often build demand for a particular product line or item by offering services that focus consumers' attention on that product. Many cosmetic companies, including

Offering an on-site cooking course can help a retailer generate store traffic as well as promote sales.

Elizabeth Arden and Shiseido, use computer simulation to provide their customers with high-tech information about skin and hair needs. Shiseido's Makeup Simulator "is able to give the customer an on-screen make-over, change hair styles . . . and add henna or highlights without physical application of the product to the customer."[9] Because of the tremendous increase in the number of "do it yourselfers," some home centers offer instructional services and classes on how to repair plumbing, hang a light fixture, and so on to promote related product lines.

Retail Service Determinants

Several factors enter into the decision about what service level to offer. Guided by the previously discussed service objectives, the retailer should consider at least the following five determinants: type of merchandise, type and size of store, location of the store, service levels of competitors, and resources of the firm.

Type of Merchandise

The type of merchandise a retailer carries dictates to some extent the services consumers expect and desire. The physical and psychological attributes of a product are perhaps the two most important determinants of what the retailer's service level should be. For example, consumers expect home delivery and installation when they buy furniture and appliance products; the products' bulk makes these necessary services for most consumers. Also, when buying appliances and many other mechanical products, most consumers look for availability of repair services before making a purchase decision. Warranties and maintenance contracts also are services most retailers offer with these types of merchandise to reduce consumers' perceived risk.

Type and Size of Store

Consumers tend to associate certain services with specific types of retail operations. Consumers generally expect department stores to be full-service retailers, whereas they perceive the discounter as either a cash-and-carry retailer or at most a limited-service retailer. Consumers expect lawn and garden shops to provide information on when and how to care for plants, jewelry stores to repair watches and appraise jewelry, and supermarkets to provide shopping carts, check cashing, bagging, and carryout service. Also, consumers look for a higher level of services from prestige- or status-conscious stores than from stores that appeal to the mass market.

A store's physical *size* also influences what service level is feasible; some services require substantial space. The type and number of services that a small retailer with limited space can offer must be restricted to those that are essential to operation or at least those that can be provided with a minimal spatial commitment.

Location of Store

A store's location can influence types of services. Depending on its location, the retailer should consider services that (1) overcome a locational deficiency, (2) fit into a locational surrounding, and (3) intensify a locational advantage. For example, retailers in central business districts of major metropolitan areas include certain services to overcome the deficiencies associated with their locations. Downtown locations often lack adequate on-site parking facilities; as a service to their customers, many such retailers arrange for free parking at public and private facilities.

To illustrate how a retailer's service levels are influenced by locational setting, consider the service requirements of some specialty shopping centers. A retailer that elects to locate in a center where quality-oriented, high-service–level retailers operate will normally have to offer a similar level of service; otherwise, the operation will not appeal to the type of customer attracted to the cluster.

A final example of a service included in a service mix to enhance a locational advantage might be a quality lakeside restaurant providing complementary pre- or postdinner cruises aboard a paddleboat.

Competitive Service Levels

Many retailers prefer to engage in *nonprice competition,* of which one form is competing with service levels. Unfortunately, this kind of competition creates a dilemma; exceeding competitors' service levels can incur additional costs that lead to higher operating margins and thus greater vulnerability to price competition. On the other hand, if the retailer offers services below that of other retailers, it is not competitive in the area of services. As a general rule, the retailer should offer a service level comparable to that of competing operations of a similar type.

Resources of the Firm

Services require resources. Each service must be based on adequate facilities and equipment, trained personnel, and sufficient capital investment. In addition to having adequate resources, the retailer must decide whether a service offering is worth the resources necessary to making the service available. To justify an investment, the retailer must determine that consumers need a given service and that any resulting sales volume more than offsets the investment.

The service mix includes all those nonproduct "extras" retailers offer consumers to enhance the merchandise mix and to facilitate purchases. The major components of the service mix include store hours, credit plans, delivery, alterations and repairs, wrapping, and customer complaints.

**THE RETAIL
SERVICE MIX**

Store Hours

The retailer in today's market does not work an eight-to-five job. Because of changing consumer life-styles, increasing competitive conditions, various legal restrictions, and additional operational requirements, the retailer must provide store hours that are convenient to the customers in its area.

Evening Hours

Evening hours from Monday through Saturday have become commonplace for most supermarkets and other retailers of necessity goods. Many supermarkets are now open twenty-four hours a day; since many supermarkets are staffed all night with stocking personnel, around-the-clock openings can be accomplished within reasonable cost constraints.[10] Likewise, for many mass merchandisers operating in community and regional shopping centers, evening hours have become an expected service. The duration of hours ranges from all night to an eight, nine, or ten P.M. closing. In part, night openings are the retailer's response to changing life-styles of consumers who find it more convenient and enjoyable to shop at night. Evening hours not only increase the cost of doing business (labor, utilities) but also increase personnel problems (individuals who do not want to work at night) and security risks (as exemplified by the number of night robberies at convenience-food stores).

Sunday Hours

The issue of **Sunday hours** is similar to night hours in all respects except for the social, religious, and legal restrictions imposed in some parts of the country. Many state and local governments have enacted laws, often referred to as "blue laws," that determine (1) whether Sunday openings are allowed, (2) what types of products can be sold on Sundays (necessities vs. nonnecessities), and (3) when and how many hours stores can be open (e.g., from one to six P.M.). In addition to legal restrictions, retailers should consider the effect Sunday hours have on their stores' images. In some communities, a retailer's image could be damaged by a Sunday opening.

Consumer Credit

"Charge it!" "Buy now, pay later!" "Easy terms available!" "Only $10 down and $10 a month!" "Financing is available!" "Four years to pay!" These notices proclaim that credit has become a basic way of life for many U.S. consumers. To a substantial majority, credit has become either an essential or an expected part of the retailer's service mix. The question for most retailers is not whether to offer credit, but what type of credit to offer.[11]

Attitudes toward credit depend to a certain extent on social class. In a study of credit card usage, researchers found that lower classes used credit cards for installment purchase, restricted use of credit cards to purchases of durable and necessity goods, and tended to search for retailers that honored their particular credit cards. In contrast, the researchers learned that upper-class consumers view credit cards more as a convenience, use them in making luxury-goods purchases, and do not seek out stores that accept their particular credit cards.

Credit Systems

The retailer can elect one of several different credit systems: in-house credit, third-party credit, and private-label credit.

In-house credit system. An **in-house credit system** is owned, operated, and managed by the retail firm. Retailers offer credit services for a variety of reasons: (1) consumers expect the service, (2) store image will be enhanced, (3) many consumers cannot afford the retailer's assortment of merchandise unless they are offered credit, (4) competitors offer credit arrangements, and (5) market and economic conditions dictate the need for credit. Offering an in-house credit plan has advantages and disadvantages for most retailers.[12] Advantages include the following:

☐ *Customer attraction.* Stores that offer credit services tend to attract customers who are more interested in product quality, store reputation, and service offerings and less interested in prices.

☐ *Customer loyalty.* Credit-granting stores more easily build repeat business, since credit customers tend to be more loyal than cash customers.

☐ *Customer goodwill.* Credit-granting stores generally have a more personal relationship with their customers and therefore become the first place the customer shops for a particular purchase.

☐ *Increased sales.* Credit services increase total sales volume because credit customers tend to buy more goods and pay higher prices than customers who do not use credit.

☐ *Sales stabilization.* Credit sales are more evenly spread throughout the month, whereas cash sales correspond more closely with those times immediately following paydays.

☐ *Market information.* Credit applications provide considerable amounts of information (age, sex, income, occupation, etc.) on the credit consumer; credit records can reveal a history of what, when, and where (which department) the customer bought.

☐ *Promotional effort.* Because credit customers are known to be customers of the store, they are an excellent foundation on which to build a mailing or telephone list for special promotions; additionally, the monthly statement credit customers receive is an effective vehicle for promotional literature.

In addition to these advantages, retailers realize the disadvantages associated with offering credit services. The most commonly cited disadvantages are those related to increased costs:

☐ *Higher operating expenses* result from additional facilities, personnel, equipment, and communications expenses necessary to provide credit services.

☐ *Costs of fees and commissions* paid to outside credit agencies that provide part or all of the retailer's credit services.

☐ *Tied-up funds* diverted to accounts receivable, thereby forcing the retailer to borrow working capital.

☐ *Bad debts,* losses from uncollectables, are part of the risk of providing credit services.

These additional costs are acceptable if they can be covered by offsetting revenues. Some retailers realize a substantial profit from their charges for credit services; Sears, for example, makes substantial profits on its retail credit operations.

Third-party credit system.   As an alternative to offering in-store credit services, many retailers use **third-party credit systems,** accepting one or more of the credit cards issued by outside institutions. Often referred to as third-party cards, the most common types are those issued by banks (MasterCard and Visa) and entertainment-card companies (American Express, Diner's Club, and Carte Blanche). Gasoline companies also issue credit cards that consumers can use at stations carrying their brands. Some shopping malls have begun to offer a mall credit card; South Coast Plaza in Costa Mesa and Fashion Island Mall in Newport Beach, both in California, are two such examples.[13]

Major advantages to accepting third-party cards are that retailers (1) do not have the problems of establishing and maintaining a credit department; (2) are relieved of the unpleasant tasks of investigating credit applications, billing customers, and pursuing collections; (3) can offer credit to consumers who otherwise would not qualify (e.g., out-of-town consumers) and thereby make sales they might have lost; and (4) can maintain a steady cash flow, since financial institutions convert credit card sales quickly and regularly into cash minus agreed-on service charges. The retailer does, however, have certain responsibilities in accepting and processing credit card sales, including filling out sales drafts properly, cooperating with financial institutions in identifying expired and stolen cards, obtaining authorization for charges over certain purchase ceilings, and submitting sales drafts to the credit agency within an agreed-on time.

The chief disadvantages for retailers that accept credit cards are the costs of the service and the depersonalization of relationships with customers. Credit agencies charge rates varying with the retailer's potential credit sales volume and several market and competitive conditions. Since the rate is negotiable, the retailer should make every effort to obtain the best possible terms. Depersonalization comes in the form of reduced store loyalty (the customer can shop anywhere the credit card is accepted) and consumers' lost feeling of "belonging" to a store in which they have a personal account.

Private-label system.   A **private-label credit system** is one that retailers offer under their name but that a bank operates and manages. The retail firm realizes most of the benefits associated with in-house credit systems while avoiding many of the problems associated with credit management. Typically, the cost of this type of system is comparable to most in-house systems, and it is an attractive option for the retailer that has had difficulty turning its credit operation into a profit center.

Credit Plans

Depending on the type of credit system, one or more of three different types of credit plans will be available to the consumer: the open account, the installment plan, and revolving credit. The retailer's decision about which and how many types of credit plans to offer depends on the customer's need for a particular type of credit balanced against the retailer's need for cash for operating expenses.

Open account. Often referred to as the "regular charge" or "open book credit," the **open-account credit** plan allows customers to buy merchandise and pay for it within a specific time period without finance charges or interest. Usually, the customer is expected to pay the full amount within thirty days of the billing date, although some retailers extend the due date to either sixty or ninety days to promote special occasions or to distinguish their credit services from the thirty-day services their competitors offer. This **deferred billing** is often used during the Christmas season as a sales promotion tool and as an incentive to finalize the sale of a major purchase (i.e., the appliance dealer who offers "ninety days same as cash"). Beyond the due date, if full payment is not received, the retailer can assess a finance charge. The retailer usually grants an open account without requiring the customer to make a down payment or to put up collateral to secure the purchase. Given the free nature of the service and its lack of formal security, retailers generally reduce both credit costs and risks by limiting open-account credit to customers who have established good credit records.

Installment credit. Most customers would find it impossible to purchase large-ticket items such as automobiles, furniture, and appliances if they could not make small down payments and spread the additional payments over several months or years. The **installment-credit** plan allows consumers to pay their total purchase price (less down payment) in equal installment payments over a specified time period. Usually, equal installment payments are due monthly, although weekly and quarterly payments are optional. Retailers prefer to receive a down payment on installment purchases that equals or exceeds the initial depreciation of the product. Some retailers require only a minimal down payment or no down payment to make the sale.

Installment-credit arrangements are legal contracts between retailers and consumers. Terms and conditions include the total amount of each payment, the number of payments, and the dates the payments are due. In addition, the contract specifies financial charges (interest, service, insurance) and penalties for late or nonpayment. Retailers carry installment accounts in one of three ways: conditional sales agreements, chattel mortgages, and lease agreements. In the **conditional sales agreement,** the title of the goods passes to the consumer conditional on full payment. The retailer can repossess the product and obtain a judgment against the consumer for any lost product value and expenses resulting from repossession. Retailers prefer the conditional sales contract since it gives them the most protection from loss.

In a **chattel mortgage agreement,** title passes to the customer when the contract is signed, but the product is secured by a lien against it for the unpaid balance. **Lease agreements** are contracts in which the customer rents a product in the present with the option to buy in the future. Consumers usually pay periodic rent, which is applied toward the purchase price.

Revolving credit. Revolving credit incorporates some of the features of both the open-account and installment plans. Of the several variations of revolving credit plans, the two most common are the fixed-term and the option-term. The **fixed-term revolving credit** plan requires the customer to pay a fixed amount on any unpaid balance at regularly scheduled intervals (usually monthly) until the amount is paid in full. Under this plan, customers have a credit limit, such as $500, and may make credit purchases up to this limit as long as they continue to pay the agreed-on fixed payment (e.g., $50) each month. People who use fixed-term revolving accounts are usually assessed a finance charge (e.g., 1.5 percent per month, or 18 percent annually) on the unpaid balance.

Option-term revolving credit gives customers two payment options. They can either pay the full amount of the bill within a specified number of days (typically 30) and avoid any finance charges, or they can make at least a minimum payment and be assessed finance charges on the unpaid balance. As with the fixed-term account, a credit line is established and customers are free to make purchases up to the established limit.

Credit Management

A retailer that decides to offer in-store credit as part of the service mix must develop a credit-management system. Although the wide range of credit management activities is beyond the scope of this text, two activities essential to successful credit management are (1) forming sound policies for granting credit and (2) determining good procedures for collecting credit accounts.

Granting credit. Before granting credit to individuals, retailers should first request that applicants complete a credit application. Whether the retailer personally investigates the applicant or uses one of the many credit bureaus, it should evaluate each individual on the basis of the **three C's of credit**: character, capacity, and capital.

Character in a credit sense refers to attributes that distinguish one individual from another in meeting obligations. Desirable traits include maturity and honesty—characteristics that indicate willingness to accept responsibility (to pay bills) regardless of the circumstances. Personal interviews, reference checks, and the applicant's credit history help the retailer evaluate this attribute.

Capacity is the measure of an individual's earning power and ability to pay. A credit applicant's income is important not only in deciding whether to extend credit, but also in determining how much credit to extend. The third indication of credit worthiness is *capital* (i.e., the applicant's tangible assets). Accumulation of capital suggests that the applicant is capable of managing financial affairs and gives the retailer hope of recovering losses if it becomes necessary to sue the customer for nonpayment.

A more sophisticated system for screening credit applications is a **credit-scoring system**—the process of replacing lending with scientific scoring. The procedures for developing a credit-scoring system follow:

> *Identifying* is an examination of good and bad credit accounts to identify characteristics associated with individuals who are good or poor credit risks. Figure 14–4 is one list of general characteristics that might be used in developing a credit-scoring system.
> *Weighting* is the weighting of each characteristic (by assigning point values) based on its ability to discriminate between good and poor credit risks.
> *Scoring* is the evaluation of credit applications by adding the points received on the various application characteristics to arrive at a total score.
> *Accepting/Rejecting* is accepting or rejecting a credit application based on minimum point score.
> *Limiting* is setting a credit limit based on the total points assigned to the application; the higher the score, the higher the credit limit.[14]

Credit collections. Most credit accounts are handled through a routine, efficient billing system without any collection problems. When credit-collection problems

FIGURE 14–4

Characteristics used in developing credit-scoring systems

Telephone at home	Bank savings account
Own/rent living accommodations	Bank checking account
Age	Zip code of residence
Time at home address	Age of automobile
Industry in which employed	Make and model of automobile
Time with employer	Geographic area of United States
Time with previous employer	Finance company reference
Type of employment	Debt-to-income ratio
Number of dependents	Monthly rent/mortgage payment
Types of credit reference	Family size
Income	Telephone area code
Savings and loan references	Location of relatives
Trade-union membership	Number of children
Age difference between man and wife	Number of other dependents
Telephone at work	Ownership of life insurance
Length of product being purchased	Width of product being purchased
First letter of last name	

Source: Noel Capon, "Credit Scoring Systems: A Critical Analysis," *Journal of Marketing* 46 (Spring, 1982): 85.

(such as slow payment, nonpayment, or incorrect payment) occur, the retailer must have policies and procedures to handle them.[15] Any credit-collection procedure entails several basic steps. First, credit accounts must be *reviewed* periodically and routinely to identify delinquent accounts. Immediate identification of delinquent accounts is critical because the more overdue the account becomes, the harder it is to collect.[16]

Second, the retailer should make every effort to *determine the reason* for the delinquency. If the customer faces unexpected financial problems, the retailer should strive to reach some mutually agreeable arrangement that will not only satisfy the debt but also preserve the debtor as a customer. On the other hand, if the customer has no intention of repaying the debt or is a poor manager of finances, the retailer should initiate actions to settle the account, either by requiring the consumer to make payments with penalties on a definite time schedule or by turning the account over to a collection agency. Eventually, a retailer realizes that some customers are no longer desirable either as credit customers or cash customers (typically, a customer whose account is far overdue will avoid the store and take cash business elsewhere). Thus, in general, credit-collection methods must be flexible enough to meet specific situations.

Delivery Service

Delivery service is one of the most controversial aspects of a service mix. In general, delivery service is difficult to plan, execute, and control. Before including delivery service in the service mix, the retailer must have a clear understanding of when to offer it, what problems it entails, under which terms and conditions it can be offered, and what type of delivery system is most appropriate to the operation.

Delivery-Service Decision

Many circumstances justify including delivery services in the service mix. (1) Delivery is practically indispensable in retailing such bulky products as furniture, appliances, building materials, and lawn products (trees and shrubs). (2) In large urban areas where customers traveling by public transportation are greatly inconvenienced by taking purchases with them, delivery is often necessary. (3) Retailers that actively solicit telephone and mail orders must provide home-delivery services. (4) Delivery services for emergency goods, such as prescription drugs, are perceived by consumers as a valuable addition to the retailer's service mix. (5) For retailers engaged in institutional sales (such as schools and hospitals), sales frequently are made and prices quoted on the basis of delivering the product to the institution's facilities. (6) Some retailers have a prestige image to protect and therefore must include delivery services in their merchandise mix.

Finally, delivery services can create a competitive advantage by providing extra time and place convenience. Domino's Pizza, Inc., has built an entire chain based on the firm's willingness to deliver. Quick Flix Video has gone one up on Domino's by offering home delivery for a movie/pizza combination.[17]

Delivery-Service Problems

The problems associated with delivery service are substantial. One of the most difficult problems is immediacy. When consumers purchase a product, they want immediate possession, with delivery either the same day or within a short period. It is virtually impossible for the retailer to provide immediate delivery without increasing costs.

A second major problem involves "not-at-homes." Delivery personnel face a recurring problem of what to do when the customer is not at home and must (1) leave the package on the doorstep, (2) leave the package with a neighbor, or (3) call back. Some retailers attempt to reduce this problem by telephoning the customer before delivery.

A third problem in offering delivery services is the variations in demand. The day-to-day, week-to-week, and month-to-month fluctuations in demand for delivery services seriously undermine management planning; to be always ready to handle peak delivery times is cost-prohibitive. Additional problems include damage in transit, inaccurate deliveries, and problems of security.

Delivery-Service Systems

Retailers can elect to use either an in-store system, an independent system, or a combination of the two. Each has its advantages and disadvantages. **In-store delivery systems** can be either wholly owned and operated by an individual store (private store systems) or partially owned and operated with other stores (cooperative store systems). Private in-store systems offer numerous advantages. Of all the delivery systems, they give the retailer the greatest level of control over delivery operations and the greatest flexibility in adjusting services to customer needs. The retailer can personalize delivery vehicles with its name, slogan, and other messages, and the delivery personnel work for the retailer. Properly trained delivery personnel can provide the retailer with feedback from present customers (complaints and messages) and prospects for new sales opportunities (maintenance contracts). Unfortunately, private systems are the most expensive to establish and maintain, and many retailers simply cannot afford to operate them.

Independent delivery systems are owned and operated independently from the retailer. They offer their services either on a contractual basis (consolidated systems) or on an open-to-the-general-public basis (parcel post and express services). Consolidated systems are independent firms that, for a fee, will deliver a store's packages; the fee depends on the number, size, weight, and handling characteristics of the packages. The typical consolidated operation of an independent system is to pick up the store's packages on a regularly scheduled basis, take the packages to a central facility where they are sorted for efficient routing, and deliver the packages to customers on a specific time schedule. Most consolidated delivery firms perform cash on delivery (COD) functions, make call backs, and assume full liability for damaged or lost packages. The major limitations of using consolidated services are lack of control over delivery time and inability to monitor the behavior of delivery personnel.

Express services and parcel post serve the needs of the general public. Retailers can resort to these systems when the delivery destination lies outside their delivery-service area.

Alterations and Repairs

Many retailers offer alterations and repairs both as a supplement to the sale of products and as an income-producing service. Consumers expect retailers of expensive clothing to provide alteration services, and retailers of appliances, television sets, automobiles, and other durable goods to provide repair services. Traditionally, retailers offered alteration services as part of a garment's sales price; in recent years, however, retailers have experimented with various types of alteration charges ranging from no charge for minor alterations to partial or full charge for major alterations. To facilitate product-related alterations and to justify their investment in workroom facilities, equipment, and personnel, some retailers have established income-producing tailoring operations. Retailers usually charge customers for repairs on durable goods according to the terms and conditions of product warranties and established store policies. Normally, consumers bear no charge (or at most a minimum charge) for repairs on products still under warranty or that occur within a prescribed period after the purchase date. After the warranty or policy date expires, the retailer charges the consumer for repairs on a profit-making basis. To increase their income from repair services, many chain retailers (such as Sears) offer maintenance contracts on a fixed-fee basis. In addition to creating revenues, maintenance contracts also aid retailers in fully using their repair and service departments.

The retailer that deems it necessary to provide alteration or repair services has two operation alternatives: in-store and out-of-store services. In-store alteration and repair services give the retailer all of the advantages associated with direct control of such activities; however, this alternative also presents numerous management problems and requires substantial capital investments. Out-of-store alterations are subcontracted to private-service retailers specializing in tailoring services. Retailers normally use authorized, local repair services, factory repair services, and other subcontracted private-service firms to do out-of-store repairs. Disadvantages of using out-of-store repair services are lack of control, customer inconvenience, and longer service time.

Wrapping

The three basic types of wrapping services retailers perform are bagging or sacking, store wrap, and gift wrap. Most consumers expect retailers to place purchases in a bag even when the products are prepackaged. **Bagging** (1) facilitates handling (especially when multiple purchases are involved); (2) protects purchases from inclement weather; and (3) preserves the privacy of the customer purchase. Proper bagging takes into account the size, shape, weight, and strength of the bag and the goods that go into it.

Store wrap is the wrapping of customers' purchases in a standard (color and design) wrapping paper or box. Most department and specialty stores offer this service free of charge. Store wrap not only is an additional service for many retailers but also is a way to supplement their stores' advertising programs. The retailer that incorporates its prestige name with store wrap can provide additional purchase incentives for customers who either seek a prestige gift or want their gift receivers to know the present came from a prestige store.

Gift wraps normally incorporate additional wrapping features such as bows and ribbons to distinguish them clearly from store wraps. Because of increased costs of materials and labor, the customer normally is charged an additional fee for gift-wrapping services.

Wrapping services are handled on either a departmental or a centralized basis. **Department wrapping** is performed by either the salesperson who makes the sale or the department cashier and wrapper. The advantages of having the salesperson wrap the merchandise are convenience for the customer, the opportunity for the salesperson to make an extra sale, and enhancement of the store's image through personalized service. Disadvantages of department wrapping are that salespeople must leave their primary job of selling and that salespeople normally do not excel at gift wrapping. Many stores perform **centralized wrapping** at one central location, but many large stores centralize wrapping on each floor. Although more cost-efficient than department wrapping, this system does represent an inconvenience for customers, who must find the wrapping desk and may have to wait in line.

Gift wrapping departments may be centralized on each floor or in one location for the whole store.

Customer Complaints

In 1962, President John F. Kennedy identified four basic consumer rights: "the right to safety, the right to be informed, the right to choose, and the right to be heard." Two of these rights, the right to be heard and to be informed, are key factors in the customer-complaint process. Customers expect to be informed of all operating policies that affect their patronage, and they expect to be heard when they want to register a complaint. While customer complaints typically are viewed negatively, especially if excessive in number, they also can be viewed positively. First, a customer who complains gives the retailer a chance to identify and correct a problem. Second, customer complaints serve as a major source of information regarding the retailer's products, services, and other merchandising activities.

Causes of Complaints

Most customer complaints result from one of three general causes: product-related, service-related, and customer-related difficulties. Product-related causes include the following:

1. *Poor-quality products*—inferior workmanship and materials that cause fading or bleeding colors, shrinking or stretching fabrics, and rusting or tarnishing metals
2. *Damaged products*—merchandise that is chipped, stained, soiled, ripped, spoiled, or scratched
3. *Incorrect products*—merchandise that is either mislabeled according to size and price or mismatched in terms of color and style
4. *Insufficient selection*—out-of-stock merchandise, discontinued merchandise, limited-line merchandise, and new merchandise

Service-related causes involve customer dissatisfaction with sales personnel and services such as checkout, delivery, workroom, and customer accounts. Complaints about sales personnel usually center around the salesperson's (1) *disposition* (indifferent, discourteous, unfriendly, pushy); (2) *incompetence* (lack of product knowledge, poor selling skills, lack of familiarity with store policies); (3) *dishonesty* (unfulfilled promises, false information, additional charges, incorrect change); or (4) *selling methods* (overselling customers by selling them too much of an item or by trading them up to a product they cannot afford). Complaints about delivery services include late, lost, and incorrect deliveries and untidy and unpleasant delivery personnel. Improper alterations, lengthy delays, and overcharges are the chief causes of complaints stemming from workroom services. Finally, improper handling of accounts irritates customers. Errors in billing, receipt of a bill after it has already been paid, and delays in receiving account statements are some of the more irksome problems.

Customers make mistakes; sometimes they are intentional, sometimes they are not. Customer mistakes are also a cause of customer-related complaints. For example, customers may purchase a product thinking it will match or fit another product they own. If it does not, they may want to return it. If the retailer does not issue a refund, then the customer surely will complain. A "change of mind" is another cause of complaint. Customers often change their minds because they later think the product is not really the style, quality, price, or color they wanted. Most consumers consider these legitimate reasons for returning goods, and they expect the retailer to make an exchange or give a refund. Questioning the customer's motives invites further customer complaints.

Alternatives for Handling Complaints

The retailer has several alternatives in handling consumer complaints. They include offering returns and refunds, making product adjustments, price adjustments, and service adjustments, and practicing good customer relations.

Returns and refunds.   Policies on returning merchandise range from "no returns" or "all sales final" to "satisfaction guaranteed or your money back." A retailer that has a no-return policy should make that policy clear by posting signs, printing the policy on sales slips, verbal statements by salespeople, or a combination of these means.

Retailers that guarantee satisfaction must decide whether to refund the customer's money in the form of cash or as a credit slip. Some retailers prefer to give cash refunds because they feel this policy creates greater customer satisfaction, relieves the store of further obligation, and frees store personnel to perform more productive work. Proponents of the credit-slip refund believe this method is better because it maintains contact with the customer and ensures a future sale and at least part of the profit from the original sale. As with the no-return policy, retailers should inform customers of any conditions or restrictions on returning merchandise and receiving refunds before the purchase is made.

Product adjustments.   Complaints about incorrect products can easily be handled by allowing customers to exchange the incorrect product for a correct one. By offering to clean, repair, alter, or exchange products, retailers can satisfy most customers' complaints about damaged products.

One way to handle consumer complaints about poor-quality products is to substitute a higher-quality product for the poor- quality product. This policy is especially appropriate when the product sold was, in fact, of lower quality than the price suggested, or when the retailer wants to protect a quality product and store image. Finally, complaints concerning insufficient selection can be handled by either (1) agreeing to stock the product, (2) explaining why the product cannot be stocked, then offering an appropriate substitute, or (3) directing the customer to a store that stocks the desired product.

Price adjustments.   Price adjustments can either be given as an allowance or as a discount on the purchase price of the product. Since it is not always possible to exchange or adjust a product that has been damaged, the retailer often can satisfy customers by reducing the price of the product to compensate for the damages. Price adjustments also can include free merchandise and discount coupons. When the retailer is obviously at fault, price adjustments are generally the most effective way to show the customer that the store is making an extra effort to correct the problem.

Service adjustments.   Retailers can handle service adjustments in much the same way as price adjustments. For example, if a consumer says that a garment alteration is unsatisfactory, the retailer should make the additional alteration free of charge. Or if a billing error shows the customer paid a bill late, any late charges or interest penalties the retailer would normally charge should be dropped.

Customer relations.   Some situations generate customer complaints for which none of the preceding adjustments are appropriate. A rude salesperson is one example. In such cases, the customer may just want to be heard or to "blow off steam." Whether the complaint is justified or not, good customer relations dictate the retailer listen carefully and politely, reassure the customer, and apologize for the situation. Who knows? The individual might be a very good customer who simply had a bad day and was set off by a minor incident. By allowing the customer to register the complaint and by handling that complaint professionally, the retailer keeps a good customer.

Systems for Handling Complaints

Customer complaints in small stores usually are handled by the store owner or manager; large stores, however, must develop a system for handling complaints. Three alternatives are the centralized system, the decentralized system, and a combination system.

Centralized complaint system.   All customer complaints are referred to a central office or complaint desk under a **centralized complaint system**. This arrangement allows the retailer to use personnel who are trained in the art of handling people. Also, the retailer can implement a more uniform policy for handling complaints and making adjustments and management receives more accurate information on complaints than if a particular department reported the complaint itself. Additional benefits of a centralized complaint system are (1) complaints are handled privately and not aired in public, and (2) complaint records can be standardized, analyzed, and used by management to correct causes of complaints. Shortcomings associated with central complaint systems focus on the fact that some customers prefer to deal with the department or salesperson from which they made their original purchase.

Decentralized complaint system.   A **decentralized complaint system** handles customer complaints at the department level. Department salespersons usually handle minor complaints and adjustments while the department manager is responsible for major complaints. Although customers generally prefer this type of system, it has its disadvantages. First, there can be considerable variation in how complaints are handled within and between departments. Second, many complaints are not reported to central management, and much of what is reported is biased. Third, commissioned salespersons are reluctant to make certain adjustments that might affect their commissions. Finally, most department personnel are not trained to handle complaints or to make adjustments.

Combination system.   In an attempt to gain the advantages of both the centralized and decentralized systems, many retailers employ a combination of the two. Customers with complaints go directly to the department involved, where most adjustments are made. When major adjustments are necessary or when the customer is dissatisfied with the department adjustment, complaining customers are directed to a central complaint office.

Guidelines for Handling Complaints

How a store handles a customer's complaint can, in many cases, be more important to the customer than the actual adjustment. Many retailers find that if they display an immediate and sincere willingness to be fair, the customer will reciprocate by being willing to accept any reasonable adjustment. There are no absolute rules or steps for handling all complaints and all customers, but the general guidelines presented in Figure 14–5 are appropriate "do's" and "don'ts" for most situations.

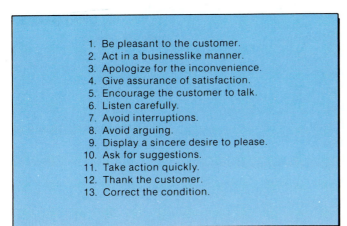

FIGURE 14–5
Guidelines for handling
complaints

1. Be pleasant to the customer.
2. Act in a businesslike manner.
3. Apologize for the inconvenience.
4. Give assurance of satisfaction.
5. Encourage the customer to talk.
6. Listen carefully.
7. Avoid interruptions.
8. Avoid arguing.
9. Display a sincere desire to please.
10. Ask for suggestions.
11. Take action quickly.
12. Thank the customer.
13. Correct the condition.

SUMMARY

Retailers offer services under two sets of circumstances. Primary services are offered as part of the principal business function. Complementary services are offered in conjunction with or as a supplement to a basic product mix. The basic problems in developing a service mix are which and how many services to offer.

Services can be classified according to their relative importance to the consumer. Essential services are basic and necessary to a particular retail operation. Expected services are not absolutely essential for operating reasons but are necessary for customer patronage reasons: The consumer expects them to be available. Optional services are neither necessary to the retailer's operation nor expected by the retailer's customers. They include all other services that distinguish the retailer's service mix.

The service mix can be developed to meet any number of objectives. Some of the more common service objectives are to (1) increase form utility, (2) facilitate time utility, (3) enhance place utility, (4) promote possession utility, (5) increase consumer convenience, (6) create a desirable store image, (7) provide customer security, (8) increase store traffic, (9) establish a competitive position, and (10) build demand. In deciding what level of service to offer, the retailer considers type of merchandise, type and size of the store, location of the store, service level of competitors, and the firm's resources.

The retailer's service mix can incorporate any number of services. Services basic to most retailing operations include store hours, credit, delivery, alterations and repairs, wrapping, and customer complaints.

KEY TERMS AND CONCEPTS

bagging
centralized complaint system
centralized wrapping system
chattel mortgage agreement
complementary services
conditional sales agreement
credit-scoring system

decentralized complaint system
deferred billing
department wrapping system
essential services
evening hours
expected services
fixed-term revolving credit

gift wrap

independent delivery system

in-house credit system

installment credit

in-store delivery system

lease agreement

open-account credit

optional services

option-term revolving credit

primary services

private-label credit system

service level

Sunday hours

store wrap

third-party credit system

three C's of credit

REVIEW QUESTIONS

1. Distinguish between a primary-service retailer and one that offers complementary services.
2. How are services classified? Describe the three classes of services and their relationship to the retailer's operation. Give examples of each type of service.
3. Identify the services the retailer should offer to increase form utility.
4. Which services might the retailer offer to promote possession utility?
5. Describe the services the retailer should use to build specific demand.
6. How does store location influence the retailer's service mix?
7. Identify the two chief disadvantages for retailers that accept third-party credit cards.
8. Does a private-label credit system differ from in-store and third-party systems? How?
9. Briefly describe the three types of credit plans.
10. List the three C's of credit and describe each.
11. Outline the basic procedures for establishing a credit-scoring system.
12. What problems face the retailer that develops and operates a home-delivery system?
13. Characterize the three basic types of wrapping services.
14. Identify the major product-, service-, and customer-related causes of complaints.
15. Describe methods for handling customer complaints.

ENDNOTES

1. Leonard L. Berry, "Editors Corner," *Retailing Issues Letter,* Center for Retailing Studies, Texas A&M University (December 1986): 4.
2. See Duane L. Davis, Joseph P. Guiltinan, and Wesley H. Jones, "Service Characteristics, Consumer Search, and the Classification of Retail Services," *Journal of Retailing* 55 (Fall, 1979): 3–23.
3. "Retailers Expand Old Services, Add New Ones to Attract Customers," *Stores* (October, 1984): 52–53.
4. Peter Geiger, "Stockquotes Served With Hamburgers," *Akron Beacon Journal,* 28 Oct. 1987, F-1.
5. Joan Berger, "In the Service Sector, Nothing Is 'Free' Anymore," *Business Week,* 8 June 1987, 144.
6. "K-Mart Automates Layaway," *Chain Store Age Executive* (September 1987): 78, 80.
7. "Debit Card Systems Gain Momentum," *Chain Store Age Executive* (January 1987): 115.
8. Dinah Witchel, "The Store As Tourist Lure," *Stores* (May 1987): 112.
9. Sandra Lee Breisch, "Cosmetic Beauty Is in the Eye of the Computer." *Advertising Age,* 2 March 1987, S-12.
10. David J. Jefferson, "Southern California Supermarket Chains to Clash by Night," *Wall Street Journal,* 23 March 1988.
11. See Robert Klonoski, "Trends in Retail Payment Methods," *Retail Control* (September 1985): 46–61.

12. See Jules Abend, "More Valuable Plastic," *Stores* (February 1988): 78–85, 88, 90, 93.

13. See Jim Seale, "Don't Go to the Mall Without It," *Stores* (May 1985): 44.

14. See Noel Capon, "Credit Scoring Systems: A Critical Analysis," *Journal of Marketing* 46 (Spring 1982): 82–91.

15. See Jules Abend, "Repair Job for Shoppers?" *Stores* (April 1988): 100–112; "Turmoil in Credit: What's Next?" *Stores* (April 1987): 86–90, 93; and "New Ways to Cut Risk," *Stores* (September 1987): 76.

16. See Peter McAllister, "'Early Warnings' on Delinquencies," *Retail Control* (March 1986): 16–27.

17. Joe Agnew, "Home Delivery Amenities Offered as Video-rental Outlets Seek Positioning," *Marketing News,* 10 April 1987, 34.

Abend, Jules. "Collections: Making 'em Pay." *Stores* (April 1985): 32–38, 40.

Abend, Jules. "Making Plastic Pay." (February 1986).

Abend, Jules. "New Ways to Cut Risk." (September 1987): 76–90.

Barnes, Nora Ganim. "The Seventh Day: Extended Hours for Shoppers." In *Developments in Marketing Science, Proceedings,* edited by J. D. Lindquist, 311–16. Academy of Marketing Science, 1984.

Bates, Albert D. "Rethinking the Service Offer." *Retailing Issues Letter* II (December 1986): 1–4.

Bates, Albert D., and Didion, Jamie G. "Special Services Can Personalize Retail Environment." *Marketing News,* 12 April 1985, 13.

Bearden, William O., and Teel, Jesse E. "An Investigation of Personal Influence on Consumer Complaining." *Journal of Retailing* 56 (Fall 1980): 3–20.

Czepiel, John A., Solomon, Michael R., and Surprenant, Carol F. *The Service Encounter.* Lexington, MA: Lexington Books, 1984.

Gill, R. B. "Debit Card at POS?—J. C. Penney's View." *Retail Control* (April–May 1984): 2–9.

Hoy, Mariea G., and Fisk, Raymond P. "Older Consumers and Services: Implications for Marketers." In *1985 AMA Educators' Proceedings,* edited by R. F. Lusch et al. 50–55. American Marketing Association, 1985.

Hutchens, Stephen P. "All Sales Final: Can Merchandise Return Policies Be a Deterrent to Patronage?" In *1985 Proceedings,* edited by J. C. Crawford and B. C. Garland, 181–83. Southwestern Marketing Association, 1985.

Jay, Lonny J. "The Value of Credit Marketing: A Senior Management Approach and Perspective." *Retail Control* (January 1984): 34–44.

Judd, L. Lynn, "Hours Open and Full-Time/Part-Time Employee Decision Areas: Do These Operating Factors Along with Competitive Situation Affect Small Retailer Success?" In *Developments in Marketing Science, Proceedings,* edited by J. D. Lindquist, 317–21. Academy of Marketing Science, 1984.

Krentler, Kathleen A., and Guiltinan, Joseph P. "Strategies for Tangibilizing Retail Services: An Assessment." *Journal of the Academy of Marketing Science* 12 (Fall 1984): 77–92.

Lyons, Thomas. "Managing The Three C's—Credit, Change, and Customer Service." *Retail Control* (January 1986): 2–15.

Morey, Richard C. "Measuring the Impact of Service Level on Retail Sales." *Journal of Retailing* 56 (Summer 1980): 81–90.

Rosen, Stuart M. "New Moves towards a Cashless Society—Overview of EFT in the United States." *Retail Control* (April–May, 1984): 10–21.

Upah, Gregory D. "Mass Marketing in Services Retailing: A Review and Synthesis of Major Methods." *Journal of Retailing* 56 (Fall 1980): 59–76.

Whalen, Bernie. "Retail Customer Service: Marketing's Last Frontier." *Marketing News,* 15 March 1985, 16, 18.

RELATED READINGS

15

Outline

ORGANIZING THE BUYING PROCESS
Formality
Centrality
Specialization

THE BUYING PROCESS

IDENTIFYING SOURCES OF SUPPLY
The Raw-Resource Producer
The Final Manufacturer
The Wholesaling Intermediary
The Resident Buying Office
International Sourcing

SURVEYING SOURCES OF SUPPLY
The Buying Plan
The Resource File

CONTACTING SOURCES OF SUPPLY
Vendor-Initiated Contacts
Retailer-Initiated Contacts

EVALUATING SOURCES OF SUPPLY
Evaluation Criteria
Evaluation Methods

NEGOTIATING WITH SOURCES OF SUPPLY
Negotiating the Price
Negotiating the Service

BUYING FROM SOURCES OF SUPPLY
Buying Strategies
Buying Methods

Objectives

☐ Discuss the various ways the retailer can organize the buying process.

☐ Identify alternative sources of supply and channel options for procuring the product mix.

☐ Explain the methods and procedures for initiating and maintaining supply contacts.

☐ Discuss the criteria for evaluating and methods for negotiating with sources of supply.

☐ Discuss the strategies for deciding how many sources of supply should be used in securing merchandise.

☐ Describe the buying methods used in the actual purchasing of merchandise.

Buying Process: Buying Merchandise Assortments

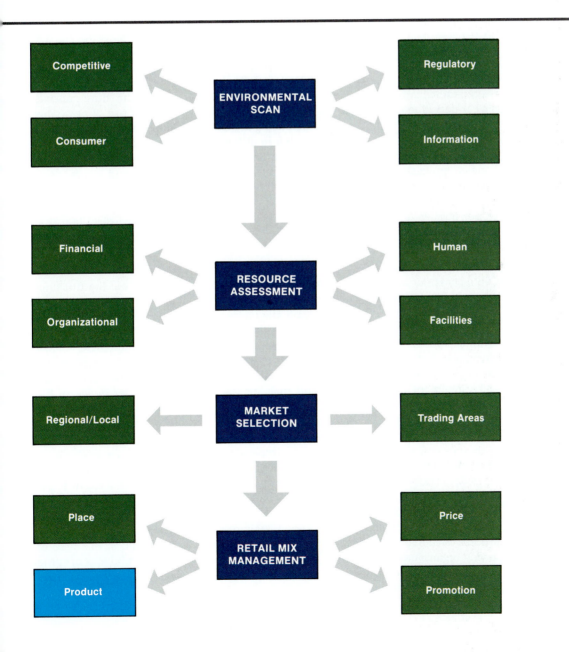

The second stage in the merchandising process is to secure the merchandise mix, which includes the buying process and the procurement process. The buying process is the focus of this chapter; the following chapter takes up the procurement process. Before examining the buying process, this chapter examines the various ways the retailer can organize the buying process.

ORGANIZING THE BUYING PROCESS

Retail buying can be viewed as "the decision-making process through which the retail buyer identifies, evaluates, and selects merchandise for resale to the consumer."[1] To complete the buying task efficiently and in a timely way, a retailer must establish a buying organization, which requires decisions about how formal, centralized, and specialized the organization should be.

Formality

The first decision is how formal the buying structure should be. A **formal buying organization** has a separate department or division to handle the buying function and related merchandising activities. Used by large retailers, the formal structure presents a clear definition of the department's authority and permits greater use of personnel trained in the buying process. Formal buying structures, however, are generally more costly to establish and to maintain. **Informal buying organizations** incorporate the buying process into the existing organizational structure, where the task of buying is handled by existing store personnel. Because of their lower costs and greater flexibility, informal buying organizations are used mainly by smaller retailers. Shortcomings of informal buying structures include lack of clearly defined authorities and responsibilities and lack of coordination between various buying activities and personnel.

Centrality

Centrality is not an organizational issue for the single-unit retailer, but the multiunit retailer must decide to handle the buying process with either a centralized or decentralized structure. In **centralized buying,** the retailer gives a central office the authority and responsibility to buy merchandise, rather than leaving the decision to each individual store in the multiunit chain. A central buying office allows the retailer to take advantage of discount structures through volume purchases, coordinate and control the buying process for the entire chain, use full-time buying specialists, gain preferential treatment from suppliers, and maintain a consistent customer image of the store's merchandise and quality. On the other hand, central buying hinders adaptability to local market needs. Additional problems include information lags, time delays, and poor morale because of the distance between the buying office and the local units and the formal nature of the buying organization. Sears, for example, is reorganizing its buying organizations (fashion merchandise) in the belief that "getting hot styles into the stores quickly is more important than Sears' traditional efforts to get suppliers to make high-quality (private-label) merchandise for good prices."[2]

Decentralized buying is structured and conducted at the local level. Each store or group of stores within a certain geographic market is responsible for the buying process. Adaptability to local market needs is the major advantage in this type of buying organization. Lack of control, inconsistency between stores, and loss of some economies of scale in purchasing are the main shortcomings of buying structures developed around local autonomy.

Specialization

The final consideration in establishing the buying organization is specialization. Some retailers prefer to have each buyer specialize in one or a few related merchandise lines—**specialized buying**; others find it necessary to have a few buyers secure all the merchandise lines—**generalized buying**. Higher costs are the principal disadvantage of specialized buying, whereas lower costs are the primary benefit of generalized buying. In turn, greater buying skills and product and market knowledge are associated with specialization, while less-developed skills and less knowledge are found in a generalized buying organization.

The buying process is the retailer's first step in getting merchandise into the store. Primary concerns are determining (1) what sources of supply are available and under what terms and conditions; (2) how to contact and evaluate various suppliers; and (3) how, when, and where to negotiate with and buy from alternative supply sources. The buying process should follow, in sequence, the six steps in Figure 15–1, which provide the structure for this chapter.

THE BUYING PROCESS

The first step in the buying process is to identify the available sources of supply. From these sources, the retailer must decide which channel to use in procuring each merchandise line. In some cases, a direct channel to the manufacturer or original producer (e.g., farmer) is preferred. In other cases, an indirect or extended supply channel using one or more intermediaries—often referred to as *middlemen*—is desired. Specifically, the retailer can select from any one or a combination of the following sources of supply:

IDENTIFYING SOURCES OF SUPPLY

- ☐ Raw-resource producers
- ☐ Manufacturers
- ☐ Intermediaries
- ☐ Resident buying offices

The Raw-Resource Producer

Under certain circumstances, the retailer may elect to obtain supplies directly from the raw-resource producer. Large food retailing chains frequently bypass traditional supply sources in their efforts to secure fresh fruits and vegetables and to obtain raw materials for their private-label brands. Both large and small food retailers often secure stocks of some specialty food items (e.g., ethnic foods) directly from local producers. Buying food products directly from the raw-resource producer offers a retailer the advantages of increased speed and reduced handling, both of which are important in getting these perishables to the store fresh and with minimal damage. Other products that retailers buy directly from raw-resource producers include lumber, some construction materials, and other bulky materials that incur extra expense if handled by additional intermediaries.

The Final Manufacturer

Recently, large retailing organizations have emerged that have the volume to consider direct purchasing from manufacturers. Where direct buying is available and feasible, several advantages can accrue to the retailer. Obtaining *fresher products* is cited as one benefit of buying directly from the manufacturer. Merchandise procured from the

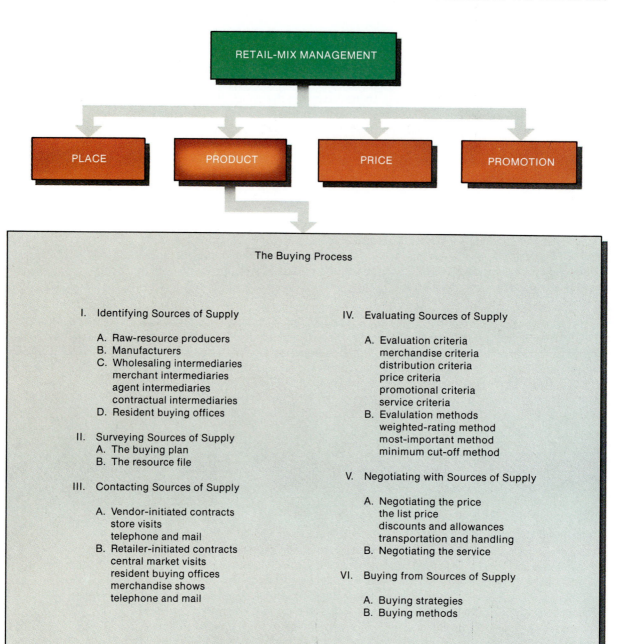

FIGURE 15–1
Developing and implementing the buying process

manufacturer is frequently packaged and shipped directly from the production line. *Quicker delivery* is the second benefit that retailers derive from making direct purchases. Direct channels of distribution are generally faster than indirect channels in processing initial orders, whereas wholesalers are usually faster on fill-in orders. Direct purchases are almost a necessity for highly perishable fashion and fad items. The third advantage of using the manufacturer as a source of supply is *lower price*. Eliminating the wholesaler and taking on the intermediary's functions enable the retailer to reduce certain costs and realize savings. Fourth, manufacturers can give retailers *more information* about their product lines than wholesalers do, because manufacturers' salespeople specialize in selling only their products, whereas wholesalers' salespeople sell product lines of several manufacturers.

The fifth advantage of the manufacturer-to-retailer channel is *better adjustment*. Direct relationships between manufacturers and retailers lead both to more lenient adjustment policies and to quicker adjustment responses on products that the retailer's customers return. Most adjustment negotiations can be conducted more efficiently in face-to-face meetings than by going through third parties (wholesalers). Finally, direct purchases permit the retailer to order and secure goods made to its *specifications*. Many large chain operations (e.g., J. C. Penney and Sears) have a large percentage of their goods made to their specifications and identified with their names. A retailer who is trying to develop a product line tailored to the needs of specific target markets may see specification buying as the best alternative for meeting those needs.

The Wholesaling Intermediary

The third alternative source of supply is wholesaling intermediaries that position themselves in the distribution channel between the manufacturer and the retailer. Their role in facilitating the transfer of goods between manufacturers and retailers varies, depending on the nature of their operations as well as the functions and services they are willing to provide. Most intermediaries do not provide the full range of wholesaling functions—buying, selling, breaking bulk, assortment creation, stocking, delivery services, credit extension, information and consultation, and title transfer (see Figure 15–2). Instead, they tend to specialize in one or a limited number of these functions. Based on the number and type of functions, wholesaling intermediaries fall into several groups. Figure 15–3 identifies these groups of wholesalers. Selection of one of these types depends on the retailer's specific needs.

Merchant Intermediaries

Merchant intermediaries are wholesalers that are directly involved in the purchase and sale of goods as they move through the channel of distribution. What distinguishes merchant intermediaries from agent intermediaries is that merchants take title to the goods they deal in, while agents do not assume ownership. As illustrated in Figure 15–3, merchant intermediaries can be classified as full-function and limited-function operations. For many small and medium-sized retailers that do not have the volume of sales to buy directly from the manufacturer, merchant intermediaries represent the most important source of supply.

Full function.   **Full-function merchant intermediaries** generally perform a full range of wholesaling functions. Based on the width of their product lines, three types of full-function merchant intermediaries can be identified. The **general merchandise wholesaler** handles a number of different and often unrelated product lines with no one product line being dominant. Typically, the product lines are nonperishable,

Buying tasks. Wholesalers act as purchase agents when they anticipate the merchandise needs of retailers and their customers. By locating appropriate sources of supply and securing merchandise that is suitable to the retailer's needs, the wholesaler greatly enhances the retailer's buying and procurement processes.

Selling tasks. Wholesalers help simplify buying procedures by having salespersons calling at the retailer's place of business. Wholesaling intermediaries help reduce the retailer's cost of securing goods by: (1) eliminating some trips to the market, and (2) assuming some of the responsibilities (e.g., order follow-up, self-stocking), for getting the merchandise onto the retailer's displays.

Credit-extending tasks. Many wholesaling intermediaries finance part or all of a retailer's inventory. The most common credit extension is the setting of the date when the net price of an invoice is due in full. By providing 30, 45, 60, or more days to pay an invoice without charges, the wholesaler is in effect financing the retailer's inventory. Consignment and memorandum selling wherein the retailer does not pay for the merchandise until it is sold is still another form of extending credit. In addition, many wholesalers make available to retailers short-, intermediate-, and long-term loans that can be used as working and fixed capital.

Informing tasks. Marketing research and source information are two important functions provided by the wholesaler. Many large wholesaling operations engage in an ongoing effort to determine marketplace needs and conditions. By passing this information on, retailers have reference points for examining their market performances and adjusting their marketing programs. On the source side, the wholesaler's unique position within the channel allows him to provide useful information of products, manufacturer's programs, supply sources, and activities of competitors.

Consulting tasks. Wholesalers provide their customers with a host of various advisory services. The more common consultant services deal with accounting, advertising, personnel training, financial and legal advice, location analysis, inventory control, and facilities planning.

Title-transferring tasks. Free-and-clear title to products is essential to the exchange process. Merchant wholesalers that own the goods they deal in assume the responsibility for transfer of payments and the management of title exchange. Agent wholesalers that do not take title to the goods facilitate the exchange of title by providing or arranging for the services necessary to the title-exchange process.

Bulk-breaking tasks. A quantity gap occurs between manufacturer's need to produce and sell in larger quantities and the retailer's need to buy in smaller quantities. Wholesaling intermediaries help bridge this quantity gap by: (1) buying in car- or truck-load quantities, (2) performing break-in bulk activities, and (3) selling smaller quantities (e.g., case lots) to retailers. This bulk-breaking function helps reduce the cost of doing business by reducing inventory carrying and handling costs.

Assortment-creating tasks. An assortment gap exists between manufacturers that need (manufacturing economies of scale) to provide and sell a limited line of identical or nearly identical products and retailers that must offer the consumer a wider selection of products. Wholesalers can fill this gap by buying the limited product lines and items of many different manufacturers and combining these lines and items into appropriate assortments. The retailer's quest for either mass- or target-market appeal is greatly enhanced by the availability of diversified product assortments.

Stocking tasks. Retailers often have limited stockroom space and inventory investment capital. Wholesalers provide an invaluable service by reducing the space and capital needed for retail stock. This reduces the need for facilities and inventory carrying costs for the retailer. The local nature of wholesalers also enhances the time and place availability of products for restocking purposes.

Delivery tasks. Quick and frequent deliveries by the wholesaler help avoid or replenish stockout conditions that result in lost sales. A timely delivery system is one service a wholesaler provides that aids the retailer in holding down in-store inventories that are required to meet customer expectations. Reliable deliveries are also an integral part in reducing safety stock and the risk and investment associated with such stock.

FIGURE 15–2
Wholesaling functions

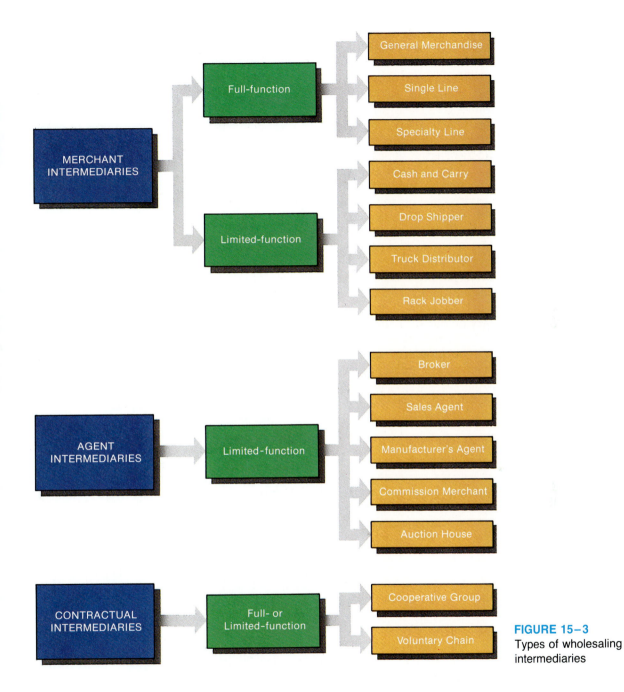

FIGURE 15–3
Types of wholesaling intermediaries

staple goods, including hardware, household durables, personal-care products, and electrical, plumbing, and automotive supplies. **Single-line wholesalers** limit their activities to one general product line (e.g., either hardware, drugs, groceries, or dry goods), while **specialty-line wholesalers** restrict their activities to one specialty line within a general line of products (e.g., frozen foods).

Limited function. As the name implies, **limited-function merchant intermediaries** limit their activities to certain wholesaling functions, in the belief that many retailers are only interested in having those functions provided and do not want to pay for services that are neither needed nor used.

Based on the functions they perform, there are several types of limited-function merchant intermediaries. The **cash-and-carry wholesaler,** for example, is the discount supermarket of the wholesaling industry because the retailer must (1) go to the wholesaler's place of business, (2) select and assemble the order, (3) check out at a central station, (4) pay cash for the assembled order, and (5) load and transport the order. Staple groceries, hardware, and variety goods are the most commonly stocked product lines of the cash-and-carry wholesaler.

Drop shippers are wholesaling operators that normally distribute bulky products, such as lumber and building materials, that are expensive to transport and handle. The drop shipper operates out of an office, takes retail orders by phone or mail, passes the orders on to the producer, and arranges to have the order shipped directly to the retailer.

The third type of limited-function intermediary is the **truck distributor,** which essentially operates its business out of a truck. By carrying inventory on the truck, the driver/salesperson can travel an established sales route and perform the sales and delivery functions almost simultaneously. Truck distributors are important sources of supply for many fast-moving perishable food products (e.g., produce, bakery, and dairy products), hardware, and variety-goods lines.

The **rack jobber** operates in much the same way as the truck distributor, but the rack jobber usually furnishes the racks or shelves for displaying merchandise. In addition, they are responsible for stocking the racks, building attractive displays, and pricing the merchandise. In return, the retailer furnishes floor or shelf space, acts as the sales agent, and collects the money from the customer.

This kind of display is typical of a wholesaler who operates as a rack jobber.

Agent Intermediaries

Agent intermediaries specialize in buying and selling merchandise for others. They facilitate the exchange process between manufacturer and retailers by bringing them together. The two distinguishing characteristics of agent intermediaries are (1) they do not take title to the goods they deal in and (2) they normally provide only a limited number of functions. Also, agent intermediaries usually work on a commission basis, may have either an intermittent or continuous working relationship with clients, and normally do not represent both buyer and seller in the same transaction.

Brokers are agent intermediaries whose primary function is to bring prospective buyers and sellers together to complete a transaction. *Information* is the broker's stock-in-trade. Seasonal products (food) and unusual products (technical products or used goods) for which general market information is lacking are the most common product lines a broker handles.

Sales agents are agent intermediaries that assume the entire marketing function for a manufacturer. In effect, the sales agent becomes the manufacturer's marketing department. The sales agent works predominantly in such industries as textiles, home furnishings, canned foods, apparel, and metals.[3]

The **manufacturers' agent** is essentially the sales organization for several manufacturers within a prescribed market territory. Normally an agent carries complementary product lines from several manufacturers as opposed to product lines that compete directly. Manufacturers' agents can be valuable sources of supply for such product lines as furniture and home furnishings, electrical and plumbing products, construction equipment and supplies, dry goods, apparel, and accessories.

Commission merchants can be an important source of supply for retailers interested in securing certain types of dry goods and agricultural products (e.g., fruits and vegetables). The typical commission-house operator takes physical possession of goods, provides storage and handling, and acts as the selling agent for the producer.

The principal function of the **auction house** is to provide a place where producers and retailers can meet and complete a sales transaction. By providing the physical facilities for producers to display their products and retailers to inspect them, the auction house plays an important role in the wholesaling of used cars and agricultural products.

Contractual Intermediaries

To combat the numerous competitive advantages of large chain organizations, many small retailers have entered into contractual arrangements with these wholesalers, known as **contractual intermediaries**. Typically, the retailer agrees to purchase a certain amount of merchandise from the wholesaler in return for considerations. Lower prices are the most important considerations, although contractual arrangements often spell out other services that the wholesaler will supply (e.g., merchandising and promotional services). The lower prices are made possible by the fact that the wholesaler has several retailers under contract, thereby permitting the wholesaler to realize economies of scale similar to chain organizations.

The two types of contractual intermediaries are **cooperative groups** and **voluntary chains** (see Chapter 3). Some contractual intermediaries operate as full-function wholesalers, whereas others limit the functions they provide.[4] Super Valu Stores, Inc., the nation's largest wholesaler, calls itself a "retail support company." The most important form of support is helping retailers expand their business through bigger, more competitive stores. Super Valu offers independent retailers advantages only chains are supposed to have: low prices, up-to-date stores, good locations, and sophisticated operations. To aid retailers, Super Valu employs retail counselors who patrol stores, detect trouble spots, and offer advice. For particular problems, retailers can call on specialists.[5]

The Resident Buying Office

Resident buying offices are organizations specializing in the buying function and located in major wholesaling and producing markets. Their central-market location puts the resident buyer in an excellent position to serve as the retailer's "eyes and ears" on supply conditions. The principal services resident buyers offer are information and buyer assistance. They provide information on (1) the availability of products; (2) the reliability of suppliers; (3) the present and future market and supply trends; and (4) the special deals, prices, promotions, and services that various suppliers offer. Buyer-assistance services include locating sources of supply, making initial contact with suppliers, aiding in sales negotiations by using their clout as representatives of several retailers, arranging delivery and payment schedules, and following up on orders to ensure fast and timely arrival of merchandise at the retailer's store.[6]

The two general types of buying offices are the **store-owned buying office** and the **independent buying office**. Figure 15−4 identifies and characterizes each of these resident buyers. Although resident buying offices are most commonly associated with the central apparel markets of New York, Dallas, and Los Angeles, other central markets are also populated with resident buyers; for example, because High Point,

FIGURE 15–4
Types of resident
buyers

Store-owned resident buying offices	Private	Owned and operated by and for an individual out-of-town retailer
		Decreasing in importance due to the lack of economies of scale in buying
	Associated	Owned and operated by and for a group of out-of-town retailers
		Increasing in importance due to the potential economies of scale in buying
	Chain	Owned and operated by and for retail chains and department-store ownership groups
		Offers advice and information to individual stores in the chain and to the chain's central buying office
Independent resident buying offices	Salaried	Owned and operated by an independent for clients that typically sign a one-year contract
		Larger retailers are usually charged a fee equal to about 0.5 percent of the retailer's annual sales, while smaller retailers are charged a minimum flat fee
	Merchandise broker	Owned and operated by an independent for both retailers and producers
		The producer pays the commission (3 to 5 percent on net sales) rather than the retailer

Source: Adapted from William R. Davidson, Alton F. Doody, and Daniel J. Sweeney, *Retailing Management*, 4th ed. (New York: Ronald Press, 1975), 386–87.

North Carolina, is the capital of the U.S. furniture industry, several resident buying offices are located there.

International Sourcing

Amalfi shoes, Louis Vuitton handbags, Lowenbrau beer, Outback Red sportswear, Yves St. Laurent fragrances, Esprit de Corp clothing, Café au Chocolat coffee, Yellow Cab Co. apparel—is it American or is it foreign? Brand names are often misleading; nevertheless, international sources of supply are an integral part of most buying programs. There is hardly a product category that some retailer does not secure from some foreign source. The complexity of issues surrounding foreign goods and international sourcing is beyond the scope of this discussion; however, retailers often cite numerous advantages in support of overseas buying. First, foreign markets offer opportunities to discover and obtain unique and distinctive products (styling, materials, workmanship, and handcrafting) that will help retailers establish a differentiated advantage in merchandise assortments. Second, in most product categories, cost structures (goods, handling, and transportation) are equal to and often better than domestic sources. Third, foreign vendors are more willing and able to adjust production to retailers' market and operating needs; domestic sources are often hampered by labor, governmental, and other restrictions in adjusting the production schedule. This greater flexibility is considered by many fashion retailers to be more significant than many of the price-structure benefits associated with foreign sources. Finally, in many product categories, foreign products have a real or imaginary status of quality and prestige; upscaled wearing apparel, wines, home electronics, and automobiles are a few examples.

There are risks associated with international sourcing. Potential risks include (1) higher buying costs resulting from travel expenses, (2) legal complications caused by export/import regulations, (3) financial risks caused by foreign currency exchange rates, (4) supply contingency risks in some foreign areas where governmental and political environments are unstable or should the U.S. government become more protective, and (5) social risk in the form of a "Buy America" backlash when the domestic economy turns down.

A retailer can obtain foreign merchandise through an **importer**—a U.S.-based commission wholesaler who represents retailers in the buying process. They provide services ranging from simply handling import dues to acting as a complete buying organization. Retailers can also use **commissionaires,** who operate full and limited buying offices within one or more foreign countries. Some retailers have "taken things into their own hands." The Limited and Charming Shoppes have developed *international programmed sourcing*—an international buying organization consisting of a network of foreign suppliers who are contracted to produce merchandise against specific orders from their parent company, as well as from other buyers. Mast Industries, a commercial division of The Limited, employs a worldwide network of 150 contract-production facilities to supply customers of The Limited and its many different retailing formats.[7] "Somewhere on this earth, no matter what the hour, there are associates of Mast inspecting quality, explaining specifications, or working at any one of the dozens—a multitude—of separate tasks that enabled them to grow to a global sourcing network."[8]

Many retail buyers are deluged with merchandise offerings from potential supply sources. Thus, the retailer must develop an initial screening procedure to identify sources that will best suit the operation's needs. An initial screening procedure calls for a *buying plan* and a *resource file*.

SURVEYING SOURCES OF SUPPLY

The Buying Plan

A buying plan is essential for securing the desired merchandise. To avoid such basic mistakes as buying the wrong merchandise and overbuying and underbuying a merchandise line, the retailer should have a clear idea of "what type" of merchandise to buy. Before contacting supply sources and engaging in the buying process, the buyer should formulate guidelines covering the quality, style, and price lines that are consistent with the store's image and customers' needs. A good buying plan establishes guidelines not only for merchandise but also for the terms and conditions under which that merchandise is acceptable. (See Chapter 17 for a more detailed discussion.)

The Resource File

To prepare for the buying process, the retailer should establish and maintain a resource file on all potential merchandise suppliers. The resource file should contain a sufficient amount of information to allow the buyer to conduct the initial screening of suppliers. Those who do not comply with the retailer's buying plan guidelines can be eliminated immediately from further consideration. Some resource files also rate suppliers' past performances. Retailers often cross-reference by firm and merchandise lines.

CONTACTING SOURCES OF SUPPLY

The third step in the buying process is to contact the potential sources of supply. Although most retailers have preferred sources, each retailer should strive to maintain as many supply-source contacts as possible. Contacts for a potential sales transaction can be initiated by either the vendor or the retailer.

Vendor-Initiated Contacts

Vendor-initiated contacts include store visits by sales representatives and telephone and mail-order solicitations.

Store Visits

Sales calls at the retailer's place of business represent the most common method of selling staple merchandise. Store visits are also used to sell some fashion goods to medium-sized and small retailers, which usually lack the resources to go to the market. From the retailer's viewpoint, store visits by supplier representatives offer the benefits of (1) saving time and money traveling to the market, (2) avoiding the strenuous market-search process, (3) allowing easy in-store access to inventory and sales records for reference purposes, and (4) permitting consultation with other store personnel before placing an order.

The primary limitations of store visits are that the retailer does not have the opportunity to (1) simultaneously compare the merchandise lines of several producers and (2) gain a "feel" for what is going on in the industry through the interaction that occurs with other retailers and vendors at trade shows and central markets.

Telephone and Mail

Some vendors use telephone and mail contacts to prospect for customers, to make appointments for store visits, to follow up on orders, and to check on the needs of existing accounts. Some vendors prefer telephone contacts because of their personal, two-way nature; others make extensive use of the mail to accomplish specific contact objectives.

Retailer-Initiated Contacts

Like vendors, retailers make initial contacts for products they need. Visiting central markets and resident buying offices, attending merchandise shows, and making telephone and mail inquiries are the four ways retailers seek vendors' products and services.

Central-Market Visits

A central market is a geographic area or city that is a dominant source of supply for a particular type of merchandise. Within these central markets are concentrated the selling offices and merchandise showrooms of a large number of suppliers. In one visit the retailer can review and compare the merchandise offerings of several suppliers. Frequently, suppliers help retailers in their reviews and comparisons by setting up permanent displays in a central facility. The furniture mart in Chicago and the

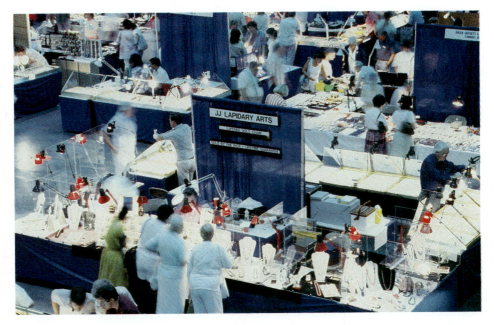

A central market, like this Gift Mart, allows retailers to see and compare many suppliers' merchandise.

apparel mart in Dallas are examples of these types of facilities. Retailers can inspect the merchandise personally, make contacts with a wide variety of suppliers, and interact with and exchange ideas with suppliers and other retailers.

Resident Buying Offices

Resident buying offices are associated with central markets. These offices allow retailers to maintain contacts with existing suppliers on a continuing basis while they prospect for and make contact with new supply alternatives.

Merchandise Shows

Merchandise shows or trade fairs are periodic displays of many suppliers' merchandise lines in one place at one time. Usually, a group of suppliers gets together and stages a show at a hotel or some other central facility such as a merchandise mart or convention facility. Typical merchandise shows feature a general type of merchandise (e.g., toys, furniture, or some type of wearing apparel); however, multiline showings are also common. Merchandise showings can be either national, regional, or local. The advantages and disadvantages of merchandise shows are basically the same as those of central markets.

Telephone and Mail

Retailers use telephone and mail contacts to make initial inquiries on the availability of and to place last-minute orders, reorders, and orders for fill-in merchandise. When the retailer is familiar with the supplier and the merchandise, telephone and mail contacts are efficient and relatively safe; however, telephone and mail orders to unknown suppliers can be quite risky, since the retailer is unable to inspect the merchandise or determine how reliable the supplier is in meeting delivery dates and sales terms. Retailers often use telephone and mail orders to place small orders, resulting in higher per-unit transportation and handling costs.

EVALUATING SOURCES OF SUPPLY

After identifying and contacting several sources of supply, the retailer must then evaluate each supplier to determine how consistent its operating characteristics are. This third step of the buying process requires evaluation criteria and methods to rank the relative capabilities of each supply alternative to serve the retailer's needs.

Evaluation Criteria

Criteria for evaluating potential suppliers are merchandise criteria, distribution criteria, price criteria, promotion criteria, and service criteria.

Merchandise Criteria

The first consideration in evaluating alternative sources of supply is what merchandise the supplier offers. The suitability, availability, and adaptability of the suppliers' merchandise lines are three common merchandise criteria. *Suitability* refers to how well the merchandise fits the needs of the retailer's customers. Suitability can be judged on the basis of assortment factors such as brand, style, and price, as well as

FIGURE 15–5
Perceived risk and corresponding consumer uncertainties

Type of Risk	Consumer Uncertainty
1. *Functional*—the capability of the merchandise to function as expected	Will it work? Is it durable? Will it perform better than the competition?
2. *Financial*—the value received versus the price-utility surrendered	What is the priority in the allocation of limited financial resources? Is it worth the sacrifice of price-utility? Can I afford it?
3. *Social*—poor choice will result in embarrassment before peers	Will my peers approve? Will my family approve? Will it please others, whose opinions I value?
4. *Psychological*—poor choice will damage the ego	Will this merchandise make me feel good? Will others, family, and peers be impressed? Do I deserve this merchandise? Am I capable of making the right choice? What are the consequences of the wrong choice?
5. *Physical*—the risk of self-damage and harm to others	Will it be safe? How badly might I and others be hurt? What effect will it have on my own environment and the environment of others?
6. *Temporal*—the value received versus the value of time and effort expended	What are my time priorities? Do I have enough time? Is the time sacrificed worth the material gain?

Source: Ernest H. Risch, *Retail Merchandising* (Columbus, OH: Merrill, 1987) 66.

individual factors such as uniqueness, originality, and durability. Suitable merchandise is also judged according to aesthetics (e.g., fabric, color, and print) and quality (e.g., construction, fit, and crafting).[9] One interesting perspective of consumers' needs that every retail buyer should keep in mind when making buying decisions is the amount of risk consumers associate with the purchase of a particular item (see Figure 15–5).

If the retailer deems the merchandise suitable, then *availability* becomes the next criterion. The buyer must first find out whether the supplier will accept an order. If so, will the merchandise be available in the appropriate quantities, sizes, styles, and colors? Merchandise availability may in fact be based on the size of the order; for example, many suppliers establish minimum quantities that retailers must order to purchase merchandise from them.

The third merchandise criterion is *adaptability*—the supplier's willingness to make necessary changes in the product to meet the needs of the retailer and its customers. Adaptability may involve (1) producing products to the retailer's specifications, (2) placing the retailer's private label on the product, and (3) adjusting production (color, sizes, styles) to take advantage of fast-moving items or incorporating new trends into existing merchandise lines.

Distribution Criteria

Because delivery delays are a concern to all retailers, an important evaluation criterion is how well suppliers perform their *distribution* and *delivery* functions. Past performance is usually a good indication of future performance. Also of interest to most retailers is the degree of *exclusiveness* the supplier offers in particular lines of merchandise—whether the product is offered on an exclusive (one retailer per market), selective (few retailers per market), or intensive (many retailers per market) basis. Exclusiveness is an important criterion for some retailers and products (specialty stores and goods) and of little importance to other stores and products (discounters and convenience goods).

Additional distribution and delivery policies the retailer should consider for potential suppliers are (1) whether delivery services are offered, (2) terms and conditions of the delivery service, (3) order size and assortment constraints, (4) initial-order processing time, (5) reorder processing time, and (6) ease and flexibility of placing an order. Figure 15–6 lists more criteria that could be used to evaluate a supplier's distribution performance.

Price Criteria

Price criteria center around two considerations: price to the consumer and price to the retailer. Regarding the price to the consumer, the major issues the retailer should evaluate are price appropriateness and price maintenance. As discussed, the retail selling price must be appropriate to the retailer's target market. Price *appropriateness* should be measured in terms of value (i.e., offering the consumer the best quality at the best price). This price–quality relationship can include any number of price–quality combinations. Price appropriateness for the prestige retailer is offering consumers top-quality merchandise at a prestige price; for the discounter, acceptable quality at the lowest price constitutes price appropriateness.

Price *maintenance* is the supplier's policy of maintaining the retail selling price at or above a certain level. Some suppliers insist that their customers (the retailers) sell their merchandise at a suggested retail price. For a high-volume discounter that relies heavily on price appeal substantiated by price comparisons, price-maintenance policies are simply unacceptable in most cases.

FIGURE 15–6

Supplier evaluation: Using distribution criteria

Major Category	Subcategory
Product availability	Line item availability Product group availability Invoice fill Cases/units
Order cycle time	Order entry Order processing Total cycle time
Consistency	In order cycle time In shipment dispatch In transit time In arrival time In warehouse handling
Response time	Order status Order tracing Backorder status Order confirmation Product substitution Order shortages Product information requests
Error rates	Shipment delays Order errors Picking & packing errors Shipping & labeling errors Paperwork errors
Product/shipment related malfunction	Damaged merchandise Merchandise refusals Claims Returned goods Customer complaints
Special handling	Transshipment Expedited orders Expedited transportation Special packaging Customer backhauls

Source: Louis W. Stern and Adel I. El-Ansary, *Marketing Channels*, 2d ed. (Englewood Cliffs, NJ: Prentice-Hall, 1983) 161.

The second group of price considerations concerns what price the retailer must pay for the merchandise. Perhaps the most important consideration is whether the price will permit the retailer to take a sufficient markup to cover expenses, make a profit, and still be competitive in the marketplace. (Price negotiation will be discussed shortly.)

Promotional Criteria

Many merchandise lines require a considerable amount of promotional support to be successfully marketed. The *type* and *amount* of promotional assistance the retailer can expect from a supplier are therefore important evaluation criteria. Promotional assistance assumes many different forms, including advertising allowances, cooperative advertising, in-store demonstrations, free display materials, and various consumer inducements such as premiums, coupons, contests, and samples. Also, the extent to which the supplier supports the sale of merchandise through national and/or local advertising is an important factor. Ultimately, the essential question for the retailer is "Does the supplier help me sell?"

Service Criteria

Besides the various types of merchandise, distribution, price, and promotional supports, some suppliers provide some or all of the following supplementary services:

- ☐ Financing and credit services
- ☐ Return privileges
- ☐ Warranty and repair services
- ☐ Sales force training
- ☐ Accounting services
- ☐ Inventory planning and control
- ☐ Prepackaging, prelabeling, and preticketing
- ☐ Markdown insurance
- ☐ Display units, fixtures, and signs
- ☐ Store facilities design services

The extent to which the retailer might consider some of these services in evaluating supply sources depends on its need for them. While any one of these services can help the retailer reduce either operating expenses or capital investment, they also make the retailer more dependent on the supplier who furnishes the service. Care must be taken to determine what strings are attached.

Evaluation Methods

To effectively evaluate alternative sources of supply, retailers must systematically assess each store using objective methods. Three methods are the weighted-rating method, the single-most-important criterion method, and the minimum-cutoff method.

The Weighted-Rating Method

The **weighted-rating method** is a procedure for evaluating supply alternatives by assigning weighted values to each of a set of evaluation criteria. Although several weighted-rating procedures have been devised, the "decision matrix approach to vendor selection" developed by John S. Berens illustrates the method.[10]

Step 1: Criteria selection. This step entails selecting criteria to evaluate sources of supply that are most relevant to the retailer and its relationship to potential suppliers.

Step 2: Criteria weighting. Predetermined weights (or levels of importance) are assigned to each evaluation criterion. Frequently, this weighting process is accomplished by simply rank-ordering all criteria from most to least important and assigning the highest value to the criterion deemed most important and subsequent lower values to those that are less important.

Step 3: Supplier selection. This is a procedure for choosing which potential suppliers to include in the evaluation.

Step 4: Supplier rating. In this step, each of the selected suppliers is rated on the basis of each evaluation criterion. By comparing each supplier to all other suppliers for each criterion, the retailer can assign a minimal rating to each supplier.

Step 5: Weighted rating. Each supplier's rating is multiplied on each evaluation criterion (step 4) by the criterion weight (step 2) to obtain the weighted rating for each supplier. To obtain the overall weighted rating for each supplier, simply add the weighted rating of each criterion.

The retailer starts by selecting the source that received the highest weighted rating and attempts to secure the necessary commitments from that supplier. If more than one source is needed or if the highest-rated source is not available, the retailer simply proceeds down the weighted-rating list until all the needed supply sources are secured. Figure 15–7 illustrates Berens' weighted-rating method.

The Single-Most-Important Criterion Method

As the name implies, some retailers evaluate and select suppliers on the basis of the **single-most-important criterion**. This method is similar to the weighted-rating method in that the retailer completes the criteria-selection, criteria-weighting, and supplier-selection steps, then compares suppliers and judges one superior according to the single-most-important criterion. If no supplier is judged superior on the basis of this criterion, then the evaluation procedure continues to the second-most-important criterion, the third, and so on, until one supplier emerges as superior.

FIGURE 15–7
Decision matrix approach to supplier selection (source: John S. Berens, "A Decision Matrix Approach to Supplier Selection," *Journal of Retailing,* 47, no. 4 [Winter 1971–1972]; 52)

	Criteria Weight (Step 2)	Supplier A		Supplier B		Supplier C		Supplier D		Supplier E	
Criterion 1: Supplier Can Fill Reorders	6	3	18	2	12	4	24	1	6	0	0
Criterion 2: Markup Is Adequate	4	2	8	4	16	3	12	0	0	1	4
Criterion 3: Customers Ask for the Line	1	1	1	2	2	4	4	3	3	0	0
Criterion 4: Supplier's Line Has Significant Changes from Season to Season	2	3	6	4	8	2	4	1	2	0	0
Criterion 5: Supplier's Line Contributes to Fashion Leadership	5	2	10	1	5	0	0	3	15	4	20
Criterion 6: Supplier's Line is Cut to Fit Customers Well	2	1	2	0	0	3	6	4	8	2	4
Criterion 7: Supplier Advertises Line in Local Media	1	0	0	1	1	2	2	4	4	3	3
Supplier TOTAL SCORES			45		44		52		38		31

The Minimum-Cutoff Method

The **minimum-cutoff method** recognizes that it is not always possible to determine the precise importance of each criterion. It is usually possible, however, to establish some minimum standard or cutoff point for each evaluation criterion. Using this method, the retailer (1) selects the criteria for inclusion in the evaluation, (2) establishes a minimum-cutoff standard for each criterion, (3) compares each supplier to the minimum cutoff on each criterion, (4) eliminates all suppliers that fall below the minimum-cutoff standard on any criterion, and (5) chooses among suppliers that have exceeded the minimum cutoff on all criteria. This method can be combined with the single-most-important criterion method to produce an even more exacting supplier-evaluation technique.

The fourth step in the buying process is active negotiation with suppliers identified in the evaluation step as potentially suitable sources. In the retailer–supplier relationship, the two most common issues subject to negotiation are *price* and *service*.

NEGOTIATING WITH SOURCES OF SUPPLY

Negotiating the Price

In contrast to the fixed prices the final consumer encounters on most products at the retailer's store, the price the retailer pays for the same merchandise is usually subject to negotiation. While any number of factors can conceivably influence the price the retailer pays, three factors play dominant roles: (1) list price, (2) discount and allowance terms, and (3) transportation and handling terms.

The Starting Point: List Price

Price negotiations usually start with the supplier's basic price list. For administrative convenience, most suppliers establish their pricing structures around basic **list prices** that they use for an extended time period. By adjusting their list prices upward or downward using various types of "add-ons" and "discounts," suppliers can avoid publishing frequently revised price lists while at the same time they can make necessary price accommodations for individual retail customers.

As the starting point for negotiation, the basic list price is a crucial element in estimating the supplier's "final" price to the retailer. Since some suppliers publish what are, in effect, inflated list prices, substantial differences in the final price can result because of large variations in discounts and allowances as well as transportation and handling terms.

Discount and Allowance Terms

The final selling price to the retailer is the difference between the supplier's list price and the negotiated discounts and allowances. The principal types of discounts are trade, quantity, seasonal and cash discounts, and promotional allowances.

Trade discounts. A trade discount is a form of compensation that the buyer may receive for performing certain services (functions) for the supplier. Also referred to as a functional discount, the trade discount is usually used by suppliers selling merchandise through catalogs and is based on a quoted list price. The supplier offers one price to all potential buyers and makes price changes simply by adjusting the amount of the trade discount offered to any given buyer. The size of the trade discount depends on the type, quantity, and quality of the services the potential buyer is willing to provide. Therefore, variations in trade discounts are legally justifiable on the basis of the different costs associated with doing business with different buyers. If the buyer is instrumental in helping the supplier realize certain savings, part of those savings are passed along to the buyer in the form of larger trade discounts.

Trade discounts come in single and chain forms. The **single trade discount** is expressed as a single percentage adjustment (e.g., 50 percent) to the supplier's list price. For example, a product with a list price of $200 less a 40 percent trade discount (which would amount to an $80 trade discount) costs the retailer $120 ($200 × .40 = $80; $200 − $80 = $120). A trade discount can also be calculated using a chain of discounts. Expressed as a series of percentages (e.g., 40 percent, 20 percent, 10 percent), the **chain trade discount** is applied to the list price in successive order. The first percentage discount is calculated on the original list price, the second percentage discount is calculated on the value resulting from the first calculation, and so on until each percentage discount is taken into account. A product listed at $300 less a 40/20/10 percent discount costs the retailer $129.60, since altogether that represents a discount of 56.8 percent; for example:

$$
\begin{array}{rl}
\text{list price} = \$\quad 300.00 & (\$300 \times 40\% = \$120) \\
\underline{-120.00} & \\
180.00 & (\$180 \times 20\% = \$\ 36) \\
\underline{-36.00} & \\
144.00 & (\$144 \times 10\% = \$\ 14.40) \\
\underline{-\quad 14.40} & \\
\text{retailer's price} = \$\quad 129.60 &
\end{array}
$$

The purpose of expressing the trade discount in the form of a chain is to facilitate offering different discounts to different buyers. The buyer that performs many services for the supplier receives the entire discount chain (40 percent, 20 percent, 10 percent), while the buyer that performs a limited number of services is offered only part of the chain (40 percent, 20 percent, or possibly only 40 percent).

Quantity discounts.   Suppliers offer quantity discounts to retailers as an inducement to buy large quantities of merchandise. Large order quantities help reduce the supplier's selling, handling, billing, transporting, and inventory costs. Some of the cost savings are passed along to the buyer in the form of quantity discounts. Quantity discounts represent an additional way to reduce the price of the merchandise for the retailer. At the same time, however, buying large quantities normally increases the retailer's operating expenses, ties up operating capital, and creates additional inventory-control problems. The retail buyer must also be aware of the potential risk of overbuying and then having to mark down the overstocked merchandise.

Quantity discounts can be expressed and calculated in several different ways. They can be based on either the dollar value of the total order or on the number of units (or cases) in the order. Quantity discounts can also be handled as a percentage reduction from list price or simply expressed in some form of a schedule with unit or dollar sales corresponding to a particular dollar discount amount. A different approach to quantity discounts is to quote a carload or truckload price. Any order less than a carload or a truckload is adjusted by a system of "add-ons"; for example, a retailer placing a less-than-carload order is quoted the carload unit price, plus a certain percentage (e.g., 6 percent) of that price as an add-on. Given the numerous methods for calculating quantity discounts, the retailer should take the time to verify exactly what type and how much of a quantity discount the supplier is offering.

Three types of quantity discounts—noncumulative, cumulative, and free merchandise—are common. A **noncumulative quantity single discount** is based on a single order or shipment. The supplier uses this type of discount to encourage the retailer to increase the size of an order—the bigger the order, the bigger the absolute discount. Quantity discounts that apply to several orders or shipments placed with the supplier over an extended period (usually a year) are referred to as **cumulative quantity discounts**. Not only do these discounts apply to several orders, but usually the amount of the discount increases as the total (accumulated) order size increases. The supplier's purpose for applying cumulative discounts is to encourage return trade by reducing the price of merchandise on subsequent orders. *Free merchandise* is also a form of quantity discount. The "13" dozen, whereby the supplier offers one free dozen for every 12 dozen ordered, is a common way to give the retailer free merchandise instead of a price reduction or a cash payment.

Seasonal discounts.   **Seasonal discounts** are price reductions given to buyers who are willing to order, receive, and pay for goods during the "off season." To even out production throughout the year, many manufacturers of seasonal goods offer seasonal discounts. For example, a retailer will be granted a seasonal discount on Christmas merchandise if it accepts early delivery in spring rather than in the fall. Although the retailer can realize a savings in the cost of merchandise by taking seasonal discounts, the savings must be viewed in light of (1) additional inventory costs and problems; (2) greater risks resulting from price changes, style changes, and merchandise depreciation; and (3) restricted use of investment capital already tied up in the merchandise.

Cash discounts.   A **cash discount** is one given for making prompt payment. To encourage retailers to pay their bills before the due date, the supplier sometimes permits the retailer to deduct a certain percentage discount from the net invoice price. When negotiating cash discounts and related payment terms, the retailer needs to consider three factors: net invoice price, discount amount, and dating terms.

The first consideration in negotiating cash discounts is to establish what constitutes the net invoice price. As the base for calculating cash discounts, the net invoice price is crucial in determining the dollar amount of the discount. The **net invoice price** is the net value of the invoice or the total invoice minus all other discounts (trade, quantity, seasonal, etc.). An exception may occur when the supplier allows the transportation charges to be included in the net invoice figure. Depending on trade practices, the inclusion of transportation charges may be open for negotiation; if so, it is obviously to the retailer's advantage to have them included.

The second factor the retailer must consider is the **discount amount**. While a 2 percent cash discount is common in many trades, the rate ranges from no cash discounts to whatever the supplier is willing to allow. The amount of the cash discount is standardized in some industry trades, and both the retailer and supplier are generally bound by the trade standards. In other trades, the cash discount amount is totally negotiable. Some retailers insist on a cash discount and automatically deduct a standard discount if payment is made within a specific time period (usually 10 days). They take the discount regardless of the terms expressed in the supplier's invoice.

Dating terms are as significant in negotiating cash discounts and payment conditions as the net invoice price and the discount amount. The importance of dating terms is that they (1) determine the cash discount period or the amount of time the retailer has to take advantage of the cash discount and (2) provide the invoice due date or the amount of time the retailer has to pay the net invoice price in full. Ten days is the most common cash discount period, while thirty days from the dating of the invoice is a fairly standard invoice due date. Both cash-discount periods and invoice due dates vary, however, depending on the particular situation and on the retailer's ability to negotiate dating terms.

The two general classes of dating terms are immediate and future. Sometimes suppliers insist on **immediate dating,** allowing no time for the cash discount or extra time for the invoice payment. Prepayment and cash on delivery (COD) are two examples of immediate dating. **Prepayment dating** means the retailer must make payment when the order is placed. Suppliers use prepayment terms when two circumstances occur simultaneously: (1) the retailer is either unknown or unreliable (bad credit rating) and (2) the merchandise is customized or highly perishable. **Cash on delivery** terms are enforced when the retailer is either unknown or unreliable, but when the merchandise can be easily sold if returned to the supplier.

Future dating is the practice of allowing the retailer more time to take advantage of the cash discount or to pay the net amount of the invoice. In essence, it encourages the retailer to delay payment and helps in short-term financing of inventory. Figure 15–8 describes several types of future dating.

One additional negotiating issue regarding cash discounts is *anticipation,* or an extra cash discount for paying the net invoice before the cash-discount period expires. It is an amount the retailer may take in addition to the cash discount. The anticipation amount depends on the number of days the invoice is paid before the last day of the discount period; for example, paying the invoice on the fourth day of a ten-day cash-discount period entitles the retailer to deduct six days of anticipation at a pre-viously agreed-on daily discount rate. Large retailers as well as those with surplus cash available use anticipation extensively.

Most experts recommend that retailers take every cash discount available, be-cause most cash discounts yield an equivalent annual interest rate far in excess of the yield most other investments produce. Also, the yield on most cash discounts is more than enough to cover the interest on funds borrowed to meet the time requirement of the cash-discount period.

FIGURE 15–8
Types of future-dating terms

FUTURE DATING TERMS	SELECTED EXAMPLES	EXPLANATION OF EXAMPLES	
		Cash Discount Terms	Net Invoice Terms
Net	Net, 30	no cash discount allowed	net amount due within 30 days of invoice date
Date of Invoice (DOI)	2/10, net 30	2-percent discount within 10 days of invoice date	net amount due within 30 days of invoice date
End of Month (EOM)	2/10, net 60, EOM	2-percent discount within 20 days of the first day of the month following the invoice date	net amount due within 60 days of the first day of the month following the invoice date
Receipt of Goods (ROG)	4/10, net 45, ROG	4-percent discount within 10 days after receiving the goods at the retailer's place of business	net amount due within 45 days after receiving the goods at the retailer's place of business
Extra	3/10-60 extra, net 90	3-percent discount within 70 days of invoice date	net amount due within 90 days of invoice date

Promotional allowances.   To gain the retailer's cooperation in promotional activities, the supplier frequently offers a promotional allowance. **Promotional allowances,** which reduce the price retailers pay suppliers for merchandise, include advertising allowances, preferred selling space, free display materials, and merchandise deals. *Advertising allowances* are discounts retailers earn by advertising the supplier's products in the local media. In essence, the retailer assumes part or all of the supplier's local advertising function and is compensated by the supplier for money spent and services performed in the form of an advertising allowance. Retailers give vendors *preferred selling space* in return for a price reduction. A variation of this type of space consideration is the "slotting allowance"—admission fees paid by manufacturers to get their product on crowded shelves.[11] Preferred sales areas include (1) a freestanding display in a high-traffic aisle, (2) an end-of-aisle display, (3) a high-exposure area near a checkout counter, or (4) a special window display. In some cases, the more preferred the selling space, the greater the allowance. Retailers also use *free display materials* in the form of counter, window, and floor displays, signs, banners, and shelf strips, as well as various types of giveaways. These materials help to increase sales, reduce selling costs, and earn allowances from suppliers. Promotional allowances also can take the form of *merchandise deals* in which the supplier substitutes free merchandise for monetary allowances as compensation for performing promotional functions. As with all other discounts, promotional allowances must be judged on a cost–benefit basis.

Transportation and Handling Terms

The retailer's actual laid-in cost of merchandise also depends on which party assumes the transportation charges and handling responsibilities. In negotiating transportation and handling terms, the retailer must consider all of these issues: Who pays transportation charges? Who bears transportation charges? Where does the title exchange hands? Who is responsible for filing claims? The payer and the bearer of transportation charges may or may not be the same person; for example, to facilitate delivery speed, the supplier may pay transportation charges when the goods are loaded at the factory but charge them back to the retailer on the invoice. In such cases the retailer ultimately bears the cost of transportation. Equally important is the point at which title to the merchandise is transferred from the supplier to the retailer. The party that has title while the goods are in transit is responsible for bearing any insurance costs that might be needed above the liability of the carrier to cover loss. The location where title exchange occurs also influences which party is responsible for filing and collecting any damage claims against the carrier. Damage claims not only can be expensive to collect in some cases but can also occupy a considerable amount of the retailer's time. Figure 15–9 illustrates the six most common expressions of transportation and handling terms. As a note of caution, however, transportation terms are characterized by a variety of expressions (e.g., the terms *plant* or *factory* are often substituted for *origin; store* or *retailer* may be used instead of *destination*). Therefore, retailers should not hesitate to ask for clarification of any expression they do not fully understand.

Negotiating the Service

In addition to price, the various types and levels of services the supplier provides also are subject to negotiation. In some cases, a service is fairly standard with only minor adjustments allowed; in other cases, certain services are totally negotiable. The discussion on evaluating sources of supply identified ten different supplier services. Although services may be available, the retailer may not receive some or any of them without actively seeking them as part of the buying process. The terms and conditions

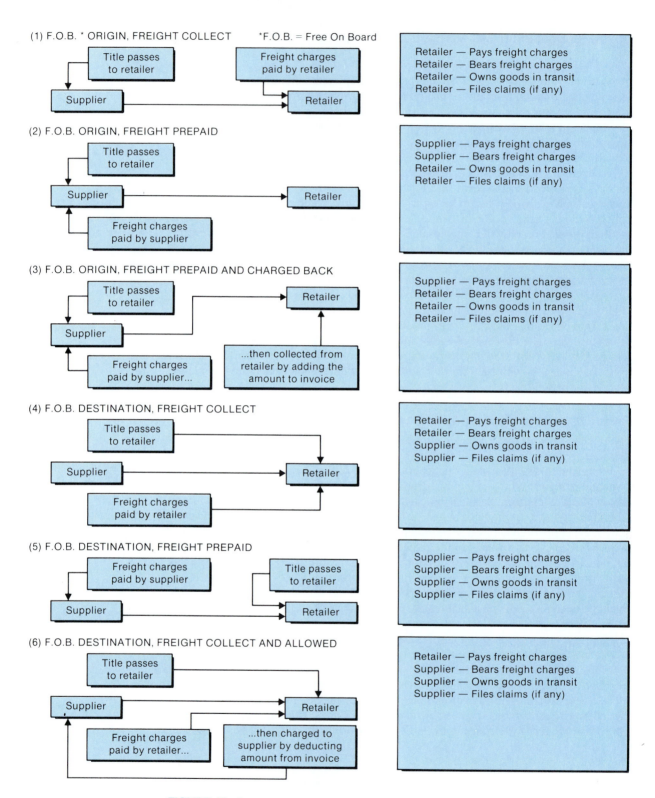

FIGURE 15–9

Transportation terms and conditions (source: adapted from Murray Krieger, *Practical Merchandising Math for Everyday Use* [New York: National Retail Merchants Association, 1980], 4) for any one of these ten services must be detailed before purchase if the retailer expects the supplier to provide them.

The final step in the retailer's buying process is the actual purchase of the merchandise. Two issues to consider are buying strategies and buying methods.

Buying Strategies

In deciding how many different sources of supply to use in securing the store's merchandise, the retailer can elect to pursue one of two buying strategies: concentrated or dispersed.

Concentrated Buying

With a **concentration strategy,** the retailer decides to use a limited number of suppliers, believing it leads to lower total costs and preferential treatment. By concentrating purchases, the retailer can lower the laid-in cost of the merchandise by taking advantage of quantity discounts and lower transportation rates. Operating expenses can be lower, since ordering, receiving, and processing of merchandise are more efficient with fewer suppliers. Equally important, many retailers believe that if they become a preferred customer by concentrating their purchases, they can expect to receive special considerations for merchandise and supplier services.

Dispersed Buying

Proponents of the **dispersion strategy** believe that concentrated buying is "concentrated risk," because it is dangerous to "put all your eggs in a few baskets." By spreading orders over many suppliers, these retailers believe they can (1) obtain a greater variety of merchandise, (2) be made aware of "hot" items, (3) ensure backup sources of supply, and (4) promote competitive services from different supply sources. Retailers must make the decision to use a concentration or a dispersion strategy in light of their individual situations. Generally, retailers of staple merchandise tend to concentrate their purchases, whereas retailers of fashion merchandise usually elect a less-concentrated approach.

Buying Methods

Retailers use several buying methods, depending on their circumstances. They include regular, consignment, memorandum, approval, and specification buying.

Regular Buying

Retailers use regular buying to secure the vast majority of their merchandise lines. **Regular buying** involves the systematic cutting and issuing of purchase orders and reorders. The entire buying process is conducted in conjunction with the merchandise budget and the inventory-control process. Purchases are mechanical and automatic. Most staple goods and many fashion goods can be handled by this method.

Consignment Buying

Consignment buying is an arrangement whereby the supplier retains ownership of the merchandise shipped to the retailer, and the retailer (1) displays the merchandise, (2) sells it to the final consumer, (3) deducts an agreed-on percentage commission, and (4) remits the remainder to the supplier. Merchandise not sold within a prescribed time is returned to the supplier. This method of buying is usually used when the merchandise is expensive, new, or of such a high-risk nature that the extent and duration of demand are relatively unknown.

Memorandum Buying

Memorandum buying is essentially a variation of consignment buying. The main difference is that the title to the merchandise exchanges hands when it is shipped to the retailer. The retailer retains the right to return to the supplier any unsold merchandise and to pay for the merchandise after it has been sold. The retailer's purpose for assuming title is to gain more control in setting the selling price to the final consumer.

Approval Buying

When merchandise is shipped to the store before the final purchase decision has been made, the retailer is buying on approval. Before the retailer can sell the merchandise it must secure ownership. **Approval buying** allows the retailer to inspect the merchandise before making the purchase decision and to postpone any purchase until physical possession has been secured. Postponing possession can result in lower inventory carrying costs, more time to take advantage of cash discounts, and more time to prepare a merchandising program for the goods.

Specification Buying

Many large retail organizations want some of their merchandise made to their specifications. Specifications can range from minor changes in existing lines of merchandise to complete specifications covering raw materials, design, quality, labeling, and packaging. Through **specification buying,** the retailer can acquire merchandise that is unique and distinctive from that of competitors and that is thus personalized. Usually, specification buying involves considerable negotiation between retailer and supplier, and ordering lead times are quite long.

SUMMARY

The buying process is the first stage in the retailer's efforts to get merchandise into the store. It involves the six steps of identifying, surveying, contacting, evaluating, negotiating with, and buying from sources of supply.

The first step of identifying sources of supply is to establish what type of channel to use in procuring each merchandise line. The retailer has several options in selecting sources of supply, including various types of raw-resource producers, manufacturers, intermediaries, and resident buying offices.

The second step, surveying sources of supply, involves determining which sources of supply are most appropriate for the retailer's operation. It provides a means by which an initial screening of supply sources can be made. The surveying step requires the retailer to develop and maintain a buying plan and a resource file.

Contacting sources of supply is the third step in the buying process. Contacts can be initiated by either the vendor or the retailer. Vendor-initiated contacts include store visits by vendor salespeople or mail and telephone solicitations. Retailers contact sources of supply by visiting central markets, using resident buying offices, attending merchandise shows, and making telephone and mail inquiries.

The fourth step in the buying process is evaluating various alternative suppliers. Suppliers can be evaluated on the basis of (1) the suitability, availability, and adaptability of the merchandise they offer; (2) the exclusiveness and policies associated with the supplier's distribution system; (3) the appropriateness of the supplier's price and policies regarding price maintenance; (4) the type and amount of promotional assistance; and (5) the type and amount of supplementary services. Three methods for evaluating supply sources are the weighted-rating method, the single-most-important criterion method, and the minimum-cutoff method.

Negotiating with sources of supply is the fifth step in the buying process. Negotiation involves discussing various issues of concern to both the retailer and the supplier. The two most common issues subject to negotiation are price and service. Price negotiations start with the supplier's list price and those discounts and allowances taken to adjust the list price. The most common price adjustments are trade, quantity, seasonal, and cash discounts, along with promotional allowances. Also of concern are various transportation and handling terms that affect the retailer's laid-in cost of the new merchandise.

The final step in the buying process is actual purchase of the merchandise from several suppliers, using various buying methods. The retailer can elect to concentrate purchases with a few suppliers or disperse them among many suppliers. In the actual buying process, the retailer can buy merchandise using a regular, consignment, memorandum, approval, or specification method of buying.

KEY TERMS AND CONCEPTS

agent intermediary
approval buying
auction house
broker
cash-and-carry wholesaler
cash discount
cash on delivery (COD)
centralized buying
chain trade discount
commission merchant
commissionaire
concentration strategy
consignment buying
contractual intermediary
cooperative group
cumulative quantity discount
dating terms
decentralized buying
discount amount
dispersion strategy
drop shipper
formal buying organization
full-function merchant intermediaries
future dating
generalized buying
general merchandise wholesaler
immediate dating
importer

independent buying office
informal buying organization
limited-function merchant intermediaries
list price
manufacturers' agent
memorandum buying
merchant intermediaries
minimum-cutoff method
net invoice price
noncumulative quantity single discount
prepayment dating
promotional allowances
rack jobber
regular buying
resident buying office
sales agent
seasonal discount
single-line wholesaler
single-most-important criterion method
single trade discount
specialized buying
specialty-line wholesaler
specification buying
store-owned buying office
truck distributor
voluntary chain
weighted-rating method

REVIEW QUESTIONS

1. How formal should the retailer's buying organization be?
2. Describe the relative strengths and weaknesses of a centralized buying organization.
3. Identify the conditions under which retailers buy directly from the manufacturer.
4. How are full-function merchant wholesalers distinguished from one another?
5. Identify and describe the four types of limited-function merchant wholesalers.
6. Distinguish between an agent intermediary and a merchant intermediary.
7. Compare and contrast the two types of contractual intermediaries.
8. What type of information and buyer assistance services does the resident buying office provide?
9. From the retailer's viewpoint, what are the benefits of having vendor sales representatives make store visits?
10. Define merchandise show.
11. How can the retailer evaluate the merchandise offered by a given supplier? Identify and discuss the evaluation criteria.
12. What distribution and delivery policies and standards should the retailer consider when evaluating a particular supplier?
13. Describe the minimum-cutoff method of supplier evaluation.
14. Identify the starting point for price negotiations between retailers and suppliers.
15. What would be the retailer's price if a product had a list price of $40 and a trade discount structure of 30/20/5?
16. How does a cumulative quantity discount differ from a noncumulative discount?
17. List the two general classes of dating terms. Discuss each class.
18. What are promotional allowances? Describe their four common forms.
19. What issues should the retailer consider when negotiating transportation and handling terms?
20. Describe the two buying-strategy options open to the retailer when deciding how many different sources of supply to use in securing the store's merchandise.
21. Identify and briefly describe the five buying methods a retailer might use.

ENDNOTES

1. Richard Ettenson and Janet Wagner, "Retail Buyers' Saleability Judgments: A Comparison of Information Use Across Three Levels of Experience," *Journal of Retailing* 62 (Spring 1986): 42.
2. Francine Schwadel, "Sears Expected to Reorganize Buying Staff," *The Wall Street Journal,* 24 Feb. 1988, 1.
3. See Renee D. Howerton and Teresa A. Summers, "Apparel Sales Representatives: Perceptions of Their Roles and Functions," *The FIT Review* 4 (Spring 1988): 10–18.
4. See Kenneth G. Hardy and Allan J. Magrath, "Buying Groups: Clout for Small Businesses," *Harvard Business Review* (September–October 1987): 16–23.
5. Bill Saporito, "Super Valu Does Two Things Well," *Fortune,* 18 April 1983: 114.
6. See Clyde Ellison, Jr., "Auditing Imports," *Retail Control* (November 1986): 45–55.
7. Roger D. Blackwell and W. Wayne Talarzyk, "Lifestyle Retailing: Competitive Strategies," *Journal of Retailing* 59 (Winter 1983): 14.
8. The Limited, promotional brochure.
9. Elizabeth C. Hirschman, "An Exploratory Comparison of Decision Criteria Used by Retail Buyers," in *Retail Patronage Theory,* eds. R. F. Lusch and W. R. Darden (Norman, OK: Center for Economic and Management Research, The University of Oklahoma, 1981), 3.
10. John S. Berens, "A Decision Matrix Approach to Suppliers' Selection," *Journal of Retailing* 47 (Winter 1971): 52.
11. Laurie Freeman and Janet Meyers, "Grocer 'Fee' Hampers New Product Launches," *Advertising Age,* 3 Aug. 1987, 1, 60.

Banting, Peter M. and Blenkhorn, David L. "Toward More Standardized Terminology in Retail Buying." In *Developments In Marketing Science, Proceedings,* edited by N. K. Malhotra and J. M. Hawes, 227–231. Academy of Marketing Science, 1986.

Bello, Daniel C. "Retailer Buying Strategies at Merchandise Marts." In *1986 AMA Educators' Proceedings,* edited by T. Shimp, 178–183. American Marketing Association, 1986.

Brill, Jack. "New Opportunities for a Competitive Edge." *Retail Control* (September 1986): 44–55.

Brown, James R., Lusch, Robert F., and Muehling, Darrel D. "Conflict and Power-Dependence Relations in Retailer–Supplier Channels." *Journal of Retailing* 59 (Winter 1983): 53–80.

Dilts, Jeffrey C. "A Cross-Channel Comparison of Channel Conflict." In *1985 AMA Educators' Proceedings,* edited by R. F. Lusch et al. 166–71. American Marketing Association, 1985.

Ettenson, Richard and Wagner, Janet. "Retail Buyers' Saleability Judgments: A Comparison of Information Use Across Three Levels of Experience." *Journal of Retailing* 62 (Spring 1986): 41–63.

Hutt, Michael D. "The Retail Buying Committee: A Look at Cohesiveness and Leadership." *Journal of Retailing* 55 (Winter 1979): 87–97.

Johnson, Jean L., Koenig, Harold F., and Brown, James R. "The Bases of Marketing Channel Power: An Exploration and Confirmation of Their Underlying Dimensions." In *1985 AMA Educators' Proceedings,* edited by R. F. Lusch et al. 160–65. American Marketing Association, 1985.

Levy, Michael, and van Breda, Michael. "A Financial Perspective on the Shift of Marketing Functions." *Journal of Retailing* 60 (Winter 1984): 23–42.

"Planning Systems Put Buyers in Their Place—The Market." *Chain Store Age Executive* (July 1985): 93–94.

"Retail Distribution." *Forbes* 17 Jan. 1980, 176–82.

Smith, Rick, and Chavie, Rick. "More Effective Buying Using State-of-the-Art Techniques." *Retail Control* (August 1984): 42–49.

16

Objectives

☐ Identify all the activities involved in physically getting the merchandise into the store and onto the shelves.

☐ Describe the necessary procedures for placing and writing a purchase order and ensuring that each order is properly processed.

☐ Design and explain an effective in-store system for receiving, checking, marking, and stocking incoming merchandise.

☐ Discuss the procedures for processing suppliers' invoices and returning defective merchandise.

Procurement Process: Procuring Merchandise Assortments

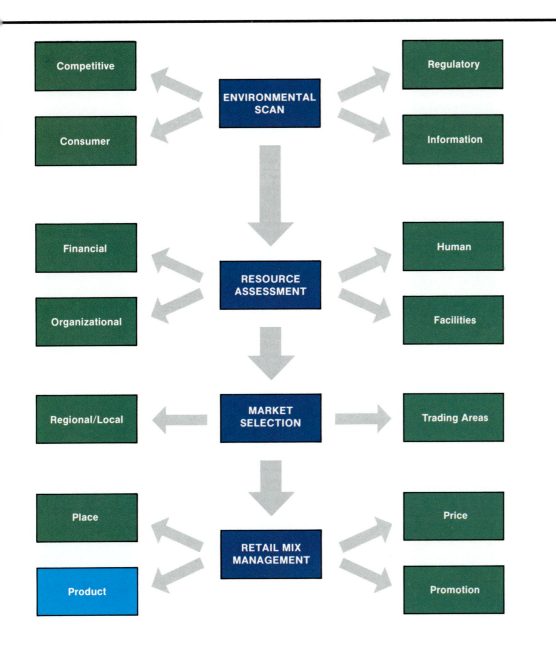

Once the retail buyer has completed the buying process, the next stage in securing the merchandise mix is *procurement*. The **procurement process** involves all the activities of physically getting the merchandise into the store and onto the shelves.

THE PROCUREMENT PROCESS

Too many retailers focus on the buying process and fail to devote sufficient time and attention to the actual procurement of the merchandise. Close control and supervision of the procurement process are as important to the retailer's profit picture as careful buying. For the buyer to secure the merchandise desired in the way intended, procedures for controlling procurement must be developed and maintained. The four basic steps in the procurement process are illustrated in Figure 16–1. In chronological order, they are ordering and following up, receiving and checking, marking and stocking, and paying and returning.

ORDERING AND FOLLOWING UP

The first step in physically procuring the retailer's merchandise is to place a purchase order and then follow up on that purchase order to ensure that it is processed properly and efficiently.

Ordering

The buyer often faces a variety of circumstances that determine which of many different types of orders must be placed. Ordering procedures might involve placing orders (1) with different suppliers at different levels in the channel of distribution; (2) at different times to accommodate past, present, and future needs; (3) for either regular or special merchandise; and (4) with complete or partial specification of terms and conditions of sale. Figure 16–2 identifies and briefly describes seven types of orders.

Manual Purchase-Order System

Retailers can place merchandise orders orally or in writing. Because oral agreements in some states are legally binding only up to some stated limit and are subject to vastly different interpretations, retailers should have them accurately transcribed into written form at the earliest possible time. Orders placed by telephone or in person (such as at central markets or at merchandise shows) are a convenient means of establishing the initial agreement; however, most retailers believe it is necessary to follow up oral agreements with written orders to prevent future misunderstandings. When placing a written order, the buyer can use a form provided by the supplier or one provided by the retailer. It is generally recommended that retailers use their own forms whenever possible.

The **order form,** as a legally binding contract when signed by both parties, specifies the terms and conditions under which the transaction is to be conducted. These terms and conditions usually are stated on both the front and back of the order form. The front of the order form usually contains the following standard information:

- ☐ Retailer description—the complete name and address of the retailer and names and telephone numbers of persons to be contacted should a problem occur
- ☐ Supplier description—the complete name and address of the supplier and the names and telephone numbers of persons to be contacted should a problem occur

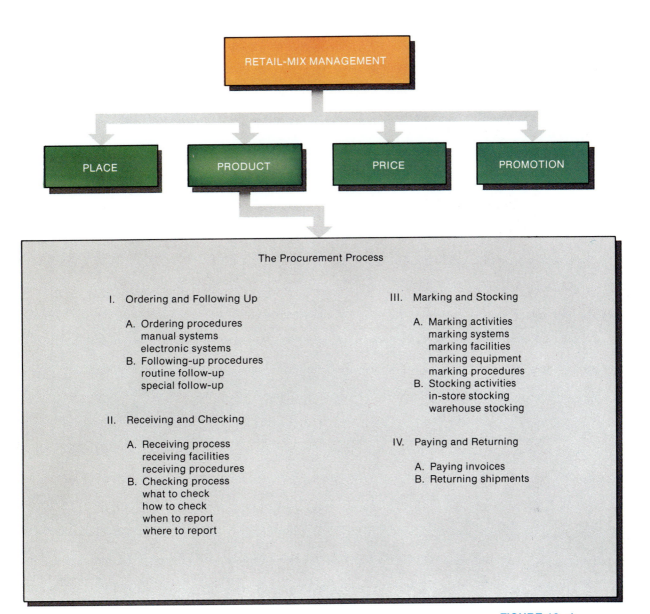

FIGURE 16-1
Structuring and implementing the procurement process

☐ Order number—a serial number used for filing the order and for future reference

☐ Store and department number—a number that identifies the store and/or department for which the merchandise is being secured

☐ Order date—the date an order was sent to or placed with the supplier; important in determining how long it takes a supplier to process an order

☐ Delivery date—the date an order is to be shipped; important because the retailer can refuse to accept merchandise shipped before that date

☐ Cancellation date—the date after which the retailer reserves the right to cancel merchandise that has not been received

☐ Discount terms—a complete listing and description of all negotiated discounts that apply to the order

Regular orders: Orders placed by the buyer directly with the vendor. Involves ordering regular stock items with complete specifications as to terms and conditions of sale and delivery.

Reorders: Orders placed with existing supplier for previously purchased goods, usually under terms and conditions specified by the original order.

Advance orders: Orders placed in advance of both the normal buying season and the immediate needs of the retailer. Involves ordering regular stock items in anticipation of receiving preferred treatment.

Back orders: Orders placed by the buyer for merchandise that was ordered but not received on time. Involves orders that the supplier intends to ship as soon as goods are available.

Blanket orders: Orders placed with suppliers for merchandise for all or part of a season. Involves ordering merchandise without specifying such assortment details as sizes, colors, and styles and such delivery details as when and how much to ship. Requisitions against the blanket order will be placed as the need for the merchandise arises.

Open orders: Orders placed with central market representatives (e.g. resident buyers) to be filled by whatever supplier the representative considers best suited to fill the order.

Special orders: Orders placed with suppliers for merchandise not normally carried in stock or for specially manufactured merchandise. May involve specification buying.

FIGURE 16–2
Types of orders

☐ Transportation terms—a complete description of all shipping and handling terms, including transportation charges, methods and modes of transportation, place of delivery, handling and insurance arrangements, methods of labeling, packaging requirements, and so on
☐ Merchandise description—a complete description of the merchandise including class, style, color, unit price, total price, order quantities, and other information serving to identify the merchandise
☐ Miscellaneous information—a complete description of any additional requirements in terms of ticketing information, instructions for receiving, checking, and marking merchandise, reorder agreements, invoicing arrangements, and so on
☐ Authorized signatures—the required signatures of individuals authorized to place an order; usually the signature of either the store buyer, merchandise manager, or both

The back side of the retailer's order form usually contains a standardized statement of the general conditions under which the supplier will be held legally responsible if it accepts the order.

An equally important issue in writing the order is the distribution of order copies. The size and complexity of the retailer's organization determine the number of copies the retailer should make and distribute. Large retail organizations may distribute as many as seven copies; small retail organizations normally make only three—one for the supplier and two for internal store accounting and processing purposes.

Electronic Purchase-Order System

Several technological developments for improving purchase-order management via computer linkages have emerged during the last several years; one of these is the **electronic purchase-order (EPO) system**.[1] Retail managers now have a variety of options for structuring their EPO system. Figure 16–3 illustrates the most common structures retailers and vendors use in exchanging electronic purchase-order and invoice data. The options follow.

Mail linkages.   Purchase-order and invoice data are transcribed onto magnetic tape or diskettes and transmitted between retailers and vendors via the mail. This is a practical option for communicating a large volume of information when time is not critical.

Telephone linkages.   Purchase-order and invoice data are communicated between the retailer's computer and the vendor's computer via the telephone. The *point-to-point* option involves arranging transmission schedules and common protocols to allow direct computer-to-computer interchange of data.[2] The *dial-up* option involves the storage of retailer orders and vendor invoices in on-line files and allowing each party dial-up access to these files. K Mart's dial-up system works something like this: (1) store manager electronically sends purchase orders to K Mart headquarters; (2) store order is "homogenized" in the ordering system; (3) consolidated purchase orders for each store are available each morning; and (4) each vendor has an assigned path and time slot for calling K mart headquarters to obtain orders.[3]

Third-party clearing houses.   A third-party data processing company makes arrangements to (1) receive orders and invoices, (2) sort them by addressees, (3) store them on-line, and (4) allow subsequent access by authorized addressees. This method allows use of a standardized machine language to establish a bridge for common communication, thereby eliminating the need for separate and distinct methodologies among various vendors and retailers.

To the retailer, the advantages of the EPO system include more effective inventory management, more effective open-to-buy systems (see Chapter 18), and reduction of ordering lead times, thereby improving in-stock positions and stock turnovers while reducing inventory carrying costs.

Following Up

To be sure the right order is received in the right place at the right time, the retailer needs follow-up procedures. Following up an order is also necessary to make a purchase contract legally binding. In most cases, the original copy of the purchase order, which is sent to the supplier, constitutes a legal *offer to buy*. No purchase contract exists, however, until the seller *accepts* the buyer's offer. Therefore, the first step in following up an order is to determine whether the supplier has accepted the order. The retailer should maintain adequate records, including the supplier's formal notification of acceptance for each order. Suppliers usually notify the retailer of their acceptance by returning the acknowledgment copy of the order form or by using their own acceptance forms. Follow-up procedures also include checking the supplier's

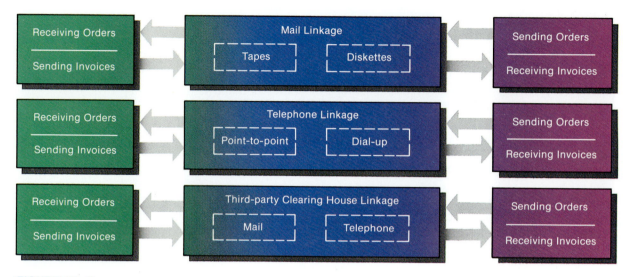

FIGURE 16–3
Electronic purchase-order systems

acceptance form to determine whether the supplier has made any changes in the order; the retailer may be legally bound to a changed order unless it is corrected in writing. Retailers use both routine and special procedures in following up an order.

Routine Follow-Up

Routine follow-up procedures are used to check for order acceptance and discrepancies between the retailer's original order and the supplier's acceptance. Various types of filing systems are used to "flag" purchase orders that have not been checked. The buyer manually or electronically reviews the files frequently to determine which orders require additional attention. Routine procedures also are used to check the progress of orders for merchandise that are considered either extremely important or overdue. After identifying these important or overdue orders, the buyer contacts the supplier to check their status. The buyer routinely sends either a postcard, a personal letter, or a telegram, or, if circumstances are urgent, makes a telephone call.

Special Follow-Up

There are **special follow-up** procedures if the importance of the order merits them. These special procedures usually involve the use of a field expediter (e.g., resident buyer) who personally visits the supplier. Personal visits generally are seen as the strongest method available for pressuring the supplier to meet its obligations.

Once the order has been placed and received, the retailer must efficiently process incoming shipments to ensure their timely arrival on the sales floor. Figure 16–4 illustrates in-store handling tasks for incoming merchandise shipments.

RECEIVING AND CHECKING

Receiving is the actual physical exchange of goods between the retailer and the supplier's transporting agent. It is the point at which the retailer takes physical possession of the goods. **Checking** is the process of determining whether the supplier has shipped what the retailer ordered and whether the shipment has arrived in good condition.

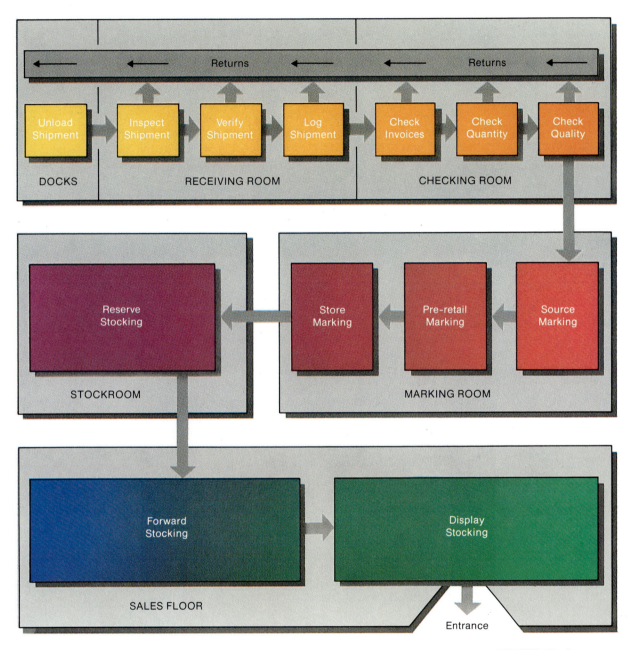

FIGURE 16—4
The in-store merchandise-handling process

Receiving Process

Retailers receive their merchandise in a variety of ways. The nature of the retailer's business along with the physical facilities dictates to a large extent how goods are brought into the store. Large stores usually require more elaborate receiving facilities and procedures than do small stores. Merchandise that is either large and bulky or that is ordered in large quantities needs a greater amount of space within the receiving center. Also, high-value merchandise requires greater control and security than low-value merchandise. Whatever the particular situation, receiving facilities and procedures should be designed to meet the store's individual needs.

Receiving Facilities

Retailers can receive merchandise shipments through either the front door (customer entrance) or the back door. Generally, the retailer should avoid front-door receiving because it interferes with the smooth flow of customer traffic; receiving, checking, and stocking areas are located in the back of the store; there is greater likelihood of damaged shipping cartons as well as damaged sales floor display fixtures; and it creates problems in trying to maintain a clean sales floor.

The typical back-door receiving operation consists of an unloading area and a receiving area. The area devoted to unloading should permit easy maneuverability and facilitate careful handling. Unloading docks must be large enough to allow forklift trucks to handle bulky merchandise and quantity shipments that arrive on pallets. Some retailers also have mechanical unloading devices such as chutes, roller conveyors, and overhead conveyor systems.

Usually located adjacent to the unloading area on the store's ground floor, the receiving area should be large enough to permit easy maneuverability, to allow inspection of incoming shipments, and to act as a holding area for merchandise awaiting transfer to the checking room. The receiving room layout should facilitate inspection of incoming packages and cartons.

Receiving Procedures

The responsibility for receiving merchandise in large stores usually is delegated to a full-time receiving clerk who is held accountable for any errors in receiving goods and documenting the receipt. Receiving responsibilities in small stores often are assumed by either the store manager, assistant manager, or one of the sales personnel. In addition to the responsibility of controlling incoming merchandise, the receiving department also must control the flow of outgoing merchandise to the sales floor. Store sales personnel should not be allowed to remove merchandise from the receiving room until it has been properly processed, which normally involves inspecting, verifying, and logging incoming shipments.

Inspecting shipments. The first step in inspecting incoming merchandise is to arrange the shipment so that each package (box or carton) in the shipment is clearly visible. Next, a visual inspection of the exterior of each package is conducted to determine whether the package has been damaged (crushed, punctured) or opened (broken seal). If a package has been badly damaged or opened, the receiving clerk should refuse to accept the shipment unless the carrier's employee agrees to witness the visual inspection of the contents of the package. Packages that are slightly damaged may be accepted, but before signing for the shipment, the receiving clerk should make a notation of the damage on all transportation and receiving documents to facilitate processing of any future damage or loss claims by both the store and the supplier.

Verifying shipments. After inspecting the shipment for visual damage, the receiving clerk should make several verifications. First, the clerk must verify that the shipment was ordered by consulting the receiving department's file of purchase orders or a log (schedule) of incoming shipments. Second, the completeness of the shipment must be verified. Sometimes suppliers ship only partial orders; in such cases, the retailer may or may not decide to accept shipment depending on its needs at the time. Third, the receiving clerk should verify that the actual makeup of the shipment is the same as that described on the *bill of lading* (a transportation document between shipper and carrier that serves as a receipt for the goods tendered to the carrier). The number

Retailers have four possible methods for checking quantities of incoming shipments.

of cartons in the shipment and the weight of each carton should also be checked to see if they correspond to the bill of lading. Fourth, freight charges sometimes are verified by comparing the total weight of the shipment with various rate schedules. Finally, additional verification might include recording the name and address of the supplier and the carrier, the name of the person making the delivery, and the delivery date.

Logging shipments.   To facilitate and organize the processing of incoming shipments, each shipment is logged in a receiving record and assigned a receiving number. The **receiving record** and number follow the shipment through the checking, marking, and stocking steps of the procurement process and serve as a quick reference should problems arise. The accounting department also uses the record to verify shipment before invoices are paid. Further, the record is a source of identification if the merchandise must be returned.

Checking Process

After inspecting, verifying, and logging the shipment, the retailer must check the merchandise contained in the shipment. While the merchandise can be checked in the receiving room, most retailers prefer to have a separate area or room (if space permits) for this task. Checking involves opening each package, removing the merchandise, and examining it. Accessibility to the receiving area and to the marking and stocking rooms must be considered in locating the checking room. The ideal layout is a straight line—receiving room to checking room to marking to stocking rooms.

What to Check

The retailer can make three checks to ensure it has received what was ordered: an invoice, a quantity, and a quality check. In the **invoice check,** the retailer compares the invoice with the purchase order. The invoice is the supplier's bill and the document that itemizes particulars of the shipment in terms of merchandise assortment, quantity, and price. It also identifies the terms of the sale, delivery terms, and the amount due for payment. Checking personnel must determine whether the retailer's purchase order exactly matches the supplier's invoice.

During the **quantity check,** the checking personnel unpack and sort each package to check the actual physical contents of each package against the purchase order, the invoice, or both. Essentially, the checker sorts each package by style, size, and color (or other assortment factors) and makes a physical count to determine whether the package contains the same number of units as listed on the invoice and purchase order. Any shortages, overages, or substitutions are noted and reported to the buyer or merchandise manager. It is not uncommon for some suppliers to ship substitute merchandise if they are out of the merchandise that was ordered. Equally common are honest mistakes in filling the order: shipping the wrong assortment of styles, sizes, and colors is to be expected on occasion.

The third check is the **quality check,** which actually involves two separate checks. First, the merchandise is examined for any damage that is obviously the result of shipping. This kind of damage is the responsibility of the carrier and the insurer of the shipment. The second check is for imperfections in the merchandise and for lesser-quality merchandise than the retailer ordered. Regular checking personnel can detect merchandise that has either been damaged in shipment or has obvious imperfections (cracked, stained, scratched, torn); however, detecting lower-than-ordered quality creates problems. Usually, if checking personnel suspect that merchandise might be of lower quality than what was ordered, they should inform either the buyer or the merchandise manager, who makes the final determination on the quality.

How to Check

The retailer can use one of four methods to check the quantity of incoming shipments: the direct check, the blind check, the semiblind check, and the combination check. In a **direct check,** the retailer checks off from the invoice, which lists all the ordered and shipped items, each group of items as they are counted. If the invoice is not available and the merchandise is needed on the sales floor, the retailer can make a direct check against the purchase order to verify the quantity. Speed and simplicity are the principal advantages of the direct check. The **blind check** is a procedure in which the checker lists and describes each merchandise group on a blank form and then counts and records the number of items in each group. The checker may also record any additional information deemed pertinent. Next, the buyer, merchandise manager, or some other knowledgeable person compares the checker's list and descriptions with the invoice or purchase order to determine whether there are any discrepancies. Generally, the blind method is the most accurate for checking incoming shipments, but it is also the most expensive because of the additional time and labor involved.

The **semiblind check** provides the checker with a list and description of each merchandise group in the shipment but not the quantities for each group. The checker must physically count and record the number of items in each merchandise group. The semiblind method has the advantages of being both reasonably fast and accurate. The **combination check** method is simply using the direct check method when the supplier's invoice is available and the blind or semiblind check method when the retailer does not have the supplier's invoice.

When to Report

It is extremely important that the retailer promptly report any damages or discrepancies to the appropriate person on completion of the checking process. The retailer must report or return unwanted merchandise immediately to receive prompt and fair adjustments. The longer the goods are left in the store, the more difficult it becomes to receive satisfactory adjustments on claims.

Where to Report

The retailer should immediately notify the appropriate supplier of discrepancies between (1) the supplier's invoice and the retailer's purchase order, (2) the supplier's invoice and the quantity check, or (3) the quality ordered and the quality received.

MARKING AND STOCKING

Marking is affixing to merchandise the information necessary for stocking, controlling, and selling. Customers want information on the price, size, and color of merchandise before they are willing to buy, and the retailer needs to know when and from where the merchandise was secured, its cost, and where it goes to maintain proper inventory and record controls. **Stocking** includes all the activities associated with in-store and between-store distribution of merchandise. Stocking may involve moving merchandise to the sales floor for display or to the reserve or stocking rooms for storage.

Marking Activities

The facilities, equipment, procedures, and personnel for marking merchandise should be tailored to the volume and type of merchandise. Small, hand-, and mechanically operated marking systems usually are sufficient for most small retail operations. More sophisticated mechanical and electronic systems are more appropriate for large retailing organizations with sufficient merchandise volume to justify the expense. Regardless of which system is installed, it is essential to develop and maintain controlled marking procedures. First, well-marked merchandise is necessary for customer selection. Customers need informative, easy-to-read tags to make their merchandise selections without the aid of the store's sales personnel. Second, clearly and informatively marked merchandise also can aid in the selling activities of store personnel; they also are useful when sales personnel stock and organize sales floor displays. Third, well-marked merchandise aids sales personnel in handling returns and adjustments. Finally, good marking procedures permit better inventory control. One of the first steps a retailer should take in organizing a stock and record-control system is to ensure that all incoming merchandise is properly marked.

Marking Systems

There are a number of ways to physically mark merchandise. The three most common marking systems are source marking, preretailing, and store marking. **Source marking** is the system by which the retailer authorizes the manufacturer or supplier to mark the merchandise before shipping it to the store. The merchandise is marked either with preprinted tickets sent to the supplier by the retailer or with tickets printed by the manufacturer based on information supplied by the retailer. Source marking reduces both in-store marking expenses and the time it takes to get the merchandise onto the sales floor. A standard tag code and format enables the retailer to make very effective use of electronic data processing equipment.

Preretailing is a retail buying practice of deciding the selling price of merchandise before it is purchased and recording that price on the store's copy of the purchase order so the store's "markers" can put the selling price on the merchandise as soon as it comes through the doors. Store personnel who are responsible for marking merchandise can do so on its arrival without contacting the store buyer.

Store marking is the practice of having store personnel mark all merchandise after the store has received it. It also is used to complete the marking process initiated in the preretailing system. When using store marking, the retailer must invest in marking facilities and equipment and establish marking procedures.

Marking Facilities

Merchandise should be marked before it reaches the sales floor. The most common problems associated with marking merchandise on the sales floor are (1) a greater frequency of errors, slower performance, and poorer-quality work; (2) a lack of security for marking tags and equipment left unsupervised; (3) a loss of sales because sales personnel were busy marking merchandise; (4) a messy-appearing sales floor; and (5) the interference with a smooth customer traffic flow as a result of the marking activities.

Marking Equipment

Merchandise can be marked by means of hand, mechanical, and electronic equipment. The size and nature of the retailer's operation often determine which type of equipment is most appropriate.

Hand marking.   Hand marking is done with grease pencils, ink stamps, and pens. The desired information is marked directly on either the merchandise or its package, or on a gummed label, string tag, or pin ticket attached to the merchandise. Hand marking is the least desirable method of marking merchandise because it (1) is more time-consuming, (2) results in more marking errors, and (3) lacks permanence and neatness. Further, price security is jeopardized, since grease and ink markings can be blotted out, smeared, and easily changed.

Mechanical marking.   Mechanical equipment can produce tags and tickets in both printed (human-readable language) and punched (machine-readable language) forms. Marking machines offer the advantages of fewer errors, faster speed, greater permanence, improved legibility, and a higher level of price security than hand marking. Also, more information can be placed on smaller tags using mechanical as opposed to hand marking.

Electronic marking.   Technological advancements in electronic (computer-controlled) equipment have generated a wave of new marking procedures that are compatible with various **point-of-sale (POS)** systems. Electronic marking devices can code prices onto tickets and tags that can be quickly and automatically read and processed by optical scanning equipment or **optical character recognition** (OCR) systems. Optical scanners usually are employed at checkout counters, where they read all the information on the ticket or tag and transmit it to the store's computer system for further processing (e.g., for inventory control and accounting records). While the checkout counter wand is the most common type of optical scanner used in general merchandise retailing, fixed-slot scanners (checkout counters with built-in laser beams that read tags as the merchandise is passed over the beam) are the predominate system in the supermarket industry. Kroger Supermarkets are currently experimenting with a checkout system that allows consumers to scan their own purchases; Figure 16–5 describes the system.

Marking Procedures

In deciding on marking systems, facilities, and equipment, the retailer must decide what and how much information to place on the tag, where and how to attach the tag to the merchandise, and when to use bulk marking.

Coding merchandise tags.   Most retailers want more than just price information on their merchandise tags. The retail price, along with size, color, and style, should

The Check-Robot utilizes a flat-top scanner, a touch-sensitive video display monitor, a conveyor belt, and a sensing mechanism used for security purposes.

The consumer scans each item in her shopping basket and then places it on a conveyor belt which is activated by the scanner. Overhead on the monitor, the product identification and price are displayed for the last five items scanned, scrolling upward as more items are added. The groceries move down the conveyor belt through a metal archway to a bagging area where a Kroger bagger is stationed.

After all items have been scanned, the consumer brings the receipt to a nearby payment station and tenders her bill.

At the consumer's disposal are all the functions a cashier would enjoy on a traditional POS terminal, but instead, on the touch-sensitive screen. There is a subtotal button and a button that allows the option of voicing the prices.

If a consumer comes up against a bar code that won't scan, she merely presses the numbers of the code into the video monitor, just as a cashier would do on a POS terminal. The product description and price are displayed just as if the item were scanned.

Coupons are accommodated in a rather simple way. "There's a button right beside the price [on the screen] that says 'coupon'." "When you touch that, it highlights that item on the screen and puts an asterisk next to the item on the receipt. This helps the cashier verify the product was purchased; the amount of the coupon is subtracted at the time payment is made."

Source: Reprinted by permission from "The Ultimate in Self-Service: Scan Your Own," *Chain Store Age Executive* (June 1987), p. 53. Copyright © Lebhar-Friedman Inc. 425 Park Avenue, New York, NY 10022.

FIGURE 16–5
The ultimate in self-service: Self-service scanning

appear on the tag in such a way that customers can easily identify this information. The department, supplier, and merchandise class are most frequently identified by means of the National Retail Merchants Association's classification system. The last three informational requirements (receiving date, stocking date, and cost of the merchandise) are placed on the tag in coded form to disguise the information from the customers.

With the installation of optical scanners, many retailers have elected to use a standardized marking system. These universal vendor marking (UVM) systems involve coding merchandise tags with a machine-readable code that is sponsored by one or more trade associations. In the past, the National Retail Merchants Association (NRMA) sponsored the **optical character recognition-font A (OCR-A)** code, which is equally human and machine readable. The second standardized code in common use is the **universal product code (UPC)**. Used largely within the supermarket industry, the UPC is a bar code system that identifies both the product and the manufacturer. Recently, there has been a tremendous increase in the acceptance and popularity of UPC; as a result, the NRMA endorses it as the preferred marking system for all merchandise.[4] "No UPC. No PO" (purchase order) is a sign that is posted at Toys 'R' Us headquarters.[5] To help in the transition from OCR-A to UPC, a *dual-technology* vendor marking system is available (see Figure 16–6).

Many retailers have their own customized marking system. Receiving and stocking dates, for example, are coded using a transformation of the date by addition, subtraction, multiplication, or division. A receiving date of 10-12-80 could be transformed to 40-42-110 by adding 30 to the month, day, and year. Reversing their position (to 110-42-40) can further disguise the dates.

Two common types of cost codes are word and symbol codes. **Word cost codes** use a 10-letter word or words in which no letter is repeated. Some popular

word codes are MAKE PROFIT, MONEY TALKS, and REPUBLICAN. Each letter in the word code is assigned a single-digit number. For example,

$$\begin{matrix} \text{M} & \text{O} & \text{N} & \text{E} & \text{Y} & & \text{T} & \text{A} & \text{L} & \text{K} & \text{S} \\ 1 & 2 & 3 & 4 & 5 & & 6 & 7 & 8 & 9 & 0 \end{matrix}$$

To use such a cost code, the retailer would code EYES on the price tag for a merchandise item that costs $45.40. **Symbol cost codes** use easy-to-recognize symbols as direct substitutes for numbers. The main limitations of symbol codes are that they take longer to write than either letters or numbers, and the marker is usually less familiar with the symbols and thus prone to make mistakes.

Attaching merchandise tags. Price tags are attached by strings, pins, snaps, gummed labels, and heat seals. To prevent price tag switching, retailers should attach tags so that customers cannot easily remove them without damaging or destroying the tag; at the same time, store personnel must be able to remove the tag at the point of sale without damaging the merchandise. Visibility and consistency are the key considerations in deciding where to place tags on the merchandise. When merchandise is marked in the same place, both customers and store employees can readily locate the tag. Visibility and consistency prevent unnecessary opening of packages, maintain cleaner and neater displays, and reduce wear and tear on merchandise.

Re-marking merchandise tags. Re-marking merchandise often becomes necessary because of damage, obsolescence, or an increase in the wholesale price. In re-marking merchandise, the retailer should set strict policies on how markdowns are to be shown. Some retailers manually re-mark merchandise on the sales floor by crossing out the old price and adding the new price to the ticket. While this policy permits the customer to identify the price as a reduced price, it also identifies the merchandise as being somewhat undesirable, at least at the former price. Manual re-marking also increases the opportunity for consumer fraud—the retailer that re-marks with a red ballpoint pen is inviting some customers to do a little re-marking of their own. Other retailers prefer to send the merchandise back to the marking room for re-marking and to replace the old price tag with a new one. Re-marking in the marking room allows for both greater security and greater accuracy. Attaching new price tags for merchandise that has been marked down offers the retailer the opportunity to sell the merchandise at a lower price without the negative connotation of its being inferior.

When re-marking merchandise to reflect price increases, retailers should remove the old price tag and replace it with a new one. Covering up the price simply invites the customer to peek at the old one. It also is an invitation to remove the new tag. More important, all customers will be somewhat dissatisfied with the merchandise and the store knowing that they had to pay a higher price.

Bulk marking. Retailers frequently elect to use bulk marking on merchandise that is characterized by low unit value, high turnover, and suitable size and shape for bin, rack, or table displays. Individual marking is too expensive for many hardware items, variety goods, candies, and toiletries. **Bulk marking** involves simply placing similar merchandise with the same price in a display and attaching one price card to the display. It can save time in marking and speed the delivery of merchandise to the sales floor. Technology is also coming to bulk-marking procedures—electronically programmable shelf labels (see Figure 16–7).

Stocking Activities

Once the merchandise has been marked, the retailer must decide where to stock the merchandise. The retailer can use an in-store or warehouse stocking plan or some combination of the two plans.

In-Store Stocking

The primary goal in stocking is to move the merchandise as close as possible to its selling point. To accomplish this goal, most retailers follow the policy of **in-store stocking**, maximizing the amount of display and forward stock and minimizing the

---

Prices of more than 500 items will change today at Bauersfeld's supermarket in Topeka, Kan., but the clerks won't have to peel outdated labels off the shelves.

Instead, they will change the prices electronically, plugging a hand-held computer into programmable labels clipped to the store's shelves. The computer sends a signal to a microchip in the molded plastic label, which then displays the new price in half-inch-high liquid crystal numerals.

Such devices are part of the grocery industry's continuing effort to reduce overhead with technology. Already more than half of the nation's supermarkets have electronic scanners at checkouts to ring up prices of bar-coded packages. Programmable shelf labeling promises to trim labor costs further and allow quicker price changes than are now possible.

FIGURE 16–7
Electronically programmable shelf label

Source: from Richard Gibson, "Electronic Price Labels Tested in Supermarkets," *The Wall Street Journal*, 31 March 1988. Reprinted by permission of *The Wall Street Journal* © Dow Jones & Company 1988. All rights reserved.

amount of stock in reserve. **Display stock** is stock placed on various display fixtures that customers can directly examine. **Forward stock** is backup stock that is temporarily stored on the sales floor near its selling department. Forward stock may be carried in perimeter storage areas around the department or in drawers or cupboards beneath the sales floor display fixtures. **Reserve stock** is backup stock held in reserve, usually in a central stockroom. Because reserve stocks frequently create access problems for sales personnel, most retailers prefer to limit the amount of stock in these areas. Reserve stocks usually are converted to forward or display stocks as quickly as possible.

Warehouse Stocking

Warehouse stocking is often used in addition to or in place of in-store display, forward, and reserve stocking. Warehouse stocking is necessary or at least more efficient for certain types of merchandise or under certain operating conditions. Bulky products such as furniture and appliances usually require warehouse stocking, because the retailer must limit the amount of display stock on the sales floor. Forward stocking is generally prohibitive for such products. Disassembled products that are sold in their cartons are usually picked up by the consumer at a warehouse delivery door or delivered to the customer's home. Seasonal products typically are held in warehouses until the appropriate selling season.

Many retailers prefer using central warehouse and distribution centers that serve several stores because of the operating conditions associated with chain store operations. The receiving, checking, marking, and stocking functions are initially accomplished at these regional facilities, then the merchandise is distributed to individual stores. Central facilities often are more efficient, based on the economies of scale that large retailers can realize in ordering, transporting, and processing incoming merchandise and in using modern, expensive facilities and equipment. The key to an effective distribution center is to move merchandise, not store it.[6]

Regardless of where stocking occurs, three elements are necessary to ensure its success: *accessibility, security,* and *controllability.* Stocks must be accessible to authorized personnel to maintain the flow of merchandise to the final consumer. Strict policies and procedures are necessary to ensure security of the merchandise, but they should not be unduly cumbersome. When temporary stockouts occur on the sales floor, sales personnel should be able to replenish display stocks from either forward or reserve stocks with minimal time and effort. Security and controllability go hand in hand. To avoid unacceptable shrinkage levels, merchandise must be secured from customer theft, employee pilferage, damage from dirt, dust, and the elements, and misplacement. Essentially, security involves limited access to the merchandise, good housekeeping, and careful maintenance of records.

PAYING AND RETURNING

Paying Invoices

Paying involves the procedures for processing and settling suppliers' invoices. In large organizations, the accounting department is responsible for making payments. The owner, manager, or bookkeeper in small retail establishments assumes the responsibilities of rendering payments. Most retailers prefer to pay invoices after they have received and checked the merchandise, especially when dealing with an unknown supplier or suppliers whose return and adjustment policies on damaged merchandise and incorrect shipments are either restrictive or unknown. Sometimes invoices must be paid before receiving and checking to take full advantage of cash discounts that were negotiated.

This kind of stocking fixture maximizes the amount of display and forward stock.

Returning Shipments

Returns occur when a retailer does not accept all or part of a shipment and sends some or all of the merchandise back to the supplier. The retailer must carefully determine whether there are legitimate reasons for the returns. Unfair returns along with unfair cancellations are two key causes of friction between suppliers and retailers. Unfairly returning merchandise jeopardizes good relationships between supplier and retailer.

When returns are justified, retailers should use their own return forms. The retailer typically fills out the form in triplicate and sends the original copy to the supplier with the returned merchandise. The buyer retains the second copy, and the accounting department holds the third copy. It is, however, a good idea to contact the supplier before processing the return form and returning the merchandise. Most suppliers have their own return procedures, and retailers can save considerable time and effort by working out prior agreements on returns. Depending on the nature of the complaint and the reason for the return, the supplier may elect either to credit the retailer's account, ship replacement merchandise, or refuse to make an adjustment on the grounds that the return is unfair.

SUMMARY

The procurement process includes all the physical operations associated with getting merchandise into the store and onto the shelves. The four basic steps in procurement are ordering and following up, receiving and checking, marking and stocking, and paying and returning.

Retailers must develop the necessary procedures for ordering merchandise—in either oral or written form—and for following up on those orders, which is necessary to make a purchase contract legally binding. Receiving is the physical exchange of goods between the retailer and the supplier's transporting agent. Retailers must plan facilities and procedures for receiving, inspecting, verifying, and logging incoming shipments. Checking is the process of determining whether the supplier has shipped what the retailer ordered and whether it has arrived in good condition. Personnel are trained to know what and how to check merchandise and when and where to report problems.

Marking is affixing to the merchandise the information necessary for stocking, controlling, and selling it. Marking systems that retailers use include source marking, preretailing, and store marking. Retailers must decide what and how much information to place on merchandise tags, where and how to attach tags to merchandise, and how to re-mark merchandise. Stocking includes the activities associated with in-store and between-store distribution of merchandise. The primary goal of stocking is to move the merchandise as close as possible to its selling point.

Paying involves the procedures for processing and settling the supplier's invoice. Returning merchandise becomes necessary when there is a legitimate reason for not accepting the supplier's shipment.

KEY TERMS AND CONCEPTS

blind check	procurement process
bulk marking	quality check
checking	quantity check
combination check	receiving
direct check	receiving record
display stock	reserve stock
electronic purchase-order (EPO) system	returns
forward stock	routine follow-up
in-store stocking	semiblind check
invoice check	source marking
marking	special follow-up
optical character recognition-font A (OCR-A)	stocking
order form	store marking
paying	symbol cost codes
point of sale (POS)	universal product code (UPC)
preretailing	warehouse stocking
	word cost codes

REVIEW QUESTIONS

1. When is an order form a legally binding contract?
2. Describe the options retailers have in structuring their electronic purchase-order system.
3. Describe the strongest follow-up method available to the retailer for putting pressure on suppliers to meet their obligations.
4. Why should the retailer avoid front-door receiving?
5. Identify the three basic activities normally associated with proper receiving procedures. Describe each activity.
6. The retailer makes three checks to see that it has received what was ordered. What are the three checks?
7. How might the retailer check quantities of incoming shipments?
8. Describe the three most common marking systems.
9. Explain why hand marking is the least desirable method of marking merchandise.
10. What are the two most common standardized marking systems for coding merchandise tags?

11. Using the word code REPUBLICAN, what is the cost of a merchandise item with the code BANE?
12. When is bulk marking used?
13. Discuss the options a retailer has for in-store stocking.
14. List three guidelines for developing a stocking plan.
15. When should the retailer pay invoices?

ENDNOTES

1. See Jules Abend, "Computer Links," *Stores* (June 1984): 75.
2. See Gary Robins, "EDI: Closing the Loop." *Stores* (April 1988): 53–62.
3. See "At K-Mart: Nearly 200 Vendors Now on a Direct Electronic Purchase Order System: How It Is Working," *Stores* (May, 1981): 50–52.
4. See "Goal for PLG: Pre-Ticketing With UPC." *Stores* (March 1988): 30–32 and Jules Abend, "Tracking UPC Growth," *Stores* (September 1987): 52, 57–64, 70.
5. Judith Graham, "Bar Codes Becoming Universal," *Advertising Age,* 18 April 1988, 36.
6. See Jules Abend, "Moving Goods Faster," *Stores* (October 1987): 60–69.

RELATED READINGS

Abend, Jules. "UPC + OR = JIT Inventory." *Stores* (May 1987): 44–54.
Abend, Jules. "OR: Changing the OC." *Stores* (April 1988): 89–95.
Clarke, William L. "Integrating the Logistics of Merchandise Management." (June/July 1987): 21–30.
Corr, Fitzhugh L. "Scanners in Marketing Research: Paradise (Almost)." *Marketing News,* 4 Jan. 1985, 1, 15.
Fox, Harold W. "Scanners in Supermarkets: Past, Present, and Prospects." In *1984 Proceedings,* edited by J. R. Lumpkin and J. C. Crawford, 56–59. Southwestern Marketing Association, 1984.
Harris, Brian F., and Mills, Michael K. "The Impact of Item Price Removal on Grocery Shopping Behavior." *Journal of Retailing* 56 (Winter 1980): 73–93.
Jackson, Gary B., and Racer, Miriam J. "Shopper Attitude Related to the Use of the Electronic Scanner in Grocery Stores." In *1985 Proceedings,* edited by J. C. Crawford and B. C. Garland, 189–91. Southwestern Marketing Association, 1985.
Joseph, Anthony. "Centralized Versus Store-Controlled Merchandise Replenishment." *Retail Control* (April–May 1985): 2–21.
Lund, Daulatram B. "Food Retailers' Perception of Supermarket UPC Scanner Checkout Systems." In *Developments in Marketing Science, Proceedings,* edited by N. K. Malhotra and J. M. Hawes, 21–25. Academy of Marketing Science, 1986.
Miller, J. Joseph. "The Retailers' View of Just-in-Time and Quick Response." *Retail Control* (September 1987): 11–19.
Pommer, Michael D., Berkowitz, Eric N., and Walton, John R. "UPC Scanning: An Assessment of Shopping Response to Technological Change." *Journal of Retailing* 56 (Summer 1980): 25–44.
Robins, Gary. "Better Service – POS = Faster Shopper Checkout." *Stores* (February 1988): 71–75.
Schulz, David P. "Just-in-Time Systems." *Stores* (April 1985): 28–31.
Woodruff, Robert A. "Merchandise Processing Systems." *Retail Control* (September 1982): 2–11.

17

Objectives

- ☐ Discuss the need for merchandise planning as an essential tool in ensuring that both the customer's merchandise needs and the retailer's financial requirements are satisfied.

- ☐ Plan an acceptable balance between merchandise inventories and sales.

- ☐ Devise and use a merchandise budget in the dollar planning of the retailer's investment in merchandise inventory.

- ☐ Devise and use a merchandise list in the unit planning of the retailer's merchandise assortment and support.

Merchandise-Planning Process: Planning Merchandise Budgets and Lists

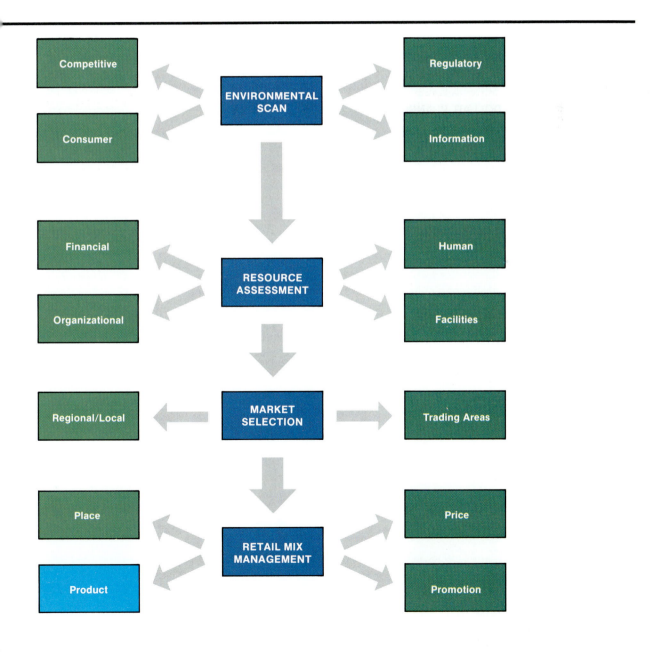

The previous four chapters examined the first two stages in the merchandising process, developing and securing the merchandise mix. The third stage of the merchandising process concerns managing the merchandise mix, which Chapters 17 and 18 discuss. For reasons of organizational simplicity, merchandise management will be examined after the basic activities associated with developing and securing the merchandise mix are identified. In practice, however, managing the merchandise mix coincides with developing and securing it.

THE MERCHANDISE-MANAGEMENT PROCESS

A sound policy for managing merchandise is essential to enable the retailer to offer the right product in the right place at the right time in the right quantities and at the right price. The basic ingredients of the merchandise-management process are illustrated in Figure 17–1. As portrayed, **merchandise management** focuses on planning and controlling the retailer's inventories. **Merchandise planning** consists of establishing objectives and devising plans for obtaining those objectives. The planning process normally includes both dollar planning in terms of merchandise budgets and unit planning in terms of merchandise lists. **Merchandise control** involves designing dollar and unit inventory information and analysis systems for collecting, recording, analyzing, and using merchandise data to determine whether the stated objectives have been achieved. In summary, planning is the process of establishing performance guidelines, whereas control is the process of checking on how well management is following those guidelines. The remainder of this chapter is devoted to the merchandise-planning process; the next chapter examines the topic of merchandise control.

MERCHANDISE PLANNING

The overall objective of merchandise planning is to satisfy both the customer's merchandise needs and the retailer's financial requirements. To accomplish that objective, the retailer must devise merchandise plans that create an acceptable balance between merchandise inventories and sales. This inventory-to-sales balance requires the retailer to plan each merchandise category carefully regarding (1) inventory investment, (2) inventory assortment, and (3) inventory support.

Inventory investment involves planning the total dollar investment in merchandise inventory so that the firm can realize its financial objectives. **Inventory assortment** is planning the number of different product items (brand, style, size, color, material, and price combinations) the retailer should stock within a particular product line and determining whether this assortment is adequate to meet the merchandise-selection needs of the firm's targeted consumers. **Inventory support** refers to planning the number of units the retailer should have on hand for each product item to meet sales estimates (e.g., stocking 100 six-packs of Coca-Cola in the 12-ounce can). By

FIGURE 17–1
The merchandise-management process

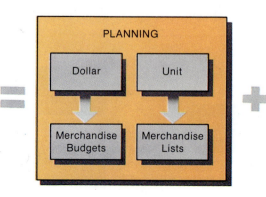
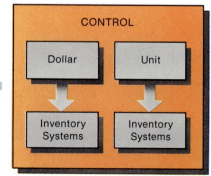

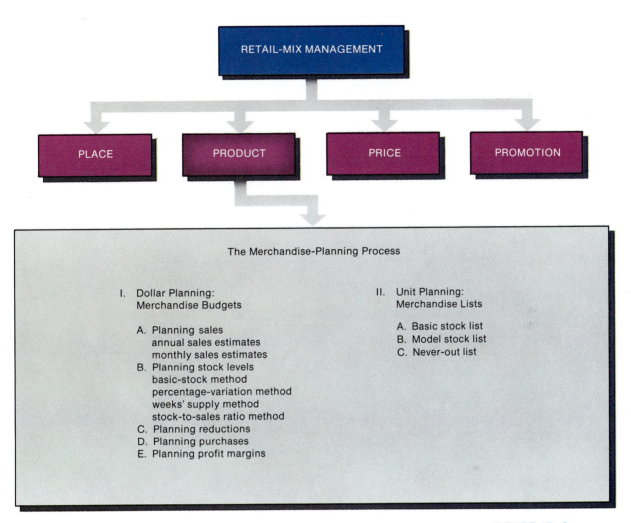

FIGURE 17–2
Developing and implementing the merchandise-planning process

carefully planning the investment, assortment, and support aspects of merchandise inventories, the retailer can take a major step toward the merchandising objective of "customer satisfaction at a profit."

Both dollar and unit planning are essential if the retailer expects to balance inventory investment, assortment, and support. Inventory investment is the focus for dollar planning, whereas unit planning centers on the retailer's inventory assortment and support. Figure 17–2 illustrates the major concerns in developing and implementing the retailer's merchandise-planning process.

DOLLAR PLANNING: MERCHANDISE BUDGETS

Dollar planning is largely a financial-management tool that retailers use to plan the amount of total value (dollars) inventory they should carry. It answers the inventory question of how much the retailer should invest in merchandise during any specified period. Dollar planning is accomplished through a **merchandise budget**—a financial plan for managing merchandise inventory investments. The merchandise budget consists of five stages:

1. Planning sales
2. Planning stock levels

3. Planning reductions
4. Planning purchases
5. Planning profit margins

To facilitate merchandise planning and preparation of the merchandise budget, most retailers use a form that summarizes basic budgetary information for a given merchandise grouping during a specified period. Figure 17−3 illustrates a common form for preparing the merchandise budget.

Planning Sales

The starting point in developing the merchandise budget is sales planning. It is absolutely necessary to accurately forecast future sales; if future sales are incorrectly estimated during this initial stage, then all other aspects of the merchandise budget

FIGURE 17−3

Form for preparing a merchandise budget (BOM, beginning-of-the-month stock)

SIX-MONTH MERCHANDISE BUDGET

Date _____   Department _____

		Aug.	Sept.	Oct.	Nov.	Dec.	Jan.	Total
Sales	Last Year							
	Planned							
	Adjusted							
	Actual							
BOM Stock Levels	Last Year							
	Planned							
	Adjusted							
	Actual							
Reductions	Last Year							
	Planned							
	Adjusted							
	Actual							
Purchases	Last Year							
	Planned							
	Adjusted							
	Actual							
Initial Markup %	Last Year							
	Planned							
	Adjusted							
	Actual							

(stock levels, reductions, purchases, profit margins) will reflect this initial error and will require the retailer to adjust the budget throughout its application.

Before making sales estimates, the retailer must select the control unit for which the projections will be made. The **control unit** is the merchandise grouping that serves as the basic reporting unit for various types of information (e.g., past, current, and future sales). The retailer can elect to estimate future sales for an entire store, for a merchandise division or department, or for an individual product line or item. The discussion of the product mix in Chapter 13 identified three possible control units: merchandise groups, merchandise classes, and merchandise categories. To increase accuracy in estimating future sales and to obtain a greater degree of control throughout the entire budgetary process, retailers generally prefer narrowly defined control units. Therefore, using merchandise categories (specific lines of products that are directly comparable and substitutable, such as blenders) as the basic control unit is recommended because it is generally much easier to aggregate information (summing merchandise categories into merchandise classes and groups) than it is to disaggregate information (breaking down merchandise groups into classes and categories).

Annual Sales Estimates

An examination of the retailer's past sales records is the starting point for making sales forecasts for each merchandise category (control unit). By plotting the actual sales for each control unit over the last few years, the retailer can identify past sales patterns and gain some insight into possible future sales trends. This approach to sales estimates is generally referred to as *time-series forecasting*. It represents a simple, inexpensive, and widely used method for obtaining reasonably reliable estimates of sales in the near future. Time- series forecasting is generally quite appropriate for staple merchandise, somewhat less appropriate for fashionable merchandise (those fashions in a ford or classic life cycle), and totally inappropriate for faddish merchandise.

For purposes of illustration, Figure 17—4 presents a department store's six-year sales experience (1984 to 1989) with automatic-drip coffee makers and electric blenders. Past sales for these two merchandise categories reveal some interesting patterns. While both have experienced sales increases, the amount and stability of the increases are noticeably different. The store's past blender sales reveal a small yet

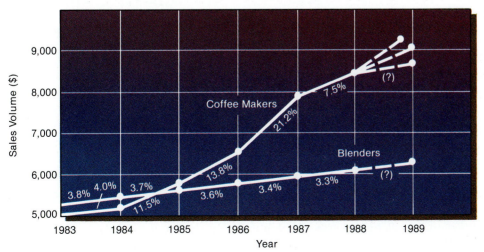

FIGURE 17—4
Five-year sales record for automatic-drip coffee makers and electric blenders

steady increase in dollar sales. Looking at changes in the percentage increase in sales per year, we see that sales are increasing but at a decreasing rate. These figures suggest that the blender is in the maturity stage of its product life cycle and that sales are fairly stable and predictable, at least in the near future. The past sales pattern for coffee makers shows both large and small dollar and percentage increases, together with drastic changes from one year to the next. Viewing the overall pattern of coffee maker sales, the retailer could conclude that this product has passed through the growth stage of its product life cycle and done so fairly erratically at that. (Look at the percentage increase in sales. Sales increasing at an increasing rate are indicative of a product in the growth stage of the product life cycle.) In 1989, however, sales of coffee makers began to show increasing sales at a decreasing rate—a possible sign that the product is entering its maturity stage. Thus, because of the erratic changes in the rate of sales of coffee makers and the data's suggestion that the product *might* be entering its maturity stage, the retailer's 1990 sales estimates for coffee makers are likely to be much less accurate than sales estimates for blenders.

Annual sales for each merchandise category are estimated largely by means of judgmental or qualitative methods. Two such methods are the fixed and variable adjustment procedures.

Fixed adjustment method.   With the fixed adjustment method, the retailer adjusts last year's sales by some fixed percentage to estimate the coming year's sales. The direction (plus or minus) and the size (the exact percentage) of the adjustment are based on the retailer's past sales experience with each merchandise category. For example, based on the past sales trend for electric blenders shown in Figure 17–4, the department store's forecaster might well expect a 3.2 percent increase in sales for 1990 in the absence of extenuating circumstances that might strongly influence the sale of blenders. The fixed adjustment method usually works reasonably well in estimating future sales if a clear and stable sales trend has been established. When past sales patterns are erratic, however, a fixed percentage adjustment is inappropriate.

Equally inappropriate is the "beat last year's sales" approach for calculating next year's sales estimates. Some retailers simply estimate future sales by using a fixed percentage (e.g., 4, 6, 8 percent) that will yield sales estimates above last year's sales performance. This approach does not recognize that various merchandise categories are in different stages of their product life cycles. While some are in the growth stage (accelerated sales growth), others may be in the maturity (declining sales growth) or decline (decreased sales) stages of the cycle. Beating last year's sales may be an appropriate sales goal for the store as a whole, but it is not an appropriate sales-estimating method for an individual category of merchandise.

Variable adjustment method.   The second method for estimating annual sales is the variable adjustment method. As with the fixed adjustment method, the forecaster usually starts with an examination of the past sales history of the merchandise category. Based on the sales history, the forecaster determines a percentage change (e.g., 6 percent) that appears reasonable. The figure is then adjusted upward or downward by a degree that depends on the nature of the merchandise and its exposure and sensitivity to environmental influences. To make these adjustments, the retailer might consider the following external environmental factors: (1) the general prosperity of local and national markets; (2) rate of inflation; (3) chances for recessionary developments; (4) discernible trends (growth or decline) in the size of the target market population; (5) changes in the demographic makeup of the population (e.g., age, income, family structure, etc.); (6) developing legal and/or social

Step 1: Tracking the past

Select the variable to be forecast, forecasting horizon, and level of data (annual, quarterly, monthly)

Find the most recent value of the variable that is available

Collect historical data on the variable at the required level

Step 2: Extrapolating the past

Select an extrapolation model (constant percentage, absolute change, and so on)

Assume no change in external factors

Identify underlying patterns in historical data

Extrapolate past patterns into future, assuming past patterns continue

Step 3: Finding causal factors

Identify major factors in environment that affect the forecast variable (past and future)

Assess the past impact of each factor (direction and magnitude) on the forecast variable

Step 4: Making the forecast

Assess whether past impact of environmental factors on the forecast variable will be the same in future

Estimate future impact of the factors on the forecast variable for the forecasting horizon

Modify the extrapolation in Step 2 to obtain final forecast

FIGURE 17−5

Four-step judgmental forecasting process (source: Reprinted with permission from Steven W. Hartley and William Rudelius, "How Data Format and Problem Structure Affect Judgmental Sales Forecasts: An Experiment," *1986 AMA Proceedings,* ed. Terence A Shimp [American Marketing Association, 1986], 297)

restrictions; (7) changing patterns of competition (e.g., type, size, and merchandising strategies); and (8) changing consumer preferences and life-styles. Internal factors to consider in adjusting annual sales estimates include (1) changes in the amount and location of shelf or floor space devoted to the merchandise category; (2) changes in the amount and type of planned promotional support; and (3) changes in basic operating policies (e.g., longer store hours or higher levels of service).

In summary, the **annual sales estimate** for a particular merchandise category equals the previous year's sales plus or minus a fixed or variable percentage adjustment. The adjustment factor is a blend of forecaster judgment, experience, and analytical skill. Figure 17−5 provides a four-stage recap of how to conduct a judgment forecast.

Monthly Sales Estimates

Retail planning periods typically are based on one-month or several-month periods; for example, some retailers estimate sales for products for the three-month winter season or the six-month fall/winter season. The best operational estimate for budgetary planning purposes is **monthly sales estimates**. Estimating monthly sales involves three steps: (1) making annual sales estimates; (2) determining estimated monthly sales; and (3) adjusting monthly sales estimates using a monthly sales index.

Step 1: Making annual sales estimates. To make monthly sales estimates, the forecaster starts with annual sales estimates, as discussed.

Step 2: Determining average estimated monthly sales. The second step in estimating monthly sales is to allocate the annual sales estimate derived in step 1 on a monthly basis. One way to make this allocation is to determine average estimated monthly sales by dividing the annual sales estimate by the number of months in a year (12). This figure would be a reasonably reliable estimate of monthly sales if we could assume that sales were evenly distributed over the 12 months of the year.

Step 3: Adjusting average estimated monthly sales. Average estimated monthly sales are adjusted according to a *monthly sales index* based on past monthly sales records. The purpose of this adjustment is to obtain a *planned monthly sales figure,* the final estimate of each month's sales that the retailer will use throughout the budgetary process. By indexing past monthly sales, the forecaster can establish a sales norm for an "average month" by which all other monthly sales can be judged. The average month is represented by an index value of 100. Any month with an index below 100 represents monthly sales below the norm; above-average sales are represented by index values exceeding 100. For example, a monthly sales index of 76 indicates that sales for that month are 24 (100 − 76) percent below the average. An index value of 181 denotes an above-average sales performance of 81 (181 − 100) percent.

Procedures for calculating the monthly sales index are shown in Figure 17−6. The monthly sales index is obtained by dividing the actual monthly sales by average

FIGURE 17−6
Procedures for calculating the monthly sales index

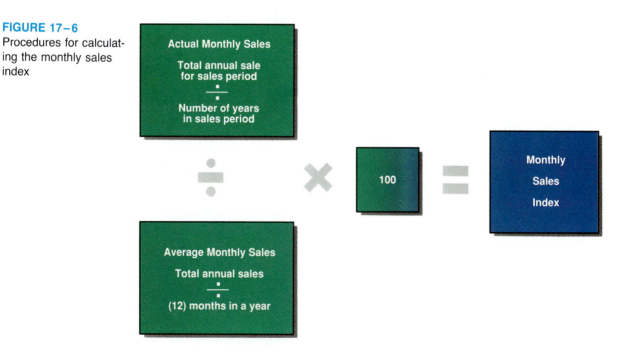

Month	Actual Monthly Sales ($)	Monthly Sales Index
January	3,400	24
February	3,600	26
March	6,800	49
April	7,000	50
May	23,800	170
June	27,200	194
July	6,600	47
August	7,200	51
September	10,600	76
October	8,800	63
November	25,400	181
December	41,400	296
Total annual sales	168,000	
Average monthly sales	14,000	
Average monthly index		100

FIGURE 17–7

Example of calculating the monthly sales index (Men's and women's watches)

monthly sales and multiplying by 100. An example of calculating the monthly sales index is presented in Figure 17-7. We see that the actual monthly sales for men's and women's watches is highly seasonal; the sales peaks correspond to the May/June graduation and December holiday seasons. Average monthly sales are obtained by dividing the total annual sales by 12 (months in a year); in the example, $168,000 divided by 12 equals $14,000. January's monthly sales index of 24 was calculated by dividing $3,400 (actual monthly sales) by $14,000 (average monthly sales) and multiplying by 100. The remaining eleven monthly sales indexes were calculated in the same manner. Once the monthly sales index has been calculated, it can be used to adjust future (estimated) annual and average monthly sales to obtain planned monthly sales—a basic element in all the stock-planning methods to be discussed next. *Planned monthly sales* are obtained by multiplying the *average estimated monthly sales* (see Step 2) by the *monthly sales index* (see Step 3).

Planning Stock Levels

The second stage in developing a merchandise budget involves planning appropriate stock levels for a specific sales period. Ideally, the retailer's stock plan should (1) meet sales expectations, (2) avoid out-of-stock conditions, (3) guard against overstock conditions, and (4) keep inventory investment at an acceptable level. Although it is extremely difficult to devise a plan to achieve all these objectives, four methods can serve the retailer in planning stock requirements. They are the basic stock method, the percentage variation method, the week's supply method, and the stock/sales ratio method.

The Basic Stock Method

The **basic stock method** is designed to meet sales expectations and avoid out-of-stock conditions by beginning each month with stock levels that equal the estimated sales for that month plus an additional basic stock amount that serves as a "cushion" or

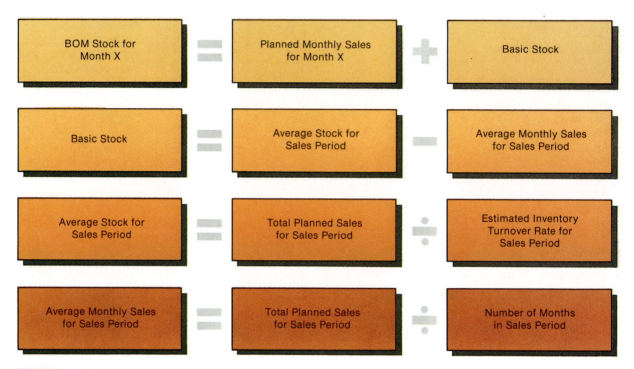

FIGURE 17–8

The basic stock method for determining BOM stock

"safety stock" in the event that actual sales exceed estimated sales. The safety stock also protects the retailer against stockouts if future shipments of merchandise are delayed or arrive damaged and must be returned to the vendor. On the negative side, safety stock means that the retailer has a larger investment in inventory and greater inventory carrying costs. Retailers that use the basic stock method want to ensure minimum stock levels for a particular merchandise category. Generally, retailers that operate stores and departments with low inventory turnover are most likely to use this method.

The basic stock method involves calculating the beginning-of-the-month stock (BOM stock) for each month of the sales period. The BOM stock is computed by adding a basic stock amount to each of the planned monthly sales as determined in the sales-planning stage of the budgetary process. For example, let's assume that the department manager for the jewelry department of Selmer's Department Store is in the process of planning stocks for the upcoming Christmas season (October, November, and December). Using the basic stock method, the department manager would plan the BOM stock for each of the three months (sales period) using the procedures outlined in Figure 17–8.

To illustrate the basic stock method, we continue with the watch example; Figure 17–9 reconstructs the three-month Christmas sales period of October, November, and December. Based on past sales records, the retailer knows that the turnover rate (number of times the average stock on hand is sold during a given time period) for watches during this three-month sales period has averaged about two. Using the information in Figure 17–9, BOM stock is determined for the month of October in the following manner:

average monthly sales for
October, November, December = $81,000 ÷ 3 = $27,000

Sales Period	Planned Monthly Sales ($)[1]	BOM Stock Using Basic Stock Method ($)	BOM Stock Using Percentage Variation Method ($)
Oct.	9,450	22,950	27,337.50
Nov.	27,150	40,650	40,905.00
Dec.	44,400	57,900	53,460.00
Total	81,000	—	—

FIGURE 17–9
BOM stock for men's and women's watches (jewelry department, Selmer's Department Store)

$$\text{average stock for October, November, December} = \$81,000 \div 2 = \$40,500$$

$$\text{basic stock} = \$40,500 - \$27,000 = \$13,500$$

$$\text{BOM stock for October} = \$9,450 + \$13,500 = \$22,950$$

As shown, a basic or safety stock of $13,500 is added to each month's planned sales to arrive at the BOM stock. The BOM stocks for November and December are shown in Figure 17–9. When actual sales either exceed or fall short of planned sales for a given month, the retailer can easily adjust the amount of overage or shortfall to bring the next month's BOM stock back to its calculated level (in this case, $13,500).

The Percentage Variation Method

The **percentage variation method** uses a procedure that attempts to adjust stock levels in accordance with actual variations in sales. BOM stock is increased or decreased from average stock for the sales period by one half of the percentage variation in planned monthly sales for that month from the average monthly sales for the sales period. The calculating procedures for the percentage variation method are shown in Figure 17–10.

$$\text{BOM stock for October} = \$40,500 \times \frac{1}{2}\left(1 + \frac{\$9,450}{\$27,000}\right) = \$27,337.50$$

The BOM stocks for November and December have been calculated and are shown along with the October BOM stock in Figure 17–9.

Retailers prefer to use the percentage variation method with merchandise categories characterized by a high turnover rate (usually exceeding six times per year) because it results in less stock fluctuation than use of the basic stock method.

FIGURE 17–10
The percentage variation method for determining BOM stock

* Calculating procedures for average stock and average monthly sales were reviewed in the previous discussion of the basic stock method.

The Week's Supply Method

The **week's supply method** is a stocking plan that determines stock levels in direct proportion to sales. As a means to plan stocks on a weekly basis, this method uses a desired annual stock turnover rate to establish the amount of stock necessary to cover a predetermined number of weeks. If the manager of Selmer's jewelry department thinks an annual stock turnover rate of eight is both desirable and feasible, determining stock for the start of the Christmas sales period (October) would be done as shown in Figure 17–11. Using the data in Figure 17–9,

number of weeks
to be stocked $=\ 52 \div 8 = 6.5$ weeks

average weekly
sales $= \$180{,}000 \div 52 = \$3{,}462$

BOM stock
for October $= \$3{,}462 \times 6.5 = \$22{,}503$

Having determined the number of weeks' supply to stock (6.5 weeks) and the average weekly sales ($3,462), stock levels can be replenished frequently and regularly (e.g., weekly or biweekly) before stock shortages occur. The principal limitation of this method is that during weeks with a slow stock turn (below annual rate), there will be an excessive accumulation of stock. Therefore, this method is most appropriate for retailers whose merchandise categories show stable sales and stable stock turnover rates.

The Stock/Sales Ratio Method

The **stock/sales ratio method** is another method retailers use to determine BOM levels. The assumption behind this method is that the retailer should maintain a certain ratio of goods on hand to planned monthly sales. This ratio could be 2:1, 3:1, or any other appropriate relationship. A stock/sales ratio of 2:1 means the planned monthly sales of $5,000 would require $10,000 of stock. The key to using this method is finding a dependable stock/sales ratio, for which the best source is the retailer's own past record—provided that it has been kept in sufficient detail over a reasonable length of time. Stock/sales ratios also can be obtained from various trade sources, such as the National Retail Merchants Association's annual publication *Department Merchandising and Operating Results of Department and Specialty Stores.*

FIGURE 17–11
The week's supply method of determining BOM stock

FIGURE 17–12
Stock/sales ratio method of determining BOM stock

To illustrate this method, let's assume that past sales records for Selmer's jewelry department reveal that a 2:1 stock/sales ratio is desirable. Based on the planned monthly sales cited in Figure 17–9, the BOM stock for October would be calculated as shown in Figure 17–12.

$$\text{BOM stock for October} = \$9,450 \times 2 = \$18,900$$

Using the same procedures, the BOM stock for November would be $54,000, while December's BOM stock would be $88,800.

Planning Reductions

The third stage in developing the merchandise budget is to plan reductions. **Retail reductions** can be defined as the difference between the merchandise item's original retail value and its actual final sales value. This difference is the result of three factors: markdowns, discounts, and shortages. **Markdowns** are reductions in the original retail price for the purpose of stimulating the sale of merchandise. The amount of markdown can vary considerably depending on the type of merchandise and the conditions under which it is sold. Figure 17–13 shows typical markdown percentages for department store operation. **Discounts** are reductions in the original retail price that are granted to store employees as special fringe benefits and to special customers (e.g., clergy, senior citizens, disadvantaged consumers) in recognition of their special status. **Shortages** are reductions in the total value of the retailer's inventory as a result of shoplifting, pilfering, and merchandise being damaged and misplaced. Department store shortages range from less than one percent for cosmetics and drugs to 2.7 percent for female apparel (see Figure 17–13). (Markdowns are discussed fully as a pricing strategy in Chapter 19; employee discounts were discussed in Chapter 8 in conjunction with employee compensation. The problems of shoplifting and pilfering were discussed in Chapter 9, and stock shortages receive additional treatment in the next chapter.)

Product Category	Markdowns (%)	Stock Shortage (%)
Female apparel	26.3	2.7
Female accessories	13.5	3.3
Men's and boy's apparel and accessories	21.3	2.1
Infant and children's clothing and accessories	22.2	1.8
Shoes	23.9	1.0
Cosmetics and drugs	1.7	0.8
Recreation	12.8	2.6
Home furnishings	14.4	1.5
All other merchandise	13.6	2.6

FIGURE 17–13
Markdown and stock shortages for department stores, 1986

Source: David P. Schulz, "New MOR: New Data," *Stores* (January 1988): 123. Reprinted by permission of *Stores*. Copyright by National Retail Merchants Association.

Planning for reductions is necessary for several reasons. First, the major purpose of the merchandise budget is to outline the retailer's total dollar investment in inventory. Therefore, any occurrence that might reduce the value of that inventory should be accounted for to give the retailer an accurate inventory investment picture. Second, the merchandise budget calls for an estimate of stock levels in dollar amounts; without reduction planning, the retailer's proposed stock levels might be inadequate to meet expected sales levels. Finally, reduction planning is necessary if the retailer is to plan future purchases accurately. Estimating reductions is a key input variable into the planned-purchases formulas.

Planning reductions essentially involves making a percentage-of-sales (dollars) estimate for each of the three major reduction factors: markdowns, discounts, and shortages. These percentage estimates are made on the basis of past experience or obtained from trade sources. To be consistent with sales and stock-level planning, reduction estimates should be made in retail dollars on a monthly basis for a particular merchandise category. Continuing our watch example, if the retailer's past records reveal that for the month of October men's and women's watches experienced average monthly markdowns of 6 percent and discounts and shortages averaged 1.5 percent and 2.5 percent, respectively, then the total planned reductions for October would be 10 percent of planned monthly sales, or $945 (see Figure 17–9). Having determined a monthly estimate of reductions, the retailer can proceed to plan purchases.

Planning Purchases

Planning purchases constitutes the fourth stage in developing a merchandise budget. In this stage, the retailer plans the dollar amount of merchandise that must be purchased for a given time period (e.g., a month or a season) in view of planned sales and reductions for that period as well as the planned stock levels at the beginning of the period and the desired stock levels at the end of the period. (The ending stock usually equals the beginning stock for the next period.) The format for calculating planned purchases for a monthly planning period is as follows:

```
    planned monthly sales
  + planned monthly reductions
  + desired end-of-the-month stock
  ─────────────────────────────────
  = total stock needs for the month
  − planned beginning-of-month stock
  ─────────────────────────────────
  = planned monthly purchases
```

For illustration, let's assume that the manager of Selmer's jewelry department is planning the October purchases of men's and women's watches. From our previous discussions we have the following information concerning October: (1) planned monthly sales estimated at $9,450 (see Figure 17–9); (2) planned monthly reductions estimated at 10 percent of sales of $945; (3) desired end-of-the-month stock of $40,500 (the beginning-of-the- month stock for November—see Figure 17–9); (4) planned beginning-of-the-month stock of $22,500 (see Figure 17–9). Given this information, the planned purchases for the month of October are

planned monthly sales	$ 9,450
+ planned monthly reductions	945
+ desired end-of-the-month stock	$40,650
= total stock needs for the month	$51,045
− planned beginning-of-the-month stock	22,950
= planned monthly purchases	28,095

The planned monthly purchases of $28,095 were computed in terms of retail prices. To find out what the manager must spend in terms of cost prices, the retailer must multiply the retail value ($28,095) by the cost equivalent (the percentage of the retail price that is the manager's cost). For example, if merchandise costs are 60 percent of the retail price, then the manager can plan to make purchases totaling $16,857 at cost prices ($28,095 × .60).

The planned monthly purchase value represents the retailer's additional merchandise needs for that month—how much merchandise must be purchased and made available during that month. It does *not* tell the retailer when those purchases should be made. Order-processing requirements, delivery schedules, and other considerations demand that some of the planned purchases for a month may have to be ordered far in advance. The timing of purchases depends on a number of internal (retailer) and external (supplier) conditions. (Purchase-order timing is discussed more fully in the next chapter.)

Planning Profit Margins

An integral part of developing the merchandise budget is to allow for a reasonable profit by ensuring an adequate dollar **gross margin**—the difference between cost of goods sold and net sales. An adequate dollar gross margin must cover the operating expenses associated with buying, stocking, and selling the merchandise, as well as produce an acceptable operating profit. Department store gross margins typically run from around 47 to 48 percent for women's apparel accessories to 32 to 33 percent for recreation, leisure, and hobby merchandise. The procedures for determining dollar gross margin and operating profit are as follows:

$$
\begin{array}{rl}
 & \text{net sales (\$)} \\
- & \underline{\text{cost of goods sold (\$)}} \\
= & \text{gross margin (\$)} \\
- & \underline{\text{operating expenses (\$)}} \\
= & \text{operating profit (\$)}
\end{array}
$$

Retailers attempt to achieve an adequate gross margin and operating profit by planning an **initial markup percentage**—the percentage difference between the cost of the merchandise and its original retail price—that will cover expenses, profits, and reductions. The formula for calculating the initial markup percentage is shown in Figure 17–14.

Sales and reduction estimates are obtained from the sales and reduction planning stages of the merchandise budget. Expense estimates are based on past experience as revealed by expense records. After making sales, reduction, and expense estimates, the retailer can then establish a realistic profit objective. To facilitate easy planning, reductions, expenses, and profits are estimated as a *percentage of sales*. For example, in planning the required initial markup percentage on men's and women's watches for the coming year (1990), the manager of Selmer's jewelry department has estimated total annual sales of $180,000, reductions at 10 percent of sales or $18,000, and anticipated expenses at 20 percent of sales or $36,000. Further, assuming that the manager desires a profit objective of 12 percent of sales or

FIGURE 17–14

Procedure for calculating required initial markup percentage

$21,600, which is considered both feasible and acceptable, the manager calculates the required initial markup on watches:

$$\text{required initial} \atop \text{markup percentage} = \frac{\$36{,}000 + \$21{,}600 + \$18{,}000}{\$180{,}000 + \$18{,}000} = 38.2\%$$

The same formula can be used when expenses, profits, reductions, and sales are expressed in percentage terms (sales equals 100 percent). For example,

$$\text{required initial} \atop \text{markup percentage} = \frac{20\% + 12\% + 10\%}{100\% + 10\%} = 38.2\%$$

This required initial markup percentage represents an overall average for a merchandise category (e.g., watches). As long as this category average is maintained, the actual initial markup on any individual merchandise item (a watch of a particular brand, style, and price) can vary from the average to adjust to different demand conditions, competitive circumstances, and other external and internal merchandising factors. (A more in-depth discussion of markup and gross margin appears in Chapter 19.)

In summary, the merchandise budget is the sequential dollar planning of sales, stock levels, reductions, purchases, and profit margins. By carefully planning the dollar investment in merchandise inventory, the retailer is developing a blueprint of what must be accomplished to realize a desired profit and other financial goals. The retailer's merchandise budget also sets the financial standards against which to measure actual performance.

UNIT PLANNING: MERCHANDISE LISTS

Unit planning is an operational management tool to plan the merchandise assortment and support. It is directed at determining the amount of inventory the retailer should carry by item and by units and answers the inventory questions of how many product items (assortment) and how many units of each item (support) to stock. Unit planning involves the use of several *merchandise lists*—a set of operational plans for managing total selection of merchandise. Based on the type of merchandise the retailer carries, one or more of the following three merchandise lists will apply.

1. Basic stock list—for planning staple merchandise
2. Model stock list—for planning fashion merchandise
3. Never-out list—for planning key items and best-sellers

Merchandise lists essentially represent the "ideal" stock for meeting the consumer's merchandise needs in terms of assortment and support.

Basic Stock List

The **basic stock list** is a planning instrument retailers use to determine the assortment and support for staple merchandise. **Staples** are product items for which sales are either very stable or highly variable but very predictable. In either case, estimates of the required assortment of merchandise items and the number of support units for each item can be made with a relatively high degree of accuracy. Thus, in planning for staple merchandise, the retailer can develop a very specific stocking plan. The basic stock list is a schedule or listing of "stock-keeping units" (SKU) for staple merchandise. A **stock-keeping unit** is a merchandise category for which separate records (sales and stock) are maintained; an SKU can consist of a single merchandise item or a group of items. The basic stock list usually identifies each SKU in precise terms. A retailer can use the following product characteristics to distinguish clearly an SKU of staple merchandise: (1) brand name, (2) style or model number, (3) product or package size, (4) product color or material, (5) retail and/or cost price of the product, and (6) manufacturer's name and identification number. In addition to a complete listing of SKUs, the basic stock list also contains a detailed description of the stock position for each SKU by stock levels (merchandise support, or total number of units). Also, this description of stock support normally identifies (1) a minimum stock level to be on hand, (2) actual stock on hand, (3) amount of stock on order, (4) planned sales, and (5) actual sales. Stock support information is recorded on a standardized form at regular and frequent intervals (e.g., quarterly or monthly). Figure 17–15 illustrates one of several possible forms for recording the information contained in a basic stock list.

The importance of carefully maintaining a basic stock list cannot be overstated. Most merchandise departments, including those that are fashion oriented, contain at least some product items that are basic staples. Examples are black nylon socks and white cotton briefs in the men's wear department. Given the "essential" character of staple merchandise in the consumer's buying behavior patterns, close supervision over the stock position of staples is absolutely necessary. The simple fact that consumers expect an adequate supply of staple merchandise makes it all the more

FIGURE 17–15
A basic stock list form

Stock Keeping Unit		Vendor Description			Merchandise Description						Stock Description				
Number	Name	Manuf. Name	Manuf. I.D.	Brand	Style/ Model	Material	Color	Size	Price R	C		Quarters 1	2	3	4
											MS				
											PS				
											AS				
											OH				
											OO				
											MS				
											PS				
											AS				
											OH				
											OO				
											MS				
											PS				
											AS				
											OH				
											OO				
											MS				
											PS				
											AS				
											OH				
											OO				

Key: R = Retail Price   PS = Planned Sales   OH = Stock on Hand
C = Cost Price   AS = Actual Sales   OO = Stock on Order
MS = Minimum Stock

important to have an adequate supply. Many staple items have no totally satisfactory substitutes for many consumers; a stockout of a particular staple forces the consumer to look elsewhere for the item. By being unable to meet the consumer's need for a basic staple, the retailer not only loses the sale but also damages the store's assortment image and strains the customer's goodwill. Additionally, the customer, in the process of looking elsewhere, may decide to switch to a competitor whose stock of staples is well maintained.

Model Stock List

Stock planning for fashion merchandise is accomplished through use of the **model stock list**—a schedule or listing of SKUs for fashion merchandise. The model stock list differs from the basic stock list because it defines each SKU in general rather than precise terms. Common criteria in identifying a model SKU are *general price lines* ("better dresses" at $100, $150, and $200 or "moderate dresses" at $40, $60, and $80); *distribution of sizes* (misses 8, 10, 12, 14, and 16); *certain basic colors* (black cocktail dresses or navy-blue blazers); *general style features* (long and short sleeve dresses or crew neck, v-neck, and turtleneck sweaters); and *product materials* (wool, cotton, and polyester dresses). The more general character of each SKU in a model stock plan reflects the transience of fashion merchandise, which represents only the currently prevailing style. The likelihood of style changes within a short period and the high probability that market demand (sales) will fluctuate considerably within any selling season require a more general approach to stock planning. If the model stock list calls for 300 "better dresses" equally distributed among the $100, $150, and $200 price lines, the retailer is still free to adapt to specific fashion trends that are currently stylish. In the initial planning of model stock lists, desired support quantities for each SKU are established on the basis of past sales experience. The exact distribution of those quantities among the various assortment features (e.g., colors, styles, and materials) is left to the buyer's judgment about what is and will be appropriate for the store's customers. In essence, the model stock list provides general guidelines on the size and composition of an ideal stock of fashion merchandise, without specifying the exact nature of the merchandise assortment or support.

The form used to plan the model stock list differs somewhat from the basic stock list form. First, the vendor description is usually absent or abbreviated. Second, the merchandise description is more generalized. Finally, the stock description is frequently more detailed, breaking down each season (quarter) into desired stock levels at various times within the season: beginning of the season, seasonal peak, and end of the season.

Never-Out List

The **never-out list** is a specially created list of merchandise items that are identified as key items or best-sellers for which the retailer wants extra protection against the possibility of a stockout. As a result of the high level of demand for these items, many retailers establish rigid stock requirements. For example, a retailer might specify that 99 percent of all items on the never-out list must be on hand and on display at all times. Stockouts of these key items result in permanent loss of sales. Typically, the consumer simply will not wait to purchase best-sellers. Never-out lists can include fast-selling staples, key seasonal items, and best-selling fashion merchandise. The integrity of the never-out list is preserved through regular and frequent revision. The importance of the never-out list is underscored by the fact that many chain organizations expect individual store managers to have a near-perfect record in maintaining the stock levels for merchandise on the list. Even a moderate number of stockouts of merchandise on the list is considered an indication of poor management.

SUMMARY

Establishing merchandise objectives and devising tactics for obtaining the objectives are the focal point for the merchandise-planning process. The planning process normally includes both dollar planning, in terms of merchandise budgets, and unit planning, as accomplished through merchandise lists. Satisfying consumers' needs and ensuring retailers' profits are the principal reasons for planning the merchandise mix. The retailer must carefully plan inventory investment (the total dollar amount invested in merchandise), inventory assortment (the number of different products stocked within a particular product line), and inventory support (the number of units to be stocked for each product item).

Dollar planning is accomplished by means of a merchandise budget—a financial plan for managing merchandise inventory investments—that requires the retailer to consider (1) sales, (2) stock levels, (3) reductions, (4) purchases, and (5) profit margins. The retailer uses unit planning to determine the amount of inventory to carry in terms of items (assortment) and units (support). A merchandise list—a set of operational plans for managing the retailer's total selection of merchandise—is used in unit planning. Based on the type of merchandise the retailer carries, one or more of the following lists are appropriate: basic stock list (for planning staple merchandise), model stock list (for planning fashion merchandise), and never-out list (for planning key items and best-sellers).

KEY TERMS AND CONCEPTS

annual sales estimates

basic stock list

basic stock method

control unit

discounts

dollar planning

gross margin

initial markup percentage

inventory assortment

inventory investment

inventory support

markdowns

merchandise budget

merchandise control

merchandise management

merchandise planning

model stock list

monthly sales estimates

never-out list

percentage variation method

retail reductions

shortages

staples

stock-keeping unit (SKU)

stock/sales ratio method

week's supply method

REVIEW QUESTIONS

1. Distinguish among the three concepts of inventory investment, assortment, and support.
2. What is a merchandise budget? Identify the five stages in developing a merchandise budget.
3. Why does the author recommend the use of merchandise categories as the basic control unit in making sales estimates?
4. How does the variable adjustment method differ from the fixed adjustment method of estimating annual sales?
5. David Ostrem is the manager of the Shoe Shack and is responsible for making sales estimates and placing orders for new stock. Because of seasonality of sales, David is required to make monthly sales estimates. Given an annual sales estimate of $9,000 for 1990 and the past sales record for children's dress shoes (see sales record), calculate the planned monthly sales for 1990—the final sales figure David will use in the budgetary planning process.

The Shoe Rack Monthly Sales Record:* Children's Dress Shoes					
	1985	1986	1987	1988	1989
Jan.	400	400	500	600	600
Feb.	300	400	400	500	700
March	300	400	500	600	800
April	800	800	900	1,000	1,200
May	700	700	800	800	800
June	400	500	600	500	700
July	200	300	300	500	700
Aug.	600	600	600	700	800
Sept.	900	1,100	1,400	1,500	1,800
Oct.	500	700	600	700	800
Nov.	400	500	500	600	700
Dec.	700	800	900	1,000	1,200

*Rounded to the nearest hundred.

6. Gina Lewis is the department manager of the "better dresses" department. Having estimated planned monthly sales for the upcoming year, Gina must now plan the appropriate stock levels for the fall season. To obtain a better idea of the stock that will be needed, Gina has decided to calculate BOM stock for each month using both basic stock and percentage variation methods. Using an estimated inventory turnover rate of two, calculate the BOM stock for each month using both methods.

Planned Monthly Sales

August	$32,000
Sept.	$18,000
Oct.	$10,000

7. A hardware retailer estimates its total annual sales for plumbing equipment to be $72,000 and hopes to achieve an annual stock turnover rate of six. Using the week's supply method, calculate the BOM stock for January.
8. What are retail reductions? Identify and describe the cause of retail reductions.
9. How are planned monthly purchases determined?
10. Given the following information, calculate the required initial markup percentage:

1. Sales — $240,000
2. Expenses — 22 percent of sales
3. Reductions — 8 percent of sales
4. Desired profit — 14 percent of sales

11. What is an SKU? How are SKUs distinguished from one another?
12. Basic stock lists are used as a planning instrument for what type of merchandise?
13. Characterize the model stock list. What criteria are used in identifying a model stock-keeping unit?
14. What are never-out lists used for?

RELATED READINGS

Abend, Jules. "New AIM." *Stores* (March 1982): 54–59.

Abend, Jules. "PCs, Easier Software." *Stores* (August 1985): 25–30.

Bernstein, Joseph E. "Inventory Shortage and the 'Back Burner'." *Retail Control* (December 1984): 50–57.

Joseph, Anthony M. "Inventory Planning and Control for Improved Profitability." *Retail Control* (October 1984): 21–39.

Lesser, Jack A., and Schwartz, Martin L. "The Effect of Stock-Out on Retail Store Customers." In *Marketing Comes of Age, Proceedings,* edited by David M. Klein and Allen E. Smith, 142–45. Southern Marketing Association, 1984.

McGinnis, Michael A., Gable, Myron, and Madden, R. Burt. "Improving the Profitability of Retail Merchandising Decisions—Revisited," *Journal of the Academy of Marketing Science* 12 (Winter–Spring 1984): 49–57.

Schary, Philip B., and Christopher, Martin. "The Anatomy of a Stock-Out." *Journal of Retailing* 55 (Summer 1979): 59–70.

Shipp, Ralph D., Jr. *Retail Merchandising,* 2d ed. Boston: Houghton Mifflin Co., 1985.

Staples, William, and Swerdlow, Robert. "Planning and Budgeting for Effective Retail Merchandise Management." *Journal of Small Business Management* (January 1978): 1–6.

Wilson, Cyrus C., and Haueisen, William D. "Retail Information Systems Can Help Provide Profits Needed for Growth." *Marketing News,* 7 March 1980, 4, 14–15.

18

Outline

INVENTORY-INFORMATION SYSTEMS
Inventory Information
Inventory Systems
Inventory Valuation

INVENTORY-ANALYSIS SYSTEM
Stock Turnover
Return on Inventory Investment
Open-to-Buy

Objectives

☐ Describe the need for merchandise control in maintaining a planned balance between the retailer's merchandise inventory and sales.

☐ Outline the method for collecting and procedures for processing merchandise data.

☐ Discuss the methods and procedures for valuing the retailer's inventories.

☐ Explain the methods and procedures for evaluating past merchandising performances.

☐ Identify the methods and procedures for making future merchandise decisions.

Merchandise-Control Process: Controlling Merchandise-Inventory Systems

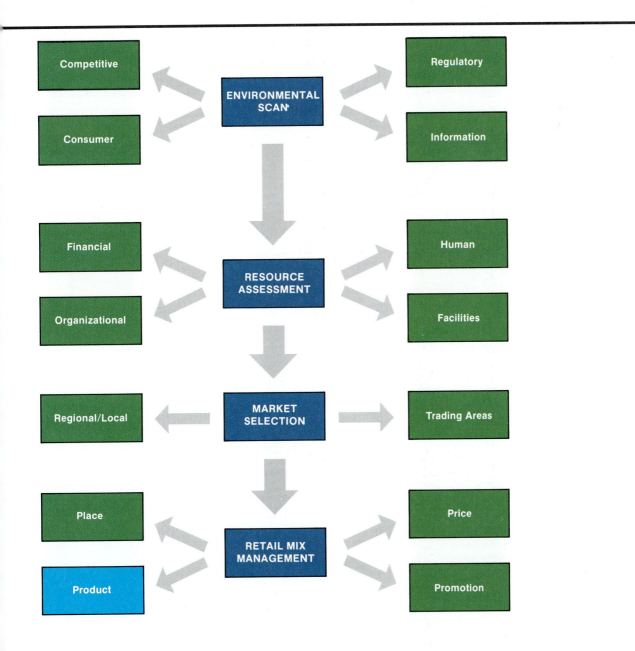

Merchandise control is the process of designing and maintaining inventory systems for controlling the planned balance between inventory and sales. "Inventory control provides the necessary parameters to the planning process."[1] As illustrated in Figure 18–1, merchandise control can be viewed as the sum of two types of inventory systems: an inventory-information system and an inventory-analysis system. The **inventory-information system** is the set of methods and procedures for collecting and processing merchandise data pertinent to the planning and control of merchandise inventories. The **inventory-analysis system** includes methods for evaluating the retailer's past merchandising performance and decision-making tools for controlling future merchandising activities. As with merchandise planning, merchandise control relies on the retailer's inventory information and analysis systems to control inventory investment as well as inventory assortment and support.

The retailer's merchandise controls must be able to supplement the basic merchandising decisions of buying, stocking, and selling. A well-conceived merchandise-control system can aid in the merchandise decision-making process by providing essential information and analysis on both the right amount (dollars) and the right quantity (units) to buy, stock, and sell. It also provides a better position to (1) prevent

FIGURE 18–1
Developing and implementing the merchandise-control process

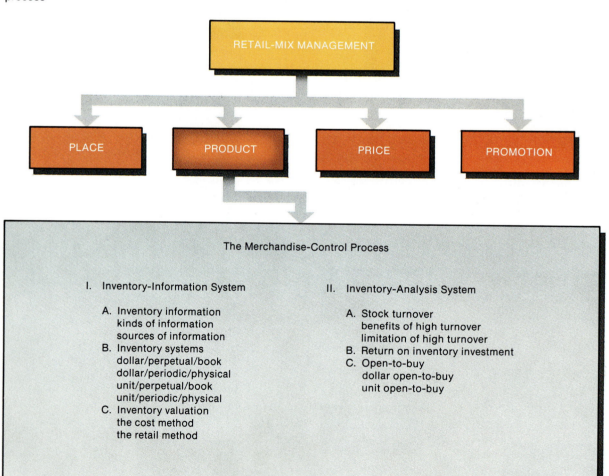

RETAIL-MIX MANAGEMENT

PLACE   PRODUCT   PRICE   PROMOTION

The Merchandise-Control Process

I. Inventory-Information System

  A. Inventory information
    kinds of information
    sources of information
  B. Inventory systems
    dollar/perpetual/book
    dollar/periodic/physical
    unit/perpetual/book
    unit/periodic/physical
  C. Inventory valuation
    the cost method
    the retail method

II. Inventory-Analysis System

  A. Stock turnover
    benefits of high turnover
    limitation of high turnover
  B. Return on inventory investment
  C. Open-to-buy
    dollar open-to-buy
    unit open-to-buy

stockouts, which result in lower profits resulting from lost sales and reduced store loyalty because of customer dissatisfaction, and (2) avoid overstocks, which lower profits because of higher inventory carrying costs and greater risks of markdowns.

To control their inventories effectively, retailers must have an efficient means of obtaining information on the inventories' past and current status. An adequate inventory-information system is a prerequisite to planning and controlling future merchandising activities. Before examining the major types of inventory-information systems, let's consider the kinds of information retailers need for controlling inventories and sources for that information.

**INVENTORY-
INFORMATION
SYSTEMS**

Inventory Information

Kinds of Information

Merchandise investment and merchandise assortment and support are the principal elements the retailer wants to control. To complement merchandise planning, the retailer's inventory-information system must be capable of providing both dollar control and unit control. **Dollar control** considers the "value" of merchandise and attempts to identify the dollar amount of investment in merchandise. Dollar control requires the retailer to collect, record, and analyze merchandise data in terms of dollars. **Unit control** deals not with dollars but with the number of different product items (assortment) and the number of units stocked within each item (support). It is the number of physical units (sales, purchases, and stock levels) recorded and analyzed. Both dollar and unit control are essential for the retailer who needs investment information for profit control and assortment information for stock control.

Sources of Information

The retailer's source of inventory information is the inventory system. Inventory systems differ depending on when (perpetually or periodically) inventory is taken and how (book or physical) it is taken. Based on these two factors, inventory procedures can be classified as either perpetual book inventory systems or periodic physical inventory systems.

A **perpetual book inventory** refers to a system of inventory taking and information gathering on a continuous or ongoing basis using various accounting records to compute stock on hand at any given time. The purchase, sales, and markdown figures needed to calculate stock on hand are derived from internal accounting records that must be kept current if the computed book inventory is to correctly reflect the retailer's true stock position. In summary, a perpetual book inventory represents an up-to-the-minute, -day, or -week accounting system in which all transactions that affect inventory are considered as they occur or shortly thereafter. Its major advantage is that the retailer can determine stock on hand as required by operating conditions and the need for inventory information.

A **periodic physical inventory** refers to a system of gathering stock information intermittently (usually once or twice a year) using an actual physical count and inspection of the merchandise items to compute sales for the period since the last physical inventory. Limitations of a periodic physical inventory system are the time-consuming process of making an actual, physical count of each merchandise item and the fact that most retailers have faster, easier, and more time-saving methods for obtaining sales information. Nevertheless, a physical inventory must be taken at least once a year for income tax reporting purposes. A physical count of the retailer's inventory also is necessary to determine stock shortages (book inventory minus physical inventory). Finally, for the small retailer that can afford neither the electronic data processing equipment nor the accounting personnel to maintain a sophisticated accounting system, a periodic physical inventory is the only alternative.

Inventory Systems

The major types of inventory-information systems used in merchandise control are (1) dollar/perpetual/book, (2) dollar/ periodic/physical, (3) unit/perpetual/book, and (4) unit/periodic/physical. These four systems are based on the kinds of information the retailer needs and the methods and sources for obtaining that information.

Dollar/Perpetual/Book

Dollar control using a **dollar/perpetual/book inventory** system provides the retailer with continuous information on the amount of inventory (dollars) that should be on hand at any given time as determined by internal accounting records. The basic procedures for calculating a perpetual book inventory in dollars are as follows:

$$
\begin{array}{rl}
 & \text{beginning stock on hand} \\
+ & \text{purchases} \\
\hline
= & \text{total stock handled} \\
- & \text{sales} \\
+ & \text{markdowns} \\
\hline
= & \text{ending stock on hand}
\end{array}
$$

Dollar control systems express values either in terms of retail prices or cost prices. To simplify the discussion of dollar control, all values are considered at retail price.

In the preceding formulation, the beginning stock-on-hand value is the ending stock-on-hand value from the preceding accounting period. Merchandise data concerning purchases, sales, and markdowns are obtained from the appropriate internal accounting records. The computed ending stock on hand is the dollar value of the retailer's inventory, provided no shortages have occurred as a result of customer shoplifting, employee pilfering, or other causes that would reduce the value of the merchandise on hand. To determine actual stock shortages, the retailer would have to check the book inventory by taking a physical inventory. Many retailers use an estimated shortage percentage (e.g., 2 percent) based on past experience to adjust the ending stock-on-hand value perpetually. A final adjustment is then made at the end of the season or year by conducting a physical count and valuation of the merchandise.

The primary limitation of a perpetual book inventory for controlling dollar investment in merchandise is the need to obtain accurate and timely merchandise information. A complete up-to-the-minute information system capable of reporting all relevant transactions (purchases, sales, and markdowns) as they occur is necessary. While this limitation creates few problems for large retailers that can afford and justify the expense of sophisticated information-reporting systems, the expenses involved in establishing and maintaining such systems often are prohibitive for the small retailer. On a more promising note, the increasing capabilities and decreasing prices of personal computers are making the perpetual book inventory system a reality for many small and medium-sized retailers.

Dollar/Periodic/Physical

A **dollar/periodic/physical inventory** system for dollar control provides the retailer with periodic information on the amount of inventory (dollars) actually on hand at a given time as determined by a physical count and valuation of the merchandise. It permits the retailer to compute the dollar amount of sales since the last physical count. A periodic physical inventory system for dollar control requires a less complex system for reporting merchandise information. However, it provides less timely and less useful information. A periodic physical inventory usually is computed at designated intervals (monthly, quarterly, or semiannually) using the following basic procedure:

$$
\begin{array}{l}
\text{ beginning stock on hand} \\
+\ \underline{\text{purchases}} \\
=\ \text{total stock handled} \\
-\ \underline{\text{ending stock on hand}} \\
=\ \text{sales and markdowns} \\
-\ \underline{\text{markdowns}} \\
=\ \text{sales}
\end{array}
$$

The beginning stock on hand is the value of the ending stock on hand brought forward from the previous accounting period. Internal purchases and markdown records are used to determine the dollar amount of purchases and markdowns since the last accounting. The ending stock-on-hand figure is derived from a physical count and valuation of the merchandise inventory. The sales figure is computed as shown and incorporates the value of whatever shortages have occurred.

Most retailers have easier and more timely means to obtain sales information; however, as mentioned, the periodic physical inventory system can be used to determine sales figures for merchandise groupings that are not part of the sales-reporting system.

Unit/Perpetual/Book

A perpetual book inventory system for unit control—a **unit/perpetual/book inventory** system—involves continuous recording of all transactions (e.g., number of units sold or purchased), which changes the unit status of the retailer's merchandise inventory. Each unit transaction is posted as it occurs or shortly thereafter (e.g., on a daily basis). Perpetual unit control provides a running total of the number of units of a given type that are flowing into and out of the store or department and helps the retailer continuously control the balance between units on hand and unit sales. In other words, this system allows the retailer to develop and maintain the required merchandise assortment and support necessary to meet consumers' selection expectations. Perpetual unit control systems are maintained manually or through various automatic recording systems.

Manual systems.   A manual system of perpetual unit control is maintained by the retailer's accounting personnel, who continuously record merchandise data on standard forms. Figure 18–2 illustrates one such form, as well as the basic information needed to maintain a daily perpetual book inventory in units. To determine stock on hand, the accountant simply adds the number of units received during the accounting period and subtracts the number of units sold. For example, to determine the ending stock on hand for October 9 (see Figure 18–2):

beginning stock on hand (from Oct. 7)	8 units
+ units received (Oct. 9)	+12 units
= total stock on hand	20 units
− units sold (Oct. 9)	− 1 unit
= ending stock on hand (Oct. 9)	=19 units

In this example, the beginning stock on hand is the ending stock on hand for October 7. The number of units received into stock is obtained from records furnished by the receiving department or clerk. Information on the number of units sold can be gathered by means of a number of manual systems, such as (1) *point-of-sale-tallies* (sales personnel keep track of the number of units sold by making a tally mark on a merchandise list after each sale); (2) *price-ticket stubs* (sales personnel remove information stubs from price tickets when the merchandise is sold and collect, sort, and tally the number of units sold); and (3) *cash-register stubs* (sales personnel remove information stubs from receipts before giving them to customers; these stubs are then used to determine the number of units sold).

FIGURE 18–2

A standardized form used in maintaining a unit/perpetual/book inventory system

Merchandise Item: 12-Inch Portable T.V., G.E., Model 71			
Date	Merchandise Received	Merchandise Sold	Stock on Hand
10-2			10
10-3	10	0	20
10-4	0	1	19
10-5	0	4	15
10-6	0	2	13
10-7	0	5	8
10-9	12	1	19
10-10	0	2	17
10-11	0	3	14
10-12	0	4	10
10-13	0	0	10
10-14	0	0	10
10-16	0	2	8
10-17	0	1	7
10-18	10	0	17
10-19	0	3	14
10-20			
10-21			
10-23			
10-24			
10-25			
10-26			
10-27			
10-28			
10-30			
10-31			

Automatic systems.   Automatic systems of perpetual unit control accomplish the same tasks as manual systems except they are a faster, more timely, and more accurate means of obtaining inventory information. Computer-based electronic data processing equipment allows the retailer to convert automatically merchandise data on sales, purchases, and stocks into useful information for planning and controlling merchandise assortment and support. A *tag system* uses prepunched merchandise tags containing basic assortment information that are attached to each merchandise item. These tags are collected when the item is sold and sent to a data processing facility where the information is fed into the computer. *Card systems* are similar to tag systems, except sales personnel record assortment information directly onto punch cards or scanner cards, which are then fed into the data processing system and used for unit control purposes. *Point-of-sale (POS) systems* use cash registers or terminals capable of transmitting assortment information (e.g., style, price, color, material) directly to the central data processing facility as the sale is being recorded. A number of different methods can be used to record sales and assortment information in a point-of-sale system. Two common methods are (1) *optical scanners,* which read codes (e.g., Universal Product Code) that have been premarked or imprinted on the merchandise item or package, and (2) *terminal keys,* which transmit data directly to the computer when sales personnel depress them. Point-of-sale systems are becoming the dominant form of gathering merchandise information.[2] Figure 18–3 identifies the various ways that different types of retailers are using POS systems.

Both manual and automatic perpetual book inventory systems are used in unit control to obtain information regarding the assortment and support status of the retailer's inventory. Manual systems generally are used to control assortment and

FIGURE 18–3

Ways that POS systems are used: Merchandise and inventory by segment, 1986

Type of Function, Merchandise and Inventory	Discount /Mass Merchandise	Department	Specialty Hard Goods	Specialty Soft Goods
Markdowns	52%	60%	55%	57%
Transfers	28	27	50	41
Big-ticket processing	12	11	34	8
Ticket-generation requests	4	9	16	5
Receipts	28	22	50	38
Purchases	20	16	34	16
Physical inventory	36	24	42	20
Price changes	24	44	58	36
Price look-up	48	26	58	16
SKU data capture	92	77	61	76
Special order printing	8	4	21	3
Inquiry for stock availability in warehouse or other stores	20	7	26	5
Automatic ordering and delivery for customers	12	4	16	2
Picking ticket generation	8	4	18	8
Trade-in of merchandise	16	11	26	17
Merchandise exchange	36	56	42	54
Merchandise credits and refunds	72	66	55	66

(POS, point-of-sale; SKU, stock-keeping unit)

Source: "NRMA's New POS Study," *Stores* (April 1987): 68. Reprinted by permission of *Stores.* Copyright by National Retail Merchants Association.

support of merchandise items characterized by a high unit value and a short selling season (e.g., men's and women's wearing apparel and accessories). Manual systems are considered appropriate for fashionable merchandise because sales can be easily recorded by number of units and unit reorders. Manual systems are not practical for small, fast-selling staples for which rapid turnover would prohibit a timely and accurate record of sales, purchases, and stocks. With the advent of automatic systems, however, perpetual book inventory systems are becoming a realistic alternative for controlling the assortment and support for staple items.

Unit/Periodic/Physical

Unit control also can be achieved by making a periodic physical check on the status of the retailer's inventory—**unit/periodic/physical inventory**. For example, the department manager may be assigned to monitor stock levels for all merchandise items within the department at regular intervals. Stock levels are monitored by a visual inspection or a physical count.

Visual inspection.   For a visual inspection, stock-control personnel visually examine the stock of each item to determine whether sales have depleted the stock to the point of reordering. Several methods can determine at a glance the general condition of the stock; for example, display or storage bins can be divided into quarters, with each quarter having the capacity to hold a certain number of units. When a designated number of quarters (e.g., two) are empty, the person responsible for stock control reorders merchandise to refill the bin. Another example of visual stock control is placing merchandise (e.g., hardware items) on a sequentially numbered pegboard (e.g., 1 to 25). When the stock reaches a certain level, say 10, then 15 units are reordered. Visual inspection is a reasonably appropriate inventory-information system for staple merchandise of low unit value that the retailer can quickly obtain from suppliers.

Physical count.   The second method of monitoring stock levels and determining unit sales is a physical count—actually counting and recording the number of units on hand at regular intervals. The retailer attempts to determine the number of units sold since the last physical count by adding purchases during the intervening period to the beginning stock on hand and then subtracting the ending stock on hand obtained from the current physical count. For example, to determine monthly unit sales for a merchandise item for which the retailer began the month with 300 units on hand, purchased 80 units during the month, and ended the month with 190 units (as determined by physical count), the following computations are necessary:

	beginning monthly stock on hand	300 units
+	monthly purchases	+ 80 units
=	total stock handled during the month	=380 units
−	ending monthly stock on hand	−190 units
=	monthly sales (including shortages)	=190 units

A physical counting system is considerably more time-consuming and expensive than the visual inspection method. The retailer, however, can collect sales information for a given specific period and can determine the relationship between sales and stocks at the time of the physical count. A stock-counting system also is generally used for staple goods of a low per-unit value.

Inventory Valuation

A major financial concern of every retailer is determining the actual worth of the inventory on hand. How the retailer establishes the value of the inventory can have a profound effect on the outcome of various financial statements (e.g., the income statement and the balance sheet). Knowing the true value of inventories is also an essential element in sound financial planning and control. Retailers can value their inventories at cost (what they paid for the merchandise) or at retail (what they can sell the merchandise for). This section examines the cost and retail methods of inventory and reviews the relative strengths and weaknesses of each method.

The Cost Method

Small retailers generally prefer the **cost method of inventory valuation** because it is easy to understand, easy to implement, and requires a limited amount of record keeping. The retailer simply values merchandise inventory at the original cost to the store each time a physical inventory is taken. One of two procedures typically is used in computing the cost value of merchandise items. First, the original cost can be coded on the price tag or merchandise container using either a word or symbol code (see the discussion of marking procedures in Chapter 16). When taking physical inventory, the retailer records the cost and the number of units for each merchandise item. Multiplying the two yields the total cost value for each type of item.

The second procedure is to imprint a serialized reference number on each price tag corresponding to an itemized merchandise stock-control list containing the per-unit cost of each item. Again, the retailer can compute total cost values by multiplying the number of units obtained during the physical count by the per-unit cost as shown on the control sheet.

A major problem of the cost method occurs when the retailer procures various shipments at different times during inflationary periods. If the wholesale price of an inventory item remained constant, the retailer's costs for various shipments of the same product would be identical. Unfortunately, constant wholesale prices are the exception, and fluctuating wholesale prices are usually the rule. While the rate of inflation can vary significantly, the mere fact that inflation exists creates a problem (the extent of the problem depends on the rate of inflation), with different shipments of identical products being purchased at different wholesale prices (cost to retailer). The retailer then must decide which cost value to use. FIFO (first-in, first-out) and LIFO (last-in, first-out) are two inventory costing methods used to resolve this dilemma.

The FIFO method.   The **FIFO (first-in, first-out) method** assumes that merchandise items are sold in the order in which they are purchased; that is, older stock is sold before newer stock that was purchased at a later date. The cost of the oldest units in stock determines the retailer's cost of goods sold. From an operational viewpoint of maintaining the freshness of merchandise in stock, FIFO makes good sense and is the operating practice of most retailers. From a financial accounting viewpoint, however, during inflationary periods the FIFO method results in an overstatement of profits, thereby increasing the firm's tax liability (see Figure 18–4).

The LIFO method.   "Under **LIFO—the last-in, first-out method**—recent acquisition costs are used to price inventory (even though in actuality, the inventory bought last is not sold first)."[3] The cost of the newest units in stock determines the retailer's cost of goods sold. During a rising market (increasing wholesale prices), the LIFO method

What would you call a technique that enabled a small business to reduce its tax bill and increase its cash flow without any additional investment? Unbelievable? Too good to be true?

Accountants would call this method LIFO—last in, first out—one of two methods of valuing inventory. LIFO values business inventory based on the cost of the last item placed into stock. The other method of evaluation, FIFO—first in, first out—places a value on inventory based on the cost of the first item placed in stock. During inflationary times, the last items purchased are more expensive, and under LIFO these items are assumed to be sold first. In effect, this method eliminates the inflation rate from the inventory's value.

The use of LIFO to value inventory results in lower "paper" profits, which in turn reduces the firm's taxable income. The business (or its owner) pays less income tax and net cash flow is greatly improved. But, since reported profits are lower, the small firm's ability to borrow money and attract investors also is lessened. However, a recent IRS ruling overcomes this disadvantage. The IRS will allow a business to show the value of its inventory under both the LIFO and FIFO methods. In effect, the owner can use LIFO for tax purposes and FIFO for reporting purposes.

To calculate the savings from using LIFO, the firm simply takes its ending inventory, multiplies it by the rate of inflation, and multiplies the result by the marginal tax rate.* For example, suppose a firm has 10,000 units in inventory that cost $3.00 each at the beginning of the year and $5.00 at the year end. Sales revenue was $70,000. The following table compares the income tax savings gained by using the LIFO technique to value inventory.

	FIFO	LIFO
sales revenue	$70,000	$70,000
cost of goods sold	30,000	50,000
gross profit	40,000	20,000
income tax*	$ 8,000	$ 4,000

Income tax savings = $8,000 − $4,000 = $4,000

*Marginal tax rate = 20%

Clearly, LIFO can improve the typical small firm's financial position. The rules on converting to LIFO are very confusing, and the assistance of a professional is required to decipher them. The benefits of switching to LIFO are worth the effort. In fact, tax expert John Klug calls LIFO "one of the greatest weapons in the artillery of the business taxpayer."

Adapted from "LIFO Saves." Reprinted with permission, INC. magazine, (Jan. 1981). Copyright © 1981 by INC. Publishing Company, 38 Commercial Wharf, Boston MA. 02110.

FIGURE 18–4

LIFO (last-in, first-out) versus FIFO (first-in, first-out)

results in tax savings as a result of lower gross profits (see Figure 18–4). For LIFO to be advantageous to the firm, the following conditions are appropriate: "high inflation, a level of markdowns that does not exceed the benefits of inflation, and rising inventory costs."[4] To determine the savings from LIFO, the retailer can use the formula shown in Figure 18–5. The ending inventory value is obtained from the retailer's inventory system, whereas the rate of inflation is determined using one or more price indexes. "Almost all large-volume department stores and many discount, specialty and drug chains use the Department Store Inventory Price Indexes established by the Bureau of Labor Statistics as an indication of inflation."[5] The accounting department computes the marginal tax rate using tax tables prepared by the Internal Revenue Service.

Although the cost method is simple, it does have several disadvantages. First, a cost valuation of inventory requires a physical count of the merchandise, and the need to count and decode prices is both time-consuming and costly. Second, the cost method does not provide a book inventory of what merchandise ought to be on hand. Therefore, the retailer has no means to determine shortages. (Remember, shortages equal book inventory minus physical inventory.) Finally, the cost method

FIGURE 18–5
Computing savings
from using LIFO

is often untimely, because physical inventory is usually taken only once or twice a year. As a result, the retailer cannot prepare weekly, monthly, and quarterly financial statements. Semiannual or annual financial statements are inadequate for effective planning and control for many retailers. The disadvantages of the cost method can be largely overcome if the retailer elects to employ the retail method of inventory valuation.

The Retail Method

The **retail method of inventory valuation** allows the retailer to estimate the cost value of an ending inventory for a particular accounting period without taking a physical inventory. Essentially, the retail method is a book inventory system whereby the cost value for each group of related merchandise (e.g., a department) is based on its retail value (selling price). By determining the percentage relationship between the total cost and the total retail value of the merchandise available for sale during an accounting period, the retailer can obtain a reliable estimate of the ending inventory value at cost. To use the retail method, the retailer must make the following calculations: (1) the total merchandise available for sale, (2) the cost complement, (3) the total retail deductions, and (4) the ending inventory at retail and cost values.

Total merchandise available. The total merchandise available for sale is illustrated in the following example:

	Cost ($)	Retail ($)
beginning inventory	120,000	200,000
+ net purchases	80,000	140,000
+ additional markons	—	2,000
+ freight charges	4,000	—
= total merchandise available	204,000	342,000

As shown, beginning inventory and purchase figures are kept both at cost and at retail values. The beginning inventory is the ending inventory brought forward from the previous accounting period, obtained from the stock ledger that the accounting department maintains. Net purchases represent all purchases the retailer made during the accounting period minus any returns to the vendor. A purchase journal is used to record all purchase transactions. Any additional markons taken since setting the original retail price are added to the retail value of the inventory to reflect the market value of the merchandise. A price-change journal is maintained to keep track of additional markons as well as markdowns and other changes in the original retail selling price. Finally, freight charges, obtained from the purchase journal, are added to portray the true cost of the merchandise correctly.

Cost complement. The cost complement is the average relationship of cost to retail value for all merchandise available for sale during an accounting period. In essence, it is the complement of the cumulative markup percentage. The cost complement is computed as follows:

$$\text{cost complement} = \frac{\text{cost value of inventory}}{\text{retail value of inventory}}$$

Using the previous example in which the value of the total merchandise available for sale equaled $204,000 at cost and $342,000 at retail, then

$$\text{cost complement} = \frac{\$204,000}{\$342,000} = .5965$$

In this example, the retailer's merchandise cost is, on the average, equal to 59.65 percent of the retail value of the merchandise.

Retail deductions.   The third step in the retail method of inventory valuation is to determine the total merchandise available for sale. Retail deductions include merchandise that has been sold, marked down, discounted, stolen, and lost. Total retail deductions are obtained by adding all the deductions, reducing the retail value of the merchandise that was available for sale. To continue our illustration,

	sales for period	$160,000
+	markdowns	$ 30,000
+	discounts	$ 10,000
+	shortages (estimated)	$ 2,000
=	total retail deductions	$202,000

The sales figure for the accounting period represents both cash and credit sales and is obtained from the retailer's sales journal. The amount of markdowns taken during the accounting period and the amount of the discounts granted to employees and special customers can be secured from the price-change journal. Because shortages resulting from shoplifting, employee pilfering, and lost merchandise cannot be determined without a physical inventory, the retailer usually estimates the shortage figure based on past experience.

Ending inventory value.   The final step in implementing the retail method is to determine the value of ending inventory at retail and at cost. The retail value of ending inventory is computed by subtracting total retail deductions from total merchandise available for sale at retail. In our example,

	total merchandise available at retail	$342,000
−	total retail deductions	$202,000
=	ending inventory at retail	$140,000

The cost value of ending inventory is calculated by multiplying the ending inventory at retail by the cost complement in the following manner:

$$\begin{array}{lll} \text{ending inventory} & = \text{ending inventory} & \times \text{ cost} \\ \text{at cost} & \text{at retail} & \text{complement} \end{array}$$

$$\begin{array}{l} \text{ending inventory} = \$140,000 \times .5965 = \$83,510 \\ \text{at cost} \end{array}$$

While the figure $83,510 is only an estimate of the true cost value of the ending inventory, it is sufficiently reliable to allow the retailer to estimate both the cost of goods sold and gross margin for the accounting period. To complete our example:

	total merchandise available at retail	$204,000
−	ending inventory at retail	$83,510
=	cost of goods sold	$120,490

	sales for the period	$160,000
−	cost of goods sold	$120,490
=	gross margin	$39,510

Although the retail method has the disadvantages of requiring the retailer to keep more records (stock ledger and sales, purchases, and price-change journals) and use averages to estimate cost values, its advantages are numerous. The retail method forces the retailer to "think retail" in that it highlights both retail and cost figures. Second, frequent and regular calculations of various financial and operating statements are possible as a result of the availability of cost and retail information. These statements are essential to good financial planning and control and allow the retailer to adjust more quickly to changing market conditions. Third, when the retail method is used, physical inventories are taken in retail prices, thereby eliminating the costly, time-consuming job of decoding cost prices. Recording physical inventory in retail prices greatly simplifies the process and encourages a more frequent physical count of stock. Fourth, the retail method facilitates planning and control on a departmental basis. Sales, purchases, inventories, and price-change information are recorded by department and can be used to evaluate each department's performance. Fifth, by providing a book figure on what inventory should be on hand, the retail method allows the retailer to determine shortages each time a physical inventory is taken. Sixth, the retail method facilitates planning for insurance coverage and collecting insurance claims by providing an up-to-date valuation of inventory.

Given the many advantages of the retail method of inventory valuation, it is not surprising that large departmentalized and chain store retailers use it extensively to gain tighter control over their various operating units.

INVENTORY-
ANALYSIS
SYSTEM

Inventory information is only useful when it provides the retailer with insights into past mistakes and with foresight for future planning. Merchandise data collected and processed by the inventory-information system can be used to evaluate past performances and to plan future actions. A determination of stock turnover and return on inventory investment are the principal methods for evaluating the retailer's past performance in controlling merchandise inventories. The dollar and unit open-to-buy methods are two of the more important tools for controlling future merchandising activities.

Stock Turnover

Stock turnover is the rate at which the retailer depletes and replenishes stock. Specifically, stock turnover is defined as the number of times during a specific period (usually annual) that the average stock on hand is sold.

Stock turnover rates can be calculated in both dollars (at retail or at cost) and units. The formulas for figuring stock turnover rates are shown in Figure 18–6. (Data

FIGURE 18–6
Computing stock turn-
over rates

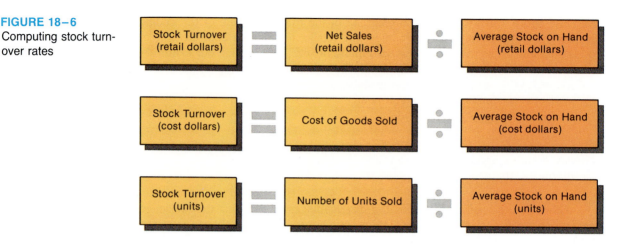

on net sales, cost of goods sold, and number of units sold are obtained from the inventory-information system.) **Average stock** on hand for any time period is defined as the sum of the stock on hand at the beginning of the period, at each intervening period, and at the end of the period divided by the number of stock listings. For example, the average stock at retail for the summer season of June, July, and August would be calculated as follows:

June 1	$60,000
July 1	$40,000
August 1	$50,000
August 31	$35,000
total inventory:	$185,000

$$\text{average stock} = \frac{\text{total inventory}}{\text{number of listings}}$$

$$\begin{array}{c}\text{average stock}\\(\text{June}-\text{August})\end{array} = \frac{\$185,000}{4} = \$46,250$$

If the net sales (retail dollars) for the three-month summer season were $220,000, then the stock turnover rate at retail would be

$$\begin{array}{c}\text{stock turnover}\\\text{at retail}\end{array} = \frac{\text{net sales}}{\text{average stock on hand}}$$

$$\begin{array}{c}\text{stock turnover}\\\text{at retail}\\(\text{June}-\text{August})\end{array} = \frac{\$220,000}{\$\ 46,250} = 4.76$$

Benefits of High Turnover

High stock turnover rates generally reflect good merchandise planning and control. Several benefits accrue to retailers with a high rate of stock turnover. They include the following: (1) *Fresher merchandise:* With a rapid stock turnover there is more frequent replacement of merchandise and, therefore, a continuous flow of new and fresh merchandise into the store. (2) *Fewer markdowns and less depreciation:* A fast stock turnover is associated with a faster rate of sales and, therefore, reduced losses resulting from style or fashion obsolescence and soiled or damaged merchandise. (3) *Lower expense:* A quick stock turnover helps to reduce inventories and, therefore, reduce such inventory expenses as interest and insurance payments, storage costs, and taxes on inventory; it also helps to reduce promotional costs, since a new and fresh selection of merchandise tends to more easily sell itself. (4) *Greater sales:* A rapid stock turnover allows the retailer to adjust the merchandise assortment according to the changing needs of the target market and, therefore, to generate more customer interest and a greater sales volume. (5) *Higher returns:* A rapid stock turnover resulting in an increase in sales and a corresponding decrease in stocks will generate a higher return on inventory investment, hence, a more productive and efficient use of the retailer's capital.

Increasing the rate of stock turnover requires the retailer to control the size and content of its inventory. The retailer must carefully balance inventory investment for greater profit with inventory assortment and support for adequate customer selection. Strategies for increasing stock turnover include (1) limiting merchandise assortment to the most popular brands, styles, sizes, colors, and price lines; (2) reducing merchandise support by maintaining a minimum reserve or safety stock; (3) clearing out slow-moving stock through price reductions; and (4) increasing the promotional effort in an attempt to increase sales.

Limitations of High Turnover

A high rate of stock turnover is not without its problems. Excessively high stock turns can mean the retailer is buying in too-small quantities. If so, then the retailer is (1) not taking full advantage of available quantity discounts; (2) adding to the costs of transportation and handling; and (3) increasing accounting costs by processing too many orders. Another potential problem with high stock turnover is the danger of losing sales because of stockouts.

Return on Inventory Investment

"Merchandise assortments must be effective if the retail store is to prosper. An effective assortment is one that creates good financial returns."[6]

The second method for evaluating past performance in controlling merchandise inventories is **gross margin return on inventory** (GMROI)—the ratio of gross margin dollars to the average stock on hand. This ratio tells the retailer the dollar investment in inventory needed to achieve a desired gross profit (gross margin dollars).[7] Specifically, return on inventory investment can be expressed as shown in Figure 18–7. Essentially, return on inventory investment concerns the relationship between stock turnover and profitability. The importance of this ratio is that it allows the retailer to

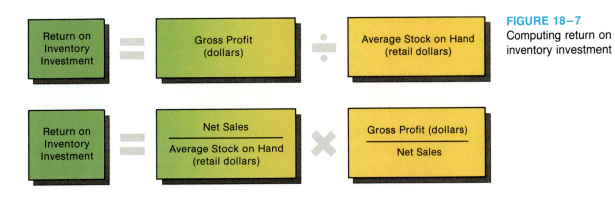

FIGURE 18–7
Computing return on inventory investment

FIGURE 18–8
Determining gross margin return on selling space

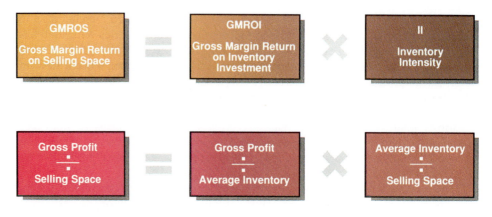

evaluate past and future effects of turnover on a store's (or department's) profitability. Before initiating plans to increase the stock turnover rate, the retailer should first determine how a higher stock turnover rate might affect profitability.

The GMROI concept can be expanded to include planning and controlling stock levels and assortments in terms of their space productivity. Gross margin return on selling space (GMROS) involves the retailer in designing effective merchandise assortments by planning assortments "at the stock-keeping unit (SKU) level with special consideration given to the gross profit, inventory investment, sales and space attributable to each SKU. . . . The SKUs that contribute most to the effectiveness of the

FIGURE 18–9
An assortment planning matrix (source: based on Robert F. Lusch, "Two Critical Determinants of Retail Profitability and Productivity," *Retailing Issues Letter* 2, no.1 [Zale Corporation in conjunction with the Center for Retailing Studies, Texas A&M University, 1986]:2)

GMROI- GROSS MARGIN RETURN ON INVESTMENT

	LOW	HIGH

(II) Inventory Intensity — LOW	Competitive Assortments
	
	Low GMROI, low II
	Poor performers
	Poor space productivity
	Assortment strategy:
	   trim and hold at competitive parity
	
	Example:
	   Linens and domestics in Discount Department Store
		Inventory Effective Assortments
		
		High GMROI, low II
		Reasonable performers
		Reasonable space productivity
		Assortment strategy:
		   maintain and manage at consumer demand levels
		
		Example:
		   Stationery and school supplies in Discount Department Stores

HIGH	Space Effective Assortments
	
	Low GMROI, high II
	Reasonable performers
	Reasonable space productivity
	Assortment strategy:
	   maintain and manage at consumer demand levels
	
	Example:
	   Cameras and accessories in Discount Department Store
		Golden Assortments
		
		High GMROI, high II
		Excellent performers
		Excellent space productivity
		Assortment strategy:
		   build and protect to gain competitive advantage
		
		Example:
		   Costume jewelry in Discount Department Store

assortment plan are those that have a high inventory investment per unit of space they occupy (inventory intensity)."[8] Figure 18–8 illustrates how to compute GMROS. The GMROS concept can be used to construct an assortment planning matrix to assist the retailer in making SKU decisions. As suggested in Figure 18–9, the most desirable assortment strategy is to gain a competitive edge by protecting and building "golden assortments" (high GMROI investment and high inventory intensity).

> [However], the competitive realities of the marketplace dictate that a retailer must plan the store's total assortment to have a mix of these four categories with the goal being to maximize the number of SKUs in golden assortments. Each SKU or group of similar SKUs should be monitored regularly to determine if one of the three "hot" buttons of space productivity (gross margin, sales-to-stock ratio, inventory intensity) can be pushed to improve its performance.[9]

Open-to-Buy

Open-to-buy is one of the retailer's most important tools for controlling future merchandise inventories. This tool helps the retailer decide how much to buy. **Open-to-buy** is the amount of new merchandise the retailer can buy during a specific time period without exceeding the planned purchases for that period. Open-to-buy represents the difference between what the retailer plans to buy and what it has already bought—planned purchases minus purchase commitments. Open-to-buy applies to both dollar and unit control. Dollar open-to-buy sets a financial constraint on the retailer's buying activities, whereas unit open-to-buy controls assortment and support in the buying process.

Open-to-buy is a versatile control tool. The retailer can use it to control purchase activities on a daily, weekly, or monthly basis. Also, open-to-buy can help control purchases of any classification or subclassification of merchandise. As a control tool, it allows the retailer to allocate purchases so stocks are maintained at predetermined levels by either the merchandise budget (dollar planning and control) or a merchandise list (unit planning and control).

Dollar Open-to-Buy

Dollar open-to-buy is used to determine the amount of money the retailer has to spend for new merchandise at any given time. It can be calculated and recorded at both retail and cost prices. To calculate **dollar open-to-buy at retail** prices for any day of a monthly period, the buyer starts with planned monthly purchases and subtracts purchase commitments already made during the month. Figure 18–10 shows the steps for determining dollar open-to-buy at retail. To obtain **dollar open-to-buy at cost,** the buyer simply multiplies open-to-buy at retail by the complement of the initial markup percentage. Figure 18–10 shows the formula for determining open-to-buy at cost.

To illustrate, a buyer for a women's apparel department is planning a trip to the market on April 15 and wants to know how much she can buy without exceeding the budget. Examination of the merchandise budget for April reveals that planned sales for the month were $70,000, while reductions (shortages, markdowns, and discounts) were $4,000. Inventory records reveal that the store started the month with $60,000 worth of inventory and plans call for an ending inventory of $50,000. A review of purchase orders indicates that the department has made purchase commitments of $14,000 since the beginning of the month. Given an initial markup percentage of 50 percent on retail, the buyer calculates the dollar open-to-buy to be $50,000 at retail and $25,000 at cost. These figures were obtained by first calculating planned purchases for April ($70,000 + $4,000 + $50,000 − $60,000 = $64,000), then subtracting all purchase commitments ($14,000) made through the 15th of the

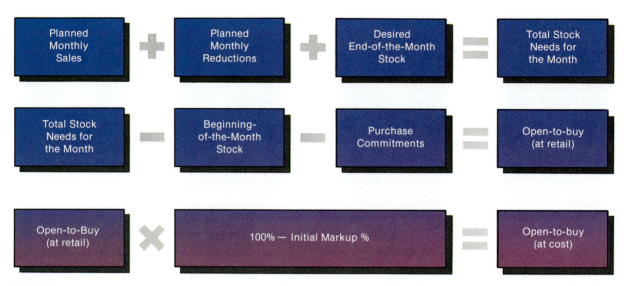

FIGURE 18–10

Computing dollar open-to-buy at retail (top) and open-to-buy at cost (bottom)

month. Figure 18–11 illustrates a form for calculating a weekly dollar open-to-buy by means of a slightly different format, one commonly used by small retailing organizations for computing their open-to-buy position regularly and frequently.

Unit Open-to-Buy

For the retailer engaged in unit control, unit open-to-buy is a successful and necessary tool in preventing stockouts and overstocking. Unit open-to-buy is most frequently used to control inventories of staple merchandise. This method lends itself to formal and systematic procedures for reordering merchandise that has well-established and predictable sales trends. **Unit open-to-buy** calculations involve two steps: (1) determining maximum inventory and (2) computing the unit open-to-buy quantity.

Step 1: Determine maximum inventory. **Maximum inventory** is the number of merchandise units the retailer needs to cover expected sales during the reorder and

FIGURE 18–11

A form for computing dollar open-to-buy on a weekly basis (source: Mary D.Troxell, *Retail Merchandise Mathematics—Principles and Procedures* [Englewood Cliffs, NJ: Prentice-Hall, 1980], 254)

The Boutique Dollar Open-to-buy				
Department _____ Week Ending _____				
1. Physical inventory on hand this Monday				
2. On order this Monday				
3. Total inventory and on order (lines 1 plus 2)				
4. Planned sales this week (Monday thru Saturday)				
5. Planned closing physical inventory at end of this week (Saturday)				
6. Planned on order at end of this week				
7. Planned total closing inventory and on order at end of this week (lines 5 plus 6)				
8. Planned total closing inventory and on order and planned sales for this week ending Saturday (lines 7 plus 4)				
9. Open to buy for this week (lines 8 minus 3)				

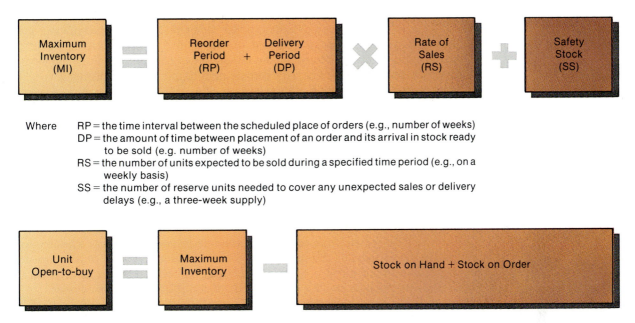

Where RP = the time interval between the scheduled place of orders (e.g., number of weeks)
DP = the amount of time between placement of an order and its arrival in stock ready
to be sold (e.g. number of weeks)
RS = the number of units expected to be sold during a specified time period (e.g., on a
weekly basis)
SS = the number of reserve units needed to cover any unexpected sales or delivery
delays (e.g., a three-week supply)

FIGURE 18–12
Computing unit open-to-buy

delivery periods plus a safety stock for either unexpected sales or problems in securing the merchandise. The formula for determining maximum inventory is shown in Figure 18–12.

As an illustration, a hardware retailer reorders a staple item of merchandise every six weeks, expecting that delivery will take three weeks. Based on past experience, the hardware retailer expects to sell approximately 40 units a week and considers a two-week safety stock necessary. The maximum inventory (MI) for the merchandise is 440 units. It is calculated as follows:

$$\begin{aligned} MI &= (6 \text{ weeks} + 3 \text{ weeks}) \times 40 \text{ units} + 80 \text{ units} \\ &= (9 \text{ weeks}) \times 40 \text{ units} + 80 \text{ units} \\ &= 360 \text{ units} + 80 \text{ units} \\ &= 440 \text{ units} \end{aligned}$$

The hardware retailer therefore must stock 440 units to cover the reorder period and delivery period and to ensure a safety stock capable of covering two weeks' sales if the reorder is delayed or sales are higher than expected.

Step 2: Compute unit open-to-buy. Maximum inventory represents the number of merchandise units the retailer is open-to-buy if there is no stock on hand or stock on order. Unit open-to-buy is defined as maximum inventory minus stock on hand and stock on order. The computation formula is shown in Figure 18–12. Suppose our hardware dealer determines that it had 210 units on hand (obtained from the inventory-information system) and 90 units on order (obtained from purchase orders). Then,

$$\text{open-to-buy} = 440 - (210 + 90) \text{ (or 140 units)}$$

The systematic nature of unit open-to-buy permits easy computerization of this control tool.

SUMMARY

Merchandise control involves designing dollar- and unit-inventory-information and -analysis systems for collecting, recording, analyzing, and using merchandise data to control the planned balance between the retailer's merchandise inventory and sales. Merchandise control is the necessary complement to merchandise planning.

An inventory-information system is a set of methods and procedures for collecting and processing merchandise data that are pertinent to planning and controlling merchandise inventories. Depending on the kind of information needed and the available sources of that information, the retailer can elect to use (1) a dollar/perpetual/book system, (2) a dollar/periodic/physical system, (3) a unit/perpetual/book system, or (4) a unit/periodic/physical system. An essential element in dollar control is knowing the true value of inventories. The two methods of inventory valuation are the cost method and the retail method. The cost method is simpler, whereas the retail method provides more timely and useful information.

The inventory-analysis system includes methods for evaluating the retailer's past merchandising performance as well as the decision-making tools available for controlling future merchandising activities. Stock turnover analysis and return on inventory investment ratios are used to evaluate the retailer's past performance. Dollar and unit open-to-buy are key methods of controlling future inventories.

KEY TERMS AND CONCEPTS

average stock	maximum inventory
cost method of inventory valuation	merchandise control
dollar control	open-to-buy
dollar open-to-buy at cost	periodic physical inventory
dollar open-to-buy at retail	perpetual book inventory
dollar/periodic/physical inventory	retail method of inventory valuation
dollar/perpetual/book inventory	stock turnover at cost
first-in, first-out (FIFO) method of costing inventories	stock turnover at retail
gross margin return on inventory (GMROI)	stock turnover in units
inventory-analysis system	unit control
inventory-information system	unit open-to-buy
last-in, first-out (LIFO) method of costing inventories	unit/periodic/physical inventory
	unit/perpetual/book inventory

REVIEW QUESTIONS

1. Describe the concerns of dollar and unit control.
2. What distinguishes perpetual book inventory from periodic physical inventory?
3. How is a dollar/perpetual/book inventory determined?
4. What is the purpose of a dollar/periodic/physical inventory system?
5. What types of manual and automatic systems are used to gather information on the number of units sold?
6. How are stock levels monitored in a unit/periodic/physical inventory system? Briefly describe each method.
7. What are the two procedures for calculating the cost value of merchandise items?
8. Describe the FIFO and LIFO methods of costing inventories.
9. What are the disadvantages of the cost method of inventory valuation?
10. Using the retail method of inventory valuation, how does the retailer obtain a reliable estimate of the ending inventory value at cost?

11. What is the cost-complement factor in the retail method of inventory valuation?
12. List the advantages of the retail method of inventory valuation.
13. How are dollar (at retail and at cost) and unit stock turnover rates computed?
14. What are the benefits and limitations of high stock turnover rates?
15. Why is the return on inventory investment ratio important?
16. What is open-to-buy?
17. What are the procedural steps for determining dollar open-to-buy?
18. What is maximum inventory? How is it computed? What role does it have in determining unit open-to-buy?

ENDNOTES

1. William L. Clarke, "Integrating The Logistics of Merchandise Management," *Retail Control* (June/July 1987): 26.
2. See "NRMA's New POS Study," *Stores* (April 1987): 67–74 and "Point-of-Sale '86: A New Study," *Stores* (November 1986): 88–90.
3. "LIFO Survey Shows It's Here to Stay," *Chain Store Age Executive* (January, 1984): 32.
4. Ibid.
5. Ibid.
6. Robert F. Lusch, "Two Critical Determinants of Retail Profitability and Productivity," *Retailing Issues Letter* 2 (Zale Corporation in conjunction with the Center for Retailing Studies, Texas A&M University, 1986): 1.
7. See Daniel J. Sweeney, "Improving the Profitability of Retail Merchandising Decisions," *Journal of Marketing* 37 (January, 1973): 60–68.
8. Lusch, "Two Critical Determinants," 1.
9. Ibid., 2.

RELATED READINGS

Berlin, Peter D. "Using Retail Method of Inventory to Reduce Shrinkage."*Retail Control* (March 1984): 41–45.
Brame, Ken. "Merchandise Unit Control for Better Profitability." *Retail Control* (September 1984): 41–46.
Bunton, B. James, and Sycamore, Robert J. "What's Wrong with the Retail Method?" *Retail Control* (November 1982): 35–56.
Congdon, Robert J. "What's the Best Way to Capture Item Numbers?" *Retail Control* (December 1983): 13–18.
Fink, Michael M. "On-Line Big Ticket System at Wickes Furniture." *Retail Control* (December 1984): 32–49.
Gilberg, Mitchell. "Create Open-to-Buy Plans the Easy Way." *Retail Control* (December 1984): 21–31.
Greco, Alan J. "The Integration of Short and Long Range Planning for Retailers Through Expanded Point-of-Sale Based Information Systems."In *Developments in Marketing Science, Proceedings,* edited by J. D. Lindquist, 348. Academy of Marketing Science, 1984.
Joseph, Anthony M. "Maximizing the Returns on Your Merchandise Investment." *Retail Control* (August 1985): 26–42.
Lake, Marjorie A. "Strategies for Spreading OTB Timing!" *Stores* (April 1982): 19–23.
Levy, Michael, and Ingene, Charles A. "Using Residual Income Analysis (RIA) to Make Merchandising Decisions." *Retail Control* (January 1985): 27–41.
Mason, J. Berry, and Mayer, Morris L. "Retail Merchandise Information Systems for the 1980's."*Journal of Retailing* 56 (Spring 1980): 36–76.
Paxton, Daniel. "GMROI: The Axis of Retail Profit Planning." *Retail Control* (November 1983): 2–24.
Rothman, Marian Burk. "Expanding the Concept of Inventory Management." *Stores* (June 1979): 55–62.

19

Outline

SETTING THE RETAIL PRICE
Price-Setting Objectives
Price-Setting Determinants
Price-Setting Methods
Price-Setting Policies

ADJUSTING THE RETAIL PRICE
Discount Adjustments
Markon Adjustments
Markdown Adjustments
Markdown Strategies
Markdown Control

Objectives

☐ Set specific, measurable price objectives consistent with the needs of both the consumer and the retailer.

☐ Assess the impact of demand, competition, cost, product, and legal considerations on the retailer's price-setting activities.

☐ Describe the methods by which retailers set their prices.

☐ Differentiate the numerous policies supplementing and modifying retail price-setting methods.

☐ Explain the need to adapt prices to the changing external and internal environmental conditions of the retail firm.

☐ Differentiate among the three basic types of price adjustments.

☐ Identify the necessities of price markdowns and explain the factors that determine when and how great a price markdown should be taken.

Price Strategy: Establishing the Retail Price

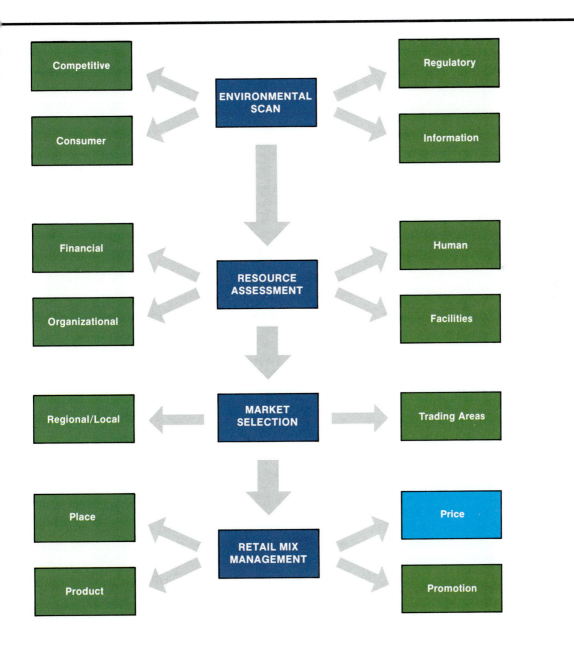

The right price is one that consumers are willing and able to pay and retailers are willing to accept in exchange for merchandise and services. The right price allows the retailer to make a fair profit while providing the consumer with value satisfaction before, during, and after the sale. For the retailer, "effective pricing can be achieved with neither a rule of thumb nor a mathematical formula. It is, like advertising, a creative process. It requires both insight to identify buyer segments and imagination to design pricing strategies that distinguish among them."[1] From the consumer's viewpoint, price can act as a forceful attraction or as an absolute repellent in the consumer's store-selection process. It can also serve as either an incentive or a deterrent in the decision to buy. Some consumers consider price the most important criterion in selecting stores and products; others are far less sensitive to price. Retailers view prices in terms of (1) profitability, or how much they will have left after covering the merchandise cost and operating expenses; (2) sales volume, or how many merchandise units they can sell at various prices; (3) consumer traffic, or how many consumers they can attract to the store using various price levels or strategies; and (4) store image, or what type of image they will project to consumers through different price levels, policies, and strategies.

This chapter examines price-setting objectives, determinants, methods, and policies as well as the various means of adjusting retail prices: discounts, markons, and markdowns. Figure 19–1 illustrates the pricing concerns of the retail manager.

SETTING THE RETAIL PRICE

Price-Setting Objectives

In any decision-making process, the decision maker should establish objectives. Price setting is no exception. Before the retailer can effectively establish prices consistent both with the firm's requirements and the consumer's expectations, it should set specific, measurable objectives based on well-thought-out pricing guidelines. Retail price objectives are generally categorized in three groups: sales objectives, profit objectives, and competitive objectives.

Sales Objectives

Retailers usually state sales objectives in terms of either sales volume or market share. The primary reason for setting **sales-volume objectives** is to achieve future sales growth or to maintain current sales levels. Sales growth in the form of "beating last year's sales" by some percentage is a common objective for many retailers. How appropriate this kind of pricing objective is ultimately depends on its effect on profits. Retailers can set prices to increase dollar sales volume, but if those prices fail to generate sufficient revenues to more than offset additional costs, the net result could be reduced profit levels.

Market-share objectives are price-setting goals that retailers set to increase or maintain their share of the total market. Many retailers prefer market-share objectives to sales objectives because the former represent a relative measure of how well they are performing in the market compared to competitors. Put another way, market share is a measure of the retailer's sales position relative to all competitors in the same trading area, in terms of percentage share of total sales for that trading area. When total sales within a trading area are expanding or contracting, the retailer's market share is a better reflection than a total sales measurement of what the store has accomplished.

If *market-share growth* is the principal objective in setting prices, the retailer must realize that any increase in percentage share of the market will come at the

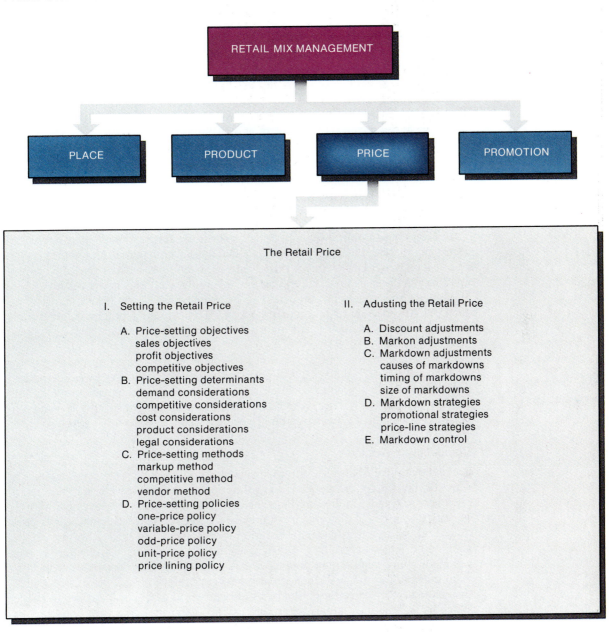

FIGURE 19-1
Setting and adjusting
the retail price

expense of one or more of its competitors. Therefore, some type of aggressive action and retaliatory pricing actions should be anticipated from competitors seeking to protect their share of the market. As a pricing objective, market-share growth may be a preferred goal for a new and expanding product market rather than for an older one, because many competitors in the former situation are more interested in increasing their sales as opposed to their market share. In mature and stable product markets, however, *market-share maintenance* is generally the more accepted pricing objective. Price-cutting activities in mature markets force competitors to meet the new price, lowering profit margins for all concerned.

Profit Objectives

Profit maximization and target return on investment and on net sales are retailers' three most-cited profit objectives for guiding price-setting decisions. **Profit-maximization objectives** seek the highest possible profit through pricing and other merchandising activities. In practice, a profit-maximization objective has several limitations. First, a retailer might have to maximize profits at the expense of other members of the channel (wholesalers and manufacturers). This kind of activity will lead to conflict within the marketing channel. Second, for many people, profit maximization has negative connotations of "price gouging" and excessive profits. Third, if the retailer were to achieve excessive profits, it is likely that additional competitors would be attracted into the trade area. Finally, because of inability to obtain perfect information, the retailer can never know if maximum profit objectives have been achieved.

Target return objectives are profit objectives for guiding price-setting decisions. Target returns are usually expressed as a certain percentage return on either capital investment or net sales. *Return on investment* (ROI) is a ratio of profits to capital investments (facilities, fixtures, equipment, inventory, etc.). ROI is a measure of how efficiently a retailer is using investment to generate profits. The retailer may wish, for example, to earn a target return of 10, 15, or 20 percent; a 15 percent return simply means the retailer wants to earn a net profit of 15 percent for every dollar of capital invested.

Return on net sales (ROS) is the percentage value derived by dividing dollar profit by net sales. To achieve this targeted return, retailers set prices by using markup percentages large enough to cover all appropriate operating expenses (payroll, rent, utilities, professional services, etc.), plus the desired dollar profit per unit needed to generate the targeted percentage return on net sales.

Competitive Objectives

Competitive price objectives also take several forms, including (1) meeting competition, (2) preventing competition, and (3) nonprice competition. Some retailers simply follow the leader in their price-setting activities; their price objectives can best be described as meeting their major competitor's price.[2] Certain retailers within a given trade area act as price leaders for some product lines. The price followers simply adjust their prices accordingly. Other retailers take preventing competition as their pricing objective and set their prices low enough to discourage additional competitors from entering the market. Finally, some retailers prefer to avoid price competition; they would rather compete on the basis of better product or service offerings, better locations and facilities, greater promotional efforts, or any other merchandising activities except price.

Price-Setting Determinants

Each retailer faces several considerations in trying to establish a selling price that will both sell the merchandise and offer a profitable return. The retailer should examine demand, competitive, cost, product, and legal factors.

Demand Considerations

In setting a price, retailers should consider not only economic costs but noneconomic factors as well. Consumers' perceptions of and reactions to different prices must be taken into account before making price-setting decisions. Some consumers' buying behavior closely reflects the law of demand; consumers will buy more products at lower prices than at higher prices. The retailer must consider the effects of different price levels on consumer demand. This effect is called elasticity of demand.

Price elasticity of demand is a measure of the effect a price change has on consumer demand (i.e., the number of units sold). Demand elasticity describes the relationship between a percentage change in price and a percentage change in quantity sold. The formulas for computing demand elasticity are shown in Figure 19–2. A demand elasticity greater than 1 is referred to as *elastic demand*—a condition in which a change in price strongly influences consumer demand. For example, consumer demand is more elastic for stock-up items (nonperishable goods like soap, toothpaste, canned foods, etc.) than for non–stock-up items (perishables and low usage rate goods).[3] *Inelastic demand* occurs when a change in price has little or no influence on consumer demand. A demand elasticity of less than 1 represents an inelastic situation. A demand elasticity of 1 represents *unitary elasticity* whereby changes in price are exactly offset by changes in demand. A good way to remember the difference between elastic demand and inelastic demand is to consider the consumer's degree of *sensitivity* to a price change. Inelastic demand means that consumers are relatively insensitive to a change in price, whereas under elastic demand conditions they are sensitive to price changes.

To illustrate how to calculate price elasticity of demand, suppose a restaurant raises its price for a sirloin steak dinner from $10 to $14 and experiences a sharp drop in orders for the sirloin dinner (from 800 to 400) in the first month. The elasticity of demand for this menu item is computed as follows:

$$\text{percentage change in quantity} = \frac{400}{800} = 500\%$$

$$\text{percentage change in price} = \frac{4}{10} = 40\%$$

$$\text{demand elasticity} = \frac{50\%}{40\%} = 1.25$$

The computed elasticity of 1.25 indicates that the demand for sirloin steak dinners is elastic. A $4 increase in price had a major effect on consumer demand (50% decrease) for this particular menu item.

In some cases, changing the price of a merchandise item will change the demand for not only that item but also a different item. *Cross-elasticity of demand*

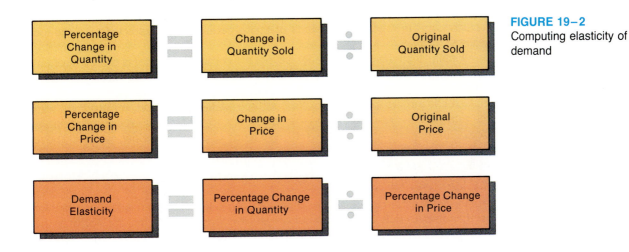

FIGURE 19–2
Computing elasticity of demand

occurs when a change in the price of one product results in a change in demand for another product. For example, the demand for a complementary product (e.g., film) may decrease as a result of increased prices and reduced demand for the product it complements (e.g., cameras). A different result can occur between "substitute" products. In this situation, cross-elasticity of demand might produce an increased demand for tea as the price of coffee rises. Retailers must watch the price–demand interplay between products closely so as to avoid costly pricing errors.

Although it would be virtually impossible to formally determine the price elasticity of demand for each merchandise line carried, the retailer should develop a "feel" for which products are highly sensitive to changes in price. Knowing whether a product is generally elastic, inelastic, or unitary in demand is one of several important factors a retailer must understand in setting a retail price in harmony with the target market's demand.

Competitive Considerations

Because a retailer does not operate in a vacuum, it is imperative to consider competitors' pricing actions in setting prices. Although prices need not equal those of competitors, the retailer should provide consumers with a price difference they can accept and justify based on differences in service, location, and product-mix factors. In response to tough competition from T. J. Maxx stores and Hit or Miss shops, Marshalls discount apparel stores fought back by selling more lower-priced goods; the result of this strategy was that customers believed quality was deteriorating. "Marshalls is trying to re-establish its image by emphasizing its name brands, renovating stores, and redesigning merchandise displays."[4]

Excessive price competition among retailers in the form of pricing "wars" usually does not benefit any of the parties, and retailers must realize that price competition is one of the least distinctive forms of competition. A retailer's price cuts can be instantaneously offset by competitors that easily match the lower price. Given the relative brevity of price competition (because of the high likelihood of precipitating price reprisals), retailers must consider alternative forms of competition (product, service, promotion, and so on) before engaging in aggressive price-setting activities.[5] To increase sales at the expense of profits is not a wise pricing strategy, at least not over the long run.

The freedom a retailer enjoys in setting prices depends on estimates of its competitive position. A retailer that judges its competitive position as strong because of a distinctive retail mix, highly loyal consumers, or a unique store image has greater freedom in price-setting decisions. On the other hand, "me-too" retailers that lack distinctiveness in the nonprice areas of their operations are restricted to a me-too pricing strategy.

Finally, the retailer must recognize that the competitor's price is more important for some merchandise items than for others. First, the retailer must closely consider products that consumers purchase frequently and the supplier distributes intensively because consumers can easily make price comparisons. Second, for products with high unit value—big-ticket items—retailers need to seriously consider competitors' prices. The retailer can set prices for these kinds of products below, with, or above those of competitors, depending on the type of price image desired.

Cost Considerations

A major determinant in any price-setting decision is the cost the retailer must pay for merchandise. In defining merchandise cost, it is important to include not only the actual cost of the merchandise but also all costs incurred in getting the merchandise into the store and preparing it for sale. Retailers determine merchandise costs by following the procedure outlined in Figure 19–3. Calculating merchandise cost this way gives the retailer a more accurate picture of the true cost. For many retailers, merchandise cost is both a reference and starting point for price-setting decisions. Their approach to the pricing problem is cost-oriented; they set the retail selling price of a product at a level high enough to cover not only the cost of the merchandise but also the fixed and variable expenses associated with merchandising the product plus an additional profit margin.

Product Considerations

Retailers should not make price-setting decisions without considering the product's characteristics. Different products can command different prices at different times and in different locations.

Retailers must first consider *product perishability* and its associated risks. Perishable products often require higher initial prices to cover markdowns that become necessary as the product loses its marketability. Product perishability takes several forms:

☐ *Physical perishability*—loss of marketability resulting from physical damage or deterioration of the product
☐ *Style or fashion perishability*—a loss of marketability as a result of style, fashion, or model obsolescence (as in being "out of style" or "the old model")
☐ *Seasonal perishability*—loss of marketability because the product is out of season
☐ *Competitive perishability*—loss of marketability as a result of the aggressive actions of competitors, such as a pricing war

It is also worth noting that a retailer may decide to set a lower initial price on some highly perishable products to move them out before a loss in marketability occurs; for example, a retailer might place a low price on a quart of fresh strawberries during the strawberry-picking season.

Product quality, whether perceived or real, is another major product determinant the retailer should examine before setting a price. Depending on the price/quality image the retailer wants to project, one of several possible pricing strategies can be used. Figure 19–4 illustrates nine possible pricing strategies based on product quality. From this figure, we see that the retailer can assume quite a number of roles in offering a particular product-quality level at various price levels.

FIGURE 19–3
Determining merchandise cost

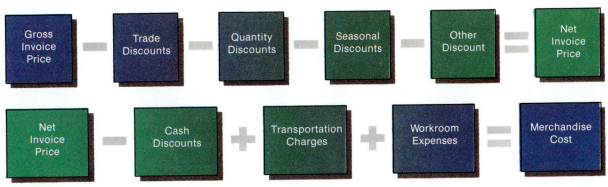

FIGURE 19–4
Product-quality consid-
erations in price-setting
decisions (source:
Phillip Kotler, *Principles
of Marketing*
[Englewood Cliffs, NJ:
Prentice-Hall, 1980],
402)

FIGURE 19–4
Product-quality considerations in price-setting decisions (source: Phillip Kotler, *Principles of Marketing* [Englewood Cliffs, NJ: Prentice-Hall, 1980], 402)

Product uniqueness is a characteristic that retailers can exploit to realize a premium price. Consumers who seek something different tend to be insensitive to price and therefore willing to pay higher prices for products that exhibit originality.[6]

Legal Considerations

Price-setting decisions are subject to numerous legal constraints. According to law, any pricing activity that any governmental agency considers to be a present or probable restraint on trade or an unfair trade practice can be illegal. Price setting is perhaps the most regulated aspect of the retailer's business. (The legalities of pricing were discussed in Chapter 5.)

Price-Setting Methods

Price-setting decisions are both an art and a science. A policy of setting low prices might well produce high sales volumes but inadequate profit margins. High prices usually allow for excellent profit margins; however, the merchandise must be sold before those profits can be realized. Knowing when a price is too high or too low is an art that comes with the experience of being in the business. Nevertheless, certain price-setting methods blend the art of experience with the science of retail mathematics.

Markup Method of Pricing

Markup is the difference between the cost of the merchandise and its retail price. Although markup appears to be a relatively simple concept, it incorporates several complex relationships expressed in a variety of ways.

Dollar markup. **Dollar markup** is a cost-oriented approach to setting prices wherein the retailer adds to the cost of the merchandise a dollar amount large enough to cover related operating expenses and to provide a given dollar profit. The basic dollar relationships between merchandise cost, retail price, and markup are best expressed as follows:

$$\text{retail} = \text{cost} + \text{markup}$$
$$\text{cost} = \text{retail} - \text{markup}$$
$$\text{markup} = \text{retail} - \text{cost}$$

With these formulas, the retailer can solve any dollar markup problem. Dollar markup is most frequent on big-ticket items; for example, the owner of a jewelry store that has paid $3,000 for a diamond ring and prices it at $4,000 is just as likely to think in terms of a $1,000 markup as a 25-percent markup on retail or a 33.33-percent markup on cost.

Percentage markups. **Percentage markups** usually are calculated to facilitate the process of setting prices and to permit comparisons between merchandise lines and departments. In calculating percentage markups, the retailer must first determine the markup base. Markups can be calculated on the cost of the merchandise or on the retail selling price. Formulas for calculating percentage markups are illustrated in Figure 19–5. Suppose, for example, that a hardware retailer pays $80 for a power lawnmower that sells at retail for $150. The retailer's percentage markup on cost would be 87.5 percent, whereas on retail it is 46.7 percent. The calculations are as follows:

$$\text{markup percentage at cost} = \frac{\$150 - \$80}{\$80} = 87.5\%$$

$$\text{markup percentage at retail} = \frac{\$150 - \$80}{\$150} = 46.7\%$$

In practice, retailers prefer to compute markups on the retail base for several reasons:

☐ *Psychological reasons.* A retail-based markup is always smaller than a cost-based markup; therefore, it is more acceptable to consumers who desire smaller markups.
☐ *Comparison reasons.* A retail-based markup facilitates comparisons between store operations and trade statistics because trade-association statistics generally are reported by percentage of net sales.
☐ *Inventory reasons.* Markup on retail is consistent with the retail method of inventory.
☐ *Emphasis reasons.* A retail-based markup encourages the retailer to think in terms of retail prices and their resulting profits.

Given its popularity, we will focus on retail-based markups for the remainder of our discussion.

Cumulative markups. Retailers find a cumulative markup on a group of merchandise items (e.g., a product line) useful in daily operations. This cumulative markup cannot be computed by averaging the individual markups on each merchandise item in the group; instead, the retailer must calculate **cumulative markup** based on the

FIGURE 19–5
Determining markup percentage (at cost or at retail)

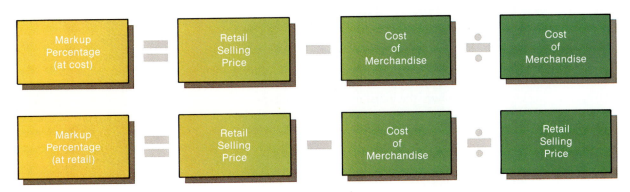

weight each item contributes to the total markup of all the items in the merchandise group. To illustrate, the buyer for the men's department of a large specialty store wants to determine the cumulative markup on a stock of men's summer suits. A check of inventory and purchase records for the month of June reveals that the month started with an inventory costing $20,000 that retails for $40,000. Additional purchases costing $16,000 and retailing for $30,000 have been added since the beginning of the month. The total cost and retail value of the merchandise follows:

	Cost	Retail
beginning stock	$20,000	$40,000
additional purchases	+$16,000	+$30,000
total stock	$36,000	$70,000

The cumulative markup percentage at retail is computed as

$$\text{markup percentage at retail} = \frac{\text{retail (\$)} - \text{cost (\$)}}{\text{retail}}$$

$$= \frac{\$70,000 - \$36,000}{\$70,000} = 48.6\%$$

Using the cumulative markup percentage, the retailer can adjust markup plans throughout the merchandising season.

Up to this point, we have discussed markup in general terms as the difference between the cost of merchandise and its retail price; however, we must now distinguish among three kinds of markup: the initial markup, the maintained markup, and the gross margin.

Initial and maintained markups. **Initial markup** refers to the difference between merchandise cost and the original retail price. Stated differently, it represents the first markup placed on a merchandise item. Rarely, however, does the retailer receive the initial markup for each item within a merchandise line because of the retail reductions that decrease the original retail price set for the item. Retail reductions take the form of shortages resulting from merchandise that is lost or stolen, discounts granted to employees and special customers, and markdowns that sometimes become necessary to sell merchandise that has lost some of its marketability.

A **maintained markup** is the difference between gross merchandise cost and actual selling price. Stated differently, maintained markup equals initial markup minus all retail reductions; that is, initial markup is what the retailer originally hoped to receive, and maintained markup is what the retailer actually received. Although retailers do not usually expect to gain the full initial markup on merchandise sales, they still need to use initial markup as a profit-margin planning tool.

The **initial markup percentage** is the key element in guiding the retailer's price-setting decisions. Essentially, this pricing strategy establishes the initial markup percentage—and therefore the retail price—to achieve a specified target profit. The basic formula for calculating the initial markup percentage is shown in Figure 19–6. As shown, the initial markup percentage equals the sum of the operating expenses, operating profit, alterations cost, and retail reduction, divided by the sum of the net sales and retail reduction. The initial markup must be large enough to cover store operating expenses and retail reductions as well as to provide a profit and to cover any alteration costs. Alteration costs (e.g., hemming trousers, assembling products, etc.) are added because they represent a legitimate expense the retailer incurs in making the merchandise more marketable.

As a brief illustration of the initial markup percentage formula, consider the following problem. A sporting goods retailer wants to know the appropriate initial markup percentage on a new line of tennis rackets. Planning records reveal these figures: (1) estimated operating expenses of 28 percent, (2) planned operating profit of 12 percent, (3) estimated alteration cost (e.g., stringing rackets) of 4 percent, (4) expected shortages of 2 percent, (5) planned markdowns of 4 percent, and (6) estimated employee discounts of 1 percent. Using the preceding formula, the initial markup percentage should be as follows:

$$\text{initial markup \%} = \frac{28\% + 12\% + 4\% + 7\%}{100\% + 7\%}$$

$$= \frac{51}{107} = 47.7\%$$

To determine the actual percentage markup realized after the foregoing computations have been completed, the retailer can use the maintained markup percentage formula expressed in Figure 19–6. For example, the retailer had originally planned for an initial markup of 40 percent, and retail reductions amounting to 8 percent actually occurred:

$$\text{maintained markup \%} = .40 - [.08(1.00 - .40)]$$

$$= .352 \text{ or } 35.2\%$$

The retail reduction percentage is adjusted because it was based on net sales, while the initial markup percentage was based on the original retail price.

Gross margin.   Gross margin refers to the difference between net sales and total merchandise costs. As such, it is closely related to maintained markup (net sales minus gross merchandise costs). The differences between gross margin and maintained markup or between total merchandise cost and gross merchandise costs are

FIGURE 19–6
Computing the initial and maintained markup percentage

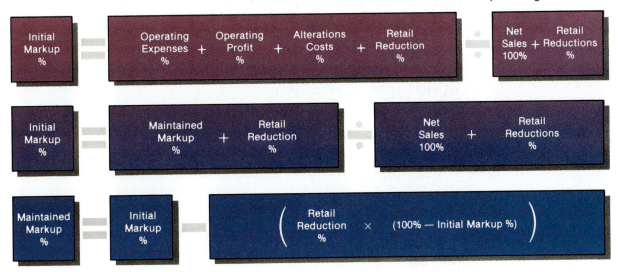

adjustments for cash discounts and alteration costs. This difference can be illustrated as follows:

gross margin   = maintained markup + cash discounts − alteration costs

maintained markup = gross margin   − cash discounts + alteration costs

If there were no cash discounts or alteration costs, then gross margin would equal maintained markup.

Competitive Pricing Method

A competitive pricing method means the retailer sets prices in relation to competitors' prices. It is largely a judgmental price-setting method whereby the retailer uses competitive prices as reference points for price-setting decisions. Competitive price setting is popular among some retailers because it is simple to administer: the basic decision rules are to price either below, at, or above competitors' price levels.

Pricing below competition.   One price-setting alternative is **pricing below the competition**. Mass merchandisers, such as hypermarkets, superstores, and discounters, attempt to undersell competitors. Pricing below competition is a price-setting policy aimed at generating large dollar revenues to achieve a desired dollar target return. In other words, these retailers practice a low-price, high-volume, high-turnover pricing strategy.

To successfully sell merchandise at low prices and still generate sufficient profit margins calls for certain merchandising strategies. To price below competition, the retailer not only must secure merchandise at a lower cost, but must also keep operating expenses as low as possible. The lower-price retailer usually stocks and sells "presold" or "self-sold" merchandise, thereby reducing advertising and personal selling expenses. Typically, these retailers sell name brands at the lowest prices to build traffic and to promote a low-price image. Low-price retailers stock private brands of many standard items that consumers cannot easily compare to other retailers' private brands and on which they can receive high margins at the lower prices. These retailers keep their service offerings at the minimum levels necessary to sell the merchandise; any nonessential services they offer carry a separate, additional charge. Their physical facilities are spartan and project an austere image. In addition, the structure of the store's management organization is generally flat (the number and specialization of managers are minimal and general). Generally speaking, the profit strategy of the retailer that elects to price below competition is to keep expenses low to keep prices low; this in turn attracts consumers and generates a profitable sales level through rapid inventory turnover rates.

Pricing with competition.   The second alternative method of competitive price setting open to the retailer is selling a merchandise item at the "going" or traditional price within the store's general trading area. **Pricing with the competition** implies that the retailer has, in general, elected to de-emphasize the price factor as a major merchandising tool and instead decided to compete on a location, product, service, and promotion basis. Competitive price parity does not necessarily imply that the retailer matches every price exactly. Usually, this policy involves setting prices that are within an acceptable range of the competitive standard. Small price discrepancies, especially if they reflect proportional variances in service levels, either go unnoticed or are accepted by consumers.

Pricing above competition. Some retailers attempt to differentiate themselves by setting prices above the going trading-area price. Although the higher-priced stores do not expect to achieve the turnover rates of their lower-priced competitors, they do expect their products to make a substantially *greater per-unit profit* than the lower-priced retailer's products.

Strategically, if the retailer chooses **pricing above the competition,** then it must include several of these consumer benefits: (1) many free services, (2) higher-quality merchandise, (3) exclusive merchandise, (4) personalized sales attention, (5) plusher shopping atmosphere, (6) full staffing in all functional areas of store operations, (7) prestige image, (8) superconvenient locations, and (9) longer store hours. In other words, the retailer of higher-priced merchandise must provide consumers with a *total product* having functional, aesthetic, and service features that give consumers the psychological benefits they expect from buying, using, and possessing the product. Many exclusive specialty shops and some department stores engage in price-setting strategies that establish prices above those of less-prestigious competitors.

Vendor Pricing Method

A third price-setting alternative is to let the manufacturer or wholesaler determine the retail price. This type of price setting assumes the form of a "suggested retail price." Vendors suggest retail prices by supplying the retailer with a price list, printing the price on the package, or affixing a price tag to the merchandise. While they are not legally required to use the suggested retail price, many retailers think it represents a fair estimate of the going market price for certain products.

Some manufacturers believe they have a vested interest in trying to maintain retail prices for their products at or above certain levels or within a set range of prices. For products consumers view as having a strong price–quality relationship, maintaining price is essential to the product's image as a quality piece of merchandise. Also, price maintenance creates a reasonable price consistency among similar retail outlets within a trading area. Finally, if the manufacturer permits certain retailers to reduce prices below certain levels, other high-margin retailers may decide to eliminate the product from their merchandise assortment.

Although the vendor method of setting prices does relieve the retailer of that difficult task, it is not appropriate for many products and many retailers. As guidelines for retailers, the vendor's suggested price is not appropriate when (1) it fails to provide a sufficient margin to cover merchandise costs, store operating expenses, and an adequate profit; (2) it fails to stimulate sufficient sales; (3) it simply is not competitive with merchandise of a similar quality; or (4) it fails to provide the retailer's customers with the value they deserve.

Price-Setting Policies

Retailers are also guided by a number of price-setting policies that supplement and modify price-setting methods. For example, a retailer may set prices by using the markup method. The established retail price (e.g., $40) is then modified to accommodate an odd-pricing policy (e.g., $39.95). This section discusses several price-setting policies: the one-price policy, the variable-price policy, the multiple-price policy, odd-pricing, unit pricing, and price lining.

One-Price Policy

Most U.S. retailers follow a **one-price policy,** charging *all* customers the same price for the same product under similar circumstances. In contrast to many foreign consumers, most U.S. consumers are accustomed to paying the established price marked on the merchandise. Price "haggling" or "bargaining" is usually limited to big-ticket items, such as automobiles and appliances, and to used merchandise. Bargaining over the price for big-ticket items often centers on the allowance the customer can receive for a trade-in.

A one-price policy has its advantages. First, it greatly facilitates the speed at which each transaction can be made. Second, a one-price policy helps simplify the retailer's various accounting records. Third, it substantially reduces the retailer's need for sales personnel and makes a self-service strategy possible. The major weakness in the one-price policy is lack of flexibility; that is, it does not allow the retailer to readily adjust prices to the customer's purchase motives (e.g., economy).

Variable-Price Policy

A **variable-price policy** allows the customer to negotiate the final selling price. The best bargainers receive the lowest prices. Retailers that use variable pricing deal in merchandise with one or more of the following characteristics: (1) high initial mark-ups, (2) need for personal selling, (3) unstandardized or specialized product features, (4) service requirements, and (5) infrequent purchase rates. Variable pricing gives the retailer price flexibility and increases its ability to adjust to the consumer's purchase motivations, but it can increase the retailer's labor costs, selling time, and dissatisfaction among any customers who were unable to negotiate the same low price as some other customers.

Multiple-Price Policy

A **multiple-price policy** attempts to increase both unit and dollar sales volume. This pricing strategy gives customers a discount for making quantity purchases; that is, the retailer offers a reduced price if consumers are willing to purchase several units at the multiple-unit price. For example, the retailer can price a can of peas at $.50 each or three for $1.37. Essentially, multiple-unit pricing is a form of psychological pricing, in that many consumers have been conditioned to expect a bargain price if they buy in multiple quantities.

Multiple pricing suggests that the consumer is getting a bargain by buying in quantity, which may not always be true.

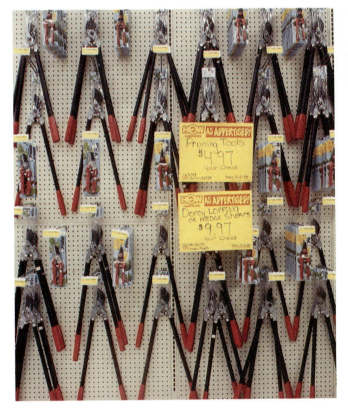

Odd pricing leads the consumer to perceive an item's cost as substantially lower than it would be at an even price.

Retailers commonly use multiple-unit pricing with products purchased regularly and frequently and characterized by a low per-unit price. Supermarkets, for example, use multiple pricing to stimulate sales for basic staples such as canned goods, paper products, and soft drinks. Multiple-unit pricing also is used occasionally to clear out merchandise that has lost some of its marketabililty, as when a clothing store prices men's suits at two for $199 (regularly $150 each) during an end-of-season sale.

Odd-Pricing Policy

Odd pricing is the strategy of setting prices that end in odd numbers (e.g., $.49, $1.99, $9.95, and $29.50). By setting prices below even-dollar amounts, the retailer is relying on the psychological ploy that consumers perceive odd prices as substantially below even prices (e.g., $2.95 is perceived to be considerably less than $3.00). The theory is that consumers will think of a $2.95 price in terms of $2.00 rather than $3.00.

The strategy of odd pricing varies with the general price level of the product.[7] Products with low per-unit prices (under $5) are odd priced at one or two cents below an even price (e.g., $.49, $1.99, and $3.98). As the per-unit price increases, products are priced at odd values that represent a greater reduction from even prices. For example, products ranging in price from $10 to $20 tend to be odd priced at $9.95 or $19.95—a five-cent differential. Nine- and five-dollar odd endings are common among big-ticket items (e.g., $199 and $495). While nine and five are the most common odd-price endings, retailers also use three and seven to project a bargain-price image.

Unit-Pricing Policy

Given the multiplicity of package sizes and shapes together with the diversity of price tags and product labels, many consumers cannot determine which purchase is the best value for the money. As a result, some retailers have initiated a unit-pricing system to eliminate this uncertainty. **Unit pricing** is the retailing practice of posting prices on a per-unit-measurement basis. By stating the price per ounce, pound, quart, or yard for each brand, the retailer helps the consumer compare prices among products of different sizes, shapes, and quantities. Per-unit price tags are usually posted on shelf facings directly above or below the product. Maintaining a unit price system usually means that the retailer will incur additional time, labor, equipment, and material expenses.

Price-Lining Policy

The objective of a **price-lining** policy is to direct retail prices at a targeted consumer group. To accomplish this objective, the retailer must perform two tasks. First, the retailer must identify the appropriate pricing zone for each targeted consumer group. A **pricing zone** is a range of prices that appeals to a particular group of consumers either for *demographic reasons* (e.g., income or occupation); *psychographic reasons* (e.g., life-style or personality); *product usage reasons* (e.g., heavy or light users); or *product benefit reasons* (e.g., economy, function, or sociability). Usually, retailers identify price zones in broad terms; for example, economy price range, intermediate or family price range, and prestige or luxury price range. Although most retailers tend to focus on one broadly defined price range, some retailers try to cover more than one range (e.g., middle-to-high) but rarely try to appeal to all three ranges. Attempting to cover the entire price range would defeat the target-marketing objective of a price-lining strategy.

    Pricing lines are *specific pricing points established within pricing zones.* Assume, for example, that a specialty store retailer has identified three pricing zones for men's suits: (1) the low-range suit (under $100), (2) the middle-range suit ($100 to $200), and (3) the high-range suit (above $200). Also suppose the retailer has targeted the middle-price-range consumer as the one to whom it wishes to appeal. Then, the retailer might establish price lines at $119.95, $159.95, and $189.95. The use of price lines is commonly associated with shopping goods and in particular with wearing apparel. Figure 19–7 illustrates one hypothesized example of the potential range of pricing zones and points within the fashion apparel industry for department store operations.

    A price-lining policy has several advantages for both consumer and retailer. Advantages for the consumer are that (1) it facilitates comparison among merchandise items and (2) it reduces shopping confusion and frustration and helps the consumer make purchase decisions. For the retailer, price lining (1) simplifies the personal selling effort, (2) makes advertising and sales promotion more effective, (3) increases the chances of trading up the customer to the next price, (4) creates an image of good merchandise depth and support, and (5) simplifies the buying process, because the buyer secures only merchandise that can be profitably priced at a given pricing point.

    A price-lining policy also creates some difficulties. If the retailer does not carefully establish pricing points, it is likely to project to consumers an image of inadequate merchandise assortment and consequently eliminate customers who are either above or below the price lines they seek. A second potential problem is that retailers find it extremely difficult to reduce one line without reducing all lines. To do so destroys the carefully planned spread between all price lines. Price lining also makes

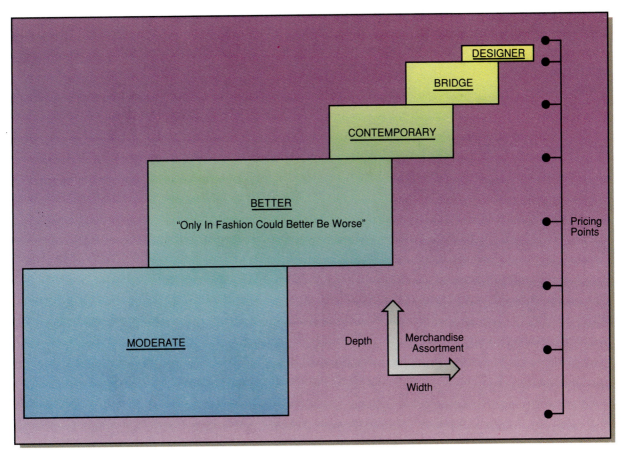

*Michael Gross, fashion writer for the *New York Times*.

FIGURE 19–7
Conceptualization of various pricing zones and pricing points for fashion apparel within a department store product mix

it easier for competitors to develop successful competitive-pricing strategies. A limited number of price lines might well aid competitors in planning counter-price strategies. Finally, during times of rising costs, it is difficult to maintain price lines without reducing product quality.

Price adjustments are one means for the retailer to adapt to changing external and internal environmental conditions. Retailers often find it necessary to adjust prices either upward or downward. The three basic types of adjustment are discounts, markons, and markdowns.

ADJUSTING THE RETAIL PRICE

Discount Adjustments

In the previous discussion on developing the merchandise budget (see Chapter 17), we examined the role of markdowns, discounts, and shortages in planning retail reductions. **Discounts** were defined as reductions in the original retail price, granted to store employees as special fringe benefits and to special customers (e.g., clergy, senior citizens, and some disadvantaged consumers) in recognition of their special circumstances. Regardless of the reason for granting the discount, each discount given represents a downward adjustment in price, and as such has a direct impact on profit margins. Employee discounts are a customary privilege in many retail organizations. They represent a supplementary means of compensating employees and are frequently used as a motivational tool. Customer discounts are granted to special consumer segments for a number of reasons. Drugstores frequently give "golden-agers" discounts to customers over the age of 65. Sales to other business or professional organizations are often made at a discount price.

Markon Adjustments

Retailers use the term *markon* in a variety of ways. Here, however, **markon** refers to markups taken after the initial selling price has been established. In essence, a markon represents an additional markup and an upward adjustment in the initial selling price. Upward adjustments are needed to cover increases in wholesale prices and operating expenses as well as to correct consumers' quality perceptions of merchandise. When consumers believe the quality of a product is questionable because of its low price, retailers sometimes can correct this misconception by increasing the price, thereby taking advantage of the perceived price–quality relationship. Retailers also take additional markons when the demand for an item is high and consumer price sensitivity for the item is low.

Markdown Adjustments

A **markdown** is a downward adjustment in the original selling price of a merchandise item. A markdown represents the difference between what the merchandise was originally valued at and what it actually sells for. Markdowns, together with shortages and employee and customer discounts, are the three major factors retailers consider in planning retail reductions (see Chapter 17). Retailers use both dollars and percentages to express markdowns. "All men's slacks reduced $5!" is a typical dollar markdown expression. Per-unit **markdown percentages** are computed as a percentage of the reduced selling price or as a percentage of the original selling price. The latter expression is generally referred to as the off-retail markdown percentage.

The formula for computing per-unit markdowns as a percentage of the reduced price is shown in Figure 19–8. For example, a dress originally priced at $30 is reduced to $20; the markdown as a percentage of the reduced price would be ($30 − $10)/$20 or 50 percent. This procedure is generally preferred for expressing reduced prices.

The **off-retail markdown percentage** formula is also shown in Figure 19–8. The off-retail markdown percentage on the same dress would be 33.33 percent or ($30 − $20)/$30.

FIGURE 19–8
Determining markdown percentage

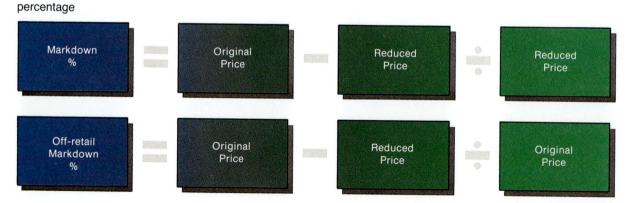

Causes of Markdowns

Retailers must take markdowns for a number of reasons, some of which are beyond the retailer's control. In other cases, markdowns are caused by errors in the retailer's judgment. Markdown causes can be categorized as buying-, selling-, and operational-related.

Buying-related causes.   Many markdowns result from retailers' errors in buying or procuring merchandise. Price reductions are often necessary to adjust for errors in the assortment, support, and quality of merchandise the retailer purchased, as well as for mistakes in timing of purchases and selection of suppliers.

Assortment errors occur when the retailer buys brands, styles, models, sizes, colors, and materials that do not match what consumers want to buy. Assortment errors are serious not only because they necessitate markdowns, but also because they can require major price reductions to move the merchandise. Very attractive prices are typically the only way to sell merchandise the consumer does not really want.

Support errors are quantity errors that result when the retailer buys too much merchandise. Overbuying and overstocking certain merchandise items cause the retailer to tie up capital that could be invested in more profitable merchandise. Support errors occur when the retailer fails to plan sales, stocks, and purchases adequately or fails to execute the plans outlined on the merchandise budget and merchandise list.

Timing errors occur when retailers secure merchandise at the wrong time; they fail to match retail inventories with what their consumers want when they want it. In these cases, markdowns become necessary because the retailer faces surplus merchandise at the end of a selling season. Reordering at the height of a selling season and late shipments are two common causes for surplus merchandise.

Misjudging the quality of merchandise consumers expect is another reason retailers take markdowns. To move merchandise with unacceptable materials or workmanship, retailers must reduce prices.

The final buying-related cause of markdowns is the retailer's *selection of suppliers*. The retailer should evaluate the service-performance levels of each supplier. Late, incorrect, and damaged shipments all contribute to the retailer's need to take price reductions.

Selling-related causes.   Even buying and securing the right merchandise in the right quantity at the right time are not enough to avoid unplanned price reductions; retailers must also control their selling activities. Selling-related causes of markdowns include errors in pricing, attempts to stimulate sales or to gain competitive price parity, and various policies and practices relating to the sale of merchandise.

A *pricing error* is any set price that does not create customer interest in the merchandise. Initial prices can be set too high or too low. High prices result in lost sales because consumers' perceptions of value are not satisfied. Low prices result in customer concern over quality. In either case, price adjustments are needed to match customers' perceptions of value and quality.

Retailers frequently use markdowns to *stimulate sales*. They may use this purposeful reduction of prices to attract additional consumer traffic into the store, to introduce a new line of merchandise, to boost customer interest during a slack sales period, to reduce inventories on slow-moving merchandise, or for a host of other reasons. Sales-stimulation markdowns can take the form of loss or low-price leaders, special or promotional prices, a multiunit pricing scheme, or the use of coupons and premiums.

Sometimes retailers use markdowns to achieve *competitive parity*. Direct and indirect competitors that sell the same (or similar) merchandise at lower prices have a comparative shopping advantage over other retailers in their trading areas. Retailers take markdowns to achieve competitive price parity when they cannot justify the price differential on the basis of additional customer services, unique store-image characteristics, or general convenience factors such as time and place utility.

Selling policies also can create conditions that lead to markdowns. A policy of "aggressive selling" (e.g., trading the customer up to higher-priced merchandise, selling the customer more than is desired, making false or misleading claims about product performance) can lead to an above-average rate of merchandise returns. It may be late in the selling season by the time the merchandise makes it back to the sales floor, and the retailer must reduce prices to clear the merchandise out by the end of the season. Some retailers engage in "umbrella merchandising"—stocking a limited number of high-fashion merchandise items, such as designer clothing and limited editions, to display merchandise that creates or enhances the store's contemporary image. Retailers often stock this promotional merchandise knowing that much of it will require drastic price reductions to be sold. Another policy that leads to markdowns is "assortment maintenance"—the image-building policy of carrying a complete selection until late into the selling season—that requires markdowns in the form of clearance sales. Finally, a selling policy that encourages customers to take home merchandise and is supported by a liberal return policy increases the likelihood of taking markdowns.

Operationally related causes.   In a retail store's day-to-day operations, both internal and external circumstances arise that create the need for some type of corrective action in the form of a price reduction. Two such circumstances are market shifts and distressed merchandise.

Market shifts are changes in demand levels for a particular merchandise line. Faddish and fashion merchandise often have fast and sometimes unexpected changes in both level and duration of customer acceptance. Introduction of a new product or a new brand can have unsettling effects on the demand for existing products already in stock. The demand for seasonal merchandise is highly dependent on having near-average climatic conditions. A mild winter, for example, can seriously reduce the demand for winter sporting equipment.

By its very nature, *distressed merchandise* requires price reductions. Merchandise that becomes damaged, dirty, or shopworn must be marked down to compensate the purchaser for the obvious reduction in value. Odd lots (e.g., a set with one or more pieces missing) also require markdowns.

Timing of Markdowns

An important issue for every retailer is *when* to take markdowns.[8] Opinions differ; some retailers prefer to take early markdowns, but others feel that a policy of late markdowns is the more profitable strategy.

Early markdowns.   **Early markdowns** reduce the selling price of a merchandise item when either of two conditions is present: (1) there is a notable slack in the rate of sales for that item or (2) the item has been in stock for a specific time period (e.g., six weeks). Proponents of early markdowns cite a number of advantages. (1) *Fresher stock:* Early markdowns help make room for new merchandise by weeding out slow movers, thereby freeing investment capital and selling and storage space. (2) *Smaller markdowns:* Early markdowns reduce the size of the markdown required to sell the merchandise because some demand for the item still remains, and because the chances of the item's becoming shopworn are substantially reduced. (3) *Reduced selling expenses:* Early markdowns promote rapid clearance of merchandise without the additional advertising and personal selling expenses normally associated with major sale promotion campaigns. (4) *Increased customer traffic:* Early markdowns encourage customers to take advantage of reduced prices (both advertised and un-advertised specials) because of the continuous availability of marked-down merchandise. (5) *Reduced selling risks:* Early markdowns permit sufficient time to take a second and possibly a third price reduction in one selling season if they become necessary to move the merchandise. (6) *Heightened market appropriateness:* Early markdowns prevent repetitive showing of dated merchandise at regular prices. Market appropriateness is extremely important in selling fashion merchandise. Many fashion-oriented consumers are willing to buy only new arrivals at full prices, and they expect a continuous influx of new merchandise. Other fashion-oriented consumers are willing to buy fashion merchandise that is well along in the fashion cycle only if the price has been reduced.

Early markdowns are most frequent among large department stores and medium-priced specialty retailers who are very promotion oriented.

Some retailers have an early-markdown policy that takes markdowns on a routine basis. **Automatic markdown** policies reduce prices by a fixed percentage at regular intervals. Automatic markdowns are generally taken without regard to how well the merchandise is selling. Waldenbooks is experimenting with an automatic markdown program that operates as follows:

> The books will be discounted in three steps. When a book has been in the store for 60 days, the price will be reduced. After another 30 days, the price will be reduced again. Depending on the original price of the book, there will be a third reduction 120 days after the book entered the store. As prices are reduced, the books will be moved from one area of the store to another.[9]

Late markdowns.   **Late markdowns** maintain the original selling price until late in the selling season, at which time a major clearance sale is held. A policy of taking late markdowns is most common with smaller specialty retailers and the more prestige- or status-oriented stores. Late-markdown advocates stress these advantages: (1) *They preserve exclusive image.* Late markdowns help prestige retailers preserve a store image of high quality and exclusiveness by not mixing sale-priced goods with regular-priced merchandise and by not mixing regular, prestige-oriented customers with bargain-seekers during the normal course of the selling season. (2) *They encourage creative selling.* Late markdowns allow sufficient time for the retailer to experiment with different selling approaches. By displaying the merchandise in different places and ways, the retailer can often influence the demand for that item. (3) *They allow "late bloomers."* Late markdowns allow each merchandise line a trial sales period of sufficient duration to realize the line's full potential. Some lines of merchandise simply take longer to catch on. (4) *They reduce purchase postponement.* Late markdowns discourage customers from waiting until the merchandise item is placed on sale before making a purchase. (5) *They create the "big event."* Late markdowns allow the retailer to accumulate large quantities of regularly stocked merchandise for a major clearance sale. Because of its infrequency and the fact that the clearance sale incorporates regularly stocked merchandise, the potential promotional impact is great enough to create the "big event."

Retailers can use several compromise markdown strategies. For example, some take early markdowns on certain merchandise lines (e.g., highly seasonal items) and late markdowns on other lines (e.g., staple merchandise). Other retailers schedule clearance sales for the last selling day of each month.

Size of Markdowns

The purpose of a markdown is to increase the customer's incentive to buy the merchandise. Each markdown, therefore, should be large enough to attract customers' attention and induce them to buy. At the same time, unnecessarily deep markdowns will adversely affect the retailer's profit margins. There are no hard and fast rules for determining the size of a markdown. Some retailers believe in making the first "bath" count; that is, they take deep initial markdowns, thereby reducing the need for later, more drastic markdowns. Other retailers think taking several shallow markdowns is the best approach to clearing merchandise with the least-negative impact on profit margins. Some retailers are making more extensive use of the "straw man" policy schemes—"a phony regular price which is quickly lowered, the sale price which is what the retailer actually expects to sell at, and deeper markdowns, as necessary, to clear the merchandise out."[10]

The degree of physical, fashion, or seasonal perishability strongly influences the size of the markdown. Highly perishable merchandise (e.g., a particular fashion near the end of its fashion cycle or a seasonal product approaching the end of the season) typically requires substantial markdowns as part of the clearance effort. Fashionable and seasonal items often require initial markdowns of 25 to 50 percent, whereas 10- to 15-percent markdowns on staple merchandise usually are sufficient to create customer interest.

The original retail selling price of the merchandise influences the size of the markdown needed to generate customer interest. For example, a $5 markdown on a $100 item would hardly be sufficient to attract additional buyers. On the other hand, that same $5 markdown on a $20 item is perhaps more than enough to clear the item out of stock. On average, the retailer must reduce the price at least 15 percent to create customer attention.

The amount of markdown the retailer takes also depends on the time in the selling season. Early in the selling season the retailer can take smaller markdowns knowing that, if the merchandise fails to sell at the reduced price, there is still time to take additional markdowns. Late markdowns must usually be deeper to stimulate sales.

Several additional factors determine the size of the markdown. For example, the need for substantial markdowns often depends on the number of units in stock that require clearance, the need for space (storage and selling), and the need for investment capital. A retailer facing a drastic overstock may decide that the only way to correct the situation is to take drastic markdowns. A continuous flow of incoming merchandise means that the retailer must have adequate storage and selling space. Finally, old merchandise represents a major source of funds for many retailers. To gain immediate use of the funds, the retailer will need to take substantial markdowns.

Markdown Strategies

Retailers use many pricing strategies that incorporate markdowns either directly or indirectly. Clearance sales are examples of direct markdowns. Indirect price reductions are best exemplified by the retailer's use of coupons, premiums, and trading stamps. The following discussion examines some of the more common pricing strategies that either directly or indirectly incorporate the markdown concept.

Promotional Pricing Strategies

All promotional pricing strategies have at least one thing in common: They are designed to draw consumers into the store where, it is hoped, they will purchase not only reduced merchandise but also regularly priced merchandise. To this end, retailers use a variety of promotional pricing strategies. Typical are sale prices, prices with coupons and premiums, leader prices, and special-purchase prices.

Sale prices. "Sales" are an everyday occurrence in most retail markets. Retailers cite a variety of reasons for holding sales, such as clearances, liquidations, and closeouts. Retailers also use several different occasions for conducting a sale: seasonal sales, anniversary sales, and holiday sales. Overuse of "sales" is making it "increasingly difficult for retailers to get off the price-cutting merry-go-round. . . . Retailers unwittingly are teaching consumers that they shouldn't buy something until it's placed on sale unless they absolutely, desperately need it."[11] Some retailers conduct sales that are either brand specific or are not specifically oriented toward any particular product or brand.

The actual markdown or price reduction is expressed in a variety of ways. Reduced sale prices are expressed as (1) a certain dollar or percentage value "off" the original selling price, (2) as a multiple-unit price (e.g., three for $9.97), or (3) as a fraction of the original selling price.

Coupons. Coupons are sales promotion devices in the form of redeemable cards (e.g., direct mail) or cut-outs (e.g., newspapers) that allow the customer to purchase specific merchandise at a reduced price. Although coupons issued by the manufacturer represent a reduced price for the consumer, they do not represent a markdown for the retailer, because the manufacturer reimburses the retailer for any payments made to customers. Coupons issued by the retailer *do* represent markdowns, however, because the retailer bears the cost of the difference between the original and reduced selling price.

Premiums. Premiums include free merchandise or merchandise that has been drastically reduced. Retailers normally offer premiums to consumers after they have completed some requirement (such as test driving an automobile, filling out a form, or buying a certain dollar amount of merchandise). In a general sense, the cost to the retailer of premiums represents an indirect markdown.

Leader pricing. **Leader pricing** is the strategy of selling key merchandise items below their normal markup or, in some cases, even below the retailer's merchandise costs (negative markup). As with other promotional prices, the main objective of leader pricing is to attract consumers to the store in the hope that they also will purchase other merchandise that has normal markups.[12] Although leader merchandise contributes very little profit on a per-unit basis, its indirect contribution to total dollar profit can be substantial if the retailer makes anticipated additional sales on high-profit items. To be effective, leader merchandise should include well-known (frequently national brands), widely used items priced low enough to attract most income groups and to be easily recognized as a bargain.[13] Supermarkets, in weekly advertised specials, often use meat, dairy, and bakery products as leader merchandise.

Leader pricing strategies differ depending on the extent of the markdown and the retailer's purpose in attracting the potential customer. The three types of leader pricing strategies are low-leaders, loss-leaders, and bait-leaders.

Low-leaders are prices set below the customary selling price but above the retailer's actual cost of the merchandise. Customer attraction is the principal objective of the low-leader strategy. Low-leaders also generate some gross profit, thereby contributing to operating expenses and possibly to operating profit.

Loss-leaders are prices reduced to or below the retailer's cost of the merchandise. Such drastic price cuts aim to improve substantially the store's customer traffic. To make loss-leaders profitable, sales of regular-priced merchandise must be great enough to more than offset the losses generated by the sale of loss-leaders. Some retailers' extensive use of loss-leader pricing has generated considerable criticism by those who maintain that it is basically an unfair trade practice with the intent to injure competition (see Chapter 5).

A **bait-leader** is an extremely attractive advertised price on merchandise that the retailer does not intend to sell; the attractive advertised price is "bait" to get the customer into the store. Having accomplished this, the retailer attempts to switch the customer from the merchandise featured in the advertisement to merchandise priced at full markup—hence the common description for this pricing strategy as "bait and switch." Retailers use numerous ploys to switch the customer to more expensive merchandise. In the first step, called the *trade-off,* the retailer tries to disinterest the customer in the advertised bait merchandise. The trade-off can be handled by (1) *persuasion* (convincing customers that the bait merchandise is of extremely inferior quality and a poor value even at the sharply reduced price); (2) *refusal* (refusing to sell the merchandise on the grounds that it is unsafe, unhealthy, or unsupported [e.g., without warranties] by either the retailer or the manufacturer); and (3) *stockouts*

Coupons the retailer issues represent a markdown, whereas retailers are reimbursed for manufacturers' coupons.

(informing the customer that the advertised merchandise was in very short supply and all units were sold before the customer's visit). The second task is trading up the customer to more expensive merchandise by stressing the higher quality of the substitute merchandise, the better services the customer will receive (delivery, installation, wrapping, repairs, etc.), the easy availability of credit, and any other appeal judged to be effective in convincing the baited customer. (The legal nature of "bait and switch" was discussed in Chapter 5.)

Special-purchase pricing.   A **special-purchase price** is a low advertised price on merchandise the retailer has purchased at reduced prices. Because these promotional prices are initially set below the retailer's customary price for such merchandise, indirectly they represent a markdown pricing strategy. The purpose for special-purchase pricing is the same as for most promotional pricing: to generate customer traffic. The legalities of *first* establishing a going market price is the most commonly cited reason for not directly advertising special purchases as reduced in price. Special-purchase pricing is most often associated with large chain-store retailers that enjoy buying economies of scale.

Price-Line Adjustment Strategies

For the retailer whose original price-setting strategies included pricing zones (a range of prices) and pricing lines (at specific pricing points), markdown adjustments create a slightly different price-reduction problem. Shallow markdowns usually involve reducing the price of an item from one pricing point within a pricing zone to a lower pricing point within the same zone and may be adequate for small clearance sales to dispose of a limited number of units. Deep markdowns are taken by moving a merchandise line from a pricing point in one zone to a pricing point in a lower pricing zone. Deep markdowns become necessary when the retailer considers the merchandise inappropriate for the targeted customer within the original pricing zone but possibly suited to the value expectations of targeted customers within a lower pricing zone.

The second issue in making price-line adjustments is whether to inform the customer that a markdown adjustment has been made. The retailer may decide to drop a merchandise item from one price point to a lower pricing point without informing customers of the item's markdown condition simply by replacing the old price tag with a new price. If the retailer believes it is beneficial for the customer to know about the price reduction, there are two ways to communicate the information: re-mark the old price tag so that the reduction is shown on the original tag or mark the merchandise down to an "off" pricing point. For example, a merchandise item can be reduced from its original pricing point of $29.95 to $24.00 rather than to the next lower pricing point of $19.95. Consumers perceive this even-ending pricing point as a reduced price.

Markdown Control

Some markdowns are inevitable, the natural result of the risks retailers assume in going into business. An extremely low markdown percentage could indicate that the retailer is not assuming sufficient risks to take advantage of emerging market opportunities. On the other hand, excessive markdowns are often indicative of poor planning and control procedures. By carefully planning sales, stock levels, purchases, and profit margins, the retailer can control to a reasonable extent both the amount and the timing of markdowns. To facilitate **markdown control** many retailers require their buyers to maintain records on the causes or reasons for taking markdowns on a particular merchandise item. Careful analysis of these records allows the retailer to take corrective action when necessary and detect excessive markdowns.

SUMMARY

Retailers view prices in terms of their ability to generate profits, sales, and consumer traffic, as well as how they affect the store's image. In setting retail prices, the retailer can elect to be guided by profit, sales, or competitive objectives. A number of factors influence the retailer's price-setting decisions, including demand, competitive, cost, product, and legal considerations.

Retail price-setting methods include those that are cost oriented (markups), competition oriented, and vendor oriented.Retailers often use numerous different pricing policies in refining their price-setting tactics. For example, retailers can use a one-price policy, a variable-price policy, a multiple-unit policy, odd pricing, unit pricing, and price lining as guidelines for their stores' prices.

Retailers use price adjustments as adaptive mechanisms to accommodate changing market conditions and operating requirements. Both upward and downward adjustments are needed from time to time to adapt to the dynamic retailing environment. Three common types of price adjustments are discounts, markons, and markdowns.

The three general causes for markdowns are buying related (e.g., assortment, support, and timing errors as well as misjudgment of merchandise quality and problems associated with suppliers); selling related (e.g., attempts to stimulate sales, to achieve competitive parity, and to correct improper selling policies); and operational related (e.g., market shifts and distressed merchandise). Some retailers prefer to take early markdowns, whereas others believe late markdowns are more profitable. The size of the markdown depends on the type of merchandise, the price of the item, and the time in the selling season. Markdown pricing strategies include promotional strategies (sales, coupons, premiums, price leaders, and special-purchase prices) and price-line adjustment tactics. To avoid excessive and unnecessary markdowns, the retailer must establish markdown control policies.

KEY TERMS AND CONCEPTS

automatic markdown	markdown percentage
bait-leader	markdowns
competitive price objectives	market-share objectives
cumulative markup	markons
discounts	multiple-price policy
dollar markup	odd pricing
early markdowns	off-retail markdown percentage
gross margin	one-price policy
initial markup	percentage markup
initial markup percentage	price elasticity of demand
late markdowns	price lining
leader pricing	pricing above competition
loss-leader	pricing below competition
low-leader	pricing line
maintained markup	pricing with competition
markdown control	pricing zone

profit-maximization objectives
sales-volume objectives
special-purchase pricing

target return objectives
unit pricing
variable-price policy

1. When might the retailer prefer a market share maintenance objective over a market share growth objective?
2. Why might profit maximization be an inappropriate pricing objective?
3. Describe how target return-pricing objectives are expressed.
4. What does price elasticity of demand measure? What are the three types of demand elasticity?
5. From a product perspective, when are competitive price levels a more important pricing consideration?
6. Discuss how merchandising costs are determined.
7. Identify and discuss the several forms of product perishability.
8. Identify the formulas for calculating percentage markup at retail and at cost. Why do most retailers prefer markups based on retail?
9. Compare and contrast the initial and maintained markups.
10. Which merchandising strategies are essential to a successful below-competition pricing strategy?
11. Discuss when the vendor's suggested selling price is not appropriate.
12. Identify the strengths and weaknesses of a one-price policy.
13. What are pricing zones and pricing lines?
14. List the advantages to the consumer and to the retailer of a price-lining policy.
15. Who receives discount adjustments and why?
16. Define markons. When are they applied?
17. Describe the two methods for computing markdowns.
18. Briefly describe the four selling-related causes of markdowns.
19. Cite the advantages of early markdowns.
20. What size markdown should the retailer take?
21. Describe typical promotional pricing strategies used by the retailer.
22. Differentiate among low-, loss-, and bait-leaders.

1. Thomas Nagle, "Pricing as Creative Marketing," *Business Horizons* (July/August 1983): 15.
2. See Lynn L. Judd and Barry T. Lewis, "Do Retailer Pricing Strategies and the Perceived Competitive Situation Influence Retailing Success," in *Developments in Marketing Science, Proceedings,* eds. J. M. Hawes and G. B. Glisan (Academy of Marketing Science, 1987): 296–300.
3. David S. Lituack, Rogert J. Calantone, and Paul R. Warshaw, "An Examination of Short-term Retail Grocery Price Effects," *Journal of Retailing* 61 (Fall 1985): 10.
4. Frank McCoy, "Melville's New Crew Aims to Get Back to Speed," *Business Week,* 13 July 1987, 94.
5. See Robin T. Peterson, "Price Cutting Can't Be Sole Strategy," *Marketing News,* 23 Oct. 1987, 10, 12.
6. Thomas T. Nagle, *The Strategy of Tactics of Pricing* (Englewood Cliffs, NJ: Prentice-Hall, 1987): 59.
7. "Penny Pricing Facing Pinch From Nickel Discounts: Restaurant Study," *Marketing News,* 11 April 1986, 14.
8. See Michael Levy, "How to Determine When to Take Markdowns and How Much They Should Be," *Retail Control* (January 1987): 35–48.
9. Cynthia Crossen, "Waldenbooks to Cut Some Book Prices in Stages in Test of New Selling Tactic," *The Wall Street Journal,* 29 March 1988, 30.

10. Leonard L. Berry, "Multidimensional Strategies Can Combat Price Wars," *Marketing News,* 31 Jan. 1986, 10.
11. Ibid.
12. See Rockney G. Walters and Heikki J. Rinne, "An Empirical Investigation into the Impact of Price Promotions on Retail Store Performance," *Journal of Retailing* 62 (Fall 1986): 237–66.
13. See Gerard J. Tellis, "Beyond the Many Faces of Price: An Integration of Pricing Strategies," *Journal of Marketing* 50 (October 1986): 146–60.

RELATED READINGS

Aaker, David A., and Ford, Gary T. "Unit Pricing Ten Years Later: A Replication." *Journal of Marketing* 47 (Winter 1983): 118–22.

Blattberg, Robert C., Epen, Gary D., and Lieberman, Joshua. "A Theoretical and Empirical Evaluation of Price Deals for Consumer Nondurables." *Journal of Marketing* 45 (Winter 1981): 116–29.

Bode, Ben, Koerts, Johan, and Thurik, A. Roy. "On Storekeepers' Pricing Behavior." *Journal of Retailing* 62 (Spring 1986): 98–110.

Carlson, Phillip G. "Fashion Retailing: The Sensitivity of Rate of Sale to Markdown." *Journal of Retailing* 59 (Spring 1983): 67–78.

Carlson, Phillip G. "Fashion Retailing: Reorder Window and Markdown Threshold." *Retail Control* (September 1983): 52–57.

Frazier, Robert M. "Reducing Markdowns for Increased Profitability." *Retail Control* (March 1985): 2–26.

Grant, R. M. "On Cash Discounts to Retail Customers: Further Evidence." *Journal of Marketing* 49 (Winter 1985): 145–46.

Halsband, Albert. "Implementing a Price Change Management System." *Retail Control* (April–May 1984): 22–43.

Hisrich, Robert D., and Peters, Michael P. "Increasing Consumer Price Awareness: Implications for Retail Management and Public Policy." In *Marketing: The Next Decade, Proceedings,* edited by D. M. Klein and A. E. Smith, 115–118. Southern Marketing Association, 1985.

Lambert, Zarrel V. "Perceived Prices as Related to Odd and Even Price Endings." *Journal of Retailing* 51 (Fall, 1975): 13–22.

Lucas, Stephen R., Miles, Benton E., and Williamson, Nicholas C. "An Exploratory Study of Retailers' Perceptions of Issues Related to the Viability of the Offer of Cash Discounts." In *Developments in Marketing Science, Proceedings,* edited by J. M. Hawes and G. B. Glisan, 274–77. Academy of Marketing Science, 1987.

McElroy, Bruce F., and David A. Aaker. "Unit Pricing Six Years after Introduction." *Journal of Retailing* 55 (Fall, 1979): 44–57.

Prestwich, Leonard. "Measuring Price Increase Due to Shortage in Department Store Retailing." *Retail Control* (June/July 1987): 55–63.

Riesz, Peter C. "Price versus Quality in the Marketplace—1961–1975." *Journal of Retailing* 54 (Winter 1978): 15–28.

Rothenberg, Marvin J. "New Approaches and the Information in Retail Prices." *Journal of Retailing* 63 (Fall 1987): 279–97.

Whalen, Bernard F. "Strategic Mix of Odd, Even Prices Can Lead to Increased Retail Profits." *Marketing News,* 7 March 1980, 24.

20

Objectives

☐ Describe the communication process and discuss its impact on retail promotions.

☐ Identify and define the five major components of the retailer's promotion mix.

☐ Discern the role of retail advertising in attracting, informing, and motivating consumers.

☐ Specify and analyze the components necessary for planning a successful retail advertising program.

☐ Delineate the organizational structures and the advertising functions necessary for accomplishing an effective advertising program.

☐ Discuss the instruments and methodologies for evaluating advertising effectiveness.

Advertising Strategy: Directing the Advertising Function

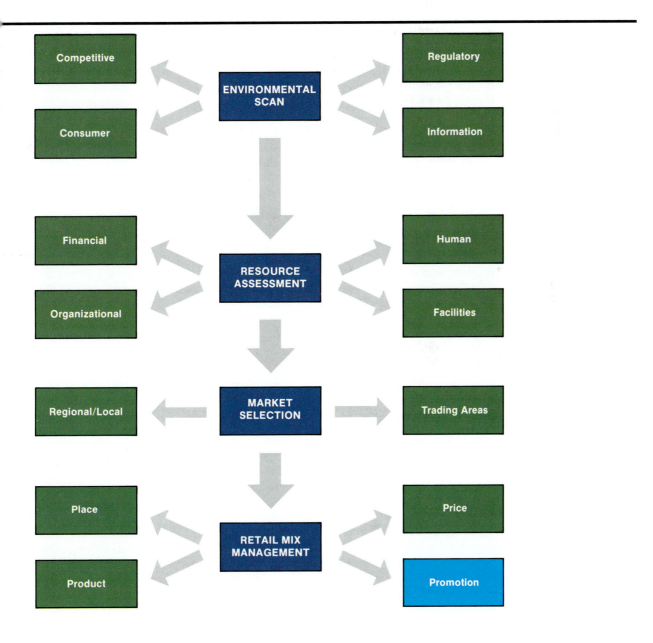

Unlike most other businesses, retailers do not generally take their product to market. Instead, they rely on consumers to take the initiative of visiting their stores or placing an order by phone or mail. Most consumers will not take this initiativeunless they are in some way motivated to do so. Before consumers will visit a particular store, however, they must be aware of its existence, know its location, and have some idea of what is available inside. They also may want information about prices they must pay, the terms of sale they can expect, services available, and store hours. In addition, consumers need to be persuaded that a particular retailer's offering is most suited to their needs. Effective retailers supply this information and persuasion, generally through their retail promotional efforts.

RETAIL PROMOTIONS

The fourth element in the retail mix is promotion. **Promotion** involves both providing the consumer information regarding the retailer's store and its product—service offering as well as influencing consumer perceptions, attitudes, and behavior toward the store and what it has to offer. As implied in the definition, promotion is both an informative and persuasive communication process; therefore, it is useful to view the retailer's promotional efforts from the standpoint of the communication process. For example, Consolidated Stores Corp., operator of Odd Lots and Big Lots closeout stores, uses newspaper ads that stress its good prices (persuasive communications) "but instead of just listing merchandise and prices, the ads tell exactly why the manufacturer closed out the goods. That way, customers won't suspect that the products are irregular, damaged, or counterfeit" (informative communications).[1]

The Communication Process

The **communication process** involves transmitting meaningful messages between senders (i.e., retailers) and receivers (i.e., target consumers). Figure 20—1 illustrates the communication process and its participants (senders and receivers), processes (encoding and decoding), and acts (transmission and feedback).

The *source* of the communication process is the **sender**—a retailer that wants to inform or persuade a select group of consumers (**receivers**) about the benefits of an idea (e.g., lower prices, quality merchandise, high fashion, fast service, or contemporary image). To be effective, the message must be **encoded** into messages using signs and symbols (e.g., words, displays, pictures, or gestures) that (1) promote understanding of the idea, (2) attract attention of the intended audiences, (3) stimulate needs felt by the intended audiences, and (4) suggest a course of action for need satisfaction. Having developed an effective message, the sender must then select the most appropriate communication channel or *medium* (e.g., salespeople, newspapers, magazines, radio, television, direct mail, in-store displays, and sales promotions) for **transmitting** the message to consumers targeted as the most suitable **receivers** of the message. The receiver or target audience is the intended destination of the sender's message and the object of the sender's promotional efforts (e.g., creating awareness, generating interest, and initiating behavioral change).

Upon reception of the message, the receiver **decodes** it and interprets its meaning either correctly or incorrectly, depending on how well the message was encoded and the decoder'sexperience and skill with the communication process. After the decoding process has been completed, the receiver may or may notreact (e.g., visit the store, phone in an order, or do nothing).The nature of the receiver's *response* or lack of it is then communicated back to the sender as **feedback**. The information gained through the feedback mechanism is vital in developing and encoding new ideas for future promotions. A final element in the communication process is

FIGURE 20–1
The communication
process

SENDER
A retailer that wants to communicate an idea (e.g., price, selection, convenience, image, service etc.) to a targeted group of consumers

ENCODING
The process by which the sender translates the idea into clearly understandable messages using signs and symbols (e.g., words, pictures, displays, numbers, gestures etc.

FEEDBACK
The act of communicating the receiver's response to the sender's message via actions (e.g., purchases and attitude changes) or inactions

TRANSMISSION
The act of transmitting the sender's message to targeted receivers using various communication channels (salespeople, mass media, displays, catalogs etc.)

DECODING
The process by which the receiver interprets the sender's message, understands its meaning and plans appropriate responses

RECEIVER
An audience that is the target of the sender's message and the object of the sender's actions

𝒩 = noise

noise—anything that occurs during the communication process that distracts senders or receivers, interferes with the encoding and decoding activity, or interrupts the transmission or feedback process (see Figure 20–1).

The Promotion Mix

The retailer's promotion mix comprises various combinations of the five basic promotional elements: advertising, personal selling, store displays, sales promotions, and publicity. The remainder of this chapter is devoted to a look at the advertising function, Chapter 21 discusses personal selling, and Chapter 22 examines the issues surrounding store displays, sales promotions, and publicity.

Retailers inform consumers about their stores, merchandise, services, or ideas and persuade consumers to accept their point of view or direct them toward desirable courses of action. To develop and implement the promotion mix, retailers use some combination of these elements:

☐ **Advertising**—indirect, impersonal communication carried by a mass medium and paid for by an identified retailer

☐ **Personal selling**—direct, face-to-face communication between a retail salesperson and a retail consumer

PROMOTION TYPE / CHARACTERISTIC	ADVERTISING	PERSONAL SELLING	STORE DISPLAY	SALES PROMOTION	PUBLICITY
MODE OF COMMUNICATION	Indirect Nonpersonal	Direct Face-to-face	Direct Nonpersonal	Indirect Nonpersonal	Indirect Nonpersonal
REGULARITY OF ACTIVITY	Regular	Regular	Regular	Irregular	Irregular
FLEXIBILITY OF MESSAGE	Unvarying Uniform	Personalized Tailored	Unvarying Uniform	Unvarying Uniform	Beyond Retailer's Control
DIRECTNESS OF FEEDBACK	Indirect Feedback	Direct Feedback	Indirect Feedback	Indirect Feedback	Indirect Feedback
CONTROL OF MESSAGE CONTENT	Controllable	Controllable	Controllable	Controllable	Uncontrollable
IDENTITY OF SPONSOR	Identified	Identified	Identified	Unidentified	Identified
COST PER CONTACT	Low to Moderate	High	Varies	Varies	No Cost

FIGURE 20–2
Characteristic profile of types of promotion (source: adapted from William Zikmund and Michael d'Amico, *Marketing* [New York: John Wiley & Sons, 1984], 494)

☐ **Store displays**—direct, impersonal in-store presentations and exhibitions of merchandise together with related information
☐ **Sales promotions**—direct and indirect impersonal inducements that offer an extra value to consumers
☐ **Publicity**—indirect, impersonal communication (positive or negative) carried by a mass medium that is neither paid for nor credited to an identified sponsor

Figure 20–2 compares the general characteristics of each type of promotion.

RETAIL ADVERTISING

Retail advertising includes all paid forms of impersonalcommunications about stores, merchandise, service, or ideas by an identified retailer. Its purpose is to favorably influenceconsumers' attitudes and perceptions about the store, its merchandise, and its activities, and to induce sales directly or indirectly. To distinguish it from publicity, advertising is described as a *paid* form of communication. Advertising is impersonal because the message is delivered through the public medium to many consumers simultaneously, which distinguishes it from personal selling (see Figure 20–2).

Understanding How Advertising Works

Consumers go through a series of steps, at varying rates, before they are motivated to accept something such as a store or a product and to take the action to patronize the business or buy the product they have accepted. Communications theorists have

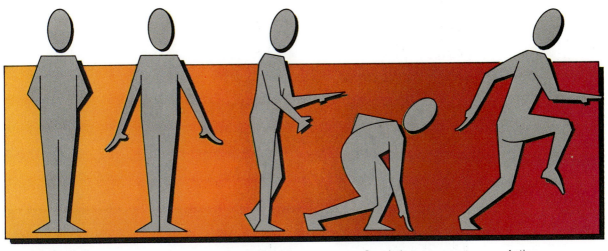

| Unawareness | Awareness | Comprehension | Conviction | Action |

FIGURE 20–3

The DAGMAR consumer-adoption model (source: adapted from Russell H. Colley, *Defining Advertising Goals for Measured Advertising Results* [New York: Association for National Advertisers, Inc., 1961], 46–69)

proposed several models of this personal "adoption" process, most of which are similar. The model presented here is known as **DAGMAR (defining advertising goals for measured advertising results)**. Developed by Russell Colley, the model describes a sequence of steps through which prospective customers move from total unawareness of a store and its offering to store patronage and purchase (action).

As Figure 20–3 illustrates, several steps intervene between unawareness and action (or store selection). Through advertising, the retailer can help consumers move to *awareness* of the store and its offerings; to *comprehension* or understanding of the store and its image, price structure, services, and so on; to *conviction* or favorable attitudes toward the store. To build awareness and comprehension, each time Wal-Mart enters a new market, they precede the opening with a "pre-awareness campaign" using TV and print advertisements one month before the doors open. When an outlet opens, Wal-Mart does monthly direct mailings and weekly newspaper inserts to obtain continuing favorable consumer response.[2] Although advertising cannot accomplish this process alone (other aspects of the retailer's marketing mix also play important roles in moving customers through this behavioral sequence), it plays a major role, particularly in the awareness and comprehension steps.

Advertising affects a large number of people simultaneously with a single message because of the mass media it uses. Although it is itself a mass form of communication (and therefore impersonal), the ultimate effects of advertising are often magnified by personal communications among consumers. This phenomenon, known as the **two-step flow of communications**, is illustrated in Figure 20–4.

The first step in the process is the communications flow from media to opinion leaders. (**Opinion leaders** are persons whose attitudes, opinions, preferences, and actions affect others.) The second step is word-of-mouth communications from opinion leaders to others (followers). This communication may occur through personal conversations (a "fashionable" woman tells her friends where she bought her new coat) or through nonverbal personal communications (the friends notice the label in her coat). Regardless of how the second step takes place, it is crucial to the influence advertising has on consumers.

An obvious implication of the two-step flow theory is that retail advertising should reach opinion leaders. Unfortunately, this is not an easy task, because opinion leaders are not easy to locate. A retailer may be able to locate opinion leaders through

FIGURE 20–4

Two-step flow model of communications

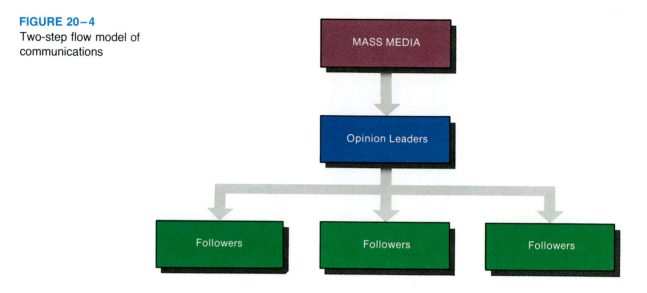

observation; for example, a women's fashion retailer may read in the newspaper the names of the sponsors and participants in style shows put on by a women's club, then write to or call these potential opinion leaders and invite them to select some merchandise. If they are satisfied, the retailer would ask them to "pass the word." Other methods of working with opinion leaders include the following: (1) create opinion leaders out of certain people by supplying them with free merchandise and information; (2) work through influential persons in the community, such as disc jockeys, television personalities, and class presidents; and (3) create advertising that depicts people having conversations about one's store or products.

Identifying Types of Advertising

Retail advertising has two basic purposes: to get customers into the store and to contribute to the store's image. The first purpose is immediate: Today's advertising brings buyers into the store tomorrow, tomorrow's advertising brings them the next day, and so on. To accomplish this, the store must give buyers some specific reason to come to the store now. Retailers also want long-run, or delayed, results from advertising. They want customers to know "who" the store is in relation to competitors and the community as a whole. They also want customers to be favorably inclined to shop at the store because of its image. Accordingly, retailers undertake two kinds of advertising: product and institutional.

Product Advertising

Product advertising presents specific merchandise for sale and urges customers to come to the store immediately to buy. This indirect form of advertising helps to create and maintain the store's reputation through its merchandise. Product advertising themes center around promoting merchandise that is new, exclusive, and of superior quality and design as well as around themes relating to complete assortments and merchandise events. Announcements of sales, special promotions, or other immediate-purpose advertising are other types of product advertising.

Save $60 And A Trip To Guangzhou.

Cheung Settee, 45" in width, has plenty of room for two. And snugly seats three.
Regular Price $159.99, Sale **$129.88.**

Cheung Table. 20"W x 40"L x 17"H. Regular Price $69.99, Sale **$59.88.**

Cheung Armchair is perfect for catnaps.
Regular Price $79.99, Sale **$59.88.**

Cushions sold separately. Selection may vary by store.

The Cheung Group pictured above was handmade in the town of Guangzhou, China. A very nice place to visit, but geographically inconvenient for wicker furniture shopping. Pier 1, on the other hand, is close by and has The Cheung Group on sale this week. Stop by and see its honey-colored finish and its long-lasting lacquer coating. Feel its sturdy, tightly woven construction. And choose from dozens of colorful seat cushions. By doing so, you'll save yourself $60. And a very long, tiring trek to Guangzhou.

Pier 1 imports®

A Place To Discover.™

This product advertisement offers specific merchandise (wicker furniture) and urges customers to buy immediately so as to save $60. (Courtesy of The Richards Group)

Institutional Advertising

Institutional advertising sells the store generally as an enjoyable place to shop. Through institutional advertising, the store helps to establish its image as a fashion leader, price leader, leader in offering wide merchandise selection, superior service, or quality, or whatever image the store chooses to cultivate. To "neutralize" the junk food misconception about its food, McDonald's ran a series of magazine ads stressing the nutritional value of its food.[3] (The FDA later required McDonald's to curb these ads.) In reality, practically all of a store's product advertising should communicate its institutional image as well. The art, copy, typography, and logotype of product advertising all help to convey store image.

Cooperative Advertising

Another way a retailer might undertake product advertising economically is to take advantage of **cooperative advertising**. Manufacturers prepare print and broadcast advertising material of their own products and allow the retailer to insert its store name and address in the ad, then manufacturer and retailer split the cost of media space or time to run the ad. Usually the cost split is 50:50, although the percentages vary. Some manufacturers also make direct-mail advertising of their products available to retailers to distribute to their customers. Sometimes the material is free to the retailer, or the manufacturer may charge a nominal fee.

Developing an Advertising Strategy

Like all other retail mix operations, advertising, to be effective, must be done within the framework of an overall plan. A comprehensive advertising program, like any other well-managed project, must be systematically planned, organized, executed, and controlled. In other words, the retailer must (1) determine what it wishes to accomplish with advertising, (2) establish the organizational structure necessary for implementing objectives, (3) develop a means for reaching these objectives, and (4) measure the degree to which it met the objectives. At the minimum, an advertising strategy should consist of the components shown in Figure 20–5.

PLANNING THE ADVERTISING FUNCTION

Planning the advertising function involves (1) a statement of objectives and (2) developing a budget.

Determining Advertising Objectives

Objectives—statements of results the retailer wishes to achieve—are the most essential requirement for effective advertising planning. Effective planning is next to impossible without established goals of desired end results.

Nature of Advertising Objectives

All retailers should have two types of objectives for their advertising effort. The first type of objectives are the broad, overall aims, the institution's *policy objectives,* such as achieving a high level of sales or profits over a sustained period while at the same time promoting the total image of the institution. The second type, *operational objectives,* are established for specific time periods, for particular products, for the store as a whole, or for specific advertising campaigns. Ideally, advertising goals should be specific, measurable, and realistic (e.g., to increase the 1990 in-store customer traffic count by 10 percent over 1989).

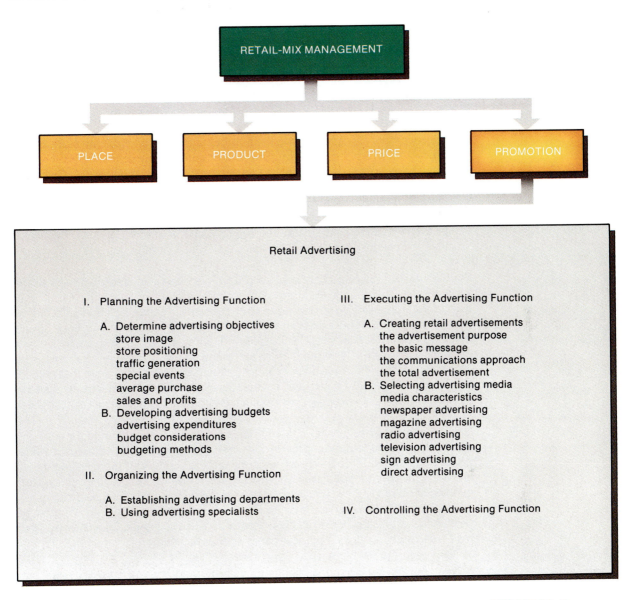

FIGURE 20–5
Developing and imple-
menting the advertising
function

Types of Advertising Objectives

Store image.   To acquire and keep regular customers, every store needs to be thought of as unique in some way by its target market. The retailer may wish to establish an image by size (large), merchandise specialization (Early American furniture store), clientele ("designer" lines for "discriminating" shoppers), fashion leadership or merchandise quality (always presenting fashion "news"), or by price levels (not being undersold on products with well-known prices). Frequently, department stores use "fashion umbrella ads," in which they illustrate the latest or newest fashion merchandise. The purpose of the ads is not to sell a particular number of units "but to show that the store is first with something, such as a style, an item or a concept."[4]

Store positioning. *Positioning* is a term advertisers use in reference to attempts to get the market to think of the store in a certain way in relation to its competition. Wendy's now-famous television ad, "Where's the beef?" was an extremely successful commercial that positioned Wendy's as the restaurant with the large burger, one with more beef than the competitive products offered by McDonald's (Big Mac) or Burger King (The Whopper).[5]

Traffic generation. *Traffic* refers to the number of people who visit the store and the frequency with which they visit. In general, the more consumers who visit the store, the greater the store's sales. Retailers can generate traffic in many ways. One of the surest methods is to provide customers with a special purpose for visiting, which can be achieved through sales, "theme" promotions (such as bridal seminars), special-merchandise showings, demonstrations, and so forth, each of which must be advertised. The retailer can measure the results of efforts to produce traffic by actually counting the number of people who enter the store.

Special events. Sales-promotional events are planned in advance, oriented around some theme, and coordinated through merchandising, store decoration, and advertising. One of retailing's most famous special events is Dallas's Nieman-Marcus annual "Fortnight," a two-week fall happening featuring a unique theme. For example, the store may create an exotic atmosphere of some foreign country complete with displays and sales of rare and exclusive merchandise. The event induces many customers to visit the store out of curiosity, many of whom make purchases totally unrelated to the special advertised event. Measurable objectives might be evaluated by head counts or average number of purchases during the course of the promotion.

Increasing average purchases. Many retailers believe the most fruitful method for expanding sales is to induce present customers to buy more. Retailers can identify present customers through charge account records, by asking them to register, by recording names and addresses from personalized checks, and in other ways. These people have already demonstrated a measure of favor toward the store by buying, so concentrated efforts to induce them to buy more may be one of the greatest potential payoffs to advertising. Most retailers attempt to accomplish this objective by direct-mail invitations to sales or by new-merchandise showings.

Sales. Advertising is intended to contribute to expanded sales. Some retailers therefore express advertising objectives in terms of sales (e.g., increase average monthly sales for the shoe department by 10 percent over last year). The major limitation of such a broad sales objective for advertising is that many factors (e.g., prices, merchandise quality) affect sales besides advertising. Thus, it is not recommended that retailers state advertising objectives in terms of sales, because advertising alone should not shoulder the burden of achieving a desired sales level.

Developing Advertising Budgets

Executing the advertising campaign requires spending money. Therefore, determining the advertising appropriation is the next step in developing a comprehensive advertising plan. Although many retailers use the terms *appropriation* and *budget* synonymously, *appropriation* refers to the total expenditure for advertising undertaken in a time period, whereas *budget* refers to the allocation of the total expenditure across departments, merchandise lines, advertising media, and planning periods such as weeks, months, and seasons.

(Opposite page) This advertisement promotes the store's image as a long-established business that remains up-to-date ("serving cool customers for 100 years"). (Courtesy of Fallon McElligott)

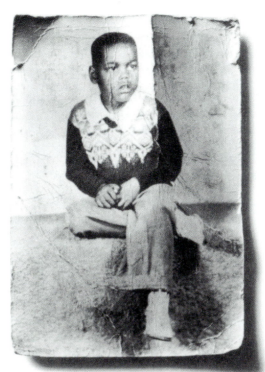

Walt Frazier, 1955

Even as a kid I had an eye for colors and style. Even my cool demeanor was evident. But things are not always the way they seem, and it was many years later before I felt cool and confident in front of a camera.

Walt Frazier

Bloomingdale's has been serving cool customers for 100 years.

It wouldn't be the same without you.

Advertising Expenditures

Most retailers consider the following as advertising expenses: (1) space and time costs in print and broadcast media; (2) advertising-department salaries and travel and entertainment expenses; (3) cost of advertising consultants; (4) advertising research services; (5) media costs for contests, premiums, and sampling promotions; (6) direct-mail advertising to consumers; and (7) storage of advertising materials. Other expenditures that some retailers include as advertising expenses are catalogs, advertising office supplies, point-of-sale materials, window display installation services, consumer contest awards, product tags, signs on company-owned vehicles, public relations, and other consultants.

Budget Considerations

Budgeting, as defined here, refers to the process of dividing the total advertising appropriation into its various components; in other words, splitting up the advertising "pie." **Advertising budget** allocations are made on the basis of departments, merchandise lines, media, and time periods. At different times, the store will want to feature different items in its product line and de-emphasize promotion of others items. Some stores choose to promote high-markup, low-turnover items heavily and de-emphasize lower-markup, higher-turnover items. Others may elect either to introduce a new line or to achieve a higher market penetration in a given line. Retailers can select from among several different advertising media, depending on their objectives and strategies. The retailer must determine how much of the total advertising appropriation to devote to each of the media (e.g., radio, newspapers) to make those expenditures more efficient.

Finally, most retailers advertise more at certain times and less at others. Some advertise extensively before and during heavy buying periods, while others attempt to offset slack periods with heavier advertising. Most retailers develop quarterly and monthly advertising budgets, but others develop extremely short-run budgets such as two-week intervals.

Budgeting Methods

Retailers use many methods to determine their advertising budgets. These range in sophistication from little more than guesswork to highly sophisticated techniques.

Educated-guess method.   Some small sole proprietors depend on intuition and practical experience to develop an advertising budget—**the educated-guess method**. The retailer simply looks at last year's sales and advertising expenditures, determines what it hopes to accomplish this year, considers other necessary expenditures, and chooses an amount to spend on advertising next year. This method is little better than no method at all, because more sophisticated methods are available that are not much more difficult.

Percentage-of-sales method.   One of the most widely used methods of determining the advertising appropriation is the **percentage-of-sales method**. To develop a budget with this method, the retailer takes a predetermined percentage of either the previous year's sales or the estimated sales for the coming year to calculate how much to spend on advertising. The percentage figure is based on either the "traditional" figure the company has taken in the past, personal "insight," or an industry average. Figure 20–6 provides some advertising/sales ratios for selected types of retailers. After determining the total advertising budget, the retailer then allocates the budget according to sales by departments, merchandise lines, and time periods.

(Opposite page) An advertisement for a "Fortnight" at Nieman-Marcus. (Courtesy of Nieman-Marcus/Dallas)

Agency: Neiman-Marcus/Dallas
Creative Direction: Laura Rivers
Art Direction/Art: Phil French

Client: Neiman-Marcus
Copy: Ed Taussig

A GERMAN FORTNIGHT

OCTOBER 17-NOVEMBER 5. CELEBRATING 300 YEARS OF GERMAN IMMIGRATION IN NORTH AMERICA.

Succumb to the outrageous luxury of Baden-Baden. ■ Where Napoleon III and the Kaiser along with their courts summered and "took the cure" — the legendary waters of the river Oos. ■■ We've recaptured the famous spa in Cosmetics. ■ With its own Lancaster Beauty Farm with lotions, scrubs, masques and massage creams to cleanse and purify body and facial skin. ■ And Ralph Lauren makeup artists to make a healthy glow more glowing. ■■ Ah, what wonders these waters work. ■ Complimentary makeovers by Ralph Lauren and Lancaster teams, daily. ■■■ Lancaster facials, 30.00. Make your appointment: 741-6911, ext. 2101, First Floor, Downtown.

Neiman-Marcus

Downtown Dallas Special Fortnight Hours:
Monday through Friday, 9:30 a.m. to 8:00 p.m.; Saturday, 9:30 a.m. to 5:30 p.m.

FIGURE 20-6
Advertising-Sales
Ratios, 1986

Selected Types of Retailers	Ad Dollars as Percentage of Sales (%)
Apparel and accessory stores	2.4
Catalog showrooms	3.5
Convenience stores	0.4
Department stores	3.1
Jewelry stores	5.1
Shoe stores	1.8
Variety stores	2.3

Source: "Ad–Sales Ratios by Industry Compiled." Reprinted with permission from the October 12, 1987 issue of *Advertising Age*, p. 50. Copyright © by Crain Communications, Inc.

The percentage-of-sales method is popular among retailers because it is simple; unfortunately, it has no logical tie-in with achieving advertising objectives. Moreover, the percentage-of-sales method fails to consider changes in population, competitive activity, and other environmental factors that affect every business. Thus, although this method has widespread appeal because it is easy to understand and apply, it is a questionable way to set advertising budgets.

Competitive parity method.   Some retailers set their advertising appropriation at the amount they estimate their most important competitors are spending—the **competitive parity method**. By monitoring the amount of advertising Retailer B is doing and estimating its costs, Retailer A may determine its appropriation and even allocate the appropriation across time periods, media, and merchandise in the same proportions as B.

There are three basic problems with the competitive parity method. First, Retailer A is estimating the amount Retailer B has spent in the *past* to estimate how much to spend in the *future*. In general, little relationship could be expected between how much one store spent for advertising *last* year and how much another should spend *next* year. Second, Retailer B may not allocate its total promotional dollars in the same way as A. B may de-emphasize advertising and emphasize in-store personal selling. If A bases its advertising appropriation on B's expenditures, it may underadvertise without compensating for B's in-store effort. Third, A has no way of knowing whether B's allocation method is appropriate for B, much less for A, and B's advertising expenditures certainly bear little direct relation to A's sales, profit objectives, market position, or share of the market.

Objective and task method.   One of the most logical methods of advertising appropriation and budgeting is the **objective and task method**, by which retailers follow a four-step process:

1. Establish the objectives for advertising.
2. Determine the type and amounts of advertising necessary to accomplish these objectives.
3. Determine the overall cost of the advertisement.
4. Schedule the advertisements day by day.

The last step allows for budgeting the total appropriation across media, product lines, and time periods.

As discussed earlier, advertising objectives should be specific and measurable. As an example, assume that one of the retailer's advertising objectives is as follows: "By November 30 of this year, 50 percent of all women in our trading area who are 25 or older and who have household incomes over $25,000 will give our store name when asked 'Which store in town sells the best women's coats?' " To reach this objective, the retailer must perform certain tasks, such as producing advertisements, selecting the necessary media for reaching the stated target market, determining how many ads to run in each mediumselected, and when (time of month, week, day) to run the ads. After establishing all the tasks necessary to meet the objective(s), the retailer adds the cost to perform each task. This sum is the retailer's advertising budget.

The objective and task budgeting method offers several strengths. First, advertising expenditures are based on specifically stated objectives, not on "guesstimates" or competitors' advertising expenditures. Second, this method forces the retailer into *planning* an advertising strategy and becoming a part of it. Third, it helps the retailer create criteria against which to measure performance.

Day-to-day advertising functions include deciding which products to promote, developing copy and artwork, and scheduling and placing ads in the media. How the store is organized to execute these functions depends on its size and the funds available for specialized personnel to perform the functions.

ORGANIZING THE ADVERTISING FUNCTION

Establishing Advertising Departments

The owner-manager or one of the partners in small sole proprietorships and partnerships must handle the advertising function. With so many other store duties to perform, it is unlikely that this person will be an expert in advertising production. Thus, the main function is to establish advertising objectives, appropriations, and budgets and to work with outside advertising specialists—usually freelancers, media representatives, and advertising agencies. Representatives of newspapers, radio, and television can and will produce finished print and broadcast advertising and offer advice on media placement and scheduling.

Large stores have small advertising departments with an advertising manager who supervises a few artists, copywriters, and production specialists. The manager usually is responsible for establishing objectives, appropriations, budgets, and scheduling and for working with store merchandise managers and other managers to determine what will be promoted and how. This is usually the person who interacts with outside specialists in agencies and the media. Because most retailers advertise primarily in newspapers, the artists and copywriters spend most of their time developing newspaper copy. The production specialists arrange for the advertisements to be either engraved or made camera-ready for newspaper printing. Broadcast advertising usually is produced with the help of agencies or personnel from the television and radio stations.

The largest stores are likely to have a complete advertising and sales promotion department. A **sales promotion director** usually is responsible for supervising and coordinating the activities of an advertising manager, a display manager, and a special events, publicity, or public relations coordinator. The **advertising manager** performs all the advertising activities described and supervises an art director, copy chief, and production manager. The **sales promotion manager** works with merchandise managers to develop and coordinate advertising, promotion, and displays with sales and special promotions. Even in the largest stores, in-house advertising production is likely to be print oriented; however, large stores often use the services of an advertising agency for broadcast production and scheduling.

Using Outside Advertising Specialists

Freelancers, advertising agencies, and media representatives are the three principal advertising specialists available to the retailer. An **advertising freelancer** might be an artist, copywriter, or photographer who produces advertising on a part-time basis. Freelancers usually operate alone, but sometimes have a small staff, charge a fee or an hourly rate for work, and work on their own premises or at the retailer's store. **Media representatives** are the employees of newspapers and radio or television stations whose principal job is to sell advertising space and time. These specialists also can arrange to produce the retailer's advertisements. Usually, newspapers do not charge for production and take compensation only for the space they sell. Radio stations normally do not charge for production, only for time, but charge a production fee for the tapes they make if they are broadcast on other stations. Television stations generally charge a fee for producing commercials in addition to the air time. Although **advertising agencies** produce the majority of national advertising, most retailers do not use them.

EXECUTING THE ADVERTISING FUNCTION

Few retailers become directly involved in creating advertising. Nonetheless, all must be able to distinguish good, effective advertising from poor, ineffective advertising. This section introduces the basic process of creating advertising. For simplicity, we limit discussion to newspaper advertising, the most common kind of retail advertising.

Creating Retail Advertisements

There are as many processes for creating ads as there are creators of ads. In general, though, the creator of an advertisement must take into account the following steps for developing an effective ad:

1. Determine the purpose of the advertisement.
2. Decide on the basic message.
3. Select the communications approach.
4. Develop the total advertisement, part by part.

The Purpose of the Advertisement

An individual advertisement can have one or more purposes, such as promoting the store as a whole, making customers aware of a special event, focusing on a single product, or highlighting several products. Regardless of the purpose for a single advertisement, all advertising has some degree of "institutional" content as well. To achieve the double benefit of special-purpose advertising and institutional advertising, the retailer should select a special theme, product, or combination of products to feature but should always maintain the same style in advertisements.

The Basic Message

Two basic elements in persuasive communications such as advertising are *what is said* and *how it is said*—substance and style. Too many advertisers concentrate on style and forget about substance, but the substance must be clear before advertising can be effective. Stipulating the basic **advertisement message** is determining what to

MY, MY. THE CLIENT'S REALLY LOOKING FORWARD TO YOUR PRESENTATION.

Maybe this time, just once, he'll have an open mind. But then again, well, he's always been one to make snap judgements.

To sell that proposal, your staff is going to need every slight advantage, every bit of confidence. Who knows? Maybe they need Juster's.

We offer an unique Corporate Clothing Program that can make their business wardrobes work harder. You know, give them that little extra edge. Help them wrestle with those unnerving corporate situations. And come out on top.

When your company participates, your employees receive a seminar on proper business dressing, personal consultation, special tailoring services, plus other valuable incentives. Call us at 333-1431, and ask how this exclusive program can work for you.

Juster's. We can give your employees' clothing the right kind of bite.

SURVIVAL OF THE FITTEST **Juster's**

Nicollet Mall, Southdale, Brookdale, Ridgedale, Rosedale, Highland Village.

Targeting customers' wants and needs and showing how a product can satisfy wants and needs combine to create an advertisement's appeal. (Courtesy of Miller Meester/ DBK & O) say. Most retail advertising messages are quite simple: "Ours is a high-fashion store"; "Our women's coats are of highest quality"; "Our meat selection is the best in town." But the message should not be pulled out of thin air. Instead, it should be based on the target customer's wants and needs and the ability of the advertised product to *satisfy* those wants and needs. The combination of these two is the advertising *appeal*. If, for example, the advertiser thinks its target customers are concerned not with the quality of a coat but with its social acceptability, then the basic appeal of the message should be "Fashionable women wear this coat," not "This coat will last for five years." Note that both messages stress the *benefit* consumers derive from buying and not the *features* of the coat from which they derive the benefit. Although the retailer's advertisement can point out that a coat has a double-stitched lining (a product feature), the resulting benefit (the lining is unlikely to separate from the coat) is the basic message the retailer should stress.

The Communications Approach

In determining the **communications approach,** the advertiser turns attention from *what* to say to *how* to say it. Most messages can be effectively communicated by either a rational or an emotional approach. The *rational* approach uses facts, narrative, and logical reasoning to persuade the consumer. The *emotional* approach appeals to the consumer's sense of aesthetics, ego, or feelings. For example, a tire dealer may effectively use a rational approach to promote snow tires ("You can get there on time—even if you wake up to snow") or it may arouse a husband's fear and protective instincts by depicting a solemn wife and two wide-eyed children under the headline, "Are you sure they'll get home tonight?" Although both approaches can be effective, advertising practitioners believe the emotional approach is more effective.

The Total Advertisement

After the retailer determines the message and approach, it must then develop the total advertisement. The **total advertisement** consists of several components: headline, illustration, copy, logotype or "signature," and layout (the visual arrangement). Although each component has a specific purpose, they work together to accomplish the ad's basic purpose: *to motivate the consumer to action.* An advertisement's layout, illustration, and headline all work to capture the consumer's attention and to create *awareness.*

Layout.   The principal purpose of an ad's **layout** is to capture attention and guide consumers through all parts of the advertisement. Several other layout considerations merit attention. For example, one old advertising rule of thumb is that the principal focal point of the layout should fall five eighths from the top. Sparse illustrations with lots of white space suggest quality and prestige, whereas cluttered ads suggest discounting and a price appeal.

Headline.   An ad's **headline** performs several functions besides getting attention. It should motivate the reader to review the remainder of the ad by providing news ("Blatt's Biggest Sale Ever!"), selecting readers ("Now You Can Get Organized"), and arousing curiosity ("Color TV for a Dollar a Day? Want to Know More?"). In general, the more original or unique the headline, the better. The headline must be coordinated, however, with the remainder of the advertisement's basic message. In fact, the headline condenses the basic advertising message, telling the reader essentially what is to come.

Illustration.   **Illustrations** help build consumer comprehension. The most common illustration is a drawing or a photograph of the product. The illustration can depict the product alone, isolate certain product features or details, show the product in context (such as illustrating a sofa in a completely furnished living room), depict the product in use, or illustrate how a consumer can derive a benefit from the product.

Copy.   The **copy**—what is actually said in the advertisement—helps develop consumer comprehension, conviction, and action. In brief, good advertising copy should be simple and readable, yet vivid in word selection; it should be conversational in tone, interesting, enthusiastic, informative, point out benefits, and suggest action. Effective copy can be brief or lengthy; however, the chance that anyone will read long copy is remote.

Logotype.   The **logotype,** or *logo* in common usage, is the store's distinctive "signature" that appears in all advertising. It usually is coordinated with the store's sign, with its point-of-purchase advertising, labels, shopping bags, and so forth. Done in a distinctive style, script, or type, the logo identifies the store in the consumer's mind in much the same way that a trademark identifies a product or company. The store's logo should be carefully designed, since it may have a significant impact on consumers. Most retailers use the same logo for all their advertising, although some stores vary their logos depending on the products they advertise. A logo is effective when it suggests the store's "character" or the nature of the retailer's merchandise. For example, a women's sportswear store might use a "lazy" script for a logotype, whereas an early-American furniture store might choose an antique type of script. A good logo communicates the store's personality and product offerings.

Selecting Advertising Media

The retailer's advertising message must be carried to the market by some communications vehicle, called advertising *media*. The retailer can select from among *print media,* such as newspapers, shopping publications, and magazines; *broadcast media,* such as radio and television; *sign media,* such as outdoor and transit; and *miscellaneous media,* including point-of-purchase media and advertising specialties, such as calendars or ashtrays. The retailer also can choose to become its own medium and use direct advertising to the consumer through mailed or hand-delivered letters, circulars, and catalogs.

Selecting advertising media is not easy. The retailer must choose the medium or media that will best communicate the advertising message to the greatest number of consumers in the retailer's target market at the lowest cost. To accomplish these tasks, large retailers usually employ several media over a given time and must select the best media for their purposes based on an understanding of the strengths and weaknesses of each medium.

Media Characteristics

There are many characteristics to consider in choosing advertising media. Some media are costly, some are inexpensive; some communicate a given message well, others poorly; some present the message continuously, others are instantaneous.

Communication effectiveness refers to a medium's ability to deliver the desired impact to the target market. Print media show consumers pictures and words they can see and read. With radio, consumers can only listen to the message, whereas television allows them to both see and hear the retailer's communication. The print media are generally thought to be effective with an intelligent audience, whereas the broadcast media are more effective with a less intelligent audience. Newspapers and radio stimulate quick attention to a retailer's current offering, whereas television and magazines create long-term images in the consumer's mind.

Geographic selectivity is a medium's ability to "home in" on a specific geographic area such as a city and its surrounding area. This is an important media characteristic to a retailer, because most customers live in the local area. A medium that delivers the message to many people outside the retailer's market has a high degree of "wasted" circulation, viewership, or listenership, since these people are unlikely to buy from that retailer. Of the major media, local newspapers and local radio and television stations offer the retailer reasonably good geographic selectivity.

Audience selectivity refers to the medium's ability to present the message to a certain target audience within a population. Most magazines appeal to people with special interests, such as antique collectors, golfers, and electronics hobbyists. Radio stations also have a high degree of audience selectivity because their programming formats (e.g., country and western music, classical music, rock) appeal to distinct groups of consumers. Television also can be highly selective when individual programs are considered. On the whole, people who watch "Monday Night Football" have different interests from those who watch "Days of Our Lives." Newspapers, on the other hand, do not have a selective audience; they appeal to groups with a wide array of interests and socioeconomic profiles. Audience selectivity can be increased by placing ads in strategic locations *within* a newspaper (for example, an ad for a sporting goods store in the sports section).

Flexibility refers to the number of different "things" the advertiser can do in the medium. Direct mail, for example, allows the advertiser to enclose money, coupons, pencils, postage-paid envelopes—in fact, practically anything, limited only by the advertiser's ingenuity. Radio, on the other hand, can provide words, music, and sound, but nothing more.

Impact refers to how well a medium stimulates particular behavioral responses within the target market. Television and magazines are better than other media in building store images, for example, whereas newspapers and the yellow pages of a telephone directory are better at generating immediate purchase behavior.

Prestige is the amount of status consumers attach to a medium. In general, consumers attribute more prestige to advertising in print media than broadcast media. Naturally, the prestige of print media varies with the individual publication (e.g., the *New Yorker* versus *Mad* magazine). Broadcast media are thought to be less prestigious in general because of the typically "lowbrow" nature of most programming.

Immediacy is the medium's ability to present a timely or newsworthy message. Radio announcements, for example, can be prepared today and aired tomorrow, whereas magazines require one to three months' notice in advance of the issue date. Newspapers also need very little lead time (usually 24 hours) to place a retailer's ad. If a snow or ice storm hits a city one day, knocking out electrical power, retailers can advertise oil lamps and butane stoves the next day. A medium's ability to deliver a retailer's message *immediately* helps the retailer when external events present instant opportunities to the business.

Life means the length of time the announcement continues to "sell." Broadcast announcements are gone in an instant and must be repeated to be effective, but a newspaper ad may "live" for several hours while people read the paper. Ads in magazines, which people read leisurely, may continue to "live" for several weeks, since consumers leave them in their homes and re-expose themselves to them over a long period of time.

Coverage refers to the percentage of a given market that a medium reaches. A newspaper might be read by 70 to 90 percent of adults in a certain city, whereas only a fraction of the same market may be reached by a "hard rock" FM radio station. Although coverage is often an important criterion in reaching a market, it must be considered in light of audience selectivity.

Cost should be viewed in both absolute and relative terms. Absolute cost is the amount of money a retailer must pay to run an advertisement in a medium; for example, the cost of a full-page ad in a newspaper might be $2,000 for one day. *Relative cost* is the number of dollars the retailer spends to reach a specific number of people; for example, if the full-page newspaper ad reaches 300,000 people, then the relative cost is $6.67 per 1,000 readers. If, on the other hand, the retailer spends $250 on a radio ad, much less money is spent in absolute terms, but if the message is heard by only 25,000 people, then the relative cost would be $10.00 per 1,000 listeners. Therefore, retailers should compare relative costs as well as absolute costs in selecting media. Once again, audience selectivity and "wastage" are among the criteria to consider in making final media selections.

Frequency refers to the number of times the same viewer or reader may be exposed to the same advertisement. A consumer might pass an outdoor poster twice daily for 90 days, whereas a radio spot might be broadcast a dozen times before a person hears it once. Similarly, consumers are likely to read newspapers only once per day but see a magazine ad in one issue several times.

Newspaper Advertising

Newspapers have always made up the bulk of retail advertising, probably because their local nature fits the retailer's desire for geographic coverage, prestige, and immediacy. In addition, newspapers are a "participative" medium that people read partly for the advertising; in fact, many consumers use newspapers as a shopping guide. As mentioned, retailers gain some measure of audience selectivity by advertising in specific sections of the paper, such as the sports, society, and financial sections. The cost of **newspaper advertising** is neither the highest nor the lowest of the available media.

By size and format, newspapers are classified as either standard or tabloid. Most large newspapers are standard; that is, they are about 23.5 inches deep and eight columns wide, with each column about 2 inches wide. Tabloid newspapers are smaller "booklet" papers, five columns wide by about 14 inches deep, or about half the size of standard newspapers. The *New York Daily News* is an example of a tabloid newspaper.

Newspapers also are classified as dailies and weeklies, although some "dailies" are published only four to six days a week, and some "weeklies" are published two or three times per week. Newspapers may be metropolitan, community, or shopping newspapers. Metropolitan newspapers are circulated over an entire metropolitan area (e.g., the *New York Times*), whereas community newspapers are published for a portion of a city or a suburb (e.g., *Newsday,* the Long Island newspaper). Shopping newspapers are comprised mostly of retail and classified advertising.

Newspapers sell two kinds of advertising space: *classified* and *display*. Classified advertising is carried in a special section and used only by certain kinds of retailers, such as automobile dealers. Most retailers, however, use display advertising, which is spread throughout the newspaper. The basic unit of space the retailer buys from the newspaper is *agate line* (or "line" in common use). An agate line is one column wide and 1/14 of an inch deep. Fourteen lines of space thus equals one *column inch,* the basic space unit for smaller papers. (The width of a column is not a factor in calculating newspaper space.) One full page of advertising equals about 2,400 lines or approximately 172 column inches, depending on the size of the paper.

Newspapers publish their rates on *rate cards* that they make available to customers. A retailer that buys newspaper space one time with no stipulations would pay the paper's *open rate*. Few retailers, however, actually pay the open rate, since the cost of newspaper space generally decreases with the quantity bought and increases as the retailer improves the "quality" of its advertising by specifying a particular position in the paper or by using color.

Most retailers that advertise regularly make *space contracts* with the newspaper, by which the retailer agrees to use a certain amount of space over the year and to pay a certain amount per line that is lower than the paper's open rate for the same space. The lower rate is simply a quantity discount. A retailer that advertises heavily in a newspaper can receive up to 40 percent off the open rate in a large space contract. If at the end of the year it becomes apparent that the store will not use the amount of space for which it contracted, the paper will "short rate" the retailer, charging more for subsequent space so that the retailer averages the normal rate for the total space used during the year. If the retailer uses more space than it contracted for, the paper will give a rebate at the end of the year. This rebate represents a lower rate for more space used.

Unless otherwise specified, newspaper rates are "ROP" (run of the paper), meaning the paper will put the ad wherever it sees fit in composing the paper. This is not necessarily undesirable, because newspapers, like other businesses, want to satisfy their customers. They therefore do the best they can to make up an attractive paper and place advertising where it fits best. A retailer who is willing to pay a premium called a *position charge* can, however, specify a position in the paper. The retailer can then specify the first three pages, the sports, society, or financial section, or even a specific page. Some retailers even rent a certain space permanently. For ROP ads, newspapers generally place larger ads closer to the front of a section and smaller ads nearer the back.

Most newspapers can print in color, and color advertising is becoming more common. Needless to say, the retailer pays more for color, and the more color used, the more the retailer pays. Many newspapers also can insert preprinted color advertisements.

Newspaper rate structures are determined by circulation: The greater the circulation, the higher the rates, and vice versa. A paper's paid and unpaid circulation is audited by the Audit Bureau of Circulations, which publishes a report of circulations throughout the paper's city and its retail trading zone, the area beyond the city proper for which the city is a trade center. To compare newspapers' advertising rates, which vary widely, advertisers commonly use a calculation called the *milline rate,* which is the paper's cost of getting a line of advertising to a million people. The formula for the milline rate follows:

$$\text{milline rate} = \frac{\text{line rate} \times 1,000,000}{\text{circulation}}$$

Magazine Advertising

Few retailers advertise in consumer magazines. Although magazines do offer a high degree of prestige, audience selectivity, and impact (when used correctly), they generally lack geographic selectivity, which is what the vast majority of retailers require. Because magazines' advertising rates, likenewspapers', are based on total circulation, a retailer that places an ad must pay for wasted circulation outside its trading area. Thus, a Kansas City retailer that advertises in a nationally circulated magazine pays to advertise not only to Kansas City residents but also to readers in Maine and Louisiana. To offset this disadvantage, many magazines publish regional editions (same editorial matter, different advertising) for certain geographic areas (e.g., Southwest) and major cities (e.g., New York). City and regional magazines have grown in both number and circulation, and the greater geographic selection of these magazines makes them a more feasible advertising medium for some retailers.

Magazines also require a considerable period of time between publication date and the date advertising materials must be available. Magazines therefore do not accommodate the immediate-response advertising that makes up the majority of retail business. Most retailers that use magazines are either nationwide chains or stores with branches in several nearby cities.

Magazine advertising space usually is bought in pages and fractions, such as half page, one-third page, or two-thirds page. Generally, the only premium positions are inside the front cover, the inside and outside of the back cover, opposite the table of contents, and the center spread. Magazine rates, like newspaper rates, are based on circulations, and the rate structures, circulations, facts of publication, and publication requirements are published in *Standard Rate and Data Service*. Magazines' rates are compared by a calculation known as cost per thousand (CPM). As briefly described earlier, it is computed as follows:

$$CPM = \frac{\text{cost of page} \times 1,000}{\text{circulation}}$$

If a full-page black and white advertisement in a magazine costs $5,000 and the circulation is 750,000, then CPM = $5,000 × 1,000/750,000 = $6.67. As with newspapers, one magazine may have a higher cost per page but a lower CPM than another, depending on their relative circulations.

Radio Advertising

Americans own about five radio receivers per household, and American retailers have used radio extensively almost since its inception. Among its advantages are low cost and a high degree of geographic and audience selectivity. Although radio broadcasters claim otherwise, sound alone is not a very good communications medium. Therefore, advertisers should stick with a simple message, make it easy to remember (hence the radio "jingle"), and repeat the message frequently.

Like other media advertising rates, radio rates are based on audience sizes. *Coverage* is the geographic area over which the station's signal can be heard; *audience* refers to the number of people who actually listen.

Some 50,000-watt "clear-channel" radio stations broadcast over a large geographic area, including many areas outside the retailer's market area. *Regional* stations cover smaller geographic areas that are much larger than a typical city. *Local* stations (1,000 watts or less) broadcast a signal that usually does not carry further than about 25 miles, and most listeners are clearly in the retailer's market area.

As mentioned, radio stations appeal to highly specialized audiences because of their programming: rock and roll stations, easy-listening stations, classical music stations, all-news stations, or talk-show stations (see Figure 20–7). Moreover, radio listeners are much more station-loyal than television viewers, who switch freely from one channel to another. Radio is particularly important to drivers, who have their radios tuned in about 62 percent of their "drive time"; peak drive times are 7 to 9 A.M. and 4 to 6 P.M.

Radio advertising is sold as either *network* radio (buying from several stations that air joint programming) or *spot* radio (bought from individual stations). Because

FIGURE 20–7
Radio executives predict the hottest formats (source: "New Tools, New Tunes," *Advertising Age,* 11 July 1983, M11, and Ted Bolten Associates and Mc-Gavren Guild Radio/ "Radio Trends: Insiders Looking Out," a 1982 study based on response of 314 radio executives of stations represented by Mc-Gavren Guild)

	All	Station managers	Program directors	Sales personnel
Adult contemporary	34%	36%	35%	30%
Rock/AOR	9	6	11	10
Beautiful music	1	2	1	
Big band	1	1	1	
Black				2
Classical				2
Country	16	16	15	17
Easy rock	1		1	
Jazz			1	
Mellow music			1	
MOR	1	1	1	2
Music of your life	2	2	2	2
News	1	2		
News/talk	5	3	5	6
Oldies/nostalgia	1		2	
Personality	2	2	1	4
Service radio				2
Talk	1	2	1	
Top 40	2	2	4	2
Urban contemporary	1	1	1	4
Dependent of market	2	4	1	
No answer	18	21	16	15

most retailers want to advertise in one city only, most buy spot radio announcements. Stations divide their total air time into classes, usually labeled AAA, AA, A, B, and C, with the best times being early morning (6 to 10 A.M.) and late afternoon (3 to 7 P.M.). Generally, the fewest people listen at night, so this time is the cheapest. Spot announcements usually are sold in one-minute, thirty-second, and ten-second periods for a certain number of repetitions (e.g., 15, 50, or 150 times). Retailers often buy weekly "package plans" for a number of repetitions of a message of a certain duration over a certain time class; for example, retailers can select 20 thirty-second announcements in class AA time for a week. They also can buy joint sponsorship of certain programs, such as the daily stock market report. *Standard Rate and Data Service* lists radio stations' packages and rates and describes their programming.

Radio rates are based on audience size. Estimates of the number and characteristics of listeners at certain times of the day are made by companies like The Pulse, Inc., and American Research Bureau. These statistics are sold to radio stations, which in turn make them available to potential advertisers. The retailer, as an advertiser, can write its own radio copy and have the station "produce" it—provide the announcer and develop a musical background and whatever sound effects are needed. Normally, the station does not charge for this service if the retailer runs the message on the producing station.

Television Advertising

Television is the most glamorous and conspicuous advertising medium in this country. Reaching about 99 percent of all U.S. homes, this medium garners a large amount of advertising dollars but not from retailers. Typically, only the larger chain organizations have the budgets to support **television advertising** (see Figure 20–8).

Although television is an excellent communications medium, its high cost constraints also eliminate all but the largest retailers from using it regularly. Moreover, preparing of television commercials requires expertise that store advertising departments do not usually have, so most retailers depend onadvertising agencies to produce and place their television commercials. Television stations also will produce commercials for a fee.

Like radio time, television time is sold as network or spot time. Unlike radio, the majority of television programming originates from the major networks. Since most retailers' markets are localized, again only the largest nationwide chains can buy network television time. Most retailers buy spot announcements from local stations. In contrast to the number of radio stations, only a few television stations operate in most cities.

Television time rate structures and measurements of audience size on which rates are based are quite complex. A complete discussion is beyond the scope of this book; the reader is referred to any standard advertising text. In general, television stations divide their time into classes based on size of audience at a given time. The larger the audience, the higher the cost of advertising time. *Prime time,* when most people watch television, is 7:30 to 11 P.M. on the East and West coasts and 6:30 to 10 P.M. in the Midwest. *Fringe time* comprises the hours immediately preceding and following prime time. *Daytime* and *late nighttime,* the least expensive times, are when the fewest people watch television. Advertising rates, therefore, are lowest during the times with few viewers and highest during prime time, which normally attacts the most viewers.

Local stations sell spot announcements in and around programming at certain times, as well as packages of announcements much like radio packages. As in almost all media, television stations allow advertisers a quantity discount; the greater the number of repetitions, the lower the cost per repetition. The retailer can buy one-minute, thirty-second, and ten-second spots (or combinations of these), or it may buy partial sponsorship of the station's local programming.

The sizes of local stations' television audiences are measured by firms such as the A. C. Nielsen Company and the American Research Bureau. By means of diaries, electronic recording devices, and interviews, these companies estimate the number of people in the station's market area watching various television programs. With these figures, station managers can compute a CPM figure in much the same way that newspapers compute their CPMs. Television and radio stations have a special problem, however; viewership and listenership figures vary with the same program on a day-to-day and week-to-week basis and also vary from one program to another.

McDonald's "Mac Tonight" (Davis, Johnson, Mogul & Colombatto; Ian Leach): The idea was to stress dinner. The method in this :30 was to adapt the foot-tapping music of "Mack the Knife" to McDonald's lyrics and have it played by a smiling figure with a half-moon head seated at the piano. Festive amusement park background is replete with McDonald's and Coke signs and a giant rotating mock-up of a McD.L.T. McDonald's regional operators' agency handled this one, and its West Coast success led to spot going national. Third-quarter earnings up 14%, which the company credited partly to the spot. AA's adWatch ranked it No. 1 in recall for September.

McDonald's "Daddy's Little Girl" (Leo Burnett USA; Steve Horn Productions): Dad, after picking up young daughter and friends after the dance, is persuaded to take them to McDonald's because "all the cute boys" will be there. As father follows girls into entrance, daughter stops: "Dad! You're not coming in?" 'Course not, says Pop. He eats his burger in the station wagon. Daughter, sipping Coke, waves to him surreptitiously through window. A story designed, says McD., to strengthen the emotional bond with the public.

McDonald's "The New Kids" (Leo Burnett USA; Harmony Pictures): It's a tender tale of a senior citizen's first day of work at McDonald's. The young crew, taken aback at his age, is soon impressed with his prowess: "Sure you've never done this before?" On returning home, wife asks him how it went. Reply: "Don't know how they got along without me." For McDonald's, one planned recruitment result: A flood of senior-citizen job applications.

Southland Corp.'s 7-Eleven "Dabney/-Chicken" (W.B. Doner & Co.; Elite Films): Actor Dabney Coleman has some good-natured fun positioning 7-Eleven as the store for key commodities like eggs, milk and soft drinks. Opens with Dabney in henhouse selling merits of eggs. As cackling grows loud, he angrily shouts, "Quiet!" Silence, as camera freezes on hens. At end, he apologizes to hen for "getting a little emotional." Slogan: At 7-Eleven, "Even good prices come easy." So does Dabney.

Frederick & Nelson department store (R, Seattle) "Great Department Store" (Cole & Weber; Paul Hopkins/Sue Mowrer): "What makes a great department store?" asks voice-over as a colorful, appealing array of products parades past—perfume to designer fashion to furniture. Contributing mightily to the atmosphere is the Gershwin music, in vogue for other advertisers, too, in 1987 (United Airlines among them). Screen and voice-over sew it up: "One of the great department stores—Frederick & Nelson."

Amoco Silver gasoline "Lone Ranger-Prospector" (DMB&B; Yarbrough & Co.): Launching a new midgrade unleaded gas, Amoco uses Lone Ranger and reference to his horse, Silver, to associate with the product name. It's a light-hearted spoof of the Lone Ranger as, after gassing up, he rides off into the sunset in his Jeep, shouting, "Hi-yo, Silver, awa-a-y." With all that aging and nostalgic audience, awareness of the new gas hit 62%.

Source: Merle Kingman, "Music is the Magic for Most of the Best." Reprinted with permission from the March 14, 1988 issue of *Advertising Age*, p. 5-8. Copyright © by Crain Communications, Inc.

Thus, for any one program, it is sensible to calculate an average audience size. A way to calculate CPM for a television station is shown here:

$$\text{CPM} = \frac{\text{average of a minute's advertising} \times 1,000}{\text{average audience size}}$$

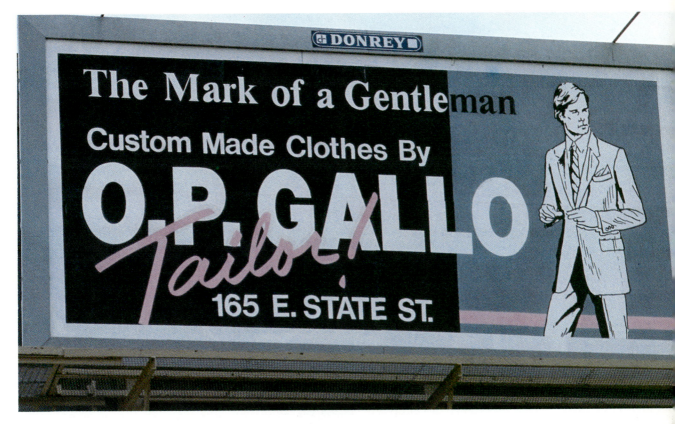

Sign advertising can be effective and relatively inexpensive.

Sign Advertising

Retailers use outdoor advertising media extensively, especially posters, bulletins, and spectaculars. **Sign advertising** gives retailers impact, coverage, frequency, geographic selectivity, and a long life for a relatively low CPM. As described by experts, "out-of-home scores well in segmentation. . . it permits geographic targeting of specific groups. And it has the added advantage not only of reaching target audiences but also frequently exposing them to the ad message . . . [and it] has the lowest cost per-thousand impressions of any medium."[6] Outdoor signs, however, are good for presenting only a short reminder message, perhaps the store name, an illustration, and a few words of copy.

Outdoor signs are owned or leased by local "plant operators" that install the advertisers' messages and are responsible for maintaining the signs and the surrounding areas. The three basic outdoor signs are the thirty-sheet, 12- by 25-foot *poster* that most people call a "billboard," *painted bulletins,* and outdoor *spectaculars.* Painted bulletins are signs approximately 14 by 48 feet on which the advertising message is actually painted in sections by an artist working from a miniature. When the advertisement is painted in sections, the advertiser can remove the message to another location. Outdoor spectaculars are nonstandardized, custom-made signs that use elaborate lighting, falling water, rising steam, billowing smoke, and other techniques to attract consumers' attention. Although these signs have higher attention value, they are quite costly to produce.

Outdoor signs usually are bought in "showings" for periods of time of ninety days and up. A number 100 showing is a number of signs sufficient for a daily exposure of the message to a population equal to that of the market area. Other showing sizes are number 75, 50, 25, and 150; a showing size of 75, for example, means that the number of signs will expose the advertiser's message to 75 percent of the market area. The number of signs in a showing is not fixed. Fewer signs are necessary if they are exposed to heavy traffic, whereas more signs are needed if they are exposed to light-traffic areas. The Traffic Audit Bureau, Inc., audits, by markets, the "circulation" of posters and bulletins (the amount of traffic passing by) and publishes the results in *The Audited Circulation Values of Outdoor Advertising*. The medium's prices are based on these circulation figures. The CPM of outdoor advertising can be computed as follows:

$$\text{CPM} = \frac{\text{rental of all showings bought per month} \times 1{,}000}{\begin{array}{c}\text{number of cars passing by in a month}\\ \times \text{ average number of passengers in the car}\\ \text{(the "auto load factor")}\end{array}}$$

Transit advertising includes car cards, exterior displays, and station posters. *Car cards* are the posters (usually 11 by 28 inches) displayed on interior wall racks in buses, subway trains, and the cars of rapid transit systems. *Exterior displays,* which vary in size, are the advertisements shown on the outside of buses, cars, and taxis. *Station posters* are signs displayed in the interiors of subway, railroad, and rapid-transit stations.

Advertisers buy transit advertising from transit-advertising companies, also known as *operators,* which function much the same as outdoor plant operators. Car cards normally are sold in *runs*. A full run is two cards in every bus, car, and so forth in the market. Half runs and quarter runs are also possible. The rate structure in transit advertising is similar to that of outdoor advertising, because it is based on the volume of traffic passing through bus and train routes. The rates for exterior or traveling displays and station posters are not standardized but, as for outdoor showings, are based on the number of people who view them. The CPM for transit advertising is calculated in the same way as for outdoor media. Like outdoor advertising, transit advertising is relatively inexpensive.

Direct Advertising

Direct advertising is a medium that retailers use extensively to communicate their product offerings to a select group of consumers. The retailer creates an advertisement and distributes it directly to consumers through the mail or through personal distribution of circulars, handbills, and other printed matter. Although direct advertising is expensive in terms of CPM, it is the most selective medium, since the ads are read only by people the retailer selects. It also is a personal form of advertising and extremely flexible. Direct advertising can include pictures, letters, records, pencils, coins, coupons, premiums, samples, and any other gifts the retailer chooses to include.

Retailers may choose to distribute direct advertising to their charge customers or other known or potential customers, or they may buy a mailing list from "mailing-list houses," which sell lists for a certain charge per thousand names. The variety of these lists is astonishing, ranging from magazine subscribers to professional groups to hobbyists to owners of certain products. The retailer never sees these lists; instead, advertising pieces are sent to the mailing-list house, which addresses and mails them. Some retailers prepare their own direct advertising, whereas others choose agencies to prepare it and arrange for distribution. The cost of direct-mail advertising is also measured by the CPM criterion:

$$\text{CPM} = \frac{\text{cost of preparing and distributing advertising} \times 1{,}000}{\text{total number of recipients}}$$

Unlike most other advertising media, the effectiveness of direct advertising can be directly measured if the advertisement calls for a response or an order. By dividing the total sales resulting from customer responses by the total cost of preparing and distributing the direct-advertising materials, the retailer can establish a measure of the cost per sale or response for this promotion.

CONTROLLING THE ADVERTISING FUNCTION

To establish some measure of control over its advertising effort, the retailer must evaluate the effects of advertising. The retailer must first establish specific, measurable advertising objectives, then acquire or develop instruments and methodologies to determine whether those objectives were met. As mentioned, advertising objectives can be stated in terms of either sales or communications levels. Because sales are affected by factors both internal and external to the retailer's operations, meaningful measurements of **advertising effectiveness** are difficult to make, especially in the long run. Short-run advertising objectives can be measured broadly, however, if we assume very few changes occur in the short run (one day to a week). If noticeable changes do occur in this short run, then the retailer must temper its evaluation of advertising effectiveness in light of this information or consider the evaluation a failure. Given that external and internal factors remain relatively stable, the retailer can make a gross measurement of its advertising's sales effectiveness in two ways. (1) For all advertising messages designed to stimulate immediate sales (such as coupons, half-price sales, etc.), the retailer can measure dollar sales increases, increases in number of purchases, increases in store traffic, and so on against those for a comparable period (e.g., last year at the same time or last week). (2) For any direct-advertising campaign, the retailer can measure in-store and out-of-store inquiries, sales increases, or traffic increases. Increases in sales, consumer traffic, and number of purchases are all important success measurements for advertising. An even more appropriate measure of success of a retail promotion, though, is to compare the gross profits from additional sales generated by the promotion to the cost of the promotion.[7] One method for obtaining this measurement is shown in Figure 20–9.

Advertising designed to achieve communications objectives should be measured over the long run. Changes in customer awareness, attitudes, perceptions, and behavioral intentions toward the store should be measured either by personal interviews or mail surveys. In this case, the retailer must use both pretest and posttest measurement to establish possible changes in consumers' opinions of the store.

SUMMARY

Promotion is the fourth element in the retail mix. It involves providing consumers with information about the retailer's store and its offering and influencing their perceptions, attitudes, and behavior. Promotion is also closely related to the communication process, because transmitting meaningful messages through the retailer's promotion mix involves the five major components of advertising, personal selling, store displays, sales promotion, and publicity. Managing the retail advertising function consists of planning, organizing, executing, and controlling advertising strategies. Advertising works for the retailer by prompting individual consumers to move

FIGURE 20–9
The effectiveness of advertising (source: Irwin Broh, "Measure Success of Promotions with In-Store Customer Surveys," *Marketing News,* 13 May 1983, 17)

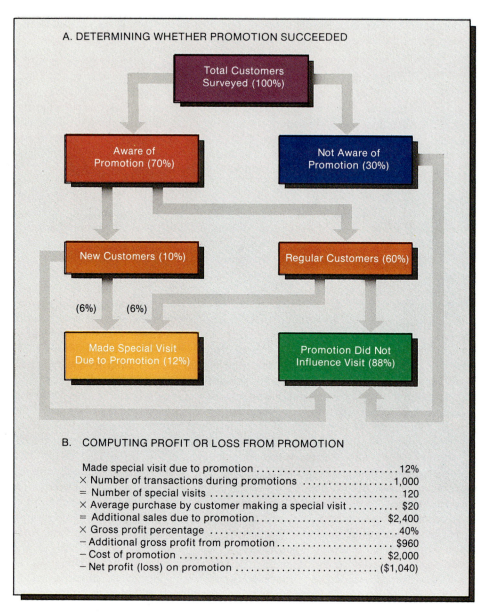

A. DETERMINING WHETHER PROMOTION SUCCEEDED

Total Customers Surveyed (100%)

Aware of Promotion (70%)

Not Aware of Promotion (30%)

New Customers (10%)

Regular Customers (60%)

(6%)   (6%)

Made Special Visit Due to Promotion (12%)

Promotion Did Not Influence Visit (88%)

B. COMPUTING PROFIT OR LOSS FROM PROMOTION

Made special visit due to promotion 12%
× Number of transactions during promotions 1,000
= Number of special visits 120
× Average purchase by customer making a special visit $20
= Additional sales due to promotion $2,400
× Gross profit percentage 40%
– Additional gross profit from promotion $960
– Cost of promotion $2,000
– Net profit (loss) on promotion . . . . ($1,040)

through the adoption process and by stimulating the two-step flow of mass communications.

In developing advertising plans, the retailer sets advertising objectives, identifies the types of advertising it must conduct, and develops advertising appropriations and budgets. Retail advertising takes the form of product advertising, institutional advertising, or some combination of the two. The advertising appropriation is the total amount spent on advertising, whereas the budget is the allocation of this appropriation across departments or across merchandise lines, time periods, and advertising media. Advertising appropriation and budgeting methods include the educated-guess, the percentage-of-sales, the competitive parity, and the objective and task methods.

Organizing and executing the advertising function depends heavily on store size and available funds. Small stores rely heavily on outside advertising specialists, whereas large stores normally have a sales promotion and advertising manager to supervise artists, copywriters, publicity directors, and display managers. In addition, this manager works with store merchandise managers and outside advertising specialists.

Executing the advertising function consists of creating advertisements and selecting advertising media. The retailer must determine the purpose of the advertisement, create the basic message, develop the communications approach, and finalize the total advertisement. A total print advertisement consists of layout, headline, illustration, copy, and logotype. Retailers use newspapers, consumer magazines, radio, television, sign media, direct advertising, and numerous other miscellaneous media.

Advertising control, the job of evaluating advertising effectiveness, consists of determining what to measure and how to measure it. The retailer may choose either sales or communications measures and from among numerous methods of measuring advertising effectiveness.

KEY TERMS AND CONCEPTS

advertisement message
advertising
advertising agencies
advertising budgets
advertising effectiveness
advertising freelancer
advertising manager
audience selectivity
communication effectiveness
communication process
communications approach
competitive parity method
cooperative advertising
copy
cost
coverage
DAGMAR
decoding
direct advertising
educated-guess method
encoding
feedback/
flexibility
frequency
geographic selectivity
headline
illustration
immediacy
impact

institutional advertising
layout
life
logotype
magazine advertising
media representative
newspaper advertising
noise
objective and task method
opinion leaders
percentage-of-sales method
personal selling
prestige
product advertising
promotion
publicity
radio advertising
receivers
sales promotion
sales promotion director
sales promotion manager
senders
sign advertising
store displays
television advertising
total advertisement
transmission
two-step flow of communications

REVIEW QUESTIONS

1. Identify and briefly describe the various participants, processes, and acts of the communication process.
2. Describe the five elements of the promotion mix.
3. How is product advertising different from institutional advertising?
4. Discuss the purpose of an advertising objective aimed at store positioning.
5. What considerations should the retailer take into account when allocating advertising budgets?
6. Discuss the problems associated with the competitive parity method of determining advertising budgets.
7. Describe the four-step objective and task method of determining the retailer's advertising budget.
8. Do retailers make extensive use of advertising agencies? Why or why not?
9. In developing the basic advertising message, the retailer is concerned with which two issues?
10. Which two general communication approaches are used to convey the retailer's message?
11. List the five components of a total advertisement and define each component.
12. Which media characteristics do retailers consider when selecting the most appropriate types of media for communicating with their consumers?
13. Newspapers sell two kinds of advertising space. What are they? How is newspaper space measured?
14. Explain the following newspaper advertising concepts: open rate, space contract, ROP, and position charge.
15. How are newspaper rate structures determined?
16. Identify the positive and negative aspects of magazine advertising from the retailer's viewpoint.
17. How is radio advertising sold?
18. From the retailer's perspective, what are the positive and negative characteristics of television advertising?
19. What are the three types of outdoor advertising? Describe each type.

ENDNOTES

1. Stephen Phillips, "Can the Closeout King Unload Its Woes?" *Business Week,* 7 Dec. 1987, 94.
2. Laurie Freeman, "Wal-Mart Blankets Wisconsin," *Advertising Age,* 17 Aug. 1987, 26MW.
3. Scott Hume, "McDonald's Heavy in Print for Nutrition," *Advertising Age,* 19 Jan. 1987, 2.
4. "Ad Effectiveness: Can It Be Calculated?" *Chain Store Age Executive* (September 1987): 66.
5. David Kettlewell, "Positioning, Not Sales, Is Real Value of Wendy's Ad," *Format* (June 1984): 1.
6. Richard Edel, "Segmentation Attracts New Product Categories," *Advertising Age,* 12 May 1986, S-1.
7. Irwin Broh, "Measure Success of Promotions with In-Store Customer Surveys," *Marketing News,* 13 May 1983, 17.

RELATED READINGS

Allaway, Arthur, Mason, J. Barry, and Brown, Gene. "An Optimal Decision Support Model for Department-Level Promotion Mix Planning." *Journal of Retailing* 63 (Fall 1987): 215–42.

Bearden, William O., Lichtenstein, Donald R., and Teel, Jesse E. "Comparison Price, Coupon, and Brand Effects on Consumers, Reactions to Retail Newspaper Advertisements." *Journal of Retailing* 60 (Summer 1984): 11–34.

Gardner, Meryl P., and Houston, Michael J. "The Effects of Verbal and Visual Components of Retail Communication." *Journal of Retailing* 62 (Spring 1986): 64–78.

George, Richard J., and Lord, John B. "Supermarket Promotional Strategies: What's Hot and What's Not." In *Developments in Marketing Science, Proceedings,* edited by N. K. Malhotra, 299–302. Academy of Marketing Science, 1985.

Green, Paul E., Mahajan, Vijay, Goldberg, Stephen M., and Kedia, Pradeep K. "A Decision Support System for Developing Retail Promotional Strategy." *Journal of Retailing* 59 (Fall 1983): 116–43.

Higie, Robin A., Feick, Lawrence F., and Price, Linda L. "Types and Amount of Word-of-Mouth Communications About Retailers." *Journal of Retailing* 63 (Fall 1987): 260–78.

Moriarty, Mark. "Feature Advertising—Price Interaction Effects in the Retail Environment." *Journal of Retailing* 59 (Summer 1983): 80–98.

"Outdoor Is In! By The Boards." *Stores* (May 1982): 57–65.

Rust, Roland T. *Advertising Media Models: A Practical Guide.* Lexington, MA: Lexington Books, 1985.

Teel, Jesse E., and Bearden, William O. "A Media Planning Algorithm for Retail Advertisers." *Journal of Retailing* 56 (Winter 1980): 23–29.

21

Outline

THE EFFECTIVE SALESPERSON
Physical Traits
Personality Traits
Individual Skills
Message-Presentation Skills

THE RETAIL SELLING PROCESS
Preparing for Customers
Prospecting for Customers
Contacting the Customer
Presenting the Merchandise
Handling Objections
Closing the Sale

Objectives

☐ Explain why the basis for personal selling is good communications.

☐ Identify the traits and skills of a good salesperson.

☐ Name and discuss the seven steps of the retail selling process.

☐ Describe procedures for training, motivating, and evaluating salespeople.

Selling Strategy: Handling the Personal Selling Process

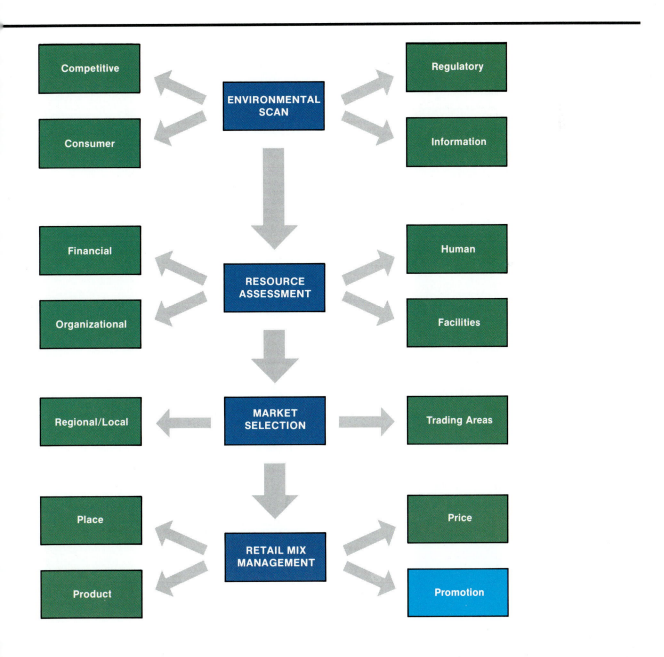

"In a product's long journey from the producer to the customer, the last two feet are the most important. That 'last two feet' is the distance across the sales counter."[1] Retail selling is a special kind of selling whereby the customer comes to the store with a general or specific need in mind. The retail salesperson must close the sale while the customer is still in the store; otherwise, the sale might be lost forever.[2]

Personal selling is, perhaps, the most important element in the store image-creating process. Salespeople are usually the first people in the store to interact with customers on a face-to-face basis; thus, they have tremendous influence on how consumers perceive a store. In sum, salespeople are a significant factor in enhancing or detracting from the consumer's total impressions of a retail store.

FIGURE 21–1
Developing and managing the personal selling effort

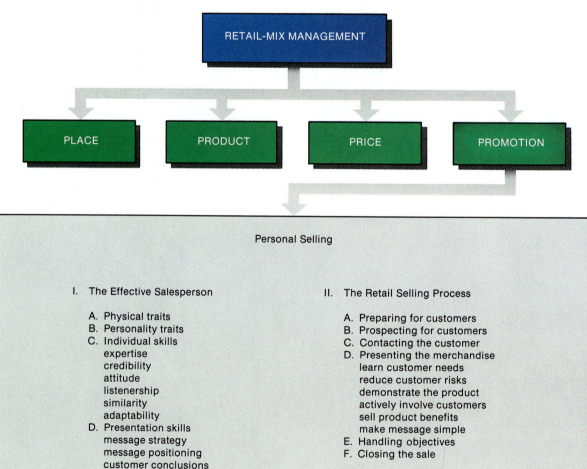

RETAIL-MIX MANAGEMENT

PLACE   PRODUCT   PRICE   PROMOTION

Personal Selling

I. The Effective Salesperson

  A. Physical traits
  B. Personality traits
  C. Individual skills
    expertise
    credibility
    attitude
    listenership
    similarity
    adaptability
  D. Presentation skills
    message strategy
    message positioning
    customer conclusions
    customer participation
    message appeals
  E. The "super" salesperson

II. The Retail Selling Process

  A. Preparing for customers
  B. Prospecting for customers
  C. Contacting the customer
  D. Presenting the merchandise
    learn customer needs
    reduce customer risks
    demonstrate the product
    actively involve customers
    sell product benefits
    make message simple
  E. Handling objectives
  F. Closing the sale

III. Retail-Sales Management

  A. Training salespeople
  B. Motivating salespeople
  C. Evaluating salespeople

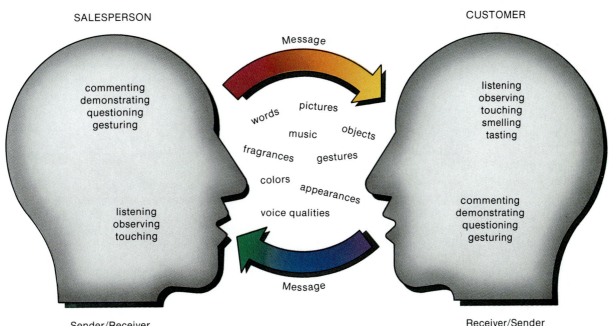

SALESPERSON

CUSTOMER

commenting
demonstrating
questioning
gesturing

listening
observing
touching

Message

words   pictures

music   objects

fragrances   gestures

colors   appearances

voice qualities

listening
observing
touching
smelling
tasting

commenting
demonstrating
questioning
gesturing

Message

Sender/Receiver

Receiver/Sender

FIGURE 21–2
A communications
model of the
customer–salesperson
interaction (a partial
adaptation from Robert
F. Spohn and Robert
Y. Allen, *Retailing*
[Reston, VA: Reston
Publishing, 1977], 236)

This chapter covers personal selling as a communication process, the characteristics of a good salesperson, the steps in the retail selling process, how to train salespeople, and how to evaluate their performance. The issues and concerns associated with managing the retailer's personal selling efforts are shown in Figure 21–1.

The basis for *all* personal selling is personal communications. Communication is *not* something you do *to* someone, but something you do *with* someone. **Personal communication** is the process of exchanging ideas and meanings with other people. Although one person is listening, even that person is active, not passive, in every communications situation. Figure 21–2 shows the basic elements of the communications interaction between a customer and a salesperson.

The model also illustrates that both customer and salesperson are simultaneously sending and receiving information. The transmission and reception of information comes in many forms, such as words, objects, fragrances, colors, gestures, appearances, music, and voice qualities, to name but a few modes. With all of these communications channels occurring at the same time, a good salesperson must be a good listener and observer and adapt quickly to each moment in the selling situation.

Whether a salesperson is an "order getter" or an "order taker," certain qualities or characteristics are needed to be effective. **Order getters** must be aggressive to obtain sales. They must persuade customers that what they are selling is best for them. **Order takers** simply comply with customers' requests for certain types of merchandise. The more difficult job (and more rewarding) is order getting. Although most of the characteristics described in this section apply more to the order getter, they are traits that can also help order takers to be successful. Characteristics of an effective salesperson fall into four categories: physical traits, personality traits, individual skills, and message-presentation skills.

**THE EFFECTIVE
SALESPERSON**

Physical Traits

Although there may be a fine line between **physical traits,** such as personal grooming and hygiene, and personality traits, they are sufficiently different to discuss separately. Clean clothing, shined shoes, clean, well-groomed hair, clean teeth and fresh breath, a well-shaven, clean-smelling body, and a pleasant smile are essential. Of course, these physical features can quickly be negated by an unpleasant personality.

Personality Traits

Personality traits are individual characteristics people acquire over a lifetime. These traits become an inherent part of a person through prior learning. Good salespeople have developed personality traits of sociability, curiosity, imagination, creativity, enthusiasm, sincerity, ambition, and reliability. Good salespeople get along with people, want to know, want to try new ways, want to do something different, have great interest in their work, are honest about their work and dealings with others, want to achieve certain self-imposed objectives, and state the truth about the product they sell.

Individual Skills

One can develop **individual selling skills** if one is willing to work on them. Based on research, several skills an individual can acquire are (1) perceived expertise, (2) perceived credibility, (3) positive attitude, (4) good listenership, (5) salesperson–customer similarity, and (6) adaptability.

Expertise

Salespeople whom customers **perceive as expert** have a much greater chance of making a sale than salespeople whom customers perceive as having less expertise. People who are high in expertise are those who are more qualified than others to speak on a particular topic. Salespeople with special education or training, information, and knowledge to talk about the product they sell have the expertise to be effective at their job. The key word in this discussion, however, is *perceived*. No matter how expert the salesperson, selling effectiveness depends on whether the customer *perceives* the person as an expert. Studies suggest that expertise must be communicated to each customer to effectively increase sales.

Credibility

Similarly, how effective a salesperson will be in making a sale depends partly on how **credible the customer perceives** the person to be. The more credible a salesperson is perceived to be, the more sales are likely to be made. A credible salesperson is believable, trustworthy, and honest in dealing with customers. Research in this area shows strong evidence of the persuasive powers of people who are perceived as credible.

Attitude

A salesperson is more effective with a positive rather than a negative attitude toward himself or herself, the message (and product), and the customer. A **positive attitude** means self-confidence, not arrogance. Successful salespeople have confidence in their abilities to do their job. A salesperson also must have a positive attitude toward the product and what is said about it. If the salesperson does not believe in the product, why should the customer? Finally, a salesperson must have a positive attitude toward customers, demonstrated by paying careful attention to what the customer says, showing respect for the customer, and not "talking down" to the customer.

Listening Skills

Salespeople too often overlook **listening skills**. Some sales clerks are so busy talking and listening to themselves that they fail to listen to their customers. Failure to be a good listener can lead to lost sales. If they do not listen carefully, salespeople cannot determine customers' needs, wants, or preferences. Good listening skills not only improve the salesperson's chances of making a sale but also can provide feedback through the salesperson to top management about changes that might be made in store policies, merchandise lines, and a variety of other aspects of store operations. Figure 21–3 presents some guidelines for developing good listening skills.

Similarity

"People are persuaded more by a communicator they perceive to be similar to themselves," one expert pointed out. Salespersons who can quickly discover a **salesperson–customer similarity** can capitalize on this common characteristic to enhance their chances of making the sale. A salesperson can detect similarities by asking questions, listening, and observing. For example, if the customer is accompanied by children and the salesperson is a parent, the subject can be brought up in conversation. Or, if through conversation one learns that the customer is a student, professor, or staff member at the local university, the salesperson should mention the fact—if it is true—that he or she buys season tickets to all the games, attends the plays, supports the university, or whatever. The more specific the similarities, the better. *Perceived similarity* can be based on personality, dress, race, skin color, religion, politics, interests, group affiliations, and many more attributes. Clever salespersons quickly determine similarities between themselves and their customers and use them in casual talk.

FIGURE 21–3
Guidelines for developing good listening skills

1. Do not only listen to the words themselves, but also watch carefully for non-verbal cues to the real intentions of the customer.
2. Practice being interested in what customers have to say. Remember you are not always the most interesting person around.
3. Be sensitive to the customer's personal pronouns, such as "I", "we", "you", "us" and "our". These are cues to things that really interest the customer.
4. Do not be distracted by peculiarities in the speech of the customer.
5. Establish eye contact with customer.
6. Ask clarifying questions to test your understanding of a message.
7. Shut up and listen when the customer wants to talk.
8. Relax. Try not to give the customer the impression that you are just waiting to jump in and start talking.
9. Do not assume you understand the customer's problem or need. Keep listening while they keep talking.
10. Listen for ideas, not just words.

Source: Ronald B. Marks, *Personal Selling*, 2d ed. (Boston: Allyn and Bacon, Inc., 1985), 130–31.

A perceived salesper-
son—customer similar-
ity enhances the
chance of making a
sale.

Adaptability

Good salespeople demonstrate adaptability to differences in customer types. Figure 21−4 shows the types of customers that salespeople will encounter and suggests how they should react to each type. Salespeople must learn to identify customer types and adapt accordingly, without losing their own identity.

Message-Presentation Skills

Through training, salespeople can develop **skills in message presentation** that will help them become more persuasive and increase sales.

Message Strategy

Salespeople can present merchandise to customers either by explaining only the product's strengths and benefits (one-sided message) or by describing the product's weaknesses as well as strengths (two-sided message). Although it might sound strange to mention a product's weaknesses to customers (or the strength of competitors' products), this strategy works under certain circumstances. When consumers are not knowledgeable about a product, however, the general rule is to present a one-sided message; that is, to be more persuasive and produce more sales, it is better to tell them only about benefits, advantages, and strengths. When customers lack product knowledge, they are unable to comprehend product weaknesses and will become confused if the salesperson tries to explain them. Therefore, to this audience, sell *only the strong points of the product.*

On the other hand, if the salesperson is presenting a product to a customer who is very knowledgeable about the product, the best strategy is to explain the product's strengths as well as its weaknesses or to describe both the product's strengths and the competing products' strengths. Since the customer is knowledgeable about the product, he or she will have already recognized the weakness in the merchandise or

Basic Types of Customer	Basic Characteristic	Secondary Characteristic	Other Characteristics	What Salesperson Should Say or Do
Arguer	Takes issue with each statement of salesperson	Disbelieves claims, tries to catch salesperson in error	Cautious, slow to decide	Demonstrate; show product knowledge; use "Yes, but . . ."
Chip on shoulder	Definitely in a bad mood	Indignation; angry at slight provocation	Acts as if being deliberately baited	Avoid argument; stick to basic facts; show good assortment
Decisive	Knows what is wanted	Customer confident choice is right	Not interested in another opinion—respects sales person's brevity	Win sale—not argument; sell self; tactfully inject opinion
Doubting Thomas	Doesn't trust sales talk	Hates to be managed	Arrives at decision cautiously	Back up merchandise statements by manufacturers' tags, labels; demonstrate merchandise; let customer handle merchandise
Fact-finder	Interested in factual information—detailed	Alert to sales person's errors in description	Looks for actual tags and labels	Emphasize label and manufacturer's facts; volunteer care information
Hesitant	Ill at ease—sensitive	Shopping at unaccustomed price range	Unsure of own judgment	Make customer comfortable; use friendliness and respect
Impulsive	Quick to decide or select	Impatience	Liable to break off sale abruptly	Close rapidly; avoid oversell, overtalk; note key points
Look around	Little ability to make own decisions	Anxious—fearful of making a mistake	Wants sales person's aid in decision—wants adviser—wants to do "right thing"	Emphasize merits of product and service, "zeroing" in on customer-expressed needs and doubts
Procrastinator	I'll wait 'til tomorrow	Lacks confidence in own judgment	Insecure	Reinforce customers' judgments
Silent	Not talking—but thinking!	Appears indifferent but truly listening	Appears nonchalant	Ask direct questions—straightforward approach
Think it over	Refers to need to consult someone	Looking for another adviser	Not sure of own uncertainty	Get agreement on small points; draw out opinions; use points agreed upon for close

Source: C. Winston Borgen, *Learning Experiences in Retailing* (Santa Monica, CA: Goodyear Publishing), 293.

FIGURE 21–4

Customer types and what salespersons should say or do

the strengths of other retailers' products. Do not, therefore, insult the customer's product knowledge or intelligence. Instead, salespeople should admit to *minor* weaknesses in a brand or *minor* strengths in those of competitors. Customers will respect the salesperson's honesty and he or she will be more credible to them. When using the two-sided message, one's own merchandise "wins"—there are fewer weaknesses in one's merchandise or fewer strengths in competitors' brands.

Message Positioning

Salespeople should place their strongest selling points at the beginning (opening) and the end (closing) of the message, *never* in the middle. Psychologists tell us that people remember the beginning and ending of a message better than the middle. Salespeople, therefore, should always capture the customer's attention with strong points of the merchandise at the beginning of the sales presentation and summarize those points in the closing.

Customer Conclusions

The general selling rule is to draw a conclusion in the sales presentation, summarizing reasons the product is right for the customer. Unfortunately, many customers cannot add together the logical statements they hear to why they should purchase the merchandise. Therefore, the salesperson should do it for them by quickly summarizing major points and telling them (in conclusion) why they should buy. The exception to this rule is when one encounters highly intelligent people who can easily draw conclusions for themselves and drawing a conclusion insults the intelligence of the prospective buyer.

Customer Participation

Salespeople are more likely to sell a product when they can get the prospective buyer to try it as they explain its benefits. Psychologists tell us that *active participation* not only helps consumers learn the benefits of a product but also helps persuade them to purchase it. The rule in retail selling is to let customers touch, feel, smell, taste, and hear the product. Get them to take a test drive, taste the sausage, smell the ham, feel the power as they maneuver the dials, play the video game, see how the diamond ring looks on the hand. Customers' active involvement and participation with the product in the store is a powerful selling technique—perhaps the most effective way to present the "message."

Message Appeals

All people have emotions, and the "heart" often rules the mind. Salespeople must recognize and use their customers' emotions to good advantage. We all would like to believe we make buying decisions rationally and logically, but usually we do not. Instead, we purchase most products largely on an emotional basis. Given these emotional aspects of purchase behavior, salespeople should acquire the skill of describing their merchandise in emotional terms.

THE RETAIL SELLING PROCESS

Several basic steps occur in every selling situation. The length of time that a salesperson takes in each step depends on the product, the customer, and the selling situation. The seven steps of the retail selling process appear in Figure 21–5.

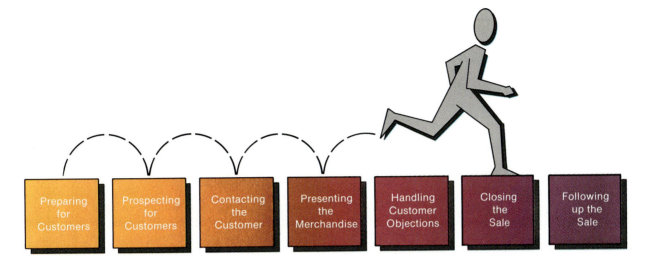

| Preparing for Customers | Prospecting for Customers | Contacting the Customer | Presenting the Merchandise | Handling Customer Objections | Closing the Sale | Following up the Sale |

FIGURE 21–5
The seven steps of the retail selling process

Preparing for Customers

Preparing for the customer is the first step in the selling process. In this stage, the salesperson does the *preliminary* work necessary for effective interaction with the customer. This stage can be subdivided into long-run preparation and short-run preparation.

In long-run preparation, the salesperson learns store policies and procedures and gains knowledge about the merchandise. These learning activities include becoming familiar with store operating procedures, return policies, and guarantees; learning to operate merchandise that the store (or department) sells; and knowing manufacturer warranties—to name but a few. Short-term preparations are daily and weekly activities, including learning what merchandise is currently in stock; which items are on sale; recent changes in store policies and operating procedures; changes that have occurred in new styles, fashions, and models of merchandise; and dozens of other day-to-day store happenings.

Prospecting for Customers

Prospecting is the process of finding people who are *willing* to buy the merchandise a store has to offer and are *able* to pay for that merchandise. Salespeople learn through experience how to spot good prospects. Good prospects generally display more interest in the merchandise than poor prospects who are "just browsing." A variety of behavioral cues set good prospects apart from the poor prospects; for example, carrying several bags of merchandise from other stores is often a clue to a shopper's interest in making additional purchases.

Prospecting is particularly important when the store is full of customers. An alert salesperson can single out prime prospects and not waste time with browsers. When the store is not busy, salespeople should attend to everyone, including weak prospects to build possible future business and enhance the store's image of concern for its customers.

Contacting the Customer

Initial impressions are important determinants in successfully making a sale. A warm smile and an appearance of genuine interest in customers and their needs are parts of a good initial impression. At the beginning of the contact, the salesperson should make an opening comment that quickly captures the buyer's attention and arouses interest. Further, the first words should be positive and should stimulate any needs the customer might be displaying. If a woman is holding up a blouse to examine, the salesperson might open by saying, "That blouse certainly would look nice on you. Would you like to try it on?" This opening compliments the woman's taste in clothing, stimulates her need to "look nice," and requests her to take an *action* (try it on). A simple "May I help you?" is a routine, worn-out phrase that almost invites the customer to turn down the request.

Openings should be original and appropriate to the situation. Consider the following examples of customer situations and potential salesperson responses.

Situation 1: Customer looking at a home video game.

☐ *Preferred opening* Salesperson: "Press this button like this [salesperson turns game on], and the game's all set to go. Why don't you try your luck?"
☐ *Nonpreferred opening* Salesperson: "Do you need some help in how to operate this thing?" Customer: "[Gads, he thinks I'm stupid or something.] No, I was just looking."

Situation 2: Woman looking at a coat in an exclusive, high-fashion women's clothing store.

☐ *Preferred opening* "That's 100-percent mink. Please let me help you on with it to see how it looks and feels."
☐ *Nonpreferred opening* "Want some help?" Customer: "[She thinks I don't know how to put on a coat!] No, thank you."

Situation 3: Shopper looking at a telephone in a phone center store.

☐ *Preferred opening* "That phone will make a call for you if simply one button is pressed. Look how easy it is to operate."
☐ *Nonpreferred opening* "Are you interested in a phone?"

In summary, a salesperson's opening statement at the point of initial contact can determine whether conversation will continue and, therefore, whether the sale can be made. A good opening should attract the customer's attention, arouse interest, stimulate a customer need, and be original to the situation. A poor opening is generally one the customer can answer with a yes or a no. In a selling situation, a good beginning is usually necessary for a happy ending (the sale).

Presenting the Merchandise

After making initial contact, the salesperson is in a position to present the merchandise and the sales message. How the salesperson should present the merchandise depends on the customer. Because customers are not identical, the salesperson's presentations should not be identical; instead, they should be tailored to the individual and the circumstances. Some basic guidelines can help the salesperson make a good presentation. Remember, however, that salespeople must continually exercise their creativity to adapt to particular customers and circumstances.

Learn the Customer's Needs and Wants

To know what merchandise to show, the salesperson must learn what the customer needs and wants. Asking key questions and listening attentively help the salesperson to determine what merchandise the store has that might meet those needs and wants. "When questions are asked at the right time and the right place, they are

FIGURE 21–6
Guidelines on how to
ask questions

1. Start with broad questions and move toward narrower questions. Broad, open-ended questions are less threatening than narrow, specific questions.
2. Listen to everything the customer says.
3. Keep questions simple and focused. Use one idea at a time.
4. Ask sensitive questions in a nonthreatening way (e.g., "How much were you planning to spend?" not "How much can you afford?"). If you must ask a very personal question, always explain why.
5. Always ask questions that are easy to answer! Studies show that people would rather answer a question when they agree than voice their objections.
6. Turn the statements your customer makes into questions to clarify or reinforce feelings. "So, Tuesday would be best for you, is that right?"
7. Use questions to develop the presentation! "You mentioned that your present car needs repairs. What types of repairs does it need?" Explain the advantages of a new car.
8. Use caution when leading clients with questions. Always respect the intelligence of your prospect.
9. Use questions to give information. "Are you aware of our 90-days same as cash policy?"

Source: Nido R. Quebein, "The Power of Asking Questions." *Personal Selling Power* (January/February 1988): 20–21.

powerful tools for raising your customer response level."[3] Questions allow the salesperson to (1) discover important information that is useful in closing the sale, (2) demonstrate genuine interest in the customer, (3) move the customer toward active involvement in the sales process, (4) correct any misconceptions about the product or the store, and (5) develop rapport with the customer.[4] Figure 21–6 provides guidelines in how to ask questions. "The pay in selling is far greater for asking the right questions than for knowing the right answer—a closed mouth gathers no foot."[5] At this point, the salesperson must closely observe the customer's reactions to each piece of merchandise shown to determine the level of product interest; that is, whether the product is a "must have," "should have," or "would be nice to have" item. The salesperson can also, in this initial presentation, determine whether to try trading up—attempting to sell higher-quality, higher-priced merchandise or to sell a larger quantity than the customer originally intended to buy. The salesperson may believe the customer would be better satisfied with more durable, stronger, lighter, heavier, bigger, or softer materials or may think the customer needs a larger quantity to complete the job or to save money. Because customer need satisfaction is a goal of the retailer, then determining customer needs and wants is a logical first step in presenting and selling merchandise.

Reduce Customers' Perceived Risk

Customers run the risk that the product they buy might not perform correctly, might fall apart or break down, might embarrass them in a social setting (a "gold" necklace chain turns the neck green), or might be unsafe. These concerns are particularly strong for high-cost items; refrigerators, washers, cars, sets of tires, houses, and television sets represent substantial outlays of money and therefore risk. Perceived risk takes the form of financial, physical, or social risk. Therefore, products with high perceived risk must be accompanied by assurances of satisfactory performance. The

Successful retail sales representatives demonstrate the product and actively involve the customer.

salesperson should stress the manufacturer's warranty, the retailer's money-back guarantee, the retailer's in-house repair facilities, the dependable brand name, and so on. This selling situation might also be an opportunity for the salesperson to trade up the customer to higher-quality merchandise to reduce perceived risk and thus make the sale.

Demonstrate the Product

Some products lend themselves to demonstration better than others, but virtually all products can be demonstrated somehow. Demonstrating the merchandise means the customer sees the product in action—its features, benefits, and possible advantages. While demonstrating the product, the salesperson should point out the unique features and benefits to reinforce what the customer is seeing. A product can often sell itself, particularly if the salesperson helps a little. Demonstrations can also help reduce some customers' perceived risk in purchasing the product.

Actively Involve the Customer

Get customers actively involved with the product! Have them touch, smell, taste, hear, and feel it. "Push the accelerator and feel the power, *experience* its smooth ride, *listen* to the quiet of the engine and the outside air, *touch* the soft velour seats," a car salesperson might say while the customer is actually using, controlling, and experiencing the product.

Chances of persuading customers to buy a product improve greatly when they actively interact with it. A good salesperson points out how the product affects the customer's five senses ("Smell the manly scent of this cologne." "Taste the rich flavor of this coffee." "Feel the softness of this sweater.") The more of the customer's senses a salesperson can stimulate, the greater the chance of a sale.

Sell Product Benefits, Not the Product

"In the factory we produce cosmetics; in the store we sell the promise and hope of beauty!" "We don't sell the steak, we sell the sizzle." What all manufacturers, retailers, and salespeople must realize is that they don't sell physical products, but the physical, social, and psychological *benefits* they provide consumers. People don't buy lawn mowers, they buy trim lawns. People don't buy ¼-inch drill bits, they buy ¼-inch holes. Customers buy, in effect, the end result (the benefit), not the product for the product's sake. Therefore, salespeople should sell benefits. Encyclopedia sales representatives learned this idea a long time ago—"We provide your children with *educational* materials, not encyclopedias. Don't you think your child's education is important?"

Make the Message Simple

Too often salespeople present merchandise in *technical* terms and phrases that the average customer does not understand. As a result, many customers are frightened off or confused and a sale is lost. Good salespeople present the product message in words that are clear and understandable to the customer. The salesperson must be ready to adapt quickly to each consumer's level of understanding and sophistication. Sometimes the salesperson must use analogies and speak simply; for other customers, the salesperson might engage in technical conversation. The sales-message level should be geared to the customer's product-knowledge level. Thus a "golden rule" is to *communicate the message at the customer's level of understanding and knowledge.* Salespeople should not talk "over their customers' heads" or insult their intelligence by speaking too simply.

Handling Objections

Consumers who do not purchase a product immediately after the merchandise presentation are likely to have perceived "stumbling blocks," objections to buying the product. A salesperson must anticipate objections and know how to handle each type. Figure 21–7 summarizes techniques of handling customer objections. Customer objections are of five kinds: product, price, place (store), timing, and salesperson.

Some consumers think the *product* is just not right for them. It is too big, too small, too heavy, too light, does not look right on them, is too simple, too complex, or one of a host of other objections. The salesperson must be creative and adaptable in handling objections. If the customer says "This doesn't look right on me," it probably means "My friends (family, co-workers, boss, etc.) wouldn't like it." A creative salesperson counters with reasons the customer's reference groups might well approve of this merchandise. This approach reinforces the customer's self-image and gives supporting approval from others for making the purchase. In other cases, customers may object to the product by saying they are not sure it will perform as it should, to which the salesperson should reiterate the proven record of the product, its warranties, and store guarantees.

Price is a common customer objection that takes two forms. First, the customer really wants the product but doesn't have the cash to pay for it. In this case, the salesperson can emphasize the store's easy credit terms ("You can buy this washing machine for only $10 a month"). In other cases, the customer does not consider the product worth the price; for these customers, the salesperson must emphasize product value, perhaps by mentioning that competitors' prices are about the same even though their products do not have comparable features, warranties, or guarantees.

Customers may not like the *store* itself. An advertisement or a display caught their eye, they came into the store and saw something they liked, but they usually don't shop in this store or "a store like this" and therefore feel uncomfortable buying here. To meet this kind of objection, the salesperson must assure customers of the integrity of the store, its management, and its merchandise.

Putting the purchase off (*timing*) is another objection salespeople frequently encounter. Customers might not know exactly why they don't want to buy now; they

FIGURE 21–7
Summary of objection-handling techniques

Method	When to Use	How to Use
Head-on	With objections arising from incorrect information	Salespeople directly, but politely, deny the truth of the objection; to avoid alienating prospects, it is helpful to offer proof
Indirect denial	With objections arising from incorrect information	Salespeople never directly tell prospects that they are wrong, but still manage to correct the mistaken impression
Compensation	With valid objections, but where compensating factors are present	Salespeople agree with prospects initially, but then proceed to point out factors that outweigh or compensate for the objection (for this reason, it is often called the "yes, but" technique)
"Feel, felt, found"	With emotional objections, especially when prospects have retreated from their adult ego states, and when the prospect fails to see the value of a particular feature and benefit	Salespeople express their understanding for how prospects feel, indicate that they are okay since others have also felt that way, but have found their fears to be without substance
Boomerang	When the objection can be turned into a positive factor	Salespeople take the objection and turn it into a reason for buying
Forestalling	With any type of objection	From prior experience, salespeople anticipate an objection and incorporate an answer into the presentation itself, hoping to forestall the objection from ever coming up

Source: Ronald B. Marks, *Personal Selling* (Boston: Allyn and Bacon, Inc., 1985), 326.

just don't. Customers usually use the "timing" objection to conceal their real objections. Thus, this type of objection is difficult for salespeople to handle, since they do not understand its underlying motives. Handling this objection is "groping in the dark." Nevertheless, the salesperson can emphasize the need to buy immediately ("The sale ends today at this extraordinarily low price" or "There are only a few left in stock"). Any statement indicating the urgency to buy now might overcome this objection.

One last possible customer objection can be to the *salesperson*. Shifty eyes, long hair, short hair, conservative dress, wild dress, garlic on the breath, or any number of other "faults" may turn away a customer. Whatever the reason, the salesperson is often unlikely to detect it. If the salesperson guesses that this is the objection, he or she should direct the customer's attention to the product—its benefits, its advantages, or its need-fulfilling capacities—or turn the sale over to another salesperson.

Closing the Sale

Closing the sale (suggesting that the customer make the purchase) is the "natural" conclusion to the selling process. *Timing* in the closing stage, however, is critical. Customers often provide verbal or physical (body language) cues that suggest they might be ready to make a purchase. Figure 21–8 identifies several physical and verbal cues for potential closing opportunities. In timing the closing, the salesperson must adapt to the individual customer and circumstances. Some customers do not want to be rushed into making a final decision; others don't want to wait too long to have the sales person begin to close. Still other customers do not know how to make the decision or won't make the decision without help. In this latter situation, the salesperson must *tell* them to make the purchase. These people need someone to make decisions for them. In other cases, customers definitely make up their own minds and don't want to be pushed. In dealing with customers like these, the salesperson can remind them of their need and how the merchandise meets that need, restate the advantages and benefits of the merchandise, and explain why they must buy now and not put off the decision.

Skilled salespeople have developed several closing techniques that move the customer toward the purchase decision. After the customer has examined several pieces of merchandise, for example, the salesperson usually can determine which one or two merchandise items the customer prefers. To avoid confusing the customer and to aid in the final decision, the salesperson should put away the less-preferred items. If the customer has tried on seven rings, the five or six least-preferred rings should be put back in their cases. "I can tell this is the one you really like the most," the salesperson might say. "May I wrap this for you? Will this be cash or charge?" Figure 21–9 identifies seven of the more common closing techniques.

FIGURE 21–8

Spotting closing cues

Physical cues provided by customers

1. The customer closely reexamines the merchandise under consideration.
2. The customer reaches for his billfold or opens her purse.
3. The customer samples the product for the second or third time.
4. The customer is nodding in agreement as the terms and conditions of sale are explained.
5. The customer is smiling and appears excited as he or she admires the merchandise.
6. The customer intensely studies the service contract.

Verbal cues provided by customers

1. The customer asks "Do you offer free home delivery?"
2. The customer remarks "I always wanted a pair of Porsche sunglasses."
3. The customer inquires "Do you have this item in red?"
4. The customer states "This ring is a real bargain."
5. The customer exclaims "I feel like a million bucks in this outfit!"
6. The customer requests "Can you complete the installation by Friday?"

Technique	Definition	Example
Direct close	The salesperson asks the customer directly for the order	"Can I write this order up for you?"
Assumptive close	The salesperson assumes the customer is going to buy and proceeds with completing the sales transaction	"Would you like to have this gift wrapped?"
Alternative close	The salesperson asks the customer to make a choice in which either alternative is favorable to the retailer	"Will this be cash or charge?"
Summary/agreement close	The salesperson closes by summarizing the major features, benefits, and advantages of the product and obtains an affirmative agreement from the customer on each point	"This dishwasher has the features you were looking for"—YES "You want free home delivery"—YES "It is in your price range"—YES "Let's write up the sale."
Balance-sheet close	The salesperson starts by listing the advantages and disadvantages of making the purchase and closes by pointing out how the advantages outweigh the disadvantages	"This dishwasher is on sale; it has all the features you asked for, you have 90 days to pay for it without any financial charges, and we will deliver it free. Even though we can not deliver it until next week, now is the time to buy."
Emotional close	The salesperson attempts to close the sale by appealing to the customer's emotions (love, fear, acceptance, recognition)	"The safety of your children could well depend on this smoke alarm. Now is the time to get it installed."
Standing-room-only close	The salesperson tries to get the customer to act immediately by stressing that the offer is limited	"The sale ends today." "This is the last one we have in stock."

FIGURE 21–9

Types of closing techniques

Another aspect of closing a sale is to show customers other merchandise that complements the item they are going to buy. This technique is called **suggestive selling**. If the customer is buying a sport coat, the salesperson can suggest a shirt and tie that are a "perfect" match for the coat. Suggestive selling is a service to customers who might not have thought of purchasing complementary items to enhance the appearance or use of their intended purchase. Both customers and salespeople benefit from suggestive selling when the additional items represent true benefits for the customer.

Next, the salesperson must perform several *administrative* tasks in closing the sale, such as ringing up the sale on the cash register, checking the accuracy of the address and other parts of the check the customer may present, verifying the customer's credit card, and boxing, bagging, or wrapping the merchandise. Finally, closing the sale is not complete until the salesperson has said thank you, asked the customer to come back, and has said good-bye. This phase in closing the sale is called *developing good will,* and repeat business depends on it!

A good salesperson continues to sell the customer *after* the sale. The sale is not over once the customer has walked out the door. Many customers are happy about their purchases at the time they buy them, but later begin to doubt the wisdom of their buying decision. The "doubt" phase usually affects consumers who have made a substantial investment of time, effort, and money. A salesperson might follow up the sale by assuring customers they have made the right decision, the merchandise is of good quality, their friends and relatives will approve, and the store and manufacturer back the merchandise. Salespeople have three ways to follow up a sale: (1) writing a letter to the customer, (2) telephoning the customer, and (3) personally visiting the customer. A personal visit is out of the question for most salespeople because it involves so much time away from work, so with certain exceptions, telephone calls or letters are the best options for following up a sale. Letters are more effective in reducing postpurchase doubt because customers can read letters at their convenience. Therefore, the rule on sales follow-up is to send the customer a letter.

Jordan Marsh, the Boston area department store, has a unique sales—follow-up procedure called "I Guarantee It." It works this way:

> All sales associates are supplied with business cards with their name and department telephone number and reply cards for suggestions, which they hand to every customer with whom they come in contact. Imprinted on the card is the "I Guarantee It!" pledge which states: "It has been a pleasure assisting you today. I hope I was able to make your visit to Jordan Marsh a pleasant experience. If you are dissatisfied with your purchase in any way, please bring it to my attention. I guarantee your personal satisfaction in our merchandise and service. Thank You."[6]

SUMMARY

Personal selling is a communication process between salesperson and customer. Communication is a two-way process in which both members actively exchange ideas and meanings. The characteristics of a good salesperson generally can be divided into physical traits, personality traits, individual skills, and message-presentation skills.

Steps in the retail selling process are (1) preparing for the customer, (2) prospecting for customers, (3) contacting the customer, (4) presenting the merchandise, (5) handling objections, (6) closing the sale, and (7) following up the sale. A good salesperson prepares well for the sale even before greeting the customer, then adapts throughout the sale to each customer and set of store circumstances as they arise at the time.

In all, salespeople are perhaps the retailer's most valuable asset. They interact face-to-face with customers to make the sale and to project the kind of image the retailer desires. Thus, an investment in salespeople is a wise decision.

KEY TERMS AND CONCEPTS

adaptability of salesperson
alternative close technique
assumptive close technique
balance-sheet close technique
boomerang method
compensation method
direct close technique
emotional close technique

feel, felt, found method
forestalling method
head-on method
indirect denial method
individual selling skills
listening skills
message-presentation skills
order getter

order taker   positive attitude

perceived credibility   salesperson–customer similarity

perceived expertise   standing-room-only close technique

personal communication   suggestive selling

personal selling   summary/agreement close technique

personality traits   trading up

physical traits

REVIEW QUESTIONS

1. How are personal selling and personal communications related?
2. What are some of the personality traits of a good salesperson?
3. Describe the role of salesperson expertise and credibility in the selling process.
4. How can a salesperson improve listening skills?
5. How does salesperson–customer similarity affect the selling process?
6. When should a salesperson use a one-sided sales message? When is a two-sided sales message appropriate?
7. Where should the strongest selling points be positioned within a sales message?
8. Should the salesperson draw conclusions for the customer? Are there any exceptions?
9. How can salespeople integrate emotional terms into a sales presentation?
10. What should the salesperson determine in prospecting for customers?
11. Which three forms of perceived risk are part of each customer purchase? How can a retail salesperson reduce perceived risks?
12. What should the retail salesperson sell?
13. What are the most common methods for handling customer objections? Give an original example of each technique.
14. When should a salesperson attempt to close a sale?
15. Describe the various types of closing techniques available to the salesperson. Give an original example of each technique.
16. What is the best option for following up a sale? Why?

ENDNOTES

1. David L. Kurtz, H. Robert Dodge, and Jay E. Klopmaker, *Professional Selling*, 4th ed. (Plano, TX: Business Publications, 1985): 365.
2. See Ronald B. Marks, *Personal Selling*, 2d ed. (Boston: Allyn & Bacon, 1985): 374.
3. Nido R. Quebein, "The Power of Asking Questions," *Personal Selling Power* (January/February 1988): 20–21.
4. Ibid.
5. Hank Trisler, "Stop Telling—Start Selling," *Personal Selling Power* 7 (September 1987): 20.
6. "How Jordan Marsh People 'Guarantee It'," *Stores* (September 1985): 68.

RELATED READINGS

Avila, Ramon. "Predicting Salesperson Success Using Personal and Personality Characteristics: A Theoretical Framework." In *Developments in Marketing Science, Proceedings*, edited by N. K. Malhotra, 242–46. Academy of Marketing Science, 1985.

Dubinsky, Alan J., and Howe, Vince. "Empirical Dimensionality of the Retail Sales Job." In *AMA Educators' Proceedings*, edited by R. W. Belk et al., 158–61. American Marketing Association, 1984.

Dubinsky, Alan J., and Levy, Michael. "Ethics in Retailing: Perceptions of Retail Salespeople." *Journal of the Academy of Marketing Science* 13 (Winter 1985): 1–16.

Farah, John J. "What Makes a Good Salesperson?" In *Developments in Marketing Science, Proceedings,* edited by J. C. Rogers, III, 334–38. Academy of Marketing Science, 1983.

Fedder, Curtis J. "The Art of Listening Is Really a Skill That Has to Be Learned." *Marketing News,* 28 Aug. 1987, 17.

Levy, Michael, and Dubinsky, Alan J. "Identifying and Addressing Retail Salespeople's Ethical Problems: A Method and Application." *Journal of Retailing* 59 (Spring 1983): 46–66.

Skinner, Steven J., Dubinsky, Alan J., and Donnelly, James H., Jr. "The Use of Social Bases of Power in Retail Sales." *Journal of Personal Selling & Sales Management* 4 (November 1984): 48–56.

Solomon, Michael R. "The Wardrobe Consultant: Exploring the Role of a New Retailing Partner." *Journal of Retailing* 63 (Summer 1987): 110–28.

Stretch, Shirley M., Strickler, Susan C., Harp, Shelly S., and Horridge, Patricia E. "Insights into Selling Service Priority in Department Stores." In *Marketing in an Environment of Change, Proceedings,* edited by R. L. King, 88–91. Southern Marketing Association, 1986.

Vaccaro, Joseph P. "Best Salespeople Know Their ABC's (Always Be Closing)." *Marketing News,* 28 March 1988, 10.

Weitz, Barton A. "Effectiveness in Sales Interaction: A Contingency Framework." *Journal of Marketing* 45 (Winter 1981), 85–103.

22

Outline

Objectives

- [ ] Discuss the unique contribution of visual merchandising, sales incentives, and publicity to communicating the retailer's merchandising messages to consumers.
- [ ] Plan and construct an effective in-store display.
- [ ] List many innovative sales-incentive tools and describe how they attract customers and stimulate purchases.
- [ ] Explain how to plan favorable publicity and manage unplanned publicity.

Promotions Strategy: Managing Retail Displays, Sales Incentives, and Publicity

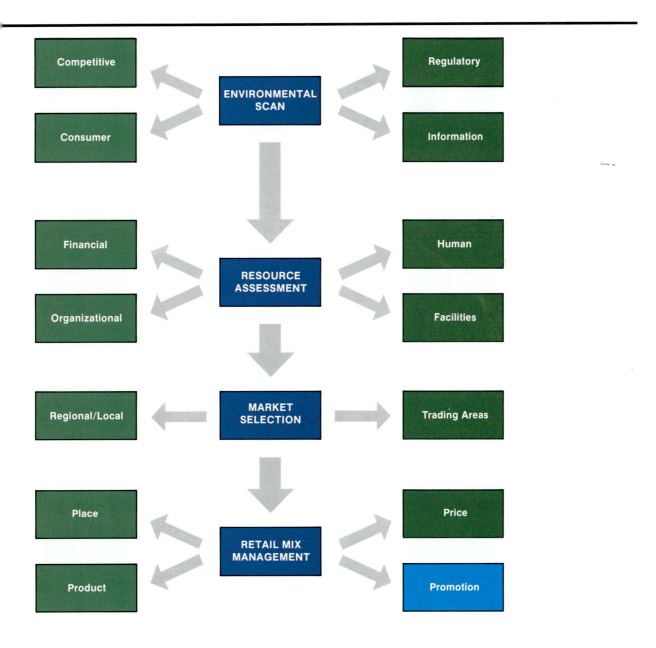

To supplement the advertising program, the retailer must offer in-store promotional support, provide special purchase inducements, and capitalize on public events that affect the store and its personnel. This chapter examines the role of visual merchandising (retail displays), sales incentives, and publicity as part of the retailer's total promotional effort. Figure 22–1 outlines these issues.

VISUAL MERCHANDISING

FIGURE 22–1
Developing and implementing retail displays, sales promotions, and publicity campaigns

Advertising may attract consumers to the store, but it is primarily the retailer's visual displays that make the sale after the consumer is in the store. Retail displays are nonpersonal, in-store presentations and exhibitions of merchandise together with related information. In practice, retail displays are used (1) to maximize product exposure, (2) to enhance product appearance, (3) to stimulate product interest, (4) to exhibit product information, (5) to facilitate sales transactions, (6) to ensure product security, (7) to provide product storage, (8) to remind customers of planned purchases, and (9) to generate additional sales of impulse items.

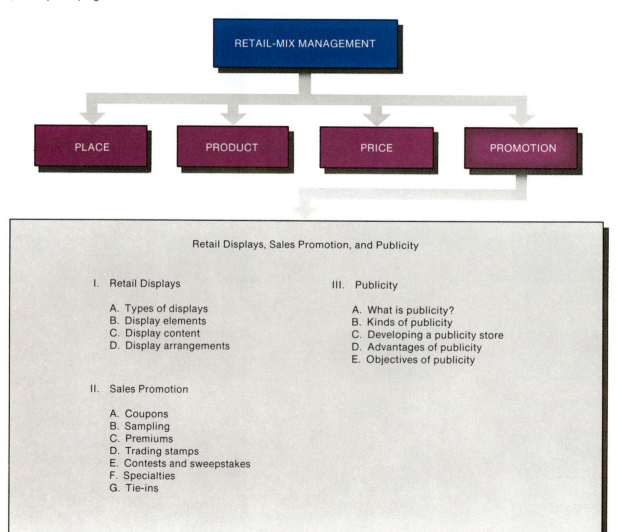

RETAIL-MIX MANAGEMENT

PLACE   PRODUCT   PRICE   PROMOTION

Retail Displays, Sales Promotion, and Publicity

I. Retail Displays

  A. Types of displays
  B. Display elements
  C. Display content
  D. Display arrangements

II. Sales Promotion

  A. Coupons
  B. Sampling
  C. Premiums
  D. Trading stamps
  E. Contests and sweepstakes
  F. Specialties
  G. Tie-ins

III. Publicity

  A. What is publicity?
  B. Kinds of publicity
  C. Developing a publicity store
  D. Advantages of publicity
  E. Objectives of publicity

"Merchandise displays must gain the attention of consumers, provide proper balance, be constructed in proper proportion, be hard-hitting, and convey their message quickly. The consumer only spends an average of 11 seconds observing a display."[1] In addition, retail displays are essential ingredients in creating the store's shopping atmospherics, because the sight, sound, touch, taste, and scent appeals are largely the result of in-store displays. Every business has a personality, and each display should contribute to expressing the store's personality: be it black and white Art Deco or soft and earthy Mom and Pop.[2] (Refer to the section on creating store image and buying atmosphere in Chapter 9.) Here we will discuss types of interior displays and their content and arrangements.

Types of Displays

Store interiors are the sums of all the displays designed to sell the retailer's merchandise. While retail displays can be classified in various ways, we shall identify four general types of displays: selection, special, point-of-purchase, and audiovisual.

Selection Displays

Nearly all the merchandise for which retailers rely on self-service and self-selection selling is presented to the consumer in the form of **selection displays**. These mass displays typically occupy rows of stationary aisle and wall units (shelves, counters, tables, racks, and bins) designed to expose the complete assortment of merchandise to the consumer. Selection display units are generally "open" to promote merchandise inspection. Their primary functions are to provide customer access to the store's merchandise and to facilitate self-service sales transactions. As a rule, retailers use selection displays to exhibit their normal, everyday assortments of convenience and shopping goods. Effective selection displays should present the merchandise in (1) logical selling or usage groupings; (2) a simple, well-organized arrangement; (3) a

A selection display

clean, neat condition; (4) an attractive, informative setting; and (5) a safe, secure state. Customer convenience and operational efficiency are the watchwords for good selection displays.

Special Displays

A **special display** is a notable presentation of merchandise designed to attract special attention and make a lasting impression on the consumer. Special displays use highly desirable in-store locations, special display equipment or fixtures, and distinctive merchandise.

Placing special displays in highly desirable locations ensures maximum exposure for the display and its merchandise, thereby significantly affecting the number of units sold.[3] End-of-aisles, counter tops, checkout stands, store entrances and exits, and freestanding units in high-traffic areas are all preferred locations for attracting special attention from shoppers. Unique combinations of display equipment (counters, tables, racks, shelves, bins, mobiles) and display fixtures (stands, easels, millinery heads, forms, set pieces) help create a dramatic setting that will attract consumer attention and build shopper interest. The choice of display equipment and fixtures depends on the merchandise, the amount of space available, and the effect sought.

A special display

Although store location and display equipment and fixtures are extremely important in constructing a special display, the key to successful display merchandising is the merchandise itself. Special displays highlight merchandise that can attract customers into the store, build the store's image, improve sales volume, or increase net profits. Special displays therefore are reserved for advertised, best-selling, high-margin, and high-fashion merchandise, together with product items suitable to impulse and complementary buying behavior. Merchandise selected for special displays should also lend itself to good display techniques, which create a favorable sight, sound, taste, touch, or scent appeal.

Point-of-Purchase Displays

A **point-of-purchase (POP) display** is a particular type of special display. Retailers make heavy use of POP materials to stimulate immediate purchase behavior. The POPs are often the first and last chance retailers and manufacturers have to tell customers about merchandise. The importance of POP displays is suggested by the fact that "80.7% of supermarket and drugstore shoppers make their final purchasing decisions in the store. Shoppers also say 60.4% of their supermarket purchases aren't planned."[4] Point-of-purchase displays include items such as counter displays, window displays, shelf extenders, grocery-cart ads, floor-stand displays, dumpbins, end-aisle stands, banners, shelf talkers, clocks, counter cards, sniff teasers, and video-screen displays. Point-of-purchase displays are designed to attract customer attention and interest, reinforce the store's creative theme, and fit in with the store's interior decoration.

In recent years, retailers have begun to "program" their on-site promotions. The idea is to stage a sequence of steps that lead the prospective customer from some point outside the store to the ultimate point of making a purchase decision. Grocers

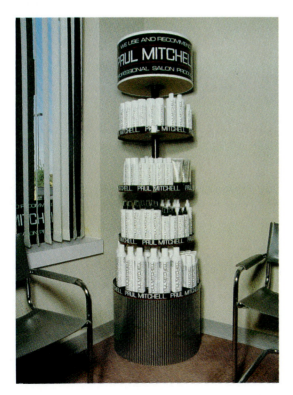

A point-of-purchase display

An audiovisual display

have been particularly active in using POP materials to increase their sales. Promotional materials such as handbills, bag stuffers, and window signs remind shoppers of what they saw advertised in the local newspapers. Counter decorations include hanging dummy products, manufacturers' signs, and price signs. To draw attention to special sales, some retailers use in-store microphones; K mart, for example, announces its "blue light specials" over a public-address system. Each K mart department is supposed to announce a "special sale" on an item for fifteen minutes each day. The purpose of this kind of promotion is to keep customers in the store to "shop around." K mart's experience has been that people will "hang around all day" to get a "blue light special." Thus, such POP promotion not only increases store traffic but maintains it for longer periods of time. Finally, POP displays make the store a more exciting and fun place to shop. This latter benefit can well mean the difference between a loyal customer or one that shops around.[5]

Audiovisual Displays

The trend in fashion retailing is to make a video statement by applying current technology to stimulate consumer purchases. Retailers now use **visual merchandising, audio merchandising,** and/or **audiovisual merchandising** to sell products. Three key applications of audiovisual merchandising are (1) to display the depth and breadth of product lines (e.g., Florsheim Express Shops can show all shoe sizes and styles); (2) to use kiosks to explain the benefits of different products (e.g., Best Products, a catalog showroom, uses kiosks to help merchandise electronic products); and (3) to provide customers with basic price information (e.g., customers at Zale's jewelers can view video displays to determine price and quality ranges before seeing a salesperson).[6] These display approaches use technology to "speak" to and to "show" the consumer available merchandise. Devices include *shelf talkers* (tape recordings describing the merchandise audibly); rear-screen projections (slide projectors that present wide-screen, color pictures of the merchandise and its use); and audiovisual displays (a combination of sound and videotape or slides to present the product's story). As technology changes, so will sales promotions.

Display Elements

To communicate the desired message effectively, the retailer must carefully consider and plan each element of a display. Display elements include the merchandise, shelf display areas or window display, props, colors, background materials, lighting, and signs.[7] The retailer must consider the contrast, repetition, motion, harmony, balance, rhythm, and proportion of each display to draw attention to it (see Figure 22–2).

Display Content

Display content is the type and amount of merchandise to be set off. Cluttered displays of unrelated merchandise attract little attention and are ineffective in stimulating customer interest. To ensure good display content, many retailers confine their efforts to one of three groupings.

Unit groupings of merchandise highlight a separate category of product items (e.g., shoes, shirts, cocktail dresses, or handbags). Unit groupings contain merchandise that is almost identical (e.g., five black leather handbags of different sizes) or closely related (e.g., three red leather handbags and five brown suede bags). **Related groupings** of merchandise are ensemble displays that present accessory items along with the featured merchandise; for example, a mannequin may be dressed in a matching sportswear outfit with sporting accessories (e.g., tennis racket and bag). The principal idea behind the inclusion of accessory items is to remind the customer

FIGURE 22–2
Developing an attractive display

Display elements must be evaluated to determine how well and if they attract and hold the attention of passersby.

Contrast is one way to attract attention. Contrast is achieved by using different colors, lighting, form (size and shape), lettering, or textures.

Repetition attracts consumer attention by duplicating an object to reinforce and strengthen the impression. By displaying 20 tennis rackets, the image is created of a store with a wide assortment of merchandise in that category.

Physical motion is a powerful attention getter, as is dominance. If an item is much larger than other items in a display, it will be the dominant item and will draw attention to the entire display.

Once attention has been harnessed, the next step is to direct that attention to the intended message. Harmony and graduation frequently are used to accomplish this.

Harmony refers to the unification of merchandise, lighting, props, shelf space, and showcards to create a pleasing effect. Balance, emphasis, rhythm, and proportion work to focus attention on the central point.

Formal balanced displays in which one side is duplicated by the other tend to produce feelings of dignity, neatness, and order. Informally balanced displays in which one side does not exactly match the other tend to generate excitement and are less stuffy.

Rhythm refers to the eye's path after initial contact with the display. The objective is to hold the eye until the entire display is seen.

Design specialists use vertical lines to create the image of height, strength, and dignity. Horizontal lines connote calmness, width, and sophistication; diagonal lines create action, and curved lines suggest continuity and femininity.

Proportion concerns the relative sizes of the display's various objects. Attention can be directed to the desired focal point by arranging items in a graduated pattern from the small to the large.

The proportion concept also involves the positioning of objects in patterns. Popular display patterns include pyramids, steps, zigzags, repetition, and mass.

The image of height and formality is created with pyramids, while the zigzag is a popular method of displaying clothing to create an aura of excitement.

Repetition arrangements are used primarily in shelf merchandising situations. Merchandise items are placed equidistant from one another in a straight, horizontal line.

The mass arrangement is the placement of a large quantity of merchandise in either neatly stacked lines or in jumbled dump bins to convey the image of a sale item.

Source: Ray Marquardt, "Merchandise Displays Are Most Effective When Marketing, Artistic Factors Combine," *Marketing News,* 16 August 1983, 3.

A unit grouping display

of a need for more than the featured item; in other words, the retailer is using suggestive selling. A display of either unit or related groupings should contain an odd number of product items. Consumers perceive an odd number of items as more intriguing; hence, the items attract more attention and create a more dramatic setting. When displaying an even number of merchandise items (e.g., a set of eight stemmed glasses), it is recommended that one item be set apart from the rest or differentiated in some other way (e.g., elevated).

   Theme groupings display merchandise according to a central theme or setting. Themes provide a focus in planning displays and are useful vehicles around which the five sensory appeals can be employed. The number of possible display themes is unlimited. For example, there are product themes ("Shoes complete the appearance"), seasonal themes ("Swing into spring"), patronage themes ("Cheaper by the dozen"), usage themes ("Mealtime magic"), occasion themes ("Along the bridal path"), color themes ("Pastel softness"), life-style themes ("The swinging singles set"), holiday themes ("Santa approved"), as well as themes based on historical, current, and special events.

A related grouping (ensemble) display

Display Arrangements

Display arrangement is organizing display merchandise into interesting, pleasing, and stimulating patterns. Haphazard arrangement of merchandise items can substantially reduce a display's effectiveness. Selection displays are simply arranged in some well-organized fashion, but special-display merchandise frequently is presented in one of four definite arrangement patterns: the pyramid, zig-zag, step, or fan arrangement. Figure 22–3 illustrates these patterns.

Pyramid arrangements are triangular displays of merchandise in vertical (stacked) or horizontal (unstacked) form. "The pyramid begins at a large or broad base and progresses up to an apex, or point, at the highest level."[8] The vertical pyramid can be two or three dimensional and is well suited to displaying boxed and canned merchandise; it also represents efficient use of space. The base of a horizontal pyramid is placed in the rear of the display to achieve the proper visual perspective. When displaying different-sized merchandise items, larger items are positioned at the base and the smallest item occupies the apex. Figure 22–3(a) illustrates the use of pedestal displayers arranged in a pyramid fashion—an effective arrangement pattern for window, counter, and table displays.

Zig-zag arrangements are modified pyramids that zig and zag their way to the apex of the display. No two display levels are at the same height. This arrangement

A theme display

is less monotonous than the pyramid; it is perceived to be more fluid and graceful, and perhaps more feminine. A zig-zag pattern of pedestal displayers (such as the one shown in Figure 22–3[b]) is especially appropriate for displaying women's jewelry, cosmetics, small apparel items, and shoes.

Step arrangements are essentially that: a series of steps. "Step arrangements lead the eye in a direct line; they begin at a low point on one side of a display area and progress directly to a higher point on the opposite side of that area."[9] Typically, step displays are constructed so that the base of each step increases in area (see Figure 22–3[c]); the larger base area is used to display accessory items, while the steps are used for the featured merchandise. The step arrangement is well suited to displaying a wide variety of merchandise.

Fan arrangements spread up and out from a small base, thereby directing the viewer's eyes upward and outward. Figure 22–3(d) illustrates this inverted-pyramid arrangement. The fan pattern is appropriate for displaying merchandise ranging from clothing goods to sporting goods.

SALES INCENTIVES

Retailers use the term *sales incentive* in many different ways. A common usage includes all promotional activities other than advertising, personal selling, and publicity as sales incentives or sales promotions. This text defines **sales incentive** as any direct or indirect nonpersonal inducement that offers extra value to the consumers. Retailers use these "extras" to supplement advertising, personal selling, and other merchandising activities. Typically, sales incentives are temporary offers extended to

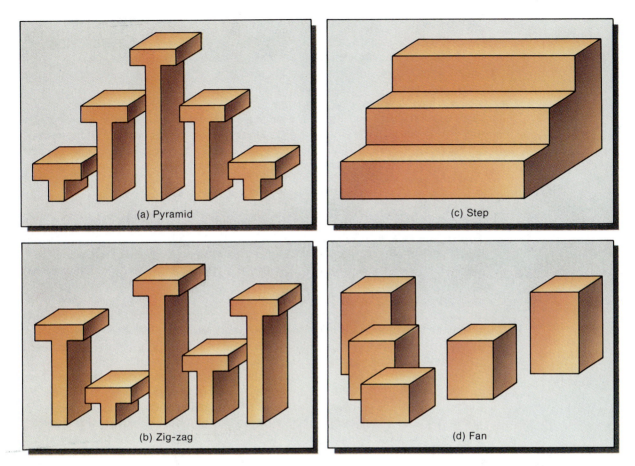

FIGURE 22–3
A gallery of display arrangements

the customer to stimulate an immediate response—the purchase of a good or service. Sales incentives are targeting activities in that they are directed at triggering particular customer actions.

Coupons

Coupons are manufacturer or retailer certificates that give consumers a price reduction on specific kinds of merchandise. Consumers obtain coupons from newspapers, magazines, mail, on and in packages, door-to-door, and in-store advertising supplements. **Couponing** attracts customers to the store. Shoppers come into the store to purchase the "bargain" but usually end up buying other merchandise as well.

Couponing is popular with consumers and is a relatively low-cost sales incentive program; however, it also has its problems. First, everyone is into the act. With billions of coupons distributed each year, it becomes more difficult to gain customer attention and to get "one up" on competitors. A second problem is in coupon distribution. In-pack coupons, for example, only create repurchases by current users, not new users, which is a major objective in couponing.[10] One study shows that 47 percent of frequent coupon redeemers use coupons for brands they would have bought anyway.[11] Third, misredemption (illegal redemption) is a major problem. Fourth, complex coupons (e.g., self-destruct, sticky, multiple purchase, and size-specification coupons) add significantly to handling time at checkout counters, and often consumers misunderstand these coupons.[12]

Sampling

Sampling involves giving the customer a free trial or sample of the product; it gets the customer involved with the product through hands-on experience. Trial use invites active participation, which can quickly lead to a customer purchase decision; however, only some products should be sampled. The kinds of products retailers can sample have low unit cost, are small in size, and are subject to high repeat sales. Supermarkets hand out samples of sausage; bakeries provide sample pastries; Hickory Farms places cheese and crackers at convenient points throughout its stores so customers can sample them. Sampling is generally quite expensive, but because it gives customers direct experience and involvement with the product, it is thus a powerful tool to induce purchases.

Premiums

A **premium** is a merchandise item given to the consumer free of charge or at a substantial price reduction as an inducement to purchase another product or to participate in an activity, or both. Essentially, a premium is a bonus or gift given to a qualified customer. A customer purchase is the most common way to qualify for a premium; however, premiums are sometimes given for visiting the store or participating in an activity (e.g., taste-testing a new product). Store visits and participation events are often referred to as "traffic-building premiums." Several types of premiums involve retailers with manufacturers in this kind of effort to create sales incentives: self-liquidating, direct or value pack, mail-in, and continuing premiums.

Self-liquidating premiums require the consumer to pay something for the premium; typically, the consumer must pay an amount sufficient to cover the costs associated with the premium. Successful self-liquidating premiums are merchandise items that usually cannot be obtained elsewhere, and their uniqueness makes them valued gifts that consumers perceive to be worth considerably more than what they have to pay for them. The cosmetic industry in concert with many department and specialty store retailers provides an excellent example of self-liquidating premium offers. These offers take the form of purchase with purchase (PWP) and gift with purchase (GWP) premiums, which account for a large percentage of cosmetic and fragrance sales.[13] These PWP and GWP premiums might consist of garment bags, overnight totes, sunglasses, billfolds, ties, and other apparel items complete with the insignias of the company or designer (e.g., Calvin Klein, Ralph Lauren, and others). Creating and maintaining customer sales and return trade was the goal of McDonald's offer of "Garfield" coffee cups for $.99 each time a customer purchased a breakfast item. The customer had to make several trips to McDonald's to get a full set of cups because a different cup was available each week for four weeks.

Direct premiums or value packs are free gifts given to the customer at the time of purchase. The gift can be (1) attached to the product package, "on packs"; (2) contained in the product package, "in packs"; (3) found adjacent to the product package, "near packs"; or (4) provided in special decorator packages with the product, "container-packs." To the extent that these direct premiums generate store traffic and ensure rapid product turnover, they are desirable additions to both the retailers' and manufacturers' sales incentive program. When direct premiums require additional shelf space, however (e.g., near-packs), special handling (e.g., on-packs), or result in other cost-generating activities, the retailer must closely evaluate the cost–benefit aspects.

Mail-in premiums require the customer to send in a proof-of-purchase to receive a free gift. This type of premium encourages first-time or repeat purchases;

however, given the extra effort required of the customer, it has limited acceptance on the part of the general consuming public. But if the retailer does not have to get involved with processing and handling the mail-in offer, this type of premium is still another weapon in a successful sales incentive arsenal.

Continuity premiums require the customer to make repeat purchases of products and services to benefit from the premium offer. This kind of premium is offered as part of a continuous, on-going sales incentive program. The customer's length and degree of involvement usually determines the value of the gift; longer and greater involvement results in bigger and better gifts. The most common type of continuity premiums are trading stamps. Sperry and Hutchinson (S&H) Green stamps and Quality Stamp Company are two organizations that are working to revive this once important sales incentive tool that enjoyed peak popularity in the 1960s.[14] Pressure-sensitive stamps, more convenient stamp collection books, and better gift selection catalogs are some of the improvements for enhancing the image of this kind of inducement and convincing both retailers and consumers to return to trading stamps as a buyer reward system.

Competing with trading stamps is a new type of continuity premium—the frequent buyer program. This format gives customers bonus points for each purchase, with the number of points corresponding to the amount of purchase. Zayre's, the discount store, has its "Frequent Z" program:

> Customers get 3,000 bonus points for joining the program, then 100 points for each dollar they spend in Zayre discount department stores. The points may be redeemed for gifts in the Frequent Z catalog. "There's just no points in shopping anywhere else" is the theme of TV spots. . . . The gift catalog, which is handled by a separate fulfillment house, includes such items as an Anne Klein quartz watch and a Simmons hide-a-bed. Consumers would have to rack up 7.8 million points for a trip to Hawaii.[15]

Sears is also experimenting with its version of a frequent buyer program; Bonus Club shoppers can get incentives ranging from $5 gift certificates to automobiles.[16]

Contests and Sweepstakes

Contests and **sweepstakes** are theme-based sales incentive programs designed to create a special event that generates customer involvement with the store and its merchandise. Contests are promotional activities in which participants compete for rewards; successful participants are selected on the basis of their skill in completing a particular task (e.g., designing a store advertisement or completing a puzzle).

Sweepstakes are promotions in which customers win prizes based on chance. For the sweepstakes to be legal, however, the customer cannot be required to risk money for a chance; the major requirement is that the customer fill out an entry form to have a chance to win. Sweepstakes involve pure chance and minimal effort for entrants. Because of relaxation in "games of chance" laws, more retailers are turning to sweepstakes in their sales promotion programs.

> The growth and variety of sweepstakes are endless. There is the "straight" sweepstakes, where the winning entry blank is pulled out of a crowded drum of hopefuls. And the "matching" sweepstakes, where numbers or symbols are matched to a preselected number or symbol.
>
> Then there is the "instant win" (rub-off or wash-off) variety of sweepstakes —the hottest item right now. And let us not forget the "programmed learning" type of sweepstakes, where the entrant is required to give back some information from a label, package or advertisement, with winners chosen from the "correct" entries.[17]

Specialty Advertising

The Specialty Advertising Association defines **specialty** advertising as a useful article of merchandise that is imprinted with an advertisement and given to the customer without obligation. Specialty items can range from inexpensive key chains to expensive travel bags. To be successful, a specialty should be useful, fashionable, and appropriate for the targeted consumer. A good rule for the retailer to remember about a specialty item is that the store's name will be on the item; hence, the item should be consistent with the store's image.

Tie-ins

Sales incentive **tie-ins** are another approach to attracting attention to a store's offerings. McDonald's, for example, tied in with Paramount Pictures to offer Star Trek meals: "children's meals in boxes with Star Trek designs on the outside and space-age plastic toys inside."[18] Such tie-ins can benefit both parties; in this case, McDonald's was "hitchhiking" on the potential success of the movie, Star Trek. Sears used a national television campaign to promote "its exclusive collection of children's clothing, bedding, watches, and plush animals tied to and coinciding with the opening of 'An American Tail,' Steven Spielberg's first animated film."[19] Successful tie-ins can generate excitement, enthusiasm, and sales, but if the tie-in (such as a movie) bombs, the retailer can suffer.

Tie-ins assume a variety of forms. Besides a tie-in with an entertainment event, tie-ins can occur in conjunction with national holidays, special occasions, sporting events, local celebrations, annual conventions, unusual events, and other products, to name but a few ways. The purpose of tie-ins is to capitalize on the excitement generated by momentary trends or events. They are by definition transient—how many people today would buy a coffee mug with a bicentennial decal (1776–1976) on it?

Tie-ins of complementary merchandise have several advantages:

- □ *Increased awareness.* By promoting two or more compatible pieces of merchandise, the retailer can attract more attention than by promoting a single piece of merchandise.
- □ *Increased readership.* Readership of advertising sales promotion literature will increase, particularly if there is a logical tie-in between the merchandise.
- □ *Reinforced image.* Where there are natural "go-togethers," the image of the store's merchandise can be reinforced because of the combined benefits the consumer will derive from using both pieces of merchandise together.
- □ *Cross-brand trial.* If customers are loyal to one brand of a store's merchandise, they are likely to try the complementary merchandise because of the "promotional marriage."
- □ *Cost-efficiency.* Retailers can save money by promoting tie-ins; that is, two or more pieces of merchandise can be promoted together, achieving a synergistic effect.

PUBLICITY

Publicity is one of the tools of public relations. It can be defined as positive or negative communication that is indirect, nonpersonal, is carried by a mass medium, and is neither paid for nor credited to an identified sponsor. A key concern to the retailer regarding publicity is that the firm has no control over *what* is said (the message), *how* it is said (the presentation), *to whom* it is said (the audience), and *how often* it is said (the message frequency). Nevertheless, publicity plays an important supportive role in enhancing and augmenting product and store advertising. "Publicity's nonpaid source lends a level of credibility unavailable to advertiser sponsored messages, producing a heightened potential for informative and persuasive impact."[20] Hence, it behooves the retailer to appreciate both the positive and negative results of good and bad publicity. A positive story can greatly enhance the retailer's image; on the other hand, that positive image can be negated by one incidence of negative publicity. Although retailers cannot control publicity, they can take steps to gain favorable publicity and to lessen the impact of negative publicity.

Kinds of Publicity

Publicity can be either planned or unplanned. **Planned publicity** means the retailer exercises some control over the news item. Regarding **unplanned publicity,** the retailer simply responds to the uncontrollable events as they occur. Planned publicity includes press releases, press conferences, photographs, letters to the editor, editorials, and special events (see Figure 22–4). Large retailers typically send out dozens of news releases about their stores and activities. Further, they use press conferences to describe major new events that might be of interest to the public. Pictures and

---

FIGURE 22–4
What makes an event "special"?

Special events don't necessarily equal participating in an auto show or sponsoring a rock tour—not all sponsorships are special events. As might be expected, the line between special events and other promotion techniques can be fuzzy. But, there are distinct characteristics common to all promotions that fall under the classification of special events:

- A special event is in most cases a leisure pursuit, either sports or something that fits within the broad definition of the arts.
- It involves some form of public participation on the part of the audience—attending a fest, competing in a triathlon—as opposed to seeing an ad or reading about a product.
- Unlike ad campaigns, which may run as long as they are effective, special events occur within a prescribed time frame and have a definite opening and closing.
- An event is independently legitimate; it can stand on its own merits apart from any sponsor. Furthermore, the event does not form part of the primary commercial function of the sponsoring body (but there is usually some link between the sponsoring organization and the event). In other words, horse races are not special events because they are the chief business of their sponsor, the track authority. So too, for sweepstakes, coupons and premiums. While they may be nifty promotions, they are created exclusively to step up direct sales of their sponsor's product and can not stand alone.

On the other hand, the New York City Marathon is a special event because it is an entity apart from sponsor Manufacturers Hanover Trust, and running is not the chief function of the bank.

- The sponsoring body of a special event expects a return on its investment. While foundations often support charitable and civic ventures, they rarely sponsor a special event.
- The bulk of publicity derived from a special event happens spontaneously, usually within an editorial, not an advertising, context. This is quite different from advertising where mentions are specifically placed and paid for.

Source: Reprinted with permission of *Advertising Age*, 18 April 1983. Copyright Crain Communications Inc.

drawings are useful for showing store-expansion plans, new equipment to better serve customers, and so forth; these are generally newsworthy items that bring attention to the retailer. These approaches to gaining favorable publicity are subject to the whims of the news media, because they select what they consider newsworthy. The media, however, do have space or time to fill, and persistence and continually disseminated media releases increase the likelihood of favorable coverage.

Developing a Publicity Story

To develop a publicity story, the retailer first must identify the *kinds* of stories the media accepts and the *criteria* they use to make decisions. This step gives retailers basic ideas on which to develop stories.

FIGURE 22–5
Guidelines for obtaining successful placement of publicity stories

1. **Know deadlines**. Time governs every newspaper. News events should be scheduled, whenever possible, to accommodate deadlines.
2. **Generally write, don't call.** Reporters are barraged by deadlines. They are busiest right around deadline time, late afternoon for morning newspapers and morning for afternoon papers. Thus, it's preferable to mail or messenger news releases rather than trying to explain them over the telephone. Also, follow-up calls to reporters to "make sure you got our release" should be avoided. If reporters are unclear on a certain point, they'll call to check.
3. **Direct the release to a specific person or editor.** Newspapers are divided into departments—business, sports, style, entertainment, and the like. The release directed to a specific person or editor has a greater chance of being read than one addressed simply to "editor."
4. **Make personal contact.** Knowing a reporter may not result in an immediate story, but it can pay residual dividends. Those who know the local weekly editor or the daily, city editor have an advantage over colleagues who don't. Also, when a reporter uses your story idea, follow up with a note of commendation—particularly on the story's accuracy.
5. **Don't badger.** Newspapers are generally fiercely independent about the copy they use. Even a major advertiser will usually fail in getting a piece of puffery published. Badgering an editor about a certain story is bad form. So is complaining excessively about the treatment given a certain story. Worst of all, it achieves little to act outraged when a newspaper chooses not to run a story.
6. **Use "exclusives" sparingly.** Sometimes public relations people promise "exclusive" stories to particular newspapers. The exclusive promises one newspaper a "scoop" over its competitors. For example, practitioners will frequently arrange to have a visiting executive interviewed by only one local newspaper. While the chances of securing a story are heightened by the promise of an exclusive, there is a risk of alienating the other papers. Thus, the exclusive should be used sparingly.
7. **When you call, do your own calling**. Reporters and editors generally don't have assistants. Most do not like to be kept waiting by a secretary calling for the boss. Public relations professionals should make their own initial and follow-up calls. Letting a secretary "handle" a journalist can alienate a good news contact.

Source: Fraser P. Seitel, *The Practice of Public Relations,* 2nd ed. (Columbus, OH: Merrill, 1984), 340–42.

Stories that depict new and unusual events, store innovations, improvements in working conditions, new store openings, and stories that are currently important to the public often attract the interest of the news media. Publicity must also be newsworthy, somewhat unusual, appeal to a broad cross section of the public, and must be truthful. Publicity stories are more effective if they are dramatic or emotional and if they show action or human interest through photographs and illustrations.

Retailers increase the chance of successfully placing news releases and other publicity items if they adapt to the operational methods and personal references of the targeted media. Figure 22–5 lists guidelines for successfully placing news stories with newspapers. Most of the guidelines are equally important when dealing with magazines, radio, and television personnel.

SUMMARY

Visual merchandising, sales incentives, and publicity are effective retail promotional tools. They stimulate quick customer action to purchase, and they influence customer attitudes toward and images of the store and its merchandise.

As in-store visual presentations of the merchandise, retail displays assume a key role in creating a shopping atmosphere and enhancing the consumer's buying mood. Depending on their objectives, retailers use a variety of methods to present merchandise, including selection, special, point-of-purchase, and audiovisual displays. To ensure effective displays, retailers plan merchandise exhibits by controlling content (unit, related, and theme groupings) and arrangements (pyramid, zig-zag, step, and fan patterns).

Coupons, sampling, premiums, contests, sweepstakes, specialties, and tie-ins are among the many devices retailers use to communicate with customers about their store and their merchandise. Sales incentive approaches are limited only by the retailer's imagination. With ongoing technological innovations, businesses are creating growing numbers of sales incentive tools to stimulate customer interest in their merchandise.

Publicity is another important part of a retailer's promotion program. Good publicity can bring attention to a retailer and its merchandise and help build a good store reputation and sales. Bad publicity can ruin a retailer. A retailer therefore must learn how to manage its publicity.

KEY TERMS AND CONCEPTS

audio merchandising

audiovisual display

contests

continuity premiums

couponing

direct premiums

fan arrangements

mail-in premiums

planned publicity

point-of-purchase (POP) display

premiums

publicity

pyramid arrangements

related groupings

sales incentives

sampling

selection display

self-liquidating premiums

special display

specialties

step arrangements

sweepstakes

theme groupings

tie-ins

unit groupings

unplanned publicity

visual merchandising

zig-zag arrangements

REVIEW QUESTIONS

1. What merchandising objectives might a retailer achieve through in-store displays?
2. What is the primary function of a selection display?
3. Special displays should be reserved for what type of merchandise?
4. Identify the types of items that are appropriate for a point-of-purchase display.
5. What display elements should the retailer consider in creating attention-getting displays? Briefly explain each element.
6. Describe the three types of display content and give an example of each type.
7. Which four arrangement patterns are used in store displays? Describe each arrangement.
8. What is a sales incentive?
9. What is the primary purpose of sampling?
10. Compare and contrast the various types of premiums.
11. What is the difference between a contest and a sweepstakes? Describe the four types of sweepstakes retailers use.
12. Identify the advantages of tie-in promotions.
13. What doesn't the retailer control in publicity-related stories?

ENDNOTES

1. Ray Marquardt, "Merchandise Displays Are Most Effective When Marketing, Artistic Factors Are Combined," *Marketing News,* 19 Aug. 1983, 3.
2. Dinah Witchel, "NRMA Honors Joe Cicio," *Stores* (June 1986): 52.
3. Jean Paul Gagnon and Jane T. Osterhaus, "Research Note: Effectiveness of Floor Displays on the Sales of Retail Products," *Journal of Retailing* 61 (Spring 1985): 115.
4. Lisa Phillips, "POP Enriched by Impulse Food Buying," *Advertising Age,* 17 Nov. 1986, S-25.
5. Joe Agnew, "POP Displays Are Becoming a Matter of Consumer Convenience," *Marketing News,* 9 Oct. 1987, 14.
6. Cyndee Miller, "Trend in Fashion Retailing Is to Make a Video Statement," *Marketing News,* 4 Dec. 1987, 14.
7. Marquardt, "Merchandise Displays," 3.
8. See Kenneth Mills and Judith Paul, *Visual Merchandising* (Englewood Cliffs, NJ: Prentice-Hall, 1983): 37.
9. Ibid.
10. Kevin Higgins, "Couponing's Growth Is Easy to Understand," *Advertising Age,* 8 Sept. 1984, 12.
11. Marji Simon, "Survey Probes Strengths, Weaknesses of Promotions," *Marketing News* (June 1984): 4.
12. P. Rajan Varadarajan, "Issue of Efficient Coupon Handling and Processing Pits Manufacturers Against Retailers, Coupon Clearinghouses," *Marketing News* (September 1984): 13.
13. See Dottie Enrico, "GWP and PWP: Pros and Cons," *Stores* (September 1986): 63–68.
14. Diane Schneidman, "Trading Stamps Face Redemption as Viable Marketing Tool," *Marketing News,* 13 Feb. 1987, 1, 28.
15. Janet Meyers, "Zayre Will Target Frequent Buyers in Bonus Program," *Advertising Age,* 14 Oct. 1987, 7.
16. Francine Schwadel, "Sears Plans to Offer Promotional Prizes to Frequent Buyers," *Wall Street Journal,* 1 March 1988.
17. Eileen Norris, "Everyone Will Grab at a Chance to Win," *Advertising Age,* 22 Aug. 1983, 10.
18. "McDonald's Plans Next Film Tie," *Advertising Age,* 11 Feb. 1980, 44.
19. Sara E. Stern, "Sears Line Tails New Spielberg Film," *Advertising Age,* 3 Nov. 1986, 33.
20. Daniel L. Sherrell and R. Eric Reidanback, "A Consumer Response Framework for Negative Publicity: Suggestions for Response Strategies," *Akron Business and Economic Review* 17 (Summer 1986): 37.

Achabal, Dale D., McIntyre, Shelby H., Bell, Cheryl H., and Tucker, Nancy. "The Effect of Nutrition P-O-P Signs On Consumer Attitudes and Behavior." *Journal of Retailing* 63 (Spring 1987): 9–24.

Babakus, Emin, Cunningham, William, and Tat, Peter. "An Examination of Some Attitudinal Dimensions of Coupon Redemption." In *Marketing in an Environment of Change, Proceedings,* edited by R. L. King, 71–74. Southern Marketing Association, 1986.

Chapman, Randall G. "Assessing the Profitability of Retailer Couponing with a Low-Cost Field Experiment." *Journal of Retailing* 62 (Spring 1986): 19–40.

Dhebar, Anirudh, Neslin, Scott A., and Quelch, John A. "Developing Models for Planning Retail Sales Promotions: An Application to Automobile Dealerships." *Journal of Retailing* 63 (Winter 1987): 333–64.

"Display Makers Serve Two Masters." *Marketing News,* 7 Dec. 1984, 15, 19.

Gagnon, Jean Paul, and Osterhaus, Jane T. "Effectiveness of Floor Displays on the Sales of Retail Products." *Journal of Retailing* 61 (Spring 1985): 104–16.

George, Richard J., and Lord, John B. "Alternative Retailer Couponing Strategies: Consumer Reactions and Marketing Implications." In *Developments in Marketing Science, Proceedings,* edited by J. D. Lindquist, 306–10. Academy of Marketing Science, 1984.

Higgins, Kevin. "Couponing's Growth Is Easy to Understand: It Works." *Marketing News,* 28 Sept. 1984, 12–13.

Jenkins, Roger L., and Samiee, Saeed. "Retail Patronage Profile: Rebate Users versus Non-Users." In *Developments in Marketing Science, Proceedings,* edited by J. M. Hawes and G. B. Glisan, 291–95. Academy of Marketing Science, 1987.

Kopp, Robert J. "Premiums Provide Great Impact, But Little Glamour." *Marketing News,* 7 June 1985, 12, 14.

Marlow, Nancy D., and Marlow, Edward K. "Coupons: A Review of the Literature." In *Marketing Comes of Age, Proceedings,* edited by David M. Klein and Allen E. Smith, 149–52. Southern Marketing Association, 1984.

Massey, Tom K., Jr., and Engelbrecht, James W. "The Semantic Effect of Shelf Signs on Product and Store Perception: A Preliminary Investigation." In *Marketing: The Next Decade, Proceedings,* edited by D. M. Klein and A. E. Smith, 232–34. Southern Marketing Association, 1985.

Moore, H. Frazier, and Kalupa, Frank B. *Public Relations: Principles, Cases, and Problems.* 9th ed. Homewood, IL: Richard D. Irwin, 1985.

Moriarty, Mark M. "Retail Promotional Effects on Intra- and Inter-brand Sales Performance." *Journal of Retailing* 61 (Fall 1985): 27–47.

Pegler, Martin M. *The Language of Store Planning and Display.* New York: Fairchild Books, 1984.

Pegler, Martin M. *Visual Merchandising and Display.* New York: Fairchild Books, 1984.

Reibstein, David J., and Traver, Phyllis A. "Factors Affecting Coupon Redemption Rates." *Journal of Marketing* 46 (Fall 1982): 102–13.

Reiling, Lynn. "Video Shock Gives Retailer Low-Cost Promotional Boost." *Marketing News,* 1 Feb. 1985, 22, 24.

Roth, Laszlo. *Display Design.* Englewood Cliffs, NJ: Prentice-Hall, 1980.

Schababb, George A. "The Trial Effectiveness of Coupons." *The Nielsen Researcher* 1 (Summer 1987): 14–19.

Schmitz, Robert A. "The Long-Term Relationship Between Retail Trade Promotion and Brand Sales Share." *The Nielsen Researcher* 1 (Summer 1987): 8–13.

Seitel, Fraser P. *The Practice of Public Relations.* Columbus, OH: Merrill, 1984.

Spalding, Lewis A. "Taped for Success." *Stores* (May 1985): 23–24, 29–30, 32.

Varadarajan, P. Rajan. "Horizontal Cooperative Sales Promotion: A Framework for Classification and Additional Perspectives." *Journal of Marketing* 50 (April 1986): 61–73.

RELATED READINGS

PART SIX
Additional Considerations: Judging and Exploring Opportunities

23

Objectives

☐ Identify the unique characteristics that distinguish service retailers from goods retailers.

☐ Describe the importance of service retailers in our nation's economy.

☐ Discern and discuss the various types of service retailers and their operations.

☐ Explain the factors involved in offering the right service in the right way in the right place at the right time at the right price by the right appeal.

☐ Use the strategic service vision to integrate both the service retailers' external (customer) and internal (employee) functions.

Service Retailers: Exploring Growth Opportunities

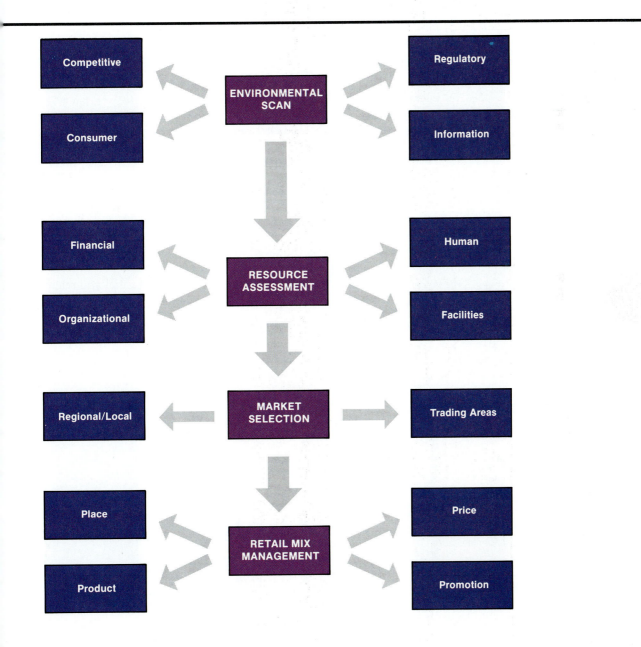

T he retailing of services involves most of the same problems and decisions associated with the retailing of goods. Many of the merchandising and operating strategies and tactics discussed in the previous twenty-two chapters therefore are equally applicable to service retailers, with appropriate modifications. This chapter describes the nature and types of service retailing, identifies its distinguishing characteristics, and discusses the issues surrounding the development of appropriate service blends and integration of marketing and operating strategies.

THE NATURE OF SERVICE RETAILING

What is a **service**? The definition of service is rather illusive because of the concept's multifaceted nature. Depending on the environmental and temporal context, a service could be many different activities to different people at different times. There is no standard or commonly accepted definition of service within the context of business or retailing operations. Nevertheless, Figure 23–1 attempts to illustrate the multifaceted nature and complex, interactive character of retail services. As shown, a retail service can be any of the following:

- ☐ An intangible process that is provided to inform a client (e.g., a lawyer's advice on what and what not to say in court)
- ☐ A variable performance that is orchestrated to entertain a patron or fan (e.g., a concert by The Boss, Bruce Springsteen)
- ☐ An inseparable procedure that is provided to benefit a patient (e.g., a cardiovascular surgeon who performs open-heart surgery)
- ☐ A perishable event that is created to amuse a customer (e.g., a water slide at an amusement park)
- ☐ A profitable task that is developed to satisfy a traveller (e.g., a slot machine in the lobby of a hotel)
- ☐ A communicable act that is produced to educate a student (e.g., an interesting lecture by your professor)
- ☐ A host of any other combination of elements and examples that you might think of

It is obvious, then, that retail services can be defined and characterized along many different dimensions.

FIGURE 23–1
What is a service?

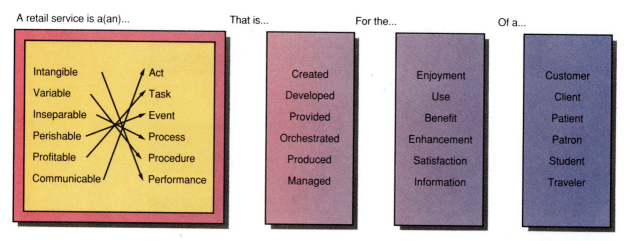

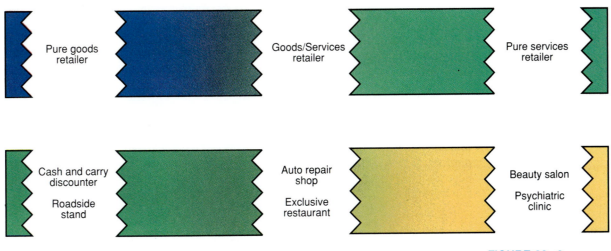

FIGURE 23–2
The goods–service continuum for ultimate consumers

Who provides services? Individuals, groups, and organizations are all service providers. Although we tend to think of services as face-to-face interactions between individuals (e.g., doctor–patient, consultant–client, student–tutor), some services are essentially the collective efforts of a group (e.g., jazz quartet, car wash attendants, basketball team) or an organization (hospital, museum, employment agency). The customer's particular situation and need determines whether an individual or collective effort is required to develop the service package.

How do **service retailers** differ from **goods retailers**? Goods retailers emphasize physical objects; service retailers emphasize "people, ideas, and information instead of things."[1] There is no clear distinction between goods and service retailers; rather, "it is generally accepted that there is a continuous spectrum running from a pure good to a pure service. Many goods companies are building service related benefits into their projects and many service companies deliver goods as part of the bundle of benefits they provide to consumers."[2] Figure 23–2 illustrates the goods–services continuum for the ultimate consumer.

On the **pure goods** ends of the continuum are retailers who provide no services whatever. One example might be the roadside vegetable stand that doesn't even provide a formal parking area; another example is the farmer's market that requires customers to bring their own containers and harvest their own products. As a point of fact, even retailers who emphasize goods retailing usually provide essential services necessary to successful operation of business (e.g., parking, bagging, and store hours).

At the other end of the continuum are primary-service retailers, which concentrate on rendering a service; the core of the business is a service. Like goods retailers, primary-service retailers often supplement their core-service offering with both complementary services and goods (e.g., a psychiatrist who provides medication for the patient and bills the patient at the end of the month).

At the midpoint of the continuum (see Figure 23–2) are retail businesses that have an equal or near-equal emphasis on goods and services. A special dining occasion is special because of the quality and presentation of the food, the attentiveness and courtesy of the waiter, and the atmospherics and comfort of the room and table. When an individual patronizes a fast-food restaurant like McDonald's, is it for good food or fast service? It depends on the circumstances—with or without children, seeking a quick lunch or a leisure dinner.

THE IMPORTANCE OF SERVICES

How important are services? In many respects, services represent the most important part of our nation's economy. "Service is no longer an industrial by-product, a sector that generates no wealth but 'simply moves money around' as some economists have scoffed. . . . Service has become a powerful economic engine in its own right—the fast track of the new American economy."[3] More than 60 million Americans are employed in one of the many service sectors; by 1995, total service sector employment will be 75 million. "Nine out of 10 jobs created between now and 1995 are expected to be in services."[4] When one considers that the combined total output of all the various service sectors accounts for nearly 70 percent of the gross national product, the importance of services becomes quite obvious.[5] The United States has become the first nation to have a predominantly service-oriented economy, and there is every reason to believe the boom in the service economy will continue.

THE TYPES OF SERVICE RETAILERS

The complex, multifaceted nature of services allows an equally complex, multifaceted classification system. Like goods retailers, service retailers can be classified according to the character of the service, its organizational structure and operating characteristics, the type of channel relationships and level of integration, the firm's size and ownership arrangements, and the type and degree of customer contact. By whatever criterion we group and identify service retailers, a mutually exclusive classification system is impossible. For our purposes, this chapter examines two of the more common schemes based on character of the service offered and the operating characteristics.

Services Offered

The U.S. Department of Commerce, through the Bureau of Census, classifies services-oriented activities into four major categories: (1) Transportation, Communication, and Public Utilities; (2) Finance, Insurance, and Real Estate; (3) Public Administration; and (4) Services. The first three categories are self-explanatory, but the services category requires further explanation; it is broken down as follows:

- □ *Lodging places*—hotels, motels, rooming and boarding houses, sporting and recreational camps, trailer parks and camp sites
- □ *Personal services*—laundry and dry cleaners, linen and diaper service, carpet and upholstery cleaning, photographic studios, beauty and barber shops, shoe repair, funeral homes and crematoriums, reducing salons and health clubs, tax services, and other personal services
- □ *Business services*—advertising, credit reporting and collections, blueprinting and photocopying, commercial photography, art and graphics, cleaning and maintenance services, employment agencies, computer, data processing, research and development, management and administrative, public relations, security services, equipment rental or leasing, testing laboratories, and other business services
- □ *Automotive services*—car, truck, trailer and recreational vehicle rentals, auto and truck repairs, parking facilities, car washes
- □ *Repair services*—radio, TV, appliances, and furniture repair, farm machinery, lawn and garden equipment, and watch, clock and jewelry repair
- □ *Motion pictures*—motion picture production and distribution
- □ *Amusement and recreation services*—dance group halls and studios, live theaters, radio and TV production, symphony orchestras, opera companies, music organizations and presentations, sporting establishments and clubs,

golf courses and amusement parks, carnivals and circuses, museums and art galleries, and other entertainment and attractions
- ☐ *Health services*—offices of health professionals, medical and dental labs, and outpatient care facilities
- ☐ *Legal services*—offices of lawyers and other legal aid services
- ☐ *Educational services*—libraries, business and vocational schools, schools, and other educational services
- ☐ *Social services*—job training and rehabilitation, child day-care, residential care, and individual and family social services
- ☐ *Noncommercial institutions*—noncommercial museums, art galleries, and botanical and zoological gardens
- ☐ *Membership organizations*—business, professional, civic, social, and fraternal organizations
- ☐ *Miscellaneous services*—architectural, engineering, surveying, accounting, auditing, scientific, and research organizations

For a more detailed description and classification of the service categories, check the most recent *Census of Service Industries* in your local school library.

Operating Characteristics

Service retailers can be classified on their degree of reliance on equipment in performing the service and on the level of skill required by the service provider.[6] As seen in Figure 23–3, *equipment-based service retailers* rely heavily on equipment, and skill levels range from a totally automated service provider (e.g., automatic teller machines) to highly skilled airline pilots. *People-based service retailers* are highly

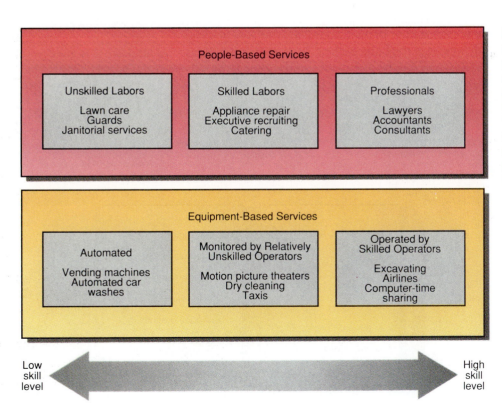

FIGURE 23–3

Classifying service retailers: Based on operating characteristics (source: Based on Dan R. E. Thomas, "Strategy Is Different in Service Businesses," *Harvard Business Review*" [July–August 1978], 161)

dependent on an individual to perform the service; that individual may be an un-skilled provider (e.g., janitor) or a highly skilled professional (e.g., surgeon).

THE RIGHT SERVICE BLEND

Understanding the unique characteristics inherent in services is prerequisite to developing successful marketing plans. As is the case with goods retailers and the right merchandising blend (see Chapter 1), service retailers must develop a service blend that is right for their customers. Figure 23–4 identifies the six ingredients of the **right service** blend and the major goal of each ingredient. This discussion reviews the major issues facing the service retailer and includes examples of unique and successful applications within the service industry.

Offering The Right Service: Add Tangibility

If you can see, hear, smell, touch, and taste what you have purchased, it is more a good than a service; if you cannot see, hear, smell, touch, and taste your purchase, it is more a service than a good. "It is whether the essence of what is being bought is tangible or intangible that determines its classification as a good or a service."[7] Physical features (size, shape, workmanship, etc.) determine to a considerable extent how well a good will function; one can evaluate these features before making a purchase. A service is not distinguished by physical features; hence, consumers have a difficult time judging the service before making the purchase, and in many cases, they have little or no tangible evidence to take away with them to show they have made a purchase or gained something of ongoing utility. Memories from a concert, ideas from a lecture, impressions from a funeral, and excitement from a game are not tangible. Thus a major marketing problem for every service retailer is to add a greater degree of **tangibility** to the firm's services.

At the center of every demand for a service is the core benefit or benefits sought by the consumer. In the financial investments industry, for example, the investor at any one time might be looking for investment security, opportunity, direction, convenience, or special treatment (see Figure 23–5). Whatever the sought benefit, the service provider must find some way to "tangibilize" the offer—to help the customer visualize and mentally grasp the core service concept. The service offering can be made tangible by (1) providing representations of the service, (2) creating physical and mental symbols for the service, (3) developing name or brand recognition for businesses or service lines, and (4) adding extra peripheral services or supplementary goods.

FIGURE 23–4
The right service blend—Ingredients and goals

Offering the right service...	Add tangibility
In the right way...	Control variability
In the right place...	Bridge inseparability
At the right time...	Overcome perishability
At the right price...	Enhance profitability
By the right appeal...	Increase communicability

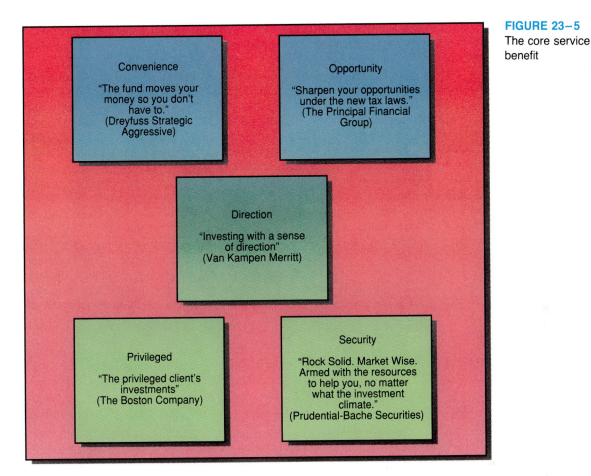

FIGURE 23–5
The core service benefit

A *visual representation* of the service and its positive attributes (benefits) can notably enhance the tangibility of the service offer. An architect who provides a scale model of the proposed building or facility has created a tangible substitution for design ideas and concepts that might not otherwise be appreciated or understood. When that same architect provides a complete set of architectural plans and specifications, the consumer has sufficient information to make a good judgment and correct decisions before, during, and after the purchase. Examples of visual concept representations are (1) an information systems analyst's schematic drawing of a proposed information flow, (2) a management consultant's organization chart demonstrating the reporting relationships (line and staff) within an organization, (3) an interior design specialist's sketches illustrating a room layout, and (4) a professor's diagram (handout) portraying a concept or idea. These examples not only are visual, but they also provide the customer with something to hold.

Symbols, both *physical* and *mental,* can be used to achieve tangibility of a service and its benefits. A classic example of physical symbolization is the "plastic credit card"; it represents credit (i.e., money and purchasing power) and a whole lot more (*status*—plain, silver, gold cards; *convenience*—cash, check, charge cards; and *security*—limited liability and cashless crime target). Mental symbols can be equally effective in creating service-offering tangibility. "Hands (Allstate), rocks (Prudential), umbrellas (Traveler's), and blankets (Nationwide) are used to more effectively communicate what insurance can provide people; they are devices used to make the service more easily grasped mentally."[8] The American "eagle," the Christian "cross," and the "scales" of justice are three examples of symbols that may be associated with both physical and mental imagery.

Service identification and differentiation often depend on linking a specific image or concept with a specific brand name. Adding tangibility through *name association* is the focus of this tactic. Names can be associated with service type, quality, convenience, cost (price), status, and a host of other identities. Consider the associations with these service names and brands: child care (Kinder-Care and LaPetite Academy), auto care (Jiffy Lube and Grease Monkey), home care (Molly Maid and Tailor-Maid), health care (MetLife and Kaiser-Permanente), emergency health care (Rapid Response and Med Center), car rental (Budget and Nationwide), automatic teller machines (Green Machine and Money Station), air travel (American Airlines and Trans World Airlines), freight transportation (Overnite and Roadway)—the potential list of service branding examples is almost endless. A variation of the service branding strategy is to offer new services in association with a well-known name. Sears, for example, has created a financial services conglomerate in association with its retail operations. Sears has also branched into insurance (Allstate), real estate (Coldwell Banker), stock brokerage (Dean Witter Reynolds), and credit card (Discover). Bank One, a large financial institution in Ohio, is experimenting with a financial services superstore that includes full-range banking, insurance, real estate, and brokerage services.

A more tangible service can be created through *service-line extensions*—adding extra peripheral services or supplementary goods. SAS advertises itself as "the business airline" with a focus on transcontinental flights to Europe. In the copy of a recent advertisement in *Business Week*, SAS has made tangible its basic service, air transportation, using both extra services and goods. The ad copy reads as follows:

> **SAS EuroClass.** It's the intercontinental business class with a style all its own. In the interest of everyone's comfort, we've removed a whole row of seats. Our cabins are smaller and more intimate, but you get more space, more legroom and seats that recline 33% further. And, for the first time, you get a choice. You can either enjoy the best traditional service—with a leisurely meal, a movie and plenty of attention. Or you can opt for a new way of flying in our secluded sleep/work class cabin. By night, it's almost like home. After we've served you a quick meal, we'll bed you down with proper sheets. Home comforts, indeed. We do everything short of singing you a lullaby. (That might disturb the peace.) There's no smoking in this cabin. And no movie. We won't even bother you with breakfast unless you ask for it. By day, the cabin is an "office in the sky." We'll give you what you need to do some work—everything from overhead film to typewriters. We'll even give you peace and quiet. If you need something we'll be there. Otherwise, we won't bother you. We believe that this kind of choice is the future of long-distance flying. So why not enjoy tomorrow's way of flying today? And tonight, too, for that matter.

In the Right Way: Control Variability

Services tend to be people-oriented activities on both the production and consumption side of the service-exchange process. As a result of the people-intensive nature of this process, service providers have considerable latitude in deciding and providing various service levels; services can range from totally standardized to totally customized activities. For example, a college course in business administration can range from the totally customized independent study to the highly standardized mass classroom lecture (see Figure 23–6). Whatever level of service is selected, the service retailer must offer service in the **right way**—must control the process to ensure that

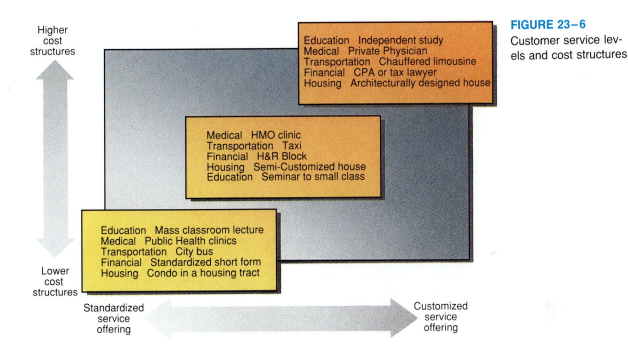

FIGURE 23-6

Customer service levels and cost structures

the level of service matches the value of the service. Which is more valuable as an educational experience: a mass lecture, a seminar, or an independent course? What does each course cost the student? Does the service level equal the value level? In these cases, controlling **variability** means finding a match between customer service levels and customer cost structures.

The quality and consistency of services can also vary considerably because of the various skill levels and degrees of automation employed in the production and delivery of a service. Adding to the degree of variability are the personal attributes and attitudes of the service provider and how these are conducted in providing service (e.g., the doctor's bedside manner, the courtesy of the hotel bell captain, or the efficiency of the bank teller). Controlling service variability in this case requires that management ensure customer satisfaction by first ensuring employee satisfaction through high motivation and constructive training. Good personnel management is critical to successful retail service operations. (This issue is elaborated on in the last section of this chapter.)

In the Right Place: Bridge Inseparability

Inseparability is the typical exchange mode in the service industry; that is, under typical conditions a service is produced and consumed simultaneously (e.g., a lecture by a professor, a cleaning by a dental hygienist, and an actress's live performance)—the right place is anywhere the provider and consumer are together. Simultaneous production and consumption means that the service provider is often physically present when consumption occurs.[9] In cases where service production and consumption can be separated, intermediaries (service agents) can facilitate the exchange process. Depending on the degree of inseparability of production and consumption, service retailers can use either a direct- or indirect-channel delivery system. Service-delivery system options are shown in Figure 23-7.

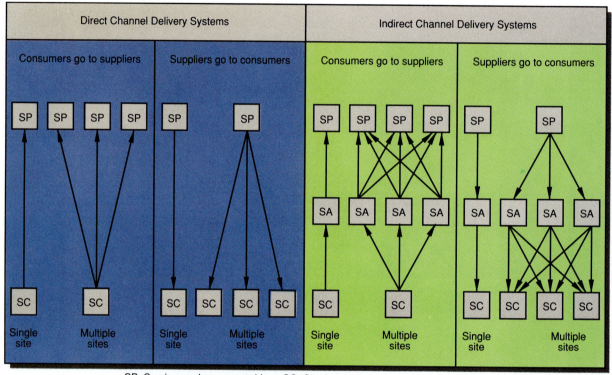

SP=Service producer or provider   SC=Service consumer   SA=Service agent

FIGURE 23–7
Types of service delivery systems

The *direct-channel delivery system* is a one-on-one relationship between service producer and service consumer. It is used when the service cannot be separated from the producer. Direct-channel delivery options (see Figure 23–7) include consumer to supplier and supplier to consumer channels.

The *consumer to supplier channel* (1) requires the consumer to go to a single site for the service (e.g., hospital for surgery) or (2) allows the consumer to select one of several sites (e.g., emergency medical care chain). The *supplier to consumer channel* (1) delivers the service to a single site (e.g., home lawn care) or (2) provides the service at any one of several locations (e.g., tailoring service at home, office, or club).

The *indirect-channel delivery system* involves a facilitating agent between producer and consumer. It is used when the service can be separated from the producer. Like direct channels, the service-exchange process can be initiated by the consumer's going to the producer or the producer's going to the consumer (see Figure 23–7); single and multiple outlets also are found within the indirect channel option. A representative sample of common service intermediaries associated with indirect delivery systems includes travel, ticket, and employment agents and stock, real estate, and insurance brokers. A travel agent with a single location may have only one option in selecting an airline (e.g., a feeder airline) when booking a flight from one small airport to another. The same agent or an agent with several locations has multiple options (airlines), however, when booking flights between New York and Chicago. A service supplier (local symphony orchestra) may elect to sell tickets through (1) an exclusive ticket sales agent with one (e.g., downtown) location, (2) an exclusive ticket sales agent with several ticket outlets, or (3) several ticket sales agents who may have one or more outlets.

At the Right Time: Overcome Perishability

Neither time nor a service can be put into storage and carried as inventory. The value (revenue-producing abilities) of services is defined temporally; a service is offered at a particular time. After that **right time** has passed without the service being used, the value of that service is lost forever. Classic examples of service **perishability** are described this way: "What is the value of an empty airplane seat on yesterday's flight or the unused appointment time because of a no-show?" Fluctuating demand is a key contributing factor to the high degree of service perishability; when demand stabilizes, the perishable character of services is greatly reduced. Offering the right services at the right time requires service retailers to strive to balance and synchronize their supply of services to the demand for their services. Demand—supply synchronization can be accomplished by adjusting demand, adjusting supply, or adjusting both demand and supply.

Adjusting and synchronizing the demand for a service retailer's output might be achieved by means of the following:

Incentive systems

Reservation systems

Reminder systems

Punishment systems

Incentive systems can shift demand from peak times to off-peak periods. Incentives take the form of (1) "lower prices" for lower demand periods (e.g., afternoon movie or late-night flight); (2) "quantity discounts" for patronage during off periods (e.g., two-nights' lodging for the price of one night during the weekend); (3) "product extras" for off-peak service (e.g., complimentary dessert for the early-bird dinner); and (4) "service extras" to reshape demand patterns (free late-fall cleanup with each annual summer lawn-care program). *Reservation systems* can schedule supply to meet customer demand to maximize the service provider's output and to minimize customer uncertainty and confusion. Doctors, dentists, hair stylists, and auto care centers are but a few examples of service retailers who schedule their time carefully and fully. *Reminder systems* are used to contact customers immediately before scheduled service time to verify day and time of appointment and to avoid any perishable "down time" for the service retailer. Reminders usually are conducted the day before the appointment. *Punishment systems* charge customers for missed appointments or appointments that were cancelled too late for rescheduling the service-provider's time. Full and partial charges might be levied.

There are several tactics for altering supply capacities to better match demand patterns. One service-retailing expert recommends the following:

☐ Use part-time employees and perform only essential tasks during peak demand periods.

☐ Train employees to perform multiple jobs so they can switch from one to another as demand dictates.

☐ Use paraprofessionals so that professionals can concentrate on duties requiring their expertise (e.g., parabankers who do legwork, solve routine problems, and handle clerical duties).

☐ Substitute equipment for human labor to make the service system more productive (e.g., automated car washes and computer-prepared income tax returns).[10]

At the Right Price: Enhance Profitability

Service providers often are divided into profit and nonprofit enterprises. Nonprofit businesses (e.g., educational, religious, charitable, and civic organizations) strive to meet social and public interest goals, while services-for-profit retailers seek financial gain. Our concern in this discussion is limited to the for-profit service retailer. Managing labor, equipment, and facility costs while obtaining the **right price** are the key elements in the service retailer's **profitability** equation. Unlike the goods retailer, "cost-of-goods-sold" is not a major profit determinant. Controlling labor cost is usually the single most important contribution the labor-intensive service-retailer can make to ensure satisfactory profits.

The service retailer's price is often not a price; rather, price is expressed in terms of a fee, charge, rent, tariff, contribution, commission, admission, donation, tuition, interest, rate, offering, or retainer. Regardless of what it is called, the service retailer's price is important because it takes on greater emphasis as a result of the intangibility of the service offering. Correctly or incorrectly, price often is used as the most important indicator of the quality of service.

Price determinants and price-setting methods for service retailers are similar to those of goods retailers. Depending on the circumstances, the service retailer might use demand-based, cost-plus, and/or competitive-oriented pricing strategies and tactics. (A review of these strategies and tactics, discussed in Chapter 19, will be helpful.)

By the Right Appeal: Increase Communicability

Creating the **right appeal** is the same for service retailers as it is for goods retailers; it involves the three-step process of presenting the *right message* to the *right audience* through the *right media*, which add up to **communicability**.

The right message addresses the concerns of the targeted consumer. Service retailers can make a service, patronage, or price appeal. *Service appeals* emphasize the rightness of the service offering in meeting the consumer's needs. Unfortunately, as a result of the intangible nature of most service offerings, it is often quite difficult to communicate the exact nature, the true value, the extra dimensions, the full benefit, and a host of other attributes that comprise a service offering. The persuasive and informative communication process becomes quite challenging when the object of the promotion is an idea, task, event, process, procedure, or performance. Developing a service appeal usually centers on building name-brand recognition and creating an image the customer can visualize. *Patronage appeals* are somewhat more tangible messages; they emphasize the rightness of the service provider's facilities, location, and operating hours. *Price appeals* are a major promotional element for some service retailers. For example, an advertised competitive price is essential to the success of auto repair, home cleaning, lawn care, travel, recreational, and entertainment firms. In the professional services field (medical, dental, and legal), price appeals were (and in some cases still are) considered unprofessional, unethical, and/or low class. These restrictions on price advertising are rapidly disappearing as more and more professional services firms become market-oriented chain organizations (e.g., Hyatt Legal Services or The Dental Center at Sears). Service retailers use both "logical" (a factual presentation) and "emotional" (an appeal to feelings) approaches to presenting their message in the right way.

The highly tangible, variable, personal, and perishable nature of most services requires that service retailers target their promotional appeals. The *right audience* is the individual or targeted group of individuals who can use a particular type of service at a particular time. Few service concepts (e.g., freedom? health? salavation? security?) can be effectively targeted and promoted to a mass audience. Although general demand for a service concept might be created through promotional appeals to mass markets, specific demand for a particular provider's service's must be created through tailored appeals to targeted audiences.

People, customers, and employees should be the focal point of all strategic planning for service retailers. In the retail service industry, customer satisfaction at a profit often equates to employee satisfaction through high motivation. High-contact service business activities require highly integrated marketing and operating functions. It is not enough to strike some type of a balance between the customer's service needs and the service retailer's operating requirements; these two functional areas must be coordinated and integrated into a single strategic plan. One such plan was developed by Professor James Heskett of the Harvard Business School. His plan is two-part: the externally oriented strategic service vision and the internally oriented strategic vision.[11]

THE RIGHT SERVICE STRATEGY

The **externally oriented strategic service vision** is directed at planning and integrating the service provider's marketing and operating functions for the benefit of the service consumer. As identified in Figure 23–8, the externally oriented strategic service vision model consists of the basic elements to be integrated and the integrative links that bridge the various marketing and operating elements. Professor Heskett describes the *strategic service vision* as follows:

> The need of most service organizations to plan as well as to direct marketing and operations as one function has led to the formation in leading companies of what I call a *strategic service vision*. Its elements consist of identification of a target market segment, development of a service concept to address targeted customers' needs, codification of an operating strategy to support the service concept, and design of a service delivery system to support the operating strategy. . . . A company naturally tries to position itself in relation to both the target market and the competition. The links between the service concept and the operating strategies are those policies and procedures by which the company seeks to maximize the difference between the value of the service to customers (the service concept) and the cost of providing it. This difference, of course, is a primary determinant of profit. And the link *between the operating strategy* and the *service delivery system* is the integration achieved in the design of both.[12]

Integrating customer-oriented functions is not enough to ensure success. Employees also must be fully integrated into the process. To repeat, most services are people-based on both the consumption and production side of the exchange process; hence, the service retailer must also have an **internally oriented strategic service vision**. "High-performance service companies have gained their status in large measure by turning the strategic service vision inward by targeting groups of employees as well as customers."[13] This inner-directed vision is shown in Figure 23–9. It differs from the outer-directed vision mainly in that the focus of planning and integrating is on the firm's employees and not its customers.

The integrative elements in Figures 23–8 and 23–9 are guidelines for planning, implementing, and directing a strategy that will ensure a service team effort in targeting various markets.

FIGURE 23–8
Externally oriented strategic service vision

Target market segments	Positioning	Service concept	Value-cost leveraging	Operating strategy	Strategy-systems integration	Service delivery system
What are common characteristics of important market segments?	How does the service concept propose to meet customer needs?	What are important elements of the service to be provided, stated in terms of results produced for customers?	To what extent are differences between perceived value and cost of service maximized by:	What are important elements of the strategy?	To what extent are the strategy and delivery system internally consistent?	What are important features of the service delivery system, including:
What dimensions can be used to segment the market?	How do competitors meet these needs?	How are these elements supposed to be perceived by the target market segment? By the market in general? By employees as a whole?	Standardization of certain elements?	Operations? Financing? Marketing? Organization? Human resources? Control?	Can needs of the strategy be met by the delivery system?	The role of people? Technology? Equipment? Layout? Procedures?
Demographic? Psychographic?	How is the proposed service differentiated from competition?		Customization of certain elements?	On which will the most effort be concentrated?	If not, what changes must be made in:	What capacity does it provide?
How important are various segments?	How important are these differences?	How do customers perceive the service concept?	Emphasizing easily leveraged services?	Where will investments be made?	The operating strategy?	Normally? At peak levels?
What needs does each have?	What is good service?	What efforts does this suggest in terms of the manner in which the service is:	Management of supply and demand?	How will quality and cost be controlled?	The service delivery system?	To what extent does it:
How well are these needs being served?	Does the proposed service concept provide it?	Designed? Delivered? Marketed?	Control and quality through—	Measured? Incentives? Rewards?	To what extent does the coordination of operating strategy and service delivery system ensure:	Help ensure quality standards? Differentiate the service from competition?
In what manner? By whom?	What efforts are required to bring customer expectations and service capabilities into alignment?		Rewards? Appeal to pride? Visibility and supervision? Peer group control? Involving the customer? Effective use of data?	What results will be expected versus competition in terms of:	High quality? High productivity? Low cost?	Provide barriers to entry by competitors?
			To what extent does this effort create barriers to entry by potential competition?	Quality of service? Cost profile? Productivity? Morale and loyalty of servers?	High morale and loyalty of servers? To what extent does this integration provide barriers to entry to competition?	

Basic element

Integrative element

FIGURE 23–9
Internally oriented strategic service vision

Target employee group	Positioning	Service concept	Value-cost leveraging	Operating strategy	Strategy-systems integration	Service delivery system
What are common characteristics of important employee groups? What dimensions can be used to describe these employee groups? Demographic? Psychographic? How important are each of these groups to the delivery of the service? What needs does each group have? How well are these needs being served? In what manner? By whom?	How does the service concept propose to meet employee needs? How do competitors meet such needs? How are relationships with employees differentiated from those between competitors and their employees? How important are these differences? What is "good service" to employees? Does the proposed service concept provide it? What efforts are required to bring employee expectations and service capabilities into alignment?	What are important elements of the service to be provided, stated in terms of results produced for employees and the company? How are these elements supposed to be perceived by the targeted employee group? How are these elements perceived? What further efforts does this suggest in terms of the manner in which the service is: Designed? Delivered?	To what extent are differences between returns to employees and the level of effort they put forth maximized by: The design of the service concept? The design of the elements of the operating strategy? Job design? The leveraging of scarce skills with a support system? The management of supply and demand? Control of quality through– Rewards? Appeal to pride? Visibility? Supervision? Peer group control? Involving the customer in the delivery of the service? Effective use of data?	How important is direct human contact in this provision of the service? To what extent have employees been involved in the design of the service concept and operating strategy? How desirable is it to: Increase employee satisfaction? Increase employee productivity? What incentives are provided for: Quality? Productivity? Cost? How does the strategy address employee needs for: Selection? Assignment? Development? Evaluation? Compensation? Association?	To what extent are the strategy and the delivery system for serving important employee groups internally consistent? To what extent does the integration of operating strategy and service delivery system ensure: High quality? High productivity? Low cost? High morale and "bonding" of the target employee group?	What are important features of the service delivery system, including: The role of people? Technology? Equipment? Layout? Procedures? What does it require of target employee groups? Normally? At peak periods of activity? To what extent does it help employees: Meet quality standards? Differentiate their service from competitors? Achieve expectations about the quality of their work life?

(Source: Reprinted by permission of *Harvard Business Review.* "Lessons in the Service Sector" by James L. Heskett [March-April 1987]. Copyright © 1987 by the President and Fellows of Harvard College; all rights reserved.)

Basic element

Integrative element

SUMMARY

A service is a multifaceted concept involving several activities performed by an individual or group of individuals for the benefit of a customer or group of customers. Service retailers differ from goods retailers in that the former emphasize people, ideas, and information, whereas the latter focus on physical things and objects. The nation's service industry is the most important sector of the economy; it is the principal employer of the nation's workforce and accounts for nearly 70 percent of the gross national product.

Service retailers are classified by the Department of Commerce into four major categories: (1) transportation, communications, and public utilities, (2) finance, insurance, and real estate, (3) public administration, and (4) services (lodging, personal, business, automotive, repair, motion pictures, amusement and recreation, health, legal, educational, social and various miscellaneous groupings). Services also can be classified according to operating characteristics, such as equipment-based and people-based service retailers.

The right service blend consists of six essential ingredients. The ingredients and their associated goals include offering the right service (add tangibility) in the right way (control variability) in the right place (bridge inseparability) at the right time (overcome perishability) at the right price (enhance profitability) by the right appeal (increase communicability).

The right service strategy requires that the service retailer plan and integrate the marketing and operations functions for both the firm's customers and its employees. The inner- and outer-directed strategic service visions provide the necessary guidelines for developing the service retailer's strategic plans.

KEY TERMS AND CONCEPTS

communicability	right appeal
externally oriented strategic service vision	right place
goods/services retailer	right price
inseparability	right service
internally oriented strategic service vision	right time
perishability	right way
primary service retailer	service
profitability	tangibility
pure goods retailer	variability

REVIEW QUESTIONS

1. Develop three original definitions and examples of a retail service.
2. Who provides services?
3. Distinguish service retailers from goods retailers. Give an original example of a pure-goods and a pure-service retailer.
4. Identify two additional examples for each of the various types of equipment-based and people-based service retailers.
5. Outline the issues of concern in offering the right service and adding tangibility.
6. Give additional original examples of physical and mental symbols of service organizations.
7. Discuss the problem of service variability and how the service retailer might control this problem.
8. Describe the channel delivery system operations available to the service retailer.
9. Why are services perishable? Cite three examples.

10. Identify and describe the systems service retailers use to synchronize demand and supply.
11. Express the concept of price in other terms or language.
12. What is typically the most important factor in determining the price of a service?
13. Describe the process of increasing communicability by the right appeal.
14. Why is it important to integrate both the marketing and operating functions internally and externally?

RELATED READINGS

1. James L. Heskett, "Lessons in the Service Sector," *Harvard Business Review* (March–April 1987): 126.
2. John E. G. Bateson, "Retailing and Services Marketing: Friends or Foes?" *Journal of Retailing* 61 (Winter 1985): 11.
3. Steven K. Beckner, "The Boom That Won't Quit," *Nation's Business* 74 (April 1986): 27.
4. Ibid.
5. Ibid.
6. See Christopher H. Lovelock, "Classifying Services to Gain Strategic Marketing Insights," *Journal of Marketing* (Summer 1983): 9–20.
7. Leonard L. Berry, "Services Marketing Is Different," *Business* (May–June 1980): 25.
8. Ibid., 27.
9. Ibid.
10. Ibid., 28.
11. See James L. Heskett, "Lessons in the Service Sector," *Harvard Business Review* (March–April 1987): 118–126.
12. Ibid., 119.
13. Ibid., 119–120.

ENDNOTES

Agnew, Joe. "Hotel Industry Focusing on High-Quality Rooms." *Marketing News,* 1 Feb. 1988, 1, 24.

Benuay, Susan. "Presto! The Convenience Industry: Making Life a Little Simpler." *Business Week,* 27 April 1987, 86–90, 92–94.

Berry, Leonard L. "Big Ideas in Services Marketing." *Journal of Consumer Marketing* (Spring 1986): 47–51.

Berry, Leonard L., Parasuraman, A., and Zeithamal, Valarie A. "Synchronizing Demand and Supply in Service Businesses." *Business* 34 (October–December 1984): 35–36.

Bloom, Paul N. "Effective Marketing to Professional Services." *Harvard Business Review* 62 (September–October 1984): 102–110.

Bolis, K. J. "The Structure of Service Firms and Their Market Policies." *Strategic Management Journal* 4 (1983): 251–61.

Dunn, Dan T., Jr., Thomas, Claude A., and Young, Robert F. "Banking: The Marketing Battle Heats Up." *Business* 34 (January–March 1984): 3–12.

George, William R. "The Retailing of Services—A Challenging Future." *Journal of Retailing* (Fall 1977): 88–89.

Ivey, Mark. "Hi, I'm Goofy. Come Ski With Me." *Business Week,* 15 Feb. 1988, 58–60.

Kelley, J. Patrick, and George, William R. "Strategic Management Issues for the Retailing of Services." *Journal of Retailing* 58 (Summer 1982): 26–43.

Kelley, Robert E. "Poorly Served Employees Serve Customers Just as Poorly." *Wall Street Journal,* 12 Oct. 1987.

Kotler, Philip, and Bloom, Paul N. *Marketing Professional Services.* Englewood Cliffs, NJ: Prentice-Hall, 1984.

Lovelock, Christopher H. "Classifying Services to Gain Strategic Marketing Insights." *Journal of Marketing* (Summer, 1983): 9–20.

Lovelock, Christopher H. *Services Marketing* Englewood Cliffs, NJ: Prentice-Hall, 1984.

Nasar, Sylvia. "Good News for Productivity." *Fortune,* 10 Dec. 1984, 40–50.

Parasuraman, A., Zeithami, Valarie A., and Berry, Leonard L. "A Conceptual Model of Service Quality and Its Implications for Future Research." *Journal of Marketing* (Fall, 1985): 44.

"Physician Sell Thyself." *Fortune,* 1 April 1985, 109–110.

Shoestack, Lynn, "Breaking Free From Product Marketing." *Journal of Marketing* (April 1977): 73–80.

Thomas, Dan R. E. "Strategy Is Different in Service Business." *Harvard Business Review* (July–August 1978): 158–65.

Ticer, Scott. "Why Holiday's Mike Rose Deserves a Holiday." *Business Week,* 16 May 1988, 64.

Upah, Gregory D. "Mass Marketing in Service Retailing: A Review and Synthesis of Major Methods." *Journal of Retailing* 56 (Fall 1980): 59–76.

Zeithmal, Valerie A., Parasuraman, A., and Berry, Leonard L. "Problems and Strategies in Services Marketing." *Journal of Marketing* (Spring 1985): 33–46.

24

Objectives

☐ Distinguish personal attributes and personality traits essential to the successful retailer.

☐ Judge the opportunities associated with a retailing career.

☐ Assess one's own personal strengths and weaknesses as applicable to the retailing field.

☐ Plan a successful employment-search process.

☐ Decide whether one is the kind of person who can successfully start and run an independent retail business.

Retailing Careers: Judging Career Opportunities

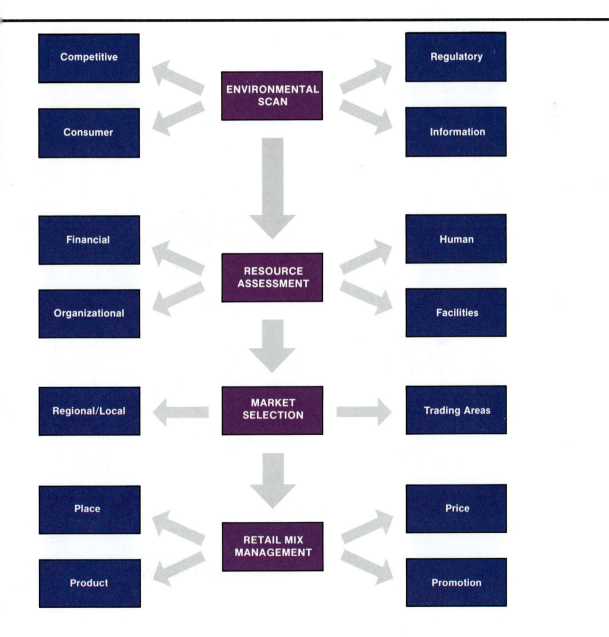

So you want to consider being a retailer? Or at least you might want to consider entering the retailing field. This chapter provides a glimpse of what it is like to be in retailing. You will discover some of the joys and, yes, also some of the frustrations involved in the retailing field. You will learn that people must have special characteristics to be successful retailers. You will read about employment opportunities, ownership opportunities, employment features in a retailing career, and the personal attributes of retailers. After you have read this chapter, you can decide—is retailing for you?

RETAILER ATTRIBUTES AND PERSONALITIES

Whether a neophyte or a veteran, an independent entrepreneur or a chain store employee, the individual engaged in retailing must have certain personality traits and attributes to succeed in the marketplace. Some of the more successful retailer personality types include the people pleaser, the risk taker, the problem solver, the decision maker, and the retail entrepreneur.

The People Pleaser

The retailer is in the people business. No other type of business deals so directly with so many people in such a variety of ways. Successful retailers have a genuine interest in and general liking for *people*. "People-pleasing" retailers can "read" their customers' minds, guess their wants and needs, anticipate their likes and dislikes, understand their hopes and fears, and adapt to their customers' viewpoints. As **people pleasers**, retailers can talk with their customers in a common language. Successful merchandising is largely a matter of good communications.

Finally, people-pleasing retailers can appreciate their customers, empathize with them, and recognize their motives. Thus, people pleasers are retailers who understand people, recognize their problems, know their goals, and try to satisfy their needs. To be a successful retailer, one must be able and willing to please people.

The Risk Taker

Risks are an inherent part of any business, and retailing is no exception. There are risks in deciding what merchandise to stock, where to locate, how many and which markets to serve, how extensive a product line to offer, and which and how many services to provide. Because no retailer can precisely determine what every customer wants or provide everything that all competitors are doing better, risks are simply unavoidable in retailing. The **risk taker** not only is willing to assume the inherent chances of going into business but is able to tell a good merchandising risk from a bad one. A successful risk taker can reduce risk by gathering and analyzing pertinent information.

The Problem Solver

The marketing minded retailer not only understands retailing problem situations but enjoys solving them—is an active **problem solver**. As discussed in Chapter 1, retailing can be described as a problem of how to satisfy customers at a profit. Therefore, the retailer must have the capacity, determination, and stamina to overcome all the barriers associated with any problem-solving situation. A typical retail operation faces a wide diversity of problems, ranging from the physical problems of getting the merchandise into the store and onto the shelves to the mental and emotional problems of handling dissatisfied and vocal customers. Regardless of the situation, the retailer must be prepared to solve not only routine problems but also unusual ones. What's more, the retailer should enjoy it!

The Decision Maker

Of the large number of managerial decisions a retailer faces, the range of possible choices in each decision can be equally broad. Retailers must make daily decisions about locations, facilities, merchandise, prices, promotions, and service, and they must make periodic decisions about staff, suppliers, and investors. Not everyone is willing or able to make these decisions under pressure of time and with limited knowledge of the marketplace. To the marketing minded **decision maker,** making choices under adverse and uncertain conditions is natural. The decision maker must understand and adapt daily to a changing marketplace. Such a person's strength lies in the ability and desire to make moment-by-moment and year-by-year decisions on a continual basis. People pleaser, risk taker, problem solver, and decision maker: the successful retailer must be all these and more.

The Retail Entrepreneur

A retail **entrepreneur** organizes, manages, and assumes the responsibilities of running a retail business. Although the term entrepreneur generally refers to an individual, the concept of entrepreneurship is actually appropriate to all retail organizations, since entrepreneurial skills are needed in all successful retailing careers. Like most skills, entrepreneurship exists in degrees. The following list of ten entrepreneurial attributes are important in creating an organizational culture that enhances the retailer's chances for success:

- ☐ Take risks but always be careful to minimize exposure. Take reasonable risks based on a clear evaluation of the expected and unexpected.
- ☐ Focus on opportunities rather than on problems, and make the primary focus customer needs rather than internal interests or limitations.
- ☐ Constantly seek improvement. It is the keystone of productivity, profitability, and customer satisfaction.
- ☐ Keep a clear head when it comes to your perception of reality. Be impressed with productivity and not appearances.
- ☐ Emphasize personal contact. Stay in touch with employees at all levels. Recognize the importance of your own example, emphasizing an open-door policy and personal contact as a leadership style.
- ☐ Keep things simple. Complex solutions in themselves don't necessarily produce incremental profits but often reduce opportunities.
- ☐ Allow for some level of ambiguity. Everything need not be tightly wrapped in a neat package or carefully explained in a manual.
- ☐ Court both change and flexibility to find improved service opportunities and increased efficiencies. Understand that every opportunity has an elusive life and is a moving target.
- ☐ Discourage focus on the negative, which will tend to produce a fear of failure and squelch the entrepreneurial spirit.
- ☐ Be purposeful and communicate the vision. The entrepreneurial spirit feeds off purposeful pursuit. There is a driving passion to make each opportunity work when everyone understands the corporate direction and the focus on consumers.[1]

No single measurement is appropriate for all individuals, and no one test measures all the attributes a retailer needs to be successful in retailing. Two psychologists, however, have developed what they deem indicators of what makes a successful retailing entrepreneur. A summary of this test of entrepreneurial mental skills and attitudes is shown in Figure 24–1.

The entrepreneurial skills of people-pleasing, decision-making, problem-solving, and risk-taking people, together with the abilities for organizing and managing, can be acquired to a degree in a formal learning situation, such as a college classroom, or in an informal learning situation, such as a work setting. Most people learn entrepreneurial skills in both ways.

FIGURE 24–1
Testing the entrepre-
neurial you

Your psychological makeup can play a strong role in making your business a success or a failure. Here are some questions based on ideas supplied by Richard Boyatzis and David Winter, two psychologists who have studied the entrepreneurial character. The questions are designed to reveal whether you have entrepreneurial attitudes. Even if no answer fits your feelings precisely, choose the one that comes closest. (The answers to these questions are provided in the chapter summary.)

1. If you have a free evening, would you most likely (a) watch TV, (b) visit a friend, (c) work on a hobby?
2. In your daydreams, would you most likely appear as (a) a millionaire floating on a yacht, (b) a detective who has solved a difficult case, (c) a politician giving an election night victory speech?
3. To exercise, would you rather (a) join an athletic club, (b) join a neighborhood team, (c) do some jogging at your own pace?
4. When asked to work with others on a team, which would you anticipate with most pleasure? (a) Other people coming up with good ideas, (b) cooperating with others, (c) getting other people to do what you want.
5. Which game would you rather play? (a) Monopoly, (b) roulette, (c) bingo.
6. Your employer asks you to take over a company project that is failing. Would you tell him that you will (a) take it, (b) won't take it because you're up to your gills in work, (c) give him an answer in a couple of days when you have more information?
7. In school, were you more likely to choose courses emphasizing (a) fieldwork, (b) papers, (c) exams?
8. In buying a refrigerator, would you (a) stay with an established, well-known brand, (b) ask your friends what they bought, (c) compare thoroughly the advantages of different brands?
9. While on a business trip in Europe, you are late for an appointment with a client in a neighboring town. Your train has been delayed indefinitely. Would you (a) rent a car to get there, (b) wait for the next scheduled train, (c) reschedule the appointment?
10. Do you believe people you know who have succeeded in business (a) have connections, (b) are more clever than you are, (c) are about the same as you but maybe work a little harder?
11. An employee who is your friend is not doing his job. Would you (a) take him out for a drink, hint broadly that things are not going right and hope he gets the message, (b) leave him alone and hope he straightens out, (c) give him a strong warning and fire him if he doesn't shape up?
12. You come home to spend a relaxing evening and find that your toilet has just overflowed. Would you (a) study your home repair book to see if you can fix it yourself, (b) persuade a handy friend to fix it for you, (c) call a plumber?
13. Do you enjoy playing cards most when you (a) play with good friends, (b) play with people who challenge you, (c) play for high stakes?
14. You operate a small office-cleaning business. A close friend and competitor suddenly dies of a heart attack. Would you (a) reassure his wife that you will never try to take away any customers, (b) propose a merger, (c) go to your former competitor's customers and offer them a better deal?

Source: Marlys Harris, "The Entrepreneur—Do You Have What It Takes?" *Money* 7 (March, 1978), 52.

The ideas in this book have built on and expanded whatever entrepreneurial skills you have and given you new insights into the world of retailing and the entrepreneurial spirit that people need to launch prosperous retailing careers.

To judge career opportunities in different fields, one should investigate the employment features for each career path. We will discuss several key aspects of a retailing career: employment security, employee compensation, working conditions, career advancement, and job satisfaction.

EMPLOYMENT ASPECTS OF A RETAILING CAREER

Employment Security

Employment in the retail sector offers the capable individual a high level of job security. Several factors account for this security. First, although all economic sectors suffer during a recession, the decline in retail employment is notably less than employment losses in either the manufacturing or wholesaling sectors. Even during recessionary periods, consumers continue to buy. They do, however, become more selective in making purchases. Second, the large number of employment opportunities in retailing creates a high level of job mobility, and increased mobility generally results in increased job security. The third factor accounting for the high level of job security in retailing is "transferability of skills." Good merchandising skills can easily be transferred from one department to another within a firm, from one type of retailer to a different retailing operation, and even from retailing firms to wholesaling and manufacturing companies. This transferability of skills is essentially an extension of the mobility factor. Because skills transferability increases the number of employment opportunities, it thereby increases present job security.

Employee Compensation

Retail salaries vary considerably, ranging from minimum wage for lower-echelon, part-time employees to competitive salaries for upper-echelon managers. Where starting retail salaries are somewhat lower than those in other industries, the multitude of managerial levels within most retailing organizations provide opportunities for rapid advancement and can often result in a higher salary for the retail manager in just a few years. Equally important, retailing is a geographically dispersed industry in which a large number of middle- and upper-level managerial positions offer very attractive salaries and benefits. Also, for the prospective employee with limited formal education, entry to higher-salaried positions in retailing is not education-oriented but productivity-oriented (e.g., based on ability to generate profits or sales). Finally, there is the opportunity for self-employment. (The potential returns for owning and operating one's own business are discussed later in the chapter.)

Working Conditions

Retail working conditions have their pluses and minuses. On the plus side, the retail employee enjoys the benefits of a variety of work assignments, a number of pleasant work environments, and a host of people-oriented work relationships. If "variety is the spice of life," then the prospective employee should find a retailing career attractive. The variety of work assignments stems from two factors. First, continuously changing economic conditions, regular changes in merchandising seasons, and the attraction of new and old customers make the retail business highly dynamic. These conditions foster new and interesting challenges for the retail employee. Second, the natural progression in training retail management personnel requires that the employee gain experience with all aspects of business. Typical retail training programs involve experiences with merchandising (e.g., buying and selling responsibilities); operations management (e.g., inventory planning and control responsibilities); sales promotion (e.g., advertising and retail display responsibilities); and personnel management (e.g., recruiting and training store personnel). Figure 24–2 illustrates these programs.

The pleasant work environment is the result of the retailer's efforts to create a *buying atmosphere*. Contrasted with the sterile atmosphere of most offices, the opportunity to work in an exciting and stimulating store environment is a definite plus of retail employment. Many individuals find that "action is where the people are." Given the people-oriented nature of the retailing business, individuals who crave action should find a retailing career very rewarding.

The most commonly cited minuses of a retailing career concern working hours. Of particular concern are the questions of how long and when employees work. While lower-echelon positions have a "normal" work week of 40 hours, the aspiring management trainee should expect to work considerably longer. Compared to the hours expected at lower-level managerial positions in other businesses, however, the retail manager's work week is reasonable. The longer retail store hours of recent years have resulted in more supervision during nonstandard working times. Because of these extended hours, both management and nonmanagement personnel are expected to work off-hours (such as evenings), off-days (such as weekends), and some off-times (such as holidays).

Career Advancement

The opportunities for rapid advancement in retailing result from several interacting factors: the number of retail establishments, the diversity of retailing positions, and the number of managerial levels. The number of retail establishments is large and expanding. As a result, managerial positions abound. For the ambitious and talented, finding potential positions for career advancement is not difficult. Equally important in finding a career environment where rapid advancement is possible is a job market characterized by a diversity of positions. Retailing has enough diversity to allow all individuals to seek and to foster a career niche best suited to their talents (see Figure 24–3). Additionally, upward mobility need not be hampered by an individual's getting locked into a particular type of job that suits neither one's talents nor one's aspirations.

The third factor contributing to an accelerated rate of advancement is the typical retail organization's large number of managerial levels. Consider, for example, the managerial levels one might find in a department store chain: assistant department manager, department manager, assistant merchandise and/or promotions manager, assistant store manager, store manager—and upward into the various district, regional, and national managerial positions. The aspiring retail manager does not have to wait for a chance at the one big career break. Making small yet steady career advancements gives the retail manager greater control over future opportunities and greater satisfaction from current job responsibilities.

Consider a final note: retailing offers women some of the best opportunities for professional advancement in the business world. These opportunities arise in part from women's power as the majority of customers at many stores. The belief that women managers have both greater understanding of women shoppers' needs and greater ability for developing meaningful relationships with this group of customers has created a career path for women in retailing that can definitely be characterized by rapid advancement.

FIGURE 24–2

Retail training programs: A variety of work experiences—the Sears model (source: *Retail Management Careers*, Sears Merchandise Group, company brochure, 9)

You will first receive **basic sales training** in a division to become familiar with its merchandise, basic selling techniques, register operations, and other sales floor procedures. You will also receive an initial overview of the **division manager's responsibilities.**

In **installed sales** you will learn about sales floor and in-the-home activities of selling home-improvement merchandise — such as roofing, fencing, and kitchens — and how to coordinate them with the activities of installers and Sears credit and customer service departments.

Display introduces you to principles of merchandise arrangement and presentation, methods of space allocation, promotional displays, signing, and fixturing.

Merchandising will help you understand store merchandising responsibilities: the concepts of gross profit and mark-up on inventory, and techniques for their improvement; merchandising systems; and reports of merchandising results.

In **catalog sales** you will become familiar with sales activities of the catalog counter and telephone sales unit, types of catalogs, the processing of orders, and the catalog delivery system.

Customer convenience center functions include:

Customer service, which will involve you with delivery, installation, and repair services, as well as Sears policies and practices in maintaining customer satisfaction.

Credit sales, where you will learn about credit policies, types of accounts, credit sales promotions, processing applications, credit authorization procedures, and helping customers with credit-related problems.

The group merchandise offices will acquaint you with the development of merchandising objectives and plans, assortment and pricing structures, merchandise ordering and replenishment procedures, and the systems used to maintain balanced merchandise inventories.

In **receiving and shipping** you will learn the functions of receiving, price marking, distribution, and shipping of merchandise, and how their procedures relate to inventory control.

In the **auto center** you will become familiar with merchandising and operating aspects of automotive service as well as techniques and procedures for the sale of tires, batteries, and accessories.

Operating acquaints you with budgeting and control of expenses, methods of safeguarding store properties and inventories, sources of store income, and analysis of the profit and loss statement.

In **accounting** you will develop an understanding of Sears accounting systems and how results of store operations are accumulated and reported. You will also learn accounting's role in inventory control and preservation of store assets.

In **personnel** you will learn about employment practices, training, benefits, employee relations, salary administration, and personnel scheduling.

You will complete your training with an assignment in a selling department to gain on-the-job experience in the activities of **division management.**

694

STORE MANAGEMENT

BUYING

Trainee
General orientation to the retailing industry and the specifics of our operations through both classroom work and extensive on-the-job experience.

Sales Manager
Responsible for running a complete selling area in a store, including merchandise presentation, supervision of sales personnel, customer service, inventory control, and all other aspects of running a business.

Assistant Buyer
Learning to be a Buyer through assisting a Buyer in planning, acquiring, pricing, distributing, and promoting a category of merchandise for all stores of a division.

Group Manager
Responsible for executing merchandising plans for several departments in a store and reaching sales goals; supervises, trains, and develops sales managers.

Buyer
Responsible for planning, selecting, acquiring, pricing, distributing, and promoting merchandise for all stores of a division. With experience, buying responsibilities increase.

Merchandise Manager
Similar to Group Manager's position but with responsibility for expanded merchandise categories; coordinates the efforts among differerent departments; acts as major liaison between store executives and buyers.

Store Manager
Responsible for the total operation of a store, including merchandising, operations, and personnel; responsible for community relations, overall image of the store, and providing leadership in planning and goal setting.

Merchandise Administrator
responsible for conceptualizing and planning overall buying in several related merchandise classifications for a division; coordinates, develops, and evaluates the work of buyers, with responsibility for profits.

Senior Vice President for Merchandising
Responsible for developing and overseeing divisional objectives and policies in buying, merchandise planning, advertising, promotion, and systems for large sectors of the business; direct responsibility for the overall profitability of those sectors.

FIGURE 24–3
Retail management: A diversity of career paths—the R. H. Macy & Co. model (source: *Your Career Planning Workbook*, R. H. Macy & Co., Inc.)

Job Satisfaction

Many aspects of a retailing career can provide job satisfaction. Some of the aspects already mentioned are the diversity of job responsibilities, potential for rapid advancement, opportunities to work with people, challenges of a continually changing environment, and competitive levels of compensation. Others are the freedom to use one's initiative, quick recognition of one's abilities, and continuous opportunities to demonstrate leadership.

The nature of a retail store's operating and merchandising activities gives employees and managers a considerable degree of independence. The opportunity for motivated individuals to use their initiative in assuming responsibilities and making meaningful decisions is rewarding and tends to promote considerable job satisfaction. Retailing careers provide many opportunities for people who want the freedom to "do their thing." Most store managers, for example, are responsible for "running their own show." Their responsibilities extend to all facets of the business: merchandising, operations, personnel, promotions, and finance.

Retailing offers ample opportunities to demonstrate one's talents and abilities and have those talents and abilities recognized. Most people need feedback before they can judge how satisfied they are with their performance. Where else can one get a daily rating of job performance? Large retailing organizations compute sales, expense, and profit figures daily, by means of electronic data processing systems, for each operating unit. In smaller retailing organizations, the relative sales and profit positions of various operating units usually are known through more informal means. In either case, the timely feedback affords career-minded people opportunities to demonstrate their abilities and to communicate their successes to their superiors who are directly responsible for career advancements.

The opportunity to assume a leadership role is a key factor to job satisfaction for some individuals. The people-intensive nature of retailing offers unlimited occasions for leadership-minded people to "stand out" rather than "fit in."

Finally, many people relate job satisfaction at least in some degree to the status or image of their field of endeavor within the general business community. In recent years, as retailers have become a dominant force in the marketing and distribution of goods, their status has reached parity with other business careers. Successful retailing requires the same professional skills as any other business, a fact now widely recognized throughout the business community.

EMPLOYMENT OPPORTUNITIES

Employment choices are among the most important decisions people make and represent long-term commitments with profound effects on professional, personal, and family lives as well as general life-styles. Therefore, it behooves anyone to approach an employment choice with the utmost preparation. The first step in planning for employment is to assess one's personal strengths and weaknesses, hopes and aspirations, and career goals and objectives. Each prospective employee needs to make a life audit and a career audit before engaging in an employment search.

Making a Personal Assessment

The Life Audit

For understandable reasons, no one has your best interest at heart as much as you do. No one can know and understand you or your abilities, interests, and aspirations as well as you. Unfortunately, many individuals do not really know themselves well because they have never taken the time to assess what they want and expect out of life. A **life audit** is an attempt to seek insight into one's true feelings about one's abilities and aspirations. A form of self-analysis, a life audit involves simply answering truthfully a series of questions about one's expectations. No prescribed set of questions is appropriate for every life audit; however, the audit should include questions regarding family issues, personal values, general attitudes, basic beliefs, and personal goals and objectives. A life audit gives people a better self-understanding and helps them decide whether they might be successful and happy in the world of retailing.

The Career Audit

To start and maintain a successful career, you need a career plan that includes necessary strategies and tactics for success. To develop a career plan, you should first conduct a **career audit**. Figure 24—4 illustrates a career audit, a set of twenty questions that many executive recruiters believe will help you discover yourself and your career aspirations. These questions not only are useful in developing initial career plans, but also can serve as guidelines to continually evaluate career assets and liabilities. One of the most difficult aspects of a job search, especially for recent college graduates, is determining what job function is most interesting to them.[2]

After making both a life and a career audit, the final step in a personal assessment is to identify life and career goals. For clarity and future reference, you should write down these goals and file them in a secure place. Although your goals will undergo many modifications during your life and career, specifying goals in writing forces you to assess what you want as of now.

Securing a Retail Position

After you have completed a personal assessment, you are then ready to secure a retail position—the **employment-search process**. Because of the many and various

FIGURE 24—4
Twenty questions to ask in making a career audit

> 1. Do I work better in a large or small corporation?
> 2. How important is geographic location to me? To my family?
> 3. Am I a loner, or do I work better as a member of a group?
> 4. Am I more comfortable following than leading?
> 5. Do I analyze better than I execute?
> 6. Am I an innovator?
> 7. Do I work more successfully under pressure?
> 8. Am I a good planner?
> 9. Am I a good listener?
> 10. Do I think well on my feet?
> 11. Do I express myself well orally? In writing?
> 12. What characteristics do I admire in others?
> 13. Which function of my job do I perform most effectively?
> 14. Which do I perform least effectively?
> 15. What do I enjoy doing most?
> 16. In the past six months, what accomplishment has most satisfied me? Which has been the most difficult?
> 17. What have I done to correct my shortcomings?
> 18. What level of responsibility do I aspire to in five years?
> 19. What should I be earning then?
> 20. How will I achieve these levels?

Source: Robert Ankerson, "Marketing a New Product," *MBA: Master In Business Administration* (October, 1975), 28.

employment opportunities in retailing, the strategies and tactics of a search for a retail position must be systematic and comprehensive. This discussion covers how to identify prospective employers, obtain a personal interview, prepare for an interview, and participate in the interview.

Identifying Prospective Employers

Prospective employer identification is a process of organizing opportunities. The four steps include listing employment criteria, ranking employment criteria, scaling employment preferences, and matching job preferences with prospective employers.

Step 1: Listing employment criteria. In the initial stages of an employment search, you must determine the general conditions under which you are willing to accept a job, that is, your **employment criteria**. Although the particulars of any job (e.g., salary) are determined during actual employment negotiation, you may have certain preconditions regarding employment. Common preconditions involve location, organization, and position. For personal, professional, and many other reasons, you may prefer or need to work in a particular part of the country or in a particular state or city. You should also list any preconditions regarding the kind of organization for which you are willing to work. Representative organizational preconditions might include the size of the firm, type of organization (e.g., independent vs. chain organization), and nature of the operation (e.g., department, specialty, or discount organization). Finally, you should include a list of any preconditions regarding positions you are willing or unwilling to accept. For example, you should consider your interest (or lack of interest) in accepting a position in such areas as merchandising, operations management, sales promotion, or personnel.

Step 2: Ranking employment criteria. Not all the criteria identified in Step 1 will necessarily be equally important to you. Step 2 of the prospective employer-identification process therefore requires that you rank each of the employment criteria according to importance. You may judge some criteria extremely important or essential (e.g., for family reasons you must find a job in the greater Chicago area); others might be preferences but not absolutely essential (e.g., you prefer to work in the merchandising area for a large department store). Finally, you might view other criteria as not important but a definite plus (e.g., the opportunity to work in a particular merchandising department—women's apparel). By ranking employment criteria, you develop a concrete means of judging employment opportunities.

Step 3: Scaling employment preferences. The third step in identifying prospective employers is to develop a preference scale of employment opportunities. This step requires developing general job descriptions for first, second, and third preference levels. For example, your most-preferred job description might be an assistant manager of a women's apparel department in a major Chicago metro-area department store, preferably somewhere in the northwest part of the city. On the other end of the scale, your least-preferred job description might be the same type of job in an out-of-state location. After you have developed two or three general job descriptions for each of the three preference levels, you will be ready for the final stage of your employer-identification process.

Step 4: Matching job preferences with prospective employers. Now that you have listed, ranked, and scaled your preferences, the final step in the employer-identification process is to match those preferences with prospective employers. The matching process consists of compiling a list of jobs and screening that list of pro-spective employers according to your scaled preferences.

It will be to your benefit to explore all possible sources in compiling a **jobs list**. The campus placement office is a logical starting point, as it represents one of the most fruitful sources for good leads for potential employment. It also provides a number of services (e.g., setting up personal interviews) that can greatly facilitate your employment-search process. By checking with your placement office frequently and regularly, you will be able to keep your jobs list updated. You also need to system-atically check the employment sections of local and national newspapers as well as trade and professional journals, magazines, and newspapers. Federal equal employ-ment opportunity requirements have made these publications a good source for locating employment opportunities. Commercial employment agencies are still an-other source. Before making any commitments to one of these agencies, however, be sure you fully understand what services they provide and under what conditions and terms. You can obtain additional job leads by sending inquiries to the personnel departments of retail firms you believe have the potential to offer the kind of em-ployment you desire. Finally, some of the best leads to employment opportunities come through personal contacts. Professors, friends, relatives, and social and pro-fessional acquaintances often provide an inside track to opportunities.

Screening a jobs list is a fairly routine procedure if you have carefully completed the previous step in the employment- search process—scaling employment prefer-ences. Jobs-list screening involves (1) reducing your jobs list to employment oppor-tunities that meet your minimum requirements for employment and then (2) rank ordering the remaining jobs on the list according to your preferences. This screening results in a list of available and acceptable employment opportunities rank ordered from most to least desirable.

Obtaining a Personal Interview

Personal interviews are a way for retailers to question and observe job applicants in a face-to-face situation. Most retailers consider interviews essential to hiring. One short interview with the store's personnel manager is usually all that is necessary for lower-echelon positions. By contacting the personnel department and complet-ing an application form, qualified applicants normally will be granted a personal inter-view.

The **personal interview process** for most managerial positions is much more involved. Typically, it involves a series of personal interviews with various managers at different levels. Although it is necessary to be successful at each of these interviews, getting the *initial* interview is the most crucial step because without it nothing else happens. Obtaining the initial interview can be quite simple or extremely difficult. The method you use to get the first interview depends on the circumstances surrounding the job (e.g., type and level of the position) and the firm's employment practices (e.g., where and how they recruit). There are several methods for obtaining the initial interview with retailing firms. They include (1) obtaining an on-campus interview schedule from the school placement office and scheduling an interview through that office; (2) contacting the store's personnel office and making arrangements for the initial interview; (3) asking personal contacts to set up a personal interview; and (4) writing brief letters and making telephone calls and personal visits to one or more of the firm's managers to discuss possible employment opportunities. Once you have arranged a personal interview, you must carefully prepare for the interview to in-crease your chances for success.

Preparing for a Personal Interview

Lack of preparation is perhaps the most common error applicants make in the personal-interview process. It is foolish for anyone to spend several years in college preparing for a career and then fail to spend several hours preparing for the key interview that could very well launch a career with the right firm. Preparing for a personal interview involves getting to know something about the firm interviewing you and helping the firm in its efforts to get to know you.

Before the interview, you should do some research on the firm. Your ability to talk knowledgeably about the firm and its activities will pay substantial dividends during the actual interview. Preparation not only will make a favorable impression on the interviewer, but will also allow you to answer and to ask meaningful questions. Your information search on the firm should help you to discuss the firm's organizational structure, market positions, merchandising strategies, financial positions, and future prospects. Examining various trade magazines, industrial directories, and other reference books can provide a good general picture of the firm and its operations.

To help the firm get to know you, you will need to prepare a résumé, which should include (1) a brief statement of personal data (e.g., name, address, telephone number, marital status, date of birth, health status, and physical condition); (2) a brief outline of educational experience (i.e., type of degree, name of school, date of graduation, major and minor fields of study, class ranking, scholarships, honors, awards, and extracurricular activities); (3) a short history of work experience (i.e., a list of jobs, position and responsibilities, names of employers, and dates of employment); and (4) a summary of other activities, interests, and skills that support your professional credentials. Also, you might wish to include a list of references and a short statement of your career objectives. In preparing a résumé, the following guidelines are helpful:

1. *Be concise.* The purpose of a résumé is to stimulate the interviewer's interest and not to tell your life story. A one-page résumé is sufficient to create this interest. If interviewers want to know more, they will ask for more information and clarification.
2. *Be factual.* Experienced interviewers will recognize résumé "puffery" and generally take a dim view of it. A statement of a few real accomplishments is received much more favorably than a list of artificial ones.
3. *Be professional.* A well-organized, neatly produced résumé is an excellent "scene setter" for your personal interview. A poorly organized résumé with confusing layout, typographical errors, misspellings, and blurred or messy photocopying make a definite statement about your abilities to organize and to produce good work.

As a final note, you must recognize that it is your responsibility to establish and verify the time and place for each interview. Missing or being late to an interview is rarely excusable, regardless of the reason. You should therefore plan for unforeseen delays to ensure getting to your interview on time.

Taking a Personal Interview

The interview situation varies according to the interviewer's personal preferences. Some interview situations are conducted formally in a structured question-and-answer format. Other interview situations are informal, conducted without any apparent structure. Figure 24–5 outlines the typical stages and topics of an initial interview. Whether the interview is formal or informal, your ability to read the interview situation and to react accordingly will determine your success. All interviews,

FIGURE 24–5

Stages and topics covered during the initial interview (stages 2 and 3 are the most important parts of the interview)

Stages	Interviewer Topics	Interviewer Looks for
1. First impressions	Introduction and greeting Small talk about traffic conditions, the weather, the record of the basketball team	Firm handshake, eye contact Appearance and dress appropriate to the business, not campus, setting
2. Your record	*Education* Reasons for choice of school and major Grades: effort required for them Special areas of interest Courses enjoyed most and least, reasons Special achievements, toughest problems Value of education as career preparation Reaction to teachers High school record, SAT scores *Work Experience* Nature of jobs held Why undertaken Level of responsibility reached Duties liked most and least Supervisory experience Relations with others *Activities and Interests* Role in extracurricular, athletic, community, and social service activities Personal interests—hobbies, cultural interests, sports	Intellectual abilities Breadth and depth of knowledge Relevance of course work to career interests Special or general interest Value placed on achievement Willingness to work hard Relation between ability and achievement Reaction to authority Ability to cope with problems Sensible use of resources (time, energy, money) High energy level, vitality, enthusiasm Leadership ability; interest in responsibility Willingness to follow directions Ability to get along with others Seriousness of purpose Ability to motivate oneself, to make things happen Positive "can do" attitude Diversity of interests Awareness of world outside the laboratory Social conscience; good citizenship
3. Your career goals	Type of work desired Immediate objectives Long-term objectives Interest in this company Other companies being considered Desire for further education/training Geographical preferences and limitations Attitude toward relocation Health factors that might affect job performance	Realistic knowledge of strengths and weaknesses Preparation for employment Knowledge of opportunities Seriousness of purpose; career-oriented rather than job-oriented Knowledge of the company Real interest in the company Work interests in line with talents Company's chance to get and keep you
4. The company	Company opportunities Where you might fit Current and future projects Major divisions and departments Training programs, educational and other benefits	Informed and relevant questions Indications of interest in answers Appropriate but not undue interest in salary or benefits

Stages	Interviewer Topics	Interviewer Looks for
5. Conclusion	Further steps you should take (application form, transcript, references) Further steps company will take, outline how application handled, to which departments it will be sent, time of notification of decision Cordial farewell	Candidate's attention to information as a sign of continued interest

Source: Reprinted with permission from *Peterson's Business and Management Jobs 1985*, © 1984 by Peterson's Guides, Inc., P.O. Box 2123, Princeton, New Jersey 08540. 1986 edition available at bookstores or direct from the publisher.

formal or informal, usually have four parts: (1) rapport building—a few minutes of chit-chat to open the interview; (2) questions and answers—information exchange; (3) the sell—applicant outlines what he or she can do for the retailer while the retailer explains the opportunities available with the organization; and (4) the close—each party, if favorably impressed, tries to end the interview on a positive note.[3] No absolute rules apply in taking a personal interview, but the guidelines that follow are useful in most situations.

Dress appropriately.   The job or position for which you are interviewing will provide you with cues on how to dress. Do not overdress or underdress for the occasion.

Be prepared for openers.   Many interviewers like to open their interviews with broad questions such as "What do you expect out of life?" "Why do you want to work for our firm?" "Where do you want to be in your career 10 years from now?" or "What do you think you can do for our company?" (Additional questions usually asked during the personal interview process are shown in Figure 24–6.)

Be relaxed.   Interviewers expect a reasonable amount of nervousness; however, excessive nervousness may well suggest to the interviewer that you are unable to handle pressure situations. Avoid nervous gestures. On the other hand, avoid appearing so relaxed or "laid back" that you give the impression of being disinterested in the interview or the job.

Listen carefully.   Let the interviewer guide the interview, at least during the initial stages. Interviewers provide cues as to how they want to conduct the interview and what they want to talk about. Also, by listening carefully, you will be able to fully understand the nature of the questions and thus give better responses.

Ask questions.   If you want a job with the interviewer's company, you should be able to show your interest by asking intelligent questions about the firm.

Be informative.   You should answer the interviewer's questions fully and quickly but avoid talking too much or too fast. Most of the interviewer's questions will require more than a yes or no answer; however, you should avoid telling your life story, boasting about your accomplishments, and complaining about your problems.

FIGURE 24–6

Fifty most-asked interview questions

The Endicott Survey, published by the Placement Center of Northwestern University, periodically updates its original list of questions most commonly asked of college graduates at interviews. Variations of that list have appeared in many publications.

1. What are your long-range and short-range goals and objectives, when and why did you establish these goals, and how are you preparing yourself to achieve them?
2. What specific goals, other than those related to your occupation, have you established for yourself for the next 10 years?
3. What do you see yourself doing five years from now?
4. What do you really want to do in life?
5. What are your long-range career objectives?
6. How do you plan to achieve your career goals?
7. What are the most important rewards you expect in your career?
8. What do you expect to be earning in five years?
9. Why did you choose the career for which you are preparing?
10. Which is more important to you, the money or the type of job?
11. What do you consider to be your greatest strengths and weaknesses?
12. How would you describe yourself?
13. How do you think a friend or a professor who knows you well would describe you?
14. What motivates you to put forth your greatest effort?
15. How has your education prepared you for a career?
16. Why should I hire you?
17. What qualifications do you have that make you think that you will be successful?
18. How do you determine or evaluate success?
19. What do you think it takes to be successful in a company like ours?
20. In what ways do you think you can make a contribution to our company?
21. What qualities should a successful manager possess?
22. Describe the relationship that should exist between a supervisor and subordinates.
23. What two or three accomplishments have given you the most satisfaction? Why?

Be somewhat aggressive. It is better to be perceived as a little too aggressive rather than too passive. In terms of aggressiveness, the right impression to portray might be that you are a "mover" but not a "shaker."

Be honest. Answer questions as truthfully as you can. Interviewers recognize that everyone has strengths and weaknesses. Frankly admitting a weakness adds credibility to the statements you make about your strengths. Admitting a weakness also makes you appear more trustworthy to the interviewer.

Following these guidelines greatly improves one's chances for a successful interview. One last point: If you can make the interviewer feel comfortable and at ease, then you have gone a long way toward getting a second interview and possibly a position with that company.

FIGURE 24–6
continued

24. Describe your most rewarding college experience.
25. If you were hiring a graduate for this position, what qualities would you look for?
26. Why did you select your college or university?
27. What led you to choose your field of major study?
28. What academic subjects did you like best? Least?
29. Do you enjoy doing independent research?
30. If you could do so, would you plan your academic study differently?
31. What changes would you make in your college or university?
32. Do you think that your grades are a good indication of your academic achievement?
33. What have you learned from participation in extracurricular activities?
34. Do you have plans for continued study? (Graduate students may be asked: Why did you decide to pursue an advanced degree?)
35. In what kind of work environment are you most comfortable?
36. How do you work under pressure?
37. In what part-time or summer jobs have you been most interested? Why?
38. How would you describe the ideal job for you following graduation?
39. Why did you decide to seek a position with this company?
40. What do you know about our company?
41. What two or three things are most important to you in your job?
42. Are you seeking employment in a company of a certain size? Why?
43. What criteria are you using to evaluate the company for which you hope to work?
44. Do you have a geographical preference? Why?
45. Will you relocate? Does relocation bother you?
46. Are you willing to travel?
47. Are you willing to spend at least six months as a trainee?
48. Why do you think you might like to live in the community in which our company is located?
49. What major problem have you encountered and how did you deal with it?
50. What have you learned from your mistakes?

Source: Reprinted with permission from *Peterson's Business and Management Jobs, 1985*, © 1984 by Peterson's Guides, Inc., P.O. Box 2123, Princeton, New Jersey 08540. 1986 edition available at bookstores or direct from the publisher.

OWNERSHIP OPPORTUNITIES

Regardless of their income, many people who work for others feel they are living a hand-to-mouth, paycheck-to-paycheck existence. According to one old adage, the only way to get ahead is to get other people to work for you or to get money working for you—the idea is that income and perhaps job satisfaction are limited when you work for someone else. Many people find that self-employment is the answer to a better income, greater independence, a more rewarding career, and an improved life-style. Many people think that going into business for themselves is the only way they can fully realize their hopes and aspirations. To have a chance at realizing their personal, career, and life goals, these individuals are willing to assume the considerable burdens and risks of owning and operating their own businesses.

The preceding chapters fully discussed the factors necessary for a successful retail operation. With that background in mind, consider whether *you* are the kind of person who could succeed as an independent retailer. To help assess this possibility, take the self-evaluation test in Figure 24–7; it should give you some insight into whether you have the personal attributes to become an independent retailer. If, after taking the self-evaluation test, you decide that you do have what it takes to be an independent retailer, three options are open to you: (1) starting a new business; (2) buying an existing business; or (3) securing a franchise. Each option has advantages and disadvantages that you should fully explore. Figure 24–8 compares issues surrounding the decision to start a new business or buy an existing one. The principal concerns associated with securing a franchise are outlined in Figure 24–9.

FIGURE 24–7

Do you have what it takes to be an independent retailer?

Under each question, check the answer that says what you feel or comes closest to it. Be honest with yourself.

Are you a self-starter?
- [ ] I do things on my own. Nobody has to tell me to get going.
- [ ] If someone gets me started, I keep going all right.
- [ ] Easy does it, man. I don't put myself out until I have to.

How do you feel about other people?
- [ ] I like people. I can get along with just about anybody.
- [ ] I have plenty of friends—I don't need anyone else.
- [ ] Most people bug me.

Can you lead others?
- [ ] I can get most people to go along when I start something.
- [ ] I can give the orders if someone tells me what we should do.
- [ ] I let someone else get things moving. Then I go along if I feel like it.

Can you take responsibility?
- [ ] I like to take charge of things and see them through.
- [ ] I'll take over if I have to, but I'd rather let someone else be responsible.
- [ ] There's always some eager beaver around wanting to show how smart he is. I say let him.

How good an organizer are you?
- [ ] I like to have a plan before I start. I'm usually the one to get things lined up when the gang wants to do something.
- [ ] I do all right unless things get too goofed up. Then I cop out.
- [ ] You get all set and then something comes along and blows the whole bag. So I just take things as they come.

How good a worker are you?
- [ ] I can keep going as long as I need to. I don't mind working hard for something I want.
- [ ] I'll work hard for a while, but when I've had enough, that's it, man!
- [ ] I can't see that hard work gets you anywhere.

Can you make decisions?
- [ ] I can make up my mind in a hurry if I have to. It usually turns out O.K., too.
- [ ] I can if I have plenty of time. If I have to make up my mind fast, I think later I should have decided the other way.
- [ ] I don't like to be the one who has to decide things. I'd probably blow it.

Can people trust what you say?
- [ ] You bet they can. I don't say things I don't mean.
- [ ] I try to be on the level most of the time, but sometimes I just say what's easiest.
- [ ] What's the sweat if the other fellow doesn't know the difference?

Can you stick with it?

☐ If I make up my mind to do something, I don't let *anything* stop me.
☐ I usually finish what I start—if it doesn't get fouled up.
☐ If it doesn't go right away, I turn off. Why beat your brains out?

How good is your health?

☐ Man, I *never* run down!
☐ I have enough energy for most things I want to do.
☐ I run out of juice sooner than most of my friends seem to.

Now count the checks you made.

How many checks are there beside the *first* answer to each question? _____
How many checks are there beside the *second* answer to each question? _____
How many checks are there beside the *third* answer to each question? _____

If most of your checks are beside the first answer, you probably have what it takes to run a business. If not, you're likely to have more trouble than you can handle by yourself. Better find a partner who is strong on the points you're weak on. If many checks are beside the third answer, not even a good partner will be able to shore you up.

Source: *Checklist for Going into Business,* Small Marketers Aids No. 71, Small Business Administration (October, 1976), 4–5.

FIGURE 24–7
continued

FIGURE 24–8
To start or buy?

Should I start my own business from scratch or should I purchase an existing business? These are the two alternatives facing the potential small business manager. If the business is started fresh, there are these advantages:

1. You can create a business in your own image. The business is not a made-over version of someone else's place, but it is formed the way you think it should be.
2. You do not run the risk of purchasing a business with a poor reputation that you would inherit.
3. The concept you have for the business is so unusual that only a new business is possible.

The creation of a new business also has some substantial drawbacks. Some of the disadvantages include:

1. Too small a market for your product or service.
2. High cost of new equipment.
3. Lack of a source of advice on how things are done and who can be trusted.
4. Lack of name recognition. It may take a long time to persuade customers to give your business a try.

Buying an existing business also has advantages and disadvantages. The major advantages are:

1. A successful business may provide the buyer with an immediate source of income.
2. An existing business may already be in the best location.
3. An existing business already has employees who are trained and suppliers who have established ties to the business.
4. Equipment is already installed and the productive capacity of the business is known.
5. Inventories are in place, and suppliers have extended trade credit which can be continued.
6. There is no loss of momentum. The business is already operating.
7. You have the opportunity to obtain advice and counsel from the previous owner.
8. Often, you can purchase the business you want at a price much lower than the cost of starting the same business from scratch.

FIGURE 24–8
continued

Purchasing an existing business can have some real drawbacks, such as the following:

1. You can be misled, and end up with a business that is a "dog."
2. The business could have been so poorly managed by the previous owner that you inherit a great deal of ill will.
3. A poorly managed business may have employees who are unsuited to the business or poorly trained.
4. The location of the business may have become, or is becoming, unsuitable.
5. The equipment may have been poorly maintained or even be obsolete.
6. Change can be difficult to introduce in an established business.
7. Inventory may be out of date, damaged, or obsolete.
8. You can pay too much for the business.

To avoid buying a business that cannot be made profitable, investigate six critical areas:

1. Why does the owner wish to sell? Look for the real reason and do not simply accept what you are told.
2. Determine the physical condition of the business. Consider the building and its location.
3. Conduct a thorough analysis of the market for your products or services. Who are your present and potential customers? You cannot know too much about your customers. Conduct an equally thorough analysis of your competitors, both direct and indirect. How do they operate and why do customers prefer them?
4. Consider all of the legal factors which might constrain the expansion and growth of the business. Become familiar with zoning restrictions.
5. Identify the actual owner of the business and all liens that might exist.
6. Using the material covered in previous chapters, analyze the financial condition of the business.

The business can be evaluated on the basis of its assets, its future earnings, or a combination of both. Don't confuse the value of a business with its price. Price is determined through negotiation. The bargaining zone represents that area within which agreement can be reached.

Source: Norman M. Scarborough and Thomas W. Zimmerer, *Effective Small Business Management* (Columbus: Charles E. Merrill Publishing Co., 1984), 130–31.

FIGURE 24–9
A retail franchise: Is it for you?

The Franchisor and the Franchise

1. Is the potential market for the product or service adequate to support your franchise? Will the prices you charge be in line with the market?
2. Is the market's population growing, remaining static, or shrinking? Is the demand for your product or service growing, remaining static, or shrinking?
3. Is the product or service safe and reputable?
4. What will the competition, direct or indirect, be in your sales territory? Do any other franchisees operate in this general area?
5. Is the franchise international, national, regional, or local in scope? Does it involve full- or part-time involvement?
6. How many years has the franchisor been in operation? Does it have a sound reputation for honest dealings with franchisees?
7. How many franchise outlets now exist? How many will there be a year from now? How many outlets are company-owned?
8. How many franchisees have failed? Why?
9. What services and assistance will the franchisor provide? Training programs? Advertising assistance? Financial aid? Are these one-time programs or are they continuous in nature?
10. Will the firm perform a location analysis to help you find a suitable site?

FIGURE 24–9
continued

11. Will the franchisor offer you exclusive distribution rights for the length of the agreement, or may it sell to other franchises in this area?

12. What facilities and equipment are required for the franchise? Who pays for construction? Is there a lease agreement?

13. What is the total cost of the franchise? What are the initial capital requirements? Will the franchisor provide financial assistance? Of what nature? What is the interest rate? Is the franchisor financially sound enough to fulfill all its promises?

14. How much is the franchise fee? **Exactly** what does it cover? Are there any continuing fees? What additional fees are there?

15. Does the franchisor provide an estimate of expenses and income? Are they reasonable for your particular area? Are they sufficiently documented?

16. Does the franchisor offer a written contract which covers all the details of the agreement? Have your attorney and your accountant studied its terms and approved it? Do **you** understand the implications of the contract?

17. What is the length of the franchise agreement? Under what circumstances can it be terminated? If you terminate the contract, what are the costs to you? What are the terms and costs of renewal?

18. Are you allowed to sell the franchise to a third party? If so, will you receive the proceeds?

19. Is there a national advertising program? How is it financed? What media are used? What help is provided for local advertising?

The Franchisee—You

20. Are you qualified to operate a franchise successfully? Do you have adequate drive, skills, experience, education, patience, and financial capacity? Are you prepared to work hard?

21. Are you willing to sacrifice some autonomy in operating a business to own a franchise?

22. Can you tolerate the financial risk?

23. Are you genuinely interested in the product or service you will be selling?

24. Has the franchisor investigated your background thoroughly enough to decide you are qualified to operate the franchise?

25. What can this franchisor do for you that you cannot do for yourself?

Source: Norman M. Scarborough and Thomas W. Zimmerer, *Effective Small Business Management* (Columbus: Charles E. Merrill Publishing Co., 1984), 101–2.

SUMMARY

Successful retailers have a "mind for marketing." They like people and enjoy working with them. They understand the risks associated with any business enterprise and are willing to assume those risks. They are challenged by problems and enjoy solving them. And, they are willing to make decisions and to accept the responsibility that goes with making them. These people-pleasing, risk-taking, problem-solving, and decision-making personality traits are best summed up in the skills of the retail entrepreneur.

Figure 24–1 showed some of the indicators of entrepreneurial attitudes. (Note: The best answers to these questions are [1] c, [2] b, [3] c, [4] a, [5] a, [6] c, [7] a, [8] c, [9] a, [10] c, [11] c, [12] a, [13] b, and [14] c. Score one point for each correct answer. Questions 1, 2, 3, 7, 9, and 12 suggest whether you are a realistic problem solver who can run a business without constant help from others. Questions 5, 6, and

8 probe whether you take calculated risks and seek information before you act. Questions 4, 10, 13, and 14 show whether you, like the classic entrepreneur, find other people satisfying when they help fulfill your need to win. Question 11 reveals whether you take responsibility for your destiny—and your business. If you score between 11 and 14 points, you could have a good chance to succeed. If you score from 7 to 10 points, you'd better have a superb business idea or a lot of money to help you out. If you score 7 or less, stay where you are.)

The employment aspects of a retailing career involve (1) above-average employment security; (2) competitive compensation in managerial positions and below-average compensation in lower-echelon positions; (3) a variety of work assignments; (4) pleasant work environment; (5) opportunities for rapid advancement; and (6) the satisfaction of using one's initiative, the quick recognition of one's abilities, and the opportunity to demonstrate leadership.

Employment opportunities in retailing are numerous and diverse. Finding a retail position, however, requires preparation and planning. Before starting the employment-search process, one must make a personal assessment consisting of life and career audits. These audits help identify personal and professional strengths and weaknesses as well as clarify one's hopes and aspirations. The audits also provide direction for developing personal and professional goals and objectives.

The employment-search process consists of identifying prospective employers and obtaining, preparing for, and taking personal interviews. To identify possible employers, prospective employees should list and then rank their employment criteria, scale their employment preferences, and match their job preferences with prospective employers.

Methods for getting a personal interview include contacting the school placement office or the store's personnel office, using personal contacts to set up interviews, and writing letters and making phone calls or personal visits to the appropriate store managers. Before an interview, the applicant should prepare a résumé and conduct research on the firm.

Finally, common sense is the best rule for taking a personal interview. Other helpful guidelines are to dress appropriately, be prepared for openers, be relaxed, listen carefully, ask questions, be informative, be somewhat aggressive, and be honest.

Each year, thousands of people start retail businesses, hoping to realize personal and professional goals they cannot achieve by working for someone else. Some people have what it takes to own and operate a business successfully, whereas others probably do not. The self-evaluation test in Figure 24—7 provides some insight into whether an individual has what it takes. (If you have not already taken the test, do so now.) Your instructor can guide discussion on the answers you give to help you assess your probable success at operating a business of your own.

KEY TERMS AND CONCEPTS

career audit	jobs list
decision maker	life audit
employment criteria	people pleaser
employment preferences	personal interview process
employment-search process	problem solver
entrepreneur	risk taker

1. Identify the characteristics of a people pleaser.
2. Describe the factors that account for the relatively high level of job security in the retail-management field.
3. Why might a retailing career be described in terms of the old adage "variety is the spice of life"?
4. Identify and discuss the numerous opportunities for rapid career advancement in the field of retailing.
5. Describe a life audit.
6. Describe briefly the four steps in identifying prospective employers.
7. What are the various options open to the prospective employee in obtaining an initial interview with a retail firm?
8. Identify the information you should include on your resume.
9. Cite the eight guidelines for taking a personal interview.
10. What are the advantages and disadvantages of starting your own business from scratch?

1. Donald Zale, "The Need to Rekindle the Entrepreneurial Spirit," *Retailing Issues Letter* (Center for Retailing Studies, Texas A&M University, September 1986): 2.
2. Susan Bernard, "Your Job Search Countdown," *Business Week's Careers* 3 (October/Winter Preview 1985): 96.
3. Marilyn M. Kennedy, "How To Win the Interview Game," *Business Week's Careers* 5 (September 1987): 17.

"A Career in Advertising." *Stores* (May 1987): 102–103.
Cohen, William A. "A Tentative Model for Student Self-Marketing." In *1985 AMA Educators' Proceedings,* edited by R. F. Lusch et al., 110–13. American Marketing Association, 1985.
Donaghy, William C. *The Interview—Skills and Applications.* Glenview, IL: Scott, Foresman & Co., 1984.
Frisbie, Gil A., and Petroshius, Susan M. "Career Perceptions and Influencing Factors on Business Students' Choice of Major." In *1985 AMA Educators' Proceedings,* edited by R. F. Lusch et al., 99–104. American Marketing Association, 1985.
Gaedeke, Ralph, and Tootelian, Dennis. *Small Business Management.* Glenview, IL: Scott, Foresman & Co., 1984.
Goldgehn, Leslile A., and Soares, Eric. "Marketing Our Students: An Emphasis on Communication Skills." In *1985 AMA Educators' Proceedings,* edited by R. F. Lusch et al., 105–9. American Marketing Association, 1985.
Levitt, Julie G. *Your Career: How to Make It Happen.* Cincinnati, OH: South-Western Publishing Co., 1985.
Olm, Kenneth, and Eddy, George G. *Entrepreneurship and Venture Management.* Columbus, OH: Merrill, 1985.
Peterson's Business Management Jobs 1988. Princeton, NJ: Peterson's Guides, 1988.
Stevenson, Howard H., Roberts, Michael J., and Grousbeck, H. Irving. *New Business Ventures and the Entrepreneurs.* 2d ed. Homewood, IL: Richard D. Irwin, 1985.
Winer, Leon. "Many Students Seek the Skills Successful Entrepreneurs Need." *Marketing News,* 18 July 1986, 30.

CASE 1

The Case Assignment: Creating the Right Match

Dale M. Lewison and Jon Hawes, the University of Akron

It was time to face reality. It was do or die time for Ralph Reed, Lindsay Barta, and Bob Prentice. The case analysis that Dr. Rebecca Palmer assigned ten weeks ago was due in three weeks. Class policy in Retail Management—705 was that all late papers were discounted two percentage points per day regardless of the reason. "Old Palmer" was a hardnose.

The procrastinating trio sat around the large rear table in "The Pit," the now-famous eatery in the old student center. Having spent the last two hours reviewing the information in the case, it was time to get down to business.

Bob: Look, all we have to do is to find the right match between a camera store and its customers.

Lindsay: Your problem statement is a bit generalized. According to the text, the right match is finding an acceptable balance between the retailer's right merchandise blend of products, quantities, places, times, prices, and appeals and the consumer's right choice.

Ralph: How do we know what the right choice is?

Lindsay: By analyzing and interpreting the psychographic customer types shown in Exhibits 1, 2, and 3. Keep in mind that most of our grade is based on analysis and interpretation of the case situation.

Bob: OK, let me see if I got this straight. For each of the three customer types, we are to develop a merchandising blend or plan. Does it have to include each one of the six "rights" for the three "customers"?

Lindsay: That's right. Better safe than sorry.

Ralph: I have ideas for the right product, price, or appeal, but what do you do for the right quantity or time?

Bob: Be creative, I guess.

Lindsay: OK, I have a test tomorrow, so let's decide who's going to do what.

Ralph: Each one of us can take a customer type and develop the merchandising blend for it. We can meet in two weeks and edit each other's work.

Lindsay: That's OK with me, but remember each of us had better do a good job because we will be out of time in two more weeks.

Bob: Let's make a specific list of things to do for each customer type and merchandising ingredient.

Ralph: Just follow the text, be creative, and develop specific recommendations.

Lindsay: Bob, you take the professional customer (Exhibit 1—1), Ralph, the striver (Exhibit 1—2), and I will cover the underachiever (Exhibit 1—3).

Bob: One last time, we are to develop an appropriate merchandising blend for our customer type.

Ralph: Keep in mind that we are to develop a blend that would be used by a specialty camera store.

Bob: I think we should get as creative as possible. For example, I am going to develop a newspaper advertisement, the layout—the whole thing.

Ralph: Good idea. Do whatever you think it will take to get an A.

Lindsay: Boy, look who is getting ambitious, but if you are willing to shoot for an A, so am I.

Bob: Two weeks from today. We've been slow out of the gate, let's finish strong.

ASSIGNMENT

☐ Assume the responsibilities of Ralph, Lindsay, and Bob.

EXHIBIT 1–1

Customer profile: The professional

1. Market share equals 15.1 percent of active owners.
2. Professional occupations.
3. Male "baby boomers."
4. Not people oriented, low in emotionalism and social interaction.
5. Do not view photography as important in social and family situations.
6. Photography interest stems from high involvement with camera.
7. Prefer manually controllable camera.
8. Uninfluenced by where others buy their camera.
9. Least motivated by low price.
10. More likely to notice print photo advertising and less likely to notice electronic advertising.
11. Strong ego involvement with camera.
12. Interested in objects rather than people.
13. Interested in high-performance equipment.
14. Newest camera is 35-mm SLR programmable.
15. Camera store is most likely outlet for new camera purchases.
16. More likely to photograph scenery, flowers, and nature.
17. Most likely to have entered a photo contest, earned money in some way related with photography and taken photo lessons.
18. Responsible for 25.4% of all film exposures.
19. Most likely to choose drug stores and mail order for their processing.
20. Above-average user of one-hour processing.
21. Below-average user of mini labs.
22. Picture quality major factor in choosing a processing outlet.
23. Above-average users of different finishing services.
24. A high outlet return rate in purchasing accessories after initial camera purchase.
25. Overall, the highest rate of accessory purchases.

Source: Glenn S. Omura, *Photo Consumer Life-styles* (Jackson, MI: Photo Marketing Association International, 1986), 4–13.

EXHIBIT 1–2
Customer profile: The strivers

1. Market share equals 8.6 percent of active owners.
2. Extremely high achievement oriented.
3. Very materialistic and creative.
4. Love high-tech consumer products.
5. Very people oriented, emotional, and compassionate toward children.
6. Have fewest children per household.
7. Like to take pictures that are different and difficult to shoot.
8. Believe picture taking is an important way to demonstrate affection.
9. Willing to pay a premium for a camera that allows them to be more creative.
10. Tend to be store loyal.
11. Prefer shops that cater to photo experts.
12. Relish personal attention at stores.
13. Patronize stores that show them how to be more professional and creative.
14. Prefer finishers that automatically correct for bad exposures.
15. Would take more pictures if finishers would provide further assistance, such as creating special effects.
16. Most likely to incorporate photography into their life-styles.
17. True photography enthusiasts, not just camera hobbyists.
18. Recall print media better than electronic advertising.
19. More likely to shop department stores and drug stores for any type of merchandise.
20. Not as price sensitive and are value conscious, enjoy negotiating lower prices, but want the best they can get.
21. 35-mm programmable most popular camera.
22. Interested in picture quality, ease of operation, versatility, and technological sophistication.
23. Camera stores are favorite outlet for camera purchases.
24. Expect greater quality reputation, service, knowledgeable staff, product selection from their outlet.
25. More likely to take photos at large gatherings.
26. More likely to take pictures to give as gifts.
27. Greatest finishing profit potential on a per household basis.
28. Most likely to choose drug stores as their finishing outlet, but camera stores are also popular finishings outlets.
29. Expect more of their finishing outlet than any other group—picture quality, added services, knowledgeable staff, personalized attention, convenient location, turnaround time, and selection of photo and nonphoto merchandise.
30. More likely to use ancillary finishing services of all types.
31. Good one-hour processing potential customers.
32. More likely to use non-mini lab outlets.
33. Heavy buyers of camera accessories.

Source: Glenn S. Omura, *Photo Consumer Life-styles* (Jackson, MI: Photo Marketing Association International, 1986), 4–13.

EXHIBIT 1-3
Customer profile: The
underachiever

1. Market share equals 13.6 percent of active owners.
2. High self-confidence, yet least likely to engage in do-it-yourself projects, hence name of market segment.
3. Economic rationality ranks high in their value hierarchy—enjoy seeking the best possible deal.
4. Greater proportion of women.
5. High need for control.
6. Prefer simple equipment, do not believe that expensive and sophisticated cameras are needed to capture important emotions in photographs.
7. Prefer professional photos of loved ones because they do not trust their own photographic abilities.
8. Like finishers to automatically correct their pictures for poor exposures.
9. Want finishers to help record children's development by offering such aid as printed dates on photos.
10. Little involvement with cameras so long as they get good pictures.
11. Respond to appeals that emphasize simplicity and "you can do it."
12. Most sensitive to price.
13. Least able to recall photo advertising.
14. Better recall on TV ads.
15. Word of mouth important.
16. Outlet does not need a strong photo image.
17. Lowest in profit potential for cameras as a result of price sensitivity.
18. Prefer cameras for ease of operation, low price, low film cost, and picture quality.
19. Favorite camera is 110, but can be traded up to a range finder, also interested in disc and instant camera.
20. Most likely to buy from discount store, but some chance at buying at camera store to upgrade camera.
21. Low finishing profit potential.
22. Drug stores primary outlet for finishing but also other low-cost outlets.
23. Modest ancillary finishing potential.
24. Below average in purchase of camera accessories.
25. Above average in use of frames and albums.

Source: Glenn S. Omura, *Photo Consumer Life-styles* (Jackson, MI: Photo Marketing Association International, 1986), 4-13.

CASE 2

What Happened to the Department Store? Seeking New Strategies and Tactics

Dale M. Lewison and Jon Hawes, the University of Akron

RETAIL WEEKLY   January 10, 1989

What's Happening to Department Stores

At the turn of the century, department stores had positioned themselves for absolute dominance of the retail market. Through mergers and integration, these retail organizations became large conglomerate corporations capable of dominating many supply markets. As a dominant retail force, department stores established the competitive position by which all other retailers were judged. There, dominance continued into the post–World War II period and through the 1960s. By the early 1970s, however, department stores were being outflanked by savvy competitors whose specialty and/or value-discount business formats were delivering more and better goods for the money. Now, while total retail sales continue to increase, the conventional department store market share is decreasing. In addition, specialty stores have passed department stores in profitability, and discounters have drawn about even with department store operations.

Many conventional department stores have become so aggressive in price promotions that it is almost impossible to distinguish them from discounters. By employing this suicidal pricing practice, department stores can expect the continuing loss of consumer confidence, the steady decline of operating profits, and an ever-stiffening of competitive actions. So, What's happening to department stores? One answer is that they have forgotten the other five "rights" of merchandising (product, quantity, place, time, and appeal) in their never-ending quest for cheaper prices.

by Jeb Brown, Senior Staff Writer

One more trade article lamenting the downturn in department store fortunes. It seemed to Stan Morris that he had read essentially the same article five times in the last couple of months. As an associate in the firm Retail Associates International, a consulting organization specializing in strategic retail planning, Morris had a vested interest in department store futures; he was one of the firm's principle resident experts on department store strategies and tactics. What troubled Morris was that everyone was an expert on the fact that department stores seemed to have entered the late maturity stage of the retail life cycle. These armchair experts, however, seemed to have very few concrete suggestions for reviving the industry. Perhaps that was why Stan had been so busy lately; if everyone had a workable answer for reviving the department store business, Morris might've been out of work.

It was time for Morris to prepare the firm's annual report on the state of the department store industry. Given that each of Retail Associates International's twenty-four department store clients pays an annual fee of $20,000 for this report and the right to access the firm's extensive research files on all aspects of retailing, Morris had better be able to identify the specific causes for the woes of department store retailing. More importantly, some constructive strategies and tactics for overcoming past problems and promoting the growth and revitalization of the industry would be absolutely essential to the report's credibility. One comment that Morris read in Brown's article especially rang true: Department stores need to place less emphasis on price promotions and pay greater attention to the other five merchandising "rights."

ASSIGNMENT

☐ Assume the role of a student who has a summer internship with Retail Associates International. Stan Morris has asked you to conduct a library search to find trade and other articles that (1) identify specific merchandising and operational problems within the department store industry and (2) identify specific merchandising and/or operating strategies and tactics that might aid in overcoming the problems of department store retailing.

☐ Prepare a well-organized written report to Morris on your findings. You might want to think of future employment opportunities and make your own recommendations, fully supported by a complete rationale.

PART TWO: ENVIRONMENTAL SCAN

CASE 3

Ray's Super: Responding to Competitive Threats

Jeffrey Dilts, the University of Akron

BACKGROUND

"We can't make money on groceries," Ray Henry said, reacting to the recent price war that had turned the grocery business upside down. Henry was a manager of a moderate-sized (20,000 square feet) supermarket operation located in a middle- to upper-income suburban area of the community. Until recently, the operation had managed to generate a reasonable return. New competition had begun to squeeze profits, however.

The area's economy was recovering from a recession that had reduced the population by seven percent as a result of job layoffs. Decreased volume placed greater importance on price competition. "Almost every trick of the trade was employed," Henry said, "including double and triple coupon redemptions." As a result, increases in area food prices were substantially below the national norm.

In the face of high labor costs, grocery chains attempted to negotiate wage concessions to improve profitability. Unsuccessful in this endeavor, National Groceries pulled out of the market, closing eight stores—including three large-scale super stores that had opened during the past two years.

Sav-More, a regional grocery wholesale operation, responded by opening three of the former National super stores and converting five of its existing area stores to a super discount warehouse format. An "Every Day Low Prices" policy on all items replaced weekly specials and double- and triple-coupons promotions. Sav-More advertising claimed price cuts on approximately 8,000 items, with the biggest cuts in packaged foods and paper goods.

Competitors, for the most part, responded in kind by cutting prices across the board. Overnight, the cost of a basket of 30 commonly purchased items had been reduced by an average of $7.89 in a majority of area stores.

CURRENT SITUATION

Concerned about the turn of events, Henry noted that "If this continues, I won't be able to stay in business." He suspected that the average purchase made in his store had declined, largely as a result of reduced volume for packaged goods. Revenues generated by perimeter departments, such as the deli and produce, appeared to be maintaining their previous levels.

Henry was not at a loss for alternatives; his personnel had recommended various solutions. He had to determine which action would help maintain customer patronage and build sales.

Mary Walle, assistant manager and part owner, had suggested an immediate price cut across the board to regain volume. Alice Dunlap, produce manager, disagreed because she thought such action would adversely affect profitability. Based on her previous management experience with a national chain, Dunlap argued that the size of the present store was not sufficient to generate the volumes necessary to be profitable at the lower margins suggested. Alternatively, she recommended that the operation build on its strengths in perishables and personal service.

Ray Nader, head butcher, agreed that the operation could differentiate itself from competitors by employing service departments. "The main attraction of warehouse operations is price, not service," he commented. Accordingly, he recommended expanding the service areas to include a specialty fish department, based on customer suggestions. "The margin on specialty items and perishables can make up for the volume lost on low-margin packaged groceries," Nader pointed out.

ASSIGNMENT

- ☐ Evaluate the alternatives described in this situation. Under what conditions would one alternative be more appropriate than another?
- ☐ What action would you recommend that Ray Henry take? Explain.

CASE 4

Quinn's Department Store: Using Leased Departments

Dan Gilmore, the University of Akron

In her five years as president of Quinn's Department Stores, Janet Spalding had continued the local chain's successful strategy of catering to the upper-end consumer market with high-quality, distinctive merchandise, excellent service, and innovative product and marketing techniques. Sales growth at the flagship store downtown and the six branch stores in area shopping malls had been impressive under Spalding's leadership, attributable in part to her ability to identify and support profitable changes and innovations that maintained the stores' fashionable image and her ability to develop better ways to meet customer needs.

In this tradition, Spalding and other company executives had recently decided to add a new food department and accompanying "café" in the downtown store.

Though many of the details had yet to be finalized, the plan called for the department to offer a variety of fancy, gourmet, and hard-to-find food and wine items, including many imported goods. Complementing this shop would be a delicatessen serving specialty salads and light meals for take-home or on-premise dining inside an open-store "sidewalk café." The atmosphere of both the mini-grocery and café was planned to exude fashionable elegance and feature expensive fixtures, lighting, and displays.

Spalding was convinced the concept would work. A few department stores in other areas of the country had been successful with similar ventures, and Spalding felt that Quinn's customer base would be especially receptive to the new offering, particularly since no grocery retailers in the downtown area offered the type of foods Quinn's planned to carry. "This department will have great appeal to the upscale shoppers whom we serve, provide them with an extra service not currently available in our market area, and make Quinn's a more enjoyable and distinctive place to shop," Spalding had told upper management at a recent meeting.

But although the store executives generally agreed that the new department was right for Quinn's, they differed considerably as to whether the grocery and deli should be run entirely by company personnel or should be created and managed by an outside operator on a lease basis. "Leased departments" have been used by retailers for many years, particularly by department stores in such product areas as shoes, jewelry, millinery, books, and photography. After a period of decline in the early 1980s, these leased departments have enjoyed a resurgence of popularity in recent years.

Under most lease agreements, customers are unable to distinguish leased departments from store-owned ones. These departments, however, are operated by the lessee, who is responsible for buying and pricing its merchandise, hiring its employees, and managing daily operations. In return for a monthly rental and/or a percentage of department sales, the leasing store typically provides services such as delivery, credit, payroll, accounting, utilities, and space lighting to the lessees. Many lessees are national companies that have departments in hundreds of different stores, though some operate on a much smaller regional or local basis.

Alex Archwell, Quinn's vice president of marketing, favored leasing the new department, and had already conducted some preliminary discussions with a food retailer in a nearby city who operated several specialty food stores that were similar in style and merchandise to that considered by Quinn's. Though this company had never operated a leased department, its owner was enthusiastic about the prospect.

"Janet, these guys are just what we need to make a success of this thing," Archwell told his boss. "While I think the idea is great, what do we know about food retailing? For instance, I can see significant problems in inventory management. I think leasing will enable us to provide the service we want as well as make a profit—with considerably less risk."

Barbara Roberts, manager of the downtown store, disagreed. "Who knows and can serve our customers better than we can?" she asked. "Isn't that one of the reasons we've avoided any lease agreements in the past, such as in shoes or jewelry? Besides, I think the quality of our in-store management is one of the chief factors in Quinn's success, and putting outsiders in control of even one of our departments is asking for trouble."

Janet Spalding had always had great faith in both Archwell's and Roberts's judgment, and recognized that each of them raised important points regarding the decision to lease or not lease the new department. She also realized that the new department's eventual success might well depend on making the right choice about leasing. Earlier, she had been so confident that the fancy foods and sidewalk café idea would work in the main store that she had already thought about how long it would be before she could introduce similar departments in Quinn's branch stores. Now she realized that she would have to take a closer look at the practice of leasing and its desirability for Quinn's fancy foods department and café.

ASSIGNMENT

☐ Assume Janet Spalding has asked you, a new Quinn's employee with college coursework in retailing, to help her analyze this situation. What do you see as the pros and cons of leased departments?
☐ What decision would you recommend to Janet Spalding for Quinn's fancy foods department and sidewalk café? Justify your decision.
☐ If Quinn's decides to lease the new department, what can management do in terms of its relationship with the lessee to help ensure the project's long-term success?

CASE 5

Doug's Video: Developing Competitive Positioning Strategies Based on Consumer Patronage Behavior

Ken Mast and Dale M. Lewison, the University of Akron

Doug Deitz's story was not unlike that of many other New Englanders who successfully survived the migration to the sunbelt of many types of manufacturing. Deitz had graduated from high school in the late 1940s, taken a job in a textile mill, enlisted in the Army Reserve, spent two years on active duty during the Korean conflict, and then returned to the mill. When the mill headed south in the sixties, Deitz took advantage of his G.I. bill and completed an associate degree in business.

He started his retailing career with a family-owned department store. Failure of the department store management to follow the movement into shopping centers led to the sale of the store to a chain. It became apparent to Deitz that the new management favored persons with baccalaureate degrees. When Deitz realized how long it was going to take him to complete his degree on a part-time basis, he regretted his decision not to continue his education at the time he'd completed the associate degree. As others with less experience received promotions to buying responsibility, Deitz sought a change of scenery and obtained more managerial responsibility in the employ of a discount store chain. He worked for two different discount chains until two years ago, when, with the benefit of an inheritance from his parents, he acquired a video store.

Although Deitz benefitted from the growing popularity of video rentals and the sale of video equipment, the success of his business seemed to indicate that he had more managerial talent than former employers had perceived. Proof of self-perception is the additional success Deitz achieved in providing unique and profitable video services. His first service was the videotaping of houses for sale. The tapes were sold to the more progressive area realtors who used it to screen home buyers' interests. Since it benefitted both the realtors and the prospective home buyers, it had been highly successful. Recently, he had expanded the video service to include videotapes of homes and contents for insurance purposes. Although the insurance service didn't generate the volume or the regular revenues of the realtor service, it did not require any additional investment in equipment and staff. The only added cost was for promotion; therefore, it represented the addition of a complementary line of service.

Doug's Video was located in a community shopping center complex that had been built as part of a relatively new housing development. The introduction and expansion of local high-tech industries had created a mini-boom for the local economy. New people were being attracted by these high-tech firms because job salaries in the $50,000 to $100,000 range were common. These high-income families constituted the majority of the home buyers in the housing development surrounding the shopping center. Additional retailers in the complex were a junior department store, a large super-food store,

a dry cleaner, a bakery, a hardware store, a small pharmacy, three apparel stores, a pizza/sub shop, and a delicatessen.

The video-rental business generated a fairly lively traffic volume into the store. Deitz's prior expansion of services had taken advantage of existing products and staff abilities but only indirectly of the high-volume in-store traffic. Because all systems seemed to be "go" in terms of the local economy, Deitz was seriously considering some type of expansion.

One expansion idea was to add a complementary line of merchandise that would fit into the current business format and capitalize on the high in-store traffic generated by the video rental business. The addition of a complete line of cameras and accessories was a product-extension strategy that Deitz felt he and his staff could handle within current operating abilities. The buying and merchandising aspects of adding new camera and accessory lines did not create any major obstacles. What concerned Deitz was developing a business format that would be competitive with other retailers and consistent with consumer patronage behavior. Recently, Deitz had obtained from a vendor an excellent trade survey on what factors influenced consumer choice of outlet for camera purchases. As revealed in the survey, the importance of patronage factors varies for different types of retailers (see Exhibit 5–1). The discount store camera customer is different from the department store customer. Through experience, Deitz learned that "competitive positioning" is often a key variable in introducing a new product or service. A quick mental survey of local retailers who sell cameras revealed that Deitz will face each of the six types of competitors identified in the trade report.

ASSIGNMENT

☐ Based on the consumer patronage behavior for camera purchases, develop three competitive positioning strategies Deitz might pursue in establishing his camera department. Analyze each strategy and make a recommendation.

☐ Based on your competitive positioning recommendation, identify key merchandising tactics that Deitz should use to successfully introduce this new line of products.

EXHIBIT 5–1 Patronage factors

Retail Setting	Rank	Influencing Factor	Outlet Rating	Overall Average
Discount store	1	Low price	5.77	5.36
	2	Services offered	4.92	5.08
	3	Quality reputation	4.59	5.00
	4	Knowledgeable sales staff	4.40	5.03
	5	Selection of photo goods	4.12	4.44
	6	Close to home or work	4.07	3.90
	7	Selection of other goods	3.60	2.83
	8	Attractive atmosphere	3.25	3.07
Camera store	1	Knowledgeable sales staff	5.84	5.03
	2	Services offered	5.73	5.08
	3	Quality reputation	5.64	5.00
	4	Selection of photo goods	4.91	4.44
	5	Low price	4.80	5.36
	6	Close to home or work	4.00	3.90
	7	Attractive atmosphere	3.15	3.07
	8	Selection of other goods	2.19	2.83
Mail order	1	Low price	5.81	5.36
	2	Quality reputation	5.40	5.00
	3	Selection of photo goods	5.00	4.44
	4	Services offered	4.68	5.08
	5	Knowledgeable sales staff	4.44	5.03
	6	Close to home or work	2.75	3.90
	7	Selection of other goods	2.16	2.83
	8	Attractive atmosphere	2.00	3.07
Department store	1	Low price	5.36	5.36
	2	Services offered	5.18	5.08
	3	Knowledgeable sales staff	4.98	5.03
	4	Quality reputation	4.97	5.00
	5	Selection of photo goods	4.25	4.44
	6	Close to home or work	4.15	3.90
	7	Attractive atmosphere	3.46	3.07
	8	Selection of other goods	3.19	2.83
Catalog showroom	1	Low price	5.73	5.36
	2	Services offered	4.90	5.08
	3	Quality reputation	4.80	5.00
	4	Knowledgeable sales staff	4.63	5.03
	5	Selection of photo goods	4.60	4.44
	6	Close to home or work	3.81	3.90
	7	Attractive atmosphere	3.41	3.07
	8	Selection of other goods	3.34	2.83
Discount camera store	1	Low price	5.56	5.36
	2	Knowledgeable sales staff	5.26	5.03
	3	Quality reputation	4.79	5.00
	4	Services offered	4.69	5.08
	5	Selection of photo goods	4.64	4.44
	6	Close to home or work	3.36	3.90
	7	Attractive atmosphere	2.39	3.07
	8	Selection of other goods	1.87	2.83
Overall factors	1	Low price		5.36
	2	Services offered		5.08
	3	Knowledgeable sales staff		5.03
	4	Quality reputation		5.00
	5	Selection of photo goods		4.44
	6	Close to home or work		3.90
	7	Attractive atmosphere		3.07
	8	Selection of other goods		2.83

Source: *1985 Consumer Photographic Survey* (Jackson, MI: Photo Marketing Association International): 21.

DINKs, DINKdom, and No DINKerbells: Targeting Consumer Life Cycles and Life-Styles*

Dale M. Lewison and Douglas Hausknecht, the University of Akron

Who are the DINKs? They are *Double Income, No-Kids* couples who work a combined 100-hour-plus workweek and earn a combined salary that is notably higher than either their "dual-income, with kids" or "single-income, no kids" counterparts. Nevertheless, there is a class system even within this limited consumer segment. Philip Kotler, professor of marketing at Northwestern, divides DINKs into upper and lower classes: U-DINKs and L-DINKs. "No doubt, while the L-DINKs are rushing to graduate from K mart to Marshall Field, the U-DINKs will be deserting the Banana Republic for Abercrombie & Fitch."

Where is DINKdom? Is it a place or a state of mind or is it both? DINKdom for the U-DINKs is often an architect-designed house in a pricier suburb or a refurbished gentrified flat in a trendy urban neighborhood. For the L-DINK, home is the best residential area within reach of a stretched pocketbook. DINKdom is also a state of mind, it is a desire for security, privacy, a nest, the finer things, and Persian duck in pomegranate sauce. But beware, it could also be a transitory state—"the moment before tradition sets in."

No DINKerbells means children are not desired in the near future. DINKs are not ready "to give up the quality time that is necessary to devote to their careers and transfer that to children." However, if the recent mini-baby boom among the thirtyish crowd is any indication, DINKs may find that "children may be the next pleasure source after they have tried everything else."

Never fear, if DINKs disappear, there are several snappy target market acronyms to take their place (e.g., TIPS—*Tiny Income, Parents Supporting* and NINKs—*No Income, No Kids*).

ASSIGNMENT

☐ Prepare a report titled "Merchandising Strategies for *Double-Income, No Kids* couples." The report should profile the key psychological, personal, and social factors that influence the buying behavior of this consumer segment. The report should make specific recommendations regarding the most appropriate product, price, place, and promotional strategies that retailers should follow in targeting this unique market segment.

---

*This case is based on Christine Gorman and Bill Johnson, "Here Come the DINKs," *Time*, 20 April 1987, 75–76.

Tri-State Audio-Video

Joseph McCafferty, the University of Akron

BACKGROUND

Karen Barta, owner and operator of Tri-State Audio-Video, had enjoyed considerable success as an independent retailer of consumer electronics. The mainstay of Tri-State's product mix had been high-quality stereos and television sets. Using value (quality products at reasonable prices) as the principal merchandising strategy, Barta had expanded her operation to include four outlets in the tri-state market area: two stores in south-central Michigan and two stores in northeast Indiana. Current expansion plans include opening new Tri-State Audio-Video outlets in northwest Ohio.

CURRENT SITUATION

Barta had a 10 o'clock appointment with her attorney, K. L. Kovach. A number of issues had surfaced recently that necessitated some sound legal advice. Of primary concern to Barta was her potential liability stemming from manufacturers' warranties. She wanted to determine her responsibility under the Magnuson-Moss Warranty Act. Tri-State offered no warranties on any items sold. With manufacturers' warranties, Tri-State acted strictly as an intermediary between its customers and the producer. When a customer bought a product from Tri-State and returned it within the time period allowed by the manufacturer's warranty, Barta's policy was to make sure the product returned to the manufacturer and to make sure the customer was satisfied with whatever adjustment the manufacturer made. To date, Barta had never been asked to refund a customer's money because the manufacturer was unable to repair or refused to replace a defective product. On reflection, this liability issue had never been much of a problem in the past because she'd always dealt with well-known manufacturers that had quality reputations to protect.

Today's visit concerned Barta's plans to sell compact disk players, one of the hottest items on the market. Her new concern with warranty liability arose because none of her current suppliers market a compact disk player and the only available supplier is a relatively new company called Compact Disk Corporation (CDC). CDC offered Barta an exclusive dealership for the tri-state area. Barta was worried over a recent article in a West Coast newspaper citing various problems consumers were having with CDC's products and CDC's inability to provide quick and satisfactory repairs.

To facilitate the discussion with her lawyer, Barta brought along all the literature she'd received from CDC. Of particular interest was the CDC warranty statement. As described in the literature, CDC offered a "Full 90-Day Warranty," which guaranteed the CDC compact disk player will not have defects in materials or workmanship for 90 days from date of original purchase. CDC will repair or replace the defective part free of charge if the defective product is delivered prepaid to CDC Service

Division, 435 Johns Ave., Surfside, California. The full warranty statement also included a clause stating that CDC will not be responsible for any "consequential or incidental" damages. In addition to the full warranty, CDC also offered a "limited warranty" on defects in the product's turntable. This warranty simply stated that coverage begins 90 days after the original purchase and lasts for one year after original purchase. It also stated that no "consequential or incidental" damages are recoverable from the manufacturer under this warranty. To benefit from the warranty, the customer had to send the turntable to the manufacturer in California. The last paragraph in CDC's warranty stated that after 90 days from purchase, there are no implied warranties of merchantability or fitness. After a brief discussion, Kovach advised Barta not to sign any contract with CDC until she received Kovach's written assessment of Tri-State's liability exposure.

ASSIGNMENT

☐ Assume the role of K. L. Kovach. What possible role could state laws play in determining the applicability of consumer warranties, in light of the Magnuson-Moss Warranty Act? What parts of CDC's warranty would be disallowed by the Magnuson-Moss Warranty Act and what might be Barta's potential liability under this warranty? Prepare a written report.

CASE 8

Is It Bait and Switch, or Is It Trading Up?

Joseph McCafferty, the University of Akron

BACKGROUND

The morning edition of the *Cleveland Gazette* carried two sales advertisements featuring special promotions on color television sets. Prough Home Centers, a chain of home appliance stores with eighty-four outlets in fourteen states, ran an advertisement featuring repossessed color televisions:

PROUGH HOME CENTERS
"The Professionals in Home Appliances"
Saturday Only
Repossessed, Repaired, Resold
COLOR TELEVISIONS
At Rock Bottom Prices
Starting at $99.95
LIKE NEW

The second advertisement was placed by The World of Entertainment, a specialty electronics store chain with outlets in eight states; it featured deep discounting of new, brand-name color televisions:

THE WORLD OF ENTERTAINMENT
Proudly Presents
NEW, NAME-BRAND, FAMILY-SIZE
COLOR TELEVISIONS
$279.95
"We Buy Straight From the Factory"
DON'T MISS THIS DEAL
SALE ENDS SOON

CURRENT SITUATION

The Johnsons' Experience

Dave and Carol Johnson, a newlywed couple, had been holding off purchasing a new color television until the right sale came along. The Prough Home Center ad caught Dave's attention. The price of $99.95 seemed almost too good to be true. Since the Johnsons lived only six blocks from the nearest outlet, they decided to check out what specific items were available. While Carol reminded Dave that the advertisement did specify "repossessed" color televisions, Dave dismissed Carol's comment, saying "At $99.95, who cares! So long as we can get a couple of good years of trouble-free service out of it, I'll be happy."

Entering the store, the Johnsons were met by Kathy O'Brian, a top performer in the store's sales department. Dave told O'Brian they had seen Prough's newspaper advertisement, and he expressed an interest in seeing which sets were available. O'Brian informed the Johnsons that although the used sets were in good working order, many of the models had nicks and scratches and the lower-priced sets were generally smaller portable models with even more wear and tear. To support her statement, O'Brian explained that the set advertised for $99.95 was a 12-inch, two-year-old model. Dave replied that he expected as much, but would still like to see the selection of used sets.

As they started to the back of the store where the used sets were on display, O'Brian stopped them at a 14-inch Sony with remote control. "You know," she said, "this is the best set in the store. It's also the best value. This color portable comes complete with remote control and automatic tuning. The regular price on this Sony is $499 but it is currently on sale for $399, terms are 90 days same as cash. Also, Sony has a great limited warranty, so you would not have to worry about any major repair bills. I really think this set offers excellent value. You really should consider taking advantage of this offer." As a commissioned salesperson, O'Brian stood to benefit financially from the sale of a more expensive set.

"We really would like to look at the used sets if we could," Dave said.

"Sure," O'Brian replied. "I just wanted to show you an opportunity to make a real value purchase. Personally, I feel the smart buy is a new set because there is very little risk with such a purchase."

"What risk?" Carol asked.

"Well, as you would expect, the manufacturers' warranties are no longer in force on the used sets," O'Brian replied. "And the store's guarantee is limited to 30 days." Seeing that this final clincher had sold the Johnsons, O'Brian hurriedly started writing up the sales contract on the new Sony.

The Criss's Experience

The same day across town, Betty Criss was skimming the *Cleveland Gazette*. The sales promotion advertisement by The World of Entertainment caught Betty's eye. Betty and her husband, Dick, had been watching television on a portable set for a long time, and she thought it was time to get a big 24-inch console television. When Betty saw The World's offer of "family-size" color televisions for "$279.95," she knew the time to buy a new color television had come. Dick Criss expressed some concern about this "almost too good to be true deal" but agreed to accompany Betty to the local outlet in Leipply Square.

Betty walked confidently into The World of Entertainment that night and expressed interest in the color television console she had seen advertised. Bob Sproat, department manager, led Betty and Dick to a 19-inch color portable. "This is it! This is as family size as you can get," Sproat said. "We've been having trouble with the picture on this one all day, so let's see if I can get one in for you now."

Much to Sproat's delight, Betty's face shriveled at the sight of this family-size portable. The truth was that The World of Entertainment had none of these sets in stock at the moment and the earliest Sproat could get one with an immediate order was 60 days, if he was lucky. He sensed an excellent opportunity to unload one of the many big console sets in stock. "This portable set has a very limited manufacturer's warranty, and the store's guarantee is limited to 30 days. You've already seen the tough time I've had getting a clear picture. This particular model has already given us nothing but trouble. I doubt that it would last more than a couple of years, if that long."

Sproat stepped around the set on sale to a big color console on display in an adjacent setting. Betty's face lit up. Sproat kicked his sales pitch into high gear. "Look at this beautiful console. It's got a great finish and would complement the decor of any home. The manufacturer's warranty is excellent, and we have a full service department to support the warranty. It's a bit more in price than the one on sale, but look at how much more you're getting. At this price, I think we can even throw in a remote control. Personally, I would hate to see you get stuck with that other troublemaker when I can let you walk out of here today with this set." After extolling all the virtues of the big console, Sproat tried once again to get a clear picture on the portable but without success.

As Betty and Dick stared at the fuzzy picture, Sproat whipped out a sales contract and started filling in the necessary information. Within 20 minutes, Betty and Dick were driving home with a new 24-inch console in the back of the station wagon. "I thought he said he would deliver this thing," Dick said. "For $625.95 you would think he would at least have it delivered."

"He would have," Betty replied, "but they wouldn't be able to deliver it until the end of next week."

ASSIGNMENT

☐ Discuss the legal implications concerning the two sales experiences. What remedies might each family attempt, if any?

☐ Discuss the moral and ethical implications of the advertising and selling techniques employed by each retailer. Look at the transaction from both sides. Do retailers and consumers really deal at arm's length (with equal knowledge of the product and its value)?

PART THREE: RESOURCE ASSESSMENT

CASE 9

The Family Shoe Shop

Dale M. Lewison, the University of Akron

BACKGROUND

The Family Shoe Shop was an independently owned and operated shoe store located in a large regional shopping center. R. P. Evans, the proprietor, had organized the store around three departments: 1,800 square feet of selling space are devoted to men's shoes, 1,600 square feet for women's shoes, and 1,200 square feet for the children's department.

CURRENT SITUATION

Each year Evans faced the task of completing the store's annual income statement. With this year's gross sales totaling $250,000, Evans hoped to end the year with a greater operating profit than last year's $39,800. An examination of the current year's sales records shows that 8,450 sales transactions and an average investment in inventory of $88,000 were required to generate the $250,000 figure. Further examination of various records provided Evans with the following information: (1) The store opened the year with $48,000 of inventory. (2) The beginning inventory was supplemented throughout the year by net purchases of $112,000. (3) The year ended with an inventory on hand conservatively valued at $36,000. (4) Workroom costs of $1,000 were incurred in preparing the products for sale, and $4,000 was spent on transportation charges in getting the products to the store. (5) The store earned a $2,000 cash discount by paying for the goods as soon as the invoice was received.

One figure that greatly disturbed Evans was the $1,100 in goods returned by customers. In addition, he had to make allowances totaling $250 for damaged merchandise.

Another of Evans's major concerns was operating expenses. After a concerted effort to control this year's operating expenses, he hoped that a lower expense figure would substantially improve his profit picture. Records kept by natural divisions revealed the following expenses:

Payroll	$26,000
Advertising	3,000
Taxes	1,700
Supplies	900
Services purchased	500
Unclassified	100
Travel	350
Communications	550
Insurance	2,600
Pensions	1,100
Depreciation	1,450
Professional services	3,500
Donations	250
Bad debts	400
Equipment	600
Real property rentals	36,000

In addition to these operating expenses, Evans was concerned about the $2,500 interest payments to the First Republic Bank. Something would have to be done to reduce the principal on that business loan. If nothing else worked out, at least the income from the candy machine increased 100% from $75 last year to $150 this year.

ASSIGNMENT

☐ Given the information in the case, lend Evans a hand by developing a complete income statement.

CASE 10

The Island Shops Franchise: Making A Financial Investment Decision

Dan Gilmore, the University of Akron

CURRENT SITUATION

Penny Shaheen and her husband listened intently to the presentation being given to them in their home by a representative of The Island Shops, a chain of franchised clothing outfits in the Midwest that featured casual Hawaiian and safari-style clothing and accessories. The franchise was of the business-format type, which meant that it provided not only the right to do business under The Island Shops name but also a standardization of store design and operations as well as assistance at some specified level in such areas as management training, accounting, merchandising, site location, and many others. The representative, Debra Long, was here because Penny had called the company after seeing a franchise opportunity ad in a well-known national business publication. Though she had called the firm on little more than a whim, Penny had been considering for some time the idea of leaving her present job and starting her own business. She had read that franchising might be a good choice for achieving this goal, and The Island Shops advertisement had sounded quite appealing.

"The fact that you have no retail management experience, Mrs. Shaheen, should not be of concern," said Long shortly after she began her presentation. "Believe me, our complete training and assistance program will enable you to learn successful operating procedures with little difficulty. That's one of the great advantages of franchising."

She went on to explain that becoming an Island Shops store owner, or franchisee, required payment of

EXHIBIT 10–1
Disclosure statement as of 1 February 1988

Name of Company: The Island Shops, Inc.
310 Riverside Drive
Rock Island, IL 50432
(242) 555-6812

The Island Shops is a wholly owned subsidiary of Omega, Inc., San Jose, California.

Description of operations: Franchised and company-owned retail clothing stores. The Island Shops, typically located in shopping malls and plazas, carry an exciting line of Hawaiian and safari-style clothing and accessories for men and women.

Number of stores: Twenty franchise stores and five company-owned stores in five states.

Number of franchises sold in 1987: Fourteen.

In business since: 1985.

Managerial assistance provided: Initial and continuing management assistance in the areas of general retail management, accounting merchandising, site selection, lease negotiations, and advertising is provided franchisees at company expense.

EXHIBIT 10–2
Income statement
for year ending
31 December 1987

Total revenue (stores, royalties, franchise sales)	$2,912,000
Cost of goods sold	$1,450,000
Income from operations	$1,462,000
Administrative and other expenses	$ 720,000
Net income before taxes	$ 742,000

List of franchises: 1543 Boucher Blvd.
Indianapolis, IN 49202
(315) 555-9123
Owner: Jim Plezak

(The remaining franchisees were listed)

an initial franchise fee of $60,000, plus the ability to secure an additional $40,000 of capital. On top of that, continuing royalty fees of 3 percent of gross sales were required.

"Our franchise fee is somewhat high for this type of store," Long conceded. "But that is more than balanced by the low royalty fees we collect." She noted that McDonald's, for instance, charges franchisees an 11.5 percent royalty fee plus another 4 percent for advertising.

As required by Federal Trade Commission law, Long gave Penny a franchise disclosure statement, or prospectus. This document must give detailed information concerning 20 subjects of interest to potential franchise investors, such as terms of sale, any continuing fees, operating restrictions, and a variety of financial and business figures, including a company balance sheet, income statement, and a statement of changes in financial position. A copy of a sample franchise contract must also be attached. (A selected sample of the information in the disclosure statement for The Island Shops is provided in Exhibits 10–1 and 10–2.)

"I know it's a lot to think over," said Long, "but you'll need to make a decision rather quickly. You are just one of many people we're interviewing, and only one franchise is available in this area. I can give you a week, but after that I'm afraid someone else will snap up this opportunity. Long continued, "I've been impressed by our meeting here, however. If you can meet our capital requirements, I can say with near certainty you will be selected as this area's Island Shops franchisee."

Penny had never been to an Island Shops store, but the concept did sound appealing. She had purchased a Hawaiian outfit herself recently and knew that this type of clothing was currently quite popular.

"Let me tell you, these stores are hot," said Long. "The merchandise really moves. Everybody is inter-

ested in this type of clothing now, as some of our other franchisees can tell you. I would suggest if you want to find out more about the stores that you call Jim Huscroft in Toledo or Alice Schaub in Ft. Wayne. They're both fairly typical of our owners and very easy to talk to."

The presentation lasted nearly two hours, after which Penny and her husband felt they knew a great deal about both the chain and the opportunity. Long had been informative and thorough. Having read a little bit about franchise deals, they were pleased about several aspects of the opportunity, including the low royalty payments and Long's promise that the outlet would have an exclusive territory; that is, no other company stores would be opened in their defined territory during the first five-year contract.

As she was leaving, Long said, "You know, not many franchisors can advertise in the type of prestigious publication like the one in which you saw our ad. I think that tells you something about our company's commitment to quality." Then she added, "And one more thing—please review our standard contract. I think you'll find it is written quite favorably for franchisees."

After Long left, Penny and her husband talked things over. The opportunity sounded great, but it was an awfully big decision to make in a short time. Penny was unhappy with her insurance job, though as a district manager for claims adjustment she was earning nearly $40,000 per year. But her job dissatisfaction, combined with the desire she had always had to own her own retail clothing business, made the offer attractive. The Shaheens decided they could raise the required capital without too much strain and that if the store were successful, their return on the investment would be substantial. Both agreed, nevertheless, that they had a lot to think over and do in the next week before making a decision.

THE ISLAND SHOPS' PROSPECTUS

Some of the information contained in The Island Shops' prospectus given to Penny Shaheen is provided in Exhibits 10–1 and 10–2.

ASSIGNMENT

☐ If you were Penny Shaheen, what steps would you take to help you make your decision? Outline a

plan, including what you would do and why, for making a franchise investigation and investment decision.

☐ Critique the proposal and presentation given by Debra Long and The Island Shops from an investor's perspective. Are there any actions, evidence, or statements that you feel are misleading or a cause for concern?

CASE 11

The Jones Boycott: A Community Complains About Personnel Policies

Gary B. Frank, the University of Akron

Larry Mason turned to George Paul and said, "This is getting serious, George!"

Paul nodded decisively. "Yes, I think it's time to call in the lawyers on this, Larry. I don't know if we are right or wrong; I'm not even sure if it matters. In my mind there are at least two issues we must consider: legal and ethical. In any case, you will have to continue to manage the West Side store somehow, even if Reverend Jones makes good on his threat of a boycott. I'm sorry, Larry, that we didn't take this matter seriously enough two months ago when this whole mess got started."

BACKGROUND

The "mess" that George Paul was bemoaning had begun as a complaint by the Reverend Thadeous S. Jones to Larry Mason, manager of the West Side Market. Specifically, the Reverend Jones had first called on Larry Mason after one of his parishoners, Aaron Washington, had talked to the Reverend about his failure to get a job at the store. When Washington had applied, one of the assistant managers told him not to bother filling out an application. The assistant manager had responded as he did because the store had just filled the last of its vacant positions, but his choice of words was unfortunate. Washington took the statement to mean that he was not welcome to apply because he was black.

The Reverend Jones arrived at the store on the assistant manager's day off, and Mason had no idea what had happened. After listening to the complaint, Mason said, "I'm sure there was some mistake by Mr. Washington. We're an equal opportunity employer, we have many black employees, and we've never discouraged blacks from applying at any of our stores."

The Reverend Jones looked around, then said, "Yes. Well I see that a couple of your baggers are black, but that's all I see. Mr. Washington is a qualified butcher, a

man with a family to support, and I guess you thought he was probably too old to bag groceries for you."

The confrontation might have been resolved at that point, but the Reverend Jones's sarcasm had not been lost on Larry, and he'd had a bad day already. He concluded the conversation by saying, "Reverend Jones, we're a good employer. We stand by our record. And I'm sorry if that doesn't suit you."

The next Sunday the Reverend talked at length from his pulpit about the need for his congregation to support employers that provided meaningful and dignified jobs to the members of the community—and to walk an extra block to shop at stores where the owners weren't just "trying to make a dollar off our people."

That statement may have been unfair as applied to West Side Market, but it did echo the concerns of many of the congregation. The west side was the older section of town, which had been largely abandoned by whites as they moved to the suburbs. For 30 years the west side had been predominately black; however, the tone of the community had started to change in the last six or eight years.

"Gentrification" had hit the west side as young, urban professionals rediscovered the magnificent older homes of the district and the convenience of the sector's proximity to both the central business district and the riverside bars and clubs. These young professionals had an impact on the area's business mix as trendy bars and health clubs started to displace older businesses. To many of the black businesspeople on the verge of retirement, the chance to sell out at the highest prices in memory was a godsend; but for others in the community, fear of losing employment made the changes unwelcome.

In this climate, the West Side Market became the unwitting center of community tension. The West Side Market had taken over and remodeled a market that had stood vacant for four years. The new store did not displace anyone, and the competition that it provided the single existing food market had resulted in lower food prices in the neighborhood. But in the heat of the current social controversy, the beneficial impact of the West Side Market was ignored. The situation escalated as community rallies were held by the Reverend Jones. The news media covered these events, and in the course of two months, the West Side Market's hiring practices became an open topic of community discussion.

So, as George Paul discussed these events with Mason, he had good cause for concern. Opening the new store had extended him financially, but his initial projections had been that the store would break even within a couple of years. An organized boycott, however, even for a few weeks, would force him to close the store, with ruinous losses.

CURRENT SITUATION

Very disturbed, George Paul met with his lawyer, Justin Stanhope. After hearing the facts, Stanhope responded, "George, you're my friend, and I hate to see you in a bind, but I have to warn you that your problem may be more than community relations. I'm somewhat surprised that you haven't already had a call from the Equal Employment Opportunity Commission. But I've dealt with the Reverend Jones before, and I know he has strong feelings about community self-help. So, maybe the Reverend Jones has done you a favor that neither you nor he recognize yet. Reverend Jones pulls a lot of weight in that community, and you made a mistake in not meeting with him before this got so far out of hand. At the same time, I think he can be a reasonable man. He's intelligent, and he truly cares for his community. If you can get him cooled off, you might be able to discuss this whole affair more rationally. As to whether you have a legal problem, I can't answer you yet. We need more facts to go on."

At this point, Paul jumped back into the conversation. "Justin, you know I'm always willing to call in the legal eagles when I'm in over my head. At the same time, I know from past experience what you folks charge. What with opening the new store, I'm in a real cash bind. Is there anything I can do to help put together these facts?"

"Well George, I did give a speech a while back to the Small Business Association that covered some of the problems in equal employment opportunity law. If you like, I'll have my secretary run off a copy for you. After you've gone through it, give me a call. I should caution you, though, that the speech was very general, and the law in this area changes rapidly."

Paul took the speech home that night and read it carefully. The text of this speech is shown in Exhibit 11–1.

After reading the speech, Paul called the manager of the West Side store. "Larry, we need to get together tomorrow morning. Meet me at 9:00 in my office. I've got some material I want you to read. And it's going to mean that you'll have to do a bunch of digging through your personnel files."

The next morning while Mason was in his office, Paul called Stanhope. "Justin, I read your speech. I'm going to have the West Side manager pull together the figures for adverse-impact analysis. But we're at somewhat of a loss. We could analyze things six ways to Sunday, and we need some direction."

"Well George, you're right. If you do get hit with an EEOC charge, they will probably go on a fishing expedition that covers all your personnel policies. If that does happen, we will need to present your best case—and that may mean breaking the data down by store, or trying to lump all the stores together if that gives us better bottom-line figures. But don't get carried away yet. For now, you aren't facing a charge, and what you want to do is placate Reverend Jones. After we've done our own analysis of your personnel records, it may be helpful to lay the facts before Reverend Jones. For the analysis, I suggest you focus on the West Side Market's hiring data, and break it down into supervisory/nonsupervisory by male/female and racial categories. Also, don't accuse me of trying to drum up business, but we might want to set up a review of all of your personnel policies just in case your problem worsens."

"Justin, I think you're right. I had no idea this EEOC stuff was so far reaching. It's time to take a close look at our personnel policies. But one question, how can we validate our policies?"

"George, you're jumping the gun. Don't worry about that yet. Let's see what develops. And get me that data as soon as you can."

Within several days, Larry Mason collected the personnel data on the store's first four months of operation, organized them into the suggested categories, and sent the result to Justin Stanhope's office. These data are shown in Exhibit 11–2 on p. 730.

ASSIGNMENT

Advise George Paul on the following issues:

☐ From a legal perspective, does he have basis for concern? Support your answer with a detailed analysis of the data presented.

☐ How should George Paul resolve the problem? What specific actions do you recommend?

☐ What are the ethical issues in this case? How should these issues be resolved? Is there a conflict between the "most ethical" course of action and the objectives of West Side Market?"

EXHIBIT 11–1
Equal employment and
the law (presented to
the Small Business As-
sociation by Justin
Stanhope)

I'm pleased to be here this afternoon, and I believe the subject you have asked me to cover is a timely one. At one time only major corporations seemed to have to worry about equal opportunity employment, but that is no longer the case. The impact of the law is being felt by increasing numbers of small firms. Both the public and employees are far more knowledgeable about their rights. And fewer employees feel disloyal if they pursue those rights.

Most of you try to be fair in all aspects of your employment practices. As businesspeople you know that "fairness" is just good business practice. You recognize that if you limit employment to one class of people, you miss out on good potential employees. And you recognize that the morale of your current employees will be adversely affected if you act in a capricious, arbitrary, or discriminatory fashion. So I know that all of you try to follow a "Golden Rule" policy in the way you treat employees and applicants. However, despite your best intentions, you can inadvertently violate the law if you don't understand it. This is especially the case in the area of equal employment opportunity law.

So, today I'm going to give you a brief overview of the law and the associated administrative process. Since our time is limited, I will focus on Title VII of the Civil Rights Act of 1964, although you should be aware that there are numerous other pieces of antidiscrimination law.

The thrust of Title VII is put forth in Section 703 where it states that it shall be unlawful for an employer ". . . to limit, segregate or classify his employees in any way which would deprive or tend to deprive any individual of employment opportunities or otherwise adversely affect his status as an employee because of such individual's race, color, religion, sex or national origin."

That's a fairly simple statement, but note how far reaching it is in terms of your employment practices. It affects recruiting, hiring, performance appraisal, promotions, job transfers, and indeed all of your personnel policies and actions.

As businesspeople you wish to comply with the law, but in the early days after enactment, what constituted discrimination was often unclear. And employers often wondered what their defense would be if faced by a discrimination charge. Today, even though we see a continuing case-by-case development and interpretation of the law, business does have some general guides to follow. In 1978, the major federal equal employment opportunity enforcement agencies jointly issued the Federal Uniform Guidelines on Employee Selection Procedures. These guides are significant to you for three reasons:

1. They apply across most of the federal statutes and executive orders that may affect you.
2. They give an operational definition of employment discrimination so that you can monitor whether you are likely to have broken the law.
3. They lay out the defenses you have if you are the target of an EEO action.

We will talk about the latter two points at some length; but first, you must recognize that the law has never said that you must hire or retain unqualified employees. What Title VII does say is that if you are not able to identify qualified employees, you can't make your personnel decisions based upon race, sex, religion, or national origin.

Now, with regard to an operational or working definition of discrimination, the 1978 guides established what is known as the 4/5ths or 80% rule. Previous case law had developed the concept of adverse impact to define discrimination. Under the concept of adverse impact, if the effect of your employment practices led to disproportionate selection of a group, you had discriminated. But the employer did not know how equally balanced its labor force had to be to protect itself from a discrimination charge. Now, under the 80% rule, the employer has an advance guide to what constitutes adverse impact, and therefore this allows the employer to self-monitor actions. Slide 1 will show you how this works.

	Slide 1		
	Applied	Hired	Percentage Selected
Blacks	42	4	9.5%
Whites	215	35	16.3%

Highest Rate	16.3%
Times 80%	× .8%
Level below which adverse impact is demonstrated:	12.04%

To use the 80% rule in adverse-impact analysis, we need to identify applicant groups and have historic information on numbers applying and selected. We identify the group with the highest selection rate and multiply that rate by .8. If the selection rate for any other group is less than the result—here less than 12%—there is demonstrated adverse impact and the employer is held to have discriminated. The burden of proof to justify his actions then falls on the employer. You should note two facts:

1. The illustration we used was simplified. You would have a more complex analysis by the time you had included whites, blacks, American Indians, Asians, and Hispanics, cross categorized by male or female. Moreover, almost any identifiable group might claim protected status.

2. You are under a strong record-keeping requirement. The legitimacy of your selection procedure will depend on the outcome of the adverse-impact analysis. If you don't have records, there is a strong presumption of adverse impact.

At this point, assuming you have done adverse-impact analysis and have found that you have violated the 80% rule, you may choose to change your selection policies, or you may be ordered to change them. However, if you feel your selection methods are justified, the 1978 Uniform Guides tell you how to defend what you have done. The guides discuss multiple validation methods, but the process essentially amounts to a demonstration that the standards you have used are job related and are justified by business necessity.

Remember, the law does not require you to hire or maintain unqualified people. The law does require that an employer have the burden of proof to show that these qualifications are necessary for the job if they result in adverse impact.

The actual validation methodologies are quite complex and beyond the limits of our time today. I do caution you, though, that it is very difficult to validate procedures after you are the target of an EEO suit. In that case, your only hope is if you had previously conducted a full job analysis that identified the knowledge, skills, and abilities that each job required, and your selection procedures were based on these critical work behaviors.

If you are unable to justify your practices, you may be forced to modify your policies. You also may be liable for hefty back-pay settlements. The good news is that most cases are settled out of court through compromise. Due to limited resources, the EEOC has been forced to rely on voluntary compliance and negotiated settlements. If a charge is brought to the EEOC, it will make at least two attempts to get a voluntary settlement between you and the parties who have brought the charge. If that fails, it is still unlikely the EEOC will carry the suit against you unless your case is very blatant, involves large numbers, or covers new legal ground—the commission doesn't have the personnel to press every case. And, the affected employees or applicants are not likely to sue by themselves unless they can get backing from some outside group such as the American Civil Liberties Union.

Even though this is the case, it is not something you want to risk because you can't tell in advance which cases the EEOC will press all the way to court. Consequently, your best course of action is to mount a pre-emptive defense in depth. By this, I mean that you should build into your personnel policies protective measures such as:

1. Conduct job analyses of your positions.
2. From the job analyses, construct selection procedures that are based on critical job behaviors.
3. Monitor the outcome, and if you find that you are getting close to the 80% limit, change your policies.
4. Finally, federal enforcement agencies are increasingly taking a "holistic" approach in that they watch for good-faith efforts on behalf of the employer. So you should try to communicate in every way possible to your employees and job applicants that you are an equal opportunity employer, and follow through with actions that back your words.

If you do all this, it still won't totally protect you from individual charges of discrimination, but it will go a long way in preventing a class action, and that is a significant accomplishment.

Position	Current Employees Black		White		Applicants Black		White	
	M	F	M	F	M	F	M	F
Supervisory								
Store Manager			1		2		7	2
Asst. Mgr. (Produce Mgr.)			1		1		5	
Asst. Mgr. (Stockperson)			1		2		6	
Butcher			1		3		5	
Deli and bakery		1					4	3
Nonsupervisory								
Meat cutters	2		3		6		12	2
Stockers	1		3		12	4	25	4
Produce	1		2		5	1	12	
Deli and bakery		3		2	3	12	1	8
Checkers		3		4		17		14
Baggers	4	1	2		24	6	20	5

CASE 12

The Case of the Organic Gardener: Investigating Various Forms of Business Ownership

Ken Mast and Jon Hawes, the University of Akron

Gareth Reed was known for his melons. Actually, Reed was known and respected by people who practiced organic gardening. Organic gardeners use only natural fertilizers and forms of insect control. Compost, natural or dehydrated manures, and dehydrated seaweed are some of the fertilizers; bug traps using feromes, powders or sprays using reotenone or pyrethrens, and side-by-side planting or combinations of vegetables or flowers and vegetables are all means of insect control.

Reed had graduated with a bachelor's degree in biology and, after a couple of false starts, had become a medical laboratory technician. He had enjoyed doing the individual tests in serology, hematology, and blood chemistry. One blood specimen, however, could now be run through an automatic "hemoanalyzer," which performed several diagnostic tests. The loss of opportunity for individual investigation had diminished his enthusiasm for that line of work.

Reed had learned that a lawn and garden store he occasionally patronized was for sale because the owner was ill. He knew of no lawn and garden store within a 30-mile radius of this store that carried a full line of organic gardening products and seeds that were not treated with chemicals or poisons to repel birds and other unwanted scavengers. He presently had to drive 40 miles to patronize his preferred source of organic garden supplies but figured that not all organic gardeners were as persnickety as himself. Thus, he figured he could enhance the business of the store that was for sale by carrying a full line of organic gardening supplies. He was known and respected throughout the county among an informal network of organic gardeners.

Reed felt pretty comfortable with the prospect of the operations aspect of a lawn and garden store because he had worked in a hardware store part-time for many years. Of some concern was the fact that he had not taken any business courses in college, and he had never been involved in the financial aspects of running a business. There was also the issue of raising the necessary capital if he were to try to buy the business from the present owner.

Reed stopped in the store one day on his way home from work. He talked with the owner and his wife, the Mofits, who had living quarters in the back of the store. It was around closing time, and when the owners became convinced that Reed's interest was more than a casual inquiry, they closed for the day and invited him to ask any questions he wished. While Mrs. Mofit prepared supper, Mr. Mofit showed Reed the financial records and even quoted his asking price. When Reed expressed concern, Mr. Mofit indicated that he and Mrs. Mofit would consider staying on as partners with the "right" person.

As a result of his visit with the Mofits, Reed decided to do some further investigation. A high school classmate, Kim Falanga, was a managing partner in a highly successful certified public accounting firm. Reed arranged an appointment and was pleased to find Falanga cordial, professional, and well prepared to discuss all financial aspects of retail ventures similar to and including lawn and garden stores. She asked some questions that he hadn't really thought about, and he felt embarrassed by some of his attempts at answers. He was surprised that she encouraged him to formally develop a proposal for funding along guidelines that she provided. His surprise turned to amazement when she hinted that she might personally be interested in investing in such a venture.

Another surprise developed when he contacted a number of fellow organic gardeners. His purpose was merely to ascertain their interest in a more accessible source of full-line organic gardening supplies. He discovered not only interest but also inquiries about investing and in one instance, an inquiry regarding part-time employment. One thing led to another and eventually to a meeting at his house of organic gardeners who had expressed unexpected interest beyond just a closer source of supplies. Among this group united by a common interest in organic gardening was a lawyer who was knowledgeable and helpful in explaining the advantages

and disadvantages of general and limited partnerships as well as corporations. Although no consensus was established as to the form of ownership, only a couple of those present appeared to have any reservations about some type of financial interest in the venture. No one indicated dollar amounts, but there were indications that all were reasonably well established financially.

After everyone left, Reed pondered his situation. He wasn't sure he could raise enough money to buy the lawn and garden store by liquidating his own resources. Even if he could, the risk would be high since everything he had would be invested in the store. Furthermore, selling his house would leave him without a place to garden. He could rent a plot of ground, but he hated the thought of parting with all that compost-rich dirt he had carefully nurtured over the years.

His discussion with the Mofits had revealed little interest on their part in carrying a full line of organic supplies. Mr. Mofit claimed that even the limited organic supplies he carried didn't "move very fast." As for Kim Falanga, he wistfully wondered if the heart of an organic gardener could somehow beat within the lapels of her tailored business suits. Her polished nails had probably never turned the handle of a compost maker. The "organic group" was long on enthusiasm, but other than the lawyer, appeared to have relatively little business experience that would compensate for Reed's relative inexperience with financial management.

ASSIGNMENT

☐ Outline the advantages and disadvantages of the alternative forms of business ownership available to Gareth Reed.

☐ Rank the form of business that you perceive to be best for Reed based on the information provided. Justify your ranking.

☐ What additional information, if any, do you believe would be particularly helpful if you were the person in Reed's garden shoes?

CASE 13

Aubrey Creations, Inc.: Managing a Direct-Marketing Salesforce

Jon Hawes, the University of Akron

BACKGROUND

Aubrey Creations, founded in 1978, sold a line of fashion jewelry (most items under $50) through the party-plan method. To attract a base of customers who were more likely to make repeat purchases, Aubrey McDonald

had developed an extensive line of exceptionally high-quality skin-care products. The Aubrey Beauty Collection was introduced in 1981. Prices currently ranged from as low as $1.95 for a single item to $111.75 for the Total Look Collection.

Total revenues for Aubrey Creations during the last year were under $10 million. Operations were limited almost entirely to the United States, and approximately 2,000 sales consultants were involved in selling the products through the party-plan method. The company recently had increased its recruitment efforts for sales consultants. Many of the leading members of this industry belonged to the Direct Selling Association, a trade organization that (among other activities) enforces a strict code of ethical business conduct. Aubrey Creations, Inc., was an active member of this organization.

CURRENT SITUATION

Aubrey McDonald, founder and CEO of Aubrey Creations, had "an opportunity." As for all firms in the direct-selling industry, sales revenues for Aubrey Creations tended to flatten when the economy picked up. Recent improvements in the economy had created this "opportunity," and Aubrey was searching for ways to overcome the recent decline in sales.

There is a simple explanation for the inverse relationship between sales revenues of firms in the direct-selling industry and GNP. More than in any other field, business in the direct-selling industry depends on the number and the intensity levels of salespeople. Few customers actively search for the products of direct-selling companies. These types of sales often require a great deal of personal selling effort to persuade people to make a purchase. Consequently, when a direct-selling organization's sales force is reduced in number and/or the existing sales force becomes less active, revenues usually decline.

During periods of reduced overall economic activity, the sales forces of direct-selling companies often grow dramatically as people attempt to supplement family incomes by working in this field. When the economy improves, however, people often return to full-time employment in other industries or reduce the intensity of their sales efforts in direct-selling organizations.

At Aubrey, sales consultants arranged with hosts to sponsor parties in their homes. The host received free products for encouraging ten to fifteen friends to attend the party, often referred to as the "show" or "booking." Sales consultants seldom attempted to sell both the jewelry and skin-care product lines at a particular party. The central event of a skin-care booking involved a complete makeover (at no charge) for one of the guests.

Besides selling products, sales consultants were also involved in building a sales organization. They recruited people to work in their sales organization and received a commission for all the sales made by these recruits.

Sales consultants earned income based on the level of their sales and the sales of their recruits. Incomes varied widely, but a few consultants made over $100,000 in 1985. In addition, Aubrey Creations sponsored several incentive programs to reward sales consultants who reach a certain level of sales. The top prize was a new Cadillac. Many other rewards, incentives, contests, and recognition were also provided. The highlight of each year was a national conference.

ASSIGNMENT

- ☐ Outline a plan of action to minimize the negative effects of an improving economic climate on the sales force of Aubrey Creations.
- ☐ Develop some motivational strategies that would be appropriate regardless of the general economic conditions.
- ☐ Suggest improvements in the compensation plan and reward structure for the sales force.

CASE 14

Braddock's Department Stores: Facing Up to the Growing Retail Labor Crunch

Dan Gilmore, the University of Akron

As president of Braddock's Department Stores, a chain of nine stores in central and southern California, Amy Whitmeyer's time was usually spent dealing with sales volume promotions, marketing and merchandising strategies, and long-term planning. Lately, another problem was developing that required attention—the increasing shortage of sales, clerical, and management personnel. In many areas of the country, particularly on the East and West Coasts, the personnel shortage problem was acute; it was hampering store operations and impeding growth. Reasons for this shortage were many, but among the most prominent were (1) shrinking numbers of people in the sixteen- to twenty-four-year-old age group, which traditionally staffed most lower-level retail positions; (2) the rapid growth of the retail sector in terms of job creation; and (3) the low wages, poor working conditions, and meager benefits associated with lower-echelon positions.

Whitmeyer feared that the labor crunch would soon affect Braddock's. She was especially concerned because the turnover rate among both sales and management personnel at the company was already high. Nearly 40 percent of the individuals hired for Braddock's management trainee program were not with the company after one year, a figure similar to that of much of the industry. No detailed check of why this rate was so high had been completed by the company, but someone from Human Resources told Whitmeyer that many management trainees quit because they were unable to adjust to the hard first year of the job training (e.g., long hours, weekend hours, physical work, dealing with customers). After a year or two, things became easier; many trainees leave before then, however, although company data showed that within a few years, Braddock's managers have greater opportunities and better compensation than many other firms or industries (i.e., jobs in banking and insurance) offered.

Whitmeyer was studying a report supplied by the Human Resources Department that outlined most of Braddock's personnel policies. As expected, the report showed that for lower-level sales and clerical employees, Braddock's hired primarily high-school and college students to work part-time; however, a few did work full time. The firm usually relied on walk-in applicants to fill lower-level positions, or used newspaper want ads if the need was great enough. For store and corporate management positions, Braddock's hired only college graduates who entered the firm's management-training program. These trainees were chosen from unsolicited applications and also from the twice-yearly recruiting trips to the two local universities.

The report also contained some of the gloomy projections about personnel shortages the company could experience in coming years. It warned that the pool of candidates from which the company now drew its applicants was contracting and that there would be increasing competition with other retailers for available candidates. The report also discussed the turnover problem within the company. Though Braddock's had not conducted studies on the problems particular to its own employee turnover, the Human Resources department had been looking at some research that showed that although pay and benefits were important components of an employee's decision to stay with a retail firm, other factors were influential. Specifically, the report identified five factors especially important to lower level employees:

1. Skill variety—the number of skills and talents the job requires
2. Task identity—the degree to which an employee does a job from beginning to end with a visible outcome

3. Task significance—the impact of that job on other people
4. Autonomy—the freedom and independence an employee has to determine his or her own work procedures
5. Feedback—the direct information an employee receives about the effectiveness of his or her performance

In short, the report said these psychological aspects of the job could be as important as monetary ones for retaining and motivating sales and clerical employees who felt their jobs were not valued by the company and that they were treated poorly by their supervisors.

The report concluded that wages and benefits would probably have to be raised for both management and lower-level employees to attract and retain the employees the company would need in coming years. Whitmeyer, however, felt this would not be sufficient. She realized that although Braddock's would have to increase the monetary aspects of the job, everyone in the business, including many of Braddock's competitors, would be forced to do the same to compete with other industries for employees. The net result would be that while wages, and therefore costs, would be higher than at present, the personnel shortage would probably remain.

Whitmeyer was convinced that it would be necessary to come up with some creative techniques for attracting employees and keeping them with the company. She realized the company couldn't overhaul its personnel policies overnight, but she thought it had better start preparing now before Braddock's found it had stores full of customers—and not enough employees to service them.

ASSIGNMENT

Take the role of Braddock's SPO (senior personnel officer). Whitmeyer has asked you to prepare a report dealing with the following issues:

☐ Evaluate Braddock's recruitment process for both management and sales employees. In light of the predicted retail labor shortage, what actions can you suggest to improve the process?

☐ The employee turnover rate is high for Braddock's. Identify possible causes. What policies or practices can you recommend that might help retain both sales and management employees? Be creative.

☐ Now you have come up with some solid suggestions for improving the recruiting, retaining, and motivation of employees for Braddock's. Whitmeyer will also want to know what disadvantages the company might run into if the firm adopts your suggestions. Help her out.

Fallis Foods: Investigating an Innovative Store Layout

Charles R. Patton, Pan American University, and Dale M. Lewison, the University of Akron

BACKGROUND

Steve Fallis had a right to be proud. As the owner and manager of the largest independent supermarket in Hopkinsville, Indiana, Fallis had enjoyed remarkable success over the last ten years. As of last year, Fallis Foods had captured a 21-percent market share. Given that there were six supermarkets in the greater Hopkinsville area, he was quite pleased with his store's performance. Nevertheless, Fallis had no intention of resting on his laurels. For Fallis Foods to maintain its current share of the food market and have any chance of improving its market share will require considerable forward planning effort. In Fallis's mind, innovation is a major ingredient in any successful plan for the future.

In recent weeks, Fallis had given a great deal of thought to making some innovative changes in the store's layout, specifically, assembling product lines into more natural groupings and locating these natural groupings within a concentrated area of the store. Bakery products, for example, were currently assembled into a number of different groupings scattered throughout the store. In the past, Fallis Foods had followed the conventional wisdom of displaying bakery products using the grouping and locating practices of competitive supermarkets. Fallis thought, however, that regrouping bakery products into one large group and placing it at a single location could provide the store's customers with a more convenient shopping experience; it could also provide Fallis Foods with a distinctive merchandising practice and possibly a small but significant competitive advantage.

CURRENT SITUATION

Monday morning, Fallis decided to audit the store's current practices in merchandising bakery products. Armed with a blueprint of the store's layout (see Exhibit 15–1) and a clipboard, he collected the following information on the in-store groupings and locations of bakery products.

1. In-Store Bakery Shop

A separate in-store bakery was installed at considerable expense two years ago. It carried a full line of freshly baked breads, rolls, cakes, pies, donuts, pastries, cookies, and other specialty bakery items. This department had above-average markups and operating expenses. It required several full-time employees (bakers and salesclerks). Strict supervision was necessary to avoid too many "stales" that must be sold at reduced prices or given away to charity (see location A in Exhibit 15–1).

2. Commercial Bakery Goods

Fallis had a full gondola of commercially baked breads, rolls, and pastries delivered by national and regional vendors (bakeries) that provided the full range of services normally associated with such rack jobbers. They stocked the shelves, priced the merchandise, accepted returns of "stales," and provided other inventory control functions. This section was a carbon copy of the commercial bakery goods section found in most supermarkets. This section was known to have a high traffic count and was located at some distance from the store's "scratch" bakery shop (see location B in Exhibit 15–1).

3. Frozen Bakery Products

A growing line of bakery products were those displayed in the open, chest-type frozen-food cabinets. This assortment of frozen bakery products included mostly nationally advertised, brand-name items (e.g., Sara Lee, Morton, and Rich's). While the assortment emphasis was on dessert items and pastries, there were several brands of frozen bread and roll dough that require baking by the consumer (see location C in Exhibit 15–1).

4. Commercial Cookies

A large section of one gondola was devoted to packaged cookies. This product line was dominated by a few large national brands (e.g., Keebler, Nabisco, Duncan Hines, and Archway). To date, cookies baked by the store's bakery had limited success competing against these long-established commercial products (see location D in Exhibit 15–1).

5. Commercial Cake Mixes

A large section of one gondola was devoted to commercial cake mixes (e.g., Duncan Hines, Betty Crocker, and Pillsbury). These were well-established product lines that offer considerable variety of flavors. To promote complementary sales, cake frostings were located adjacent to the cake mixes (see location E in Exhibit 15–1).

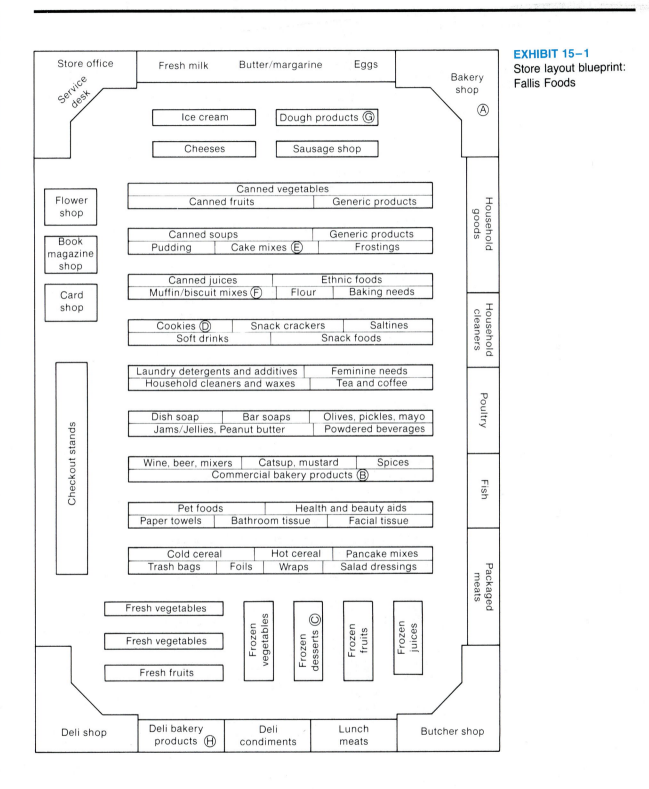

EXHIBIT 15–1
Store layout blueprint:
Fallis Foods

Store office

Fresh milk   Butter/margarine   Eggs

Bakery shop (A)

Service desk

Ice cream   Dough products (G)

Cheeses   Sausage shop

Flower shop

Book magazine shop

Card shop

Canned vegetables
Canned fruits | Generic products

Canned soups | Generic products
Pudding | Cake mixes (E) | Frostings

Canned juices | Ethnic foods
Muffin/biscuit mixes (F) | Flour | Baking needs

Cookies (D) | Snack crackers | Saltines
Soft drinks | Snack foods

Laundry detergents and additives | Feminine needs
Household cleaners and waxes | Tea and coffee

Dish soap | Bar soaps | Olives, pickles, mayo
Jams/Jellies, Peanut butter | Powdered beverages

Wine, beer, mixers | Catsup, mustard | Spices
Commercial bakery products (B)

Pet foods | Health and beauty aids
Paper towels | Bathroom tissue | Facial tissue

Cold cereal | Hot cereal | Pancake mixes
Trash bags | Foils | Wraps | Salad dressings

Checkout stands

Household goods

Household cleaners

Poultry

Fish

Packaged meats

Fresh vegetables

Fresh vegetables

Fresh fruits

Frozen vegetables

Frozen desserts (C)

Frozen fruits

Frozen juices

Deli shop | Deli bakery products (H) | Deli condiments | Lunch meats | Butcher shop

EXHIBIT 15–2
A shopping scenario

Driving home from work, Rita Thomas realized that she did not have any dessert to serve after the evening meal. Since Harold really appreciated having dessert, Rita decided to pop in at Fallis Foods to pick up something. Pie seemed like a good idea. Upon entering the store, Rita proceeded to travel around the store in her normal counter-clockwise pattern. Deciding to investigate all the possibilities, Rita made the following stops and was faced with the following choices:

Stop 1: Frozen-food cases (location C in Exhibit 1)
    Choice 1: Frozen 8-inch pies, six varieties, mostly nationally advertised brands, must be thawed before eating.
    Choice 2: Frozen 9-inch pies, three varieties, local and regional brands, must be baked before serving.
    Choice 3: Frozen 5-inch pies (two to three servings), four varieties, must be baked before serving.
    Choice 4: Frozen individual pie pieces, individually wrapped, three varieties, must be thawed and warmed before serving.
    Choice 5: Frozen pie crusts, individual and multiple packs, three sizes (tart 4-inch, standard 8-inch, and family 9-inch), must be thawed, filled, and baked before serving.

Stop 2: Commercial bakery-goods section (location B in Exhibit 1)
    Choice 1: Prepackaged pies, baked by local and regional bakeries, standard 8-inch size, one day old, seven varieties, lowest prices, ready-to-eat.
    Choice 2: Prepackaged pies, national brands, individual sizes, four varieties, ready-to-eat.
    Choice 3: 8-count box of pie-like product called Little Debbie, individual servings that are individually wrapped, one variety, ready-to-eat.

Stop 3: Commercial cake mixes (location E in Exhibit 1)
    Choice 1: Packaged pie crust mixes, requiring additional ingredients, must be mixed and formed into pie crust, very reasonable.
    Choice 2: Packaged pie filling mixes, requiring preparation, nine varieties.

Stop 4: In-store bakery shop (location A in Exhibit 1)
    Choice 1: Freshly baked pies, five varieties, baked on premises, standard 8-inch size, more expensive, ready-to-eat.
    Choice 2: Freshly baked tarts, three varieties, baked on premises, individual servings, quite expensive, ready-to-eat.

Stop 5: Refrigerated dough products (location G in Exhibit 1)
    Choice 1: Refrigerated pie crusts, ready-to-use, require filling, may or may not be baked, standard 8-inch size, pie dough and graham cracker base.
    Choice 2: Refrigerated pie dough, must be rolled out and shaped, requires baking.

Stop 6: Canned goods section (see Exhibit 1)
    Choice 1 Canned pie fillings, six varieties, ready-to-use, very inexpensive.

Having made her whirlwind tour of the store, Rita was somewhat exhausted from all the rushing about, and even more confused at all the choices. Her original intention was to simply buy a pie for tonight's dessert, but the problem is which pie in what form and flavor and at what price?

6. Commercial Muffin, Biscuit, and Bread Mixes

A six-foot section of one gondola was stocked with muffin, biscuit, and homemade bread mixes. Many local competitors placed all "mixes" together. Fallis Foods, however, had traditionally followed customer belief that muffin, biscuit, and bread mixes are more commonly associated with flour (see location F in Exhibit 15–1).

7. Refrigerated Dough Products

A large, open, chest-type refrigerator was used to display a complete selection of refrigerated dough products. Items in this product line included preformed pie crusts, breakfast pastries, bread dough, refrigerated desserts, and biscuit and roll doughs (see location G in Exhibit 15–1).

8. Deli Bakery Products

To complement the store's complete deli department, a small wall display was devoted to deli bakery products, such as specialty breads and rolls (see location H in Exhibit 15–1).

Having completed the audit and a review of its findings, Fallis had arrived at several tentative conclusions. First, the store offered an extensive selection of bakery products. Until now, he'd never realized the extent of the variety and assortment of products currently stocked in the various bakery departments. The total number of possible choices facing the customer was almost staggering. Fallis wondered whether this extensive selection was necessary. Did it meet customers' needs for selection or did it simply confuse them? Thinking about this issue, Fallis developed a hypothetical shopping scenario that he thought might be a fairly typical experience (see Exhibit 15–2). The more he thought about it, the more he believed there was a strong likelihood of overkill in the selection of bakery goods currently offered in his store.

Fallis also thought the bakery goods category appeared to have considerable duplication, perhaps too much. For example, is it necessary to stock both frozen and refrigerated pie crusts? Do customers perceive these two items to be different, and if so, is the difference important? Also, are all the various product brands and package sizes necessary? For Fallis, the issue of duplication needed close attention.

Fallis's final conclusion centered on the issue of multiple locations for bakery products. The seven or eight current locations certainly must have some negative implications for customer convenience. For example, the

several widely scattered locations must hinder the customer's ability to make price, brand, quality, and other relevant comparisons without considerable backtracking through the store. Multiple locations might also hinder customers from finding the particular item they were looking for. In sum, the arrangement could confuse and irritate the customer.

Each of these tentative conclusions seemed to support Fallis's contention that a more efficient, effective way to merchandise bakery products would be to regroup and relocate all the goods into one concentrated bakery department. The more he thought about the idea, the more he liked it. Before making a final decision or drawing up any plans, however, Fallis decided to contact Spatial Interactions, Inc. (SII), a consulting firm specializing in spatial problems associated with retailing operations (e.g., retail location and store layout and design). After discussing the idea at some length with Anne Duff, President of SII, Fallis was convinced that an in-depth study of the issues surrounding his idea was essential before proceeding with any direct action. He provided Duff with a copy of the audit and a blueprint of the store's layout. He also agreed to cooperate with SII researchers assigned to the project. Fallis spent the next few hours discussing with Duff the particulars of the study. They agreed on a limited study that would accomplish the following:

1. Identify the pros and cons of regrouping all the store's bakery products into one concentrated location. The pro and con statements should be made from two perspectives: (a) retail merchandising and operations and (b) consumer buying behavior.
2. Recommend, based on the pro and con statements, what course of action would be most advisable for Fallis Foods (supported by a complete rationale statement).
3. Develop a store layout and design plan for remodeling the store that would incorporate a concentrated bakery-products section. The plan also should consider regrouping and relocating other product categories (e.g., beverages) and any recommendations related to this issue. (Note: this plan is to be developed regardless of the recommendation presented.)

ASSIGNMENT

☐ Assume the role of a project research director for SII. Duff has assigned the Fallis Foods project to you. A comprehensive report, complete with supporting graphics, is due in two months.

Hoffmann-La Roche, Inc.

Jon Hawes, the University of Akron

Drug abuse is one of our most serious social problems and an important factor to corporations seeking to increase employees' productivity. Experts estimate that 10 to 23 percent of American workers use dangerous drugs while on the job. Employee drug abuse has been estimated to cost American industry $33 billion per year. Obviously, from social and competitive perspectives, U.S. firms are interested in reducing drug abuse among the work force.

Drug-abuse testing is seen as a legitimate means for screening prospective employees (nearly one third of the Fortune 500 companies do this) and for discouraging drug use by current employees. Several pharmaceutical companies now manufacture drug-abuse tests, and others are considering entry into this potentially lucrative market. In fact, a recent study indicated that the market potential for drug-abuse testing has been increasing by 10 to 15 percent annually and could grow to $220 million by 1991.

Hoffmann-La Roche, Inc., located in Nutley, New Jersey, has already entered the market for drug-abuse testing. The company currently sells about $20 million per year in various drug-testing products. It recently introduced a service known as Abuscreen and has begun promoting it as 99 percent accurate in testing for the presence of marijuana, LSD, amphetamines, cocaine, morphine, barbiturates, and methaqualone.

The high reliability of Hoffmann-La Roche's drug-abuse testing is extremely important in marketing these services. The company's reputation, experience, and comprehensive services to potential customers are also important factors that have enabled Hoffmann-La Roche to sell its services to the 1984 Olympics, the U.S. Department of Defense, and many other organizations. Although price is a concern, most of the prospective corporate clients place greater emphasis on the quality of the drug-abuse tests.

Hoffmann-La Roche recently launched a new subsidiary called Diagnostic Dimensions, which markets comprehensive services to fight drug abuse in the work force. It offers training programs, employee education and counseling, and other services to help companies help their employees.

ASSIGNMENT

Assume the role of the Director of Human Resources for an eighty-unit chain of specialty apparel shops. The president of the firm believes that many of the personnel problems (e.g., employee pilferage, poor employee morale, customer complaints, and store security) are often drug-related. Although there is no exact information on what percentage of the firm's employees might be using drugs, national averages provide some guidance. Because you are the person responsible for managing personnel problems, the president has asked you to prepare a report on the following:

- [ ] Is drug usage a security problem?
- [ ] Should the firm initiate a drug-testing program?
- [ ] How might a drug-testing program be administered?
- [ ] What actions should be taken if an employee is found to be using drugs?

Southwestern Supermarkets: Responding to an Extortion Threat

Jon Hawes, the University of Akron, and George Glisan, Illinois State University

BACKGROUND

It was a telephone call that Mike Kelly really didn't want to take. It was 11:00 A.M., and he'd been busy helping unload a shipment of frozen food. Nevertheless, the caller was insistent, so Mike took the call.

"People are going to die," the voice on the other end of the line said.

"What?" Kelly said in disbelief. "Is this some kind of crank call?"

"No. People are going to die unless you give us $60,000. We have poisoned the food in three Southwestern stores in Waco, and unless you give us the money, your customers are going to die from poison. We'll get back to you with details when you deliver the money. Talk to your boss about the money, but you better not call the police!"

Kelly was dumbounded. Needless to say, in his four

years as manager of a Southwestern Supermarket, he'd never dealt with a situation like this. He took a moment to collect his thoughts, then called his boss as the extortionist had demanded. Cheryl Bault, vice president of sales, took the news calmly. Bault said she would be in the store within the hour and that Kelly should keep the matter secret until she arrived.

Bault immediately called George Powell, president of the chain of 152 supermarkets, to inform him of the situation. Powell told her to go to the store and do her best to ensure the safety of Southwestern's customers. The resources of the chain were at Bault's disposal, he told her.

Bault went to the store and asked Kelly to repeat everything he could remember from the phone call. She asked Kelly if any store employees had recently been fired or if he could think of anyone else who might have a reason to make such a threat. Kelly drew a blank. As far as he knew, the six Southwestern Supermarkets in Waco were highly respected members of the business community and enjoyed good relations with the public. No one had been fired from his store within the past six months.

At 12:30 P.M. the extortionist called again. He talked with Bault and again stated that people were going to die unless Southwestern Supermarkets complied with his demands. This time, however, the extortionist informed Bault that no one had been exposed to the poison yet. In fact, he said there would be no danger for the next two days.

Bault then called Powell, and they discussed the latest developments. The president authorized Bault to pay $60,000 but said that the police should be brought into the situation.

Bault then called the police, and several plainclothes detectives were dispatched to the store. When the extortionist called back at 3:45 P.M., Bault told him that Southwestern was willing to pay the $60,000, but that the police would handle delivery of the cash. After a brief outburst of rage, the extortionist hung up. He called back, however, and the negotiations continued over the next thirty-six hours. Several brief telephone conversations were conducted; the extortionist hung up each

time after a couple of minutes for fear of the call's being traced. Ultimately, the arrangements were finalized. In the meantime, the police had been examining food in Southwestern's Waco stores for signs of foul play but had found no evidence of poisoning.

The police delivered the money at 1:00 P.M., two days after Kelly had received the first call from the extortionist. Even though the extortionist's demands were followed, the money was still in the designated location at 5:00 A.M. the next morning. This was unexpected and caused the police and Southwestern executives great concern.

CURRENT SITUATION

The two-day period of safety the extortionist had originally promised had now passed. What should Southwestern do? The executives conferred and decided to close all six Southwestern Supermarkets in Waco immediately. Virtually all stock except canned goods was taken to the city dump under armed guard. More than 1.3 million pounds of groceries were plowed into the landfill.

The company quickly began restocking the shelves of the six Waco stores and reopened four days later. Sales soon reached normal levels, and customer reaction was reported to be extremely favorable.

ASSIGNMENT

Assume that you were part of Southwestern's management team and justify your solutions to each of these issues:

- [ ] What would have been your reaction to this extortion threat?
- [ ] Would you have informed the police?
- [ ] Would you have kept the stores open during the negotiations?
- [ ] Would you have agreed to pay the $60,000?
- [ ] When the extortionist failed to retrieve the money, would you have dumped the goods of all six local stores?

CASE 18

The Electronic Mall: Identifying and Evaluating Market Areas*

Dale M. Lewison and John Thanopoulos, the University of Akron, and Charles R. Patton, Pan American University

"I think your mall is excellent!" "I think your mall is a wonderful place, and I will be shopping here often." "I've used The Mall frequently and have found the service to be excellent—keep up the good work." "What a great idea. Now I will not have to go throughout our fair city looking for gifts for those I know little about. This is my first time on board, and I am looking forward to browsing again." "I would first like to say I'm very impressed with The Mall."

The above are but a few of the encouraging customer comments received by the Mall Manager. In this case, the mall is The Electronic Mall, a shop-at-home service that enables personal computer owners to purchase goods and services via computer. This videotex shopping mall is owned and operated by CompuServe Incorporated of Columbus, Ohio. The Mall is open 24 hours a day, 365 days a year, and offers thousands of brand-name products at the touch of a keystroke.

Shoppers enter The Electronic Mall using a personal computer and a telephone modem. Shoppers can browse The Mall by keying in "This week's Mall News," a comprehensive product index or a directory of all Mall merchants. Questions are promptly answered by the Mall Manager, an online representative. To make a purchase, the customer keys in the selected product together with his or her credit card number. The system reviews the selection and captures the order. Orders are then sent to a designated address via Express Mail or some other delivery service. Buyers receive an electronic receipt, which is sent to their own online mailboxes. If a customer has a question about a product or a bill, he or she can send a message directly to the merchant, who will respond via electronic mail.

The Mall layout and design may not look like a "bricks and mortar" facility, but it is organized into departments. A retailer can focus on one department or display merchandise in several departments. The Mall is layed out into sixteen departments: (1) apparel and accessories, (2) automotive, (3) books and periodicals, (4) gifts and novelties, (5) computing, (6) gourmet and flowers, (7) hobbies and toys, (8) merchandise and electronics, (9) online services, (10) premium merchants, (11) music and movies, (12) health and beauty, (13) financial, (14) travel and entertainment, (15) office supplies, (16) sports and leisure.

Electronic shopping, a phenomenon of the Information Age, is one of the ways retailers are reaching a lucrative market of busy consumers who want to shop at home. It is a direct-marketing technique that takes the store to the market rather than attracting the market to the store.

ASSIGNMENT

- ☐ Identify and delineate the market area for The Electronic Mall.
- ☐ Profile and characterize the typical consumer (i.e., targeted market) who patronize The Mall.
- ☐ List and describe the advantages and disadvantages of this mall location for the consumer and for the retailer.
- ☐ Describe the type of retailing format (products, prices, promotions) that is most compatible with this type of mall. Explain.

---

*Materials for this case were obtained from promotional brochures, press releases, and advertisements supplied by CompuServe Incorporated of Columbus, Ohio.

Jacobson's Dilemma: Location of a "Fancy" Restaurant

J. B. Wilkinson, the University of Akron

BACKGROUND

Up to now, George Jacobson had felt pretty good about all his decisions and activities in starting his own restaurant. Jacobson had been a military chef in the officers' mess at Fort Belvoir but had recently retired after 22 years in the service. Too young at 45 to simply "take it easy," Jacobson decided to start a restaurant in Smithville, a central city in a three-county SMSA (Standard Metropolitan Statistical Area). The restaurant was positioned as a plush, moderately expensive lunch and dinner and cocktail bar type of restaurant featuring continental cuisine. Two shopping center locations were under consideration: Pinnacle Plaza and Hidden Valley Shopping Mall. Both intramall locations were comparable in terms of size/space, rent, and traffic, but Jacobson suspected that the shopping centers might differ considerably in terms of trading area characteristics.

CURRENT SITUATION

Having spent the last three weeks collecting and organizing data on each retail center and its trading area, Jacobson believed he was ready to evaluate each center's potential as a location for a fancy restaurant. The data he'd compiled concerned the locational attributes of each center, the population and income characteristics of surrounding census tracts, and the retail tenant mix within the city and each of its major retailing centers.

Location Characteristics

Exhibit 19–1 shows the location of both shopping malls in Smithville. Pinnacle Plaza (MRC 1) draws Smithville shoppers primarily from the area north of U.S. Route 72 (Census Tracts 2.01, 2.02, 3.01, 3.02, 4.01, 4.02, 5.01, 5.02, 5.03, 6.01, 6.02, 7.01, 7.02, 8, 11, and 13), while Hidden Valley (MRC 3) attracts Smithville shoppers primarily from areas south of State Route 1 (Census Tracts 19.01, 19.02, 19.03, 20, 21, 22, 23, 24, 25.01, 25.02, 26, 27.01, 27.02, 28.01, 28.02, 29.01, and 29.02). In addition, Pinnacle Plaza attracts shoppers from northern areas outside Smithville. Mountain View (pop. 30,000) is 40 miles north of Smithville on State Route 52; Pikesville (pop. 10,000) is 20 miles north on Mountain Pike; and Jolson (pop. 15,000) is 25 miles north on U.S. Route 254. The mountainous areas to the east of Smithville are relatively unpopulated; however, Hidden Valley attracts shoppers from southern areas outside Smithville, notably Dover (pop. 30,000), which is 25 miles southwest of Smithville on State Route 1 and Marshall (pop. 25,000), which is 15 miles away on U.S. Route 254.

Population/Income Characteristics

Exhibit 19–2 contains selected population and income characteristics for all census tracts that comprise each of the shopping centers' primary drawing areas.

Major Retail Center Characteristics

The retail store mix characteristics of the major retail centers (i.e., Pinnacle Plaza and Hidden Valley), the central business district of Smithville, the City of Smithville, and the Smithville SMSA are shown in Exhibit 19–3, which also indicates the number of competitors.

Additional Information

Additional information that George Jacobson collected included the following:

1. Approximately 8 percent of family median income is spent on dining out *(Expenditure Patterns of the American Family)*.
2. Average sales per eating and drinking place in the United States were $172,000, with approximately 5.0 eating and drinking places per 1,000 households in the United States in 1977 *(U.S. Bureau of the Census and Census of Retail Trade, 1977)*.
3. Pinnacle Plaza had approximately 16,000 square feet of floor space allocated to eating and drinking establishments. The eating and drinking establishments in Hidden Valley occupied approximately 55,000 square feet (estimated by Jacobson).
4. The number of eating and drinking establishments in the market areas of Pinnacle Plaza and Hidden Valley was 100 and 94, respectively (estimated by Jacobson).

ASSIGNMENT

☐ Assume the role of a consultant and advise George Jacobson. Which location do you recommend as the preferred site for his restaurant? Provide Jacobson with a complete justification for your recommendation.

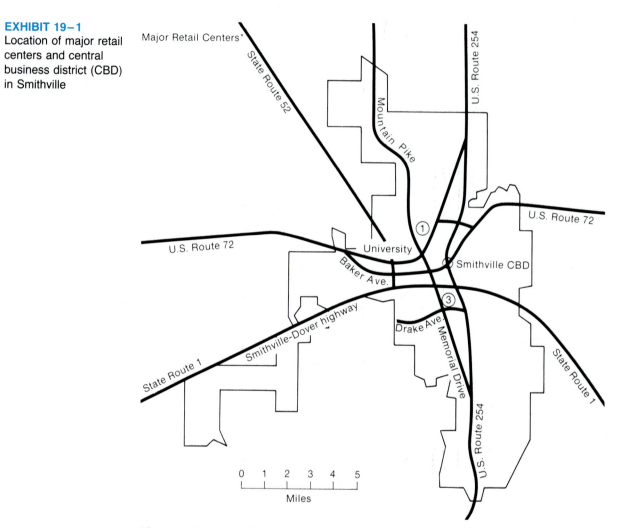

EXHIBIT 19–1
Location of major retail centers and central business district (CBD) in Smithville

Major Retail Centers*

State Route 52

U.S. Route 254

Mountain Pike

U.S. Route 72

University

Baker Ave.

Smithville CBD

Smithville-Dover highway

Drake Ave.

Memorial Drive

State Route 1

U.S. Route 254

State Route 1

0 1 2 3 4 5
Miles

*Concentration of retail stores (located inside the MSA but outside the CBD) having at least $5 million in retail sales and at least 10 retail establishments, one of which was classified as a department store (SIC 531).

EXHIBIT 19–2

Population/income characteristics for selected census tracts, Smithville SMSA, 1980

	SMSA	Smithville City	Tract 2.01	Tract 2.02	Tract 3.01	Tract 3.02
AGE						
Total persons	308,593	142,513	821	4,255	5,313	4,335
3 and 4 years	8,274	3,572	21	83	172	147
16 yrs and over	230,134	107,383	624	3,588	3,741	2,944
18 yrs and over	217,498	101,377	590	3,433	3,482	2,718
21 yrs and over	198,327	92,294	527	2,242	3,148	2,478
60 yrs and over	38,970	15,076	120	273	387	241
62 yrs and over	33,840	12,844	100	229	314	205
Median	29.1	28.9	26.7	21.4	25.9	25.1
INCOME in 1979						
Households	106,369	50,790	292	854	1,601	1,228
Median	$15,472	$17,843	$11,023	$16,741	$16,542	$17,476
Mean	18,678	21,424	16,716	17,899	19,419	18,501
Families	84,881	38,746	238	743	1,405	1,101
Median	$17,565	$20,920	$11,989	$16,956	$17,181	$17,816
Mean	20,739	24,179	18,810	18,236	20,110	19,054
Per capita income	$6,488	$7,661	$6,055	$3,921	$5,789	$5,284

	Tract 4.01	Tract 4.02	Tract 5.01	Tract 5.02	Tract 5.03	Tract 6.01	Tract 6.02
AGE							
Total persons	813	3,970	2,401	3,291	2,409	1,917	2,716
3 and 4 years	27	124	69	105	73	31	55
16 yrs and over	538	2,724	1,685	2,263	1,704	1,438	2,058
18 yrs and over	492	2,519	1,552	2,110	1,577	1,329	1,921
21 yrs and over	453	2,296	1,401	1,887	1,437	1,192	1,749
60 yrs and over	26	214	121	163	130	132	228
62 yrs and over	21	168	95	139	108	101	203
Median	26.4	27.1	25.2	26.9	29.7	29.7	30.3
INCOME in 1979							
Households	224	1,167	698	970	737	591	928
Median	$22,262	$21,427	$22,917	$15,794	$19,480	$23,995	$22,567
Mean	21,789	23,367	24,088	17,270	22,309	25,411	21,905
Families	203	1,053	665	843	649	534	825
Median	$22,841	$22,361	$24,063	$16,599	$19,234	$24,750	$23,511
Mean	22,284	24,211	24,695	17,956	21,738	26,440	22,944
Per capita income	$5,582	$6,888	$6,952	$5,211	$6,757	$7,431	$7,484

EXHIBIT 19–2, *continued*

	Tract 7.01	Tract 7.02	Tract 8	Tract 11	Tract 13	Tract 19.01	Tract 19.02
AGE							
Total persons	4,136	2,095	2,858	1,950	4,130	3,105	820
3 and 4 years	117	54	78	67	77	64	16
16 yrs and over	3,057	1,615	2,176	1,346	3,333	2,378	600
18 yrs and over	2,885	1,540	2,076	1,260	3,209	2,213	543
21 yrs and over	2,612	1,437	1,930	1,156	2,856	2,100	510
60 yrs and over	254	401	421	353	280	412	53
62 yrs and over	201	373	373	314	218	335	38
Median	25.8	31.3	28.9	26.6	26.7	37.9	37.2
INCOME in 1979							
Households	1,447	847	1,126	602	1,729	1,076	249
Median	$16,865	$11,911	$11,458	$6,463	$17,899	$31,303	$40,510
Mean	18,333	14,316	13,347	8,490	19,003	38,551	42,356
Families	1,124	523	755	433	993	925	249
Median	$18,289	$17,557	$12,392	$7,262	$20,040	$35,428	$40,510
Mean	20,079	18,269	14,744	9,604	21,617	42,738	42,356
Per capita income	$6,332	$5,873	$5,245	$2,742	$8,067	$13,652	$12,573

	Tract 19.03	Tract 20	Tract 21	Tract 22	Tract 23	Tract 24	Tract 25.01
AGE							
Total persons	2,084	2,555	5,207	2,961	5,793	5,011	2,125
3 and 4 years	24	50	192	96	141	156	67
16 yrs and over	1,630	2,207	3,896	2,357	4,451	3,766	1,679
18 yrs and over	1,494	2,151	3,728	2,291	4,255	3,606	1,626
21 yrs and over	1,406	2,051	3,406	2,103	3,870	3,143	1,445
60 yrs and over	240	675	1,039	378	617	239	171
62 yrs and over	178	582	942	336	511	185	142
Median	40.8	43.2	28.0	27.5	28.1	24.8	25.6
INCOME in 1979							
Households	713	1,197	2,133	1,182	2,209	2,014	1,054
Median	$44,430	$16,720	$7,339	$13,921	$14,857	$13,187	$11,217
Mean	48,089	17,735	8,939	16,446	16,644	14,861	14,056
Families	665	825	1,322	768	1,593	1,389	541
Median	$44,430	$16,720	$ 9,855	$15,211	$16,632	$15,578	$12,792
Mean	50,245	20,697	10,345	17,510	18,533	16,510	15,620
Per capita income	$16,262	$8,304	$3,693	$6,617	$6,425	$5,994	$7,116

EXHIBIT 19–2, *continued*

	Tract 25.02	Tract 26	Tract 27.01	Tract 27.02	Tract 28.01	Tract 28.02	Tract 29.01
AGE							
Total persons	1,886	4,513	2,021	7,111	3,469	1,953	7,154
3 and 4 years	52	65	26	156	72	75	179
16 yrs and over	1,490	3,714	1,633	5,265	2,606	1,403	4,993
18 yrs and over	1,430	3,546	1,525	4,872	2,483	1,323	4,586
21 yrs and over	1,331	3,338	1,420	4,552	2,293	1,221	4,262
60 yrs and over	96	736	242	496	245	92	311
62 yrs and over	69	641	184	391	192	69	241
Median	26.2	37.8	43.7	32.8	29.5	27.9	31.2
INCOME in 1979							
Households	882	1,915	642	2,442	1,341	674	2,140
Median	$15,745	$22,789	$38,125	$32,167	$23,260	$23,351	$30,607
Mean	18,189	26,480	38,404	35,217	24,504	25,510	32,549
Families	523	1,294	599	2,061	917	569	2,006
Median	$15,993	$27,753	$39,489	$34,769	$29,275	$25,474	$31,073
Mean	15,886	31,292	40,016	38,500	29,242	27,489	33,214
Per capita income	$8,494	$11,223	$12,718	$12,008	$9,588	$8,563	$9,609

	Tract 29.02
AGE	
Total persons	3,908
3 and 4 years	126
16 yrs and over	2,674
18 yrs and over	2,505
21 yrs and over	2,339
60 yrs and over	125
62 yrs and over	109
Median	28.5
INCOME in 1979	
Households	1,172
Median	$26,654
Mean	27,211
Familes	1,068
Median	$27,165
Mean	27,882
Per capita income	$8,376

EXHIBIT 19–3
Characteristics of major retail centers and central business district in the Smithville SMSA, 1977

SIC Code	Kind of Business	Standard Metropolitan Statistical Area	City	Central Business District	Major Retail Centers	
					No. 1	No. 3
	Retail stores					
	Number	2,574	1,208	158	48	77
	Sales (1,000)	941,530	(D)	111,086	43,221	66,452
54, 58, 591	Convenience goods stores					
	Number	810	379	35	10	20
	Sales (1,000)	(D)	(D)	8,562	8,269	10,245
53, 56, 57 594	Shopping goods stores					
	Number	726	375	73	33	40
	Sales (1,000)	239,539	(D)	43,066	34,095	36,511
52, 55, 59 ex. 591, 4, 6	All other stores					
	Number	1,038	454	50	5	17
	Sales (1,000)	(D)	(D)	59,458	857	19,696
58	Eating and drinking places					
	Number	332	214	20	4	13
	Sales (1,000)	69,875	53,303	5,203	(D)	(D)

PART FIVE: RETAIL MIX MANAGEMENT

CASE 20

The Limited, Inc.: Considering a New Location Strategy

Dale M. Lewison and Jon Hawes, the University of Akron

The Limited, Inc., has become the leading force in American retailing by offering apparel tailored to the tastes and life-styles of fashion-conscious contemporary consumers. By positioning itself as the dominant specialist in the fashion apparel market through multiple retail formats and state-of-the-art distribution system, The Limited, Inc., has become one of the top achievers across all industries in the United States. A basic operating principle is the firm's pursuit of excellence "to offer the absolute best customer shopping experience anywhere—the best stores—the best merchandise—the best merchandise presentation—the best customer service—the best 'everything' that a customer sees and experiences."

In the "quest for the best", The Limited is currently considering a new "cluster location strategy" that would group several or possibly all of its various retailing formats within one shopping mall. For example, within one

EXHIBIT 20-1
The Limited, Inc., retailing formats

Limited Stores—consists of 711 stores in every major market with an average store size of 4,000 square feet. The Limited specializes in medium-priced fashion apparel that complements the tastes and life-styles of contemporary women, 20 to 40 years of age.

Limited Express—offers the latest, most creative international assortment of sportswear and accessories designed to appeal to spirited women on the cutting edge of world fashion. Store designs and merchandise displays offer fashion-forward women (aged 15 to 25) an exciting place to shop. There are currently 348 stores in most major markets with an average size of 2,600 square feet.

Lane Bryant—with 631 stores averaging over 4,000 square feet, Lane Bryant is the foremost retailer of women's special-size apparel—fashions for sizes 14 and up. The format's ability to supply special-size customers with attractive and fashionable sportswear, ready-to-wear, intimate apparel, and accessories has resulted in a pattern of continuous expansion.

Victoria's Secret—offers an international lingeries collection, which provides contemporary women with imaginative, high-fashion designer intimate apparel through retail and mail-order divisions. With 236 stores averaging 1,900 square feet, the goal set for this division is to bring intimate apparel out of the basement and into the vanguard of fashion.

Lerner Stores—fashion-forward sportswear, coats, dresses, and accessories at popular and budget prices. With 770 stores in every major market with an average size in excess of 6,000 square feet, Lerner is the nation's largest specialty retailer under a single trade name.

Sizes Unlimited—offers sportswear, dresses, and accessories, sizes 14 and up, priced below similar goods in most department and specialty stores. Sizes Unlimited offers a wide assortment of first-quality merchandise, nationally known brand labels and private labels, at prices that appeal to the value-conscious customer. The 398 stores average 3,500 square feet and can be found in most major markets.

Henri Bendel—represents the best in international designer clothing and accessories. The store occupies a unique position at the apex of the fashion world (57th Street in Manhattan). It provides the ultrasophisticated customer with merchandise of incomparable style and quality. Henri Bendel plans to open stores in the top 40 markets in the nation.

shopping mall The Limited, Inc., could create a store cluster comprised of: (1) a Limited store, (2) Limited Express, (3) Victoria's Secret, (4) Lane Bryant, (5) Lerner Store, (6) Sizes Unlimited, and (7) Henri Bendel. Exhibit 20-1 profiles each of The Limited, Inc.'s retailing formats.

ASSIGNMENT

Evaluate the proposed "cluster location strategies." As a location consultant, would you recommend it to Leslie H. Wexner, Chairman of The Limited, Inc.? Defend your recommendation. Assume Wexner wants you to develop two different "cluster" prototypes: (1) for an upscale shopping mall in southern California catering to upper-income consumers and (2) for a typical middle-class shopping center in St. Louis. Provide supporting rationale for your prototypes.

CASE 21

Clemente Cleaners: Evaluating Site Accessibility

Dale M. Lewison, the University of Akron, and Charles R. Patton, Pan American University

BACKGROUND

Clemente Cleaners had occupied the same location on the northwest corner of Johnston Avenue and Oak Park Boulevard for the last twenty-seven years. Bart Clemente, owner and operator of Clemente Cleaners, originally selected the site because he thought it represented a convenient stop for customers commuting between Walnut Valley, a large suburb, and the central business district of Omaha. Customers could drop off their cleaning on the way to work and pick it up on the way home. The selection of the Johnston Avenue site proved to be one of the best business decisions Clemente ever made. For twenty-seven years, Clemente Cleaners serviced the commuting public, and he enjoyed the benefits of a successful business.

Two years ago, the Metro Traffic Engineering Department made a complete study of the numerous traffic problems that commuters were experiencing during their weekday work trips to and from the central city. After considerable deliberation, a decision was made to convert two of the major traffic arteries into one-way streets. Washington Avenue was designated a one-way westbound artery leading into the central business district, while Johnston Avenue was designated an eastbound traffic artery out of the city (Exhibit 21–1).

While the realignment of traffic arteries marked the end of numerous traffic problems, it also represented the beginning of a substantial decline in revenues for Clemente Cleaners. Although the store remained reasonably profitable, many of Clemente's long-time commuter customers found it more convenient to go elsewhere.

Many of Clemente's customers from Walnut Valley had frequently commented on their satisfaction with

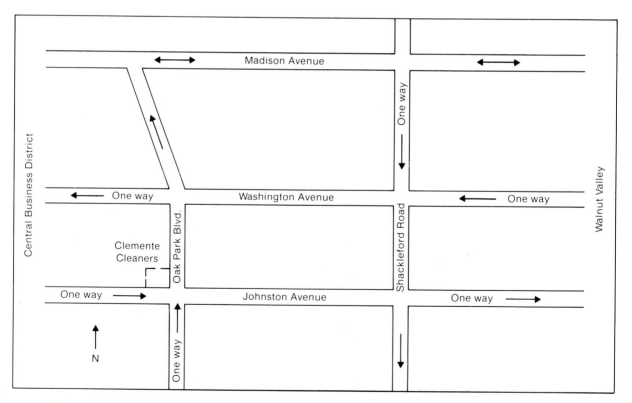

EXHIBIT 21–1
New traffic artery pattern

EXHIBIT 21–2
The proposed Madison Avenue site

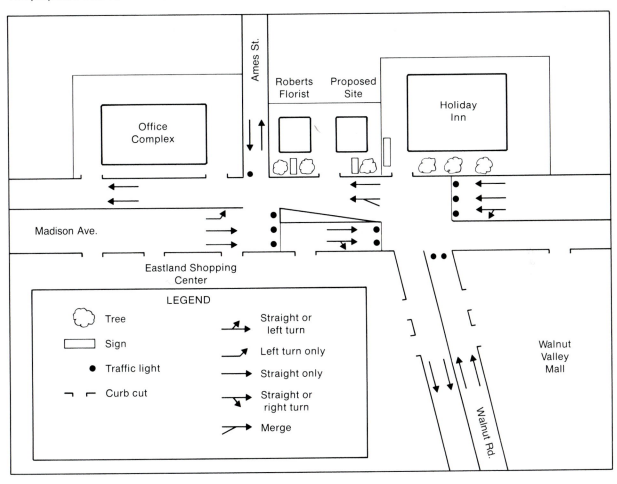

Clemente Cleaners and expressed their potential support should Bart Clemente decide to open a second conveniently located outlet in Walnut Valley. Unfortunately, good locations are hard to find in Walnut Valley, but after a ten-month search, Clemente found a Madison Avenue site that he thought might be appropriate (Exhibit 21–2).

From his service records, Clemente determined that a large number of his former customers live within one mile of the site. Most of these customers would have to pass the site on their shopping trips to Walnut Valley Mall and Eastland Shopping Center. Walnut Valley Mall was a large regional center anchored by Sears, J. C. Penney, and two large local department stores. A large discount store and a catalog showroom were the principal tenants of Eastland Shopping Center. In Clemente's mind, there was no question that the site's trading area contained sufficient business potential to support his proposed venture. What troubled him was the site itself. While the existing building was adequate for his needs, he would have to share the parking lot (eight parking spaces) with Robert's Florist. In addition, Clemente was somewhat concerned with the site's accessibility.

CURRENT SITUATION

Clemente's option on the site expired at the end of the month. Hence, he had to make a decision soon. Having limited experience in site analysis, Clemente decided to engage the services of Professor Kristine Michaels, head of the marketing department at the local state university. Michaels agreed to investigate the site accessibility issue and to make appropriate recommendations. She also agreed to address the issue of whether Clemente should exercise the rent, lease, or buy clause of his option.

ASSIGNMENT

☐ Assume the role of Professor Michaels. First, prepare a written report on the pros and cons of the site's accessibility and make whatever recommendations you think are appropriate. Second, prepare a report on the pros and cons of renting, leasing, and buying a location and make a recommendation to Clemente regarding this issue. Be sure to provide adequate support and rationale for your recommendations.

CASE 22

Lockner's Department Store: The Role of a Toy Department

George Prough and Dale M. Lewison, the University of Akron

INTRODUCTION

For the last forty years, Lockner's Department Store had been recognized as one of the leading retail merchandisers in the midwestern city of Plains, Iowa (1987 population, 175,000). The area is expected to continue above-average population growth for the next 20 years. During the last four decades, Lockner's had built a reputation as an upscale retailer of quality merchandise. By carefully designing the firm's total merchandising program, Lockner's management had generally been successful in appealing to both middle- and upper-class consumers. Over the last five years, sales and profit objectives for most merchandise departments were met or exceeded. The one exception to this is the toy department. For Betty Lockner, founder and president of the store, this situation was simply unacceptable.

LOCKNER'S MERCHANDISING STRATEGY

The Product–Service Mixes

Good quality, high style, and an excellent variety of brand-name merchandise were hallmarks of the firm's product mix. To help differentiate its product mix from competitive product offerings, Lockner's featured a number of top-quality private labels in several different product lines. Also, a variety of specialty and imported goods not commonly found in competitive stores were an integral part of Lockner's product strategy. To enhance its image as an upscale, full-line department store and as a one-stop shopping store, Lockner's carried a deep assortment of brands, models, styles, and colors for most product lines.

Excellent service was another key ingredient in the store's merchandising program. Lockner's offered a complete service mix with a variety of credit, delivery, and wrapping plans, and alterations, repair, and layaway services. All essential and expected services were provided free or, in a few cases, at a minimal fee.

The Promotional–Place Mixes

Lockner's promotional strategy was directed at enhancing the store's prestige image. To do so, local newspaper advertisements focused on appeals stressing product selection and quality, service offerings, and shopping atmosphere.

Product advertisements featuring a few carefully selected items were used to inform customers of new and special merchandise. The store also ran numerous institutional advertisements that attempted to communicate the message that "Lockner's is *the* place to shop." After a customer had been attracted to the store, considerable attention was given to capitalizing on the traffic, through such promotional tools as attractive and accessible displays, special effects, and promotional demonstrations.

The store was located on the newly opened Hub Mall, an open-air pedestrian mall in downtown Plains. The area featured many renovated or new specialty and more fashion-oriented shops. Lockner's was completely renovated inside and out at the same time as the mall. Both the area and the store were accessible to the area's population and offered a pleasurable and exciting shopping environment not found anywhere nearby.

THE TOY INDUSTRY

Estimates of sales in the toy industry are in the neighborhood of $2 billion annually. Department stores typically sell about 13 percent of all toys, games, and hobby items. Sales in department stores, however, indicate that they sell a higher than average share of dolls and educational and scientific toys.

Toys are product items with interesting life cycles. Both the level and duration of consumer acceptance can vary substantially from one toy line to another. Toys range from faddish product items whose life expectancy is short (several months) to classics like Monopoly and Scrabble that remain popular for decades. Frequently, the general nature of the life cycle for a particular new toy can be explained by the toy's origin. Currently, many new toy ideas originate in popular movies or television programs; hence, the life expectancy depends on the level and duration of popularity for these entertainment vehicles. For instance, Strawberry Shortcake products once enjoyed tremendous success, but since the demise of the television program, popularity of these products has declined considerably. In contrast, Star Wars toys have enjoyed tremendous popularity for several years, and sales are expected to continue at fairly substantial levels as a result of plans to continue sequels into the 1990s.

Technologically and socially, the toy industry has undergone considerable change during the last few decades. On the technological front, toys have evolved dramatically from the cornhusk dolls of the seventeenth century. Today, computer technology has had a major impact on toys and games in the sense that many computer games and software for home computers have broadened the appeal of such "toys" to all age groups. The old rule that toys appeal only to young children no longer applies. Computer and board games also offer people the opportunity to exercise their analytical prowess by making key decisions that affect the outcome of the game. For all age groups, the trend appears to be away from passive games of chance to more active games of skill and decision making.

Socially, toys have evolved with the social values and moods of the country. As exemplified by the Fisher Price line, educational values are often preeminent for parents shopping for toys for younger children. Today, motives for purchasing toys include not only entertainment value but the belief that toys can play an important role in children's mental, physical, and creative development. Contemporary social values are also reflected in the type of toys purchased. In past years, dolls only cried "Mama"; today, dolls have more extensive vocabularies, are often anatomically correct, and can perform a number of biological functions. Further, as roles of men and women are redefined, so too are toys and toy buying. Boys are increasingly accepting dolls (Star Wars figures, G.I. Joe figures, He-Man figures, Cabbage Patch dolls, etc.), and girls are increasingly becoming active in sports.

The toy industry is highly competitive; of the estimated 125,000 toy items produced each year, approximately 12,000 achieve a high level of customer acceptance. Of the 12,000 that do gain wide acceptance, only a few return to the same level of public acceptance the following year. Thus, knowing what is and what is not a hot item is vital to survival in the toy industry.

Product offerings are planned by toy manufacturers in April, and production levels are set at that time. Product competition takes several forms. Toy manufacturers compete for the rights to produce toy items that are expected to succeed (e.g., Star Wars toys), for the development of new products, and for the development of additional product features and options for existing toys. Manufacturers' representatives, printed materials, and trade shows are the major promotional vehicles for obtaining orders from wholesalers and retailers. Orders for toys are accepted from April through August and are filled on a first-come, first-served basis. Because the manufacturer produces a preset number of a given toy, it is essential that wholesalers and retailers place orders for "hot" items early. Advertising is vitally important at both local and national levels. To create product awareness and to promote product and brand preference, toy manufacturers advertise heavily on television during Saturday mornings and on other programs directed toward children. At the local level, manufacturers and retailers often run cooperative newspaper or other local advertising to inform customers about which stores have the product and their prices.

Clearly the major target market for toys is the youth market. Children with allowances and some with babysitting, yardwork, and other income represent a strong economic force. In addition, children play an "influencer" role in the family. Demand for a particular toy depends heavily on the ability of children to influence parents to purchase that item. A number of research studies show the following:

1. Children are strongly influenced by television commercials; in three out of four cases, preferred toys had recently been seen on television.
2. Peer groups are strong influences of toy preference for many children (this influence occurs in the form of the "two-step flow of communication"—television advertisements to playmates or peers who buy the product and then influence their friends to buy it, too).
3. Younger children attempt to influence parental purchasing more frequently than do older children.
4. The frequency of parents' giving in to a child's requests for a particular toy increases with the age of the child.
5. Parents are preferred twice as much as peers as a source of product information even by adolescent children.
6. Mothers are the general purchasing agent for most families; they therefore make the majority of actual toy purchases.

MIKE ROGERS'S SITUATION

In February Mike Rogers, toy department manager for Lockner's Department Store, contemplated the toy department's role in the firm's overall merchandising strategy. The toy department has been used as a seasonal "leader" department; that is, its primary function was to attract consumers into the store during the Christmas season by offering an excellent selection of popular toys at competitive prices. During the rest of the year, the toy department was largely neglected both by Lockner's management and by Lockner's customers. At these times, Lockner's stocks seasonal toys plus a variety of the most popular toys, and prices are kept competitive.

Lockner's toy stock during the nonholiday seasons consists primarily of the most popular toys and dolls. Rogers had never bought many board games, European specialty toys, specialty and collectable dolls, or the more extraordinary toys. Instead, he'd chosen to stay with the basics except for the seasonal promotions.

Recently, Rogers wondered whether a new role for the toy department might be worth considering. Rogers believed it would be appropriate to review the department's overall situation with the idea of identifying strategy alternatives and making possible recommendations for a new merchandising role for the toy department.

ASSIGNMENT

☐ What options are available for the future selling season?

☐ Identify the merchandising role you would adopt for Lockner's toy department and justify your selection.

CASE 23

Cironi's Sewing Center: Merchandising-Mix Decisions Based on Financial Analysis

J. B. Wilkinson and Joseph P. McCafferty, the University of Akron

In July of 1987, Tony Cironi, owner and manager of Cironi's Sewing Center, faced what he considered to be the most difficult decision since the start of his business in 1985. Over the past two years, sales of Singer sewing machines had not been adequate to cover the costs of the business and provide a decent living income. Without the income from repairs and maintenance of sewing machines, the business would have actually operated at a loss in both 1986 and 1987 (Exhibit 23–1).

Part of the problem could be attributed to the declining trend for home sewing and to shrinking profit margins on Singer sewing machines caused by low-cost imports. The location of the store in Akron, Ohio, was a contributing factor, however. Since the late 1970s, Akron had been the scene of a severe local recession caused by high unemployment rates and a declining industrial base. Local competition was fierce, especially among retailers of consumer durables. Price-cutting on sewing machines had been particularly prevalent. Sears sometimes advertised a basic zigzag-stitch machine in a cabinet for $99. Jo Ann Fabrics often advertised "matching the price of any local competitor on Singer sewing machines." During the past two years, Cironi had been forced into "price and deal" advertising on Singer sewing machines just to stay in business. The impact on his profits had been ruinous. Whereas Singer dealers in other market areas could realize a 40 percent margin on selling price, he had averaged only 25 percent. As a result, Cironi had decided to diversify his business and add a merchandise line with better profit potential.

EXHIBIT 23–1

Cironi's Sewing Center: Statement of income for the years ending 31 December 1986 and 1987

	1986		1987	
Sales revenue		$120,000		$125,000
Less cost of sales		90,000		93,000
Gross profit		30,000		32,000
Rent and utilities	9,310		9,825	
Depreciation	3,120		3,120	
Advertising	8,310		8,500	
Salaries (part-time employee)	12,500		13,000	
Miscellaneous expense	6,760	(40,000)	5,555	(40,000)
Operation income		(10,000)		(8,000)
Other income (repair and maintenance)		18,625		17,825
Total income before taxes		$ 8,625		$ 9,825

Other dealers in similar circumstances had been adding such merchandise lines as home entertainment products (including video rentals), microwave ovens, waterbeds, ceiling fans, vacuum cleaners, small electric appliances, fabrics, and furniture. As far as Cironi could determine, the choice of which line to add was not clear. Dealer preference and the characteristics of local competitors seemed to influence the choice. Also, some dealers had added popular or "fad" items and then dropped the products when consumers lost interest in them. Based on the experience of a few friends who were sewing machine dealers, Cironi decided to investigate the possibility of adding one of the following product lines: vacuum cleaners, stereo equipment, and fabrics/sewing notions/patterns. He also toyed with the idea of adding additional lines of sewing machines. Although this latter option would not be a diversification strategy, it appealed to Cironi for personal reasons.

BACKGROUND

Tony Cironi had been a Singer salesman in a company-owned Singer store in Akron before 1980. During that year, Singer began a program to close, convert to dealerships, or reconfigure more than 150 retail outlets, including the store in which Cironi worked. On 11 October 1980, the Singer board of directors approved a program to completely restructure the company's sewing machine manufacturing operations and distribution systems. Some 2,000 company-owned outlets in North America and Europe were either closed or converted to dealerships. In the Akron area, Jo Ann Fabrics, a chain of fabric stores, was licensed to sell Singer sewing machines, and Cironi got a job in the Jo Ann Fabrics Akron store as a manager of the newly formed department for Singer sewing machines. Jo Ann Fabrics offered little opportunity for advancement, however, and less attractive employee benefits than Singer. In 1982, Cironi approached Singer for a dealer license and received permission to open a dealership in Akron. By 1982, though, the outlook for a Singer dealership was discouraging. The sewing machine industry and Singer, the largest sewing machine firm in the world, were in deep trouble. In the words of Singer chairman Joseph Flavin, "If there is a smokestack industry, it's sewing machines. The sewing machine is 130 years old. Anybody can make one. They're made all over the world. The patents are all gone. You don't have anything unique and you have little growth."

The Industry

In 1982, the U.S. sewing machine industry was composed of approximately thirty-two firms employing some 8,500 workers. The industry produces household sewing machines for occasional use in supplying cloth-

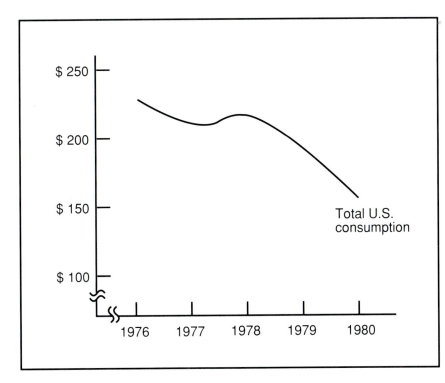

$ 250

$ 200

$ 150

$ 100

1976   1977   1978   1979   1980

Total U.S. consumption

EXHIBIT 23-2
U.S. consumption of household sewing machines, 1976 to 1980 (in millions) (source: Robert C. Skinner, U.S. International Trade Commission, *Summary of Trade and Tariff Information—Sewing Machines (1976–80)* [Washington, D.C.: U.S. Government Printing Office, September 1981] 1–30.)

ing and home accessories, industrial sewing machines for the apparel industry, and sewing machine parts. Estimated U.S. production in 1982 was $347 million, up 14 percent from $305 million in 1978. The bulk of 1982 production was accounted for by parts (57 percent), followed by industrial machines (25 percent), and household machines (17 percent). Estimated U.S. consumption of these products increased from $430 million in 1978 to $473 million in 1980 and then fell to $414 million in 1982. The decline was primarily due to declining demand for household sewing machines.

The U.S. market for household sewing machines peaked in 1974, and the European market had stopped growing in 1976. Between 1974 and 1982, industry analysts estimated that total unit sales in the U.S. consumer sewing machine market declined by approximately 50 percent. As shown in Exhibit 23–2, U.S. consumption of household sewing machines declined from $223 million in 1978 to $159 million in 1982. Imports accounted for approximately 69 percent of this volume throughout the period.

In 1979, Singer commissioned a study to explain these disturbing trends. The study, prepared by economist Norma Pace, indicated that "only 18 percent of females aged 16 to 24 will own machines in 1985, compared with an estimated 46 percent in 1970. The drop in the 25- to 29-year-olds is even more dramatic, with only 31 percent owning machines in 1985 in these age brackets, as compared with 79 percent in 1970" (see

Exhibit 23–3). The traditional market for household sewing machines had been women between the ages of 18 and 29 who use a sewing machine to make clothing and home furnishings. During this time, however, women in these age brackets took jobs and therefore had less time for sewing. Also, as rising costs forced clothing manufacturers to low-cost, overseas locations, clothing prices actually rose less than the overall inflation rate, which further blunted the incentive to sew at home.

In 1978, the same trends became apparent in Singer's European markets, and in 1979 Singer decided to shrink its sewing machine business by closing nearly all of its U.S. and European manufacturing plants and either closing company-owned retail stores or converting them to outsider-owned dealerships. In its 1979 annual report, Singer stated that "[this] program was adopted to address the continuing losses in the company's consumer sewing operations in these markets of the developed world and in its worldwide industrial sewing operations."

CURRENT SITUATION

Throughout the summer, Cironi collected information about the profitability and feasibility of adding one of the following merchandise lines to his business: vacuum cleaners, stereo equipment, fabrics/sewing notions/patterns, and other brands of sewing machines.

EXHIBIT 23–3

U.S. machine ownership (women 16 to 29 years of age) (source: adapted from Thomas O'Hanlon, "Behind the Snafu at Singer," *Fortune*, 5 November, 1979, 77.)

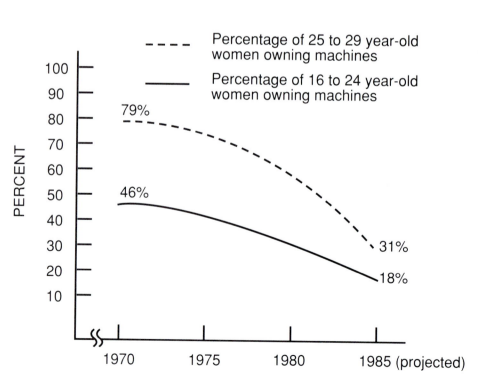

Percentage of 25 to 29 year-old women owning machines

Percentage of 16 to 24 year-old women owning machines

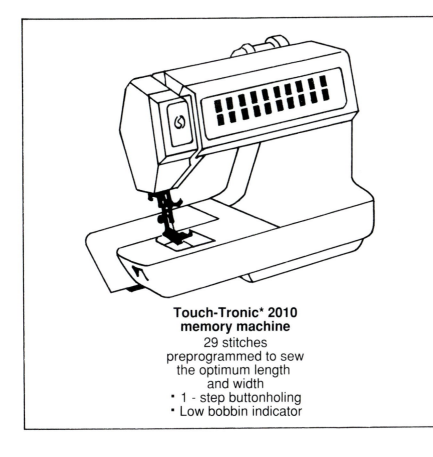

EXHIBIT 23–4
Singer Touch-Tronic
2010 Memory Machine

**Touch-Tronic* 2010
memory machine**
29 stitches
preprogrammed to sew
the optimum length
and width
• 1 - step buttonholing
• Low bobbin indicator

Availability of appropriate merchandise would be no problem. Cironi had decided that quilting fabrics and supplies would be attractive to sewing hobbyists, and such merchandise could be obtained from sales reps of textile manufacturers. Distributorships for Hoover vacuum cleaners and Sony stereo equipment were readily available. Because many customers asked about the quality European machines, Cironi looked into the possibility of distributing any of the European brands. Only Bernina and Elna distributorships were immediately available to his business in Akron.

Singer Sewing Machines

The current line of Singer household sewing machines was priced from $99 to $1,299 and consisted of approximately ten models. At the bottom of the line was a basic zigzag machine; top-of-the-line models were solid-state electronic machines with instant touch-panel pattern selection and one-step, built-in buttonholer. The Touch-Tronic 2010 model shown in Exhibit 23–4 was priced at $1,299 and was well regarded by serious sewers. At the present time, the Singer line of sewing machines occupied the entire 1,800 square feet of selling space. The inventory turnover ratio was eight.

Bernina and Elna Sewing Machines

By adding additional lines of sewing machines, Cironi could offer shoppers one-stop shopping. Most shoppers were either first-time buyers or had bought a sewing machine ten to twenty years earlier. Unless a buyer was well informed, the range (brands, models, and price levels) and complexity of the new machines were confusing. To reduce anxiety, sewing machine buyers typically visited several dealers before making a decision. Cironi felt he would increase his chances of "getting the sale" by offering more choice and by providing comparative information about several good lines of sewing machines. Also, becoming a dealer for additional lines of sewing machines would facilitate his access to repair parts and training. Cironi's Sewing Center had gained a good reputation in Akron for sewing machine repair, and customers often brought in Bernina, Elna, White, Pfaff, and other makes for repair.

Bernina was willing to offer Cironi an exclusive dealership in Akron for a 25-mile radius. Elna had three other dealers in Akron. In contrast, there were six other Singer dealers in Akron, one of which had four outlets. Price ranges for Bernina and Elna machines are shown in Exhibit 23–5. Estimated productivity and profitability

EXHIBIT 23–5
Suggested retail prices
for selected brands of
sewing machines, 1982

Brand Name	Suggested Retail Price Range	Brand Name	Suggested Retail Price Range
Bernina	$649–$1,099	New Home	$249–$1,250
Brother	$140–$ 900	J.C. Penney	$100–$ 300
Elna	$599–$1,219	Pfaff	$499–$1,249
Kenmore (Sears)	$ 96–$1,000	Riccar	$400–$1,000
Montgomery Ward	$145–$ 590	Singer	$110–$1,299
Necchi	$280–$1,150	Viking	$599–$1,449
Nelco	$400–$ 700	White	$299–$ 699

ratios for the two lines combined are shown in Exhibit 23–6.

Hoover Vacuum Cleaners

Approximately 75 percent of all sewing machine dealers also sold vacuums. Price-cutting on vacuums was vicious, however. The markup on Hoover vacuums was only 15 percent, and there were at least 29 Hoover dealers in Akron. This was not surprising, since Hoover's world headquarters was located less than thirty minutes away.

After conversations with other dealers, Cironi's best estimate on sales per square foot was $1,250, but this was based on carrying the full line, priced from $70 to $350. With aggressive selling, the inventory turnover ratio could be twelve.

Repair of Hoover vacuums was "easy" but "dirty." Several dealers had quite a repertoire of stories about how customers mistreated vacuum cleaners. A large inventory of parts was necessary to handle the repair volume.

Sony Stereos

The possibility of adding a line of stereos was attractive to Cironi. A dealer friend in Cleveland had recently dropped Singer sewing machines in favor of home entertainment products, and he helped Cironi estimate productivity and profitability figures for Sony stereo equipment (Exhibit 23–6). He also told Cironi about compact disk players. Industry experts regarded compact disk players as one of the most complex products ever de-

signed for consumers. Barring some unforeseen problem, compact disk players would completely replace electronic stereo systems. By getting a Sony dealership, Cironi could hope to share the huge market that would eventually develop for compact disk players.

Certain aspects of selling stereo equipment were not so attractive. Stereo buyers shopped around for stereo equipment and sometimes "put together" systems with components from different manufacturers. Also, a stereo was regarded by many buyers as only one part of a home entertainment center. Cironi was not sure that one brand of only stereo equipment would satisfy shoppers' needs. If Cironi's Sewing Center were forced to carry additional products and brands, he felt that the store would either lose its identity as a sewing machine center or experience the effects of a confused retail image.

Stereo equipment also required "salesmanship" and a commitment to the product. Warranty and repair service was required of dealers. Cironi, however, would have to farm out most of this to an appliance repair outlet since he had no experience with stereo equipment. Furthermore, there were twelve Sony dealers in Akron.

Quilting Fabrics

Quilting fabrics would enjoy year-long demand by sewing hobbyists, who use them to make knickknacks for the house. Of all the product lines under consideration, quilting fabrics would have the greatest compatibility with sewing machines. Productivity and profitability estimates for quilting fabrics are shown in Exhibit 23–6. Competitor statistics for quilting fabrics could not be ac-

EXHIBIT 23–6
Productivity and profit-
ability ratios for
selected merchandise
lines

	Quilting Fabrics and Supplies	Hoover Vacuums	Sony Stereos	Bernina and Elna Sewing Machines
Gross profit (percent)	45%	15%	35%	45%
Inventory turnover	2×	12×	17×	14×
Sales per square foot	$100	$1,250	$1,075	$350
Selling space (sq. ft.)	250	144	100	400

curately determined, but there were 34 established, full-line fabric stores in Akron.

Several problems relative to fabrics had occurred to Cironi. First, fabrics had a low turnover, which meant tying up working capital for long periods. From past experience, Cironi knew that selling fabric required a lot of time. Customers often wanted advice about pattern requirements, and the measuring, cutting, and notion selection activities could take up a considerable amount of time. Also, other dealers who had been successful with specialty fabrics (quilting, lingerie, drapery, and the like) emphasized the need for lessons and display to achieve high profits.

On the other hand, quilting attracted serious sewers who might buy an expensive high-quality sewing machine. Carrying quilting fabrics would bring these hobbyists into the store on a regular basis.

QUESTIONS

☐ What criteria would you use to evaluate the merchandise lines? Why?
☐ Which merchandise line would you select? Why?

The authors thank Bob Barnes, owner of Barnes Sewing Center in Akron, Ohio, for technical information regarding sewing centers.

CASE 24

J. Rogers Department Stores Company: Evaluating a New Merchandising Program

Dale M. Lewison and Jon Hawes, the University of Akron

BACKGROUND

Rogers's Emporium was established in 1907 by John Rogers. The firm's present-day image as one of the leading retail merchandisers in the southwestern United States is based on the founder's early recognition of the potential market demand for upscale merchandise that emerged during the oil boom years. As old "J.R." used to say, "give the customers what they want, but always make a profit." This guiding principle has always served as the firm's basic merchandising and operating policy and has given it a national reputation as a unique and profitable merchandiser of a wide variety of unusual and everyday products and services.

The firm was reorganized into J. Rogers Department Stores Company in 1952. Its success has been attributed largely to its adherence to the policy of "gross margin maintenance." It is and always has been the company's operating goal to obtain an overall 40-percent gross margin for each of its stores. The following gross margin objectives were established for each of the store's general merchandise categories: 50 percent for wearing apparel, 60 percent for accessories, 30 percent for household goods, 30 percent for household furnishings, 40 percent for consumer electronics, and 40 percent for sporting goods.

Currently, the J. Rogers Department Stores Company operated three full-line department stores at Great Plains Mall, Parkside Mall, and Southland Mall. By March of this year, the company's new store in Dixieland Mall would be open and in full operation. As with the three current stores, the new outlet would be a full-service department store appealing to the area's middle- and upper-class consumers.

As the general merchandise manager (GMM) for the last five years, Louise Stouch had been directly responsible for overseeing most of the major buying decisions for all three stores. During her tenure as GMM, Louise's track record had been outstanding as judged by the criterion of achieving the expected 40-percent overall gross margin. Each of the major merchandise categories and most of the individual product lines realized the expected gross margins. One of the more important exceptions has been Great Western Clothing Company's line of men's suits, The Naturals. Gross margins realized on The Naturals have varied considerably, and unsatisfactory performance levels have characterized this product line in three of the last five years. A review of Great Western's other product lines carried by J. Rogers, however, revealed a sales and gross margin performance that met or exceeded the firm's expectations. This latter fact would suggest the need to maintain good relationships with the Great Western Clothing Company.

CURRENT SITUATION

With the rapidly approaching summer buying season, Stouch needed to make an immediate decision whether to continue to carry The Naturals line of men's suits. She'd already received next year's proposed merchandising program for The Naturals (see Exhibits 24–1 and 24–2) from Sharon Neidert, national sales manager for

EXHIBIT 24–1

Ms. Louise Stouch
General Merchandise Manager
J. Rogers Department Stores
400 East Plains Ave
Dallas, Texas 78041

Dear Ms. Stouch:

A new season is upon us, and we at Great Western Clothing Company are excited about our new merchandising program for The Naturals. The new program entails numerous changes, and we believe these changes will provide you with the opportunity to realize a substantial increase in unit sales at profitable levels. With the opening of your new store and the quantity discount structure of the new merchandising program, we think it would be in your best interest to place a unit order in excess of 300 units. Our sales representative, Jeb Works, will call on you shortly to finalize your order. As always, we are looking forward to working with you and your organization.

Sincerely,

Sharon Neidert
National Sales Manager
Great Western Clothing Company

Great Western Clothing Company. Before making any decision regarding The Naturals, a comprehensive comparative analysis between last year's merchandising program (Exhibit 24–3) and the new proposed program seemed in order. Skimming the new program, Stouch noticed a number of significant changes, which might be sufficient to ensure the 50-percent gross margin expectations that have not always been realized in the past. Pressed for time, she decided to ask the assistant GMM, Cheryl Nader, to conduct the comparative analysis and to recommend possible courses of action.

ASSIGNMENT

Assume the role of Cheryl Nader and develop a comprehensive comparative analysis report for each year of The Naturals merchandising program. After discussing the project with Louise Stouch, you have agreed to include the following items in the report:

☐ A determination of the realized gross margin for the first year's program. Sales records will show that 190 units were ordered and sold. Expense records will show that the average transportation cost per unit is 4 percent of list price, the average transit insurance cost per unit is 1 percent of list price, and the average alteration cost per unit is 1 percent of list price.

☐ A determination of the expected gross margin for the second year's program at various estimated unit sales levels (e.g., 175, 200, 250, and 300 units).

☐ A statement of the advantages and disadvantages of the first year's program as compared to the second year's program.

☐ A description of the alternative courses of action that are open to the company regarding the second year's program.

☐ A recommendation and justification of which alternative the company should pursue.

Product class	Men's apparel
Product line	The Naturals—mix and match suits
Product items	The summer Naturals are available as separate pieces and can be sold in any coat–slack combination (mix and match) Solid and patterned coats are available in standard sizes 30 to 48 and long sizes 40–48 Slacks are available in standard waist sizes A standard length allows the slack to be altered to the customer's dimensions
Merchandising program	
List price	Coat: $90 Slack: $30
Discount structure	
Trade (chain)	Coat: 30%, 15%, 10% Slack: 25%, 10%, 5%
Quantity (noncumulative)	Coat: 0% per unit—1–99 units 1% per unit—100–199 units 4% per unit—200–299 units 8% per unit—300 or more units Slack: 0% per unit—1–199 units 1% per unit—200–299 units 4% per unit—300 or more units
Cash	2/10, net thirty days
Promotional allowance	Coat: 0% per unit—1–199 units .5% per unit—200–299 units 1.5% per unit—300 or more units Slack: 0% per unit—1–299 units 1% per unit—300 or more units
Shipping terms	FOB origin, freight prepaid
Reorder delivery time	Two to three weeks
Minimum reorder quantity	One dozen

EXHIBIT 24–2

Second-year merchandising program for The Naturals, Great Western Clothing Company

EXHIBIT 24–3
First-year merchandis-
ing program for The
Naturals, Great West-
ern Clothing Company

Product class	Men's apparel
Product line	The Naturals—two-piece suits
Product items	The summer Naturals are available in four solid colors
	The Naturals are cut in contemporary fashion and are available in standard suit sizes of 30–48
Merchandising program	
List price	Suit: $100
Discount structure	
Trade (chain)	Suit: 30%, 15%, 10%
Quantity (cumulative)	Suit: 0% per unit—1–99 units
	1% per unit—100–199 units
	4% per unit—200–299 units
	7% per unit—300 or more units
Cash (EOM)	2/10, net 30 days
Promotional allowances	Suit: .5% per unit
Shipping terms	FOB destination, freight prepaid
Reorder delivery time	One to two weeks
Minimum reorder quantity	One dozen
Return privilege	5% of ordered stock

CASE 25

"Dear Manager": Coping With Consumer Complaints

Douglas Hausknecht, the University of Akron

Bill Baker was having a trying morning. The dog got into the trash (again), the bakery didn't have the muffins he wanted, and traffic was backed up all the way into the city. Bill tried to shake off these annoyances as he prepared to open the store.

The morning at Rich's Friendly Appliances seemed to be going better when the mail came at 10:30. As manager, Baker had the responsibility of dealing with the various invoices, product announcements, payments, and the like as they came in each day. Rarely were there any real letters, except those from customers complaining about one thing or another. In his four years with the store, Baker could remember only one letter that complimented and thanked the store for its efforts. Today's mail was no exception. Mixed in with notices promising manufacturer support for another "truckload" sale and some booklets on Toast/Bake/Microwave ovens were several letters from customers. These he saved for last.

After having coffee and a danish, Baker settled in to read the letters. The first was from Baltimore and came in a hand-addressed envelope (Exhibit 25–1). "Hey

lady, we all got problems," Baker thought as he read the letter. "Forget the autobiography and tell me the problem." He checked the Recent Sales file for the ticket and discovered that the washer was a relatively low-price but comparatively high-margin item. There were no notations on the delivery slip. "Well, what do you want?" Baker wondered as he finished reading the letter. "I'm certainly not going to send you a hundred bucks for this." Just then, the telephone rang and he set the letter aside until later.

After rescheduling a couple of deliveries, Baker returned to the mail. The next letter had been typed on obviously good-quality stationery with a civic group's letterhead (Exhibit 25–2). The amount of money demanded got his attention right away. "A $265 rebate?" Baker fumed, "That's a pretty big chunk of this week's profit." As he was finishing the letter, one of the saleswomen came in and told him that she could close a sale if the store could "throw-in" an icemaker. "No way," he exploded, "do you know how much those things cost us?" The saleswoman was surprised at this response but returned to the customers. She was

EXHIBIT 25—1

3900 Southwestern Blvd.
Apt. 31-C
Baltimore, MD 21227

6/13/87

Rich's Appliances
Glen Burnie, MD 21220

Dear Managers,

I really didn't want to write this letter, but my sister-in-law said to. We really like the washer we bought, so that's not the problem.

With three kids, my husband and myself we do a lot of cleaning. It was bad enough carrying the stuff around here in the building. The machines kept breaking down and getting dirty. Half the time only 3 washers were working and you'd have to wait for a turn.

They finally got new machines here. But it costs $2.00 to wash and dry a load of clothes. I guess we could use the clothesline out back, but I hate to leave my stuff out there unless I'm watching it and you know I can't do that and watch the kids too.

We decided to get a washer and dryer cause they give us the hook-ups and the place. We saved up so we could put half down on the washer first. After we get that paid for we'll save up for the dryer.

When we came in, the salesgirl (Trudy was her name) was so very nice. She helped us figure out what we needed and what was a good buy. The one we got wasn't on special, but it seemed like a good price. We were so pleased that delivery and hook-up were only a little bit extra.

The people came out right on time to install the washer. (I was surprised that a woman was one of them.) They brought it in and hooked it to the water and the drain and we started a load. Everything seemed to work then and it has really worked well ever since.

I was so proud of the new washer that I asked Mrs. Webb, our manager, to come in and see it. She said it looked like a "good, basic machine." We had some coffee and store-bought cookies.

When she was leaving, Mrs. Webb saw a hole in the plaster wall and a tear in the staircase rug leading to the utility room. She told me that part of the lease was a damage deposit and we'd have to pay for repairs when we moved out unless we fixed it ourselves.

I had just cleaned that staircase the day before because I knew your men (people it turns out) were coming the next day. There wasn't a hole or a tear then, I'm sure about it. They must have happened when the washer was delivered. I didn't watch too close, as I was trying to keep Nancy, our youngest, out of the way.

When I told my sister-in-law she said to call the store. Trudy didn't know what to do about it and said you weren't in. She said to write to you because you are so busy when you are there.

I wasn't going to bother you, but Mrs. Webb said it might cost $100 to get these things fixed right. We don't plan to move anytime soon, why else would I buy a washer and dryer, but that is a lot of money for something we didn't do. I'm sure you'll take care of this.

Thank you for your help,

Mrs. F. (Christine) Albenasi

EXHIBIT 25–2

SUNNY HEIGHTS
NEIGHBORHOOD ASSOCIATION
Potomac, MD

June 11, 1987

Rich's Friendly Appliances
Glen Burnie Mall
Glen Burnie, MD 21220

To the manager:

As a recent purchaser of a refrigerator from your store, I must vehemently protest the quality which I received. The icemaker which is installed in the QwikChill 500 simply does not keep up with my family's needs. I am therefore requesting a credit in the amount of half of the original purchase price (i.e., $265 out of $529).

Since the refrigerator was purchased and delivered in April, we have never accumulated more than a half tub of ice cubes. While we seldom run out completely, the quantity produced forces my family to constrain its use of ice. We believe this to be completely unacceptable.

This refrigerator was needed for its ice-making ability. Because it is only able to make a half tub, I feel that it is worth only half the price. In addition, I have already invested over $400 of my own time in shopping for, helping your people install, and trying to improve the performance of the refrigerator. As you can see, there is no way that I can come out even on this exchange, but I'm willing to be reasonable and settle for $265.

Please send a check, by the end of this month, to my home address:

54 Crabcake Ln.
Potomac, MD 21407

I have no desire to invest any additional time in shopping for a different refrigerator. I am convinced this is the best you can do.

Thank you,

James Flavin, President

JF:mtp

pleased that Baker came out of the office and helped to close the sale with a half-price offer on the icemaker.

After a few more telephone calls, Baker finally read the third letter (Exhibit 25–3). It dealt with a bottom-of-the-line microwave that sold well at a small margin. "A new glass tray will eat me up on that item," he thought. Checking the inventory, which showed ten in stock, he saw that the gross mark-up was only $17.35.

After reading the final letter, another threat to sue (Exhibit 25–4), Baker was exhausted. He wasn't even sure how to react. He closed the office door, sat back in his chair, and spread the four letters in front of him and mused about his possible responses.

ASSIGNMENT

- ☐ How should Bill respond to each letter?
- ☐ Is responding to customer calls and letters an adequate way to monitor consumer satisfaction? Suggest other methods.
- ☐ What operational changes are indicated by these letters?

EXHIBIT 25–3

William Baker, Manager
Rich's Friendly Appliances
Glen Burnie Mall
Glen Burnie, MD 21220

295 Forest Ave.
Dorsey, MD 21076
June 13, 1987

Dear Mr. Baker:

I'm writing to request a replacement glass tray for the microwave oven (Triton #31RS) which I purchased and which was delivered on the 10th of this month. When my husband and I opened the carton, we found the tray had a crack running through about 2/3 of its length. I also did not receive the recipe book promised in the advertisement.

I hope the items are in stock, or at least available readily in the area. If so, perhaps we can have this problem cleared up by the end of the week.

Since the oven was delivered to me, I assume that these replacement items can also be delivered. I will telephone you Friday A.M. to check on progress.

Sincerely,

Ellen Cole

EXHIBIT 25–4

Rich's Friendly Appliances
Glen Burnie Mall
Glen Burnie, MD 21220

1313 Mockingbird Ln
Laurel, MD 21250
June 13, 1987

Sir:

What's the matter with you guys? Why can't I get any decent service. I've had it with this oven and now I want it replaced.

I bought this house early in 1986, when they were building it. Since I was living alone, my friends suggested that I have a microwave oven installed instead of a regular oven. I even came down to your fine (Ha!) store and picked one out and paid extra so the contractor would substitute.

Well, let me tell you it's been nothing but trouble. No matter how many different things I try, everything is always undercooked or overcooked. Sometimes the stuff I defrost is half-cooked before I'm ready to use it.

The builder is no longer in business, but this isn't really his fault. I want you to come out and replace this piece of junk with a real, electric oven. I also want my $100 back.

If I don't have this by the end of the month, I'm going to get a lawyer and sue you. I'll also have you shut down for selling things that don't do what they are supposed to. I'll be waiting to hear from you.

(signed) Frank Martin

CASE 26

Don't Give an Inch: Handling Returns and Adjustments

Dale M. Lewison and Jon Hawes, the University of Akron

Date: Thursday, 7 April 1989, 4:35 P.M.
Scene: Retail Sales Floor, Quality Auto Service Centers
Characters: Mike and Jackie Buckholzer, a married couple and customers; Pam Adams, Retail Sales Associate

ACTION

Mike: Let me get this straight. The four, all-season, steel-belted radials are on sale for $49.95 each—or a total of $200.

Pam: About $200 plus tax, plus balancing, and alignment.

Mike: What about the tire-protection plan? What does it cost?

Pam: That is $79.95.

Jackie: According to this [pointing to sign], the protection plan includes the initial alignment and wheel balance.

Pam: That's right.

Mike: So, the four tires plus the protection plan will be close to $300 with tax.

Pam: A few dollars less.

Jackie: Let's have them check and see if they can find out what's causing the rattle under the left rear side of the car.

Pam: Well, let's have the service people put it up on the rack and check it out.

Date: Thursday, 7 April 1989, 5:08 P.M.
Scene: Auto Service Floor, Quality Auto Service Centers

Characters: Mike and Jackie Buckholzer, customers; Pam Adams, Retail Sales Associate; John Zee, Mechanic

Date: Friday, 8 April 1989; 9:23 A.M.
Scene: Buckholzer Residence, Kitchen Phone
Characters: Jackie Buckholzer, customer; Ben Reeves, Service Manager

ACTION

Pam: John, let's put this Stanza up on the rack and check it out. The Buckholzer's are concerned with some noise coming from the left rear side.

John: [After inspecting the undercarriage of the car.] Look at this exhaust system. The muffler and tail pipe are all hanging loose. The exhaust system clamps have all rusted through. Two of them have already broken and another is about to. Both the muffler and the tail pipe are almost rusted through.

Mike: What's all that going to cost me?

John: Around $100, but we'll have to check the price with Tri-County Nissan. Look at this. [John demonstrates that the left front tire has some play in it.]

Jackie: What does that mean?

John: It means that you are going to have to replace it; sooner or later you will have trouble with it. Also, it will cause uneven wear on the new tire.

Mike: What about the other side? Does it need to be replaced also?

John: [After inspecting it.] No. It's fine, see, there's no play in this wheel.

Mike: How much does a new strut cost?

John: On these smaller cars, you have to replace the whole strut assembly. I'll have to check the price tomorrow morning when Tri-County Nissan opens up, but with parts and labor, it shouldn't be more than $100.

Jackie: Well, Mike, there goes your new golf bag.

Mike: And there goes your new dress, Jackie.

Pam: Mr. Buckholzer, where can we contact you tomorrow morning? As soon as we check on the prices for the exhaust system and strut assembly, we will call you with a total estimate.

Mike: I have an early morning appointment but I should be back in my office from 9 A.M. to 11 A.M. My telephone number is 555-4646.

Pam: OK, we'll get hold of you then. The service manager will call you before we proceed.

Jackie: When will the car be ready?

Pam: Tomorrow afternoon.

Mike: Pam, we'll pick it up around 4 P.M. Well, Jackie, we planned on $250, and it's going to cost twice what we planned on.

ACTION

Jackie: Buckholzer Residence.

Ben: Hello, Mrs. Buckholzer, this is Ben Reeves, Service Manager for Quality Auto Service Centers. I haven't been able to reach your husband at work. I have the estimate of the repairs that were discussed.

Jackie: Well, how much will it cost?

Ben: It'll be $490 for the exhaust system, struts, valve stems, grease seals, and labor.

Jackie: That includes everything—$490 is the total bill?

Ben: That's it.

Jackie: OK, go ahead. When can we pick it up?

Ben: Late afternoon.

Date: Friday, 8 April 1989; 4:47 P.M.
Scene: Auto Service Floor, Quality Auto Service Centers
Characters: Mike and Jackie Buckholzer, customers; Adam, Mechanic

ACTION

Jackie: Look, there's our car. It's still up on the rack with the wheels off.

Mike: When will the Stanza be done?

Adam: In about an hour, maybe a little longer.

Jackie: We can't wait that long. We're expected for dinner.

Mike: I suppose we'll have to make another trip up here tomorrow. Can we pick it up tomorrow?

Adam: Yeah, that will give me plenty of time to get it done.

Date: Saturday, 9 April 1989; 12:43 P.M.
Scene: Retail Sales Floor, Quality Auto Service Centers
Characters: Mike and Jackie Buckholzer, customers; Tim Harmon, Retail Sales Associate; Ben Reeves, Service Manager

ACTION

Mike: I'm here to pick up my car.

Tim: Your last name, please.

Mike: Buckholzer, Mike.

Tim: Will it be charge or cash? [Tim keys up the terminal and receives a printed invoice.] The total comes to $800.08.

Mike:	There must be some mistake. The estimate was $490.
Tim:	*Let me check. [Tim again keys up the terminal and obtains the same results.]* No, $800.08 is the total. See here.

4	R13 Z2 tires @ 49.30	197.20
1	Tire protection plan	79.95
4	New Valve Stems @ 2.00	8.00
1	LF Bearing FWD	22.60
2	Gas Strut Assemblies @ 91.00	182.00
1	Repack four wheel bearings	26.00
2	Front grease seals @ 8.00	16.00
1	Muffler	200.26
	Sales Tax	36.97
	TOTAL	800.08

Jackie:	I did not authorize this. The total cost for everything was $490, and that is all I authorized, and that is all we are paying.
Tim:	Let me get the service manager.
Ben:	Is there some problem?
Mike:	Yes, there is. We had repairs completed on our car that were not authorized.
Ben:	[Examining the terminal printout and the work order.] Yes, Mrs. Buckholzer, you authorized this work. You see, Mr. Buckholzer, I tried to call you at your office but couldn't reach you, so I called your wife and informed her of the charges and she authorized them.
Jackie:	I authorized $490, not $800. Thursday night your mechanic told us that it would be about $500 for everything.
Ben:	It is, $490 for parts and labor.
Mike:	No. The $490 includes the tires plus the protection plan plus the repairs.
Ben:	No, the $490 is only for the repairs. The tires are totally separate.
Jackie:	That's not what you said. I asked you what the total bill was, and you said $490, including everything.
Ben:	We operate the service business separate from tire sales. What you agreed to pay for the tires is a separate issue. I only deal with repair and installation services.
Mike:	How is a customer to know that you treat these two businesses separately? Let me talk to the manager.
Ben:	I am the manager on the weekend. The store manager is not in today.
Mike:	Call him at home.
Ben:	I can't do that.

Mike:	I would like to talk to someone else, other than yourself. I don't believe you can be objective about this since you were involved.
Ben:	You'll have to wait until Monday.
Mike:	All right. But we need the car. My daughters are waiting for my wife.
Ben:	I can't let you have the car unless you pay the full amount.
Jackie:	It's our car, and your mistake. I have people waiting for me up at the mall.
Ben:	I can't help that.
Mike:	I will pay the $490 we agreed to and come in on Monday to talk to the manager.
Ben:	No, you will have to pay the full amount.
Mike:	Check your records. Less than six months ago I bought four new tires and a protection plan from you on my other car. I live in a new home, less than two miles from here. I'm not about to skip town over $300.
Ben:	That's beside the point. I will have to have the $800 or I can't release the car.
Jackie:	I need the car, and I'm taking it.
Ben:	If you do, I will call the police and have you arrested.
Mike:	It's our car. Is this the level of service you provide? Call the police right now. We'll let them decide.
Ben:	No, I am not going to call the police unless you take the car.
Mike:	Then call the manager or his boss or someone in charge.
Tim:	Ben, I think you'd better call someone.
Ben:	Keep out of this. I'll take care of it.
Mike:	OK, I find your product and service unacceptable. Your sign says my satisfaction is guaranteed. I am not satisfied. So restore my car to its original form, and I will be on my way.
Ben:	I can't do that.
Mike:	What the hell can you do? You can't call a manager or anyone else. You can't restore my car. You can't quote prices or provide the services you agreed to.
Jackie:	We have to pick the kids up.
Mike:	I will be back on Monday to talk to the manager. When I do, I do not intend to accept anything except my car in its original form. I do not want your tires, struts, exhaust system, or anything else.

Date:	Monday, 11 April 1989; 9:21 A.M.
Scene:	Store Manager's Office, Quality Auto Service Centers
Characters:	Mike Buckholzer, angry customer; George Wills, Store Manager

Mike: . . . and that is basically the problem I had with your product, service, and service manager. I want my car restored. . . .

George: Mr. Buckholzer. . .

ASSIGNMENT

Assume the role of George Wills, Store Manager:

☐ How would you resolve the problem with Mr. Buckholzer? Develop various scenarios for resolving the issue, and identify the pros and cons for the store and for the customer. What would be your best offer to Mr. Buckholzer?

☐ Who is right? Who is wrong? Why?

☐ Evaluate Ben Reeves's performance in handling this complaint situation.

☐ What suggestions would you make for improving the complaint handling process?

☐ Are there other suggestions you could make for improving the store's operations?

CASE 27

Apex Stores: A Buy-American Campaign

Dan Gilmore, the University of Akron

Alexander Ferris, president and chief executive officer of Apex Stores, Inc., was preparing for the 10:00 meeting he had called of top executives in each of the corporation's four divisions. Each division represented one of the four retail store chains owned by Apex.

1. Fashion Works is a chain of twenty-six stores throughout Ohio, Michigan, Indiana, and Illinois that carry low- to medium-priced apparel for men and women.
2. Style Corner is an eighteen-store division featuring higher-priced women's fashions in the same Midwest market served by Fashion Works.
3. Minerva's is an upscale, fashionable chain of twenty-one women's clothing stores located along the West Coast.
4. Cray's is a midpriced department store chain consisting of sixteen units primarily operating in the Midwest, although there were plans for expansion into Pennsylvania, New York, and Maryland. Cray's carries a full line of men's and women's clothing, cosmetics, home electronics, furniture, appliances, housewares, and toys.

When the executives were all assembled in his office at Apex's Chicago headquarters, Ferris outlined his new plan that he was considering for all four of the company's divisions. He wanted to institute a policy of buying the goods sold in Apex's stores from American manufacturers whenever possible, whereas in the past, purchases had always been made without regard to country of origin.

"In recent years, I've noticed a rising percentage of our overall purchases have been from foreign suppliers," Ferris said. "I think this is a trend that needs to be stopped. Concern about the U.S. trade deficit with foreign countries is growing, and I believe we have some responsibility to do our part to reduce imports."

But Ferris admitted that his idea was not driven solely by patriotic fervor. He thought that American consumers were increasingly sensitive to a product's country of origin and that they would react quite favorably to Apex's campaign to sell as many American-made goods as possible. Ferris was also confident that this move by Apex would take advantage of other national efforts to promote products made in America.

One promotion effort, sponsored primarily by the U.S. textile industry, was launched in the mid-1980s under the auspices of the Crafted with Pride in the USA Council. The council developed an extensive ad campaign using celebrity spokespersons—working for free—proclaiming "It matters to me" and pointing to made-in-America labels on their clothing. Another independent group leads the Buy American Campaign, a nonprofit, grass-roots organization that uses its annual advertising budget of several million dollars to tout American-made goods in general. In addition, several other store chains and manufacturers had recently adopted "buy-American" promotions or policies.

"I think the time is right for us to have a Buy American policy of our own," Ferris told the executives. "I believe we should make a public promise to buy American-manufactured goods whenever we can, and set some target, such as 75 percent of total purchases, to be reached in some chosen time period, such as one year. I'm open to negotiation on the specific details, but I'm convinced that we must take some step in this direction. Please do some research on how this will affect your divisions, and report back to me with your analysis and recommendations in two weeks."

The division presidents didn't speak as they left the office and headed down the hallway to the elevator. Once inside, however, they immediately began to discuss their boss's idea. "I was certainly not expecting that," said Erin Dietrick, head of Fashion Works. "I was just reading the other day that the National Retail Merchants Association has been lobbying Congress to keep international trade as open as possible, for the benefit of consumers."

"Yes, that's true, but several large chains, like K mart, WalMart, and The Limited, have recently adopted buy-American campaigns of one sort or another," noted Jayne Hardin, the Style Corner's president. Responded Richard Bellows of Cray's Department Stores, "I don't care what anyone else is doing. This will certainly make my buyers' jobs a heck of a lot tougher, whatever the specifics turn out to be."

All of them agreed that whatever decision was made, it needed to be based on sound business principles, not just emotion. The question they faced was whether a buy-American campaign was really a good idea for Apex Stores, Inc.

ASSIGNMENT

☐ As mentioned in the case, several large retailers have developed buy-American purchasing policies in the past several years. What do you see as the advantages and disadvantages of these strategies?

☐ From a retail buyer's point of view, how would you feel about your company decision to announce a percentage of purchases that will be made from American suppliers within a year? How might it affect your job? Your career?

☐ If a buy-American policy is chosen for Apex Stores, should it be the same for all four divisions? What arguments can you offer in favor of employing a different strategy for each chain?

CASE 28

Showcase Gallery: Exploring Supplier Relationships

Jeffrey Dilts, the University of Akron

BACKGROUND

Frank Smith just finalized a deal for a store facility that would become the future "Showcase Gallery." Smith had always wanted to open his own furniture store in the community and had the opportunity to do so when the previous owner of a home furnishings store retired. The investment involved a 14,000-square-foot facility in a growing, high-income suburban area. He financed the venture through previous savings and investments by his family.

Smith had a working knowledge of the furniture trade, having been employed for eleven years as a manufacturer's representative in the industry. He brought to the venture a knowledge of case goods and upholstery and experience in interior design—a level of knowledge not often found among retail personnel.

The opportunity to work for himself, to be his own boss, had always been Smith's dream. Consequently, he placed great importance on operational autonomy. Having experienced the other half of the dealer–supplier relationship, however, Smith recognized that his autonomy might have to be tempered somewhat to achieve benefits possible only through mutual cooperation.

CURRENT SITUATION

With the purchase of the retail facility, Smith first had to decide which type of dealer–supplier arrangement would be most appropriate for his needs and the firm's

future success. He had three alternatives: conventional arrangements, programmed merchandising, and business-format franchising. As he examined each option, Smith realized that his decision not only would have significance in developing trade relations but also could have a major impact on his performance as a dealer. Smith mentally reviewed the implications of each dealer–supplier arrangement.

Conventional Arrangement

With a conventional arrangement, Smith would deal with many suppliers. The highly fragmented furniture industry consists of many dealers and manufacturers, and dependence of any one firm on another is accordingly low. Consequently, a conventional arrangement tended to involve a relatively less enduring, loosely aligned relationship. Smith had observed that dealers were often suspicious of suppliers and did not cooperate fully for fear of becoming locked into a relationship.

Despite the potential problems, some dealers felt this arrangement gave them greater operational flexibility in serving their customers. They were not confined to particular styles or price points offered by a particular manufacturer; instead, they were able to adapt quickly to the changing needs of the community by working with a large number of suppliers to provide an appropriate product assortment that would have broad appeal to various customer groups.

Programmed Merchandising

Programmed merchandising arrangements are a second alternative. This type of relationship would require Smith to establish several formal or implied licensing agreements with a select number of primary suppliers. These supplier-developed arrangements are tailor-made programs designed to generate greater dealer commitment for one or more of the supplier's product lines. To encourage strong dealer commitment, the supplier offers selected retailers customized programs such as in-store merchandising assistance, advertising allowances, discount structures, and sales promotional support.

In return for the right to handle the supplier's merchandise line and to benefit from the privileges of the supplier's programs, Smith would be expected to limit his involvement with competitive products and to commit significant resources to support each of the supplier's merchandise lines. Support requirements include maintaining a minimum level of inventory investment in each line of merchandise and committing a minimum amount of floor space to permanent display of the supplier's products. Smith also would be expected to cooperate in supplier-initiated programs such as factory-authorized sales and other special sales promotions.

Business-Format Franchise

Colony House, a business-format franchise, was the third alternative that Frank investigated. This option involved a tightly knit dealer–supplier arrangement in which Colony House (the franchisor) would provide Frank (the franchisee) with a patterned way of doing business. Colony House would provide a total store concept. This concept included a plan for store layout and design, a complete line of merchandise, a comprehensive merchandising program, and a detailed operations manual. Colony House's total store concept was highly coordinated to achieve a sharply focused image that appeals to a targeted group of consumers. Product assortments included early and traditional American furniture and home accessory items. In contrast to the industry's frequent style changes, Colony's continuity of established merchandise lines enabled customers to purchase coordinated furniture pieces over an extended period.

The initial investment for a standard 12,000-square-foot operation would be approximately $250,000. Because Frank already had an existing facility, Colony House would require that he alter the exterior and interior of the building to make it consistent with the Colony House image. In return, Colony would provide architectural plans, training, and merchandising backup. Although no franchise fee was required, an annual fee (5 percent of sales) would be charged for promotional support.

Colony House believed that strong commitment was necessary for the formulated concept to succeed. Consequently, it screened retail applicants closely to determine their compatibility with Colony House. It reviewed each applicant's background, personality, and business philosophy. Franchisees, although independent businesses, were expected to adhere very closely to Colony's recommendations regarding store operations and merchandising.

ASSIGNMENT

- [ ] Outline the advantages and disadvantages of each supplier–dealer arrangement.
- [ ] Recommend the most suitable supplier–dealer arrangement for Frank Smith and explain the rationale for your recommendation.
- [ ] Advise Smith as to how your recommendation will influence his trade relations and store performance.

CASE 29

Itty-Bitty Baby Boutique: Selecting an Inventory-Valuation System

J. B. Wilkinson, the University of Akron

BACKGROUND

Recent changes in the federal tax law authorized by the Economic Recovery Act of 1981 prompted many trade journals to publish articles about the new regulations that simplify the last in, first out (LIFO) method of inventory valuation used by retailers. Consequently, Millie Marie Baker, owner of Itty-Bitty Baby Boutique, was rethinking her use of the "traditional" retail method of inventory valuation that estimates ending inventory at lower of cost or market (LCM).

CURRENT SITUATION

Early in June of 1982, Baker consulted Bill Truly, senior auditor for B. S. Cheatum & Co., for an opinion. His response is shown in Exhibits 29–1 to 29–4.

ASSIGNMENT

- [ ] Advise Baker based on Truly's comments. Should she switch to dollar-value LIFO? Why or why not?

EXHIBIT 29–1
Auditor's analysis

B. S. Cheatum & Co.
MEMORANDUM

DATE: 5 July 1982
TO: Ms. Millie Baker, Owner
             Itty-Bitty Baby Boutique
FROM: Bill Truly, Senior Auditor
             B. S. Cheatum & Co.
RE: Possible LIFO Election

Your request for a formal comparison of current inventory valuation procedures to an appropriate dollar-value LIFO method for Itty-Bitty Baby Boutique has received careful consideration. Because Itty-Bitty is a specialty store that carries a full line of infant apparel and some baby furniture and equipment, we believe that use of the Department Store Inventory Price Index for "Infants' Wear" will be acceptable to the IRS. The following comparison is premised on this assumption.

To demonstrate the value of dollar-value LIFO to your business, we reconstructed your 1981 income statement as it would have been if dollar-value LIFO had been elected for that year. Schedule 1 [Exhibit 29–2] is a simplified version of your 1981 income statement. Schedule 2 [Exhibit 29–3] explains determination of 1981 ending inventory under the retail method, lower of cost or market inventory valuation model. Schedule 3 [Exhibit 29–4] illustrates the calculations necessary to estimate ending inventory under dollar-value LIFO using 1981 data. Notice that the cost ratio used to reduce the inventory increment to cost is based on purchases and is the complement of the net markon percentage: cumulative markon less markdowns expressed as a percentage of retail. The relevant BLS Department Store Inventory Price Indexes for Infants' Wear are shown below.

	Infants' Wear	
	Price Index (Jan. 1941 = 100)	Percentage of Change from Jan. 19XX to Jan. 19XX + 1
Jan. 1980	378.8	
Jan. 1981	420.7	11.1
Jan. 1982	444.7	5.7

In this illustration, your base year would begin 1 January 1981. Consequently, the January 1981 price index represents 100.0, and the adjusted price index for any year ended 31 December 19XX is found by dividing the following January index by the January 1981 index. The adjusted price index for the year ended 31 December 1981 is 105.7 (444.7/420.7) and is used to determine the 1981 ending inventory in base year retail dollars.

Notice that the retail value of ending inventory that was found for the LCM model is reduced to base-year cost (at retail) by dividing with the adjusted LIFO price index (105.7/100). An incremental inventory layer occurs if ending inventory at base-year cost exceeds the previous year's ending inventory at base-year cost. A decrement occurs if ending inventory at base-year cost is less than the previous year's ending inventory at base-year cost. When a decrement occurs, previous inventory layers must be liquidated in reverse order. Increments or decrements are first determined with base-year retail dollars and then converted to relevant current-year retail dollars by the appropriate LIFO price index and then adjusted to cost using the cost ratio. Ending inventory is the sum of base-year inventory at base-year cost and the increments, if any, at current relevant-year costs.

For the year ended 31 December 1981, ending inventory under the "traditional" retail method, LCM, was $370,000. Ending inventory at LIFO cost would have been $351,328. It follows that cost of sales is $1,080,000 under the LCM model and $1,098,672 under dollar-value LIFO. However, LIFO is a cost method. If you had elected LIFO for the year ended 31 December 1981, the beginning inventory would have had to be restated to cost. The $350,000 beginning inventory is stated at lower of cost or market. We estimate that a positive adjustment of $68,800 would have been required. This adjustment would reduce the LIFO cost of sales to $1,029,872. Thus, gross margin would have been $770,128 under LIFO. At a marginal tax rate of 50 percent, your tax bill would have been $25,064 more under dollar-value LIFO.

It is difficult to project what your 1982 dollar-value LIFO experience might be. We do estimate that you would have to restate 1982 beginning inventory to cost. That adjustment is likely to be around $74,000. Also, we are concerned about your expected markdowns as a percentage of sales. The LCM model allows you to reduce ending inventory to lower of cost or market. Dollar-value LIFO only removes the effects of inflation. Which is best for you? Do you expect high markdowns as a percentage of sales in the future? Another consideration is your ability to correctly predict sales and plan for inventory levels sufficient to prevent decrements. Inventory decrements under LIFO cause older costs (lower costs in periods of inflation) to enter the calculation of cost of sales. As a result, most businesses control inventory levels carefully to prevent liquidation of previous inventory layers.

We advise you to consider this decision carefully. Expected price level changes, inventory levels, and markdowns are important factors in estimating the financial advantage of electing dollar-value LIFO.

Please let us know your decision as soon as possible.

Schedule 1: 1981 Income Data for Itty-bitty Baby Boutique

Net sales	$1,800,000
less cost of sales (1)	1,080,000
Gross profit	720,000
less operating expense	666,000
Operating profit	$ 54,000

Notes:
(1) Cost of sales is computed as follows: Beginning inventory (at cost) + Purchases (at cost) − Ending inventory (at cost). Ending inventory for Itty-bitty was valued at lower of cost or market using the retail method. These computations are shown in Schedule 2.

EXHIBIT 29–2
Schedule 1: 1981 Income Data

EXHIBIT 29-3
Schedule 2: 1981 end-
ing inventory, LCM
model

Schedule 2: Determination of 1981 Ending Inventory Using Retail Method, LCM Model

	At Cost	At Retail	Cost Ratio
Inventory, Jan. 1, 1981	$ 350,000	$ 698,000	
Purchases	1,100,000	2,200,000	
Net additional markups		2,000	
Total (incl. beginning inv.)	$1,450,000	$ 2,900,000	.50
Deduct:			
Sales		(1,800,000)	
Net markdowns		(360,000)	
Ending inventory at LCM	$ 370,000 (1)	$ 740,000	

Notes:
(1) Ending inventory at LCM was found by reducing ending inventory at retail to cost through application of the cost ratio. The cost ratio for the LCM model is computed by dividing total merchandise available for sale at cost by total merchandise available for sale at retail before markdowns.

EXHIBIT 29-4 Schedule 3: 1981 ending inventory, LIFO method

Schedule 3: Determination of 1981 Ending Inventory Using the Dollar-Value LIFO Method

Steps:

1. Price index for the year ended December 31, 1981 (Jan. 1, 1981 = 100) is 105.7.

2. Computation of cost ratio and ending inventory at retail.

	At Cost	At Retail	Cost Ratio
Inventory, Jan. 1, 1981	$ 350,000	$ 698,000	
Purchases	1,100,000	2,200,000	
Net additional markups		2,000	
Net markdowns		(360,000)	
Total (excl. beginning inv.)	1,100,000	1,842,000	.60
Total (incl. beginning inv.)	1,450,000	2,540,000	
Deduct:			
Sales		(1,800,000)	
Ending inventory at retail		$ 740,000	
Ending inventory at cost	$ 444,000		

3. Computation of ending inventory at LIFO cost.

	At Cost	At Retail
Ending inventory at retail deflated to base year retail $		$ 700,095 (1)
Base layer: At base yr. cost / At base yr. retail	$ 350,000	(698,000)
Increment (or decrement) at base-year retail		2,095
Increment (or decrement) at current-year retail		2,214 (2)

EXHIBIT 29–4 *continued*

Increment (or decrement) at current-year cost	1,328(3)
Total ending inventory at LIFO cost	$ 351,328

Notes:
(1) $740,000/1.057
(2) $2,095 × 1.057
(3) $2,214 × .60

CASE 30

Dude's Duds: Pricing a New Product Line

Jon Hawes, the University of Akron

BACKGROUND

Dude's Duds was a large, well-known clothing store chain with more than 400 retail outlets located throughout the United States and Canada. Appealing to teenagers and young adults, Dude's success was based largely on the firm's ability to market faddish and fashionable merchandise at reasonable, competitive prices. Although Dude's Duds stocked a limited selection of national manufacturers' brands (e.g., Levi's and Haggar) to enhance its store image and to generate consumer traffic, the vast majority of each outlet's merchandise consists of the firm's own private retailer brands. To ensure a reliable source of supply for their private labels, Dude's Duds purchased the Fashion-Plus Clothing Company (FPCC) in 1978. At the time of the takeover, FPCC was a well-established national manufacturer of high-quality, fashionable apparel. FPCC's product mix consisted of a wide line of both men's and women's wearing apparel.

CURRENT SITUATION

The recent increase in the popularity and acceptance of Western wearing apparel by many diverse consumer groups throughout all market areas of the country prompted Ralph West, general merchandise manager for Dude's Duds, to investigate the possibility of adding a new line of men's Western-style shirts. Preliminary results of that investigation led West to conclude that such a line would appeal to the consumer group that the firm identified as "the swingers"—a consumer market segment that wants faddish and stylish clothing of good quality but has a discretionary income requiring moderate prices. To West, adding a new line of men's Western shirts would make good merchandising sense, but the production staff at Fashion-Plus ultimately will decide whether the new line is feasible given the price, cost, and profit constraints under which it must produce the product.

Although Fashion-Plus was a wholly owned subsidiary of Dude's Duds, Inc., FPCC's management was responsible for making all production decisions. To determine the feasibility of new product lines, Bill Morris, manager for new product development, needed to collect the necessary information to make a cost and break-even analysis, to project expected profits, and to recommend a suggested retail price as well as a manufacturer's price (the price that Fashion-Plus should charge Dude's Duds). Having spent two weeks collecting data, Morris believed he now had the necessary information to make the required evaluations of the new Western shirt project. Before proceeding with his analysis, he reviewed the information he had collected (Exhibit 30–1).

ASSIGNMENT

☐ Assume that Bill Morris was unexpectedly called out of town, and he has asked you to prepare the analysis and written report on the feasibility of the project. Then make a recommendation for the pricing strategy he should use. At a minimum, your analysis should include a cost analysis (variable cost per shirt, fixed cost allocation for the line, and total cost per shirt); a break-even analysis in units and dollars; a determination of the manufacturer's price and suggested retail price; and a statement of expected profit the company can derive from the new line.

EXHIBIT 30–1

Data gathered by manager for new product development

1. Several competitors have introduced similar lines of men's Western shirts. Market research indicates that these lines are selling at a brisk pace at competitive retail stores for the following prices:

Retail Selling Price	No. of Times Observed
$14.00	2
$15.00	7
$16.00	5
$17.00	3

2. Dude's Duds will apply a 40 percent initial markup on the retail selling price of shirts.

3. Production costs for the new shirts were estimated as follows:

Cloth	$2.20 per shirt
Buttons	$ .05 per shirt
Thread	$ .05 per shirt
Direct labor	20 minutes per shirt
Shipping weight	2 pounds per packaged shirt

4. Basic marketing costs for introducing the new line of shirts are estimated to be $300,000 the first year if a penetration pricing policy is used or $340,000 if a skimming pricing policy is employed.

5. A large company, FPCC has fifteen production facilities strategically located throughout the United States. Last year, the average round-trip distance from FPCC production facilities to Dude's Duds outlets was 225 miles. Current plans are to produce the new line of shirts at each of FPCC's production facilities.

6. An examination of FPCC's annual report reveals the following information:

Managerial salaries	$ 1,500,000
Rent and utilities expense	$ 1,200,000
Transportation costs (1,250,000 miles)	$ 750,000
Depreciation on plant and equipment	$ 1,300,000
Other overhead	$ 2,000,000
Direct labor costs (2,000,000 hours)	$ 8,000,000
Total company sales	$45,000,000
Average order size	1,000 pounds

7. The Karen Behrens Market Research Corporation was hired to develop a sales forecast for the new line of Western shirts. Their research findings estimate that if a skimming pricing policy were used, Dude's Duds could expect to sell approximately 110,000 to 130,000 shirts. Under a penetration-type policy, the Behrens organization estimates a unit sales volume of approximately 130,000 to 150,000 shirts.

Free Bacon or Only $1.49: Testing Price Offerings

Dale M. Lewison and Douglas Hausknecht, the University of Akron

The fast-food industry usually confronts a sales slump during the first quarter of each year. During this period, when the frequency of customer visits declines, competitors in the hamburger segment of the industry attempt to boost total sales, to improve customer counts, and to increase average sales by offering reduced prices on their smaller-size, lower-price hamburgers.

In planning for this predictable downturn in sales, Wendy's International, the fourth largest hamburger chain, decided one year to try a different competitive product strategy by offering a "quality sale," that is, a create-a-meal deal that involved a more upscaled product item, the bacon cheeseburger. The intended target market was adult males, eighteen to twenty-five years of age, and known to be heavy fast-food users. The problem was how to express and portray the sales terms to the consumer. Should the meal deal be expressed as a value-enhancement offer or a price-reduction offer? Wendy's management wanted to test the two price expressions in the following manner. The value enhancement offer was to be expressed as follows:

"FREE BACON"—Order a Bacon Cheeseburger
and Get the Bacon Free

The rationale behind this offer was that *free* would enhance readership of Wendy's ads and would be perceived more favorably because the total value of the offer would appear to be worth more than the actual savings as a result of the consumer belief of getting something for nothing.

The price-reduction offer was to be expressed as:

ONLY $1.49—Get Our Bacon Cheeseburger
Special for Only $1.49

The belief that the customers would find a concrete dollar amount easier to relate to than a free offer was the basic premise for this kind of offer.

ASSIGNMENT

Assume the role of an account manager for Wendy's sales promotion agency:

☐ Develop a hypothesis as to which of the two price offers will be most effective in achieving a favorable customer response. Support your hypothesis with a complete rationale for your beliefs.

☐ Develop and conduct a market test of the two sales promotion offers suggested by Wendy's management to determine which is the more effective. Report your findings and analysis.

☐ Identify two variations for each of the price expressions—value enhancement and price reductions. Conduct a market test on your suggestions and report your results.

Campbell Clothiers: Assessing an Advertising Opportunity

Ken Mast and Dale M. Lewison, the University of Akron

BACKGROUND

Campbell Clothiers was a local chain of specialty stores that offered an extensive selection of men's and women's sporting and casual apparel and accessories. By appealing to the upscale tastes of middle- and upper-class consumers for fashionable casual and sporting apparel, Gabe and Sandy Campbell had successfully expanded their operation to include nine stores in northeastern Ohio. The success of Campbell Clothiers could be attributed to a number of merchandising factors. Campbell's was known for its unique offering of high-quality product lines, plush yet exciting store atmo-

spherics, friendly and competent salespeople, and image-building promotions.

Campbell's tended to limit its product selection to middle- and upper-pricing lines and points. The store's January and July clearance sales, however, were almost legendary in the local area as a value-packed sales promotion. Although each of these factors had been an important ingredient in Campbell's successful merchandising blend, the store's management team believed the most important overall success ingredient was the organization's commitment to maintaining and cultivating its image of exclusivity. At Campbell Clothiers, exclusive meant being unique, selective, different, tasteful, and distinctive in all its merchandising activities.

CURRENT SITUATION

The morning had started peacefully for Jacqueline Theiss, sales promotion manager for Campbell Clothiers. As usual, it did not stay that way. Campbell's new sportswear buyer, Kris Kovach, burst into Theiss's office:

Kris: Jacqueline, I just heard that Michizuki cancelled its sponsorship of the Super Bowl of Golf. This is a great opportunity to promote our new line of men's and women's sportswear by Outdoor World! A 20-percent-off sale would really draw in customer traffic.

Jacqueline: What makes you think that?

Kris: Surely, WWTV is going to have to unload a lot of local air time in a hurry. If we act fast I know we can get some prime-time slots at bargain rates. A sale this early in the season would really attract some attention.

Jacqueline: Where do you propose we get the money for this unexpected blessing? Not to mention that two weeks is hardly enough time to plan, to schedule, to shoot, and to edit a commercial.

Kris: You must have some money stuck away somewhere. And I've already checked with Outdoor World, and they have several canned commercials available for a small fee. All we would have to do is add our sales promotional message and store identification to the end of the film.

Jacqueline: Assuming we can find the money, which is a big assumption, and these canned commercials are available and acceptable, is it worthwhile to spend this kind of money on this particular product line?

Kris: You bet it is! Outdoor World is a well-known national brand, it offers something for both men and women, and we have sufficient stock in all our stores to support this kind of sales promotion.

Jacqueline: Well, Kris, I have a meeting in five minutes. Let me think about it, and I'll get back to you with a decision by tomorrow afternoon.

Kris: OK, but we have to act fast or we'll lose this opportunity. I'd really appreciate your support on this. It can be a successful campaign.

After her ten o'clock meeting and lunch, Theiss contacted her account representative at WWTV and learned that Michizuki had in fact cancelled its sponsorship of the Super Bowl of Golf. Theiss was offered a 30-percent discount off the rate book price for local spots during the tournament. The minimum number of thirty-second spots was six: four spots on Saturday and two spots on Sunday. In a quick mental calculation, Theiss determined the total minimum cost would be approximately $30,000 for air time. She indicated her interest in the spots and informed the account representative that she would make a decision within twenty-four hours.

The considerable time constraints surrounding the decision and numerous other pressing business matters led Theiss to seek help from Tyler Scott, the advertising manager for Campbell Clothiers. In the lengthy discussion that ensued, Theiss identified several key issues.

1. The $30,000 minimum price tag for air time would consume about 40 percent of Campbell's reserve advertising budget set aside each year for unexpected situations. It would leave a $45,000 reserve for the remainder of the year. This assumes that the expected $5,000 needed for producing the commercial and paying the fees asked by Outdoor World could be found elsewhere.

2. Kris Kovach had already spent most of her entire promotional budget, and an examination of her promotional expenditures revealed inadequate support of the Outdoor World line of sportswear. Through luncheon and grapevine conversations, Theiss discovered that the line was not selling as well as had been expected and that Kovach was feeling a great deal of heat from the general merchandise manager.

3. Although the Super Bowl of Golf is the single most important local sporting event during the year, its appeal is still limited to a rather select group of customers.

4. WWTV is a satellite station affiliate of the national network that has broadcasting rights to the Super Bowl of Golf. WWTV is a UHF station whose broadcast signal provides only partial coverage of the company's nine store trading areas. Specifically, WWTV provides 100 percent coverage of five store trading areas, 50 percent coverage of two store trading areas, and little or no coverage for two trading areas.

With the key issues of concern identified, Scott agreed to drop everything and study the entire situation. He thought that by noon the next day he could recommend possible alternative courses of action.

ASSIGNMENT

☐ Assume Tyler Scott's role. Write a report outlining the various alternative courses of action. Recommend which alternative the company should pursue, and provide a complete justification for your recommendation.

The Case of Mary Adams

Scott Cevasco and Jon Hawes, the University of Akron

Mary Adams had just celebrated her youngest child's eighth birthday. She was bored with "just being a housewife" and wanted to work part-time. Her husband, an electrician, thought it would be nice to have the extra money, especially during the slack periods of the year for electricians.

Trecaso's Jewelry was a small but elegant jewelry store. Traditionally, the store had been operated by family members. Robert Trecaso and his son Tony had continued to operate the business since Robert's father died over ten years ago. The Trecasos now realized that the jewelry store was growing rapidly and that other employees were needed. They had known Adams for many years from church activities and asked her if she would like to work for them. Adams accepted the job eagerly and began the next week.

Adams loved jewelry, and this enthusiasm showed when she interacted with customers. As she learned more and more about the business, her sales levels continued to increase. The Trecasos were delighted with Adams's progress. The business ran smoothly—sales increased each quarter.

After about a year and a half, Adams's attitude began to change. She thought she should receive fringe benefits other than health insurance and a two-week vacation. She also wanted an increase in her salary beyond minimum wage. The Trecasos said they would like to start a retirement plan, among other possible fringe benefits, but sales for the last half of the year had not met expectations, and they consequently stated that they could not afford to meet Adams's demands.

Adams yelled back, "That's not fair, you promised me!" None of the Trecasos remembered promising anything. They had only said that they wanted to offer these benefits if they could afford to do so.

After this incident, Adams's sales began to decline. She lost interest in customers and moped around the store. She also made mistakes on almost everything she was asked to do. She did not record bank deposits correctly. She sent checks for the wrong amounts to the wrong wholesalers. She also set up the display counters in disarray. The Trecasos were afraid to let her do anything because she did everything incorrectly. They could not understand this because they were the same tasks she had previously done so effectively.

The Trecasos knew they had to do something. They tried to talk to her about these mistakes, but Adams only said, "I'll be more careful the next time." They were afraid to threaten her with termination because she was extremely sensitive to criticism. Also, they really needed the extra person with the Christmas season starting in a month. They also knew it was difficult to hire someone they could trust. The Trecasos scheduled a meeting to discuss how to deal with Mary Adams.

ASSIGNMENT

- [ ] How important is personal selling in the promotion mix for a store such as Trecaso's Jewelry?
- [ ] What basic personal selling tasks does Mary Adams perform?
- [ ] Is following up the sale likely to be an important step in the personal selling process as far as Mary Adams is concerned?
- [ ] What do you think of the Trecasos' efforts to train and develop, compensate, and motivate Mary Adams?
- [ ] What should the Trecasos do to help Mary Adams?

Photo-Imaging Centers: Promoting a New Product/Service Through Visual Merchandising

Dale M. Lewison, Jon Hawes, and James Muir, the University of Akron

Historically, the success of the specialty camera store business depended on several factors: (1) a highly technical product that was at the leading edge of technology; (2) a knowledgeable salesforce who could educate, train, and service the customer; (3) the limited or exclusive distribution of branded merchandise; and (4) pricing points that allowed sufficient margins to support a high level of customer service. In the 1970s, the retail camera market changed drastically; automatic cameras requiring low user-skill levels eliminated much of the need for

EXHIBIT 34–1

PIC's merchandising
system

Phase 1 Customer Attraction	Phase 2 Customer Information	Phase 3 Customer Decision
Use the advertising and publicity elements of the promotional mix to create an awareness of and an interest in the Home Decorating Studio and complementary components of PIC's product–service mix	Use the visual merchandising and store display elements of the promotional mix to promote consumer comprehension and understanding of the Home Decorating Studio and complementary components of PIC's product–service mix	Use of personal selling and sales promotion elements of the promotion mix to ensure consumer conviction and patronage of the Home Decorating Studio and complementary components of PIC's product–service mix

highly trained salespeople and specialized camera equipment service mixes. The 1970s also saw the mass distribution of all types of cameras and associated accessories, which in turn encouraged price reduction as a major competitive merchandising strategy. With declining sales volume and reduced profit margins, specialty camera stores were forced to change their marketing approach. There were essentially two strategic choices: (1) Become a discount specialty camera store emphasizing price, or (2) develop a unique specialty product–service mix to appeal to the more service-oriented customer.

Photo-Imaging Centers (PIC), a full-line specialty camera and photo supplier retailer, operated three retail mall outlets within the greater metro area. Faced with the destructively competitive dynamics of the local market, PIC's management team elected to pursue a strategic course of action that would incorporate a unique combination of products with a complete mix of photographic and imaging services. A particular tactic of the overall strategy was to develop the product–service concept of the "Home Decorating Studio."

PIC's Home Decorating Studio was a product–service

EXHIBIT 34–2

PIC's merchandising
objectives

Phase 1: Customer attraction

1. Develop a print (newspaper) and broadcast (radio) advertising campaign that will create general consumer awareness of and interest in PIC's Home Decorating Studio—a new product–service offering.
2. Develop a publicity campaign that will promote and increase public traffic for PIC's "Photographic Art Gallery"—an image-building cultural center.

Phase 2: Customer information

1. Plan an in-store visual exhibition of PIC's Home Decorating Studio that illustrates the various types of products and services that comprise this integrated merchandising system.
2. Plan in-store displays of complementary products that can be merchandised in conjunction with or as supplements to the products and services that comprise the Home Decorating Studio.

Phase 3: Customer decision

1. Devise a personal selling process that will assist store sales personnel in securing customer involvement with the Home Decorating Studio by developing techniques for customer prospecting, customer contact, merchandise presentation, handling objections, and sales closure.
2. Devise sales promotion incentives that will help induce potential customers to make a positive decision regarding their involvement with the Home Decorating Studio.

EXHIBIT 34–3
PIC's store layout

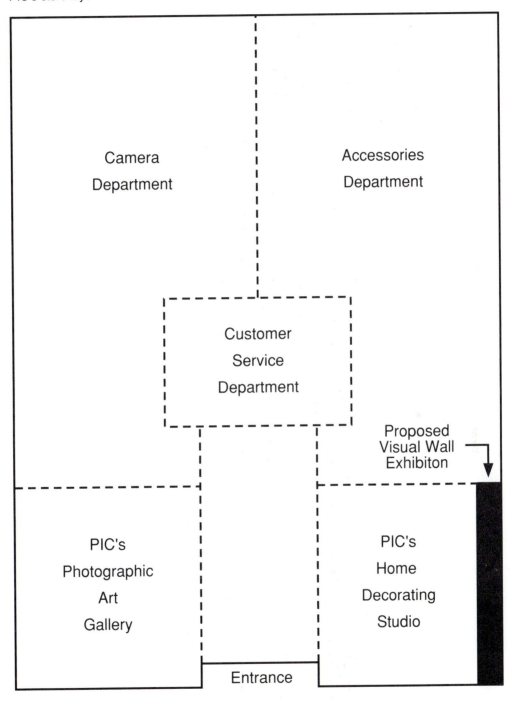

EXHIBIT 34–4

PIC's proposed visual merchandising wall display

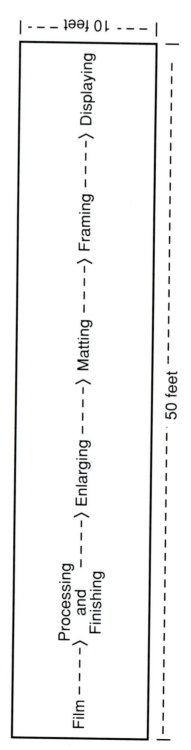

Film – – – –⟩ Processing and Finishing – – – –⟩ Enlarging – – – –⟩ Matting – – – –⟩ Framing – – – –⟩ Displaying

|– – – – 10 feet – – – –|

|– – – – – – – 50 feet – – – – – – – –|

concept based on the idea that individuals can decorate their home using their own personal photographic art. Both skilled and unskilled photographers can take photographs that could be turned into decorative art with the proper professional guidance and enhancement from PIC. This type of product–service line would be substituted for the now-popular poster and pop-art types of decor. The Home Decorating Studio offered a combination of products and services that represented a complete cycle of potential sales. The cycle began with the sale of various types of film, proceeding to film processing and finishing, to photographic enlargements that could be professionally matted and framed.

It was PIC's belief that once customers became involved with this system, they would become dependent on PIC for the entire process. Equally important was the fact that individuals would have personal involvement with and pride in a home decor that they had done themselves. If PIC's professional touch could enhance the customer's art decor, there would be considerable potential for return trade. An additional benefit of the particular concept was that it represented a component of the business with high margins, thereby making PIC less dependent on camera equipment sales at the narrower margins. This new offering would also attract new customers who could be enticed to make purchases of complementary product and service lines.

To enhance the image of PIC as a leader in quality photographic imagery, a new department was added to each store—PIC's Photographic Art Gallery. The department displayed and sold the photographic art of professional, well-known local and state photographers. The work of good amateur photographers also was displayed and sold. The monthly "showing of the featured artist" gained PIC favorable publicity and had been an excellent vehicle for drawing new customers into the stores.

To launch the "Home Decorating Studio" concept, PIC developed a three-phase merchandising system (see Exhibit 34–1) supported by a general statement of goals (see Exhibit 34–2). The standardized store layout for each of PIC's outlets is shown in Exhibit 34–3.

The problem facing the management team was to plan Phase 2 of PIC's merchandising system. More specifically, the team was concerned with Part 1 of Phase 2—designing the in-store visual exhibition of the various types of products and services that comprise the integrated merchandising system. The visual exhibition (see Exhibit 34–4) was planned as a wall display 50 feet long and 10 feet high (floor to ceiling).

ASSIGNMENT

☐ Assume the role of an outside consultant who specializes in visual merchandising and retail displays. PIC's management team has asked you to develop two alternative wall display layouts that would meet the information objectives identified in Phase 2, Customer Information. Each alternative display should provide both the visual and verbal information the customer needs to fully appreciate and understand the entire home decorating concept. The complete line of products (e.g., film or frames) and services (e.g., finishing or enlarging) (see Exhibit 34–4) must be incorporated into each alternative display. As part of the final report, PIC expects scaled diagrams of the alternative displays and a complete verbal description of each display and its strengths and weaknesses.

CASE 35

Audiomobile, Inc.: Developing a Sales Incentive Program

Dale M. Lewison and Douglas Hausknecht, the University of Akron

Audiomobile, Inc., specialized in the sale, installation, and service of car stereos, phones, and burglar alarm systems. The firm's president, Joyce Barta, was always interested in finding new products or services that might help expand the business or improve the productivity of the firm's facilities, equipment, and labor force. The auto after-market could be a bit seasonal; hence, the right complementary product or service line could help fill in the slow periods. Last year, Barta added a complementary service that she felt was ideally suited to her operation: auto detailing—the process of making cars look like new by means of advanced cleaning and polishing techniques. The process is called *detailing* because it gets all the details normal car cleaning misses, from the roof to the tires, inside and out.

To introduce and to inform potential customers of the new service, Barta (1) added the service to the list of services identified in her half-page yellow pages ad; (2) ran one four-column-inch advertisement for four weeks in the sports section of the local newspaper; (3) installed a new outdoor sign; and (4) hung two point-of-sale placards. In addition, sales and service people attempted suggestive selling to all customers who visited the store for one of the other services. To assist in the suggestive selling effort, Barta had a brochure printed that identified the specific detailing services that were performed on each car.

Although the auto detailing service generated a respectable trade, Barta was still somewhat disappointed. Potential customers always seemed to be somewhat hesitant to buy the service. She discussed the situation with her father-in-law, Professor Mike Lewis. He suggested that perhaps some sort of sales incentive might be needed to overcome the observed hesitancy and to move the potential customer toward a favorable decision. Coupons, premiums, contests, and sweepstakes were just a few of the sales incentives they discussed.

Lewis agreed to use the problem as a project during the fall semester of his retailing class; it would be the least he could do in return for the two complementary detailings that Barta had done for him.

ASSIGNMENT

☐ You are part of a student group in Professor Lewis's Retailing course. Develop three sales incentive programs that would help Joyce Barta overcome sales resistance. Each program should be complete regarding objectives, operating procedures, artwork, and so on.

CASE 36

Sweatmate Ltd.

George Prough, the University of Akron

BACKGROUND

Janet McGill had been working for the last ten months as advertising director for Sweatmate Ltd., a manufacturer of home exercise equipment. Sweatmate's overall marketing efforts had been reasonably successful, resulting in a market share of about 6 percent of the home exercise equipment market. Industry experts said that Sweatmate's success was largely due to its product line, which they say is certainly above average in all respects. The company's products were sold through department stores, sports specialty stores, and discount stores. No sales efforts were being directed at health spas or recreation and fitness centers, and none were planned.

CURRENT SITUATION

Part of McGill's efforts during the last ten months involved analyzing the existing advertising program. The national advertising seemed fine. Sweatmate was running magazine ads in some of the better known sport and fitness publications aimed at the household market. Brand awareness was about at the levels expected, roughly the same as that for most other competitors in the same market position as Sweatmate.

The more McGill looked, however, the more it became clear to her that there were some problems with the local and store advertising. About five years ago, John Occhino, her predecessor, had begun a cooperative advertising program. The program encouraged stores to develop ads featuring Sweatmate products either as the entire ad or as a portion of the ad. Sweatmate then reimbursed the store for 50 percent of the media costs associated directly with the Sweatmate products. Thus, if

the store spent $250 on the advertisement and the Sweatmate products' section of the ad occupied half the space or time of the ad, Sweatmate reimbursed the store $125. In addition, Sweatmate sent stores camera-ready copies of line drawings of the products as well as the Sweatmate trademarked logo for use in the newspaper ads. A store then used these and developed its own ad, either in the store's advertising department, with the store's ad agency or with the retail advertising department of the local newspaper. The maximum annual reimbursement allowance was 5 percent of the store's purchases from Sweatmate during that year.

In looking through the cooperative advertising files, McGill found that mainly larger stores took advantage of the program. Many had their own advertising departments or made extensive use of local advertising, especially newspapers. Because of that, few of the ads looked alike or coincided in timing with Sweatmate's national advertising. The ads lacked consistency because Sweatmate's customers, the stores, controlled them.

ONE RETAILER'S PERSPECTIVE

McGill also found several letters from some of the smaller retailers complaining about the advertising program. She knew that small stores that had no advertising departments, no ad agency, and no large budget might not use the current system. McGill decided to pull one of these letters and determine the small retailer's view of the program.

She found the file of Baker's Sports Shop, a sporting goods store in Salem, Indiana. Included in the file was correspondence with Jon Baker, the store's owner. The correspondence indicated that Baker had tried to use the existing cooperative program but found it unsatisfactory.

Baker's letters indicated that in his small market there were no major stores to promote Sweatmate products. As a result, local awareness of the brand was quite limited. His budget was not large enough to give Sweatmate products the kind of visibility needed to build brand awareness, so Baker did little in the way of using, let alone featuring, Sweatmate products in the store's advertising. In addition, Baker sometimes had found that the artwork provided by Sweatmate was the wrong size. (Sweatmate required ads to be a prescribed minimum size.)

Another complaint Baker voiced was that Sweatmate, in requiring the ad to be done by the stores, provided very little real assistance to those stores. He wanted more help. Baker believed that if Sweatmate could provide complete ads (artwork plus copy) for use by the stores, then his store would be better able to sell Sweatmate products. Brand awareness could be built up, and the stores and the products would do better.

A POSSIBLE SOLUTION

McGill thought she knew what Baker wanted. A quick phone call to Baker's Sports Shop confirmed this. He wanted completed newspaper ads with a place at the bottom of the ad for imprinting the names of the local dealers that carried Sweatmate products. The ad would be product oriented rather than store oriented; it would give local dealers a chance to place their name, address, store hours, and similar information in an allotted space in the ad; and the stores would need to do little or no work in getting the ad placed locally. McGill and Baker also discussed the possibility of a total media cooperative effort, using radio, Yellow Pages, outdoor, and whatever other advertising possibilities came to mind. In all these efforts, the cooperating stores would pay a minimal fee for their involvement in the cooperative activity.

McGill wasn't sure what to do next. The annual marketing and advertising plans were due soon. The old system of letting the customers control the retail advertising for Sweatmate worked well but only in portions of the total retail spectrum. A dealer-controlled system might offer some benefits in traditionally neglected areas. McGill had two weeks to make her decision.

ASSIGNMENT

☐ What are the benefits and costs of customer-controlled and dealer-controlled cooperative advertising programs?

☐ What do you recommend that McGill do?

PART SIX: RETAIL SPECIALTIES

CASE 37

James Travel

George Prough and Jeffrey Dilts, the University of Akron

BACKGROUND

After starting James Travel in 1974, Leron James was concerned about the direction he should take with his agency. Back then the agency business had been a lot more fun. James had felt much closer to his customers, and he'd known many by name. He also liked the personal interaction, the chance to get to know people and provide them with quality travel services. This preference had always guided his methods of doing business, and he'd tried to make his agency and the travel agents who worked there more conscious of service to customers, of advising them of the many options available, not just acting to write them tickets. A number of other travel agencies in town seemed to be just ticketing agencies, writing up tickets requested by their customers but providing little else in the way of advice or the full range of services that an agent could provide.

INDUSTRY CHANGES

Numerous changes had occurred in the travel industry, significantly influencing the nature of the travel agency business. The airlines were deregulated in 1978, and in the years that followed, major changes occurred regarding air travel. More people were traveling now than ever before, partly because of the periodic airfare wars, frequent flyer programs, and other similar incentives. For many of these people, however, the role of the travel agent was simply that of a ticketer. These people called the agent with a specific flight schedule in mind (and only that) and asked for the lowest fare. The agent had almost no interaction with the individual and could offer little in the way of advice. In addition, the amount of money or commission made by the travel agent on booking a discount airline ticket was very low. In fact, on some of the real supersaver fares, James and other agents claimed they actually lost money. Because many of these travelers shop around for the lowest fare, the chances of James Travel gaining any degree of store loyalty from such customers was quite low.

One other effect of airline deregulation was an increase in the number of ticketing options. Many airlines now compete for the most profitable routes, so competition in these areas is intense. Other airlines have attempted to carve out particular niches for themselves. Overbooking in this situation is a common problem. The travel agent facing this will find not only many alternatives available but also a dramatic number of daily changes in the form of cancelled flights, flight changes, flight delays, and the like, all of which have made dealings with the airlines hectic indeed.

Another significant change occurred in 1985, when the effects of the Competitive Marketing Case began to be felt. This case brought an end to the Civil Aeronautics Board (CAB) and resulted in deregulation of the sale of airline tickets. This meant that instead of dealing only with travel agents, airlines could now deal with any retail organization that adhered to that carrier's standards. After nearly 40 years worth of exclusivity, agents were now faced with newer forms of competition, including such possibilities as banks, hotels, retail chain stores, Ticketron and other ticketing outlets, vending machine-type distribution, and others. Not only were these competitors new to the travel agency business, but they also brought with them newer and often unusual methods of competing. As a result, travel agents have been undergoing a period of great confusion and uncertainty regarding the new competitive forces from their suppliers (air and other carriers) and from their markets as well.

As has been true with other deregulated industries, the travel agency business has seen a shift in emphasis in the size of travel agencies. As was seen in the banking and financial industry following its deregulation, the travel agency business has been undergoing a period of merger, acquisition, and reformulation of strategies. The June 1986 special Louis Harris Survey issue of *Travel Weekly*, the major weekly newspaper of the travel industry, reported that the market was being increasingly dominated by either small, specialized agencies, or large agency networks, or mega-agencies. Small agencies often have prospered because of their local nature or because they have acquired some strong (though small) defensible specialized niche in the market. On the other

extreme, large mega-agencies have been acquiring many medium-sized agencies, while other medium-sized agencies have been forming networks or consortia to give them buying power and market clout in the form of standardized marketing and advertising efforts around the country as well as the ability to make appeals to very large corporate and other clients. This posed a problem for many medium-sized agencies such as James Travel who were caught in the middle of all this. The overall share of the travel market for medium-sized agencies (those with annual sales of between $2 million and $5 million) declined from 43 percent in 1983 to 38 percent in 1986.

THE TYPICAL TRAVEL AGENT

The Louis Harris survey of travel agents conducted in 1986 and included in the special June issue of *Travel Weekly* reported the following facts about the typical travel agency:

Annual sales volume was $1.9 million.
Business travel (including combined business–pleasure travel) accounted for 53 percent of all bookings, and purely personal–pleasure travel was 47 percent.
Of total bookings, air represents 62 percent; cruises (the fastest growing category), 14 percent; hotel bookings, 10 percent; car rentals, 7 percent; rail travel, 3 percent; and motorcoach and miscellaneous bookings, 4 percent.

Travel agents such as James Travel act as retailers of tickets for travel and as counselors of the various options available to the traveler. They can provide services ranging from simply issuing tickets to assembling a complete itinerary related to travel (including nearly all aspects of the travel plans). They generate sales revenues on the commissions they receive when ticketing the various components of the travel plans or when charging fees for particular services.

THE SITUATION FACING JAMES TRAVEL

James Travel was located in an urban area of nearly 900,000 people in the northeastern United States. The area had grown lately at about the same pace as the national average, and the demographic and economic makeup of the area were about typical in terms of the demographics, and slightly upscale in terms of the socioeconomic characteristics.

By reading the trade publications available to many travel agents, James and his son Shaun had become more aware of the recent changes facing travel agents around the country. In May of 1988 they attended a series of workshops on strategic planning in the travel industry, and returned with great enthusiasm to begin developing plans for their agency. Over the course of that summer, they studied the performance of James Travel over the previous ten years. Of special significance were the following findings:

1. Growth in agency bookings increased dramatically during the early years, but lately had slowed to a pace parallel to that of the industry and also parallel to that experienced in general in their market.

2. Sales in 1987 were $2.3 million, giving James Travel a market share in their target area of 2.1 percent. This put them slightly above average in terms of share in the area they served. Though James Travel served a wider community than the surrounding community at large, James and his son estimate that the surrounding community contains a total of approximately seventy travel agents.

3. In 1977, James Travel's business/pleasure ratio was approximately 51 to 49 percent. Although this was somewhat below the national level, it was not troublesome, because this had not been a focus. In 1987, this figure had dropped to 47 to 53 percent, in part reflecting the loss of business travelers to the mega-agencies and the networks that had made special attempts to gather such business.

4. Ten-year performance figures show some changes in the makeup of James Travel's business. These are shown in Exhibit 37–1.

Because of deregulation and the changes in competition, James felt that it would be difficult to predict activities of the near future with any certainty. He did have some information, however. And always an optimist, he'd generally been pleased with his progress. He'd put a lot of himself into this business. Although the long hours away from home may have cost him his marriage (his wife had divorced him four years previously), he'd seen his agency grow and prosper. He wanted to continue to make things happen.

Last year, one of the local agencies with whom James Travel had been competing had signed an agreement with Travel World, a huge national mega-agency that provides management, marketing, and promotional assistance for its local members. Now under the Travel World name, that agency had been running big local ads featuring Travel World's excellent graphics and strong bargain-oriented copy. Partly in response to this strong marketing effort, the travelers who want discount air-

fares seemed to be going to this agency in significant numbers. Their airfare bookings were up nearly 15 percent over the prior year's figures. James estimated that he'd lost some business to this agency but not too much. He'd never tried too hard to appeal to the discount traveler and suspected that a lot of the growth in Travel World's sales came from infrequent travelers and from the other agencies in town who specialized more in discounted air fares.

THE DECISION FACING THE JAMESES

James and his son both felt that some strategic decisions should be made regarding the direction James Travel should take. They were too aggressive and too proud of their agency to let it sit still. Competition had increased dramatically, especially in the area of discount air travel. With Travel World's strong resources, high visibility, and obvious focus in the area of discounting, James and his son both did not think that the discount airfare market would likely change except to continue moving toward Travel World. With the newer forms of competition likely to make inroads into the travel agency business, there was further incentive to make significant changes and to make those changes before the competitive situation became too clouded.

The Jameses thought that James Travel might be able to join forces with some other larger mega-agency such as Travel World or some other consortium of agencies. This would increase James Travel's market clout. But they would then have to give up some autonomy and might have to change their name and identity to satisfy the requirements of the association.

They alternatively thought that James Travel could focus its marketing on some specific niche or on a differentiating aspect of the agency to establish it with a position of strong defense against the newer forms of competition. And there may be other options that James and his son hadn't yet considered.

ASSIGNMENT

☐ What strategic direction do you think is appropriate for James Travel? Support your decision.

Sales Sources	1977(%)	1987(%)
Air travel	68	53
Cruise	8	18
Hotel	10	11
Car rentals	5	6
Rail	4	5
Motorcoach and misc.	5	7
Total	100	100

EXHIBIT 37–1
James Travel: Percentage of sales, 1977 to 1987

NAME INDEX

SUBJECT INDEX